Everyday Evidence:
A Practical Approach
2nd, Edition

D1385206

Professor Charles H. Rose III
Professor of Excellence in Trial Advocacy
Director, Center for Excellence in Advocacy
Stetson University College of Law

2nd Edition

Copyright Practice Ready Press, December 2016
An Imprint of CHR Publishing
All Rights Reserved

"[W]e shall be better and braver and less helpless if we think that we ought to enquire, than we should have been if we indulged in the idle fancy that there was no knowing and no use in seeking to know what we do not know;– that is a theme upon which I am ready to fight, in word and deed, to the utmost of my power."

PLATO, mathematician and philosopher, (427?–347 BC)[1]

"In seeking wisdom, the first step is silence, the second listening, the third remembering, the fourth practicing, the fifth—teaching others."

IBN GABIROL, poet and philosopher (AD 1022–1058)[2]

"If you hold a cat by the tail you learn things you cannot learn any other way."

Mark Twain, author and humorist (1835-1910)[3]

---

[1] PLATO, *MENO* 56 (Benjamin Jowett trans., Digireads.com 2005). Plato's exact date of birth is unknown.

[2] *THE PAINTER'S KEYS*, http://www.painterskeys.com/auth_search.asp?name=Ibn+Gabirol.

[3] LEARNSTREAMING, http://learnstreaming.com/50-quotes-about-learning/

2nd Edition Acknowledgements

   This book was written for my students - past, present, and future. Professors live to teach, and I have been blessed to have some of the best students one could ever hope for. At the end of the day their desire to learn has forever been the difference.

   As always I thank my wife Pamela. She remains my guiding light, teaching me yet again those things that truly matter. The mistakes within, and I am sure that there are many (most grammatical I hope), are of course, my own.

   Enjoy!

   Charles H. Rose III
   December 2016

1st Edition Acknowledgements

Few things in life are ever done in a vacuum, and this book is no exception. While it has been a labor of love, it would have never been possible without the love and support of my wife Pamela, my two children Laura and Charlie, my colleagues at Stetson University College of Law, and the students for whom it is written. The handprints of my students can be found on every page. It is my hope that in some small way future students benefit from the trials and tribulations of those who have come before.

We stand on the shoulders of everyone that ever crosses our lives, I have been blessed in that regard as well. The mistakes within, and I am sure that there are many (most grammatical I hope), are of course, my own.

Enjoy!

Charles H. Rose III
July 2012

Dedication:

"For my students, past, present and future - you make the teaching of law a joy instead of a burden."

Chapter 1: A Practical Approach

*Evidence is an area of substantive law that only makes true sense when
discovered, developed, and applied through the rubric of trial practice.*

INTRODUCTION

This text is a practically organized, focused, user-friendly book. Each chapter
discusses the development of the law, reviews the major cases, and discusses problems
presented in real world situations. Supplemental materials include photos, diagrams,
presentation slides, and instructional videos. It emphasizes learning everyday evidence
using a practical approach. We will discuss the historical development of the rules to
develop context and understanding, identify the most important cases for the substantive
doctrine, and apply what we have learned through the use of problems.

My primary goal is to help you learn to evaluate and resolve practical evidentiary
problems using the types of materials and situations you will confront in practice. These
real world scenarios are presented as problems that put you in the shoes of the lawyer
encountering the issue, making you decide what to do, and why. While the book includes
excerpts from relevant evidentiary teaching cases, the focus is on solving problems by
using the substantive explanations of the law found in the text in conjunction with the
applicable rules. This approach cross-references the skill of trial practice and evidentiary
doctrine holistically – teaching evidence by mirroring the way it is applied. We will deal
with the same basic evidentiary decisions routinely confronting practicing lawyers and
judges in courts every day.

It is impossible to cover all of the evidentiary issues that practicing lawyers confront
in a text of this size. We can however, cover the core traditional topics of evidence –
relevance, character, foundations, impeachment, experts and hearsay. These are the
subjects trial lawyers must understand to be successful - they also happen to form the vast

majority of evidence questions found on the multi-state bar examination (MBE). You will learn to recognize and evaluate evidentiary dilemmas, internalizing methods of analysis that carry over into practice. The book offers detailed, contextualized information about selected cases, problems, and stories. By the time we are done you will have a three-dimensional picture of the issues, ensuring competency when dealing with similar issues in the future. The multimedia resources included provide additional opportunities to grow your knowledge base, placing your understanding of evidence in context.

CENTRAL THEMES

You hold in your hands a book designed to combine the skill, law and art of evidentiary law into a collective whole that assists you in becoming the best advocate possible through out all stages of litigation. It is based on the idea that to effectively understand evidentiary rules you must take a practical approach. The video located at http://www.youtube.com/user/TRIALADVOCACY is a short summary of the subjects you will be exposed to as you study the basics of evidentiary law in this book.

PRELIMINARY MATTERS

The chapter on preliminary matters begins by addressing the need for an evidentiary code, the policy considerations when drafting such rules, and the historical development of evidentiary law. Once we've taken a stroll through the foundational reasons behind evidentiary law, we identify the rights and responsibilities of the parties involved in the process.

We will look at the applicable rules, focusing on Federal Rules of Evidence(FRE) 103, 104, and 105. These rules tell us what happens when we make evidentiary errors at trial. They also identify the rights, responsibilities, and duties of both counsel and the court. A careful analysis is necessary to properly understand when to object, how to object, and why it matters.

You must fully understand the limitations placed upon the judiciary by the Federal rules of Evidence. These guidelines form the basis of how we determine the power and limitation of the judge and understanding them allows you to move on to mastering issues of both persuasion and proof. This chapter deals with the counsel's responsibilities, limitations placed upon the judge, and duties of the jury. It explains judicial notice, when it applies, how it applies, and its effect at trial.

Once you understand the rights and responsibilities of the parties involved in litigation we will turn to a discussion of burdens of proof and persuasion, taking an in-depth look at each of the rules addressing burdens of proof and burdens of persuasion as they relate to actual courtroom situations. There are subtle differences, depending on the cause of action in a civil case, or the existence of a criminal proceeding, and the ability to understand and use those differences for the benefit of your client's case is the difference between competency and mastery of the process.

The Federal Rules of Evidence are designed, at least in part, to deal with two very different proceedings-civil and criminal. The type of case is crucial because the procedural and constitutional issues raised can be quite different between the two. Once you are aware of this tension within the FRE you are more likely to read the rules with it in mind. Doing this allows you to determine which constituency within the legal community in all likelihood drafted that particular rule. An understanding of the policy behind a particular Rule of Evidence gives us an advantage when fashioning arguments to the court that they will be accepted.

RELEVANCE, PROBATIVE VERSUS PREJUDICIAL

In the next chapter we deal with relevancy. The Federal Rules of Evidence(FRE) are built on this basic concept. There are two ways to look at questions of relevancy. The first is to consider the *logical* implication of the existence of the evidence, this is logical relevancy and is dealt with in FRE 401. Logical relevancy is a very low threshold standard and courts have broadly applied it in favor of admission. Fortunately, most admissibility questions are not decided based upon FRE 401.

The true focus of relevancy is found in FRE 403. This rule is referred to throughout evidentiary literature as *the balancing test*. We will identify the substantive structure of the language within this rule, and then attempt to apply it in real world situations. Legal relevancy begins with the idea that pieces of information may very well have logical significance, but for a variety of reasons - some of them practically based and some of them policy-based, we are not going to allow that evidence to be heard by the jury. This is a completely different approach from what you would find in a civil law system. The common law doctrine of evidence routinely removes from consideration evidence that is logically relevant.

DISCUSSION PROBLEM 1-1

1. Should we exclude evidence that is logically consistent with the issues before the court? Why?

2. What would be some of the benefits of allowing all relevant evidence to be heard by the jury?

3. What would be some of the disadvantages? Which do you prefer? Why?

The federal rules of evidence are designed to be rules of inclusion, meaning that unless there is a specifically identified prohibition against admissibility the court should consider it to be generally admissible. The rest of the Federal Rules of Evidence are designed to address those specific instances where for some reason we want to prevent access to the information in question.

Many of the rules we will discuss could fairly be described as rules of "super relevancy." These rules address specific types of witnesses or situations. Examples include character of witnesses, prior convictions, expert witnesses, and statements made outside of the court.

As we study FRE 403, and the other rules that address specific instances and types of evidence, keep in mind that FRE 403 is the fallback position for the court. In other words, it serves as the final screen through which evidence must pass before it can be admitted. A proper understanding of the rule is crucial from a practical perspective, and you cannot understand evidentiary law as a doctrine unless you fully grasp the policy and procedural reasons behind the implementation of this rule.

CHARACTER MATTERS

After we discuss relevancy we will move into a specific set of rules that are designed to address the character of the accused and the victim in both civil and criminal cases. Character evidence is one of the more confusing doctrines found in evidentiary law, in part because of its historical development within our legal system. This chapter is designed to remove the confusion, shining a clear light of logic and process on the development and application of the character rules of evidence.

When you begin your study of character evidence later in the text you should focus with particular attention on the individual whose character is being offered, as well as the person who is offering it, and the method by which they are attempting to prove the character trait in question. These three questions form the core of all character evidence issues dealt with in a criminal case concerning the accused and the victim. The same thing is true for civil proceedings, where the plaintiff and respondent are involved. You will learn though that there is a difference between civil and criminal cases that must always be considered when dealing with character evidence. Determining whether you are involved in a civil or criminal proceeding is a seminal question when applying character evidence in a US court.

We will discuss opening the door to character evidence, who can walk through when the door is opened, and how to admit character evidence for a non character theory of relevancy. To properly grasp these concepts we will spend time with FRE 404(A), FRE 404(B), and FRE 405. When we are done with our discussion of character evidence, you will understand how character evidence works from a doctrinal perspective. You will also be able to apply it in real world situations. This ability to apply evidentiary law in real world situations is a core value in my approach, and we will use the real world to learn evidence practically.

OFFERING EXHIBITS

Offering exhibits deals with the three primary types of evidence that are available for use at trial. They are fungible, non-fungible, and demonstrative. We will take a very practical approach in this chapter, identifying the overarching Federal rule of evidence that addresses authentication, and then providing several real-world examples of the foundation rules in action. Authentication and foundation are subjects best learned through application. The substantive doctrine revolves around showing that the item in question is what it claims to be. By the time we reach the chapter on offering exhibits you will realize that at least a part of that question is answered using FRE 401 and FRE 403.

Unless there is a specific rule that trumps FRE 403, it will always be considered as part of the process in determining the admissibility of evidence. The very issues that are found in the discussion of FRE 403 are present in the application of FRE 901 and FRE 902 dealing with authentication and foundations.

DEALING WITH WITNESSES

After we have completed our discussion of admitting exhibits, we will then shift our focus and address how evidentiary law empowers lawyers to deal with witnesses as they testify. We will look at issues of competency in the beginning of our discussion about witnesses, and then identify the ground rules about who can ask questions and how they may be asked. The Federal rules of evidence dealing with competency of witnesses and control of the courtroom by the judge are an excellent starting point for understanding how a lawyer interacts with the witness under the applicable evidentiary doctrine, but they are nothing more than the foundation for what follows – impeachment.

After we understand the players involved a large portion of our discussion in this chapter will revolve around the doctrine of impeachment. Depending upon whom you ask, evidentiary scholars can identify as few as four or as many as 15 different ways to impeach the witness. What that should mean to you at this point is that impeachment is a very important process within the trial. Lawyers use impeachment to test the credibility of witnesses. Credibility is always a question residing in the forefront of the jury's mind. We will walk through different theories of impeachment, looking at their historical basis, their current statutory enactment, doctrines of impeachment from the common law allowed in the federal courts, and then complete our discussion with examples of how to impeach.

Much like our discussion regarding offering evidence in the preceding chapter, it will be helpful to understand how these rules apply by looking at them in action. We will use real-world examples and problems so that you can play with the rules and grasp how they work in the real world. After we have looked at ways to impeach witnesses we will then move on to a discussion of the most powerful witness in trial today-experts.

WHEN EXPERTS SPEAK

Our discussion of expert witnesses will follow the substantive law found within the federal rules of evidence, while also focusing on recent Supreme Court jurisprudence in this area. At the close of our study in this chapter you will not only understand the substantive law, you will be able to translate the substantive law into formulating questions that allow you to admit evidence, or arguments that may assist you in excluding the testimony of a supposed expert.

Topics that we will address include what type of expert opinions are helpful, the proper basis for an expert's opinion, how to get the court to let the expert testify, structuring the presentation of the expert witness, and properly dealing with experts that do not support your side. Once we have developed a full understanding of how expert witnesses work within the federal rules of evidence we will move to a subject that can be both confusing, aggravating, and phenomenally interesting-the doctrine of hearsay.

HEARSAY – CAN WE TALK?

Hearsay doctrine deals with admitting statements at trial for the truth of what they assert when they were made before the trial and are now being repeated. Evidence at trial is admitted primarily through the testimony of witnesses' firsthand knowledge. These witnesses testify as to their personal observations, and are not allowed to speculate about what others may have observed, seen, or thought. An entire doctrine of law has been developed to deal with those instances when the witness is asked a question about which they do not have personal knowledge. Normally, when the witness is testifying to what they heard someone else say, or what they themselves said at some other time, there must be a reason under evidentiary law to allow that type of statement which is not based on firsthand knowledge. This is how the doctrine of hearsay developed.

There is a very simple equation that we will learn in this text that is the starting point for all hearsay analysis. First, was a statement made? That seems like a relatively straightforward question, but in all actuality it can be a difficult thing to decide. We will address when a statement is not a statement, and when action can be the equivalent of verbal conduct. For now you should remember that the first question asked is, was a statement made?

The second line of inquiry, after we have determined that the statement was made, is who made it? The identity of the person making the statement becomes a crucial component in the analysis of whether it fits into one of the hearsay exclusions or exceptions identified in the federal rules of evidence. After we have determined the identity of the individual who made the statement, we must turn to the third question that we need to ask - what was the purpose of the statement?

When we combine these three questions and consider them in light of hearsay doctrine, it becomes much easier to posit whether a particular statement should be admitted substantively for the truth of the matter asserted therein. Let me say that again, hearsay concerns itself with out of court statements offered for the truth of the matter asserted within the statement itself. This is the core issue surrounding hearsay doctrine, and lies at the heart of every moment at trial when the witness wants to say someone else said something at some other time.

Once we have identified the initial analysis of whether hearsay should apply, we will then take a look at all the different ways in which hearsay statements may potentially come into evidence. These doctrines include (1) it was not an assertion, (2) it is being offered for a non-hearsay use, (3) there is a particular exclusion that applies under FRE 801, (4) a hearsay exception applies when the availability of the declarant is not material, or (5) a hearsay exception applies were counsel must first establish that the declarant is unavailable. Keep these five areas of hearsay doctrine in mind as we continue through our study of the rules of evidence.

Other evidentiary issues will be addressed, but substantive chapters are not dedicated to those subjects. Issues such as best evidence, duplicates versus originals and the like are best addressed in concert with other rules. The subjects chosen for this book are based on the issues that practicing trial lawyers must master. Additionally, they also focus on the majority of subjects historically tested on the national multi-state bar examination. Mastery of these subjects is the core component on the path to understanding evidence. This text is designed to accomplish exactly that result.

STRUCTURE OF THIS BOOK

Stylistic decisions

This text quickly and efficiently identifies the specific law necessary to increase your ability to understand and apply evidentiary rules. It begins with a discussion of the substantive rule to be learned, explaining the history of the law behind the rule, and then provides cases that either defined or developed the rule, and then finishing with the application of the rule to real world scenarios through problems and examples.

Several different learning techniques are employed throughout the text. You will observe call out boxes with quotes, as well as call out boxes that identify fundamental principles of the law from a policy, history, and practical perspective. Once you know them inside and out you will be able to automatically address any evidentiary issue that might arise in court. Understanding and possessing these skills at a fundamental checklist level gets the mechanics out of the way, allowing you to focus on the persuasive power of the evidence.

> *This is an example of the type of call out box you might expect to see....*

You will know you have reached a new level of competency when you no longer worry about how to ask the next question and are instead "in the moment" listening to the answer of the witness and crafting questions that lead to the goal of examination, confident that you can handle any evidentiary issue that is raised. That is true empowerment of the lawyer and this text takes an approach maximizing your ability to focus on becoming better immediately.

The text identifies and discusses the substantive law first, working through a clear discussion of the rule and the policy behind it. We will then reinforce the information you aver received by teaching through a review of the truly important case law, and by applying the law in real world problems.

A Holistic Approach

A fundamental goal of this book is to remove the mystery so that we can get about the business of discussing the reality of evidentiary law. We will accomplish this by taking elements of many different resources and bringing them together in a way that makes the whole greater than the sum of its parts. What do I mean by that? In the past when studying evidence you might have a case book filled with cases from which you were to apply the Socratic method. To support your understanding of that casebook you might buy an outline, hornbook, or some other resource to explain the black letter law. Finally, to ensure that you can properly apply the law you might use flash cards, computer-based lessons, or workbooks. In this book we will combine the black letter law, the relevant Supreme Court jurisprudence, and practical problems to ensure that you learn "evidence in context." Each section of the text will discuss the law from a substantive perspective, provide you with the opportunity to analyze cases where appropriate, and then present you with practical problems and examples of evidentiary law in action. The goal is to immerse you in the process so that when you are done you will not only understand the policies behind evidentiary law, but might be able to use it in service to client.

> *Learning law in the context of how it is applied works. You will find that your understanding of evidentiary law will deepen as your understanding of how a trial works develops.*

CONCLUSION

The process of learning how to deal with evidentiary issues at trial will require you to rediscover the human being lurking beneath your lawyerly exterior, while developing the fundamental skills that will allow you to practice law. You should not abandon the ability to think like a lawyer that you learned through the Socratic Method. You must merely combine it with the ability to again think like a human being.

When you are done with this book you will be able to do both. To lose your humanity in a search for academic or professional excellence is both shortsighted and foolish. Many of the approaches to evidentiary law in this text are grounded in the idea that where the law is applied matters a great deal in your understanding of it. The techniques offered in this book are predicated on the belief that the type of person you are at your core matters in your development as a lawyer. This book provides a way for you to develop a mastery of evidentiary law while remembering and honoring the humanity of everyone involved. In the process it will also help make you a superior lawyer.

-Notes-

Chapter 2: Preliminary Matters

WHY HAVE AN EVIDENCE CODE?

Evidentiary law lies squarely at the unique intersection of substance and practice. Because the rules of evidence govern the conduct of the trial, they are often applied quickly, under a great deal of stress, and sometimes without much thought. When you have finished this book I hope that you will have developed the ability to think quickly, deeply, and clearly, about evidentiary issues and their application.

Although there is a great deal of substantive doctrine, both constitutional and otherwise, contained within the foundations of evidence law in the United States, the vast majority of it is primarily procedural in nature. What do I mean by this? Evidence is a process used to control and manage the presentation of information at trial. You should think of it as the rules of the game controlling actions by counsel, witnesses, and the court. Evidence functions in much the same way for trial as the rules of criminal and civil procedure do for the pretrial process. The rules of evidence manage the relative risks and rewards of admitting or excluding information to or from the jury. They control the actions of counsel and oversee the adversarial process. In a very real sense your understanding of how evidentiary law works directly has an impact on your ability to be persuasive at trial.

In order to properly argue for the particular application of a rule of evidence you must understand the logical underpinnings beneath the applicable evidentiary rule. While many different arguments have been put forward explaining the need for a set of evidentiary rules, there are three primary arguments that I believe you should understand. A knowledge of them will assist you in forming the correct motion, objection, or argument, that will allow you to shape the message received by the jury.

Juries

The legal system has a love and hate relationship with juries. The jury serves as the finder of fact in many cases, accepting and rejecting evidence based upon credibility determinations formed in the minds of individual with the jury and then expressed collectively as a verdict. Unfortunately, lawyers are less than certain about the ability of the jury to properly discharge the duties the system places upon it. While we do trust the jury to sort through issues of proof, credibility, and weight we do not completely trust them. The need to trust the jury, when coupled with our inability to do so, has resulted in the growth of evidentiary law that is designed to control; without completely limiting, the amount of information the jury receives during a trial.

For example, most of our Hearsay doctrine, a topic we will discuss in great degree later in this text, revolves around the idea that we cannot trust juries to properly weigh the evidentiary value assigned to statements made out of court when they are offered for the truth asserted, in other words, contained within them. In this same vein, the evidentiary rules regarding character are built around a simple premise that juries will place too much weight on character evidence. We fear that juries will be inclined to improperly consider character evidence both for reasons of proof and punishment.

This distrust of juries is the "issue behind the issue" whenever the court is trying to decide whether some types of evidence should be considered. While the jury has the power to decide questions of fact, we worry they will make those decisions based upon issues that we do not want them to consider. The court is always concerned with whether the jury appropriately weighed the information fairly. The evidentiary rules are designed to reduce or prevent the possibility of *unfair prejudice* in the jury's deliberations. A valid argument exists that all the rules of evidence are nothing more than specific restrictions and developments upon the basic concepts outlined in the rules addressing legal and logical relevance, specifically 401, 402, and 403. We will discuss these at length through out the pages of this book.

Controlling the Process

While the rules of evidence are designed to limit and control the amount of information that is presented to the jury (finder of fact), they also have the very real function of controlling the process by which admissible evidence is considered. Along with being worried about process, we are also concerned with finality. Finality means that the results of the case will withstand any appellate process or review.

The rules of evidence give the court the ability to control the scope and duration of trials. Society needs lawsuits to be resolved within a reasonable time frame, and with a final result that we can rely upon. This need for timely process and finality is important, and supports the outcome of trials even when such outcomes are less than perfect. These rules give the judge the power to control and organize the dispute. That ability to control includes sequences of proof and the examination of witnesses (FRE 611), as well as the exclusion of evidence based upon its cumulative nature, danger of confusion, or waste of time (FRE 403). These rules work in concert with others are designed to ensure accurate fact finding by the jury.

Many of the rules designed to ensure accurate fact-finding will be discussed throughout this text, to include authenticating documents and exhibits ("referred to by trial lawyers as laying a foundation"), the Best Evidence doctrine (requiring content of a writing to be proved by the writing itself), and the basis for a witness' testimony (usually personal knowledge). Each of these are examples of rules used to ensure accuracy. Think of them as rules of quality control in the trial process.

Policy Considerations

We use evidentiary law to control the process, manage our concern about jury prejudice, and to support substantive policies agreed upon by society. A place where you see this is the setting of presumptions and burdens of proof. One can readily see how identifying a different burden of proof or the presumption as to who has the duty to prove can have an immediate and long-lasting impact on not only the way in which the trial goes forward, but ultimately upon who prevails. These rules regarding burdens of proof and presumptions are nearly as important as purely substantive principles. How might this work?

Let's say we have a negligence action in a civil court. One of our goals might be to increase or decrease the likelihood of recovery by a plaintiff when they have been partially to blame. In tort courses, this concept is often referred to as comparative contributory negligence. You should remember that a state that uses contributory negligence bars recovery by the plaintiff if they contributed to the cause of their injury. A state that uses comparative negligence apportions responsibility and then apportions recovery based upon that comparative negligence. This is an example of how the substantive law can control issues of recovery. The same thing could be determined using burdens of proof and persuasion.

In many civil cases, the burden of persuasion, or proof, is a preponderance of the evidence standard–often referred to as the lowest burden of proof. Many different scholars have attempted to describe preponderance of evidence, but for our purposes let's imagine that we have a scale with absolutely equal weight on either side, whatever you place on one side, no matter how slight in weight, if it moves the scale in the direction of one side or the other it is sufficient to meet that burden that preponderance of the evidence standard.

Using our earlier example of a plaintiff in a negligence action, we could increase or decrease that plaintiff's chances of prevailing at trial by adopting a different burden of proof - such as clear and convincing, or, by placing some burden of persuasion on the defendant or plaintiff as to a specific subordinate issue in the case. For example, if the defendant had the burden of proving plaintiff's negligence it could increase the likelihood of the plaintiff winning recovery. On the other hand, if we required a burden of proof on the plaintiff to show due care we might reduce the ability of the plaintiff to prevail. In each of these examples nothing has changed other than the burden of proof. Nonetheless, it has a very real effect on the ability of one side or the other to prevail at trial. As we continue through this discussion of evidentiary law, take the time to ask yourself what is happening behind the scenes? Is this a procedural rule designed to control the process? Is this a rule designed to prevent the jury from unfairly deciding the case? Is it perhaps an attempt to modify substantive issues with evidentiary law? When you can see which of these factors is in play you will better understand the method behind the madness.

HISTORICAL DEVELOPMENT

It was not always this way. The journey of evidentiary law began in the common law, meandered through issues of constitutionality, and transformed into an evidentiary code in 1975. Before 1975, it was a common law process that was uniquely malleable to the formation of local rules on a case-by-case basis. While most jurisdictions had addressed specific matters such as: privileges, admissibility of business records, or aspects of impeachment through statute, a comprehensive code was longer in coming to the fore and slow to gain acceptance. Much of the need for a comprehensive evidentiary code grew out of the complexities of modern life and the sheer weight of precedence. There was a need for some degree of uniformity, or at least commonality of language and approach in dealing with evidentiary issues at trial.

Although it was a long time coming, the successful adoption of the code was a sea change. At common law, the rules of evidence were designed to limit the amount of information that was presented to the jury. The codified federal rules of evidence took exactly the opposite approach, suddenly the rules were designed to ensure admissibility unless specifically prohibited, a one hundred and eighty degree turn around from

JOHN H. WIGMORE
Dean of Northwestern University School of Law
From a painting by Arvid Nyholm

Dean John Henry Wigmore, father of American evidence, from a painting by Arvid Nyholm.

the common law tradition of excluded unless specifically allowed.

The intent behind the creation of the rules is important when arguing to the court how they should be interpreted and applied. The rules were drafted to prevent undue "prejudice" to either party. This belief in the need for fairness, as well as a recognition that prejudice, while being part of the process, should not be unfairly prejudicial, has historical, sociological, and legal underpinnings. We will discuss this at length when dealing with relevancy, but for now you should take as a given that the evidentiary rules are designed to prevent waste of time; ensure that information used in the case meets the minimum standard of reliability; and to get all reliable and relevant evidence before the fact finder for consideration.

Multiple attempts were made to codify evidence law in the United States before the adoption of the Federal Rules of Evidence. One of the two early great evidentiary giants, Dean Wigmore, while still a young man, wrote an early code in 1909. Most consider his effort to be a cumbersome, lengthy and, ultimately, an impractical document. It did not achieve any practical success, but it did serve to show that perhaps evidentiary law could be codified.

The American Law Institute proposed the Model Code of Evidence in 1945. Professor Edmund Morgan drafted this document for ALI, and he spent a good portion of his career defending his approach. He did not agree with many of the positions taken by Dean Wigmore, and instead drafted a code that was quite radical and extremely technical. For instance, he favored getting rid of the hearsay doctrine, and when viewed in comparison with the modern Commercial Code its complexity is readily apparent. The ALI Model Code of 1945 was never adopted in any jurisdiction.

While other efforts are of interesting historical significance, the adoption of the California Evidence Code in 1965, truly signaled the arrival of the modern evidentiary era. It is a comprehensive statutory scheme that was written by a public commission and enacted by the legislature. This highly successful code made important modifications to the common law tradition.

The Federal Rules of Evidence were designed to make evidence law accessible and understandable. It has become the most influential body of American evidence law. The 68 short provisions of these rules set forth the majority of the law of evidence in language that is easy to read and for the most part relatively free of cross referencing that often make such codes too complex and technical.

DISCUSSION PROBLEMS 2-1

1. What were the primary reasons for the promulgation of the federal rules of evidence? Have those purposes been met? Should the rules easily adapt to the particular facts of the case to ensure more information goes to the fact finder, or would they work better if they are most often used as rigid tools to keep relevant evidence out of the courtroom?

2. Should advocates use FRE 102 to support an argument for the admission or exclusion of evidence? How literally should this rule be read? How would you use it?

3. Given the concerns regarding juries, why do we apply the same rules to trials by judge alone?

How was this accomplished? It is a wonderful example of what can happen when members of the bench, bar, and academia come together under a common purpose and with clear guidelines. These rules are an excellent example of drafting that is both filled with common sense and created contextually to accomplish goals inside and outside the courtroom.

A distinguished Advisory Committee of practitioners, judges, and law professors appointed by the United States Supreme Court proposed the Federal Rules of Evidence. Albert Jenner (a prominent Chicago trial attorney) chaired the committee, and the late Professor Edward Cleary (then of the University of Illinois) took on the task of drafting the rules. The Committee worked for more than eight years. They produced two published drafts that were publicized among members of the bench and bar for comment. They then provided a suggested final version that the Supreme Court accepted and transmitted to Congress pursuant to the enabling act.

A primary reason for the success of the Rules is their brevity and simplicity. They are the *bones of evidentiary law* in the United States, and they serve as an excellent structure to use when mastering the subject. They apply in federal courts across the land in both criminal and civil cases, and generally they apply regardless of whether federal or state law supplies the rule of decision. As of 2009, more than 40 states have adopted evidentiary codes based in whole or in part on these rules. Even where states have not adopted them they are still often cited for their underlying principles in appellate opinions dealing with the law of evidence.

These rules were not passed unmodified by Congressional activity. The Watergate scandal was in full force when they were presented to Congress. Then President Nixon was making claims of Executive Privilege and the privilege provisions in the Rules attracted immediate attention by a Congress that was not inclined to overlook the issues accompanying privilege. Many members of Congress saw the Rules as an encroachment by the other branch—an infringement of legislative prerogative by the judiciary. In response to those concerns Congress held hearings and prepared committee reports The proposed rules were scrutinized, changed, and finally enacted as a statute. Changes included the deletion of the privilege rules and in their place adopted a single provision (FRE 501) leaving privilege to common law evolution. Congress also rejected a proposal to admit prior inconsistent statements by testifying witnesses for both their substantive and impeachment value. They did this by defining prior inconsistent statements under FRE 613 as "not hearsay."

For many years the occasional changes in the Rules came either from other committees or from Congress. In 1993, however, the Supreme Court appointed an Advisory Committee on Evidence Rules, which undertook the process of review and revision, proposing amendments to many Rules that were adopted. This process continues through this day, although some changes have statutory limitations, such as proposed changes to the rules on privileges, and cannot be enacted without Congressional approval.

ERRORS IN ADMITTING & EXCLUDING EVIDENCE
Basics of FRE 103

Attorneys use FRE 103 to preserve appellate arguments concerning whether the court erred in admitting evidence at trial. To preserve a challenge to the admission or exclusion of evidence by the trial judge, the attorney must first make a timely objection to the evidence, a motion, or request that the court strike objectionable testimony from the record. A request that testimony be stricken is often accompanied by a request that the finder of fact be instructed to disregard that testimony.

Objections have both tactical and strategic value, but from an evidentiary perspective they are designed to accomplish several different goals. The primary goal of objections are to assist the trial court in avoiding errors concerning the admissibility or exclusion of evidence by providing a method whereby the court is placed on notice and given an opportunity to reconsider its ruling – taking corrective measures when necessary. Objections also allow the proponent of the evidence to properly perfect proof issues so that the decision of the court is upheld. Finally, requiring parties who wish to oppose the admission of evidence to affirmatively make the record serves a systemic interest because it allows for fair opportunities to litigate admissibility issues, but limits those opportunities appropriately.

By placing the decision of whether to object in the hands of the parties, fairness in the litigation process is increased. The additional standard of objections not made being waived assists in creating finality as to the verdict. Both of these values are served by this particular rule of evidence. Because lawyers are tasked with the job of informing the court as to violations of the evidentiary rules concerning admissibility and exclusion of evidence, they also can waive those issues. The two powers go hand in hand.

Rule 103. Rulings on Evidence

(a) Preserving a Claim of Error. A party may claim error in a ruling to admit or exclude evidence only if the error affects a substantial right of the party and:

(1) if the ruling admits evidence, a party, on the record:

(A) timely objects or moves to strike; and

(B) states the specific ground, unless it was apparent from the context; or

(2) if the ruling excludes evidence, a party informs the court of its substance by an offer of proof, unless the substance was apparent from the context.

(b) Not Needing to Renew an Objection or Offer of Proof. Once the court rules definitively on the record — either before or at trial — a party need not renew an objection or offer of proof to preserve a claim of error for appeal.

Once Judge rules it is preserved

(c) Court's Statement About the Ruling; Directing an Offer of Proof. The court may make any statement about the character or form of the evidence, the objection made, and the ruling. The court may direct that an offer of proof be made in question-and-answer form.

(d) Preventing the Jury from Hearing Inadmissible Evidence. To the extent practicable, the court must conduct a jury trial so that inadmissible evidence is not suggested to the jury by any means.

(e) Taking Notice of Plain Error. A court may take notice of a plain error affecting a substantial right, even if the claim of error was not properly preserved.

Motions to strike become necessary when evidence has been admitted conditionally, admitted improperly, or the objection could not be heard or considered by the court in sufficient time to prevent the fact finder from hearing the inadmissible evidence. To preserve the appellate issue in situations where the court conditionally admitted evidence, the opposing party must move to strike once the offering party has failed to satisfy a condition that the court relied upon when conditionally admitting the evidence. The party that initially objected to the admissibility of the conditionally accepted evidence must make such a motion when it becomes clear that the condition upon which the judge based admissibility failed. A party must also move to strike if the judge admits evidence and it later appears that the evidence should not have come in, or if the evidence comes in so quickly that there was no time to object in advance.

Failing to object or move to strike constitutes waiver, effectively placing the evidentiary issue in question outside of potential appellate review. While the general rule is that failing to object or move to strike waives the issue on appeal, the door may not be closed completely. The injured party may still obtain relief if they can persuade a reviewing court that the mistake amounted to plain error. For purposes of this type of appellate issue the party arguing for appellate review of the evidentiary issue has the burden of showing that the error in question was very serious, obvious, and essentially devastating. Failure to object to evidence, or to move to strike improperly admitted evidence, allows the finder of fact and the trial judge to consider it to the extent it may be relevant.

The objecting party has a duty to promptly make necessary objections that are accompanied by a brief statement of the grounds for the objection. A timely objection is one that is made when the grounds first become apparent. This usually means that an objection must be made after the opposing counsel asks the question and before it is answered, unless the witness answers before an objection can be properly made, is unresponsive in their answer, or gives an answer that appeared proper at the time but is later found to be improper. Absent these conditions a motion to strike will not normally be granted by the court if the party making such a motion had not previously objected before the answer was given.

The objecting party must state the reason or grounds for the objection so that the court can properly rule. In certain instances, it may become necessary for the lawyer to cite a specific provision of evidentiary law. While most trial judges do not normally require rote memorization of evidentiary doctrine, they do require that the objection identify in general terms the evidentiary rule that has allegedly been violated. This requirement means that general objections as to fairness, materiality, and the like will generally not be sufficient when they do not properly identify the substantive rule.

Trial lawyers understand that there are many valid reasons to object at trial that are at best tangentially related to specific evidentiary issues of exclusion or admissibility. Objections can interrupt damaging testimony, disrupt the rhythm of the witness' testimony, convey outrage, disgust or boredom with the current testimony, or perhaps give counsel time to form a more cogent evidentiary objection. Occasionally, a general objection will preserve an evidentiary issue for appeal, but normally that only happens when the appellate court concludes that there is no possible ground upon which the evidence in question could have been admitted. On the other hand, general objections that are sustained will be found valid by the appellate court if any possible basis for sustaining it exists within the record. General objections may have valid advocacy reasons, but they are rarely effective from an evidentiary perspective.

While the general rule under FRE 103 is that a statement of the grounds should accompany the objection, such a statement will not be necessary if the reason for the objection is "apparent from the context" of the testimony. This may be the case when the parties have previously argued the issue either at trial or during a motion in limine. It also happens when the flow of the testimony makes it apparent what issue is being addressed, or when the issue in question is so elementary that it is obvious from the context of the question and answer. Counsel would do well, however, to not rely upon the "apparent from the context" language, and should, all things being equal, always state their basis when objecting. Similarly, once an objection has been made to a particular line of questioning, the objecting party can make a standing objection to that line of inquiry, obviating the need for continued objections on a question-by-question, and answer-by-answer, basis.

While it used to be an open question whether an objection raised before trial needed to be made at trial, recent changes to FRE 103 now make it clear that an objection need not be raised again if the court has already made "a definitive ruling on the record," either "at or before trial." It is still the responsibility of the parties that argued the motion to ensure that there was a definitive pretrial ruling concerning the objection or motion. If the judge reserves ruling or avoids ruling then the change to FRE 103 will not preserve the issue if it is not raised during the trial itself. A conservative advocate will take the time to strategically and tactically renew objections, especially when there is any doubt whether the prior action by the trial court was definitive. It is important that lawyers listen carefully to what the trial judge says when dealing with these issues during pretrial motions and when ruling on objections.

Waiver

An advocate may very well decide, based upon their theme and theory of the case, to forgo a valid objection and accept the impact of the evidence that is admitted by not objecting. This makes perfect sense in an adversarial system that stresses party responsibility. The lawyer knows that the decision to object, or to not object, may very well have an impact on the admissibility of evidence, but that knowledge becomes part of the choices that are made in forming the case theory. This approach is allowed under the waiver provisions of FRE 103. When courts talk about this approach on the part of litigants they often refer to it as either invited error, or opening the door to otherwise potentially inadmissible evidence.

"Invited error" occurs when a party questions a witness and the answer is proper, or responsive, to the posed question. If the answer also contains something that might otherwise be inadmissible, the questioner is stuck with the answer since they posed the question to begin with. The doctrine is based upon the idea that if you have control of the question, then you must bear the weight of the answer. You can think of it as a garbage in, garbage out rule.

"Opening the door," on the other hand, describes what happens when, in response to one party introducing evidence, the other party introduces evidence to refute or contradict the evidence initially proffered by the other side. This is often a matter of case analysis and litigation strategy. When the first party chooses to make it an issue, it is reasonable to expect the response from the other side. When the initial party objects to the response, often because they did not completely reason through the impact of the counter response, the court will often cite to the

> In a very real sense the attitude of the court practically speaking is you get what you paid for when you make it an issue.

"opening of the door" when overruling the objection. This same counterproof, if initially offered by a party without the door having been opened, would normally not be admissible.

At the core of this issue is an idea that when you invite the issue, or open the door – either through opening statement, closing argument, direct or cross, you cannot later raise an objection to a response that is based upon your initial actions. In a very real sense the attitude of the court practically speaking is you get what you paid for when you make it an issue. Most courts allow these two doctrines to overlap, even using the terms interchangeably when addressing these issues.

Think of it this way, if you introduce evidence you have made it relevant, allowing other parties to introduce similar evidence, such as evidence to contradict it, form questions for witnesses based upon that evidence, as well as attempt to both rebut or limit the evidence initially offered.

Now none of this means that the door is always opened. Sometimes a witness will run, giving unresponsive answers, answers that are broader than the question asked. In those instances, the advocate who asked the question should not be barred from objecting to the testimony, or to have waived the ability to object if the other side attempts to offer evidence based upon that nonresponsive or overbroad answer. This often happens during cross-examination of an opposing witness, or through direct examination of a hostile witness, which often occurs in civil cases where the plaintiff calls the defendant. It makes sense to not punish the questioner when the witness does not answer the question posed. The advocate should be held accountable for their trial strategy, but they should not be responsible for answers that do not follow the rules.

Offers of Proof

When the trial judge excludes evidence the party that loses the ruling must preserve the issue on appeal by making an offer of proof. This offer of proof occurs after the objection or motion has been stated with sufficient grounds, and the court has ruled against the party attempting to enter the evidence. Under FRE 103 an adequate offer of proof must be made, unless one of the exceptions applies. The absence of an offer of proof places the decision of the court in a category other than plain error. The court needs the offer of proof in order for the record of trial to be sufficiently complete to properly disclose the error made by the trial judge in excluding the evidence. The language often preceding the offer of proof usually goes something like this:

> "Your honor I wish to make an offer of proof (usually made outside the presence of the jury). But for your ruling on this objection, I proffer that this witness would have testified as follows...."

The attorney then goes on to state the specific factual information that would have been provided to the finder of fact but for the court's ruling. In the best case scenario the attorney would call the witness in question to the stand, outside the presence of the jury, and make the offer through the testimony of the witness. In practice the judge will rarely allow this approach in most jurisdictions.

Offers of proof allow the trial judge to "reevaluate his decision considering the actual evidence to be offered," and help the reviewing court decide whether "exclusion affected the substantial rights" of the offering party. Appellate courts are particularly interested in offers of proof, claiming that assessing error is virtually impossible without such offers.

Another way to think about offers of proof is to consider how they fit into the process. You make them when witnesses are testifying and there is an objection. You also make them when arguing a motion before the court. In both instances you are not only telling the judge what it is you are trying to do, you are also telling the judge that if he doesn't agree with you the appellate court might!

By beginning with this position, the lack of an offer of proof places the burden on the shoulders of the appellant to show that the excluded evidence affected a substantial right without sufficient information present in the record of trial to support such a position.

Despite the general rule for an offer of proof, it is not required if the context makes the evidentiary issue apparent on its face. The appellate court will look at the questions posed, the answers given, and both the substance and form of those questions and answers. When sufficient clarity exists by considering the testimony, the reasons for having an offer of proof have already been met.

An adequate offer of proof will identify the type and content of the evidence, identifying its use and relevancy. When it is the only evidence available the proponent of the evidence will have to establish the sufficiency and competency of the proffered evidence. When an offer of proof fails to give the court sufficient information to evaluate it the court will normally consider it too vague, or general in nature, and discount it.

DISCUSSION PROBLEM 2-2:
Making an Offer

You represent a young college student who is charged with driving under the influence. If convicted she faces the loss of her license for over 1 year, and potential jail time. At issue in the case is the validity of the BAC test. You have brought to court an expert in the field who is available to testify. If allowed to testify she will say that she reviewed the maintenance logs of the Breathalyzer machine and it is is her expert opinion that the machine could not have possibly been functioning properly on the day of the test due to the overdue maintenance procedures that had not been performed. She can identify those procedures and discuss the impact of the failure to perform each in detail. When she takes the stand to testify the prosecution objects to the validity of her testimony. Before you can you make a proffer to the court the judge sustains the objection and tells you to call your next witness.

How do you respond? Identify with specificity what you would do and say to the court, with appropriate reference to relevant evidentiary rules and factual predicates. When preparing your response you should consider:

1. How do you address this with the court?

2. What is your best argument to make this evidence admissible?

3. If the judge does not allow the witness to testify what should you do? Why? What is the reason for your suggested approach? What rule of evidence supports what you want to do?

Pretrial Rulings on Motions in Limine

Courts routinely rule in advance on evidence objections when requested by a party in a pretrial "motion in limine" (a Latin phrase meaning "at the threshold"). Although counsel are not required to seek pretrial rulings, it is often advantageous to the theme and theory of their case to do so. You should consider pretrial rulings and motions practice as a more formalized process for identifying and resolving evidentiary issues before trial.

FRE 104 establishes the authority of the judge to decide questions of admissibility in a motions hearing. This rule gives the judge authority to make decisions during motions without regards to the limitations on admissibility that the other federal rules of evidence might place upon the offered evidence. The only limitation on what evidence the judge may consider is found in the rule on privileges. The courts have determined that we will not destroy the privilege protections when deciding motions.

The rule also allows for the conditional admissibility of evidence even though counsel has not yet established that it will be relevant. Conditional relevancy exists so that the court can control the flow of the trial and keep cases moving forward promptly. It also reflects the modernization of trial process as part of the federal rules of evidence. Finally, the rule allows the accused to testify for the limited purpose of addressing the subject of the motion without otherwise waiving his right to silence in a criminal case.

While FRE 104 authorizes the trial judge to decide preliminary issues of admissibility, the impact of that authority, and the limitations upon its exercise are discussed in FRE 103. FRE 103 establishes that once the judge rules conclusively on an issue raised during a motion hearing that issue is preserved on appeal for the losing side. Before this recent change to the Federal Rules of Evidence the losing party was required to object when the evidence addressed during the pretrial motion was admitted at trial.

Rule 104. Preliminary Questions

(a) **In General.** The court must decide any preliminary question about whether a witness is qualified, a privilege exists, or evidence is admissible. In so deciding, the court is not bound by evidence rules, except those on privilege.

(b) **Relevance That Depends on a Fact.** When the relevance of evidence depends on whether a fact exists, proof must be introduced sufficient to support a finding that the fact does exist. The court may admit the proposed evidence on the condition that the proof be introduced later.

(c) **Conducting a Hearing So That the Jury Cannot Hear It.** The court must conduct any hearing on a preliminary question so that the jury cannot hear it if:

(1) the hearing involves the admissibility of a confession;

(2) a defendant in a criminal case is a witness and so requests; or

(3) justice so requires.

(d) **Cross-Examining a Defendant in a Criminal Case.** By testifying on a preliminary question, a defendant in a criminal case does not become subject to cross-examination on other issues in the case.

(e) **Evidence Relevant to Weight and Credibility.** This rule does not limit a party's right to introduce before the jury evidence that is relevant to the weight or credibility of other evidence.

Pretrial rulings are a tool that both advocates and the court can use to settle evidentiary disputes without interrupting the flow of the trial, or what is more important, as a way to identify themes and theories that are based upon evidence that the court will admit. Evidentiary decisions by the court have an immediate impact upon case analysis and presentation – pretrial motions allow the litigants to identify what is, and what is not, potentially admissible. Trial judges are often reticent to rule on issues prospectively though, and often they will reserve ruling before trial. Also, just because the judge has ruled one way during pretrial motions, the losing party is not barred from raising the issue again during the trial itself, particularly when the evidence presented to the jury conflicts with, or changes from, the offer of proof or evidence presented during the motion.

There are only a few instances in which litigants must raise objections by pretrial motion, but those are normally identified by specific rules of procedure applicable in that particular jurisdiction. Other types of pretrial motions that are normally raised include rulings on issues of impeachment of potential witnesses who have convictions, evidence of prior sexual activity in sexual assault cases and motions attempting to exclude character evidence of the victim or accused.

EVIDENTIARY ERRORS

Harmless Error

These issues concerning the admission or exclusion of evidence are important because during the appellate review process the court is going to apply a harmless error standard to the evidentiary rulings.

While multiple scholars and members of the bench have addressed harmless error, in a nutshell it means that the court must determine, after the fact (through the appellate process) whether a mistaken ruling as to the admission or exclusion of evidence affected a substantial right of the convicted person. This after the fact analysis is problematic, and trial lawyers should not trust the appellate court to change outcomes based upon mistakes.

Five general guidelines addressing harmless error were adopted by the court in *Kotteakos v. United States,* they are:

(1) a "technical violation of an evidentiary rule should not serve as the basis for determining that a substantial right was violated, unless that technical violation had an impact on the outcome of the trial.

(2) When making the determination as to whether or not the error was harmless, the appellate court should consider the record in its entirety, it is improper to focus solely on the violation itself.

(3) The focus of the court is on whether or not the alleged error impacted the outcome of the trial – not the degree of proof available to the court as to the conviction.

(4) Precedent does not rule when dealing with harmless error, instead the court should use prior cases to assist in interpreting the present case on its own merits, not those of others.

(5) The focus must be on whether the error had an impact on the judgment at trial.

The appellate court should not speculate on what the outcome of a new trial might be with a different evidentiary ruling.

While the moving party has the burden of showing that evidentiary error was committed during the trial, practically speaking that burden is always connected to the follow on argument that the error alleged affected the judgment of the court. When briefing such issues both the appellant and appellee have similar burdens when briefing and arguing these points. Regardless of the local rules, it is best for the moving party to approach these issues as though they bear the burden of establishing the effect of error.

These appellate issues are made problematic by the existence of judicial discretion on the part of the trial judge. Examples of that discretion include determinations of the balancing test under FRE 403 (where the judge weighs the probative value of the evidence against the substantial danger of unfair prejudice), and what is more important, when making preliminary findings of fact upon which to base rulings, as allowed under FRE 104(a). These types of issues are normally reviewed at the appellate level by applying clear error doctrine.

Even when an error is made, the court can cure it during the trial. One common means of doing this is to properly instruct the jury with a *limiting instruction* that explains for what purposes evidence may be considered, directing that it be disregarded in certain instances, or by explaining it in other ways. When confronted with proper limiting instructions appellate courts will normally conclude that limiting instructions render any error in admitting evidence harmless. Other potential cures of evidentiary mistakes by the court include outcomes that establish that improperly admitted or excluded evidence was not considered by the fact finder, or the presence of other evidence that rebutted or neutralized the improperly admitted evidence. This fighting fire with fire approach has met with almost universal approval and use when courts confront this issue. Finally, in a criminal case a grant of mistrial would cure such issues because of the double jeopardy standard.

When thinking about error attorneys should take care to remember that if you invited the error to begin with you will have to live with it at the appellate level. This has an immediate impact on trial strategy, witness preparation, and methods of proof.

REVERSIBLE AND PLAIN ERROR

"Reversible error" is a mistake made at trial affecting a substantial right in such a serious way that that relief from the judgment is warranted. In other words, error is reversible as opposed to harmless when it affected the outcome of the trial. Courts usually define reversible error in the negative, focusing on how it is in fact "not harmless error." "Plain error" is more egregious than reversible error. It is obvious, egregious, serious, or some combination of those factors. When plain error occurs it is something that the judge should not have done, and the burden is not on counsel to have first objected. Think of it this way, some things are just not allowed to happen, and when they do there must be consequences – usually vacation of the judgment.

Plain error allows the court to note and correct errors sua sponte, either during the trial itself or in response to a post trial motion. They serve as a safety valve for the system. It is usually described in broad terms by the court, focusing on the overarching fact that the error in question is found in a mistake that is obvious on its face. Plain error attacks the very root of the justice system and must be dealt with when identified. The party that raises the issue has the burden of establishing that the mistake qualifies as plain error. When doing a review of these issues the court is confined to the record. Finally, appellate courts look carefully to see if the error was the result of a tactical decision made by the attorney. If there is a hint that such is the case they will not find plain error. The courts use it sparingly, if at all.

CONSTITUTIONAL ERROR

Unlike normal harmless error, a separate test exists for harmless error when it concerns a potential constitutional right of the accused. This special harmless error standard requires reversal unless the court believes beyond a reasonable doubt that the error did not affect the verdict. This standard was not always the case, and at one time it was believed that constitutional error, by its very nature, could not be harmless and when it was present automatic reversal was required. That is no longer the case.

The Supreme Court put that view to rest in *Chapman v. California*, which considered and rejected an automatic reversal rule for all constitutional errors. The court held instead that "some constitutional errors" may be "so unimportant and insignificant" in the setting of the case that they may be "deemed harmless." *Chapman* has greatly changed the analysis of constitutional error, creating a subcategory of analysis that did not exist before. It effectively expanded the category of harmless error, and subsequent decisions by the court have made it clear that most constitutional errors that involve evidentiary issues are judged under a harmless error standard. This heightens the focus that must be paid to evidentiary errors at trial, because the ability to overturn the finality of the verdict has been lessened by this series of cases.

If anything, *Chapman* and its progeny recognize that trials are human endeavors that will never be perfect. Examples of harmless constitutional error include:

(1) denying the right of confrontation as it pertains to cross examination,

(2) admitting hearsay in violation of the confrontation clause,

(3) admitting competing statements by codefendants identifying one another in violation of *Bruton,*

(4) commenting on the right of the accused to remain silent,

(5) admitting statements taken in violation of Miranda,

(6) admitting evidence that violated the accused's 4th amendment rights and the exclusionary rule found under *Mapp,*

(7) admitting evidence that violates either the accused's right to post offense silence, 6th amendment right to counsel and admitting confessions that violated the voluntariness doctrine.

It is important to note that nothing in these cases establishes a holding that all constitutional errors are subject to the harmless error standard. They do recognize that some constitutional issues can never be treated as harmless, and for those instances automatic reversal is still appropriate. Examples include:

(1) erroneous instructions on intent, or

(2) conclusive presumptions that reduce the need of the government to prove an element of a charged offense.

Finally, even though a harmless error standard now exists for constitutional issues, the court must determine to a beyond a reasonable doubt that the constitutional error did not affect the outcome of the trial.

DISCUSSION PROBLEMS 2-3

1. Do you agree with the Court's position that some constitutional errors do not matter? Explain your reasoning.

2. How might the categories of harmless error, reversible error, and constitutional error, impact your decisions at trial? Should they?

3. To what extent should appellate review standards affect trial decisions? Explain.

INITIAL ISSUES OF ADMISSIBILITY

What the Court Decides

Both the language and subsequent interpretation of FRE 104(a) are clear – the trial judge determines issues concerning admissibility of evidence, qualifications of witnesses, and privileges. In making those determinations the court is not constrained by the rules of evidence. The court is given this ability because the issues in question are "legal" in nature and therefore, within the purview of the judge.

When deciding these legal questions, the trial judge also decides factual questions that allow the court to rule on the legal issues. In other words, they make factual decisions to the extent necessary to allow them to render an opinion on the legal importance of the issue at hand. How does this work?

One of the legal questions that the court might need to determine is whether a proffered piece of testimony is admissible under the hearsay doctrine when it is clearly an out of court statement that the proponent is offering for the truth of the matter asserted. To determine whether the proffered statement meets the requirements of a hearsay exception, the court would have to consider the factual circumstances having an impact on how, when, or why the statement was made. To consider those circumstances the court would have to accept competing factual versions. This fact finding by the court is necessary for the limited purpose of making a legal conclusion and is authorized under FRE 104(a).

The court routinely addresses both factual and legal issues when considering and ruling on questions about admissibility, relevancy, impeachment, hearsay, and Best Evidence. Preliminary questions of admissibility in these situations can run the gamut from mostly legal to mostly factual, but in either instance FRE 104(a) gives the court the ability to decide them.

Rule 104. Preliminary Questions

(a) In General. The court must decide any preliminary question about whether a witness is qualified, a privilege exists, or evidence is admissible. In so deciding, the court is not bound by evidence rules, except those on privilege.

(b) Relevance That Depends on a Fact. When the relevance of evidence depends on whether a fact exists, proof must be introduced sufficient to support a finding that the fact does exist. The court may admit the proposed evidence on the condition that the proof be introduced later.

(c) Conducting a Hearing So That the Jury Cannot Hear It. The court must conduct any hearing on a preliminary question so that the jury cannot hear it if:

> (1) the hearing involves the admissibility of a confession;
> (2) a defendant in a criminal case is a witness and so requests; or
> (3) justice so requires.

The initial determination of whether a piece of evidence is relevant to the case at bar is made by the judge. There are normally two types of evidence that may be proffered, either "circumstantial" or "direct" evidence. When confronted with either type the judge must ask whether the evidence being offered makes a consequential fact more or less likely than it would be without the evidence. Although this determination is legal in nature, and properly within the purview of the trial judge, she looks at the question of relevancy in much the same way that the jury will. Initially, the judge asks how the proffered evidence will impact the proffered facts of the case. When answering that question the judge is supposed to consider his or her own life experiences and common sense. However, the judge, when making this determination, is also asking whether the proffered evidence will potentially have that effect on the decision making of a reasonable juror.

Judges also make what might be called "legal relevancy" decisions, meaning that they decide whether the probative value of a piece of evidence is outweighed by the substantial danger of unfair prejudice or confusion under FRE 403. These decisions are necessary because we realize that sometimes just because a piece of evidence is logically relevant does not necessarily mean that the jury should hear it. Sometimes there are very good legal policy reasons to prevent them from doing so. This rule allows the court to make that decision.

Decisions of legal relevancy are also made concerning impeachment of witnesses; which are questions of "admissibility." A classic example is the question of whether a witness' conviction for theft should be known by the jury to assist them in determining the witness' truthfulness. Judges are empowered to decide these preliminary questions under FRE 104(a). When a judge decides if a proffered statement fits a hearsay exception they often must make decisions of fact.

Judges decide, for example, whether proffered statements fit standard hearsay exceptions and in doing so they may have to decide factual questions. Judges also decide whether various evidentiary prerequisite conditions are satisfied, such as the declarant being unavailable to testify in a hearsay exception ruling, or the existence of corroboration. They also determine whether a statement or other conduct should even be considered hearsay, an important decision if it looks like the actor or speaker lacked assertive purpose or that what he said or did is to be used to prove something other than what was asserted.

Four basic procedural issues are implicated when dealing with preliminary questions presented to the judge. Practically speaking, should the jury observe the proceedings? Which party bears the burden of proof? What standard of proof applies? Do the Rules apply on these preliminary questions? We can find the answer to the first question posed, as well as the last, in FRE 104. However, the question does become more complicated when the accused testifies on preliminary issues – then the court must also determine the extent to which those statements of the accused can be used at other points in the proceedings.

FRE 104(c) requires hearings outside of the jury's presence on the admissibility of confessions, when the accused is a witness (if he requests), and when "the interests of justice require." The language was left vague in the belief that detailed treatment is not feasible and that practical concerns may militate against excluding the jury, particularly if evidence on preliminary matters is likely to be introduced on the merits.

Rule 104. Preliminary Questions

(c)   Conducting a Hearing So That the Jury Cannot Hear It.
The court must conduct any hearing on a preliminary question so that the jury cannot hear it if:

(1) the hearing involves the admissibility of a confession;

(2) a defendant in a criminal case is a witness and so requests; or

(3) justice so requires.

Rule 103. Rulings on Evidence

(c) Court's Statement About the Ruling; Directing an Offer of Proof. The court may make any statement about the character or form of the evidence, the objection made, and the ruling. The court may direct that an offer of proof be made in question-and-answer form.

Attorneys should read FRE 104(c) with FRE 103(c), which tells courts to conduct proceedings to the extent practicable to "prevent inadmissible evidence from being suggested to the jury" by offers of proof or otherwise. In practice, offers and objections tend to merge with the determination of preliminary matters, particularly if the judge asks for something beyond a short statement by the proponent and the adversary in resolving evidence issues. It is sometimes appropriate to exclude juries when parties explain or expand on objections or offers of proof, particularly if either party feels that just hearing the discussions about admissibility will unfairly prejudice the jury.

There are obvious reasons to hold hearings on admissibility outside of the jury's presence: One is to keep from exposing the jury to evidence that might ultimately be excluded, otherwise why bother with the hearing? The other is to keep the objecting party from having to incur additional risks (beyond those that come with objecting) by making arguments needed to support objections. These concerns often require excluding the jury from hearings on the admissibility of hearsay where the judge normally considers the statement itself in deciding whether it fits an exception. For similar reasons, preliminary questions on privilege claims should often be resolved outside the hearing of the jury.

On the other hand, preliminary questions on matters like personal knowledge of a witness or authentication of physical evidence are less likely to require this precaution and are less likely to create unfair prejudice. Often the judge is only answering a question of conditional relevancy under FRE 104(b), meaning that the judge would only be asking whether there was enough evidence to support a jury's finding – and that is a standard that is relatively easy to meet. Exposing the jury to the foundational facts and surrounding arguments on such points is not likely to be risky, even if the evidence is ultimately not admitted. Finally, much of the evidence and argument on these points relate to weight and credibility as well, and of course such matters are for juries to assess.

Rule 104. Preliminary Questions

(b) Relevance That Depends on a Fact. When the relevance of evidence depends on whether a fact exists, proof must be introduced sufficient to support a finding that the fact does exist. The court may admit the proposed evidence on the condition that the proof be introduced later.

The proponent normally bears the burden of proof on preliminary matters relating to admissibility of evidence. This makes sense, both from a traditional and ease of application perspective. The offering party is normally the party best situated to explain and justify the evidence proffered, and should be in the position to best assist the court in determining initial questions of admissibility. It also follows our tradition that the party requesting the court to do something has the burden of showing why the court should do it. Finally, this goes hand in hand with an adversarial system and works well in that format. Parties offering hearsay, establishing personal knowledge, qualifications of experts, basis of expert opinions, and applying the Daubert standard to the testimony of experts – these are all examples of burdens of proof.

Privilege issues are the opposite, with the burden resting on the one who would exclude, for they must show that a privilege applies. If that initial burden is met, then the party seeking to overcome the privilege bears the burden of showing some exception applies. Sometimes the privilege claimant has the benefit of presumptions that help carry the burden, other times they do not. For example, the authority of a lawyer to assert the attorney-client privilege on behalf of his client is presumed, and private spousal conversations are presumed to be confidential.

The preponderance standard applies to most court-determined preliminary questions (those relating to admissibility, witness competency, and privileges). This standard applies to preliminary questions in civil cases and to preliminary questions affecting evidence offered by both the prosecutor and the defendant in criminal cases.

The United States Supreme Court settled these standards in a series of decisions. In *Bourjaily v. United States,* the court held that the government bears the burden of establishing the predicate facts for the exception of a hearsay statement by a preponderance of the evidence. In *Huddleston v. United States* the Court brushed off any suggestion that the government needed to satisfy a higher standard when offering prior crimes evidence under FRE 404(b). The Court has repeatedly adopted this standard for important constitutional issues relating to evidence. We will look further at these cases when discussing hearsay and character evidence.

If proffered evidence is being offered conditionally, the proponent of the evidence need only establish enough proof of the fact in questions so that a reasonable jury might find it exists. Conditional relevancy is a difficult standard to truly understand and apply, made all the more so by the fact that questions of this nature rarely require specific jury instructions. Although there is little case law on what the standard of proof is for these issues, it is probably a preponderance of the evidence standard, given that the one area where it has been addressed is authentication, and the court did adopt a preponderance standard in that instance.

Everyday Evidence: A Practical Approach

Rule 404. Character Evidence; Crimes or Other Acts

(b) Crimes, Wrongs, or Other Acts.

(1) *Prohibited Uses.* Evidence of a crime, wrong, or other act is not admissible to prove a person's character in order to show that on a particular occasion the person acted in accordance with the character.

(2) *Permitted Uses; Notice in a Criminal Case.* This evidence may be admissible for another purpose, such as proving motive, opportunity, intent, preparation, plan, knowledge, identity, absence of mistake, or lack of accident. On request by a defendant in a criminal case, the prosecutor must:

(A) provide reasonable notice of the general nature of any such evidence that the prosecutor intends to offer at trial; and

(B) do so before trial — or during trial if the court, for good cause, excuses lack of pretrial notice.

FRE 104(a) does not bind the judge with evidentiary rules when making preliminary decisions, except for when the court is deciding an issue of privilege. When a claim of privilege is made, if the reason for the hearing is to determine the validity of the claim of privilege, the court may require the disclosure of the allegedly privileged material, except for material that is allegedly privileged based upon a claim of improper self incrimination.

Rule 104. Preliminary Questions

(a) In General. The court must decide any preliminary question about whether a witness is qualified, a privilege exists, or evidence is admissible. In so deciding, the court is not bound by evidence rules, except those on privilege.

FRE 104(a), which says the judge "is not bound by the rules of evidence" (other than privileges) in deciding questions of admissibility, changed traditional practice of requiring separate predicate facts to prove the admissibility of a hearsay statement. The language of the rule can be read to mean that judges can find preliminary facts like conspiracy and agency by relying on the statement. In the setting of coconspirator statements the Supreme Court decided in the *Bourjaily* case that the judge may indeed look at the statements in determining the issue of conspiracy, reasoning that out-of-court statements are not necessarily unreliable (they are only "presumed unreliable") and that the "sum" of all the relevant pieces of evidence (including the statement being offered) "may well be greater than its constituent parts."

In 1998, the coconspirator exception was amended to adopt the *Bourjaily* holding, including the hint in *Bourjaily* that at least *some* independent evidence should still be required. At the same time, the exceptions for authorized admissions and for admissions by agents were amended to adopt the *Bourjaily* approach, meaning that the statement itself can be considered in deciding whether the necessary conditions are satisfied, but independent evidence is also required. We will visit both of these cases again when we discuss Hearsay.

THE JURY DECIDES

FRE 104(b) establishes that the jury has the responsibility of deciding whether a condition of fact has been fulfilled when determining the relevancy of that piece of evidence. This allows juries to sort out the fragmented stories that are told by counsel, empowering them to connect those fragments when making their decisions as the finder of fact. FRE 104(b) codified the approach that separate items of evidence may be interdependent, making accepting or rejecting one item an action that would increase or decrease the importance of another. FRE 104(b) confirms that juries play a vital role in assessing such matters of conditional facts. Practically speaking, it is what juries are charged to accomplish, and without this approach it would be difficult to accomplish. Under this rule the jury can hear pieces of evidence from different witnesses under the theory that when they are taken together their relevancy becomes evident, being conditional upon other facts proven.

Unfortunately, conditional relevancy is deeply problematic. In even the simplest trials, much of the evidence may only make sense when considered by the jury in conjunction with other evidence. The ability to stop the trial and continuously instruct the jurors about this decision making process would be practically impossible. Instead, we take on faith the ability of the jury to connect such conditional facts, once the court has allowed their presence in the trial.

The jury also considers issues of authentication under FRE 104(b). The framers of the federal rules made it clear that questions on authenticity of documentary evidence and identification of other kinds of real evidence are examples of conditional relevancy for the jury to resolve under FRE 104(b).

Rule 104. Preliminary Questions

(b) Relevance That Depends on a Fact. When the relevance of evidence depends on whether a fact exists, proof must be introduced sufficient to support a finding that the fact does exist. The court may admit the proposed evidence on the condition that the proof be introduced later.

FRE 104(b) also allows the jury to determine whether a witness satisfies the personal knowledge requirement of FRE 602. The side calling the witness establishes, in the initial phase, of the direct that the witness personally observed the acts or occurrences about which he is to testify. If the opposing party objects as to the witness' knowledge the question becomes one for the jury to decide - the judge plays a screening role envisioned by FRE 104(b): The witness will be allowed to testify if the judge concludes that enough evidence of knowledge is offered to enable a reasonable jury to conclude that he had that knowledge. The threshold is not high, and even a brief chance to observe suffices. Normally if this objection is raised, the best practice is for the judge to not allow questioning to proceed until the offering party makes a sufficient showing to support the necessary finding of personal knowledge by the jury.

Rule 602. Need for Personal Knowledge

A witness may testify to a matter only if evidence is introduced sufficient to support a finding that the witness has personal knowledge of the matter. Evidence to prove personal knowledge may consist of the witness's own testimony. This rule does not apply to a witness's expert testimony under Rule 703

LIMITING INSTRUCTIONS

As a practical matter, almost every piece of evidence that is admitted at trial is properly used for some purpose, but potentially improperly used for others. The tool used by the court to ensure that the evidence admitted at trial is properly used is a limiting instruction under FRE 105.

Rule 105. Limiting Evidence That Is Not Admissible Against Other Parties or for Other Purposes

If the court admits evidence that is admissible against a party or for a purpose — but not against another party or for another purpose — the court, on timely request, must restrict the evidence to its proper scope and instruct the jury accordingly.

There are several different reasons for the potential improper use of evidence at trial. Consider for a moment that many of the restrictions on the use of evidence come from evidentiary rules governing hearsay, impeachment, and various aspects of relevancy. These restrictions allow for some uses of the proffered evidence, but not others. Additionally, modern trials often involve multiple claims, charges, and defenses, each resting on substantive case theories that in turn make different kinds of evidence relevant or irrelevant, important or unimportant. The reality of complex litigation requires such a rule. Finally, out-of-court statements that do not qualify for a hearsay exception or exclusion may nonetheless be allowed for limited purposes. Common appropriate uses include impeachment, establishing verbal acts, and explaining the effect that the out-of-court statement had on the listener or declarant. Such statements are also often admitted to show the basis for expert testimony even when they cannot be used to prove what they assert as a hearsay statement.

Among the methods of impeachment, some bring serious problems of limiting the use of the evidence to its proper purpose. Prior inconsistent statements are one example. They are typically admissible to show vacillation but not to prove what they assert. By the same token, prior bad acts or convictions are often usable to suggest that the witness is untruthful, but if the witness is also either the accused or victim in a criminal case, or the respondent or plaintiff in a civil case were the character rules apply, the bad acts and convictions cannot be used to show he committed the charged crime or committed the tort or other act underlying a civil claim or defense. We will discuss this propensity rule in the chapter addressing character evidence of parties at trial. Impeachment by contradiction often involves evidence that would otherwise be excluded under some Rule or constitutional restriction. It is admissible only to refute something the witness has said (and suggest more generally that he should not be believed) and not to prove other points that it might naturally tend to prove.

Evidence is routinely admissible against one defendant but not another in a criminal case, and courts routinely admit such evidence with limiting instructions. The Supreme Court supports this approach, identifying it as necessary to the jury system. The court criticized "unfounded speculation" that jurors might disregard limiting instructions. Courts in criminal trials routinely admit prior convictions of one of several codefendants and real evidence like guns or demonstrative evidence like photographs that are linked only to one defendant. In those cases, the courts rely on limiting instructions to guide the jury, and only occasionally do the unwanted "spillover effects" require such evidence to be excluded altogether.

FRE 105 requires the trial judge, upon request, to restrict evidence to its proper purpose when evidence is admissible against one party but not others, or for some purpose but not others. The task to ask for such instructions rests on the shoulders of the counsel, and not the court. Normally failure to give limiting instructions, when counsel has not requested it, is not reversible error. Occasionally, the evidence in question is so obviously admissible for only a limited purpose and so clearly possible of creating serious prejudice to the opponent that there are reversals on the basis of the plain error doctrine even in the absence of a request for instructions, but that is not the norm.

The timing of limiting instructions may be critical. Normally the judge has discretion either immediately to instruct or to include limiting instructions with the general charge at the end of the case. Sometimes courts require immediate instructions on the ground that the passage of time and accumulation of other evidence make it hard to accomplish the intended purpose at the end of the case.

Normally the judge will not give limiting instructions unless requested, and should also not insist on giving instructions if the intended beneficiary objects. Still, the discretion of the court on this issue is quite broad, and sometimes the judge may give limiting instructions over objection. The court should, however, solicit and respect the views of counsel on the desirability of instructions, to protect the role of counsel in assessing the risk of jury misuse of the evidence, as required by their function under the rules.

DISCUSSION PROBLEM 2-4
Asking for a Limiting Instruction

During direct examination your witness testified that she had never seen the defendant before the night he allegedly assaulted her. On cross examination the defense counsel impeached your witness, the alleged victim, with a prior inconsistent statement she made to her best friend. About two weeks after the alleged assault the alleged victim told her friend that she had met the defendant a few weeks before a local dance club. You objected, but the judge overruled your objection and allowed the testimony for purposes of impeachment only.

How do you respond? Identify with specificity what you would do and say to the court, with appropriate reference to relevant evidentiary rules and factual predicates. When preparing your response you should consider:

1. How do you address this with the court?

2. What specific issues did you consider when deciding how to deal the possibility of a limiting instruction?

3. What impact will this jury instruction have on your case? How? Why?

RULE OF COMPLETENESS
The Rule of Completeness—When and How, Limits

When parts of a written or recorded statement are offered, as opposed to the entire statement, FRE 106 entitles opposing parties to introduce other parts of the statement that helps place in context the portions of the statement that has already been introduced.

The additional portion may be offered immediately after the statement is first mentioned, during cross-examination of the testifying witness, or later, through the testimony of other witnesses.

FRE 106 goes further - it entitles other parties to require their proponent, as part of the original presentation, to include other parts of the writing or recorded statement that ought in fairness to be considered with the parts that the proponent wants to use. The idea behind this rule comes from an understanding that sometimes waiting until later is just not good enough, context matters when making determinations of credibility about statements. Finally, the contextual data is more easily understood if it is provided contemporaneously. FRE 106 allows the court to interrupt a party's presentation to permit the other side to insist that other relevant parts of a statement be offered, and in effect to offer them.

> **Rule 106. Remainder of or Related Writings or Recorded Statements**
>
> If a party introduces all or part of a writing or recorded statement, an adverse party may require the introduction, at that time, of any other part — or any other writing or recorded statement — that in fairness ought to be considered at the same time.

All of this is allowed, even though there may very well be good reasons that the proponent of the statement only wishes to offer part of the statement. Such reasons may include relevancy – either legal or logical, exigencies of proof, or when part of the writing may be admissible while another part may not. In these instances FRE 106 may not require that the rest of the statement be admitted. The court should focus on the reason cited for completing the statement. The purpose of FRE 106 is not to insist on completeness as an end in itself, but to allow others to insist on admitting enough to put a statement in context.

FRE 106 does not apply to statements not memorialized in permanent form. However, fairness in presenting evidence of other statements may require courts to observe the common law principle of completeness, and courts sometimes invoke it in this setting. That approach is justified under ordinary notions of relevancy found in FRE 401-403, and reflects the common law idea that completeness should extend to statements that have not been written or recorded.

The completeness rule applies to letters and records, recordings, and documents. This rule applies to medical records in civil cases offered to prove diagnosis, treatment, condition, or for those used as the basis for expert testimony. It applies where selective use of some passages while ignoring others might mislead the finder of fact if not corrected through the use of the rule of completeness. The rule of completeness also applies to depositions and other prior testimony offered at trial.

When impeaching a witness with prior inconsistent statements, the general rule is that impeachment by showing a prior inconsistency on some point does not pave the way for showing a prior consistent statement on the same point (the inconsistency remains). The completeness doctrine will also apply in circumstances where the inconsistent statement was isolated from a larger statement in such way that its use is misleading during the impeachment.

If the state is attempting to admit portions of the accused's statement(s) while omitting others, the accused may request that the court require the prosecutor who wants to offer parts of the admission or confession to introduce at the same time both the incriminating and self-serving or exculpatory parts that should in fairness be heard and considered contemporaneously. If the prosecutor introduces only a portion, while also deleting self-serving or exculpatory remarks that the accused wishes to have heard by the jury, the rule of completeness requires the court to allow the additional remarks. FRE 106 applies if the statement is written or recorded, regardless of whether it admits all necessary elements of guilt (a confession in the fullest sense) or only states some relevant fact (an ordinary admission).

FRE 106 applies not only to different parts of the same statement, but to different statements, recognizing that mechanical interpretations of what makes a statement or what must be shown to reach an adequate understanding of a statement are not helpful in applying this rule. FRE 106 authorizes the court, when asked to do so by the adverse party, to require the proponent to introduce not only the recorded statement they wish to introduce, but also other written or recorded statements that should in fairness be considered. If the proponent fails to do so the court should allow the adverse party to admit the statement(s) in question.

JUDICIAL NOTICE

Judicial Notice of Facts

Litigants use judicial notice to establish the existence of a fact necessary to support their case without using the formal means of evidentiary proof. It is, in a very real sense, a substitute process for admitting evidence, relying on the ability of the court to take notice of certain types of facts that are not in controversy. The concept of judicial notice was created at the common law to avoid the time and expense of proving facts that are not contestable. Using judicial notice benefits all the parties involved, to include the court and litigants.

FRE 201 addresses the scope and procedures for taking judicial notice in federal courts. Many state courts have adopted similar provisions. FRE 201(a) establishes that the rule governs judicial notice of adjudicative facts. This rule is not designed, and should not be used, for legislative or basic facts.

Rule 201. Judicial Notice of Adjudicative Facts

(a) Scope. This rule governs judicial notice of an adjudicative fact only, not a legislative fact.

FRE 201(b) allows a court to take judicial notice of an adjudicative fact where it is "not subject to reasonable dispute" either because it is "generally known" (for example,

Chicago is located in the state of Illinois) or readily verifiable by reliable sources (May 5, 1961, was a Friday).

Rule 201. Judicial Notice of Adjudicative Facts

(b) Kinds of Facts That May Be Judicially Noticed. The court may judicially notice a fact that is not subject to reasonable dispute because it:

> (1) is generally known within the trial court's territorial jurisdiction; or

> (2) can be accurately and readily determined from sources whose accuracy cannot reasonably be questioned.

FRE 201(c) establishes that the court may take judicial notice sua sponte, while FRE 201(d) forces the court to take judicial notice when requested by a party and supplied with the necessary information. FRE 201(e) guarantees the parties an opportunity to be heard on the propriety of taking judicial notice. It gives litigants that wish to object to the taking of judicial notice a specific means to do so. FRE 201(f) allows judicial notice to be taken at any stage of the proceeding. Under this rule a judge can take notice of adjudicative facts only during trial, during pretrial, and post trial proceedings, as well as on appeal.

Rule 201. Judicial Notice of Adjudicative Facts

(c) Taking Notice. The court:

> (1) may take judicial notice on its own; or

> (2) must take judicial notice if a party requests it and the court is supplied with the necessary information.

(d) Timing. The court may take judicial notice at any stage of the proceeding.

(e) Opportunity to Be Heard. On timely request, a party is entitled to be heard on the propriety of taking judicial notice and the nature of the fact to be noticed. If the court takes judicial notice before notifying a party, the party, on request, is still entitled to be heard.

(f) Instructing the Jury. In a civil case, the court must instruct the jury to accept the noticed fact as conclusive. In a criminal case, the court must instruct the jury that it may or may not accept the noticed fact as conclusive.

In order for the notice to be effective during a jury trial the judge must inform the jury by instruction of the fact to be noticed. FRE 201(g) lays out the form that the instruction should take and establishes that notice of adjudicative facts is binding in civil cases and permissive in criminal cases. It is important to not that judicial notice in a criminal case cannot shift the burden of proof as to any element of an offense.

While FRE 201 does not directly apply to the determination of preliminary questions of fact affecting the admissibility of evidence, courts often follow the provisions of 201 when doing so. Think of it as a logical construct that is used in a permissive fashion to guide the thought process of the court when determining the admissibility of certain preliminary evidentiary issues. Similarly, it is not used during preliminary examinations in criminal cases, probation revocations, or sentencing hearings, which are exempted from application of the Federal Rules of Evidence by FRE 1101(d).

Rule 1101. Applicability of Rules

(d)   **Exceptions.** These rules — except for those on privilege — do not apply to the following:

      (1)   the court's determination, under Rule 104(a), on a preliminary question of fact governing admissibility;

      (2)   grand-jury proceedings; and

      (3)   miscellaneous proceedings such as:

            ·extradition or rendition;

            ·issuing an arrest warrant, criminal summons, or search warrant;

            ·a preliminary examination in a criminal case;

            ·sentencing;

            ·granting or revoking probation or supervised release; and

            ·considering whether to release on bail or otherwise.

Indisputability of the Adjudicative Fact Required

FRE 201(b) allows the court to take judicial notice of adjudicative facts that are "not subject to reasonable dispute." This standard serves as a preventive one, significantly limiting the facts that are subject to notice. It is required, at least in part, because of the effect of taking notice. Notice of adjudicative facts is binding in civil cases, and improper notice in criminal cases can be harmful. Binding notice has the effect of reducing the adversarial nature of the process while infringing on the right to trial by jury.

While the rule does not define "Adjudicative facts," the Advisory Committee's Note cites a useful definition: "[A]djudicative facts are those to which the law is applied in the process of adjudication. They are the facts that normally go to the jury in a jury case." In other words these are the facts that the jury must use to assist in determining the outcome of the case.

Think of them as the answers to the basic questions of who, what, when, where, how and with what motive or intent. This is a key point, the facts that courts take judicial notice of should be adjudicative in nature, although courts have frequently taken judicial notice of facts that do not meet this definition. Facts concerning dates, tide tables, phases of the moon, boundaries, and world history are often subjects of judicial notice, while they may not be directly related to the litigants, they are often helpful to the jury in determining the credibility of more on point adjudicative facts. They are, nonetheless, easily determinable and not subject to argument. The courts do routinely take notice of them under FRE 201 for practical reasons as much as anything else – it makes the trial go smoother.

Given this preference for taking judicial notice of facts that are not technically adjudicative in nature, it is best to consider adjudicative facts as those facts that are necessary to prove or are used to prove a question of fact as distinguished from a question of law. In other words, if the court did not take notice of the fact in question, someone would need to prove it.

The party requesting notice of the adjudicative fact bears the burden of proving the standard of FRE 201(b) is satisfied. The opponent may object, offering evidence that the matter is subject to reasonable dispute. Notice may be taken upon a finding of indisputability as to the fact in question, or refused if a reasonable dispute exists as to the factual nature of the proffered fact. The reach of the ability to take notice applies to the adjudicative facts "generally known" within the territorial jurisdiction of the trial court. This is not a universal knowledge requirement.

General knowledge can be established by showing that the fact is generally known by well-informed persons within the district, or even within the geographical subdivision of the district where the case is being tried. Although the personal experience or private knowledge of the judge is not a proper foundation for judicial notice, trial judges occasionally overlook this well-established rule.

This standard covers a large area of knowledge, including current events, geography, language, word usage, history, politics, economic conditions, and other similar facts as the court may determine. Sometimes the trial court will take notice of facts that are not normally even adjudicative in nature. It is noteworthy that one area where courts are loathe to take notice involves the mental state or intent of an individual.

FRE 201(b)(2) authorizes judicial notice of facts beyond reasonable dispute because they are subject to accurate and ready verification. The court and litigants may use resources whose accuracy cannot reasonably be questioned. This does not yet include Wikipedia, but even online resources may suffice in assisting the parties in determining whether the proffered fact is beyond dispute. The courts have taken notice of a veritable plethora of verifiable facts, including: geography, science, history, hard sciences, politics, government records and regulations, dates, languages, learned treatises, court records and files, administrative records, agency records, and the outcome of previous adjudicative proceedings. They have also taken judicial notice of general principles underlying well-recognized scientific instruments, tests or procedures, or the acceptance of such tests or procedures in the scientific community. The case law clearly shows that courts take judicial notice, sometimes when the fact is not even clearly adjudicative in nature.

The party requesting notice bears the burden of providing a source on which notice can be based, and establishing that the provided source's accuracy cannot be questioned. Historically courts have been reluctant to treat newspapers as such a source, and decisions are split on the issue of whether websites qualify.

The source identified and proffered need not qualify for admission separately under the FRE. This is allowed because FRE 201 replaces formal proof. It is analogous to the resolution of a question preliminary to the admissibility of evidence under FRE 104(a). Just as under FRE 104(a), parties can offer their proof and counterproof on the propriety of taking notice without being constrained by the rules of evidence, except the rules of privilege. The court can consult additional sources it finds reliable in deciding whether the proof satisfies the requirements of FRE 201(b). Whatever sources are used in determining whether judicial notice will be taken should be clearly stated in the record of trial.

TAKING NOTICE

The starting point in analyzing this rule is to remember that a trial judge has discretion to take judicial notice under FRE 201(c) whether the parties request it. The rule is drafted to accommodate the exercise of judicial prerogative, but the courts usually will not take judicial notice if a party indicates a preference for offering evidence on the point based upon their case analysis.

Sometimes the court does not have discretion, but must take notice. FRE 201(d) establishes that judicial notice will be taken when a party requests it and supplies the court with the necessary information to establish the indisputability of the proffered fact. This allows parties that wish to use judicial notice to rely on it as a method of establishing reasonably indisputable facts at trial. Judicial notice functions as a shortcut removing the need for formal proof, and neither the source itself nor secondary evidence used to verify its accuracy is required to meet the admissibility standards that would normally be applied before admitting such evidence.

There is not a specific notice requirement for judicial notice, and the rule is designed to prevent automatic error if the judge fails to provide notice. The rule also allows for counsel to be given an opportunity to be heard when they request judicial notice.

A court may take judicial notice at a party's request or on its own initiative. If a party requests notice, the request itself constitutes notice to the adverse party, and no additional notice requirements are necessary. Given this fact, the only real chance for notice to not be provided occurs when the court takes judicial notice sua sponte. Requests to be heard on issues of judicial notice must be made in a timely matter, and can be either oral or in writing. The Rule specifies no time period, but timeliness should be construed to mean as soon as it is reasonable, considering the stage and schedule of the proceedings. Usually these issues are not controversial, often being so firmly in the scope of FRE 201 that a hearing is not requested or required.

INSTRUCTING THE JURY

FRE 201(g) is one of the few provisions in the Federal Rules of Evidence that draws a significant distinction between civil and criminal proceedings. In civil cases, once the court has taken judicial notice of an adjudicative fact the court instructs the jury to accept the fact judicially noticed. This is not the case in criminal cases, where the fact judicially noticed does not bind the jury. It functions instead as a permissible inference or comment on the evidence that the jury is allowed, but not required, to accept as conclusive any fact judicially noticed. The jury is free to disregard and ignore it.

Effects of Judicial Notice

Once judicial notice is taken in a civil case the opposing party cannot present evidence rebutting the fact noticed. This makes sense, given that allowing such rebutting evidence would undermine the purpose of judicial notice, permitting the very irrational results that judicial notice rules are designed to help prevent. If parties' wish to challenge a fact noticed it must occur during the hearing process allowed under FRE 201(3). Once the court has judicially noticed an adjudicative fact a litigant cannot challenge the court's decision by presenting contrary evidence to the jury and cannot urge the jury to disregard a judicially noticed fact.

FRE 201(g) provides that judicial notice is not conclusive in criminal cases, but functions instead as a permissive inference. Opposing parties in criminal cases are not explicitly barred from presenting evidence rebutting judicially noticed facts in criminal cases, but such presentations might best be served during the initial hearing under FRE 201(e). However, given the ability of the jury to ignore the court, it may well make sense at trial to present such evidence to jury, although the court may not appreciate it.

Judicial Notice of Law

Sometimes courts take judicial notice of laws that apply in a particular case. The determination of controlling law is a classic judicial function undertaken so that the court can make proper legal rulings and instruct the jury at the conclusion of the trial. There is not a specific rule allowing for this, but it is authorized by rules of procedure and the common law.

At common law, the term "judicial notice" was used to distinguish between law that was considered known by the court and law that the parties had to prove. A court would take "judicial notice" of domestic law, relieving the parties of the burden of offering formal proof. When the issue was one of foreign law, formal proof was generally required, usually in the form of authenticated copies of cases and statutes, affidavits, and testimony of expert witnesses.

Under the current view applied in most courts, if parties must establish applicable law, the court makes the determination rather than the jury, allowing informal proof not subject to the rules of evidence. Often a statute or rule of procedure specifically authorizes the court to take judicial notice of a particular law, relieving the parties of the burden of formally proving such law, saving the court time and the litigants' money. In federal courts, the scope of judicial notice of law and the procedures for taking such notice are regulated by case law, statutes, and the Federal Rules of Civil and Criminal Procedure. Federal courts take judicial notice of the United States Constitution, federal statutes, and federal case law, as well as the constitutions, statutes, and case law of every state of the union.

During the twentieth century, there has been a steady trend toward expansion of the categories of law subject to "judicial notice." Despite this fact, the rules governing judicial notice of law remain an incomplete hodgepodge of cobbled together procedures. State statutes are sometimes silent on issues such as pleading the law, notice, informing the parties of notice, as well as the evidentiary standards govern proof of law offered by the parties.

BURDENS & PRESUMPTIONS

Civil Cases - Burdens of Pleading, Production, and Persuasion

1. Pleadings

Burdens are one of the most troublesome areas of evidentiary law to teach effectively. Courts react to the requests of litigants, so we normally talk in terms of the litigants carrying certain burdens when requesting a court order or judgment. This can create issues, particularly when sliding down the slippery slope of how to define and impose burdens on the parties involved. There are three primary areas where this can occur – pleadings, production, and persuasion.

The burden of pleading is really not a difficult one to understand and implement. The improvement in legal drafting has resulted in claims and defenses that are set out in a straightforward manner. Most questions and answers are plain and clear, amendments are allowed. One of the results of this is that motions to dismiss for failure to state a claim or motions for judgment on the pleadings are rarely successful. The discovery process, as opposed to the pleadings process, drives trials much more in the current legal environment. Many jurisdictions have pattern books that take the mystery out of pleadings, and those that don't often have statutes or regulations that accomplish the same function.

Sometimes though, courts will use pleading rules as a method to achieve faster results. This reflects the growing reliance upon expanded statutory schemes and rights, with a preference by the court to use those to control the process of litigation. Some courts are beginning to experiment again with heightened pleading requirements. They understand how relaxed pleadings rules can both prolong cases and force settlements due to litigation pressures as opposed to the litigation itself. Despite these attempts by the lower courts, the United States Supreme Court has clearly identified its disapproval of such efforts.   Nevertheless, some statutory schemes still impose additional pleading burdens to accomplish goals identified within the statute.

Eventually litigants shift from the pleadings process to the trial process, where two burdens come in to play – burdens of proof and burdens of persuasion. The term "burden of proof" embraces two related but different concepts that come into play at trial. One is the burden of producing evidence. The other is the burden of persuasion.

2. Production and Persuasion

When the trial begins, the party bearing the burden of producing evidence normally also has the burden of persuasion. When a party bears the burden of producing evidence, they run the risk of losing automatically (on a motion to dismiss or for judgment as a matter of law) if they cannot offer sufficient evidence to enable a reasonable person to find in their favor. Once the party satisfies their burden of producing evidence supporting their case, the party has earned the right to have the fact finder consider and weigh the produced evidence. Ordinarily burdens of pleading, producing evidence, and persuading the trier of fact are all cast on the same party because of the way in which the suit has been plead. The pleadings produce a helpful guide to the way in which trial burdens are allocated.

When a party bears the burden of persuasion, they can only win when the evidence they produce at trial seems more likely true than not – depending upon the burden of proof required by the action. Courts refer to this burden of persuasion (proof) as one that never shifts. It is normally addressed in jury trials during arguments and instructions.

3. The Burden of Production

The burden of production is the requirement that the party attempting to prevail at trial must introduce sufficient evidence to support findings of fact in their favor. Plaintiffs normally carry both the burden of production and the burden of persuasion at trial. Meeting the burden of production prevents the opposing side from terminating the case by seeking and receiving a directed verdict at the close of the plaintiff's case. This is often referred to as having established a prima facie case. Failure to do so means that there was not a sufficiency of evidence produced, and a judgment as a matter of law is usually the result. When that occurs the court takes the decision away from the fact finder.

Once the party with the burden of production meets their burden, their opposing counsel must now produce evidence to counter the evidence already produced, otherwise they lose. How much evidence must be offered during the opposing counsel's case to avoid a directed verdict in favor of the plaintiff is a confusing question that many jurisdictions struggle with. They vary in both the quantum and quality of evidence that must be produced by the opposing side. The terms cogent and compelling are often used, but they are not uniformly applied across jurisdictions within the federal system.

4. The Burden of Persuasion

On most issues in the typical civil trial, the burden of persuasion rests on the plaintiff, who must prove the elements of her case, although the defendant bears the burden of persuasion on affirmative defenses. A party carries the burden of persuasion by introducing evidence that persuades the judge or jury to find that they have presented facts necessary to prevail. Ordinarily, a party must first carry the burden of production on claims or defenses on which she bears the burden of persuasion. Whether she has done so is a question of law for the judge to decide, as a matter of sufficiency of the evidence. The court addresses this as a question of law - when opposing counsel raises the issue after the close of the plaintiff's case. The question as to whether or not the plaintiff carried the burden of persuasion is a question of fact that the finder of fact, the jury in jury trials and the bench in judge alone trials, as a matter of weight of the evidence.

The burden of persuasion becomes most important when the proof is in and the parties rest their cases. It is the issue that is addressed in the jury instructions and the burden that is argued during closings. The burden of persuasion in civil cases is defined as a preponderance of the evidence. This standard applies unless there is some special important individual interest or right that is at stake. For a plaintiff to prevail she must prove each element of her case by a preponderance of the produced evidence. Under this standard the jury must be persuaded that the elements are more probably proved than not proved.

The preponderance standard is the most generous or lenient standard possible. It is satisfied if the factfinder believes by the thinnest conceivable margin that the points to be proved are so, and anything less would not be a standard of proof at all. The volume of evidence produced is not relevant; its quality is – in other words, how persuasive was the testimony.

While the preponderance standard is normally applied in civil cases, in certain types of cases a higher standard of "clear and convincing evidence" applies. Those include civil commitment cases, termination of parental rights, and deportation and denaturalization cases, where the Court has found that due process requires more persuasive proof. Additionally, our common law tradition typically requires proof to satisfy a similar high standard in cases claiming fraud or undue influence, suits to set aside or reform a contract for fraud or mistake, suits on oral contracts to make a will or seeking to establish the terms of a lost will, suits for specific performance of an oral contract, and in other special situations involving disfavored claims or defenses.

Presumptions

Presumptions require the finder of fact to draw conclusions based upon certain facts. Once the basic facts are established, the trier of fact must find the presumed fact, unless other evidence is produced tending to disprove it. Presumptions do have the effect of shifting the burden of production to the party that would be negatively affected by the presumption. When enough counterproof has been offered, the presumption disappears and it becomes a question of fact for the jury. In other words, once the basic facts of a presumption are established, it controls, unless evidence to the contrary is offered and accepted by the court.

The general rule in the federal system is that presumptions do not affect the burden of persuasion (only the burden of production). Thus FRE 301 says a presumption "does not shift" to the other side "the burden of proof in the sense of the risk of nonpersuasion."

FRE 301 applies only in cases "not otherwise provided for by Act of Congress." This language exempts federal statutory presumptions, and the courts may give such presumptions greater effect than FRE 301 would normally allow under the evidentiary rule.

Civil presumptions act in much the same way as burdens of production and persuasion. Just like those burdens, presumptions assist the court in implementing substantive policies making claims or defenses easier or harder to maintain, ensuring parties with better access to proof will produce it, providing relief to parties less able to obtain evidence, establishing what is most likely to be true anyway, and resolving cases where definitive proof is unavailable.

FRE 302 stands for the proposition that state presumptions are matters of substance rather than procedure for *Erie* purposes when they bear on elements of claims or defenses that are governed by state law. In such cases, FRE 302 requires federal courts to give state presumptions the same effect state law would give them. This provision virtually assumes that federal courts under *Erie* recognize and apply state presumptions because they are substantive law. Many common presumptions bear on elements of claims or defenses and fit the terms of FRE 302. The phrase "element of a claim or defense" in FRE 302 should be construed to encompass any fact providing direct support of elements even if the fact itself is not directly related to the element.

Beyond a Reasonable Doubt

American jurisprudence requires a higher standard of proof in criminal case, in part because the consequences of an erroneous verdict include loss of liberty or even life. A fundamental value inherent in our legal system is that criminal trials must safeguard against the wrongful conviction of the innocent even at the price of sometimes allowing the guilty to go free.

The common law developed a standard that the state must prove an accused guilty "beyond a reasonable doubt." Because this standard was so widely accepted by case law, statutes, and state constitutions, the issue seldom arose whether it was required as a component of due process guaranteed by the federal constitution. In the *Winship* case, the Supreme Court finally addressed the question and held that "the Due Process Clause protects the accused against conviction except upon proof beyond a reasonable doubt of every fact necessary to constitute the crime with which he is charged."

It is generally agreed that the beyond reasonable doubt standard applies to each element of the crime but not to each piece of evidence offered to prove an element. This standard does not apply to preliminary questions that the trial judge decides under FRE 104(a), such as whether a witness qualifies as an expert, or an out-of-court statement fits a hearsay exception, or a confession was voluntary.

Presumptions in Criminal Cases

Courts and legislatures have created what are often called "presumptions," which, because of constitutional constraints, may only operate as inferences. They have been designed to help prosecutors carry the heavy burden imposed on the state in criminal cases. For example, mens rea can be very difficult to prove with direct evidence. Despite that fact, intent may be strongly "suggested" by the actions of the defendant. Many jurisdictions recognize this fact, and allow for a presumption inferring mens rea based upon an inference of intent that is established by certain behaviors. In such a situation, if the state offers evidence proving the charged act, they may be entitled to an instruction that a person usually intends the natural and probable consequences of his voluntary actions.

It can be difficult to correctly frame a presumption instruction because such instructions may not serve as a substitute for evidence that was not admitted, or improperly enhance or supplement proffered evidence to the point that it goes beyond the probative force normally associated with the proffered evidence. Even the mildest language that urges or reassures the jury may create an improper presumption. As a result courts have multiple concerns about presumptions in criminal cases and they are viewed with suspicion – dragons tend to inhabit them, and dragons can be dangerous.

Some improper effects noted from presumption instructions include:

> (1)   Diluting or undercutting the requirement of proof beyond a reasonable doubt;
>
> (2)   serving as an adverse comment on the fact that the accused has not testified, or
>
> (3)   depriving the accused of the right to a jury trial on important factual issues.

Each of these potential improper effects from a presumptions instruction create mistrial issues, or winning appellate arguments. What is more important, they would deny the accused the constitutional right to a fair trial. When statutes required or invited these instructions, it raises questions about legislative determination (or predetermination) of points that courts rightly think they should decide, such as the sufficiency of evidence.

-Notes-

Chapter 3: Logical and Legal Relevancy

FUNDAMENTALS

Your entire study of evidentiary law can fairly be placed under the heading of relevancy. Relevancy permeates any discussion of evidentiary law, and is the predicate question that must be answered before we address other potential bars to admissibility. It is also the last question raised before evidence is usually admitted. We will continually ask ourselves about the relevancy of evidence throughout this text.

FRE 401, 402 and 403 address logical and legal relevancy. These are rules of logical and legal relevance. Relevancy is the first and last question asked in most court situations. FRE 401 identifies the logical relevancy standard. When determining whether the proffered evidence is relevant the court will consider both its logical and legal relevance. Logical relevance is a low threshold requirement. FRE 401 requires that evidence having any tendency to make the existence of a fact that is of consequence to the determination or the action more probable or less probable than it would be without the evidence is logically relevant.

- The first step to admit evidence is one of logical relevancy

- If evidence is not relevant, it is not admissible. Relevancy is thus the primary threshold determination that must be made for each item of proffered evidence. FRE 402 establishes that evidence that is not relevant is not admissible, it works in tandem with FRE 401 to establish and enforce the logical relevancy standard.

- Evidence that does not meet the logical relevancy test is **NOT** admissible

FRE 402 establishes that relevant evidence is admissible except as otherwise provided by the Constitution of the United States, federal statutes, other provisions of the Federal Rules of Evidence, or other rules prescribed by the Supreme Court. Such rules include the Federal Rules of Civil Procedure and Federal Rules of Criminal Procedure.

- Logical evidence **IS** admissible unless not allowed by a specific law/rule

The Constitution recognizes relevant evidence may be excluded when it is obtained in violation of constitutional guarantees. The Federal Rules of Evidence contain numerous exclusionary provisions, and various federal statutes prohibit disclosure of certain types of evidence, such as unlawfully obtained wiretap evidence. The Federal Rules of Civil Procedure and Federal Rules of Criminal Procedure contain several evidentiary provisions as well. The connection between procedural and evidentiary rules is not uncommon. Trial lawyers must understand these interconnected doctrines to competently represent others in court.

The Federal courts treat relevancy as a procedural rather than substantive question. Because of this, even in proceedings where state law supplies the rule of decision, FRE 402, unlike some other evidence rules such as presumptions under FRE 302, privileges under 501, and competency under FRE 601, all of which defer to state law when in federal court. Federal standards of relevancy generally control.

Legal relevancy deals with what is commonly referred to as the 403 balancing test. Evidence having only the slightest probative force is more likely to be excluded under FRE 403 on grounds of unfair prejudice, confusion of the issues, misleading the jury, undue delay, waste of time, or needless presentation of cumulative evidence. It often helps to visualize the 403 balancing test as a "teeter totter" from grade school. On one side of the scale you have the potential probative value of the evidence proffered. The fulcrum of the teeter-totter is the ***substantial danger of***. On the other side of the teeter-totter you have several different folks who might be on the board. They include unfair prejudice, waste of time and confusion of the issues.

This balancing act takes place on a day-to-day basis in courtrooms across the nation. It forms the core concept of legal relevancy and applies throughout the FRE unless otherwise noted in the specific rule. FRE 403 reads as follows:

> ### Rule 403. Excluding Relevant Evidence for Prejudice, Confusion, Waste of Time, or Other Reasons
>
> The court may exclude relevant evidence if its probative value is substantially outweighed by a danger of one or more of the following: unfair prejudice, confusing the issues, misleading the jury, undue delay, wasting time, or needlessly presenting cumulative evidence.

When dealing with evidence courts are concerned with both the "weight" the evidence is given by the finder of fact, and the initial "admissibility" decision made by the judge. Relevancy is mainly a question of admissibility and is different from the related issues of weight and sufficiency. "Weight" describes the persuasive force assigned to the evidence by the trier of fact once it has been admitted.

"Sufficiency" refers to the quantum and persuasive force of evidence necessary to take an issue to the jury. A party must produce evidence sufficient to support a finding in its favor to avoid a directed verdict, dismissal, or similar adverse order. Article IV of the Federal Rules of Evidence does not address questions of weight or sufficiency of evidence; it deals with logical and legal relevancy.

Usually the court determines relevancy. *See FRE 402*. In deciding whether the proffered evidence supports the inference claimed by the offering party (proponent), the court may draw upon its own knowledge, experience, and judgment. In Federal Court the judge may consider otherwise inadmissible evidence when determining the admissibility of other evidence. Examples of that happening include when counsel present the court with additional information, including scientific studies, publications, and even expert testimony, to establish connections that might not be apparent or to disprove relationships that are not correct. Parties are not restricted by the rules of evidence other than rules of privilege when providing information to the court to assist it in determining admissibility. FRE 104(a) gives the court this ability.

Consider the following U.S. Supreme Court case dealing with FRE 403. As you read ask yourself, is it helpful in understanding how the rule is supposed to work? What are the boundaries of relevancy? Do we really need any evidentiary rule other than relevancy?

SUPREME COURT SPEAKS - OLD CHIEF V. U.S.

Johnny Lynn OLD CHIEF, Petitioner,

v.

UNITED STATES

No. 95-6556.

Argued Oct. 16, 1996.

Decided Jan. 7, 1997.

Justice SOUTER delivered the opinion of the Court.

Subject to certain limitations, 18 U.S.C. § 922(g)(1) prohibits possession of a firearm by anyone with a prior felony conviction, which the Government can prove by introducing a record of judgment or similar evidence identifying the previous offense. Fearing prejudice if the jury learns the nature of the earlier crime, defendants sometimes seek to avoid such an informative disclosure by offering to concede the fact of the prior conviction. The issue here is whether a district court abuses its discretion if it spurns such an offer and admits the full record of a prior judgment, when the name or nature of the prior offense raises the risk of a verdict tainted by improper considerations, and when the purpose of the evidence is solely to prove the element of prior conviction. We hold that it does.

In 1993, petitioner, Old Chief, was arrested after a fracas involving at least one gunshot. The ensuing federal charges included not only assault with a dangerous weapon and using a firearm in relation to a crime of violence but violation of 18 U.S.C. § 922(g)(1). This statute makes it unlawful for anyone "who has been convicted in any court of, a crime punishable by imprisonment for a term exceeding one year" to "possess in or affecting commerce, any firearm...." "[A] crime punishable by imprisonment for a term exceeding one year" is defined to exclude "any Federal or State offenses pertaining to antitrust violations, unfair trade practices, restraints of trade, or other similar offenses relating to the regulation of business practices" and "any State offense classified by the laws of the State as a misdemeanor and punishable by a term of imprisonment of two years or less." § 921(a)(20).

The earlier crime charged in the indictment against Old Chief was assault causing serious bodily injury. Before trial, he moved for an order requiring the Government "to refrain from mentioning-by reading the Indictment, during jury selection, in opening statement, or closing argument-and to refrain from offering into evidence or soliciting any testimony from any witness regarding the prior criminal convictions of the Defendant, *except* to state that the Defendant has been convicted of a crime punishable by imprisonment exceeding one (1) year." He said that revealing the name and nature of his prior assault conviction would unfairly tax the jury's capacity to hold the Government to its burden of proof beyond a reasonable doubt on current charges of assault, possession, and violence with a firearm, and he offered to "solve the problem here by stipulating, agreeing and requesting the Court to instruct the jury that he has been convicted of a crime punishable by imprisonment exceeding one (1) yea[r]." He argued that the offer to stipulate to the fact of the prior conviction rendered evidence of the name and nature of the offense inadmissible under Rule 403 of the Federal Rules of Evidence, the danger being that unfair prejudice from that evidence would substantially outweigh its probative value. He also proposed this jury instruction:

"The phrase 'crime punishable by imprisonment for a term exceeding one year' generally means a crime which is a felony. The phrase does not include any state offense classified by the laws of that state as a misdemeanor*176 and punishable by a term of imprisonment of two years or less and certain crimes concerning the regulation of business practices.

"[I] hereby instruct you that Defendant JOHNNY LYNN OLD CHIEF has been convicted of a crime punishable by imprisonment for a term exceeding one year."

While Old Chief's proposed instruction was defective even under the law as he viewed it, the instruction actually given was erroneous even on the Government's view of the law. The District Court charged, "You have also heard evidence that the defendant has previously been convicted of a felony. You may consider that evidence only as it may affect the defendant's believability as a witness. You may not consider a prior conviction as evidence of guilt of the crime for which the defendant is now on trial."

This instruction invited confusion. First, of course, if the jury had applied it literally there would have been an acquittal for the wrong reason: Old Chief was on trial for, among other offenses, being a felon in possession, and if the jury had not considered the evidence of prior conviction it could not have found that he was a felon. Second, the remainder of the instruction referred to an issue that was not in the case. While it is true that prior-offense evidence may in a proper case be admissible for impeachment, even if for no other purpose, Fed. Rule Evid. 609, petitioner did not testify at trial; there was no justification for admitting the evidence for impeachment purposes and consequently no basis for the District Court's suggestion that the jurors could consider the prior conviction as impeachment evidence. The fault for this error lies at least as much with Old Chief as with the District Court, since Old Chief apparently sought some such instruction and withdrew the request only after the court had charged the jury.

The Assistant United States Attorney refused to join in a stipulation, insisting on his right to prove his case his own way, and the District Court agreed, ruling orally that, "If he doesn't want to stipulate, he doesn't have to." At trial, over renewed objection, the Government introduced the order of judgment and commitment for Old Chief's prior conviction. This document disclosed that on December 18, 1988, he "did knowingly and unlawfully assault Rory Dean Fenner, said assault resulting in serious bodily injury," for which Old Chief was sentenced to five years' imprisonment. The jury found Old Chief guilty on all counts, and he appealed.

The Ninth Circuit addressed the point with brevity:

"Regardless of the defendant's offer to stipulate, the government is entitled to prove a prior felony offense through introduction of probative evidence. *See United States v.*

Breitkreutz, 8 F.3d 688, 690 (9th Cir.1993) (citing *United States v. Gilman,* 684 F.2d 616, 622 (9th Cir.1982)). Under Ninth Circuit law, a stipulation is not proof, and, thus, it has no place in the FRE 403 balancing process. *Breitkreutz,* 8 F.3d at 691-92."

. . . . .

"Thus, we hold that the district court did not abuse its discretion by allowing the prosecution to introduce evidence of Old Chief's prior conviction to prove that element of the unlawful possession charge." *1 (C.A.9, May 31, 1995) (unpublished), App. 50-51, judgt. order reported at 6 F.3d 75 (1995)."

We granted Old Chief's petition for writ of certiorari, 516 U.S. 1110, 116 S.Ct. 907, 133 L.Ed.2d 840 (1996), because the Courts of Appeals have divided sharply in their treatment of defendants' efforts to exclude evidence of the names and natures of prior offenses in cases like this. Compare, *e.g., United States v. Burkhart,* 545 F.2d 14, 15 (C.A.6 1976); *United States v. Smith,* 520 F.2d 544, 548 (C.A.8 1975), cert. denied, 429 U.S. 925, 97 S.Ct. 328, 50 L.Ed.2d 294 (1976); and *United States v. Breitkreutz,* 8 F.3d 688, 690-692 (C.A.9 1993) (each recognizing a right on the part of the Government to refuse an offered stipulation and proceed with its own evidence of *United States v. Poore,* 594 F.2d 39, 40-43 (C.A.4 1979); *United States v. Wacker,* 72 F.3d 1453, 1472-1473 (C.A.10 1995); and *United States v. Jones,* 67 F.3d 320, 322-325 (C.A.D.C.1995) (each holding that the defendant's offer to stipulate to or to admit to the prior conviction triggers an obligation of the district court to eliminate the name and nature of the underlying offense from the case by one means or another). We now reverse the judgment of the Ninth Circuit.

II. A.

As a threshold matter, there is Old Chief's erroneous argument that the name of his prior offense as contained in the record of court, Rule 402 of the Federal Rules of Evidence. Rule 401 defines relevant evidence as having "any tendency to make the existence of any fact that is of consequence to the determination of the action more probable or less probable than it would be without the evidence." Fed. Rule Evid. 401. To be sure, the fact that Old Chief's prior conviction was for assault resulting in serious bodily injury rather than, say, for theft was not itself an ultimate fact, as if the statute had specifically required proof of injurious assault. But its demonstration was a step on one evidentiary route to the ultimate fact, since it served to place Old Chief within a particular sub-class of offenders for whom firearms possession is outlawed by § 922(g)(1). A documentary record of the conviction for that named offense was thus relevant evidence in making Old Chief's § 922(g)(1) status more probable than it would have been without the evidence.

Nor was its evidentiary relevance under Rule 401 affected by the availability of alternative proofs of the element to which it went, such as an admission by Old Chief that he had been convicted of a crime "punishable by imprisonment for a term exceeding one year" within the meaning of the statute. The 1972 Advisory Committee Notes to Rule 401 make this point directly:

"The fact to which the evidence is directed need not be in dispute. While situations will arise which call for the exclusion of evidence offered to prove a point conceded by the opponent, the ruling should be made on the basis of such considerations as waste of time and undue prejudice (see Rule 403), rather than under any general requirement that evidence is admissible only if directed to matters in dispute." Advisory Committee's Notes on Fed. Rule Evid. 401, 28 U.S.C.App., p. 859. ☞This is Relevant — try 403

If, then, relevant evidence is inadmissible in the presence of other evidence related to it, its exclusion must rest not on the ground that the other evidence has rendered it "irrelevant," but on its character as unfairly prejudicial, cumulative or the like, its relevance notwithstanding.

Viewing evidence of the name of the prior offense as relevant, there is no reason to dwell on the Government's argument that relevance is to be determined with respect to the entire item offered in evidence (here, the entire record of conviction) and not with reference to distinguishable sub-units of that object (here, the name of the offense and the sentence received). We see no impediment in general to a district court's determination, after objection, that some sections of a document are relevant within the meaning of Rule 401, and others irrelevant and inadmissible under Rule 402.

B.

The principal issue is the scope of a trial judge's discretion under Rule 403, which authorizes exclusion of relevant evidence when its "probative value is substantially outweighed by the danger of unfair prejudice, confusion of the issues, or misleading the jury, or by considerations of undue delay, waste of time, or needless presentation of cumulative evidence." Fed. Rule Evid. 403. Old Chief relies on the danger of unfair prejudice.

Petitioner also suggests that we might find a prosecutor's refusal to accept an adequate stipulation and jury instruction in the narrow context presented by this case to be prosecutorial misconduct. The argument is that, since a prosecutor is charged with the pursuit of just convictions, not victory by fair means or foul, any ethical prosecutor must agree to stipulate in the situation here. But any ethical obligation will depend on the construction of Rule 403, and we have no reason to anticipate related ethical lapses once the meaning of the Rule is settled.

definition

1.

The term "unfair prejudice," as to a criminal defendant, speaks to the capacity of some concededly relevant evidence to lure the factfinder into declaring guilt on a ground different from proof specific to the offense charged. See generally Advisory Committee's Notes on Fed. Rule Evid. 403, 28 U.S.C.App., p. 860.

Reason as to why unfair

Such improper grounds certainly include the one that Old Chief points to here: generalizing a defendant's earlier bad act into bad character and taking that as raising the odds that he did the later bad act now charged (or, worse, as calling for preventive conviction even if he should happen to be innocent momentarily). As then-Judge Breyer put it, "Although ... 'propensity evidence' is relevant, the risk that a jury will convict for crimes other than those charged-or that, uncertain of guilt, it will convict anyway because a bad person deserves punishment-creates a prejudicial effect that outweighs ordinary relevance." 681 F.2d 61, 63 (C.A.1 1982). Justice Jackson described how the law has handled this risk:

"Courts that follow the common-law tradition almost unanimously have come to disallow resort by the prosecution to any kind of evidence of a defendant's evil character to establish a probability of his guilt. Not that the law invests the defendant with a presumption of good character, *Greer v. United States,* 245 U.S. 559, 38 S.Ct. 209, 62 L.Ed. 469, but it simply closes the whole matter of character, disposition and reputation on the prosecution's case-in-chief. The state may not show defendant's prior trouble with the law, specific criminal acts, or ill name among his neighbors, even though such facts might logically be persuasive that he is by propensity a probable perpetrator of the crime. The inquiry is not rejected because character is irrelevant; on the contrary, it is said to weigh too much with the jury and to so over persuade them as to prejudge one with a bad general record and deny him a fair opportunity to defend against a particular charge. The overriding policy of excluding such evidence, despite its admitted probative value, is the practical experience that its disallowance tends to prevent confusion of issues, unfair surprise and undue prejudice." *Michelson v. United States,* 335 U.S. 469, 475-476, 69 S.Ct. 213, 218-219, 93 L.Ed. 168 (1948)

Rule of Evidence 404(b) reflects this common-law tradition by addressing propensity reasoning directly: "Evidence of other crimes, wrongs, or acts is not admissible to prove the character of a person in order to show action in conformity therewith." Fed. Rule Evid. 404(b). There is, accordingly, no question that propensity would be an "improper basis" for conviction and that evidence of a prior conviction is subject to analysis under Rule 403 for relative probative value and for prejudicial risk of misuse as propensity evidence. Cf. 1 J. Strong, McCormick on Evidence 780 (4th ed.1992) (hereinafter McCormick) Rule 403 prejudice may occur, for example, when "evidence of convictions for prior, unrelated crimes may lead a juror to think that since the defendant already has a criminal record, an erroneous conviction would not be quite as serious as would otherwise be the case").

As for the analytical method to be used in Rule 403 balancing, two basic possibilities present themselves. An item of evidence might be viewed as an island, with estimates of its own probative value and unfairly prejudicial risk the sole reference points in deciding whether the danger substantially outweighs the value and whether the evidence ought to be excluded. Or the question of admissibility might be seen as inviting further comparisons to take account of the full evidentiary context of the case as the court understands it when the ruling must be made. This second approach would start out like the first but be ready to go further. On objection, the court would decide whether a particular item of evidence raised a danger of unfair prejudice. If it did, the judge would go on to evaluate the degrees of probative value and unfair prejudice not only for the item in question but for any actually available substitutes as well. If an alternative were found to have substantially the same or greater probative value but a lower danger of unfair prejudice, sound judicial discretion would discount the value of the item first offered and exclude it if its discounted probative value were substantially outweighed by unfairly prejudicial risk. As we will explain later on, the judge would have to make these calculations with an appreciation of the offering party's need for evidentiary richness and narrative integrity in presenting a case, and the mere fact that two pieces of evidence might go to the same point would not, of course, necessarily mean that only one of them might come in. It would only mean that a judge applying Rule 403 could reasonably apply some discount to the probative value of an item of evidence when faced with less risky alternative proof going to the same point. Even under this second approach, as we explain below, a defendant's Rule 403 objection offering to concede a point generally cannot prevail over the Government's choice to offer evidence showing guilt and all the circumstances surrounding the offense.

It is important that a reviewing court evaluate the trial court's decision from its perspective when it had to rule and not indulge in review by hindsight. See, for example, *United States v. O'Shea,* 724 F.2d 1514, 1517 (C.A.11 1984), where the appellate court approved the trial court's pretrial refusal to impose a stipulation on the Government and exclude the Government's corresponding evidence of past convictions because the trial court had found at that stage that the evidence would quite likely come in anyway on other grounds.

While our discussion has been general because of the general wording of Rule 403, our holding is limited to cases involving proof of felon status. On appellate review of a Rule 403 decision, a defendant must establish abuse of discretion, a standard that is not satisfied by a mere showing of some alternative means of proof that the prosecution in its broad discretion chose not to rely upon.

The first understanding of the Rule is open to a very telling objection. That reading would leave the party offering evidence with the option to structure a trial in whatever way would produce the maximum unfair prejudice consistent with relevance. He could choose the available alternative carrying the greatest threat of improper influence, despite the availability of less prejudicial but equally probative evidence. The worst he would have to fear would be a ruling sustaining a Rule 403 objection, and if that occurred, he could simply fall back to offering substitute evidence. This would be a strange rule. It would be very odd for the law of evidence to recognize the danger of unfair prejudice only to confer such a degree of autonomy on the party subject to temptation, and the Rules of Evidence are not so odd.

Rather, a reading of the companions to Rule 403, and of the commentaries that went with them to Congress, makes it clear that what counts as the Rule 403 "probative value" of an item of evidence, as distinct from its Rule 401 "relevance," may be calculated by comparing evidentiary alternatives. The Committee Notes to Rule 401 explicitly say that a party's concession is pertinent to the court's discretion to exclude evidence on the point conceded. Such a concession, according to the Notes, will sometimes "call for the exclusion of evidence offered to prove [the] point conceded by the opponent...." Advisory Committee's Notes on Fed. Rule Evid. 401, 28 U.S.C.App., p. 859. As already mentioned, the Notes make it clear that such rulings should be made not on the basis of Rule 401 relevance but on "such considerations as waste of time and undue prejudice (see Rule 403)...."

The Notes to Rule 403 then take up the point by stating that when a court considers "whether to exclude on grounds of unfair prejudice," the "availability of other means of proof may ... be an appropriate factor." Advisory Committee's Notes on Fed. Rule Evid. 403, 28 U.S.C.App., p. 860. The point gets a reprise in the Notes to Rule 404(b), dealing with admissibility when a given evidentiary item has the dual nature of legitimate evidence of an element and illegitimate evidence of character: "No mechanical solution is offered. The determination must be made whether the danger of undue prejudice outweighs the probative value of the evidence in view of the availability of other means of proof and other facts appropriate for making a decision of this kind under 403." Advisory Committee's Notes on Fed. Rule Evid. 404, 28 U.S.C.App., p. 861.

Thus the notes leave no question that when Rule 403 confers discretion by providing that evidence "may" be excluded, the discretionary judgment may be informed not only by assessing an evidentiary item's twin tendencies, but by placing the result of that assessment alongside similar assessments of evidentiary alternatives.

2.

In dealing with the specific problem raised by § 922(g)(1) and its prior-conviction element, there can be no question that evidence of the name or nature of the prior offense generally carries a risk of unfair prejudice to the defendant. That risk will vary from case

[handwritten margin note: court considers: are there other means of proof?]

[handwritten margin note: we don't want bad character reasoning]

to case, for the reasons already given, but will be substantial whenever the official record offered by the Government would be arresting enough to lure a juror into a sequence of bad character reasoning. Where a prior conviction was for a gun crime or one similar to other charges in a pending case the risk of unfair prejudice would be especially obvious, and Old Chief sensibly worried that the prejudicial effect of his prior assault conviction, significant enough with respect to the current gun charges alone, would take on added weight from the related assault charge against him.

It is true that a prior offense may be so far removed in time or nature from the current gun charge, and any others brought with it, that its potential to prejudice the defendant unfairly will be minimal. Some prior offenses, in fact, may even have some potential to prejudice the Government's case unfairly. Thus an extremely old conviction for a relatively minor felony that nevertheless qualifies under the statute might strike many jurors as a foolish basis for convicting an otherwise upstanding member of the community of otherwise legal gun possession. Since the Government could not, of course, compel the defendant to admit formally the existence of the prior conviction, the Government would have to bear the risk of jury nullification, a fact that might properly drive the Government's charging decision.

The District Court was also presented with alternative, relevant, admissible evidence of the prior conviction by Old Chief's offer to stipulate, evidence necessarily subject to the District Court's consideration on the motion to exclude the record offered by the Government. Although Old Chief's formal offer to stipulate was, strictly, to enter a formal agreement with the Government to be given to the jury, even without the Government's acceptance his proposal amounted to an offer to admit that the prior-conviction element was satisfied, and a defendant's admission is, of course, good evidence. See Fed. Rule Evid. 801(d)(2)(A).

[handwritten margin note: But does it say for what crime?]
[handwritten note: He did admit it.]

Old Chief's proffered admission would, in fact, have been not merely relevant but seemingly conclusive evidence of the element. The statutory language in which the prior-conviction requirement is couched shows no congressional concern with the specific name or nature of the prior offense beyond what is necessary to place it within the broad category of qualifying felonies, and Old Chief clearly meant to admit that his felony did qualify, by stipulating "that the Government has proven one of the essential elements of the offense." As a consequence, although the name of the prior offense may have been technically relevant, it addressed no detail in the definition of the prior-conviction element that would not have been covered by the stipulation or admission. Logic, then, seems to side with Old Chief.

[handwritten note: What element? That he was a felon?]

3.

There is, however, one more question to be considered before deciding whether Old Chief's offer was to supply evidentiary value at least equivalent to what the Government's own evidence carried. In arguing that the stipulation or admission would not have carried equivalent value, the Government invokes the familiar, standard rule that the prosecution is entitled to prove its case by evidence of its own choice, or, more exactly, that a criminal defendant may not stipulate or admit his way out of the full evidentiary force of the case as the Government chooses to present it. The authority usually cited for this rule is *Parr v. United States*, 255 F.2d 86 (CA5), cert. denied, 358 U.S. 824, 79 S.Ct. 40, 3 L.Ed.2d 64 (1958), in which the Fifth Circuit explained that the "reason for the rule is to permit a party 'to present to the jury a picture of the events relied upon. To substitute for such a picture a naked admission might have the effect to rob the evidence of much of its fair and legitimate weight.'" <u>255 F.2d, at 88</u> (quoting <u>*Dunning v. Maine Central R. Co.*, 91 Me. 87, 39 A. 352, 356 (1897)</u>).

This is unquestionably true as a general matter. The "fair and legitimate weight" of conventional evidence showing individual thoughts and acts amounting to a crime reflects the fact that making a case with testimony and tangible things not only satisfies the formal definition of an offense, but tells a colorful story with descriptive richness. Unlike an abstract premise, whose force depends on going precisely to a particular step in a course of reasoning, a piece of evidence may address any number of separate elements, striking hard just because it shows so much at once; the account of a shooting that establishes capacity and causation may tell just as much about the triggerman's motive and intent. Evidence thus has force beyond any linear scheme of reasoning, and as its pieces come together a narrative gains momentum, with power not only to support conclusions but to sustain the willingness of jurors to draw the inferences, whatever they may be, necessary to reach an honest verdict. This persuasive power of the concrete and particular is often essential to the capacity of jurors to satisfy the obligations that the law places on them. Jury duty is usually unsought and sometimes resisted, and it may be as difficult for one juror suddenly to face the findings that can send another human being to prison, as it is for another to hold out conscientiously for acquittal. When a juror's duty does seem hard, the evidentiary account of what a defendant has thought and done can accomplish what no set of abstract statements ever could, not just to prove a fact but to establish its human significance, and so to implicate the law's moral underpinnings and a juror's obligation to sit in judgment. Thus, the prosecution may fairly seek to place its evidence before the jurors, as much to tell a story of guiltiness as to support an inference of guilt, to convince the jurors that a guilty verdict would be morally reasonable as much as to point to the discrete elements of a defendant's legal fault. Cf. <u>*United States v. Gilliam*, 994 F.2d 97, 100-102 (CA2)</u>, cert. denied, <u>510 U.S. 927, 114 S.Ct. 335, 126 L.Ed.2d 280 (1993)</u>.

But there is something even more to the prosecution's interest in resisting efforts to replace the evidence of its choice with admissions and stipulations, for beyond the power of conventional evidence to support allegations and give life to the moral underpinnings of law's claims, there lies the need for evidence in all its particularity to satisfy the jurors' expectations about what proper proof should be. Some such demands they bring with them to the courthouse, assuming, for example, that a charge of using a firearm to commit an offense will be proven by introducing a gun in evidence. A prosecutor who fails to produce one, or some good reason for his failure, has something to be concerned about. "If [jurors'] expectations are not satisfied, triers of fact may penalize the party who disappoints them by drawing a negative inference against that party." Saltzburg, A Special Aspect of Relevance: Countering Negative Inferences Associated with the Absence of Evidence, 66 Calif. L.Rev. 1011, 1019 (1978) (footnotes omitted). Expectations may also arise in jurors' minds simply from the experience of a trial itself. The use of witnesses to describe a train of events naturally related can raise the prospect of learning about every ingredient of that natural sequence the same way. If suddenly the prosecution presents some occurrence in the series differently, as by announcing a stipulation or admission, the effect may be like saying, "never mind what's behind the door," and jurors may well wonder what they are being kept from knowing. A party seemingly responsible for cloaking something has reason for apprehension, and the prosecution with its burden of proof may prudently demur at a defense request to interrupt the flow of evidence telling the story in the usual way.

Cf. Green, "<u>The</u> ("[E]videntiary rules ... predicated in large measure on the law's distrust of juries [can] have the unintended, and perhaps ironic, result of encouraging the jury's distrust of lawyers. The rules do so by fostering the perception that lawyers are deliberately withholding evidence" (footnote omitted)). The fact that juries have expectations as to what evidence ought to be presented by a party, and may well hold the absence of that evidence against the party, is also recognized in the case law of the Fifth Amendment, which explicitly supposes that, despite the venerable history of the privilege against self-incrimination, jurors may not recall that someone accused of crime need not explain the evidence or avow innocence beyond making his plea. See, *e.g.,* The assumption that jurors may have contrary expectations and be moved to draw adverse inferences against the party who disappoints them undergirds the rule that a defendant can demand an instruction forbidding the jury to draw such an inference.

In sum, the accepted rule that the prosecution is entitled to prove its case free from any defendant's option to stipulate the evidence away rests on good sense. A syllogism is not a story, and a naked proposition in a courtroom may be no match for the robust evidence that would be used to prove it. People who hear a story interrupted by gaps of abstraction may be puzzled at the missing chapters, and jurors asked to rest a momentous decision on the story's truth can feel put upon at being asked to take responsibility knowing that more could be said than they have heard. A convincing tale can be told with economy, but when economy becomes a break in the natural sequence of narrative evidence, an assurance that the missing link is really there is never more than second best.

evidentiary depth? ...4. eh... not good enough

This recognition that the prosecution with its burden of persuasion needs evidentiary depth to tell a continuous story has, however, virtually no application when the point at issue is a defendant's legal status, dependent on some judgment rendered wholly independently of the concrete events of later criminal behavior charged against him. As in this case, the choice of evidence for such an element is usually not between eventful narrative and abstract proposition, but between propositions of slightly varying abstraction, either a record saying that conviction for some crime occurred at a certain time or a statement admitting the same thing without naming the particular offense. The issue of substituting one statement for the other normally arises only when the record of conviction would not be admissible for any purpose beyond proving status, so that excluding it would not deprive the prosecution of evidence with multiple utility; if, indeed, there were a justification for receiving evidence of the nature of prior acts on some issue other than status (*i.e.,* to prove "motive, opportunity, intent, preparation, plan, knowledge, identity, or absence of mistake or accident," Fed. Rule Evid. 404(b)), Rule 404(b) guarantees the opportunity to seek its admission. Nor can it be argued that the events behind the prior conviction are proper nourishment for the jurors' sense of obligation to vindicate the public interest. The issue is not whether concrete details of the prior crime should come to the jurors' attention but whether the name or general character of that crime is to be disclosed. Congress, however, has made it plain that distinctions among generic felonies do not count for this purpose; the fact of the qualifying conviction is alone what matters under the statute. "A defendant falls within the category simply by virtue of past conviction for any [qualifying] crime ranging from possession of short lobsters, *see* 16 U.S.C. § 3372, to the most aggravated murder." *Tavares,* 21 F.3d, at 4. The most the jury needs to know is that the conviction admitted by the defendant falls within the class of crimes that Congress thought should bar a convict from possessing a gun, and this point may be made readily in a defendant's admission and underscored in the court's jury instructions. Finally, the most obvious reason that the general presumption that the prosecution may choose its evidence is so remote from application here is that proof of the defendant's status goes to an element entirely outside the natural sequence of what the defendant is charged with thinking and doing to commit the current offense.

not really making case

doesn't harm anything for jurors or state [handwritten note in margin]

Proving status without telling exactly why that status was imposed leaves no gap in the story of a defendant's subsequent criminality, and its demonstration by stipulation or admission neither displaces a chapter from a continuous sequence of conventional evidence nor comes across as an officious substitution, to confuse or offend or provoke reproach.

Given these peculiarities of the element of felony-convict status and of admissions and the like when used to prove it, there is no cognizable difference between the evidentiary significance of an admission and of the legitimately probative component of the official record the prosecution would prefer to place in evidence. For purposes of the Rule 403 weighing of the probative against the prejudicial, the functions of the competing evidence are distinguishable only by the risk inherent in the one and wholly absent from the other. In this case, as in any other in which the prior conviction is for an offense likely to support conviction on some improper ground, the only reasonable conclusion was that the risk of unfair prejudice did substantially outweigh the discounted probative value of the record of conviction, and it was an abuse of discretion to admit the record when an admission was available. What we have said shows why this will be the general rule when proof of convict status is at issue, just as the prosecutor's choice will generally survive a Rule 403 analysis when a defendant seeks to force the substitution of an admission for evidence creating a coherent narrative of his thoughts and actions in perpetrating the offense for which he is being tried.

There may be yet other means of proof besides a formal admission on the record that, with a proper objection, will obligate a district court to exclude evidence of the name of the offense. A redacted record of conviction is the one most frequently mentioned. Any alternative will, of course, require some jury instruction to explain it (just as it will require some discretion when the indictment is read). A redacted judgment in this case, for example, would presumably have revealed to the jury that Old Chief was previously convicted in federal court and sentenced to more than a year's imprisonment, but it would not have shown whether his previous conviction was for one of the business offenses that do not count, under § 921(a)(20). Hence, an instruction, with the defendant's consent, would be necessary to make clear that the redacted judgment was enough to satisfy the status element remaining in the case. The Government might, indeed, propose such a redacted judgment for the trial court to weigh against a defendant's offer to admit, as indeed the Government might do even if the defendant's admission had been received into evidence.

The judgment is reversed, and the case is remanded to the Ninth Circuit for further proceedings consistent with this opinion.

It is so ordered.

* * * * *

DISCUSSION PROBLEMS 3-1

1. Do you agree with Justice Souter's analysis of how FRE 403 should apply in this case?

2. Why should we allow the defense to use FRE 403 to prevent the state from offering evidence that is both relevant and admissible?

3. Are there other evidentiary rules that might better handle the issues present in Old Chief? If not, should there be? What type of rule would you propose to deal with these issues?

Now that we have reviewed how the U.S. Supreme Court dealt with relevancy let's take some time and consider the following problems dealing with legal relevancy. As you go through these problems consider why you want to admit the evidence and the competing arguments for its exclusion. Imagine the interplay between opposing counsel and the court as they discuss allowing testimony to establish these alleged facts. Who would initially object to the testimony? When would they do so? Should this be an objection that is saved for trial, or is it sufficiently important, or required to be raised in a pretrial motion? What are the benefits and weaknesses of each approach?

DISCUSSION PROBLEM 3-2
The Convenience Store Robbery

The Facts: Ms. Sarah James is suing Police Officer Jerry Jones for violating her sons' civil rights when he shot and killed them while they were leaving a convenience store after robbing it during the early morning hours of November 1st. Officer Jones was getting out of his cruiser to enter the convenience store to fill his thermos with coffee. He had a history with the James boys and recognized them when they came running out of the front door of the store. Officer Jones shot and killed both brothers in the convenience store parking lot. At the civil trial officer Jones' defense attorney is attempting to admit evidence of the James boys' propensity for misusing guns under the theory that Jones' choice to use deadly force when dealing the with the James boys was justified because he had a reasonable belief that the brothers posed a serious threat to his safety. In support of this theory the defense wishes to offer three different pieces of evidence:

> The first piece of evidence the defense wishes to offer is a cross-burning the James brothers conducted in an African-American community. According to one of the boys who allegedly participated in the burning, the James brothers fired a .44 Magnum into the air six times after the cross had been lit. After the cross began to burn, the brothers ran back to a white area of town and hid with guns in anticipation of retaliatory acts from the African-American community. Although no weapons charges were filed against the brothers, one of them was charged with disorderly conduct. This incident was investigated by a Lieutenant Record, who reported directly to Jones during that time.

> The second piece of evidence arose from an accidental shooting where Jimmy Collins shot himself in the leg. Although there was no evidence that the gun belonged to the James brothers, they were present at the shooting. Jones worked that case, and testified that the shooting was an accident.

> The third piece of evidence came from an investigation of an armed robbery at a restaurant. While Jones was investigating the robbery he learned that the girlfriend of one of the James Boys had been bragging about how he was involved in the robbery. No

charges were brought against the James brothers as a result of Jones' investigation of that case.

The plaintiff's attorney for Ms. James objects to the use of the evidence.

1.   What are the best arguments for admissibility of each piece of evidence?

2.   What are the best arguments for excluding each piece of evidence?

3.   How should the judge rule?

4.   Why?

Problem 3-3 is based upon a wrongful death suit filed by Charissa Washington against Rebecca Hartwell. Consider the following introductory information before proceeding to the problem.

Background Information: The children were black. The driver was white. The community was outraged. It was a media circus. Was it one vehicle, two or three? A van? A dark blue Honda? A Toyota? Or was it all three? The witnesses couldn't agree. The car sped away as a horrified crowd of about 200 emptied into the street and began shouting in outrage. Children's shoes and sandals were scattered on the pavement. Next to a puddle of blood was a pillow left behind by paramedics who had treated one of the victims. Were the non-working streetlights also to blame? Did someone hide the car? Was DNA removed from the evidence? What were the unsupervised children doing in a high-traffic area at night? Who would pay? After being sought for days, a high-profile criminal defense attorney, Steve Levine, finally announced that the driver would come forward. That driver was Rebecca Hartwell, a 28 year old citizen of Pelican Bay, Calusa County.

On March 21, 20XX-2 at approximately 7:15 PM Ms. Rebecca Hartwell was driving her midnight blue Toyota Echo. She was traveling north on 39th Street. It is undisputed that at some point her car hit at least two of the four children crossing the street. She also fled the scene of the accident. The hit-and-run crash killed two brothers, aged 14 and 3, and seriously injured a 2-year-old boy and a 7-year-old girl. The 3-year-old boy was caught underneath the grill of Ms. Hartwell's car and drug approximately 150 feet before his body worked loose and came to rest in the middle of 39th street. The Toyota then fled the scene of the accident.

The criminal case has ended. Judge Jerry Parker oversaw the prosecution for negligent homicide that resulted in a hung jury on July 13, 20XX-1. The prosecution's office has indicated that they have no intention of retrying the case, citing evidentiary concerns and proof difficulties. Steve Levine contends that the nature of this trial caused the hung jury to have the effect of a dismissal with prejudice. The state's office has publicly stated that they disagree with that assessment.

A civil case has been filed alleging both wrongful death and defamation. After filing answers and affirmative defenses to the Complaint, civil defense counsel moved for a change of venue. The Motion was denied.

DISCUSSION PROBLEM 3-3
Rebecca's Dilemma

You are the plaintiff attorney in the civil case of *Washington v. Hartwell.* Your assigned investigator has returned the following factual summary concerning the Reckless Driving offense for which Rebecca Hartwell was convicted on January 21, 20XX-10:

On July 4th, 20XX-11 Rebecca Hartwell was driving home from a party she had attended celebrating the 4th of July. At the party she drank three wine coolers. She drove to the party and also drove home. While driving home late that night, around 11 PM she was driving north on 87th street when a homeless man stepped out in front of vehicle. She struck the man, injuring him severely. She stopped her car immediately and went out to help the homeless man. While she was assisting him the police arrived. Smelling alcohol on Ms. Hartwell they conducted Field Sobriety Test (FST) which she failed. She later gave a breathalyzer sample that registered .016, twice the legal limit. She was charged with DUI which she plead down to the offense of Reckless Driving. You want to get this information before the jury.

1. What is your best argument to make this evidence admissible?

2. How will the defense attorney likely respond?

3. How will you counter that defense response?

4. What process will the judge use to decide admissibility?

5. How will the judge likely rule?

6. What will you do if the judge does not rule in your favor?

Problem 3-4 is based upon a murder trial. The state has indicted Brandi Alexander for the murder of her husband Chris Alexander. Consider the following introductory information before proceeding to the problem.

Background Information: Brandi Alexander was accused of the shooting and killing of her husband, Chris Alexander, on the night of June 3, 20XX-2. Chris Alexander, 32, was having multiple extramarital affairs and was allegedly talking on a cell phone with one of his lovers, a woman named Nikki Long, less than two minutes before he was shot to death in his living room. The Alexander's two children, Ariel and Jasmine, were asleep in a nearby bedroom at the time of their father's murder.

A gunshot residue test was performed on Brandi the night of the shooting. It found one particle of gunshot residue on the back of her left hand. The murder weapon was a . 45 caliber pistol and has not been found. One neighbor heard gunshots but did not see a car fleeing, while another said she heard the screeching wheels of a car right after the shooting. The alleged motive for the murder is jealously, vengeance, and a $250,000 insurance policy. The defendant argued at the first trial that either an intruder, or possibly another jilted lover, killed Chris. Brandi Alexander was convicted January 9, 20XX-1 and sentenced her to life in prison.

Ten months later, the circuit court threw out her conviction and ordered a new trial, citing discrimination in the jury selection process by the prosecution.

DISCUSSION PROBLEM 3-4
Don't You Dare Cheat on Me!

You are the prosecutor in *State v. Alexander*. Your investigator has uncovered evidence that 15 years ago the defendant, Brandi Alexander, was involved in a serious relationship with a young man. He cheated on her. After she learned about his cheating she confronted him at his home. She kicked him in the genital area multiple times, causing massive hematomas to his body. He refused to press charges. You have extrinsic evidence of these events. Are these events admissible?

1. Identify the theory of admissibility.

2. How will the defense respond?

3. What will be your counter response?

4. How will the judge rule?

5. Why will the judge rule that way?

CONCLUSION

In this chapter we have developed our understanding of logical and legal relevancy, the core concept around which all evidentiary issues rotate. Now that we have studied, the law, discovered the law, and then applied the law of relevancy, let's move on to an in depth discussion and understanding of how a person's individual character traits may be offered at trial.

Chapter 4: Character Always Matters

INTRODUCTION

As used in the Rules, "character" means a person's disposition or propensity to engage or not engage in various forms of conduct. Character is a trait of the person's personality that is thought to have predictive power. The connection between a character trail and its predictive power follows the type of logical reasoning that people apply in their day-to-day lives. If you have a tendency to do something in certain situations, you are more likely to have acted in accordance with that trait in a specific situation. This is called propensity evidence.

Because our common sense sees the causal connection between past conduct and future activity, those not familiar with evidentiary law would expect that courts would routinely rely upon prior conduct when trying to determine whether someone charged with an offense committed it. American jurisprudence has gone in the opposite direction. Our concerns about the potential unfairly prejudicial impact of character evidence has lead us to greatly proscribe the time and circumstances under which it may be admitted, and by whom. Consider the words of one of the fathers of American evidentiary law, James Bradley Thayer, when describing how character evidence works. His words from 1898 are as true as the day they were published:

At once, when a man raises his eyes from the common law system of evidence, and looks at foreign methods, he is struck with the fact that our system is radically peculiar. Here, a great mass of evidential matter, logically important and probative, is shut out from the view of the judicial tribunals by an imperative rule, while the same matter is not thus excluded anywhere else....[W]e alone have generated and evolved this large, elaborate, and difficult doctrine.[4]

Our evidentiary law was forged in the crucible of common sense and the vast experience of our common law heritage.[5] At its best it balances competing values with great dexterity; at its worst we are left scratching our heads and wondering why we cannot fashion a more rational and cogent way to deal with the very human dynamics of the law. Nowhere is this more true than in the development and application of the evidentiary rules regarding character.

Character evidence is one spot where the rules ebb and flow with societal concerns and an always-developing understanding of what it means to be human. The developments of evidentiary rules within the Federal Rules of Evidence that address character are examples of where common sense, social science, and public policy go hand in hand.

The issue then becomes what sort of balance should be used to weigh the legitimate probative importance of the evidence against the danger of its improper use by the jury and how effectively trial judges use their authority to exclude for undue prejudice to regulate the danger of prejudice when persistent advocates do their utmost to find a legitimate basis for the admission of evidence reflecting badly on character and to persuade the court that the dangers of prejudice are outweighed by the legitimate benefits

---

[4] James Bradley Thayer, *A Preliminary Treatise on Evidence at the Common Law*, 1, 2 (Boston: Little, Brown and Company 1898) [hereinafter *Thayer on Evidence*].

[5] *Id.* at 4 (stating, "It is attending to practical ends. Its rules originate in the instinctive suggestions of good sense, legal experience and sound practical understanding; and they are seeking to determine, not what is or is not probative, but rather passing by that inquiry, what, among really probative matters, shall, nevertheless, for this or that practical reason, be excluded and not even heard by the jury." *Id.*).

of the evidence (a concise explanation of how character evidence is, or is not, admitted at trial).[6]

Character evidence deals with the internal beliefs, value systems and development of an individual as reflected by their conduct. To properly understand the logical and legal relevance of propensity character evidence one must understand what personality is, how it affects a person's actions and to what degree it is in turn influenced by particular situations. To understand how character and conduct interact with one another we must consider how they developed.

Professor John Wigmore explained the relationship between character trait and behavior as follows: "A defendant's character . . . as indicating the probability of his doing or not doing the act charged, is essentially relevant."[7] This explanation of the relevancy of character traits was a reflection of common sense nurtured by several centuries of legal experience. His view reflected experience and common sense: inquiring into a person's character is relevant when weighing his or her actions through the presentation of character traits at trial. Relevancy based upon common sense or the social sciences does not necessarily equate to admissibility, but it is an initial hurdle that evidence must clear. When deciding whether the character trait is sufficiently relevant to be potentially admissible, courts very quickly become concerned with an improper use of character evidence by the jury.

The idea that a person on trial should only be judged based upon their acts regarding the case at bar is a time honored shibboleth of American and Anglo jurisprudence. This traditional treatment of character evidence comes from our common law heritage,[8] and represents a core American value. From a societal perspective we believe that a person should be judged based upon what they have done, not who they are. You can trace this sense of independence and self-reliance back to the founding of the United States. The founding fathers rejected many elements of European thought, particularly the reliance upon a civil system of law derived from earlier canon law.

The prohibition in common law against the use of character evidence to prove a person acted in a predictable manner based upon a perceived character trait extends back to the 1600's.[9] Several important cases during that time developed the proposition that we should judge an individual based upon what he or she may have or have not done, not what he may or may not be. This common law position was unique, and served as a signpost marking the continued separation of the secular (common) law from canon law. From a western civilization perspective, common law and canon law had previously worked together and relied upon each other. This relationship between common law and canon law developed many of the great facets of our current criminal justice system, including one of the most famous, the privilege against self-incrimination.[10]

---

[6] John H. Wigmore, *Wigmore on Evidence*, § 54.1, 1152 (rev. Tillers 1983).

[7] Wigmore, *Wigmore revised supra* note 3, § 55, at 1157.

[8] Wigmore, *Wigmore on Evidence supra* note 3, § 8, at 107 – 114 (2d ed. 1923).

[9] Department of Justice, Office of Legal Policy, *'Truth in Criminal Justice Series Office of Legal Policy: The Admission of Criminal Histories at Trial*, 22 U. Mich. J.J. Ref. 707, 771, n.1, (1989); *also* Wigmore, *Wigmore on Evidence*, at 109 (2.ed.).

[10] Id *supra* note 3 at 109(2 ed.). "[A] fourth important principle, wholly independent in origin, here also arose and became fixed by the end of this period – the privilege against self incrimination. The creature, under another form, of the canon law, under which it had a long history of its own, it was transferred, under stress of political turmoil, into the common law, and thus, by a singular contrast, came to be the most distinctive feature of our trial system. About the same period (the 1600s) an equally distinctive feature, the rule against using an accused's character, became settled."

     Everyday Evidence: A Practical Approach

Canon law was inquisitorial,[11] relying upon a panel of judges to determine the outcome of controversies. An underlying belief of canon law was that the more information available to the finder of fact the more reliable and truthful the final decision. This system required access to all relevant facts to ensure that the judges could determine a truthful outcome. Canon law presupposed that truth is determinable, and accepted the burden that the business of settling controversies is the discovery of truth. The belief that a trial should be the search for an ultimate identifiable and ascertainable truth still forms the fundamental basis for most civil law systems in Europe.

Canon law generally accepted as a given that the character of the individuals involved was relevant to the issue in controversy. That belief ensured that inquiries into the character of the individual were not only permissible but encouraged. This treatment of character evidence is still followed in European civil court systems. Canon law's approach to the use of character evidence did not cross over into common law.[12]

The decision at common law to not follow the position taken by canon law in dealing with character evidence was based on the importance of the jury system and competing views of how the use of character evidence would have an impact on a fact finder's decision-making process. Common law viewed character evidence as being too prejudicial and feared that the jury would be unduly influenced by it while canon law posited that the more logically relevant information the finder of fact had the closer to the truth the decision making process would come.

When dealing with the issues surrounding character evidence, using an analogy can be helpful in driving home the considerations that compete with one another when determining whether character evidence should be admissible at trial. Consider the following problem:

DISCUSSION PROBLEM 4-1:

The Case of the Missing Cookies

A parent comes home from a hard day at work to find a shattered cookie jar lying on the middle of the floor in the kitchen. Broken cookies are scattered everywhere. The shards of pottery that made up the cookie jar are spread across the linoleum. There are three children who live in this house. One is a young 6-year-old who has an incredible sweet tooth. This child has never met a cookie that they did not like. The second child is a health nut. They never eat anything that is not good for them, and are often quite sanctimonious about it. The third child is just your average run-of-the-mill kid, sometimes they eat sweets, and sometimes they don't.

Who is Most Likely to Take the Cookies? Why?

If you are the parent in this situation, do you consider the character traits of your children when trying to decide who broke the cookie jar? The vast majority of us would say that we do. If you think about it for a moment that makes sense. We live our daily lives with the idea that past behavior can help us in predicting future behavior. From the

---

[11] Ken Pennington, Law, *Criminal Procedure, Dictionary of the Middle Ages: Supplement 1*, at 309-320 (New York: Charles Scribner's Sons-Thompson-Gale, 2004).

[12] Wigmore, *Wigmore on Evidence*.

---

standpoint of running our life and dealing with other folks, this belief works just fine, but when using it to determine guilt or innocence of the criminal setting, it has the effect of allowing us to convict someone for who they are instead of for what they've done. That is not an acceptable standard under our jurisprudential philosophy. This means the use of character evidence at trial can be counterintuitive. We know that it's helpful in predicting future behavior much of the time, and, we know that it's so helpful that it may overwhelm the evidence that is or is not present and serve as the basis for conviction. If you are the person on trial, most would agree that you would prefer to be convicted for what you have done as opposed to who you are. The character rules of evidence are designed to ensure that it takes evidence and not reputation to convict someone at trial.

U.S. SUPREME COURT SPEAKS - MICHELSON V. U.S.

The United States Supreme Court has considered this issue of character evidence and propensity. Consider the following U.S. Supreme Court case dealing with FRE 404. As you read, ask yourself, is it helpful in understanding how the rule is supposed to work? What are the boundaries of character evidence? Do you agree with the construct of the court? What do you think of the dissent?

69 S.Ct. 213
Supreme Court of the United States
MICHELSON
v.
UNITED STATES.
No. 23. Argued Oct. 14, 15, 1948. Decided Dec. 20, 1948.

Hosang **Michelson** was convicted of bribing a federal revenue agent. Judgment of conviction was affirmed by the Circuit Court of Appeals, 165 F.2d 732, and defendant brings certiorari.

Affirmed.

Mr. Justice RUTLEDGE and Mr. Justice MURPHY, dissenting.

On Writ of Certiorari to the **United States** Court of Appeals for the Second Circuit

Mr. Justice JACKSON delivered the opinion of the Court.

In 1947 petitioner **Michelson** was convicted of bribing a federal revenue agent. The Government proved a large payment by accused to the agent for the purpose of influencing his official action. The defendant, as a witness on his own behalf, admitted passing the money but claimed it was done in response to the agent's demands, threats, solicitations, and inducements that amounted to entrapment. It is enough for our purposes to say that determination of the issue turned on whether the jury should believe the agent or the accused.

On direct examination of defendant, his own counsel brought out that, in 1927, he had been convicted of a misdemeanor having to do with trading in counterfeit watch dials. On cross-examination it appeared that in 1930, in executing an application for a license to deal in second-hand jewelry, he answered 'No' to the question whether he had theretofore been arrested or summoned for any offense.

Defendant called five witnesses to prove that he enjoyed a good reputation. Two of them testified that their acquaintance with him extended over a period of about thirty years and the others said they had known him at least half that long. A typical examination in chief was as follows:

'Q. Do you know the defendant **Michelson**? A. Yes.

'Q. How long do you know Mr. **Michelson**? A. About 30 years.

'Q. Do you know other people who know him? A. Yes.

'Q. Have you have occasion to discuss his reputation for honesty and truthfulness and for being a law-abiding citizen? A. It is very good.

'Q. You have talked to others? A. Yes.

'Q. And what is his reputation? A. Very good.'

These are representative of answers by three witnesses; two others replied, in substance, that they never had heard anything against **Michelson**.

On cross-examination, four of the witnesses were asked, in substance, this question: 'Did you ever hear that Mr. **Michelson** on March 4, 1927, was convicted of a violation of the trademark law in New York City in regard to watches?' This referred to the twenty-year-old conviction about which defendant himself had testified on direct examination. Two of them had heard of it and two had not.

To four of these witnesses the prosecution also addressed the question the allowance of which, over defendant's objection, is claimed to be reversible error:

'Did you ever hear that on October 11th, 1920, the defendant, Hosang **Michelson**, was arrested for receiving stolen goods?'

None of the witnesses appears to have heard of this.

The trial court asked counsel for the prosecution, out of presence of the jury, 'Is it a fact according to the best information in your possession that **Michelson** was arrested for receiving stolen goods?' Counsel replied that it was, and to support his good faith exhibited a paper record which defendant's counsel did not challenge.

The judge also on three occasions warned the jury, in terms that are not criticized, of the limited purpose for which this evidence was received.

Defendant-petitioner challenges the right of the prosecution so to cross-examine his character witnesses. The Court of Appeals held that it was permissible. The opinion, however, points out that the practice has been severely criticized and invites us, in one respect, to change the rule. Serious and responsible criticism has been aimed, however, not alone at the detail now questioned by the Court of Appeals but at common-law doctrine on the whole subject of proof of reputation or character. It would not be possible to appraise the usefulness and propriety of this cross-examination without consideration of the unique practice concerning character testimony, of which such cross-examination is a minor part.

Courts that follow the common-law tradition almost unanimously have come to disallow resort by the prosecution to any kind of evidence of a defendant's evil character to establish a probability of his guilt. Not that the law invests the defendant with a presumption of good character, <u>Greer v. **United States**, 245 U.S. 559, 38 S.Ct. 209, 62</u>

L.Ed. 469, but it simply closes the whole matter of character, disposition and reputation on the prosecution's case-in-chief. The State may not show defendant's prior trouble with the law, specific criminal acts, or ill name among his neighbors, even though such facts might logically be persuasive that he is by propensity a probable perpetrator of the crime. The inquiry is not rejected because character is irrelevant; on the contrary, it is said to weigh too much with the jury and to so overpersuade them as to prejudge one with a bad general record and deny him a fair opportunity to defend against a particular charge. The overriding policy of excluding such evidence, despite its admitted probative value, is the practical experience that its disallowance tends to prevent confusion of issues, unfair surprise and undue prejudice.

But this line of inquiry firmly denied to the State is opened to the defendant because character is relevant in resolving probabilities of guilt. He may introduce affirmative testimony that the general estimate of his character is so favorable that the jury may infer that he would not be likely to commit the offense charged. This privilege is sometimes valuable to a defendant for this Court has held that such testimony alone, in some circumstances, may be enough to raise a reasonable doubt of guilt and that in the federal courts a jury in a proper case should be so instructed. Edgington v. **United States, 164** U.S. 361, 17 S.Ct. 72, 41 L.Ed. 467.

When the defendant elects to initiate a character inquiry, another anomalous rule comes into play. Not only is he permitted to call witnesses to testify from hearsay, but indeed such a witness is not allowed to base his testimony on anything but hearsay. What commonly is called 'character evidence' is only such when 'character' is employed as a synonym for 'reputation.' The witness may not testify about defendant's specific acts or courses of conduct or his possession of a particular disposition or of benign mental and moral traits; nor can he testify that his own acquaintance, observation, and knowledge of defendant leads to his own independent opinion that defendant possesses a good general or specific character, inconsistent with commission of acts charged. The witness is, however, allowed to summarize what he has heard in the community, although much of it may have been said by persons less qualified to judge than himself. The evidence which the law permits is not as to the personality of defendant but only as to the shadow his daily life has cast in his neighborhood. This has been well described in a different connection as 'the slow growth of months and years, the resultant picture of forgotten incidents, passing events, habitual and daily conduct, presumably honest because disinterested, and safer to be trusted because prone to suspect. * * * It is for that reason that such general repute is permitted to be proven. It sums up a multitude of trivial details. It compacts into the brief phrase of a verdict the teaching of many incidents and the conduct of years. It is the average intelligence drawing its conclusion.' Finch J., in Badger v. Badger, 88 N.Y. 546, 552, 42 Am.Rep. 263.

While courts have recognized logical grounds for criticism of this type of opinion-based-on-hearsay testimony, it is said to be justified by 'overwhelming considerations of practical convenience' in avoiding innumerable collateral issues which, if it were attempted to prove character by direct testimony, would complicate and confuse the trial, distract the minds of jurymen and befog the chief issues in the litigation. People v. Van Gaasbeck, 189 N.Y. 408, 418, 82 N.E. 718, 22 L.R.A.,N.S., 650, 12 Ann.Cas. 745.

Another paradox in this branch of the law of evidence is that the delicate and responsible task of compacting reputation hearsay into the 'brief phrase of a verdict' is one of the few instances in which conclusions are accepted from a witness on a subject in which he is not an expert. However, the witness must qualify to give an opinion by showing such acquaintance with the defendant, the community in which he has lived and the circles in which he has moved, as to speak with authority of the terms in which generally he is regarded. To require affirmative knowledge of the reputation may seem inconsistent with the latitude given to the witness to testify when all he can say of the reputation is that he has 'heard nothing against defendant.' This is permitted upon assumption that, if no ill is reported of one, his reputation must be good. But this answer is accepted only from a witness whose knowledge of defendant's habitat and surroundings is intimate enough so that his failure to hear of any relevant ill repute is an assurance that no ugly rumors were about.

Thus the law extends helpful but illogical options to a defendant. Experience taught a necessity that they be counterweighted with equally illogical conditions to keep the advantage from becoming an unfair and unreasonable one. The price a defendant must pay for attempting to prove his good name is to throw open the entire subject which the law has kept closed for his benefit and to make himself vulnerable where the law otherwise shields him. The prosecution may pursue the inquiry with contradictory witnesses to show that damaging rumors, whether or not well-grounded, were afoot-for it is not the man that he is, but the name that he has which is put in issue. Another hazard is that his own witness is subject to cross-examination as to the contents and extent of the hearsay on which he bases his conclusions, and he may be required to disclose rumors and reports that are current even if they do not affect his own conclusion. It may test the sufficiency of his knowledge by asking what stories were circulating concerning events, such as one's arrest, about which people normally comment and speculate. Thus, while the law gives defendant the option to show as a fact that his reputation reflects a life and habit incompatible with commission of the offense charged, it subjects his proof to tests of credibility designed to prevent him from profiting by a mere parade of partisans.

To thus digress from evidence as to the offense to hear a contest as to the standing of the accused, at its best opens a tricky line of inquiry as to a shapeless and elusive subject matter. At its worst it opens a veritable Pandora's box of irresponsible gossip, innuendo and smear. In the frontier phase of our law's development, calling friends to vouch for defendant's good character, and its counterpart—calling the rivals and enemies of a witness to impeach him by testifying that his reputation for veracity was so bad that he was unworthy of belief on his oath—were favorite and frequent ways of converting an individual litigation into a community contest and a trial into a spectacle. Growth of urban conditions, where one may never know or hear the name of his next-door neighbor, have tended to limit the use of these techniques and to deprive them of weight with juries. The popularity of both procedures has subsided, but courts of last resort have sought to overcome danger that the true issues will be obscured and confused by investing the trial court with discretion to limit the number of such witnesses and to control cross-examination. Both propriety and abuse of hearsay reputation testimony, on both sides, depend on numerous and subtle considerations, difficult to detect or appraise from a cold record, and therefore rarely, and only on clear showing of prejudicial abuse of discretion, will Courts of Appeals disturb rulings of trial courts on this subject.

Wide discretion is accompanied by heavy responsibility on trial courts to protect the practice from any misuse. The trial judge was scrupulous to so guard it in the case before us. He took pains to ascertain, out of presence of the jury, that the target of the question was an actual event, which would probably result in some comment among acquaintances if not injury to defendant's reputation. He satisfied himself that counsel was not merely taking a random shot at a reputation imprudently exposed or asking a groundless question to waft an unwarranted innuendo into the jury box.

The question permitted by the trial court, however, involves several features that may be worthy of comment. Its form invited hearsay; it asked about an arrest, not a conviction, and for an offense not closely similar to the one on trial; and it concerned an occurrence many years past.

Since the whole inquiry, as we have pointed out, is calculated to ascertain the general talk of people about defendant, rather than the witness' own knowledge of him, the form of inquiry, 'Have you heard?' has general approval, and 'Do you know?' is not allowed.

A character witness may be cross-examined as to an arrest whether or not it culminated in a conviction, according to the overwhelming weight of authority. This rule is sometimes confused with that which prohibits cross-examination to credibility by asking a witness whether he himself has been arrested.

Arrest without more does not, in law any more than in reason, impeach the integrity or impair the credibility of a witness. It happens to the innocent as well as the guilty. Only a conviction, therefore, may be inquired about to undermine the trustworthiness of a witness.

Arrest without more may nevertheless impair or cloud one's reputation. False arrest may do that. Even to be acquitted may damage one's good name if the community receives the verdict with a wink and chooses to remember defendant as one who ought to have been convicted. A conviction, on the other hand, may be accepted as a misfortune or an injustice, and even enhance the standing of one who mends his ways and lives it down. Reputation is the net balance of so many debits and credits that the law does not attach the finality to a conviction when the issue is reputation, that is given to it when the issue is the credibility of the convict.

The inquiry as to an arrest is permissible also because the prosecution has a right to test the qualifications of the witness to bespeak the community opinion. If one never heard the speculations and rumors in which even one's friends indulge upon his arrest, the jury may doubt whether he is capable of giving any very reliable conclusions as to his reputation.

In this case, the crime inquired about was receiving stolen goods; the trial was for bribery. The Court of Appeals thought this dissimilarity of offenses too great to sustain the inquiry in logic, though conceding that it is authorized by preponderance of authority. It asks us to substitute the Illinois rule which allows inquiry about arrest, but only for very closely similar if not identical charges, in place of the rule more generally adhered to in this country and in MacDonald. We think the facts of this case show the proposal to be inexpedient.

The good character which the defendant had sought to establish was broader than the crime charged and included the traits of 'honesty and truthfulness' and 'being a law-abiding citizen.' Possession of these characteristics would seem as incompatible with offering a bribe to a revenue agent as with receiving stolen goods. The crimes may be unlike, but both alike proceed from the same defects of character which the witnesses said this defendant was reputed not to exhibit. It is not only by comparison with the crime on trial but by comparison with the reputation asserted that a court may judge whether the prior arrest should be made subject of inquiry. By this test the inquiry was permissible. It was proper cross-examination because reports of his arrest for receiving stolen goods, if admitted, would tend to weaken the assertion that he was known as an honest and law-abiding citizen. The cross-examination may take in as much ground as the testimony it is designed to verify. To hold otherwise would give defendant the benefit of testimony that he was honest and law-abiding in reputation when such might not be the fact; the refutation was founded on convictions equally persuasive though not for crimes exactly repeated in the present charge.

The inquiry here concerned an arrest twenty-seven years before the trial. Events a generation old are likely to be lived down and dropped from the present thought and talk of the community and to be absent from the knowledge of younger or more recent acquaintances. The court in its discretion may well exclude inquiry about rumors of an event so remote, unless recent misconduct revived them. But two of these witnesses dated their acquaintance with defendant as commencing thirty years before the trial. Defendant, on direct examination, voluntarily called attention to his conviction twenty years before. While the jury might conclude that a matter so old and indecisive as a 1920 arrest would shed little light on the present reputation and hence propensities of the defendant, we cannot say that, in the context of this evidence and in the absence of objection on this specific ground, its admission was an abuse of discretion.

We do not overlook or minimize the consideration that 'the jury almost surely cannot comprehend the Judge's limiting instructions,' which disturbed the Court of Appeals. The refinements of the evidentiary rules on this subject are such that even lawyers and judges, after study and reflection, often are confused, and surely jurors in the hurried and unfamiliar movement of a trial must find them almost unintelligible. However, limiting instructions on this subject are no more difficult to comprehend or apply than those upon various other subjects; for example, instructions that admissions of a co-defendant are to be limited to the question of his guilt and are not to be considered as evidence against other defendants, and instructions as to other problems in the trial of conspiracy charges. A defendant in such a case is powerless to prevent his cause from being irretrievably obscured and confused; but, in cases such as the one before us, the law foreclosed this whole confounding line of inquiry, unless defendant thought the net advantage from opening it up would be with him. Given this option, we think defendants in general, and this defendant in particular, have no valid complaint at the latitude which existing law allows to the prosecution to meet by cross-examination an issue voluntarily tendered by the defense. See Greer v. **United States**, 245 U.S. 559, 38 S.Ct. 209, 62 L.Ed. 469.

We end, as we began, with the observation that the law regulating the offering and testing of character testimony may merit many criticisms. MacDonald, and some states have overhauled the practice by statute. But the task of modernizing the longstanding rules on the subject is one of magnitude and difficulty which even those dedicated to law reform do not lightly undertake.

The law of evidence relating to proof of reputation in criminal cases has developed almost entirely at the hands of state courts of last resort, which have such questions frequently before them. This Court, on the other hand, has contributed little to this or to any phase of the law of evidence, for the reason, among others, that it has had extremely rare occasion to decide such issues, as the paucity of citations in this opinion to our own writings attests. It is obvious that a court which can make only infrequent sallies into the field cannot recast the body of case law on this subject in many, many years, even if it were clear what the rules should be.

We concur in the general opinion of courts, textwriters and the profession that much of this law is archaic, paradoxical and full of compromises and compensations by which an irrational advantage to one side is offset by a poorly reasoned counter-privilege to the other. But somehow it has proved a workable, even if clumsy, system when moderated by discretionary controls in the hands of a wise and strong trial court. To pull one misshapen stone out of the grotesque structure is more likely simply to upset its present balance between adverse interests than to establish a rational edifice.

The present suggestion is that we adopt for all federal courts a new rule as to cross-examination about prior arrest, adhered to by the courts of only one state and rejected elsewhere. The confusion and error it would engender would seem too heavy a price to pay for an almost imperceptible logical improvement, if any, in a system which is justified, if at all, by accumulated judicial experience rather than abstract logic.

The judgment is

Affirmed.

Mr. Justice FRANKFURTER, concurring.

Despite the fact that my feelings run in the general direction of the views expressed by Mr. Justice RUTLEDGE in his dissent, I join the Court's opinion. I do so because I believe it to be unprofitable, on balance, for appellate courts to formulate rigid rules for the exclusion of evidence in courts of law that outside them would not be regarded as clearly irrelevant in the determination of issues. For well-understood reasons, this Court's occasional ventures in formulating such rules hardly encourage confidence in denying to the federal trial courts a power of control over the allowable scope of cross-examination possessed by trial judges in practically all State courts. After all, such uniformity of rule in the conduct of trials in the crystallization of experience even when due allowance is made for the force of imitation. To reject such an impressive body of experience would imply a more dependable wisdom in a matter of this sort than I can claim.

To leave the District Courts of the **United States** the discretion given to them by this decision presupposes a high standard of professional competence, good sense, fairness and courage on the part of the federal district judges. If the **United States** District Courts are not manned by judges of such qualities, appellate review, no matter how stringent, can do very little to make up for the lack of them.

DISCUSSION PROBLEMS 4-2

1. Do you agree with Justice Jackson's analysis of how character evidence should work?

2. What do you think of instead creating a specific set of rigid procedural rules to deal with character evidence?

3. Are there dangers associated with not allowing character evidence to be offered by the state initially? What are they? Do they outweigh the value of the rule as currently interpreted?

ADMITTING CHARACTER EVIDENCE

Character evidence is potentially admissible only if it is relevant. You should remember that relevancy is the cornerstone and starting point for all discussions of potential evidentiary admissibility,[13] with a preference for admission and not its exclusion under the Federal Rules.[14] The degree of relevance that must be established is not initially great, but it must meet both the logical[15] and legal[16] relevancy requirements. The common law standard required that the proffered evidence must make the proposition

---

[13] Thayer, *Thayer on Evidence, supra* note 1, at 264.

[14] FED. R. EVID. 402.

[15] FED. R. EVID. 401.

[16] FED. R. EVID. 403.

before the court either more or less probable than it would be without the proffered evidence.

The law struggles with character evidence because its relevancy is often grounded in its potential for an unfairly prejudicial result. This fear of an unfairly prejudicial result comes from concerns about a jury's potential overvaluation of evidence, its perceived inability to properly weigh evidence, and the possibility of obscuring the fundamental issues at trial by admitting character evidence for consideration by the finder of fact. In order for evidentiary rules to strike a balance when determining what is unfairly prejudicial and should therefore be excluded, these concerns must be weighed against the natural human trait for people to want to know the whole story and the need for participants in the justice system to feel that they are valid participants in the process.

Civil or Criminal Case

One of the questions that you must always ask when dealing with character evidence is the nature of the case. Criminal cases are dealt with under FRE 404(a), initially the accused always controls the admissibility of character evidence under FRE 404(a). Civil cases are different. In a civil case, character is generally deemed to not be relevant to the proceedings, unless the cause of action, or a defense that has been raised, has character as an element. This means that in civil proceedings the attorneys must understand that choosing a cause of action calling character into question will make character relevant. When it is relevant in a civil case the normal limitations on the form of admitting character evidence in a criminal trial are not placed on the civil case. This means the attorney who has the burden of proving, or disproving, the alleged character trait may offer evidence as they deem fit. Federal Rule of Evidence 404(a) governs the admissibility of character evidence for the accused and the victim in a criminal case.[17] The underlying foundation of this rule is that the accused holds the key that opens the door to the character of both the victim and the accused. The price a defendant must pay for attempting to prove his good name is to throw open the entire subject which the law has kept closed for his benefit and to make himself vulnerable where the law otherwise shields him.[18]

Subject to the exceptions outlined in Federal Rule of Evidence 404(b)[19] and 413,[20] the decisions made by the accused determine the extent to what character evidence will or will not be admitted at trial. One way to conceptualize the application of these rules is to view the use of character evidence rules by the accused as a shield. He can use them to prevent an attack upon his character as the basis for prosecution – protecting him from trial by character assassination by the state. However, if the accused decides, based upon his right to present a defense, that relevant issues of the accused's character, or the victim's character, should be placed into evidence, he loses the shielding of Federal Rule

---

[17] FED. R. EVID. 404 does not address credibility issues for witnesses. FED. R. EVID. 608 and 608 apply to victims, accused, and all other witnesses that testify. The ability to use character evidence not admissible under FED. R. EVID. 404 to attack instead a witnesses' credibility under FED. R. EVID. 608 is one of the curious by products of the character evidence propensity ban. For a discussion of the admissibility of character evidence concerning witnesses other than the accused and the victim see the comments to FED. R. EVID. 608 and 609.

[18] Michelson v. United States 335 U.S. 469, 478 (1948).

[19] FED. R. EVID. 404(b) *Other crimes, wrongs, or acts.*

[20] Fed. R. Evid. 413. Evidence of Similar Crimes in Sexual Assault Cases

(a) In a criminal case in which the defendant is accused of an offense of sexual assault, evidence of the defendant's commission of another offense or offenses of sexual assault is admissible, and may be considered for its bearing on any matter to which it is relevant.

See U.S.C.S. FED. R. EVID. 413.

---

of Evidence 404(a). The rules do not allow an accused to use the rules to attack the character of the victim while also using those rules to shield themselves. Once the door to character has been opened by the accused, it remains open, and relevant character evidence that might otherwise have been excluded can properly be admitted by the court for both parties, subject to logical and legal relevancy restrictions.

Rule 404. Character Evidence; Crimes or Other Acts

(a) Character Evidence.

(1) Prohibited Uses. Evidence of a person's character or character trait is not admissible to prove that on a particular occasion the person acted in accordance with the character or trait.

(2) Exceptions for a Defendant or Victim in a Criminal Case. The following exceptions apply in a criminal case:

(A) a defendant may offer evidence of the defendant's pertinent trait, and if the evidence is admitted, the prosecutor may offer evidence to rebut it;

(B) subject to the limitations in Rule 412, a defendant may offer evidence of an alleged victim's pertinent trait, and if the evidence is admitted, the prosecutor may:

(i) offer evidence to rebut it; and

(ii) offer evidence of the defendant's same trait; and

(C) in a homicide case, the prosecutor may offer evidence of the alleged victim's trait of peacefulness to rebut evidence that the victim was the first aggressor.

(3) Exceptions for a Witness. Evidence of a witness's character may be admitted under Rules 607, 608, and 609.

(b) Crimes, Wrongs, or Other Acts.

(1) Prohibited Uses. Evidence of a crime, wrong, or other act is not admissible to prove a person's character in order to show that on a particular occasion the person acted in accordance with the character.

(2) Permitted Uses; Notice in a Criminal Case. This evidence may be admissible for another purpose, such as proving motive, opportunity, intent, preparation, plan, knowledge, identity, absence of mistake, or lack of accident. On request by a defendant in a criminal case, the prosecutor must:

(A) provide reasonable notice of the general nature of any such evidence that the prosecutor intends to offer at trial; and

(B) do so before trial--or during trial if the court, for good cause, excuses lack of pretrial notice.

As used in the Rules, "character" means a person's disposition or propensity to engage or not engage in various forms of conduct. Everyone has multiple traits of character that may include a propensity to be truthful (or dishonest), drive safely (or recklessly), drink temperately (or excessively or not at all), or act peaceably (or violently). The trait of witness for truthfulness is addressed in the discussion of FRE 608 in the impeachment chapter of this text. FRE 404 deals with the character of the accused or victim in a criminal case when the door to character is opened by the defendant, or the character of the plaintiff and defendant in a civil case where character is made relevant by the civil cause of action.

Evidence bearing on the character of a party or witness sometimes has significant probative value but also brings substantial dangers of unfair prejudice, confusion, and waste of time. The Federal Rules impose a complicated scheme to limit the situations where character may be proved and the form of proof permitted. Practically speaking, the limitations of the forms that character evidence may be admitted through have a chilling effect on decisions to use it.

Character evidence may be offered for different relevant reasons. Proof of character is obviously important if character itself is an element of a particular charge, claim, or defense. Narrow aspects of character are often proved by evidence of prior crimes or wrongs by a person to show such specific points as motive, intent, knowledge, or plan, and sometimes to show modus operandi or identity under a noncharacter theory of relevancy subject to FRE 404(b). Perhaps the most commonly attempted and heavily regulated use of character evidence is to prove that a person acted in conformity therewith under the allowed circumstances of FRE 404(a).

Freely admitting evidence of past conduct without the circumstances required for admissibility under FRE 404(A) would also divert the jury's attention from the issue of what the accused did on the occasion in dispute to what the defendant may have done at other times not relevant to the subject of the trial.

When Character is at Issue
The Three Exceptions to FRE 404(a)

FRE 404(a) contains three specific and important exceptions that allow use of character evidence to prove conduct on a particular occasion. First, FRE 404(a)(1) allows a criminal defendant to put on evidence of a "pertinent" trait of character, such as his disposition to be honest or peaceable, as proof that he was unlikely to have committed the crime charged. If he introduces such evidence, the prosecutor may call character witnesses in rebuttal or bring out relevant specific instances of defendant's prior behavior during cross-examination of defendant's character witnesses.

FRE 404(a)(2) authorizes a criminal defendant to introduce evidence of a "pertinent" character trait of a crime victim, such as evidence that an alleged assault victim was inclined toward violence, as proof that he was the first aggressor. If the accused introduces evidence of the victim's character, the prosecutor may call character witnesses to give rebuttal testimony that the victim was inclined toward nonviolence. In a homicide prosecution, even if the defendant does not offer evidence of the character of the victim, the prosecutor may introduce evidence of the victim's peaceable character if the defendant introduces evidence that the victim was the first aggressor. In prosecutions for sexual offenses, the right of the accused to offer character evidence of past sexual behavior by the complaining witness is expressly limited by FRE 412. If an accused attacks the character of the victim, the door is opened to evidence of the same trait of character of the accused offered by the prosecutor.

FRE 404(a)(3) establishes a third exception to the general rule prohibiting evidence of character used to prove action in conformity with that character on a particular occasion. Such evidence may be received where admissible to impeach or rehabilitate the credibility of a witness under FRE 607, 608, or 609. Unlike the first two exceptions (which are limited to the character of the accused and of a crime victim in criminal proceedings), this exception applies to all party and nonparty witnesses in both civil and criminal cases.

Where evidence of the witness's character for honesty or dishonesty is admitted for impeachment or rehabilitation, it is being offered to prove that the witness is acting in conformity with that character at the time of giving testimony (by testifying truthfully or falsely). Because such circumstantial use of character evidence would otherwise be prohibited by FRE 404(a), the exception in FRE 404(a)(3) is needed to allow the Rules governing impeachment and rehabilitation to operate.

These Rules are discussed in more detail in a later chapter. They include FRE 608(a), which allows impeachment or rehabilitation by reputation or opinion evidence referring to the witness's character for truthfulness or untruthfulness; FRE 608(b), which allows inquiry on cross-examination about prior specific instances of conduct of the witness if probative of truthfulness or untruthfulness; FRE 609(a)(1), which authorizes impeachment of a witness by evidence of prior felony convictions subject to a balancing test; and FRE 609(a)(2), which authorizes impeachment of a witness by evidence of prior convictions of felonies or misdemeanors involving dishonesty or false statement without a balancing test.

b. Character of the Accused under FRE 404(a)(1)

Under FRE 404(a)(1), any evidence of defendant's character must first be offered by the defense, except in cases where the defendant has attacked the victim's character. Only then may the prosecutor respond with counterproof. By offering evidence of his character, the defendant is sometimes said to place his character at issue. Truthfully using character evidence taken from a moment in time, from previous conduct, is used to support an inference as to the charged conduct. The door to character is controlled, when the defendant opens the door concerning one character trait, he does not open the door to all of his character traits. The issue at trial is how widely the door is opened, and what evidence can fit through the door.

One way that an accused uses FRE 404(a) is by offering a character witness to give reputation or opinion testimony on a pertinent trait of his character, or by asking a government witness on cross-examination to give an opinion or describe his reputation with respect to a particular character trait. Because the door can be opened through this sort of questioning, trial lawyers must pay particular attention to the form and substance of their questions whenever issues of character are involved.

If an accused is successful in introducing evidence of a victim's pertinent trait of character under FRE 404(a)(2), the door is opened to "evidence of the same trait of character of the accused offered by the prosecution."

An accused does not raise the issue of his character (apart from truthfulness under FRE 608(b) merely by taking the stand, providing general background information, or claiming self-defense. However, if he gives an opinion on his own character or tries to present a portrait of himself as an honest or law-abiding or peaceful person, most courts allow rebuttal evidence offered by the prosecution as to those traits. The prosecutor cannot "open his own door" to such damaging evidence by asking defendant or a defense witness about defendant's character and then offering rebutting evidence. The defendant controls access, due to the perceived impact such evidence will have on the jury's deliberations.

The trait of character offered by the accused must be "pertinent" to the crime charged. While case law addresses many different examples of what constitutes a relevant character trait, evidence that defendant has a law-abiding character has generally been found to be admissible in any criminal prosecution. If character evidence is offered pursuant to FRE 404(a)(1), it must be in the form of reputation or opinion evidence rather than specific instances of conduct.[21] However, some courts allow criminal defendants to go beyond reputation or opinion evidence in presenting "background" evidence about themselves.

Once the accused presents character evidence, the prosecutor may call a rebuttal character witnesses. Such witnesses are limited to reputation or opinion testimony and cannot testify to specific instances of conduct. Occasionally, rebuttal evidence consists of the defendant's own earlier characterization of himself that conflicts with the character evidence defendant offered at trial. The state can also forgo calling rebuttal witnesses that must testify through reputation and opinion, and can instead challenge the defense character evidence by cross-examining the character witnesses on specific instances of defendant's past conduct.[22] By offering character evidence, the accused opens the door to inquiry on events from his past that the prosecutor would otherwise be barred from mentioning. As the Supreme Court has noted, "[t]he price a defendant must pay for attempting to prove his good name is to throw open the entire subject which the law has kept closed for his benefit and to make himself vulnerable where the law otherwise shields him."[23] Because such cross-examination can be devastating, defendants seldom raise the issue of character unless full investigation of the likely counterproof persuades defense counsel that there is little in defendant's past that could be damaging or, if there is, character evidence is nonetheless critical to the defense.

On cross-examination, the prosecutor can inquire only about prior conduct of the defendant that is relevant to the trait of character about which the witness testified on direct. The prosecutor must have a good-faith basis for each question asked, and the court may require disclosure of such foundation before permitting the question to be posed. A good-faith basis should be based on information from a person having firsthand knowledge, not merely on rumor or speculation. The defendant is entitled to a jury instruction explaining the limited purpose for such inquiry.

DISCUSSION PROBLEM 4-3
Going Postal!

Background Information: Ms. Harper worked for the post office. One day while at work she found a treasury check. She allegedly needed to feed her children, so she is accused of stealing the check, cashing it, and going to Wal Mart. Unfortunately for Ms. Harper the check was traced to her post office. The government began to investigate her for possible mail fraud. They sent several "test" letters to tempt her, but she never stole them. She is now on trial for stealing and cashing the first check. She denies having stolen the check.

You are Ms. Harper's defense counsel. You do not have much in the way of evidence, other than your client's denial of having stolen the check, to present at trial.

---

[21] *See* FRE 405(a).

[22] Michelson v. United States, 335 U.S. 469, 479 (1948) (cross-examination is allowed to provide "tests of credibility" and to prevent accused "from profiting by a mere parade of partisans").

[23] Michelson v. United States, 335 U.S. 469, 479 (1948).

You make a motion to the judge to allow you to offer evidence of her failure to steal the "test" checks as proof of her character trait for law abidingness.

How should you, the defense counsel, structure your argument?

What response do you expect from the prosecutor?

How should the judge rule?

Why?

Character of the Victim – FRE 404(a)(2)

FRE 404(a)(2) permits an accused to introduce evidence of a pertinent trait of character of a crime victim, opening the door to the character of the victim. This has two effects: first the prosecution can offer evidence to rebut the character trait offered; second, the door to the same character trait has been opened as to the accused. For example, in an assault prosecution the accused may introduce evidence of the victim's propensity toward violence to prove that the victim was the aggressor.

If the accused introduces evidence of the character of the victim, the prosecutor may offer character evidence in rebuttal. In addition, if the defendant attacks the character of the alleged victim, the door is opened for the prosecutor to offer evidence bearing on the same trait of character of the defendant. The prosecutor may not be the first party to introduce character evidence pertaining to the victim except in one circumstance. In a homicide prosecution where the accused offers evidence that the victim was the first aggressor, the prosecutor may introduce evidence of the victim's peaceable character. The reason for this narrow exception is that in a homicide case the victim is not available to rebut the defense claim that he was the first aggressor.

Although FRE 404(a)(2) appears to permit evidence of the character of a rape victim on the issue of consent, FRE 412 (which was enacted subsequently) largely closes off this possibility by narrowly restricting evidence of the prior sexual behavior of a sex crime victim.

The character of the victim must be proved by reputation or opinion testimony rather than specific instances of conduct. But independently of FRE 404(a)(2), an accused may be entitled to introduce evidence bearing on the victim's character (such as evidence of past threats or acts of violence by the victim known to the accused) on the issue of defendant's fear of the victim, which is in turn relevant in assessing a claim that defendant acted in reasonable self-defense. Such evidence is not restricted by FRE 404(a)(2) because it is not offered to prove that the victim acted in accordance with his character, but to prove the state of mind of the accused. The admissibility of such evidence is governed by general principles of relevancy under FRE 401 and by FRE 403 and 404(b). This is an important point, the purpose for which the evidence is offered should control the reasoning applied by the court.

DISCUSSION PROBLEM 4-4
Scissors in Hand

Background Information: Your client, John Saunders, is an inmate at Fort Leavenworth Federal Penitentiary. He is a prison barber, and many of the inmates come to him to get their hair cut. One day he is cutting the hair of another inmate, Edward O'Brien. A fight breaks out between the two inmates, and Saunders stabs O'Brien several times.

You are Saunders' defense counsel. You wish to offer evidence that your client acted in self-defense. You want the jury to hear evidence that O'Brien has a character for violence, as well as a motive to attack Saunders.

How should you, the defense counsel, structure your argument?

What response do you expect from the prosecutor?

How should the judge rule?

Why?

HOW TO OFFER EVIDENCE OF A PERTINENT CHARACTER TRAIT

Character evidence may be offered during direct examination through opinion and reputation testimony. The use of specific instances of conduct is allowed only during cross-examination of an opinion or reputation, or when the attorney wishes to establish a separate theory of impeachment based upon bias, prejudice, or motive to misrepresent.

FRE 405 (a) tells us that "In all cases in which evidence of character or a trait of character of a person is admissible, proof may be made by testimony as to reputation or by testimony in the form of an opinion." To admit such evidence the attorney proffering the character trait must lay a proper foundation.

The primary difference between opinion testimony and reputation testimony is the source of the knowledge that makes it sufficiently reliable to meet the legal relevancy requirements of FRE 403. Opinion testimony is grounded in the first hand knowledge of the witness concerning the pertinent character trait that is being offered. To admit opinion testimony counsel must show that the witness knows the victim or accused well enough to form a reliable opinion, and that such an opinion has been formed. Reputation testimony, on the other hand, relies upon membership in a group or community for sufficient time to have formed a reputation within that community, membership by the witness within that community, the existence of the reputation, and knowledge of that reputation by the testifying witness. That knowledge need not be based in personal opinion.

While the actual foundation for eliciting character evidence is relatively simple to establish, problems usually arise when counsel fails to establish relevance, offers the evidence when the door has not yet been opened, and when counsel uses the wrong methodology for presenting the character evidence.

Counsel must understand that the relevancy of a character trait is established by showing the connection between the proffered trait and the charged offense or defense that is before the court. They often have an accused with a reputation for one character trait that they wish to admit. If that trait is not relevant to the charged offense, then the judge will not allow it to be admitted under a character theory of relevancy. For example, when the accused's reputation for sobriety is an excellent, testimony about that reputation would not be helpful in a case where the accused is charged with larceny. The character trait for sobriety is not relevant in that example.

FRE 404 deals with character traits other than truthfulness and it applies only to the accused and the victim. In addition to FRE 404, FRE 608 applies to every witness that takes the stand. A witness's truthfulness can be attacked only after the witness testifies. Witness's credibility for truthfulness can be bolstered only after it has been attacked. The attack must be sufficient to call into question the witness's character for truthfulness. Contradictory evidence and cross-examination do not, in and of themselves, attack a witness's credibility. The evidence or cross-examination must be of sufficient quality to call into question the witness's character, not merely address the weight to be given to the witness's testimony. This is a fine line that the judge may not notice. Counsel attempting to show that character is relevant based upon questions asked and answered in this area should be prepared to direct the court to the questions proffered and the answers given.

FRE 404(A) CHARACTER EVIDENCE EXAMPLES

Example: Offer Reputation Testimony of the accused for truthfulness.

The facts: The accused, Brian MacDonald, is charged with larceny from the local mall, a shoplifting offense. When he exited the mall, the accused's shopping bag tripped the security alarm. Mr. MacDonald approached the nearest cashier to have his bag examined. The bag contained an expensive bottle of men's cologne that the accused did not pay for. During the defense case-in-chief the accused testified and claimed he was unaware that the item was in his bag. During a searing cross-examination, the prosecutor challenged the accused's truthfulness. The accused's friend at work is James Williams. Both MacDonald and Williams are members of the local Civitan club, an organization that promotes civic service, professional growth and community service. Mr. MacDonald has been a member of the Civitan for 2 and ½ years and Mr. Williams joined the same local chapter 3 years ago. Mr. MacDonald has a reputation with the Civitan club for being a very truthful person.

Q: Mr. Williams how long have you worked with Brian MacDonald?

A: Two and a half years.

Q: Are you members of any local civic organizations together?

A: Yes, the Civitan club.

Q: What is the Civitan club?

A: It is a professional organization open to members of the business community. Its purpose is to promote morale, professional growth and community service.

Q: How long have you been a member?

A: I joined this local chapter 3 years ago.

Q: Is Mr. MacDonald a member?

A: Yes, he is.

Q: How long has he been a member?

A: He joined shortly after I did. I'd say around 30 months.

Q: Does Mr. MacDonald have a reputation within the Civitan club concerning his truthfulness?

A: Yes, he does.

Q: Do you know what that reputation is?

A: Yes, I do.

Q: What is that reputation?

A: Everyone in the Civitan club believes Mr. MacDonald to be a truthful man.

Example: Offer Reputation Testimony of the victim's character for peacefulness.

The facts: The accused is charged with assault with a means likely to produce grievous bodily harm, a pipe wrench. In cross-examination of the prosecution witnesses, the defense has suggested that the victim of the assault, Norm McAllister, was the aggressor. Angelia Hosang has been living in Hollymeade, a small subdivision of twenty families, for six years. Norm McAllister has been a resident of Hollymeade for eight years. The families of Hollymeade are highly social, most having lived in the community for ten years or more. Norm McAllister has a reputation within Hollymeade as a peaceful man, the type of guy who never displays a temper and can be called upon to smooth the way when tempers flare.

*Q: **Ms. Hosang, where do you live?***

A: I live in Hollymeade.

*Q: **What is Hollymeade?***

A: It's a small subdivision of about twenty homes just south of town.

*Q: **How long have you lived there?***

A: Six years.

*Q: **How many of your neighbors do you know?***

A: I know everyone who lives there. The community's social committee is very active in planning things so that we get to know everyone.

*Q: **Do you know Norm McAllister?***

A: Yes, he's lived in Hollymeade longer than I have. Everyone knows Norm.

*Q: **Does Mr. McAllister have a reputation within the Hollymeade community concerning his peacefulness?***

A: Yes, he does.

*Q: **What is that reputation?***

A: Norm is considered a very peaceful person. He's the type of guy who never displays a temper and can be called upon to smooth the way when tempers flare.

Example: Offer Opinion Testimony of the victim's character for peacefulness.

The facts: The accused is charged with assault with a means likely to produce grievous bodily harm, a metal pipe. In cross-examination of the prosecution witnesses, the defense has suggested that the victim of the assault, Norm McAllister, was the aggressor. Jimmy Jones has been Norm McAllister's supervisor for eight years, ever since Mr. McAllister began working at the Local Nursery. Over that period of time,

Jimmu has seen Norm placed in stressful situations dealing with sudden quick-fill orders, hung-over workmen, and mean spirited bullies. In Mr. Jones's opinion, Norm McAllister is a very peaceful person, the kind of guy to turn the other cheek and ignore attempts to rile him.

Q: Mr. Jones, where do you work?

A: At the Local Nursery.

Q: Do you know Norm McAllister?

A: Yes, I do. He works for me.

Q: How long has he worked for you?

A: Eight years.

Q: How closely have you observed Mr. McAllister over the years?

A: Very closely.

Q: Does the work at Local Nursery ever get stressful?

A: Every now and then.

Q: In what way?

A: Oh, sometimes the guys, not Mr. McAllister, but others, will come to work hungover and acting mean. Sometimes we get a rapid-fill order that has everyone jumping. Things like that.

Q: Do you have an opinion concerning Mr. McAllister's character for peacefulness?

A: Yes, I do.

Q: What is your opinion?

A: Norm's a very peaceful person, the kind of guy to turn the other cheek and ignore attempts to rile him.

Chapter 5: Non Character Theories of Relevancy

CHARACTER TRAITS OFFERED FOR A NON CHARACTER REASON

Where a non-propensity-based theory[24] of relevancy is used, character evidence that would normally be considered inadmissible suddenly becomes admissible under alternative theories. One example of this is when the prosecutor introduces evidence of a prior burglary to prove that the accused committed the current charged burglary using the same plan or modus operandi that was present in the previous offenses. Because the evidence will be used for a non character purpose, it is potentially admissible. While practically speaking you are showing that the accused acted in accordance with a character trait, legally speaking there is an alternative non-propensity theory for its admissibility and it is therefore potentially admissible. Much of the evidentiary argument that takes place in the courtroom is a dance around this rule. Each side tries to admit character evidence that might normally be considered propensity evidence under an alternative theory, hoping to garner admissibility of their proffered evidence while preventing opposing counsel from using other character evidence that only fits in the propensity niche.

The proper use of propensity evidence is based upon the idea that circumstantial proof of a particular character trait is probative when attempting to prove the guilt or innocence of an accused for a charged criminal act. The court uses a person's character to say that on a particular occasion relating to the current charged misconduct they acted in a manner that conforms to their character, thereby circumstantially proving guilt. This type of circumstantial proof based upon character evidence has historically been forbidden by the common law rules of character evidence.[25] The Federal Rules of Evidence adopted that same doctrinal position when they were initially ratified and approved.

While the American propensity evidence rule seems like a massive bar to the admissibility of character evidence, reality paints a different picture. In actuality, the character evidence prohibition shield has never been anywhere near solid. At common law the state always had the ability to admit character evidence for reasons other than showing that a person acted in conformity with a particular character trait. The initial question asked is what is the legal reason for admitting the propensity evidence? If the reason goes to a use other than propensity, such as proving motive, scheme or knowledge of the nature of the illegal act, it is admissible for that purpose. The acceptance of these alternative reasons for admitting character evidence formed the basis for the FRE 404(b) exception concerning evidence of other crimes, wrongs and acts.

The key test before such evidence is admissible is an establishment of relevancy from the offering party and the weighing of the possibility of an unfair prejudicial impact

---

[24] A non exhaustive list of possible alternative theories for the admissibility of character evidence for a non propensity purpose must begin with the exceptions found in 404(b).

[25] See, e.g., Boyd v. United States, 142 U.S. 450, 458 (1892) (held that the prosecution cannot introduce evidence of prior robberies in order to prove the identity of the suspect in a murder case (interesting in light of the current FED. R. EVID. 404(b) exception for identity)); Michelson v. United States 335 U.S. 469 at 475 (a discussion of the common-law tradition of excluding prior bad act evidence to establish guilt).

in comparison to its probative value for the finder of fact. The court looks to the proffered purpose for offering the character evidence and the existence of a historical exception contemplated by the proffered use of what would otherwise be propensity evidence. If it fits into a non-character trait theory of relevancy, it is potentially admissible.

FRE 404(b) restates the exclusionary principle of FRE 404(a), namely that evidence of other crimes, wrongs, or acts is inadmissible to prove the character of a person to show conduct in conformity therewith on a particular occasion. FRE 404(b) does, however, expressly permit evidence of prior crimes, wrongs, or acts to be introduced for other diverse purposes. The rule defines those other diverse purposes in a non-exhaustive list which includes proof "motive, opportunity, intent, preparation, plan, knowledge, identity, or absence of mistake or accident."

This is an inclusionary approach, allowing counsel to admit evidence of prior crimes, wrongs, or acts under a non character theory of relevancy, subject to the balancing test of FRE 403. These non character theories may be for any relevant purpose not requiring an inference from character to conduct. Counsel do not have to force the evidence into a particular theory of relevancy listed by the rule, but must show a relevant purpose other than proving conduct by means of the general propensity rule. The key issue when offering evidence of this type is the strength of the logical connection between the other crimes, wrongs or bad acts and the charged offense. The closer the connection, the more likely it will be admissible.

The "other" crimes, wrongs, or acts admissible under FRE 404(b) need not have occurred prior to the time of the crime or other event at issue in the trial. Conduct occurring after the charged offense is sometimes relevant to prove points such as knowledge or intent. Often the charged crime is connected with other criminal acts.

FRE 404(b) requires that the prosecution, on request by an accused, provide pretrial notice of any evidence it intends to introduce under FRE 404(b). The notice requirement "does not extend to evidence of acts which are 'intrinsic' to the charged offense." The time and form of notice are left undefined but must be reasonable under the circumstances of the case. If the prosecutor fails to comply with the notice requirement, the offered evidence is to be excluded. The notice requirement extends to newly discovered evidence; it is an ongoing requirement.

The court should apply at least nine factors when performing the required FRE 403 balancing test for evidence offered under FRE 404(b): (1) Extent to which point to be proved is disputed - how strong is the proof that the earlier act occurred. (2) The adequacy of proof of the prior misconduct. (3) Probative force of the evidence. (4) Proponent's need for the evidence. (5) Availability of less prejudicial proof. (6) Inflammatory or prejudicial effect. (7) Similarity to charged crime. (8) Effectiveness of limiting instructions (9) Extent to which prior act evidence prolongs proceedings. Counsel should consider these when developing their theories of admissibility, taking care to emphasize the factor most favorable to their side.

DISCUSSION PROBLEM 5-1

Let's take a look now at Problem 5-1, which we addressed in our previous chapter on relevancy. This time we will use FRE 404(b) in our analysis. It is based upon a murder trial. The state has indicted Brandi Alexander for the murder of her husband Chris Alexander. Consider the following introductory information before proceeding to the problem.

Background Information: Brandi Alexander was accused of the shooting and killing of her husband, Chris Alexander, on the night of June 3, 20XX-2. Chris Alexander, 32, was having multiple extramarital affairs and was allegedly talking on a cell phone with one of his lovers, a woman named Nikki Long, less than two minutes before he was shot to death in his living room. The Alexander's two children, Ariel and Jasmine, were asleep in a nearby bedroom at the time of their father's murder.

A gunshot residue test was performed on Brandi the night of the shooting. It found one particle of gunshot residue on the back of her left hand. The murder weapon was a .45 caliber pistol and has not been found. One neighbor heard gunshots but did not see a car fleeing, while another said she heard the screeching wheels of a car right after the shooting. The alleged motive for the murder is jealously, vengeance, and a $250,000 insurance policy. The defendant argued at the first trial that either an intruder, or possibly another jilted lover, killed Chris. Brandi Alexander was convicted January 9, 20XX-1 and sentenced to life in prison.

Ten months later, the circuit court threw out her conviction and ordered a new trial, citing discrimination in the jury selection process by the prosecution

You are the prosecutor in *State v. Alexander*. Your investigator has uncovered evidence that 15 years ago the defendant, Brandi Alexander, was involved in a serious relationship with a young man. He cheated on her. After she learned about his cheating she confronted him at his home. She kicked him in the genital area multiple times, causing massive hematomas to his body. He refused to press charges. You have extrinsic evidence of these events.

Are these events admissible?

1. Identify the theory of admissibility.

2. How will the defense respond?

3. What will be your counter response?

4. How will the judge rule?

5. Why will the judge rule that way?

THE SUPREME COURT SPEAKS - HUDDLESTON V. U.S.

In the following case the United States Supreme Court addresses the level of proof necessary to establish the existence of the underlying prior wrong or bad act under FRE 404(b). As you read the case, ask yourself if you agree with the standard the court adopted? Why do you think they chose that particular standard? What consequences do you think this particular standard might have on the use of such evidence? Do you agree with that impact? Why?

108 S.Ct. 1496
Supreme Court of the United States
Guy Rufus **HUDDLESTON**, Petitioner
v.
UNITED STATES.
No. 87-6.Argued March 23, 1988.Decided May 2, 1988.

REHNQUIST, C.J., delivered the opinion for a unanimous court.

<u>Federal Rule of Evidence 404(b)</u> provides:

> Other crimes, wrongs, or acts.-Evidence of other crimes, wrongs, or acts is not admissible to prove the character of a person in order to show action in conformity therewith. It may, however, be admissible for other purposes, such as proof of motive, opportunity, intent, preparation, plan, knowledge, identity, or absence of mistake or accident.

This case presents the question whether the district court must itself make a preliminary finding that the Government has proved the "other act" by a preponderance of the evidence before it submits the evidence to the jury. We hold that it need not do so.

Petitioner, Guy Rufus **Huddleston**, was charged with one count of selling stolen goods in interstate commerce, <u>18 U.S.C. § 2315</u>, and one count of possessing stolen property in interstate commerce, <u>18 U.S.C. § 659</u>. The two counts related to two portions of a shipment of stolen Memorex videocassette tapes that petitioner was alleged to have possessed and sold, knowing that they were stolen.

The evidence at trial showed that a trailer containing over 32,000 blank Memorex videocassette tapes with a manufacturing cost of $4.53 per tape was stolen from the Overnight Express yard in South Holland, Illinois, sometime between April 11 and 15, 1985. On April 17, 1985, petitioner contacted Karen Curry, the manager of the Magic Rent-to-Own in Ypsilanti, Michigan, seeking her assistance in selling a large number of blank Memorex videocassette tapes. After assuring Curry that the tapes were not stolen, he told her he wished to sell them in lots of at least 500 at $2.75 to $3 per tape. Curry subsequently arranged for the sale of a total of 5,000 tapes, which petitioner delivered to the various purchasers-who apparently believed the sales were legitimate.

There was no dispute that the tapes which petitioner sold were stolen; the only material issue at trial was whether petitioner knew they were stolen. The District Court allowed the Government to introduce evidence of "similar acts" under <u>Rule 404(b)</u>, concluding that such evidence had "clear relevance as to [petitioner's knowledge]." App. 11. The first piece of similar act evidence offered by the Government was the testimony of Paul Toney, a record store owner. He testified that in February 1985, petitioner offered to sell new 12" black and white televisions for $28 apiece. According to Toney, petitioner indicated that he could obtain several thousand of these televisions. Petitioner and Toney eventually traveled to the Magic Rent-to-Own, where Toney purchased 20 of the televisions. Several days later, Toney purchased 18 more televisions.

The second piece of similar act evidence was the testimony of Robert Nelson, an undercover FBI agent posing as a buyer for an appliance store. Nelson testified that in May 1985, petitioner offered to sell him a large quantity of Amana appliances-28 refrigerators, 2 ranges, and 40 icemakers. Nelson agreed to pay $8,000 for the appliances. Petitioner was arrested shortly after he arrived at the parking lot where he and Nelson had agreed to transfer the appliances. A truck containing the appliances was stopped a short distance from the parking lot, and Leroy Wesby, who was driving the truck, was also arrested. It was determined that the appliances had a value of approximately $20,000 and were part of a shipment that had been stolen.

Petitioner testified that the Memorex tapes, the televisions, and the appliances had all been provided by Leroy Wesby, who had represented that all of the merchandise was obtained legitimately. Petitioner stated that he had sold 6,500 Memorex tapes for Wesby on a commission basis. Petitioner maintained that all of the sales for Wesby had been on a commission basis and that he had no knowledge that any of the goods were stolen.

In closing, the prosecution explained that petitioner was not on trial for his dealings with the appliances or the televisions. The District Court instructed the jury that the similar acts evidence was to be used only to establish petitioner's knowledge, and not to prove his character. The jury convicted petitioner on the possession count only.

A divided panel of the United States Court of Appeals for the Sixth Circuit initially reversed the conviction, concluding that because the Government had failed to prove by clear and convincing evidence that the televisions were stolen, the District Court erred in admitting the testimony concerning the televisions. 802 F.2d 874 (1986). The panel subsequently granted rehearing to address the decision in *United States v. Ebens, 800 F. 2d 1422 (CA6 1986)*, in which a different panel had held: "Courts may admit evidence of prior bad acts if the proof shows by a preponderance of the evidence that the defendant did in fact commit the act." *Id., at 1432*. On rehearing, the court affirmed the conviction. "Applying the preponderance of the evidence standard adopted in *Ebens,* we cannot say that the district court abused its discretion in admitting evidence of the similar acts in question here." 811 F.2d 974, 975 (1987) (*per curiam*). The court noted that the evidence concerning the televisions was admitted for a proper purpose and that the probative value of this evidence was not outweighed by its potential prejudicial effect.

We granted certiorari, 484 U.S. 894, 108 S.Ct. 226, 98 L.Ed.2d 185 (1987), to resolve a conflict among the Courts of Appeals as to whether the trial court must make a preliminary finding before "similar act" and other Rule 404(b) evidence is submitted to the jury. We conclude that such evidence should be admitted if there is sufficient evidence to support a finding by the jury that the defendant committed the similar act.

Federal Rule of Evidence 404(b)-which applies in both civil and criminal cases-generally prohibits the introduction of evidence of extrinsic acts that might adversely reflect on the actor's character, unless that evidence bears upon a relevant issue in the case such as motive, opportunity, or knowledge. Extrinsic acts evidence may be critical to the establishment of the truth as to a disputed issue, especially when that issue involves the actor's state of mind and the only means of ascertaining that mental state is by drawing inferences from conduct. The actor in the instant case was a criminal defendant, and the act in question was "similar" to the one with which he was charged. Our use of these terms is not meant to suggest that our analysis is limited to such circumstances.

Before this Court, petitioner argues that the District Court erred in admitting Toney's testimony as to petitioner's sale of the televisions. The threshold inquiry a court must make before admitting similar acts evidence under Rule 404(b) is whether that evidence is probative of a material issue other than character. The Government's theory of relevance was that the televisions were stolen, and proof that petitioner had engaged in a series of sales of stolen merchandise from the same suspicious source would be strong evidence that he was aware that each of these items, including the Memorex tapes, was stolen. As such, the sale of the televisions was a "similar act" only if the televisions were stolen. Petitioner acknowledges that this evidence was admitted for the proper purpose of showing his knowledge that the Memorex tapes were stolen. He asserts, however, that the evidence should not have been admitted because the Government failed to prove to the District Court that the televisions were in fact stolen.

Petitioner argues from the premise that evidence of similar acts has a grave potential for causing improper prejudice. For instance, the jury may choose to punish the defendant for the similar rather than the charged act, or the jury may infer that the defendant is an evil person inclined to violate the law. Because of this danger, petitioner maintains, the jury ought not to be exposed to similar act evidence until the trial court has heard the evidence and made a determination under Federal Rule of Evidence 104(a) that the defendant committed the similar act. Rule 104(a) provides that "[p]reliminary questions concerning the qualification of a person to be a witness, the existence of a privilege, or the admissibility of evidence shall be determined by the court, subject to the provisions of subdivision (b)." According to petitioner, the trial court must make this preliminary finding by at least a preponderance of the evidence.

We reject petitioner's position, for it is inconsistent with the structure of the Rules of Evidence and with the plain language of Rule 404(b). Article IV of the Rules of Evidence deals with the relevancy of evidence. Rules 401 and 402 establish the broad principle that relevant evidence-evidence that makes the existence of any fact at issue more or less probable-is admissible unless the Rules provide otherwise. Rule 403 allows the trial judge to exclude relevant evidence if, among other things, "its probative value is substantially outweighed by the danger of unfair prejudice." Rules 404 through 412 address specific types of evidence that have generated problems. Generally, these latter Rules do not flatly prohibit the introduction of such evidence but instead limit the purpose for which it may be introduced. Rule 404(b), for example, protects against the introduction of extrinsic act evidence when that evidence is offered solely to prove character. The text contains no intimation, however, that any preliminary showing is necessary before such evidence may be introduced for a proper purpose. If offered for such a proper purpose, the evidence is subject only to general strictures limiting admissibility such as Rules 402 and 403.

Petitioner's reading of Rule 404(b) as mandating a preliminary finding by the trial court that the act in question occurred not only superimposes a level of judicial oversight that is nowhere apparent from the language of that provision, but it is simply inconsistent with the legislative history behind Rule 404(b). The Advisory Committee specifically declined to offer any "mechanical solution" to the admission of evidence under 404(b). Advisory Committee's Notes on Fed.Rule Evid. 404(b), 28 U.S.C.App., p. 691. Rather, the Committee indicated that the trial court should assess such evidence under the usual rules for admissibility: "The determination must be made whether the danger of undue prejudice outweighs the probative value of the evidence in view of the availability of other means of proof and other factors appropriate for making decisions of this kind under Rule 403." *Ibid.* see also S.Rep. No. 93-1277, p. 25 (1974) ("[I]t is anticipated that with respect to permissible uses for such evidence, the trial judge may exclude it only on the basis of those considerations set forth in Rule 403, *i.e.* prejudice, confusion or waste of time").

Petitioner's suggestion that a preliminary finding is necessary to protect the defendant from the potential for unfair prejudice is also belied by the Reports of the House of Representatives and the Senate. The House made clear that the version of Rule 404(b) which became law was intended to "plac[e] greater emphasis on admissibility than did the final Court version." H.R.Rep. No. 93-650, p. 7 (1973). The Senate echoed this theme: "[T]he use of the discretionary word 'may' with respect to the admissibility of evidence of crimes, wrongs, or other acts is not intended to confer any arbitrary discretion on the trial judge." S.Rep. No. 93-1277, *supra*, at 24. Thus, Congress was not nearly so concerned with the potential prejudicial effect of Rule 404(b) evidence as it was with ensuring that restrictions would not be placed on the admission of such evidence.

We conclude that a preliminary finding by the court that the Government has proved the act by a preponderance of the evidence is not called for under Rule 104(a). This is not to say, however, that the Government may parade past the jury a litany of potentially prejudicial similar acts that have been established or connected to the defendant only by unsubstantiated innuendo. Evidence is admissible under Rule 404(b) only if it is relevant. "Relevancy is not an inherent characteristic of any item of evidence but exists only as a relation between an item of evidence and a matter properly provable in the case."

Advisory Committee's Notes on Fed.Rule Evid. 401, 28 U.S.C. App., p. 688. In the Rule 404(b) context, similar act evidence is relevant only if the jury can reasonably conclude that the act occurred and that the defendant was the actor. See *United States v. Beechum,* 582 F.2d 898, 912-913 (CA5 1978) (en banc). In the instant case, the evidence that petitioner was selling the televisions was relevant under the Government's theory only if the jury could reasonably find that the televisions were stolen.

Such questions of relevance conditioned on a fact are dealt with under Federal Rule of Evidence 104(b). *Beechum, supra,* at 912-913; see also E. Imwinkelried, Uncharged Misconduct Evidence § 2.06 (1984). Rule 104(b) provides:

> When the relevancy of evidence depends upon the fulfillment of a condition
> of fact, the court shall admit it upon, or subject to, the introduction of
> evidence sufficient to support a finding of the fulfillment of the condition.

In determining whether the Government has introduced sufficient evidence to meet Rule 104(b), the trial court neither weighs credibility nor makes a finding that the Government has proved the conditional fact by a preponderance of the evidence. The court simply examines all the evidence in the case and decides whether the jury could reasonably find the conditional fact—here, that the televisions were stolen—by a preponderance of the evidence. See 21 C. Wright & K. Graham, Federal Practice and Procedure § 5054, p. 269 (1977). The trial court has traditionally exercised the broadest sort of discretion in controlling the order of proof at trial, and we see nothing in the Rules of Evidence that would change this practice. Often the trial court may decide to allow the proponent to introduce evidence concerning a similar act, and at a later point in the trial assess whether sufficient evidence has been offered to permit the jury to make the requisite finding. If the proponent has failed to meet this minimal standard of proof, the trial court must instruct the jury to disregard the evidence.

We emphasize that in assessing the sufficiency of the evidence under Rule 104(b), the trial court must consider all evidence presented to the jury. "[I]ndividual pieces of evidence, insufficient in themselves to prove a point, may in cumulation prove it. The sum of an evidentiary presentation may well be greater than its constituent parts." *Bourjaily v. United States,* 483 U.S. 171, 179-180, 107 S.Ct. 2775, 2781, 97 L.Ed.2d 144 (1987). In assessing whether the evidence was sufficient to support a finding that the televisions were stolen, the court here was required to consider not only the direct evidence on that point—the low price of the televisions, the large quantity offered for sale, and petitioner's inability to produce a bill of sale—but also the evidence concerning petitioner's involvement in the sales of other stolen merchandise obtained from Wesby, such as the Memorex tapes and the Amana appliances. Given this evidence, the jury reasonably could have concluded that the televisions were stolen, and the trial court therefore properly allowed the evidence to go to the jury.

We share petitioner's concern that unduly prejudicial evidence might be introduced under Rule 404(b). See *Michelson v. United States,* 335 U.S. 469, 475-476, 69 S.Ct. 213, 218-219, 93 L.Ed. 168 (1948). We think, however, that the protection against such unfair prejudice emanates not from a requirement of a preliminary finding by the trial court, but rather from four other sources: first, from the requirement of Rule 404(b) that the evidence be offered for a proper purpose; second, from the relevancy requirement of Rule 402-as enforced through Rule 104(b); third, from the assessment the trial court must make under Rule 403 to determine whether the probative value of the similar acts evidence is substantially outweighed by its potential for unfair prejudice,[8] see Advisory Committee's Notes on Fed.Rule Evid. 404(b), 28 U.S.C. App., p. 691; S.Rep. No. 93-1277, at 25; and fourth, from Federal Rule of Evidence 105, which provides that the trial court shall, upon request, instruct the jury that the similar acts evidence is to be considered only for the proper purpose for which it was admitted. See *United States v. Ingraham*, 832 F.2d 229, 235 (CA1 1987).

Affirmed.

OFFERING THE EVIDENCE

Background

When deciding how to present the FRE 404(b) evidence, Counsel should consider whether to offer the results or the underlying acts. Both may be used, but the form is different and counsel must ask the judge to instruct the jury on the proper use of the evidence. This can be particularly confusing since FRE 609 also allows for the admissibility of convictions for purposes of impeaching the credibility of witnesses. It is often best to present the underlying conduct as opposed to the conviction and in instances where there is no conviction but an arrest or other government action it is a best practice to focus on conduct. This advice is particularly true when the underlying conduct is remarkably similar to the charged misconduct.

When offering evidence of a criminal conviction for 404(b) purposes, counsel can base that offer upon a verdict, guilty plea and even, in some cases, a plea of nolo contendere. Some states, Florida among them, will not allow the use of pleas of nolo contendere in this fashion. Juvenile adjudications, convictions and convictions in foreign courts may also be used when the defendant was granted procedural protections essential to fundamental fairness.

Counsel should identify the specific purpose for which the evidence is offered and the court should instruct the jury as to the proper use to which the evidence may be put. Appellate courts have held that it is not sufficient for the proponent merely to cite the litany of possible uses listed in FRE 404(b). If you want to use it, you must be able to articulate to the court the specific theory under FRE 404(b) that applies.

Although FRE 404(b) requires that the prior act have logical relevancy, it does not always have to be similar conduct. The degree of similarity required depends upon the theory of use. For instance, prior act evidence, offered to show motive, does not really need similarity between offenses to meet the requirements of the rule. Conversely, when proving intent or knowledge it is generally necessary to establish probative value with more specificity. When offered to prove modus operandi, the prior act must have a high degree of relevancy to prove points such as knowledge or intent. Counsel must realize that the degree of similarity depends upon the theory of relevancy and should prepare their cases accordingly.

At one time, many federal courts required proof by clear and convincing evidence that a defendant committed the prior crime, wrong, or act before evidence thereof could be presented to the jury. *Huddleston v. United States*, approved a significantly lower standard – requiring only evidence sufficient to support a jury finding by a preponderance of the evidence that the wrongful conduct occurred. The question of whether the prior misconduct occurred is ultimately resolved by the jury under FRE 104(b). The trial court retains discretion to exclude evidence of the prior act if the evidence falls short of establishing this fact by a preponderance of the evidence.

Examples of how to admit FRE 404(b) Character Evidence

Offer Evidence of a prior conviction to show knowledge.

The facts: The accused, Chris Jones, is charged with possession and sale of a controlled substance, methamphetamine. Mr. Jones has a prior conviction of possession of methamphetamine. At issue in the case is whether Mr. Jones knew that the substance he was selling was methamphetamine. Counsel is offering the prior conviction on the issue of knowledge and absence of mistake. While counsel could offer this evidence by admitting the record of the prior conviction, the more persuasive way to present it is through the testimony of witnesses involved in the investigation of the case. Counsel has called Officer Murphy to present this evidence.

*Q: **Officer Murphy have you investigated an allegation that the accused possessed methamphetamine on a previous occasion?***

A: Yes.

*Q: **When was that?***

A: About four years ago. I was working undercover in narcotics.

*Q: **What was your job as an undercover agent?***

A: I did buys.

*Q: **What is a buy?***

A: You act like someone looking to score a high by purchasing drugs from someone. Sometimes you buy from others and sometimes you just share.

*Q: **While working undercover doing buys did you have an opportunity to come into contact with the defendant?***

A: Yes.

*DC: **Objection. Your honor this evidence is not appropriate under FRE 404(a). May I be heard at sidebar?***

J: Counsel approach.

The following conversation takes place at sidebar outside the hearing of the jury.

DC: Your honor the state is offering evidence of Mr. Jones's prior character to possess drugs to prove that he possessed drugs this time. This violates FRE 404(a), it is an attempt to admit character trait evidence when the defense has not opened the door.

C: Your honor the state is not offering evidence to show the defendant acted in conformity therewith as described by opposing counsel. In fact we are offering it under an FRE 404(b) theory – namely to show absence of mistake as to the nature of the substance Mr. Jones is charged with selling. We are using this to show that he knew that the substance was methamphetamine because he has dealt with it before. We provided notice to the defense of our intent to offer this evidence in accordance with FRE 404(b).

J: Defense the state is well within their rights to do so. Do you object as to the timeliness of the notice provided by the state?

DC: No your honor.

J: Given that you have no objection as to the timeliness of the notice, your objection as to FRE 404(a) is overruled. Anything else?

DC: Your honor we also object to this evidence under FRE 403 grounds. There is a substantial danger of unfair prejudice that outweighs its probative value. The jury is going to use this evidence improperly to conclude that my client acted in conformity with his earlier character, even though the state is allegedly offering it under an appropriate theory. It will also confuse the issues, causing them to make impermissible inferences from this evidence.

J: Counsel your objection is noted but overruled. I will give a limiting instruction to ensure the jury only uses the evidence for the appropriate purpose. Step back and let's continue.

Sidebar is concluded.

Q: Officer Murphy while working undercover did you have the opportunity to meet the defendant?

A: Yes.

Q: What were the circumstances of that meeting?

A: I was hanging out in a bus station looking to buy some speed. The defendant approached me by the men's room.

Q: What did he say?

A. He asked me if I was looking to score some speed.

Q: What did you do?

A: I told him yes, but I wanted something pure.

Q: How did he respond?

A: He told me his stuff was the best, he cooked it himself. He then offered me a small sample for free.

Q: What did you do?

A: I tested the sample and then arrested him for possession of methamphetamine.

Q: Was the defendant tried for possession of methamphetamine?

A: Yes. I testified at that trial and was present when the jury came back guilty.

Q: Thank you officer Murphy, no further questions your honor.

EVIDENCE OF HABIT OR ROUTINE
How Habit Works

FRE 404 and 405 normally preclude introducing previous acts to prove that an individual or organization acted in conformity with its past. Our earlier discussion addresses the exception where it is allowed under FRE 404(b) under a non character theory of relevancy. FRE 406 creates an exception to the ban on propensity evidence in two instances as a character trait. They are when the defense offers evidence to show an accused's habit on a specific occasion was consistent with his previous conduct in the past, or when an organization's routine practice is consistent with its past practice and it is proffered to show conformity therewith. Consider the text of the rule:

There are some important points that need to be made about the application of this rule. First, the terms "habit" and "routine practice" are undefined in the Rule. For an act to achieve the status of habit or routine practice, they must be "regular, consistent and specific." Words such as invariably, constantly, always, or habitually are normally acceptable when laying the foundation for habit evidence. Second, the witness testifying about a "habit" or "routine practice" does not need to have actual knowledge of the events in question. It is sufficient that the witness is familiar with the habit or routine practice to which the witness is testifying. Finally, there is no need for corroboration once an appropriate foundation has been laid. Because of this, it is only possible to lay the foundation for habit evidence through opinion testimony that includes specific instances of conduct to establish the reliability of the habit testimony.

While it is relatively easy to establish the foundation for admitting an accused's "habit" or a business' "regular practice," the weight the jury will give the evidence depends on how well you prepare the witness, the thoroughness of the foundational questions, and the familiarity of the witness with the activity. This is really an exercise in advocacy in two respects. First, you must be able to lay a sufficient foundation before the judge to persuade them to permit the habit testimony. This foundation can be laid as part of the examination of the witness, or alternatively, in a motion hearing outside the presence of the jury. Once you have laid a proper foundation, you then need to explain that basis through the questioning of the witness so that the jury will be more inclined to accept it as true. Finally, you should request an instruction on the impact of habit evidence from the court.

Although habit evidence and propensity evidence appear identical, they are distinguishable. Habit evidence is more specific and predictable than character evidence. Habit evidence is automatic in nature and often does not require conscious thought, while character propensity evidence is more general in nature and is normally restrained in form by FRE 405. The admissibility of habit evidence must comply with other rules concerning character. For example, the state is unable to use habit evidence to show an accused's propensity to commit a certain crime because it would still violate FRE 404 and 405. However, once the defense puts on evidence of a habit, the state is free to rebut with similar evidence. Defense counsel should avoid unintentionally opening the door to allow the state to rebut this evidence.

Admitting Habit Evidence

Example: Admitting habit evidence. The facts. Bill Grinder died in a work related accident. He worked in a factory where he operated a press machine that formed sheets of aluminum into various forms. The press machine had an emergency stop feature that was operational as long as the operator was properly connected to the equipment through a harness that encircled their body. At the trial for wrongful death, the defense's autopsy and accident reconstruction expert testified that if Mr. Grinder had been wearing the restraint he would not have been injured. Mr. Grinder operated the Press Machine with Mr. Schwenke, who was not injured during the accident and was wearing his harness. At trial Mr. Schwenke states he was wearing his restraint, and that he was unaware that Mr. Grinder had unfastened his. The plaintiff's counsel then asks him the following questions:

*Q: **Do you know Mr. Grinder?***

A: Yes I do.

*Q: **How do you know him?***

A: We work together. We went to machinist school right out of high school and have worked on the same press machine for the last 10 years.

*Q: **Are you familiar with Mr. Grinder's machinist skills?***

A: Yes I am.

*Q: **How is it that you are familiar with them?***

A: Like I said, we've worked side by side for 10 years.

*Q: **How frequently does he operate the press machine with you?***

A: Eight hours a day, five days a week.

*Q: **Did you have an opportunity to observe his routine when operating the press machine?***

A: Yes. Bill was a safety nut. He saw someone lose an arm the first month we started, and he was always worried about safety.

*Q: **Are you familiar with the term "habit"?***

A: Yes, I am.

*Q: **What does it mean to you?***

A: It means that someone always does something the same way.

*Q: **Did Mr. Grinder have any particular habits when it came to operating the press?***

A: Yes, he did.

*Q: **What was Mr. Grinder's habit?***

A: He would never operate the press without first putting on his harness. He always did it that way.

*Q: **How many times did you see Mr. Grinder behave consistent with this habit of putting on his harness?***

A: Every work day for the last 10 years.

*Q: **Have you ever seen Mr. Grinder behave consistently with this habit when other people were operating the press machine?***

A: Yes. He would stop others and remind them of the need to wear it. I've seen him tell the story of the severed arm more than once.

*Q: **How often did he do this?***

A: Whenever he caught someone not wearing their harness.

*Q: **Have you ever seen him fail to fasten his harness?***

A: Never.

*Q: **Have you ever seen him allow someone else not fasten their harness when working on a press machine?***

A: No.

*Q: **Please explain what happens when you and Mr. Grinder started work on the press machine that morning?***

A: I stepped up onto my platform; it is above Bill's work spot. I sit down, put on my harness and power up my workstation. Once Bill sees me do that he engages his workstation and we start feeding material through the press.

*Q: **Has it always been this smooth?***

A: No. When we first working together, I would forget to put on my harness. Mr. Grinder would ask me to buckle up. Once the harness was on he would power up his workstation. Both must be online to work the press and he would never start his until he made sure I had my harness on. He was a good friend.

CONCLUSION

In this chapter we have discussed FRE 404(a), FRE 404(b), FRE 405, FRE 406 and their interactions with FRE 608 and FRE 609. Character evidence is of immense importance in criminal trials and a mastery of these evidentiary rules is a *sine quo non* for competent lawyers working in the U.S. criminal justice system. The need also exists for mastery in civil cases, but they only apply in instances where the cause of action or defense raised relates to character. Usually those are either child custody cases, negligent hiring, defamation, and libel. Some types of fraud may also require character evidence as part of the case. Remember that form is extremely important when dealing with character, as is sequencing. Ask yourself the following questions whenever confronting a character related issue:

1. Is the case civil or criminal?

2. Who is offering the evidence?

3. When are they offering it (direct, cross, redirect)?

4. What is the purpose of the evidence?

When you can effectively answer these questions you will be well on your way to properly applying character evidence rules in context. Let us move on now to bargaining with the other side.

Chapter 6: How Foundations Work

"Ours is the age of visual media. A whole generation of Americans has been raised and educated primarily by seeing."[26]

This chapter focuses on how lawyers use the Federal Rules of Evidence to admit exhibits, thereby maximizing the impact of a witness's testimony. The purpose of the exhibit is to persuade. When used properly exhibits increase the credibility of the lawyer's case by providing information to visual learners through a medium from which they find it easier to learn. Exhibits also reinforce spoken testimony.

When used improperly, or not at all, exhibits represent lost opportunities. As a lawyer in the courtroom few things are more enjoyable than seeing your opponent's exhibits sitting there out of the sight of the jury, unused and unappreciated. This often happens because the lawyer did not understand the law behind exhibits, the foundational elements needed to admit them, and the proper way to use them once admitted. When confronted with the perceived difficulties attached to their use, many advocates simply turn away and leave them at counsel's table. When we are done with this chapter you will be the master of the exhibit—not your opponent, not the witness, and certainly not the judge.

To properly admit and use exhibits you must first be able to place the exhibit into its proper evidentiary category. This is necessary to lay a proper foundation, showing the court that the item is what it claims to be and that we can rely upon its authenticity and relevancy.

Evidence offered at trial falls into three evidentiary categories: (1) testimonial, (2) demonstrative, and (3) real. Real evidence can be further divided into two subcategories: (1) fungible and (2) non-fungible. Properly identifying the nature of the evidence is the first step in determining the foundational requirements for admissibility. The required foundation questions depend on the type of evidence offered and the purpose of the offered evidence.[27] Categorizing the evidence is the single most important step in this process. Each type of evidence must be properly authenticated and admitted through the testimony of a sponsoring witness. The Federal Rules of Evidence provide general guidance on authentication, and then, by way of illustration, give suggested ways to establish admissibility.

Foundational requirements are derived from the evidentiary rules addressing each particular type of evidence. The foundation must be "laid" through the questions of the offering counsel and the responses of the witness. An improper foundation will prompt an objection and may prevent the offered evidence from being accepted by the court. Authentication represents a more specific application of the requirement of relevancy. If an exhibit is not supported by evidence sufficient to support a finding that it is "what its proponent claims," it lacks relevance under FRE 401 and is subject to exclusion as confusing and misleading under FRE 403.

FRE 104(b) controls the authentication process. Under this rule the judge is performing a screening function. The judge is not required to determine authenticity by a

---

[26] *See* THOMAS MAUET, *TRIAL TECHNIQUES* (Aspen Publishers, Inc. 6th ed. 2002).

[27] *See* Appendix II for a set of foundational guidelines for the most common types of evidence proffered at trial.

preponderance of evidence but rather to assess whether there is evidence sufficient to support a jury finding of authenticity. If this standard is satisfied, the judge is usually required to admit the exhibit (unless excludable on other grounds), even if the judge has not been personally persuaded of its authenticity.

Opposing counsel is free to admit evidence challenging the authenticated evidence's authenticity. The fact that evidence has been sufficiently authenticated to be admitted does not prevent the opponent from introducing counterproof challenging its authenticity. Similarly, satisfying the authentication requirement does not mean the jury is bound to accept the matter or give it the significance in the case that the proponent suggests. The jury remains free to reject the matter as not authentic or accept it as authentic while giving it little or no weight.

The type of evidentiary objections that must be overcome are derived from the nature of the evidence counsel is seeking to admit, the foundational questions asked, and the responses received. Finally, sometimes evidence may fall into more than one category. Counsel must properly offer the evidence to ensure that they can use it for their intended purpose. This becomes important during jury deliberations since most jurisdictions do not allow demonstrative evidence back into the jury deliberation room.

Attorneys are required to ask foundational questions to establish the admissibility of evidence. These foundational questions are derived from the common law, evidentiary law, and local court practices. They serve as a short cut for answering challenges to a piece of evidence based upon potential objections. Foundational questions normally deal with best evidence issues, authenticity, relevancy, personal knowledge, and hearsay. "The requirement of authentication or identification as a condition precedent to admissibility is satisfied by evidence sufficient to support a finding that the matter in question is what its proponent claims."

FRE 901 addresses authentication. For example, only a witness with personal knowledge of the scene may authenticate a diagram. They must be able to testify that the diagram is a "fair and accurate" depiction of the scene in question. The proponent of the diagram should ensure that the witness also explains labels and other markings present on the diagram before admitting it and using it.

Regardless of the type of proffered evidence, it is the judge who determines the sufficiency of the authentication. That issue is a question of fact under Federal Rule of Evidence 104(a). Along with the authentication requirement, the proponent of demonstrative evidence must be prepared to respond to other evidentiary objections raised by opposing counsel that may bar the admissibility of the evidence. An easy acronym to use when addressing possible evidentiary objections to exhibits is BARPH. Counsel should always lay all foundational elements when dealing with exhibits. These foundational questions can be used to not only authenticate the evidence, but to persuade the jury that the evidence is worthy of consideration.

Let us use our earlier example of a diagram to discuss how you would admit it. First the diagram must be shown to the sponsoring witness, giving them the opportunity to examine it. Next you should ask the witness if the diagram is a "fair and accurate" depiction of the scene at that time. Unless exact distances are crucial the diagram need not be to scale, although this is a common objection that you will have to deal with if you have not created a diagram that is to scale. The lack of scale may be established on either direct or cross-examination. If the diagram is drawn to scale, it should be noted on the record and the scale clearly shown on the diagram.

Foundation 1 - Diagrams

Once you have established that the diagram is relevant and authentic, you offer it into evidence. You must then use it in the testimony of the witness and publish it to the jury. Publication may be accomplished in a variety of ways. You can provide copies to the jury, blow the exhibit up so that everyone may see it, or place it in a location where the jury is able to reference as the witness testifies. The Federal Rule of Evidence from which this foundation process derives can be found in the illustrative examples of FRE 901(b).

The following questions normally meet the foundational requirement for various types of exhibits. Each jurisdiction may modify or rearrange these foundational questions, but they serve as a competent and thorough basis from which to begin. Remember, they are based primarily on the illustrative examples found in FRE 901(b). As you read them carefully, note the specific differences for each type of exhibit. The foundational requirements vary because the evidentiary rules necessary to authenticate the evidence and establish its relevancy are influenced by the physical nature of the offered exhibit. If you consider FRE 901(b)(4) below that makes perfect sense.

A witness who attests that the photograph accurately and fairly depicts the scene in question authenticates a photograph. There is no need to address the mechanics of exposing or developing the film or the working condition of the camera. Also, it is important to note that a photograph does not need to be authenticated by the photographer, but must be authenticated by a witness with personal knowledge of the scene depicted in the photograph.

Foundation 2 - Photographs

Non-fungible evidence is evidence having a unique characteristic that allows it to be identified by individuals who have personal knowledge of that unique characteristic. The nature of the unique characteristic is not identified by the rules of evidence, but in practice it is a relatively common sense rule. The person who initially takes custody of the evidence has the opportunity to observe the evidence carefully. They look for indications of uniqueness. Such indications might include a serial number on a weapon, a nick in a particular location on the blade of a knife, the nature of a scratch or disfiguring mark on the piece of evidence.

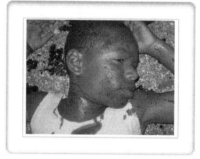

Additionally, relatively common items can be given unique characteristics by the individual taking them into custody. The classic example of this is when the police officer places her initials on the butt of a weapon seized at the crime scene. Conversely, fungible evidence is evidence that does not have a unique characteristic rendering it readily identifiable. Fungible evidence requires additional foundational steps before it can be admitted, usually involving some type of chain-of-custody. Examples of non-fungible evidence include a gun with a serial number or other unique items seized for their evidentiary value.

Sometimes a non-fungible piece of evidence also contains fungible evidence. Consider the scenario of a bloody knife seized at the crime scene. The knife will have some unique characteristic that will allow the police officer testifying at trial to properly identify it—the blood does not. If the police intend to test the blood for DNA identification they must safeguard that blood from the moment it is taken into custody. Certain procedures must be followed to ensure that the fungible blood is what it purports to be—blood taken from the knife found at the scene of the crime. These are referred to as chain-of-custody documents. Before the court would allow a witness to testify as to the nature of that blood, the judge must be satisfied that the blood has not been adulterated either intentionally or unintentionally. That concern does not exist as to the knife because it has unique characteristics making it an identifiable non-fungible piece of evidence— you can mark it in a manner that lets you ensure it is controlled. But, while you cannot mark the blood in order to ensure it remains in the state that it was when collected, but you can create both procedures that safeguard the fungible evidence and documents that verify those procedures.

Foundation 3 - Non-Fungible Evidence

Because the blood does not have unique characteristics, a court will be concerned with the chain-of-custody documents that establish that the blood has not been tampered with. The offering party must lay the foundation for the chain-of-custody documents first, admitting them subject to a relevancy connection to the case.

Fungible evidence has the potential to be easily modified, adulterated, or replaced by people having access to it. To guarantee its relevance and authenticity, fungible evidence must be carefully guarded to prevent contamination or destruction. As part of the process in laying the foundation for the admissibility of fungible evidence the offering party must first establish that the fungible evidence has been properly safeguarded against potential contamination. Chain-of-custody procedures accomplish this purpose. To admit fungible evidence, the chain-of-custody documents relating to the evidence must be offered and admitted before the fungible evidence itself can be offered and admitted.

Establishing a proper chain-of-custody for fungible evidence is a condition precedent to its admissibility. This is a precise and important skill that a competent trial attorney must master. Improperly authenticated evidence may result in crucial evidence being excluded that could deal a fatal blow to your case. While this skill is important, it is relatively easy to master. All that is required is attention to the local rules of court, an understanding of how the rules of evidence have an impact on foundational questions, and a commitment to preparation that includes taking examples of foundational requirements for your intended exhibits into court with you and having them readily available if you run into difficulties.

Once counsel establishes the authenticity of a business record, they must next establish that the contents of the chain-of-custody document are admissible as an exception to the hearsay rule, usually under the business records exception found in FRE 803(6). After laying the foundations for the fungible evidence and the chain-of-custody documents, counsel can then move to admit both into evidence.

Let us now consider how other rules of evidence and the procedures involved in admitting exhibits create additional legal issues and advocacy opportunities.

THE LAW OF EXHIBITS – VOIR DIRE & OBJECTIONS

When an exhibit is offered into evidence opposing counsel must decide whether to object. In your initial thought process you should consider how allowing this evidence to be admitted will affect your chosen theme and theory. If it doesn't hurt, let it in, especially if you have found a way to make it work to your advantage. If it does hurt, opposing counsel may: (1) voir dire on the exhibit, (2) object as to the foundation, or (3) object based upon BARPH.

Opposing counsel may request to voir dire the witness on the exhibit for the purposes of developing an objection to the exhibit's admissibility. This voir dire about an exhibit is a cross-examination of the witness that is limited in scope to questions addressing only the potential admissibility of the exhibit. Questions concerning the weight that the evidence might be given are outside the scope of the voir dire and should instead be asked during normal cross examination of the witness. Since voir dire on an exhibit occurs during the direct examination of a witness by opposing counsel, judges are careful to restrict the scope of voir dire on exhibits. Save your questions designed to attack the weight that the exhibit should be given for your cross examination.

A common objection often made during the voir dire is that it is "outside the scope of the direct." When a judge sustains this objection you can be confident that she perceives that you are asking questions about weight and not admissibility. Another common objection is "Your honor that goes to weight, and not admissibility." That is another way of saying "outside the scope" that is accepted in most jurisdictions. Normally, questions asked during voir dire on the exhibit will not be allowed during cross, but creative counsel can easily tie what was earlier an admissibility issue to a greater weight issue later. If counsel chooses to not request voir dire on an exhibit then they must either agree to its admission or object.

When counsel stands and says: "Objection, insufficient foundation," the judge must either rule on the objection, or respond to the objecting counsel by asking how the foundation is insufficient. If the court sustains the objection without an explanation, the proponent of the exhibit may inquire for the reasons for the ruling under the rules of evidence. When the objection is other than foundational, the counsel opposing admissibility should stand and say "Objection," and then give a BRIEF statement of the grounds for the objection without testifying with a rambling objection that is really designed to make arguments to the jury. The judge will either rule on the objection or ask the proponent of the exhibit how they respond to opposing counsel's objection. If the court sustains the objection, the proponent is not barred from continuing to attempt to lay an adequate foundation to get the exhibit into evidence.

THE APPELLATE COURT SPEAKS - U.S. V. COLLINS

The following case deals with the admissibility of photographs and cell phone information in a gruesome murder case. As you read through it ask yourself if you are persuaded with the court's reasoning, or is something else happening underneath the surface. Pay particular attention to the impact that FRE 403 has in the court's analysis. Does that support your understanding of how the rules work together? How would you defend your answer?

U.S. v. Collins
368 Fed.App. 517 (2010)

Joe Lewis Collins was convicted by a jury of conspiracy to commit murder and murder of a government witness under 18 U.S.C. § 1512(a)(1)(A) and (k). On this direct appeal, he challenges his convictions based on two evidentiary rulings. As to the first ruling, we find no error. As to the second ruling, we assume without deciding that error was committed, but we conclude that any error was harmless. AFFIRMED.

I. BACKGROUND

"We recite the facts in the light most favorable to the verdict." *United States v. Olis,* 429 F.3d 540, 541 n. 1 (5th Cir.2005). Levon Edmond and Kathleen Nelson (who are sisters), along with Nelson's boyfriend Roosevelt Walker and their mutual friend Joe Lewis Collins (the appellant in this case), were involved in a fraud conspiracy. The four forged settlement claims and recruited false claimants under the Pigford-Glickman litigation. Once the false claimants received settlement checks, Edmond, Nelson, Walker, and Collins would take a cut of the money. Clovis Reed, one of their recruits, received a $50,000 settlement check in March 2001, but Edmond and Nelson stole the check. Reed reported the check as stolen, and the FBI started an investigation. Edmond and Nelson were indicted in February 2003 on federal charges of forgery and conversion of Reed's check, and Reed was to be the key witness for the prosecution. However, before the case could proceed, Reed was murdered. As she drove home from work on the evening of April 2, 2003, Reed was ambushed, allegedly by Walker and Collins. Broken glass, matching that from a broken window in Reed's car, was found along the route from her job to her home in Canton, Mississippi. Her body was discovered in a secluded, wooded area, approximately 50 miles south of Canton, on April 4 by Luther Crownover, a beekeeper who was checking his hives. Her head and hands had been cut off, and they were never recovered.

The FBI investigated Reed's death and eventually charged Edmond, Nelson, Walker, and Collins with her murder. Edmond pled guilty to conspiracy to murder a government witness and, in exchange for a twenty-five year sentence, agreed to testify against her co-conspirators. After a joint trial, Nelson and Walker were convicted; both received life sentences. Collins was indicted for one count of conspiracy to commit murder, under 18 U.S.C. § 1512(k), and one count of murder of a government witness, under 18 U.S.C. § 1512(a) (1)(A). At the jury trial, the main issue was whether the prosecution could link Collins to Reed's death, as he did not dispute the cause of her death. Edmond testified that Collins came up with the idea to kill Reed in order to prevent exposure of the fraud scheme, **admitted** on several occasions he killed Reed by strangling her with his belt, and bragged about amputating Reed's head and hands. Collins was convicted on both counts and received two life sentences.

On appeal, Collins raises two evidentiary issues. First, he challenges the admission of six **photographs** of Reed's body where it was discovered and during the autopsy. Second, he contends that Edmond was improperly allowed to testify that Collins used a particular cell phone without first establishing her basis of knowledge.

II. STANDARD OF REVIEW

As Collins properly objected at trial to both evidentiary issues, on appeal we review for abuse of discretion. *United States v. Fields,* 483 F.3d 313, 354 (5th Cir.2007). "A trial court abuses its discretion when it bases its decision on an erroneous view of the law or a clearly erroneous assessment of the evidence." *United States v. Caldwell,* 586 F.3d 338, 341 (5th Cir.2009). Should we find an abuse of discretion has occurred, we conduct a harmless error analysis and affirm unless the error affected Collins's substantial rights. *United States v. Ragsdale,* 426 F.3d 765, 774-75 (5th Cir.2005); *see also* FED.R.CRIM.P. 52(a) ("Any error, defect, irregularity, or variance that does not affect substantial rights must be disregarded."). An error affects substantial rights if it affects the outcome of the district court proceedings. *United States v. Olano,* 507 U.S. 725, 734, 113 S.Ct. 1770, 123

L.Ed.2d 508 (1993). The Government bears the burden of showing that any error was harmless beyond a reasonable doubt. *Id.*

III. DISCUSSION

A. Photographs

[the government] offered six **photographs** of Clovis Reed's body-two at the site where it was discovered, and four at the autopsy. The district court **admitted** all six **photographs** over Collins's objection. During the Government's case-in-chief, the prosecutor objections based on Federal Rule of Evidence 403 (Rule 403). Collins argues that the six **photographs** of Reed's dismembered body lacked relevance because he offered to stipulate to all the facts reflected in the **photographs** and the photos therefore offered no information in addition to facts already offered through live testimony. Collins argues that their prejudicial effect therefore substantially outweighed any probative value and the trial court abused its discretion in **admitting** them. The district court did not conduct a Rule 403 balancing analysis on the record; however, Collins did not request one. *See United States v. Alarcon,* 261 F.3d 416, 424 (5th Cir.2001) ("Normally, the trial court must explicitly perform [the Rule 403 balancing] analysis on the record; however, if the party objecting to the admission fails to request the analysis, the trial court need not perform it on the record." (citation omitted)).

1. The Legal Standard

Rule 403 provides that: "Although relevant, evidence may be excluded if its probative value is substantially outweighed by the danger of unfair prejudice, confusion of the issues, or misleading the jury, or ... needless presentation of cumulative evidence." FED.R.EVID. 403. The scope of Rule 403 is quite narrow, *Fields,* 483 F.3d at 354, and it is "not designed to 'even out' the weight of the evidence." *Baker v. Canadian Nat'l / Ill. Cent. R.R.,* 536 F.3d 357, 369 (5th Cir.2008); *see also* FED.R.EVID. 401 advisory committee's note ("The fact to which the evidence is directed need not be in dispute."). In the Fifth Circuit, "**admitting** gruesome **photographs** of the victim's body in a murder case ordinarily does not rise to an abuse of discretion where those photos have nontrivial probative value." *Fields,* 483 F.3d at 355. "On appellate review of a Rule 403 decision, a defendant must establish abuse of discretion, a standard that is not satisfied by a mere showing of some alternative means of proof that the prosecution in its broad discretion chose not to rely upon." *Old Chief v. United States,* 519 U.S. 172, 183 n. 7, 117 S.Ct. 644, 136 L.Ed.2d 574 (1997).

In *Old Chief,* the Supreme Court stated that "[i]f ... relevant evidence is inadmissible in the presence of other evidence related to it, its exclusion must rest not on the ground that the other evidence has rendered it 'irrelevant,' but on its character as unfairly prejudicial, cumulative or the like, its relevance notwithstanding." 519 U.S. at 179, 117 S.Ct. 644. Although when "one party stipulates to a disputed fact, the stipulation conclusively proves that fact," *Caldwell,* 586 F.3d at 342, "a criminal defendant may not stipulate or **admit** his way out of the full evidentiary force" of the Government's case, *Old Chief,* 519 U.S. at 186, 117 S.Ct. 644. The Government is faced with a "need for evidence in all its particularity to satisfy the jurors' expectations about what proper proof should be," and because the Government bears the burden of proof, it "may prudently demur at a defense request to interrupt the flow of evidence telling the story in the usual way." *Id.* at 188-89, 117 S.Ct. 644.

We addressed a similar set of facts in *United States v. Caldwell,* 586 F.3d at 342-43. There, a defendant charged with possession of child pornography argued that the publication of several brief excerpts from child pornography videos found on his computer was unfairly prejudicial, as he offered to stipulate that the videos contained child pornography. *Id.* at 342. We rejected that argument, concluding that *Old Chief* "turn[s] on the contribution of the challenged evidence to the overall narrative of the Government's case." *Id.* at 343. Because "child pornography is graphic evidence that has force beyond simple linear schemes of reasoning," the language of the stipulation did not have the same evidentiary value as "actually seeing the particular explicit conduct of the specific minors." *Id.*

We also addressed similar facts in *United States v. Fields,* where we considered a Rule 403 challenge to thirty-two **photographs** of a murder victim's body, both at the site where it was discovered and during the autopsy. 483 F.3d at 354. We concluded that the **photographs** were "highly probative" and "necessary to rebut [the defendant's] arguments" that the Government failed to produce any physical evidence linking him to the crime. *Id.* at 355. The crime scene photos showed the body "in an advanced state of decomposition and ... subject to animal predation"; they helped "explain why little physical evidence was found: because it had been carried away by animals or worn away by the elements." *Id.* at 354, 355. The crime scene photos also corroborated witness testimony that the defendant **admitted** dragging the victim's body. *Id.* at 355. The autopsy photos "helped the jury understand the medical examiner's testimony" and supported the Government's theory on the cause of death. *Id.* at 355-56. We rejected the defendant's contention that several individual photos should have been excluded because "some of the points made by the photos were not in dispute," concluding that the Government needed the **photographs** to demonstrate "that the body had decomposed too much for any physical evidence to be found," a point made "more effectively with images than it would have been with vague generalizations about the difficulty in processing weeks-old crime scenes." *Id.* at 356. We also declined to engage in "strict scrutinizing" of the district court's Rule 403 decision. *Id.*

1. *Probative Value of Crime Scene Photos*

The two crime scene **photographs** depict information valuable to the Government's case; they clarify oral testimony and illustrate the condition of Reed's body and the scene where her body was left. The first **photograph** depicts the body lying in a clearing surrounded by a wooded area. It is difficult to tell that the photo depicts a human body, as Reed's head and hands have been removed. The second **photograph** shows a close-up of the body, and the individual wounds are more clearly visible.

These two photos were first **admitted** during Luther Crownover's testimony. Crownover, a beekeeper, discovered Reed's body; in his testimony, he referred to the photos as he described the discovery and where the body was located. Crownover testified that he observed "what [he] assumed was an animal carcass ... that someone had started butchering" across the fence from a line of his bee hives. He related that he approached the carcass because he thought it was "going to attract flies and birds and was going to be a problem ... with the odor for several weeks probably," so he "climb[ed] over the fence and [went to] go see if [he] could move it further into the woods." However, once he approached and bent over the carcass, he realized it was a human body. While looking at the two photos, Crownover testified that Reed's body was only clothed in underwear at the time of discovery, although he did not know it was underwear at the time. He testified that he "thought it was possibly just a rag or something someone had used to drag this carcass out, because at that time [he] still didn't know it was a human body." He stated that the second photo in particular reflected the condition of Reed's body at the time he discovered her. Crownover also testified that the area, flat and marshy, had once been an old farm road for wagons and that there were no homes within a quarter mile or more.

Donnie McGovern, the Simpson County Sheriff's Office investigator who responded to Crownover's 911 call, also testified about the two **photographs**. McGovern identified the photos as depicting "the body that was reported ... by Mr. Luther Crownover," and he stated that the body was located down a trail, 194 feet to the east of Old River Road (a paved street), and about fifteen feet north of a deer stand. He used the second photo to indicate where the deer stand was located in relation to the body. He also testified that while the trail was visible from Old River Road during daytime hours, the trail would not be visible at night and the body was not visible from the road.

Like in *Fields,* the two **photographs** help explain why no physical evidence was found linking Collins to the murder-a point Collins repeatedly leaned on at trial. The photos show that Reed's body was left outside, in the elements, in only her underwear. Whoever committed the crime had removed the clothing and the parts of Reed's body most likely to retain traces of physical evidence. The two **photographs** also corroborate the medical examiner's testimony that Reed was killed at another location and then dumped on the trail, as there was only a small amount of blood at the dump site. While the probative value of the two crime scene **photographs** either was or could have been brought out through testimony at trial, we have consistently held that "[t]he fact to which the evidence is directed need not be in dispute," and Rule 403 "does not ban *per se* all duplicative evidence." *Fields,* 483 F.3d at 356 (citations and internal quotation marks omitted). The two crime scene photos have nontrivial probative value.

1. *Probative Value of Autopsy Photos*

The four autopsy **photographs** also convey information vital to the Government's case. All four photos helped the jury understand the medical examiner's testimony regarding the results of the autopsy. In particular, one **photograph** depicts a broad view of Reed's upper back, neck, and left *522 arm. The decapitation wound is the focus of this photo. Distinct cut marks are visible; the wounds have a slight green discoloration; and the deepest wound shows significant maggot larval infestation. Small bits of leaves, grass, and dirt are visible on her back, and her upper back shows scrape marks. This photo was introduced as Dr. Hayne, the medical examiner, testified as to his findings on the cause and time of death. This photo helped illustrate the condition of Reed's body and why Dr. Hayne could not reach a more definite finding as to the cause of death. Dr. Hayne testified that, following the autopsy, he "favored cranial cerebral trauma" as the cause of Reed's death but could not come to a "definitive conclusion [ ]." He explained that, other than her head and hands, Reed's body was intact; as a result, he "reasonably excluded any other cause of death." He "did not see evidence that [would allow him to] conclude that strangulation had occurred," and he felt that injury to the head was the most likely cause of death. Dr. Hayne stated that the "multiple abrasions or scrapes of the skin ... [,] linear in configuration [were] indicative of a body being dragged." Because of the "significant maggot larval infestation," the "minimal green discoloration" in the wounds, and the lack of "significant skin slippage"-all visible in the autopsy photo-Dr. Hayne set the time of death at around 36 to 48 hours prior to the amputation of Reed's head and hands. He also opined that the amputations occurred post-mortem, because no significant hemorrhage or bleeding was present in the injured tissue. The fact that Dr. Hayne's testimony was largely uncontested does not rob it of its relevancy or its importance to the Government's case. *See United States v. Bowers,* 660 F.2d 527, 530 (5th Cir.1981) (per curiam) ("[T]he mere fact that [a defendant] stipulate[s] with the government as to the cause of death [does] not preclude the government from offering proof on that issue."). The first autopsy photo clearly has non-trivial probative value to the Government's case.

Three other autopsy photos show Dr. Hayne comparing Reed's wounds to a Kaiser blade. The Government offered these three photos to support and explain Dr. Hayne's testimony that he believed that a Kaiser blade was the weapon used to decapitate Reed. He testified that he reached this conclusion because this type of blade has a "nonsharpened [sic] edge" but still had "mass to it or weight to deliver enough force to produce these injuries." According to Dr. Hayne, the three photos demonstrate "the potential correlation between a weapon such as a Kaiser blade and the inflicted injuries on the decedent." Specifically, the photos reflected Dr. Hayne's conclusion that "the curvature and the depth" of the wounds matched the type of injuries that a Kaiser blade might inflict. 3 Dr. Hayne also opined that "it would take a considerable amount of force to inflict [the] type[ ] of injuries" suffered by Reed, and that he favored a man, rather than a woman, as the perpetrator.

At trial, Collins objected to Dr. Hayne's testimony on the probable correlation between the Kaiser blade and the wounds on relevancy grounds, as the state did not offer any evidence linking Collins to a Kaiser blade. However, the district court overruled the objection, and Collins does not appeal that ruling. Collins contends that these three comparison **photographs** are irrelevant because they depict post- mortem injuries, not related to the cause of death. However, the comparison photos clearly help explain Dr. Hayne's testimony-unchallenged on appeal-regarding the correlation between the wounds and the Kaiser blade. As such, the photos have nontrivial probative value.

1. *Prejudicial Effect*

Collins argues that the admission of the six **photographs** unfairly prejudiced the jury against him. While all six **photographs** are, in fact, shocking and gruesome, the district court acted within its discretion by **admitting** them into evidence. The "general, conclusory language of [a] stipulation" to the facts and circumstances of Reed's murder and the disposal of her body "does not have the same evidentiary value as actually seeing the particular" crime scene and the condition of the body. *Cf. Caldwell,* 586 F.3d at 343. The **photographs** are graphic evidence with force beyond simple linear schemes of reasoning. Within reasonable limits, the prosecution is entitled to present its case through the evidence it deems most appropriate. *See Old Chief,* 519 U.S. at 187-88, 117 S.Ct. 644. Furthermore, the district court's questions to the jury panel during voir dire and the instructions to the audience 5 helped to limit any prejudicial impact. Collins argues extensively that "this specific photo or that specific photo was used to make points that might also have been made with other evidence or with another specific photo"; however, we cannot engage in "strict scrutinizing ... when reviewing a trial court's Rule 403 balancing decision." *Cf. Fields,* 483 F.3d at 356. Given the deference required by the standard of review, we find that any prejudicial effect did not substantially outweigh the nontrivial probative value of the six **photographs**; therefore, the trial court did not abuse its discretion in **admitting** the photos.

B. Testimony About the Cell Phone

At trial, the Government's case turned on whether they could successfully link Collins to Reed's murder-a link that relied in large part upon circumstantial evidence. In particular, the Government presented evidence on the location of four cell phones on April 2 and 3, 2003. Three of the cell phones were clearly linked to Edmond, Nelson, and Walker-each one's name was registered to the phone in the phone company's records. The fourth phone was a demonstration phone that Nelson had stolen from a Sprint store; phone company records did not list a registered owner. Using phone records and information from cell phone towers, the Government showed that the four cell phones placed numerous calls amongst each other throughout the night of April 2 and into the morning of April 3. The locations and times of the calls roughly corresponded to the locations where Reed was attacked and her body was abandoned. In particular, the fourth phone moved from the area where Reed's car window was broken (around 1:40 a.m.), to the area where Reed's body was recovered (between 3:15 and 3:30 a.m.), and then to the area around the

InTown Suites in Jackson, Mississippi, where Collins was staying (around 5:15 a.m.). After 5:15 a.m. on April 3, the fourth phone was not used again for two weeks.

Edmond testified on direct examination that she knew Collins had used the fourth phone, but that she did not know whether he used the phone on the night of the murder. The exchange on direct examination went as follows:

Q: [by prosecutor] How are you familiar with a stolen Sprint phone?

A: It was a cell phone that my sister, Kathleen, took from the Sprint store.

Q: [by defense counsel] I object. Your Honor, I'm going to object unless there's a basis of knowledge laid.

Q: [by prosecutor] How would you know Kathleen took a phone from the Sprint store?

A: I was with her when she took it. Q: Okay. *And what happened to that phone, if you know?*

A: *She had that phone that night, but I don't know exactly, you know.*

Q: *Do you know who might have used that phone?* Q: [by defense counsel] Again, objection unless there's a

basis- A: Mr.-

THE COURT: I sustain the objection. I sustain the objection to the form of the question "might have used."

Q: [by prosecutor] *Do you know who used that phone?* A: Mr. Joe- Q: [by defense counsel] Same objection, your Honor. THE COURT: She can answer.

A: *Mr. Collins.* Q: [by prosecutor] Okay. *But you don't know if he had it*

that night. A: *I can't say.* Q: All right.

Q: [by defense counsel] Your Honor, I want to move to strike her answer earlier because there's been no basis of knowledge for her earlier answer.

THE COURT: I'll let you cross-examine on that point.

(emphases added). Defense counsel did not cross-examine Edmond on the basis for her knowledge. Collins argues that the district court abused its discretion in allowing this testimony, as the Government failed to establish that Edmond had personal knowledge that Collins had used the fourth phone. At oral argument, Collins clarified that he challenges Edmond's basis of knowledge that he used the fourth cell phone between the time Nelson stole it and the night of Reed's murder, and he argues he was prejudiced because without the testimony linking him to the phone, the evidence regarding the location and movement of the four cell phones would not have come in.

Rule 602 states that "[a] witness may not testify to a matter unless evidence is introduced sufficient to support a finding that the witness has personal knowledge of the matter. Evidence to prove personal knowledge may, but need not, consist of the witness'[s] own testimony." FED.R.EVID. 602. The proponent of testimony bears the burden of establishing that a witness has personal knowledge. *Burton v. Banta Global Turnkey, Ltd.*, 170 Fed.Appx. 918, 923 n. 4 (5th Cir.2006). "[A] witness to a fact which can be perceived by the senses must have had an opportunity to observe, and must have actually observed the fact." 1 MCCORMICK ON EVIDENCE § 10 (5th ed. 1999). However, the threshold for **admitting** testimony under Rule 602 is fairly low; if "reasonable persons could differ as to whether the witness had an adequate opportunity to observe, ... the witness's testimony should come in, and the jury will appraise his opportunity to know in evaluating the weight of the testimony." *Id.*

Arguably, Edmond had the opportunity to observe whether Collins used the fourth cell phone, as she, Collins, Walker, and Nelson were mutual friends and spent a lot of time together, especially in the weeks leading up to the murder. However, assuming without deciding that the district court abused its discretion by allowing Edmond to testify that Collins had used the fourth cell phone *before* that night, that error was harmless, because it did not affect the outcome of the district court proceedings. Edmond expressly stated that she did not know who used the phone on the night of the murder, and her testimony regarding his alleged prior use of the phone was brief and equivocal.

Where "other extensive evidence" supports the jury's verdict, an error does not affect a defendant's substantial rights. *United States v. Cooks,* 589 F.3d 173, 180 (5th Cir.2009); *United States v. Clark,* 577 F.3d 273, 288 (5th Cir.2009) (finding that any evidentiary error would have been harmless "given the overwhelming evidence of [the defendant's] guilt"). Here, the record contained extensive circumstantial evidence that allowed the jury to infer that Collins used the fourth phone on the night of the murder and that he acted with Edmond, Nelson, and Walker in planning and carrying out Reed's murder. For example, the evidence from the phone records shows that the fourth phone was located directly in the vicinity of the InTown Suites, where Collins was staying, when the last call was made in the early morning of April 3. Edmond testified that she, Nelson, Walker, and Collins were all good friends. In fact, Edmond paid for Collins's room at the InTown Suites in the weeks leading up to Reed's murder, and Walker often stayed with Collins at the InTown Suites. Walker and Collins both initially told FBI investigators that they had been playing dominoes together on the night of the murder; however, both men eventually gave inconsistent statements that undercut the initial joint alibi. Collins also offered investigators a notebook with domino scores to support the claim that he and Walker had been in his room at the InTown Suites on April 2, but an FBI handwriting analyst determined that the date for the April 2 game had been altered-it was originally marked as April 3. Reed's body was recovered from an isolated location, approximately a mile and a half from a house where Collins lived for seventeen years.

In addition, the jury heard Edmond's testimony that Collins was involved in the fraud scheme; he hatched the idea to kill Reed to prevent her from testifying; he **admitted** to strangling Reed with his belt; he asked Edmond and Nelson to clean up Reed's car and gave them directions to the abandoned car; he and Walker dumped Reed's body off Old River Road; he bragged about cutting off Reed's hands and head and called himself the "Little Butcher"; he told Edmond, on the day the local news reported the discovery of Reed's body, not to ask about the contents of a bag in the backseat of his car (which Edmond presumed contained Reed's head and hands); and he repeatedly exhorted the others to keep their stories straight and suggested alibis to tell the police. *See United States v. Setser,* 568 F.3d 482, 494-95 (5th Cir.2009) (finding improper admission of expert testimony was harmless error where government presented "considerable" evidence against defendant and where improper testimony only made up two lines of testimony in an extended trial). Where, as here, extensive evidence supports the jury's verdict, any error did not affect the outcome of the district court proceedings; Collins's substantial rights were not affected; and, therefore, any error was harmless.

I. **CONCLUSION**

For the foregoing reasons, we AFFIRM the conviction below. AFFIRMED.

DISCUSSION PROBLEMS 6-1

1. How do the lessons concerning presumptions and burdens of proof and persuasion play into this case?

2. What about relevancy?

3. Is the interconnected nature of the federal rules of evidence a weakness or a strength? Explain.

ADMITTING EXHIBITS

There are a variety of ways to approach admitting exhibits at trial, most of which are either derived from the customary practices of the particular local jurisdiction or promulgated in the local rules of court. Advocates must also take the time to ascertain the particular local rules that are "unwritten" when preparing exhibits. Customs of the court are just that—customs. An advocate should not refrain from approaching the court and requesting that they be allowed to use an exhibit in a particular fashion.

These issues are normally addressed during pretrial conferences with the court or by the experience of doing it wrong and being reprimanded. While both methods are effective, the former is much more enjoyable than the latter. There are no surprises when it comes to exhibits so there is no valid reason for counsel to attempt exhibit by ambush. Show them to the judge and opposing counsel. Address any concerns about their relevancy and authenticity and then use them—often.

Advocates following these steps will ensure that the exhibit is not only admitted, but used in a persuasive fashion. These fundamental steps serve as the guideline for properly handling the exhibit in a manner that removes potential objections, ensures that proper foundations are laid; and allows the jury to focus on the viability of the exhibit.

This list should be copied by the advocate and placed prominently in their trial notebooks for continued use. Once the advocate is familiar with the list, the only portion that changes is the fifth step, and that particular section changes based upon the nature of the exhibit proffered. This text contains sample foundation questions for the most common forms of exhibits admitted at trial.[28] Now, let us look at some examples to see this list in action.

Sample Foundations

The following two examples show how to apply the law and techniques discussed in this chapter. Note the degree of control and direction that the advocate has over their witness even though this is direct examination. You are able to sprinkle a certain number of leading questions during direct examination when you are laying a foundation for the admissibility of an exhibit. When used artfully these leading questions reinforce control, establish pace and let the witness know with little to no uncertainty the direction that the advocate wishes to take. Mastery of the applicable Federal Rules of Evidence will create a deeper understanding of the necessary steps that must be taken to get this sort of information before the jury, where it can continue to persuade long after closing arguments are completed.

---

[28] *See* Appendix II.

Sample Diagram Foundation

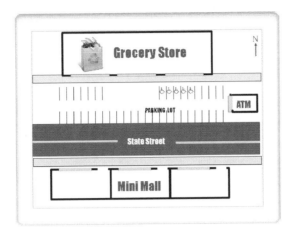

Prosecution Exhibit 1 for ID

Q: Mr. Witness, WHERE did the robbery occur?

A: At the ATM machine located in the grocery store parking lot across from the Mini-Mall on State Street.

Q: Please look at the diagram located on the easel to your left, marked Prosecution Exhibit 1 for identification. Do you recognize it?

A: Yes.

Q: WHAT is it?

A: It is a diagram of the area around the ATM machine where I was robbed.

Q: HOW do you recognize it?

A: I've lived in this neighborhood for fifteen years and have done most of my ATM banking through that machine for the last eight years. I am very familiar with that area.

Q: HOW often do you use this ATM?

A: I used it about three times a week for the last eight years before the robbery. Since the robbery I haven't been able to go back to that spot.

Q: Is this diagram a fair and accurate representation of the area around the ATM?

A: Yes, it looks good to me.

This completes the foundation of an unmarked diagram. If the diagram has been pre-marked by counsel, it is now necessary to have the witness explain the labels that have been superimposed on various objects on the diagram. That explanation could go as follows:

Q: Mr. Witness, HOW did you get to the ATM on the night of the robbery?
A: I drove my car there.

Q: WHERE did you park your car when you got there?
A: In the grocery store parking lot on State Street, about 40 feet from the ATM Machine.

Q: Is the position of your parked car shown on this diagram, P.E. 1 for ID?
A: Yes, it is shown as a car with the word "Car" next to it on the diagram.

Q: HOW is the ATM machine marked on the diagram?
A: There is a picture of a building with the letters "ATM" next to it.

Q: You testified earlier that it was dark outside when you arrived at the ATM. Was the area around the ATM also dark?
A: No. It was lit fairly well by the streetlight located about fifteen feet from the ATM.

Q: Please point out the location of the street lamp for the jury.
A: Okay. There is a picture of a street lamp which is labeled "Light" on the diagram.

Q: Mr. Witness, what happened after you arrived at the ATM?
A Well, my friend stayed in the car and I went to the machine to withdraw some cash. As I was entering my PIN number, a man in a ski mask came around the side of the machine and pointed a gun at me. He said that he would kill me if I didn't give him all my money.

Q: [To the Judge] Your honor, request permission to have the witness approach the diagram.
J: Go ahead.

Q: Using the blue marker, please place an "X" where you were standing when the masked man approached you.
A: All right.

Q: The witness marked P.E. 1 for ID, as directed. Now using the red marker, draw an arrow to indicate the approach used by the gunman before he robbed you.
A: Right here.

Q: [To the Judge] The witness marked P.E. 1 for ID with a red arrow as directed.

Counsel may offer the diagram into evidence at this time or any time before passing the witness. The diagram may not be further marked after it is admitted. Opposing counsel may ask that the judge instruct the jury that the diagram is not to scale.

SAMPLE PHOTOGRAPH FOUNDATION

Q: Mr. Witness, where do you work?
A: I work at the grocery store on State Street across from the Mini-Mall.

Q. [To the Judge] I am showing opposing counsel what has previously been marked as Prosecution Exhibit-1 for Identification. *(Show it to opposing counsel.)* Your Honor, may I approach the witness? [Most jurisdictions require counsel to do this when initially approaching each witness, but you usually only need to ask once per witness.]
J: You may approach the witness counsel.

Q: I now hand you P.E.-1 for Identification. What is it?
A: It is a picture of the ATM Machine located in our grocery store parking lot.

Q: How do you recognize it?
A: I have worked at that store as the assistant manager in charge of the night shift for the last twelve years. I was there when it was installed and have used it many times. I took this picture of the machine at the request of the store owner about 6 months ago. We were worried about the safety of our customers when they used it.

Q: From what angle was this photograph taken?
A: The picture is slightly left of center from the front of the ATM machine where customers use it.

Q: Does this photo fairly and accurately depict the ATM Machine as it appeared six months ago?
A: Absolutely.

Q: Your Honor, I offer P.E.-1 for Identification into evidence as P.E.-1.

If the judge sustains an objection do not allow it to fluster you. Simply regroup and go through your foundational questions again. If the judge sustains another foundational objection it sometimes helps to show the judge that you are actually reading the foundational questions from an approved example in your jurisdiction. You can take the drudgery that is sometimes associated with laying foundations for exhibits and turn it into yet another opportunity for persuasive advocacy.

CONCLUSION

Proper use of exhibits is a fundamental skill for both cross and direct examination. Applying the skills discussed in this chapter, in concert with our earlier discussions concerning authentication and foundation, will empower you to competently deal with a tremendous component of persuasion at trial—visuals. It also serves as the third component in our basic understanding of witness testimony. Let us shift our focus now to dealing with the law, opposing counsel and the judge—objections.

Chapter 7: Objections

HOW TO OBJECT

Objections are an area of trial work where the lawyer must develop an ability to act instinctually in response to the violation of an evidentiary rule. To develop this skill, the lawyer must learn the key phrases or situations that foreshadow a violation of an evidentiary rule and the moments in trial where they are most likely to occur. Most new lawyers list objections as one of the areas of trial practice with which they are least comfortable. This discomfort comes from the fast-paced nature of objections during the trial and the lack of connectivity between evidentiary law and trial skills when the lawyer first learned evidence and trial advocacy. Fortunately, both of these issues can be overcome through practice and study.

The first step along the path to mastering objections is to identify objectionable questions and evidence in the context of the moment in trial where they are going to arise. This process begins during case analysis and continues throughout the trial. The lawyer should review all prior statements of the noticed witness, identify the potential fungible and non-fungible evidence that the witness may be used to admit, and review carefully any interview notes. This review process should focus on potential evidentiary issues that may occur. Counsel should note those issues, forecast how opposing counsel may object, and then identify their potential response to counsel's objection. Potential objections that are always relevant when a witness is testifying include the best evidence rule, authentication (when exhibits are involved), relevancy, personal knowledge (the lack thereof) and hearsay.

Once you learn how to do this, it is simply a matter of then deciding whether the question is objectionable and whether it is to your advantage to object. Case analysis should assist you in determining when you want to fight over an objectionable piece of evidence or testimony and when letting it go will help your case. You should always evaluate the situation before deciding whether to object. Ask yourself if the evidence is probably going to come in anyway? For example, if the objection is strictly to a lack of proper foundation, your objection will merely allow opposing counsel to fix the problem, making additional advocacy points while doing so. If that is the case why object? You may wind up keying jury members to the importance of evidence upon which you would rather they not focus.

The ability to make and respond to objections is a key skill for the lawyer. To properly exercise this skill you must not only understand the rules of evidence, but also have a system that allows you to recall needed information amidst the heat of trial. This is an advocacy skill that is reactionary in most situations, in that you are responding to the actions of opposing counsel. You can plan for that reaction, using the actions described above as a checklist. It is a skill that develops through practice. A list of common objections and the corresponding rules of evidence in your trial notebook will help you prepare to properly execute this skill. One such possible list is included as an appendix to this book.29 Others are for sale by third party vendors in a variety of forms and jurisdictions. The ones produced by Elex Publishers are particularly useful.30

Practice with the rules is another step toward competency in the area of trial advocacy. You should not despair; making good objections is a skill you can develop.

---

[29] *See* Appendix II.

[30] *See* http://www.elexpublishers.com.

Given that most evidentiary rulings by the court are reviewed at the appellate level under an abuse of discretion standard, this is an important skill to have so you may win this battle at trial.

AN APPELLATE COURT SPEAKS

995 F.2d 982
United States Court of Appeals,
Tenth Circuit.
UNITED STATES of America, Plaintiff-Appellee,
v.
Lorenzo Jesus MEJIA-ALARCON, Defendant-Appellant.
No. 91-2048.June 7, 1993.

Opinion

EBEL, Circuit Judge.

On December 5, 1990, a jury found the defendant-appellant, Lorenzo Jesus Mejia-Alarcon (Mejia), guilty of one count of conspiracy to possess with intent to distribute heroin, one count of possession of heroin with intent to distribute, and one count of carrying or using a firearm in relation to a drug-trafficking crime. The counts arose from an undercover operation conducted by the Drug Enforcement Administration and the Las Cruces-Dona Ana County Metro Narcotics Unit. During the investigation, Agent Frank Ruiz negotiated three purchases of heroin from Mejia's co-defendant, Carlos Galaviz.

On direct appeal, Mejia contends that the district court erred (1) in permitting the prosecution to impeach him with a prior conviction and (2) in failing to ascertain on the record whether Mejia voluntarily and knowingly consented to a stipulation entered by his counsel that admitted that the substance found in Mejia's car was heroin and that the weights in the laboratory reports were accurate. In addition, Mejia filed a supplemental pro se brief in which he contended that he had been denied his Sixth Amendment right to effective assistance of counsel at trial.

As to the first contention, we hold that although the district court erred in admitting the prior conviction, the error was harmless. As to the second contention, we hold that the district court did not err in failing to provide more explicitly on the record that Mejia entered the stipulation knowingly and voluntarily. Last, we hold that Mejia's ineffective assistance of counsel claim fails as to the errors he has alleged on direct appeal.

I. FACTS

Agent Ruiz of the Las Cruces-Dona Ana County Metro Narcotics Unit was working undercover in the summer of 1990 in a heroin-trafficking investigation conducted by his narcotics unit and the United States Drug Enforcement Agency. While undercover, Agent Ruiz arranged to purchase heroin from Mejia's co-defendant, Carlos Galaviz, on three occasions.

During the first transaction, Galaviz told Agent Ruiz that a man named "Lorenzo" was involved in the heroin trafficking scheme. Agent Ruiz understood Galaviz to be saying that Lorenzo was the "main man." "Lorenzo" is Mejia's first name.

Mejia drove Galaviz to the second transaction, which took place on August 23, 1990. The buy took place at the Desert Sun Lounge in Las Cruces, New Mexico. While Galaviz and Agent Ruiz completed the purchase in Agent Ruiz's car, Mejia waited inside the lounge.

When Agent Ruiz asked Galaviz who was with him, Galaviz responded that it was "Lorenzo." Although Galaviz denied that it was the Lorenzo who was the "main man," he did say that Mejia knew "what's going on." Agent Ruiz testified that drug traffickers typically do not readily identify their suppliers. Once inside Agent Ruiz's car, Galaviz told Agent Ruiz that he had "the stuff" in the car he had come in, but that he had to get the keys from Lorenzo. He went into the bar, got the keys from Mejia, and then retrieved a package of heroin from the car.

On September 8, 1990, Mejia drove Galaviz first to Juarez, Mexico, and then to a Whataburger in Las Cruces, where the third drug transaction between Agent Ruiz and Galaviz was to take place. Agent Ruiz testified that the heroin involved was coming from Juarez. Mejia often traveled to Juarez to visit relatives and to buy cheap sodas for his wife's daycare center. Agents arrested both Mejia and Galaviz at the Whataburger. Upon an inventory search of Mejia's car after his arrest, agents found 200 grams of heroin on the floorboard of the passenger's side. On the driver's side, agents found a loaded weapon, the receipt for which they found in Mejia's wallet.

Mejia was charged in a superseding indictment on October 24, 1990, with one count of conspiracy to possess with intent to distribute heroin in violation of 21 U.S.C. § 841(a)(1) and (b)(1)(B), 21 U.S.C. § 846, and 18 U.S.C. § 2; one count of possession of heroin with intent to distribute in violation of 21 U.S.C. § 841(a)(1) and (b)(1)(B) and 18 U.S.C. § 2; and one count of carrying or using a firearm in relation to a drug-trafficking crime in violation of 18 U.S.C. § 924(c)(1), 21 U.S.C. § 846, and 18 U.S.C. § 2.

On December 5, 1990, a jury in the District of New Mexico found Mejia guilty on all three counts. Mejia was sentenced to concurrent, 70-month sentences on the drug counts and a consecutive 60-month sentence on the gun-possession count. In addition, Mejia was sentenced to two four-year terms and one three-year term of supervised release, all to run concurrently.

Mejia appeals, asserting the following errors occurred below: (1) that the district court erred in permitting the prosecution to impeach him with a prior conviction, (2) that the district court erred in failing to ascertain on the record whether Mejia voluntarily and knowingly consented to a stipulation that admitted that the substance found in Mejia's car was heroin and that the weights in the laboratory reports were accurate, and (3) that he was denied his Sixth Amendment right to effective assistance of counsel at trial. We will address each contention in turn.

II. ADMISSION OF THE PRIOR CONVICTION

At a pretrial hearing, Mejia moved in limine to exclude the admission of his prior conviction for the unauthorized acquisition and possession of food stamps. The court denied the motion in limine, ruling that the government could use the conviction to impeach Mejia if he testified, apparently on the ground that the conviction was for a crime of dishonesty or false statement under Federal Rule of Evidence 609(a)(2). At trial, Mejia made no further objection to the admission of the prior conviction. In fact, Mejia's counsel brought the conviction out on direct examination of Mejia, presumably to lessen its impact. Mejia now contends that the district court erred in admitting the conviction. We will first discuss whether Mejia waived his objection and then will assess the merits of his contention that evidence of his prior food-stamp conviction was inadmissible.

A. *Waiver*

As an initial matter, the government contends that Mejia's motion in limine was insufficient to preserve his objection to the prior food-stamp conviction and that we should therefore review its admission only for plain error. *See generally United States v.*

Jordan, 890 F.2d 247, 250 (10th Cir.1989) (noting the general rule that if appellant failed to object at trial, appellate review is only for plain error).1 We disagree.

A pretrial motion in limine to exclude evidence will not always preserve an objection for appellate review. *See United States v. Sides,* 944 F.2d 1554, 1560 (10th Cir.), *cert. denied,* 502 U.S. 989, 112 S.Ct. 604, 116 L.Ed.2d 627 (1991). However, a motion in limine may preserve an objection when the issue (1) is fairly presented to the district court, (2) is the type of issue that can be finally decided in a pretrial hearing, and (3) is ruled upon without equivocation by the trial judge. *See Greger v. Int'l Jensen, Inc.,* 820 F.2d 937, 941-42 (8th Cir.1987); *Palmerin v. City of Riverside,* 794 F.2d 1409, 1413 (9th Cir.1986); *Sprynczynatyk v. General Motors Corp.,* 771 F.2d 1112, 1118-19 (8th Cir.1985), *cert. denied,* 475 U.S. 1046, 106 S.Ct. 1263, 89 L.Ed.2d 572 (1986); *American Home Assurance Co. v. Sunshine Supermarket, Inc.,* 753 F.2d 321, 324-25 (3d Cir.1985). "When counsel diligently advances the contentions supporting a motion [in limine] and fully apprises the trial judge of the issue in an evidentiary hearing, application of the rule [requiring parties to reraise objections at trial] ... make[s] little sense." *Sides,* 944 F.2d at 1560. In such circumstances, parties are entitled to " 'treat th[e] ruling as the law of the case' " and to rely on it. *Cook v. Hoppin,* 783 F.2d 684, 691 n. 2 (7th Cir.1986) (quoting *United States v. Rios,* 611 F.2d 1335, 1339 n. 4 (10th Cir.1979)).

Permitting motions in limine to preserve objections in such circumstances is consistent with the elimination of formal exceptions under modern procedural rules. Although Federal Rule of Evidence 103(a)(1) requires parties to make "timely" objections, this provision must be construed in light of Federal Rule of Criminal Procedure 51, which states that formal exceptions are unnecessary. Requiring a party to renew an objection when the district court has issued a definitive ruling on a matter that can be fairly decided before trial would be in the nature of a formal exception and therefore unnecessary. *See American Home,* 753 F.2d at 324 (applying same reasoning in the context of a civil case and Federal Rule of Civil Procedure 46); *Palmerin,* 794 F.2d at 1413 (same); *see also* Fed.R.Crim.P. 51 advisory committee's note 1 (stating that Fed.R.Crim.P. 51 and Fed.R.Civ.P. 46 are "practically identical" and "relate[ ] to a matter of trial practice which should be the same in civil and criminal cases in the interest of avoiding confusion"). Thus, as the Third Circuit notes, the question is whether an objection at trial would have been more in the nature of a formal exception or in the nature of a timely objection calling the court's attention to a matter it need consider. *American Home,* 753 F.2d at 324.

Furthermore, we believe that an absolute rule holding that motions in limine may never preserve an objection is a trap for the unwary, who sensibly rely on a definitive, well-thought-out pretrial ruling on a subject that will not be affected by the evidence that comes in at trial. Moreover, requiring the renewal of objections after a definitive ruling may be a needless provocation to the trial judge, not to mention a distracting interruption during the trial.

Consequently, we apply a three-part test to determine whether it was necessary for an objecting party to renew the objection at trial. First, we ask whether the matter was adequately presented to the district court. *See Palmerin,* 794 F.2d at 1413 (requiring that the subject of the objection be fully explored during the hearing on the motion in limine); *see also Sprynczynatyk,* 771 F.2d at 1119 (noting the matter was fully briefed and argued); *American Home,* 753 F.2d at 324-25 (noting that the motion in limine set forth reasons, including case citations, to support the exclusion of the evidence and that the district court held a hearing at which it considered counsel's arguments); *Sides,* 944 F.2d at 1560 (suggesting that a motion in limine may preserve an objection "where counsel diligently advances the contentions supporting a motion and fully apprises the trial judge of the issue in an evidentiary hearing"). Here, we find that Mejia's counsel adequately argued the issue of whether Mejia's prior food-stamp conviction was admissible under Rule 609(a)(2).

Second, we determine whether the issue is of the type that can be finally decided in a pretrial hearing. That is, some evidentiary issues are akin to questions of law, and the decision to admit such evidence is not dependent upon the character of the other evidence admitted at trial. *See e.g., Sprynczynatyk,* 771 F.2d at 1118-19 (holding that motion in limine preserved objection to post-hypnosis recollection and noting that "[i]t was not a typical motion in limine situation where a hypothetical question is posed whose nature and relevance is unclear before trial"); *see also Cook,* 783 F.2d at 690-91 & n. 2 (holding that the plaintiff's motion in limine to exclude statements in medical records on hearsay grounds preserved objection). On the other hand, some admission decisions are very fact-bound determinations dependent upon the character of the evidence introduced at trial. *See, e.g., Palmerin,* 794 F.2d at 1411-12 (distinguishing two prior Ninth Circuit cases, one in which a motion in limine preserved an objection and one in which it did not, on the ground that in the latter, the issue was "highly dependant upon the trial context" while in the former "[t]he objection was adequately covered by the motion *in limine*"); *United States v. Cobb,* 588 F.2d 607, 612-13 (8th Cir.1978) (stating that a party should ordinarily renew at trial an objection to the admission of a conviction older than ten years under Fed.R.Evid. 609(b), because the decision to admit it rests on "specific facts and circumstances" adduced at trial, and Fed.R.Evid. 609(b) requires a balancing of the probative value against the prejudicial effect of the old conviction), *cert. denied,* 440 U.S. 947, 99 S.Ct. 1426, 59 L.Ed.2d 636 (1979).

Mejia's motion in limine presented an evidentiary issue akin to a question of law: whether Mejia's food-stamp conviction qualified as a crime of dishonesty under Rule 609(a)(2).2 Mejia was therefore entitled to rely on the district court's ruling that the conviction was admissible, as long as the ruling was definitive.

This brings us to the third requirement for reliance on a motion in limine: that the district court's ruling must be definitive. *See e.g., Greger,* 820 F.2d at 941; *Palmerin,* 794 F.2d at 1413 (noting the district court's ruling was "explicit and definitive" and that "[t]here was no hint that the ruling might be subject to reconsideration"); *Sprynczynatyk,* 771 F.2d at 1118 ("The district court's denial of the motion was not made conditionally or with the suggestion that the matter would be reconsidered."); *American Home,* 753 F.2d at 325; *see also Doty v. Sewall,* 908 F.2d 1053, 1056 (1st Cir.1990) (holding that "a pretrial motion in limine is not sufficient to preserve an issue for appeal where the district court declines to rule on the admissibility of the evidence until the evidence is actually offered"); *cf. United States v. Miles,* 889 F.2d 382, 384 (2d Cir.1989) (per curiam) (holding that a ruling made before direct examination of a witness regarding admissibility of the witness's prior conviction did not preserve the objection, as the district court had explicitly indicated that the ruling was not final and should be renewed). Here, the district court unequivocally ruled that the prior food-stamp conviction was admissible, and Mejia was entitled to rely on that ruling.

McEwen v. City of Norman, 926 F.2d 1539 (10th Cir.1991), is not inconsistent with our holding today that an adequately presented motion in limine may preserve an objection if it concerns an issue that can be and is definitively ruled upon in a pretrial hearing. In *McEwen,* the district court expressly reserved ruling on the plaintiff's motion in limine until trial. *Id.* at 1543. When the court finally ruled at trial that the objected-to expert testimony would be admitted, the plaintiff failed to renew the objection-even though the district court invited the plaintiff to make a record on the ruling. *Id.* The only contemporaneous objection the plaintiff made during the expert's testimony was unrelated to the objection raised on appeal. *See id.* at 1543, 1544. Because the district court in *McEwen* expressly declined to issue a definitive pretrial ruling, the plaintiff was required under the test we have enunciated today to renew the objection at trial.

Despite our holding today, we stress that "[u]nder the best of circumstances, counsel must exercise caution in relying exclusively upon rulings made in connection with pretrial motions *in limine* as the basis for preserving claims of error in the admission and exclusion of evidence." *Sides*, 944 F.2d at 1559 (citation omitted). Prudent counsel will renew objections at trial, because the three-part test we enunciate today carries with it the inherent risk that the appellate court might find that the objection was of the type that must be renewed and that the party, by relying on the motion in limine, has waived the objection. Indeed, most objections will prove to be dependent on trial context and will be determined to be waived if not renewed at trial.

B. *Admissibility of the Food-Stamp Conviction*

Having decided that Mejia properly preserved his claim, we now address the merits. We hold that the district court erred in admitting the food-stamp conviction under Federal Rule of Evidence 609(a)(2). Mejia was convicted of acquiring and possessing food coupons having a value of $500 in a manner not authorized by law. He committed the crime by selling four chrome pick-up truck wheels to an undercover Department of Agriculture agent. This food-stamp conviction simply does not qualify as a crime of dishonesty or false statement under this Circuit's construction of Rule 609(a)(2).

Rule 609(a)(2) permits the admission of prior convictions for crimes involving dishonesty or false statement for the purpose of attacking the credibility of a witness.[5] We have narrowly defined the term "dishonesty and false statement" as used in Rule 609(a)(2). As we have previously noted, the adoption of Rule 609 was the culmination of a trend in judicial decisions toward restricting the use of prior convictions for impeachment purposes. *United States v. Wolf*, 561 F.2d 1376, 1380 (10th Cir.1977). "Although it may be argued that any willful violation of the law ... evinces a lack of character and a disregard for all legal duties, including the obligations of an oath, Congress has not accepted that expansive legal theory" and "has 'narrowly defined' the offenses comprehended by Rule 609(a)(2)." *United States v. Millings*, 535 F.2d 121, 123 (D.C.Cir.1976). The Conference Committee Report on the rule specified the type of crimes contemplated by the rule:

By the phrase "dishonesty and false statement" the Conference means crimes such as perjury or subordination of perjury, false statement, criminal fraud, embezzlement, or false pretense, or any other offense in the nature of crimen falsi, the commission of which involves some element of deceit, untruthfulness, or falsification bearing on the accused's propensity to testify truthfully.

H.R.Conf.Rep. No. 1597, 93d Cong., 2d Sess. 9, *reprinted in* 1974 U.S.C.C.A.N. pp. 7051, 7098, 7103. Nor do we believe that the inclusion of the term "crimen falsi" in the Conference Committee Report broadens the category of crimes admissible under Rule 609(a)(2). As the District of Columbia Circuit has noted, even in its broadest sense, the term "crimen falsi" has encompassed only those crimes characterized by an element of deceit or deliberate interference with the truth. *United States v. Smith*, 551 F.2d 348, 362-63 & n. 26 (D.C.Cir.1976). Thus, relying on the Conference Committee Report, we have held that to be admissible under Rule 609(a)(2), the prior conviction must involve "some element of deceit, untruthfulness, or falsification which would tend to show that an accused would be likely to testify untruthfully." *United States v. Seamster*, 568 F.2d 188, 190 (10th Cir.1978).

Consequently, we have held that crimes like burglary, robbery, and theft are not automatically admissible under Rule 609(a)(2), *Seamster*, 568 F.2d at 190, but that a conviction for making false and misleading statements in the sale of securities is, *United States v. O'Connor*, 635 F.2d 814, 818-19 (10th Cir.1980). We have also held that a conviction for making false claims to the United States government is a crime of dishonesty or false statement. *Wolf*, 561 F.2d at 1381. And in *United States v. Mucci*, 630 F.2d 737 (10th Cir.1980), we held that issuing a bad check *while knowing it will be dishonored* is a crime of dishonesty or false statement. *Id.* at 743; *accord United States v. Kane*, 944 F.2d 1406, 1412 (7th Cir.1991); *United States v. Rogers*, 853 F.2d 249, 252 (4th Cir.), *cert. denied*, 488 U.S. 946, 109 S.Ct. 375, 102 L.Ed.2d 364 (1988); *United States v. Livingston*, 816 F.2d 184, 190 (5th Cir.1987).

Furthermore, we have suggested that the trial court may look beyond the elements of an offense that is not considered a per se crime of dishonesty to determine whether the particular conviction rested upon facts establishing dishonesty or false statement. *See United States v. Whitman*, 665 F.2d 313, 320 (10th Cir.1981); *Seamster*, 568 F.2d at 191. For example, in *Whitman*, we held that a grand larceny conviction stemming from a land fraud scheme was a crime of dishonesty, because the larceny was committed by false pretenses rather than by stealth. 665 F.2d at 320.

However, neither the elements of the offense for which Mejia was convicted nor any evidence concerning the way it was committed support the district court's conclusion that the conviction was admissible as a crime of dishonesty or false statement under Rule 609(a)(2). The crime for which Mejia was apparently convicted-unauthorized acquisition and possession of food stamps under 7 U.S.C. § 2024B-DOes not include an element of deceitfulness or untruthfulness. Nor did the government show that Mejia acquired the food-stamps in a deceitful manner: to the contrary, the Presentence Report indicated that Mejia acquired the stamps simply by giving an undercover Department of Agriculture agent four chrome pick-up truck wheels in exchange for the stamps. Thus, Mejia's conviction for illegally acquiring and possessing food stamps does not appear to bear on the likelihood that he would testify truthfully any more than would a burglary conviction imposed for the illegal acquisition of other goods. The district court therefore erred in admitting Mejia's prior food-stamp conviction under Rule 609(a)(2).11

Having determined that the district court erred in admitting the prior conviction, we must now consider whether the error was harmless. Because the defendant alleges no constitutional error, we will apply the harmless-error analysis of *Kotteakos v. United States*, 328 U.S. 750, 66 S.Ct. 1239, 90 L.Ed. 1557 (1946). Under *Kotteakos*, a non-constitutional error is harmless unless it had a "substantial influence" on the outcome or leaves one in "grave doubt" as to whether it had such effect. 328 U.S. at 765, 66 S.Ct. at 1248; *United States v. Rivera*, 900 F.2d 1462, 1469 (10th Cir.1990) (en banc). We must therefore gauge whether the admission of Mejia's food-stamp conviction " 'substantially influenced' the jury's verdict in the context of the entire case against him." *United States v. Short*, 947 F.2d 1445, 1455 (10th Cir.1991) (citing *United States v. Williams*, 923 F.2d 1397, 1401 (10th Cir.1990), *cert. denied*, 500 U.S. 925, 111 S.Ct. 2033, 114 L.Ed.2d 118 (1991)), *cert. denied*, 503 U.S. 989, 112 S.Ct. 1680, 118 L.Ed.2d 397 (1992).

We do not believe that the admission of the food-stamp conviction substantially influenced the jury's verdict. The food-stamp conviction had only modest impeachment value, at best. Mejia's counsel brought out the conviction during direct examination of Mejia, without going into any detail. The food-stamp conviction was not drug-related or weapons-related, as were the charges in the instant case, thus reducing the potential for prejudice. The prosecutor's reference in closing arguments to Mejia's "criminal conviction" was brief and did not go into the details of the conviction. On the other hand, evidence of Mejia's guilt was considerable. We therefore find that the court's admission of the prior food-stamp conviction was harmless.

III. FAILURE TO ASCERTAIN MEJIA'S CONSENT TO THE STIPULATION

Mejia also contends that the trial court erred in failing to determine on the record that Mejia understood and voluntarily consented to a stipulation entered into by his trial counsel and the government. In the stipulation, which was discussed in open court at some length and then read into the record, Mejia's trial counsel agreed that the substance found in Mejia's car on September 8, 1990, was heroin and that the weights in the laboratory report were accurate. Mejia was in court during the discussion and introduction of the stipulation. The record reflects that Mejia speaks and understands a small amount of English and that he had an interpreter present during at least part of the trial. Mejia never objected to the stipulation.

However, Mejia did not sign or in any other way expressly assent on the record to the stipulation. Because Count II charged Mejia with possession of heroin with intent to distribute, possession of heroin was a fact essential to the proof of the crime. Mejia contends that because the stipulation constituted a waiver of his right under _In re Winship,_ _397 U.S. 358, 90 S.Ct. 1068, 25 L.Ed.2d 368 (1970),_ to have the government prove every element of the crime beyond a reasonable doubt, the court should have determined on the record whether Mejia understood and voluntarily entered into the stipulation.

Because Mejia did not object to the stipulation at trial, we review only for plain error. _United States v. Herndon, 982 F.2d 1411, 1416 (10th Cir.1992)._

Certainly, we would prefer that a district court address the defendant directly before accepting a stipulation that goes to one or more elements of the government's case in order to ascertain whether the defendant understood the stipulation and entered it voluntarily, and to determine whether the stipulation has a factual basis. _Herndon, 982 F. 2d at 1418._ However, we have held that a district court's failure to do so does not constitute plain error, nor does it deprive the defendant of due process, at least where the defendant was present in court and represented by counsel at the time of the stipulation. _Herndon, 982 F.2d at 1418._ On the facts of this case, we hold that Mejia's due process rights to a fair trial were not violated when the district court accepted the stipulation and read it to the jury without establishing more explicitly that Mejia understood it and agreed with it.

IV. INEFFECTIVE ASSISTANCE OF COUNSEL

Mejia filed a supplemental pro se brief raising a third issue: that his trial counsel was constitutionally ineffective. He asks us to stay his appeal and remand the ineffectiveness issue to the district court for factual findings on the claim.

As a general matter, however, this Circuit does not stay proceedings on direct appeal to permit the district court time to make factual findings on ineffective assistance claims; rather, we hold that ineffective assistance of counsel claims are ordinarily inappropriate to raise on direct appeal because the necessary fact finding can best be done on collateral attack. See _Osborn v. Shillinger, 861 F.2d 612, 623 (10th Cir.1988); Beaulieu v. United States, 930 F.2d 805, 807 (10th Cir.1991)._ We therefore reject Mejia's contention that we should remand the case to the district court for further factual findings.

There are, however, rare cases where the record is sufficiently complete to enable a fair evaluation of the ineffectiveness claim on direct appeal, as where the claim is confined to matters found in the trial record or does not merit further factual inquiry. _Beaulieu, 930 F. 2d at 807._ Mejia's assertion that the failure to object at trial to the prior food-stamp conviction constituted deficient performance is such a claim. To prove a claim of ineffective assistance of counsel, Mejia must show that counsel's performance was deficient and prejudicial. _United States v. Clonts, 966 F.2d 1366, 1369-70 (10th Cir.1992)_ (citing *Strickland v. Washington,* 466 U.S. 668, 687, 691-92, 104 S.Ct. 2052, 2066-67, 80 L.Ed.2d 674 (1984)). Mejia has not shown that counsel's failure to object to the conviction was either. As we held earlier in this opinion, trial counsel's motion in limine was sufficient to preserve the objection to the prior conviction for appeal; thus, Mejia was not prejudiced by any waiver of the objection. Moreover, there is no suggestion that even if counsel re-raised the objection, the district court would have reversed its prior ruling and excluded the conviction. We also note that Mejia's counsel made a reasonable, tactical decision to bring the conviction in during direct examination of Mejia, presumably to "lessen the sting." Most importantly, we held today that any error in admitting the conviction was harmless. Consequently, we hold that Mejia has failed to establish that his trial counsel's failure to renew the objection was either deficient or prejudiced him. His ineffective assistance of counsel claim on this issue therefore has no merit.

Similarly, we have held that there was no plain error when the district court accepted the stipulation pertaining to the quantities and nature of the drugs seized. Mejia has not alleged that the stipulation was involuntary in fact. In the absence of an allegation that the stipulation was false and involuntary, Mejia does not allege an adequate predicate for an ineffective counsel claim. It is not clear what other claims of ineffective counsel Mejia may wish to raise, but we limit our holding on this appeal to a ruling that Mejia is not entitled to relief for ineffective assistance of counsel based upon the two substantive issues raised in this appeal.

V. CONCLUSION

We AFFIRM Mejia's conviction. In doing so, we hold that the district court erred in admitting Mejia's food-stamp conviction, but that the error was harmless. We further hold that the district court did not plainly err in accepting from Mejia's counsel the stipulation as to the identity and weight of the heroin. Finally, we hold that Mejia has failed to sustain an ineffective counsel claim as to the two alleged errors asserted on direct appeal.

DISCUSSION PROBLEMS 7-1

1. This case was decided before the changes to FRE 103. Do you agree with the analysis of the court?

2. How is the reasoning of the court reflected in the current rule?

3. What practice makes the most sense regarding pretrial motions? Should the rules for preserving objections be different? Why?

THE SKILL OF OBJECTIONS

Objections are both strategic and tactical. A thorough case analysis and preparation of your direct and cross examinations will alert you to possible objections from opposing counsel, as well as arm you with objections to make when opposing counsel is examining a witness. These objections are planned in depth and fall into the strategic category. Others arise in the heat of the moment and more fairly can be said to fall into the tactical category of objections. Sometimes something will simply not sound right and you will be on your feet objecting while still formulating the specific basis for your objection.

One aspect of objecting that you may consider is whether an objection will cause your opponent to lose momentum or get flustered. While it is improper to make an objection solely to disrupt your opponent, it is proper to object whenever you have a good faith basis. Be cautious in this area. Tactical objections may work against you by making you appear overly contentious to the jury. It may also annoy the judge. Consider the judge to be a sleeping lion: if you are going to poke it with a stick, make sure it is on an issue that matters and the reaction that you get is not too severe.

The mechanics of making an objection depend upon your local jurisdiction and the preferences of the trial judge. Some judges will require you to state the basis and the applicable rule of evidence. Others only need to hear the word "objection," and they will start to interrogate opposing counsel. Be aware, especially as defense counsel, that appellate courts will often find waiver of an issue if the objection is not sufficiently specific. This may sometimes require a citation to relevant case law. Some judges will try to get counsel to agree or simply will listen to evidentiary arguments and never rule. Lawyers must be prepared to force the issue of a final ruling when that happens. Waiver occurs in some jurisdictions if the objection is not renewed each time the disputed evidence or testimony is offered. Conversely, you can request that the judge note your continuing objection to evidence of the same type. When in doubt—object!

When you hear an objection you should think about what you just said and why it may be objectionable. Reasons might include: (1) how the question was phrased (leading, argumentative, vague, ambiguous, compound); (2) what you were asking the witness (answered a question that you already asked, gave a conclusion or opinion that is improper, answered with hearsay, gave a narrative response, disclosed privileged information); or perhaps (3) you have gotten ahead of yourself (assuming a fact not in evidence, incomplete or improper foundation, bolstering a witness before credibility is attacked). Wait to hear what the judge says. He may overrule the objection outright. If he invites a response, state your position. If the problem is a matter of phrasing or you tried to enter evidence before the foundation was complete, ask for leave to rephrase the question or to complete the foundation. If you do not understand the objection, but the point that you were attempting to make was critical, ask the judge for clarification before responding.

Whenever opposing counsel violates the rules of evidence as to either the form of the question or the nature of the evidence they are attempting to admit, you must decide whether to object. You should consider whether the theme and theory you identified through case analysis will be aided by your objection. It is also appropriate to use objections to assist you in preventing your opponent from furthering their theme and theory. If either of these two predicate possibilities exist, then it may be appropriate to object.

On the other hand, if it does not hurt your case, consider passing on the potential objection, especially if you have found a way to make the objectionable issue work to your advantage. If you are not sure, but it simply does not sound right when you hear it, then consider using BARPH.

An alternative to BARPH is to structure your objections for maximum persuasion. The judge is your target, so stop and think for a moment of how the objections might appear from the judge's perspective. We will use something as simple as a letter that talks about the lack of character of the accused for our example. Let us say that the alleged victim in a homicide case wrote the letter. The defense counsel who is trying to keep this evidence out has a variety of objections potentially available. The order in which she chooses to raise these objections is crucial, as is her ability to properly identify the relevant evidentiary rule and the policy reasons supporting it. Consider the following:

Prosecutor (P): Ma'am I hand you what has been marked as PE-1 for ID. Do you recognize it?

Witness (W): Yes.

P: What is it?

W: It is a letter written by my dear sweet murdered daughter. She was talking about her sorry husband in it.

Defense (D):   [To the Judge] Objection, this violates 403. May I be heard?

Judge (J): Briefly counsel.

D: Your honor this note has a high probability of unfairly prejudicing my client. Any probative value is substantially outweighed by the danger of unfair prejudice.

J: Overruled. You may proceed, State.

P: I offer PE-1 for ID into evidence as PE-1.

J: Admitted as marked.

Consider what would have happened if the young defense counsel had planned her objections to create a greater degree of concern about the ultimate substantial danger of unfair prejudice. In order to accomplish this she needs to stack and arrange her objections so that she gets the judge's attention. It might go like this:

Prosecutor (P): Ma'am I hand you what has been marked as PE-1 for ID. Do you recognize it?

Witness (W): Yes.

P: What is it?

W: It is a letter written by my dear sweet murdered daughter. She was talking about her sorry husband in it.

Defense (D): [To the Judge] Objection, may I be heard?

Judge (J): Briefly counsel. Basis?

D: Your honor counsel has not laid a proper foundation.

J: Overruled. You may proceed, State.

D: Objection, best evidence rule.

J: Explain.

D: Your honor this letter is a copy of an original that is not available for comparison.

J: I'm going to overrule that objection as well. You may proceed, State.

D: Objection - authentication. May I be heard?

J: All right counsel.

D: Your honor the state has not properly authenticated this letter to show that it was in fact written by the alleged victim. We would request they do so before you admit it.

J: Okay. Lay a foundation, State.

P: [State lays a foundation] I offer...

D: Objection, authentication and hearsay.

J: Counsel, I am overruling the authentication objection. State, how do you respond to the hearsay objection?

P: Your honor it is a dying declaration.

D: Your honor, how can a letter be a dying declaration? The state has not laid sufficient foundation to support that hearsay exception.

J: I disagree, counsel. Objection as to hearsay is overruled.

D: Objection, impermissible character evidence.

J: Counsel this getting old. How is this letter impermissible character evidence?

D: It relates alleged prior misconduct by my client that the jury could improperly consider as propensity evidence. FRE 404(a) is clearly designed to prevent this. Further more, your honor, we have not opened the door to character evidence in this case.

J: How do you respond, State?

P: Your honor, we offer it under the 404(b) exception and request a limiting instruction to the jury as to its permissible use under 105.

J: Based upon that offer I overrule the objection.

D: Your honor, may I be heard?

J: Extremely briefly counsel.

D: Your honor, we have established concerns with admitting this letter that include foundation and authentication under FRE 901, hearsay under FRE 804 and impermissible character evidence under 404(a). Although you have overruled each of these objections their cumulative effect is to point out quite clearly the substantial danger of unfair prejudice to my client if this letter is admitted. We request you exclude it under 403.

J: [rubbing his eyes] Counsel, I'll consider your objection over lunch. We are in recess.

The defense counsel in this second example may very well lose the 403 objection, but they have made an excellent record. They have also raised so many concerns that the judge may decide to exclude this piece of evidence. This technique is useful when you want to send the signal to the judge that this particular issue is important and worthy of careful consideration. This approach will only work if you save it for the right moment. If you throw every objection available out indiscriminately then the judge will eventually tune you out.

Another danger exists if you have a judge that either prefers or requires that you state every relevant objection to a piece of evidence when raising an objection about that evidence. Lawyers must know the local court's preference on this issue. While the preference of the judge is not dispositive on whether you raise all issues at one time, it may be that you need to do so to get the judge's attention. When that is the case you still stack your objections, but you just make a complete stack at one time.31

---

[31] Many thanks to the honorable Christina Habas, one of the best judges teaching for NITA. Her honor's comments on this section were extremely valuable. She has also donated two sections to Stetson's Online Advocacy Resource Center discussing storytelling and jury selection. Her presentation on Jury Selection is the best I have ever seen. Thanks, Tina!

Regardless of whether you are BARPHing or stacking, you should stand and say "objection" and then briefly state the basis for your concern. You should focus on the judge and her reactions, never looking at opposing counsel. The judge will either rule on your objection outright or ask opposing counsel to respond. Listen carefully both to what opposing counsel says and the judge's response. If opposing counsel cannot give the judge a valid basis to overrule the objection then you should remain silent. Do not snatch defeat from the jaws of victory when objecting by talking too much. If you lose the objection you can make an offer of proof, and, when necessary, refer back to that objection when attempting to admit or suppress other evidence.

Along with dealing with objections off the cuff, the superior lawyer will plan for potential objections in depth on those important, if not dispositive, legal and factual issues identified during case analysis. This is accomplished by: (1) identifying potentially objectionable issues through case analysis; (2) researching the basis and strength of your objection (with favorable case law identified and prepared); (3) analyzing potential responses by opposing counsel; and then (4) preparing your counter-response.

This type of in-depth planning creates the sense on the part of the judge that you know what you are talking about. They will take you seriously because their primary concern is protecting the record. When you can get inside of the decision-making loop the judge uses to protect the record you are well on your way to winning the evidentiary battle over objections.

THE LAW OF OBJECTIONS

There are two general types of trial objections, form and substance. "Objections to Form" attack the way counsel asked the question. FRE 611(a) and (c) empowers the trial court to control the mode and order of interrogation and to limit the use of leading questions. "Objections to Substance" attack the admissibility of the testimony elicited. All of these objections are derived directly from the law of evidence. The most common objections are outlined below with the form of the objection, an explanation of the basis for the objection, possible responses to the objection by a trial judge or by opposing counsel and, where applicable, more recent federal decisions addressing the objection.

Objections to Form

Lawyers often identify objections to form based upon "feel." They listen for questions that are either not properly formed or are not sufficiently focused based upon the rules of evidence and norms of practice in their jurisdiction. Lawyers can avoid objection to form by using questions that are allowed under FRE 611. A nice place to begin conceptually is with the concept that bad questions are objectionable and should be avoided.

Ambiguous, Confusing or Unintelligible Question – FRE 611(a)

Objection: *The question is ambiguous/confusing/unintelligible.*

Response: *I will rephrase.*

Explanation: A question is ambiguous if it may be interpreted in several ways, or if it is so vague or unclear that it may confuse the jury, judge, or the witness.

Argumentative Question - FRE 611(a)

Objection: *The question is argumentative.*

Response: *Rephrase the question.*

Explanation: A question is argumentative if it is an attempt to make an argument to the jury, to summarize, draw inferences from, or comment on the evidence, or to ask the witness to testify as to his own credibility. A question can also be argumentative if it is unduly hostile or sarcastic.

Asked and Answered or Unduly Repetitious - FRE 403, 611(a)

Objection: *The witness has already answered the question.*

Response: *The witness has not yet answered this particular question.*

Explanation: Repetitious questions are unlikely to elicit additional evidence of probative value. *See U.S. v. Collins*, 996 F.2d 950, 952 (8th Cir. 1993), cert. denied, 510 U.S. 956 (1993) (objection to question posed during re-direct examination on basis that it had been asked and answered on direct examination sustained).

Assumes Facts Not in Evidence - FRE 601, 611(a)

Objection: *Assumes facts not in evidence.*

Responses: *(1) The existence of this fact may be inferred from evidence which has been admitted; (2) if permitted to answer the fact will be in evidence; or (3) the fact will be proved during the testimony of Witness X. We will "tie it up" later.*

Explanation· A question that assumes facts not yet in evidence effectively allows counsel to testify as to those facts without personal knowledge.

Multifarious; Compound Question - FRE 611(a)

Objection: *Compound Question.*

Response: *I will rephrase the question.*

Explanation: A question combining more than one inquiry is likely to be confusing and misleading to both the witness and the fact-finder.

Harassing the Witness - FRE 403, 611(a)(3)

Objection: *Harassing the witness.*

Response: *I will rephrase the question.*

Explanation: A question that is asked to harass or embarrass a witness, for example, a question that unnecessarily delves into a witness's personal life, is impermissible.

Leading Question - FRE 611(c)

Objection: *Leading.*

Responses: *(1) The question is not a leading question simply because it elicits a yes or no answer. It is generally to elicit preliminary or background information from a witness through leading questions, (2) the witness is an adverse party, or the witness is hostile, (3) leading questions are allowed of one's own witnesses on cross examination if the witness is called by the adverse party, or (4) I'll rephrase the question.*

Explanation: A leading question is one that suggests to the witness the answer desired by the examiner. Leading questions are generally impermissible on direct examination.

Calls for Narrative Answer - FRE 403, 611(a)

> Objection: *I object. The question calls for narrative testimony and deprives us of an Objection: Calls for a narrative. Counsel is trying to admit inadmissible evidence.*
>
> Response: *I will rephrase the question.*

Explanation: Narrative, unspecific, or long "rambling" answers are not per se objectionable, but are likely to contain hearsay or other inadmissible evidence to which counsel is deprived of an opportunity to object. *See U.S. v. Pless*, 982 F.2d 1118, 1123 (7th Cir. 1992) ("there is nothing particular, unusual, or incorrect, in a procedure of letting a witness relate pertinent information in a narrative form as long as it stays within the bounds of pertinence and materiality").

Mischaracterizes or Misquotes the Witness or Prior Evidence - FRE 611(a).

> Objection: *I object. The question mischaracterizes, misstates, or misquotes the prior testimony...*
>
> Response: *I'll rephrase the question.*

Explanation: Questions that misquote previous testimony or evidence are likely to mislead or confuse the jury.

Objections to Substance
Objections as to substance address evidentiary issues dealing with the portions of the Federal Rules of Evidence dealing with admitting or excluding evidence. These include questions of character, authenticity, credibility, relevancy, impeachment and hearsay. These are the types of objections that have a greater potential impact upon those issues in controversy that must be proven at trial. These are the types of objections that are not waived if you were to fail to make them during a deposition. New lawyers should think of them as being objections that have more potential for a prejudicial impact if they are not properly raised and addressed.

Lack of Authentication – FRE 901, 902

> Objection: *I object. The evidence has not been properly authenticated.*
>
> Response: *The item is sufficiently authenticated by _____ (a method listed in Rule 901(b)).*

Examples of sufficient authentication include:
- Testimony of a witness with knowledge.
- Non-expert opinion on the genuineness of handwriting.
- Comparison by trier-of-fact or expert witness to authenticated specimens.
- Distinctive characteristics of the item offered.
- Voice identification by opinion based upon hearing the voice under circumstances connecting it with the alleged speaker.
- Public records or reports.
- The item is self-authenticating under FRE 902.

Examples of self-authenticating evidence under FRE 902 include:
- Domestic public documents under seal.

- Domestic public documents not under seal if officer certifies that the signature is genuine.
- Foreign public documents.
- Certified copies or public records.
- Official publications.
- Newspapers and periodicals.
- Acknowledged or notarized documents.
- Commercial paper and related documents.

Explanation: Authentication is not satisfied if insufficient evidence has been offered to support a finding that the matter in question is what its proponent claims is it. *See U.S. v. McGlory*, 968 F.2d 309, 328-29 (3d Cir. 1992), cert. denied, 507 U.S. 962 (1993) (to show authenticity there must be a prima facie showing of authenticity to the court; the jury will ultimately determine the authenticity of the evidence).

Best Evidence Not Offered - FRE 1001, 1002, 1003, 1004.

Objection: *I object. The evidence is not the best evidence.*

Response: *The evidence qualifies as an original, or as a duplicate.*

Explanation: The best evidence rule requires the original writing, recording, or photograph to prove the content of the writing, recording, or photograph. FRE 1001 defines original and duplicate. An "original" is the writing or recording itself, any counterpart intended to have the same effect, the negative or print therefrom if the evidence is a photograph, and any printout or other output shown to accurately reflect the data of an original that is stored in a computer.

A "duplicate" is a counterpart produced by the same impression as the original, or from the same matrix, or by means of photography, including enlargements and miniatures, or by mechanical or electronic re-recording, or by chemical reproduction, or by other equivalent techniques." Duplicates are admissible to the same extent as originals.

Response: *The rule is inapplicable because the proponent is not seeking to prove the content of the item.*

Response: *The original is not obtainable and secondary evidence is therefore admissible.*

Explanation: Secondary evidence is admissible if the original has been lost or destroyed except for when the loss or destruction was done in bad faith by the proponent. Other examples for when secondary evidence is admissible from FRE 1004 include: (1) the original is unobtainable by any available judicial process or procedure, (2) the original is under the control of the opponent and the opponent does not produce the original when put on notice that it will be subject of proof at a hearing, (3) the item is offered for a collateral purpose. *See U.S. v. Haddock*, 956 F.2d 1534, 1545 (10th Cir. 1992), cert. denied, 506 U.S. 828 ("due to modern and accurate reproduction techniques, duplicates and originals should normally be treated interchangeably").

Improper Use of Character Evidence - FRE 404, 405, 608

Objection: *I object. The question calls for inadmissible character evidence.*

Response: *The person's character trait is "in issue."*

Explanation: A person's character is "in issue" when it is an element of a charge, claim, or defense. For example, in a claim of negligent entrustment, the trait of incompetence of the person to whom the defendant entrusted the dangerous instrumentality to is an element of the claim and is "in issue." Proof of character may then be made by opinion or reputation testimony, or by evidence of specific instances of conduct. Character evidence is generally inadmissible to show that a person acted in conformity with that character on a particular occasion. Character evidence may be proved only by reputation or opinion testimony, not by specific acts, except where a trait of the person's character is "in issue," or for the purpose of impeachment or rehabilitation on cross examination.

Objection: *I object. Evidence of specific acts is impermissible to prove character.*

Response: *The character evidence is offered for the purpose of impeachment or rehabilitation on cross-examination and is therefore admissible under FRE 608.*

Explanation: A witness that has testified as to the character of a person may be asked on cross examination about specific acts of that person in the form of "have you heard?" or "do you know?" questions to test the factual basis of their testimony on direct examination. A witness may always be asked on cross examination about specific instances of his or her own conduct that are probative of untruthfulness. Counsel must have a good faith basis for making the inquiry (FRE 608).

Objection: *I object. The question calls for inadmissible character evidence.*

Response: *The person's character trait is "in issue" because it is an element of a charge, claim, or defense.*

Explanation: The specific act is offered to prove something other than character. Evidence of other crimes, wrongs, or acts may be admissible to prove motive, opportunity, intent, preparation, plan, knowledge, identity, or absence of mistake or accident (FRE 404(b)). *See U.S. v. Roberts*, 887 F.2d 534 (5th Cir. 1989) (character trait was in issue on a question of whether defendant formed the requisite intent, and evidence of personality traits was therefore properly admitted); *U.S. v. McGuiness*, 764 F. Supp. 888 (S.D.N.Y. 1991) (evidence of defendant's previous refusal to accept bribes not admissible to prove character of defendant and action in conformity with that character); *U.S. v. Nazarenus*, 983 F.2d 1480 (8th Cir. 1993) (extrinsic evidence of defendant's driving habits inadmissible to impeach defendant as specific acts may not be proved by extrinsic evidence for the purpose of attacking or supporting the witness's credibility) (FRE 608(b)).

Bolstering the Credibility of a Witness - FRE 607, 608, 801(d)(1)(B)

Objection: *I object. Counsel is bolstering the witness.*

Response: *The witness's credibility has been attacked and this evidence is proper rehabilitation.*

Explanation: FRE 608(a) permits evidence of a witness's character for truthfulness only after the witness's character for truthfulness has been attacked. Bolstering refers to a proponent's attempt to offer otherwise inadmissible character evidence solely to enhance his witness's credibility when the witness has not yet been impeached. *See U.S. v. Hedgcorth*, 873 F.2d 1307, 1313-1314 (9th Cir. 1989), cert. denied, 493 U.S. 857 (1989) (testimony as to defendant's character for truthfulness properly excluded where government had not attacked defendant's character for truthfulness).

Impeachment on a Collateral Matter - FRE 403, 608

Objection: *I object. Extrinsic evidence of specific instances is inadmissible to impeach a witness on collateral matters.*

Responses: *(1) The extrinsic evidence is independently relevant to a substantive issue in the case, (2) the evidence is offered to prove bias, which is not a collateral matter, or (3) evidence of specific acts of a witness are admissible when offered to prove something other than a witness's untrustworthy character.*

Explanation: This objection arises most commonly when a party seeks to impeach a witness by introducing extrinsic evidence that contradicts an answer given by the witness. *See U.S. v. Abel*, 469 U.S. 45 (1984) (bias is not collateral); *Foster v. General Motors Corp.*, 20 F.3d 838, 839 (8th Cir. 1994) (evidence relevant to a material issue is admissible).

Conclusion of Law or Ultimate Issue - FRE 701, 702, 704

Objection: *I object. The witness is testifying to an ultimate issue.*

Response: *The expert or lay witness has knowledge or expertise of the matter, and the evidence is helpful. An adequate foundation has been laid.*

Explanation: Testimony phrased in conclusory terms is less helpful than testimony that provides information to the jury so that it may draw its own conclusions. Conclusions of law are generally inadmissible. Lay or expert witness testimony must be based on the lay witness's perception or must be within the scope of the expertise of an expert witness, and must be helpful to the fact finder. Opinions on an ultimate issue are generally admissible (FRE 704). *See U.S. v. Lockett*, 919 F.2d 585, 590 (9th Cir. 1990) (expert opinions about guilt or innocence inadmissible); *Kostelecky v. NL Acme Tool/NL Industries, Inc.*, 837 F.2d 828, 830 (8th Cir. 1988) ("evidence that merely tells the jury what result to reach is not sufficiently helpful to the trier of fact to be admissible").

Cross Examination beyond the Scope of Direct - FRE 611(b)

Objection: *I object. The question asked goes beyond the scope of the matters raised on direct.*

Response: *The question is permissible because the subject matter of direct includes all inferences and implications arising from direct.*

Explanation: Cross examination that raises subjects not raised on direct is generally inadmissible.

Cumulative - FRE 403

Objection: *I object. The evidence is cumulative.*

Response: *A party has a right to present a persuasive case and the cumulative evidence concept should not interfere with that right.*

Explanation: If the evidence is needlessly cumulative or repetitious, it may be excluded. *See Davis v. Mason County*, 927 F.2d 1473 (9th Cir. 1991), cert. denied, 502 U.S. 899 (1991) (testimony of expert witness properly excluded on ground that two other experts had testified on the same topic).

Hearsay - FRE 801, 802, 803, 804

Objection: *I object. The question calls for hearsay.*

Responses: *(1) The statement is not hearsay because it is not offered to prove the truth of the matter asserted, (2) the statement is not hearsay under the rules... (3) I am offering it for a non-hearsay purpose, or (4) the statement is hearsay, but is specifically exempted by the rules...*

Explanation: Hearsay is inadmissible unless it falls within an established exception. Key exceptions, as listed in FRE 801, 803 and 804, include:

- Prior statements by witness
- Admissions by party-opponent offered against party-opponent
- Present sense impressions
- Excited utterances
- Statement of the declarant's then existing state of mind
- Statements for the purpose of medical diagnosis or treatment
- Recorded recollections
- Records of regularly conducted activity
- Public records and reports
- Learned treatises
- Former testimony of unavailable declarant
- Statement under belief of impending death where the declarant is unavailable
- Statement against interest of an unavailable declarant

Impermissible Hypothetical Question - FRE 705

Objection: *I object. Counsel is posing a hypothetical question that contains facts not in evidence.*

Response: *A hypothetical question need not refer to all of the relevant facts in evidence. The witness is an expert witness, and an expert may base an opinion on facts that are not admitted into evidence, as long as they are the type reasonably relied upon by experts in forming opinions on the subject.*

Explanation: A hypothetical question is inadmissible if it contains facts that are not already in evidence, that will not be introduced before the close of evidence, or that are not reasonably drawn from such facts. *See Toucet v. Maritime Overseas Corp.*, 991 F.2d 5, 10 (1st Cir. 1993) (a hypothetical question should include only those facts suggested by the evidence).

Witness is Incompetent or Lacks Personal Knowledge - FRE 601-606

Objection: *I object. The witness is incompetent or lacks sufficient capacity to testify, or no showing has been made that the witness has personal knowledge about this matter.*

Responses: *(1) Rule 601 abolishes objections to a witness's competence, (2) The witness is competent under state law, (3) A personal assertion by the witness is sufficient to show personal knowledge, (4) I will ask additional questions sufficient to lay the foundation to establish personal knowledge.*

Explanation: All persons are presumed competent to testify except as otherwise provided in the rules. However, incompetence of a witness may be the basis for an objection in two situations: where state law supplies the rule of decision with respect to an element of a claim or defense, and the witness is incompetent under state law; or where insufficient evidence has been introduced to support a finding that the witness has personal knowledge of the matter. *See U.S. v. Phibbs*, 999 F.2d 1053 (6th Cir. 1993) (admission of testimony from witness with history of mental problems was not error as all persons are presumed competent to testify); *Kemp v. Balboa*, 23 F.3d 211 (8th Cir. 1994) (nurse not allowed to testify because she lacked personal knowledge as to the facts stated in medical records which she had not prepared).

Misleading - FRE 403

Objection: *I object. The evidence will mislead the jury. Or, if a bench trial: I object, the evidence is misleading.*

Response: *The probative value of the evidence outweighs the danger of misleading the jury or the court.*

Explanation: The danger of misleading the jury usually refers to the possibility that the jury will attach undue weight to the evidence. If the probative value of the evidence is substantially outweighed by the danger of misleading the jury, the evidence may be excluded. *See Rogers v. Raymark Indus.*, 922 F.2d 1426 (9th Cir. 1991) (evidence of observations taken at defendant's asbestos plant was properly excluded because plaintiff's complaint was based on activities at a different plant and there was no evidence of similarity among the plants).

Prejudicial Effect Outweighs Probative Value - FRE 403

Objection: *I object. The probative value of this evidence is outweighed by the danger of unfair prejudice.*

Response: *All probative evidence is prejudicial. The rule does not afford protection from evidence that is merely detrimental to a party's case. In this instance the probative value of the evidence outweighs the danger of unfair prejudice.*

Explanation: Evidence is unfairly prejudicial if it suggests a decision on an improper basis, most commonly an emotional basis. If the probative value of the evidence is substantially outweighed by the danger of unfair prejudice, the evidence may be excluded. *See U.S. v. Skillman*, 922 F.2d 1370, 1374 (9th Cir. 1990), cert. dism'd, 502 U.S. 922 (1991) (rule only protects against evidence that is unfairly prejudicial).

Confusion of the Issues - FRE 403

Objection: *I object. The evidence will confuse the issues.*

Response: *The probative value of the evidence outweighs the risk of confusion.*

Explanation: Evidence is confusing if it tends to distract the jury from the proper issues of the trial. If the probative value of evidence is outweighed by the danger of confusion, it may be excluded. See *Ramos-Melendez v. Valdejully*, 960 F.2d 4, 6 (1st Cir. 1992) (evidence of other suits properly excluded as distracting the jury from the issues at hand).

Privilege - FRE 501

Objection: *I object. The question calls for privileged information.*

Response: *The privilege asserted is not one created by constitution, court, or state rule, or one recognized by common law. The communication at issue is not privileged.*

Explanation: Privileged information based on the attorney-client privilege, doctor patient privilege, spousal privilege, and other privileges recognized by Common or statutory law is inadmissible. Privilege law is generally governed by the principles of common law as interpreted by the United States courts, but in civil actions, state privilege law applies with respect to an element of a claim or defense as to which state substantive law governs.

The privilege has been waived. *See U.S. v. Moscony*, 927 F.2d 742, 751 (3d Cir. 1991), cert. denied, 501 U.S. 1211 (1991) (although Congress did not enact the Supreme Court's proposed privilege rules which discussed individual privileges, courts often refer to those rules for guidance).

Speculation - FRE 602, 701, 702

Objection: *I object. The question calls for the witness to speculate.*

Response: *I will rephrase the question to establish the witness's personal knowledge or basis for the witness's statement.*

Explanation: A question which asks a witness to speculate as to what occurred or what caused an event may conflict with the requirement that a witness have personal knowledge of a matter testified to, or in the case of an expert witness, may be an impermissible attempt to elicit an opinion beyond the scope of the witness's expertise.

CONCLUSION

In this chapter we have discussed the various types of objections that counsel can make at trial. We have looked at them individually while also attempting to begin to see how they might connect to one another through the course of an actual trial. You need to understand each objection from a legal perspective initially, so that you use it appropriately when the moment demands it. Let's move on now to some specific means of impeachment. As we work our way through the next chapter make sure that you focus on the specific and the general. It is through understanding the initial rule individually that you will begin to develop an understanding of how and when to connect them with others.

-Notes-

Chapter 8: How Impeachment Works

IMPEACHMENT
Understanding Impeachment

This chapter on impeachment builds upon the skills of case analysis, basic questioning techniques, and cross examination previously discussed. It is the next step a lawyer takes in developing a thorough set of cross examination skills. Think of it as a subset of cross examination driven by the rules of evidence and your own common sense. Mastering the law behind these methods of impeachment, the human element is always present when confronting someone about a lie, and the theories of contradiction and omission allowed for at common law will ensure you are prepared to deal with a witness that misstates the truth. Remember, most, if not all, witnesses make that mistake to some degree during direct examination.

One of the three goals during cross examination is to establish facts that build up the credibility of your witnesses and decrease the credibility of your opponent's witness. Impeachment is the tool lawyers use to accomplish this goal. The fundamental purpose of impeachment is to discredit the witness as a reliable source of information. Lawyers must use all the skills developed for cross examination, including case analysis, goal questions and physicality.

There are seven common methods of impeachment. Most evidentiary texts only identify the five forms of impeachment in the Federal Rules of Evidence; at least two others exist at common law. We will limit ourselves to these generally accepted methods of impeachment in this chapter. There are some common legal and practical considerations that must be addressed before choosing which type of impeachment to employ. Initially you must know everything that the witness knows, and what the witness does not know, to be successful during impeachment. You will only be in this position if you have prepared sufficiently, a continuing case analysis is the best means available to a lawyer to guarantee sufficient knowledge to ensure success. There are seven primary means of impeachment. Each has a slightly different legal basis, and the manner in which you accomplish each type of impeachment is tied to the reason you are legally allowed to impeach the witness.

When a witness testifies, his credibility becomes an issue. Because credibility is intrinsically tied to testifying it is always logically relevant. The limitations of the Federal Rules of Evidence on impeachment establish the degree to which the credibility of a witness is legally relevant. Lawyers must be able to articulate how a particular fact or set of facts tends to impeach the credibility of a witness and satisfy the logical relevancy requirements of the Federal Rules of Evidence. Remember that probative impeachment evidence that is both logically and legally relevant may be excluded by the judge based on FRE 403 if its probative value is substantially outweighed by the danger of unfair prejudice, confusion of the issues, waste of time or due to its cumulative nature.

Witness credibility has three facets at trial—bolstering, impeachment, and rehabilitation. Lawyers are not allowed to bolster the believability of their witness by offering to prove the witness's character for truthfulness before it has been attacked through impeachment by opposing counsel. Bolstering is generally prohibited. Lawyers are permitted to accredit the witness by eliciting general background information and qualifications as a preliminary step of direct examination. This is an essential step for expert witnesses.

After a witness has been impeached the proponent may attempt to rehabilitate his credibility by giving him the opportunity to explain or deny an apparent inconsistency, prior bad act, or prior untruthfulness. Impeachment is not limited to opposing counsel. Under FRE 607 "the credibility of a witness may be attacked by any party, including the party calling the witness."

For reasons of judicial economy, certain matters offered for impeachment of a witness may not be proven by extrinsic evidence because they raise questions that are too collateral to the issues in the trial. If courts allowed this sort of inquiry, examinations would consist of mini-trials within trials. This is referred to as the Collateral Fact Rule. If a matter is deemed collateral, the court will only permit inquiry on cross examination. Prior untruthful acts of the witness are generally considered collateral, whereas prior convictions and proof of bias are rarely collateral. When an issue is collateral, extrinsic proof cannot be offered to establish the veracity of the impeachment. Some forms of impeachment may be proven by extrinsic evidence while others only permit inquiry on cross examination. Regardless of which impeachment technique is used, counsel must have a good faith belief that the impeaching facts are true.

These techniques are designed to create tension by building suspense and sparking the interest of the jury, while suggesting the answer that everyone expects. There is nothing wrong with that expectation during impeachment—provided you can deliver on the expectation. You must make certain that you have the available resources to impeach the witness when they stray from the good or bad facts that you identified through your case analysis. This point is crucial. If the witness challenges you and the law allows you to respond to that challenge—you must. Failure to properly control empowers the witness, weakens your theme and theory of the case, and calls into question your credibility as a lawyer in the eyes of the fact-finder.

Preparing Impeachment

Impeachment is not an end in itself. Counsel must always analyze not only whether impeachment of a particular witness will help their case, but how it will help the case. A clear theory of your case and your opponent's case is critical before you can adequately determine whether an impeachment is warranted and will be effective. An effective impeachment depends upon accurate knowledge of the law, good technique, and projection of the right attitude. Counsel should always strive for clarity and simplicity because clarity and simplicity will assist the jury in understanding and using the impeachment for its proper evidentiary purpose.

If the witness has testified in a way that exposes him to impeachment, consider whether clarification or refreshing his recollection will accomplish the same purpose that a full-blown impeachment would produce. If the witness has hurt your case and you decide to impeach him, you must further consider what tone and style of impeachment will be most effective. If the witness is cocky, partisan, or simply lying, then a hard-hitting, aggressive tone may be appropriate. If the witness seems sincere, then a gentler approach may be warranted.

THE LAW OF CROSS EXAMINATION AND IMPEACHMENT

FRE 611 addresses witnesses and establishes the manner and scope of witness testimony during cross examination. While FRE 611 governs the form of cross examination questions, many other evidentiary rules also impact your ability to impeach witnesses. You must understand the legal doctrine behind the rules governing impeachment. You should begin your inquiry by developing a deeper basis of knowledge concerning prior untruthful acts under FRE 608(b), prior convictions under FRE 609, and prior inconsistent statements under FRE 613.

Additionally you must master the common law concerning bias, motive, and defects in capacity to observe, recall, or relate information. An in-depth study of these evidentiary rules is beyond the capacity of this text, but in the following pages, when each type of impeachment is discussed, the rule and the fundamental questioning steps you must take to establish a valid impeachment under that particular legal basis will be provided.

Using the text will make you competent, but it will not make you superior when it comes to impeachment. Impeachment is legally relevant activity at trial because the rules of evidence and the common law make it so. The law of evidence allows you to specifically point out certain defects in the testimony of witnesses. You should consider the evidentiary rules mentioned above and sprinkled throughout this chapter as examples of the legal relevance standard that must exist before the court will allow you to impeach.

THE SUPREME COURT SPEAKS-ADMITTING CONVICTIONS AT TRIAL

Consider the following Supreme Court case dealing with admitting convictions at trial. As you read it ask yourself, is this a government friendly, defense friendly, or advocate neutral ruling? What effect does the court's ruling have on subsequent decisions to admit this type of evidence? Do you agree with the court's position? Why?

120 S.Ct. 1851
Supreme Court of the United States
Maria Suzuki **OHLER**, Petitioner,
v.
UNITED STATES.
No. 98-9828.
Argued March 20, 2000.Decided May 22, 2000.

Chief Justice <u>REHNQUIST</u> delivered the opinion of the Court.

Petitioner, Maria **Ohler**, was arrested and charged with importation of marijuana and possession of marijuana with the intent to distribute. The District Court granted the Government's motion *in limine* seeking to admit evidence of her prior felony conviction as impeachment evidence under <u>Federal Rule of Evidence 609(a)(1)</u>. **Ohler** testified at trial and admitted on direct examination that she had been convicted of possession of methamphetamine in 1993. The jury convicted her of both counts, and the Court of Appeals for the Ninth Circuit affirmed. We agree with the Court of Appeals that **Ohler** may not challenge the *in limine* ruling of the District Court on appeal.

Maria **Ohler** drove a van from Mexico to California in July 1997. As she passed through the San Ysidro Port of Entry, a customs inspector noticed that someone had tampered with one of the van's interior panels. Inspectors searched the van and discovered approximately 81 pounds of marijuana. **Ohler** was arrested and charged with importation of marijuana and possession of marijuana with the intent to distribute. Before trial, the Government filed motions *in limine* seeking to admit **Ohler's** prior felony conviction as character evidence under <u>Federal Rule of Evidence 404(b)</u>and as impeachment evidence under <u>Rule 609(a)(1)</u>. The District Court denied the motion to admit the conviction as character evidence, but reserved ruling on whether the conviction could be used for impeachment purposes. On the first day of trial, the District Court ruled that if **Ohler** testified, evidence of her prior conviction would be admissible under <u>Rule 609(a)(1)</u>. App. 97-98. She testified in her own defense, denying any knowledge of the marijuana. She also admitted on direct examination that she had been convicted of possession of methamphetamine in 1993. The jury found **Ohler** guilty of both counts, and she was sentenced to 30 months in prison and 3 years' supervised release. *Id., at* 140-141.

On appeal, **Ohler** challenged the District Court's *in limine* ruling allowing the Government to use her prior conviction for impeachment purposes. The Court of Appeals for the Ninth Circuit affirmed, holding that **Ohler** waived her objection by introducing evidence of the conviction during her direct examination. 169 F.3d 1200 (C.A.9 1999). We granted certiorari to resolve a conflict among the Circuits regarding whether appellate review of an *in limine* ruling is available in this situation. 528 U.S. 950, 120 S.Ct. 370, 145 L.Ed.2d 289 (1999). See *United States v. Fisher,* 106 F.3d 622 (C.A.5 1997) (allowing review); *United States v. Smiley,* 997 F.2d 475 (C.A.8 1993) (holding objection waived). We affirm.

Generally, a party introducing evidence cannot complain on appeal that the evidence was erroneously admitted. See 1 J. Weinstein & M. Berger, Weinstein's Federal Evidence § 103.14, p. 103-30 (2d ed. 2000). Cf. 1 J. Strong, McCormick on Evidence § 55, p. 246 (5th ed. 1999) ("If a party who has objected to evidence of a certain fact himself produces evidence from his own witness of the same fact, he has waived his objection"). **Ohler** seeks to avoid the consequences of this well-established commonsense principle by invoking Rules 103 and 609 of the Federal Rules of Evidence. But neither of these Rules addresses the question at issue here. Rule 103 sets forth the unremarkable propositions that a party must make a timely objection to a ruling admitting evidence and that a party cannot challenge an evidentiary ruling unless it affects a substantial right.[1] The Rule does not purport to determine when a party waives a prior objection, and it is silent with respect to the effect of introducing evidence on direct examination, and later assigning its admission as error on appeal.

Rule 609(a) is equally unavailing for **Ohler**; it merely identifies the situations in which a witness' prior conviction may be admitted for impeachment purposes. The Rule originally provided that admissible prior conviction evidence could be elicited from the defendant or established by public record during cross-examination, but it was amended in 1990 to clarify that the evidence could also be introduced on direct examination. According to **Ohler**, it follows from this amendment that a party does not waive her objection to the *in limine* ruling by introducing the evidence herself. However, like Rule 103, Rule 609(a) simply does not address this issue. There is no question that the Rule authorizes the eliciting of a prior conviction on direct examination, but it does no more than that.

Next, **Ohler** argues that it would be unfair to apply such a waiver rule in this situation because it compels a defendant to forgo the tactical advantage of pre-emptively introducing the conviction in order to appeal the *in limine* ruling. She argues that if a defendant is forced to wait for evidence of the conviction to be introduced on cross-examination, the jury will believe that the defendant is less credible because she was trying to conceal the conviction. The Government disputes that the defendant is unduly disadvantaged by waiting for the prosecution to introduce the conviction on cross-examination. First, the Government argues that it is debatable whether jurors actually perceive a defendant to be more credible if she introduces a conviction herself. Brief for United States 28. Second, even if jurors do consider the defendant more credible, the Government suggests that it is an unwarranted advantage because the jury does not realize that the defendant disclosed the conviction only after failing to persuade the court to exclude it. *Ibid.*

Whatever the merits of these contentions, they tend to obscure the fact that both the Government and the defendant in a criminal trial must make choices as the trial progresses. For example, the defendant must decide whether or not to take the stand in her own behalf. If she has an innocent or mitigating explanation for evidence that might otherwise incriminate, acquittal may be more likely if she takes the stand. Here, for example, **Ohler** testified that she had no knowledge of the marijuana discovered in the van, that the van had been taken to Mexico without her permission, and that she had gone there simply to retrieve the van. But once the defendant testifies, she is subject to cross-examination, including impeachment by prior convictions, and the decision to take the stand may prove damaging instead of helpful. A defendant has a further choice to make if she decides to testify, notwithstanding a prior conviction. The defendant must choose whether to introduce the conviction on direct examination and remove the sting or to take her chances with the prosecutor's possible elicitation of the conviction on cross-examination.

The Government, too, in a case such as this, must make a choice. If the defendant testifies, it must choose whether or not to impeach her by use of her prior conviction. Here the trial judge had indicated he would allow its use,[3] but the Government still had to consider whether its use might be deemed reversible error on appeal. This choice is often based on the Government's appraisal of the apparent effect of the defendant's testimony. If she has offered a plausible, innocent explanation of the evidence against her, it will be inclined to use the prior conviction; if not, it may decide not to risk possible reversal on appeal from its use.

Due to the structure of trial, the Government has one inherent advantage in these competing trial strategies. Cross-examination comes after direct examination, and therefore the Government need not make its choice until the defendant has elected whether or not to take the stand in her own behalf and after the Government has heard the defendant testify.

Ohler's submission would deny to the Government its usual right to decide, after she testifies, whether or not to use her prior conviction against her. She seeks to short circuit that decisional process by offering the conviction herself (and thereby removing the sting) and still preserve its admission as a claim of error on appeal.

But here **Ohler** runs into the position taken by the Court in a similar, but not identical, situation in *Luce v. United States*, 469 **U.S.** 38, 105 S.Ct. 460, 83 L.Ed.2d 443 (1984), that "[a]ny possible harm flowing from a district court's *in limine* ruling permitting impeachment by a prior conviction is wholly speculative." *Id.*, at 41, 105 S.Ct. 460. Only when the Government exercises its option to elicit the testimony is an appellate court confronted with a case where, under the normal rules of trial, the defendant can claim the denial of a substantial right if in fact the district court's *in limine* ruling proved to be erroneous. In our view, there is nothing "unfair," as **Ohler** puts it, about putting her to her choice in accordance with the normal rules of trial.

Finally, **Ohler** argues that applying this rule to her situation unconstitutionally burdens her right to testify. She relies on *Rock v. Arkansas*, 483 **U.S.** 44, 107 S.Ct. 2704, 97 L.Ed. 2d 37 (1987), where we held that a prohibition of hypnotically refreshed testimony interfered with the defendant's right to testify. But here the rule in question does not prevent **Ohler** from taking the stand and presenting any admissible testimony which she chooses. She is of course subject to cross-examination and subject to impeachment by the use of a prior conviction. In a sense, the use of these tactics by the Government may deter a defendant from taking the stand. But, as we said in *McGautha v. California*, 402 **U.S.** 183, 215, 91 S.Ct. 1454, 28 L.Ed.2d 711 (1971):

"It has long been held that a defendant who takes the stand in his own behalf cannot then claim the privilege against cross-examination on matters reasonably related to the subject matter of his direct examination.... It is not thought overly harsh in such situations to require that the determination whether to waive the privilege take into account the matters which may be brought out on cross-examination. It is also generally recognized that a defendant who takes the stand in his own behalf may be impeached by proof of prior convictions or the like.... Again, it is not thought inconsistent with the enlightened administration of criminal justice to require *760 the defendant to weigh such pros and cons in deciding whether to testify."

For these reasons, we conclude that a defendant who preemptively introduces evidence of a prior conviction on direct examination may not on appeal claim that the admission of such evidence was error.

The judgment of the Court of Appeals for the Ninth Circuit is therefore affirmed.

It is so ordered.

DISCUSSION PROBLEMS 8-1

1. Are you convinced by the court's reasoning as to the relationship between 103 and 609?

2. What is the impact of this decision? Who should control the introduction of impeachment evidence? Why?

3. Do you agree that the primary purpose of FRE 609 does not include concealment? If you were going to modify the rule what would you propose? Why?

HOW IMPEACHMENT WORKS
Prior Untruthful Acts

FRE 608(b) permits counsel to impeach a witness by cross-examining her concerning certain prior bad acts. Only those prior acts, which are probative of the witness's character for truthfulness, may be used to impeach under this rule. Impeachment by prior untruthful acts is limited to cross examination. When you impeach for this purpose extrinsic evidence is not allowed. If the witness denies or minimizes the deceptive nature of the act for which you are attempting to impeach her, you cannot use extrinsic evidence to refute her answer, or to establish the untruthful nature of the witness's prior act. You are stuck with her answer.

Although extrinsic evidence is not admissible to prove the prior untruthful act, counsel may be required to disclose the basis for believing that the act occurred. The inability to articulate a good faith basis for an inquiry under FRE 608(b) may result in a mistrial or other judicial sanction. Additionally, the judge may forbid inquiry into prior untruthful acts if they violate the requirements of FRE 403. The most common objections raised when lawyers attempt to impeach a witness with prior untruthful bad acts deal with the fact that the impeachment is either unduly prejudicial or a waste of time. Judges pay particular attention to this issue when the individual being impeached is the defendant.

There are several ways to approach the prior untruthful act. If you know the witness will admit the prior act, it may be possible to impeach with a few direct, dramatic questions. More commonly, you will need to pursue a more oblique approach, committing the witness to specific facts surrounding the prior incident before confronting her with the specific untruthful act. If you demonstrate to the witness your knowledge of the prior act through detailed, succinct, leading questions, she will be reluctant to deny your account. It is especially difficult for the witness if your questions refer to witnesses who could corroborate your allegations. The witness doesn't understand that you are barred from presenting extrinsic proof of the prior untruthful act. The subtle handling of documents during cross examination may also lead the witness to believe that you possess documentary proof of the prior act.

Since you are not permitted to present extrinsic evidence of the prior bad act, you are stuck with the witness's denial. You may, however, test the witness's commitment to his denial. An initial denial may need clarification to ensure that you are referring to the same event as the witness. If you persist after a denial, you may draw an "asked and answered" objection from opposing counsel. Be prepared to explain to the judge that you are simply attempting to refresh the witness as to the surrounding facts or clarifying the incident to which you are referring.

Special care is warranted when using prior bad acts to impeach the accused in a criminal case. You should alert the judge and opposing counsel as to your intent to impeach the accused with such information. This is appropriate given the requirements of both FRE 103 and FRE 104. This gives the opposing counsel an opportunity to object to such impeachment prior to cross examination. The judge will appreciate the opportunity to weigh the matter in advance outside the presence of the jury. Since the judge is the gatekeeper in determining whether you will be allowed to ask these questions it makes perfect sense to not try and hide the ball.

DISCUSSION PROBLEM 8-2

Background Information: In a trial for conspiracy to distribute cocaine, the defense attempts to cross examine two state regarding their past drug use. One witness has suffered no ill effects from their drug use, but the other witness has suffered memory loss and blackouts from alcohol use, and alcohol use with cocaine.

1. How should the judge rule?

2. What evidentiary law applies?

3. Why?

Example of Prior Untruthful Acts Impeachment

Q: Isn't it true that you once lied to your insurance company by filing an incorrect claim about an allegedly stolen car stereo?
A: I don't know what you are talking about.

Q: GEICO refused to renew your car insurance recently, isn't that correct?
A: They canceled it because I had too many points on my license.

Q: You filed a claim with GEICO based on the alleged theft of your car stereo, right?
A: Right.

Q: At the time you filed the claim your policy was still in effect?

A: Yes.

Q: GEICO refused to pay your claim?
A: Yeah, they refused.

Q: Your car stereo was never stolen?
A: No.

Q: Isn't it true that you filed a false claim for your car stereo with GEICO?
A: No.

Q: It's true isn't it that GEICO canceled your policy right after you claimed your stereo was stolen?
A: No.

Q: We can at least agree that GEICO canceled your policy after you filed your stolen stereo claim?
A: Yes. But that was not the reason they cancelled it.

You have probably gone as far as you can go with this impeachment. If the jury has been following you, they should get the clear impression that this witness is not truthful.

Prior Convictions

The admissibility of prior untruthful acts is normally decided during a motion in limine. Resolution of issues of admissibility under FRE 609 often requires judicial balancing. Both the proponent and the opponent of the witness should consider a motion in limine to obtain a ruling prior to trial so that they can make tactical decisions regarding the examination of the witness based upon potential impeachment. On the other hand, counsel may consider waiting for the other side to raise the issue of the prior conviction if they believe it to be clearly admissible. In some jurisdictions discovery rules may require disclosure of this information even if you do not seek a ruling through a motion in limine. The impeaching party can choose the form of impeachment. Options include eliciting the fact of the conviction on cross examination, admitting into evidence an authenticated record of the conviction, or by testimony of someone present when the witness was convicted.

This rule permits counsel to use either cross examination or extrinsic evidence to prove the prior conviction. When the witness admits the facts pertaining to the conviction on cross examination, however, the judge may exclude further evidence on the grounds that it is cumulative. While there is more than one way to prove a prior conviction, cross examination of the witness about the conviction is the preferred method. If the witness denies, mischaracterizes, or minimizes the nature of the conviction, then the impeachment value of the record is magnified. Always be prepared to do it both ways. When preparing for possible impeachment with a conviction remember that a properly certified record of conviction is a self-authenticating document and needs no sponsoring witness. If opposing counsel objects to the record of conviction on hearsay grounds, cite to FRE 803(8); that should be sufficient to overcome a hearsay objection.

It is important to note that most courts do not permit counsel to explore the details of the prior conviction. Getting in the conviction itself is enough for impeachment, but the details do not come in, i.e. you cannot ask what led her to commit the crime of the past conviction, etc. Some courts permit proof of the sentence imposed. The record of previous conviction usually indicates the sentence imposed. If the record is admissible, then cross examination about the sentence imposed should also be admissible. Determine how far the judge will permit you to go by asking him during the pretrial hearing.

When sorting out which convictions may be used to impeach a witness under FRE 609, it is helpful to sort the convictions into either crimes of dishonesty and false statement (usually referred to as crimen falsi crimes) and all other crimes. Crimen falsi crimes are admissible to impeach any witness, including the accused, regardless of the punishment authorized or imposed. Convictions for other crimes depend upon whether the crime was punishable by death or confinement in excess of one year. If so, impeachment by conviction may be admissible subject to the discretion of the court. The law of the jurisdiction in which the conviction was obtained governs the determination of maximum punishment. Maximum punishment is determined based upon the statutory possibility, not the actual punishment received. For instance, a conviction for robbery that carried a maximum sentence of five years would be a qualifying conviction, even if the court only sentenced the accused to less than one year confinement.

The "other crimes" category of convictions is subject to judicial balancing under FRE 403 for all witnesses other than the accused when determining admissibility. When the accused is the witness then his conviction is admissible for impeachment purposes only if the judge determines that the probative value outweighs the prejudicial effect to the accused.[32] For convictions other than crimen falsi crimes there is a 10-year window. If the conviction was obtained or the sentence of confinement, to include any probation, was completed more than 10 years ago it is not admissible for impeachment purposes. However, the judge can still admit such evidence if the proponent of the evidence gives written notice and the judge determines that the probative value of the evidence substantially outweighs the prejudicial effect.

Note that this test differs from the normal FRE 403 balancing test, with a preference for excluding the evidence under this standard. Keep in mind that pendency of an appeal will not render such convictions inadmissible, but pardon, annulment, or certificate of rehabilitation may bar use of such evidence. It is also important to note that evidence of juvenile adjudications is generally not admissible.

DISCUSSION PROBLEMS 8-3

Background Information: The accused is facing trial for interstate transportation of stolen goods. His counsel has made a motion to exclude evidence of his client's prior convictions for possession of a stolen vehicle and receipt of stolen goods. The defense argues that FRE 403 applies to FRE 609 and that the court should suppress his earlier convictions if he takes the stand to testify.

1. How should the trial judge rule?

2. What is the relationship between FRE 609 and FRE 403?

3. Where did you find support for your interpretation of that relationship?

Example where the witness admits to the previous conviction
Q: Mr. Bones, isn't it true that you were convicted in state court nine years ago?

---

[32] See FRE 609(a)(1).

A: *Yes.*

Q: **That court convicted you for filing a false claim with the state unemployment agency?**
A: *Yes, sir.*

Q: **And you were convicted of making a false claim for lying on several forms filed with the state?**
A: *Yes.*

Q: **Nothing further, your honor.**

Example where the witness is not inclined to admit to the earlier conviction
Q: **Are you the same Mr. Bones who was previously convicted in federal court in December 20XX?**
A: *Well, I don't know if it was a federal court.*

Q: **Isn't it a fact that you were convicted of conspiracy to destroy the original manuscript of the Declaration of Independence in 20XX?**
A: *It should have never been signed!*

Q: **Please answer the question. Were you convicted of conspiracy to destroy the Declaration of Independence?**
A: *No, I was not.*

Q: **Isn't it a fact that you were sentenced to five years confinement for conspiracy to destroy the Declaration of Independence?**
A: *Uh, no, it was only two years.*

Q: **So, you now admit that you were convicted of that crime?**
A: *Well, yes, but it wasn't a "federal" court I wasn't sentenced to five years in jail.*

Q: **Your honor, the state moves to admit P.E.-10 for ID into evidence as P.E.-10.**
J: *Defense?*

D: **We object to this exhibit on the grounds of hearsay and lack of authentication.**
J: *State?*

Q: **Your honor P.E.-10 for ID is a self-authenticating document under FRE 902(4) and also falls within the hearsay exception under FRE 803(8).**

J: The objection is overruled. P.E.-10 for ID will be admitted as P.E.-10. You may proceed.

Q: **I am handing the witness P.E.-10. Mr. Bones, this is an official record of your conviction. Please take a moment to read block "5e" of that record of conviction. Tell the court what block f states as the sentence you were given for the conspiracy to destroy the Declaration of Independence.**
A: *It says that I was sentenced to five years confinement.*

Q: **Thank you. Nothing further.**

Prior Inconsistent Statements

FRE 613 governs the use of the prior inconsistent statements (PIS) for impeachment purposes. When impeaching under this rule you can use the inconsistency established through the impeachment to argue witness credibility in closing argument. You may not use the impeachment to suggest an alternative factual position – unless the witness adopts your position or an additional evidentiary rule allows for the admittance of the out-of-court statements that form the basis of your impeachment. The form of the PIS can be varied. Possible options include written statements, transcripts of prior testimony, oral statements made by the witness, omissions of a material nature from a prior statement, and assertive or communicative conduct. The focus of the inquiry is whether you have a good faith basis to believe that the statement was made by the witness. If you do then it is potentially impeachment material.

Before FRE 613 was adopted a common law requirement existed that you had to give the witness an opportunity to see the prior written statement before you could cross examine them on its contents. While FRE 613 disposed of this requirement, some state jurisdictions still expect it. You should check your local rules before impeaching without first showing the written statement to the witness. In any event, you must disclose the written statement to opposing counsel upon their request. Most competent counsel routinely request disclosure of all impeachment materials during discovery. When impeachment occurs under the auspices of FRE 613 it is admitted for the limited purpose of showing a lack of credibility. If the impeaching counsel wishes to argue that evidence substantively then it must also either be adopted as fact by the witness or be otherwise admissible under an appropriate hearsay rule.

The PIS may be admitted as extrinsic evidence only if (1) the witness denies making the prior statement or denies that it is inconsistent, (2) the inconsistency goes to a non-collateral matter, and (3) the statement is otherwise admissible under the hearsay rules. If the witness acknowledges the prior statement, then it is not allowed into evidence because it has been adopted by the witness. If counsel is able to introduce the prior statement the witness must be given the opportunity to explain or deny the statement.

When a PIS is used, the judge shall give a limiting instruction to the jury upon request by the opposing party. The PIS is not substantive evidence and cannot be relied upon to prove an element of the offense or a defense. The statement, if admitted, will be accompanied by a limiting instruction from the judge stating it can be considered only on the issue of the witness's credibility. A PIS offered solely to impeach the witness under FRE 613 is hearsay and not admissible for the truth of the matter contained therein. However, a PIS is not hearsay if the declarant and the witness are the same and the prior statement was made under oath and subject to cross examination.[33] A PIS is also not hearsay if it is a party-opponent admission.[34]

When conducting PIS impeachment on cross examination, lawyers use the three-step process commonly referred to as the "3 C's." The order of the three steps may vary depending on the witness, but in most situations they (1) commit the witness to their in-court testimony, (2) credit the earlier statement of the witness, and (3) confront the witness with the inconsistency. The degree to which each step in the "3 C's" is emphasized depends upon the strength of the available information. It may be you can spend a great deal of time crediting the earlier statement because of the circumstances

---

[33] *See* FRE 801(d)(1)(A).

[34] *See* FRE 801(d)(2).

under which it was made. Other times the difference between the prior statement and the current in-court testimony is so great that you spend a good deal of time working on the confrontation. You choose which to emphasize based on your case's strength and the reason for the impeachment.

Consider the following examples:

Witness impeaches himself. Lawyers may highlight the relevant portion of the witness's statement, mark the document as an exhibit for identification (always coordinate with the court reporter when marking an exhibit in advance), and present the document to the witness. The witness will then identify the document and confirm that it is his statement. Counsel may confront the witness with the conflicting language by having the witness read aloud the portion that counsel selected. Counsel may also have the witness read the preceding question (if the statement is in question-and-answer format) and then his own answer to that question. Be sure to control the witness during this maneuver. Focus the witness to do exactly what you want with clear, succinct and direct words.

Lawyer impeaches the witness. Lawyers may simply have the witness confirm the existence of the prior statement, reinforce its credibility, and verify the conflicting testimony by quoting it to the witness. This approach removes the necessity of fumbling with the document, since it does not need to be handed to the witness.

Graphic aid impeaches the witness. Lawyers may wish to convert the documentary statement into a clear graphical aid and then project the document onto a screen. This way the jurors themselves can see the words that damn the witness.

Statement impeaches the witness. When the witness denies making the statement, and the statement does not relate to a collateral matter, counsel may, after the witness has departed, present another witness who overheard the witness's out-of-court statement or who took the written statement from the witness. In such a case, the statement may be admitted for the limited purpose of showing that it was made, unless the statement is admissible as substantive evidence (*see* FRE 801).

The important facts lawyers should rely upon while validating the prior statement vary, depending on the form of the statement. If the prior statement was a sworn statement, then it is important to elicit the fact that the witness had the opportunity to review the statement, initialed each page, took an oath, and signed his name.

When should a lawyer impeach? A good rule of thumb is to impeach only on significant inconsistencies. Juries understand that there will be minor variations in detail each time a human tells a story. Repeated attempts to call the witness a liar on the basis of these variations will be perceived as overreaching, rather than effective impeachment of the witness's credibility. Lawyers should make certain there is a true factual inconsistency rather than a mere semantic difference. Care should also be taken to ensure that the ability to prove the prior inconsistent statement exists when the rules will allow for the admission of extrinsic evidence to prove the inconsistency. Any evidence used to do so must meet other evidentiary requirements.

Bias and Motive

Bias, prejudice, or any motive to misrepresent may be shown to impeach the witness either by the witness or by evidence otherwise adduced. Such evidence is relevant because it may show that the witness is not an impartial observer or witness of the truth. As long as the impeaching counsel can articulate a theory of why the witness may be predisposed to favor the other side, the evidence should be admissible. Common law allows this under the theory of bias, prejudice or motive. Each of these issues is not collateral to the testimony of the witness, even when the witness in question is not the victim.

The foundation that must be laid for bias, motive, or prejudice is case-specific and does not require any specific foundational elements. Lawyers can prove bias, prejudice, or motive to lie by direct or circumstantial evidence. To impeach the witness, counsel must persuade the fact-finder that the witness has some reason to perceive or recall events in a skewed manner, or to abandon his oath and become a partisan for one side.

Evidence of bias is not limited only to cross examination of the witness. While the best evidence often may be concessions from the witness himself, supplemental proof may be necessary to give it full impact. Counsel will ordinarily be given wide latitude in proving facts that establish bias. Even if the witness admits his bias, or facts from which bias may be inferred, the judge may permit extrinsic evidence of the same facts, unless such evidence is cumulative. For example, if the witness acknowledges his friendship with the accused, the judge may still allow other witnesses to drive the fact home with specific examples of acts of friendship.

When deciding whether to impeach with bias or motive to lie, lawyers must remember that they cannot use it if they do not have it. Assumptions and stereotypes will not suffice. Successful bias impeachment is developed through thorough pretrial investigation and case analysis. Interview every witness, talk to neighbors and social contacts. Ask your investigators to assist with this effort, even though it goes beyond element-based evidence gathering. You need to know as much as possible to prepare for effective impeachments in this area. You should begin this process by asking yourself why the witness is saying something that other evidence contradicts. People are untruthful for a reason, even when they are not aware of it themselves.

Impeaching witnesses about issues that are obvious to everyone in the courtroom is wasted time. We all know that mothers love their sons. What benefit is received by impeaching a mother about her familial love when she has testified? It may have been pointed out to the jury, but does it matter? Without evidence to the contrary there is little if any reason to belabor the obvious. It is better to subtly establish facts from which bias can be inferred, rather than confronting the witness directly. Establish the predicate facts that add up to bias, prejudice or motive to lie, but "do the math" for the jury during closing argument. However, sometimes the relationship creating the bias can be developed in a very persuasive fashion. Consider the following bias impeachment questions for a jailhouse snitch that has cut a deal with the government:[35]

You just testified against my client, Johnny.

How long have you been in prison now?

How long is your sentence?

So you have _____ amount of time left to do?

You have family?

You have children?

---

[35] This line of questioning was birthed when watching Joshua Karton perform an outstanding demonstration on impeachment at Stetson's Teaching Advocacy Skills Conference.

You miss them?

You have pictures of them in your cell?

What time of year do you miss them most?

They miss you?

Is there anything more important to you than your kids?

Wouldn't you like to hold them in your arms again as a free man?

But that won't happen until you get out?

You might get out sooner now?

After you've testified against Johnny?

It must have been very hard for you to do this?

Family is a powerful motivator, isn't it?

You can hear the sorrow in the voice of the impeaching attorney. The regret at the situation in which the snitch finds himself and the implicit argument that anyone in such a situation must be biased in favor of finding and providing information that would shorten the amount of time before they could hold their children again.

On the other hand if the attorney chooses to just ask the bias question and is foolish enough to ask the witness to sum it up they will, but the lawyer will not like their math. Witnesses usually respond with a dramatic reaffirmation of their oath or a statement of their heartfelt pain in admitting mistakes for the good of the "truth." Control is the better approach. Consider the following example:

Q: Mr. Jones, you and the defendant, Mr. Smith, work on the same line in the cardboard factory?

A: Yes.

Q: You are both quality control inspectors on the end of the line?

A: Yes.

Q: What is your current position on the line?

A: I am the assistant quality control manager.

Q: You are the assistant quality control manager. Who is the quality control manager?

A: Mr. Smith.

Q: How long have you been his assistant?

A: About eight years.

Q: You got the job when Mr. Smith recommended you for it?

A: Yes.

Q: Who writes your quarterly employee reports?

A: Mr. Smith does.

Q: You work with him on a daily basis?

A: Yes.

Q: You and the defendant are a good quality control team?

A: Best in the plant.

Q: You and the defendant spend time together after work?

A: Sure, all the time.

Q: You go to movies together?

A: Sometimes.

Q: You go to ball games together?

A: We've been to a few.

Q: You are both on the company softball team?

A: Yes.

Q: You guys practice year round, don't you?

A: Yes.

Q: In fact you are the team's star catcher?

A: Yes.

Q: And the defendant is your pitcher?

A: He's the best.

Q: You get along well with Mr. Smith, don't you?

A: What do you mean?

Q: You are good friends?

A: Yes.

Q: He's one of your best friends, isn't he?

A: I guess so.

Q: And you certainly don't want him to go to jail, do you?

A: No.

Q: You don't believe he should be tried, do you?

A: No.

Q: You weren't in the bowling alley the night Mr. Smith hit Mr. Johnson with a spare bowling pin?

A: No.

Q: All you know about the incident has been told to you by Mr. Smith?

A: I guess so.

Defects in Capacity
Common Law

While there is not a specific federal rule of evidence that addresses the ability of counsel to impeach a witness based upon defects in observation, such defects are not collateral and inquiry is generally permissible. When lawyers prepare the cross examination of a witness who will provide testimony about a visual observation they must consider both the internal and the external factors that may affect the accuracy of such testimony. Internal factors are those physical and mental aspects of the witness that may have impacted their ability to fully and accurately observe, recall, or relate the questioned events.

External factors are factors that exist outside of the witness but that had an impact on the ability of the witness to observe the questioned events. The lawyer calling the witness will normally try to emphasize the positive internal and external factors supporting the credibility of the witness's observations. They may also try to remove the sting of negative factors by fronting them on direct. When impeaching, lawyers should try to demonstrate as many unreliable factors as possible and arrange them in a way that impacts the overall credibility of the witness's testimony. The following rules of evidence, when read in concert with one another, provide the legal support for impeachment on defects of capacity.

The most obvious example of internal physiological factors is poor eyesight, usually combined with a failure to wear prescription eye wear. Other visual factors include color blindness, physical disabilities, age, and night vision. Sometimes a witness has prior training that increases their ability to adequately recall and relate incidents they have observed. The classic example is an experienced police officer or other trained observers. Internal psychological factors include perception, memory and the witness's ability to communicate.

Perception is effected by a variety of factors, such as distorted focus on certain elements of the scene to the exclusion of others. Examples of this type of distorted focus include a preoccupation with the weapon in an assault rather than the facial features of the assailant. Personal expectations, such as bias, stereotypes, interpretations and assumptions also affect the perceptual process. This has led courts to develop model instructions to jurors to assist them in weighing the credibility of eyewitness identifications.

External or environmental factors include such things as exposure time, line of sight, obstructions, lighting, weather, speed of movement, and distance. The traumatic nature of the event observed is also an important external factor that may have an impact on the witness's ability to observe or remember. Lawyers weave external and internal factors together, pointing out to the jury those issues that call into question the validity of the testimony of the witness. This is an artful way of saying that the witness believes what they are telling you, but you should not. When done properly impeachment as to defects in capacity allow you to persuade the jury to not believe a witness without ever needing to call the witness a liar. They are instead merely mistaken. This is an easier position to take and a more realistic bar to reach for during this type of cross examination.

Because these types of impeachment need not be as confrontational as when an attorney directly challenges the truthfulness of a witness, lawyers should carefully consider the tone they choose to adopt while examining the witness. It is not necessary to adopt a hostile or sarcastic tone when cross examining a witness who is called to testify as to a visual observation. A friendly tone may produce better results in most cases. Even if the witness has given testimony that is adverse to counsel's cause, the goal of such cross examination is simply to elicit facts that affect the witness's ability to observe, interpret, and recall relevant facts accurately, not to beat them up on the stand.

Witnesses are naturally reluctant to concede the inaccuracy of their observations and recollections, especially after they have testified on direct. Lawyers should avoid the temptation to ask a question that directly challenge the accuracy of the witness by reciting the factors bearing on accuracy and then challenging the witness to agree that his original report or testimony was wrong. Besides being argumentative, such ultimate questions usually produce unsatisfactory responses. When confronted with a direct challenge, most witnesses forcefully reassert the certainty of their observations and memory. As a general rule the reliability argument should be saved for summation.

When preparing for impeachment concerning defects in capacity, counsel should take the time to carefully scrutinize the witness's prior statements. They should examine the record for statements by the witness that show a greater certainty about their observations at trial than immediately after the event when they observed it. The intervening preparation for trial can often inadvertently (or purposefully) focus the memory of the witness in a fashion not consistent with their initial unadulterated observations. These inconsistencies may not be sharp enough to clearly qualify as prior inconsistent statements, but they do tend to show that the witness has lost their objectivity over time. When necessary counsel may impeach on this issue, again without ever calling the witness a liar, but showing the jury why their current testimony is just not as useful as what they said earlier.

Example of ability to observe

The facts: A group of students in a high school classroom are listening to a lecture. Another person comes into the room and stands quietly for around 15 seconds. They then scream "I can't take it anymore," throwing a pile of papers at the feet of the teacher. They then run out of the room. A witness from the class has been called to testify about this incident on direct examination. The witness stated that they observed the unknown person and identified them as a white male, approximately 5 feet 6 inches tall and weighing around 130 pounds. The witness also stated on direct that the person's hair was blond and their eyes were green.

Q. You were seated in the classroom when the unidentified person came into the room?
A. *Yes.*

Q. There were forty-three other students in the class?
A. *If don't know. I didn't count them.*

Q. You were there in class to listen to the lecture?
A. *Yes.*

Q. Someone came into class?
A. *I believe so.*

Q. Through an entrance located about 30 feet to the right of the podium?
A. *Yes.*

Q. You were seated in the back?
A. *Yes.*

Q. There were 16 rows of students between you and the person?
A. *Yes.*

Q. How tall are you?
A. *Five feet, three inches.*

Q. You had your laptop?
A. *Yes.*

Q. That laptop is an Apple with a 19 inch screen?
A. *Yes.*

Q. You were typing?
A. *Yes, but I was paying attention.*

Q. So the screen was up?
A. *Yes.*

Q. The screen was between you and the teacher?
A. *Yes.*

Q. She was lecturing and you were typing what you heard?
A. *Correct.*

Q. You want to do well in class?
A. *Yes.*

Q. This was important to you? It might affect your grade?
A. *I guess so.*

Q. You were focused on the teacher when the person entered the room?
A. *Yes, but I did notice him.*

Q. You did not recognize him?
A. No.

Q. You noticed nothing remarkable about his clothing?
A. Nope.

Q. You didn't look closely when they first came in?
A. Well, I noticed him walk in the room.

Q. He looked like a regular student, right?
A. Right. I figured he might be late for class.

Q. He did not say anything when he walked in the room?
A. Not then, no.

Q. Your attention was focused on the lecture?
A. Yes.

Q. You were surprised when the person yelled and threw some papers on the floor?
A. We all were.

Q. After he yelled he immediately turned and left the room?
A. Yes, it happened pretty fast.

Q. They went out the same way they came in?
A. Yes.

Q. Everybody in the class was looking and whispering when this happened?
A. Yeah.

Q. You didn't stand up to get a look at him, did you?
A. No.

Q. Some of those standing blocked your view?
A. I suppose.

Q. You couldn't see the person as he left the room?
A. Well, I saw him when he threw the papers.

Q. You could not see him the whole time?
A. No.

Q. You did look at the teacher to see what she would do?
A. Yes.

Q. When was your last eye examination?
A. I think it was about two years ago.

Q. When you had your last eye examination, the doctor prescribed new glasses?
A. Yes.

Q. The doctor said your eyesight had become worse and you needed a new prescription?

A. *They were only slightly worse.*

Q. But the doctor gave you a new prescription?

A. *Yes.*

Q. You have had multiple eye examinations over the years?

A. *Yes.*

Q. Each time your prescription has changed?

A. *Yes.*

Q. It has been two years since your last eye exam?

A. *Yes.*

Impeachment by Omission

One of the most difficult types of impeachment to accomplish is impeachment by omission or "negative impeachment."[36] The other six forms of impeachment are fundamentally different in that there is another source of information that serves as the basis for the impeachment. When dealing with a situation where impeachment by omission is necessary the witness has just said something important to the case that has never been mentioned before. It is often a piece of information that may very well be case dispositive. It is also the type of fact that if the witness is being truthful, would have reasonably been disclosed at an earlier point in the process. Some jurisdictions frown upon negative impeachment as an accepted form of inquiry.[37]

While not identified by a specific evidentiary rule, impeachment by omission falls under relevancy. When the fact is non-collateral in nature opposing counsel can test the validity of the evidence, to include admitting extrinsic evidence to establish that fact in question had not been previously provided when an opportunity to do so presented itself.

The seminal decision that a lawyer must make when deciding whether to impeach by omission revolves around the nature of the omission. Impeachment by omission only works if you can set up the impeachment by pointing out the overwhelming importance of the newly disclosed fact. It has to be the type of information that the witnesses would not have kept to themselves prior to trial. Usually this means that the substance of the statement is an answer to a question that any normal person asking about the case would ask prior to trial. If the omission is not central to the case then the game is usually not worth the candle.

To effectively conduct impeachment by omission the setup of the impeachment is crucial. It is similar in nature to the process that a lawyer uses to credit the validity of an earlier statement when impeaching with a PIS. The foundation for the earlier statement is crucial. When impeaching by omission no earlier statement exists contradicting the in

---

[36] See Larry Posner and Roger Dodd, Cross-Examination: Science and Techniques, Lexis.

[37] In Florida, for example, negative impeachment is frowned upon. This is due at least in part to the fact that Florida is a state where depositions are allowed in both civil and criminal proceedings. The idea is that since a lawyer has the opportunity to depose witnesses there should never be the possibility of an omission if the lawyer has competently deposed the witness. This is a nice idea in theory, but in practice it is a "bridge too far."

court testimony. Regardless, multiple opportunities do exist to disclose the fact in question before trial. This is the key point that must be brought out in the impeachment by omission. The wind-up is critical. If not done properly the entire process falls flat. This type of impeachment can be difficult to accomplish, but when done properly the results are devastating.

In the following example of an impeachment by omission the witness has just stated on direct examination that she heard the deceased identify his attacker, the accused, while talking to him on the cell phone immediately before he was shot. This came out during testimony on direct examination. The witness has never stated this fact before. She was previously interviewed by two different detectives, testified at the grand jury hearing and has been interviewed by both the state prosecutor and the criminal defense attorney. After picking his jaw up from the floor the defense attorney proceeds as follows:

Q: Mrs. Jones, you just told us on direct examination that you heard Mr. Smith identify his shooter, the defendant, immediately before he was shot?

A: Yes.

Q: You were on the phone with Mr. Smith at the time?

A: Yes.

Q: You could hear him?

A: Yes.

Q: He identified his attacker?

A: Yes.

Q: You then heard the gunshots?

A: The line went dead?

Q: You did not call 911?

A: No.

Q: You did speak with the police eventually?

A: Yes.

Q: They called you?

A: Yes.

Q: They told you they got your number from the deceased's phone?

A: Yes.

Q: They asked to interview you?

A: Yes.

Q: They came to your home?

A: Yes.

Q: You met with the police?

A: Yes.

Q: You met with them twice?

A: Yes.

Q: You answered their questions?

A: Yes.

Q: You wanted to help?

A: Yes.

Q: They told you they got your number from the deceased's phone?

A: Yes.

Q: They asked to interview you?

A: Yes.

Q: They came to your home?

A: Yes.

Q: You met with the police?

A: Yes.

Q: You met with them twice?

A: Yes.

Q: You answered their questions?

A: Yes.

Q: You wanted to help?

A: Yes.

Q: You were truthful?

A: Yes.

Q: They talked with you several hours each time?

A: Yes.

Q: **You gave a statement each time?**
A: *Yes. Well I signed a statement, they typed it.*

Q: **The cops typed it?**
A: *Yes.*

Q: **But you reviewed it?**
A: *Yes.*

Q: **You initialed the top of each page?**
A: *Yes.*

Q: **The bottom of each page?**
A: *Yes.*

Q: **You signed it?**
A: *Yes.*

Q: **Promised it was truthful?**
A: *Yes.*

Q: **Complete?**
A: *Yes.*

Q: **Fair?**
A: *Yes.*

Q: **Accurate?**
A: *Yes.*

Q: **You never told them you heard the deceased identify the accused as the shooter?**
A: *I told them but they didn't write it down.*

Q: **This was a murder investigation?**
A: *Yes.*

Q: **You identified the killer?**
A: *Yes.*

Q: **It is your testimony now that you told the investigating officer in a homicide case who the killer was but they never wrote it down in your statement?**

A: Yes.

Q: When you reviewed the statement you didn't add it?
A: No. I missed it.

Q: You missed it. Is that why you didn't tell the grand jury about it?
A: I was nervous that day and forgot. The state's attorney never asked either.

Q: You never told me when I interviewed you?
A: Yes I did.

Q: Just like you told the police officer?
A: Yes.

Q: Told them both times?
A: Yes.

This is probably as much as a lawyer could do with this particular witness. The idea that she never told anyone this terribly important fact is not credible. The next step would be to call the detectives who took the sworn statements and use them to verify what the witness said, the manner in which the statement was taken, and the investigative steps taken as a result of those interviews. When done there is little, if any chance, that the jury believes this witness.

It should be clear now that the devil is in the details. When done properly not only is the witness's credibility irreparably damaged, but closing argument just got a boost as well. Let us move on now to impeachment by contradiction, a similar but somewhat different evidentiary approach.

Impeachment by Contradiction

This form of impeachment[38] exists at common law. It occurs when a witness makes an in-court statement that differs from either their out-of-court statements or out-of-court actions. When this occurs, and the issue is one that is not collateral, extrinsic evidence is allowed to prove the contradiction. This type of impeachment is not effective when the lawyer has not done a thorough and continuing case analysis. They cannot stand up and effectively impeach on an issue by contradiction when you have not identified those key disputed questions of fact in light of your case theme and theory.

Impeachment by contradiction calls into question the specific in court statement and casts doubt on all aspects of the witness's testimony. You cannot use impeachment by contradiction when the issue is collateral. Case analysis and preparation ensure that you have identified a non-collateral issue for impeachment by contradiction. The trap for this type of impeachment is set on cross examination. You use cross to force contradiction.

---

[38] Professor Chris Behan, Southern Illinois School of Law, discusses this type of impeachment in his presentation at http://www.law.stetson.edu/arc, found in Stetson's Online Advocacy Resource Center. I commend it to you. Thanks, Chris!

Either the witness agrees with your version of the fact in controversy or you impeach them with the information that contradicts them. You control the entire process. This approach supports the closing argument identified during your case analysis and can be devastating.

The cross examination of Detective Mark Fuhrman[39] in the O.J. Simpson murder trial, including the follow-on extrinsic evidence establishing the contradiction, destroyed the credibility of Detective Fuhrman in general, and specifically called into question the evidence he collected during the investigation of Nicole Brown-Simpson's murder. Remember when F. Lee Bailey inquired as to whether Detective Furman used a racial epithet in the last ten years? He responded no, opening the door to the additional witnesses that sank the state's case. This is a classic example of impeachment by contradiction that also contained elements of bias, motive to lie and general witness credibility. It became the linchpin of the successful defense of O.J. Simpson, at least in that case.

CONCLUSION

This chapter fleshed out our understanding of the evidentiary law controlling methods of impeachment. When you consider these rules considering the tasks that they are designed to control the rules concerning impeachment begin to fit together in a way that increases your understanding of both their application, and the thought behind it. As you continue to apply these rules in courtroom situations you begin to see the interconnected nature of each rule to the other. Eventually you should understand not only the connection between evidentiary rules concerning impeachment, but the overall weblike structure within which all the evidentiary rules exist.

Let us move on now to what happens when we offer expert witnesses.

---

[39] *See* http://www.criminology.fsu.edu/crimemedia/lecture1.html.

-Notes-

Chapter 9: Expert Witnesses

INTRODUCTION

Expert witnesses occupy a special place at trial. They are one of the few witnesses allowed to testify without any personal knowledge, and their opinions can speak to the ultimate issues in the case. Lawyers must bring all of their skills to the task of properly questioning an expert. Judges treat them differently under the rules, and their testimony carries more weight with juries. In a world where technology is king, experts reign supreme.

When accepted by the court the testimony of the expert is often dispositive. The expert witness is very much like a genie in a lamp—within their world they have phenomenal cosmic power, but their living space is very limited. Displaying the expert to maximum effect is the goal of direct examination; controlling and differentiating expert testimony is often the goal of cross. FRE 611 controls both of those processes, but the Federal Rules of Evidence governing the use of experts, in combination with U.S. Supreme Court jurisprudence, provides the substance that drives the form of the questioning by counsel when experts testify.

Unlike normal lay witnesses, an expert's purpose is to assist the jury in understanding evidence or in determining a fact at issue in the case. They are able to accomplish these twin goals because they possess scientific, technical, or other specialized knowledge that gives them the ability to make sense of complex and counter intuitive subjects, explaining them to the finder of fact in a way that makes sense.

Establishing the source of an expert's expertise, the first step in admitting their opinions, involves qualifying the expert witness by laying a foundation meeting the requirements of FRE 702. There are two threshold questions that must be established: (1) does the witness possess sufficient scientific, specialized or technical knowledge, and (2) will the expert's knowledge assist the trier of fact in determining a complex or counter intuitive issue in the case? If both of these questions can be answered affirmatively through the testimony of the witness then they may be accepted by court and allowed to testify.

Let us now consider in greater depth the seven steps an attorney must take to use an expert as well as the law that allows them to do so.

When presenting an expert witness a lawyer must: (1) tell the jury why the expert is here, (2) establish conclusively the foundations for the expertise of the expert, (3) tender the expert as an expert in the specific area identified to the jury and for which the foundation is laid, (4) ask the expert to provide the major opinions needed, (5) explore the specific basis for these opinions (usually research or learned treatises in the field of expertise), (6) diffuse weaknesses, and then, (7) restate the main opinion. Following these seven steps will competently prepare and present expert testimony that is tied to your case theme and theories. To do so you must spend significant time educating yourself on the way in which your expert's testimony will assist the jury in understanding the issues in controversy. That assistance begins with qualifying the expert witness. The first step in accomplishing this is to fully understand how the qualification process works and the steps to take to lay appropriate foundations for the admissibility of your expert's testimony.

Qualifying and Tendering an Expert Witness

Lawyers must master the legal issues surrounding the admissibility of expert testimony and the substantive knowledge necessary to present and test the validity of the expert's conclusions.

To accomplish this, lawyers combine advocacy principles, legal principles, and substantive knowledge when dealing with expert witnesses. The core legal principles regulating expert testimony fall into three primary categories: (1) will the expert be allowed to testify, (2) what is permissible testimony, and (3) how broad is the scope of cross examination of the expert witness. Qualifying an expert witness is the first step an advocate masters to ensure the court will allow the expert to testify as an expert. The witness must first be qualified by reason of knowledge, skill, experience, training, or education in a field of specialized knowledge. FRE 703 lays out the basis for qualifying an expert:

The first step to qualify an expert in accordance with FRE 703 is to call the witness to the stand and elicit testimony about his or her credentials. This may be avoided if opposing counsel is willing to stipulate to the expert's qualifications. Most lawyers rarely stipulate to their expert's qualifications, preferring to use the qualification requirement to show the jury the credentials of the witness. It is much more effective to allow the jury to hear the impressive credentials of the expert witness instead of a cold, dispassionate, and unemotional instruction from the judge that "the witness is qualified as an expert. Consider the following example of how to qualify an expert witness:

Q: Investigator Price, please identify yourself to the jury.
A: My name is Investigator Ray Price, I work at the United States Army Criminal Investigative laboratory.

Q: Is that the Army equivalent of NCIS or the FBI?
A: Yes.

Q: How long have you been in law enforcement?
A: I spent my first 20 years as an agent investigating crimes in a regional office. I have been working at USACIL as an analyst for the last 15 years. So I guess that's 35 years total.

Q: What are your primary duties at USACIL?
A: I have spent the last 10 years in the firearms division. My particular expertise is in ballistics data for handguns.

Q: What do you do at USACIL?
A: I identify weapons, reconstruct shooting scenes, test weapons, conduct ballistic tests and gunshot residue testing, to include splatter identification.

Q: Over the course of your 35 year career how many ballistic tests have you conducted?
A: I've lost count. At least several hundred.

Q: What specialized training have you received in ballistics testing?
A: I attended the FBI lab in Quantico, Virginia as a student many years ago. I have gone back for yearly updates. For the last 5 years I have been honored to serve as one of their senior ballistics instructors teaching new agents how to conduct ballistic testing.

Q: Have you testified about ballistics testing in court?

A: Yes.

Q: How many times?
A: Approximately 59 times.

Q: Were you accepted as an expert in ballistics by the court on those 59 occasions?
A: Yes.

After establishing the credentials of the expert the lawyer must officially tender them to the court and have them accepted before they are able to provide expert level testimony. When tendering the witness, the expert should be offered with sufficient specificity to clearly identify their area of expertise. The devil is in the details. When offering a witness as an expert, the court may allow opposing counsel to voir dire as to the foundation of the witness's expertise. Consider the following example:

Q: Your honor I offer Investigator Price has an expert in ballistic testing for handguns.
J: Objection?
D: Your honor may I voir dire for the purposes of forming an objection?
J: Briefly counsel. Please limit your inquiry to qualifications.

Attacking Qualifications of an Expert Witness

Preparation is the key for effective voir dire when attacking the credentials of an expert or when attempting to limit the scope of an expert's court-accepted expertise. When preparing to voir dire in this situation, attorneys address each of the following issues long before the witness takes the stand. First they need to know the subject area of the expert. Effective voir dire of an expert witness requires that the lawyer understand the subject matter. They should also review all documentation within the file and that was received through discovery. Finally the lawyer must develop an understanding of how the available evidence ties into the testimony of the expert.

Counsel must carefully identify the basis of the expert's testimony. Did he perform any tests or is he merely commenting on the work of others? That type of comment often raises quality control issues. Has he interviewed everyone involved? Did he spend sufficient time familiarizing himself with the case? Is he basing his theories or opinion solely on government-provided evidence or has he conducted his own tests? Is he aware of the defense's alternative theory; if not, why not? Is he a "professional" expert? The answers to these questions provide fruitful grounds to challenge either the qualifications of the witness or the validity of their testimony. Consider the following example:

Q: Investigator Price you conduct ballistic tests as part of your duties at USACIL.
A: Yes.

Q: You did not conduct any tests in preparation for testifying today?
A: Correct.

Q: You reviewed tests that another lab conducted?
A: Yes.

Q: You were not present for those tests?
A: No I was not.

Q: You would have performed some of those tests differently?
A: Yes, but that doesn't mean their results were not valid.

Q: You reviewed work you did not do?
A: Yes.

Q: You cannot tell us conclusively that proper testing procedures were followed based upon your own direct observation?
A: No I cannot.

Q: Your honor we object to this witness, he has no personal knowledge and is merely serving has a mouthpiece for what would otherwise be inadmissible hearsay.

J: Response?

P: Your honor we have laid a proper foundation for this witness's expertise under FRE 702. Personal knowledge is not required for expert witness testimony.

J: Defense?

D: Your honor while we concede that personal knowledge is not a requirement for expert witnesses, in this instance the state is using this witness to pass through hearsay that is not otherwise admissible.

J: A point I am sure you will bring out on cross examination. The witness is accepted as an expert.

Occasionally an attorney may strategically decide not to voir dire the expert, or even attack their testimony. Choosing to voir dire an expert that is qualified assists opposing counsel in verifying the expertise of their chosen witness. Consider the following exchange concerning an expert in animal pathology. The following is the presentation of an expert witness, a veterinarian, by the plaintiff's attorney, to testify in a tort case regarding intentional neglect of a horse:

J: Call your first witness.

P: Thank you, Your Honor. The Plaintiff will call Dr. Frank Mellish.

J: [To Dr. Mellish] Come forward and I'll swear you in.

J: Raise your right hand. Do you solemnly swear that the testimony you are about to give in the cause now pending is the truth, so you help you God?
W. I do.

J: Please watch your step, be seated and spell your last name for the court reporter.

W. My last name is Mellish, M-E-L-L-I-S-H.

P: Doctor. Please state your full name and occupation for the record.
W: Frank Mellish, and I'm a Professor at Enormous State University and a Diagnostic Pathologist at the ESU Center for Population and Animal Health.

P: Do your duties include performing pathological examinations on horses?
W: Yes.

P: How long have you been doing this?
W: Since 2002.

P: Approximately how many pathological examinations have you performed on horses during that period of time?
W: At least probably 250.

P: Why do you conduct these examinations?
W: Usually it is to determine the cause of death or to look for infectious diseases that might affect the population.

P: Doctor, in March of 2007, did you perform a pathological examination on a horse sent in by the County Animal Control Agency?
W: Yes, I did.

P: Your Honor, I would move for Dr. Frank Mellish to be recognized by the Court as an Expert in the field of pathology.

J: Any objection?

D: I'd like to voir dire, Your Honor. I don't believe that's been established.

The following is the voir dire by the defense of the plaintiff's expert witness that was presented to the court:

D: Doctor, do you have a curriculum vitae here with you today?
W: No, I don't.

D: Do you have one in your file back at your office?
W: Yes, I do.

D: And what is your educational—what is your degree?
W: I have a doctorate in Veterinary Medicine from Enormous State University. I have nine years of clinical practice. I did a residency in anatomic pathology at ESU and I have a Ph.D. in comparative pathology from Vine Covered University.

D: Have you been published in any kind of scholarly journals or written any books. Anything of that nature?
W: Yes.

D: How many articles have you written, specifically?
W: Approximately 10 are currently published.

D: For veterinary-type journals or …?
W: Veterinary journals.

D: And how long have you been doing pathological evaluations?
W: As a Board Certified Pathologist, since 2002.

D: You're Board Certified as a Pathologist?
W: As a Veterinary Pathologist.

D: Okay. So you've been with ESU since September 5th of 2006. Is that correct?
W: Correct.

D: How many pathology evaluations have you done at Enormous State University since September of 2006?
W: In the area of necropsies, I've probably done in the vicinity of 50 a month since then. That would be, what, 450.

D: And you're talking about all sorts of animals?
W: All sorts of animals. That's correct.

D: Your Honor, I have no other questions of Dr. Mellish at this moment.

P: We renew our motion, Your Honor.

J: I am going to grant the motion based on the background criteria of the witness for purposes of preliminary examination. You may continue.

P: Thank you.
If you had any doubts about the qualifications of this expert witness they have been obliterated by the voir dire that covered all of the additional foundational elements of expertise not covered when the witness was tendered. Ouch.

Proper preparation will allow an attorney to effectively use the voir dire process to break up the rhythm of the opponent's case, confuse the basis of the expert's opinion, and limit the expert's opinion while putting forth an alternative theory for their client. Preparation is the key to effective voir dire and cross examination of any witness, particularly one that is an expert.

Providing the Major Opinion

After the judge accepts the witness as an expert you should focus on previewing the major opinion. This is the crux of the opinion that identifies the expert's conclusions. Think of it as the bottom line up front. What follows after the opinion is rendered is a follow up with an in depth discussion of how the opinion was realized.

Q: Investigator Price, as an expert in ballistics, have you formed an opinion concerning the slugs that were retrieved from the decedent's corpse?
A: Yes.

Q: What is that opinion?
A: The slugs in question were fired by a .357 magnum revolver belonging to the accused in this case.

Q: To what degree of certainty can you state this opinion?

A: I have no doubt concerning the weapon which fired the rounds retrieved from the victim's body.

Q: Investigator Price I'd like to talk with you now about the basis for your opinion. How did you come to this conclusion?

Establishing the Basis for the Major Opinion

The next step would be to further explore the evidence, procedures and results from the testing either reviewed or conducted by the expert witness. During this section of the direct examination the expert witness shines. This is their time to make certain that the jury is getting a show. The expert should teach, engage and explain. This is the moment in the direct where counsel bring in the supporting documentations, research, tests, treatises, and the like, that support the relevant opinions of your expert.

Diffusing Weaknesses

Advocates use the techniques of primacy and recency when dealing with the weaknesses of an expert's opinion. They should honestly disclose any shortcomings in the opinion, but are not required to highlight them is such a fashion that they negatively impact the relevant portions of the opinion that assist their case. Those weaknesses are sandwiched between strengths in a way that increases credibility while minimizing the damage.

Restating the Major Opinion

The final wind up of the direct examination of the expert is when the expert restates the opinion that was first given, but with a more developed statement of that opinion, connecting it to the basis previously mentioned.

THE LAW OF EXPERT WITNESSES

Expert Witness or Expert Assistance?

Deciding how and when to employ experts is a tactical and strategic decision that has factual, theoretical, and legal implications. One of the first decisions counsel must make is how to categorize the expert. If the expert is a member of the defense team and is brought on to assist in understanding the case, they are covered by attorney-client privilege and their comments, reports they produce and their conversations with the client are not discoverable by the opposing side. Once they are made a witness however, the attorney-client privilege dissipates.

This creates a potential problem for attorneys who do not consider that possibility ahead of time. They could wind up disclosing things you do not want to or, alternatively, having an expert they cannot turn into a witness because the disclosure of privileged information would destroy the case. If this issue is thought out ahead of time during case analysis, it can, to a certain extent be ameliorated through careful planning.

Rule 702. Testimony by experts

> If scientific, technical, or other specialized knowledge will assist the trier of fact to understand the evidence or to determine a fact in issue, a witness qualified as an expert by

knowledge, skill, experience, training, or education, may testify thereto in the form of an opinion or otherwise.

FRE 104(a) establishes that the trial judge decides preliminary questions concerning the relevance, propriety and necessity of expert testimony, the qualification of expert witnesses, and the admissibility of his or her testimony. The courts have provided judges with six factors that they must consider. They are:

- **Qualified Expert**. To give expert testimony, a witness must qualify as an expert by virtue of his or her "knowledge, skill, experience, training, or education." *See* FRE 702.

- **Proper Subject Matter**. Expert testimony is appropriate if it would be "helpful" to the trier of fact. It is essential especially if the trier of fact could not otherwise be expected to understand the issues and rationally resolve them. *See* FRE 702.

- **Proper Basis**. The expert's opinion may be based on admissible evidence "perceived by or made known to the expert at or before the hearing" or inadmissible hearsay if it is "of a type reasonably relied upon by experts in the particular field in forming opinions or inferences upon the subject. . . ." The expert's opinion must have an adequate factual basis and cannot be simply a bare opinion. *See* FRE 702 and 703.

- **Relevant**. Expert testimony must be relevant. *See* FRE 402.

- **Reliable**. The expert's methodology and conclusions must be reliable. *See* FRE 702.

- **Probative Value**. The probative value of the expert's opinion, and the information comprising the basis of the opinion, must not be substantially outweighed any unfair prejudice that could result from the expert's testimony. *See* FRE 403.

The Expert's Qualification to Form an Opinion

During a trial, the concepts of knowledge, training, and education foundation can be established in the following ways. Counsel must show the following with every expert witness. This information is normally found in the curriculum vitae of the expert and is fertile grounds for foundational questions during the direct examination. Qualifications are normally discussed while laying the foundation for the acceptance of an expert during direct examination.

Rule 702. Testimony by experts

> ....a witness qualified as an expert by knowledge, skill, experience, training, or education, may testify thereto in the form of an opinion or otherwise.

Examples of fertile areas used to establish the qualifications of an expert witness include degrees attained from educational institutions, other specialized training in the field, licenses for practice in their field, practical experience (if applicable) for a long period of time, teaching experience in the field, the witness's publications, membership in professional organizations, honors or prizes received, and previous expert testimony.

Skill and Experience Foundation – The following examples explain ways to lay the foundation for an expert with specialized knowledge.

- Testimony by FBI agent concerning his "crime scene analysis" of a double homicide. Testimony included observations that killer was an "organized individual" who had planned and spent some time in preparation for crime, was familiar with crime scenes and victims, and acted alone. Such evidence was not too speculative for admission under FRE 702.

- In another instance, a judge erred when he refused to allow the defense clinical psychologist to testify about the relevance of specific measurements for a normal prepubertal vagina, solely because the psychologist was not a medical doctor. As the court noted, testimony from a qualified expert, not proffered as a medical doctor, would have assisted the jury in understanding the government's evidence.

- A judge did not err in qualifying a highway patrolman who investigated over 1,500 accidents as an expert in accident reconstruction.

Proper Subject Matter ("Will assist the fact-finder")

The current standard is whether the testimony assists the trier of fact, not whether it embraces an "ultimate issue" so as to usurp the jury's function. At the same time, ultimate-issue opinion testimony is not automatically admissible. Opinions still must be relevant and helpful as determined through Rules 401-403 and 702.

Rule 704. Opinion on Ultimate Issue

> Testimony in the form of an opinion or inference otherwise admissible is not objectionable because it embraces an ultimate issue to be decided by the trier of fact.

One recurring problem is that expert should not opine that a certain witness's rendition of events is believable or not. We are skeptical about whether any witness could be qualified to opine as to the credibility of another. **An expert may not become a "human lie detector."** Questions like whether the expert believes the victim was raped, or whether the victim is telling the truth when she claimed to have been raped (i.e. was the witness truthful?) are impermissible. However, the expert *may* opine that a victim's testimony or history is consistent with what the expert's examination found, and whether the behavior at issue is *typical* of victims of such crimes. Focus on symptoms, not conclusions concerning veracity.

Consider the following applications of this rule:

- A judge improperly applied "necessary testimony" standard rather than a "helpful testimony" standard in excluding forensic psychiatrist expert testimony that accused did not form specific intent to kill or injure children. The court noted that the federal rules of evidence liberally allow for expert testimony that will assist the trier of fact.

- In one case the court held that the expert's focus should be on whether children exhibit behavior and symptoms consistent with abuse, but was reversible error to allow social worker and doctor to testify that the child-victims were telling the truth and were the victims of sexual abuse. **Questions such as whether the victim's behavior is consistent with individuals who have been raped, or whether injuries are consistent with a child who has been battered, however, are permissible.** For example an expert may testify as to what symptoms are found among children who have suffered sexual abuse and whether the child-witness has exhibited these symptoms. However, testimony that expert explained to the child the importance of being truthful and, based on child's responses, recommended further treatment, was an affirmation that expert believed the victim, which improperly usurped the responsibility of the fact-finder. In this instance the court ruled that the expert went too far.

- In another case a government expert testified that preteen and teenage boys (the victims) were the least likely group to report abuse because of shame and embarrassment and fear of being labeled a homosexual. She opined that false allegations from that group were "extremely rare" and outside of her clinical experience. Such testimony was improperly admitted, although harmless.

- On the other hand, a social worker's testimony that a rape victim was not vindictive and wanted to stay away from the accused was not improper comment on credibility.

- On appeal for the first time, the defense objected to testimony of government expert on "child abuse accommodation" syndrome. Defense claimed that it amounted to labeling the accused as an abuser and vouching for the credibility of the victims because the expert got all her information from the victims. The appellate court rejected that argument and noted that the expert testimony was limited to factors and that the facts of this case were consistent with those factors.

- A defendant was charged with indecent acts with his daughter. The defendant made a partial confession to the police and at trial stated that any contact with his daughters was not of a sexual nature. On rebuttal the government called an expert in child abuse who testified that, in her opinion, the victim suffered abuse at the hands of her father. The defense did not object. On appeal the court noted that error was not constitutional. Nonetheless, the court held the error had a substantial influence on the findings and reversed the conviction.

Basis for the Expert's Testimony

The language of the rule is broad enough to allow three types of bases: facts personally observed by the expert; facts posed in a hypothetical question; and hearsay reports from third parties. **Expert testimony must be based on the facts of the case, but not necessarily the firsthand observations of the expert.**

Rule 703 provides:

> "The facts or data in the particular case upon which an expert bases an opinion or inference may be those perceived by or made known to the expert, at or before the hearing. If of a type reasonably relied upon by experts in the particular field in

forming opinions or inferences upon the subject, the facts or data need not be admissible into evidence."

In an example, the fact that an expert did not interview or counsel the victim did not render the expert unqualified to arrive at an opinion concerning rape trauma syndrome. The defense objected to the social worker's opinion that the victim was exhibiting symptoms consistent with rape trauma accommodation syndrome and suffered from PTSD on the basis that the opinion was based solely on observing the victim in court, reading reports of others and assuming facts as alleged by the victim were true. Objection went to weight to be given expert opinion, not admissibility.

If the expert opinion is based on personal observations, then the foundational elements must include: (1) where and when the expert witness observed the fact, (2) who was present, (3) how the expert witness observed the fact, and (4) a description of the observed fact. These facts may not even necessarily be found within the record of the court. Facts presented out-of-court (non-record facts), are allowed if they are "of a type reasonably relied upon by experts in the particular field" (this is allowed even if inadmissible because it is not being offered for its truth but the expert's testimony based on that evidence).

It is also permissible for expert opinions to be based on hearsay reports by third parties. "The rationale in favor of admissibility of expert testimony based on hearsay is that the expert is fully capable of judging for himself what is, or is not, a reliable basis for his opinion. This relates directly to one of the functions of the expert witness, namely to lend his special expertise to the issue before him." *United States v. Sims*, 514 F.2d 147, 149 (9th Cir). Beware: there is a potential problem of smuggling in otherwise inadmissible evidence.

Compare these to *Hutchinson v. Groskin*, 927 F.2d 722 (2d Cir. 1991) (testimony that expert's opinion was "consistent with" prognoses of three non-testifying physicians, not disclosed during discovery, conveyed hearsay testimony to the jury) with *Primavera v. Celotex Corp.*, 608 A.2d 515 (Pa. Super. Ct. 1992) (sustaining expert's reliance on hearsay reports since they were the kind of data ordinarily used by practitioners, and because the expert *used* the reports to arrive at and explain his opinion, not as a "mere conduit or transmitter" of the hearsay).

Relevance and Reliability

Expert testimony, like any other testimony, must be relevant to an issue at trial to be admissible. *Daubert v. Merrell Dow Pharmaceuticals, Inc.* 509 U.S. 579 (1993) and FRE 401 and 402 establish the baseline requirements for admissible expert testimony. In *Daubert,* the Supreme Court held that nothing in the Federal Rules indicates that "general acceptance" is a precondition to admission of scientific evidence. Instead, the rules assign the task to the judge to ensure that expert testimony rests on a reliable basis and is relevant. The judge assesses the principles and methodologies of such evidence pursuant to FRE 104(a).

THE U.S. SUPREME COURT SPEAKS – BASIS OF THE EXPERT OPINION

113 S.Ct. 2786

Supreme Court of the United States
William **DAUBERT**, et ux., etc., et al., Petitioners,
v.
MERRELL **DOW** PHARMACEUTICALS, INC.
No. 92–102.Argued March 30, 1993
Decided June 28, 1993

Vacated and remanded.

Chief Justice Rehnquist filed opinion concurring in part and dissenting in part in which Justice Stevens joined.

BLACKMUN, J., delivered the opinion for a unanimous Court with respect to Parts I and II–A, and the opinion of the Court with respect to Parts II–B, II–C, III, and IV, in which WHITE, O'CONNOR, SCALIA, KENNEDY, SOUTER, and THOMAS, JJ., joined. REHNQUIST, C.J., filed an opinion concurring in part and dissenting in part, in which STEVENS, J., joined, *post*, p. ——.

Opinion

Justice BLACKMUN delivered the opinion of the Court.

In this case we are called upon to determine the standard for admitting expert scientific testimony in a federal trial.

I

Petitioners Jason **Daubert** and Eric Schuller are minor children born with serious birth defects. They and their parents sued respondent in California state court, alleging that the birth defects had been caused by the mothers' ingestion of Bendectin, a prescription antinausea drug marketed by respondent. Respondent removed the suits to federal court on diversity grounds.

After extensive discovery, respondent moved for summary judgment, contending that Bendectin does not cause birth defects in humans and that petitioners would be unable to come forward with any admissible evidence that it does. In support of its motion, respondent submitted an affidavit of Steven H. Lamm, physician and epidemiologist, who is a well-credentialed expert on the risks from exposure to various chemical substances. Doctor Lamm stated that he had reviewed all the literature on Bendectin and human birth defects—more than 30 published studies involving over 130,000 patients. No study had found Bendectin to be a human teratogen (*i.e.,* a substance capable of causing malformations in fetuses). On the basis of this review, Doctor Lamm concluded that maternal use of Bendectin during the first trimester of pregnancy has not been shown to be a risk factor for human birth defects.

Petitioners did not (and do not) contest this characterization of the published record regarding Bendectin. Instead, they responded to respondent's motion with the testimony of eight experts of their own, each of whom also possessed impressive credentials. These experts had concluded that Bendectin can cause birth defects. Their conclusions were based upon "in vitro" (test tube) and "in vivo" (live) animal studies that found a link between Bendectin and malformations; pharmacological studies of the chemical structure of Bendectin that purported to show similarities between the structure of the drug and that of other substances known to cause birth defects; and the "reanalysis" of previously published epidemiological (human statistical) studies.

The District Court granted respondent's motion for summary judgment. The court stated that scientific evidence is admissible only if the principle upon which it is based is " 'sufficiently established to have general acceptance in the field to which it belongs.' " 727 F.Supp. 570, 572 (S.D.Cal.1989), quoting *United States v. Kilgus,* 571 F.2d 508, 510 (CA9 1978). The court concluded that petitioners' evidence did not meet this standard. Given the vast body of epidemiological data concerning Bendectin, the court held, expert opinion which is not based on epidemiological evidence 584 ***584** is not admissible to establish causation. 727 F.Supp., at 575. Thus, the animal-cell studies, live-animal studies, and chemical-structure analyses on which petitioners had relied could not raise by themselves a reasonably disputable jury issue regarding causation. Petitioners' epidemiological analyses, based as they were on recalculations of data in previously published studies that had found no causal link between the drug and birth defects, were ruled to be inadmissible because they had not been published or subjected to peer review.

The United States Court of Appeals for the Ninth Circuit affirmed. 951 F.2d 1128 (1991). Citing *Frye v. United States,* 54 App.D.C. 46, 47, 293 F. 1013, 1014 (1923), the court stated that expert opinion based on a scientific technique is inadmissible unless the technique is "generally accepted" as reliable in the relevant scientific community. 951 F. 2d, at 1129–1130. The court declared that expert opinion based on a methodology that diverges "significantly from the procedures accepted by recognized authorities in the field ... cannot be shown to be 'generally accepted as a reliable technique.' " *Id.,* at 1130, quoting *United States v. Solomon,* 753 F.2d 1522, 1526 (CA9 1985).

The court emphasized that other Courts of Appeals considering the risks of Bendectin had refused to admit reanalyses of epidemiological studies that had been neither published nor subjected to peer review. 951 F.2d, at 1130–1131. Those courts had found unpublished reanalyses "particularly problematic in light of the massive weight of the original published studies supporting [respondent's] position, all of which had undergone full scrutiny from the scientific community." *Id.,* at 1130. Contending that reanalysis is generally accepted by the scientific community only when it is subjected to verification and scrutiny by others in the field, the Court of Appeals rejected petitioners' reanalyses as "unpublished, not subjected to the normal peer review process and generated solely for use in litigation." *Id.,* at 1131. The court concluded that petitioners' evidence provided an insufficient foundation to allow admission of expert testimony that Bendectin caused their injuries and, accordingly, that petitioners could not satisfy their burden of proving causation at trial.

We granted certiorari, 506 U.S. 914, 113 S.Ct. 320, 121 L.Ed.2d 240 (1992), in light of sharp divisions among the courts regarding the proper standard for the admission of expert testimony. Compare, *e.g., United States v. Shorter,* 257 U.S.App.D.C. 358, 363–364, 809 F.2d 54, 59–60 (applying the "general acceptance" standard), cert. denied, 484 U.S. 817, 108 S.Ct. 71, 98 L.Ed.2d 35 (1987), with *DeLuca v. Merrell* **Dow** *Pharmaceuticals, Inc.,* 911 F.2d 941, 955 (CA3 1990) (rejecting the "general acceptance" standard).

II. A

In the 70 years since its formulation in the *Frye* case, the "general acceptance" test has been the dominant standard for determining the admissibility of novel scientific evidence at trial. See E. Green & C. Nesson, Problems, Cases, and Materials on Evidence 649 (1983). Although under increasing attack of late, the rule continues to be followed by a ****2793** majority of courts, including the Ninth Circuit.

The *Frye* test has its origin in a short and citation-free 1923 decision concerning the admissibility of evidence derived from a systolic blood pressure deception test, a crude precursor to the polygraph machine. In what has become a famous (perhaps infamous) passage, the then Court of Appeals for the District of Columbia described the device and its operation and declared:

> "Just when a scientific principle or discovery crosses the line between the experimental and demonstrable stages 586 *586 is difficult to define. Somewhere in this twilight zone the evidential force of the principle must be recognized, and while courts will go a long way in admitting expert testimony deduced from a well-recognized scientific principle or discovery, *the thing from which the deduction is made must be sufficiently established to have gained general acceptance in the particular field in which it belongs.*" 54 App.D.C., at 47, 293 F., at 1014 (emphasis added).

Because the deception test had "not yet gained such standing and scientific recognition among physiological and psychological authorities as would justify the courts in admitting expert testimony deduced from the discovery, development, and experiments thus far made," evidence of its results was ruled inadmissible.

The merits of the *Frye* test have been much debated, and scholarship on its proper scope and application is legion. Petitioners' primary attack, however, is not on the content but on the continuing authority of the rule. They contend that the *Frye* test was superseded by the adoption of the Federal Rules of Evidence. We agree.

We interpret the legislatively enacted Federal Rules of Evidence as we would any statute. *Beech Aircraft Corp. v. Rainey,* 488 U.S. 153, 163, 109 S.Ct. 439, 446, 102 L.Ed.2d 445 (1988). Rule 402 provides the baseline:

> "All relevant evidence is admissible, except as otherwise provided by the Constitution of the United States, by Act of Congress, **2794 by these rules, or by other rules prescribed by the Supreme Court pursuant to statutory authority. Evidence which is not relevant is not admissible."

"Relevant evidence" is defined as that which has "any tendency to make the existence of any fact that is of consequence to the determination of the action more probable or less probable than it would be without the evidence." Rule 401. The Rule's basic standard of relevance thus is a liberal one.

Frye, of course, predated the Rules by half a century. In *United States v. Abel,* 469 U.S. 45, 105 S.Ct. 465, 83 L.Ed.2d 450 (1984), we considered the pertinence of background common law in interpreting the Rules of Evidence. We noted that the Rules occupy the field, *id.,* at 49, 105 S.Ct., at 467, but, quoting Professor Cleary, the Reporter, explained that the common law nevertheless could serve as an aid to their application:

> " 'In principle, under the Federal Rules no common law of evidence remains. "All relevant evidence is admissible, except as otherwise provided...." In reality, of course, the body of common law knowledge continues to exist, though in the somewhat altered form of a source of guidance in the exercise of delegated powers.' " *Id.,* at 51–52, 105 S.Ct., at 469.

We found the common-law precept at issue in the *Abel* case entirely consistent with Rule 402's general requirement of admissibility, and considered it unlikely that the drafters had intended to change the rule. *Id.,* at 50–51, 105 S.Ct., at 468–469. In *Bourjaily v. United States,* 483 U.S. 171, 107 S.Ct. 2775, 97 L.Ed.2d 144 (1987), on the other hand, the Court was unable to find a particular common-law doctrine in the Rules, and so held it superseded.

Here there is a specific Rule that speaks to the contested issue. Rule 702, governing expert testimony, provides:

> "If scientific, technical, or other specialized knowledge will assist the trier of fact to

understand the evidence or to determine a fact in issue, a witness qualified as an expert by knowledge, skill, experience, training, or education, may testify thereto in the form of an opinion or otherwise."

Nothing in the text of this Rule establishes "general acceptance" as an absolute prerequisite to admissibility. Nor does respondent present any clear indication that Rule 702 or the Rules as a whole were intended to incorporate a "general acceptance" standard. The drafting history makes no mention of *Frye,* and a rigid "general acceptance" requirement would be at odds with the "liberal thrust" of the Federal Rules and their "general approach of relaxing the traditional barriers to 'opinion' testimony." *Beech Aircraft Corp. v. Rainey,* 488 U.S., at 169, 109 S.Ct., at 450 (citing Rules 701 to 705). See also Weinstein, Rule 702 of the Federal Rules of Evidence is 589 ***589*** Sound; It Should Not Be Amended, 138 F.R.D. 631 (1991) ("The Rules were designed to depend primarily upon lawyer-adversaries and sensible triers of fact to evaluate conflicts"). Given the Rules' permissive backdrop and their inclusion of a specific rule on expert testimony that does not mention " 'general acceptance,' " the assertion that the Rules somehow assimilated *Frye* is unconvincing. *Frye* made "general acceptance" the exclusive test for admitting expert scientific testimony. That austere standard, absent from, and incompatible with, the Federal Rules of Evidence, should not be applied in federal trials.

B

That the *Frye* test was displaced by the Rules of Evidence does not mean, however, that the Rules themselves place no limits on the admissibility of purportedly scientific evidence. Nor is the trial judge disabled from screening such evidence. To the contrary, under the Rules the trial judge must ensure that any and all scientific testimony or evidence admitted is not only relevant, but reliable.

The primary locus of this obligation is Rule 702, which clearly contemplates some degree of regulation of the subjects and theories about which an expert may testify. "*If scientific,* technical, or other specialized *knowledge will assist the trier of fact* to understand the evidence or to determine a fact in issue" an expert "may testify *thereto.*" (Emphasis added.) The subject of an expert's testimony must be "scientific ... knowledge." The adjective " scientific" implies a grounding in the methods and procedures of science. Similarly, the word "knowledge" connotes more than subjective belief or unsupported speculation. The term "applies to any body of known facts or to any body of ideas inferred from such facts or accepted as truths on good grounds." Webster's Third New International Dictionary 1252 (1986). Of course, it would be unreasonable to conclude that the subject of scientific testimony must be "known" to a certainty; arguably, there are no certainties in science. See, *e.g.,* Brief for Nicolaas Bloembergen et al. as *Amici Curiae* 9 ("Indeed, scientists do not assert that they know what is immutably 'true'—they are committed to searching for new, temporary, theories to explain, as best they can, phenomena"); Brief for American Association for the Advancement of Science et al. as *Amici Curiae* 7–8 ("Science is not an encyclopedic body of knowledge about the universe. Instead, it represents a *process* for proposing and refining theoretical explanations about the world that are subject to further testing and refinement" (emphasis in original)). But, in order to qualify as "scientific knowledge," an inference or assertion must be derived by the scientific method. Proposed testimony must be supported by appropriate validation—*i.e.,* "good grounds," based on what is known. In short, the requirement that an expert's testimony pertain to " scientific knowledge" establishes a standard of evidentiary reliability.

Rule 702 further requires that the evidence or testimony "assist the trier of fact to understand the evidence or to determine a fact in issue." This condition goes primarily to relevance. " Expert testimony which does not relate to any issue in the case is not relevant and, ergo, non-helpful." 3 Weinstein & Berger ¶ 702[02], p. 702–18. See also *United States v. Downing*, 753 F.2d 1224, 1242 (CA3 1985) ("An additional consideration under Rule 702—and another aspect of relevancy—is whether expert testimony proffered in the case is sufficiently tied to the facts of the case that it will aid the jury in resolving a factual dispute"). The consideration has been aptly described by Judge Becker as one of "fit." *Ibid.* "Fit" is not always obvious, and scientific validity for one purpose is not necessarily scientific validity for other, unrelated purposes. See Starrs, *Frye v. United States* Restructured and Revitalized: A Proposal to Amend Federal Evidence Rule 702, 26 Jurimetrics J. 249, 258 (1986). The study of the phases of the moon, for example, may provide valid scientific "knowledge" about whether a certain night was dark, and if darkness is a fact in issue, the knowledge will assist the trier of fact. However (absent creditable grounds supporting such a link), evidence that the moon was full on a certain night will not assist the trier of fact in determining whether an individual was unusually likely to have behaved irrationally on that night. Rule 702's "helpfulness" standard requires a valid scientific connection to the pertinent inquiry as a precondition to admissibility.

That these requirements are embodied in Rule 702 is not surprising. Unlike an ordinary witness, see Rule 701, an expert is permitted wide latitude to offer opinions, including those that are not based on firsthand knowledge or observation. See Rules 702 and 703. Presumably, this relaxation of the usual requirement of firsthand knowledge—a rule which represents "a 'most pervasive manifestation' of the common law insistence upon 'the most reliable sources of information,' " Advisory Committee's Notes on Fed.Rule Evid. 602, 28 U.S.C.App., p. 755 (citation omitted)—is premised on an assumption that the expert's opinion will have a reliable basis in the knowledge and experience of his discipline.

Faced with a proffer of expert scientific testimony, then, the trial judge must determine at the outset, pursuant to Rule 104(a),10 whether the expert is proposing to testify to (1) scientific knowledge that (2) will assist the trier of fact to understand or determine a fact in issue. This entails a preliminary assessment of whether the reasoning or methodology underlying the testimony is scientifically valid and of whether that reasoning or methodology properly can be applied to the facts in issue. We are confident that federal judges possess the capacity to undertake this review. Many factors will bear on the inquiry, and we do not presume to set out a definitive checklist or test. But some general observations are appropriate.

Ordinarily, a key question to be answered in determining whether a theory or technique is scientific knowledge that will assist the trier of fact will be whether it can be (and has been) tested. "Scientific methodology today is based on generating hypotheses and testing them to see if they can be falsified; indeed, this methodology is what distinguishes science from other fields of human inquiry." Green 645. See also C. Hempel, Philosophy of Natural Science 49 (1966) ("[T]he statements constituting a scientific explanation must be capable of empirical test"); K. Popper, Conjectures and Refutations: The Growth of Scientific Knowledge 37 (5th ed. 1989) ("[T]he criterion of the scientific status of a theory is its falsifiability, or refutability, or testability") (emphasis deleted).

Another pertinent consideration is whether the theory or technique has been subjected to peer review and publication. Publication (which is but one element of peer review) is not a *sine qua non* of admissibility; it does not necessarily correlate with reliability, see S. Jasanoff, The Fifth Branch: Science Advisors as Policymakers 61–76 (1990), and in some instances well-grounded but innovative theories will not have been published, see Horrobin, The Philosophical Basis of Peer Review and the Suppression of Innovation,

263 JAMA 1438 (1990). Some propositions, moreover, are too particular, too new, or of too limited interest to be published. But submission to the scrutiny of the scientific community is a component of "good science," in part because it increases the likelihood that substantive flaws in methodology will be detected. See J. Ziman, Reliable Knowledge: An Exploration 594 *594 of the Grounds for Belief in Science 130–133 (1978); Relman & Angell, How Good Is Peer Review?, 321 New Eng.J.Med. 827 (1989). The fact of publication (or lack thereof) in a peer reviewed journal thus will be a relevant, though not dispositive, consideration in assessing the scientific validity of a particular technique or methodology on which an opinion is premised.

Additionally, in the case of a particular scientific technique, the court ordinarily should consider the known or potential rate of error, see, *e.g., United States v. Smith,* 869 F.2d 348, 353–354 (CA7 1989) (surveying studies of the error rate of spectrographic voice identification technique), and the existence and maintenance of standards controlling the technique's operation, see *United States v. Williams,* 583 F.2d 1194, 1198 (CA2 1978) (noting professional organization's standard governing spectrographic analysis), cert. denied, 439 U.S. 1117, 99 S.Ct. 1025, 59 L.Ed.2d 77 (1979).

Finally, "general acceptance" can yet have a bearing on the inquiry. A "reliability assessment does not require, although it does permit, explicit identification of a relevant scientific community and an express determination of a particular degree of acceptance within that community." *United States v. Downing,* 753 F.2d, at 1238. See also 3 Weinstein & Berger ¶ 702[03], pp. 702–41 to 702–42. Widespread acceptance can be an important factor in ruling particular evidence admissible, and "a known technique which has been able to attract only minimal support within the community," *Downing,* 753 F.2d, at 1238, may properly be viewed with skepticism.

The inquiry envisioned by Rule 702 is, we emphasize, a flexible one.12 Its overarching subject is the scientific validity *595 and thus the evidentiary relevance and reliability— of the principles that underlie a proposed submission. The focus, of course, must be solely on principles and methodology, not on the conclusions that they generate.

Throughout, a judge assessing a proffer of expert scientific testimony under Rule 702 should also be mindful of other applicable rules. Rule 703 provides that expert opinions based on otherwise inadmissible **2798 hearsay are to be admitted only if the facts or data are "of a type reasonably relied upon by experts in the particular field in forming opinions or inferences upon the subject." Rule 706 allows the court at its discretion to procure the assistance of an expert of its own choosing. Finally, Rule 403 permits the exclusion of relevant evidence "if its probative value is substantially outweighed by the danger of unfair prejudice, confusion of the issues, or misleading the jury...." Judge Weinstein has explained: "Expert evidence can be both powerful and quite misleading because of the difficulty in evaluating it. Because of this risk, the judge in weighing possible prejudice against probative force under Rule 403 of the present rules exercises more control over experts than over lay witnesses." Weinstein, 138 F.R.D., at 632.

III

We conclude by briefly addressing what appear to be two underlying concerns of the parties and *amici* in this case. Respondent expresses apprehension that abandonment of "general acceptance" as the exclusive requirement for admission will result in a "free-for-all" in which befuddled juries are confounded by absurd and irrational pseudoscientific assertions. *596 In this regard respondent seems to us to be overly pessimistic about the capabilities of the jury and of the adversary system generally. Vigorous cross-examination, presentation of contrary evidence, and careful instruction on the burden of proof are the traditional and appropriate means of attacking shaky but admissible evidence. See *Rock v. Arkansas,* 483 U.S. 44, 61, 107 S.Ct. 2704, 2714, 97 L.Ed.2d 37 (1987). Additionally, in the event the trial court concludes that the scintilla of evidence presented supporting a position is insufficient to allow a reasonable juror to conclude that the position more likely than not is true, the court remains free to direct a judgment, Fed.Rule Civ.Proc. 50(a), and likewise to grant summary judgment, Fed.Rule Civ.Proc. 56. Cf., *e.g., Turpin v. Merrell **Dow** Pharmaceuticals, Inc.,* 959 F.2d 1349 (CA6) (holding that scientific evidence that provided foundation for expert testimony, viewed in the light most favorable to plaintiffs, was not sufficient to allow a jury to find it more probable than not that defendant caused plaintiff's injury), cert. denied, 506 U.S. 826, 113 S.Ct. 84, 121 L.Ed.2d 47 (1992); *Brock v. Merrell **Dow** Pharmaceuticals, Inc.,* 874 F.2d 307 (CA5 1989) (reversing judgment entered on jury verdict for plaintiffs because evidence regarding causation was insufficient), modified, 884 F.2d 166 (CA5 1989), cert. denied, 494 U.S. 1046, 110 S.Ct. 1511, 108 L.Ed.2d 646 (1990); Green 680–681. These conventional devices, rather than wholesale exclusion under an uncompromising "general acceptance" test, are the appropriate safeguards where the basis of scientific testimony meets the standards of Rule 702.

Petitioners and, to a greater extent, their *amici* exhibit a different concern. They suggest that recognition of a screening role for the judge that allows for the exclusion of "invalid" evidence will sanction a stifling and repressive scientific orthodoxy and will be inimical to the search for truth. See, *e.g.,* Brief for Ronald Bayer et al. as *Amici Curiae.* It is true that open debate is an essential part of both legal and scientific analyses. Yet there are important differences between the quest for truth in the courtroom and the quest for truth in the laboratory. Scientific conclusions are subject to perpetual revision. Law, on the other hand, must resolve disputes finally and quickly. The scientific project is advanced by broad and wide-ranging consideration of a multitude of hypotheses, for those that are incorrect will eventually be shown to be so, and that in itself is an advance. Conjectures that are probably wrong are of little use, however, in the project of reaching a quick, final, and binding legal judgment—often of great consequence—about a particular set of events in the past. We recognize that, in practice, a gatekeeping role for the judge, no matter how flexible, inevitably on occasion will prevent the jury from learning of authentic insights and innovations. That, nevertheless, is the balance that is struck by Rules of Evidence designed not for the exhaustive search for cosmic understanding but for the particularized resolution of legal disputes.

IV

To summarize: "General acceptance" is not a necessary precondition to the admissibility of scientific evidence under the Federal Rules of Evidence, but the Rules of Evidence—especially Rule 702—do assign to the trial judge the task of ensuring that an expert's testimony both rests on a reliable foundation and is relevant to the task at hand. Pertinent evidence based on scientifically valid principles will satisfy those demands.

The inquiries of the District Court and the Court of Appeals focused almost exclusively on "general acceptance," as gauged by publication and the decisions of other courts. Accordingly, **598* the judgment of the Court of Appeals is vacated, and the case is remanded for further proceedings consistent with this opinion.

It is so ordered.

FOR DISCUSSION

1. How would you respond to an argument that the "new" Daubert Standard is nothing more than a relaxation of the standards for scientific evidence?

2. Considering the holding in this case would you expect an increase or decrease in admissible scientific evidence?

3. What about nonscientific evidence?

THE U.S. SUPREME COURT SPEAKS – GATEKEEPING FUNCTION

118 S.Ct. 512
Supreme Court of the United States
GENERAL ELECTRIC COMPANY, et al., Petitioners,
v.
Robert K. **JOINER**, et ux.
No. 96–188.Argued Oct. 14, 1997.Decided Dec. 15, 1997

Chief Justice <u>REHNQUIST</u> delivered the opinion of the Court.

We granted certiorari in this case to determine what standard an appellate court should apply in reviewing a trial court's decision to admit or exclude expert testimony under *Daubert v. Merrell Dow Pharmaceuticals, Inc.*, 509 U.S. 579, 113 S.Ct. 2786, 125 L.Ed. 2d 469 (1993). We hold that abuse of discretion is the appropriate standard. We apply this standard and conclude that the District Court in this case did not abuse its discretion when it excluded certain proffered expert testimony.

I

Respondent Robert **Joiner** began work as an electrician in the Water & Light Department of Thomasville, Georgia (City), in 1973. This job required him to work with and around the City's **electrical** transformers, which used a mineral-oil-based dielectric fluid as a coolant. **Joiner** often had to stick his hands and arms into the fluid to make repairs. The fluid would sometimes splash onto him, occasionally getting into his eyes and mouth. In 1983 the City discovered that the fluid in some of the transformers was contaminated with polychlorinated biphenyls (PCB's). PCB's are widely considered to be hazardous to human health. Congress, with limited exceptions, banned the production and sale of PCB's in 1978. See 90 Stat.2020, 15 U.S.C. § 2605(e)(2)(A).

Joiner was diagnosed with small-cell lung cancer in 1991. He sued petitioners in Georgia state court the following year. Petitioner Monsanto manufactured PCB's from 1935 to 1977; petitioners **General Electric** and Westinghouse **Electric** manufactured transformers and dielectric fluid. In his complaint **Joiner** linked his development of cancer to his exposure to PCB's and their derivatives, polychlorinated dibenzofurans (furans) and polychlorinated dibenzodioxins (dioxins). **Joiner** had been a smoker for approximately eight years, his parents had both been smokers, and there was a history of lung cancer in his family. He was thus perhaps already at a heightened risk of developing lung cancer eventually. The suit alleged that his exposure to PCB's "promoted" his cancer; had it not been for his exposure to these substances, his cancer would not have developed for many years, if at all.

Petitioners removed the case to federal court. Once there, they moved for summary judgment. They contended that (1) there was no evidence that **Joiner** suffered significant exposure to PCB's, furans, or dioxins, and (2) there was no admissible scientific evidence that PCB's promoted **Joiner's** cancer. **Joiner** responded that there were numerous disputed factual issues that required resolution by a jury. He relied largely on the testimony of expert witnesses. In depositions, his experts had testified that PCB's alone can promote cancer and that furans and dioxins can also promote cancer. They opined that since **Joiner** had been exposed to PCB's, furans, and dioxins, such exposure was likely responsible for **Joiner's** cancer.

The District Court ruled that there was a genuine issue of material fact as to whether **Joiner** had been exposed to PCB's. But it nevertheless granted summary judgment for petitioners because (1) there was no genuine issue as to whether **Joiner** had been exposed to furans and dioxins, and (2) the testimony of **Joiner's** experts had failed to show that there was a link between exposure to PCB's and small-cell lung cancer. The court believed that the testimony of respondent's experts to the contrary did not rise above "subjective belief or unsupported speculation." 864 F.Supp. 1310, 1326 (N.D.Ga.1994). Their testimony was therefore inadmissible.

The Court of Appeals for the Eleventh Circuit reversed. 78 F.3d 524 (1996). It held that "[b]ecause the Federal Rules of Evidence governing expert testimony display a preference for admissibility, we apply a particularly stringent standard of review to the trial judge's exclusion of expert testimony." Id., at 529. Applying that standard, the Court of Appeals held that the District Court had erred in excluding the testimony of **Joiner's** expert witnesses. The District Court had made two fundamental errors. First, it excluded the experts' testimony because it " drew different conclusions from the research than did each of the experts." The Court of Appeals opined that a district court should limit its role to determining the "legal reliability of proffered expert testimony, leaving the jury to decide the correctness of competing expert opinions." Id. at 533. Second, the District Court had held that there was no genuine issue of material fact as to whether **Joiner** had been exposed to furans and dioxins. This was also incorrect, said the Court of Appeals, because testimony in the record supported the proposition that there had been such exposure.

We granted petitioners' petition for a writ of certiorari, 520 U.S. 1114, 117 S.Ct. 1243, 137 L.Ed.2d 325 (1997), and we now reverse.

II

Petitioners challenge the standard applied by the Court of Appeals in reviewing the District Court's decision to exclude respondent's experts' proffered testimony. They argue that that court should have applied traditional "abuse-of-discretion" review. Respondent agrees that abuse of discretion is the correct standard of review. He contends, however, that the Court of Appeals applied an abuse-of-discretion standard in this case. As he reads it, the phrase "particularly stringent" announced no new standard of review. It was simply an acknowledgment that an appellate court can and will devote more resources to analyzing district court decisions that are dispositive of the entire litigation. All evidentiary decisions are reviewed under an abuse-of-discretion standard. He argues, however, that it is perfectly reasonable for appellate courts to give particular attention to those decisions that are outcome determinative.

We have held that abuse of discretion is the proper standard of review of a district court's evidentiary rulings. *Old Chief v. United States*, 519 U.S. 172, 174 n. 1, 117 S.Ct. 644, 647 n. 1, 136 L.Ed.2d 574 (1997); *United States v. Abel*, 469 U.S. 45, 54, 105 S.Ct. 465, 470, 83 L.Ed.2d 450 (1984). Indeed, our cases on the subject go back as far as *Spring Co. v. Edgar*, 99 U.S. 645, 658, 25 L.Ed. 487 (1879), where we said that "[c]ases arise where it is very much a matter of discretion with the court whether to receive or exclude the evidence; but the appellate court will not reverse in such a case, unless the ruling is manifestly erroneous." The Court of Appeals suggested that _Daubert_ somehow altered this general rule in the context of a district court's decision to exclude scientific evidence. But _Daubert_ did not address the standard of appellate review for evidentiary rulings at all. It did hold that the " austere" _Frye_ standard of "general acceptance" had not been carried over into the Federal Rules of Evidence. But the opinion also said:

"That the _Frye_ test was displaced by the Rules of Evidence does not mean, however, that the Rules themselves place no limits on the admissibility of purportedly scientific evidence. Nor is the trial judge disabled from screening such evidence. To the contrary, under the Rules the trial judge must ensure that any and all scientific testimony or evidence admitted is not only relevant, but reliable." 509 U.S., at 589, 113 S.Ct., at 2794–2795 (footnote omitted).

Thus, while the Federal Rules of Evidence allow district courts to admit a somewhat broader range of scientific testimony than would have been admissible under _Frye,_ they leave in place the "gatekeeper" role of the trial judge in screening such evidence. A court of appeals applying "abuse-of-discretion" review to such rulings may not categorically distinguish between rulings allowing expert testimony and rulings disallowing it. Compare _Beech Aircraft Corp. v. Rainey,_ 488 U.S. 153, 172, 109 S.Ct. 439, 451, 102 L.Ed.2d 445 (1988) (applying abuse-of-discretion review to a lower court's decision to exclude evidence), with _United States v. Abel, supra,_ at 54, 105 S.Ct., at 470 (applying abuse-of-discretion review to a lower court's decision to admit evidence). We likewise reject respondent's argument that because the granting of summary judgment in this case was "outcome determinative," it should have been subjected to a more searching standard of review. On a motion for summary judgment, disputed issues of fact are resolved against the moving party-here, petitioners. But the question of admissibility of expert testimony is not such an issue of fact, and is reviewable under the abuse-of-discretion standard.

We hold that the Court of Appeals erred in its review of the exclusion of **Joiner's** experts' testimony. In applying an overly "stringent" review to that ruling, it failed to give the trial court the deference that is the hallmark of abuse-of-discretion review. See, _e.g., Koon v. United States,_ 518 U.S. 81, 98–99, 116 S.Ct. 2035, 2046–2047, 135 L.Ed.2d 392 (1996).

III

We believe that a proper application of the correct standard of review here indicates that the District Court did not abuse its discretion. **Joiner's** theory of liability was that his exposure to PCB's and their derivatives "promoted" his development of small- cell lung cancer. In support of that theory he proffered the deposition testimony of expert witnesses. Dr. Arnold Schecter testified that he believed it "more likely than not that Mr. **Joiner's** lung cancer was causally linked to cigarette smoking and PCB exposure." App. 107. Dr. Daniel Teitelbaum testified that **Joiner's** "lung cancer was caused by or contributed to in a significant degree by the materials with which he worked." _Id.,_ at 140.

Petitioners contended that the statements of **Joiner's** experts regarding causation were nothing more than speculation. Petitioners criticized the testimony of the experts in that it was "not supported by epidemiological studies ... [and was] based exclusively on isolated studies of laboratory animals." 3 Record, Doc. No. 46 (Defendants' Joint Memorandum in Support of Summary Judgment 3). **Joiner** responded by claiming that his experts had identified "relevant animal studies which support their opinions." 4 Record, Doc. No. 53 (Plaintiffs' Brief in Opposition to Defendants' Motion for Summary Judgment 47). He also directed the court's attention to four epidemiological studies on which his experts had relied.

The District Court agreed with petitioners that the animal studies on which respondent's experts relied did not support his contention that exposure to PCB's had contributed to his cancer. The studies involved infant mice that had developed cancer after being exposed to PCB's. The infant mice in the studies had had massive doses of PCB's injected directly into their peritoneums3 or stomachs. **Joiner** was an adult human being whose alleged exposure to PCB's was far less than the exposure in the animal studies. The PCB's were injected into the mice in a highly concentrated form. The fluid with which **Joiner** had come into contact generally had a much smaller PCB concentration of between 0-to-500 parts per million. The cancer that these mice developed was alveologenic adenomas; **Joiner** had developed small-cell carcinomas. No study demonstrated that adult mice developed cancer after being exposed to PCB's. One of the experts admitted that no study had demonstrated that PCB's lead to cancer in any other species.

Respondent failed to reply to this criticism. Rather than explaining how and why the experts could have extrapolated their opinions from these seemingly far-removed animal studies, respondent chose "to proceed as if the only issue [was] whether animal studies can ever be a proper foundation for an expert's opinion." 864 F.Supp., at 1324. Of course, whether animal studies can ever be a proper foundation for an expert's opinion was not the issue. The issue was whether *these* experts' opinions were sufficiently supported by the animal studies on which they purported to rely. The studies were so dissimilar to the facts presented in this litigation that it was not an abuse of discretion for the District Court to have rejected the experts' reliance on them.

The District Court also concluded that the four epidemiological studies on which respondent relied were not a sufficient basis for the experts' opinions. The first such study involved workers at an Italian capacitor plant who had been exposed to PCBs. Bertazzi, Riboldi, Pesatori, Radice, & Zocchetti, Cancer Mortality of Capacitor Manufacturing Workers, 11 American Journal of Industrial Medicine 165 (1987). The authors noted that lung cancer deaths among ex-employees at the plant were higher than might have been expected, but concluded that "there were apparently no grounds for associating lung cancer deaths (although increased above expectations) and exposure in the plant." *Id.,* at 172. Given that Bertazzi et al. were unwilling to say that PCB exposure had caused cancer among the workers they examined, their study did not support the experts' conclusion that **Joiner's** exposure to PCB's caused his cancer.

The second study followed employees who had worked at Monsanto's PCB production plant. J. Zack & D. Musch, Mortality ****519** of PCB Workers at the Monsanto Plant in Sauget, Illinois (Dec. 14, 1979)(unpublished report), 3 Record, Doc. No. 11. The authors of this study found that the incidence of lung cancer deaths among these workers was somewhat higher than would ordinarily be expected. The increase, however, was not statistically significant and the authors of the study did not suggest a link between the increase in lung cancer deaths and the exposure to PCB's.

The third and fourth studies were likewise of no help. The third involved workers at a Norwegian cable manufacturing company who had been exposed to mineral oil. Ronneberg, Andersen, & Skyberg, Mortality and Incidence of Cancer Among Oil-Exposed Workers in a Norwegian Cable Manufacturing Company, 45 British Journal of Industrial Medicine 595 (1988). A statistically significant increase in lung cancer deaths had been observed in these workers. The study, however, (1) made no mention of PCB's and (2) was expressly limited to the type of mineral oil involved in that study, and thus did not support these experts' opinions. The fourth and final study involved a PCB-exposed group in Japan that had seen a statistically significant increase in lung cancer deaths. Kuratsune, Nakamura, Ikeda, & Hirohata, Analysis of Deaths Seen Among Patients with Yusho—A Preliminary Report, 16 Chemosphere, Nos. 8/9, p. 2085 (1987). The subjects of this study, however, had been exposed to numerous potential carcinogens, including toxic rice oil that they had ingested.

Respondent points to *Daubert 's* language that the "focus, of course, must be solely on principles and methodology, not on the conclusions that they generate." 509 U.S., at 595, 113 S.Ct., at 2797. He claims that because the District Court's disagreement was with the conclusion that the experts drew from the studies, the District Court committed legal error and was properly reversed by the Court of Appeals. But conclusions and methodology are not entirely distinct from one another. Trained experts commonly extrapolate from existing data. But nothing in either *Daubert* or the Federal Rules of Evidence requires a district court to admit opinion evidence that is connected to existing data only by the *ipse dixit* of the expert. A court may conclude that there is simply too great an analytical gap between the data and the opinion proffered. See *Turpin v. Merrell Dow Pharmaceuticals, Inc.,* 959 F.2d 1349, 1360 (C.A.6), cert. denied, 506 U.S. 826, 113 S.Ct. 84, 121 L.Ed.2d 47 (1992). That is what the District Court did here, and we hold that it did not abuse its discretion in so doing.

We hold, therefore, that abuse of discretion is the proper standard by which to review a district court's decision to admit or exclude scientific evidence. We further hold that, because it was within the District Court's discretion to conclude that the studies upon which the experts relied were not sufficient, whether individually or in combination, to support their conclusions that **Joiner's** exposure to PCB's contributed to his cancer, the District Court did not abuse its discretion in excluding their testimony. These conclusions, however, do not dispose of this entire case.

Respondent's original contention was that his exposure to PCB's, furans, and dioxins contributed to his cancer. The District Court ruled that there was a genuine issue of material fact as to whether **Joiner** had been exposed to PCB's, but concluded that there was no genuine issue as to whether he had been exposed to furans and dioxins. The District Court accordingly never explicitly considered if there was admissible evidence on the question whether **Joiner's** alleged exposure to furans and dioxins contributed to his cancer. The Court of Appeals reversed the District Court's conclusion that there had been no exposure to furans and dioxins. Petitioners did not challenge this determination in their petition to this Court. Whether **Joiner** was exposed to furans and dioxins, and whether if there was such exposure, the opinions of **Joiner's** experts would then be admissible, remain open questions. We accordingly reverse the judgment of the Court of Appeals and remand this case for proceedings consistent with this opinion.

It is so ordered.

DISCUSSION PROBLEMS 9-1

1. To what extent did the subject matter of this lawsuit drive the court's interpretation of the standard for appellate review?

2. Compare the reasoning of Justice Stevens to that of Justice Rehnquist? Which do you find more persuasive? Why?

3. Would it make more sense to require to courts to appoint experts that are neutral? Why or why not? What might be some of the consequences of that approach?

To sum up the Joiner opinion, the role of the judge as a "gatekeeper" leads to a determination of whether the evidence is based on a methodology that is "scientific," and therefore reliable. The judgment is made before the evidence is admitted, and entails "a preliminary assessment of whether the reasoning or methodology is scientifically valid." The trial court is given broad discretion in admitting expert testimony; rulings are tested only for abuse of discretion. General Electric Co. v. Joiner, 522 U.S. 136 (1997).

Daubert Factors:

Whether the theory or technique can be and has been tested;

Whether the theory or technique has been subjected to peer review and publication;

Whether the known or potential rate of error is acceptable;

Whether the theory or technique enjoys widespread acceptance.

THE U.S. SUPREME COURT SPEAKS: Nonscientific Experts

119 S.Ct. 1167
Supreme Court of the United States
KUMHO TIRE COMPANY, LTD., et al., Petitioners,
v.
Patrick CARMICHAEL, etc., et al.
No. 97–1709. Argued Dec. 7, 1998. Decided March 23, 1999.

Justice <u>BREYER</u> delivered the opinion of the Court.

In _Daubert v. Merrell Dow Pharmaceuticals, Inc.,_ 509 U.S. 579, 113 S.Ct. 2786, 125 L.Ed.2d 469 (1993), this Court focused upon the admissibility of scientific expert testimony. It pointed out that such testimony is admissible only if it is both relevant and reliable. And it held that the Federal Rules of Evidence "assign to the trial judge the task of ensuring that an expert's testimony both rests on a reliable foundation and is relevant to the task at hand." _Id., at 597, 113 S.Ct. 2786._ The Court also discussed certain more specific factors, such as testing, peer review, error rates, and "acceptability" in the relevant scientific community, some or all of which might prove helpful in determining the reliability of a particular scientific "theory or technique." _Id., at 593–594, 113 S.Ct. 2786._

This case requires us to decide how _Daubert_ applies to the testimony of engineers and other experts who are not scientists. We conclude that _Daubert's_ general holding—setting forth the trial judge's general "gatekeeping" obligation—applies not only to testimony based on "scientific" knowledge, but also to testimony based on "technical" and "other specialized" knowledge. See <u>Fed. Rule Evid. 702.</u> We also conclude that a trial court _may_ consider one or more of the more specific factors that _Daubert_ mentioned when doing so will help determine that testimony's reliability. But, as the Court stated in _Daubert,_ the test of reliability is "flexible," and <u>*Daubert's*</u> list of specific factors neither necessarily nor exclusively applies to all experts or in every case. Rather, the law grants a district court the same broad latitude when it decides *how* to determine reliability as it enjoys in respect to its ultimate reliability determination. See <u>*General Electric Co. v. Joiner*, 522 U.S. 136, 143, 118 S.Ct. 512, 139 L.Ed.2d 508 (1997)</u> (courts of appeals are to apply "abuse of discretion" standard when reviewing district court's reliability determination). Applying these standards, we determine that the District Court's decision in this case—not to admit certain expert testimony—was within its discretion and therefore lawful.

I

On July 6, 1993, the right rear **tire** of a minivan driven by Patrick Carmichael blew out. In the accident that followed, one of the passengers died, and others were severely injured. In October 1993, the Carmichaels brought this diversity suit against the **tire's** maker and its distributor, whom we refer to collectively as **Kumho Tire**, claiming that the **tire** was defective. The plaintiffs rested their case in significant part upon deposition testimony provided by an expert in **tire** failure analysis, Dennis Carlson, Jr., who intended to testify in support of their conclusion.

Carlson's depositions relied upon certain features of **tire** technology that are not in dispute. A steel-belted radial **tire** like the Carmichaels' is made up of a "carcass" containing many layers of flexible cords, called "plies," along which (between the cords and the outer tread) are laid steel strips called "belts." Steel wire loops, called "beads," hold the cords together at the plies' bottom edges. An outer layer, called the "tread," encases the carcass, and the entire **tire** is bound together in rubber, through the application of heat and various chemicals. See generally, *e.g.,* J. Dixon, **Tires**, Suspension and Handling 68–72 (2d ed.1996). The bead of the **tire** sits upon a "bead seat," which is part of the wheel assembly. That assembly contains a "rim flange," which extends over the bead and rests against the side of the 143 ***143* tire**. See M. Mavrigian, Performance Wheels & **Tires** 81, 83 (1998) (illustrations).

Carlson's testimony also accepted certain background facts about the **tire** in question. He assumed that before the blowout the **tire** had traveled far. (The **tire** was made in 1988 and had been installed some time before the Carmichaels bought the used minivan in March 1993; the Carmichaels had driven the van approximately 7,000 additional miles in the two months they had owned it.) Carlson noted that the **tire's** tread depth, which was $^{11}/_{32}$ of an inch when new, App. 242, had been worn down to depths that ranged from $^{3}/_{32}$ of an inch along some parts of the **tire**, to nothing at all along others. *Id.,* at 287. He conceded that the **tire** tread had at least two punctures which had been inadequately repaired. *Id.,* at 258–261, 322.

Despite the **tire's** age and history, Carlson concluded that a defect in its manufacture or design caused the blowout. He rested this conclusion in part upon three premises which, for present purposes, we must assume are not in dispute: First, a **tire's** carcass should stay bound to the inner side of the tread for a significant period of time after its tread depth has worn away. *Id.,* at 208–209. Second, the tread of the **tire** at issue had separated from its inner steel-belted carcass prior to the accident. *Id.,* at 336. Third, this "separation" caused the blowout. *Ibid.*

Carlson's conclusion that a defect caused the separation, however, rested upon certain other propositions, several of which the defendants strongly dispute. First, Carlson said that if a separation is *not* caused by a certain kind of **tire** misuse called "overdeflection" (which consists of underinflating the **tire** or causing it to carry too much weight, thereby generating heat that can undo the chemical tread/carcass bond), then, ordinarily, its cause is a **tire** defect. *Id.,* at 193–195, 277–278. Second, he said that if a

tire has been subject to sufficient overdeflection to cause a separation, it should reveal certain physical symptoms. These symptoms include (a) tread wear on the **tire's** shoulder that is greater than the tread wear along the **tire's** center, *id.*, at 211; (b) signs of a "bead groove," where the beads have been pushed too hard against the bead seat on the inside of the **tire's** rim, *id.*, at 196–197; (c) sidewalls of the **tire** with physical signs of deterioration, such as discoloration, *id.*, at 212; and/or (d) marks on the **tire's** rim flange, *id.*, at 219–220. Third, Carlson said that where he does not find *at least two* of the four physical signs just mentioned (and presumably where there is no reason to suspect a less common cause of separation), he concludes that a manufacturing or design defect caused the separation. *Id.*, at 223–224.

Carlson added that he had inspected the **tire** in question. He conceded that the **tire** to a limited degree showed greater wear on the shoulder than in the center, some signs of "bead groove," some discoloration, a few marks on the rim flange, and inadequately filled puncture holes (which can also cause heat that might lead to separation). *Id.*, at 256–257, 258–261, 277, 303–304, 308. But, in each instance, he testified that the symptoms were not significant, and he explained why he believed that they did not reveal overdeflection. For example, the extra shoulder wear, he said, appeared primarily on one shoulder, whereas an overdeflected **tire** would reveal equally abnormal wear on both shoulders. *Id.*, at 277. Carlson concluded that the **tire** did not bear at least two of the four overdeflection symptoms, nor was there any less obvious cause of separation; and since neither overdeflection nor the punctures caused the blowout, a defect must have done so.

Kumho Tire moved the District Court to exclude Carlson's testimony on the ground that his methodology failed <u>Rule 702</u>'s reliability requirement. The court agreed with **Kumho** that it should act as a *Daubert*-type reliability "gatekeeper," even though one might consider Carlson's testimony as "technical," rather than "scientific." See *Carmichael v. Samyang Tires, Inc.*, 923 F.Supp. 1514, 1521–1522 (S.D.Ala.1996). The court then examined Carlson's methodology in light of the reliability-related factors that *Daubert* mentioned, such as a theory's testability, whether it "has been a subject of peer review or publication," the "known or potential rate of error," and the "degree of acceptance ... within the relevant scientific community." <u>923 F.Supp., at 1520</u> (citing *Daubert, 509 <u>U.S., at 589–595, 113 S.Ct. 2786).</u>* The District Court found that all those factors argued against the reliability of Carlson's methods, and it granted the motion to exclude the testimony (as well as the defendants' accompanying motion for summary judgment).

The plaintiffs, arguing that the court's application of the *Daubert* factors was too "inflexible," asked for reconsideration. And the court granted that motion. *Carmichael v. Samyang Tires, Inc.*, Civ. Action No. 93–0860–CB–S (S.D.Ala., June 5, 1996), App. to Pet. for Cert. 1c. After reconsidering the matter, the court agreed with the plaintiffs that *Daubert* should be applied flexibly, that its four factors were simply illustrative, and that other factors could argue in favor of admissibility. It conceded that there may be widespread acceptance of a "visual-inspection method" for some relevant purposes. But the court found insufficient indications of the reliability of

"the component of Carlson's **tire** failure analysis which most concerned the Court, namely, the methodology employed by the expert in analyzing the data obtained in the visual inspection, and the scientific basis, if any, for such an analysis." *Id.*, at 6c.

It consequently affirmed its earlier order declaring Carlson's testimony inadmissible and granting the defendants' motion for summary judgment.

The Eleventh Circuit reversed. See *Carmichael v. Samyang Tire, Inc.*, 131 F.3d 1433 (1997). It "review[ed] ... *de novo* " the "district court's legal decision to apply *Daubert.*" *Id., at 1435.* It noted that "the Supreme Court in *Daubert* explicitly limited its holding to cover only the 'scientific context,' " adding that "a *Daubert* analysis" applies only where an expert relies "on the application of scientific principles," rather than "on skill- or experience-based observation." *Id., at 1435–1436.* It concluded that Carlson's testimony, which it viewed as relying on experience, "falls outside the scope of *Daubert,*" that "the district court erred as a matter of law by applying *Daubert* in this case," and that the case must be remanded for further (non-*Daubert*-type) consideration under Rule 702. 131 F. 3d, at 1436.

Kumho Tire petitioned for certiorari, asking us to determine whether a trial court "may" consider *Daubert's* specific "factors" when determining the "admissibility of an engineering expert's testimony." Pet. for Cert. i. We granted certiorari in light of uncertainty among the lower courts about whether, or how, *Daubert* applies to expert testimony that might be characterized as based not upon "scientific" knowledge, but rather upon "technical" or "other specialized" *147* knowledge. Fed. Rule Evid. 702; compare, *e.g., Watkins v. Telsmith, Inc.,* 121 F.3d 984, 990–991 (C.A.5 1997), with, *e.g., Compton v. Subaru of America, Inc.,* 82 F.3d 1513, 1518–1519 (C.A.10), cert. denied, 519 U.S. 1042, 117 S.Ct. 611, 136 L.Ed.2d 536 (1996).

II

A

In *Daubert,* this Court held that Federal Rule of Evidence 702 imposes a special obligation upon a trial judge to "ensure that any and all scientific testimony ... is not only relevant, but reliable." 509 U.S., at 589, 113 S.Ct. 2786. The initial question before us is whether this basic gatekeeping obligation applies only to "scientific" testimony or to all expert testimony. We, like the parties, believe that it applies to all expert testimony. See Brief for Petitioners 19; Brief for Respondents 17.

For one thing, Rule 702 itself says:

"If scientific, technical, or other specialized knowledge will assist the trier of fact to understand the evidence or to determine a fact in issue, a witness qualified as an expert by knowledge, skill, experience, training, or education, may testify thereto in the form of an opinion or otherwise."

This language makes no relevant distinction between "scientific" knowledge and "technical" or "other specialized" knowledge. It makes clear that any such knowledge might become the subject of expert testimony. In *Daubert,* the Court specified that it is the Rule's word "knowledge," not the words (like "scientific") that modify that word, that "establishes a standard of evidentiary reliability." 509 U.S., at 589–590, 113 S.Ct. 2786. Hence, as a matter of language, the Rule applies its reliability standard to all "scientific," "technical," or "other specialized" matters within its scope. We concede that the Court in *Daubert* referred only to "scientific" knowledge. But as the Court there said, it referred to "scientific" testimony "because that [wa]s the nature of the expertise" at issue. *Id., at 590, n. 8, 113 S.Ct. 2786.*

Neither is the evidentiary rationale that underlay the Court's basic *Daubert* "gatekeeping" determination limited to "scientific" knowledge. *Daubert* pointed out that Federal Rules 702 and 703 grant expert witnesses testimonial latitude unavailable to other witnesses on the "assumption that the expert's opinion will have a reliable basis in the knowledge and experience of his discipline." *Id., at 592, 113 S.Ct. 2786* (pointing out that experts may testify to opinions, including those that are not based on firsthand knowledge or observation). The Rules grant that latitude to all experts, not just to "scientific" ones.

Finally, it would prove difficult, if not impossible, for judges to administer evidentiary rules under which a gatekeeping obligation depended upon a distinction between "scientific" knowledge and "technical" or "other specialized" knowledge. There is no clear line that divides the one from the others. Disciplines such as engineering rest upon scientific knowledge. Pure scientific theory itself may depend for its development upon observation and properly engineered machinery. And conceptual efforts to distinguish the two are unlikely to produce clear legal lines capable of application in particular cases. Cf. Brief for National Academy of Engineering as *Amicus Curiae* 9 (scientist seeks to understand nature while the engineer seeks nature's modification); Brief for Rubber Manufacturers Association as *Amicus Curiae* 14–16 (engineering, as an " 'applied science,' " relies on "scientific reasoning and methodology"); Brief for John Allen et al. as *Amici Curiae* 6 (engineering relies upon "scientific knowledge and methods").

Neither is there a convincing need to make such distinctions. Experts of all kinds tie observations to conclusions through the use of what Judge Learned Hand called "general truths derived from ... specialized experience." Hand, Historical and Practical Considerations Regarding Expert Testimony, <u>15 Harv. L.Rev. 40, 54 (1901)</u>. And whether the specific expert testimony focuses upon specialized observations, the specialized translation of those observations into theory, a specialized theory itself, or the application of such a theory in a particular case, the expert's testimony often will rest "upon an experience confessedly foreign in kind to [the jury's] own." *Ibid.* The trial judge's effort to assure that the specialized testimony is reliable and relevant can help the jury evaluate that foreign experience, whether the testimony reflects scientific, technical, or other specialized knowledge.

We conclude that <u>*Daubert's*</u> general principles apply to the expert matters described in <u>Rule 702</u>. The Rule, in respect to all such matters, "establishes a standard of evidentiary reliability." <u>509 U.S., at 590, 113 S.Ct. 2786.</u> It "requires a valid ... connection to the pertinent inquiry as a precondition to admissibility." <u>*Id.,* at 592, 113 S.Ct. 2786.</u> And where such testimony's factual basis, data, principles, methods, or their application are called sufficiently into question, see Part III, *infra,* the trial judge must determine whether the testimony has "a reliable basis in the knowledge and experience of [the relevant] discipline." <u>509 U.S., at 592, 113 S.Ct. 2786.</u>

B

Petitioners ask more specifically whether a trial judge determining the "admissibility of an engineering expert's testimony" *may* consider several more specific factors that *Daubert* said might "bear on" a judge's gatekeeping determination. Brief for Petitioners i. These factors include:

—Whether a "theory or technique ... can be (and has been) tested";

—Whether it "has been subjected to peer review and publication";

—Whether, in respect to a particular technique, there is a high "known or potential rate of error" and whether there are "standards controlling the technique's operation"; and

Whether the theory or technique enjoys " 'general acceptance' " within a " 'relevant scientific community.' " <u>509 U.S., at 592–594, 113 S.Ct. 2786.</u>

Emphasizing the word "may" in the question, we answer that question yes.

Engineering testimony rests upon scientific foundations, the reliability of which will be at issue in some cases. See, *e.g.,* Brief for Stephen N. Bobo et al. as *Amici Curiae* 23 (stressing the scientific bases of engineering disciplines). In other cases, the relevant reliability concerns may focus upon personal knowledge or experience. As the Solicitor General points out, there are many different kinds of experts, and many different kinds of expertise. See Brief for United States as *Amicus Curiae* 18–19, and n. 5 (citing cases involving experts in drug terms, handwriting analysis, criminal *modus operandi,* land valuation, agricultural practices, railroad procedures, attorney's fee valuation, and others). Our emphasis on the word "may" thus reflects *Daubert's* description of the Rule 702 inquiry as "a flexible one." 509 U.S., at 594, 113 S.Ct. 2786. *Daubert* makes clear that the factors it mentions do *not* constitute a "definitive checklist or test." *Id.,* at 593, 113 S.Ct. 2786. And *Daubert* adds that the gatekeeping inquiry must be " 'tied to the facts' " of a particular "case." *Id.,* at 591, 113 S.Ct. 2786 (quoting *United States v. Downing, 753 F.2d 1224, 1242 (C.A.3 1985)*). We agree with the Solicitor General that "[t]he factors identified in *Daubert* may or may not be pertinent in assessing reliability, depending on the nature of the issue, the expert's particular expertise, and the subject of his testimony." Brief for United States as *Amicus Curiae* 19. The conclusion, in our view, is that we can neither rule out, nor rule in, for all cases and for all time the applicability of the factors mentioned in *Daubert,* nor can we now do so for subsets of cases categorized by category of expert or by kind of evidence. Too much depends upon the particular circumstances of the particular case at issue.

Daubert itself is not to the contrary. It made clear that its list of factors was meant to be helpful, not definitive. Indeed, those factors do not all necessarily apply even in every instance in which the reliability of scientific testimony is challenged. It might not be surprising in a particular case, for example, that a claim made by a scientific witness has never been the subject of peer review, for the particular application at issue may never previously have interested any scientist. Nor, on the other hand, does the presence of *Daubert's* general acceptance factor help show that an expert's testimony is reliable where the discipline itself lacks reliability, as, for example, do theories grounded in any so-called generally accepted principles of astrology or necromancy.

At the same time, and contrary to the Court of Appeals' view, some of *Daubert's* questions can help to evaluate the reliability even of experience-based testimony. In certain cases, it will be appropriate for the trial judge to ask, for example, how often an engineering expert's experience-based methodology has produced erroneous results, or whether such a method is generally accepted in the relevant engineering community. Likewise, it will at times be useful to ask even of a witness whose expertise is based purely on experience, say, a perfume tester able to distinguish among 140 odors at a sniff, whether his preparation is of a kind that others in the field would recognize as acceptable.

We must therefore disagree with the Eleventh Circuit's holding that a trial judge may ask questions of the sort *Daubert* mentioned only where an expert "relies on the application of scientific principles," but not where an expert relies "on skill- or experience-based observation." 131 F.3d, at 1435. We do not believe that Rule 702 creates a schematism that segregates expertise by type while mapping certain kinds of questions to certain kinds of experts. Life and the legal cases that it generates are too complex to warrant so definitive a match.

To say this is not to deny the importance of *Daubert's* gatekeeping requirement. The objective of that requirement is to ensure the reliability and relevancy of expert testimony. It is to make certain that an expert, whether basing testimony upon professional studies or personal experience, employs in the courtroom the same level of intellectual rigor that characterizes the practice of an expert in the relevant field. Nor do we deny that, as stated in *Daubert,* the particular questions that it mentioned will often be appropriate for use in determining the reliability of challenged expert testimony. Rather, we conclude that the trial judge must have considerable leeway in deciding in a particular case how to go about determining whether particular expert testimony is reliable. That is to say, a trial court should consider the specific factors identified in *Daubert* where they are reasonable measures of the reliability of expert testimony.

The trial court must have the same kind of latitude in deciding *how* to test an expert's reliability, and to decide whether or when special briefing or other proceedings are needed to investigate reliability, as it enjoys when it decides *whether or not* that expert's relevant testimony is reliable. Our opinion in *Joiner* makes clear that a court of appeals is to apply an abuse-of-discretion standard when it "review[s] a trial court's decision to admit or exclude expert testimony." 522 U.S., at 138–139, 118 S.Ct. 512. That standard applies as much to the trial court's decisions about how to determine reliability as to its ultimate conclusion. Otherwise, the trial judge would lack the discretionary authority needed both to avoid unnecessary "reliability" proceedings in ordinary cases where the reliability of an expert's methods is properly taken for granted, and to require appropriate proceedings in the less usual or more complex cases where cause for questioning the expert's reliability arises. Indeed, the Rules seek to avoid "unjustifiable expense and delay" as part of their search for "truth" and the "jus[t] determin[ation]" of proceedings. Fed. Rule Evid. 102. Thus, whether *Daubert's* specific factors are, or are not, reasonable measures of reliability in a particular case is a matter that the law grants the trial judge broad latitude to determine. See *Joiner, supra,* at 143, 118 S.Ct. 512. And the Eleventh Circuit erred insofar as it held to the contrary.

III

We further explain the way in which a trial judge "may" consider *Daubert's* factors by applying these considerations to the case at hand, a matter that has been briefed exhaustively by the parties and their 19 *amici.* The District Court did not doubt Carlson's qualifications, which included a masters degree in mechanical engineering, 10 years' work at Michelin America, Inc., and testimony as a **tire** failure consultant in other tort cases. Rather, it excluded the testimony because, despite those qualifications, it initially doubted, and then found unreliable, "the methodology employed by the expert in analyzing the data obtained in the visual inspection, and the scientific basis, if any, for such an analysis." Civ. Action No. 93–0860–CB–S (S.D.Ala., June 5, 1996), App. to Pet. for Cert. 6c. After examining the transcript in "some detail," 923 F.Supp., at 1518–1519, n. 4, and after considering respondents' defense of Carlson's methodology, the District Court determined that Carlson's testimony was not reliable. It fell outside the range where experts might reasonably differ, and where the jury must decide among the conflicting views of different experts, even though the evidence is "shaky." *Daubert,* 509 U.S., at 596, 113 S.Ct. 2786. In our view, the doubts that triggered the District Court's initial inquiry here were reasonable, as was the court's ultimate conclusion.

For one thing, and contrary to respondents' suggestion, the specific issue before the court was not the reasonableness *in general* of a **tire** expert's use of a visual and tactile inspection to determine whether overdeflection had caused the **tire's** tread to separate from its steel-belted carcass. Rather, it was the reasonableness of using such an approach, along with Carlson's particular method of analyzing the data thereby obtained, to draw a conclusion regarding *the particular matter to which the expert testimony was directly relevant.* That matter concerned the likelihood that a defect in the **tire** at issue caused its tread to separate from its carcass. The **tire** in question, the expert conceded, had traveled far enough so that some of the tread had been worn bald; it should have been taken out of service; it had been repaired (inadequately) for punctures; and it bore some of the very marks that the expert said indicated, not a defect, but abuse through overdeflection. See *supra,* at 1172; App. 293–294. The relevant issue was whether the expert could reliably determine the cause of *this* **tire's** separation.

Nor was the basis for Carlson's conclusion simply the general theory that, in the absence of evidence of abuse, a defect will normally have caused a **tire's** separation. Rather, the expert employed a more specific theory to establish the existence (or absence) of such abuse. Carlson testified precisely that in the absence of *at least two* of four signs of abuse (proportionately greater tread wear on the shoulder; signs of grooves caused by the beads; discolored sidewalls; marks on the rim flange), he concludes that a defect caused the separation. And his analysis depended upon acceptance of a further implicit proposition, namely, that his visual and tactile inspection could determine that the **tire** before him had not been abused despite some evidence of the presence of the very signs for which he looked (and two punctures).

For another thing, the transcripts of Carlson's depositions support both the trial court's initial uncertainty and its final conclusion. Those transcripts cast considerable doubt upon the reliability of both the explicit theory (about the need for two signs of abuse) and the implicit proposition (about the significance of visual inspection in this case). Among other things, the expert could not say whether the **tire** had traveled more than 10, or 20, or 30, or 40, or 50 thousand miles, adding that 6,000 miles was "about how far" he could "say with any certainty." *Id.,* at 265. The court could reasonably have wondered about the reliability of a method of visual and tactile inspection sufficiently precise to ascertain with some certainty the abuse-related significance of minute shoulder/center relative tread wear differences, but insufficiently precise to tell "with any certainty" from the tread wear whether a **tire** had traveled less than 10,000 or more than 50,000 miles. And these concerns might have been augmented by Carlson's repeated reliance on the "subjective[ness]" of his mode of analysis in response to questions seeking specific information regarding how he could differentiate between a **tire** that actually had been overdeflected and a **tire** that merely looked as though it had been. *Id.,* at 222, 224–225, 285–286. They would have been further augmented by the fact that Carlson said he had inspected the **tire** itself for the first time the morning of his first deposition, and then only for a few hours. (His initial conclusions were based on photographs.) *Id.,* at 180.

Moreover, prior to his first deposition, Carlson had issued a signed report in which he concluded that the **tire** had "not been ... overloaded or underinflated," not because of the absence of "two of four" signs of abuse, but simply because "the rim flange impressions ... were normal." *Id.,* at 335–336. That report also said that the "tread depth remaining was $^3/_{32}$ inch," *id.,* at 336, though the opposing expert's (apparently undisputed) measurements indicate that the tread depth taken at various positions around the **tire** actually ranged from $^5/_{32}$ of an inch to $^4/_{32}$ of an inch, with the **tire** apparently showing greater wear along *both* shoulders than along the center, *id.,* at 432–433.

Further, in respect to one sign of abuse, bead grooving, the expert seemed to deny the sufficiency of his own simple visual-inspection methodology. He testified that most **tires** have some bead groove pattern, that where there is reason to suspect an abnormal bead groove he would ideally "look at a lot of [similar] **tires**" to know the grooving's significance, and that he had not looked at many **tires** similar to the one at issue. *Id.,* at 212–213, 214, 217.

Finally, the court, after looking for a defense of Carlson's methodology as applied in these circumstances, found no convincing defense. Rather, it found (1) that "none" of the *Daubert* factors, including that of "general acceptance" in the relevant expert community, indicated that Carlson's testimony was reliable, 923 F.Supp., at 1521; (2) that its own analysis "revealed no countervailing factors operating in favor of admissibility which could outweigh those identified in *Daubert,*" App. to Pet. for Cert. 4c; and (3) that the "parties identified no such factors in their briefs," *ibid.* For these three reasons *taken together,* it concluded that Carlson's testimony was unreliable.

Respondents now argue to us, as they did to the District Court, that a method of **tire** failure analysis that employs a visual/tactile inspection is a reliable method, and they point both to its use by other experts and to Carlson's long experience working for

Michelin as sufficient indication that that is so. But no one denies that an expert might draw a conclusion from a set of observations based on extensive and specialized experience. Nor does anyone deny that, as a general matter, **tire** abuse may often be identified by qualified experts through visual or tactile inspection of the **tire**. See Affidavit of H.R. Baumgardner 1–2, cited in Brief for National Academy of Forensic Engineers as *Amicus Curiae* 16 (**Tire** engineers rely on visual examination and process of elimination to analyze experimental test **tires**). As we said before, *supra,* at 1977, the question before the trial court was specific, not general. The trial court had to decide whether this particular expert had sufficient specialized knowledge to assist the jurors "in deciding the particular issues in the case." 4 J. McLaughlin, Weinstein's Federal Evidence ¶ 702.05[1], p. 702–33 (2d ed.1998); see also Advisory Committee's Note on Proposed Fed. Rule Evid. 702, Preliminary Draft of Proposed Amendments to the Federal Rules of Civil Procedure and Evidence: Request for Comment 126 (1998) (stressing that district courts must "scrutinize" whether the "principles and methods" employed by an expert "have been properly applied to the facts of the case").

The particular issue in this case concerned the use of Carlson's two-factor test and his related use of visual/tactile inspection to draw conclusions on the basis of what seemed small observational differences. We have found no indication in the record that other experts in the industry use Carlson's two-factor test or that **tire** experts such as Carlson normally make the very fine distinctions about, say, the symmetry of comparatively greater shoulder tread wear that were necessary, on Carlson's own theory, to support his conclusions. Nor, despite the prevalence of **tire** testing, does anyone refer to any articles or papers that validate Carlson's approach. Cf. Bobo, **Tire** Flaws and Separations, in Mechanics of Pneumatic **Tires** 636–637 (S. Clark ed.1981); C. Schnuth, R. Fuller, G. Follen, G. Gold, & J. Smith, Compression Grooving and Rim Flange Abrasion as Indicators of Over–Deflected Operating Conditions in **Tires**, presented to Rubber Division of the American Chemical Society, Oct. 21–24, 1997; J. Walter & R. Kiminecz, Bead Contact Pressure Measurements at the **Tire**–Rim Interface, presented to the Society of Automotive Engineers, Inc., Feb. 24–28, 1975. Indeed, no one has argued that Carlson himself, were he still working for Michelin, would have concluded in a report to his employer that a similar **tire** was similarly defective on grounds identical to those upon which he rested his conclusion here. Of course, Carlson himself claimed that his method was accurate, but, as we pointed out in *Joiner,* "nothing in either *Daubert* or the Federal Rules of Evidence requires a district court to admit opinion evidence that is connected to existing data only by the *ipse dixit* of the expert." 522 U.S., at 146, 118 S.Ct. 512.

Respondents additionally argue that the District Court too rigidly applied *Daubert's* criteria. They read its opinion to hold that a failure to satisfy any one of those criteria automatically renders expert testimony inadmissible. The District Court's initial opinion might have been vulnerable to a form of this argument. There, the court, after rejecting respondents' claim that Carlson's testimony was "exempted from *Daubert*-style scrutiny" because it was "technical analysis" rather than "scientific evidence," simply added that "none of the four admissibility criteria outlined by the *Daubert* court are satisfied." 923 F.Supp., at 1521. Subsequently, however, the court granted respondents' motion for reconsideration. It then explicitly recognized that the relevant reliability inquiry "should be 'flexible,' " that its " 'overarching subject [should be] ... validity' and reliability," and that "*Daubert* was intended neither to be exhaustive nor to apply in every case." App. to Pet. for Cert. 4c (quoting *Daubert, 509 U.S., at 594–595, 113 S.Ct. 2786).* And the court ultimately based its decision upon Carlson's failure to satisfy either *Daubert's* factors *or any other* set of reasonable reliability criteria. In light of the record as developed by the parties, that conclusion was within the District Court's lawful discretion.

In sum, Rule 702 grants the district judge the discretionary authority, reviewable for its abuse, to determine reliability in light of the particular facts and circumstances of the particular case. The District Court did not abuse its discretionary authority in this case. Hence, the judgment of the Court of Appeals is *Reversed.*

DISCUSSION PROBLEMS 9-2

1. When you read *Kumho Tire* in conjunction with *Daubert* and *Joiner* what conclusions do you reach?

2. Why are these opinions so complex? Does the court appear to struggle with these issues? What is the focus?

3. How powerful are the gatekeeping functions of the trial court? Should the decision to admit or exclude expert testimony that can be case dispositive be reviewed merely for abuse of discretion? What test would you fashion? How would it work?

It is important to note that after *Daubert,* "helpfulness" alone will not guarantee admission of evidence because it does not guarantee "reliability." The Supreme Court resolved whether the judge's gatekeeping function and the *Daubert* factors apply to nonscientific evidence. In *Kumho Tire v. Carmichael*, 526 U.S. 137 (1999), the Court held that the trial judge's gatekeeping responsibility applies to *all types* of expert evidence. The Court also held that, to the extent the *Daubert* factors apply, they can be used to evaluate the reliability of this evidence. Finally, the Court ruled that factors other than those announced in *Daubert* can also be used to evaluate the reliability of nonscientific expert evidence.

EXAMPLES OF MATTERS FOR EXPERTS

The following examples are derived from actual cases where these issues concerning expert testimony have arisen; they are not all inclusive, but serve instead as potential examples. Advocates should focus on the *Daubert* factors when determining the validity of a proposed expert.

- **Child Abuse Accommodation Syndrome**. In a trial for child sex abuse crimes, evidence was received on how the victim exhibited "Child Sexual Abuse Accommodation Syndrome" (children change or recant their stories, delay or fail to report abuse, accommodate themselves to the abuse). While such evidence is controversial, it may be admitted where it explains the abused child's delay or recantation, as was the case here.

- **Drug Testing**. Defense claimed the lab's use of gas chromatography/tandem mass spectrometry to determine the existence of LSD in urine failed under *Daubert*. The appeals court hinted that there may be problems but reversed the case because the government failed to show that the 200 picograms per milliliter established by the agency adequately accounted for innocent ingestion.

- **Dysfunctional Family Profile Evidence**. It was an error to present expert testimony that defendant's family situation was ripe for child sexual abuse, purporting to present characteristics of a family that included a child sexual abuser, then pursued a deductive scheme of reasoning that families with the profile present an increased risk of child sexual abuse and that the defendant's family fit the profile.

- In another case, there was no abuse of discretion in allowing a government expert to testify concerning a dysfunctional family "profile" and whether the defendant's family displayed any of its characteristics. The testimony went to support credibility of daughter's accusations and to explain her admitted unusual behavior. Unlike the case above, evidence here was used to explain the behavior of the victim on the assumption she was abused by *someone*, not necessarily the accused. Using "profile' evidence to explain the counter-intuitive behavioral characteristics of sexual abuse victims was permissible.

- **Eyewitness Identification.** It is an abuse of discretion, though harmless, to limit testimony concerning the unreliability of eye witness identification by preventing testimony on the inverse relationship between confidence and accuracy in identifications and theories of memory transference and transposition. The judge excluded the testimony of defense expert in eyewitness identification on FRE 403 grounds. The Court said this per se denial was an abuse of discretion, but was harmless.

- **False Confessions.** A court held that the judge did not abuse his discretion in excluding the testimony of an expert in false confessions. The court reasoned that no witness could serve as a human lie detector, and in this case the evidence was unreliable because there was no correlation between the expert's studies and the accused in this case.

- **Hypnosis.** Hypnosis can be admissible if the judge finds that the use of hypnosis was reasonably likely to result in recall compatible in accuracy to normal human memory. *Rock v. Arkansas*, 483 U.S. 44 (1987). Proponent must show by clear and convincing evidence satisfaction of the following procedural safeguards: (1) the hypnosis was conducted by an independent, experienced hypnotist; (2) the hypnotist was not regularly employed by the parties; (3) the information revealed to the hypnotist was recorded; (4) a detailed statement must be obtained from the witness in advance; and (5) only the hypnotist and subject were present during session.

- **Psychological Autopsy.** No error in allowing forensic psychologist to testify about suicide profiles and that his "psychological autopsy" revealed it was unlikely the deceased committed suicide. Applying *Daubert* and *Kumho Tire* the court affirmed the trial judge's decision to exclude an expert's opinion that the accused was not an exhibitionist. The court noted that there was no body of scientific knowledge to support the expert's claim the Minnesota Multiphasic Personality Inventory could be used to conclude that an individual was not an exhibitionist and could not have committed a crime.

- **Rape Trauma Syndrome (RTS).** RTS is a subcategory of Post-Traumatic Stress Disorder in the Diagnostic and Statistical Manual of Mental Disorders, 4th Edition (DSM-IV). The psychiatric community recognizes the DSM-IV as valid and reliable. Evidence may assist the fact-finder by providing knowledge concerning victim's reaction to assault. RTS evidence could assist the trier of fact in determining the issue of consent. This would be particularly true where such members would likely have little or no experience with victims of rape. . . [The RTS evidence] serves as a helpful tool by providing the fact-finders with knowledge regarding a victim's psychological reactions to an alleged sexual assault.)

- RTS testimony to rebut an inference a victim's conduct was inconsistent with a claim of rape where she did not fight off the attacker, made inconsistent statements concerning the assault, did not make a fresh complaint, and recounted the incident in a calm and "unnatural" manner was impermissible testimony.

- A psychologist impermissibly expressed an opinion concerning a rape victim's credibility by discussing the performance of the victim on a "Rape Aftermath Symptoms Test," (RAST) and by stating that the victim did not fake or feign her condition. The expert thus became a "human lie detector." The RAST failed to meet the requirements for admissibility of scientific testimony (lack of foundation). Despite lack of defense objection, the court found plain error and sets aside findings and sentence.

- **Sleep Disorders**. Defendant was charged with sodomizing another male while the victim was asleep. Defense wanted to admit the testimony of two experts to testify about the victim's alleged sleep disorders. The appellate court affirmed excluding the testimony under *Daubert*, as the expert's methodologies were unreliable and not helpful because the victim had not been interviewed.

CONCLUSION

The Supreme Court case law in this area reinforced both the language and comments found in the expert witness section of the Federal Rules of Evidence. It also reiterated a standard of appellate review that places the responsibility for getting this right squarely on the shoulders of the appellate court. Let us move on now to our discussion of Hearsay.

Chapter 10: Hearsay-Can We Talk

THE FUNDAMENTALS

"Hearsay is an out-of-court statement offered to prove the truth of the matter asserted." The fundamental purpose of hearsay doctrine is to exclude from the fact-finder any prior out-of-court statements of a witness, offered for its truth, unless there are sufficient guarantees of trustworthiness for the truth of those statements. In order for the hearsay doctrine to apply, the statement in question must have been intended as an assertion. At the heart of the hearsay doctrine is the conviction that out-of-court statements are generally an inferior kind of proof. Usually this conviction is explained in terms of the risks that come with relying on the word or say-so of another person, and usually these are grouped in four categories.

Any prior out-of-court statement made by a declarant, offered for the truth of its contents is hearsay. A statement can be oral or written or even nonverbal conduct, as long as it is intended as an assertion.[40] When offered for the truth asserted within these out-of-court statements they are inadmissible unless they fall into an exclusion,[41] exemption or exception to the general hearsay rule. Most of the issues concerning hearsay at trial revolve around the purpose for the proffered out-of-court statement and the identification of an acceptable theory of admissibility. Attempts by counsel to offer the prior statement of a witness raise the possibility of a hearsay objection. Counsel must be prepared to articulate a non-hearsay reason that satisfies the requirements of the Federal Rules of Evidence making the statement admissible. The categories of admissibility include: exclusions and exemptions – statements not considered hearsay by operations of law; and exceptions – where the availability of the declarant is the key to admissibility of the statement. The following chart captures the categories of potential use for out-of-court statements.

All prior out-of-court statements offered for the truth of the matter asserted will be admissible as substantive evidence at trial if they fall under FRE 801(d), FRE 803 and FRE 804. By admitting the evidence substantively under the appropriate hearsay doctrine, it can be argued as evidence in closing arguments.

Is it an Assertion

FRE 801(c) defines hearsay using the word "statement." FRE 801(a) identifies "statement" to includes any oral or written "assertion" that the declarant "intend[s]" as an assertion. Unfortunately neither the text of the Rules, or the comments, define "assertion" or "intent," but if we read them in context, assertions are human verbal behavior where a person expresses and communicates ideas or information to others. Intent is present when, through the context of the statement, the purpose is to express and communicate. Because of the nature of trials, ideas or information are acts that show who did what, events establishing what happened at an accident or crime scene, or descriptive conditions—"objective facts."

---

[40] *See* FRE 801(a) – (c) in appendix I of this text.

[41] *See* FRE 801(d) in appendix I of this text.

Rule 801. Definitions That Apply to This Article; Exclusions from Hearsay

(a) Statement. "Statement" means a person's oral assertion, written assertion, or nonverbal conduct, if the person intended it as an assertion.

(b) Declarant. "Declarant" means the person who made the statement.

(c) Hearsay. "Hearsay" means a statement that:

(1) the declarant does not make while testifying at the current trial or hearing; and

(2) a party offers in evidence to prove the truth of the matter asserted in the statement.

Hearsay doctrine not only makes allowances for facts, they are also admitted to establish the declarant's intent or other mental state, scientific theories, or opinions as to fault. It would be a mistake to suppose that hearsay only reaches what we normally call "factual statements." Although statements are usually intended to express and communicate something, we are not concerned with whether the declarant reached or hoped to reach some other person. Think of the notes that we write to ourselves – they fall into this category.

Most words spoken or written by human beings are assertive. They are used to express and communicate ideas or information through the language, and the person who speaks or writes intends such communication. While the original drafters of FRE 801 thought that words are not always assertive. When words are found to not have an assertive purpose they are not considered statements for purposes of hearsay doctrine.

Courts sometimes apply a narrow definition to the term "assertion," excluding imperatives and questions not intended to assert information. Under this view the literal or plain meaning of words might mean that the words in question may not in fact be an assertion. For example, "the man tripped on the curb" would be an assertion but not "did he trip on the curb?" or "don't trip on the curb", since questions and imperatives do not, in normal use, make any strong claim as a matter of literal meaning. It is true that the term "assertion" sometimes embodies this narrow idea. Other commentators argue against this narrow interpretation of assertions, relying upon the historical common law in supporting a broader interpretation.

In either case, deciding that a question, a command, or a string of words is a "statement" does not necessarily mean it is hearsay. To make that determination, the court looks to whether the reason the statement was offered to prove can be determined from what is asserted. To make that decision, the court must look to the proponent's purpose, the speaker's intent, and even the broader factual context in which the statement was made.

"Statement" means not only verbal expressions, but also nonverbal expressive and communicative behavior if it was intended as a substitute for words. These wordless statements (like shaking the head no, or nodding the head yes) create the same concerns about hearsay as to any other ordinary verbal communication. The Rules are consistent with the one-line definition: When wordless behavior has expressive and communicative intent or purpose, it too is subject to the hearsay doctrine. In the language of FRE 801(a), it too is a "statement," for the term reaches "nonverbal conduct of a person" that is "intended" as an assertion.

Nodding the head means "yes," shaking it means "no," and shrugging the shoulders means "I don't know" or "nothing to be done." Others types are understood, but only in context: If a person standing at the base of the County Courthouse is asked "which way is north?" and she points toward the corner barbershop, her wordless statement means "north is that way." Still others involve gestures that can best be understood in a larger setting or prior conversations: A thumbs-up gesture could mean "I got the raise," or "you made a good play," or "we made it," or "let's do it," and conveys a positive, encouraging, or praising message. A hand cupped behind the ear may mean "please say it again," or "turn up the volume," or "I can't hear." All these wordless statements are hearsay when offered to prove what they assert.

Acts that are not common nonverbal cues are usually not "statements" for purposes of FRE 801 because the alleged declarant lacks the intent to express or communicate. Conduct that might have assertive intent, making it a statement, in which case it would be hearsay if offered to prove whatever the actor sought to express. In this setting, the burden is on the objecting party to prove that the actor had the requisite intent. It is clear from the comments to the rules that the court can make an initial determination under the Rules as to whether or not a "statement" was made for purposes of the hearsay doctrine.

IS IT HEARSAY?

The following case provides an excellent example to consider when statements are statements for purpose of hearsay and when they are not. As you read it, consider FRE 801 (a) – (c).

539 F.3d 552
United States Court of Appeals,
Sixth Circuit.
UNITED STATES of America, Plaintiff-Appellee,
v.
Joshshan **CHILDS** (07-1495); Jeremiah Japeth Sims (07-1597), Defendants-Appellants.

OPINION

KENNEDY, Circuit Judge.

We **AFFIRM** both defendants' convictions.

BACKGROUND

Immediately after midnight on August 5, 1996, sixteen-year-old Chrissy Satterfield was murdered while taking a shower at her grandmother's house in Benton Township, Michigan. Satterfield was shot multiple times by someone standing on an overturned garbage can outside of the bathroom window.

Chrissy's uncle, Elmer Satterfield, heard the gunshots and saw two men jumping the side fence and running from the residence. A neighbor also heard the gunshots and saw two unidentified young black males dressed in dark clothing running from the area. Police officers responding to the scene recovered identifiable fingerprints located on the outside window ledge of the bathroom.

The case remained dormant, with few leads, until late 2001. At that time, Doreen Dortch came forward and related that the day after the murder, she overheard a conversation between her nephew, Joshshan Childs, and Jeremiah Sims, in which they discussed their involvement in the murder of Chrissy Satterfield. Based on this new information, the FBI submitted the known prints of Childs and Sims to the crime lab for comparison against the prints recovered from the murder scene. This comparison resulted in a positive fingerprints match with Childs.

In the course of the ensuing investigation, investigators contacted Jackie Love, Childs' former girlfriend. Love testified that while at a pool party during the summer of 1996, her cousin, Carolyn Ross, asked her if she knew anyone who could kill someone for her. Both Childs and Sims were present. Love testified that she initially thought Ross was joking. Later, Childs asked her if Ross was serious about having a murder committed because he might know someone who would do it.

A few weeks later, Ross again approached Love and Childs. Ross was very upset over her husband's affair with Chrissy Satterfield. Ross asked both if they would kill her husband and Chrissy Satterfield in exchange for money. A price was agreed upon. Later, Love and Childs visited the restaurant where Satterfield worked so that Childs could see what Satterfield looked like.

Immediately after this discussion, Love and Childs moved to Atlanta, Georgia. Throughout the summer, Love and Childs traveled back to Benton Harbor, Michigan about every other week to visit friends and relatives and to pick up SSI checks for Love's children. On one of these trips in mid-July of 1996, Childs and Love conducted a surveillance of the Satterfield residence.

On August 3, 1996, Love, Childs, and her children checked into a motel in Benton Harbor. Childs met Sims at the motel that night, and Love saw Sims playing with a gun. Sims spent the night at the same motel. The following day, they all went to spend the day visiting relatives. Love testified that at some point later that night she had not seen Childs in awhile.

Sometime after midnight on August 5, 1996, Love testified that she heard sirens and saw an ambulance and fire truck racing by. One of her cousins, a sister of Carolyn Ross, informed her that Chrissy had been shot. About a half hour later, Childs returned dressed in black clothing and told Love that he needed to be with people.

Later that same day, Love and Childs checked out of the motel and met Ross at a clothing store Ross owned. Love testified that she learned on the drive back to Atlanta that Ross had given Childs a large sum of cash at the store.

After receiving payment, Childs drove himself and Love to a nearby apartment complex and picked up Sims. Tonia Childs, Defendant Child's sister, saw them and Sims remarked that "we done fucked somebody up." Defendants, along with Love and her children, then left Michigan together.

After they returned to Atlanta, Sims stayed with Childs and Love until he was arrested on August 16, 1996, during a traffic stop on an outstanding warrant. Childs later confided in Love that he murdered Chrissy Satterfield and provided specific details, including how he stood on a garbage can and shot her multiple times through the bathroom window.

Investigators also interviewed both Childs and Sims about the murder and they gave conflicting accounts. Based on the information gathered, on June 29, 2005, a federal grand jury returned a two-count indictment against Childs and Sims, charging them both with conspiracy to commit murder for hire resulting in the death of Chrissy Satterfield and the underlying offense of murder for hire. Because Sims' prior statements to both law enforcement officers and the federal grand jury inculpated both Childs and Sims, on November 9, 2006, the district court severed their trials due to confrontation concerns.

Childs was tried first. The government granted Sims use and derivative use immunity pursuant to 18 U.S.C. §§ 6002 and 6003 and sought to compel him to testify at Childs' trial. Sims opposed the motion to compel his testimony, but the district court rejected his arguments and entered a compulsion order on January 5, 2007. At trial, Sims took the stand as ordered, but provided trial testimony that was wholly contradictory to the statements he had previously given to law enforcement officers and before the grand jury. Excerpts of Sims' grand jury testimony were then entered into evidence.

Childs also testified on his own behalf at his trial. On the stand, Childs admitted that he lied to the law enforcement officers who interviewed him in jail about the Satterfield murder. He also admitted that following the interview he immediately attempted to contact Jackie Love through relatives to have her falsely deny that she and Childs were in Benton Harbor at the time of the homicide. Childs denied shooting Chrissy Satterfield.

On January 12, 2007, the jury convicted Defendant Joshshan Childs on both counts of the indictment.

On January 25, 2007, Carolyn Ross and Jeremiah Sims were named in a two-count superseding indictment, charging them both with conspiracy to commit murder for hire resulting in the death of Chrissy Satterfield and charging Ross only with the underlying substantive offense of murder for hire. Defendants' trials were also severed.

Sims did not testify at his own trial. Childs, however, voluntarily agreed, against the advice of counsel for both Sims and Childs, to testify on behalf of Sims. On the stand, Childs admitted that he shot and killed Chrissy Satterfield, but claimed that no one was with him when he committed the murder. He testified that he stood on a trash can and shot her through the bathroom window. Childs also claimed that Jackie Love drove him to the location and waited in the car while he committed the murder.

On cross-examination, Childs admitted that he lied repeatedly, including under oath at his own trial. He also testified that all of Sims' prior statements given to police and before the grand jury were lies.

On February 9, 2007, the jury found Sims guilty of the crime charged.

Both Childs and Sims were sentenced to life in prison. They now timely appeal their convictions.

ANALYSIS

I.

II.

Defendant Sims next claims that the district court committed reversible error by allowing Jackie Love to testify that Carolyn Ross asked her, in the presence of both Sims and **Childs**, if she knew anyone who could kill someone for her. Sims contends that this is inadmissible hearsay. We disagree.

The district court admitted the testimony as non-hearsay under Federal Rule of Evidence 801(d)(2)(E). That rule deems a statement not to be hearsay if "[t]he statement is offered against a party and is ... a statement by a coconspirator of a party during the course and in furtherance of the conspiracy." Before admitting the out-of-court statements of co-conspirators pursuant to Rule 801(d)(2)(E), the district court must find that "it is more likely than not that the declarant and the defendant were members of a conspiracy when the hearsay statement was made, and that the statement was in furtherance of the conspiracy." _United States v. Enright, 579 F.2d 980, 986 (6th Cir.1978)_. We review for clear error the predicate factual determinations (1) that a conspiracy existed, (2) that the defendant against whom the statement is offered was a member of the conspiracy, and (3) that the hearsay statement was made in the course of and in furtherance of the conspiracy. _United States v. Gessa, 971 F.2d 1257, 1261 (6th Cir.1992)_ (en banc). We review the district court's legal conclusion, based on these factual determinations, that Rule 801(d) (2)(E) permitted the otherwise hearsay statements to be received as non-hearsay _de novo_. _Id._

Sims argues that the district court erred in allowing Jackie Love to testify about an out-of-court statement made by indicted co-conspirator Carolyn Ross at a time when Sims was not a member of the conspiracy and at a time when the conspiracy itself did not yet exist. But the requirement that out-of-court declarations by a co-conspirator be shown to have been made while the conspiracy is in progress arises only because the declaration would otherwise be hearsay. We find that Jackie Love's testimony is not hearsay at all.

"Hearsay" is defined by the Federal Rules of Evidence as "a statement, other than one made by the declarant while testifying at the trial or hearing, offered in evidence to prove the truth of the matter asserted." FED.R.EVID. 801(c). A "declarant" is one who makes a "statement," and words qualify as a "statement" only if they make an "assertion." FED.R.EVID. 801(b), (a). "A witness who testifies at trial that [someone solicited them to commit a crime] is testifying to a verbal act of which the witness has direct knowledge: the extension of the invitation." _United States v. Gordon, No. 90-1501, 1991 WL 108723, at *3 (6th Cir. June 20, 1991)_. The words allegedly spoken by the solicitor are not a "statement" because they do not constitute an "assertion." _Id._ Thus, Jackie Love's testimony that Carolyn Ross asked her if she knew anyone who could kill someone for her is admissible evidence of a verbal act. It is the fact that the declaration was made, and not the truth of the declaration, which is relevant. We therefore find that the district court did not err in admitting Jackie Love's testimony over Sims' objection. _See Russ' Kwik Car Wash, Inc. v. Marathon Petroleum Co., 772 F.2d 214, 216 (6th Cir.1985)_ ("A decision below must be affirmed if correct for any reason, including a reason not considered by the lower court.").

Moreover, even if we were to find that the district court erred in admitting the statement into evidence, any such error was harmless. We have held that "an error by a district court with respect to the admission of evidence is subject to harmless error analysis, and it is well settled that an error which is not of a constitutional dimension is harmless unless it is more probable than not that the error materially affected the verdict." _United States v. Daniel, 134 F.3d 1259, 1262 (6th Cir.1998)_. Here, we find it more probable than not that the jury would have reached the same verdict based on other evidence of Sims' involvement in the conspiracy to murder Chrissy Satterfield properly admitted at trial, without regard to Jackie Love's testimony that Carolyn Ross asked her if she knew anyone who could kill someone for her-especially since these statements did not even inculpate Sims.

. . . .

CONCLUSION

For the foregoing reasons, we **AFFIRM** both defendants' convictions.

DISCUSSION PROBLEM 10-1

1. Do you agree with the court's determination that the statement in question was not hearsay at all?

2. Why did the court choose to declare this statement to not be hearsay at all?

3. Do you agree with that holding? What impact does the holding have?

4. Is this a distinction without a difference?

Offered for a Non Hearsay Use

One common argument raised when confronted with a hearsay objection is that the proponent was not offering the statement in question for truth of the matter asserted. The follow on inquiry to that argument is a question of relevancy. If you are not offering the out-of-court statement for its truth, then what relevancy does it have for the jury – in other words, why should they be allowed to hear the out-of-court statement if the proponent does not want the jury to believe it is true? The response that is normally given is that the statement is not being offered for the truth of the alleged assertion contained within the statement, but rather to show that it was said, and that hearing it had an effect on either the declarant or the listener. The statement is being offered so that the jury understands why the declarant or listener did something next. Consider the following:

Q: Where were you sitting that night?

A: I was in the movie theater, front row.

Q: Why were you there?

A: To see the new Spielberg movie?

Q: Did anyone say anything of interest to you that night?

OC:Objection – Hearsay?

J: Response?

Q: Your honor I'm not offering for the truth of the matter asserted, but rather to explain what the witness did next. It is for effect on the listener.

J: I'll allow it. Overuled.

Q: What was said to you that night?

A: Bobby came down front and told me that my boyfriend Jimmy was making out with a girl in the balcony?

Q: After Bobby told you that what did you do?

A: I got up and went to the balcony.

Q: What did you see there?

A: I saw the defendant pick up a purse and run out of the balcony.

Q: Thank you, no further questions.

In the example above, the attorney is really not concerned with the truthfulness of the statement about the witness' boyfriend. They are offering what was said to her to explain why she got up and went to the balcony – a classic example of the non hearsay effect on the listener use of an out-of-court statement.

How does this work? When there is doubt as to the reason for the questions, opposing counsel may raise a hearsay objection, at which time the court can ask the proponent what he is trying to do. If he suggests a hearsay use, the objection should be sustained unless he can fit the statement within an exception. Even if the proponent suggests a nonhearsay use or appropriate exception, the court can still exclude the statement if a jury is likely to misuse it as hearsay. Misuse of evidence is a classic instance of "unfair prejudice" under FRE 403. This is a particular danger when the statement in question does not fit into a hearsay exception, but it is reasonable to allow it to explain effect on the listener. In those instances, it is appropriate for opposing counsel to consider requesting a limiting instruction so that the jury will not improperly consider the out-of-court statement.

Our concerns about hearsay are universal (misperception, failed memory, insincerity, narrative ambiguity), but they will always arise in a setting peculiar to the person and her statement. This explains our preference for live testimony over out-of-court statements. Remember, a statement is hearsay only if it is offered to prove what the declarant intended to assert, and the hearsay doctrine would be incoherent if what counted was the plain or literal or objective meaning of words.

Statements normally require some degree of interpretation if the court is to understand what the speaker meant to say. Most statements contain references that can only be understood in context. Usually the unfolding case provides enough contextual information to enable the court to be confident on these points, and at this level of interpretation there is usually no controversy.

It should be possible for courts competently to assess declarant's (subjective) intent. For one thing, the same contextual information that answers basic questions of reference is likely to shed light on other aspects of expressive or communicative intent. The internal logic of the hearsay doctrine makes it self-executing in an important sense. If the logical route from the statement to the point to be proved requires taking the speaker's words as intentional expressions or communications of the point, even if his main expressive or communicative intent was broader or narrower, then the hearsay doctrine applies and the statement in question should not be admitted as non hearsay.

Hearsay Exclusions

FRE 801(d) provides that certain statements are not hearsay, if (1) the declarant testifies at the trial or hearing, is subject to cross-examination concerning the statement and the statement is: (A) inconsistent with the declarant's testimony and was given under oath subject to the penalty of perjury at the trial, hearing, or other proceeding, or deposition; (B) consistent with the declarant's testimony and is offered to rebut an express or implied charge of recent fabrication or improper influence or motive; or, (C) one of identification of a person. Also, FRE 801(d)(2) provides that admissions made by a party-opponent are not hearsay if the statement is offered against the party and is: (A) the party's own statement; (B) a statement the party has manifest his adoption of or belief in its truth; (C) a statement by a person authorized by the party to make a statement concerning the subject; (D) a statement by the party's agent or servant concerning the matters within the scope of the agency/employment made during the relationship; or, (E) a statement by a coconspirator during the course of and in furtherance of the conspiracy.

Hearsay Exceptions

Exceptions to the hearsay rule are admissible based on their unique tendency to be a reliable indicator of the truth. There are two major categories of exceptions: FRE 803, where the availability of the declarant is immaterial, and FRE 804, where the declarant must be unavailable at trial before statements are admissible. Many of the rules under FRE 803 do not depend on the availability of the declarant because they are considered firmly rooted hearsay exceptions, with a long history of demonstrated reliability, to some degree these exceptions have been impacted by the recent series of U.S. Supreme Court cases dealing with the confrontation clause in criminal trials. We will address that issue in due course. For now, remember that the most common rules include:

1. FRE 803(1)   *Present sense impressions*

2. FRE 803(2)   *Excited utterance*

3. FRE 803(3)   *The "state of mind" exception*

4. FRE 803(4)   *Statements for purposes of medical diagnosis or treatment*

5. FRE 803(6)   *Business records*

ADMITTING HEARSAY STATEMENTS

Effective use of hearsay statements depends upon an accurate knowledge of the rules and the ability to identify the possible basis for admissibility of prior statements made by a witness before it is raised through witness testimony. Counsel should identify all prior statements made by a witness and evaluate whether they intend to offer it for its content. Examples of an alternative purpose include showing knowledge, effect on the listener, state of mind, what are normally referred to as a non-hearsay use for the out-of-court statement. When the statement is not offered for the truth of the matter asserting within the statement it is not hearsay.

When attempting to admit prior statements of a witness, counsel must lay the proper foundation. These steps should be identified in advance to avoid any delay or confusion at trial. The more prepared counsel is to lay a proper foundation and offer these prior statements, the more persuasive the argument for admissibility will appear to the judge, who often rules on these questions quickly. The type of foundation will depend upon whether the statement falls under a hearsay exclusion found in FRE 801, or an exemption found in FRE 803 or FRE 804. Statements offered under FRE 801(d) require the declarant to testify in the current trial. Statements offered under FRE 803 are admissible whether the declarant testifies at the current trial. Statements offered under FRE 804 require counsel to first establish the unavailability of the declarant before the hearsay exception can apply.

Counsel must always analyze prior statements made by all witnesses as well as the accused and determine if the statements will help their case. A clear theory of the case and the opponent's case is critical to this process. Additionally, counsel must understand

and be prepared to offer a non-hearsay reason to place the statement before the court, such as to impeach the credibility of a witness.

Once prior statements are admitted under any of the hearsay rules, they can be treated like any other evidence at trial. Counsel must be careful to record the judge's ruling on admissibility of prior statements and argue only those admitted as substantive evidence. Remember, statements used to impeach the witness are not admissible as substantive evidence, but are limited as to their proper use.

Assuming counsel has adequately prepared to have prior statements of a witness admitted, that is not the end of the analysis. Counsel must also consider other evidentiary rules that may impact the court's decision to admit prior statements. Counsel should consider the authenticity requirements of FRE 901, relevance under FRE 401, including the balancing requirements of FRE 403, and the best evidence rule of FRE 1002. Counsel should also be familiar with the requirements under FRE 104 concerning preliminary questions of admissibility and relevance.

CONCLUSION

Now that we have identified the fundamentals of hearsay doctrine let us move on to a discussion of how the Confrontation Clause impacts the admissibility of these out of court statements in criminal proceedings.

Chapter 11: Hearsay & the Confrontation Clause

HISTORICAL MEANING OF CONFRONTATION CLAUSE

The confrontation clause of the Sixth Amendment establishes that in criminal cases the accused has the right "to be confronted with the witnesses against him," and it is settled law that this provision applies in both federal and state courts in the same fashion.[42] This right of confrontation has great historical significance within the United States, and Great Britain but the current applicable law of confrontation traces its roots to a series of U.S. Supreme Court decisions handed down in the 1960s. That being said, an understanding of the historical background is at a minimum interesting and probably helpful as well.

Sir Walter Raleigh was prosecuted for treason in 1603 in England. His case dramatically illustrates central modern concerns underlying the right of confrontation. The crown charged him with conspiring to overthrow the reign of King James with the intent to replace him with his sister, Arabella Stuart. The most damning evidence presented against Sir Walter Raleigh came from an alleged coconspirator, Lord Cobham. The statement was "extracted" from an interrogation that was conducted in the Tower of London – not a good place to be in 1603. In that statement Cobham named Raleigh as an instigator and claimed he was raising money to back on insurrection against the king.

Raleigh denied the charges, presented a defense, and established that Cobham recanted. He argued that the statute required two witnesses and urged the court to "call my Accuser" so they might stand "face to face," conceding that a witness need not be called if he "is not to be had conveniently" but pointing out that Cobham was "alive, and in the house." The judges noted that the statute had been repealed and that the law allowed for conviction without witnesses for conspiracy where three or more had confessed to the crime. The Court sentenced Raleigh to die, but instead King James sent him to Guyana for gold. Unfortunately that expedition went badly, and eventually it became expedient for the King to execute Raleigh as a gesture of good will to the King of Spain. Raleigh was beheaded 15 years after his trial, at 66 years of age.[43]

The basic Sixth Amendment right is the ability to confront your accuser "face-to-face." Under this right the accused is entitled to be physically present, to see and hear the witnesses against him.[44] Initially this included the right to be seen by the witnesses when they testified, but that right has been eroded to some degree by additional case law that identified times when the ability to be seen was subordinated to another concern the court was dealing with – usually having something to do with the prior conduct of the accused. Those measures included protection for child abuse witnesses, and how to deal with the accused who misbehaves in court, or threatens violence to a witness.[45]

---

[42] Pointer v. Texas, 380 U.S. 400 (1965).

[43] The passages from the Raleigh trial are reported in 2 Howell's State Cases 15-20 (1803). See also Stephen, The Trial of Sir Walter Raleigh, 2 Trans. Royal Hist. Society 172 (4th Series 1919).

[44] Dowdell v. United States, 221 U.S. 325, 330 (1911) ("meet the witnesses face to face); United States v. Benfield, 593 F.2d 815, 821 (8th Cir. 1979) (confrontation "includes a face-to-face meeting at trial").

[45] Coy v. Iowa, 487 U.S. 1012 (1988) (condemning translucent screen separating teenage girl from defendant in sexual assault case, permitting defendant to see her but shielding her from seeing him); Maryland v. Craig, 497 U.S. 836 (1990) (approving remote testimony by one-way video monitor on basis of finding that child victim would be traumatized if forced to testify in court).

What we are really concerned with is the ability to cross examine the witness, and it can be argued that the presence of accused assists in that endeavor. This right to cross examination is the core right that is referred to repeatedly in the case law. The Supreme Court has held that the right to cross-examine brings with it the right to uncover basic information about the witness and raise points relating to bias.[46] At least sometimes, this right to cross-examine entails a defense right to introduce favorable hearsay by the witness.[47]

This commitment to confrontation and the value of cross examination as the core reasons for the confrontation clause creates some interesting issues when considering whether to admit hearsay – because hearsay admissions are normally not subject to cross examination. They have not been annealed in the crucible of truth created by an effective cross examination.

Since confrontation does not block admitting all hearsay, the question becomes when should it prevent the admission of hearsay and when should it not? Most of our current structures for dealing with confrontation clause and Hearsay were decided during the Warren court, with Justice Scalia leading the current court's charge in a different, or complimentary, direction.

An earlier constitutional standard of reliability for hearsay offered against the defendant that works independently of the hearsay doctrine, was developed in the *Roberts* test, which required particularized showing of reliability only for statements that do not fit a firmly rooted hearsay exception.[48] *Roberts* also told us that "firmly rooted" hearsay exceptions under the FRE did not require confrontation clause analysis because sufficient indicia of reliability existed for those statements – making a confrontation clause analysis moot.

U.S. SUPREME COURT SPEAKS-OHIO V. ROBERTS

Consider the court's approach in the following case. As you read it, ask yourself what hearsay issues are present in the case, and what issues are the court addressing? Why did the court choose those particular issues? What flowed from that decision by the court?

100 S.Ct. 2531

Supreme Court of the United States

State of **OHIO**, Petitioner,

v.

Herschel **ROBERTS**.

No. 78-756.

Argued Nov. 26, 1979.

Decided June 25, 1980.

Mr. Justice BLACKMUN delivered the opinion of the Court.

---

[46] See Alford v. United States, 282 U.S. 687 (1931) (address of witness); Smith v. Illinois, 390 U.S. 129 (1968) (name of witness); Davis v. Alaska, 415 U.S. 308 (1974) (right to expose motive); for additional discussions about the importance of cross examination and the supporting case law *see* MacCarthy on Cross Examination, (ABA publications).

[47] See Chambers v. Mississippi, 410 U.S. 284 (1973).

[48] Ohio v. Roberts, 448 U.S. 56, 66 (1980) (hearsay by nontestifying witnesses must possess "indicia of reliability" to satisfy confrontation clause; reliability "can be inferred without more" where statement fits "firmly rooted" exception; otherwise "particularized guarantees of trustworthiness" are required).

This case presents issues concerning the constitutional propriety of the introduction in evidence of the preliminary hearing testimony of a witness not produced at the defendant's subsequent state criminal trial.

I

Local police arrested respondent, Herschel **Roberts**, on January 7, 1975, in Lake County, **Ohio**. **Roberts** was charged with forgery of a check in the name of Bernard Isaacs, and with possession of stolen credit cards belonging to Isaacs and his wife Amy.

A preliminary hearing was held in Municipal Court on January 10. The prosecution called several witnesses, including Mr. Isaacs. Respondent's appointed counsel had seen the Isaacs' daughter, Anita, in the courthouse hallway, and called her as the defense's only witness. Anita Isaacs testified that she knew respondent, and that she had permitted him to use her apartment for several days while she was away. Defense counsel questioned Anita at some length and attempted to elicit from her an admission that she had given respondent checks and the credit cards without informing him that she did not have permission to use them. Anita, however, denied this. Respondent's attorney did not ask to have the witness declared hostile and did not request permission to place her on cross-examination. The prosecutor did not question Anita.

A county grand jury subsequently indicted respondent for forgery, for receiving stolen property (including the credit cards), and for possession of heroin. The attorney who represented respondent at the preliminary hearing withdrew upon becoming a Municipal Court Judge, and new counsel was appointed for **Roberts**.

Between November 1975 and March 1976, five subpoenas for four different trial dates were issued to Anita at her parents' **Ohio** residence. The last three carried a written instruction that Anita should "call before appearing." She was not at the residence when these were executed. She did not telephone and she did not appear at trial.

In March 1976, the case went to trial before a jury in the Court of Common Pleas. Respondent took the stand and testified that Anita Isaacs had given him her parents' checkbook and credit cards with the understanding that he could use them. Tr. 231-232. Relying on **Ohio** Rev.Code Ann. § 2945.49 (1975), which permits the use of preliminary examination testimony of a witness who "cannot for any reason be produced at the trial," the State, on rebuttal, offered the transcript of Anita's testimony. Tr. 273-274.

Asserting a violation of the Confrontation Clause and indeed, the unconstitutionality thereunder of § 2945.49, the defense objected to the use of the transcript. The trial court conducted a *voir dire* hearing as to its admissibility. Tr. 194-199. Amy Isaacs, the sole witness at *voir dire*, was questioned by both the prosecutor and defense counsel concerning her daughter's whereabouts. Anita, according to her mother, left home for Tucson, Ariz., soon after the preliminary hearing. About a year before the trial, a San Francisco social worker was in communication with the Isaacs about a welfare application Anita had filed there. Through the social worker, the Isaacs reached their daughter once by telephone. Since then, however, Anita had called her parents only one other time and had not been in touch with her two sisters. When Anita called, some seven or eight months before trial, she told her parents that she "was traveling" outside **Ohio**, but did not reveal the place from which she called. Mrs. Isaacs stated that she knew of no way to reach Anita in case of an emergency. App. 9. Nor did she "know of anybody who knows where she is." *Id.* at 11. The trial court admitted the transcript into evidence. Respondent was convicted on all counts.

The Court of Appeals of **Ohio** reversed. After reviewing the *voir dire*, that court concluded that the prosecution had failed to make a showing of a "good-faith effort" to secure the absent witness' attendance, as required by *Barber v. Page*, 390 U.S. 719, 722-725, 88 S.Ct. 1318, 1320-1322, 20 L.Ed.2d 255 (1968). The court noted that "we have no witness from the prosecution to testify . . . that no one on behalf of the State could determine Anita's whereabouts, [or] that anyone had exhausted contact with the San Francisco social worker." App. 5. Unavailability would have been established, the court said, "[h]ad the State demonstrated that its subpoenas were never actually served on the witness and that they were unable to make contact in any way with the witness. . . . Until the Isaacs' *voir dire,* requested by the defense, the State had done nothing, absolutely nothing, to show the Court that Anita would be absent because of unavailability, and they showed no effort having been made to seek out her whereabouts for purpose of trial." *Ibid.*

The Supreme Court of **Ohio**, by a 4-3 vote, affirmed, but did so on other grounds. 55 **Ohio** St.2d 191, 378 N.E.2d 492 (1978). It first held that the Court of Appeals had erred in concluding that Anita was not unavailable. *Barber v. Page* was distinguished as a case in which "the government knew where the absent witness was," whereas Anita's "whereabouts were entirely unknown." 55 **Ohio** St.2d, at 194, 378 N.E.2d, at 495. "[T]he trial judge could reasonably have concluded from Mrs. Isaacs' *voir dire* testimony that due diligence could not have procured the attendance of Anita Isaacs"; he "could reasonably infer that Anita had left San Francisco"; and he "could properly hold that the witness was unavailable to testify in person." *Id.,* at 195, 378 N.E.2d, at 495-496.

The court, nonetheless, held that the transcript was inadmissible. Reasoning that normally there is little incentive to cross-examine a witness at a preliminary hearing, where the "ultimate issue" is only probable cause, *id.,* at 196, 378 N.E.2d, at 496, and citing the dissenting opinion in *California v. Green*, 399 U.S. 149, 189, 90 S.Ct. 1930, 1951, 26 L.Ed.2d 489 (1970), the court held that the mere opportunity to cross-examine at a preliminary hearing did not afford constitutional confrontation for purposes of trial. See 55 **Ohio** St.2d, at 191, 378 N.E.2d, at 493 (court syllabus).3 The court distinguished *Green*, where this Court had ruled admissible the preliminary hearing testimony of a declarant who was present at trial, but claimed forgetfulness. The **Ohio** court perceived a "dictum" in *Green* that suggested that the mere opportunity to cross-examine renders preliminary hearing testimony admissible. 55 **Ohio** St.2d, at 198, and n. 2, 378 N.E.2d, at 497, and n. 2, citing 399 U.S., at 165-166, 90 S.Ct., at 1938-1939. But the court concluded that *Green* "goes no further than to suggest that cross-examination actually conducted at preliminary hearing *may* afford adequate confrontation for purposes of a later trial." 55 **Ohio** St.2d, at 199, 378 N.E.2d, at 497 (emphasis in original). Since Anita had not been cross-examined at the preliminary hearing and was absent at trial, the introduction of the transcript of her testimony was held to have violated respondent's confrontation right. The three dissenting justices would have ruled that " 'the test is the opportunity for full and complete cross-examination rather than the use which is made of that opportunity' " (citing *United States v. Allen*, 409 F.2d 611, 613 (CA10 1969)). 55 **Ohio** St.2d, at 200, 378 N.E.2d, at 498.

We granted certiorari to consider these important issues under the Confrontation Clause. 441 U.S. 904, 99 S.Ct. 1990, 60 L.Ed.2d 372 (1979).

II

A

The Court here is called upon to consider once again the relationship between the Confrontation Clause and the hearsay rule with its many exceptions. The basic rule against hearsay, of course, is riddled with exceptions developed over three centuries. See E. Cleary, McCormick on Evidence § 244 (2d ed. 1972) (McCormick) (history of rule);

id., §§ 252-324 (exceptions).4 These exceptions vary among jurisdictions as to number, nature, and detail. See, *e. g.*, Fed.Rules Evid. 803, 804 (over 20 specified exceptions). But every set of exceptions seems to fit an apt description offered more than 40 years ago: "an old-fashioned crazy quilt made of patches cut from a group of paintings by cubists, futurists and surrealists." Morgan & Maguire, Looking Backward and Forward at Evidence, 50 Harv.L.Rev. 909, 921 (1937).

The Sixth Amendment's Confrontation Clause, made applicable to the States through the Fourteenth Amendment, *Pointer v. Texas*, 380 U.S. 400, 403-405, 85 S.Ct. 1065, 1067-1068, 13 L.Ed.2d 923 (1965); *Davis v. Alaska*, 415 U.S. 308, 315, 94 S.Ct. 1105, 39 L.Ed.2d 347 (1974), provides: "In all criminal prosecutions, the accused shall enjoy the right . . . to be confronted with the witnesses against him." If one were to read this language literally, it would require, on objection, the exclusion of any statement made by a declarant not present at trial. See *Mattox v. United States*, 156 U.S. 237, 243, 15 S.Ct. 337, 340, 39 L.Ed. 409 (1895) ("[T]here could be nothing more directly contrary to the letter of the provision in question than the admission of dying declarations"). But, if thus applied, the Clause would abrogate virtually every hearsay exception, a result long rejected as unintended and too extreme.

The historical evidence leaves little doubt, however, that the Clause was intended to exclude some hearsay. See *California v. Green*, 399 U.S., at 156-157, and nn. 9 and 10, 90 S.Ct., at 1934 and nn. 9 and 10; see also McCormick § 252, p. 606. Moreover, underlying policies support the same conclusion. The Court has emphasized that the Confrontation Clause reflects a preference for face-to-face confrontation at trial, and that "a primary interest secured by [the provision] is the right of cross-examination." *Douglas v. Alabama*, 380 U.S. 415, 418, 85 S.Ct. 1074, 1076, 13 L.Ed.2d 934 (1965).6 In short, the Clause envisions

"a personal examination and cross-examination of the witness, in which the accused has an opportunity, not only of testing the recollection and sifting the conscience of the witness, but of compelling him to stand face to face with the jury in order that they may look at him, and judge by his demeanor upon the stand and the manner in which he gives his testimony whether he is worthy of belief." *Mattox v. United States*, 156 U.S., at 242-243, 15 S.Ct., at 339.

These means of testing accuracy are so important that the absence of proper confrontation at trial "calls into question the ultimate 'integrity of the fact-finding process.' " *Chambers v. Mississippi*, 410 U.S. 284, 295, 93 S.Ct. 1038, 1046, 35 L.Ed.2d 297 (1973), quoting *Berger v. California*, 393 U.S. 314, 315, 89 S.Ct. 540, 541, 21 L.Ed.2d 508 (1969).

The Court, however, has recognized that competing interests, if "closely examined," *Chambers v. Mississippi*, 410 U.S., at 295, 93 S.Ct., at 1045, may warrant dispensing with confrontation at trial. See *Mattox v. United States*, 156 U.S., at 243, 15 S.Ct., at 340 ("general rules of law of this kind, however beneficent in their operation and valuable to the accused, must occasionally give way to considerations of public policy and the necessities of the case"). Significantly, every jurisdiction has a strong interest in effective law enforcement, and in the development and precise formulation of the rules of evidence applicable in criminal proceedings. See *Snyder v. Massachusetts*, 291 U.S. 97, 107, 54 S.Ct. 330, 333, 78 L.Ed. 674 (1934); *California v. Green*, 399 U.S., at 171-172, 90 S.Ct., at 1941-1942 (concurring opinion).

This Court, in a series of cases, has sought to accommodate these competing interests. True to the common-law tradition, the process has been gradual, building on past decisions, drawing on new experience, and responding to changing conditions. The Court has not sought to "map out a theory of the Confrontation Clause that would determine the validity of all . . . hearsay 'exceptions.' " *California v. Green*, 399 U.S., at 162, 90 S.Ct., at 1937. But a general approach to the problem is discernible.

B

The Confrontation Clause operates in two separate ways to restrict the range of admissible hearsay. First, in conformance with the Framers' preference for face-to-face accusation, the Sixth Amendment establishes a rule of necessity. In the usual case (including cases where prior cross-examination has occurred), the prosecution must either produce, or demonstrate the unavailability of, the declarant whose statement it wishes to use against the defendant. See *Mancusi v. Stubbs*, 408 U.S. 204, 92 S.Ct. 2308, 33 L.Ed. 2d 293 (1972); *Barber v. Page*, 390 U.S. 719, 88 S.Ct. 1318, 20 L.Ed.2d 255 (1968). See also *Motes v. United States*, 178 U.S. 458, 20 S.Ct. 993, 44 L.Ed. 1150 (1900); *California v. Green*, 399 U.S., at 161-162, 165, 167, n. 16, 90 S.Ct., at 1936-1937, 1938, 1939, n. 16.7

The second aspect operates once a witness is shown to be unavailable. Reflecting its underlying purpose to augment accuracy in the factfinding process by ensuring the defendant an effective means to test adverse evidence, the Clause countenances only hearsay marked with such trustworthiness that "there is no material departure from the reason of the general rule." *Snyder v. Massachusetts*, 291 U.S., at 107, 54 S.Ct., at 333. The principle recently was formulated in *Mancusi v. Stubbs* :

"The focus of the Court's concern has been to insure that there 'are indicia of reliability which have been widely viewed as determinative of whether a statement may be placed before the jury though there is no confrontation of the declarant,' *Dutton v. Evans, supra,* at 89, 91 S.Ct., at 220 and to 'afford the trier of fact a satisfactory basis for evaluating the truth of the prior statement,' *California v. Green, supra,* 399 U.S., at 161, 90 S.Ct., at 1936. It is clear from these statements, and from numerous prior decisions of this Court, that even though the witness be unavailable his prior testimony must bear some of these 'indicia of reliability.' " 408 U.S., at 213, 92 S.Ct., at 2313.

The Court has applied this "indicia of reliability" requirement principally by concluding that certain hearsay exceptions rest upon such solid foundations that admission of virtually any evidence within them comports with the "substance of the constitutional protection." *Mattox v. United States*, 156 U.S., at 244, 15 S.Ct., at 340.8 This reflects the truism that "hearsay rules and the Confrontation Clause are generally designed to protect similar values," *California v. Green*, 399 U.S., at 155, 90 S.Ct., at 1933, and "stem from the same roots," *Dutton v. Evans*, 400 U.S. 74, 86, 91 S.Ct. 210, 218, 27 L.Ed.2d 213 (1970). It also responds to the need for certainty in the workaday world of conducting criminal trials.

In sum, when a hearsay declarant is not present for cross-examination at trial, the Confrontation Clause normally requires a showing that he is unavailable. Even then, his statement is admissible only if it bears adequate "indicia of reliability." Reliability can be inferred without more in a case where the evidence falls within a firmly rooted hearsay exception. In other cases, the evidence must be excluded, at least absent a showing of particularized guarantees of trustworthiness.

III

We turn first to that aspect of confrontation analysis deemed dispositive by the Supreme Court of **Ohio**, and answered by it in the negative-whether Anita Isaacs' prior testimony at the preliminary hearing bore sufficient "indicia of reliability." Resolution of this issue requires a careful comparison of this case to *California v. Green, supra.*

A

In *Green*, at the preliminary hearing, a youth named Porter identified Green as a drug supplier. When called to the stand at Green's trial, however, Porter professed a lapse of memory. Frustrated in its attempt to adduce live testimony, the prosecution offered Porter's prior statements. The trial judge ruled the evidence admissible, and substantial portions of the preliminary hearing transcript were read to the jury. This Court found no error. Citing the established rule that prior trial testimony is admissible upon retrial if the declarant becomes unavailable, *Mattox v. United States*, 156 U.S. 237, 15 S.Ct. 337, 39 L.Ed.409 (1895); *Mancusi v. Stubbs*, 408 U.S. 204, 92 S.Ct. 2308, 33 L.Ed.2d 293 (1972), and recent dicta suggesting the admissibility of preliminary hearing testimony under proper circumstances, *Barber v. Page*, 390 U.S., at 725-726, 88 S.Ct., at 1322; *Pointer v. Texas*, 380 U.S., at 407, 85 S.Ct., at 1069, the Court rejected Green's Confrontation Clause attack. It reasoned:

"Porter's statement at the preliminary hearing had already been given under circumstances closely approximating those that surround the typical trial. Porter was under oath; respondent was represented by counsel-the same counsel in fact who later represented him at the trial; respondent had every opportunity to cross-examine Porter as to his statement; and the proceedings were conducted before a judicial tribunal, equipped to provide a judicial record of the hearings." 399 U.S., at 165, 90 S.Ct., at 1938.

These factors, the Court concluded, provided all that the Sixth Amendment demands: "substantial compliance with the purposes behind the confrontation requirement." *Id., at 166, 90 S.Ct., at 1939.*[10]

This passage and others in the *Green* opinion suggest that the *opportunity* to cross-examine at the preliminary hearing-even absent actual cross-examination-satisfies the Confrontation Clause. Yet the record showed, and the Court recognized, that defense counsel in fact had cross-examined Porter at the earlier proceeding. *Id., at 151, 90 S.Ct., at 1931.* Thus, Mr. Justice BRENNAN, writing in dissent, could conclude only that "[p]erhaps" "the mere opportunity for face-to-face encounter [is] sufficient." *Id., at 200, n. 8, 90 S.Ct., at 1957.* See Note, 52 Texas L.Rev. 1167, 1170 (1974).

We need not decide whether the Supreme Court of **Ohio** correctly dismissed statements in *Green* suggesting that the mere opportunity to cross-examine rendered the prior testimony admissible. See Westen, The Future of Confrontation, 77 Mich.L.Rev. 1185, 1211 (1979) (issue is "truly difficult to resolve under conventional theories of confrontation"). Nor need we decide whether *de minimis* questioning is sufficient, for defense counsel in this case tested Anita's testimony with the equivalent of significant cross-examination.

B

Counsel's questioning clearly partook of cross-examination as a matter of *form*. His presentation was replete with leading questions, the principal tool and hallmark of cross-examination. In addition, counsel's questioning comported with the principal *purpose* of cross-examination: to challenge "whether the declarant was sincerely telling what he believed to be the truth, whether the declarant accurately perceived and remembered the matter he related, and whether the declarant's intended meaning is adequately conveyed by the language he employed." Davenport, The Confrontation Clause and the Co-Conspirator Exception in Criminal Prosecutions: A Functional Analysis, 85 Harv.L.Rev. 1378 (1972). Anita's unwillingness to shift the blame away from respondent became discernible early in her testimony. Yet counsel continued to explore the underlying events in detail. He attempted, for example, to establish that Anita and respondent were sharing an apartment, an assertion that was critical to respondent's defense at trial and that might have suggested ulterior personal reasons for unfairly casting blame on respondent. At another point, he directly challenged Anita's veracity by seeking to have her admit that she had given the credit cards to respondent to obtain a television. When Anita denied this, defense counsel elicited the fact that the only television she owned was a "Twenty Dollar . . . old model." App. 21. Cf. *Davis v. Alaska*, 415 U.S. 308, 316-317, 94 S.Ct. 1105, 1110-1111, 39 L.Ed.2d 347 (1974).

Respondent argues that, because defense counsel never asked the court to declare Anita hostile, his questioning necessarily occurred on direct examination. See *State v. Minneker*, 27 **Ohio** St.2d 155, 271 N.E.2d 821 (1971). But however state law might formally characterize the questioning of Anita, it afforded "substantial compliance with the purposes behind the confrontation requirement," *Green*, 399 U.S., at 166, 90 S.Ct., at 1939, no less so than classic cross-examination. Although **Ohio** law may have authorized objection by the prosecutor or intervention by the court, this did not happen. As in *Green*, respondent's counsel was not "significantly limited in any way in the scope or nature of his cross-examination." *Ibid.*

We are also unpersuaded that *Green* is distinguishable on the ground that Anita Isaacs-unlike the declarant Porter in *Green* -was not personally available for questioning *at trial*. This argument ignores the language and logic of *Green* :

"Porter's statement would, we think, have been admissible at trial even in Porter's absence if Porter had been actually unavailable . . . . That being the case, we do not think a different result should follow where the witness is actually produced." *Id.*, at 165, 90 S.Ct., at 1938-39.

Nor does it matter that, unlike Green, respondent had a different lawyer at trial from the one at the preliminary hearing. Although one might strain one's reading of *Green* to assign this factor some significance, respondent advances no reason of substance supporting the distinction. Indeed, if we were to accept this suggestion, *Green* would carry the seeds of its own demise; under a "same attorney" rule, a defendant could nullify the effect of *Green* by obtaining new counsel after the preliminary hearing was concluded.

Finally, we reject respondent's attempt to fall back on general principles of confrontation, and his argument that this case falls among those in which the Court must undertake a particularized search for "indicia of reliability." Under this theory, the factors previously cited-absence of face-to-face contact at trial, presence of a new attorney, and the lack of classic cross-examination-combine with considerations uniquely tied to Anita to mandate exclusion of her statements. Anita, respondent says, had every reason to lie to avoid prosecution or parental reprobation. Her unknown whereabouts is explicable as an effort to avoid punishment, perjury, or self-incrimination. Given these facts, her prior testimony falls on the unreliable side, and should have been excluded.

In making this argument, respondent in effect asks us to disassociate preliminary hearing testimony previously subjected to cross-examination from previously cross-examined prior-trial testimony, which the Court has deemed generally immune from subsequent confrontation attack. Precedent requires us to decline this invitation. In *Green* the Court found guarantees of trustworthiness in the accouterments of the preliminary hearing itself; there was no mention of the inherent reliability or unreliability of Porter and his story. See also *Mancusi v. Stubbs*, 408 U.S., at 216, 92 S.Ct., at 2314.

In sum, we perceive no reason to resolve the reliability issue differently here than the Court did in *Green*. "Since there was an adequate opportunity to cross-examine [the witness], and counsel . . . availed himself of that opportunity, the transcript . . . bore sufficient 'indicia of reliability' and afforded ' "the trier of fact a satisfactory basis for evaluating the truth of the prior statement." ' " 408 U.S., at 216, 92 S.Ct., at 2314.12

IV

Our holding that the Supreme Court of **Ohio** erred in its "indicia of reliability" analysis does not fully dispose of the case, for respondent would defend the judgment on an alternative ground. The State, he contends, failed to lay a proper predicate for admission of the preliminary hearing transcript by its failure to demonstrate that Anita Issacs was not available to testify in person at the trial. All the justices of the Supreme Court of **Ohio** rejected this argument. 55 **Ohio** St.2d, at 195 and 199, 378 N.E.2d, at 495 and 497.

A

The basic litmus of Sixth Amendment unavailability is established: "[A] witness is not 'unavailable' for purposes of the . . . exception to the confrontation requirement unless the prosecutorial authorities have made a *good-faith effort* to obtain his presence at trial." *Barber v. Page*, 390 U.S., at 724-725, 88 S.Ct., at 1322 (emphasis added). Accord, *Mancusi v. Stubbs, supra; California v. Green*, 399 U.S., at 161-162, 165, 167, n. 16, 90 S.Ct., at 1936-1937, 1938-1939, n. 16; *Berger v. California*, 393 U.S. 314, 89 S.Ct. 540, 21 L.Ed.2d 508 (1969).

Although it might be said that the Court's prior cases provide no further refinement of this statement of the rule, certain general propositions safely emerge. The law does not require the doing of a futile act. Thus, if no possibility of procuring the witness exists (as, for example, the witness' intervening death), "good faith" demands nothing of the prosecution. But if there is a possibility, albeit remote, that affirmative measures might produce the declarant, the obligation of good faith *may* demand their effectuation. "The lengths to which the prosecution must go to produce a witness . . . is a question of reasonableness." *California v. Green*, 399 U.S., at 189, n. 22, 90 S.Ct., at 1951 (concurring opinion, citing *Barber v. Page, supra*). The ultimate question is whether the witness is unavailable despite good-faith efforts undertaken prior to trial to locate and present that witness. As with other evidentiary proponents, the prosecution bears the burden of establishing this predicate.

B

On the facts presented we hold that the trial court and the Supreme Court of **Ohio** correctly concluded that Anita's unavailability, in the constitutional sense, was established.

At the *voir dire* hearing, called for by the defense, it was shown that some four months prior to the trial the prosecutor was in touch with Amy Isaacs and discussed with her Anita's whereabouts. It may appropriately be inferred that Mrs. Isaacs told the prosecutor essentially the same facts to which she testified at *voir dire* : that the Isaacs had last heard from Anita during the preceding summer; that she was not then in San Francisco, but was traveling outside **Ohio**; and that the Isaacs and their other children knew of no way to reach Anita even in an emergency. This last fact takes on added significance when it is recalled that Anita's parents earlier had undertaken affirmative efforts to reach their daughter when the social worker's inquiry came in from San Francisco. This is not a case of parents abandoning all interest in an absent daughter.

The evidence of record demonstrates that the prosecutor issued a subpoena to Anita at her parents' home, not only once, but on five separate occasions over a period of several months. In addition, at the *voir dire* argument, the prosecutor stated to the court that respondent "witnessed that I have attempted to locate, I have subpoenaed, there has been a *voir dire* of the witness' parents, and they have not been able to locate her for over a year." App. 12.

Given these facts, the prosecution did not breach its duty of good-faith effort. To be sure, the prosecutor might have tried to locate by telephone the San Francisco social worker with whom Mrs. Isaacs had spoken many months before and might have undertaken other steps in an effort to find Anita. One, in hindsight, may always think of other things. Nevertheless, the great improbability that such efforts would have resulted in locating the witness, and would have led to her production at trial, neutralizes any intimation that a concept of reasonableness required their execution. We accept as a general rule, of course, the proposition that "the possibility of a refusal is not the equivalent of asking and receiving a rebuff." *Barber v. Page, 390 U.S., at 724, 88 S.Ct., at 1322,* quoting from the dissenting opinion in that case in the Court of Appeals (381 F.2d 479, 481 (CA10 1966)). But the service and ineffectiveness of the five subpoenas and the conversation with Anita's mother were far more than mere reluctance to face the possibility of a refusal. It was investigation at the last-known real address, and it was conversation with a parent who was concerned about her daughter's whereabouts.

Barber and *Mancusi v. Stubbs, supra,* are the cases in which this Court has explored the issue of constitutional unavailability. Although each is factually distinguishable from this case, *Mancusi* provides significant support for a conclusion of good-faith effort here, and *Barber* has no contrary significance. Insofar as this record discloses no basis for concluding that Anita was abroad, the case is factually weaker than *Mancusi* ; but it is stronger than *Mancusi* in the sense that the **Ohio** prosecutor, unlike the prosecutor in *Mancusi*, had no clear indication, if any at all, of Anita's whereabouts. In *Barber*, the Court found an absence of good-faith effort where the prosecution made no attempt to secure the presence of a declarant incarcerated in a federal penitentiary in a neighboring State. There, the prosecution knew where the witness was, procedures existed whereby the witness could be brought to the trial, and the witness was not in a position to frustrate efforts to secure his production. Here, Anita's whereabouts were not known, and there was no assurance that she would be found in a place from which she could be forced to return to **Ohio**.

We conclude that the prosecution carried its burden of demonstrating that Anita was constitutionally unavailable for purposes of respondent's trial.

The judgment of the Supreme Court of **Ohio** is reversed, and the case is remanded for further proceedings not inconsistent with this opinion.

It is so ordered.

Mr. Justice BRENNAN, with whom Mr. Justice MARSHALL and Mr. Justice STEVENS join, dissenting.

The Court concludes that because Anita Isaacs' testimony at respondent's preliminary hearing was subjected to the equivalent of significant cross-examination, such hearsay evidence bore sufficient "indicia of reliability" to permit its introduction at respondent's trial without offending the Confrontation Clause of the Sixth Amendment. As the Court recognizes, however, the Constitution imposes the threshold requirement that the prosecution must demonstrate the unavailability of the witness whose prerecorded testimony it wishes to use against the defendant. Because I cannot agree that the State has met its burden of establishing this predicate, I dissent.

"There are few subjects, perhaps, upon which this Court and other courts have been more nearly unanimous than in their expressions of belief that the right of confrontation and cross-examination is an essential and fundamental requirement for the kind of fair trial which is this country's constitutional goal." *Pointer v. Texas,* 380 U.S. 400, 405, 85 S.Ct. 1065, 1068, 13 L.Ed.2d 923 (1965). Accord, *Berger v. California,* 393 U.S. 314, 315, 89 S.Ct. 540, 541, 21 L.Ed.2d 508 (1969); *Barber v. Page,* 390 U.S. 719, 721, 88 S.Ct. 1318,

1320, 20 L.Ed.2d 255 (1968); *Pointer v. Texas, supra,* 380 U.S., at 410, 85 S.Ct., at 1071 (STEWART, J., concurring); *Kirby v. United States,* 174 U.S. 47, 55-56, 19 S.Ct. 574, 577, 43 L.Ed. 890 (1899). Historically, the inclusion of the Confrontation Clause in the Bill of Rights reflected the Framers' conviction that the defendant must not be denied the opportunity to challenge his accusers in a direct encounter before the trier of fact. See *California v. Green,* 399 U.S. 149, 156-158, 90 S.Ct. 1930, 1934-1935, 26 L.Ed.2d 489 (1970); *Park v. Huff,* 506 F.2d 849, 861-862 (CA5 1975) (Gewin, J., concurring). At the heart of this constitutional guarantee is the accused's right to compel the witness "to stand face to face with the jury in order that they may look at him, and judge by his demeanor upon the stand and the manner in which he gives his testimony whether he is worthy of belief." *Mattox v. United States,* 156 U.S. 237, 242-243, 15 S.Ct. 337, 339, 39 L.Ed. 409 (1895). See also *California v. Green, supra,* 399 U.S., at 174-183, 90 S.Ct., at 1943-1948 (Harlan, J., concurring).

Despite the literal language of the Sixth Amendment,2 our cases have recognized the necessity for a limited exception to the confrontation requirement for the prior testimony of a witness who is unavailable at the defendant's trial. In keeping with the importance of this provision in our constitutional scheme, however, we have imposed a heavy burden on the prosecution either to secure the presence of the witness or to demonstrate the impossibility of that endeavor. *Barber v. Page, supra,* held that the absence of a witness from the jurisdiction does not excuse the State's failure to attempt to compel the witness' attendance at trial; in such circumstances, the government must show that it has engaged in a diligent effort to locate and procure the witness' return. "In short, a witness is not 'unavailable' for purposes of the foregoing exception to the confrontation requirement unless the prosecutorial authorities have made a good-faith effort to obtain his presence at trial." *Id.,* 390 U.S., at 724-725, 88 S.Ct., at 1322. See, *e. g., United States v. Mann,* 590 F.2d 361, 367 (CA1 1978); *United States v. Lynch,* 163 U.S.App.D.C. 6, 18-19, 499 F.2d 1011, 1023-1024 (1974); *Government of the Virgin Islands v. Aquino,* 378 F.2d 540, 549-552 (CA3 1967). See generally 5 J. Wigmore, Evidence § 1405 (J. Chadbourn rev. 1974) and cases cited therein.

In the present case, I am simply unable to conclude that the prosecution met its burden of establishing Anita Isaacs' unavailability. From all that appears in the record-and there has been no suggestion that the record is incomplete in this respect-the State's *total* effort to secure Anita's attendance at respondent's trial consisted of the delivery of five subpoenas in her name to her parents' residence, and three of those were issued after the authorities had learned that she was no longer living there. At least four months before the trial began, the prosecution was aware that Anita had moved away; yet during that entire interval it did nothing whatsoever to try to make contact with her. It is difficult to believe that the State would have been so derelict in attempting to secure the witness' presence at trial had it not had her favorable preliminary hearing testimony upon which to rely in the event of her "unavailability." The perfunctory steps which the State took in this case can hardly qualify as a "good-faith effort." In point of fact, it was no effort at all.

The Court, however, is apparently willing to excuse the prosecution's inaction on the ground that any endeavor to locate Anita Isaacs was unlikely to bear fruit. See *ante,* at 2544. I not only take issue with the premise underlying that reasoning-that the improbability of success can condone a refusal to conduct even a cursory investigation into the witness' whereabouts-but I also seriously question the Court's conclusion that a bona fide search in the present case would inevitably have come to naught.

Surely the prosecution's mere speculation about the difficulty of locating Anita Isaacs cannot relieve it of the obligation to attempt to find her. Although the rigor of the undertaking might serve to palliate a failure to prevail, it cannot justify a failure even to try. Just as *Barber* cautioned that " 'the possibility of a refusal is not the equivalent of asking and receiving a rebuff,' " 390 U.S., at 724, 88 S.Ct., at 1322 (quoting the decision below, 381 F.2d 479, 481 (CA10 1966) (Aldrich, J., dissenting)), so, too, the possibility of a defeat is not the equivalent of pursuing all obvious leads and returning emptyhanded. The duty of "good-faith effort" would be meaningless indeed "if that effort were required only in circumstances where success was guaranteed." *Mancusi v. Stubbs*, 408 U.S. 204, 223, 92 S.Ct. 2308, 2318, 33 L.Ed.2d 293 (1972) (MARSHALL, J., dissenting).

Nor do I concur in the Court's bleak prognosis of the likelihood of procuring Anita Isaacs' attendance at respondent's trial. Although Anita's mother testified that she had no current knowledge of her daughter's whereabouts, the prosecution possessed sufficient information upon which it could have at least initiated an investigation. As the Court acknowledges, one especially promising lead was the San Francisco social worker to whom Mrs. Isaacs had spoken and with whom Anita had filed for welfare. What the Court fails to mention, however, is that the prosecution had more to go on than that datum alone. For example, Mrs. Isaacs testified that on the same day she talked to the social worker, she also spoke to her daughter. And although Mrs. Isaacs told defense counsel that she knew of no way to get in touch with her daughter in an emergency, Tr. 195, in response to a similar question from the prosecutor she indicated that someone in Tucson might be able to contact Anita. *Id.*, at 198-199. It would serve no purpose here to essay an exhaustive catalog of the numerous measures the State could have taken in a diligent attempt to locate Anita. It suffices simply to note that it is not "hindsight," see *ante*, at 2544, that permits us to envision how a skilled investigator armed with this information (and any additional facts not brought out through the *voir dire*)5 might have discovered Anita's whereabouts with reasonable effort. Indeed, precisely because the prosecution did absolutely nothing to try to locate Anita, hindsight does not enhance the vista of investigatory opportunities that were available to the State had it actually attempted to find her.

In sum, what the Court said in *Barber v. Page*, 390 U.S., at 725, 88 S.Ct., at 1322, is equally germane here: "[S]o far as this record reveals, the sole reason why [the witness] was not present to testify in person was because the State did not attempt to seek [her] presence. The right of confrontation may not be dispensed with so lightly."

Both before and after the court's decision in Roberts members of the bench, bar and academia argued that the focus of the confrontation clause should be on preventing the state from building a case against the accused using out-of-court statements in place of live testimony.

When the court decided Crawford it abandoned the *Roberts* approach and adopted a version of the procedural rights theory. This theory posits that the confrontation clause bars "testimonial" hearsay from being used against criminal defendants if they are given no chance to cross examine the witness. The practical difficulty was in deciding exactly how to apply the court's holding.

The *Crawford* case is similar to other constitutional exclusionary doctrines descending from the famous decisions in *Mapp, Massiah,* and *Miranda,* which provide counterincentives against police misconduct by requiring exclusion of evidence that might otherwise be admissible.[49] However, in *Crawford* the focus was on police misconduct, but a much broader concept of preventing prosecutorial misconduct or gaming of the process. The court later addressed this, being careful to note that the

---

[49] Miranda v. Arizona, 384 U.S. 436 (1966) (doctrine based on right against self-incrimination); Massiah v. United States, 377 U.S. 201 (1964) (doctrine based on right of counsel); Mapp v. Ohio, 367 U.S. 643 (1961) (doctrine based on right against unreasonable searches and seizures).

confrontation clause "in no way governs police conduct" because it is "the trial *use* of, not the investigatory *collection* of" testimonial statements that offends the clause.[50]

THE COURT SPEAKS AGAIN - CRAWFORD V. WASHINGTON

Consider the court's approach in this follow on case to Ohio v. Roberts. As you read it, ask yourself how the court dealt with the confrontation clause issues this time? What changed? Do you find the court's reasoning persuasive? Why?

124 S.Ct. 1354
Supreme Court of the United States
Michael D. CRAWFORD, Petitioner,
v.
WASHINGTON.
No. 02-9410.
Argued Nov. 10, 2003.
Decided March 8, 2004.

Justice SCALIA delivered the opinion of the Court.

Petitioner Michael Crawford stabbed a man who allegedly tried to rape his wife, Sylvia. At his trial, the State played for the jury Sylvia's tape-recorded statement to the police describing the stabbing, even though he had no opportunity for cross-examination. The Washington Supreme Court upheld petitioner's conviction after determining that Sylvia's statement was reliable. The question presented is whether this procedure complied with the Sixth Amendment's guarantee that, "[i]n all criminal prosecutions, the accused shall enjoy the right ... to be confronted with the witnesses against him."

I

On August 5, 1999, Kenneth Lee was stabbed at his apartment. Police arrested petitioner later that night. After giving petitioner and his wife *Miranda* warnings, detectives interrogated each of them twice. Petitioner eventually confessed that he and Sylvia had gone in search of Lee because he was upset over an earlier incident in which Lee had tried to rape her. The two had found Lee at his apartment, and a fight ensued in which Lee was stabbed in the torso and petitioner's hand was cut.

Petitioner gave the following account of the fight:

"Q. Okay. Did you ever see anything in [Lee's] hands?

"A. I think so, but I'm not positive.

"Q. Okay, when you think so, what do you mean by that?

"A. I could a swore I seen him goin' for somethin' before, right before everything happened. He was like reachin', fiddlin' around down here and stuff ... and I just ... I don't know, I think, this is just a possibility, but I think, I think that he pulled somethin' out and I grabbed for it and that's how I got cut ... but I'm not positive. I, I, my mind goes blank when things like this happen. I mean, I just, I remember things wrong, I remember things that just doesn't, don't make sense to me later." App. 155 (punctuation added).

---

[50] Davis v. Washington, 547 U.S. 813 (2006).

Sylvia generally corroborated petitioner's story about the events leading up to the fight, but her account of the fight itself was arguably different-particularly with respect to whether Lee had drawn a weapon before petitioner assaulted him:

"Q. Did Kenny do anything to fight back from this assault?

"A. (pausing) I know he reached into his pocket ... or somethin' ... I don't know what.

"Q. After he was stabbed?

"A. He saw Michael coming up. He lifted his hand ... his chest open, he might [have] went to go strike his hand out or something and then (inaudible).

"Q. Okay, you, you gotta speak up.

"A. Okay, he lifted his hand over his head maybe to strike Michael's hand down or something and then he put his hands in his ... put his right hand in his right pocket ... took a step back ... Michael proceeded to stab him ... then his hands were like ... how do you explain this ... open arms ... with his hands open and he fell down ... and we ran (describing subject holding hands open, palms toward assailant).

"Q. Okay, when he's standing there with his open hands, you're talking about Kenny, correct?

"A. Yeah, after, after the fact, yes.

"Q. Did you see anything in his hands at that point?

"A. (pausing) um um (no)." *Id.,* at 137 (punctuation added).

The State charged petitioner with assault and attempted murder. At trial, he claimed self-defense. Sylvia did not testify because of the state marital privilege, which generally bars a spouse from testifying without the other spouse's consent. See Wash. Rev.Code § 5.60.060(1) (1994). In Washington, this privilege does not extend to a spouse's out-of-court statements admissible under a hearsay exception, see *State v. Burden,* 120 Wash.2d 371, 377, 841 P.2d 758, 761 (1992), so the State sought to introduce Sylvia's tape-recorded statements to the police as evidence that the stabbing was not in self-defense. Noting that Sylvia had admitted she led petitioner to Lee's apartment and thus had facilitated the assault, the State invoked the hearsay exception for statements against penal interest, Wash. Rule Evid. 804(b)(3) (2003).

Petitioner countered that, state law notwithstanding, admitting the evidence would violate his federal constitutional right to be "confronted with the witnesses against him." Amdt. 6. According to our description of that right in ***Ohio v. Roberts***, 448 U.S. 56, 100 S.Ct. 2531, 65 L.Ed.2d 597 (1980), it does not bar admission of an unavailable witness's statement against a criminal defendant if the statement bears "adequate 'indicia of reliability.' " *Id.,* at 66, 100 S.Ct. 2531. To meet that test, evidence must either fall within a "firmly rooted hearsay exception" or bear "particularized guarantees of trustworthiness." *Ibid.* The trial court here admitted the statement on the latter ground, offering several reasons why it was trustworthy: Sylvia was not shifting blame but rather corroborating her husband's story that he acted in self-defense or "justified reprisal"; she had direct knowledge as an eyewitness; she was describing recent events; and she was being questioned by a "neutral" law enforcement officer. App. 76-77. The prosecution played the tape for the jury and relied on it in closing, arguing that it was "damning evidence" that "completely refutes [petitioner's] claim of self-defense." Tr. 468 (Oct. 21, 1999). The jury convicted petitioner of assault.

The Washington Court of Appeals reversed. It applied a nine-factor test to determine whether Sylvia's statement bore particularized guarantees of trustworthiness, and noted several reasons why it did not: The statement contradicted one she had previously given; it was made in response to specific questions; and at one point she admitted she had shut her eyes during the stabbing. The court considered and rejected the State's argument that Sylvia's statement was reliable because it coincided with petitioner's to such a degree that the two "interlocked." The court determined that, although the two statements agreed about the events leading up to the stabbing, they differed on the issue crucial to petitioner's self-defense claim: "[Petitioner's] version asserts that Lee may have had something in his hand when he stabbed him; but Sylvia's version has Lee grabbing for something only after he has been stabbed." App. 32.

The Washington Supreme Court reinstated the conviction, unanimously concluding that, although Sylvia's statement did not fall under a firmly rooted hearsay exception, it bore guarantees of trustworthiness: " '[W]hen a codefendant's confession is virtually identical [to, *i.e.*, interlocks with,] that of a defendant, it may be deemed reliable.' " 147 Wash.2d 424, 437, 54 P.3d 656, 663 (2002) (quoting *State v. Rice,* 120 Wash.2d 549, 570, 844 P.2d 416, 427 (1993)). The court explained:

"Although the Court of Appeals concluded that the statements were contradictory, upon closer inspection they appear to overlap....

"[B]oth of the Crawfords' statements indicate that Lee was possibly grabbing for a weapon, but they are equally unsure when this event may have taken place. They are also equally unsure how Michael received the cut on his hand, leading the court to question when, if ever, Lee possessed a weapon. In this respect they overlap....

"[N]either Michael nor Sylvia clearly stated that Lee had a weapon in hand from which Michael was simply defending himself. And it is this omission by both that interlocks the statements and makes Sylvia's statement reliable." 147 Wash.2d, at 438-439, 54 P.3d, at 664 (internal quotation marks omitted).

We granted certiorari to determine whether the State's use of Sylvia's statement violated the Confrontation Clause. 539 U.S. 914, 123 S.Ct. 2275, 156 L.Ed.2d 129 (2003).

II

The Sixth Amendment's Confrontation Clause provides that, "[i]n all criminal prosecutions, the accused shall enjoy the right ... to be confronted with the witnesses against him." We have held that this bedrock procedural guarantee applies to both federal and state prosecutions. *Pointer v. Texas,* 380 U.S. 400, 406, 85 S.Ct. 1065, 13 L.Ed.2d 923 (1965). As noted above, *Roberts* says that an unavailable witness's out-of-court statement may be admitted so long as it has adequate indicia of reliability-*i.e.,* falls within a "firmly rooted hearsay exception" or bears "particularized guarantees of trustworthiness." 448 U.S., at 66, 100 S.Ct. 2531. Petitioner argues that this test strays from the original meaning of the Confrontation Clause and urges us to reconsider it.

A

The Constitution's text does not alone resolve this case. One could plausibly read "witnesses against" a defendant to mean those who actually testify at trial, cf. *Woodsides v. State,* 3 Miss. 655, 664-665 (1837), those whose statements are offered at trial, see 3 J. Wigmore, Evidence § 1397, p. 104 (2d ed.1923) (hereinafter Wigmore), or something in-between, see *infra,* at 1364. We must therefore turn to the historical background of the Clause to understand its meaning.

The right to confront one's accusers is a concept that dates back to Roman times. See *Coy v. Iowa,* 487 U.S. 1012, 1015, 108 S.Ct. 2798, 101 L.Ed.2d 857 (1988); Herrmann & Speer, Facing the Accuser: Ancient and Medieval Precursors of the Confrontation Clause, 34 Va. J. Int'l L. 481 (1994). The founding generation's immediate source of the concept, however, was the common law. English common law has long differed from continental civil law in regard to the manner in which witnesses give testimony in criminal trials. The common-law tradition is one of live testimony in court subject to adversarial testing, while the civil law condones examination in private by judicial officers. See 3 W. Blackstone, Commentaries on the Laws of England 373-374 (1768).

Nonetheless, England at times adopted elements of the civil-law practice. Justices of the peace or other officials examined suspects and witnesses before trial. These examinations were sometimes read in court in lieu of live testimony, a practice that "occasioned frequent demands by the prisoner to have his 'accusers,' *i.e.* the witnesses against him, brought before him face to face." 1 J. Stephen, History of the Criminal Law of England 326 (1883). In some cases, these demands were refused. See 9 W. Holdsworth, History of English Law 216-217, 228 (3d ed.1944); *e.g., Raleigh's Case,* 2 How. St. Tr. 1, 15-16, 24 (1603); *Throckmorton's Case,* 1 How. St. Tr. 869, 875-876 (1554); cf. *Lilburn's Case,* 3 How. St. Tr. 1315, 1318-1322, 1329 (Star Chamber 1637).

Pretrial examinations became routine under two statutes passed during the reign of Queen Mary in the 16th century, 1 & 2 Phil. & M., c. 13 (1554), and 2 & 3 *id.,* c. 10 (1555). These Marian bail and committal statutes required justices of the peace to examine suspects and witnesses in felony cases and to certify the results to the court. It is doubtful that the original purpose of the examinations was to produce evidence admissible at trial. See J. Langbein, Prosecuting Crime in the Renaissance 21-34 (1974). Whatever the original purpose, however, they came to be used as evidence in some cases, see 2 M. Hale, Pleas of the Crown 284 (1736), resulting in an adoption of continental procedure. See 4 Holdsworth, *supra,* at 528-530.

The most notorious instances of civil-law examination occurred in the great political trials of the 16th and 17th centuries. One such was the 1603 trial of Sir Walter Raleigh for treason. Lord Cobham, Raleigh's alleged accomplice, had implicated him in an examination before the Privy Council and in a letter. At Raleigh's trial, these were read to the jury. Raleigh argued that Cobham had lied to save himself: "Cobham is absolutely in the King's mercy; to excuse me cannot avail him; by accusing me he may hope for favour." 1 D. Jardine, Criminal Trials 435 (1832). Suspecting that Cobham would recant, Raleigh demanded that the judges call him to appear, arguing that "[t]he Proof of the Common Law is by witness and jury: let Cobham be here, let him speak it. Call my accuser before my face ...." 2 How. St. Tr., at 15-16. The judges refused, *id.,* at 24, and, despite Raleigh's protestations that he was being tried "by the Spanish Inquisition," *id.,* at 15, the jury convicted, and Raleigh was sentenced to death.

One of Raleigh's trial judges later lamented that " 'the justice of England has never been so degraded and injured as by the condemnation of Sir Walter Raleigh.' " 1 Jardine, *supra,* at 520. Through a series of statutory and judicial reforms, English law developed a right of confrontation that limited these abuses. For example, treason statutes required witnesses to confront the accused "face to face" at his arraignment. *E.g.,* 13 Car. 2, c. 1, § 5 (1661); see 1 Hale, *supra,* at 306. Courts, meanwhile, developed relatively strict rules of unavailability, admitting examinations only if the witness was demonstrably unable to testify in person. See *Lord Morley's Case,* 6 How. St. Tr. 769, 770-771 (H.L.1666); 2 Hale, *supra,* at 284; 1 Stephen, *supra,* at 358. Several authorities also stated that a suspect's confession could be admitted only against himself, and not against others he implicated. See 2 W. Hawkins, Pleas of the Crown, ch. 46, § 3, pp. 603-604 (T. Leach 6th ed. 1787); 1 Hale, *supra,* at 585, n. *(k);* 1 G. Gilbert, Evidence 216 (C. Lofft ed. 1791); cf. *Tong's Case,* Kel. J. 17, 18, 84 Eng. Rep. 1061, 1062 (1662) (treason). But see *King v. Westbeer,* 1 Leach 12, 168 Eng. Rep. 108, 109 (1739).

One recurring question was whether the admissibility of an unavailable witness's pretrial examination depended on whether the defendant had had an opportunity to cross-examine him. In 1696, the Court of King's Bench answered this question in the affirmative, in the widely reported misdemeanor libel case of *King v. Paine,* 5 Mod. 163, 87 Eng. Rep. 584. The court ruled that, even though a witness was dead, his examination was not admissible where "the defendant not being present when [it was] taken before the mayor ... had lost the benefit of a cross-examination." *Id.,* at 165, 87 Eng. Rep., at 585. The question was also debated at length during the infamous proceedings against Sir John Fenwick on a bill of attainder. Fenwick's counsel objected to admitting the examination of a witness who had been spirited away, on the ground that Fenwick had had no opportunity to cross-examine. See *Fenwick's Case,* 13 How. St. Tr. 537, 591-592 (H.C. 1696) (Powys) ("[T]hat which they would offer is something that Mr. Goodman hath sworn when he was examined ...; sir J.F. not being present or privy, and no opportunity given to cross-examine the person; and I conceive that cannot be offered as evidence ..."); *id.,* at 592 (Shower) ("[N]o deposition of a person can be read, though beyond sea, unless in cases where the party it is to be read against was privy to the examination, and might have cross-examined him .... [O]ur constitution is, that the person shall see his accuser"). The examination was nonetheless admitted on a closely divided vote after several of those present opined that the common-law rules of procedure did not apply to parliamentary attainder proceedings-one speaker even admitting that the evidence would normally be inadmissible. See *id.,* at 603-604 (Williamson); *id.,* at 604-605 (Chancellor of the Exchequer); *id.,* at 607; 3 Wigmore § 1364, at 22-23, n. 54. Fenwick was condemned, but the proceedings "must have burned into the general consciousness the vital importance of the rule securing the right of cross-examination." *Id.,* § 1364, at 22; cf. <u>Carmell v. Texas, 529 U.S. 513, 526-530, 120 S.Ct. 1620, 146 L.Ed.2d 577 (2000).</u>

Paine had settled the rule requiring a prior opportunity for cross-examination as a matter of common law, but some doubts remained over whether the Marian statutes prescribed an exception to it in felony cases. The statutes did not identify the circumstances under which examinations were admissible, see 1 & 2 Phil. & M., c. 13 (1554); 2 & 3 *id.,* c. 10 (1555), and some inferred that no prior opportunity for cross-examination was required. See *Westbeer, supra,* at 12, 168 Eng. Rep., at 109; compare *Fenwick's Case,* 13 How. St. Tr., at 596 (Sloane), with *id.,* at 602 (Musgrave). Many who expressed this view acknowledged that it meant the statutes were in derogation of the common law. See *King v. Eriswell,* 3 T.R. 707, 710, 100 Eng. Rep. 815, 817 (K.B.1790) (Grose, J.) (dicta); *id.,* at 722-723, 100 Eng. Rep., at 823-824 (Kenyon, C.J.) (same); compare 1 Gilbert, Evidence, at 215 (admissible only "by Force 'of the Statute' "), with *id.,* at 65. Nevertheless, by 1791 (the year the Sixth Amendment was ratified), courts were applying the cross-examination rule even to examinations by justices of the peace in felony cases. See *King v. Dingler,* 2 Leach 561, 562-563, 168 Eng. Rep. 383, 383-384 (1791); *King v. Woodcock,* 1 Leach 500, 502-504, 168 Eng. Rep. 352, 353 (1789); **47* cf. *King v. Radbourne,* 1 Leach 457, 459-461, 168 Eng. Rep. 330, 331-332 (1787); 3 Wigmore § 1364, at 23. Early 19th-century treatises confirm that requirement. See 1 T. Starkie, Evidence 95 (1826); 2 *id.,* at 484-492; T. Peake, Evidence 63-64 (3d ed. 1808). When Parliament amended the statutes in 1848 to make the requirement explicit, see 11 & 12 Vict., c. 42, § 17, the change merely "introduced in terms" what was already afforded the defendant "by the equitable construction of the law." *Queen v. Beeston,* 29 Eng. L. & Eq. R. 527, 529 (Ct.Crim.App.1854) (Jervis, C. J.).

B

Controversial examination practices were also used in the Colonies. Early in the 18th century, for example, the Virginia Council protested against the Governor for having "privately issued several commissions to examine witnesses against particular men *ex parte,*" complaining that "the person accused is not admitted to be confronted with, or defend himself against his defamers." A Memorial Concerning the Maladministrations of His Excellency Francis Nicholson, reprinted in 9 English Historical Documents 253, 257 (D. Douglas ed.1955). A decade before the Revolution, England gave jurisdiction over Stamp Act offenses to the admiralty courts, which followed civil-law rather than common-law procedures and thus routinely took testimony by deposition or private judicial examination. See 5 Geo. 3, c. 12, § 57 (1765); Pollitt, The Right of Confrontation: Its History and Modern Dress, 8 J. Pub.L. 381, 396-397 (1959). Colonial representatives protested that the Act subverted their rights "by extending the jurisdiction of the courts of admiralty beyond its ancient limits." Resolutions of the Stamp Act Congress § 8th (Oct. 19, 1765), reprinted in Sources of Our Liberties 270, 271 (R. Perry & J. Cooper eds.1959). John Adams, defending a merchant in a high-profile admiralty case, argued: "Examinations of witnesses upon Interrogatories, are only by the Civil Law. Interrogatories are unknown at common Law, and Englishmen and common Lawyers have an aversion to them if not an Abhorrence of them." Draft of Argument in *Sewall v. Hancock* (Oct. 1768 - Mar. 1769), in 2 Legal Papers of John Adams 194, 207 (L. Wroth & H. Zobel eds.1965).

Many declarations of rights adopted around the time of the Revolution guaranteed a right of confrontation. See Virginia Declaration of Rights § 8 (1776); Pennsylvania Declaration of Rights § IX (1776); Delaware Declaration of Rights § 14 (1776); Maryland Declaration of Rights § XIX (1776); North Carolina Declaration of Rights § VII (1776); Vermont Declaration of Rights Ch. I, § X (1777); Massachusetts Declaration of Rights § XII (1780); New Hampshire Bill of Rights § XV (1783), all reprinted in 1 B. Schwartz, The Bill of Rights: A Documentary History 235, 265, 278, 282, 287, 323, 342, 377 (1971). The proposed Federal Constitution, however, did not. At the Massachusetts ratifying convention, Abraham Holmes objected to this omission precisely on the ground that it would lead to civil-law practices: "The mode of trial is altogether indetermined; ... whether [the defendant] is to be allowed to confront the witnesses, and have the advantage of cross-examination, we are not yet told .... [W]e shall find Congress possessed of powers enabling them to institute judicatories little less inauspicious than a certain tribunal in Spain, ... the *Inquisition.*" 2 Debates on the Federal Constitution 110-111 (J. Elliot 2d ed. 1863). Similarly, a prominent Antifederalist writing under the pseudonym Federal Farmer criticized the use of "written evidence" while objecting to the omission of a vicinage right: "Nothing can be more essential than the cross examining [of] witnesses, and generally before the triers of the facts in question .... [W]ritten evidence ... [is] almost useless; it must be frequently taken ex parte, and but very seldom leads to the proper discovery of truth." R. Lee, Letter IV by the Federal Farmer (Oct. 15, 1787), reprinted in 1 Schwartz, *supra,* at 469, 473. The First Congress responded by including the Confrontation Clause in the proposal that became the Sixth Amendment.

Early state decisions shed light upon the original understanding of the common-law right. *State v. Webb,* 2 N.C. 103 (Super. L. & Eq. 1794) *(per curiam),* decided a mere three years after the adoption of the Sixth Amendment, held that depositions could be read against an accused only if they were taken in his presence. Rejecting a broader reading of the English authorities, the court held: "[I]t is a rule of the common law, founded on natural justice, that no man shall be prejudiced by evidence which he had not the liberty to cross examine." *Id., at 104.*

Similarly, in *State v. Campbell,* 30 S.C.L. 124, 1844 WL 2558 (App.L.1844), South Carolina's highest law court excluded a deposition taken by a coroner in the absence of the accused. It held: "[I]f we are to decide the question by the established rules of the common law, there could not be a dissenting voice. For, notwithstanding the death of the witness, and whatever the respectability of the court taking the depositions, the solemnity of the occasion and the weight of the testimony, such depositions are *ex parte,* and, therefore, utterly incompetent." *Id., at 125.* The court said that one of the "indispensable conditions" implicitly guaranteed by the State Constitution was that "prosecutions be carried on to the conviction of the accused, by witnesses confronted by him, and subjected to his personal examination." *Ibid.*

Many other decisions are to the same effect. Some early cases went so far as to hold that prior testimony was inadmissible in criminal cases *even if* the accused had a previous opportunity to cross-examine. See *Finn v. Commonwealth,* 26 Va. 701, 708 (1827); *State v. Atkins,* 1 Tenn. 229 (Super. L. & Eq. 1807) *(per curiam).* Most courts rejected that view, but only after reaffirming that admissibility depended on a prior opportunity for cross-examination. See *United States v. Macomb,* 26 F.Cas. 1132, 1133 (No. 15,702) (CC Ill. 1851); *State v. Houser,* 26 Mo. 431, 435-436 (1858); *Kendrick v. State,* 29 Tenn. 479, 485-488 (1850); *Bostick v. State,* 22 Tenn. 344, 345-346 (1842); *Commonwealth v. Richards,* 35 Mass. 434, 437 (1837); *State v. Hill,* 20 S.C.L. 607, 608-610 (App. 1835); *Johnston v. State,* 10 Tenn. 58, 59 (Err. & App. 1821). Nineteenth-century treatises confirm the rule. See 1 J. Bishop, Criminal Procedure § 1093, p. 689 (2d ed. 1872); T. Cooley, Constitutional Limitations *318.

III

This history supports two inferences about the meaning of the Sixth Amendment.

A

First, the principal evil at which the Confrontation Clause was directed was the civil-law mode of criminal procedure, and particularly its use of *ex parte* examinations as evidence against the accused. It was these practices that the Crown deployed in notorious treason cases like Raleigh's; that the Marian statutes invited; that English law's assertion of a right to confrontation was meant to prohibit; and that the founding-era rhetoric decried. The Sixth Amendment must be interpreted with this focus in mind.

Accordingly, we once again reject the view that the Confrontation Clause applies of its own force only to in-court testimony, and that its application to out-of-court statements *51 introduced at trial depends upon "the law of Evidence for the time being." 3 Wigmore § 1397, at 101; accord, *Dutton v. Evans,* 400 U.S. 74, 94, 91 S.Ct. 210, 27 L.Ed. 2d 213 (1970) (Harlan, J., concurring in result). Leaving the regulation of out-of-court statements to the law of evidence would render the Confrontation Clause powerless to prevent even the most flagrant inquisitorial practices. Raleigh was, after all, perfectly free to confront those who read Cobham's confession in court.

This focus also suggests that not all hearsay implicates the Sixth Amendment's core concerns. An off-hand, overheard remark might be unreliable evidence and thus a good candidate for exclusion under hearsay rules, but it bears little resemblance to the civil-law abuses the Confrontation Clause targeted. On the other hand, *ex parte* examinations might sometimes be admissible under modern hearsay rules, but the Framers certainly would not have condoned them.

The text of the Confrontation Clause reflects this focus. It applies to "witnesses" against the accused-in other words, those who "bear testimony." 2 N. Webster, An American Dictionary of the English Language (1828). "Testimony," in turn, is typically "[a] solemn declaration or affirmation made for the purpose of establishing or proving some fact." *Ibid.* An accuser who makes a formal statement to government officers bears testimony in a sense that a person who makes a casual remark to an acquaintance does not. The constitutional text, like the history underlying the common-law right of confrontation, thus reflects an especially acute concern with a specific type of out-of-court statement.

Various formulations of this core class of "testimonial" statements exist: "*ex parte* in-court testimony or its functional equivalent-that is, material such as affidavits, custodial examinations, prior testimony that the defendant was unable to cross-examine, or similar pretrial statements that declarants would reasonably expect to be used prosecutorially," Brief for Petitioner 23; "extrajudicial statements ... contained in formalized testimonial materials, such as affidavits, depositions, prior testimony, or confessions," *White v. Illinois*, 502 U.S. 346, 365, 112 S.Ct. 736, 116 L.Ed.2d 848 (1992) (THOMAS, J., joined by SCALIA, J., concurring in part and concurring in judgment); "statements that were made under circumstances which would lead an objective witness reasonably to believe that the statement would be available for use at a later trial," Brief for National Association of Criminal Defense Lawyers et al. as *Amici Curiae* 3. These formulations all share a common nucleus and then define the Clause's coverage at various levels of abstraction around it. Regardless of the precise articulation, some statements qualify under any definition-for example, *ex parte* testimony at a preliminary hearing.

Statements taken by police officers in the course of interrogations are also testimonial under even a narrow standard. Police interrogations bear a striking resemblance to examinations by justices of the peace in England. The statements are not *sworn* testimony, but the absence of oath was not dispositive. Cobham's examination was unsworn, see 1 Jardine, Criminal Trials, at 430, yet Raleigh's trial has long been thought a paradigmatic confrontation violation, see, *e.g., Campbell*, 30 S.C.L., at 130. Under the Marian statutes, witnesses were typically put on oath, but suspects were not. See 2 Hale, Pleas of the Crown, at 52. Yet Hawkins and others went out of their way to caution that such unsworn confessions were not admissible against anyone but the confessor. See *supra,* at 1360.

That interrogators are police officers rather than magistrates does not change the picture either. Justices of the peace conducting examinations under the Marian statutes were not magistrates as we understand that office today, but had an essentially investigative and prosecutorial function. See 1 Stephen, Criminal Law of England, at 221; Langbein, Prosecuting Crime in the Renaissance, at 34-45. England did not have a professional police force until the 19th century, see 1 Stephen, *supra,* at 194-200, so it is not surprising that other government officers performed the investigative functions now associated primarily with the police. The involvement of government officers in the production of testimonial evidence presents the same risk, whether the officers are police or justices of the peace.

In sum, even if the Sixth Amendment is not solely concerned with testimonial hearsay, that is its primary object, and interrogations by law enforcement officers fall squarely within that class.

B

The historical record also supports a second proposition: that the Framers would not have allowed admission of testimonial statements of a witness who did not appear at trial unless he was unavailable to testify, and the defendant had had a prior opportunity for cross-examination. The text of the Sixth Amendment does not suggest any open-ended exceptions from the confrontation requirement to be developed by the courts. Rather, the "right ... to be confronted with the witnesses against him," Amdt. 6, is most naturally read as a reference to the right of confrontation at common law, admitting only those exceptions established at the time of the founding. See *Mattox v. United States,* 156 U.S.

237, 243, 15 S.Ct. 337, 39 L.Ed. 409 (1895); cf. *Houser,* 26 Mo., at 433-435. As the English authorities above reveal, the common law in 1791 conditioned admissibility of an absent witness's examination on unavailability and a prior opportunity to cross-examine. The Sixth Amendment therefore incorporates those limitations. The numerous early state decisions applying the same test confirm that these principles were received as part of the common law in this country.

We do not read the historical sources to say that a prior opportunity to cross-examine was merely a sufficient, rather than a necessary, condition for admissibility of testimonial statements. They suggest that this requirement was dispositive, and not merely one of several ways to establish reliability. This is not to deny, as THE CHIEF JUSTICE notes, that "[t]here were always exceptions to the general rule of exclusion" of hearsay evidence. *Post,* at 1377. Several had become well established by 1791. See 3 Wigmore § 1397, at 101; Brief for United States as *Amicus Curiae* 13, n. 5. But there is scant evidence that exceptions were invoked to admit *testimonial* statements against the accused in a *criminal* case. Most of the hearsay exceptions covered statements that by their nature were not testimonial-for example, business records or statements in furtherance of a conspiracy. We do not infer from these that the Framers thought exceptions would apply even to prior testimony. Cf. *Lilly v. Virginia,* 527 U.S. 116, 134, 119 S.Ct. 1887, 144 L.Ed.2d 117 (1999) (plurality opinion) ("[A]ccomplices' confessions that inculpate a criminal defendant are not within a firmly rooted exception to the hearsay rule").

IV

Our case law has been largely consistent with these two principles. Our leading early decision, for example, involved a deceased witness's prior trial testimony. *Mattox v. United States,* 156 U.S. 237, 15 S.Ct. 337, 39 L.Ed. 409 (1895). In allowing the statement to be admitted, we relied on the fact that the defendant had had, at the first trial, an adequate opportunity to confront the witness: "The substance of the constitutional protection is preserved to the prisoner in the advantage he has once had of seeing the witness face to face, and of subjecting him to the ordeal of a cross-examination. This, the law says, he shall under no circumstances be deprived of ...." *Id.,* at 244, 15 S.Ct. 337.

Our later cases conform to *Mattox's* holding that prior trial or preliminary hearing testimony is admissible only if the defendant had an adequate opportunity to cross-examine. See *Mancusi v. Stubbs,* 408 U.S. 204, 213-216, 92 S.Ct. 2308, 33 L.Ed.2d 293 (1972); *California v. Green,* 399 U.S. 149, 165-168, 90 S.Ct. 1930, 26 L.Ed.2d 489 (1970); *Pointer v. Texas,* 380 U.S., at 406-408, 85 S.Ct. 1065; cf. *Kirby v. United States,* 174 U.S. 47, 55-61, 19 S.Ct. 574, 43 L.Ed. 890 (1899). Even where the defendant had such an opportunity, we excluded the testimony where the government had not established unavailability of the witness. See *Barber v. Page,* 390 U.S. 719, 722-725, 88 S.Ct. 1318, 20 L.Ed.2d 255 (1968); cf. *Motes v. United States,* 178 U.S. 458, 470-471, 20 S.Ct. 993, 44 L.Ed. 1150 (1900). We similarly excluded accomplice confessions where the defendant had no opportunity to cross-examine. See *Roberts v. Russell,* 392 U.S. 293, 294-295, 88 S.Ct. 1921, 20 L.Ed.2d 1100 (1968) *(per curiam); Bruton v. United States,* 391 U.S. 123, 126-128, 88 S.Ct. 1620, 20 L.Ed.2d 476 (1968); *Douglas v. Alabama,* 380 U.S. 415, 418-420, 85 S.Ct. 1074, 13 L.Ed.2d 934 (1965). In contrast, we considered reliability factors beyond prior opportunity for cross-examination when the hearsay statement at issue was not testimonial. See *Dutton v. Evans,* 400 U.S., at 87-89, 91 S.Ct. 210 (plurality opinion).

Even our recent cases, in their outcomes, hew closely to the traditional line. *Ohio v. Roberts,* 448 U.S., at 67-70, 100 S.Ct. 2531, admitted testimony from a preliminary hearing at which the defendant had examined the witness. *Lilly v. Virginia, supra,* excluded testimonial statements that the defendant had had no opportunity to test by cross-examination. And *Bourjaily v. United States*, 483 U.S. 171, 181-184, 107 S.Ct. 2775, 97 L.Ed.2d 144 (1987), admitted statements made unwittingly to a Federal Bureau of Investigation informant after applying a more general test that did *not* make prior cross-examination an indispensable requirement.

Lee v. Illinois, 476 U.S. 530, 106 S.Ct. 2056, 90 L.Ed.2d 514 (1986), on which the State relies, is not to the contrary. There, we *rejected* the State's attempt to admit an accomplice confession. The State had argued that the confession was admissible because it "interlocked" with the defendant's. We dealt with the argument by rejecting its premise, holding that "when the discrepancies between the statements are not insignificant, the codefendant's confession may not be admitted." *Id.*, at 545, 106 S.Ct. 2056. Respondent argues that "[t]he logical inference of this statementis that when the discrepancies between the statements *are* insignificant, then the codefendant's statement *may* be admitted." Brief for Respondent 6. But this is merely a possible inference, not an inevitable one, and we do not draw it here. If *Lee* had meant authoritatively to announce an exception-previously unknown to this Court's jurisprudence-for interlocking confessions, it would not have done so in such an oblique manner. Our only precedent on interlocking confessions had addressed the entirely different question whether a limiting instruction cured prejudice to codefendants from admitting a defendant's *own* confession against him in a joint trial. See *Parker v. Randolph*, 442 U.S. 62, 69-76, 99 S.Ct. 2132, 60 L.Ed.2d 713 (1979) (plurality opinion), abrogated by *Cruz v. New York*, 481 U.S. 186, 107 S.Ct. 1714, 95 L.Ed.2d 162 (1987).

Our cases have thus remained faithful to the Framers' understanding: Testimonial statements of witnesses absent from trial have been admitted only where the declarant is unavailable, and only where the defendant has had a prior opportunity to cross-examine.

V

Although the results of our decisions have generally been faithful to the original meaning of the Confrontation Clause, the same cannot be said of our rationales. **Roberts** conditions the admissibility of all hearsay evidence on whether it falls under a "firmly rooted hearsay exception" or bears "particularized guarantees of trustworthiness." 448 U.S., at 66, 100 S.Ct. 2531. This test departs from the historical principles identified above in two respects. First, it is too broad: It applies the same mode of analysis whether or not the hearsay consists of *ex parte* testimony. This often results in close constitutional scrutiny in cases that are far removed from the core concerns of the Clause. At the same time, however, the test is too narrow: It admits statements that *do* consist of *ex parte* testimony upon a mere finding of reliability. This malleable standard often fails to protect against paradigmatic confrontation violations.

Members of this Court and academics have suggested that we revise our doctrine to reflect more accurately the original understanding of the Clause. See, *e.g., Lilly*, 527 U.S., at 140-143, 119 S.Ct. 1887 (BREYER, J., concurring); *White*, 502 U.S., at 366, 112 S.Ct. 736 THOMAS, J., joined by SCALIA, J., concurring in part and concurring in judgment); A. Amar, The Constitution and Criminal Procedure 125-131 (1997); Friedman, Confrontation: The Search for Basic Principles, 86 Geo. L.J. 1011 (1998). They offer two proposals: First, that we apply the Confrontation Clause only to testimonial statements, leaving the remainder to regulation by hearsay law-thus eliminating the overbreadth referred to above. Second, that we impose an absolute bar to statements that are testimonial, absent a prior opportunity to cross-examine-thus eliminating the excessive narrowness referred to above.

In *White,* we considered the first proposal and rejected it. <u>502 U.S., at 352-353, 112 S.Ct. 736.</u> Although our analysis in this case casts doubt on that holding, we need not definitively resolve whether it survives our decision today, because Sylvia Crawford's statement is testimonial under any definition. This case does, however, squarely implicate the second proposal.

A

Where testimonial statements are involved, we do not think the Framers meant to leave the Sixth Amendment's protection to the vagaries of the rules of evidence, much less to amorphous notions of "reliability." Certainly none of the authorities discussed above acknowledges any general reliability exception to the common-law rule. Admitting statements deemed reliable by a judge is fundamentally at odds with the right of confrontation. To be sure, the Clause's ultimate goal is to ensure reliability of evidence, but it is a procedural rather than a substantive guarantee. It commands, not that evidence be reliable, but that reliability be assessed in a particular manner: by testing in the crucible of cross-examination. The Clause thus reflects a judgment, not only about the desirability of reliable evidence (a point on which there could be little dissent), but about how reliability can best be determined. Cf. 3 Blackstone, Commentaries, at 373 ("This open examination of witnesses ... is much more conducive to the clearing up of truth"); M. Hale, History and Analysis of the Common Law of England 258 (1713) (adversarial testing "beats and bolts out the Truth much better").

The *Roberts* test allows a jury to hear evidence, untested by the adversary process, based on a mere judicial determination of reliability. It thus replaces the constitutionally prescribed method of assessing reliability with a wholly foreign one. In this respect, it is very different from exceptions to the Confrontation Clause that make no claim to be a surrogate means of assessing reliability. For example, the rule of forfeiture by wrongdoing (which we accept) extinguishes confrontation claims on essentially equitable grounds; it does not purport to be an alternative means of determining reliability. See <u>Reynolds v. United States,</u> 98 U.S. 145, 158-159, 25 L.Ed. 244 (1879).

The Raleigh trial itself involved the very sorts of reliability determinations that *Roberts* authorizes. In the face of Raleigh's repeated demands for confrontation, the prosecution responded with many of the arguments a court applying *Roberts* might invoke today: that Cobham's statements were self-inculpatory, 2 How. St. Tr., at 19, that they were not made in the heat of passion, *id.,* at 14, and that they were not "extracted from [him] upon any hopes or promise of Pardon," *id.,* at 29. It is not plausible that the Framers' only objection to the trial was that Raleigh's judges did not properly weigh these factors before sentencing him to death. Rather, the problem was that the judges refused to allow Raleigh to confront Cobham in court, where he could cross-examine him and try to expose his accusation as a lie.

Dispensing with confrontation because testimony is obviously reliable is akin to dispensing with jury trial because a defendant is obviously guilty. This is not what the Sixth Amendment prescribes.

B

The legacy of *Roberts* in other courts vindicates the Framers' wisdom in rejecting a general reliability exception. The framework is so unpredictable that it fails to provide meaningful protection from even core confrontation violations.

Reliability is an amorphous, if not entirely subjective, concept. There are countless factors bearing on whether a statement is reliable; the nine-factor balancing test applied by the Court of Appeals below is representative. See, *e.g., People v. Farrell,* 34 P.3d 401,

406-407 (Colo.2001) (eight-factor test). Whether a statement is deemed reliable depends heavily on which factors the judge considers and how much weight he accords each of them. Some courts wind up attaching the same significance to opposite facts. For example, the Colorado Supreme Court held a statement more reliable because its inculpation of the defendant was "detailed," *id., at 407,* while the Fourth Circuit found a statement more reliable because the portion implicating another was "fleeting," *United States v. Photogrammetric Data Servs., Inc.,* 259 F.3d 229, 245 (C.A.4 2001). The Virginia Court of Appeals found a statement more reliable because the witness was in custody and charged with a crime (thus making the statement more obviously against her penal interest), see *Nowlin v. Commonwealth,* 40 Va.App. 327, 335-338, 579 S.E.2d 367, 371-372 (2003), while the Wisconsin Court of Appeals found a statement more reliable because the witness was *not* in custody and *not* a suspect, see *State v. Bintz,* 2002 WI App. 204, ¶ 13, 257 Wis.2d 177, ¶ 13, 650 N.W.2d 913, ¶ 13. Finally, the Colorado Supreme Court in one case found a statement more reliable because it was given "immediately after" the events at issue, *Farrell, supra,* at 407, while that same court, in another case, found a statement more reliable because two years had elapsed, *Stevens v. People,* 29 P.3d 305, 316 (Colo.2001).

The unpardonable vice of the **Roberts** test, however, is not its unpredictability, but its demonstrated capacity to admit core testimonial statements that the Confrontation Clause plainly meant to exclude. Despite the plurality's speculation in *Lilly,* 527 U.S., at 137, 119 S.Ct. 1887, that it was "highly unlikely" that accomplice confessions implicating the accused could survive **Roberts**, courts continue routinely to admit them. See *Photogrammetric Data Servs., supra,* at 245-246; *Farrell, supra,* at 406-408; *Stevens, supra,* at 314-318; *Taylor v. Commonwealth,* 63 S.W.3d 151, 166-168 (Ky.2001); *State v. Hawkins,* No.2001-P-0060, 2002 WL 31895118, ¶¶ 34-37, *6 (**Ohio** App., Dec. 31, 2002); *Bintz, supra,* ¶¶ 7-14, 257 Wis.2d, at 183-188, 650 N.W.2d, at 916-918; *People v. Lawrence,* 55 P.3d 155, 160-161 (Colo.App.2001); *State v. Jones,* 171 Or.App. 375, 387-391, 15 P.3d 616, 623-625 (2000); *State v. Marshall,* 136 **Ohio** App.3d 742, 747-748, 737 N.E.2d 1005, 1009 (2000); *People v. Schutte,* 240 Mich.App. 713, 718-721, 613 N.W.2d 370, 376-377 (2000); *People v. Thomas,* 313 Ill.App.3d 998, 1005-1007, 246 Ill.Dec. 593, 730 N.E.2d 618, 625-626 (2000); cf. *Nowlin, supra,* at 335-338, 579 S.E.2d, at 371-372 (witness confessed to a related crime); *People v. Campbell,* 309 Ill.App.3d 423, 431-432, 242 Ill.Dec. 694, 699, 721 N.E.2d 1225, 1230 (1999) (same). One recent study found that, after *Lilly,* appellate courts admitted accomplice statements to the authorities in 25 out of 70 cases-more than one-third of the time. Kirst, Appellate Court Answers to the Confrontation Questions in Lilly v. Virginia, 53 Syracuse L.Rev. 87, 105 (2003). Courts have invoked **Roberts** to admit other sorts of plainly testimonial statements despite the absence of any opportunity to cross-examine. See *United States v. Aguilar,* 295 F.3d 1018, 1021-1023 (C.A.9 2002) (plea allocution showing existence of a conspiracy); *United States v. Centracchio,* 265 F.3d 518, 527-530 (C.A.7 2001) (same); *United States v. Dolah,* 245 F.3d 98, 104-105 (C.A.2 2001) (same); *United States v. Petrillo,* 237 F.3d 119, 122-123 (C.A.2 2000) (same); *United States v. Moskowitz,* 215 F.3d 265, 268-269 (C.A.2 2000) *(per curiam)* (same); *United States v. Gallego,* 191 F.3d 156, 166-168 (C.A.2 1999) (same); *United States v. Papajohn,* 212 F.3d 1112, 1118-1120 (C.A.8 2000) (grand jury testimony); *United States v. Thomas,* 30 Fed.Appx. 277, 279 (C.A.4 2002) *(per curiam)* (same); *Bintz, supra,* ¶¶ 15-22, 257 Wis.2d, at 188-191, 650 N.W.2d, at 918-920 (prior trial testimony); *State v. McNeill,* 140 N.C.App. 450, 457-460, 537 S.E.2d 518, 523-524 (2000) (same).

To add insult to injury, some of the courts that admit untested testimonial statements find reliability in the very factors that *make* the statements testimonial. As noted earlier, one court relied on the fact that the witness's statement was made to police while in custody on pending charges-the theory being that this made the statement more clearly against penal interest and thus more reliable. _Nowlin, supra,_ at 335-338, 579 S.E.2d, at 371-372. Other courts routinely rely on the fact that a prior statement is given under oath in judicial proceedings. _E.g., Gallego, supra,_ at 168 (plea allocution); _Papajohn, supra,_ at 1120 (grand jury testimony). That inculpating statements are given in a testimonial setting is not an antidote to the confrontation problem, but rather the trigger that makes the Clause's demands most urgent. It is not enough to point out that most of the usual safeguards of the adversary process attend the statement, when the single safeguard missing is the one the Confrontation Clause demands.

C

Roberts ' failings were on full display in the proceedings below. Sylvia Crawford made her statement while in police custody, herself a potential suspect in the case. Indeed, she had been told that whether she would be released "depend[ed] on how the investigation continues." App. 81. In response to often leading questions from police detectives, she implicated her husband in Lee's stabbing and at least arguably undermined his self-defense claim. Despite all this, the trial court admitted her statement, listing several reasons why it was reliable. In its opinion reversing, the Court of Appeals listed several _other_ reasons why the statement was _not_ reliable. Finally, the State Supreme Court relied exclusively on the interlocking character of the statement and disregarded every other factor the lower courts had considered. The case is thus a self-contained demonstration of _Roberts'_ unpredictable and inconsistent application.

Each of the courts also made assumptions that cross-examination might well have undermined. The trial court, for example, stated that Sylvia Crawford's statement was reliable because she was an eyewitness with direct knowledge of the events. But Sylvia at one point told the police that she had "shut [her] eyes and ... didn't really watch" part of the fight, and that she was "in shock." App. 134. The trial court also buttressed its reliability finding by claiming that Sylvia was "being questioned by law enforcement, and, thus, the [questioner] is ... neutral to her and not someone who would be inclined to advance her interests and shade her version of the truth unfavorably toward the defendant." _Id.,_ at 77. The Framers would be astounded to learn that _ex parte_ testimony could be admitted against a criminal defendant because it was elicited by "neutral" government officers. But even if the court's assessment of the officer's motives was accurate, it says nothing about Sylvia's perception of her situation. Only cross-examination could reveal that.

The State Supreme Court gave dispositive weight to the interlocking nature of the two statements-that they were both ambiguous as to when and whether Lee had a weapon. The court's claim that the two statements were _equally_ ambiguous is hard to accept. Petitioner's statement is ambiguous only in the sense that he had lingering doubts about his recollection: "A. I could a swore I seen him goin' for somethin' before, right before everything happened .... [B]ut I'm not positive." _Id.,_ at 155. Sylvia's statement, on the other hand, is truly inscrutable, since the key timing detail was simply assumed in the leading question she was asked: "Q. Did Kenny do anything to fight back from this assault?" _Id.,_ at 137 (punctuation added). Moreover, Sylvia specifically said Lee had nothing in his hands after he was stabbed, while petitioner was not asked about that.

The prosecutor obviously did not share the court's view that Sylvia's statement was ambiguous-he called it "damning evidence" that "completely refutes [petitioner's] claim of self-defense." Tr. 468 (Oct. 21, 1999). We have no way of knowing whether the jury agreed with the prosecutor or the court. Far from obviating the need for cross-examination, the "interlocking" ambiguity of the two statements made it all the more imperative that they be tested to tease out the truth.

We readily concede that we could resolve this case by simply reweighing the "reliability factors" under **Roberts** and finding that Sylvia Crawford's statement falls short. But we view this as one of those rare cases in which the result below is so improbable that it reveals a fundamental failure on our part to interpret the Constitution in a way that secures its intended constraint on judicial discretion. Moreover, to reverse the Washington Supreme Court's decision after conducting our own reliability analysis would perpetuate, not avoid, what the Sixth Amendment condemns. The Constitution prescribes a procedure for determining the reliability of testimony in criminal trials, and we, no less than the state courts, lack authority to replace it with one of our own devising.

We have no doubt that the courts below were acting in utmost good faith when they found reliability. The Framers, however, would not have been content to indulge this assumption. They knew that judges, like other government officers, could not always be trusted to safeguard the rights of the people; the likes of the dread Lord Jeffreys were not yet too distant a memory. They were loath to leave too much discretion in judicial hands. Cf. U.S. Const., Amdt. 6 (criminal jury trial); Amdt. 7 (civil jury trial); *Ring v. Arizona,* 536 U.S. 584, 611-612, 122 S.Ct. 2428, 153 L.Ed.2d 556 (2002) (SCALIA, J., concurring). By replacing categorical constitutional guarantees with ***68** open-ended balancing tests, we do violence to their design. Vague standards are manipulable, and, while that might be a small concern in run-of-the-mill assault prosecutions like this one, the Framers had an eye toward politically charged cases like Raleigh's-great state trials where the impartiality of even those at the highest levels of the judiciary might not be so clear. It is difficult to imagine **Roberts'** providing any meaningful protection in those circumstances.

* * *

Where nontestimonial hearsay is at issue, it is wholly consistent with the Framers' design to afford the States flexibility in their development of hearsay law-as does **Roberts**, and as would an approach that exempted such statements from Confrontation Clause scrutiny altogether. Where testimonial evidence is at issue, however, the Sixth Amendment demands what the common law required: unavailability and a prior opportunity for cross-examination. We leave for another day any effort to spell out a comprehensive definition of "testimonial." Whatever else the term covers, it applies at a minimum to prior testimony at a preliminary hearing, before a grand jury, or at a former trial; and to police interrogations. These are the modern practices with closest kinship to the abuses at which the Confrontation Clause was directed.

In this case, the State admitted Sylvia's testimonial statement against petitioner, despite the fact that he had no opportunity to cross-examine her. That alone is sufficient to make out a violation of the Sixth Amendment. **Roberts** notwithstanding, we decline to mine the record in search of indicia of reliability. Where testimonial statements are at issue, the only indicium of reliability sufficient to satisfy constitutional demands is the one the Constitution actually prescribes: confrontation.

The judgment of the Washington Supreme Court is reversed, and the case is remanded for further proceedings not inconsistent with this opinion.

It is so ordered.

Chief Justice <u>REHNQUIST</u>, with whom Justice <u>O'CONNOR</u> joins, concurring in the judgment.

I dissent from the Court's decision to overrule ***Ohio v. Roberts,*** 448 U.S. 56, 100 S.Ct. 2531, 65 L.Ed.2d 597 (1980). I believe that the Court's adoption of a new interpretation of the Confrontation Clause is not backed by sufficiently persuasive reasoning to overrule long-established precedent. Its decision casts a mantle of uncertainty over future criminal trials in both federal and state courts, and is by no means necessary to decide the present case.

The Court's distinction between testimonial and nontestimonial statements, contrary to its claim, is no better rooted in history than our current doctrine. Under the common law, although the courts were far from consistent, out-of-court statements made by someone other than the accused and not taken under oath, unlike *ex parte* depositions or affidavits, were generally not considered substantive evidence upon which a conviction could be based.1 See, *e.g., King v. Brasier,* 1 Leach 199, 200, 168 Eng. Rep. 202 (K.B.1779); see also J. Langbein, Origins of Adversary Criminal Trial 235-242 (2003); G. Gilbert, Evidence 152 (3d ed. 1769).2 Testimonial statements such as accusatory statements to police officers likely would have been disapproved of in the 18th century, not necessarily because they resembled *ex parte* affidavits or depositions as the Court reasons, but more likely than not because they were not made under oath.3 See *King v. Woodcock,* 1 Leach 500, 503, 168 Eng. Rep. 352, 353 (1789) (noting that a statement taken by a justice of the peace may not be admitted into evidence unless taken under oath). Without an oath, one usually did not get to the second step of whether confrontation was required.

Thus, while I agree that the Framers were mainly concerned about sworn affidavits and depositions, it does not follow that they were similarly concerned about the Court's broader category of testimonial statements. See 2 N. Webster, An American Dictionary of the English Language (1828) (defining "Testimony" as "[a] solemn declaration or affirmation made for the purpose of establishing or proving some fact. *Such affirmation in judicial proceedings, may be verbal or written, but must be under oath* " (emphasis added)). As far as I can tell, unsworn testimonial statements were treated no differently at common law than were nontestimonial statements, and it seems to me any classification of statements as testimonial beyond that of sworn affidavits and depositions will be somewhat arbitrary, merely a proxy for what the Framers might have intended had such evidence been liberally admitted as substantive evidence like it is today.

I therefore see no reason why the distinction the Court draws is preferable to our precedent. Starting with Chief Justice Marshall's interpretation as a Circuit Justice in 1807, 16 years after the ratification of the Sixth Amendment, <u>United States v. Burr, 25 F.Cas. 187, 193 (No. 14,694)</u> (CC Va. 1807), continuing with our cases in the late 19th century, <u>Mattox v. United States, 156 U.S. 237, 243-244, 15 S.Ct. 337, 39 L.Ed. 409 (1895); Kirby *72 v. United States, 174 U.S. 47, 54-57, 19 S.Ct. 574, 43 L.Ed. 890 (1899)</u>, and through today, *e.g., <u>White v. Illinois, 502 U.S. 346, 352-353, 112 S.Ct. 736, 116 L.Ed.2d 848 (1992)</u>, we have never drawn a distinction between testimonial and nontestimonial statements. And for that matter, neither has any other court of which I am aware. I see little value in trading our precedent for an imprecise approximation at this late date.

I am also not convinced that the Confrontation Clause categorically requires the exclusion of testimonial statements. Although many States had their own Confrontation Clauses, they were of recent vintage and were not interpreted with any regularity before 1791. State cases that recently followed the ratification of the Sixth Amendment were not uniform; the Court itself cites state cases from the early 19th century that took a more stringent view of the right to confrontation than does the Court, prohibiting former testimony even if the witness was subjected to cross-examination. See *ante,* at 1363 (citing <u>Finn v. Commonwealth, 26 Va. 701, 708 (1827); State v. Atkins, 1 Tenn. 229 (Super. L. & Eq. 1807)</u> *(per curiam)*).

Nor was the English law at the time of the framing entirely consistent in its treatment of testimonial evidence. Generally *ex parte* affidavits and depositions were excluded as the

Court notes, but even that proposition was not universal. See *King v. Eriswell,* 3 T.R. 707, 100 Eng. Rep. 815 (K.B.1790) (affirming by an equally divided court the admission of an *ex parte* examination because the declarant was unavailable to testify); *King v. Westbeer,* 1 Leach 12, 13, 168 Eng. Rep. 108, 109 (1739) (noting the admission of an *ex parte* affidavit); see also 1 M. Hale, Pleas of the Crown 585-586 (1736) (noting that statements of "accusers and witnesses" which were taken under oath could be admitted into evidence if the declarant was "dead or not able to travel"). Wigmore notes that sworn examinations of witnesses before justices of the peace in certain cases would not have been excluded **73* until the end of the 1700's, 5 Wigmore § 1364, at 26-27, and sworn statements of witnesses before coroners became excluded only by statute in the 1800's, see *ibid.; id.,* § 1374, at 59. With respect to unsworn testimonial statements, there is no indication that once the hearsay rule was developed courts ever excluded these statements if they otherwise fell within a firmly rooted exception. See, *e.g., Eriswell, supra,* at 715-719 (Buller, J.), 720 (Ashhurst, J.), 100 Eng. Rep., at 819-822 (concluding that an *ex parte* examination was admissible as an exception to the hearsay rule because it was a declaration by a party of his state and condition). Dying declarations are one example. See, *e.g., Woodcock, supra,* at 502-504, 168 Eng. Rep., at 353-354; *King v. Reason,* 16 How. St. Tr. 1, 22-23 (K.B.1722).

Between 1700 and 1800 the rules regarding the admissibility of out-of-court statements were still being developed. See n. 1, *supra.* There were always exceptions to the general rule of exclusion, and it is not clear to me that the Framers categorically wanted to eliminate further ones. It is one thing to trace the right of confrontation back to the Roman Empire; it is quite another to conclude that such a right absolutely excludes a large category of evidence. It is an odd conclusion indeed to think that the Framers created a cut-and-dried rule with respect to the admissibility of testimonial statements when the law during their own time was not fully settled.

To find exceptions to exclusion under the Clause is not to denigrate it as the Court suggests. Chief Justice Marshall stated of the Confrontation Clause: "I know of no principle in the preservation of which all are more concerned. I know none, by undermining which, life, liberty and property, might be more endangered. It is therefore incumbent on courts to be watchful of every inroad on a principle so truly important." *Burr,* 25 F.Cas., at 193. Yet, he recognized that such a right was not absolute, acknowledging that exceptions to the exclusionary component of the hearsay rule, which he considered as an "inroad" on the right to confrontation, had been introduced. See *ibid.*

Exceptions to confrontation have always been derived from the experience that some out-of-court statements are just as reliable as cross-examined in-court testimony due to the circumstances under which they were made. We have recognized, for example, that co-conspirator statements simply "cannot be replicated, even if the declarant testifies to the same matters in court." *United States v. Inadi,* 475 U.S. 387, 395, 106 S.Ct. 1121, 89 L.Ed.2d 390 (1986). Because the statements are made while the declarant and the accused are partners in an illegal enterprise, the statements are unlikely to be false and their admission "actually furthers the 'Confrontation Clause's very mission' which is to 'advance the accuracy of the truth-determining process in criminal trials.' " *Id.,* at 396, 106 S.Ct. 1121 (quoting *Tennessee v. Street,* 471 U.S. 409, 415, 105 S.Ct. 2078, 85 L.Ed. 2d 425 (1985) (some internal quotation marks omitted)). Similar reasons justify the introduction of spontaneous declarations, see *White,* 502 U.S., at 356, 112 S.Ct. 736, statements made in the course of procuring medical services, see *ibid.,* dying declarations, see *Kirby, supra,* at 61, 19 S.Ct. 574, and countless other hearsay exceptions. That a statement might be testimonial does nothing to undermine the wisdom of one of these exceptions.

Indeed, cross-examination is a tool used to flesh out the truth, not an empty procedure. See *Kentucky v. Stincer*, 482 U.S. 730, 737, 107 S.Ct. 2658, 96 L.Ed.2d 631 (1987) ("The right to cross-examination, protected by the Confrontation Clause, thus is essentially a 'functional' right designed to promote reliability in the truth-finding functions of a criminal trial"); see also *Maryland v. Craig*, 497 U.S. 836, 845, 110 S.Ct. 3157, 111 L.Ed. 2d 666 (1990) ("The central concern of the Confrontation Clause is to ensure the reliability of the evidence against a criminal defendant by subjecting it to rigorous testing in the context of an adversary proceeding before the trier of fact"). "[I]n a given instance [cross-examination *75 may] be superfluous; it may be sufficiently clear, in that instance, that the statement offered is free enough from the risk of inaccuracy and untrustworthiness, so that the test of cross-examination would be a work of supererogation." 5 Wigmore § 1420, at 251. In such a case, as we noted over 100 years ago, "The law in its wisdom declares that the rights of the public shall not be wholly sacrificed in order that an incidental benefit may be preserved to the accused." *Mattox*, 156 U.S., at 243, 15 S.Ct. 337; see also *Salinger v. United States*, 272 U.S. 542, 548, 47 S.Ct. 173, 71 L.Ed. 398 (1926). By creating an immutable category of excluded evidence, the Court adds little to a trial's truth-finding function and ignores this longstanding guidance.

In choosing the path it does, the Court of course overrules ***Ohio v. Roberts***, 448 U.S. 56, 100 S.Ct. 2531, 65 L.Ed.2d 597 (1980), a case decided nearly a quarter of a century ago. *Stare decisis* is not an inexorable command in the area of constitutional law, see *Payne v. Tennessee*, 501 U.S. 808, 828, 111 S.Ct. 2597, 115 L.Ed.2d 720 (1991), but by and large, it "is the preferred course because it promotes the evenhanded, predictable, and consistent development of legal principles, fosters reliance on judicial decisions, and contributes to the actual and perceived integrity of the judicial process," *id.*, at 827, 111 S.Ct. 2597. And in making this appraisal, doubt that the new rule is indeed the "right" one should surely be weighed in the balance. Though there are no vested interests involved, unresolved questions for the future of everyday criminal trials throughout the country surely counsel the same sort of caution. The Court grandly declares that "[w]e leave for another day any effort to spell out a comprehensive definition of 'testimonial,' " *ante*, at 1374. But the thousands of federal prosecutors and the tens of thousands of state prosecutors need answers as to what beyond the specific kinds of "testimony" the Court lists, see *ibid.*, is covered by the new rule. They need them now, not months or years from now. Rules of criminal evidence are applied every day in courts throughout the country, and parties should not be left in the dark in this manner.

To its credit, the Court's analysis of "testimony" excludes at least some hearsay exceptions, such as business records and official records. See *ante*, at 1367. To hold otherwise would require numerous additional witnesses without any apparent gain in the truth-seeking process. Likewise to the Court's credit is its implicit recognition that the mistaken application of its new rule by courts which guess wrong as to the scope of the rule is subject to harmless-error analysis. See *ante*, at 1359, n. 1.

But these are palliatives to what I believe is a mistaken change of course. It is a change of course not in the least necessary to reverse the judgment of the Supreme Court of Washington in this case. The result the Court reaches follows inexorably from *Roberts* and its progeny without any need for overruling that line of cases. In *Idaho v. Wright*, 497 U.S. 805, 820-824, 110 S.Ct. 3139, 111 L.Ed.2d 638 (1990), we held that an out-of-court statement was not admissible simply because the truthfulness of that statement was corroborated by other evidence at trial. As the Court notes, *ante*, at 1373, the Supreme Court of Washington gave decisive weight to the "interlocking nature of the two statements." No re-weighing of the "reliability factors," which is hypothesized by the Court, *ibid.*, is required to reverse the judgment here. A citation to *Idaho v. Wright*, *supra*, would suffice. For the reasons stated, I believe that this would be a far preferable course for the Court to take here.

THE U.S. SUPREME COURT SPEAKS-MELENDEZ DIAZ V. MASSACHUSETTS

Consider the court's approach in this follow on case to Crawford v. Washington. As you read it, ask yourself how the court dealt with the confrontation clause issue and testimonial evidence. Are you persuaded that this test results in a truly different outcome than the test developed in Ohio v. Roberts? If there is no outcome based difference, why the change?

129 S.Ct. 2527
Supreme Court of the United States
Luis E. **MELENDEZ-DIAZ**, Petitioner,
v.
MASSACHUSETTS.
No. 07-591.
Argued Nov. 10, 2008.
Decided June 25, 2009.

Justice SCALIA delivered the opinion of the Court.

The Massachusetts courts in this case admitted into evidence affidavits reporting the results of forensic analysis which showed that material seized by the police and connected to the defendant was cocaine. The question presented is whether those affidavits are "testimonial," rendering the affiants "witnesses" subject to the defendant's right of confrontation under the Sixth Amendment.

I

In 2001, Boston police officers received a tip that a Kmart employee, Thomas Wright, was engaging in suspicious activity. The informant reported that Wright repeatedly received phone calls at work, after each of which he would be picked up in front of the store by a blue sedan, and would return to the store a short time later. The police set up surveillance in the Kmart parking lot and witnessed this precise sequence of events. When Wright got out of the car upon his return, one of the officers detained and searched him, finding four clear white plastic bags containing a substance resembling cocaine. The officer then signaled other officers on the scene to arrest the two men in the car-one of whom was petitioner Luis **Melendez-Diaz**. The officers placed all three men in a police cruiser.

During the short drive to the police station, the officers observed their passengers fidgeting and making furtive movements in the back of the car. After depositing the men at the station, they searched the police cruiser and found a plastic bag containing 19 smaller plastic bags hidden in the partition between the front and back seats. They submitted the seized evidence to a state laboratory required by law to conduct chemical analysis upon police request. Mass. Gen. Laws, ch. 111, § 12 (West 2006).

Melendez-Diaz was charged with distributing cocaine and with trafficking in cocaine in an amount between 14 and 28 grams. Ch. 94C, §§ 32A, 32E(b)(1). At trial, the prosecution placed into evidence the bags seized from Wright and from the police cruiser. It also submitted three "certificates of analysis" showing the results of the forensic analysis performed on the seized substances. The certificates reported the weight of the seized bags and stated that the bags "[h]a[ve] been examined with the following results: The substance was found to contain: Cocaine." App. to Pet. for Cert. 24a, 26a, 28a. The certificates were sworn to before a notary public by analysts at the State Laboratory Institute of the Massachusetts Department of Public Health, as required under Massachusetts law. Mass. Gen. Laws, ch. 111, § 13.

Petitioner objected to the admission of the certificates, asserting that our Confrontation Clause decision in *Crawford v. Washington,* 541 U.S. 36, 124 S.Ct. 1354, 158 L.Ed.2d 177 (2004), required the analysts to testify in person. The objection was overruled, and the certificates were admitted pursuant to state law as "prima facie evidence of the composition, quality, and the net weight of the narcotic ... analyzed." Mass. Gen. Laws, ch. 111, § 13.

The jury found **Melendez-Diaz** guilty. He appealed, contending, among other things, that admission of the certificates violated his Sixth Amendment right to be confronted with the witnesses against him. The Appeals Court of Massachusetts rejected the claim, affirmance order, 69 Mass.App. 1114, 870 N.E.2d 676, 2007 WL 2189152, *4, n. 3 (July 31, 2007), relying on the Massachusetts Supreme Judicial Court's decision in *Commonwealth v. Verde,* 444 Mass. 279, 283-285, 827 N.E.2d 701, 705-706 (2005), which held that the authors of certificates of forensic analysis are not subject to confrontation under the Sixth Amendment. The Supreme Judicial Court denied review. 449 Mass. 1113, 874 N.E.2d 407 (2007). We granted certiorari. 552 U.S. 1256, 128 S.Ct. 1647, 170 L.Ed.2d 352 (2008).

II

The Sixth Amendment to the United States Constitution, made applicable to the States via the Fourteenth Amendment, *Pointer v. Texas,* 380 U.S. 400, 403, 85 S.Ct. 1065, 13 L.Ed. 2d 923 (1965), provides that "[i]n all criminal prosecutions, the accused shall enjoy the right ... to be confronted with the witnesses against him." In *Crawford,* after reviewing the Clause's historical underpinnings, we held that it guarantees a defendant's right to confront those "who 'bear testimony' " against him. 541 U.S., at 51, 124 S.Ct. 1354. A witness's testimony against a defendant is thus inadmissible unless the witness appears at trial or, if the witness is unavailable, the defendant had a prior opportunity for cross-examination. *Id.,* at 54, 124 S.Ct. 1354.

Our opinion described the class of testimonial statements covered by the Confrontation Clause as follows:

"Various formulations of this core class of testimonial statements exist: *ex parte* in-court testimony or its functional equivalent-that is, material such as affidavits, custodial examinations, prior testimony that the defendant was unable to cross-examine, or similar pretrial statements that declarants would reasonably expect to be used prosecutorially; extrajudicial statements ... contained in formalized testimonial materials, such as affidavits, depositions, prior testimony, or confessions; statements that were made under circumstances which would lead an objective witness reasonably to believe that the statement would be available for use at a later trial." *Id.,* at 51-52, 124 S.Ct. 1354 (internal quotation marks and citations omitted).

There is little doubt that the documents at issue in this case fall within the "core class of testimonial statements" thus described. Our description of that category mentions affidavits twice. See also *White v. Illinois,* 502 U.S. 346, 365, 112 S.Ct. 736, 116 L.Ed.2d 848 (1992) (THOMAS, J., concurring in part and concurring in judgment) ("[T]he Confrontation Clause is implicated by extrajudicial statements only insofar as they are contained in formalized testimonial materials, such as affidavits, depositions, prior testimony, or confessions"). The documents at issue here, while denominated by

Massachusetts law "certificates," are quite plainly affidavits: "declaration [s] of facts written down and sworn to by the declarant before an officer authorized to administer oaths." Black's Law Dictionary 62 (8th ed.2004). They are incontrovertibly a " 'solemn declaration or affirmation made for the purpose of establishing or proving some fact.' " *Crawford, supra*, at 51, 124 S.Ct. 1354 (quoting 2 N. Webster, An American Dictionary of the English Language (1828)). The fact in question is that the substance found in the possession of **Melendez-Diaz** and his codefendants was, as the prosecution claimed, cocaine-the precise testimony the analysts would be expected to provide if called at trial. The "certificates" are functionally identical to live, in-court testimony, doing "precisely what a witness does on direct examination." *Davis v. Washington*, 547 U.S. 813, 830, 126 S.Ct. 2266, 165 L.Ed.2d 224 (2006) (emphasis deleted).

Here, moreover, not only were the affidavits " 'made under circumstances which would lead an objective witness reasonably to believe that the statement would be available for use at a later trial,' " *Crawford, supra*, at 52, 124 S.Ct. 1354, but under Massachusetts law the *sole purpose* of the affidavits was to provide "prima facie evidence of the composition, quality, and the net weight" of the analyzed substance, Mass. Gen. Laws, ch. 111, § 13. We can safely assume that the analysts were aware of the affidavits' evidentiary purpose, since that purpose-as stated in the relevant state-law provision-was reprinted on the affidavits themselves. See App. to Pet. for Cert. 25a, 27a, 29a.

In short, under our decision in *Crawford* the analysts' affidavits were testimonial statements, and the analysts were "witnesses" for purposes of the Sixth Amendment. Absent a showing that the analysts were unavailable to testify at trial *and* that petitioner had a prior opportunity to cross-examine them, petitioner was entitled to " 'be confronted with' " the analysts at trial. *Crawford, supra*, at 54, 124 S.Ct. 1354.1

III

Respondent and the dissent advance a potpourri of analytic arguments in an effort to avoid this rather straightforward application of our holding in *Crawford.* Before addressing them, however, we must assure the reader of the falsity of the dissent's opening alarum that we are "sweep[ing] away an accepted rule governing the admission of scientific evidence" that has been "established for at least 90 years" and "extends across at least 35 States and six Federal Courts of Appeals." *Post,* at 2543 (opinion of KENNEDY, J.).

The vast majority of the state-court cases the dissent cites in support of this claim come not from the last 90 years, but from the last 30, and not surprisingly nearly all of them rely on our decision in *Ohio v. Roberts*, 448 U.S. 56, 100 S.Ct. 2531, 65 L.Ed.2d 597 (1980), or its since-rejected theory that unconfronted testimony was admissible as long as it bore indicia of reliability, *id.,* at 66, 100 S.Ct. 2531. See *post,* at 2559.2 As for the six Federal Courts of Appeals cases cited by the dissent, five of them postdated and expressly relied on *Roberts.* See *post,* at 2554 - 2555. The sixth predated *Roberts* but relied entirely on the same erroneous theory. See *Kay v. United States*, 255 F.2d 476, 480-481 (C.A.4 1958) (rejecting confrontation clause challenge "where there is reasonable necessity for [the evidence] and where ... the evidence has those qualities of reliability and trustworthiness").

A review of cases that predate the *Roberts* era yields a mixed picture. As the dissent notes, three state supreme court decisions from the early 20th century denied confrontation with respect to certificates of analysis regarding a substance's alcohol content. See *post,* at 2554 (citing cases from Massachusetts, Connecticut, and Virginia). But other state courts in the same era reached the opposite conclusion. See *Torres v. State*, 113 Tex.Crim. 1, 18 S.W.2d 179, 180 (App.1929); *Volrich v. State*, No. 278, 1925 WL

<u>2473 (Ohio App., Nov. 2, 1925)</u>. At least this much is entirely clear: In faithfully applying *Crawford* to the facts of this case, we are not overruling 90 years of settled jurisprudence. It is the dissent that seeks to overturn precedent by resurrecting <u>*Roberts*</u> a mere five years after it was rejected in <u>*Crawford.*</u>

We turn now to the various legal arguments raised by respondent and the dissent.

A

Respondent first argues that the analysts are not subject to confrontation because they are not "accusatory" witnesses, in that they do not directly accuse petitioner of wrongdoing; rather, their testimony is inculpatory only when taken together with other evidence linking petitioner to the contraband. See Brief for Respondent 10. This finds no support in the text of the Sixth Amendment or in our case law.

The Sixth Amendment guarantees a defendant the right "to be confronted with the witnesses *against him.*" (Emphasis added.) To the extent the analysts were witnesses (a question resolved above), they certainly provided testimony *against* petitioner, proving one fact necessary for his conviction-that the substance he possessed was cocaine. The contrast between the text of the Confrontation Clause and the text of the adjacent Compulsory Process Clause confirms this analysis. While the Confrontation Clause guarantees a defendant the right to be confronted with the witnesses "against him," the Compulsory Process Clause guarantees a defendant the right to call witnesses "in his favor." U.S. Const., Amdt. 6. The text of the Amendment contemplates two classes of witnesses-those against the defendant and those in his favor. The prosecution *must* produce the former;[3] the defendant *may* call the latter. Contrary to respondent's assertion, there is not a third category of witnesses, helpful to the prosecution, but somehow immune from confrontation.

It is often, indeed perhaps usually, the case that an adverse witness's testimony, taken alone, will not suffice to convict. Yet respondent fails to cite a single case in which such testimony was admitted absent a defendant's opportunity to cross-examine. Unsurprisingly, since such a holding would be contrary to longstanding case law. In *Kirby v. United States,* 174 U.S. 47, 19 S.Ct. 574, 43 L.Ed. 890 (1899), the Court considered Kirby's conviction for receiving stolen property, the evidence for which consisted, in part, of the records of conviction of three individuals who were found guilty of stealing the relevant property. *Id., at 53, 19 S.Ct. 574.* Though this evidence proved only that the property was stolen, and not that Kirby received it, the Court nevertheless ruled that admission of the records violated Kirby's rights under the Confrontation Clause. *Id., at 55, 19 S.Ct. 574.* See also *King v. Turner,* 1 Mood. 347, 168 Eng. Rep. 1298 (1832) (confession by one defendant to having stolen certain goods could not be used as evidence against another defendant accused of receiving the stolen property).

B

Respondent and the dissent argue that the analysts should not be subject to confrontation because they are not "conventional" (or "typical" or "ordinary") witnesses of the sort whose *ex parte* testimony was most notoriously used at the trial of Sir Walter Raleigh. *Post,* at 2550 - 2551; Brief for Respondent 28. It is true, as the Court recognized in *Crawford,* that *ex parte* examinations of the sort used at Raleigh's trial have "long been thought a paradigmatic confrontation violation." 541 U.S., at 52, 124 S.Ct. 1354. But the paradigmatic case identifies the core of the right to confrontation, not its limits. The right to confrontation was not invented in response to the use of the *ex parte* examinations in *Raleigh's Case,* 2 How. St. Tr. 1 (1603). That use provoked such an outcry precisely because it flouted the deeply rooted common-law tradition "of live testimony in court subject to adversarial testing." *Crawford, supra,* at 43, 124 S.Ct. 1354 (citing 3 W.

Blackstone, Commentaries on the Laws of England 373-374 (1768)). See also *Crawford, supra,* at 43-47, 124 S.Ct. 1354.

In any case, the purported distinctions respondent and the dissent identify between this case and Sir Walter Raleigh's "conventional" accusers do not survive scrutiny. The dissent first contends that a "conventional witness recalls events observed in the past, while an analyst's report contains near-contemporaneous observations of the test." *Post,* at 2551 - 2552. It is doubtful that the analyst's reports in this case could be characterized as reporting "near-contemporaneous observations"; the affidavits were completed almost a week after the tests were performed. See App. to Pet. for Cert. 24a-29a (the tests were performed on November 28, 2001, and the affidavits sworn on December 4, 2001). But regardless, the dissent misunderstands the role that "near-contemporaneity" has played in our case law. The dissent notes that that factor was given "substantial weight" in *Davis, post,* at 2551, but in fact that decision *disproves* the dissent's position. There the Court considered the admissibility of statements made to police officers responding to a report of a domestic disturbance. By the time officers arrived the assault had ended, but the victim's statements-written and oral-were sufficiently close in time to the alleged assault that the trial court admitted her affidavit as a "present sense impression." *Davis, 547 U.S., at 820, 126 S.Ct. 2266* (internal quotation marks omitted). Though the witness's statements in *Davis* were "near-contemporaneous" to the events she reported, we nevertheless held that they could *not* be admitted absent an opportunity to confront the witness. *Id., at 830, 126 S.Ct. 2266.*

A second reason the dissent contends that the analysts are not "conventional witnesses" (and thus not subject to confrontation) is that they "observe[d] neither the crime nor any human action related to it." *Post,* at 2552. The dissent provides no authority for this particular limitation of the type of witnesses subject to confrontation. Nor is it conceivable that all witnesses who fit this description would be outside the scope of the Confrontation Clause. For example, is a police officer's investigative report describing the crime scene admissible absent an opportunity to examine the officer? The dissent's novel exception from coverage of the Confrontation Clause would exempt all expert witnesses-a hardly "unconventional" class of witnesses.

A third respect in which the dissent asserts that the analysts are not "conventional" witnesses and thus not subject to confrontation is that their statements were not provided in response to interrogation. *Ibid.* See also Brief for Respondent 29. As we have explained, "[t]he Framers were no more willing to exempt from cross-examination volunteered testimony or answers to open-ended questions than they were to exempt answers to detailed interrogation." *Davis, supra,* at 822-823, n. 1, 126 S.Ct. 2266. Respondent and the dissent cite no authority, and we are aware of none, holding that a person who volunteers his testimony is any less a " 'witness against' the defendant," Brief for Respondent 26, than one who is responding to interrogation. In any event, the analysts' affidavits in this case *were* presented in response to a police request. See Mass. Gen. Laws, ch. 111, §§ 12-13. If an affidavit submitted in response to a police officer's request to "write down what happened" suffices to trigger the Sixth Amendment's protection (as it apparently does, see *Davis, 547 U.S., at 819-820, 126 S.Ct. 2266; id., at 840, n. 5, 126 S.Ct. 2266* (THOMAS, J., concurring in judgment in part and dissenting in part)), then the analysts' testimony should be subject to confrontation as well.

C

Respondent claims that there is a difference, for Confrontation Clause purposes, between testimony recounting historical events, which is "prone to distortion or manipulation," and the testimony at issue here, which is the "resul[t] of neutral, scientific testing." Brief for Respondent 29. Relatedly, respondent and the dissent argue that confrontation of forensic analysts would be of little value because "one would not reasonably expect a laboratory professional ... to feel quite differently about the results of his scientific test by having to look at the defendant." *Id.,* at 31 (internal quotation marks omitted); see *post,* at 2548 - 2549.

This argument is little more than an invitation to return to our overruled decision in *Roberts,* 448 U.S. 56, 100 S.Ct. 2531, 65 L.Ed.2d 597, which held that evidence with "particularized guarantees of trustworthiness" was admissible notwithstanding the Confrontation Clause. *Id., at 66,* 100 S.Ct. 2531. What we said in *Crawford* in response to that argument remains true:

"To be sure, the Clause's ultimate goal is to ensure reliability of evidence, but it is a procedural rather than a substantive guarantee. It commands, not that evidence be reliable, but that reliability be assessed in a particular manner: by testing in the crucible of cross-examination. ... Dispensing with confrontation because testimony is obviously reliable is akin to dispensing with jury trial because a defendant is obviously guilty. This is not what the Sixth Amendment prescribes." 541 U.S., at 61-62, 124 S.Ct. 1354.

Respondent and the dissent may be right that there are other ways-and in some cases better ways-to challenge or verify the results of a forensic test. But the Constitution guarantees one way: confrontation. We do not have license to suspend the Confrontation Clause when a preferable trial strategy is available.

Nor is it evident that what respondent calls "neutral scientific testing" is as neutral or as reliable as respondent suggests. Forensic evidence is not uniquely immune from the risk of manipulation. According to a recent study conducted under the auspices of the National Academy of Sciences, "[t]he majority of [laboratories producing forensic evidence] are administered by law enforcement agencies, such as police departments, where the laboratory administrator reports to the head of the agency." National Research Council of the National Academies, Strengthening Forensic Science in the United States: A Path Forward 6-1 (Prepublication Copy Feb. 2009) (hereinafter National Academy Report). And "[b]ecause forensic scientists often are driven in their work by a need to answer a particular question related to the issues of a particular case, they sometimes face pressure to sacrifice appropriate methodology for the sake of expediency." *Id.,* at S-17. A forensic analyst responding to a request from a law enforcement official may feel pressure-or have an incentive-to alter the evidence in a manner favorable to the prosecution.

Confrontation is one means of assuring accurate forensic analysis. While it is true, as the dissent notes, that an honest analyst will not alter his testimony when forced to confront the defendant, *post,* at 2548, the same cannot be said of the fraudulent analyst. See Brief for National Innocence Network as *Amicus Curiae* 15-17 (discussing cases of documented "drylabbing" where forensic analysts report results of tests that were never performed); National Academy Report 1-8 to 1-10 (discussing documented cases of fraud and error involving the use of forensic evidence). Like the eyewitness who has fabricated his account to the police, the analyst who provides false results may, under oath in open court, reconsider his false testimony. See *Coy v. Iowa,* 487 U.S. 1012, 1019, 108 S.Ct. 2798, 101 L.Ed.2d 857 (1988). And, of course, the prospect of confrontation will deter fraudulent analysis in the first place.

Confrontation is designed to weed out not only the fraudulent analyst, but the incompetent one as well. Serious deficiencies have been found in the forensic evidence used in criminal trials. One commentator asserts that "[t]he legal community now concedes, with varying degrees of urgency, that our system produces erroneous convictions based on discredited forensics." Metzger, Cheating the Constitution, 59 Vand.

L.Rev. 475, 491 (2006). One study of cases in which exonerating evidence resulted in the overturning of criminal convictions concluded that invalid forensic testimony contributed to the convictions in 60% of the cases. Garrett & Neufeld, Invalid Forensic Science Testimony and Wrongful Convictions, 95 Va. L.Rev. 1, 14 (2009). And the National Academy Report concluded:

"The forensic science system, encompassing both research and practice, has serious problems that can only be addressed by a national commitment to overhaul the current structure that supports the forensic science community in this country." National Academy Report P-1 (emphasis in original).

Like expert witnesses generally, an analyst's lack of proper training or deficiency in judgment may be disclosed in cross-examination.

This case is illustrative. The affidavits submitted by the analysts contained only the bare-bones statement that "[t]he substance was found to contain: Cocaine." App. to Pet. for Cert. 24a, 26a, 28a. At the time of trial, petitioner did not know what tests the analysts performed, whether those tests were routine, and whether interpreting their results required the exercise of judgment or the use of skills that the analysts may not have possessed. While we still do not know the precise tests used by the analysts, we are told that the laboratories use "methodology recommended by the Scientific Working Group for the Analysis of Seized Drugs," App. to Brief for Petitioner 1a–2a. At least some of that methodology requires the exercise of judgment and presents a risk of error that might be explored on cross-examination. See 2 P. Giannelli & E. Imwinkelried, Scientific Evidence § 23.03[c], pp. 532–533, ch. 23A, p. 607 (4th ed.2007) (identifying four "critical errors" that analysts may commit in interpreting the results of the commonly used gas chromatography/mass spectrometry analysis); Shellow, The Application of *Daubert* to the Identification of Drugs, 2 Shepard's Expert & Scientific Evidence Quarterly 593, 600 (1995) (noting that while spectrometers may be equipped with computerized matching systems, "forensic analysts in crime laboratories typically do not utilize this feature of the instrument, but rely exclusively on their subjective judgment").

The same is true of many of the other types of forensic evidence commonly used in criminal prosecutions. "[T]here is wide variability across forensic science disciplines with regard to techniques, methodologies, reliability, types and numbers of potential errors, research, general acceptability, and published material." National Academy Report S-5. See also *id.,* at 5-9, 5-12, 5-17, 5-21 (discussing problems of subjectivity, bias, and unreliability of common forensic tests such as latent fingerprint analysis, pattern/impression analysis, and toolmark and firearms analysis). Contrary to respondent's and the dissent's suggestion, there is little reason to believe that confrontation will be useless in testing analysts' honesty, proficiency, and methodology-the features that are commonly the focus in the cross-examination of experts.

D

Respondent argues that the analysts' affidavits are admissible without confrontation because they are "akin to the types of official and business records admissible at common law." Brief for Respondent 35. But the affidavits do not qualify as traditional official or business records, and even if they did, their authors would be subject to confrontation nonetheless.

Documents kept in the regular course of business may ordinarily be admitted at trial despite their hearsay status. See Fed. Rule Evid. 803(6). But that is not the case if the regularly conducted business activity is the production of evidence for use at trial. Our decision in *Palmer v. Hoffman,* 318 U.S. 109, 63 S.Ct. 477, 87 L.Ed. 645 (1943), made that distinction clear. There we held that an accident report provided by an employee of a railroad company did not qualify as a business record because, although kept in the regular course of the railroad's operations, it was "calculated for use essentially in the court, not in the business." *Id., at 114, 63 S.Ct. 477.*7 The analysts' certificates-like police reports generated by law enforcement officials-do not qualify as business or public records for precisely the same reason. See Rule 803(8) (defining public records as "excluding, however, in criminal cases matters observed by police officers and other law enforcement personnel").

Respondent seeks to rebut this limitation by noting that at common law the results of a coroner's inquest were admissible without an opportunity for confrontation. But as we have previously noted, whatever the status of coroner's reports at common law in England, they were not accorded any special status in American practice. See *Crawford,* 541 U.S., at 47, n. 2, 124 S.Ct. 1354; *Giles v. California,* 554 U.S. ----, ----, 128 S.Ct. 2678, 2705-06, 171 L.Ed.2d 488 (2008) (BREYER, J., dissenting); Evidence-Official Records-Coroner's Inquest, 65 U. Pa. L.Rev. 290 (1917).

The dissent identifies a single class of evidence which, though prepared for use at trial, was traditionally admissible: a clerk's certificate authenticating an official record-or a copy thereof-for use as evidence. See *post,* at 2552 - 2553. But a clerk's authority in that regard was narrowly circumscribed. He was permitted "to certify to the correctness of a copy of a record kept in his office," but had "no authority to furnish, as evidence for the trial of a lawsuit, his interpretation of what the record contains or shows, or to certify to its substance or effect." *State v. Wilson,* 141 La. 404, 409, 75 So. 95, 97 (1917). See also *State v. Champion,* 116 N.C. 987, 21 S.E. 700, 700-701 (1895); 5 J. Wigmore, Evidence § 1678 (3d ed.1940). The dissent suggests that the fact that this exception was " 'narrowly circumscribed' " makes no difference. See *post,* at 2553. To the contrary, it makes all the difference in the world. It shows that even the line of cases establishing the one narrow exception the dissent has been able to identify simultaneously vindicates the general rule applicable to the present case. A clerk could by affidavit *authenticate* or provide a copy of an otherwise admissible record, but could not do what the analysts did here: *create* a record for the sole purpose of providing evidence against a defendant.

Far more probative here are those cases in which the prosecution sought to admit into evidence a clerk's certificate attesting to the fact that the clerk had searched for a particular relevant record and failed to find it. Like the testimony of the analysts in this case, the clerk's statement would serve as substantive evidence against the defendant whose guilt depended on the nonexistence of the record for which the clerk searched. Although the clerk's certificate would qualify as an official record under respondent's definition-it was prepared by a public officer in the regular course of his official duties-and although the clerk was certainly not a "conventional witness" under the dissent's approach, the clerk was nonetheless subject to confrontation. See *People v. Bromwich,* 200 N.Y. 385, 388-389, 93 N.E. 933, 934 (1911); *People v. Goodrode,* 132 Mich. 542, 547, 94 N.W. 14, 16 (1903); Wigmore, *supra,* § 1678.9

Respondent also misunderstands the relationship between the business-and-official-records hearsay exceptions and the Confrontation Clause. As we stated in *Crawford:* "Most of the hearsay exceptions covered statements that by their nature were not testimonial-for example, business records or statements in furtherance of a conspiracy." 541 U.S., at 56, 124 S.Ct. 1354. Business and public records are generally admissible absent confrontation not because they qualify under an exception to the hearsay rules, but because-having been created for the administration of an entity's affairs and not for the purpose of establishing or proving some fact at trial-they are not testimonial. Whether or not they qualify as business or official records, the analysts' statements here-prepared specifically for use at petitioner's trial-were testimony against petitioner, and the analysts were subject to confrontation under the Sixth Amendment.

E

Respondent asserts that we should find no Confrontation Clause violation in this case because petitioner had the ability to subpoena the analysts. But that power-whether pursuant to state law or the Compulsory Process Clause-is no substitute for the right of confrontation. Unlike the Confrontation Clause, those provisions are of no use to the defendant when the witness is unavailable or simply refuses to appear. See, *e.g., Davis,* 547 U.S., at 820, 126 S.Ct. 2266 ("[The witness] was subpoenaed, but she did not appear at ... trial"). Converting the prosecution's duty under the Confrontation Clause into the defendant's privilege under state law or the Compulsory Process Clause shifts the consequences of adverse-witness no-shows from the State to the accused. More fundamentally, the Confrontation Clause imposes a burden on the prosecution to present its witnesses, not on the defendant to bring those adverse witnesses into court. Its value to the defendant is not replaced by a system in which the prosecution presents its evidence via *ex parte* affidavits and waits for the defendant to subpoena the affiants if he chooses.

F

Finally, respondent asks us to relax the requirements of the Confrontation Clause to accommodate the " 'necessities of trial and the adversary process.' " Brief for Respondent 59. It is not clear whence we would derive the authority to do so. The Confrontation Clause may make the prosecution of criminals more burdensome, but that is equally true of the right to trial by jury and the privilege against self-incrimination. The Confrontation Clause-like those other constitutional provisions-is binding, and we may not disregard it at our convenience.

We also doubt the accuracy of respondent's and the dissent's dire predictions. The dissent, respondent, and its *amici* highlight the substantial total number of controlled-substance analyses performed by state and federal laboratories in recent years. But only some of those tests are implicated in prosecutions, and only a small fraction of those cases actually proceed to trial. See Brief for Law Professors as *Amici Curiae* 7-8 (nearly 95% of convictions in state and federal courts are obtained via guilty plea).

Perhaps the best indication that the sky will not fall after today's decision is that it has not done so already. Many States have already adopted the constitutional rule we announce today, while many others permit the defendant to assert (or forfeit by silence) his Confrontation Clause right after receiving notice of the prosecution's intent to use a forensic analyst's report, *id.,* at 13-15 (cataloging such state laws). Despite these widespread practices, there is no evidence that the criminal justice system has ground to a halt in the States that, one way or another, empower a defendant to insist upon the analyst's appearance at trial. Indeed, in Massachusetts itself, a defendant may subpoena the analyst to appear at trial, see Brief for Respondent 57, and yet there is no indication that obstructionist defendants are abusing the privilege.

The dissent finds this evidence "far less reassuring than promised." *Post,* at 2557. But its doubts rest on two flawed premises. First, the dissent believes that those state statutes "requiring the defendant to give early notice of his intent to confront the analyst," are "burden-shifting statutes [that] may be invalidated by the Court's reasoning." *Post,* at 2554, 2557 - 2558. That is not so. In their simplest form, notice-and-demand statutes require the prosecution to provide notice to the defendant of its intent to use an analyst's report as evidence at trial, after which the defendant is given a period of time in which he may object to the admission of the evidence absent the analyst's appearance live at trial. See, *e.g.,* Ga.Code Ann. § 35-3-154.1 (2006); Tex.Code Crim. Proc. Ann., Art. 38.41, § 4

(Vernon 2005); Ohio Rev.Code Ann. § 2925.51(C) (West 2006). Contrary to the dissent's perception, these statutes shift no burden whatever. The defendant *always* has the burden of raising his Confrontation Clause objection; notice-and-demand statutes simply govern the *time* within which he must do so. States are free to adopt procedural rules governing objections. See *Wainwright v. Sykes,* 433 U.S. 72, 86-87, 97 S.Ct. 2497, 53 L.Ed.2d 594 (1977). It is common to require a defendant to exercise his rights under the Compulsory Process Clause in advance of trial, announcing his intent to present certain witnesses. See Fed. Rules Crim. Proc. 12.1(a), (e), 16(b)(1)(C); Comment: Alibi Notice Rules: The Preclusion Sanction as Procedural Default, 51 U. Chi. L.Rev. 254, 254-255, 281-285 (1984) (discussing and cataloguing State notice-of-alibi rules); *Taylor v. Illinois,* 484 U.S. 400, 411, 108 S.Ct. 646, 98 L.Ed.2d 798 (1988); *Williams v. Florida,* 399 U.S. 78, 81-82, 90 S.Ct. 1893, 26 L.Ed.2d 446 (1970). There is no conceivable reason why he cannot similarly be compelled to exercise his Confrontation Clause rights before trial. See *Hinojos-Mendoza v. People,* 169 P.3d 662, 670 (Colo.2007) (discussing and approving Colorado's notice-and-demand provision). Today's decision will not disrupt criminal prosecutions in the many large States whose practice is already in accord with the Confrontation Clause.

Second, the dissent notes that several of the state-court cases that have already adopted this rule did so pursuant to our decision in *Crawford,* and not "independently ... as a matter of state law." *Post,* at 2558. That may be so. But in assessing the likely practical effects of today's ruling, it is irrelevant *why* those courts adopted this rule; it matters only *that* they did so. It is true that many of these decisions are recent, but if the dissent's dire predictions were accurate, and given the large number of drug prosecutions at the state level, one would have expected immediate and dramatic results. The absence of such evidence is telling.

But it is not surprising. Defense attorneys and their clients will often stipulate to the nature of the substance in the ordinary drug case. It is unlikely that defense counsel will insist on live testimony whose effect will be merely to highlight rather than cast doubt upon the forensic analysis. Nor will defense attorneys want to antagonize the judge or jury by wasting their time with the appearance of a witness whose testimony defense counsel does not intend to rebut in any fashion. The *amicus* brief filed by District Attorneys in Support of the Commonwealth in the Massachusetts Supreme Court case upon which the Appeals Court here relied said that "it is almost always the case that [analysts' certificates] are admitted without objection. Generally, defendants do not object to the admission of drug certificates most likely because there is no benefit to a defendant from such testimony." Brief for District Attorneys in Support of the Commonwealth in No. SJC-09320 (Mass.), p. 7 (footnote omitted). Given these strategic considerations, and in light of the experience in those States that already provide the same or similar protections to defendants, there is little reason to believe that our decision today will commence the parade of horribles respondent and the dissent predict.

* * *

This case involves little more than the application of our holding in *Crawford v. Washington,* 541 U.S. 36, 124 S.Ct. 1354, 158 L.Ed.2d 177. The Sixth Amendment does not permit the prosecution to prove its case via *ex parte* out-of-court affidavits, and the admission of such evidence against **Melendez-Diaz** was error. We therefore reverse the judgment of the Appeals Court of Massachusetts and remand the case for further proceedings not inconsistent with this opinion.

It is so ordered.

Justice THOMAS, concurring.

I write separately to note that I continue to adhere to my position that "the Confrontation Clause is implicated by extrajudicial statements only insofar as they are contained in formalized testimonial materials, such as affidavits, depositions, prior testimony, or confessions." *White v. Illinois,* 502 U.S. 346, 365, 112 S.Ct. 736, 116 L.Ed.2d 848 (1992) (opinion concurring in part and concurring in judgment); see also *Giles v. California,* 554 U.S. ----, ----, 128 S.Ct. 2678, 2693, 171 L.Ed.2d 488 (2008) (concurring opinion) (characterizing statements within the scope of the Confrontation Clause to include those that are "sufficiently formal to resemble the Marian examinations" because they were Mirandized or custodial or "accompanied by [a] similar indicia of formality" (internal quotation marks omitted)); *Davis v. Washington,* 547 U.S. 813, 836, 126 S.Ct. 2266, 165 L.Ed.2d 224 (2006) (opinion concurring in judgment in part and dissenting in part) (reiterating that the Clause encompasses extrajudicial statements contained in the types of formalized materials listed in *White, supra,* at 365, 112 S.Ct. 736. I join the Court's opinion in this case because the documents at issue in this case "are quite plainly affidavits," *ante,* at 2532. As such, they "fall within the core class of testimonial statements" governed by the Confrontation Clause. *Ibid.* (internal quotation marks omitted).

Justice KENNEDY, with whom THE CHIEF JUSTICE, Justice BREYER, and Justice ALITO join, dissenting.

The Court sweeps away an accepted rule governing the admission of scientific evidence. Until today, scientific analysis could be introduced into evidence without testimony from the "analyst" who produced it. This rule has been established for at least 90 years. It extends across at least 35 States and six Federal Courts of Appeals. Yet the Court undoes it based on two recent opinions that say nothing about forensic analysts: *Crawford v. Washington,* 541 U.S. 36, 124 S.Ct. 1354, 158 L.Ed.2d 177 (2004), and *Davis v. Washington,* 547 U.S. 813, 126 S.Ct. 2266, 165 L.Ed.2d 224 (2006).

It is remarkable that the Court so confidently disregards a century of jurisprudence. We learn now that we have misinterpreted the Confrontation Clause-hardly an arcane or seldom-used provision of the Constitution-for the first 218 years of its existence. The immediate systemic concern is that the Court makes no attempt to acknowledge the real differences between laboratory analysts who perform scientific tests and other, more conventional witnesses-"witnesses" being the word the Framers used in the Confrontation Clause.

Crawford and *Davis* dealt with ordinary witnesses-women who had seen, and in two cases been the victim of, the crime in question. Those cases stand for the proposition that formal statements made by a conventional witness-one who has personal knowledge of some aspect of the defendant's guilt-may not be admitted without the witness appearing at trial to meet the accused face to face. But *Crawford* and *Davis* do not say-indeed, could not have said, because the facts were not before the Court-that anyone who makes a testimonial statement is a witness for purposes of the Confrontation Clause, even when that person has, in fact, witnessed nothing to give them personal knowledge of the defendant's guilt.

Because *Crawford* and *Davis* concerned typical witnesses, the Court should have done the sensible thing and limited its holding to witnesses as so defined. Indeed, as Justice THOMAS warned in his opinion in *Davis,* the Court's approach has become "disconnected from history and unnecessary to prevent abuse." 547 U.S., at 838, 126 S.Ct. 2266. The Court's reliance on the word "testimonial" is of little help, of course, for that word does not appear in the text of the Clause.

The Court dictates to the States, as a matter of constitutional law, an as-yet-undefined set of rules governing what kinds of evidence may be admitted without in-court testimony. Indeed, under today's opinion the States bear an even more onerous burden than they did before *Crawford*. Then, the States at least had the guidance of the hearsay rule and could rest assured that "where the evidence f[ell] within a firmly rooted hearsay exception," the Confrontation Clause did not bar its admission. *Ohio v. Roberts*, 448 U.S. 56, 66, 100 S.Ct. 2531, 65 L.Ed.2d 597 (1980) (overruled by *Crawford*). Now, without guidance from any established body of law, the States can only guess what future rules this Court will distill from the sparse constitutional text. See, *e.g., Mendez, Crawford v. Washington* : A Critique, 57 Stan. L.Rev. 569, 586-593 (2004) (discussing unanswered questions regarding testimonial statements).

The Court's opinion suggests this will be a body of formalistic and wooden rules, divorced from precedent, common sense, and the underlying purpose of the Clause. Its ruling has vast potential to disrupt criminal procedures that already give ample protections against the misuse of scientific evidence. For these reasons, as more fully explained below, the Court's opinion elicits my respectful dissent.

I. A. 1

The Court says that, before the results of a scientific test may be introduced into evidence, the defendant has the right to confront the "analyst." *Ante,* at 2531 - 2532. One must assume that this term, though it appears nowhere in the Confrontation Clause, nevertheless has some constitutional substance that now must be elaborated in future cases. There is no accepted definition of analyst, and there is no established precedent to define that term.

Consider how many people play a role in a routine test for the presence of illegal drugs. One person prepares a sample of the drug, places it in a testing machine, and retrieves the machine's printout-often, a graph showing the frequencies of radiation absorbed by the sample or the masses of the sample's molecular fragments. See 2 P. Giannelli & E. Imwinkelried, Scientific Evidence § 23.03 (4th ed.2007) (describing common methods of identifying drugs, including infrared spectrophotometry, nuclear magnetic resonance, gas chromatography, and mass spectrometry). A second person interprets the graph the machine prints out-perhaps by comparing that printout with published, standardized graphs of known drugs. *Ibid.* Meanwhile, a third person-perhaps an independent contractor-has calibrated the machine and, having done so, has certified that the machine is in good working order. Finally, a fourth person-perhaps the laboratory's director-certifies that his subordinates followed established procedures.

It is not at all evident which of these four persons is the analyst to be confronted under the rule the Court announces today. If all are witnesses who must appear for in-court confrontation, then the Court has, for all practical purposes, forbidden the use of scientific tests in criminal trials. As discussed further below, requiring even one of these individuals to testify threatens to disrupt if not end many prosecutions where guilt is clear but a newly found formalism now holds sway. See Part I-C, *infra.*

It is possible to read the Court's opinion, however, to say that all four must testify. Each one has contributed to the test's result and has, at least in some respects, made a representation about the test. Person One represents that a pure sample, properly drawn, entered the machine and produced a particular printout. Person Two represents that the printout corresponds to a known drug. Person Three represents that the machine was properly calibrated at the time. Person Four represents that all the others performed their jobs in accord with established procedures.

And each of the four has power to introduce error. A laboratory technician might adulterate the sample. The independent contractor might botch the machine's calibration. And so forth. The reasons for these errors may range from animus against the particular suspect or all criminal suspects to unintentional oversight; from gross negligence to good-faith mistake. It is no surprise that a plausible case can be made for deeming each person in the testing process an analyst under the Court's opinion.

Consider the independent contractor who has calibrated the testing machine. At least in a routine case, where the machine's result appears unmistakable, that result's accuracy depends entirely on the machine's calibration. The calibration, in turn, can be proved only by the contractor's certification that he or she did the job properly. That certification appears to be a testimonial statement under the Court's definition: It is a formal, out-of-court statement, offered for the truth of the matter asserted, and made for the purpose of later prosecution. See *ante,* at 2531 - 2532. It is not clear, under the Court's ruling, why the independent contractor is not also an analyst.

Consider the person who interprets the machine's printout. His or her interpretation may call for the exercise of professional judgment in close cases. See Giannelli & Imwinkelried, *supra.* If we assume no person deliberately introduces error, this interpretive step is the one most likely to permit human error to affect the test's result. This exercise of judgment might make this participant an analyst. The Court implies as much. See *ante,* at 2536 - 2537.

And we must yet consider the laboratory director who certifies the ultimate results. The director is arguably the most effective person to confront for revealing any ambiguity in findings, variations in procedures, or problems in the office, as he or she is most familiar with the standard procedures, the office's variations, and problems in prior cases or with particular analysts. The prosecution may seek to introduce his or her certification into evidence. The Court implies that only those statements that are actually entered into evidence require confrontation. See *ante,* at 2531 - 2532. This could mean that the director is also an analyst, even if his or her certification relies upon or restates work performed by subordinates.

The Court offers no principles or historical precedent to determine which of these persons is the analyst. All contribute to the test result. And each is equally remote from the scene, has no personal stake in the outcome, does not even know the accused, and is concerned only with the performance of his or her role in conducting the test.

It could be argued that the only analyst who must testify is the person who signed the certificate. Under this view, a laboratory could have one employee sign certificates and appear in court, which would ***2546*** spare all the other analysts this burden. But the Court has already rejected this arrangement. The Court made clear in _Davis_ that it will not permit the testimonial statement of one witness to enter into evidence through the in-court testimony of a second:

"[W]e do not think it conceivable that the protections of the Confrontation Clause can readily be evaded by having a note-taking policeman [here, the laboratory employee who signs the certificate] *recite* the unsworn hearsay testimony of the declarant [here, the analyst who performs the actual test], instead of having the declarant sign a deposition. Indeed, if there is one point for which no case-English or early American, state or federal-can be cited, that is it." 547 U.S., at 826, 126 S.Ct. 2266.

Under this logic, the Court's holding cannot be cabined to the person who signs the certificates. If the signatory is restating the testimonial statements of the true analysts-whoever they might be-then those analysts, too, must testify in person.

Today's decision demonstrates that even in the narrow category of scientific tests that identify a drug, the Court cannot define with any clarity who the analyst is. Outside this narrow category, the range of other scientific tests that may be affected by the Court's new confrontation right is staggering. See, *e.g.,* Comment, Toward a Definition of "Testimonial": How Autopsy Reports Do Not Embody the Qualities of a Testimonial Statement, 96 Cal. L.Rev. 1093, 1094, 1115 (2008) (noting that every court post-*Crawford* has held that autopsy reports are not testimonial, and warning that a contrary rule would "effectively functio[n] as a statute of limitations for murder").

2

It is difficult to confine at this point the damage the Court's holding will do in other contexts. Consider just two-establishing the chain of custody and authenticating a copy of a document.

It is the obligation of the prosecution to establish the chain of custody for evidence sent to testing laboratories-that is, to establish "the identity and integrity of physical evidence by tracing its continuous whereabouts." 23 C.J. S., Criminal Law § 1142, p. 66 (2008). Meeting this obligation requires representations-that one officer retrieved the evidence from the crime scene, that a second officer checked it into an evidence locker, that a third officer verified the locker's seal was intact, and so forth. The iron logic of which the Court is so enamored would seem to require in-court testimony from each human link in the chain of custody. That, of course, has never been the law. See, *e.g., United States v. Lott,* 854 F.2d 244, 250 (C.A.7 1988) ("[G]aps in the chain [of custody] normally go to the weight of the evidence rather than its admissibility"); 29A Am.Jur.2d, Evidence § 962, p. 269 (2009) ("The fact that one of the persons in control of a fungible substance does not testify at trial does not, without more, make the substance or testimony relating to it inadmissible"); C.J.S., *supra,* § 1142, at 67 ("It is generally not necessary that every witness who handled the evidence testify").

It is no answer for the Court to say that "[i]t is up to the prosecution to decide what steps in the chain of custody are so crucial as to require evidence." *Ante,* at 2532, n. 1. The case itself determines which links in the chain are crucial-not the prosecution. In any number of cases, the crucial link in the chain will not be available to testify and so the evidence will be excluded for lack of a proper foundation.

Consider another context in which the Court's holding may cause disruption: The long-accepted practice of authenticating copies of documents by means of a certificate from the document's custodian stating that the copy is accurate. See, *e.g.,* Fed. Rule Evid. 902(4) (in order to be self-authenticating, a copy of a public record must be "certified as correct by the custodian"); Rule 902(11) (business record must be "accompanied by a written declaration of its custodian"). Under one possible reading of the Court's opinion, recordkeepers will be required to testify. So far, courts have not read *Crawford* and *Davis* to impose this largely meaningless requirement. See, *e.g., United States v. Adefehinti,* 510 F.3d 319, 327-328 (C.A.D.C.2008) (certificates authenticating bank records may be admitted without confrontation); *United States v. Ellis,* 460 F.3d 920, 927 (C.A.7 2006) (certificate authenticating hospital records). But the breadth of the Court's ruling today, and its undefined scope, may well be such that these courts now must be deemed to have erred. The risk of that consequence ought to tell us that something is very wrong with the Court's analysis.

Because the Court is driven by nothing more than a wooden application of the *Crawford* and *Davis* definition of "testimonial," divorced from any guidance from history, precedent, or common sense, there is no way to predict the future applications of today's holding. Surely part of the justification for the Court's formalism must lie in its predictability. There is nothing predictable here, however, other than the uncertainty and disruption that now must ensue.

B

With no precedent to guide us, let us assume that the Court's analyst is the person who interprets the machine's printout. This result makes no sense. The Confrontation Clause is not designed, and does not serve, to detect errors in scientific tests. That should instead be done by conducting a new test. Or, if a new test is impossible, the defendant may call his own expert to explain to the jury the test's flaws and the dangers of relying on it. And if, in an extraordinary case, the particular analyst's testimony is necessary to the defense, then, of course, the defendant may subpoena the analyst. The Court frets that the defendant may be unable to do so "when the [analyst] is unavailable or simply refuses to appear." *Ante,* at 2540. But laboratory analysts are not difficult to locate or to compel. As discussed below, analysts already devote considerable time to appearing in court when subpoenaed to do so. See Part I-C, *infra;* see also Brief for State of Alabama et al. as *Amici Curiae* 26-28. Neither the Court, petitioner, nor *amici* offer any reason to believe that defendants have trouble subpoenaing analysts in cases where the analysts' in-court testimony is necessary.

The facts of this case illustrate the formalistic and pointless nature of the Court's reading of the Clause. Petitioner knew, well in advance of trial, that the Commonwealth would introduce the tests against him. The bags of cocaine were in court, available for him to test, and entered into evidence. Yet petitioner made no effort, before or during trial, to mount a defense against the analysts' results. Petitioner could have challenged the tests' reliability by seeking discovery concerning the testing methods used or the qualifications of the laboratory analysts. See <u>Mass. Rule Crim. Proc. 14(a)(2) (2009)</u>. He did not do so. Petitioner could have sought to conduct his own test. See Rule 41. Again, he did not seek a test; indeed, he did not argue that the drug was not cocaine. Rather than dispute the authenticity of the samples tested or the accuracy of the tests performed, petitioner argued to the jury that the prosecution had not shown that he had possessed or dealt in the drugs.

Despite not having prepared a defense to the analysts' results, petitioner's counsel made what can only be described as a *pro forma* objection to admitting the results without in-court testimony, presumably from one particular analyst. Today the Court, by deciding that this objection should have been sustained, transforms the Confrontation Clause from a sensible procedural protection into a distortion of the criminal justice system.

It is difficult to perceive how the Court's holding will advance the purposes of the Confrontation Clause. One purpose of confrontation is to impress upon witnesses the gravity of their conduct. See <u>*Coy v. Iowa,* 487 U.S. 1012, 1019-1020, 108 S.Ct. 2798, 101 L.Ed.2d 857 (1988)</u>. A witness, when brought to face the person his or her words condemn, might refine, reformulate, reconsider, or even recant earlier statements. See <u>*ibid.*</u> A further purpose is to alleviate the danger of one-sided interrogations by adversarial government officials who might distort a witness's testimony. The Clause guards against this danger by bringing the interrogation into the more neutral and public forum of the courtroom. See <u>*Maryland v. Craig,* 497 U.S. 836, 869-870, 110 S.Ct. 3157, 111 L.Ed.2d 666 (1990)</u> (SCALIA, J., dissenting) (discussing the "value of the confrontation right in guarding against a child's distorted or coerced recollections"); see also 96 Cal. L.Rev., *supra,* at 1120-1122 ("During private law-enforcement questioning, police officers or prosecutors can exert pressure on the witness without a high risk of being discovered. Courtroom questioning, in contrast, is public and performed in front of the jury, judge and defendant. Pressure is therefore harder to exert in court").

But neither purpose is served by the rule the Court announces today. It is not plausible that a laboratory analyst will retract his or her prior conclusion upon catching sight of the defendant the result condemns. After all, the analyst is far removed from the particular defendant and, indeed, claims no personal knowledge of the defendant's guilt. And an analyst performs hundreds if not thousands of tests each year and will not remember a particular test or the link it had to the defendant.

This is not to say that analysts are infallible. They are not. It may well be that if the State does not introduce the machine printout or the raw results of a laboratory analysis; if it does not call an expert to interpret a test, particularly if that test is complex or little known; if it does not establish the chain of custody and the reliability of the laboratory; then the State will have failed to meet its burden of proof. That result follows because the State must prove its case beyond a reasonable doubt, without relying on presumptions, unreliable hearsay, and the like. See _United States v. United States Gypsum Co., 438 U.S. 422, 446, 98 S.Ct. 2864, 57 L.Ed.2d 854 (1978)_ (refusing to permit a " 'conclusive presumption [of intent],' " which " 'would effectively eliminate intent as an ingredient of the offense' " (quoting _Morissette v. United States, 342 U.S. 246, 274-275, 72 S.Ct. 240, 96 L.Ed. 288 (1952)_)). The State must permit the defendant to challenge the analyst's result. See _Holmes v. South Carolina, 547 U.S. 319, 331, 126 S.Ct. 1727, 164 L.Ed.2d 503 (2006)_ (affirming the defendant's right to "have a meaningful opportunity to present a complete defense" (internal quotation marks omitted)). The rules of evidence, including those governing reliability under hearsay principles and the latitude to be given expert witnesses; the rules against irrebutable presumptions; and the overriding principle that the prosecution must make its case beyond a reasonable doubt-all these are part of the protections for the accused. The States, however, have some latitude in determining how these rules should be defined.

The Confrontation Clause addresses who must testify. It simply does not follow, however, that this clause, in lieu of the other rules set forth above, controls who the prosecution must call on every issue. Suppose, for instance, that the defense challenges the procedures for a secure chain of custody for evidence sent to a lab and then returned to the police. The defense has the right to call its own witnesses to show that the chain of custody is not secure. But that does not mean it can demand that, in the prosecution's case in chief, each person who is in the chain of custody-and who had an undoubted opportunity to taint or tamper with the evidence-must be called by the prosecution under the Confrontation Clause. And the same is true with lab technicians.

The Confrontation Clause is simply not needed for these matters. Where, as here, the defendant does not even dispute the accuracy of the analyst's work, confrontation adds nothing.

C

For the sake of these negligible benefits, the Court threatens to disrupt forensic investigations across the country and to put prosecutions nationwide at risk of dismissal based on erratic, all-too-frequent instances when a particular laboratory technician, now invested by the Court's new constitutional designation as the analyst, simply does not or cannot appear.

Consider first the costs today's decision imposes on criminal trials. Our own Court enjoys weeks, often months, of notice before cases are argued. We receive briefs well in advance. The argument itself is ordered. A busy trial court, by contrast, must consider not only attorneys' schedules but also those of witnesses and juries. Trial courts have huge caseloads to be processed within strict time limits. Some cases may unexpectedly plead out at the last minute; others, just as unexpectedly, may not. Some juries stay out longer than predicted; others must be reconstituted. An analyst cannot hope to be the trial court's top priority in scheduling. The analyst must instead face the prospect of waiting for days in a hallway outside the courtroom before being called to offer testimony that will consist of little more than a rote recital of the written report. See Part I-B, *supra*.

As matters stood before today's opinion, analysts already spent considerable time appearing as witnesses in those few cases where the defendant, unlike petitioner in this case, contested the analyst's result and subpoenaed the analyst. See Brief for Alabama et al. as *Amici Curiae* 26-28 (testifying takes time); *ante,* at 2542 (before today's opinion, it was " 'almost always the case that analysts' certificates [we]re admitted without objection' " in Massachusetts courts). By requiring analysts also to appear in the far greater number of cases where defendants do not dispute the analyst's result, the Court imposes enormous costs on the administration of justice.

Setting aside, for a moment, all the other crimes for which scientific evidence is required, consider the costs the Court's ruling will impose on state drug prosecutions alone. In 2004, the most recent year for which data are available, drug possession and trafficking resulted in 362,850 felony convictions in state courts across the country. See Dept. of Justice, Bureau of Justice Statistics, M. Durose & P. Langan, Felony Sentences in State Courts 2004, p. 2 (July 2007). Roughly 95% of those convictions were products of plea bargains, see *id.,* at 1, which means that state courts saw more than 18,000 drug trials in a single year.

The analysts responsible for testing the drugs at issue in those cases now bear a crushing burden. For example, the district attorney in Philadelphia prosecuted 25,000 drug crimes in 2007. Brief for National Dist. Attorneys Association et al. as *Amici Curiae* 12-13. Assuming that number remains the same, and assuming that 95% of the cases end in a plea bargain, each of the city's 18 drug analysts, *ibid.,* will be required to testify in more than 69 trials next year. Cleveland's district attorney prosecuted 14,000 drug crimes in 2007. *Ibid.* Assuming that number holds, and that 95% of the cases end in a plea bargain, each of the city's 6 drug analysts (two of whom work only part time) must testify in 117 drug cases next year. *Id.,* at 13.

The Federal Government may face even graver difficulties than the States because its operations are so widespread. For example, the FBI laboratory at Quantico, Virginia, supports federal, state, and local investigations across the country. Its 500 employees conduct over one million scientific tests each year. Dept. of Justice, FBI Laboratory 2007, Message from the FBI Laboratory Director, http://www.fbi.gov/hq/lab/lab2007/ labannual07.pdf (as visited June 22, 2009, and available in Clerk of Court's case file). The Court's decision means that before any of those million tests reaches a jury, at least one of the laboratory's analysts must board a plane, find his or her way to an unfamiliar courthouse, and sit there waiting to read aloud notes made months ago.

The Court purchases its meddling with the Confrontation Clause at a dear price, a price not measured in taxpayer dollars alone. Guilty defendants will go free, on the most technical grounds, as a direct result of today's decision, adding nothing to the truth-finding process. The analyst will not always make it to the courthouse in time. He or she may be ill; may be out of the country; may be unable to travel because of inclement weather; or may at that very moment be waiting outside some other courtroom for another defendant to exercise the right the Court invents today. If for any reason the analyst cannot make it to the courthouse in time, then, the Court holds, the jury cannot learn of the analyst's findings (unless, by some unlikely turn of events, the defendant previously cross-examined the analyst). *Ante,* at 2531. The result, in many cases, will be that the prosecution cannot meet its burden of proof, and the guilty defendant goes free on a technicality that, because it results in an acquittal, cannot be reviewed on appeal.

The Court's holding is a windfall to defendants, one that is unjustified by any demonstrated deficiency in trials, any well-understood historical requirement, or any established constitutional precedent.

II

All of the problems with today's decision-the imprecise definition of "analyst," the lack of any perceptible benefit, the heavy societal costs-would be of no moment if the Constitution did, in fact, require the Court to rule as it does today. But the Constitution does not.

The Court's fundamental mistake is to read the Confrontation Clause as referring to a kind of out-of-court statement-namely, a testimonial statement-that must be excluded from evidence. The Clause does not refer to kinds of statements. Nor does the Clause contain the word "testimonial." The text, instead, refers to kinds of persons, namely, to "witnesses against" the defendant. Laboratory analysts are not "witnesses against" the defendant as those words would have been understood at the framing. There is simply no authority for this proposition.

Instead, the Clause refers to a conventional "witness"-meaning one who witnesses (that is, perceives) an event that gives him or her personal knowledge of some aspect of the defendant's guilt. Both _Crawford_ and _Davis_ concerned just this kind of ordinary witness-and nothing in the Confrontation Clause's text, history, or precedent justifies the Court's decision to expand those cases.

A

The Clause states: "In all criminal prosecutions, the accused shall enjoy the right ... to be confronted with the witnesses against him." U.S. Const., Amdt. 6. Though there is "virtually no evidence of what the drafters of the Confrontation Clause intended it to mean," _White v. Illinois, 502 U.S. 346, 359, 112 S.Ct. 736, 116 L.Ed.2d 848 (1992)_ (THOMAS, J., concurring in part and concurring in judgment), it is certain the Framers did not contemplate that an analyst who conducts a scientific test far removed from the crime would be considered a "witnes[s] against" the defendant.

The Framers were concerned with a typical witness-one who perceived an event that gave rise to a personal belief in some aspect of the defendant's guilt. There is no evidence that the Framers understood the Clause to extend to unconventional witnesses. As discussed below, there is significant evidence to the contrary. See Part II-B, _infra_. In these circumstances, the historical evidence in support of the Court's position is " 'too meager ... to form a solid basis in history, preceding and contemporaneous with the framing of the Constitution.' " _Boumediene v. Bush, 553 U.S. 723, ----, 128 S.Ct. 2229, 2251, 171 L.Ed.2d 41 (2008)_ (quoting _Reid v. Covert, 354 U.S. 1, 64, 77 S.Ct. 1222, 1 L.Ed.2d 1148 (1957)_ (Frankfurter, J., concurring in result)). The Court goes dangerously wrong when it bases its constitutional interpretation upon historical guesswork.

The infamous treason trial of Sir Walter Raleigh provides excellent examples of the kinds of witnesses to whom the Confrontation Clause refers. _Raleigh's Case_, 2 How. St. Tr. 1 (1603); see _Crawford, 541 U.S., at 44-45, 124 S.Ct. 1354_ (Raleigh's trial informs our understanding of the Clause because it was, at the time of the framing, one of the "most notorious instances" of the abuse of witnesses' out-of-court statements); _ante_, at 2534 (same). Raleigh's accusers claimed to have heard Raleigh speak treason, so they were witnesses in the conventional sense. We should limit the Confrontation Clause to witnesses like those in Raleigh's trial.

The Court today expands the Clause to include laboratory analysts, but analysts differ from ordinary witnesses in at least three significant ways. First, a conventional witness recalls events observed in the past, while an analyst's report contains near-contemporaneous observations of the test. An observation recorded at the time it is made is unlike the usual act of testifying. A typical witness must recall a previous event that he or she perceived just once, and thus may have misperceived or misremembered. But an analyst making a contemporaneous observation need not rely on memory; he or she instead reports the observations at the time they are made. We gave this consideration substantial weight in *Davis.* There, the "primary purpose" of the victim's 911 call was "to enable police assistance to meet an ongoing emergency," rather than "to establish or prove past events potentially relevant to later criminal prosecution." 547 U.S., at 822, 827, 126 S.Ct. 2266. See also *People v. Geier,* 41 Cal.4th 555, 605-609, 61 Cal.Rptr.3d 580, 161 P.3d 104, 139-141 (2007). The Court cites no authority for its holding that an observation recorded at the time it is made is an act of "witness[ing]" for purposes of the Confrontation Clause.

Second, an analyst observes neither the crime nor any human action related to it. Often, the analyst does not know the defendant's identity, much less have personal knowledge of an aspect of the defendant's guilt. The analyst's distance from the crime and the defendant, in both space and time, suggests the analyst is not a witness against the defendant in the conventional sense.

Third, a conventional witness responds to questions under interrogation. See, *e.g., Raleigh's Case, supra,* at 15-20. But laboratory tests are conducted according to scientific protocols; they are not dependent upon or controlled by interrogation of any sort. Put differently, out-of-court statements should only "require confrontation if they are produced by, or with the involvement of, adversarial government officials responsible for investigating and prosecuting crime." 96 Cal. L.Rev., at 1118. There is no indication that the analysts here-who work for the State Laboratory Institute, a division of the Massachusetts Department of Public Health-were adversarial to petitioner. Nor is there any evidence that adversarial officials played a role in formulating the analysts' certificates.

Rather than acknowledge that it expands the Confrontation Clause beyond conventional witnesses, the Court relies on our recent opinions in *Crawford* and *Davis. Ante,* at 2531 - 2532. The Court assumes, with little analysis, that *Crawford* and *Davis* extended the Clause to any person who makes a "testimonial" statement. But the Court's confident tone cannot disguise the thinness of these two reeds. Neither *Crawford* nor *Davis* considered whether the Clause extends to persons far removed from the crime who have no connection to the defendant. Instead, those cases concerned conventional witnesses. *Davis, supra,* at 826-830, 126 S.Ct. 2266 (witnesses were victims of defendants' assaults); *Crawford, supra,* at 38, 124 S.Ct. 1354 (witness saw defendant stab victim).

It is true that *Crawford* and *Davis* employed the term "testimonial," and thereby suggested that any testimonial statement, by any person, no matter how distant from the defendant and the crime, is subject to the Confrontation Clause. But that suggestion was not part of the holding of *Crawford* or *Davis.* Those opinions used the adjective "testimonial" to avoid the awkward phrasing required by reusing the noun "witness." The Court today transforms that turn of phrase into a new and sweeping legal rule, by holding that anyone who makes a formal statement for the purpose of later prosecution-no matter how removed from the crime-must be considered a "witness against" the defendant. *Ante,* at 2531 - 2532. The Court cites no authority to justify this expansive new interpretation.

B

No historical evidence supports the Court's conclusion that the Confrontation Clause was understood to extend beyond conventional witnesses to include analysts who conduct scientific tests far removed from the crime and the defendant. Indeed, what little evidence there is contradicts this interpretation.

Though the Framers had no forensic scientists, they did use another kind of unconventional witness-the copyist. A copyist's work may be as essential to a criminal prosecution as the forensic analyst's. To convict a man of bigamy, for example, the State often requires his marriage records. See, *e.g.*, *Williams v. State,* 54 Ala. 131, 134, 135 (1875); *State v. Potter,* 52 Vt. 33, 38 (1879). But if the original records cannot be taken from the archive, the prosecution must rely on copies of those records, made for the purpose of introducing the copies into evidence at trial. See *ibid.* In that case, the copyist's honesty and diligence are just as important as the analyst's here. If the copyist falsifies a copy, or even misspells a name or transposes a date, those flaws could lead the jury to convict. Because so much depends on his or her honesty and diligence, the copyist often prepares an affidavit certifying that the copy is true and accurate.

Such a certificate is beyond question a testimonial statement under the Court's definition: It is a formal out-of-court statement offered for the truth of two matters (the copyist's honesty and the copy's accuracy), and it is prepared for a criminal prosecution.

During the Framers' era copyists' affidavits were accepted without hesitation by American courts. See, *e.g., United States v. Percheman,* 7 Pet. 51, 85, 8 L.Ed. 604 (1833) (opinion for the Court by Marshall, C. J.); see also Advisory Committee's Note on Fed. Rule Evid. 902(4), 28 U.S.C.App., p. 390 ("The common law ... recognized the procedure of authenticating copies of public records by certificate"); 5 J. Wigmore, Evidence §§ 1677, 1678 (J. Chadbourn rev.1974). And courts admitted copyists' affidavits in criminal as well as civil trials. See *Williams, supra; Potter, supra.* This demonstrates that the framing generation, in contrast to the Court today, did not consider the Confrontation Clause to require in-court confrontation of unconventional authors of testimonial statements.

The Court attempts to explain away this historical exception to its rule by noting that a copyist's authority is "narrowly circumscribed." *Ante,* at 2539. But the Court does not explain why that matters, nor, if it does matter, why laboratory analysts' authority should not also be deemed "narrowly circumscribed" so that they, too, may be excused from testifying. And drawing these fine distinctions cannot be squared with the Court's avowed allegiance to formalism. Determining whether a witness' authority is "narrowly circumscribed" has nothing to do with *Crawford's* testimonial framework. It instead appears much closer to the pre-*Crawford* rule of *Ohio v. Roberts,* under which a statement could be admitted without testimony if it "bears adequate indicia of reliability." 448 U.S., at 66, 100 S.Ct. 2531 (internal quotation marks omitted).

In keeping with the traditional understanding of the Confrontation Clause, this Court in *Dowdell v. United States,* 221 U.S. 325, 31 S.Ct. 590, 55 L.Ed. 753 (1911), rejected a challenge to the use of certificates, sworn out by a clerk of court, a trial judge, and a court reporter, stating that defendants had been present at trial. Those certificates, like a copyist's certificate, met every requirement of the Court's current definition of "testimonial." In rejecting the defendants' claim that use of the certificates violated the Confrontation Clause, the Court in *Dowdell* explained that the officials who executed the certificates "were not witnesses against the accused" because they "were not asked to testify to facts concerning [the defendants'] guilt or innocence." *Id.,* at 330, 31 S.Ct. 590. Indeed, as recently as *Davis,* the Court reaffirmed *Dowdell.* 547 U.S., at 825, 126 S.Ct. 2266.

By insisting that every author of a testimonial statement appear for confrontation, on pain of excluding the statement from evidence, the Court does violence to the Framers' sensible, and limited, conception of the right to confront "witnesses against" the defendant.

C

In addition to lacking support in historical practice or in this Court's precedent, the Court's decision is also contrary to authority extending over at least 90 years, 35 States, and six Federal Courts of Appeals.

Almost 100 years ago three state supreme courts held that their state constitutions did not require analysts to testify in court. In a case much like this one, the Massachusetts Supreme Judicial Court upheld the admission of a certificate stating that the liquid seized from the defendant contained alcohol, even though the author of the certificate did not testify. _Commonwealth v. Slavski,_ 245 Mass. 405, 413, 140 N.E. 465, 467 (1923). The highest courts in Connecticut and Virginia reached similar conclusions under their own constitutions. _State v. Torello,_ 103 Conn. 511, 131 A. 429 (1925); _Bracey v. Commonwealth,_ 119 Va. 867, 89 S.E. 144 (1916). Just two state courts appear to have read a state constitution to require a contrary result. _State v. Clark,_ 290 Mont. 479, 484-489, 964 P.2d 766, 770-772 (1998) (laboratory drug report requires confrontation under Montana's Constitution, which is "[u]nlike its federal counterpart"); _State v. Birchfield,_ 342 Or. 624, 157 P.3d 216 (2007), but see _id.,_ at 631-632, 157 P.3d, at 220 (suggesting that a "typical notice requirement" would be lawful).

As for the Federal Constitution, before _Crawford_ the authority was stronger still: The Sixth Amendment does not require analysts to testify in court. All Federal Courts of Appeals to consider the issue agreed. _Sherman v. Scott,_ 62 F.3d 136, 139-142 (C.A.5 1995); _Minner v. Kerby,_ 30 F.3d 1311, 1313-1315 (C.A.10 1994); _United States v. Baker,_ 855 F.2d 1353, 1359-1360 (C.A.8 1988); _Reardon v. Manson,_ 806 F.2d 39 (C.A.2 1986); _Kay v. United States,_ 255 F.2d 476, 480-481 (C.A.4 1958); see also _Manocchio v. Moran,_ 919 F.2d 770, 777-782 (C.A.1 1990) (autopsy report stating cause of victim's death). Some 24 state courts, and the Court of Appeals for the Armed Forces, were in accord. See Appendix A, _infra._ (Some cases cited in the appendixes concern doctors, coroners, and calibrators rather than laboratory analysts, but their reasoning is much the same.) Eleven more state courts upheld burden-shifting statutes that reduce, if not eliminate, the right to confrontation by requiring the defendant to take affirmative steps prior to trial to summon the analyst. See _ibid._ Because these burden-shifting statutes may be invalidated by the Court's reasoning, these 11 decisions, too, appear contrary to today's opinion. See Part III-B, _infra._ Most of the remaining States, far from endorsing the Court's view, appear not to have addressed the question prior to _Crawford._ Against this weight of authority, the Court proffers just two cases from intermediate state courts of appeals. _Ante,_ at 2533 - 2534.

On a practical level, today's ruling would cause less disruption if the States' hearsay rules had already required analysts to testify. But few States require this. At least sixteen state courts have held that their evidentiary rules permit scientific test results, calibration certificates, and the observations of medical personnel to enter evidence without in-court testimony. See Appendix B, _infra._ The Federal Courts of Appeals have reached the same conclusion in applying the federal hearsay rule. _United States v. Garnett,_ 122 F.3d 1016, 1018-1019 (C.A.11 1997) _(per curiam); United States v. Gilbert,_ 774 F.2d 962, 965 (C.A. 9 1985) _(per curiam); United States v. Ware,_ 247 F.2d 698, 699-700 (C.A.7 1957); but see _United States v. Oates,_ 560 F.2d 45, 82 (C.A.2 1977) (report prepared by law enforcement not admissible under public-records or business-records exceptions to federal hearsay rule).

The modern trend in the state courts has been away from the Court's rule and toward the admission of scientific test results without testimony-perhaps because the States have recognized the increasing reliability of scientific testing. See Appendix B, *infra* (citing cases from three States overruling or limiting previous precedents that had adopted the Court's rule as a matter of state law). It appears that a mere six courts continue to interpret their States' hearsay laws to require analysts to testify. See *ibid.* And, of course, where courts have grounded their decisions in state law, rather than the Constitution, the legislatures in those States have had, until now, the power to abrogate the courts' interpretation if the costs were shown to outweigh the benefits. Today the Court strips that authority from the States by carving the minority view into the constitutional text.

State legislatures, and not the Members of this Court, have the authority to shape the rules of evidence. The Court therefore errs when it relies in such great measure on the recent report of the National Academy of Sciences. *Ante,* at 2536 - 2537 (discussing National Research Council of the National Academies, Strengthening Forensic Science in the United States: A Path Forward (Prepublication Copy Feb. 2009)). That report is not directed to this Court, but rather to the elected representatives in Congress and the state legislatures, who, unlike Members of this Court, have the power and competence to determine whether scientific tests are unreliable and, if so, whether testimony is the proper solution to the problem.

The Court rejects the well-established understanding-extending across at least 90 years, 35 States and six Federal Courts of Appeals-that the Constitution does not require analysts to testify in court before their analysis may be introduced into evidence. The only authority on which the Court can rely is its own speculation on the meaning of the word "testimonial," made in two recent opinions that said nothing about scientific analysis or scientific analysts.

III

In an attempt to show that the "sky will not fall after today's decision," *ante,* at 2540, the Court makes three arguments, none of which withstands scrutiny.

A

In an unconvincing effort to play down the threat that today's new rule will disrupt or even end criminal prosecutions, the Court professes a hope that defense counsel will decline to raise what will soon be known as the ***Melendez-Diaz*** objection. *Ante,* at 2542. The Court bases this expectation on its understanding that defense attorneys surrender constitutional rights because the attorneys do not "want to antagonize the judge or jury by wasting their time." *Ibid.*

The Court's reasoning is troubling on at least two levels. First, the Court's speculation rests on the apparent belief that our Nation's trial judges and jurors are unwilling to accept zealous advocacy and that, once "antagonize[d]" by it, will punish such advocates with adverse rulings. *Ibid.* The Court offers no support for this stunning slur on the integrity of the Nation's courts. It is commonplace for the defense to request, at the conclusion of the prosecution's opening case, a directed verdict of acquittal. If the prosecution has failed to prove an element of the crime-even an element that is technical and rather obvious, such as movement of a car in interstate commerce-then the case must be dismissed. Until today one would not have thought that judges should be angered at the defense for making such motions, nor that counsel has some sort of obligation to avoid being troublesome when the prosecution has not done all the law requires to prove its case.

Second, even if the Court were right to expect trial judges to feel "antagonize[d]" by *Melendez-Diaz* objections and to then vent their anger by punishing the lawyer in some way, there is no authority to support the Court's suggestion that a lawyer may shirk his or her professional duties just to avoid judicial displeasure. There is good reason why the Court cites no authority for this suggestion-it is contrary to what some of us, at least, have long understood to be defense counsel's duty to be a zealous advocate for every client. This Court has recognized the bedrock principle that a competent criminal defense lawyer must put the prosecution to its proof:

"[T]he adversarial process protected by the Sixth Amendment requires that the accused have 'counsel acting in the role of an advocate.' *Anders v. California*, 386 U.S. 738, 743, 87 S.Ct. 1396, 18 L.Ed.2d 493 (1967). The right to the effective assistance of counsel is thus the right of the accused to require the prosecution's case to survive the crucible of meaningful adversarial testing. When a true adversarial criminal trial has been conducted ... the kind of testing envisioned by the Sixth Amendment has occurred. But if the process loses its character as a confrontation between adversaries, the constitutional guarantee is violated." *United States v. Cronic*, 466 U.S. 648, 656-657, 104 S.Ct. 2039, 80 L.Ed.2d 657 (1984) (footnotes omitted).

See also ABA Model Code of Professional Responsibility, Canon 7-1, in ABA Compendium of Professional Responsibility Rules and Standards (2008) ("The duty of a lawyer, both to his client and to the legal system, is to represent his client zealously within the bounds of the law ..." (footnotes omitted)).

The instant case demonstrates how zealous defense counsel will defend their clients. To convict, the prosecution must prove the substance is cocaine. Under the Court's new rule, apparently only an analyst's testimony suffices to prove that fact. (Of course there will also be a large universe of other crimes, ranging from homicide to robbery, where scientific evidence is necessary to prove an element.) In cases where scientific evidence is necessary to prove an element of the crime, the Court's rule requires the prosecution to call the person identified as the analyst; this requirement has become a new prosecutorial duty linked with proving the State's case beyond a reasonable doubt. Unless the Court is ashamed of its new rule, it is inexplicable that the Court seeks to limit its damage by hoping that defense counsel will be derelict in their duty to insist that the prosecution prove its case. That is simply not the way the adversarial system works.

In any event, the Court's hope is sure to prove unfounded. The Court surmises that "[i]t is unlikely that defense counsel will insist on live testimony whose effect will be merely to highlight rather than cast doubt upon the forensic analysis." *Ante,* at 2542. This optimistic prediction misunderstands how criminal trials work. If the defense does not plan to challenge the test result, "highlight[ing]" that result through testimony does not harm the defense as the Court supposes. If the analyst cannot reach the courtroom in time to testify, however, a *Melendez-Diaz* objection grants the defense a great windfall: The analyst's work cannot come into evidence. Given the prospect of such a windfall (which may, in and of itself, secure an acquittal) few zealous advocates will pledge, prior to trial, not to raise a *Melendez-Diaz* objection. Defense counsel will accept the risk that the jury may hear the analyst's live testimony, in exchange for the chance that the analyst fails to appear and the government's case collapses. And if, as here, the defense is not that the substance was harmless, but instead that the accused did not possess it, the testimony of the technician is a formalism that does not detract from the defense case.

In further support of its unlikely hope, the Court relies on the Brief for Law Professors as *Amici Curiae* 7-8, which reports that nearly 95% of convictions are obtained via guilty plea and thus do not require in-court testimony from laboratory analysts. *Ante,* at 2540. What the Court does not consider is how its holding will alter these statistics. The defense bar today gains the formidable power to require the government to transport the analyst to the courtroom at the time of trial. Zealous counsel will insist upon concessions: a plea bargain, or a more lenient sentence in exchange for relinquishing this remarkable power.

B

As further reassurance that the "sky will not fall after today's decision," *ante,* at 2540, the Court notes that many States have enacted burden-shifting statutes that require the defendant to assert his Confrontation Clause right prior to trial or else "forfeit" it "by silence." *Ibid.* The Court implies that by shifting the burden to the defendant to take affirmative steps to produce the analyst, these statutes reduce the burden on the prosecution.

The Court holds that these burden-shifting statutes are valid because, in the Court's view, they "shift no burden whatever." *Ante,* at 2541. While this conclusion is welcome, the premise appears flawed. Even what the Court calls the "simplest form" of burden-shifting statutes do impose requirements on the defendant, who must make a formal demand, with proper service, well before trial. Some statutes impose more requirements, for instance by requiring defense counsel to subpoena the analyst, to show good cause for demanding the analyst's presence, or even to affirm under oath an intent to cross-examine the analyst. See generally Metzger, Cheating the Constitution, 59 Vand. L.Rev. 475, 481-485 (2006). In a future case, the Court may find that some of these more onerous burden-shifting statutes violate the Confrontation Clause because they "impos[e] a burden ... on the defendant to bring ... adverse witnesses into court." *Ante,* at 2540.

The burden-shifting statutes thus provide little reassurance that this case will not impose a meaningless formalism across the board.

C

In a further effort to support its assessment that today's decision will not cause disruption, the Court cites 10 decisions from States that, the Court asserts, "have already adopted the constitutional rule we announce today." *Ante,* at 2540, and n. 11. The Court assures us that "there is no evidence that the criminal justice system has ground to a halt in the[se] States." *Ante,* at 2540.

On inspection, the citations prove far less reassuring than promised. Seven were decided by courts that considered themselves bound by *Crawford.* These cases thus offer no support for the Court's assertion that the state jurists independently "adopted" the Court's interpretation as a matter of state law. Quite the contrary, the debate in those seven courts was over just how far this Court intended *Crawford* to sweep. See, *e.g., State v. Belvin,* 986 So.2d 516, 526 (Fla.2008) (Wells, J., concurring in part and dissenting in part) ("I believe that the majority has extended the *Crawford* and *Davis* decisions beyond their intended reach" (citations omitted)). The Court should correct these courts' overbroad reading of *Crawford,* not endorse it. Were the Court to do so, these seven jurisdictions might well change their position.

Moreover, because these seven courts only "adopted" the Court's position in the wake of *Crawford,* their decisions are all quite recent. These States have not yet been subject to the widespread, adverse results of the formalism the Court mandates today.

The citations also fail to reassure for a different reason. Five of the Court's 10 citations- including all 3 pre-*Crawford* cases-come from States that have reduced the confrontation right. Four States have enacted a burden-shifting statute requiring the defendant to give early notice of his intent to confront the analyst. See Part III-B, *supra*; Colorado: *Hinojos-Mendoza v. People,* 169 P.3d 662, 668-671 (Colo.2007), Colo.Rev.Stat. § 16-3-309 (2008) (defendant must give notice 10 days before trial); Georgia: Compare

Miller v. State, 266 Ga. 850, 854-855, 472 S.E.2d 74, 78-79 (1996) (striking down earlier notice statute requiring defendant to show good cause, prior to trial, to call the analyst), with Ga.Code Ann. § 35-3-154.1 (2006) (defendant must give notice 10 days before trial); Illinois: *People v. McClanahan,* 191 Ill.2d 127, 133-134, 246 Ill.Dec. 97, 729 N.E. 2d 470, 474-475 (2000), Ill. Comp. Stat., ch. 725, § 5/115-15 (2006) (defendant must give notice "within 7 days" of "receipt of the report"); Oregon: *State v. Birchfield,* 342 Or., at 631-632, 157 P.3d, at 220 (suggesting that a "typical notice requirement" would be lawful), see Ore.Rev.Stat. § 475.235 (2007) (defendant must give notice 15 days before trial). A fifth State, Mississippi, excuses the prosecution from producing the analyst who conducted the test, so long as it produces someone. Compare *Barnette v. State,* 481 So.2d 788, 792 (Miss.1985) (cited by the Court), with *McGowen v. State,* 859 So.2d 320, 339-340 (Miss.2003) (the Sixth Amendment does not require confrontation with the particular analyst who conducted the test). It is possible that neither Mississippi's practice nor the burden-shifting statutes can be reconciled with the Court's holding. See Part III-B, *supra.* The disruption caused by today's decision has yet to take place in these States.

Laboratory analysts who conduct routine scientific tests are not the kind of conventional witnesses to whom the Confrontation Clause refers. The judgment of the Appeals Court of Massachusetts should be affirmed.

Appendixes

A

The following authorities held, prior to *Crawford,* that the Confrontation Clause does not require confrontation of the analyst who conducted a routine scientific test: *United States v. Vietor,* 10 M.J. 69, 72 (C.M.A.1980) (laboratory drug report); *State v. Cosgrove,* 181 Conn. 562, 574-578, 436 A.2d 33, 40-41 (1980) (same); *Howard v. United States,* 473 A. 2d 835, 838-839 (D.C.1984) (same); *Baber v. State,* 775 So.2d 258 (Fla.2000) (blood-alcohol test); *Commonwealth v. Harvard,* 356 Mass. 452, 253 N.E.2d 346 (1969) (laboratory drug report); *DeRosa v. First Judicial Dist. Court of State ex rel. Carson City,* 115 Nev. 225, 232-233, 985 P.2d 157, 162 (1999) (*per curiam*) (blood-alcohol test); *State v. Coombs,* 149 N.H. 319, 321-322, 821 A.2d 1030, 1032 (2003) (blood-alcohol test); *State v. Fischer,* 459 N.W.2d 818 (N.D.1990) (laboratory drug report); *Commonwealth v. Carter,* 593 Pa. 562, 932 A.2d 1261 (2007) (laboratory drug report; applying pre-*Crawford* law); *State v. Tavares,* 590 A.2d 867, 872-873 (R.I.1991) (laboratory analysis of victim's bodily fluid); *State v. Hutto,* 325 S.C. 221, 228-230, 481 S.E.2d 432, 436 (1997) (fingerprint); *State v. Best,* 146 Ariz. 1, 3-4, 703 P.2d 548, 550-551 (App.1985) (same); *State v. Christian,* 119 N.M. 776, 895 P.2d 676 (App.1995) (blood-alcohol test); *State v. Sosa,* 59 Wash.App. 678, 684-687, 800 P.2d 839, 843-844 (1990) (laboratory drug report).

The following authorities held, prior to *Crawford,* that the Confrontation Clause does not require confrontation of the results of autopsy and hospital reports describing the victim's injuries: *People v. Clark,* 3 Cal.4th 41, 157-159, 10 Cal.Rptr.2d 554, 833 P.2d 561, 627-628 (1992) (autopsy report); *Henson v. State,* 332 A.2d 773, 774-776 (Del.1975) (treating physician's report of victim's injuries, with medical conclusions redacted); *Collins v. State,* 267 Ind. 233, 235-236, 369 N.E.2d 422, 423 (1977) (autopsy report); *State v. Wilburn,* 196 La. 113, 115-118, 198 So. 765, 765-766 (1940) (hospital record stating victim's cause of death) (citing *State v. Parker,* 7 La. Ann. 83 (1852) (coroner's written inquest stating cause of death)); *State v. Garlick,* 313 Md. 209, 223-225, 545 A.2d 27, 34 (1988) (blood test showing presence of illegal drug); *People v. Kirtdoll,* 391 Mich. 370, 385-391, 217 N.W.2d 37, 46-48 (1974) (treating physician's report describing victim's injuries); *State v. Spikes,* 67 Ohio St.2d 405, 411-415, 423 N.E.2d 1122, 1128-1130 (1981) (treating physician's report of defendant's injuries); *State v. Kreck,* 86

Wash.2d 112, 117-120, 542 P.2d 782, 786-787 (1975) (laboratory report stating that murder victim's blood contained poison).

The following authorities held, prior to *Crawford,* that the Confrontation Clause does not require confrontation of certificates stating that instruments were in good working order at the time of a test: *State v. Ing,* 53 Haw. 466, 467-473, 497 P.2d 575, 577-579 (1972) (certificate that police car's speedometer was in working order), accord, *State v. Ofa,* 9 Haw.App. 130, 135-139, 828 P.2d 813, 817-818 (1992) *(per curiam)* (certificate that breathalyzer was in working order); *State v. Ruiz,* 120 N.M. 534, 903 P.2d 845 (App. 1995) (same); *State v. Dilliner,* 212 W.Va. 135, 141-142, 569 S.E.2d 211, 217-218 (2002) (same); *State v. Huggins,* 659 P.2d 613, 616-617 (Alaska App.1982) (same); *State v. Conway,* 70 Or.App. 721, 690 P.2d 1128 (1984) (same).

The following decisions reduced the right to confront the results of scientific tests by upholding burden-shifting statutes that require the defendant to take affirmative steps prior to trial to summon the analyst: *Johnson v. State,* 303 Ark. 12, 18-20, 792 S.W.2d 863, 866-867 (1990) (defendant must give notice 10 days before trial); *State v. Davison,* 245 N.W.2d 321 (Iowa 1976), Iowa Code Ann. § 691.2 (2008) (same); *State v. Crow,* 266 Kan. 690, 974 P.2d 100 (1999) (defendant must give notice within 10 days of receiving the result and must show that the result will be challenged at trial); *State v. Christianson,* 404 A.2d 999 (Me.1979) (defendant must give notice 10 days before trial); *State v. Miller,* 170 N.J. 417, 436-437, 790 A.2d 144, 156 (2002) (defendant must give notice within 10 days of receiving the result and must show that the result will be challenged at trial); *State v. Smith,* 312 N.C. 361, 381-382, 323 S.E.2d 316, 328 (1984) (defendant must subpoena analyst); *State v. Hancock,* 317 Or. 5, 9-12, 854 P.2d 926, 928-930 (1993) (same), but see *State v. Birchfield,* 342 Or. 624, 157 P.3d 216 (reducing defendant's burden); *State v. Hughes,* 713 S.W.2d 58 (1986) (defendant must subpoena analyst); *Magruder v. Commonwealth,* 275 Va. 283, 295-300, 657 S.E.2d 113, 119-121 (2008) (defendant must "call the person performing such analysis," at the State's expense); *People v. Mayfield-Ulloa,* 817 P.2d 603 (Colo.App.1991) (defendant must give notice to State and the analyst 10 days before trial); *State v. Matthews,* 632 So.2d 294, 300-302 (La.App.1993) (defendant must give notice five days before trial).

B

The following authorities hold that State Rules of Evidence permit the results of routine scientific tests to be admitted into evidence without confrontation: *State v. Torres,* 60 Haw. 271, 589 P.2d 83 (1978) (X ray of victim's body); *State v. Davis,* 269 N.W.2d 434, 440 (Iowa 1978) (laboratory analysis of victim's bodily fluid); *State v. Taylor,* 486 S.W.2d 239, 241-243 (Mo.1972) (microscopic comparison of wood chip retrieved from defendant's clothing with wood at crime scene); *State v. Snider,* 168 Mont. 220, 229-230, 541 P.2d 1204, 1210 (1975) (laboratory drug report); *People v. Porter,* 46 A.D.2d 307, 311-313, 362 N.Y.S.2d 249, 255-256 (1974) (blood-alcohol report); *Robertson v. Commonwealth,* 211 Va. 62, 64-68, 175 S.E.2d 260, 262-264 (1970) (laboratory analysis of victim's bodily fluid); *Kreck,* 86 Wash.2d, at 117-120, 542 P.2d, at 786-787 (laboratory report stating that murder victim's blood contained poison).

The following authorities hold that State Rules of Evidence permit autopsy and hospital reports to be admitted into evidence without confrontation: *People v. Williams,* 174 Cal.App.2d 364, 389-391, 345 P.2d 47, 63-64 (1959) (autopsy report); *Henson, supra,* at 775-776 (report of physician who examined victim); *Wilburn,* 196 La., at 115-118, 198 So., at 765-766 (hospital record stating victim's cause of death); *Garlick,* 313 Md., at 223-225, 545 A.2d, at 34 (blood test); *State v. Reddick,* 53 N.J. 66, 68-69, 248 A.2d 425, 426-427 (1968) *(per curiam)* (autopsy report stating factual findings, but not opinions, of medical examiner); *People v. Nisonoff,* 293 N.Y. 597, 59 N.E.2d 420 (1944) (same).

The following authorities hold that State Rules of Evidence permit certificates, which state that scientific instruments were in good working order, to be admitted into evidence without confrontation: _Wester v. State,_ 528 P.2d 1179, 1183 (Alaska 1974) (certificate stating that breathalyzer machine was in working order); _Best v. State,_ 328 A.2d 141, 143 (Del.1974) (certificate that breathalyzer was in working order); _State v. Rines,_ 269 A.2d 9, 13-15 (Me.1970) (manufacturer's certificate stating that blood-alcohol test kit was in working order admissible under the business-records exception); _McIlwain v. State,_ 700 So.2d 586, 590-591 (Miss.1997) (same).

Taking the minority view, the following authorities interpret state hearsay rules to require confrontation of the results of routine scientific tests or observations of medical personnel: _State v. Sandoval-Tena,_ 138 Idaho 908, 912, 71 P.3d 1055, 1059 (2003) (laboratory drug report inadmissible under state hearsay rule); _Spears v. State,_ 241 So.2d 148 (Miss.1970) (nurse's observation of victim inadmissible under state hearsay rule and constitution); _State v._ ***2561** _James,_ 255 S.C. 365, 179 S.E.2d 41 (1971) (chemical analysis of victim's bodily fluid inadmissible under state hearsay rule); _Cole v. State,_ 839 S.W.2d 798 (Tex.Crim.App.1990) (laboratory drug report inadmissible under state hearsay rule); _State v. Workman,_ 2005 UT 66, ¶¶ 9-20, 122 P.3d 639, 642-643 (same); _State v. Williams,_ 2002 WI 58, ¶¶ 32-55, 253 Wis.2d 99, 118-127, 644 N.W.2d 919, 928-932 (same), but see _id.,_ at 109-117, 644 N.W.2d, at 924-927 (no confrontation violation where expert testified based on test results prepared by an out-of-court analyst).

This summary does not include decisions that find test results inadmissible because the State failed to lay a proper foundation. Rather than endorse the minority view, those cases merely reaffirm the government's burden to prove the authenticity of its evidence and the applicability of an exception to the state hearsay rule. See, _e.g., State v. Fisher,_ 178 N.W. 2d 380 (Iowa 1970) (laboratory test of victim's bodily fluid inadmissible under business-records exception because the prosecution did not show that it was kept in regular course of business); _State v. Foster,_ 198 Kan. 52, 422 P.2d 964 (1967) (no foundation laid for introduction of blood-alcohol test because the prosecution did not show that the test was conducted in the usual course of business); _Moon v. State,_ 300 Md. 354, 367-371, 478 A. 2d 695, 702-703 (1984) (blood alcohol test inadmissible because insufficient foundational evidence that the test was conducted in a reliable manner); cf. _Davis,_ 269 N.W.2d, at 440 (laboratory test of victim's bodily fluid admitted under business-records exception to state hearsay rule); _Garlick,_ 313 Md., at 215, n. 2, 223-225, 545 A.2d, at 30, n. 2, 34 (laboratory test of defendant's blood falls within "firmly rooted" hearsay exception).

Three States once espoused the minority view but appear to have changed course to some degree: _People v. Lewis,_ 294 Mich. 684, 293 N.W. 907 (1940) (hospital record describing victim's injuries inadmissible hearsay), overruled by _Kirtdoll,_ 391 Mich., at 372, 217 N.W.2d, at 39 (noting that "in its 35 year long history, _Lewis_ ... has never been relied upon to actually deny admission into evidence of a business entry record in a criminal case"), but see _People v. McDaniel,_ 469 Mich. 409, 670 N.W.2d 659 (2003) _(per curiam)_ (police laboratory report inadmissible hearsay); _State v. Tims,_ 9 Ohio St.2d 136, 137-138, 224 N.E.2d 348, 350 (1967) (hospital record describing victim's injuries inadmissible hearsay), overruled by _Spikes,_ 67 Ohio St.2d, at 411-415, 423 N.E.2d, at 1128-1130; _State v. Henderson,_ 554 S.W.2d 117 (Tenn.1977) (laboratory drug report inadmissible absent confrontation), abrogated by statute as recognized by _Hughes,_ 713 S.W.2d 58 (statute permitted defendant to subpoena analyst who prepared blood alcohol report; by not doing so, defendant waived his right to confront the analyst).

THE SUPREME COURT SPEAKS-WILLIAMS V. ILLINOIS

Consider the court's approach in the following case. This case is the most recent attempt by the court to balance the tension between the confrontation clause and scientific evidence. As you read it, ask yourself if the doctrine espoused in Crawford is still applicable. Has it moved? How much? Why? This case is an excellent example of the tensions between technology and the law. Consider also your review of expert witnesses as you review this case.

Supreme Court of the United States

SANDY WILLIAMS, Petitioner v. ILLINOIS.

No. 10-8505

Certiorari to the Supreme Court of Illinois.

Argued December 6, 2011, Decided June 18, 2012, October Term, 2011

At petitioner's bench trial for rape, Sandra Lambatos, a forensic specialist at the Illinois State Police lab, testified that she matched a DNA profile produced by an outside laboratory, Cellmark, to a profile the state lab produced using a sample of petitioner's blood. She testified that Cellmark was an accredited laboratory and that business records showed that vaginal swabs taken from the victim, L. J., were sent to Cellmark and returned. She offered no other statement for the purpose of identifying the sample used for Cellmark's profile or establishing how Cellmark handled or tested the sample. Nor did she vouch for the accuracy of Cellmark's profile. The defense moved to exclude, on Confrontation Clause grounds, Lambatos' testimony insofar as it implicated events at Cellmark, but the prosecution said that petitioner's confrontation rights were satisfied because he had the opportunity to cross-examine the expert who had testified as to the match. The prosecutor argued that Illinois Rule of Evidence 703 permitted an expert to disclose facts on which the expert's opinion is based even if the expert is not competent to testify to those underlying facts, and that any deficiency went to the weight of the evidence, not its admissibility. The trial court admitted the evidence and found petitioner guilty. Both the Illinois Court of Appeals and the State Supreme Court affirmed, concluding that Lambatos' testimony did not violate petitioner's confrontation rights because Cellmark's report was not offered into evidence to prove the truth of the matter asserted.

Held: The judgment is affirmed.

238 Ill. 2d 125, 939 N. E. 2d 268, affirmed.

JUSTICE ALITO, joined by THE CHIEF JUSTICE, JUSTICE KENNEDY, and JUSTICE BREYER, concluded that the form of expert testimony given in this case does not violate the Confrontation Clause. Pp. 10-33.

(a) Before *Crawford v. Washington*, **541 U. S. 36**, this Court took the view that the Confrontation Clause did not bar the admission of out-of-court statements that fell within a firmly rooted exception to the hearsay rule. In *Crawford*, the Court held that such statements could be "admitted only where the declarant is unavailable, and only where the defendant has had a prior opportunity to cross-examine." *Id.*, at 59. In both *Melendez-Diaz v. Massachusetts*, **557 U. S. 305**, and *Bullcoming v. New Mexico*, **564 U. S. ___**, two of the many cases that have arisen from *Crawford*, this Court ruled that scientific reports could not be used as substantive evidence against a defendant unless the analyst who prepared and certified the report was subject to confrontation. In each case, the report at issue "contain[ed] a testimonial certification, made in order to prove a fact at a criminal trial." **564 U. S., at ___ — ___.** Here, in contrast, the question is the constitutionality of allowing an expert witness to discuss others' testimonial statements if those statements are not themselves admitted as evidence. Pp. 10-13.

(b) An expert witness may voice an opinion based on facts concerning the events at issue even if the expert lacks first-hand knowledge of those facts. A long tradition in American courts permits an expert to testify in the form of a "hypothetical question," where the expert assumes the truth of factual predicates and then offers testimony based on those assumptions. See *Forsyth v. Doolittle*, **120 U. S. 73, 77.** Modern evidence rules dispense with the need for hypothetical questions and permit an expert to base an opinion on facts "made known to the expert at or before the hearing," though such reliance does not constitute admissible evidence of the underlying information. Ill. Rule Evid. 703; Fed. Rule Evid. **703.** Both Illinois and Federal Rules bar an expert from disclosing the inadmissible evidence in jury trials but not in bench trials. This is important because *Crawford,* while departing from prior Confrontation Clause precedent in other respects, reaffirmed the proposition that the Clause "does not bar the use of testimonial statements for purposes other than establishing the truth of the matter asserted." **541 U. S., at 59**, n. 9. Pp. 13-16.

(c) For Confrontation Clause purposes, the references to Cellmark in the trial record either were not hearsay or were not offered for the truth of the matter asserted. Pp. 16-27.

(1) Petitioner's confrontation right was not violated when Lambatos answered "yes" to a question about whether there was a match between the DNA profile "found in semen from the vaginal swabs of [L. J.]" and the one identified as petitioner's. Under Illinois law, this putatively offending phrase was not admissible for the purpose of proving the truth of the matter asserted — *i.e.,* that the matching DNA profile was "found in semen from the vaginal swabs." Rather, that fact was a mere premise of the prosecutor's question, and Lambatos simply assumed it to be true in giving her answer. Because this was a bench trial, the Court assumes that the trial judge understood that the testimony was not admissible to prove the truth of the matter asserted. It is also unlikely that the judge took the testimony as providing chain-of-custody evidence. The record does not support such an understanding; no trial judge is likely to be so confused; and the admissible evidence left little room for argument that Cellmark's sample came from any source but L. J.'s swabs, since the profile matched the very man she identified in a lineup and at trial as her attacker. Pp. 16-21.

(2) Nor did the substance of Cellmark's report need to be introduced in order to show that Cellmark's profile was based on the semen in L. J.'s swabs or that its procedures were reliable. The issue here is whether petitioner's confrontation right was violated, not whether the State offered sufficient foundational evidence to support the admission of Lambatos' opinion. If there were no proof that Cellmark's profile was accurate, Lambatos' testimony would be irrelevant, but the Confrontation Clause bars not the admission of irrelevant evidence, but the admission of testimonial statements by declarants who are not subject to cross-examination. Here, the trial record does not lack admissible evidence with respect to the source of the sample tested by Cellmark or the reliability of its profile. The State offered conventional chain-of-custody evidence, and the match between Cellmark's profile and petitioner's was telling confirmation that Cellmark's profile was deduced from the semen on L. J.'s swabs. The match also provided strong circumstantial evidence about the reliability of Cellmark's work. Pp. 21-25.

(3) This conclusion is consistent with *Bullcoming* and *Melendez-Diaz,* where forensic reports were introduced for the purpose of proving the truth of what they

asserted. In contrast, Cellmark's report was considered for the limited purpose of seeing whether it matched something else, and the relevance of that match was established by independent circumstantial evidence showing that the report was based on a sample from the crime scene. There are at least four safeguards to prevent abuses in such situations. First, trial courts can screen out experts who would act as conduits for hearsay by strictly enforcing the requirement that experts display genuine "scientific, technical, or other specialized knowledge" to help the trier of fact understand the evidence or determine a fact at issue. Fed. Rule Evid. **702**(a). Second, experts are generally precluded from disclosing inadmissible evidence to a jury. Third, if such evidence is disclosed, a trial judge may instruct the jury that the statements cannot be accepted for their truth, and that an expert's opinion is only as good as the independent evidence establishing its underlying premises. Fourth, if the prosecution cannot muster independent admissible evidence to prove foundational facts, the expert's testimony cannot be given weight by the trier of fact. Pp. 25-27.

(e) Even if Cellmark's report had been introduced for its truth, there would have been no Confrontation Clause violation. The Clause refers to testimony by "witnesses against" an accused, prohibiting modern-day practices that are tantamount to the abuses that gave rise to the confrontation right, namely, (a) out-of-court statements having the primary purpose of accusing a targeted individual of engaging in criminal conduct, and (b) formalized statements such as affidavits, depositions, prior testimony, or confessions. These characteristics were present in every post-*Crawford* case in which a Confrontation Clause violation has been found, except for *Hammon v. Indiana*, **547 U. S. 813**. But, even in *Hammon*, the particular statement, elicited during police interrogation, had the primary purpose of accusing a targeted individual. A person who makes a statement to resolve an ongoing emergency is not like a trial witness because the declarant's purpose is to bring an end to an ongoing threat. *Michigan v. Bryant*, **562 U. S. ___, ___**. Such a statement's admissibility "is the concern of . . . rules of evidence, not the Confrontation Clause." *Id.*, ___ — ___. The forensic reports in *Melendez-Diaz* and *Bullcoming* ran afoul of the Confrontation Clause because they were the equivalent of affidavits made for the purpose of proving a particular criminal defendant's guilt. But the Cellmark report's primary purpose was to catch a dangerous rapist who was still at large, not to obtain evidence for use against petitioner, who was neither in custody nor under suspicion at that time. Nor could anyone at Cellmark possibly know that the profile would inculpate petitioner. There was thus no "prospect of fabrication" and no incentive to produce anything other than a scientifically sound and reliable profile. *Bryant*, *supra*, at ___, ___. Lab technicians producing a DNA profile generally have no way of knowing whether it will turn out to be incriminating, exonerating, or both. And with numerous technicians working on a profile, it is likely that each technician's sole purpose is to perform a task in accordance with accepted procedures. The knowledge that defects in a DNA profile may be detected from the profile itself provides a further safeguard. Pp. 28-33.

JUSTICE THOMAS concluded that the disclosure of Cellmark's out-of-court statements through Lambatos' expert testimony did not violate the Confrontation Clause solely because Cellmark's statements lacked the requisite "formality and solemnity" to be considered "'testimonial,'" see *Michigan v. Bryant*, **562 U. S. ___, ___** (THOMAS, J., concurring in judgment). Pp. 1-16.

(a) There was no plausible reason for the introduction of Cellmark's statements other than to establish their truth. Pp. 1-8.

(1) Illinois Rule of Evidence 703 permits an expert to base his opinion on facts about which he lacks personal knowledge and to disclose those facts to the trier of fact. Under Illinois law, such facts are not admitted for their truth, but only to explain the basis of the

expert's opinion. See *People v. Pasch*, **152 Ill. 2d 133**. But state evidence rules do not trump a defendant's constitutional right to confrontation. This Court ensures that an out-of-court statement was introduced for a "legitimate, nonhearsay purpose" before relying on the not-for-its-truth rationale to dismiss the Confrontation Clause's application. See *Tennessee v. Street*, **471 U. S. 409, 417**. Statements introduced to explain the basis of an expert's opinion are not introduced for a plausible nonhearsay purpose because, to use the basis testimony in evaluating the expert's opinion, the factfinder must consider the truth of the basis testimony. This commonsense conclusion is not undermined by any historical practice exempting expert basis testimony from the rigors of the Confrontation Clause. Before the Federal Rules of Evidence were adopted in 1975, an expert could render an opinion based only on facts that the expert had personally perceived or learned at trial. In 1975, that universe of facts was expanded to include facts that the expert learned out of court by means other than his own perception. The disclosure of such facts raises Confrontation Clause concerns. Pp. 2-5.

(2) Those concerns are fully applicable here. In concluding that petitioner's DNA profile matched the profile derived from L. J.'s swabs, Lambatos relied on Cellmark's out-of-court statements that its profile was in fact derived from those swabs, rather than from some other source. Thus, the validity of Lambatos' opinion ultimately turned on the truth of Cellmark's statements. Pp. 5-7.

(b) These statements, however, were not "testimonial" for purposes of the Confrontation Clause, which "applies to `witnesses' against the accused — in other words, those who `bear testimony."' *Crawford v. Washington*, **541 U. S. 36, 51**. "`Testimony,"' in turn, is "`[a] solemn declaration or affirmation made for the purpose of establishing or proving some fact."' *Ibid.* In light of its text, the Confrontation Clause regulates only the use of statements bearing "indicia of so lemnity." *Davis v. Washington*, **547 U. S. 813,836-837, 840** (opinion of THOMAS, J.). This test comports with history because solemnity marked the practices that the Confrontation Clause was designed to eliminate, namely, the *ex parte* examination of witnesses under English bail and committal statutes. See *id.*, at 835. Accordingly, the Clause reaches "formalized testimonial materials," such as depositions, affidavits, and prior testimony, or statements resulting from "formalized dialogue," such as custodial interrogation. *Bryant, supra*, at ___. Applying these principles, Cellmark's report is not a statement by a "witnes[s]" under the Confrontation Clause. It lacks the solemnity of an affidavit or deposition, for it is neither a sworn nor a certified declaration of fact. And, although it was produced at the request of law enforcement, it was not the product of formalized dialogue resembling custodial interrogation. *Melendez-Diaz*, **557 U. S. 305**, and *Bullcoming v. NewMexico*, **564 U. S. ___**, distinguished. Pp. 8-15.

ALITO, J., announced the judgment of the Court and delivered an opinion, in which ROBERTS, C. J., and KENNEDY and BREYER, JJ., joined. BREYER, J., filed a concurring opinion. THOMAS, J., filed an opinion concurring in the judgment. KAGAN, J., filed a dissenting opinion, in which SCALIA, GINSBURG, and SOTOMAYOR, JJ., joined.

Opinion of ALITO, J.

[*1]

JUSTICE ALITO announced the judgment of the Court and delivered an opinion, in which THE CHIEF JUSTICE, JUSTICE KENNEDY, and JUSTICE BREYER join.

In this case, we decide whether *Crawford v. Washington*, **541 U. S. 36, 50** (2004), precludes an expert witness from testifying in a manner that has long been allowed under the law of evidence. Specifically, does *Crawford* bar an expert from expressing an opinion based on facts about a case that have been made known to the expert but about which the expert is not competent to testify? We also decide whether*Crawford* substantially impedes the ability of prosecutors to introduce DNA evidence and thus may effectively relegate the prosecution in some cases to reliance on older, less reliable forms of proof.

In petitioner's bench trial for rape, the prosecution called an expert who testified that a DNA profile produced by an outside laboratory, Cellmark, matched a profile produced by the state police lab using a sample of petitioner's blood. On direct examination, the expert testified that Cellmark was an accredited laboratory and that Cellmark provided the police with a DNA profile. The expert also explained the notations on documents admitted *[*2]* as business records, stating that, according to the records, vaginal swabs taken from the victim were sent to and received back from Cellmark. The expert made no other statement that was offered for the purpose of identifying the sample of biological material used in deriving the profile or for the purpose of establishing how Cellmark handled or tested the sample. Nor did the expert vouch for the accuracy of the profile that Cellmark produced. Nevertheless, petitioner contends that the expert's testimony violated the Confrontation Clause as interpreted in *Crawford*.

Petitioner's main argument is that the expert went astray when she referred to the DNA profile provided by Cellmark as having been produced from semen found on the victim's vaginal swabs. But both the Illinois Appellate Court and the Illinois Supreme Court found that this statement was not admitted for the truth of the matter asserted, and it is settled that the Confrontation Clause does not bar the admission of such statements. See *id.*, at **59-60**, n. 9 (citing *Tennessee v. Street*, **471 U. S. 409** (1985)). For more than 200 years, the law of evidence has permitted the sort of testimony that was given by the expert in this case. Under settled evidence law, an expert may express an opinion that is based on facts that the expert assumes, but does not know, to be true. It is then up to the party who calls the expert to introduce other evidence establishing the facts assumed by the expert. While it was once the practice for an expert who based an opinion on assumed facts to testify in the form of an answer to a hypothetical question, modern practice does not demand this formality and, in appropriate cases, permits an expert to explain the facts on which his or her opinion is based without testifying to the truth of those facts. See Fed. Rule Evid. **703**. That is precisely what occurred in this case, and we should not lightly "swee[p] away an accepted rule governing the admission of scientific evidence." *[*3]* *Melendez-Diaz v. Massachusetts*, **557 U. S. 305**, **330**(2009) (KENNEDY, J., dissenting).

We now conclude that this form of expert testimony does not violate the Confrontation Clause because that provision has no application to out-of-court statements that are not offered to prove the truth of the matter asserted. When an expert testifies for the prosecution in a criminal case, the defendant has the opportunity to cross-examine the expert about any statements that are offered for their truth. Out-of-court statements that are related by the expert solely for the purpose of explaining the assumptions on which that opinion rests are not offered for their truth and thus fall outside the scope of the Confrontation Clause. Applying this rule to the present case, we conclude that the expert's testimony did not violate the **Sixth**Amendment.

As a second, independent basis for our decision, we also conclude that even if the report produced by Cellmark had been admitted into evidence, there would have been no Confrontation Clause violation. The Cellmark report is very different from the sort of extrajudicial statements, such as affidavits, depositions, prior testimony, and confessions, that the Confrontation Clause was originally understood to reach. The report was produced before any suspect was identified. The report was sought not for the purpose of obtaining evidence to be used against petitioner, who was not even under suspicion at the time, but for the purpose of finding a rapist who was on the loose. And the profile that Cellmark provided was not inherently inculpatory. On the contrary, a DNA profile is evidence that tends to exculpate all but one of the more than 7 billion people in the world today. The use of DNA evidence to exonerate persons who have been wrongfully accused or convicted is well known. If DNA profiles could not be introduced without calling the technicians who participated in the preparation of the profile, economic *[*4]* pressures would encourage prosecutors to forgo DNA testing and rely instead on older forms of evidence, such as eyewitness identification, that are less reliable. See *Perry v. New Hampshire*, **565 U. S.** ___ (2012). The Confrontation Clause does not mandate such an undesirable development. This conclusion will not prejudice any defendant who really wishes to probe the reliability of the DNA testing done in a particular case because those who participated in the testing may always be subpoenaed by the defense and questioned at trial.

I. A

On February 10, 2000, in Chicago, Illinois, a young woman, L. J., was abducted while she was walking home from work. The perpetrator forced her into his car and raped her, then robbed her of her money and other personal items and pushed her out into the street. L. J. ran home and reported the attack to her mother, who called the police. An ambulance took L. J. to the hospital, where doctors treated her wounds and took a blood sample and vaginal swabs for a sexual-assault kit. A Chicago Police detective collected the kit, labeled it with an inventory number, and sent it under seal to the Illinois State Police (ISP) lab.

At the ISP lab, a forensic scientist received the sealed kit. He conducted a chemical test that confirmed the presence of semen on the vaginal swabs, and he then resealed the kit and placed it in a secure evidence freezer.

During the period in question, the ISP lab often sent biological samples to Cellmark Diagnostics Laboratory in Germantown, Maryland, for DNA testing. There was evidence that the ISP lab sent L. J.'s vaginal swabs to Cellmark for testing and that Cellmark sent back a report containing a male DNA profile produced from semen taken from those swabs. At this time, petitioner was not under *[*5]* suspicion for L. J.'s rape.

Sandra Lambatos, a forensic specialist at the ISP lab, conducted a computer search to see if the Cellmark profile matched any of the entries in the state DNA database. The computer showed a match to a profile produced by the lab from a sample of petitioner's blood that had been taken after he was arrested on unrelated charges on August 3, 2000.

On April 17, 2001, the police conducted a lineup at which L. J. identified petitioner as her assailant. Petitioner was then indicted for aggravated criminal sexual assault, aggravated kidnaping, and aggravated robbery. In lieu of a jury trial, petitioner chose to be tried before a state judge.

B

Petitioner's bench trial began in April 2006. In open court, L. J. again identified petitioner as her attacker. The State also offered three expert forensic witnesses to link petitioner to the crime through his DNA. First, Brian Hapack, an ISP forensic scientist, testified that he had confirmed the presence of semen on the vaginal swabs taken from L. J. by performing an acid phosphatase test. After performing this test, he testified, he resealed the evidence and left it in a secure freezer at the ISP lab.

Second, Karen Abbinanti, a state forensic analyst, testified that she had used Polymerase Chain Reaction (PCR) and Short Tandem Repeat (STR) techniques to develop a DNA profile from a blood sample that had been drawn from petitioner after he was arrested in August 2000. She also stated that she had entered petitioner's DNA profile into the state forensic database.

Third, the State offered Sandra Lambatos as an expert witness in forensic biology and forensic DNA analysis. On direct examination, Lambatos testified about the general process of using the PCR and STR techniques to generate *[*6]* DNA profiles from forensic samples such as blood and semen. She then described how these DNA profiles could be matched to an individual based on the individual's unique genetic code. In making a comparison between two DNA profiles, Lambatos stated, it is a "commonly accepted" practice within the scientific community for "one DNA expert to rely on the records of another DNA expert." App. 51. Lambatos also testified that Cellmark was an "accredited crime lab" and that, in her experience, the ISP lab routinely sent evidence samples via Federal Express to Cellmark for DNA testing in order to expedite the testing process and to "reduce [the lab's] backlog." *Id.*, at 49-50. To keep track of evidence samples and preserve the chain of custody, Lambatos stated, she and other analysts relied on sealed shipping containers and labeled shipping manifests, and she added that experts in her field regularly relied on such protocols. *Id.*, at 50-51.

Lambatos was shown shipping manifests that were admitted into evidence as business records, and she explained what they indicated, namely, that the ISP lab had sent L. J.'s vaginal swabs to Cellmark, and that Cellmark had sent them back, along with a deduced male DNA profile. *Id.*, at 52-55. The prosecutor asked Lambatos whether there was "a computer match" between "the male DNA profile found in semen from the vaginal swabs of [L. J.]" and "[the] male DNA profile that had been identified" from petitioner's blood sample. *Id.*, at 55.

The defense attorney objected to this question for "lack of foundation," arguing that the prosecution had offered "no evidence with regard to any testing that's been done to generate a DNA profile by another lab to be testified to by this witness." *Ibid.*

The prosecutor responded: "I'm not getting at what another lab did." *Id.*, at 56. Rather, she said, she was simply asking Lambatos about "her own testing based on [DNA] information" that she had received from Cellmark. *[*7]* *Ibid.* The trial judge agreed, noting, "If she says she didn't do her own testing and she relied on a test of another lab and she's testifying to that, we will see what she's going to say." *Ibid.*

The prosecutor then proceeded, asking Lambatos, "Did you compare the semen that had been identified by Brian Hapack from the vaginal swabs of [L. J.] to the male DNA profile that had been identified by Karen [Abbinanti] from the blood of [petitioner]?" *Ibid.*

Lambatos answered "Yes." *Ibid.* Defense counsel lodged an objection "to the form of the question," but the trial judge overruled it. *Ibid.* Lambatos then testified that, based on her own comparison of the two DNA profiles, she "concluded that [petitioner] cannot be excluded as a possible source of the semen identified in the vaginal swabs," and that the probability of the profile's appearing in the general population was "1 in 8.7 quadrillion black, 1 in 390 quadrillion white, or 1 in 109 quadrillion Hispanic unrelated individuals." *Id.*, at 57. Asked whether she would "call this a match to [petitioner]," Lambatos answered yes, again over defense counsel's objection. *Id.*, at 58.

The Cellmark report itself was neither admitted into evidence nor shown to the factfinder. Lambatos did not quote or read from the report; nor did she identify it as the source of any of the opinions she expressed.

On cross-examination, Lambatos confirmed that she did not conduct or observe any of the testing on the vaginal swabs, and that her testimony relied on the DNA profile produced by Cellmark. *Id.*, at 59. She stated that she trusted Cellmark to do reliable work because it was an accredited lab, but she admitted she had not seen any of the calibrations or work that Cellmark had done in deducing a male DNA profile from the vaginal swabs. *Id.*, at 59-62.

Asked whether the DNA sample might have been degraded *[*8]* before Cellmark analyzed it, Lambatos answered that, while degradation was technically possible, she strongly doubted it had occurred in this case. She gave two reasons. First, the ISP lab likely would have noticed the degradation before sending the evidence off to Cell-mark. Second, and more important, Lambatos also noted that the data making up the DNA profile would exhibit certain telltale signs if it had been deduced from a degraded sample: The visual representation of the DNA sequence would exhibit "specific patterns" of degradation, and she "didn't see any evidence" of that from looking at the profile that Cellmark produced. *Id.*, at 81-82.

When Lambatos finished testifying, the defense moved to exclude her testimony "with regards to testing done by [Cellmark]" based on the Confrontation Clause. *Id.*, at 90. Defense counsel argued that there was "no evidence with regards to . . . any work done by [Cellmark] to justify testimony coming into this case with regard to their analysis." *Ibid.* Thus, while defense counsel objected to and sought the exclusion of Lambatos' testimony insofar as it implicated events at the Cellmark lab, defense counsel did not object to or move for the exclusion of any other portion of Lambatos' testimony, including statements regarding the contents of the shipment sent to or received back from Cellmark. See *id.*, at 55, 56, 90. See also **385 Ill. App. 3d 359, 367-368, 895 N. E. 2d 961, 968** (2008) (chain-of-custody argument based on shipping manifests waived).

The prosecution responded that petitioner's Confrontation Clause rights were satisfied because he had the opportunity to cross-examine the expert who had testified that there was a match between the DNA profiles produced by Cellmark and Abbinanti. App. 91. Invoking Illinois Rule of Evidence 703,**[fn1]** the prosecutor argued that *[*9]* an expert is allowed to disclose the facts on which the expert's opinion is based even if the expert is not competent to testify to those underlying facts. She further argued that any deficiency in the foundation for the expert's opinion "[d]oesn't go to the admissibility of [that] testimony," but instead "goes to the weight of the testimony." App. 91.

The trial judge agreed with the prosecution and stated that "the issue is . . . what weight do you give the test, not do you exclude it." *Id.*, at 94. Accordingly, the judge stated that he would not exclude Lambatos' testimony, which was "based on her own independent testing of the data received from [Cellmark]." *Id.*, at 94-95 (alteration in original).

The trial court found petitioner guilty of the charges against him. The state court of appeals affirmed in relevant part, concluding that Lambatos' testimony did not violate petitioner's confrontation rights because the Cell-mark report was not offered into evidence to prove the truth of the matter it asserted. See **385 Ill. App. 3d, at 369, 895 N. E. 2d, at 969-970** ("Cellmark's report was not offered for the truth of the matter asserted; rather, it was offered to provide a basis for Lambatos' opinion") The Supreme Court of Illinois also affirmed. **238 Ill. 2d 125, 939 N. E. 2d 268** (2010). Under state law, the court noted, the Cellmark report could not be used as substantive evidence. When Lambatos referenced the report during her direct examination, she did so "for the limited purpose of explaining the basis for [her expert opinion]," not for the purpose of showing "the truth of the matter asserted" by *[*10]* the report. *Id.*, at 150, 939 N. E. 2d, at 282. Thus, the report was not used to establish its truth, but only "to show the underlying facts and data Lambatos used before rendering an expert opinion." *Id.*, at 145, 939 N. E. 2d, at 279.

We granted certiorari. **564 U. S.**___ (2011).

II. A

The Confrontation Clause of the **Sixth** Amendment provides that, "[i]n all criminal prosecutions, the accused shall enjoy the right . . . to be confronted with the witnesses against him." Before *Crawford*, this Court took the view that the Confrontation Clause did not bar the admission of an out-of-court statement that fell within a firmly rooted exception to the hearsay rule, see *Ohio v. Roberts*, **448 U. S. 56, 66** (1980), but in *Crawford*, the Court adopteda fundamentally new interpretation of the confrontation, right, holding that "[testimonial statements of witnesses absent from trial [can be] admitted only where the declarant is unavailable, and only where the defendant has had a prior opportunity to cross-examine." **541 U. S., at 59.** *Crawford* has resulted in a steady stream of new cases in this Court. See *Bullcoming v. New Mexico*, **564 U. S. 353** (2008); *Indiana v. Edwards*, **554 U. S. 164** (2008); *Davis v. Washington*, **547 U. S. 813**(2006).

Two of these decisions involved scientific reports. In *Melendez-Diaz*, the defendant was arrested and charged with distributing and trafficking in cocaine. At trial, the prosecution introduced bags of a white powdery substance that had been found in the defendant's possession. The trial court also admitted into evidence three "certificates of analysis" from the state forensic laboratory stating that the bags had been "examined with the following results: *[*11]* The substance was found to contain: Cocaine." **557 U. S., at 308** (internal quotation marks omitted).

The Court held that the admission of these certificates, which were executed under oath before a notary, violated the **Sixth** Amendment. They were created for "the sole purpose of providing evidence against a defendant," *id.*, at **323**, and were "'quite plainly affidavits,'" *id.*, at **330** (THOMAS, J., concurring). The Court emphasized that the introduction of the report to prove the nature of the substance found in the defendant's possession was tantamount to "live, in-court testimony" on that critical fact and that the certificates did "precisely what a witness does on direct examination." *Id.*, at **311** (internal quotation marks omitted). There was no doubt that the certificates were used to prove the truth of the matter they asserted. Under state law, "the sole purpose of the affidavits was to provide prima facie evidence of the composition, quality, and the net weight of the analyzed substance." *Ibid.* (internal quotation marks omitted and emphasis deleted). On these facts, the Court said, it was clear that the certificates were "testimonial statements" that could not be introduced unless their authors were subjected to the "'crucible of cross-examination.'" *Id.*, at **311, 317** (quoting *Crawford, supra*, at **61**).

In *Bullcoming*, we held that another scientific report could not be used as substantive evidence against the defendant unless the analyst who prepared and certified the report was subject to confrontation. The defendant in that case had been convicted of driving while intoxicated. At trial, the court admitted into evidence a forensic report certifying that a sample of the defendant's blood had an alcohol concentration of 0.21 grams per hundred milli-liters, well above the legal limit. Instead of calling the analyst who signed and certified the forensic report, the prosecution called another analyst who had not performed or observed the actual analysis, but was only familiar with *[*12]* the general testing procedures of the laboratory. The Court declined to accept this surrogate testimony, despite the fact that the testifying analyst was a "knowledgeable representative of the laboratory" who could "explain the lab's processes and the details of the report." **564 U. S., at** ___ (KENNEDY, J., dissenting) (slip op., at 1). The Court stated simply: "The accused's right is to be confronted with the analyst who made the certification." *Id.*, at ___ (slip op., at 2).

Just as in *Melendez-Diaz*, the forensic report that was "introduce[d]" in *Bullcoming* "contain[ed] a testimonial certification, made in order to prove a fact at a criminal trial." **564 U. S., at ___ — ___** (slip op., at 7-8). The report was signed by the nontestifying analyst who had authored it, stating, "I certify that I followed the procedures set out on the reverse of this report, and the statements in this block are correct. The concentration of alcohol in this sample is based on the grams of alcohol in one hundred milliliters of blood." App. in *Bullcoming*, O. T. 2010, *No. 09-10876*, p. 62. Critically, the report was introduced at trial for the substantive purpose of proving the truth of the matter asserted by its out-of-court author — namely, that the defendant had a blood-alcohol level of 0.21. This was the central fact in question at the defendant's trial, and it was dispositive of his guilt.

In concurrence, JUSTICE SOTOMAYOR highlighted the importance of the fact that the forensic report had been admitted into evidence for the purpose of proving the truth of the matter it asserted. She emphasized that "this [was] not a case in which an expert witness was asked for his independent opinion about underlying testimonial reports that were not themselves admitted into evidence." **564 U. S., at ___**(slip op., at 6) (opinion concurring in part) (citing Fed. Rule Evid. **703**). "We would face a different question," she observed, "if asked to determine the constitutionality of allowing an expert witness to discuss others' *[*13]* testimonial statements if the testimonial statements were not themselves admitted as evidence." *Id.*, at ___ (slip op., at 6).

We now confront that question.

B

It has long been accepted that an expert witness may voice an opinion based on facts concerning the events at issue in a particular case even if the expert lacks firsthand knowledge of those facts.

At common law, courts developed two ways to deal with this situation. An expert could rely on facts that had already been established in the record. But because it was not always possible to proceed in this manner, and because record evidence was often disputed, courts developed the alternative practice of allowing an expert to testify in the form of a "hypothetical question." Under this approach, the expert would be asked to assume the truth of certain factual predicates, and was then asked to offer an opinion based on those assumptions. See 1 K. Broun, McCormick on Evidence *§ 14*, p. 87 (6th ed. 2006); 1 J. Wigmore, Evidence § *677*, p. 1084 (2d ed. 1923) ("If the witness is skilled enough, his opinion may be adequately obtained upon hypothetical data alone; and it is immaterial whether he has ever seen the person, place or thing in question" (citation omitted)). The truth of the premises could then be established through independent evidence, and the factfinder would regard the expert's testimony to be only as credible as the premises on which it was based.

An early example of this approach comes from the English case of *Beckwith v. Sydebotham*, **1 Camp. 116**, **170 Eng. Rep. 897** (K. B. 1807), where a party sought to prove the seaworthiness of a ship, the *Earl of Wycombe*, by calling as witnesses "several eminent surveyors of ships who had never seen the `Earl of Wycombe.'" *Ibid.* The opposing party objected to the testimony because it relied *[*14]* on facts that were not known to be true, but the judge disagreed. Because the experts were "peculiarly acquainted" with "a matter of skill or science," the judge said, the "jury might be assisted" by their hypothetical opinion based on certain assumed facts. *Id.*, at 117, 170 Eng. Rep., at 897. The judge acknowledged the danger of the jury's being unduly prejudiced by wrongly assuming the truth of the hypothetical facts, but the judge noted that the experts could be asked on cross-examination what their opinion of the ship's seaworthiness would be if different hypothetical facts were assumed. If the party that had called the experts could not independently prove the truth of the premises they posited, then the experts' "opinion might not go for much; but still it was admissible evidence." *Ibid.*

There is a long tradition of the use of hypothetical questions in American courts. In 1887, for example, this Court indicated its approval of the following jury instruction:

"As to the questions, you must understand that they are not evidence; they are mere statements to these witnesses . . . and, upon the hypothesis or assumption of these questions the witnesses are asked to give their [opinion]. You must readily see that the value of the answers to these questions depends largely, if not wholly, upon the fact whether the statements made in these questions are sustained by the proof. If the statements in these questions are not supported by the proof, then the answers to the questions are entitled to no weight, because based upon false assumptions or statements of facts." *Forsyth v. Doolittle*, **120 U. S. 73**, 77 (internal quotation marks omitted).

Modern rules of evidence continue to permit experts to express opinions based on facts about which they lack personal knowledge, but these rules dispense with the need for hypothetical questions. Under both the Illinois *[*15]* and the Federal Rules of Evidence, an expert may base an opinion on facts that are "made known to the expert at or before the hearing," but such reliance does not constitute admissible evidence of this underlying information. **Ill. Rule Evid. 703**; Fed. Rule Evid. **703**. Accordingly, *in jury trials*, both Illinois and federal law generally bar an expert from disclosing such inadmissible evidence.**[fn2]** In bench trials, however, both the Illinois and the Federal Rules place no restriction on the revelation of such information to the factfinder. When the judge sits as the trier of fact, it is presumed that the judge will understand the limited reason for the disclosure of the underlying inadmissible information and will not rely on that information for any improper purpose. As we have noted, "[i]n bench trials, judges routinely hear inadmissible evidence that they are presumed to ignore when making decisions."*Harris v. Rivera*, **454 U. S. 339**, 346 (1981) *(per curiam)*. There is a "well-established presumption" that "*the judge [has] adhered to basic rules of procedure*," when the judge is acting as a factfinder. *Id.*, at**346-347** (emphasis added). See also *Gentile v. State Bar of Nev.*, **501 U. S. 1030**, 1078 (1991) (Rehnquist, C. J., dissenting).

This feature of Illinois and federal law is important because *Crawford*, while departing from prior Confrontation Clause precedent in other respects, took pains to reaffirm the proposition that the Confrontation Clause "does not bar the use of testimonial statements for purposes *[*16]* other than establishing the truth of the matter asserted." **541 U. S., at 59-60**, n. 9 (citing *Tennessee v. Street*, **471 U. S. 409**). In *Street*, the defendant claimed that the police had coerced him into adopting the confession of his alleged accomplice. The prosecution sought to rebut this claim by showing that the defendant's confession differed significantly from the accomplice's. Although the accomplice's confession was clearly a testimonial statement, the Court held that the jurors could hear it as long as they were instructed to consider that confession not for its truth, but only for the "distinctive and limited purpose" of comparing it to the defendant's confession, to see whether the two were identical. *Id., at* **417**.

III. A

In order to assess petitioner's Confrontation Clause argument, it is helpful to inventory exactly what Lambatos said on the stand about Cellmark. She testified to the truth of the following matters: Cellmark was an accredited lab, App. 49; the ISP occasionally sent forensic samples to Cellmark for DNA testing,*ibid.;* according to shipping manifests admitted into evidence, the ISP lab sent vaginal swabs taken from the victim to Cellmark and later received those swabs back from Cellmark, *id.*, at 52-55; and, finally, the Cellmark DNA profile matched a profile produced by the ISP lab from a sample of petitioner's blood, *id.*, at 55-56. Lambatos had personal knowledge of all of these matters, and therefore none of this testimony infringed petitioner's confrontation right.

Lambatos did not testify to the truth of any other matter concerning Cellmark. She made no other reference to the Cellmark report, which was not admitted into evidence and was not seen by the trier of fact. Nor did she testify to anything that was done at the Cellmark lab, and she did not vouch for the quality of Cellmark's work. *[*17]*

B

The principal argument advanced to show a Confrontation Clause violation concerns the phrase that Lambatos used when she referred to the DNA profile that the ISP lab received from Cellmark. This argument is developed most fully in the dissenting opinion, and therefore we refer to the dissent's discussion of this issue.

In the view of the dissent, the following is the critical portion of Lambatos' testimony, with the particular words that the dissent finds objectionable italicized:

"Q Was there a computer match generated of the male DNA profile *found in semen from the vaginalswabs of [L.J.]* to a male DNA profile that had been identified as having originated from Sandy Williams?

"A Yes, there was." *Post*, at 7 (opinion of KAGAN J.) (quoting App. 56; emphasis added).

According to the dissent, the italicized phrase violated petitioner's confrontation right because Lambatos lacked personal knowledge that the profile produced by Cellmark was based on the vaginal swabs taken from the victim, L. J. As the dissent acknowledges, there would have been "nothing wrong with Lambatos's testifying that two DNA profiles — the one shown in the Cellmark report and the one derived from Williams's blood — matched each other; that was a straightforward application of Lambatos's expertise." *Post*, at 12. Thus, if Lambatos' testimony had been slightly modified as follows, the dissent would see no

"Q Was there a computer match generated of the male DNA profile **produced by** *[*18]* **Cellmark**~~found in semen from the vaginal swabs of~~ [L.J.] to a male DNA profile that had been identified as having originated from Sandy Williams?

"A Yes, there was."**[fn3]**

The defect in this argument is that under Illinois law (like federal law) it is clear that the putatively offending phrase in Lambatos' testimony was not admissible for the purpose of proving the truth of the matter asserted — *i.e.*, that the matching DNA profile was "found in semen from the vaginal swabs." Rather, that fact was a mere premise of the prosecutor's question, and Lambatos simply assumed that premise to be true when she gave her answer indicating that there was a match between the two DNA profiles. There is no reason to think that the trier of fact took Lambatos' answer as substantive evidence to establish where the DNA profiles came from.

The dissent's argument would have force if petitioner had elected to have a jury trial. In that event, there would have been a danger of the jury's taking Lambatos' testimony as proof that the Cellmark profile was derived from the sample obtained from the victim's vaginal swabs. Absent an evaluation of the risk of juror confusion and careful jury instructions, the testimony could not have *[*19]* gone to the jury.

This case, however, involves *a bench trial* and we must assume that the trial judge understood that the portion of Lambatos' testimony to which the dissent objects was not admissible to prove the truth of the matter asserted.**[fn4]** The dissent, on the other hand, reaches the truly remarkable conclusion that the wording of Lambatos' testimony confused the trial judge. Were it not for that wording, the argument goes, the judge might have found that the prosecution failed to introduce sufficient admissible evidence to show that the Cellmark profile was derived from the sample taken from the victim, and the judge might have disregarded the DNA evidence. This argument reflects a profound lack of respect for the acumen of the trial judge.**[fn5]**

To begin, the dissent's argument finds no support in the trial record. After defense counsel objected to Lambatos' testimony, the prosecutor made clear that she was asking Lambatos only about "her own testing based on [DNA] information" that she had received from Cellmark. App. 56. Recognizing that Lambatos' testimony would carry weight only if the underlying premises could be established, the judge noted that "the issue is . . . what weight do you give the test [performed by Lambatos], not do you exclude it." *Id.*, at 94. This echoes the old statement in *Beckwith* that an expert's opinion based on disputed premises "might not go for much; but still it [is] admissible evidence." **1 Camp., at 117, 170 Eng. Rep., at 897.** Both *[*20]*the Illinois Appellate Court and the Illinois Supreme Court viewed the record in this way, and we see no ground for disagreement.**[fn6]**

Second, it is extraordinarily unlikely that any trial judge would be confused in the way that the dissent posits. That Lambatos was not competent to testify to the chain of custody of the sample taken from the victim was a point that any trial judge or attorney would immediately understand. Lambatos, after all, had absolutely nothing to do with the collection of the sample from the victim, its subsequent handling or preservation by the police in Illinois, or its shipment to and receipt by Cellmark. No trial judge would take Lambatos' testimony as furnishing "the missing link" in the State's evidence regarding the identity of the sample that Cellmark tested. See *post*, at 6 (opinion of KAGAN, J.).

Third, the admissible evidence left little room for argument that the sample tested by Cellmark came from any source other than the victim's vaginal swabs.**[fn7]** This is so *[*21]* because there is simply no plausible explanation for how Cellmark could have produced a DNA profile that matched Williams' if Cellmark had tested any sample other than the one taken from the victim. If any other items that might have contained Williams' DNA had been sent to Cellmark or were otherwise in Cellmark's possession, there would have been a chance of a mix-up or of cross-contamination. See *District Attorney's Office forThird Judicial Dist. v. Osborne*, **557 U. S. 52, 80** (2009) (ALITO, J., concurring). But there is absolutely nothing to suggest that Cellmark had any such items. Thus, the fact that the Cellmark profile matched Williams — the very man whom the victim identified in a lineup and at trial as her attacker — was itself striking confirmation that the sample that Cellmark tested was the sample taken from the victim's vaginal swabs. For these reasons, it is fanciful to suggest that the trial judge took Lambatos' testimony as providing critical chain-of-custody evidence.

C

Other than the phrase that Lambatos used in referring to the Cellmark profile, no specific passage in the trial record has been identified as violating the Confrontation Clause, but it is nevertheless suggested that the State somehow introduced "the substance of Cellmark's report into evidence." *Post*, at 8 (KAGAN, J., dissenting). The main impetus for this argument appears to be the (erroneous) view that unless the substance of the report was sneaked in, there would be insufficient evidence in the record on two critical points: first, that the Cellmark profile was based on the semen in the victim's vaginal swabs and, second, that Cellmark's procedures were reliable. This argument is both legally irrelevant for present purposes and factually incorrect.

As to legal relevance, the question before us is whether petitioner's **Sixth** Amendment confrontation right was violated, not whether the State offered sufficient foundational evidence to support the admission of Lambatos' opinion about the DNA match. In order to prove these underlying facts, the prosecution relied on circumstantial evidence, and the Illinois courts found that this evidence was sufficient to satisfy state-law requirements regarding proof of foundational facts. See **385 Ill. App. 3d, at 366-368, 895 N. E. 2d, at 967-968; 238 Ill. 2d, at 138, 939 N. E. 2d, at 275.** We cannot review that interpretation and application of Illinois law. Thus, even if the record did not contain any evidence that could rationally support a finding that Cellmark produced a scientifically reliable DNA profile based on L. J.'s vaginal swab, that would not establish a Confrontation Clause violation. If there were no proof that Cellmark produced an accurate profile based on that sample, Lambatos' testimony regarding the match would be irrelevant, but the Confrontation Clause, as interpreted in *Crawford*, does not bar the admission of irrelevant evidence, only testimonial statements by declarants who are not subject to cross-examination.**[fn8]**

It is not correct, however, that the trial record lacks admissible evidence with respect to the source of the sample that Cellmark tested or the reliability of the Cell-mark profile. As to the source of the sample, the State offered conventional chain-of-custody evidence, namely, the testimony of the physician who obtained the vaginal swabs, the testimony of the police employees who handled and kept custody of that evidence until it was sent to *[*23]* Cellmark, and the shipping manifests, which provided evidence that the swabs were sent to Cellmark and then returned to the ISP lab. In addition, as already discussed, the match between the Cellmark profile and petitioner's profile was itself telling confirmation that the Cellmark profile was deduced from the semen on the vaginal swabs.

This match also provided strong circumstantial evidence regarding the reliability of Cellmark's work. Assuming (for the reasons discussed above) that the Cellmark profile was based on the semen on the vaginal swabs, how could shoddy or dishonest work in the Cellmark lab**[fn9]** have resulted in the production of a DNA profile that just so happened to match petitioner's? If the semen found on the vaginal swabs was not petitioner's and thus had an entirely different DNA profile, how could sloppy work in the Cellmark lab have transformed that entirely different profile into one that matched petitioner's? And without access to any other sample of petitioner's DNA (and recall that petitioner was not even under suspicion at this time), how could a dishonest lab technician have substituted petitioner's DNA profile? Under the circumstances of this case, it was surely permissible for the trier of fact to infer that the odds of any of this were exceedingly low.

This analysis reveals that much of the dissent's argument rests on a very clear error. The dissent argues that Lambatos' testimony could be "true" only if the predicate facts asserted in the Cellmark report were true, and therefore Lambatos' reference to the report must have been used for the purpose of proving the truth of those facts. See *post*, at 10-11. But the truth of Lambatos' testimony, properly understood, was not dependent on the truth of any predicate facts. Lambatos testified that two DNA profiles matched. The correctness of this expert opinion, which the defense was able to test on cross-examination, *[*24]* was not in any way dependent on the origin of the samples from which the profiles were derived. Of course, Lambatos' opinion would have lacked probative value if the prosecution had not introduced other evidence to establish the provenance of the profiles, but that has nothing to do with the truth of her testimony.

The dissent is similarly mistaken in its contention that the Cellmark report "was offered for its truth because that is all such `basis evidence' can be offered for." *Post*, at

13; see also *post*, at 3 (THOMAS, J., concurring in judgment) ("[S]tatements introduced to explain the basis of an expert's opinion are not introduced for a plausible nonhearsay purpose"). This view is directly contrary to the current version of Rule **703** of the Federal Rules of Evidence, which this Court approved and sent to Congress in 2000. Under that Rule, "basis evidence" that is not admissible for its truth may be disclosed even in a jury trial under appropriate circumstances. The purpose for allowing this disclosure is that it may "assis[t] the jury to evaluate the expert's opinion." Advisory Committee's 2000 Notes on Fed. Rule Evid. **703**, *28 U. S. C. App., p. 361*. The Rule 703 approach, which was controversial when adopted,**[fn10]** is based on the idea that the disclosure of basis evidence can help the factfinder understand the expert's thought process and determine what weight to give to the expert's opinion. For example, if the factfinder were to suspect that the expert relied on factual premises with no support in the record, or that the expert drew an unwarranted inference from the premises on which the expert relied, then the probativeness or credibility of the expert's opinion would be seriously undermined. The purpose of disclosing the facts on which the expert relied is to allay these fears — to show that the expert's reasoning was not illogical, and that the weight of the expert's opinion does *[*25]* not depend on factual premises unsupported by other evidence in the record — not to prove the truth of the underlying facts.

Perhaps because it cannot seriously dispute the legitimate nonhearsay purpose of illuminating the expert's thought process, the dissent resorts to the last-ditch argument that, after all, it really does not matter whether Lambatos' statement regarding the source of the Cellmark report was admitted for its truth. The dissent concedes that "the trial judge might have ignored Lambatos's statement about the Cellmark report," but nonetheless maintains that "the admission of that statement violated the Confrontation Clause even if the judge ultimately put it aside." *Post*, at 15, n. 2. But in a bench trial, it is not necessary for the judge to stop and make a formal statement on the record regarding the limited reason for which the testimony is admitted. If the judge does not consider the testimony for its truth, the effect is precisely the same. Thus, if the trial judge in this case did not rely on the statement in question for its truth, there is simply no way around the proviso in *Crawford* that the Confrontation Clause applies only to out-of-court statements that are "use[d]" to "establis[h] the truth of the matter asserted." **541 U. S., at 59-60**, n. 9 (citing *Street*, **471 U. S. 409**).

For all these reasons, we conclude that petitioner's **Sixth** Amendment confrontation right was not violated.

D

This conclusion is entirely consistent with *Bullcoming* and *Melendez-Diaz.* In those cases, the forensic reports were introduced into evidence, and there is no question that this was done for the purpose of proving the truth of what they asserted: in *Bullcoming* that the defendant's blood alcohol level exceeded the legal limit and in *Melendez-Diaz* that the substance in question contained cocaine. Nothing comparable happened here. In this case, the *[*26]* Cellmark report was not introduced into evidence. An expert witness referred to the report not to prove the truth of the matter asserted in the report, *i.e.*, that the report contained an accurate profile of the perpetrator's DNA, but only to establish that the report contained a DNA profile that matched the DNA profile deduced from petitioner's blood. Thus, just as in *Street*, the report was not to be considered for its truth but only for the "distinctive and limited purpose" of seeing whether it matched something else. **471 U. S., at 417**. The relevance of the match was then established by independent circumstantial evidence showing that the Cellmark report was based on a forensic sample taken from the scene of the crime.

Our conclusion will not open the door for the kind of abuses suggested by some of petitioner's *amici* and the dissent. See *post*, at 10-11; Brief for Richard D. Friedman as *Amicus Curiae* 20-21. In the hypothetical situations posited, an expert expresses an opinion based on factual premises not supported by any admissible evidence, and may also reveal the out-of-court statements on which the expert relied.**[fn11]**There are at least four safeguards to *[*27]* prevent such abuses. First, trial courts can screen out experts who would act as mere conduits for hearsay by strictly enforcing the requirement that experts display some genuine "scientific, technical, or other specialized knowledge [that] will help the trier of fact to understand the evidence or to determine a fact in issue." Fed. Rule Evid. 702(a). Second, experts are generally precluded from disclosing inadmissible evidence to a jury. See Fed. Rule Evid. 703; *People v. Pasch*, **152 Ill. 2d 133, 175-176, 604 N. E. 2d 294, 310-311** (1992). Third, if such evidence is disclosed, the trial judges may and, under most circumstances, must, instruct the jury that out-of-court statements cannot be accepted for their truth, and that an expert's opinion is only as good as the independent evidence that establishes its underlying premises. See Fed. Rules Evid. **105, 703**; *People v. Scott*, **148 Ill. 2d 479, 527-528, 594 N. E. 2d 217, 236-237** (1992). And fourth, if the prosecution cannot muster any independent admissible evidence to prove the foundational facts that are essential to the relevance of the expert's testimony, then the expert's testimony cannot be given any weight by the trier of fact.**[fn12]**

IV. A

Even if the Cellmark report had been introduced for its truth, we would nevertheless conclude that there was no Confrontation Clause violation. The Confrontation Clause refers to testimony by "witnesses against" an accused. Both the noted evidence scholar James Henry Wigmore and Justice Harlan interpreted the Clause in a strictly literal sense as referring solely to persons who testify in court, but we have not adopted this narrow view. It has been said that "[t]he difficulty with the Wigmore-Harlan view in its purest form is its tension with much of the apparent history surrounding the evolution of the right of confrontation at common law." *White v. Illinois*, 502 U. S. Court concluded in *Crawford*, "was the civil-law mode of criminal procedure, and particularly its use of *ex parte* examinations as evidence against the accused." **541 U. S., at 50**. "[I]n England, pretrial examinations of suspects *[*29]* and witnesses by government officials `were sometimes read in court in lieu of live testimony.'" *Bryant*, **562 U. S., at __**(slip op., at 6) (quoting *Crawford, supra*, at **43**). The Court has thus interpreted the Confrontation Clause as prohibiting modern-day practices that are tantamount to the abuses that gave rise to the recognition of the confrontation right. But any further expansion would strain the constitutional text.

The abuses that the Court has identified as prompting the adoption of the Confrontation Clause shared the following two characteristics: (a) they involved out-of-court statements having the primary purpose of accusing a targeted individual of engaging in criminal conduct and (b) they involved formalized statements such as affidavits, depositions, prior testimony, or confessions. In all but one of the post-*Crawford* cases**[fn13]** in which a Confrontation Clause violation has been found, both of these characteristics were present. See *Bullcoming*, **564 U. S., at 308** (slip op., at 3-4) (certified lab report having purpose of showing that defendant's blood-alcohol level exceeded legal limit); *Melendez-Diaz*, **557 U. S., at 308** (certified lab report having purpose of showing that substance connected to defendant contained cocaine); *Crawford, supra*, at **38** (custodial statement made after *Miranda* warnings that shifted blame from declarant to accused).**[fn14]** The one exception occurred in *Hammon v. Indiana*, **547 U. S. 813, 829-832** (2006), which was decided together with *Davis v. Washington*, but in *Hammon* and every other post-*Crawford* case in which the Court has found a violation of

[*30] the confrontation right, the statement at issue had the primary purpose of accusing a targeted individual.

B

In *Hammon*, the one case in which an informal statement was held to violate the Confrontation Clause, we considered statements elicited in the course of police interrogation. We held that a statement does not fall within the ambit of the Clause when it is made "under circumstances objectively indicating that the primary purpose of the interrogation is to enable police assistance to meet an ongoing emergency." **547 U. S., at 822**. In *Bryant*, another police-interrogation case, we explained that a person who makes a statement to resolve an ongoing emergency is not acting like a trial witness because the declarant's purpose is not to provide a solemn declaration for use at trial, but to bring an end to an ongoing threat. See **562 U. S., at ___, ___** (slip op., at 11, 14). We noted that "the prospect of fabrication . . . is presumably significantly diminished" when a statement is made under such circumstances, *id.*, at ___ (slip op., at 14) and that reliability is a salient characteristic of a statement that falls outside the reach of the Confrontation Clause, *id.*, at ___ — ___ (slip op., at 14-15). We emphasized that if a statement is not made for "the primary purpose of creating an out-of-court substitute for trial testimony," its admissibility "is the concern of state and federal rules of evidence, not the Confrontation Clause." *Id.*, at ___ — ___ (slip op., at 11-12).

In *Melendez-Diaz* and *Bullcoming*, the Court held that the particular forensic reports at issue qualified as testimonial statements, but the Court did not hold that all forensic reports fall into the same category. Introduction of the reports in those cases ran afoul of the Confrontation Clause because they were the equivalent of affidavits made for the purpose of proving the guilt of a particular *[*31]* criminal defendant at trial. There was nothing resembling an ongoing emergency, as the suspects in both cases had already been captured, and the tests in question were relatively simple and can generally be performed by a single analyst. In addition, the technicians who prepared the reports must have realized that their contents (which reported an elevated blood-alcohol level and the presence of an illegal drug) would be incriminating.

C

The Cellmark report is very different. It plainly was not prepared for the primary purpose of accusing a targeted individual. In identifying the primary purpose of an out-of-court statement, we apply an objective test. *Bryant*, **562 U. S., at ___** (slip op., at 13). We look for the primary purpose that a reasonable person would have ascribed to the statement, taking into account all of the surrounding circumstances. ***Ibid.***

Here, the primary purpose of the Cellmark report, viewed objectively, was not to accuse petitioner or to create evidence for use at trial. When the ISP lab sent the sample to Cellmark, its primary purpose was to catch a dangerous rapist who was still at large, not to obtain evidence for use against petitioner, who was neither in custody nor under suspicion at that time. Similarly, no one at Cellmark could have possibly known that the profile that it produced would turn out to inculpate petitioner — or for that matter, anyone else whose DNA profile was in a law enforcement database. Under these circumstances, there was no "prospect of fabrication" and no incentive to produce anything other than a scientifically sound and reliable profile. *Id.*, at ___ (slip op., at 14).

The situation in which the Cellmark technicians found themselves was by no means unique. When lab technicians are asked to work on the production of a DNA profile, they often have no idea what the consequences of *[*32]* their work will be. In some cases, a DNA profile may provide powerful incriminating evidence against a person who is identified either before or after the profile is completed. But in others, the primary effect of the profile is to exonerate a suspect who has been charged or is under investigation. The technicians who prepare a DNA profile generally have no way of knowing whether it will turn out to be incriminating or exonerating — or both.

It is also significant that in many labs, numerous technicians work on each DNA profile. See Brief for New York County District Attorney's Office et al. as *Amici Curiae* 6 (New York lab uses at least 12 technicians for each case); *People v. Johnson,* **389 Ill. App. 3d 618, 627, 906 N. E. 2d 70,** 79 (2009) ("[A]pproximately 10 Cellmark analysts were involved in the laboratory work in this case"). When the work of a lab is divided up in such a way, it is likely that the sole purpose of each technician is simply to perform his or her task in accordance with accepted procedures.

Finally, the knowledge that defects in a DNA profile may often be detected from the profile itself provides a further safeguard. In this case, for example, Lambatos testified that she would have been able to tell from the profile if the sample used by Cellmark had been degraded prior to testing. As noted above, moreover, there is no real chance that "sample contamination, sample switching, mislabeling, [or] fraud" could have led Cellmark to produce a DNA profile that falsely matched petitioner. *Post,* at 21 (KAGAN, J., dissenting). At the time of the testing, petitioner had not yet been identified as a suspect, and there is no suggestion that anyone at Cellmark had a sample of his DNA to swap in by malice or mistake. And given the complexity of the DNA molecule, it is inconceivable that shoddy lab work would somehow produce a DNA profile that just so happened to have the precise genetic makeup of petitioner, who just so happened to be picked out of a lineup by the victim. The prospect is beyond *[*33]* fanciful. In short, the use at trial of a DNA report prepared by a modern, accredited laboratory "bears little if any resemblance to the historical practices that the Confrontation Clause aimed to eliminate." *Bryant, supra,* at ___ (slip op., at 2) (THOMAS, J., concurring).

* * *

For the two independent reasons explained above, we conclude that there was no Confrontation Clause violation in this case. Accordingly, the judgment of the Supreme Court of Illinois is

Affirmed.

[fn1] Consistent with the Federal Rules, **Illinois Rule of Evidence 703** provides as follows:

"The facts or data in the particular case upon which an expert bases an opinion or inference may be those perceived by or made known to the expert at or before the hearing. If of a type reasonably relied upon by experts in the particular field in forming opinions or inferences upon the subject, the facts or data need not be admissible in evidence."

[fn2] But disclosure of these facts or data to the jury is permitted if the value of disclosure "substantially outweighs [any] prejudicial effect," Fed. Rule Evid. **703,** or "the probative value . . . outweighs the risk of unfair prejudice." People v. Pasch, **152 Ill. 2d 133, 223, 604 N. E. 2d 294,** 333 (1992). When this disclosure occurs, "the underlying facts" are revealed to the jury "for the limited purpose of explaining the basis for [the expert's] opinion" and not "for the truth of the matter asserted." **Id.,** at **176, 604 N. E. 2d, at 311.**

[fn3] The small difference between what Lambatos actually said on the stand and the slightly revised version that the dissent would find unobjectionable shows that, despite the dissent's rhetoric, its narrow argument would have little practical effect in future cases. Prosecutors would be allowed to do exactly what the prosecution did in this case so long as their testifying experts' testimony was slightly modified along the lines shown above. Following that course presumably would not constitute a "prosecutorial dodge," "subterfuge," "indirection," the "neat trick" of "sneak[ing]" in evidence, or the countenancing of constitutional violations with "a wink and a nod." See *post*, at 3, 16, 17, 12 (opinion of KAGAN, J.).

[fn4] We do not suggest that the Confrontation Clause applies differently depending on the identity of the factfinder. Cf. *post*, at 14-15 (opinion of KAGAN, J.). Instead, our point is that the identity of the factfinder makes a big difference in evaluating the likelihood that the factfinder mistakenly based its decision on inadmissible evidence.

[fn5] See *post*, at 14 (opinion of KAGAN, J.) ("I do not doubt that a judge typically will do better than a jury in excluding such inadmissible evidence from his decisionmaking process. *Perhaps* the judge did so here" (emphasis added)).

[fn6] The dissent finds evidence of the trial judge's confusion in his statement that petitioner is "`the guy whose DNA, *according to the evidence from the experts*, is in the semen recovered from the victim's vagina.'" *Post*, at 14 (emphasis added). The dissent interprets the phrase "according to the evidence from the experts" as a reference to what one expert, Lambatos, said about the origin of the sample that Cellmark tested. In context, however, the judge's statement is best understood as attributing to Lambatos nothing more than the conclusion that there was a match between the two DNA profiles that were compared. The foundational facts, that one of the profiles came from the defendant and that the other came from "`the semen recovered from the victim's vagina,'" were established not by expert testimony but by ordinary chain-of-custody evidence.

[fn7] Our point is not that admissible evidence regarding the identity of the sample that Cellmark tested excuses the admission of testimonial hearsay on this matter. Compare *post*, at 5-6 (THOMAS, J., concurring in judgment), with *post*, at 14 (KAGAN, J., dissenting). Rather, our point is that, because there was substantial (albeit circumstantial) evidence on this matter, there is no reason to infer that the trier of fact must have taken Lambatos' statement as providing "the missing link."

[fn8] Applying the Due Process Clause, we have held that a federal court may determine whether a rational trier of fact could have found the existence of all the elements needed for conviction for a state offense. *Jackson v. Virginia*, **443 U. S. 307, 314** (1979), but petitioner has not raised a due process claim. And in any event, L. J.'s identification of petitioner as her assailant would be sufficient to defeat any such claim.

[fn9] See *post*, at 18 (KAGAN, J., dissenting).

[fn10] See Advisory Committee's 2000 Notes on Rule 703, at 361.

[fn11] Both JUSTICE THOMAS and JUSTICE KAGAN quote statements in D. Kaye, D. Bernstein, & J. Mnookin, The New Wigmore: Expert Evidence § *4.10.1*, pp. 196-197 (2d ed. 2011) (hereinafter New Wigmore), that are critical of the theory that an expert, without violating the Confrontation Clause, may express an opinion that is based on testimonial hearsay and may, in some circumstances, disclose that testimonial hearsay to the trier of fact. The principal basis for this criticism seems to be the fear that juries, even if given limiting instructions, will view the disclosed hearsay as evidence of the truth of the matter asserted. See *id.*, at 196, n. 36 (referring reader to the more detailed discussion in Mnookin, Expert Evidence and the Confrontation Clause After *Crawford v. Washington*, 15 J. L. & Pol'y 791 (2007)); New Wigmore *197*, and n. 39 (citing jury cases); Mnookin, *supra*, at 802-804, 811-813. This argument plainly has no application in a case like this one, in which a judge sits as the trier of fact. In the 2012 Supplement of

The New Wigmore, the authors discuss the present case and criticize the reasoning of the Illinois courts as follows:

"The problem with [the not-for-the-truth-of-the-matter argument accepted by the Illinois courts] is that Lambatos had to rely on the truth of the statements in the Cellmark report to reach her own conclusion. The claim that evidence that *the jury* must credit in order to credit the conclusion of the expert is introduced for something other than its truth is sheer fiction." New Wigmore § *4.11.6*, at 24 (2012 Supp.) (emphasis added).

This discussion is flawed. It overlooks the fact that there was no jury in this case, and as we have explained, the trier of fact did not have to rely on any testimonial hearsay in order to find that Lambatos' testimony about the DNA match was supported by adequate foundational evidence and was thus probative.

[fn12] Our discussion of the first ground for our decision cannot conclude without commenting on the Kocak case, which dramatically appears at the beginning of the dissent. In that case, a Cellmark lab analyst realized while testifying at a pretrial hearing that there was an error in the lab's report and that the DNA profile attributed to the accused was actually that of the victim. The lesson of this cautionary tale is nothing more than the truism that it is possible for an apparently incriminating DNA profile to be mistakenly attributed to an accused. But requiring that the lab analyst or analysts who produced the DNA profile be called as prosecution witnesses is neither sufficient nor necessary to prevent such errors. Since samples may be mixed up or contaminated at many points along the way from a crime scene to the lab, calling one or more lab analysts will not necessarily catch all such mistakes. For example, a mistake might be made by a clerical employee responsible for receiving shipments of samples and then providing them to the lab's technicians. What is needed is for the trier of fact to make sure that the evidence, whether direct or circumstantial, rules out the possibility of such mistakes at every step along the way. And in the usual course of authentication, defense counsel will have access to sufficient information to inquire into, question, or challenge the procedures used by a laboratory if this seems to be a prudent and productive strategy.

[fn13] Experience might yet show that the holdings in those cases should be reconsidered for the reasons, among others, expressed in the dissents the decisions produced. Those decisions are not challenged in this case and are to be deemed binding precedents, but they can and should be distinguished on the facts here.

[fn14] With respect to *Crawford*, see *Davis*, **547 U. S.**, at 840 (THOMAS, J., concurring in judgment in part and dissenting in part).

JUSTICE BREYER, concurring. *[*1]*

This case raises a question that I believe neither the plurality nor the dissent answers adequately: How does the Confrontation Clause apply to the panoply of crime laboratory reports and underlying technical statements written by (or otherwise made by) laboratory technicians? In this context, what, if any, are the outer limits of the "testimonial statements" rule set forth in *Crawford v. Washington*, **541 U. S. 36 (2004)**? Because I believe the question difficult, important, and not squarely addressed either today or in our earlier opinions, and because I believe additional briefing would help us find a proper, generally applicable answer, I would set this case for reargument. In the absence of doing so, I adhere to the dissenting views set forth in *Melendez-Diaz v. Massachu setts*, **557 U. S. 305 (2009)**, and *Bullcoming v. New Mexico*, **564 U. S. (2011)**. I also join the plurality's opinion.

I. A

This case is another in our series involving the intersection of the Confrontation Clause and expert testimony. Before trial, the prosecutions expert, Sandra Lambatos, received a copy of a report prepared by Cellmark Diagnostics Laboratory. That report reflected the fact that Cellmark technicians had received material from a vaginal *[*2]* swab taken from the crime victim, had identified semen in that material, and had derived a profile of the male DNA that the semen contained. Lambatos then entered that profile into an Illinois State Police Crime Laboratory computerized database, which contained, among many other DNA profiles, a profile derived by the crime laboratory from Williams' blood (taken at an earlier time). The computer she was using showed that the two profiles matched. Lambatos then confirmed the match.

Later, Lambatos testified at trial, where the prosecutor asked her three relevant questions. First, the prosecutor asked whether there was "a computer match generated of the male DNA profile [derived by Cellmark] found in [the] semen from the vaginal swabs . . . to [the] male DNA profile [found in the database] that had been identified as having originated from Sandy Williams"? App. 56. Since the computer had shown such a match, Lambatos answered affirmatively. *Ibid.*

Second, the prosecutor asked whether Lambatos had independently "compare[d the DNA profile that Cellmark had derived from] the semen that had been identified . . . from the vaginal swabs of [the victim] to the male DNA profile [found in the database] that had been [derived] . . . from the blood of Sandy Williams." *Ibid.* Lambatos again answered affirmatively. *Ibid.*

Third, the prosecutor asked whether, in Lambatos' expert opinion, the DNA profile derived from the semen identified in the vaginal swabs of the victim was "a match to Sandy Williams." *Id.*, at 58. Lambatos again answered affirmatively. *Ibid.*

The Confrontation Clause problem lies in the fact that Lambatos did not have personal knowledge that the male DNA profile that Cellmark said was derived from the crime victim's vaginal swab sample was in fact correctly derived from that sample. And no Cellmark expert testified that it was true. Rather, she simply relied for her *[*3]* knowledge of the fact upon Cellmark's report. And the defendant Williams had no opportunity to cross-examine the individual or individuals who produced that report.

In its first conclusion, the plurality explains why it finds that admission of Lambatos' testimony nonetheless did not violate the Confrontation Clause. That Clause concerns out-of-court statements admitted for their truth. *Ante,* at 15-16. Lambatos' testimony did not introduce the Cellmark report (which other circumstantial evidence supported) for its truth. *Ante,* at 16-21. Rather, Lambatos used the Cellmark report only to indicate the underlying factual information upon which she based her independent expert opinion. *Ibid.* Under well-established principles of evidence, experts may rely on otherwise inadmissible out-of-court statements as a basis for forming an expert opinion if they are of a kind that experts in the field normally rely upon. See Fed. Rule Evid. **703**; **Ill. Rule Evid. 703**. Nor need the prosecution enter those out-of-court statements into evidence for their truth. That, the Illinois courts held, is just what took place here. *Ante,* at 9-10.

The dissent would abandon this well-established rule. It would not permit Lambatos to offer an expert opinion in reliance on the Cellmark report unless the prosecution also produces one or more experts who wrote or otherwise produced the report. I am willing to accept the dissent's characterization of the present rule as artificial, see *post,* at 15-17 (opinion of KAGAN, J.), but I am not certain that the dissent has produced a workable alternative, see *Bullcoming, supra,* at ___ (KENNEDY, J., dissenting) (slip op., at 7) (expressing similar view).

Once one abandons the traditional rule, there would seem often to be no logical stopping place between requiring the prosecution to call as a witness one of the laboratory experts who worked on the matter and requiring the prosecution to call *all* of the laboratory experts who did so. *[*4]* Experts — especially laboratory experts — regularly rely on the technical statements and results of other experts to form their own opinions. The reality of the matter is that the introduction of a laboratory report involves layer upon layer of technical statements (express or implied) made by one expert and relied upon by another. Hence my general question: How does the Confrontation Clause apply to crime laboratory reports and underlying technical statements made by laboratory technicians?

B

The general question is not easy to answer. The California case described at the outset of the dissenting opinion helps to illustrate the difficulty. In that example, Cellmark, the very laboratory involved in this case, tested a DNA sample taken from the crime scene. A laboratory analyst, relying upon a report the laboratory had prepared, initially stated (at a pretrial hearing about admissibility) that the laboratory had found that the crime-scene DNA sample matched a sample of the defendant's DNA. But during the hearing and after reviewing the laboratory's notes, the laboratory analyst realized that the written report was mistaken. In fact, the testing showed only that the crime-scene DNA matched a sample of the victim's DNA, not the defendant's DNA. At some point during the writing of the report, someone, perhaps the testifying analyst herself, must have misread the proper original sample labeling. Upon discovering the error, the analyst corrected her testimony.

The example is useful, not simply because as adapted it might show the importance of cross-examination (an importance no one doubts), but also because it can reveal the nature of the more general question before us. When the laboratory in the example received the DNA samples, it labeled them properly. The laboratory's final report mixed up the labels. Any one of many different technicians *[*5]* could be responsible for an error like that. And the testifying analyst might not have reviewed the underlying notes and caught the error during direct examination (or for that matter, during cross-examination).

Adapting the example slightly, assume that the admissibility of the initial laboratory report into trial had been directly at issue. Who should the prosecution have had to call to testify? Only the analyst who signed the report noting the match? What if the analyst who made the match knew nothing about either the laboratory's underlying procedures or the specific tests run in the particular case? Should the prosecution then have had to call all potentially involved laboratory technicians to testify? Six to twelve or more technicians could have been involved. (See Appendix, *infra*, which lists typically relevant laboratory procedures.) Some or all of the words spoken or written by each technician out of court might well have constituted relevant statements offered for their truth and reasonably relied on by a supervisor or analyst writing the laboratory report. Indeed, petitioner's *amici* argue that the technicians at each stage of the process should be subject to cross-examination. See Brief for Innocence Network as *Amicus Curiae* 13-23 (hereinafter Innocence Network Brief).

And as is true of many hearsay statements that fall within any of the 20 or more hearsay exceptions, cross-examination could sometimes significantly help to elicit the truth. See Fed. Rule Evid. **803** (listing 24 hearsay exceptions). The Confrontation Clause as interpreted in *Crawford* recognizes, as a limitation upon a pure "testimonial statement" requirement, circumstances where the defendant had an adequate "prior opportunity to cross-examine." **541 U. S., at 59**. To what extent might the "testimonial statements" requirement embody one or more (or modified versions) of these traditional hearsay exceptions as well?*[*6]*

Lower courts and treatise writers have recognized the problem. And they have come up with a variety of solutions. The New Wigmore, for example, lists several nonexclusive approaches to when testifying experts may rely on testing results or reports by nontestifying experts (*i.e.*, DNA technicians or analysts), including: (1) "the dominant approach," which is simply to determine the need to testify by looking "the quality of the nontestifying expert's report, the testifying expert's involvement in the process, and the consequent ability of the testifying expert to use independent judgment and interpretive skill"; (2) permitting "a substitute expert to testify about forensic science results only when the first expert is unavailable" (irrespective of the lack of opportunity to cross-examine the first expert, cf. *Crawford, supra*, at 59); (3) permitting "a substitute expert" to testify if "the original test was documented in a thorough way that permits the substitute expert to evaluate, assess, and interpret it"; (4) permitting a DNA analyst to introduce DNA test results at trial without having "personally perform[ed] every specific aspect of each DNA test in question, provided the analyst was present during the critical stages of the test, is familiar with the process and the laboratory protocol involved, reviews the results in proximity to the test, and either initials or signs the final report outlining the results"; (5) permitting the introduction of a crime laboratory DNA report without the testimony of a technician where the "testing in its preliminary stages" only "requires the technician simply to perform largely mechanical or ministerial tasks . . . absent some reason to believe there was error or falsification"; and (6) permitting introduction of the report without requiring the technicians to testify where there is a showing of "genuine unavailability." See D. Kaye, D. Bernstein, & J. Mnookin, The New Wigmore: Expert Evidence, *§§ 4.10.2*, 4.10.3, pp. 202, 204, 206 (2d ed. 2010) (internal quotation marks and footnote omitted); *id., § 4.11.6*, at 24 *[*7]* (Supp. 2012).

Some of these approaches seem more readily compatible with *Crawford* than others. Some seem more easily considered by a rules committee (or by state courts) than by this Court. Nonetheless, all assume some kind of *Crawford* boundary — some kind of limitation upon the scope of its application — though they reflect different views as to just how and when that might be done.

Answering the underlying general question just discussed, and doing so soon, is important. Trial judges in both federal and state courts apply and interpret hearsay rules as part of their daily trial work. The trial of criminal cases makes up a large portion of that work. And laboratory reports frequently constitute a portion of the evidence in ordinary criminal trials. Obviously, judges, prosecutors, and defense lawyers have to know, in as definitive a form as possible, what the Constitution requires so that they can try their cases accordingly.

The several different opinions filed today embody several serious, but different, approaches to the difficult general question. Yet none fully deals with the underlying question as to how, after *Crawford*, Confrontation Clause "testimonial statement" requirements apply to crime laboratory reports. Nor can I find a general answer in *Melendez-Diaz* or *Bullcoming*. While, as a matter of pure logic, one might use those cases to answer a narrowed version of the question presented here, see *post*, at 7-8 (KAGAN, J., dissenting), those cases do not fully consider the broader evidentiary problem presented. I consequently find the dissent's response, "Been there, done that," unsatisfactory. See *post*, at 21.

Under these circumstances, I would have this case re-argued. I would request the parties and *amici* to focus specifically upon the broader "limits" question. And I would permit them to discuss, not only the possible implications of our earlier post-*Crawford* opinions, but also any *[*8]* necessary modifications of statements made in the opinions of those earlier cases.

II

In the absence of reargument, I adhere to the dissenting view set forth in *Melendez-Diaz* and *Bullcoming*, under which the Cellmark report would not be considered "testimonial" and barred by the Confrontation Clause. See also *ante*, at 28-33 (setting forth similar conclusion). That view understands the Confrontation Clause as interpreted in *Crawford* to bar the admission of "*[t]estimonial*" statements made out of court unless the declarant is unavailable and the defendant had a prior opportunity to cross-examine. **541 U. S., at 59** (emphasis added). It also understands the word "testimonial" as having outer limits and *Crawford* as describing a constitutional heartland. And that view would leave the States with constitutional leeway to maintain traditional expert testimony rules as well as hearsay exceptions where there are strong reasons for doing so and *Crawford*'s basic rationale does not apply.

In particular, the States could create an exception that presumptively would allow introduction of DNA reports from accredited crime laboratories. The defendant would remain free to call laboratory technicians as witnesses. Were there significant reason to question a laboratory's technical competence or its neutrality, the presumptive exception would disappear, thereby requiring the prosecution to produce any relevant technical witnesses. Such an exception would lie outside *Crawford*'s constitutional limits.

Consider the report before us. Cellmark's DNA report embodies technical or professional data, observations, and judgments; the employees who contributed to the report's findings were professional analysts working on technical matters at a certified laboratory; and the employees operated behind a veil of ignorance that likely prevented them *[*9]* from knowing the identity of the defendant in this case. Statements of this kind fall within a hearsay exception that has constituted an important part of the law of evidence for decades. See Fed. Rule Evid. 803(6) ("Records of Regularly Conducted Activity"); 2 J. Wigmore, Evidence §§ *1517-1533*, pp. 1878-1899 (1904) ("Regular Entries"). And for somewhat similar reasons, I believe that such statements also presumptively fall outside the category of "testimonial" statements that the Confrontation Clause makes inadmissible.

As the plurality points out, *ante*, at 28-33, the introduction of statements of this kind does not risk creating the "principal evil at which the Confrontation Clause was directed." *Crawford*, **541 U. S., at 50**. That evil consists of the pre-Constitution practice of using "*ex parte* examinations as evidence against the accused."*Ibid.* Sir Walter Raleigh's case illustrates the point. State authorities questioned Lord Cobham, the key witness against Raleigh, outside his presence. They then used those testimonial statements in court against Raleigh. And when Raleigh asked to face and to challenge his accuser, he was denied that opportunity. See *id.*, at **44**.

The Confrontation Clause prohibits the use of this kind of evidence because allowing it would deprive a defendant of the ability to cross-examine the witness. *Id.*, at **61-62**; *Mattox v. United States*, **156 U. S. 237**, 242-243 (1895). That deprivation would prevent a defendant from confronting the witness. And it would thereby prevent a defendant from probing the witness' perception, memory, narration, and sincerity. See, *e.g.*, 2 K. Broun et al., McCormick on Evidence *§ 245*, p. 125 (6th ed. 2006); E. Morgan, Some Problems of Proof Under the Anglo-American System of Litigation 119-127 (1956); 30 C. Wright & K. Graham, Federal Practice and Procedure *§ 6324*, pp. 44-49 (1997); see also M. Hale, History of the Common Law of England 258 (1713) (explaining virtues of *[*10]* confronting witness); 3 W. Blackstone, Commentaries on the Laws of England 373

(1768) (same). But the need for cross-examination is considerably diminished when the out-of-court statement was made by an accredited laboratory employee operating at a remove from the investigation in the ordinary course of professional work.

For one thing, as the hearsay exception itself reflects, alternative features of such situations help to guarantee its accuracy. An accredited laboratory must satisfy well-established professional guidelines that seek to ensure the scientific reliability of the laboratory's results. App. 59-60, 74, 86-87; see Brief for National District Attorneys Assn. et al. as *Amici Curiae* 25, n. 5 (hereinafter NDAA Brief) (noting that the standards date back 30 years); Giannelli, Regulating Crime Laboratories: The Impact of DNA Evidence, 15 J. L. & Pol'y 59, 72-76 (2007). For example, forensic DNA testing laboratories permitted to access the FBI's Combined DNA Index System must adhere to standards governing, among other things, the organization and management of the laboratory; education, training, and experience requirements for laboratory personnel; the laboratory's physical facilities and security measures; control of physical evidence; validation of testing methodologies; procedures for analyzing samples, including the reagents and controls that are used in the testing process; equipment calibration and maintenance; documentation of the process used to test each sample handled by the laboratory; technical and administrative review of every case file; proficiency testing of laboratory; personnel; corrective action that addresses any discrepancies in proficiency tests and casework analysis; internal and external audits of the laboratory; environmental health and safety; and outsourcing of testing to vendor laboratories. See Brief for New York County District Attorney's Office et al. as *Amici Curiae* 4, n. 4 (hereinafter NY County DAO Brief); see also App. to NY County DAO *[*11]* Brief A22-A49.

These standards are not foolproof. Nor are they always properly applied. It is not difficult to find instances in which laboratory procedures have been abused. See, *e.g.*, Innocence Network Brief 6-11; App. to Brief for Public Defender Service for the District of Columbia et al. as *Amici Curiae* 1a-12a; cf. Giannelli, The Abuse of Scientific Evidence in Criminal Cases: The Need for Independent Crime Laboratories, 4 Va. J. Soc. Pol'y & L. 439 (1997). Moreover, DNA testing itself has exonerated some defendants who previously had been convicted in part upon the basis of testimony by laboratory experts. See *Melendez-Diaz v. Massachusetts*, **557 U. S., at 319** (citing Garrett & Neufeld, Invalid Forensic Science Testimony and Wrongful Convictions, *95 Va. L.* Rev. 1 (2009)).

But if accreditation did not prevent admission of faulty evidence in some of those cases, neither did cross-examination. In the wrongful-conviction cases to which this Court has previously referred, the forensic experts all testified in court and were available for cross-examination. Sklansky, Hearsay's Last Hurrah, 2009 S. Ct. Rev. 1, 72-73 (cited study "did not identify *any* cases in which hearsay from forensic analysts contributed to the conviction of innocent defendants"); see Garrett & Neufeld, *supra*, at 10-12, 84, 89 (noting that cross-examination was rarely effective); see also Murphy, The New Forensics: Criminal Justice, False Certainty, and the Second Generation of Scientific Evidence, *95 Cal. L.* Rev. 721, 785-786 (2007) (suggesting need for greater reliance upon accreditation and oversight of accredited laboratories); Sklansky, *supra*, at 74 (same). Similarly, the role of cross-examination is ambiguous in the laboratory example that the dissent describes. See *post*, at 1-2. (Apparently, the report's error came to light and was corrected after cross-examination had concluded, see Thompson, Taroni, & Aitken, Author's Response, 49 J. Forensic Sci. 1202 (2003), and in any *[*12]* event all parties had received the correctly labeled underlying laboratory data, see Clarke, Commentary, *id.*, at 1201).

For another thing, the fact that the laboratory testing takes place behind a veil of ignorance makes it unlikely that a particular researcher has a defendant-related motive to behave dishonestly, say, to misrepresent a step in an analysis or otherwise to misreport testing results. Cf. *Michigan v. Bryant*, **562 U. S. ___, ___** (2011) (slip op., at 14) (discussing the "prospect of fabrication" as a factor in whether the Confrontation Clause requires statements "to be subject to the crucible of cross-examination"). The laboratory here, for example, did not know whether its test results might help to incriminate a particular defendant. *Ante, at 32-33*; cf. *Melendez-Diaz, supra*, at **310-311**; *Bullcoming*, **564 U. S., at ___** (slip op., at 14).

Further, the statements at issue, like those of many laboratory analysts, do not easily fit within the linguistic scope of the term "testimonial statement" as we have used that term in our earlier cases. As the plurality notes, in every post-*Crawford* case in which the Court has found a Confrontation Clause violation, the statement at issue had the primary purpose of accusing a targeted individual. *Ante, at 29-31*; see, *e.g.*, *Davis v. Washington*, **547 U. S. 813, 822** (2006) ("primary purpose . . . is to establish or prove past events potentially relevant to later criminal prosecution"); *Bryant, supra*, at ___ — ___ (slip op., at 11-12) ("primary purpose of creating an out-of-court substitute for trial testimony"). The declarant was essentially an adverse witness making an accusatory, testimonial statement — implicating the core concerns of the Lord Cobhamtype affidavits. But here the DNA report sought, not to accuse petitioner, but instead to generate objectively a profile of a then-unknown suspect's DNA from the semen he left in committing the crime. See *ante*, at 31-33.

Finally, to bar admission of the out-of-court records at *[*13]* issue here could undermine, not fortify, the accuracy of factfinding at a criminal trial. Such a precedent could bar the admission of other reliable case-specific technical information such as, say, autopsy reports. Autopsies, like the DNA report in this case, are often conducted when it is not yet clear whether there is a particular suspect or whether the facts found in the autopsy will ultimately prove relevant in a criminal trial. Autopsies are typically conducted soon after death. And when, say, a victim's body has decomposed, repetition of the autopsy may not be possible. What is to happen if the medical examiner dies before trial? *E.g., State v. Lackey*, **280 Kan. 190,195-196, 120 P. 3d 332, 341** (2005); see also *People v. Geier*, **41 Cal. 4th 555, 601-602, 161 P. 3d 104,136-137** (2007). Is the Confrontation Clause "'effectively'" to function "'as a statute of limitations for murder'"? *Melendez-Diaz, supra*, at **335** (KENNEDY, J., dissenting) (quoting Comment, Toward a Definition of "Testimonial": How Autopsy Reports Do Not Embody the Qualities of a Testimonial Statement, *96 Cal. L.* Rev. 1093, 1115 (2008)).

In general, such a holding could also increase the risk of convicting the innocent. The New York County District Attorney's Office and the New York City Office of the Chief Medical Examiner tell us that the additional cost and complexity involved in requiring live testimony from perhaps dozens of ordinary laboratory technicians who participate in the preparation of a DNA profile may well force a laboratory "to reduce the amount of DNA testing it conducts, and force prosecutors to forgo forensic DNA analysis in cases where it might be highly probative. In the absence of DNA testing, defendants might well be prosecuted solely on the basis of eyewitness testimony, the reliability of which is often questioned." NY County DAO Brief 10 (citing *United States v. Wade*, **388 U. S. 218, 229** (1967)); see also NDAA Brief 26 (such a holding "will also impact the innocent who may wait to be cleared from *[*14]* suspicion or exonerated from mistaken conviction"). I find this plausible. But cf. Innocence Network Brief 3. An interpretation of the Clause that risks greater prosecution reliance upon less reliable evidence cannot be sound. Cf. *Maryland v. Craig*, **497 U. S. 836, 845** (1990) ("The central concern of the Confrontation Clause is to ensure the reliability of the evidence against a criminal defendant").

Consequently, I would consider reports such as the DNA report before us presumptively to lie outside the perimeter of the Clause as established by the Court's precedents. Such a holding leaves the defendant free to call the laboratory employee as a witness if the employee is available. Moreover, should the defendant provide good reason to doubt the laboratory's competence or the validity of its accreditation, then the alternative safeguard of reliability would no longer exist and the Constitution would entitle defendant to Confrontation Clause protection. Similarly, should the defendant demonstrate the existence of a motive to falsify, then the alternative safeguard of honesty would no longer exist and the Constitution would entitle the defendant to Confrontation Clause protection. Cf. 2 Wigmore, Evidence § *1527*, at 1892 (in respect to the business records exception, "there must have been no motive to misrepresent"). Thus, the defendant would remain free to show the absence or inadequacy of the alternative reliability/honesty safeguards, thereby rebutting the presumption and making the Confrontation Clause applicable. No one has suggested any such problem in respect to the Cellmark Report at issue here.

Because the plurality's opinion is basically consistent with the views set forth here, I join that opinion in full.

[*15]

APPENDIX

This appendix outlines the way that a typical modern forensic laboratory conducts DNA analysis. See NY County DAO Brief 7-8; NDAA Brief 22-23; Innocence Network Brief 13-23; see also Dept. of Justice, Office of the Inspector General, The FBI DNA Laboratory: A Review of Protocol and Practice Vulnerabilities 6-14 (May 2004), online at http://www.justice.gov/oig/special/0405/final.pdf (as visited June 14, 2012, and available in Clerk of Court's case file). The DNA analysis takes place in three parts, through three different sets of laboratory experts: (1) a DNA profile is derived from the suspect's DNA sample, (2) a DNA profile is derived from the crime-scene DNA sample, and (3) an analyst compares the two profiles and makes a conclusion.

As many as six technicians may be involved in deriving the profile from the suspect's sample; as many as six more technicians may be involved in deriving the profile from the crime-scene sample; and an additional expert may then be required for the comparative analysis, for a total of about a dozen different laboratory experts. Each expert may make technical statements (express or implied) during the DNA analysis process that are in turn relied upon by other experts. The *amici* dispute how many of these experts the Confrontation Clause requires to be subject to cross-examination. Compare Innocence Network Brief 13-23 with NY County DAO Brief 7-8 and NDAA Brief 22-23. In charting the three-step process, the appendix first summarizes the laboratory procedures used to derive a DNA profile and then illustrates potential statements that technicians may make to explain their analysis.

JUSTICE THOMAS, concurring in the judgment. *[*1]*

I agree with the plurality that the disclosure of Cellmark's out-of-court statements through the expert testimony of Sandra Lambatos did not violate the Confrontation Clause. I reach this conclusion, however, solely because Cellmark's statements lacked the requisite "formality and solemnity" to be considered "'testimonial'" for purposes of the Confrontation Clause. See *Michigan v. Bryant*, **562 U. S. .**, (2011) (THOMAS, J., concurring in judgment) (slip op., at 1). As I explain below, I share the dissent's view of the plurality's flawed analysis.

I

The threshold question in this case is whether Cell-mark's statements were hearsay at all. As the Court has explained, "[t]he [Confrontation] Clause . . . does not bar the use of testimonial statements for purposes other than establishing the truth of the matter asserted." See *Crawford v. Washington*, **541 U. S. 36**, **60**, n. 9 (2004) (citing *Tennessee v. Street*, **471 U. S. 409**, **414** (1985)). Here, the State of Illinois contends that Cellmark's statements — that it successfully derived a male DNA profile and that the profile came from L. J.'s swabs — were introduced only to show the basis of Lambatos' opinion, and not for their truth. In my view, however, there was no plausible reason for the introduction of Cellmark's statements *[*2]* other than to establish their truth.

A

Illinois Rule of Evidence 703 (2011) and its federal counterpart permit an expert to base his opinion on facts about which he lacks personal knowledge and to disclose those facts to the trier of fact. Relying on these Rules, the State contends that the facts on which an expert's opinion relies are not to be considered for their truth, but only to explain the basis of his opinion. See *People v. Pasch*, **152 Ill. 2d 133**, **176**, **604 N. E. 2d 294**, **311** (1992) ("By allowing an expert to reveal the information for this purpose alone, it will undoubtedly aid the jury in assessing the value of his opinion"); see also Advisory Committee's Notes on Fed. Rule Evid. **703**, *28 U. S. C. App., p. 361* (stating that expert basis testimony is admissible "only for the purpose of assisting the jury in evaluating an expert's opinion"). Accordingly, in the State's view, the disclosure of expert "basis testimony" does not implicate the Confrontation Clause.

I do not think that rules of evidence should so easily trump a defendant's confrontation right. To be sure, we should not "lightly swee[p] away an accepted rule" of federal or state evidence law, *ante*, at 2 (internal quotation marks omitted), when applying the Confrontation Clause. "Rules of limited admissibility are commonplace in evidence law." Mnookin, Expert Evidence and the Confrontation Clause after *Crawford v. Washington*, 15 J. L. & Pol'y 791, 812 (2007). And, we often presume that courts and juries follow limiting instructions. See, *e.g., Street, supra*, at **415**, n. 6. But we have recognized that concepts central to the application of the Confrontation Clause are ultimately matters of federal constitutional law that are not dictated by state or federal evidentiary rules. See *Barber v. Page*, **390 U. S. 719**, **724-725** (1968) (defining a constitutional standard for whether a witness is "unavailable" *[*3]* for purposes of the Confrontation Clause); see also *Ohio v. Roberts*, **448 U. S. 56**, **76** (1980) (recognizing that *Barber* "explored the issue of *constitutional* unavailability" (emphasis added)). Likewise, we have held that limiting instructions may be insufficient in some circumstances to protect against violations of the Confrontation Clause. See *Bruton v. United States*, **391 U. S. 123** (1968).

Of particular importance here, we have made sure that an out-of-court statement was introduced for a "*legitimate*, nonhearsay purpose" before relying on the not-for-its-truth rationale to dismiss the application of the Confrontation Clause. See *Street*, **471 U. S., at 417** (emphasis added). In *Street*, the defendant testified that he gave a false confession because police coerced him into parroting his accomplice's confession. *Id.*, at **411**. On rebuttal, the prosecution introduced the accomplice's confession to demonstrate to the jury the ways in which the two confessions differed. *Id.*, at **411-412**. Finding no Confrontation Clause problem, this Court held that the accomplice's out-of-court confession was not introduced for its truth, but only to impeach the defendant's version of events. *Id.*, at **413-414**. Although the Court noted that the confession was not hearsay "under traditional rules of evidence," *id.*, at **413**, the Court did not accept that nonhearsay label at face value. Instead, the Court thoroughly examined the use of the out-of-court confession and the efficacy of a limiting instruction before concluding that the Confrontation Clause was satisfied "[i]n this context." *Id.*, at **417**.

Unlike the confession in *Street*, statements introduced to explain the basis of an expert's opinion are not introduced for a plausible nonhearsay purpose. There is no meaningful distinction between disclosing an out-of-court statement so that the factfinder may evaluate the expert's opinion and disclosing that statement for its truth. "To use the inadmissible information in evaluating the expert's testimony, the jury must make a preliminary judgment *[*4]* about whether this information is true." D. Kaye, D. Bernstein, & J. Mnookin, The New Wigmore: A Treatise on Evidence: Expert Evidence *§ 4.10.1*, p. 196 (2d ed. 2011) (hereinafter Kaye). "If the jury believes that the basis evidence is true, it will likely also believe that the expert's reliance is justified; inversely, if the jury doubts the accuracy or validity of the basis evidence, it will be skeptical of the expert's conclusions." *Ibid.***[fn1]**

Contrary to the plurality's suggestion, this common-sense conclusion is not undermined by any longstanding historical practice exempting expert basis testimony from the rigors of the Confrontation Clause. Prior to the adoption of the Federal Rules of Evidence in 1975, an expert could render an opinion based only on facts that the expert had personally perceived or facts that the expert learned at trial, either by listening to the testimony of other witnesses or through a hypothetical question based on facts in evidence. See Advisory Committee's Notes on Fed. Rule Evid. **703**, 28 U. S. C. App., p. 361; 29 C. Wright & V. Gold, Federal Practice and Procedure *§ 6271*, pp. 300-301 (1997) (hereinafter Wright); 1 K. Broun et al., McCormick on Evidence *§ 14*, p. 86 (6th ed. 2006) (hereinafter Broun); Kaye *§ 4.6*, at 156-157. In those situations, there was little danger that the expert would rely on testimonial hearsay that was not subject to confrontation because the expert and the witnesses on whom he relied were present at trial. It was not until 1975 that the universe *[*5]* of facts upon which an expert could rely was expanded to include facts of the case that the expert learned out of court by means other than his own perception. 1 Broun *§ 14*, at 87; Kaye *§ 4.6*, at 157. It is the expert's disclosure of those facts that raises Confrontation Clause concerns.**[fn2]**

B

Those concerns are fully applicable in this case. Lambatos opined that petitioner's DNA profile matched the male profile derived from L. J.'s vaginal swabs. In reaching that conclusion, Lambatos relied on Cellmark's out-of-court statements that the profile it reported was in fact derived from L. J.'s swabs, rather than from some other source. Thus, the validity of Lambatos' opinion ultimately turned on the truth of Cellmark's statements. The plurality's assertion that Cellmark's statements were merely relayed to explain "the assumptions on which [Lambatos'] opinion rest[ed]," *ante*, at 3, overlooks that the value of Lambatos' testimony depended on the truth of those very assumptions.**[fn3]** *[*6]*

It is no answer to say that *other* nonhearsay evidence established the basis of the expert's opinion. Here, Lambatos disclosed Cellmark's statements that it generated a male DNA profile from L. J.'s swabs, but other evidence showed that L. J.'s swabs contained semen and that the swabs were shipped to and received from Cellmark. *Ante*, at 5-6. That evidence did not render Cellmark's statements superfluous. Of course, evidence that Cellmark received L. J.'s swabs and later produced a DNA profile is some indication that Cellmark in fact generated the profile from those swabs, rather than from some other source (or from no source at all). Cf. *Melendez-Diaz v. Massachusetts*, **557** U. S. **305, 319** (2009) (citing brief that describes "cases of documented `drylabbing' where forensic analysts report results of tests that were never performed," including DNA tests). But the only direct evidence to that effect was Cellmark's statement, which Lambatos relayed to the factfinder. In any event, the factfinder's ability to rely on other evidence to evaluate an expert's opinion does not alter the conclusion that basis testimony is admitted for its truth. The existence of other evidence corroborating the basis testimony may render any Confrontation Clause violation harmless, but it does not change the purpose of such testimony and thereby place it outside of the reach of the Confrontation Clause.**[fn4]** I would thus conclude that *[*7]* Cellmark's statements were introduced for their truth.

C

The plurality's contrary conclusion may seem of little consequence to those who view DNA testing and other forms of "hard science" as intrinsically reliable. But see *Melendez-Diaz, supra,* at **318** ("Forensic evidence is not uniquely immune from the risk of manipulation"). Today's holding, however, will reach beyond scientific evidence to ordinary out-of-court statements. For example, it is not uncommon for experts to rely on interviews with third parties in forming their opinions. See, *e.g., People v. Goldstein,* **6 N. Y. 3d 119, 123-124, 843 N. E. 2d 727, 729-730** (2005) (psychiatrist disclosed statements made by the defendant's acquaintances as part of the basis of her opinion that the defendant was motivated to kill by his feelings of sexual frustration).

It is no answer to say that "safeguards" in the rules of evidence will prevent the abuse of basis testimony.*Ante,* at 26. To begin with, courts may be willing to conclude that an expert is not acting as a "mere condui[t]" for hearsay, *ante,* at 27, as long as he simply provides some opinion based on that hearsay. See Brief for Respondent 18, n. 4 (collecting cases). In addition, the hearsay may be the kind of fact on which experts in a field reasonably rely. See Fed. Rule Evid. **703**; *Goldstein, supra,* at **125, 843 N. E. 2d, at 731**(evidence showed that reputable psychiatrists relied upon third-party interviews in forming their *[*8]*opinions). Of course, some courts may determine that hearsay of this sort is not substantially more probative than prejudicial and therefore should not be disclosed under Rule 703. But that balancing test is no substitute for a constitutional provision that has already struck the balance in favor of the accused. See*Crawford,* **541 U. S., at 61** ("[The Confrontation Clause] commands, not that evidence be reliable, but that reliability be assessed in a particular manner: by testing in the crucible of crossexamination").

II

A

Having concluded that the statements at issue here were introduced for their truth, I turn to whether they were "testimonial" for purposes of the Confrontation Clause. In *Crawford,* the Court explained that "[t]he text of the Confrontation Clause . . . applies to witnesses' against the accused — in other words, those who `bear testimony.'" *Id.,* at **51** (quoting 2 N. Webster, An American Dictionary of the English Language (1828)). "`Testimony,'" in turn, is "`[a] solemn declaration or affirmation made for the purpose of establishing or proving some fact.'" **541 U. S., at 51**. In light of its text, I continue to think that the Confrontation Clause regulates only the use of statements bearing "indicia of solemnity." *Davis v. Washington,* **547 U. S. 813, 836-837, 840** (2006) (THOMAS, the practices that the Confrontation Clause was designed to eliminate, namely, the *ex parte* examination of witnesses under the English bail and committal statutes passed during the reign of Queen Mary. See *id.,* at **835**; *Bryant,* **562 U. S., at** ___(THOMAS, J., concurring in judgment) (slip op., at 1); *Crawford, supra,* at **43-45**. Accordingly, I have concluded that the Confrontation Clause reaches *[*9]* "`formalized testimonial materials,'" such as depositions, affidavits, and prior testimony, or statements resulting from "`formalized dialogue,'" such as custodial interrogation. *Bryant, supra,* at ___ (slip op., at 2); see also *Davis, supra,* at **836-837**.**[fn5]**

Applying these principles, I conclude that Cellmark's report is not a statement by a "witnes[s]" within the meaning of the Confrontation Clause. The Cellmark report lacks the solemnity of an affidavit or deposition, for it is neither a sworn nor a certified declaration of fact. Nowhere does the report attest that its statements accurately reflect the DNA testing processes used or the results obtained. See Report of Laboratory Examination, Lodging of Petitioner. The report is signed by two "reviewers," but they neither purport to have performed the DNA testing nor certify the accuracy of those who did. See *ibid.* And, although the report was produced at the request of law enforcement, it was not the product of any sort of formalized dialogue resembling custodial interrogation.

The Cellmark report is distinguishable from the laboratory reports that we determined were testimonial in *Melendez-Diaz*, **557 U. S. 305**, and in *Bullcoming v. New Mexico*, **564 U. S. ___** (2011). In *Melendez-Diaz*, the reports in question were "sworn to before a notary public by [the] analysts" who tested a substance for cocaine. **557 U. S., at 308.** In *Bullcoming*, the report, though unsworn, included a "Certificate of Analyst" signed by the forensic analyst who tested the defendant's blood sample. **564 U. S., at ___** (slip op., at 3). The analyst "affirmed that *[*10]* `[t]he seal of th[e] sample was received intact and broken in the laboratory,' that `the statements in [the analyst's block of the report] are correct,' and that he had `followed the procedures set out on the reverse of th[e] report.'" *Ibid.*

The dissent insists that the *Bullcoming* report and Cellmark's report are equally formal, separated only by such "minutia" as the fact that Cellmark's report "is not labeled a `certificate.'" *Post*, at 22-23 (opinion of KAGAN, J.). To the contrary, what distinguishes the two is that Cellmark's report, in substance, certifies nothing. See *supra*, at 9. That distinction is constitutionally significant because the scope of the confrontation right is properly limited to extrajudicial statements similar in solemnity to the Marian examination practices that the Confrontation Clause was designed to prevent. See *Davis*, *supra*, at **835-836** (opinion of THOMAS, J.). By certifying the truth of the analyst's representations, the unsworn *Bullcoming* report bore "a `striking resemblance,'" **547 U. S., at 837** (quoting *Crawford*, **541 U. S., at 52**), to the Marian practice in which magistrates examined witnesses, typically on oath, and "certif[ied] the results to the court." *Id.*, at **44**. And, in *Melendez-Diaz*, we observed that "`certificates' are functionally identical to live, in-court testimony, doing precisely what a witness does on direct examination." **557 U. S., at 310-311**. Cellmark's report is marked by no such indicia of solemnity.

Contrary to the dissent's suggestion, acknowledging that the Confrontation Clause is implicated only by formalized statements that are characterized by solemnity will not result in a prosecutorial conspiracy to elude confrontation by using only informal extrajudicial statements against an accused. As I have previously noted, the Confrontation Clause reaches bad-faith attempts to evade the formalized process. See *supra*, at 9, n. 5 (quoting *Davis*, **547 U. S., at 838**). Moreover, the prosecution's use of *[*11]* informal statements comes at a price. As the dissent recognizes, such statements are "less reliable" than formalized statements, *post*, at 24, and therefore less persuasive to the factfinder. Cf. *post*, at 21-22, n. 6 (arguing that prosecutors are unlikely to "forgo DNA evidence in favor of less reliable eyewitness testimony" simply because the defendant is entitled to confront the DNA analyst). But, even assuming that the dissent accurately predicts an upswing in the use of "less reliable" informal statements, that result does not "turn the Confrontation Clause upside down." *Post*, at 24. The Confrontation Clause does not require that evidence be reliable, *Crawford, supra*, at **61**, but that the reliability of a specific "class of testimonial statements" — formalized statements bearing indicia of solemnity — be assessed through cross-examination. See *Melendez-Diaz*, **557 U. S., at 309-310**.

B

Rather than apply the foregoing principles, the plurality invokes its "primary purpose" test. The original formulation of that test asked whether the primary purpose of an extrajudicial statement was "to establish or prove past events potentially relevant to later criminal prosecution." *Davis, supra,* at **822**. I agree that, for a statement to be testimonial within the meaning of the Confrontation Clause, the declarant must primarily intend to establish some fact with the understanding that his statement may be used in a criminal prosecution. See *Bryant,* **562 U. S., at** ___ (SCALIA, J., dissenting) (slip op., at 2-3). But this necessary criterion is not sufficient, for it sweeps into the ambit of the Confrontation Clause statements that lack formality and solemnity and is thus "disconnected from history." *Davis, supra,* at **838-842** (opinion concurring in judgment in part and dissenting in part); *Bryant, supra,* at ___ (opinion concurring in judgment) (slip op., at 1). In addition, a primary purpose inquiry divorced from solemnity *[*12]* is unworkable in practice. *Davis, supra,* at **839**; *Bryant, supra,* at ___ (slip op., at 1). Statements to police are often made *both* to resolve an ongoing emergency *and* to establish facts about a crime for potential prosecution. The primary purpose test gives courts no principled way to assign primacy to one of those purposes. *Davis, supra,* at **839**. The solemnity requirement is not only true to the text and history of the Confrontation Clause, but goes a long way toward resolving that practical difficulty. If a statement bears the formality and solemnity necessary to come within the scope of the Clause, it is highly unlikely that the statement was primarily made to end an ongoing emergency.

The shortcomings of the original primary purpose test pale in comparison, however, to those plaguing the reformulated version that the plurality suggests today. The new primary purpose test asks whether an out-of-court statement has "the primary purpose of accusing a targeted individual of engaging in criminal conduct." *Ante,* at 29. That test lacks any grounding in constitutional text, in history, or in logic.

The new test first requires that an out-of-court statement be made "for the purpose of proving the guilt of a*particular* criminal defendant." *Ante,* at 30 (emphasis added). Under this formulation, statements made "before any suspect was identified" are beyond the scope of the Confrontation Clause. See *ante,* at 3. There is no textual justification, however, for limiting the confrontation right to statements made after the accused's identity became known. To be sure, the **Sixth** Amendment right to confrontation attaches "[i]n . . . criminal prosecutions," at which time the accused has been identified and apprehended. But the text of the Confrontation Clause does not constrain the time at which one becomes a "witnes[s]." Indeed, we have previously held that a declarant may become a "witnes[s]" before the accused's prosecution. See *[*13]Crawford,* **541 U. S., at 50-51** (rejecting the view that the Confrontation Clause applies only to in-court testimony).

Historical practice confirms that a declarant could become a "witnes[s]" before the accused's identity was known. As previously noted, the confrontation right was a response to *ex parte* examinations of witnesses in 16th-century England. Such examinations often occurred after an accused was arrested or bound over for trial, but some examinations occurred while the accused remained "unknown or fugitive." J. Langbein, Prosecuting Crime in the Renaissance 90 (1974) (describing examples, including the deposition of a victim who was swindled out of 20 shillings by a "`cunning man'"); see also 1 J. Stephen, A History of the Criminal Law of England 217-218 (1883) (describing the sworn examinations of witnesses by coroners, who were charged with investigating suspicious deaths by asking local citizens if they knew "who [was] culpable either of the act or of the force" (internal quotation marks omitted)).

There is also little logical justification for the plurality's rule. The plurality characterizes Cellmark's report as a statement elicited by police and made by Cellmark not "to accuse petitioner or to create evidence for use at trial," but rather to resolve the ongoing emergency posed by "a dangerous rapist who was still at large." *Ante*, at 31. But, as I have explained, that distinction is unworkable in light of the mixed purposes that often underlie statements to the police. See *supra*, at 12. The difficulty is only compounded by the plurality's attempt to merge the purposes of both the police and the declarant. See *ante*, at 29; *Bryant,supra*, at ___ — ___ (majority opinion) (slip op., at 20-23).

But if one purpose must prevail, here it should surely be the evidentiary one, whether viewed from the perspective of the police, Cellmark, or both. The police confirmed the presence of semen on L. J.'s vaginal swabs on February 15, 2000, placed the swabs in a freezer, and waited until *[*14]* November 28, 2000, to ship them to Cellmark. App. 30-34, 51-52. Cellmark, in turn, did not send its report to the police until April 3, 2001, *id.*, at 54, over a year after L. J.'s rape. Given this timeline, it strains credulity to assert that the police and Cellmark were primarily concerned with the exigencies of an ongoing emergency, rather than with producing evidence in the ordinary course.

In addition to requiring that an out-of-court statement "targe[t]" a particular accused, the plurality's new primary purpose test also considers whether the statement is so "inherently inculpatory," *ante*, at 3, that the declarant should have known that his statement would incriminate the accused. In this case, the plurality asserts that "[t]he technicians who prepare a DNA profile generally have no way of knowing whether it will turn out to be incriminating or exonerating — or both," *ante*, at 32, and thus "no one at Cellmark could have possibly known that the profile that it produced would turn out to inculpate petitioner," *ante*, at 31.

Again, there is no textual justification for this limitation on the scope of the Confrontation Clause. In *Melendez-Diaz*, we held that "[t]he text of the [**Sixth**] Amendment contemplates two classes of witnesses — those against the defendant and those in his favor." **557 U. S., at 313-314.** We emphasized that "there is not a third category of witnesses, helpful to the prosecution, but somehow immune from confrontation."*Id.*, at **314.** Thus, the distinction between those who make "inherently inculpatory" statements and those who make other statements that are merely "helpful to the prosecution" has no foundation in the text of the Amendment.

It is also contrary to history. The 16th-century Marian statutes instructed magistrates to transcribe any information by witnesses that "`shall be material to prove the felony.'" See, *e.g.*, 1 Stephen, *supra*, at 219 (quoting 1 & 2 Phil. & Mary, ch. 13 (1554)). Magistrates in the 17th and *[*15]* 18th centuries were also advised by practice manuals to take the *ex parte* examination of a witness even if his evidence was "weak" or the witness was "unable to inform any material thing against" an accused. J. Beattie, Crime and the Courts in England: 1660-1800, p. 272 (1986) (internal quotation marks omitted). Thus, neither law nor practice limited *ex parte* examinations to those witnesses who made "inherently inculpatory" statements.

This requirement also makes little sense. A statement that is not facially inculpatory may turn out to be highly probative of a defendant's guilt when considered with other evidence. Recognizing this point, we previously rejected the view that a witness is not subject to confrontation if his testimony is "inculpatory only when taken together with other evidence." *Melendez-Diaz, supra*, at **313.** I see no justification for reviving that discredited approach, and the plurality offers none.**[fn6]**

    * * *

Respondent and its *amici* have emphasized the economic and logistical burdens that would be visited upon States should every analyst who reports DNA results be required to testify at trial. See, *e.g., ante*, at 32 (citing brief stating that some crime labs use up to 12 technicians when testing a DNA sample). These burdens are largely the product of a primary purpose test that reaches out-of-court statements well beyond the historical scope of the Confrontation Clause and thus sweeps in a broad range of sources on which modern experts regularly rely. The *[*16]* proper solution to this problem is not to carve out a Confrontation Clause exception for expert testimony that is rooted only in legal fiction. See *ante*, at 3. Nor is it to create a new primary purpose test that ensures that DNA evidence is treated differently. See *ibid.*Rather, the solution is to adopt a reading of the Confrontation Clause that respects its historically limited application to a narrow class of statements bearing indicia of solemnity. In forgoing that approach, today's decision diminishes the Confrontation Clause's protection in cases where experts convey the contents of solemn, formalized statements to explain the bases for their opinions. These are the very cases in which the accused *should* "enjoy the right . . . to be confronted with the witnesses against him."

[fn1] The plurality relies heavily on the fact that this case involved a bench trial, emphasizing that a judge sitting as factfinder is presumed — more so than a jury — to "understand the limited reason for the disclosure" of basis testimony and to "not rely on that information for any improper purpose." *Ante*, at 15. Even accepting that presumption, the point is not that the factfinder is unable to understand the restricted purpose for basis testimony. Instead, the point is that the purportedly "limited reason" for such testimony — to aid the factfinder in evaluating the expert's opinion — necessarily entails an evaluation of whether the basis testimony is true.

[fn2] In its discussion of history, the plurality relies on *Beckwith v. Sydebotham*, **1 Camp. 116, 170 Eng. Rep. 897** (K. B. 1807). In that case, experts were asked to render opinions on a ship's seaworthiness based on facts read into court from the sworn *ex parte* deposition of a witness who purported to have seen the ship's deficiencies. To be sure, *Beckwith* involved expert reliance on testimonial hearsay. But *Beckwith*was an English case decided after the ratification of the Confrontation Clause, and this form of expert testimony does not appear to have been a common feature of early American evidentiary practice. See 29 Wright *§ 6271*, at 300-301; 1 Broun *§ 14*, at 86-87; Kaye *§ 4.6*, at 156-157.

[fn3] Cellmark's statements were not introduced for the nonhearsay purpose of showing their effect on Lambatos — *i.e.*, to explain what prompted her to search the DNA database for a match. See, *e.g.*, 30B M. Graham, Federal Practice and Procedure *§ 7034.1*, pp. 521-529 (interim ed. 2011) (noting that out-of-court statements introduced for their effect on listener do not implicate the Confrontation Clause). The statements that Lambatos conveyed went well beyond what was necessary to explain why she performed the search. Lambatos did not merely disclose that she received a DNA profile from Cellmark. Rather, she further disclosed Cellmark's statements that the profile was "male" and that it was "found in semen from the vaginal swabs of [L. J.]." App. 56. Those facts had nothing to do with her decision to conduct a search. They were introduced for their truth.

[fn4] The plurality concludes that the Confrontation Clause would not be implicated here "even if the record did not contain any [other] evidence that could rationally support a finding that Cellmark produced a scientifically reliable DNA profile based on L. J.'s vaginal swab." *Ante*, at 22. But, far from establishing a "legitimate" nonhearsay purpose for Cellmark's statements, *Tennessee v. Street*, **471 U. S. 409, 417**(1985), a complete lack of other evidence tending to prove the facts conveyed by Cellmark's statements would completely refute the not-for-its-truth rationale. The trial court, in announcing its verdict, expressly concluded that petitioner's DNA matched the "DNA . . . in the semen recovered from the victim's vagina." 4 R. JJJ151. Absent other evidence, it would have been impossible for the trial court to reach that conclusion without relying on the truth of Cellmark's statement that its test results were based on the semen from L. J.'s swabs.

[fn5] In addition, I have stated that, because the Confrontation Clause "sought to regulate prosecutorial abuse occurring through use of *ex parte* statements," it "also reaches the use of technically informal statements when used to evade the formalized process." *Davis*, **547 U. S., at 838** (opinion concurring in judgment in part and dissenting in part). But, in this case, there is no indication that Cellmark's statements were offered "in order to evade confrontation." *Id.*, at **840**.

[fn6] The plurality states that its test "will not prejudice any defendant who really wishes to probe the reliability" of out-of-court statements introduced in his case because the person or persons who made the statements "may always be subpoenaed by the defense and questioned at trial." *Ante*, at 4. *Melendez-Diaz*rejected this reasoning as well, holding that the defendant's subpoena power "is no substitute for the right of confrontation." **557 U. S., at 324**.

JUSTICE KAGAN, with whom JUSTICE SCALIA, JUSTICE GINSBURG, and JUSTICE SOTOMAYOR join, dissenting. *[*1]*

Some years ago, the State of California prosecuted a man named John Kocak for rape. At a preliminary hearing, the State presented testimony from an analyst at the Cellmark Diagnostics Laboratory-the same facility used to generate DNA evidence in this case. The analyst had extracted DNA from a bloody sweatshirt found at the crime scene and then compared it to two control samples-one from Kocak and one from the victim. The analyst's report identified a single match: As she explained on direct examination, the DNA found on the sweatshirt belonged to Kocak. But after undergoing cross-examination, the analyst realized she had made a mortifying error. She took the stand again, but this time to admit that the report listed the victim's control sample as coming from Kocak, and Kocak's as coming from the victim. So the DNA on the sweatshirt matched not Kocak, but the victim herself. See Tr. in No. SCD110465 (Super. Ct. San Diego Cty., Cal., Nov. 17, 1995), pp. 3-4 ("I'm a little hysterical right now, but I think . . . the two names should be switched"), online at http://www.nlada.org/forensics/for_ lib/ Documents/1037341561.0/JohnIvanKocak.pdf (as visited June 15, 2012, and available in Clerk of Court's case file). In trying Kocak, the State would have to look elsewhere for its evidence. *[*2]*

Our Constitution contains a mechanism for catching such errors — the **Sixth** Amendment's Confrontation Clause. That Clause, and the Court's recent cases interpreting it, require that testimony against a criminal defendant be subject to cross-examination. And that command applies with full force to forensic evidence of the kind involved in both the Kocak case and this one. In two decisions issued in the last three years, this Court held that if a prosecutor wants to introduce the results of forensic testing into evidence, he must afford the defendant an opportunity to cross-examine an analyst responsible for the test. Forensic evidence is reliable only when properly produced, and the Confrontation Clause prescribes a particular method for determining whether that has happened. The Kocak incident illustrates how the Clause is designed to work: Once confronted, the analyst discovered and disclosed the error she had made. That error would probably not have come to light if the prosecutor had merely admitted the report into evidence or asked a third party to present its findings. Hence the genius of an 18th-century device as applied to 21st-century evidence: Cross-examination of the analyst is especially likely to reveal whether vials have been switched, samples contaminated, tests incompetently run, or results inaccurately recorded.

Under our Confrontation Clause precedents, this is an open-and-shut case. The State of Illinois prosecuted Sandy Williams for rape based in part on a DNA profile created in Cellmark's laboratory. Yet the State did not give Williams a chance to question the analyst who produced that evidence. Instead, the prosecution introduced the results of Cellmark's testing through an expert witness who had no idea how they were generated. That approach — no less (perhaps more) than the confrontation-free methods of presenting forensic evidence we have formerly banned — deprived Williams of his **Sixth** Amendment right to "confron[t] . . . the witnesses against him."

[*3]

The Court today disagrees, though it cannot settle on a reason why. JUSTICE ALITO, joined by three other Justices, advances two theories — that the expert's summary of the Cellmark report was not offered for its truth, and that the report is not the kind of statement triggering the Confrontation Clause's protection. In the pages that follow, I call JUSTICE ALITO's opinion "the plurality," because that is the conventional term for it. But in all except its disposition, his opinion is a dissent: Five Justices specifically reject every aspect of its reasoning and every paragraph of its explication. See *ante*, at 1 (THOMAS, J., concurring in judgment) ("I share the dissent's view of the plurality's flawed analysis"). JUSTICE THOMAS, for his part, contends that the Cellmark report is nontestimonial on a different rationale. But no other Justice joins his opinion or subscribes to the test he offers.

That creates five votes to approve the admission of the Cellmark report, but not a single good explanation. The plurality's first rationale endorses a prosecutorial dodge; its second relies on distinguishing indistinguishable forensic reports. JUSTICE THOMAS's concurrence, though positing an altogether different approach, suffers in the end from similar flaws. I would choose another path — to adhere to the simple rule established in our decisions, for the good reasons we have previously given. Because defendants like Williams have a constitutional right to confront the witnesses against them, I respectfully dissent from the Court's fractured decision.

I

Our modern Confrontation Clause doctrine began with *Crawford v. Washington,* **541 U. S. 36** (2004). About a quarter century earlier, we had interpreted the Clause to allow the admission of any out-of-court statement falling within a "firmly rooted hearsay exception" or carrying "particularized guarantees of trustworthiness." *Ohio* v. *[*4]* *Roberts,* **448 U. S. 56, 66** (1980). But in *Crawford,* we concluded that our old approach was misguided. Drawing on historical research about the Clause's purposes, we held that the prosecution may not admit "testimonial statements of a witness who [does] not appear at trial unless he [is] unavailable to testify, and the defendant . . . had a prior opportunity for cross-examination." **541 U. S., at 53-54**. That holding has two aspects. First, the Confrontation Clause applies only to out-of-court statements that are "testimonial." Second, where the Clause applies, it guarantees to a defendant just what its name suggests — the opportunity to cross-examine the person who made the statement. See *id.*, at 59.

A few years later, we made clear that *Crawford*'s rule reaches forensic reports. In *Melendez-Diaz v. Massachusetts,* **557 U. S. 305** (2009), the Commonwealth introduced a laboratory's "'certificates of analysis'" stating that a substance seized from the defendant was cocaine. *Id.*, at **308**. We held that the certificates fell within the Clause's "'core class of testimonial statements'" because they had a clear "evidentiary purpose": They were "'made under circumstances which would lead an objective witness reasonably to believe that [they] would be available for use at a later trial.'" *Id.*, at **310-311** (quoting*Crawford*, **541 U. S., at 51-52**). Accordingly, we ruled, the defendant had a right to cross-examine the analysts who had authored them. In reaching that conclusion, we rejected the Commonwealth's argument that the Confrontation Clause should not apply because the statements resulted from "'neutral scientific testing,'" and so were presumptively reliable. **557 U. S., at 318**. The Clause, we noted, commands that "'reliability be assessed in a particular manner'" — through "'testing in the crucible of cross-examination.'"*Id.*, at **317** (quoting *Crawford*, **541 U. S., at 61**). Further, we doubted that the testing summarized in the certificates was "as neutral or as reliable" as the *[*5]* Commonwealth suggested. Citing chapter and verse from various studies, we concluded that "[f]orensic evidence is not uniquely immune from the risk of manipulation" and mistake. **557 U. S., at 318**; see *id.*, at **319**.

And just two years later (and just one year ago), we reiterated *Melendez-Diaz*'s analysis when faced with a State's attempt to evade it. In *Bullcoming v. New Mexico*, **564 U. S. ___** (2011), a forensic report showed the defendant's blood-alcohol concentration to exceed the legal limit for drivers. The State tried to introduce that finding through the testimony of a person who worked at the laboratory but had not performed or observed the blood test or certified its results. We held that *Melendez-Diaz* foreclosed that tactic. The report, we stated, resembled the certificates in *Melendez-Diaz* in "all material respects," **564 U. S., at ___** (slip op., at 15): Both were signed documents providing the results of forensic testing designed to "'prov[e] some fact' in a criminal proceeding," *id.*, at ___ (slip op., at 14) (quoting *Melendez-Diaz*, **557 U. S., at 310**). And the State's resort to a "surrogate" witness, in place of the analyst who produced the report, did not satisfy the Confrontation Clause. *Bullcoming*, **564 U. S., at ___** (slip op., at 12). Only the presence of "that particular scientist," we reasoned, would enable Bullcoming's counsel to ask "questions designed to reveal whether incompetence . . . or dishonesty" had tainted the results. *Id.*, at ___, ___ (slip op., at 2, 12). Repeating the refrain of *Melendez-Diaz*, we held that "[t]he accused's right is to be confronted with" the actual analyst, unless he is unavailable and the accused "had an opportunity, pretrial, to cross-examine" him. *Bullcoming*, **564 U. S., at ___** (slip op., at 2).

This case is of a piece. The report at issue here shows a DNA profile produced by an analyst at Cellmark's laboratory, allegedly from a vaginal swab taken from a young woman, L. J., after she was raped. That report is identical to the one in *Bullcoming* (and *Melendez-Diaz*) in "all material *[*6]* respects." **564 U. S., at ___** (slip op., at 15). Once again, the report was made to establish "'some fact' in a criminal proceeding" — here, the identity of L. J.'s attacker. *Id.*, at ___ (slip op., at 14) (quoting *Melendez-Diaz*,**557 U. S., at 310**); see *infra*, at 20. And once again, it details the results of forensic testing on evidence gathered by the police. Viewed side-by-side with the *Bullcoming* report, the Cellmark analysis has a comparable title; similarly describes the relevant samples, test methodology, and results; and likewise includes the signatures of laboratory officials. Compare Cellmark Diagnostics Report of Laboratory Examination (Feb. 15, 2001), Lodging of Petitioner with App. in *Bullcoming v. New Mexico*, O. T. 2010,*No. 09-10876*, pp. 62-65. So under this Court's prior analysis, the substance of the report could come into evidence only if Williams had a chance to cross-examine the responsible analyst.

But that is not what happened. Instead, the prosecutor used Sandra Lambatos — a state-employed scientist who had not participated in the testing — as the conduit for this piece of evidence. Lambatos came to the stand after two other state analysts testified about forensic tests they had performed. One recounted how she had developed a DNA profile of Sandy Williams from a blood sample drawn after his arrest. And another told how he had confirmed the presence of (unidentified) semen on the vaginal swabs taken from L. J. All this was by the book: Williams had an opportunity to cross-examine both witnesses about the tests they had run. But of course, the State still needed to supply the missing link — it had to show that DNA found in the semen on L. J.'s vaginal swabs matched Williams's DNA. To fill that gap, the prosecutor could have called the analyst from Cellmark to testify about the DNA profile she had produced from the swabs. But instead, the State called Lambatos as an expert witness and had her testify that the semen on those swabs contained Sandy Williams's *[*7]* DNA:

"Q Was there a computer match generated of the male DNA profile found in semen from the vaginal swabs of [L. J.] to a male DNA profile that had been identified as having originated from Sandy Williams?

"A Yes, there was.

"Q Did you compare the semen . . . from the vaginal swabs of [L. J.] to the male DNA profile . . . from the blood of Sandy Williams?

"A Yes, I did.

"Q [I]s the semen identified in the vaginal swabs of [L. J.] consistent with having originated from Sandy Williams?

"A Yes." App. 56-57.

And so it was Lambatos, rather than any Cellmark employee, who informed the trier of fact that the testing of L. J.'s vaginal swabs had produced a male DNA profile implicating Williams.

Have we not already decided this case? Lambatos's testimony is functionally identical to the "surrogate testimony" that New Mexico proffered in *Bullcoming*, which did nothing to cure the problem identified in *Melendez-Diaz* (which, for its part, straightforwardly applied our decision in *Crawford*). Like the surrogate witness in *Bullcoming*, Lambatos "could not convey what [the actual analyst] knew or observed about the events . . ., *i.e.*, the particular test and testing process he employed." *Bullcoming*, **564 U. S., at** ___ (slip op., at 12). "Nor could such *[*8]* surrogate testimony expose any lapses or lies" on the testing analyst's part. *Ibid.* Like the lawyers in *Melendez-Diaz* and *Bullcoming*, Williams's attorney could not ask questions about that analyst's "proficiency, the care he took in performing his work, and his veracity." **564 U. S., at** ___, n. 7 (slip op., at 12, n. 7). He could not probe whether the analyst had tested the wrong vial, inverted the labels on the samples, committed some more technical error, or simply made up the results. See App. to Brief for Public Defender Service for the District of Columbia et al. as *Amici Curiae* 5a, 11a (describing mistakes and fraud at Cellmark's laboratory). Indeed, Williams's lawyer was even more hamstrung than Bullcoming's. At least the surrogate witness in *Bullcoming* worked at the relevant laboratory and was familiar with its procedures. That is not true of Lambatos: She had no knowledge at all of Cellmark's operations. Indeed, for all the record discloses, she may never have set foot in Cellmark's laboratory.

Under our case law, that is sufficient to resolve this case. "[W]hen the State elected to introduce" the substance of Cellmark's report into evidence, the analyst who generated that report "became a witness" whom Williams "had the right to confront." *Bullcoming*, **564 U. S., at** ___ (slip op., at 13). As we stated just last year, "Our precedent[s] cannot sensibly be read any other way." *Ibid.*

II

The plurality's primary argument to the contrary tries to exploit a limit to the Confrontation Clause recognized in *Crawford*. "The Clause," we cautioned there, "does not bar the use of testimonial statements for purposes other than establishing the truth of the matter asserted." **541 U. S., at 59-60**, n. 9 (citing *Tennessee v. Street*, **471 U. S. 409**, **414** (1985)). The Illinois Supreme Court relied on that statement in concluding that Lambatos's testimony was permissible. On that court's view, "Lambatos disclosed *[*9]* the underlying facts from Cellmark's report" not for their truth, but "for the limited purpose of explaining the basis for her [expert] opinion," so that the factfinder could assess that opinion's value. **238 Ill. 2d 125,150, 939 N. E. 2d 268, 282** (2010). The plurality wraps itself in that holding, similarly asserting that Lambatos's recitation of Cellmark's findings, when viewed through the prism of state evidence law, was not introduced to establish "the truth of any . . . matter concerning [the] Cellmark" report. *Ante*, at 16; see *ante*, at 2, 24-25. But five Justices agree, in two opinions reciting the same reasons, that this argument has no merit: Lambatos's statements about Cellmark's report went to its truth, and the State could not rely on her status as an expert to circumvent the Confrontation Clause's requirements. See *ante*, at 2-8 (opinion of THOMAS, J.).

To see why, start with the kind of case *Crawford* had in mind. In acknowledging the not-for-the-truth carveout from the Clause, the Court cited *Tennessee v. Street* as exemplary. See *Crawford*, **541 U. S., at 59-60**, n. 9. There, Street claimed that his stationhouse confession of murder was a sham: A police officer, he charged, had read aloud his alleged accomplice's confession and forced him to repeat it. To help rebut that defense, the State introduced the other confession into the record, so the jury could see how it differed from Street's. This Court rejected Street's Confrontation Clause claim because the State had offered the out-of-court statement not to prove "the truth of [the accomplice's] assertions" about the murder, but only to disprove Street's claim of how the police elicited his confession. *Street*, **471 U. S., at 413**. Otherwise said, the truth of the admitted statement was utterly immaterial; the only thing that mattered was that the statement (whether true or false) varied from Street's.

The situation could not be more different when a witness, expert or otherwise, repeats an out-of-court statement *[*10]* as the basis for a conclusion, because the statement's utility is then dependent on its truth. If the statement is true, then the conclusion based on it is probably true; if not, not. So to determine the validity of the witness's conclusion, the factfinder must assess the truth of the out-of-court statement on which it relies. That is why the principal modern treatise on evidence variously calls the idea that such "basis evidence" comes in not for its truth, but only to help the factfinder evaluate an expert's opinion "very weak," "factually implausible," "nonsense," and "sheer fiction." D. Kaye, D. Bernstein, & J. Mnookin, The New Wigmore: Expert Evidence § *4.10.1*, pp. 196-197 (2d ed. 2011); *id.*, § *4.11.6*, at 24 (Supp. 2012). "One can sympathize," notes that treatise, "with a court's desire to permit the disclosure of basis evidence that is quite probably reliable, such as a routine analysis of a drug, but to pretend that it is not being introduced for the truth of its contents strains credibility." *Id.*, § *4.10.1*, at 198 (2d ed. 2011); see also, *e.g., People v. Goldstein*, **6 N. Y. 3d 119, 128**, **843 N. E. 2d 727, 732-733** (2005) ("The distinction between a statement offered for its truth and a statement offered to shed light on an expert's opinion is not meaningful"). Unlike in *Street*, admission of the out-of-court statement in this context has no purpose separate from its truth; the factfinder can do nothing with it *except* assess its truth and so the credibility of the conclusion it serves to buttress.**[fn1]**

[*11]

Consider a prosaic example not involving scientific experts. An eyewitness tells a police officer investigating an assault that the perpetrator had an unusual, star-shaped birthmark over his left eye. The officer arrests a person bearing that birthmark (let's call him Starr) for committing the offense. And at trial, the officer takes the stand and recounts just what the eyewitness told him. Presumably the plurality would agree that such testimony violates the Confrontation Clause unless the eyewitness is unavailable and the defendant had a prior opportunity to cross-examine him. Now ask whether anything changes if the officer couches his testimony in the following way: "I concluded that Starr was the assailant because a reliable eyewitness told me that the assailant had a star-shaped birthmark and, look, Starr has one just like that." Surely that framing would make no constitutional difference, even though the eyewitness's statement now explains the basis for the officer's conclusion. It remains the case that the prosecution is attempting to introduce a testimonial statement that has no relevance to the proceedings apart from its truth — and that the defendant cannot cross-examine the person who made it. Allowing the admission of this evidence would end-run the Confrontation Clause, and make a parody of its strictures.

And that example, when dressed in scientific clothing, is no different from this case. The Cellmark report identified the rapist as having a particular DNA profile (think of it as the quintessential birthmark). The Confrontation Clause prevented the State from introducing that report into evidence except by calling to the stand the person who prepared it. See *Melendez-Diaz*, **557 U. S., at 310-311**; *Bullcoming*, **564 U. S., at ___** (slip op., at 2). So the State tried another route — introducing the substance of the report as part and parcel of an expert witness's conclusion. In effect, Lambatos testified (like the police officer above): "I concluded that Williams was the rapist because Cellmark, *[*12]* an accredited and trustworthy laboratory, says that the rapist has a particular DNA profile and, look, Williams has an identical one." And here too, that form of testimony should change nothing. The use of the Cellmark statement remained bound up with its truth, and the statement came into evidence without any opportunity for Williams to cross-examine the person who made it. So if the plurality were right, the State would have a ready method to bypass the Constitution (as much as in my hypothetical case); a wink and a nod, and the Confrontation Clause would not pose a bar to forensic evidence.

The plurality tries to make plausible its not-for-the-truth rationale by rewriting Lambatos's testimony about the Cellmark report. According to the plurality, Lambatos merely "assumed" that Cellmark's DNA profile came from L. J.'s vaginal swabs, accepting for the sake of argument the prosecutor's premise. *Ante*, at 18. But that is incorrect. Nothing in Lambatos's testimony indicates that she was making an assumption or considering a hypothesis. To the contrary, Lambatos affirmed, without qualification, that the Cellmark report showed a "male DNA profile found in semen from the vaginal swabs of [L. J.]." App. 56. Had she done otherwise, this case would be different. There was nothing wrong with Lambatos's testifying that two DNA profiles — the one shown in the Cellmark report and the one derived from Williams's blood — matched each other; that was a straightforward application of Lambatos's expertise. Similarly, Lambatos could have added that *if* the Cellmark report resulted from scientifically sound testing of L. J.'s vaginal swab, *then* it would link Williams to the assault. What Lambatos could not do was what she did: indicate that the Cellmark report *was* produced in this way by saying that L. J.'s vaginal swab contained DNA matching Williams's.**[fn2]** By testifying in *[*13]* that manner, Lambatos became just like the surrogate witness in *Bullcoming* — a person knowing nothing about "the particular test and testing process," but vouching for them regardless. **564 U. S., at ___** (slip op., at 12). We have held that the Confrontation Clause requires something more.

The plurality also argues that Lambatos's characterization of the Cellmark report did not violate the Confrontation Clause because the case "involve[d] a bench trial." *Ante*, at 19 (emphasis deleted). I welcome the plurality's concession that the Clause might forbid presenting Lambatos's statement to a jury, see *ante*, at 18-19; it indicates that the plurality realizes that her testimony went beyond an "assumption." But the presence of a judge does not transform the constitutional question. In applying the Confrontation Clause, we have never before considered relevant the decisionmaker's identity. See, *e.g., Davis* v. *[*14]Washington*, **547 U. S. 813** (2006). And this case would be a poor place to begin. Lambatos's description of the Cellmark report was offered for its truth because that is all such "basis evidence" can be offered for; as described earlier, the only way the factfinder could consider whether that statement supported her opinion (that the DNA on L. J.'s swabs came from Williams) was by assessing the statement's truth. See*supra*, at 9-12. That is so, as a simple matter of logic, whether the factfinder is a judge or a jury. And thus, in either case, admission of the statement, without the opportunity to cross-examine, violates the Confrontation Clause. See *ante*, at 3-4, n. 1 (opinion of THOMAS, J.).

In saying that much, I do not doubt that a judge typically will do better than a jury in excluding such inadmissible evidence from his decisionmaking process. Perhaps the judge did so here; perhaps, as the plurality thinks, he understood that he could not consider Lambatos's representation about the Cellmark report, and found that other, "circumstantial evidence" established "the source of the sample that Cellmark tested" and "the reliability of the Cellmark profile." See *ante*, at 22-23. Some indications are to the contrary: In delivering his verdict, the judge never referred to the circumstantial evidence the plurality marshals, but instead focused only on Lambatos's testimony. See 4 Record JJJ151 (calling Lambatos "the best DNA witness I have ever heard" and referring to Williams as "the guy whose DNA, according to the evidence from the experts, is in the semen recovered from the victim's vagina"). But I take the plurality's point that when read "[i]n context" the judge's statements might be "best understood" as meaning something other than what they appear to say. See *ante*, at 20, n. 6. Still, that point suggests only that the admission of Lambatos's statement was harm-less — that the judge managed to put it out of mind. After all, whether a factfinder is confused by an error is a separate *[*15]* question from whether an error has occurred. So the plurality's argument does not answer the only question this case presents: whether a constitutional violation happened when Lambatos recited the Cellmark report's findings.**[fn3]**

At bottom, the plurality's not-for-the-truth rationale is a simple abdication to state-law labels. Although the utility of the Cellmark statement that Lambatos repeated logically depended on its truth, the plurality thinks this case decided by an Illinois rule holding that the facts underlying an expert's opinion are not admitted for that purpose. See *ante*, at 14-18; *People v. Pasch*, **152 Ill. 2d 133, 175-177, 604 N. E. 2d 294, 311** (1992). But we do not typically allow state law to define federal constitutional requirements. And needless to say (or perhaps not), the Confrontation *[*16]* Clause is a constitutional rule like any other. As JUSTICE THOMAS observes, even before *Crawford*, we did not allow the Clause's scope to be "dictated by state or federal evidentiary rules." See *ante*, at 2. Indeed, in *Street*, we independently reviewed whether an out-of-court statement was introduced for its truth — the very question at issue in this case. See **471 U. S., at 413-416**. And in *Crawford*, we still more firmly disconnected the Confrontation Clause inquiry from state evidence law, by overruling an approach that looked in part to whether an out-of-court statement fell within a "'firmly rooted hearsay exception.'" **541 U. S., at 60**(quoting *Roberts*, **448 U. S., at 66**). That decision made clear that the Confrontation Clause's protections are not coterminous with rules of evidence. So the plurality's state-law-first approach would be an about-face.

Still worse, that approach would allow prosecutors to do through subterfuge and indirection what we previously have held the Confrontation Clause prohibits. Imagine for a moment a poorly trained, incompetent, or dishonest laboratory analyst. (The analyst in *Bullcoming*, placed on unpaid leave for unknown reasons, might qualify.) Under our precedents, the prosecutor cannot avoid exposing that analyst to cross-examination simply by introducing his report. See *Melendez-Diaz*, **557 U. S., at 311**. Nor can the prosecutor escape that fate by offering the results through the testimony of another analyst from the laboratory. See *Bullcoming*, **564 U. S., at** ___ (slip op., at 2). But under the plurality's approach, the prosecutor could choose the analyst-witness of his dreams (as the judge here said, "the best DNA witness I have ever heard"), offer her as an expert (she knows nothing about the test, but boasts impressive degrees), and have her provide testimony identical to the best the actual tester might have given ("the DNA extracted from the vaginal swabs matched Sandy Williams's") — all so long as a state evidence rule says that *[*17]* the purpose of the testimony is to enable the factfinder to assess the expert opinion's basis. (And this tactic would not be confined to cases involving scientific evidence. As JUSTICE THOMAS points out, the prosecutor could similarly substitute experts for all kinds of people making out-of-court statements. See *ante*, at 7.) The plurality thus would countenance the Constitution's circumvention. If the Confrontation Clause prevents the State from getting its evidence in through the front door, then the State could sneak it in through the back. What a neat trick — but really, what a way to run a criminal justice system. No wonder five Justices reject it.

III

The plurality also argues, as a "second, independent basis" for its decision, that the Cellmark report falls outside the Confrontation Clause's ambit because it is nontestimonial. *Ante*, at 3. The plurality tries out a number of supporting theories, but all in vain: Each one either conflicts with this Court's precedents or misconstrues this case's facts. JUSTICE THOMAS rejects the plurality's views for similar reasons as I do, thus bringing to five the number of Justices who repudiate the plurality's understanding of what statements count as testimonial. See *ante*, at 1, 12-15. JUSTICE THOMAS, however, offers a rationale of his own for deciding that the Cellmark report is nontestimonial. I think his essay works no better. When all is said and done, the Cellmark report is a testimonial statement.

A

According to the plurality, we should declare the Cellmark report nontestimonial because "the use at trial of a DNA report prepared by a modern, accredited laboratory `bears little if any resemblance to the historical practices that the Confrontation Clause aimed to eliminate.'" *Ante*, at 33 (quoting *Michigan v. Bryant*, **562 U. S.** ___, ___ *[*18]* (2011) (THOMAS, J., concurring in judgment) (slip op., at 2)). But we just last year treated as testimonial a forensic report prepared by a "modern, accredited laboratory"; indeed, we declared that the report at issue "fell within the core class of testimonial statements" implicating the Confrontation Clause. *Bullcoming*, **564 U. S., at** ___ (slip op., at 16) (internal quotation marks omitted); see Brief for New Mexico Department of Health, Scientific Laboratory Division as *Amicus Curiae* in *Bullcoming*, O. T. 2010, No. 09-10786, p. 1 (discussing accreditation). And although the plurality is close, it is not quite ready (or able) to dispense with that decision. See *ante*, at 29, n. 13 ("Experience might yet show that the holdings in [*Bullcoming* and other post-*Crawford*] cases should be reconsidered"). So the plurality must explain: What could support a distinction between the laboratory analysis there and the DNA test in this case?**[fn4]**

As its first stab, the plurality states that the Cellmark report was "not prepared for the primary purpose of accusing a targeted individual." *Ante*, at 31. Where that test comes from is anyone's guess. JUSTICE THOMAS rightly shows that it derives neither from the text nor from the *[*19]* history of the Confrontation Clause. See *ante*, at 14-15 (opinion concurring in judgment). And it has no basis in our precedents. We have previously asked whether a statement was made for the primary purpose of establishing "past events potentially relevant to later criminal prosecution" — in other words, for the purpose of providing evidence. *Davis*, **547 U. S., at 822**; see also *Bullcoming*, **564 U. S., at ___** (slip op., at 14); *Bryant*, **562 U. S., at ___, ___** (slip op., at 14, 29); *Melendez-Diaz*, **557 U. S., at 310-311**;*Crawford*, **541 U. S., at 51-52**. None of our cases has ever suggested that, in addition, the statement must be meant to accuse a previously identified individual; indeed, in *Melendez-Diaz*, we rejected a related argument that laboratory "analysts are not subject to confrontation because they are not `accusatory' witnesses." **557 U. S., at 313**.

Nor does the plurality give any good reason for adopting an "accusation" test. The plurality apparently agrees with JUSTICE BREYER that prior to a suspect's identification, it will be "unlikely that a particular researcher has a defendant-related motive to behave dishonestly." *Ante*, at 12 (BREYER, J., concurring); see *ante*, at 31-32 (plurality opinion). But surely the typical problem with laboratory analyses — and the typical focus of cross-examination — has to do with careless or incompetent work, rather than with personal vendettas. And as to that predominant concern, it makes not a whit of difference whether, at the time of the laboratory test, the police already have a suspect. [fn5]

[*20]

The plurality next attempts to invoke our precedents holding statements nontestimonial when made "to respond to an `ongoing emergency,'" rather than to create evidence for trial, *Bryant*, **562 U. S., at ___**(slip op., at 11); here, the plurality insists, the Cellmark report's purpose was "to catch a dangerous rapist who was still at large." *Ante*, at 31. But that is to stretch both our "ongoing emergency" test and the facts of this case beyond all recognition. We have previously invoked that test to allow statements by a woman who was being assaulted and a man who had just been shot. In doing so, we stressed the "informal [and] harried" nature of the statements, *Bryant*, **562 U. S., at ___** (slip op., at 31) — that they were made as, or "minutes" after, *id.*, at ___ (slip op., at 28), the events they described "actually happen[ed]," *Davis*, **547 U. S., at 827** (emphasis deleted), by "frantic" victims of criminal attacks, *ibid.*, to officers trying to figure out "what had . . . occurred" and what threats remained, *Bryant*, **562 U. S., at ___** (slip op., at 30) (internal quotation marks omitted). On their face, the decisions have nothing to say about laboratory analysts conducting routine tests far away from a crime scene. And this case presents a peculiarly inapt set of facts for extending those precedents. Lambatos testified at trial that "all reports in this case were prepared for this criminal investigation . . . [a]nd for the purpose of the eventual litigation," App. 82 — in other words, for the purpose of producing evidence, not enabling emergency responders. And that testimony fits the relevant timeline. The police did not send the swabs to Cellmark until November 2008 — nine months after L. J.'s rape — and did not receive the results for another four months. See *id.*, at 30-34, 51-52, 54. That is hardly the typical emergency response.

Finally, the plurality offers a host of reasons for why reports like this one are reliable: "[T]here [i]s no prospect of fabrication," *ante*, at 31 (internal quotation marks omitted); multiple technicians may "work on each DNA *[*21]* profile," *ante*, at 32; and "defects in a DNA profile may often be detected from the profile itself," *ibid.* See also *ante*, at 10-14 (opinion of BREYER, J.). But once again: Been there, done that. In *Melendez-Diaz*, this Court rejected identical arguments, noting extensive documentation of "[s]erious deficiencies . . . in the forensic evidence used in criminal trials." **557 U. S., at 319**; see *supra*, at 4-5; see also *Bullcoming*, **564 U. S., at ___**, n. 1 (slip op., at 4, n. 1) (citing similar errors in laboratory analysis); Brief for Public Defender Service for the District of Columbia et al. as *Amici Curiae* 13 (discussing "[s]ystemic problems," such as sample contamination, sample switching, mislabeling, and fraud, at "`flagship' DNA labs").

Scientific testing is "technical," to be sure, *ante*, at 1 (opinion of BREYER, J.); but it is only as reliable as the people who perform it. That is why a defendant may wish to ask the analyst a variety of questions: How much experience do you have? Have you ever made mistakes in the past? Did you test the right sample? Use the right procedures? Contaminate the sample in any way? Indeed, as scientific evidence plays a larger and larger role in criminal prosecutions, those inquiries will often be the most important in the case.**[fn6]**

[*22]

And *Melendez-Diaz* made yet a more fundamental point in response to claims of the *über alles* reliability of scientific evidence: It is not up to us to decide, *ex ante*, what evidence is trustworthy and what is not. See **557 U. S., at 317-318**; see also *Bullcoming*, **564 U. S., at ___** (slip op., at 11). That is because the Confrontation Clause prescribes its own "procedure for determining the reliability of testimony in criminal trials." *Crawford*, **541 U. S., at 67**. That procedure is cross-examination. And "[d]ispensing with [it] because testimony is obviously reliable is akin to dispensing with jury trial because a defendant is obviously guilty." *Id.*, at 62.

So the plurality's second basis for denying Williams's right of confrontation also fails. The plurality can find no reason consistent with our precedents for treating the Cellmark report as nontestimonial. That is because the report is, in every conceivable respect, a statement meant to serve as evidence in a potential criminal trial. And that simple fact should be sufficient to resolve the question.

B

JUSTICE THOMAS's unique method of defining testimonial statements fares no better. On his view, the Confrontation Clause "regulates only the use of statements bearing `indicia of solemnity.'" *Ante*, at 8 (quoting *Davis*, **547 U. S., at 836-837**). And Cellmark's report, he concludes, does not qualify because it is "neither a sworn nor a certified declaration of fact." *Ante*, at 9. But JUSTICE THOMAS's approach grants constitutional significance to minutia, in a way that can only undermine the Confrontation Clause's protections.

[*23]

To see the point, start with precedent, because the Court rejected this same kind of argument, as applied to this same kind of document, at around this same time just last year. In *Bullcoming*, the State asserted that the forensic report at issue was nontestimonial because — unlike the report in *Melendez-Diaz* — it was not sworn before a notary public. We responded that applying the Confrontation Clause only to a sworn forensic report "would make the right to confrontation easily erasable" — next time, the laboratory could file the selfsame report without the oath. **564 U. S., at ___** (slip op., at 15). We then held, as noted earlier, that "[i]n all material respects," the forensic report in *Bullcoming* matched the one in *Melendez-Diaz*. **564 U. S., at ___** (slip op., at 15); see *supra*, at 5. First, a law enforcement officer provided evidence to a state laboratory assisting in police investigations. See **564 U. S., at ___** (slip op., at 15). Second, the analyst tested the evidence and "prepared a certificate concerning the result[s]." ***Ibid***. Third, the certificate was "formalized in a signed document . . . headed a `report.'" ***Ibid*** (some internal quotation marks omitted). That was enough.

Now compare that checklist of "material" features to the report in this case. The only differences are that Cellmark is a private laboratory under contract with the State (which no one thinks relevant), and that the report is not labeled a "certificate." That amounts to (maybe) a nickel's worth of difference: The similarities in form, function, and purpose dwarf the distinctions. See *supra*, at 5-6. Each report is an official and signed record of laboratory test results, meant to establish a certain set of facts in legal proceedings. Neither looks any more "formal" than the other; neither *is* any more formal than the other. See *ibid.* The variances are no more (probably less) than would be found if you compared different law schools' transcripts or different companies' cash flow statements or different *[*24]* States' birth certificates. The difference in labeling — a "certificate" in one case, a "report of laboratory examination" in the other — is not of constitutional dimension.

Indeed, JUSTICE THOMAS's approach, if accepted, would turn the Confrontation Clause into a constitutional gee-gaw — nice for show, but of little value. The prosecution could avoid its demands by using the right kind of forms with the right kind of language. (It would not take long to devise the magic words and rules — principally, never call anything a "certificate.")**[fn7]** And still worse: The new conventions, precisely by making out-of-court statements less "solem[n]," *ante*, at 1, would also make them less reliable — and so turn the Confrontation Clause upside down. See *Crawford*, **541 U. S., at 52-53**, n. 3 ("We find it implausible that a provision which concededly condemned trial by sworn *ex parte* affidavit thought trial by *unsworn ex parte* affidavit perfectly OK"). It is not surprising that no other Member of the Court has adopted this position. To do so, as JUSTICE THOMAS rightly says of the plurality's decision, would be to "diminis[h] the Confrontation Clause's protection" in "the very cases in which the accused *should* `enjoy the right . . . to be confronted with the witnesses against him.'" *Ante*, at 16.

IV

Before today's decision, a prosecutor wishing to admit the results of forensic testing had to produce the technician responsible for the analysis. That was the result of not one, but two decisions this Court issued in the last three years. But that clear rule is clear no longer. The five Justices who control the outcome of today's case agree *[*25]* on very little. Among them, though, they can boast of two accomplishments. First, they have approved the introduction of testimony at Williams's trial that the Confrontation Clause, rightly understood, clearly prohibits. Second, they have left significant confusion in their wake. What comes out of four Justices' desire to limit *Melendez-Diaz* and *Bullcoming* in whatever way possible, combined with one Justice's one-justice view of those holdings, is — to be frank — who knows what. Those decisions apparently no longer mean all that they say. Yet no one can tell in what way or to what extent they are altered because no proposed limitation commands the support of a majority.

The better course in this case would have been simply to follow *Melendez-Diaz* and *Bullcoming*. Precedent-based decision making provides guidance to lower court judges and predictability to litigating parties. Today's plurality and concurring opinions, and the uncertainty they sow, bring into relief that judicial method's virtues. I would decide this case consistently with, and for the reasons stated by,*Melendez-Diaz* and *Bullcoming*. And until a majority of this Court reverses or confines those decisions, I would understand them as continuing to govern, in every particular, the admission of forensic evidence.

I respectfully dissent.

In responding to this reasoning, the plurality confirms it. According to the plurality, basis evidence supports the "credibility of the expert's opinion" by showing that he has relied on, and drawn logical inferences from, sound "factual premises." *Ante*, at 24. Quite right. And that process involves assessing such premises' truth: If they are, as the majority puts it, "unsupported by other evidence in the record" or otherwise baseless, they will not "allay [a factfinder's] fears" about an "expert's reasoning." *Ante*, at 24-25. I could not have said it any better.

The plurality suggests that Lambatos's testimony is merely a modern, streamlined way of answering hypothetical questions and therefore raises no constitutional issue, see *ante*, at 2, 13-15; similarly, the plurality contends that the difference between what Lambatos said and what I would allow involves only "slightly revis[ing]" her testimony and so can be of no consequence, see *ante*, at 18, n. 3. But the statement "if X is true, then Y follows" differs materially — and constitutionally — from the statement "Y is true because X is true (according to Z)." The former statement is merely a logical proposition, whose validity the defendant can contest by questioning the speaker. And then, assuming the prosecutor tries to prove the statement's premise through some other witness, the defendant can rebut that effort through cross-examination. By contrast, the latter statement as well contains a factual allegation (that X is true), which the defendant can only effectively challenge by confronting the person who made it (Z). That is why recognizing the difference between these two forms of testimony is not to insist on an archaism or a formality, but to ensure, in line with the Constitution, that defendants have the ability to confront their accusers. And if prosecutors can easily conform their conduct to that constitutional directive, as the plurality suggests, so much the better: I would not have thought it a ground of complaint that the Confrontation Clause, properly understood, manages to protect defendants without overly burdening the State.

The plurality asserts (without citation) that I am "reach[ing] the truly remarkable conclusion that the wording of Lambatos' testimony confused the trial judge," *ante*, at 19, and then spends three pages explaining why that conclusion is wrong, see *ante*, at 19-21. But the plurality is responding to an argument of its own imagining, because I reach no such conclusion. As I just stated, the trial judge might well have ignored Lambatos's statement about the Cellmark report and relied on other evidence to conclude that "the Cellmark profile was derived from the sample taken from the victim," *ante*, at 19. All I am saying is that the admission of that statement violated the Confrontation Clause even if the judge ultimately put it aside, because it came into evidence for nothing other than its truth. See *supra*, at 9-12.

Similarly, the plurality claims (still without citation) that I think the other evidence about the Cellmark report insufficient, see *ante*, at 21. But once again, the plurality must be reading someone else's opinion. I express no view on sufficiency of the evidence because it is irrelevant to the Confrontation Clause issue we took this case to decide. It is the plurality that wrongly links the two, spending another five pages trumpeting the strength of the Cellmark report, see *ante*, at 22-24, 32-33. But the plurality cannot properly decide whether a Confrontation Clause violation occurred at Williams's trial by determining that Williams was guilty. The American criminal justice system works the opposite way: determining guilt by holding trials in accord with constitutional requirements.

JUSTICE BREYER does not attempt to distinguish our precedents, opting simply to adhere to "the dissenting view set forth in *Melendez-Diaz* and *Bullcoming*." See *ante*, at 8 (concurring opinion). He principally worries that under those cases, a State will have to call to the witness stand "[s]ix to twelve or more technicians" who have worked on a report. See *ante*, at 5; see also *ante*, at 3, 16-18. But none of our cases — including this one — has presented the question of *how many* analysts must testify about a given report. (That may suggest that in most cases a lead analyst is readily identifiable.) The problem in the cases — again, including this one — is that *no* analyst came forward to testify. In the event that some future case presents the multiple-technician issue, the Court can focus on "the broader `limits' question" that troubles JUSTICE BREYER, *ante*, at 7. But the mere existence of that question is no reason to wrongly decide the case before us — which, it bears repeating, involved the testimony of not twelve or six or three or one, but zero Cellmark analysts.

Neither can the plurality gain any purchase from the idea that a DNA profile is not "inherently inculpatory" because it "tends to exculpate all but one of the more than 7 billion people in the world today." *Ante*, at 3; see *ante*, at 32. *All* evidence shares this feature: the more inculpatory it is of a single person, the more exculpatory it is of the rest of the world. The one is but the flipside of the other. But no one has ever before suggested that this logical corollary provides a reason to ignore the Constitution's efforts to ensure the reliability of evidence.

Both the plurality and JUSTICE BREYER warn that if we require analysts to testify, we will encourage prosecutors to forgo DNA evidence in favor of less reliable eyewitness testimony and so "increase the risk of convicting the innocent." *Ante*, at 13 (BREYER, J., concurring); see *ante*, at 3-4 (plurality opinion). Neither opinion provides any evidence, even by way of anecdote, for that view, and I doubt any exists. DNA evidence is usually the prosecutor's most powerful weapon, and a prosecutor is unlikely to relinquish it just because he must bring the right analyst to the stand. Consider what Lambatos told the factfinder here: The DNA in L. J.'s vaginal swabs matched Williams's DNA and would match only "1 in 8.7 quadrillion black, 1 in 390 quadrillion white, or 1 in 109 quadrillion Hispanic unrelated individuals." App. 56-57. No eyewitness testimony could replace that evidence. I note as well that the Innocence Network — a group particularly knowledgeable about the kinds of evidence that produce erroneous convictions — disagrees with the plurality's and JUSTICE BREYER's view. It argues here that "[c]onfrontation of the analyst . . . is essential to permit proper adversarial testing" and so to *decrease* the risk of convicting the innocent. Brief for the Innocence Network as *Amicus Curiae* 3, 7.

JUSTICE THOMAS asserts there is no need to worry, because "the Confrontation Clause reaches bad-faith attempts to evade the formalized process." *Ante*, at 10; see *ante*, at 9, n. 5. I hope he is right. But JUSTICE THOMAS provides scant guidance on how to conduct this novel inquiry into motive.

JUSTICE ALITO announced the judgment of the Court and delivered an opinion, in which THE CHIEF JUSTICE, JUSTICE KENNEDY, and JUSTICE BREYER join.

* * * * *

DISCUSSION PROBLEMS 11-1

1. Does this opinion settle the issues concerning admitting reports at trial without calling the individuals who conducted the scientific testing?

2. Are you more persuaded by the plurality that affirmed the case or the plurality that dissents? Why?

3. Where do you think the court will go next? What are the practical implications of this case? If you are a prosecutor, how will you proceed when needing to introduce these sorts of materials at trial? Does that approach encompass the "historical" spirit of the Federal Rules of Evidence?

CONCLUSION

The intersection of the confrontation clause and hearsay doctrine is the most recent area of evidentiary law that the U.S. Supreme Court has addressed. The change from the Roberts doctrine is substantial, and its potential impact on FRE 803 and 804 hearsay exceptions is potentially far reaching. Let us move on now and look at the current state of these hearsay exceptions. As we discuss these exceptions posit in your mind how the court might address a potential confrontation clause argument for each.

Chapter 12: Hearsay Exclusions

BY OPERATION OF LAW

"Hearsay is an out-of-court statement offered to prove the truth of the matter asserted." The fundamental purpose of the hearsay doctrine is to exclude from the fact-finder any prior out-of-court statements of a witness, offered for its truth, unless there are sufficient guarantees of trustworthiness for the truth of those statements. In order for the hearsay doctrine to apply the statement in question must have been intended as an assertion. At the heart of the hearsay doctrine is the conviction that out-of-court statements are generally an inferior kind of proof. Usually this conviction is explained in terms of the risks that come with relying on the word or say-so of another person, and usually these are grouped in four categories.

FRE 801(d) provides that certain statements are not hearsay, if (1) the declarant testifies at the trial or hearing, is subject to cross-examination concerning the statement and the statement is (A) inconsistent with the declarant's testimony and was given under oath subject to the penalty of perjury at the trial, hearing, or other proceeding, or deposition, or (B) consistent with the declarant's testimony and is offered to rebut an express or implied charge of recent fabrication or improper influence or motive, or (C) one of identification of a person. Also, FRE 801(d)(2) provides that admissions made by a party-opponent are not hearsay if the statement is offered against the party and is (A) the party's own statement, or (B) a statement the party has manifest his adoption of or belief in its truth, or (C) a statement by a person authorized by the party to make a statement concerning the subject, or (D) a statement by the party's agent or servant concerning the matters within the scope of the agency/employment made during the relationship, or (E) a statement by a coconspirator during the course of and in furtherance of the conspiracy.

Statements admissible under FRE 801 are excluded from a hearsay analysis. We realize that they are in fact out-of-court statements offered for the truth of the matter asserted therein, but by operation of the rule they are excluded, making them non hearsay. The literature and case law refer to applications of FRE 801 as both exclusions and exceptions to hearsay. This is a different term of art than exemptions under FRE 803 and FRE 804. We are so confident in the indicia of reliability, in the circumstances if you will of how these statements are made that we exclude them from hearsay. They are, however, still subject to other applicable evidentiary rules, relevant statutes and constitutional law.

THE U.S. SUPREME COURT SPEAKS

Consider the following case concerning coconspirator statements. Do you agree with the majority opinion or the dissent? What impact does this decision have on concepts of hearsay exclusion under FRE 801?

107 S.Ct. 2775

Supreme Court of the United States

William John **BOURJAILY**, Petitioner

v.

UNITED STATES.

No. 85-6725.

Argued April 1, 1987.Decided June 23, 1987.

Chief Justice REHNQUIST delivered the opinion of the Court.

Federal Rule of Evidence 801(d)(2)(E) provides: "A statement is not hearsay if ... [t]he statement is offered against a party and is ... a statement by a coconspirator of a party during the course and in furtherance of the conspiracy." We granted certiorari to answer three questions regarding the admission of statements under Rule 801(d)(2)(E): (1) whether the court must determine by independent evidence that the conspiracy existed and that the defendant and the declarant were members of this conspiracy; (2) the quantum of proof on which such determinations must be based; and (3) whether a court must in each case examine the circumstances of such a statement to determine its reliability. 479 U.S. 881, 107 S.Ct. 268, 93 L.Ed.2d 246 (1986).

In May 1984, Clarence Greathouse, an informant working for the Federal Bureau of Investigation (FBI), arranged to sell a kilogram of cocaine to Angelo Lonardo. Lonardo agreed that he would find individuals to distribute the drug. When the sale became imminent, Lonardo stated in a tape-recorded telephone conversation that he had a "gentleman friend" who had some questions to ask about the cocaine. In a subsequent telephone call, Greathouse spoke to the "friend" about the quality of the drug and the price. Greathouse then spoke again with Lonardo, and the two arranged the details of the purchase. They agreed that the sale would take place in a designated hotel parking lot, and Lonardo would transfer the drug from Greathouse's car to the "friend," who would be waiting in the parking lot in his own car. Greathouse proceeded with the transaction as planned, and FBI agents arrested Lonardo and petitioner immediately after Lonardo placed a kilogram of cocaine into petitioner's car in the hotel parking lot. In petitioner's car, the agents found over $20,000 in cash.

Petitioner was charged with conspiring to distribute cocaine, in violation of 21 U.S.C. § 846, and possession of cocaine with intent to distribute, a violation of 21 U.S.C. § 841(a) (1). The Government introduced, over petitioner's objection, Angelo Lonardo's telephone statements regarding the participation of the "friend" in the transaction. The District Court found that, considering the events in the parking lot and Lonardo's statements over the telephone, the Government had established by a preponderance of the evidence that a conspiracy involving Lonardo and petitioner existed, and that Lonardo's statements over the telephone had been made in the course of and in furtherance of the conspiracy. App. 66-75. Accordingly, the trial court held that Lonardo's out-of-court statements satisfied Rule 801(d)(2)(E) and were not hearsay. Petitioner was convicted on both counts and sentenced to 15 years. The United States Court of Appeals for the Sixth Circuit affirmed. 781 F.2d 539 (1986). The Court of Appeals agreed with the District Court's analysis and conclusion that Lonardo's out-of-court statements were admissible under the Federal Rules of Evidence. The court also rejected petitioner's contention that because he could not cross-examine Lonardo, the admission of these statements violated his constitutional right to confront the witnesses against him. We affirm.

Before admitting a co-conspirator's statement over an objection that it does not qualify under Rule 801(d)(2)(E), a court must be satisfied that the statement actually falls within the definition of the Rule. There must be evidence that there was a conspiracy involving the declarant and the nonoffering party, and that the statement was made "during the course and in furtherance of the conspiracy." Federal Rule of Evidence 104(a) provides: "Preliminary questions concerning ... the admissibility of evidence shall be determined by the court." Petitioner and the Government agree that the existence of a conspiracy and petitioner's involvement in it are preliminary questions of fact that, under Rule 104, must be resolved by the court. The Federal Rules, however, nowhere define the standard of proof the court must observe in resolving these questions.

We are therefore guided by our prior decisions regarding admissibility determinations that hinge on preliminary factual questions. We have traditionally required that these matters be established by a preponderance of proof. Evidence is placed before the jury when it satisfies the technical requirements of the evidentiary Rules, which embody certain legal and policy determinations. The inquiry made by a court concerned with these matters is not whether the proponent of the evidence wins or loses his case on the merits, but whether the evidentiary Rules have been satisfied. Thus, the evidentiary standard is unrelated to the burden of proof on the substantive issues, be it a criminal case, see _In re Winship_, 397 U.S. 358, 90 S.Ct. 1068, 25 L.Ed.2d 368 (1970), or a civil case. See generally _Colorado v. Connelly_, 479 U.S. 157, 167-169, 107 S.Ct. 515, 522-523, 93 L.Ed.2d 473 (1986). The preponderance standard ensures that before admitting evidence, the court will have found it more likely than not that the technical issues and policy concerns addressed by the Federal Rules of Evidence have been afforded due consideration. As in _Lego v. Twomey_, 404 U.S. 477, 488, 92 S.Ct. 619, 626, 30 L.Ed.2d 618 (1972), we find "nothing to suggest that admissibility rulings have been unreliable or otherwise wanting in quality because not based *176 on some higher standard." We think that our previous decisions in this area resolve the matter. See, _e.g._, _Colorado v. Connelly, supra_ (preliminary fact that custodial confessant waived rights must be proved by preponderance of the evidence); _Nix v. Williams_, 467 U.S. 431, 444, n. 5, 104 S.Ct. 2501, 2509, n. 5, 81 L.Ed.2d 377 (1984) (inevitable discovery of illegally seized evidence must be shown to have been more likely than not); _United States v. Matlock_, 415 U.S. 164, 94 S.Ct. 988, 39 L.Ed.2d 242 (1974) (voluntariness of consent to search must be shown by preponderance of the evidence); _Lego v. Twomey, supra_ (voluntariness of confession must be demonstrated by a preponderance of the evidence). Therefore, we hold that when the preliminary facts relevant to Rule 801(d)(2) (E) are disputed, the offering party must prove them by a preponderance of the evidence.

Even though petitioner agrees that the courts below applied the proper standard of proof with regard to the preliminary facts relevant to Rule 801(d)(2)(E), he nevertheless challenges the admission of Lonardo's statements. Petitioner argues that in determining whether a conspiracy exists and whether the defendant was a member of it, the court must look only to independent evidence-that is, evidence other than the statements sought to be admitted. Petitioner relies on _Glasser v. United States_, 315 U.S. 60, 62 S.Ct. 457, 86 L.Ed. 680 (1942), in which this Court first mentioned the so-called "bootstrapping rule." The relevant issue in _Glasser_ was whether Glasser's counsel, who also represented another defendant, faced such a conflict of interest that Glasser received ineffective assistance. Glasser contended that conflicting loyalties led his lawyer not to object to statements made by one of Glasser's co-conspirators. The Government argued that any objection would have been fruitless because the statements were admissible. The Court rejected this proposition:

"[S]uch declarations are admissible over the objection of an alleged co-conspirator, who was not present when they were made, only if there is proof _aliunde_ that he is connected with the conspiracy.... Otherwise, hearsay would lift itself by its own bootstraps to the level of competent evidence." _Id._, at 74-75, 62 S.Ct., at 467.

The Court revisited the bootstrapping rule in _United States v. Nixon_, 418 U.S. 683, 94 S.Ct. 3090, 41 L.Ed.2d 1039 (1974), where again, in passing, the Court stated: "Declarations by one defendant may also be admissible against other defendants upon a sufficient showing, _by independent evidence_, of a conspiracy among one or more other defendants and the declarant and if the declarations at issue were in furtherance of that conspiracy." _Id._, at 701, and n. 14, 94 S.Ct., at 3104, and n. 14 (emphasis added) (footnote omitted). Read in the light most favorable to petitioner, _Glasser_ could mean that a court should not consider hearsay statements at all in determining preliminary facts under Rule 801(d)(2)(E). Petitioner, of course, adopts this view of the bootstrapping rule. *Glasser,* however, could also mean that a court must have *some* proof *aliunde,* but may look at the hearsay statements themselves in light of this independent evidence to determine whether a conspiracy has been shown by a preponderance of the evidence. The Courts of Appeals have widely adopted the former view and held that in determining the preliminary facts relevant to co-conspirators' out-of-court statements, a court may not look at the hearsay statements themselves for their evidentiary value.

Both *Glasser* and *Nixon,* however, were decided before Congress enacted the Federal Rules of Evidence in 1975. These Rules now govern the treatment of evidentiary questions in federal courts. Rule 104(a) provides: "Preliminary questions concerning ... the admissibility of evidence shall be determined by the court.... In making its determination it is not bound by the rules of evidence except those with respect to privileges." Similarly, Rule 1101(d)(1) states that the Rules of Evidence (other than with respect to privileges) shall not apply to "[t]he determination of questions of fact preliminary to admissibility of evidence when the issue is to be determined by the court under rule 104." The question thus presented is whether any aspect of *Glasser* 's bootstrapping rule remains viable after the enactment of the Federal Rules of Evidence.

Petitioner concedes that Rule 104, on its face, appears to allow the court to make the preliminary factual determinations relevant to Rule 801(d)(2)(E) by considering any evidence it wishes, unhindered by considerations of admissibility. Brief for Petitioner 27. That would seem to many to be the end of the matter. Congress has decided that courts may consider hearsay in making these factual determinations. Out-of-court statements made by anyone, including putative co-conspirators, are often hearsay. Even if they are, they may be considered, *Glasser* and the bootstrapping rule notwithstanding. But petitioner nevertheless argues that the bootstrapping rule, as most Courts of Appeals have construed it, survived this apparently unequivocal change in the law unscathed and that Rule 104, as applied to the admission of co-conspirator's statements, does not mean what it says. We disagree.

Petitioner claims that Congress evidenced no intent to disturb the bootstrapping rule, which was embedded in the previous approach, and we should not find that Congress altered the rule without affirmative evidence so indicating. It would be extraordinary to require legislative history to *confirm* the plain meaning of Rule 104. The Rule on its face allows the trial judge to consider any evidence whatsoever, bound only by the rules of privilege. We think that the Rule is sufficiently clear that to the extent that it is inconsistent with petitioner's interpretation of *Glasser* and *Nixon,* the Rule prevails.

Nor do we agree with petitioner that this construction of Rule 104(a) will allow courts to admit hearsay statements without any credible proof of the conspiracy, thus fundamentally changing the nature of the co-conspirator exception. Petitioner starts with the proposition that co-conspirators' out-of-court statements are deemed unreliable and are inadmissible, at least until a conspiracy is shown. Since these statements are unreliable, petitioner contends that they should not form any part of the basis for establishing a conspiracy, the very antecedent that renders them admissible.

Petitioner's theory ignores two simple facts of evidentiary life. First, out-of-court statements are only *presumed* unreliable. The presumption may be rebutted by appropriate proof. See Fed. Rule Evid. 803(24) (otherwise inadmissible hearsay may be admitted if circumstantial guarantees of trustworthiness demonstrated). Second, individual pieces of evidence, insufficient in themselves to prove a point, may in cumulation prove it. The sum of an evidentiary presentation may well be greater than its constituent parts. Taken together, these two propositions demonstrate that a piece of evidence, unreliable in isolation, may become quite probative when corroborated by other evidence. A *per se* rule barring consideration of these hearsay statements during preliminary factfinding is not therefore required. Even if out-of-court declarations by co-conspirators are presumptively unreliable, trial courts must be permitted to evaluate these statements for their evidentiary worth as revealed by the particular circumstances of the case. Courts often act as factfinders, and there is no reason to believe that courts are any less able to properly recognize the probative value of evidence in this particular area. The party opposing admission has an adequate incentive to point out the shortcomings in such evidence before the trial court finds the preliminary facts. If the opposing party is unsuccessful in keeping the evidence from the factfinder, he still has the opportunity to attack the probative value of the evidence as it relates to the substantive issue in the case. See, *e.g.,* Fed.Rule Evid. 806 (allowing attack on credibility of out-of-court declarant).

We think that there is little doubt that a co-conspirator's statements could themselves be probative of the existence of a conspiracy and the participation of both the defendant and the declarant in the conspiracy. Petitioner's case presents a paradigm. The out-of-court statements of Lonardo indicated that Lonardo was involved in a conspiracy with a "friend." The statements indicated that the friend had agreed with Lonardo to buy a kilogram of cocaine and to distribute it. The statements also revealed that the friend would be at the hotel parking lot, in his car, and would accept the cocaine from Greathouse's car after Greathouse gave Lonardo the keys. Each one of Lonardo's statements may itself be unreliable, but taken as a whole, the entire conversation between Lonardo and Greathouse was corroborated by independent evidence. The friend, who turned out to be petitioner, showed up at the prearranged spot at the prearranged time. He picked up the cocaine, and a significant sum of money was found in his car. On these facts, the trial court concluded, in our view correctly, that the Government had established the existence of a conspiracy and petitioner's participation in it.

We need not decide in this case whether the courts below could have relied solely upon Lonardo's hearsay statements to determine that a conspiracy had been established by a preponderance of the evidence. To the extent that *Glasser* meant that courts could not look to the hearsay statements themselves for any purpose, it has clearly been superseded by Rule 104(a). It is sufficient for today to hold that a court, in making a preliminary factual determination under Rule 801(d)(2)(E), may examine the hearsay statements sought to be admitted. As we have held in other cases concerning admissibility determinations, "the judge should receive the evidence and give it such weight as his judgment and experience counsel." *United States v. Matlock,* 415 U.S., at 175, 94 S.Ct., at 995. The courts below properly considered the statements of Lonardo and the subsequent events in finding that the Government had established by a preponderance of the evidence that Lonardo was involved in a conspiracy with petitioner. We have no reason to believe that the District Court's factfinding of this point was clearly erroneous. We hold that Lonardo's out-of-court statements were properly admitted against petitioner.

We also reject any suggestion that admission of these statements against petitioner violated his rights under the Confrontation Clause of the Sixth Amendment. That Clause provides: "In all criminal prosecutions, the accused shall enjoy the right ... to be confronted with the witnesses against him." At petitioner's trial, Lonardo exercised his right not to testify. Petitioner argued that Lonardo's unavailability rendered the admission of his out-of-court statements unconstitutional since petitioner had no opportunity to confront Lonardo as to these statements. The Court of Appeals held that the requirements for admission under Rule 801(d)(2)(E) are identical to the requirements of the

Confrontation Clause, and since the statements were admissible under the Rule, there was no constitutional problem. We agree.

While a literal interpretation of the Confrontation Clause could bar the use of any out-of-court statements when the declarant is unavailable, this Court has rejected that view as "unintended and too extreme." *Ohio v. Roberts*, 448 U.S. 56, 63, 100 S.Ct. 2531, 2537, 65 L.Ed.2d 597 (1980). Rather, we have attempted to harmonize the goal of the Clause-placing limits on the kind of evidence that may be received against a defendant-with a societal interest in accurate factfinding, which may require consideration of out-of-court statements. To accommodate these competing interests, the Court has, as a general matter only, required the prosecution to demonstrate both the unavailability of the declarant and the "indicia of reliability" surrounding the out-of-court declaration. *Id.,* at 65-66, 100 S.Ct., at 2538-2539. Last Term in *United States v. Inadi*, 475 U.S. 387, 106 S.Ct. 1121, 89 L.Ed.2d 390 (1986), we held that the first of these two generalized inquiries, unavailability, was not required when the hearsay statement is the out-of-court declaration of a co-conspirator. Today, we conclude that the second inquiry, independent indicia of reliability, is also not mandated by the Constitution.

The Court's decision in *Ohio v. Roberts* laid down only "a general approach to the problem" of reconciling hearsay exceptions with the Confrontation Clause. See 448 U.S., at 65, 100 S.Ct. at 2538. In fact, *Roberts* itself limits the requirement that a court make a separate inquiry into the reliability of an out-of-court statement. Because " 'hearsay rules and the Confrontation Clause are generally designed to protect similar values,' **183* *California v. Green*, 399 U.S. [149, 155, 90 S.Ct. 1930, 1933, 26 L.Ed.2d 489 (1970)], and 'stem from the same roots,' *Dutton v. Evans*, 400 U.S. 74, 86, 91 S.Ct. 210, 218, 27 L.Ed.2d 213 (1970),"*id.,* at 66, 100 S.Ct., at 2539, we concluded in *Roberts* that no independent inquiry into reliability is required when the evidence "falls within a firmly rooted hearsay exception." *Ibid.* We think that the co-conspirator exception to the hearsay rule is firmly enough rooted in our jurisprudence that, under this Court's holding in *Roberts,* a court need not independently inquire into the reliability of such statements. Cf. *Dutton v. Evans,* 400 U.S. 74, 91 S.Ct. 210, 27 L.Ed.2d 213 (1970) (reliability inquiry required where evidentiary rule deviates from common-law approach, admitting co-conspirators' hearsay statements made after termination of conspiracy). The admissibility of co-conspirators' statements was first established in this Court over a century and a half ago in *United States v. Gooding,* 12 Wheat. 460, 6 L.Ed. 693 (1827) (interpreting statements of co-conspirator as *res gestae* and thus admissible against defendant), and the Court has repeatedly reaffirmed the exception as accepted practice. In fact, two of the most prominent approvals of the rule came in cases that petitioner maintains are still vital today,*Glasser v. United States,* 315 U.S. 60, 62 S.Ct. 457, 86 L.Ed. 680 (1942), and *United States v. Nixon,* 418 U.S. 683, 94 S.Ct. 3090, 41 L.Ed.2d 1039 (1974). To the extent that these cases have not been superseded by the Federal Rules of Evidence, they demonstrate that the co-conspirator exception to the hearsay rule is steeped in our jurisprudence. In *Delaney v. United States,*263 U.S. 586, 590, 44 S.Ct. 206, 207, 68 L.Ed. 462 (1924), the Court rejected the very challenge petitioner brings today, holding that there can be no separate Confrontation Clause challenge to the admission of a co-conspirator's out-of-court statement. In so ruling, the Court relied on established precedent holding such statements competent evidence. We think that these cases demonstrate that co-conspirators' statements, when made in the course and in furtherance of the conspiracy, have a long tradition of being outside the compass of the general hearsay exclusion. Accordingly, we hold that the Confrontation Clause does not require a court to embark on an **184* independent inquiry into the reliability of statements that satisfy the requirements of Rule 801(d)(2)(E).

The judgment of the Court of Appeals is

Affirmed.

Justice STEVENS, concurring.

The rule against "bootstrapping" announced in *Glasser v. United States,* 315 U.S. 60, 74-75, 62 S.Ct. 457, 467, 86 L.Ed. 680 (1942), has two possible interpretations. The more prevalent interpretation adopted by the Courts of Appeals is that the admissibility of the declaration under the co-conspirator rule must be determined *entirely* by independent evidence. The Court correctly holds that this reading of the *Glasser* rule is foreclosed by the plain language of Rule 104(a) of the Federal Rules of Evidence. That Rule unambiguously authorizes the trial judge to consider the contents of a proffered declaration in determining its admissibility.

I have never been persuaded, however, that this interpretation of the *Glasser* rule is correct. In my view, *Glasser* holds that a declarant's out-of-court statement is inadmissible against his alleged co-conspirators unless there is some corroborating evidence to support the triple conclusion that there was a conspiracy among those defendants, that the declarant was a member of the conspiracy, and that the statement furthered the objectives of the conspiracy. An otherwise inadmissible hearsay statement cannot provide the sole evidentiary support for its own admissibility-it cannot lift itself into admissibility entirely by tugging on its own bootstraps. It may, however, use its own bootstraps, together with other support, to overcome the objection. In the words of the *Glasser* opinion, there must be proof *"aliunde,"* that is, evidence from another source, that together with the contents of the statement satisfies the preliminary conditions for admission of the statement. *Id.,* at 74, 62 S.Ct., at 467.[1] This interpretation of *Glasser* as requiring some but not complete proof *"aliunde,"* is fully consistent with the plain language of Rule 104(a).[2] If, as I assume they did, the drafters of Rule 104(a) understood the *Glasser* rule as I do, they had no reason to indicate that it would be affected by the new Rule.[3]

Thus, the absence of any legislative history indicating an intent to change the *Glasser* rule is entirely consistent with the reasoning of the Court's opinion, which I join.

Justice BLACKMUN, with whom Justice BRENNAN and Justice MARSHALL join, dissenting.

I disagree with the Court in three respects: First, I do not believe that the Federal Rules of Evidence changed the long- and well-settled law to the effect that the preliminary questions of fact, relating to admissibility of a nontestifying co-conspirator's statement, must be established by evidence independent of that statement itself. Second, I disagree with the Court's conclusion that allowing the co-conspirator's statement to be considered in the resolution of these factual questions will remedy problems of the statement's unreliability. In my view, the abandonment of the independent-evidence requirement will lead, instead, to the opposite result. This is because the abandonment will eliminate one of the few safeguards of reliability that this exemption from the hearsay definition possesses. Third, because the Court alters the traditional hearsay exemption-especially an aspect of it that contributes to the reliability of an admitted statement-I do not believe that the Court can rely on the "firmly rooted hearsay exception" rationale, see *Ohio v. Roberts,* 448 U.S. 56, 66, 100 S.Ct. 2531, 2539, 65 L.Ed.2d 597 (1980), to avoid a determination whether any "indicia of reliability" support the co-conspirator's statement, as the Confrontation Clause surely demands.

I

The Court recognizes that, according to the common-law view of the exemption of a co-conspirator's statement from the hearsay definition, an offering party was required to establish, as preliminary factual matters, the existence of a conspiracy and a defendant's participation therein by evidence apart from the co-conspirator's statement. *Ante,* at 2780. In the Court's view, this settled law was changed in 1975 by the adoption of the Federal Rules of Evidence, particularly Rules 104(a) and 1101(d)(1). As the Court explains, the plain language of Rule 104(a) allows a trial court to consider any information, including hearsay, in making preliminary factual determinations relating to Rule 801(d)(2) (E). *Ante,* at 2779-2780. Thus, reasons the Court, under the Rule a trial court should be able to examine the co-conspirator's statement itself in resolving the threshold factual question-whether a conspiracy, to which the defendant belonged, existed. According to the Court, in light of Rule 104(a)'s "plain meaning" there is no need to take the "extraordinary" step of looking to legislative history for confirmation of this meaning. *Ante,* at 2780.

I agree that a federal rule's "plain meaning," when it appears, should not be lightly ignored or dismissed. The inclination to accept what seems to be the immediate reading of a federal rule, however, must be tempered with caution when, as in the case of a Federal Rule of Evidence, the rule's complex interrelations with other rules must be understood before one can resolve a particular interpretive problem. See generally Cleary, Preliminary Notes on Reading the Rules of Evidence, 57 Neb.L.Rev. 908, 908 (1978) ("[T]he answers to all questions that may arise under the Rules may not be found in specific terms in the Rules"). In addition, if the language of a rule plainly appears to address a specific problem, one *naturally* would expect legislative history (if it exists) to confirm this plain meaning. In this case, Rule 104(a) cannot be read apart from Rule 801(d)(2)(E), which was a codification of the common-law exemption of co-conspirator statements from the hearsay definition, an exemption that included the independent-evidence requirement. An examination of the legislative history of Rule 801(d)(2) (E) reveals that neither the drafters nor Congress intended to transform this requirement in any way. In sum, the Court espouses an overly rigid interpretive approach; a more complete analysis casts significant and substantial doubt on the Court's "plain meaning" easy solution.

A

In order to understand why the Federal Rules of Evidence adopted without change the common-law co-conspirator exemption from hearsay, and why this adoption signified the Advisory Committee's intent to retain the exemption's independent-evidence requirement, it is useful to review briefly the contours of this exemption as it stood before enactment of the Rules. By all accounts, the exemption was based upon agency principles, the underlying concept being that a conspiracy is a common undertaking where the conspirators are all agents of each other and where the acts and statements of one can be attributed to all. See 4 J. Weinstein & M. Berger, Weinstein's Evidence ¶ 801(d)(2)(E) [01], pp. 801-232 and 801-233 (1985) (Weinstein & Berger); Davenport, The Confrontation Clause and the Co-Conspirator Exception in Criminal Prosecutions: A Functional Analysis, 85 Harv.L.Rev. 1378, 1384 (1972) (Davenport). As Judge Learned Hand explained this in a frequently quoted remark:

"When men enter into an agreement for an unlawful end, they become ad hoc agents for one another, and have made a 'partnership in crime.' What one does pursuant to their common purpose, all do, and, as declarations may be such acts, they are competent against all." *Van Riper v. United States,* 13 F.2d 961, 967 (CA2), cert. denied *sub nom. Ackerson v. United States,* 273 U.S. 702, 47 S.Ct. 102, 71 L.Ed. 848 (1926).

Each of the components of this common-law exemption, in turn, had an agency justification. To fall within the exemption, the co-conspirator's statement had to be made "in furtherance of" the conspiracy, a requirement that arose from the agency rationale that an agent's acts or words could be attributed to his principal only so long as the agent was acting *189 within the scope of his employment. See Levie, Hearsay and Conspiracy: A Reexamination of the Co-Conspirators' Exception to the Hearsay Rule, 52 Mich.L.Rev. 1159, 1161 (1954) (Levie); 4 D. Louisell & C. Mueller, Federal Evidence § 427, p. 348 (1980) (Louisell & Mueller). The statement also had to be made "during the course of" the conspiracy. This feature necessarily accompanies the "in furtherance of" requirement, for there must be an employment or business relationship in effect between the agent and principal, in accordance with which the agent is acting, for the principal to be bound by his agent's deeds or words. See Levie, 52 Mich.L.Rev., at 1161; 4 Louisell & Mueller 337.

The final feature of the co-conspirator hearsay exemption, the independent-evidence requirement, directly corresponds to the agency concept that an agent's statement cannot be used alone to prove the existence of the agency relationship.

"Evidence of a statement by an agent concerning the existence or extent of his authority is not admissible against the principal to prove its existence or extent, unless it appears *by other evidence* that the making of such statement was within the authority of the agent or, as to persons dealing with the agent, within the apparent authority or other power of the agent" (emphasis added). Restatement (Second) of Agency § 285 (1958).

See Levie, 52 Mich.L.Rev., at 1161. The reason behind this concept is that the agent's authority must be traced back to some act or statement by the alleged principal. See 1 F. Mechem, Law of Agency § 285, p. 205 (1914).

Thus, unlike many common-law hearsay exceptions, the co-conspirator exemption from hearsay with its agency rationale was not based primarily upon any particular guarantees of reliability or trustworthiness that were intended to ensure the truthfulness of the admitted statement and to compensate for the fact that a party would not have the opportunity to test its veracity by cross-examining the declarant. See Davenport, 85 Harv.L.Rev., at 1384. As such, this exemption was considered to be a "vicarious admission." Although not an admission by a defendant himself, the vicarious admission was a statement imputed to the defendant from the co-conspirator on the basis of their agency relationship. As with all admissions, an "adversary system," rather than a reliability, rationale was used to account for the exemption to the ban on hearsay: it was thought that a party could not complain of the deprivation of the right to cross-examine himself (or another authorized to speak for him) or to advocate his own, or his agent's, untrustworthiness. See McCormick on Evidence § 262, p. 775 (E. Cleary ed. 1984). The co-conspirator "admission" exception was also justified on the ground that the need for this evidence, which was particularly valuable in prosecuting a conspiracy, permitted a somewhat reduced concern for the reliability of the statement.[4] See Saltzburg, Standards of Proof and Preliminary Questions of Fact, 27 Stan.L.Rev. 271, 303 (1975); R. Lempert & S. Saltzburg, A Modern Approach to Evidence 395 (2d ed. 1982) (Lempert & Saltzburg).

Although, under common law, the reliability of the co-conspirator's statement was never the primary ground justifying its admissibility, there was some recognition that this exemption from the hearsay rule had certain guarantees of trustworthiness, albeit limited ones. This justification for the exemption has been explained:

"Active conspirators are likely to know who the members of the conspiracy are and what they have done. When speaking to advance the conspiracy, they are unlikely to describe non-members as conspirators, and they usually will have no incentive to misdescribe the actions of their fellow members." Lempert & Saltzburg 395.

See also 4 J. Wigmore, Evidence § 1080a, p. 199 (J. Chadbourn rev. 1972) ("[T]he general idea of receiving vicarious admissions, is that where the third person was, at the time of speaking, in *circumstances that gave him substantially the same interest* to know something about the matter in hand as had the now opponent, and the *same motive* to make a statement about it, that person's statements have approximately the same testimonial value as if the now opponent had made them") (emphasis in original). And the components of the exemption were understood to contribute to this reliability. When making a statement "during the course of" and "in furtherance of" a conspiracy, a conspirator could be viewed as speaking from the perspective of all the conspirators in order to achieve the common goals of the conspiracy, not from self-serving motives. See Davenport, 85 Harv.L.Rev., at 1387. In particular, the requirement that a conspiracy be established by independent evidence also is seen to contribute to the reliability issue. Yet that requirement goes not so much to the reliability of the statement itself, as to the reliability of the process of admitting it: a statement cannot be introduced *until* independent evidence shows the defendant to be a member of an existing conspiracy. See *id.,* at 1390 ("Independent evidence of the conspiracy's existence and of the defendant's participation in it may supply inferences as to the reliability of the declaration"); Lempert & Saltzburg 395.

The Federal Rules of Evidence did not alter in any way this common-law exemption to hearsay.[5] The Rules essentially codify the components of this exemption: Rule 801(d)(2)(E) provides that the co-conspirator's statement, to be admissible against a party, must be "by a coconspirator of a party during the course and in furtherance of the conspiracy." Moreover, the exemption was placed within the category of "not hearsay," as an admission, in contrast to the hearsay exceptions of Rules 803 and 804. The Advisory Committee explained that the exclusion of admissions from the hearsay category is justified by the traditional "adversary system" rationale, not by any specific "guarantee of trustworthiness" used to justify hearsay exceptions. See Advisory Committee's Notes on Fed.Rule Evid. 801, 28 U.S.C.App., p. 717, 56 F.R.D. 183, 297 (1972); see also Note, Federal Rule of Evidence 801(d)(2)(E) and the Confrontation Clause: Closing the Window of Admissibility for Coconspirator Hearsay, 53 Ford.L.Rev. 1291, 1295, and n. 25 (1985).

More importantly, by explicitly retaining the agency rationale for the exemption, the Advisory Committee expressed its intention that the exemption would remain identical to the common-law rule and that it would not be expanded in any way. The Advisory Committee recognized that this agency rationale had been subject to criticism. The drafters of the American Law Institute's Model Code of Evidence had gone so far as to abandon the agency justification and had eliminated the "in furtherance of" requirement, observing that "[t]hese statements are likely to be true, and are usually made with a realization that they are against the declarant's interest." Model Code of Evidence, Rule 508(b) commentary, p. 251 (1942). The Advisory Committee, however, declined to accept without reservation a reliability foundation for Rule 801(d)(2)(E).

The Advisory Committee thus decided to retain the agency justification, in general, and the "in furtherance of" language, in particular, as a compromise position. It thought that the traditional exemption appropriately balanced the prosecution's need for a co-conspirator's statements and the defendant's need for the protections against unreliable statements, protections provided by the components of the common-law exemption. See 4 Weinstein & Berger ¶ 801(d)(2)(E)[01], p. 801-235. The Advisory Committee, however, expressed its doubts about the agency rationale and, on the basis of these doubts, plainly stated that the exemption should not be changed or extended: "[T]he agency theory of conspiracy is at best a fiction and ought not to serve as a basis for admissibility beyond that already established." Advisory Committee's Notes on Fed.Rule Evid. 801, 28 U.S.C.App., p. 718, 56 F.R.D., at 299. In light of this intention *not* to alter the common-law exemption, the Advisory Committee's Notes thus make very clear that Rule 801(d)(2)(E) was to include *all* the components of this exemption, including the independent-evidence requirement.

B

Accordingly, when Rule 801(d)(2)(E) and Rule 104(a) are considered together-an examination that the Court neglects to undertake-there appears to be a conflict between the fact that no change in the co-conspirator hearsay exemption was intended by Rule 801(d)(2)(E) and the freedom that Rule 104(a) gives a trial court to rely on hearsay in resolving preliminary factual questions. Although one must be somewhat of an interpretative funambulist to walk between the conflicting demands of these Rules in order to arrive at a resolution that will satisfy their respective concerns, this effort is far to be preferred over accepting the easily available safety "net" of Rule 104(a)'s "plain meaning." The purposes of *both* Rules can be achieved by considering the relevant preliminary factual question for Rule 104(a) analysis to be the following: "whether a conspiracy that included the declarant and the defendant against whom a statement is offered has been demonstrated to exist on the basis of evidence *independent of the declarant's hearsay statements* " (emphasis added). S. Saltzburg & K. Redden, Federal Rules of Evidence Manual 735 (4th ed. 1986). This resolution sufficiently answers Rule 104(a)'s concern with allowing a trial court to consider hearsay in determining preliminary factual questions, because the only hearsay not available for its consideration is the statement at issue. The exclusion of the statement from the preliminary analysis maintains the common-law exemption unchanged.

As the Court recognizes, *ante,* at 2780, in the more than 10 years since the enactment of the Federal Rules of Evidence, the Courts of Appeals, almost uniformly, have found no conflict between Rule 104(a) and the independent-evidence requirement understood to adhere in Rule 801(d)(2)(E). Indeed, some courts have rejected the suggestion that Rule 104(a) has changed this component of the common-law exemption, because, like the Advisory Committee, they recognize the incremental protection against unreliable statements that this requirement gives to defendants. See, *e.g., United States v. Bell, 573 F.2d 1040, 1044 (CA8 1978).* Yet the Court cavalierly disregards these years of interpretative experience, as well as the rich history of this exemption, and arrives at its conclusion solely on the basis of its "plain meaning" approach.

II

The Court's second argument in favor of abandonment of the independent-evidence rule might best be characterized as an attempt at pragmatic or "real world" analysis. The Court suggests that, while a co-conspirator's statement might be presumed unreliable when considered in isolation, it loses this unreliability when examined together with other evidence of the conspiracy and the defendant's participation in it. *Ante,* at 2781. In the Court's view, such a consideration of the statement will reveal its probative value, as the facts of this case demonstrate. Proceeding in this "real world" vein, the Court believes that the trial court is capable of detecting any remaining unreliability in the co-conspirator's statement and that the defendant is afforded the opportunity to point out any shortcomings of the out-of-court statement. *Ante,* at 2781.

I, too, prefer an approach that includes a realistic view of problems that come before the Court. See, *e.g., Lee v. Illinois,* 476 U.S. 530, 547-548, 106 S.Ct. 2056, 2066, 90 L.Ed.2d 514 (1986) (dissenting opinion). I am inclined, however, to remain with the traditional exemption that has been shaped by years of "real world" experience with the use of co-conspirator statements in trials and by a frank recognition of the possible unreliability of these statements.

As explained above, despite the recognized need by prosecutors for co-conspirator statements, these statements often have been considered to be somewhat unreliable. It has long been understood that such statements in some cases may constitute, at best, nothing more than the "idle chatter" of a declarant or, at worst, malicious gossip. See 4 Weinstein & Berger ¶ 801(d)(2)(E)[01], p. 801-235. Moreover, when confronted with such a statement, an innocent defendant would have a difficult time defending himself against it, for, if he were not in the conspiracy, he would have no idea why the conspirator made the statement. See *United States v. Stipe,* 517 F.Supp. 867, 871 (WD Okla.), aff'd, 653 F.2d 446 (CA10 1981) ("The dangers that an accused may be confronted with numerous statements made by someone else which he never authorized, intended, or even knew about ... cannot be ignored"). Even an experienced trial judge might credit an incriminatory statement that a defendant could not explain, precisely because the defendant had no ready explanation for it. Because of this actual "real world" experience with the possible unreliability of these statements, the Advisory Committee retained the agency rationale for this exemption in Rule 801(d)(2)(E), as well as the safeguards, albeit limited, against unreliability that this rationale provided the defendant. The independent-evidence requirement was one such safeguard.

If this requirement is set aside, then one of the exemption's safeguards is lost. From a "real world" perspective, I do not believe that considering the statement together with the independent evidence will cure this loss. Contrary to the Court's suggestion, the situation in which a trial court now commonly will rely on the co-conspirator's statement to establish the existence of a conspiracy in which the defendant participated will not be limited to instances in which the statement constitutes just another "piece of evidence," to be considered as no more important than the independent evidence. Rather, such a statement will serve the greatest purpose, and thus will be introduced most frequently, in situations where *all* the other evidence that the prosecution can muster to show the existence of a conspiracy will *not* be adequate. In this situation, despite the use of hearsay admissible under other exceptions and the defendant's and other conspirators' actions, the co-conspirator's statement will be necessary to satisfy the trial court by a preponderance of the evidence that the defendant was a member of an existing conspiracy. Accordingly, the statement will likely *control* the interpretation of whatever other evidence exists and could well transform a series of innocuous actions by a defendant into evidence that he was participating in a criminal conspiracy. This is what "bootstrapping" is all about. Thus, the Court removes one reliability safeguard from an exemption, even though the situation in which a co-conspirator's statement will be used to resolve the preliminary factual questions is that in which the court will rely *most* on the statement.

It is at least heartening, however, to see that the Court reserves the question whether a co-conspirator's statement alone, without*any* independent evidence, could establish the existence of a conspiracy and a defendant's participation in it. *Ante,* at 2782; see also *ante,* at 2783 (STEVENS, J., concurring). I have no doubt that, in this ultimate example of "bootstrapping," the ****2791**statement could not pass the preliminary factual test for its own admissibility, even under the **199* Court's reformulation. For the presumptively unreliable statement would have no corroborative independent evidence that would bring out its probative value. See *ante,* at 2781. If the statement alone could establish its own foundation for admissibility, a defendant could be convicted of conspiracy on the basis of an unsupported remark by an alleged conspirator-a result that surely the Court could not countenance and that completely cuts the exception adrift from its agency mooring.

III

The Court answers today a question left open in *United States v. Inadi,* 475 U.S. 387, 106 S.Ct. 1121, 89 L.Ed.2d 390 (1986). There, while observing that the Confrontation Clause usually required the production of a declarant or a showing of his unavailability so that his out-of-court statement could be admitted against a defendant, the Court concluded that this requirement was not constitutionally mandated in the case of a nontestifying co-conspirator's statement admitted under Rule 801(d)(2)(E). 475 U.S., at 400, 106 S.Ct., at 1129. The Court in *Inadi* did not have occasion to reach the issue of the reliability of such statements for Confrontation Clause purposes, and said so specifically. *Id.,* at 391, n. 3, 106 S.Ct., at 1124, n. 3. Today, the Court concludes that the Constitution does not require any independent "indicia of reliability" for such statements. See *ante,* at 2782. Relying upon *Ohio v. Roberts,* 448 U.S. 56, 100 S.Ct. 2531, 65 L.Ed.2d 597 (1980), the Court reasons that no such "indicia" are needed to satisfy Confrontation Clause concerns, because the admissibility of these statements " 'falls within a firmly rooted hearsay exception.' "*Ante,* at 2782, quoting *Ohio v. Roberts, supra,* at 66, 100 S.Ct., at 2539. In a footnote, the Court dismisses any suggestion that it is altering the co-conspirator **200* hearsay exemption: in its view, the exemption essentially remains the same, and what has changed is merely a "method of proof." *Ante,* at 2783, n. 4 (emphasis omitted).

In *Roberts* the Court did observe that, for Confrontation Clause purposes, "[r]eliability can be inferred without more in a case where the evidence falls within a firmly rooted hearsay exception." 448 U.S., at 66, 100 S.Ct., at 2539. To understand the significance of this statement, however, it is important to remember why hearsay exceptions satisfy the reliability concern of that Clause. The Court in *Roberts* explained that "accuracy in the factfinding process" is a central concern of the Confrontation Clause that cross-examination normally serves. *Id.,* at 65, 100 S.Ct., at 2538. This concern is sometimes satisfied when evidence is admitted under a hearsay exception, even where no cross-examination of the declarant occurs at trial. This is because " 'hearsay rules and the Confrontation Clause are generally designed to protect similar values,' " *id.,* at 66, 100 S.Ct., at 2539, quoting*California v. Green,* 399 U.S. 149, 155, 90 S.Ct. 1930, 1933, 26 L.Ed.2d 489 (1970), and because, with respect to a particular hearsay exception, there are adequate "indicia of reliability" of the out-of-court statement. These indicia serve to guarantee the trustworthiness of the declarant's statement and thus promote the accuracy of the trial-a function otherwise fulfilled by cross-examination. Thus, to answer the Confrontation Clause's concern for reliability with respect to a particular hearsay exception, one must examine what, if any, "indicia of reliability" it possesses. In addition, one must also see how "firmly rooted" the exception is, which suggests that, through experience in its use, the exception has proved to promote the "accuracy of the factfinding process." See generally Note, 53 Ford.L.Rev., at 1306-1307.

The weakness of the Court's assertion-that the Confrontation Clause concern about reliability vanishes because Rule 801(d)(2)(E)'s exemption of a co-conspirator's statement from the hearsay definition is a "firmly rooted hearsay exception"-thus becomes immediately apparent. First, as has been explained and as its inclusion under the admissions rubric would indicate, this exemption has never been justified primarily upon reliability or trustworthiness grounds and its reliability safeguards are not extensive. See also Note, 53 Ford.L.Rev., at 1311-1312. Thus, it is surprising that, without any hesitation, the Court in this case turns to the "firmly rooted hearsay exception" rationale, which is based upon a confidence in adequate "indicia of reliability."

Second, and more astounding, is the Court's reliance upon the "firmly rooted hearsay exception" rationale as it simultaneously removes from the exemption one of the few safeguards against unreliability that it possesses. The Court cannot at all escape from this contradiction by dismissing its alteration of the exception as simply a change in "method of proof." Because the "firmly rooted hearsay exception" is defined in terms of its "indicia of reliability" for Confrontation Clause purposes, a removal of one of these "indicia" significantly transforms the co-conspirator exemption in a relevant respect. In addition, this change takes away from the exemption any weight that experience with its use by courts may have given it, thus undermining its "firmly rooted" status. In sum, the Court cannot have it both ways: it cannot transform the exemption, as it admittedly does, *and* then avoid Confrontation Clause concerns by conjuring up the "firmly rooted hearsay exception" as some benign genie who will extricate the Court from its inconsistent analysis.

With such a transformation in the co-conspirator hearsay exemption having been made, the Court's reliance upon *Roberts'* language concerning the "firmly rooted hearsay exception" is utterly misplaced. Rather, the pertinent language from *Roberts* becomes the sentence following the one quoted by the Court: "In other cases [where there is no "firmly rooted hearsay exception"], the evidence must be excluded, at least absent a showing of particularized guarantees of trustworthiness." 448 U.S., at 66, 100 S.Ct., at 2539. This showing, I believe, would involve an examination of the statement in terms of the factors outlined in *Dutton v. Evans,* 400 U.S. 74, 88-89, 91 S.Ct. 210, 219, 27 L.Ed.2d 213 (1970) (plurality opinion); see also Note, 53 Ford.L.Rev., at 1302. Intellectual honesty thus demands, at the very least, that, having changed this hearsay exemption, the Court remand the case to allow the lower courts to explore any "particularized guarantees of trustworthiness" the statement might have.[11]

I respectfully dissent.

DISCUSSION PROBLEMS 12-1

1. What impact did the bootstrapping rule in *Glasser* have in this case? Are you persuaded by the dissent or majority opinion on this issue? Why?

2. Should there be an independent of the statement proof requirement before the court will recognize the existence of the conspiracy? Why?

3. Is there a practical reason that the court decided this case in a certain way? What do you think the practical issue might be? Are you persuaded by it?

HEARSAY EXCLUSIONS

Prior Inconsistent Statement by a Testifying Witness

When applied in conjunction with FRE 613, FRE 801(d)(1)(A) allows counsel to admit prior inconsistent statements by a testifying witness. To do this, counsel must establish that the statement must be inconsistent with his later trial testimony, must have been made in a proceeding or deposition where he was under oath subject to the penalty of perjury, and the speaker must be subject to cross-examination on his earlier statement.

This provision is tied to impeachment, but only in certain instances. In reaching only some inconsistent statements, FRE 801(d)(1)(A) limits the times when this rule would be called on to admit statements given out of court. The purpose was to give prosecutors the ability to deal with turncoat witnesses. From a federal point this makes sense. In federal jurisdictions the only witnesses at criminal proceedings that testify pretrial are government witnesses who testify in grand jury proceedings. Factors peculiar to government witnesses—involvement in crimes, self serving by promising to testify, yet faced with the hard task of later helping convict a defendant—make the exception especially useful to prosecutors. The text of the rule does not support substantive use of a statement when no inconsistency exists. On the other hand, the requirement is satisfied when a statement directly contradicts what the witness says at trial. However, the conflict does not have to be complete. The rule is satisfied when the conflict is by implication, only occurring in part of the statement but creates differences in the two statements, and when one is categorical and the second statement is equivocal.

Sometimes when a witness claims lack of memory it appears feigned. In those instances the prior statement will be admissible if meets the restrictions of FRE 801(d)(1) (A). This requirement for duplicity is not, however, required, and a showing of lack of memory may itself suffice for purposes of this rule.

Sometimes, despite the perceive inconsistency, similarities will otherwise exist between the in court testimony and the prior statement. This is very common, and should not serve as the basis for reason to exclude the earlier statement. Additionally, when read in conjunction with FRE 106 it is clear that it is appropriate to admit sufficient portions of the prior statement that are consistent with the in court testimony as required to give the inconsistency context. The court is careful, however, to not admit FRE 801(d)(1)(A) that differ only on minor points from the in court testimony, particularly when the differences are not on substantive matters.

To admit these prior statements substantively, the statement must be made under oath subject to penalty of perjury at a trial, hearing, other proceeding, or deposition. Case law has established that grand jury testimony satisfies this requirement, as does testimony at a preliminary hearing, prior trial, or deposition. The confrontation clause issue is satisfied if the same motive to develop cross examination existed at the previous hearing, trial or deposition.

FRE 801(d)(1)(A) is not limited to statements made at some prior step in the same proceedings in which they are offered. Statements in separate proceedings involving different parties and transactions may be allowed. The exclusion contemplates situations where an official verbatim record is routinely kept under legal authority. There is no reason to suppose the exception is limited to judicial proceedings. In fact, its concept is broad enough to include situations where a governmental agency or officer is authorized by law to put witnesses under oath and take their statements on the record, whether for purposes of adjudication, rule making, or investigation, it is reasonable to call such activities a "hearing" or "proceeding" for purposes of the exclusion.

A station house or oral declaration to law enforcement agents, even in the form of a sworn affidavit, lies outside FRE 801(d)(1)(A) because such statements are not given in "proceedings." Gathering such a statement during an investigation does not generate a verbatim transcript, and investigations do not require the acquisition of sworn statements, so the process can hardly be classified as part of a "hearing" or "proceeding" under the Rule. They are still available though, for impeachment, they just cannot be admitted substantively.

Prior Consistent Statements

FRE 801(d)(1)(B) is tied to both testifying and impeachment. It is designed to allow for an opportunity to support direct examination testimony after it has been attacked through a prior inconsistent statement on cross examination. When that occurs, and a prior consistent statement exists that was made before a motive to fabricate exists, that statement is admissible substantively under this rule.

A statement is not consistent with testimony that has not yet been given, so the exception does not apply before the speaker testifies. Testifying by itself is not enough – the exception does not simply enable parties to bolster testimony by piling on prior statements. The exception comes into play only after an impeaching attack, and the exception paves the way only for statements consistent with that part of the testimony that was attacked.

A consistent statement fits FRE 801(d)(1)(B) only if it tends to rebut an express or implied charge of "recent fabrication or improper influence or motive." This requirement means there must be an attack raising one of these charges. That attack normally occurs through impeachment by a prior inconsistent statement under FRE 613. The exclusion may not be used to prove new points not covered in the initial direct examination. FRE 801(d)(1)(B) is closely tied to initial direct and cross. It is more limited that FRE 801(d)(1)(A) and a party is not allowed to prove important details lying beyond the initial direct examination merely because the earlier statement and testimony are consistent in general tenor.

Prior Identification of the Accused

Prior identification of the accused is an exclusion to the hearsay rules. Under FRE 801 this evidence is excluded from the hearsay category by operation of law. Bolstering is usually defined as introducing evidence to enhance a witness's credibility before her credibility is attacked. One exception to this rule is that of prior identification. In most circumstances, if the witness has made an in-court identification of the accused, counsel may prove that she made a previous, out-of-court identification of the same person. FRE 801(d)(1)(C) permits the use of an ID as **substantive** evidence.

It is imperative that counsel lays a proper foundation establishing that the witness properly identified the accused in a pretrial line up. Foundational questions for hearsay exceptions should always arise from the language of the particular rule. Counsel's knowledge of the rule and the policy behind the rule empowers them to quickly and efficiently formulate appropriate foundational questions. Rather than acting as a series of magical phrases that must be repeated in a particular fashion, like a magician saying abracadabra, foundations are a common sense series of questions that reflect knowledge of the law and testimony establishing that the witness in question can meet the legal standard identified in the rule of evidence in question.

Under the FRE, counsel are allowed to ask leading questions when laying foundations, even if laying foundations during direct examination. Just because you can lead the witness does not necessarily mean that you should. The persuasive nature of a well-presented direct examination using open-ended questions that provide the appropriate foundation should not be overlooked. Counsel should always have a set of appropriate foundational questions for the specific issue.

FRE 611(a) controls modes of questioning. It states "The court shall exercise reasonable control over the mode and order of interrogating witnesses and presenting evidence so as to (1) make the interrogation and presentation effective for the ascertainment of the truth, (2) avoid needless consumption of time, and (3) protect witnesses from harassment or undue embarrassment."

FRE 611(c) tells us that "Leading questions should not be used on the direct examination of a witness except as may be necessary to develop the witness' testimony. Ordinarily leading questions should be permitted on cross-examination. When a party calls a hostile witness, an adverse party, or a witness identified with an adverse party, interrogation may be by leading questions."

Example: Admitting Prior Identification of the accused in court.

The facts. The accused, Tracy Barnes, is at trial, charged with breaking into Michelle Tucker' room and raping her on May 4th of last year. Barnes fled the scene and evaded capture. Some months after the crime, Mr. Barnes was arrested on suspicion of an unrelated offense. When the police arrested Barnes the officer conducted a search incident to arrest. He found Ms. Tucker' purse in Barnes' car. Barnes was placed in a line-up with six other individuals of similar build and appearance. Ms. Tucker was brought in for the lineup and she picked out Barnes on her second pass of the arrayed individuals.

Q. Ms. Tucker where were you on the evening of October 4th, last year?
A. I was in my apartment in the Whisper Winds apartment complex.

Q. What happened around 2 am?
A. A man broke into my room, raped me at knifepoint, and then fled.

Q. Who raped you?
A. The accused.

Q. Would you please point him out and identify him?
A. That man (the witness points at the accused).

Q. Your honor, the witness has identified the accused, Mr. Tracy Barnes. Ms. Tucker how many times have you seen the accused?
A. Three times.

Q. What were those occasions?
A. Well, I first saw him when he raped me, I see him today in court, and I saw him one other time.

Q. What was the other time?
A. At a lineup I attended in January of this year.

Q. Where did the police hold the lineup?
A. It was in the downtown precinct, on the corner of 5th and something.

Q. How was the lighting in the room?
A.   It was fine.

Q. How close were you?
A.   I was just about ten feet away.

Q. How were you facing?
A.   I was facing straight ahead, and looking at all the guys in the lineup.

Q. How long did the police give you to see the lineup?
A.   They said take as much time as I needed, but I only had to go up and down the lineup two times, so about five minutes.

Q. How many men were in the lineup?
A.   Six.

Q. How were they dressed?
A.   They all wore jeans and t-shirts.

Q. How tall were they?
A.   About the same height, around six feet.

Q. Did the police say anything about the lineup?
A.   No. They brought me in, told me to take my time, and to turn and walk out if I recognized any of them.

Q. What were the men in the lineup doing?
A.   Nothing. They just stood looking straight ahead.

Q. What happened after the lineup?
A.   The police asked if I had recognized the rapist.

Q. What did you say?
A.   I said yes, I did.

Q. Whom did you identify at the lineup?
A.   The accused, the guy I just pointed out here.

DC. Your Honor, the defense requests a limiting instruction under FRE 105 to the effect that the fact that this witness identified her alleged attacker may be used only in assessing her credibility and not as substantive evidence that the person she identified in fact attacked her.

C. **May we have a sidebar?**
J.   Approach.

C. **Your Honor, under FRE 801 we are permitted to introduce this witness's pretrial identification as substantive evidence. Thus, opposing counsel is not entitled to a limiting instruction. Furthermore, because it is admissible as substantive evidence, the jury members may also consider it on the issue of the weight to attach to the witness's credibility.**

J. The request for a limiting instruction is denied. You may continue with your questioning.

Admissions by a Party Opponent

FRE 801(d)(2)(A) creates an exception for statements by a party when offered against him in either a criminal or civil trial. It is important to note initially that the only party in a criminal proceeding is the defendant. This common sense rule makes a great deal of sense when you consider the purpose of the adversarial system. Hearsay doctrine should not protect you against your own words – you are responsible for your actions. Parties are responsible at a very basic level for the cases in which they are involved, to allow them to hide behind hearsay to prevent their statements from being admitted against them does not make sense. This is doubly so given that the parties are obviously present and can explain, deny, or rebut any such statement. Of course in criminal cases this exclusion does not apply where constitutional restrictions hold sway. In other words, you cannot us this rule to admit a statement by the defendant that was procured through a violation of the defendant's constitutional rights.

It does not matter whether a statement is written or spoken or in the form of nonverbal cues or word substitutes (pointing or nodding), even an undelivered email can be an admission. Statements qualify largely without regard to surrounding circumstances, and include statements to police, testimony or pleas from other proceedings, recorded statements, and many others. Admissions include behavior with an assertive aspect, such as handing over an object on request, which in effect says the object is the item requested. When a speaker agrees with or incorporates remarks by others we admit them under the adoptive admissions provision of this exclusion.

Just because a statement fits FRE 801(d)(2)(A) does not ensure admissibility. It may still be excludable under exclusionary provisions such as the limits against proving prior bad acts in FRE 404-405 or statutory or constitutional restrictions. Admissions are excludable under the FRE 403 balancing test. The party cannot use this rule as a sword. In other words, this exclusion works for an opposing party, but not for the party itself.

Adoptive Admissions

Under FRE 801(d)(2)(B) a statement is "not hearsay" when offered against a party who "manifested his adoption or belief in its truth." This works in much the same way as the personal admissions doctrine. While it is an exclusion to the hearsay rule, it is not absolute. Meeting the foundational requirements under the rule will not overcome a bar to admissibility that is grounded in another evidentiary rule, statute, or constitutional doctrine. The FRE 403 balancing test is applicable to this rule as well.

Adoption is clear when a party agrees to or concurs in an oral statement by another, hears and repeats it, or reads and signs a statement prepared by another. Acting in compliance with a statement by another can indicate adoption. In that instance it should make no difference whether the party against whom the statement is offered had personal knowledge of the matter asserted. By the same token, adoption does not occur if the party makes clear his disagreement with a statement spoken in their presence. Disavowal does not have the same effect.

Coconspirator statements

These statements are vicarious admissions based on the principle of agency. The basis for imputing a declarant's statement to a coconspirator is the party's relationship with the declarant. Once the relationship is demonstrated, the declarant's statements are admissible against the accused. FRE 801(d)(2)(E) exempts from the definition of hearsay "a statement made by a coconspirator of a party during the course of and in furtherance of the conspiracy."

The coconspirator exception is one of the most commonly invoked provisions in federal criminal trials. Commentators are largely critical of the exception, basing their concerns in large part upon the issues surrounding inchoate offenses, conspiracy in particular often being referred to as the "darling of prosecutors." The Supreme Court has praised it as an acceptable means for producing courtroom testimony that could not otherwise be produced. The court has gone so far as to identify the confrontation clause issue for coconspirator statements in *Crawford*, reiterating that coconspirator statements are not excludable under the confrontation clause.

Coconspirator statements are admissible against other conspirators. To admit them the prosecution must show that they were made during the course of the conspiracy, that both the accused and the declarant were participants in the conspiracy, and finally that the statement was made in furtherance of the conspiracy.

A proper foundation to admit the statement of a coconspirator must show that the statement in question was made in the course of and in furtherance of the conspiracy. Courts evaluate admissibility on a case-by-case basis. The rule does not require availability of the declarant. For instance, a police informant or coconspirator may testify and provide the necessary foundation for admission of the statement against another coconspirator. The statement of the coconspirator is attributed to the accused if the statement was made in the course and furtherance of the conspiracy. Before admitting the statement, counsel must show by a preponderance of the evidence that the conspiracy existed statements and that the accused and the declarant participated in it. If the accused joins the conspiracy after the declarant makes the statement, the accused is deemed to ratify the earlier statements and the statement may be admissible as evidence.

> *Foundational elements for coconspirator statements.*
>
> *There was a conspiracy that was in progress when the declarant made the statement. The conspiracy continues at least until the conspirators attempt to commit the crime.*
>
> *The declarant was a coconspirator.*
>
> *The declarant made the statement in furtherance of the conspiracy.*
>
> *The accused was a member of the conspiracy.*
>
> *The statement is offered against the accused.*

The judge decides whether the statement was made during the course of the conspiracy, and when the conspiracy ended. The judge in making the determination as to the existence of the conspiracy can use the proffered statement itself. It is also clear that at a minimum the conspiracy continues until the conspirators attempt to commit the crime. Additionally, once the conspirators are arrested, any statements they make are not part of the conspiracy. Because conspirators' statements are presumed unreliable and to rebut this presumption of unreliability, the conspirator statement must be corroborated with other independent, incriminating evidence. The type of statements that may be used include those made by acquitted conspirators and uncharged conspirators.

Coconspirator's statements fall within a firmly rooted hearsay exception. These firmly rooted hearsay exceptions rest upon such solid foundations that admission of virtually any evidence in those categories comports with the substance of the confrontational clause constitutional protection. These exceptions are considered "firmly rooted hearsay" and are admissible against the accused because they bear adequate "indicia of reliability." Reliability can be inferred with these statements without introducing more evidence.

Example: Lay the Foundation for a Coconspirator Statement

The facts: The accused, Dimitri Merinov, has been charged with conspiring with another, Gregory Robinson, to sell heroin. They sold heroin to an informer, Jeremiah Washington. Mr. Washington is the witness. He testifies that Merinov and Robinson sold him a bag of heroin.

Q. **Mr. Washington, where were you on the evening of August 22ⁿᵈ last year?**
A. *I was standing on the corner of Banderos Drive and 5ᵗʰ avenue.*

Q. **Who else was there?**
A. *Two other people by the names of Merinov and Robinson.*

Q. **Where are they now?**
A. *I don't know where Robinson is, but Merinov is sitting over there at that table.*

C. **Let the record reflect that the witness has identified the accused.**
J. *So noted.*

Q. **Mr. Washington, What happened while you were there?**
A. *Merinov and Robinson were making plans to sell drugs.*

Q. **What plans did they discuss?**

DC: *Your Honor, I object to that question on the ground that it calls for hearsay.*

C: *Your Honor, the witness will testify that the accused, Mr. Merinov, told Mr. Robinson to get some bags of heroin out of Merinov's car and Robinson did so. The statement is relevant to prove the existence of a conspiracy between them. That is, Mr. Merinov and Mr. Robinson agreed to commit a criminal act and that Mr. Robinson committed an over act in furtherance of the conspiracy. The statement is admissible under FRE801(d)(2) as an exemption to the hearsay rule.*

J *The objection is overruled.*

Q. **Mr. Washington, again, what plans did they discuss?**
A. They discussed selling me some drugs. Merinov told Robinson to get some bags of heroin out of Merinov's car to get them ready for sale.

Q. **What happened then?**
A. *Mr. Robinson left for a couple of minutes and then came back with some bags.*

Q. **Please describe the appearance of the bags for the jury?**
A. *They were clear, transparent Ziploc bags.*

Q. **What if anything could you see in the bags?**
A. *There was a white, powdery substance in the bag.*

Q. ***What happened next?***
A.   *Merinov took a bag of the white, powdery substance and gave it to me and I gave him $100.00.*

DC: *Your honor I renew my hearsay objection to this evidence. Counsel has not established the existence of a conspiracy sufficiently to support admitting this evidence under FRE 801.*

J   *I find that based on the evidence presented, there existed a conspiracy between Merinov and Robinson. Both parties made statement during the conspiracy that reflected their agreement to complete a drug sale to Mr. Washington. Mr. Robinson then went to the car and retrieved several Ziploc bags of white, powdery substance. His actions were overt acts in the course and furtherance of the conspiracy. The statement is admissible under FRE 801(d)(2) as an exemption to the hearsay rule.*

CONCLUSION

Now that we have dealt with issues surrounding the development of hearsay exclusion rules under FRE 801, let us move on to a discussion of Hearsay Exceptions.

Chapter 13: Hearsay Exceptions

Exceptions to the hearsay rule are admissible based on their unique tendency to be a reliable indicator of the truth. There are two major categories of exceptions: FRE 803, where the availability of the declarant is immaterial and FRE 804, where the declarant must be unavailable at trial before statements are admissible. Of the two, FRE 804 is more suspect from a reliability standpoint, and we require a specific showing of declarant unavailability before we will admit evidence under those exceptions. To date the Crawford doctrine has not been extended to FRE 804, but, as we discussed earlier, it has been applied to some, but not all, of the 803 exceptions.

Many of the rules under FRE 803 do not depend on the availability of the declarant because they are considered firmly rooted hearsay exceptions, with a long history of demonstrated reliability. To some degree these exceptions have been affected by the recent series of U.S. Supreme Court cases dealing with the confrontation clause in criminal trials, as discussed in the previous chapter. An understanding of how FRE 803 exceptions work requires us to take a look at some of the most commonly used FRE 803 exceptions. As we review them read them with an eye towards identifying what particular themes regarding reliability and admissibility may be found. The FRE 803 exceptions not specifically discussed in this text can be found, with committee comments, in chapter 14.

HEARSAY EXCEPTIONS – AVAILABILITY IMMATERIAL
FRE 803(1)

FRE 803(1) creates an exception for statements describing or explaining an event or condition if made while the speaker was perceiving it "or immediately thereafter." The idea of immediacy lies at the heart of the exception. Present sense impressions are considered trustworthy for two reasons, both resting on the time element. Consider the following case:

10 So.2d 83
Supreme Court of Florida, Division B.
TAMPA ELECTRIC CO. v. GETROST.
Oct. 13, 1942.

Opinion

THOMAS, Justice.

Appellee's action to recover damages for the death of her husband, alleged to have resulted from appellant's negligence, culminated in a verdict in her behalf. In the appeal the sufficiency of the testimony to establish liability is challenged and it is insisted that the evidence introduced by the defendant was adequate to substantiate the plea of contributory negligence. The only other question presented is the propriety of the trial court's ruling in admitting certain testimony given by a man who was, at the time of the mishap, assisting the deceased, Charles G. Getrost.

From the testimony in the case we learn that the electricity required for the white-way system of the city of Winter Haven was furnished by the appellant. The circuit became defective and the city directed one Franzman, whose duty it was to maintain the line, to make necessary repairs. Franzman employed Getrost, an experienced electrician, to do the actual work. In order to minimize, if not eliminate, any danger to Getrost from electricity while he was working on the line, a preliminary conversation over the telephone was held between him and the operator of the plant where the electricity was controlled so that the latter could recognize Getrost's voice when he gave instructions from time to time with reference to opening and closing the switch which regulated the current. Orders given by the workman were repeated by the operator to obviate any misunderstanding.

From the testimony it appears that another precautionary measure was followed at the plant to insure the line would not be energized without an express order from the person working on it. It was established that a placard bearing the name of the person doing the work was placed on the switch and that the switch was not to be operated except upon his personal instruction. Consequently, when Getrost began his task Franzman, his immediate employer, called the operator and instructed him to 'tag' the line for Getrost. Thereafter, until some one should succeed Getrost, he was the only person who could order the switch opened or closed.

The result of the trial in the circuit court depended upon the interpretation placed by the jury on the testimony of witnesses about occurrences at the plant and at the scene of the fatal injury for the period of an hour following nine-thirty in the morning. The log kept by the plant operator showed: at nine-twenty Getrost ordered the circuit closed; at nine-twenty-eight he ordered it opened; and at nine-thirty-five he ordered it closed. According to the notations on appellant's record the current was broken at ten-sixteen and 'tagged' for Franzman and Getrost and at ten-thirty-five the former called and ordered that the circuit be 'tagged' for him. It is the contention of the appellant that Getrost ordered the line energized at nine-thirty-five and that the switch was opened at ten-sixteen and labeled in the name of Franzman and Getrost because of a telephone message received then that some person had been injured.

The appellee asserts that Getrost called the appellant's plant after nine-thirty-five and instructed the operator to open the circuit, making it harmless. Testimony was introduced to show the giving of this order over the telephone and the actions of Getrost thereafter. Witnesses testified that he immediately took his assistant in a truck and drove to the office of his employer, Franzman; that the three men with slight delay returned to one of the white-way posts on which they were then working, situated, incidentally, almost directly in front of a funeral home where an ambulance was available; and that shortly thereafter as he attempted to handle the wires Getrost received a charge of electricity which killed him. There was proof that he was taken to a hospital where he arrived at approximately ten-forty-five.

Both appellant and appellee have presented their positions plausibly. If the testimony of either is considered independently of the other it is not difficult to arrive at the conclusion for which each contends. When, as appellant insists, the precautions taken at the electrical plant are considered in connection with the entries in the log it would seem that Getrost ordered the circuit energized at nine-thirty-five and some time between that hour and ten-sixteen was electrocuted, whereupon some one telephoned and ordered the circuit opened because a man had been injured. On the other hand, if the testimony of the appellee is to be given credit Getrost was killed after he had ordered the circuit opened at ten-sixteen. In these circumstances we think that we should not interfere with the verdict of the jury and the consequent judgment because there is ample evidence to support the findings, Holstun & Son v. Embry, 124 Fla. 554, 169 So. 400, and we have found nothing in the record to show bias, Carlton v. King, 51 Fla. 158, 40 So. 191, injustice or palpable wrong, McSwain v. Howell, 29 Fla. 248, 10 So. 588.

The appellant maintains that his plea of contributory negligence was substantiated by testimony that the deceased, Getrost, had failed to use the insulated gloves which his employer had furnished him and had failed to follow directions to 'ground' the wires upon which he was working. That he did not use the gloves and that he did not ground the wires were shown but it should be remembered, if the testimony of the appellee is true, that he had the right to believe that his instructions had been followed and the wires contained no electrical current at the time he was killed. We feel that the jury was justified in believing that the use of the gloves for the added precaution of determining whether any current was passing through the wires was unnecessary in view of these instructions. It was demonstrated that it would have been impractical for him to have worn the gloves at all times while he was working in the restricted space at the base of a white-way post and it does not appear to us logical that he should have been required continually to test the wires when the order to open the circuit had been received at the plant. The rules which we have given with reference to our interference with the verdict are applicable in the consideration of this question and upon it we have the same view.

The remaining question relates to the correctness of the ruling of the trial court in denying a motion to strike certain testimony of the witness Lynch who, throughout the repair work, had been assisting Getrost. On the direct examination he testified at some length about use of the telephone by Getrost immediately prior to his death at the time it was contended by appellee he made the last call to the plant with reference to disconnecting the circuit. He did not hear the conversation but watched Getrost use the telephone and when the latter rejoined him he said he had had the circuit opened.

After all this testimony had been introduced on direct examination and after cross examination had proceeded to some extent the attorney for the appellant made his motion to strike, because it was hearsay, all the testimony about a report by Getrost to his helper that he had ordered the current discontinued. Even assuming that the objection was timely made (26 R.C.L. page 1046), still we think the testimony was admissible in view of all of the circumstances. It will be recalled that these two men had been working together and the witness was entirely familiar with the procedure of telephoning the plant operator each time the line was energized or the current interrupted. He knew of the memorandum, containing the telephone number, that Getrost used in calling the plant and evidently saw him on the last occasion follow the same procedure as on previous ones. Considering the entire experience of the witness as an assistant to Getrost, his familiarity with the methods they were following and the conduct of Getrost immediately preceding the misfortune, it seems to us that the testimony cannot be said to have been improper.

We think the statement was not infected with the vices which make such declarations usually inadmissible. At the time it was uttered there was no occasion for it to have resulted from reflection or premeditation, nor was there motive to make it selfserving. Nothing in the record indicates that Getrost anticipated danger or injury until the moment he died.

We conclude that the trial judge committed no error in allowing the testimony to be introduced by applying the exception to the rule against hearsay. See Jones on Evidence, Fourth Edition, page 630, et seq.

Affirmed.

BROWN, C. J., and TERRELL and CHAPMAN, JJ., concur.

DISCUSSION PROBLEMS 13-1

1. Do you see the common law roots of the present sense impression exception in this opinion?

2. Does the court's reasoning make sense?

3. What language do they use? Why?

FRE 803(1)

A statement describing or explaining an event or condition made while the declarant perceived it or immediately thereafter is called a present sense impression. The statement must have been made at the time of the event or condition or as soon thereafter as possible. Typically, a statement of a present sense impression is offered by the declarant or through the testimony of a witness who heard it; it is a hearsay exception recognized principally because of the inference of reliability based on the contemporaneous nature of the statement. Unlike an excited utterance, it does not require a startling event. The availability of the declarant is immaterial.

The immediacy of the observation of an external event is key. This particular exceptions does not require an event that produces nervous shock or excitement, and is therefore different from the excited utterance exception, additionally, the absence of excitement supports an argument that this exception is perhaps more reliable because the speaker is not under the influence of excitement or stress as required for the FRE 803(2) exception.

Present sense impressions are trustworthy for two reasons related to timing. First, immediacy removes the risk of lack of memory, or at least reduces it to a nonissue. Second, immediacy prevents reflection, reducing the risk of intentional deception. Immediacy satisfies these two concerns of the hearsay doctrine, leaving only the risks of ambiguity and misperception to consider.

Courts deal with ambiguity and misperception by noting that the person who hears the statement perceives the event or condition, and usually later testifies about the statement and can corroborate what the speaker said. While FRE 803(1) does not require corroboration, courts often emphasize that the statement is corroborated.

The exception has three requirements. First, the statement must be contemporaneous with the event or condition—made while speaker perceives it or immediately thereafter. The time requirement is strict, for it is the major factor in assuring trustworthiness. In most cases, the statement clearly was made during those moments when speaker perceived the event or condition. The phrase "immediately thereafter" accommodates human realities: The condition or event may happen so fast that the words do not quite keep pace, and proving a true match of words and events may be impossible for ordinary witnesses.

The exception allows enough flexibility to reach statements made a moment after the fact where a small delay or "slight lapse" is not enough to allow reflection, which would raise doubts about trustworthiness. More significant delays (measured in minutes or hours, especially if the speaker made other statements in the interim) bar resort to FRE 803(1) because they do permit time for reflection and lessen or remove the assurance of trustworthiness. In this respect, the exception for present sense impressions is distinctly narrower than the one for excited utterances.

Second, the speaker must have perceived the event or condition. Perceiving usually means seeing, but it also includes hearing and other forms of sensory perception. The speaker must have perceived the matter described in his statement, or FRE 803(1) does not apply, a personal knowledge requirement.

Third, the statement must describe or explain the event or condition. Contemporaneity would not assure trustworthiness if the statement did not describe or explain the matter perceived. Most statements admitted under the exception simply assert the existence of the condition or happening of the event, and the term "describe" accurately captures the function of such statements. But some interpret, assess, or evaluate what the speaker perceives and are reached by the term "explain.

When introducing a statement of a present sense impression, counsel should be prepared for the opposition to attack the supporting credibility of the declarant, such as whether the declarant had an opportunity to reflect and modify any initial thought. Remember, the admissibility of the statement is based on the reduced likelihood that the declarant made a conscious or deliberate misrepresentation. While time is not the controlling foundational element, the statement must be made at the first available opportunity after the event.

The benefit of a statement of a present sense impression is that you don't need the person who made the statement. You only need a person who heard it. This is especially helpful when the declarant is a small child or the spouse of the accused who suddenly becomes "unavailable" at trial.

To qualify as a present sense impression, the statement must be made at the time of the event, immediately thereafter or at the first available opportunity. There is no hard and fast rule about how much time is considered "immediately thereafter." However, the contemporaneousness of the statement is crucial to its admission. Also, while corroboration is not required in the language of the rules, courts will look to any independent corroboration. The foundation by counsel should demonstrate to the court a nexus between when the statement was made and what event stimulated the statement to qualify as a present sense impression.

Example: Foundation for a Present sense impression

The facts. The witness, John Henry, was walking the two blocks from the downtown bus stop to work when he witnessed a man in a green jacket run by him into the bus station. An unidentified bystander next to him asked if he saw the man that ran past them just grab the woman's purse? Mr. Henry responded that he did not see the purse snatching and the bystander explained that he saw the guy grab the woman's black purse from her shoulder and tuck it inside his jacket then run past them into the bus station. Upon arriving in the office, approximately 10 minutes later, he went to his boss and said "On my way to the office from the bus, this lady's purse was snatched, in broad daylight." He described the details he recalled of the robber (twenty-something, white male, with long brown hair, wearing a blue jacket, jeans and sneakers) to his boss, Mr. James Jordan. He repeated what the bystander told him about the robbery. He then went to his office.

Q. Where were you on the morning of January 21st of this year, at approximately7:30 in the morning?
A. I was just outside the downtown bus station at the corner of Main and Champion Streets.

Q. Why were you there?
A. I was on my way to work. I had just gotten off the bus that arrived at the downtown stop at 7:25.

Q. Did anything unusual happen?
A. Yeah, that lady over there in the red dress got her purse snatched (pointing to the victim).

Q. What did you see?

A. *Well, the only thing I saw was this guy (pointing to the accused) run past me into the bus station just after I got outside the door.*

Q. Did you actually see the accused snatch the purse?

A. *No, I only saw him run past me. But this guy standing next to me saw it and asked me if I saw the guy take the purse.*

Q. Did he tell you he saw the robbery?

A. *Yes. He described what he saw and identified the guy that ran past us into the bus station as the robber.*

Q. Do you know the person who told you he saw the accused grab the purse?

A. *No, I didn't catch his name. He just turned to me after that guy ran by and asked me if I saw him grab the lady's purse.*

Q. Do you know if anyone else observed the purse snatching?

A. *I'm not sure, but there were several dozen people in the area going to and from the bus that time of the morning.*

Q. Did you speak to any other bystanders about the robbery?

A. No.

Q. Can you describe this person who told you about the robbery?

A. *He was a white male, maybe thirty or thirty five, about five foot four, he was dressed in a business suit. I believe I have seen him before at the downtown bus stop. He looked familiar, like I had seen him before, but I don't know him.*

Q. Where was he at the time of this robbery?

DC. <u>Objection</u>, calls for a legal conclusion.

J. Sustained. Rephrase the question, counsel.

Q. Of course your honor, where was he at the time of the "alleged" robbery?

A *He had exited the bus station in front of me, I'd say about 5 feet in front of me. We were both approximately 10 feet from the bus station door.*

Q. How was he facing?

A. *We were both heading north, away from the bus station, in the direction where the purse snatching took place, approximately 10 feet in front of him.*

Q. How much time passed from the time you observed the man run into the bus station until the unidentified bystander told you what he saw?

A. *Immediately, within seconds. I would estimate from 3-5 seconds after the accused ran by me.*

Q. Do you recall what the bystander said to you?

A. *Yes. He turned around to me and asked if I had seen the guy that just ran past us into the bus station snatch that woman's purse.*

Q. **What was his tone of voice?**
A. He was talking fast, with a surprised look on his face.

Q. **What were his gestures?**
A. *He was pointing at the man who had just run by us into the bus station.*

Q. **Did he say anything else?**
A. *Yes. When I told him I didn't see the guy grab the purse, he said the guy just walked up to the lady and grabbed her black purse off her shoulder and stuck it inside his jacket.*

Q. **What did you do then?**
A. *I just said something like, "In broad daylight," then continued the two blocks to my job.*

Q. **Did you speak to anyone at work about the event?**
A. *Yes. When I got to work approximately 10 minutes later, I went into my boss' office and told him about the purse snatching.*

Q. **What did you tell your boss?**
A. *I told him that I saw this white guy in a blue jacket, jeans and sneakers, in his twenties with long brown hair run past me into the bus station. I also repeated what the bystander told me about the robbery.*

Q. **Do you see the person that ran past you in court today?**
A. *Yes. That's him over there (pointing to the accused).*

FRE 803(2)

FRE 803(2) creates an exception for a statement by someone speaking under the stress of excitement, expressing his reaction and relating to the causal event or condition. The exception rests on the idea that spontaneous reaction is powerful enough to overcome reflective capacity, and the statement is viewed as the product of the impression made by an external stimulus. Such reactive statements are considered trustworthy because the stimulus leaves the speaker momentarily incapable of fabrication, and her memory is fresh because the impression has not yet passed from her mind.

An excited utterance is a statement made by a person, who may or may not be testifying, relating to a startling event or condition. The statement must have been made while the person was under the stress of excitement caused by the event or condition. Typically, an excited utterance is offered through the testimony of a witness who heard it; it is a hearsay exception recognized principally because of the inference of reliability.

When introducing an excited utterance as an exception to the hearsay requirement, counsel should be prepared for the opposition to attack the supporting credibility of the declarant.

The benefit of the excited utterance exception is that counsel does not need the person who actually made the statement. They only need a person who heard it. This is especially helpful when the declarant is a small child or the spouse of the accused who suddenly becomes "unavailable "at trial.

Because our vulnerabilities vary, there is no objective test for what qualifies as a triggering event under this exception. The court will address each on a case-by-case basis depending upon the experience of the particular declarant. Courts will look to the age, physical and mental condition and basis for knowing the statement to be true when evaluating whether the person was excited when making the statement.

Example: Foundation for an excited utterance

The witness, Ms. Vilma Martinez, was teaching a soccer camp to a group of youth at noon on the outdoor university fields. A group of adult men were playing soccer on the adjacent court. One of the men was striking downfield, when he was suddenly struck to the ground, a pool of blood forming around his head. Vilma was shocked and amazed. So was another man, an unidentified bystander who was playing in the game. The man was facing the action when it occurred. Vilma overheard the man say "he didn't hit him; he blocked the ball into the little guy's face!" The issue at trial is whether the victim was hit by the ball or punched by the accused.

Q. *Where were you at noon on July 29th of last year?*
A. *I was at the outdoor soccer fields at the university.*

Q. *Why were you there?*
A. *I was teaching a soccer camp to some local kids.*

Q. *Did anything unusual happen?*
A. *Yeah, I guess you could say so. A guy did get his nose broken.*

Q. *What did you see?*
A. *Well, it was pretty disgusting. Eight guys were playing four-on-four on the field next to us. One of them, a real little guy, stole the ball at half-court and was going in for a shot. A tall guy in black shorts came racing down to defend. The little guy went to shoot, when all of a sudden he collapsed, grabbing his face. He began bleeding **immediately**; wailing, and then I saw a pool of blood.*

Q. *How many people saw this?*
A. *Not including the kids at the camp, I'd say eight people in the immediate area.*

Q. *Did you notice their reaction?*
A. *Yes. We were all shocked. It happened so fast, most of us just froze in place. As soon as we looked, we could see that the little guy was injured and bleeding badly. It was an awful sight.*

Q. *Who else besides you was in the crowd looking on?*
A. *There were a number of people standing on the sidelines observing, but there was one guy in particular who stood out.*

Q. *What was his name?*
A. *I didn't get his name.*

Q. *What did he look like?*
A. *He was a white male, maybe thirty or thirty five, about five foot four, he had his shirt off, and I remember he was wearing really small black running shorts.*

Q. *Okay, where was he at the time of the "alleged" assault?*
A. *He was right in front of me, at midfield where the men were playing.*

Q. *How was he facing?*

A.   *He was looking right where the injury took place.*

Q.   **What was his condition right after the alleged assault?**
A.   *He was just like the rest of us -- shocked and amazed.*

Q.   **What was his facial expression?**
A.   *He had his mouth open. I guess he was dumbfounded at first.*

Q.   **What was his tone of voice?**
A.   *He was shouting in a loud voice.*

Q.   **What were his gestures?**
A.   *He was pointing at the man who had been on defense and gesturing wildly.*

Q.   **What was his emotional state?**
A.   *He was really excited and upset.*

Q.   **Did he say anything?**
A.   *Yes.*

Q.   **How much time had elapsed between the event and him speaking?**
A.   *About 10 seconds.*

Q.   **What did this man say about the "alleged" assault?**
A.   *He said that the fellow in the black shorts made a clean block and stuffed the soccer ball back into the little guy's face.*

FRE 803(3)

FRE 803(3) sets forth what is usually called the state-of-mind exception, and it is a provision of extraordinary importance to those in courtroom. It covers statements that shed light on present mental attitudes and inclinations of the speaker and his physical condition. In addition, it permits use of statements to prove the speaker's later conduct and facts about his last will and testament. FRE 803(3) allows that "The following are not excluded by the hearsay rule, even though the declarant is available as a witness: ... A statement of the declarant's then existing state of mind, emotion, sensation, or physical condition (such as intent, plan, motive, design, mental feeling, pain, and bodily health), but not including a statement of memory or belief to prove the fact remembered or believed unless it relates to the execution, revocation, identification, or terms of declarant's will."

While FRE 803(3) is a hearsay exception that enables the admission of significant probative evidence resulting from declarants' spontaneous and responsive statements about their own mental, emotional, or physical condition, it is often used circumstantially to prove the intent element of many crimes. The rationale for the rule is that it is unlikely that the declarant has an opportunity to fabricate, or even reflect upon, a then existing condition. There are three main types of statements under FRE 803(3): *Statements offered to prove state of mind or emotion, Statements offered to prove conduct*, and *Statements* **offered to prove present bodily condition**.

One of the most difficult things for a trial attorney to prove is a person's state of mind. The attorney must usually rely on circumstantial evidence, such as conduct, to prove a certain state of mind. Because of this difficulty, courts have been inclined to admit sincere declarations of state of mind or emotion when that state is a material issue in a case. These declarations often give the best insight into the declarant's mental or emotional condition.

Ideally, the declarant will make the statement at the pivotal time under the substantive law, often contemporaneously with the material fact at issue. For example, if at the time of an assault, the alleged victim states that he is going to kill the accused, the statement is admissible to prove self-defense.

While declarations of state of mind are normally used when state of mind itself is at issue, another use for state of mind declarations is to prove conduct through a statement of present plan, intention, or design. These declarations indicate that the declarant currently plans to engage in subsequent conduct. The fact that the declarant expressed that intent increases the probability that the declarant subsequently performed the planned act. However, the exception is not broad enough to include a declarant's hearsay statement of memory or past state of mind.

If a declarant states his or her present bodily sensation or condition, the declaration is admissible. These statements must describe the bodily condition at the time the declarant made the statement, although it is important to note that it does not matter to whom the statement is made - there is no requirement that the statement be made to a physician or a health care provider. A declarant's statement to a friend that his nose is broken and he feels sick would be admissible.

The foundation for then existing state of mental, emotional, or physical condition is relatively easy to establish. Its effectiveness, however, depends on how well it is prepared and presented in court. A benefit of a statement of then existing mental, emotional, or physical condition is that the person who made the statement does not have to testify. There is no need to establish the declarant's unavailability before the introduction of this evidence. You must, however, present the declarant, a person who heard the statement, or another admissible form of evidence (stipulation, business record, etc.) to convey the statement at trial.

The timing of the statement in relation to a current state of mind, emotion, or physical condition is what potentially makes it admissible under this hearsay exception. When offering the statements to prove state of mind or emotion, as well present bodily conditions, the statements must directly relate to the declarant's current state or condition. Conduct related statements must indicate that the declarant currently intends to engage in subsequent conduct. These statements must be forward-looking rather than statements about memory or the past to qualify under this exception. The one proviso relates to the execution, revocation, identification, or terms of a declarant's will. Some courts still admit statements under this exception under a theory of continuity of state of mind, when the time lapse between the statement and the critical event is so short that we may assume that the declarant's state of mind was the same at both times. While timing of the statement in relation to the critical event is the primary factor a court should consider in assessing reliability, the totality of the circumstances surrounding the statement must also be evaluated.

Be aware of the potential interplay between this exception and the hearsay exclusion found in FRE 801(d). Under the exclusion rule admissions by a party opponent are admissible because they are not hearsay when offered against the party who made the admission. The prosecution frequently offers statements by the accused as admissions, which are technically not hearsay under FRE 801(d). The defense cannot use the same rule to admit statements made by the accused because they are not offered against the accused. However, the defense may be able to use FRE 803(3) to introduce a statement made by the accused if it supports the defense's theory of the case.

State of mind must be relevant under FRE 403 before it can be admitted under FRE 803(3). This holds true for every hearsay exception. When offering to prove state of mind, remember that the declarant's state of mind must be at issue in the case.

Example: laying the foundation for a FRE 803(3) exception

The facts: The accused has raised a consent defense to a sexual assault case. The victim, Vicky Violet, and her best friend Shannon Sharpe, are next door neighbors in the Botany Bay apartments. On Friday night, June 16, they went to the club for some drinks and conversation. At one point, the accused approached the women, introduced himself as Ernest Frizell, and persuaded Vicky Violet to dance. In the middle of the song, Vicky returned to the table with a flushed face, telling Shannon, "That guy gives me the creeps. He is really scary. Let's leave." At that point, the two women left the club and began walking home. When they passed the Burger King, Shannon decided to get something to eat. Vicky declined the offer to stop for a bite, saying, "I am really tired. I'm going straight home and to bed. That guy at the club is still really freaking me out." Early the next morning, Shannon went into Vicky's room to find her sitting on the floor, calm but in some disarray. Shannon asked Vicky if she was okay and what happened. Vicky sobbed, "I am in a lot of pain. My insides feel as if they were ripped apart." Consider the following direct examination:

Q. Do you know Vicky Violet?
A. Yes. She and I live on the same stairwell of Botany Bay Apartments. We are good friends.

Q. Where were you the night of Saturday, June 16, of last year?
A. Vicky and I went to the club for some drinks and conversation. We walked there so we wouldn't have to drive home after drinking.

Q. How long were you and Vicky at the club?
A. Not long, we left earlier than we thought we would. I would say we were there about 90 minutes.

Q. Did you and Vicky have anything to drink?
A. Vicky had a beer and I had a Coke.

Q. What did you do after you entered the club?
A. We got our drinks and sat down at a table by ourselves and started to listen to the music.

Q. What happened next?
A. The accused (pointing to the accused) came over and asked Vicky to dance. We didn't know him at the time, but Vicky agreed and they went to dance.

Q. The witness has identified the accused by pointing to him. What did you do after they got up to dance?
A. I watched them for a few seconds. Everything seemed okay, but then I stopped watching because the dance floor was behind me. It was only about a minute later when Vicky came back to the table alone.

Q. How was Vicky acting when she came back to the table?
A. She seemed really nervous, almost shaking. She wanted to leave.

Q. *What did she say?*
A. "*That guy is giving me the creeps, he is really scary. Let's leave.*"

Q. *Was anyone else at the table at the time?*
A. *No.*

Q. *What did you do next?*
A. *We left and started walking back to the apartments. We saw the defendant walking behind us. On the way I wanted to stop at the Burger King for something to eat, so I did.*

Q. *What did Vicky do?*
A. *She said* she was really tired and was going home and straight to bed, and that the guy from the club was still "freaking" her out*. I went in the BK and Vicky kept walking towards the apartments.*

Q. *When was the next time you saw Vicky?*
A. *The next morning at about 8:00 am. I walked into her room to say hello.*

Q. *What happened next?*
A. *She was alone, sitting on the floor in kind of a daze. Her eyes were puffy – it looked like she had been crying. I asked her if she was okay and what happened.*

Q. *What did Vicky say?*
A. *She said, "*I am in a lot of pain. My insides feel ripped apart.*"*

Example #2: Admitting an alibi defense using FRE 803(3)

The facts: Between 8:00 am and 10:00 am on June 8th a laptop was stolen from a condominium. The laptop was found in the accused's apartment. The accused, Art Colter, contends that he was by himself on a 12-mile marathon training program 7:30 to 11:30 on that day, and did not return to the apartment complex until 1130. The witness, Miss Lewis, was working as the cashier at the local convenience store on June 8. When she opened 7:30 in the morning Mr. Colter was waiting at the door. As he entered, he told her, "Thanks, it's great to be out on such a beautiful day. I hate being cooped up in there." When she asked him why he was up so early on a Saturday, Walker responded, "I am training for a marathon so I'm going on a 12-mile run by myself all the way down to the River walk and back." After buying a bottle of Gatorade, Mr. Colter departed. Around 11:00, Colter reentered the convenience store with a slight limp and showing obvious signs of fatigue. When he was paying for two more bottles of Gatorade, Miss Lewis asked him how the run went. Mr. Colter told Miss Lewis, "I am really out of shape, my legs are already really sore. I've got some huge blisters on my feet." Ms. Lewis is on the witness stand. She has been called during the defense case-in-chief.

Q. *Where were you on Saturday, June 8, last year?*
A. *I was working at the convenience store from 7:30 to 4:30.*

Q. *Do you recognize the accused?*
A. *Yes.*

Q. *How do recognize him?*

A. *He is Mr. Colter. He comes in all the time. He lives across the street in a condominium.*

Q. **How often do you see him?**
A. *Just about every day that I work.*

Q. **How well do you know him?**
A. *I only know him as a customer.*

Q. **Describe what happened when you opened the convenience store on June 8 of last year.**
A. *When I opened the store for business at 7:30 Mr. Colter was at the door. He came inside and walked towards the drinks section.*

Q. **Did either of you say anything when he entered?**
A. *Yes, as he was walking inside he said, "<u>Thanks, it's great to be out on such a beautiful day. I hate being cooped up in there.</u>" I told him, "You're welcome."*

Q. **What happened next?**
A. *I went to the register. He came up to it about 30 seconds later with a big bottle of Gatorade. I asked him why he was up so early on a Saturday.*

Q. **What did he say?**
A. *He said,<u> I am training for a marathon so I'm going on a 12-mile run by myself all the way down to the River walk and back.</u>" Then he paid for the Gatorade and left.*

Q. **Was anyone else in the store at the time you two talked?**
A. *No. It was too early.*

Q. **Besides the Gatorade, was he carrying anything?**
A. *No, just the Gatorade.*

Q. **Do you recall what he was wearing?**
A. *He was wearing running shorts and addidas shoes.*

Q. **Is that the last time you saw him that day?**
A. *No, he came back into the store at about 11:30.*

Q. **How do you know it was 11:30?**
A. *I was about to put my snack in the microwave. I always eat my snack at 11:30.*

Q. **Did you notice anything different about him?**
A. *He was still in his running clothes, but they looked a little wet. He was limping, and he looked tired.*

Q. **What happened when he was in the store?**
A. *He bought two more bottles of Gatorade. I asked him how the run went.*

Q. **What did he say?**
A. *He said, "<u>I am really out of shape, my legs are already really sore.</u>" And he said that <u>he had some huge blisters on his feet.</u>*

Q.	***How long was he in the store that second time?***
A.	*Just a few minutes*

Q.	***Was anyone else in the convenience store at the time?***
A.	*Not near the register, no.*

Q.	***You said he was limping the second time you saw him. Did you detect anything like that the first time you saw him at 7:30?***
A.	*No, he seemed fine then.*

FRE 803(4)

FRE 803(4) creates an exception for statements made for purposes of getting medical treatment or diagnosis. The main reason offered to admit statements made for purposes of getting treatment is that they are trustworthy. Usually the patient makes them to his physician, and they describe past and present physical sensations relating to his condition, so risks of misperception and faulty memory are minimal. The patient knows their description helps determine treatment, so they have reason to speak candidly and carefully, and risks of insincerity and ambiguity are minimal.

A statement describing medical history, past or present symptoms or sensations or a statement of the cause of a medical problem disclosed for the purpose of treatment or diagnosis may qualify as an exception under the hearsay rule. To be admissible, the statement must be made to medical personnel or to another, so long as the statement is made for the purpose of diagnosis or treatment.

These words set a standard that is objective but broad. Where treatment is sought, the assurance of candor reaches statements pertinent to what the doctor does. In theory the subjective understanding of the speaker determines the extent to which he feels pressed to be truthful. But in practice a court cannot figure out what the speaker was thinking. Hence it is usually reasonable to assume the physician guided the interview so the two come to similar understandings of what is pertinent, and the doctor's opinion on this point deserves considerable weight. Where diagnosis was sought, the idea is to permit substantive use of statements the jury is likely to hear anyway, as part of the basis of testimony the doctor gives. Again what she considers pertinent counts heavily.

In *White v. Illinois*, 112 S. Ct.736 (1992) the Supreme Court held that statements made by a four-year-old victim for the purpose of securing medical treatment were admissible whether the victim testified, because the statement had sufficient guarantees of reliability under a firmly rooted exception to the hearsay rule. In the case of child witnesses, the foundational requirement that the statement be made for the purpose of diagnosis or treatment may be difficult. However, some courts have been willing to relax this standard in the case of very young witnesses, especially sexual abuse cases.

Typically, a statement made for purposes of medical diagnosis or treatment is offered by the declarant or through the testimony of a witness who received it. This hearsay exception is based on a presumption that a person seeking relief from a medical condition has an incentive to make accurate statements. In the case of very young children, statements made to family members or others, and later disclosed to medical personnel on behalf of the child, may be admissible.

Expansive interpretation has severely strained this exception, but it has survived the Crawford testimonial test. The exception accepts that children are like adults in being motivated to cooperate with treating physicians in describing symptoms and causes, and natural accounts that stray beyond what is strictly important in diagnosis and treatment are likely to be as trustworthy as statements focused narrowly on clinical symptoms.

Treatment of such victims turns on finding out who harmed them, since caretakers who learn that a parent or member of the household is responsible for the harm will likely take steps to place the child in foster care and arrange to counsel the child. Additionally, the identity of the perpetrator is a necessary component of follow on mental health treatment.

When introducing a statement made for purposes of medical diagnosis or treatment, counsel should be prepared for the opposition to attack the credibility of the declarant or witness, such as whether there is any bias or motive to fabricate. They should also anticipate attacks concerning whether a declarant made the statement expecting or understanding any medical benefit would result. This is especially true in sexual abuse cases with young victims.

Like other hearsay exceptions involving the declarant's state of mind or physical condition, the foundation for statements made for purposes of medical diagnosis or treatment is relatively easy to establish. Its effectiveness, however, depends on how well it is prepared and presented in court.

The benefit of a statement made for purposes of medical diagnosis or treatment is that you don't need the person who made the statement. You should, however, present the declarant or a person who received the statement, whether, a medical witness or family member. This is especially helpful when the declarant is a small child or the spouse of the accused who suddenly becomes "unavailable" at trial. The best practice is to have the statement in question delivered to the finder of fact through the mouth of someone is perceived to be impartial.

What makes this evidence admissible is the motivation of the declarant in making the statement. While there is no definitive test for what qualifies as a statement made for purposes of diagnosis or treatment, some expected medical benefit to the declarant is essential in laying a proper foundation. The courts in the case of young witnesses have relaxed this rule on multiple occasions.

While "time" is one of the factors a court should consider in assessing reliability, the entire circumstances surrounding the statement must be evaluated. Was the statement voluntarily disclosed as a result of a complaint from the declarant of a medical condition? Did the statement result from questioning about an observed condition, such as redness of vaginal area of a small child? Was the statement made to medical personnel? The key is whether the declarant made the statement anticipating some medical benefit or treatment. For young children unable to understand or appreciate the medical benefit requirement, all the details surrounding the statement must be scrutinized. Remember, the courts, are more inclined to allow some leeway with statements of children, because of their unsophisticated sense of time and the fact that they may not have immediate access to someone to whom such a statement could be made.

The same principle that supports admissibility -- the accuracy of a statement based on the incentive to get a medical benefit -- also carries limitations, such as motive to fabricate or misrepresent, which could lead to claims of coaching or otherwise improper motive to lie. Counsel should examine this carefully, especially in the case of sexual assault involving older victims. Also, while statements of the source of an injury are frequently made to investigators or law enforcement personnel, those statements generally are not admissible under this rule.

Example: Foundation for Statements for purposes of medical diagnosis or treatment

The facts: witness, Ms. Hamby, is the preschool teacher of Kathy Jean, a four-year-old student at the Sunny Acres Day Care Center. On February 12, Ms. Hamby noticed Kathy Jean refused to sit in her during story hour. When asked why she would not sit down, Kathy said it hurt her "pee-pee" when she sat in the chair. Ms. Hamby took Kathy to the bathroom and visually examined her vaginal area. It appeared red and swollen. She told Kathy she would call her mother and take her to the school nurse to look at her hurt "pee-pee." On the way to the nurse's office, Ms. Hamby asked Kathy what happened to her "pee-pee" and she responded that her mother's boyfriend, Greg, put his "pee-pee" on her "pee-pee" and she saw "white stuff" come out on her "pee-pee." Ms. Hamby telephoned Ms. Jean and advised Kathy's mother what she observed and what Kathy told her. Once she arrived at the nurse's office, Ms. Hamby told the nurse, Ms. Lancaster, that Kathy told her it hurt her "pee-pee" when she sat down and that her mother's boyfriend put "white stuff" from his "pee-pee" on her when he rubbed his on hers. The issue is the source of the injury to Kathy Jean.

Q. Where were you on Friday, February 12th of this year?
A. I was in my classroom, Room 106, at the KIDS COME FIRST preschool where I am a teacher.

Q. Is Kathy Jean in your preschool class?
A. Yes.

Q. Was she in your class on that day?
A. Yes.

Q. Did anything unusual happen with Kathy Jean on that day?
A. Yes. I noticed that she would not sit down during story hour and when I asked why, she said her "pee-pee" hurt when she sat down.

Q. Did anyone else overhear Kathy when she said this?
A. No, there were just the two of us in the corner of the classroom. My teaching assistance, Nancy, was in the far corner of the classroom with the other students

Q. What did you do when she told you her "pee-pee" hurt?
A. Well, Kathy has been a student with us for the last 2 years and I have been her teacher all that time. I know she refers to her vagina as her "pee-pee," so I thought I should take her to the bathroom and look at her vagina to see if she had an injury or some other problem that our school nurse should look at.

Q. When you took her to bathroom, what happened?
A. I pulled down her pants and her under pants and looked at her vagina. It looked red and swollen, so I decided to call her mother and take her to the nurse for a medical assessment.

Q. What happened next?
A. I put Kathy's clothes back on and told her we were going to the nurse to let her look at it. I also told her we would call her mother.

Q. Was anyone else around when you examined Kathys' vagina?
A. No. It was only the two of us in the bathroom the entire time we were there.

Q. What happened next?

A. *On the way to the nurse's office, I asked Kathy how her "pee-pee" got hurt and she said...*

Q. In the two years that you have been Kathys; teacher, have you ever taken her to the nurse before?

A. *Yes, on numerous occasions.*

Q. Could you describe some of the circumstances where you have taken her to the nurse's office?

A. *Let's see. On several occasions she has received scrapes and scratches from playing with the other children in school. On some of the occasions, my assistant or myself noticed the incident and took Kathy to the nurse. On other occasions, she has come to us crying after being scratched by one of the other students. It has never been anything serious. Our school policy is to take all children with injuries, no matter how slight, to the nurse to make a medical determination if further care is needed.*

Q. How many times in the last 2 years would you estimate this has happened?

A. *It's hard to say, but I would guess approximately 4-6 times. With toddlers and children this age, scrapes and scratches are common. Plus the kids like the "Barney" bandages that the nurse puts on their scratches.*

Q. Have there been other times that you have taken Kathy to the nurse, aside from any injuries?

A. *Yes. It is also the policy at our school that all medication is kept and administered by our nurse. Kathy has had more than one occasion, approximately 4-6 occasions that I can recall, where she has had to take medication for ear infections, colds and stuff like that. I can't be certain of the exact number, but the nurse would have the records.*

Q. So over the last two years, you would estimate that Kathy has been to the nurse's office close to a dozen times?

A. *That is correct, based on my recollection. It could be a few more or a few less.*

Q. What happened on the way to the nurse' office?

A *I asked Kathy how her "pee-pee" got hurt and she said her mother's boyfriend Greg had put his "pee-pee" on her "pee-pee" and made white stuff come out of his "pee-pee."*

Q What did you do next?

A. *I was shocked and appalled at what I was hearing. I immediately reported the circumstances, my actions and Kathy's statement to the nurse, because I felt she had just described being sexually assaulted by her mother's boyfriend. I then left Kathy in the nurse's care and used the phone in her office to call Mrs. Q. and report to her what Kathy said to me.*

Q While in the nurse's office did you hear Kathy say anything else?

A. *Yes. I heard her repeat to the nurse what she said to me about Greg putting his "pee-pee" on her "pee-pee" when asked by the nurse how she got hurt. After about 5 minutes, I had to go to the administrator's office to report what was happening and wait for Kathy's mother.*

FRE 803(5) AND FRE 612

When faced with a witness who cannot recall a particular fact, lawyers can try to refresh her memory by referring to a writing, a document, or other aid. This is commonly known as "refreshing recollection." The goal is to simply assist the witness in remembering what they already know by using a document or other object to "jog" their memory and remind them of the facts. There are few, if any, limitations on the means lawyers can use to refresh a witness's recollection. Some common aids include letters, objects, documents, magazines, newspaper clippings, income tax returns, smells, police reports, notes, photographs, prior testimony, and tape recordings.

While the limitations on the type of item that can be used are relatively small, it is important that lawyers follow the steps when refreshing recollection. The primary concern is to make certain that after the witness's memory is refreshed they testify based upon what they remember, and not what is in the document. To that end the lawyer when refreshing recollection must use certain foundational steps.

In actual practice refreshing recollection is usually accomplished as follows:

Q. **Agent Edwards, what was the address of the house where you first encountered the accused on the date of his apprehension?**

A. *I can't remember. I know it was in Niles Township, but I can't remember anything more specific.*

Q. **Is there anything you could review which would help you remember?**

A. *Yes. I made a report shortly after the apprehension.*

Q. **Agent Edwards, I'm handing you what has been marked as Prosecution Exhibit 5 for Identification, a copy of which I am handing to the defense. What is it?**

A. *It's a copy of the report I made regarding this case.*

Q. **Please read it over silently to yourself. (pause)**

Q. **I have retrieved Prosecution Exhibit 5 for Identification from the witness. Agent Edwards, does that refresh your memory?**

A. *Yes.*

Q. **What is the address of the house where you first encountered the accused on the day of his apprehension?**

A. *It was 1551 Ferndale Boulevard.*

When done properly refreshing recollection is a seamless process that allows the lawyer to remind the witness of what they already know without making a big deal out of it. It is not a disaster that the witness cannot remember, but merely a normal human reaction to a stressful situation.

The only danger areas in refreshing recollection from an objections perspective occur when lawyers fail to follow procedures. Be exact about the procedure. Withdraw the document so the witness testifies from memory (albeit her refreshed memory) and not from the piece of paper. Distinguish the use of a document to refresh memory from use of the document as a substitute for testimony, which will require an exception to the hearsay rules.

When you are refreshing memory, the testimony, not the document, is the evidence; but you still mark the document as an exhibit and it becomes part of the record although it is not admitted into evidence. You must show a copy of the document you use to refresh the witness's memory to opposing counsel. More importantly, opposing counsel can introduce into evidence the portions your witness relies upon. You must ensure that it does not contain embarrassing or unhelpful information to your case. Do not try to be sneaky and use an excerpt from a document if the full document will harm your case. Although the full document is potentially admissible, you should be careful to mask the document so that irrelevant or privileged information cannot be read. Have a masked copy and an original ready for inspection.

When you are on the opposing side, always take the time to read the entire document. Be sure to object if refreshing the witness's memory sounds unduly suggestive or prompts the witness in a way you think the jury ought to know. If you are given the opportunity to be present during an out-of-court witness refreshment, do not decline and go to lunch. You never know what you might learn. Finally, remember that even though the writing is read into evidence, it is not taken back with the jury members into deliberations unless offered by the adverse party.

Sometimes, despite your best efforts to refresh recollection you are unsuccessful. When that happens the witness cannot independently remember a particular fact about which he has been called to testify. If a written record of the earlier fact or event exists the writing may qualify as an exception to the hearsay rule and be introduced into evidence as past recollection recorded. It can then be considered substantively by the jury.[51]

To admit evidence pursuant to FRE 803(5) the lawyer must lay a proper foundation to show that the witness cannot remember, but earlier in time could remember and that a record of that memory was made. The following elements establish the foundation for introducing evidence of a past-recorded fact as an exception to the hearsay rule for a witness's present recall of that fact.

Foundation for Past Recollection Recorded:

Witness cannot remember a fact or event on the stand;

Witness had firsthand knowledge at one time;

That knowledge is reflected in a memorandum or record made at or near the time the fact or event occurred, made or adopted by the witness;

Record was accurate and complete when made;

Record is in same condition now as when made; and

Witness still cannot completely and accurately recall the fact or event even after reviewing the record.

Here is an example of a foundation by defense counsel:

Q. Mr. Simpson, did you see the automobile as it sped away?

---

[51] See Fed. R. Evid. 803(5).

A.   *I was on the ground, but I looked up and saw the license plate.*

Q.   What was the tag number?
A.   *I don't recall. I know it was a Missouri tag, but I can't remember the numbers.*

Q.   Is there anything that would help you to recall?
A.   *Yes, I thought the number would be important so I scribbled it down a few minutes later when I found some paper.*

NOTE: At this point, you would lay the same foundation you would to refresh recollection under FRE 612.

Q.   I'm handing you what's been marked as Defense Exhibit D for Identification, a copy of which I have provided the government. What is it?
A.   *It's the note I made of the license number.*

Q.   Please take a moment to read it over. (pause)

Q.   I'm retrieving Defense Exhibit D for Identification from the witness. Now, Mr. Simpson, please tell the jury the number of the license plate
A.   *Sir, I know it's going to sound strange, but I still can't remember.*

Q.   Mr. Simpson, think again about Defense Exhibit D for Identification. When did you write this note?
A.   *About 10 minutes after the car sped away with the guys who stole my wallet.*

Q.   Are you sure it is accurate?
A.   *Yes. I kept repeating the license number to myself until I had a pencil and paper.*

Q.   I'm handing you again Defense Exhibit D for Identification. Your honor, I ask the court's permission for Mr. Simpson to testify from past recollection recorded using Defense Exhibit D for Identification.

J.   *Objection?*

P.   *None.*

J.   *The witness may testify.*

Q.   Tell the jury the numbers on the license plate.
A.   *It was a Missouri plate with the number TGV 8765.*

Q.   Your honor, the defense offers Defense Exhibit D for I.D. into evidence as Defense Exhibit D and asks that it be published to the jury.

P.   *The government objects your honor. The evidence is the witness's testimony, not the actual exhibit.*

J.   *Agreed. The exhibit will not be published.*

Unlike refreshing memory, in past recollection recorded you are offering an out-of-court statement (the contents of the contemporaneous writing) as evidence for the truth of its contents. This creates a hearsay issue that is not present when the memory is merely refreshed. The focus of analysis is on the ultimate source of the information. If it comes from the witness's memory then there is no hearsay issue, although there may very well be potential cross examination concerning defects in capacity.

If the source of the information is an out-of-court statement then there is a hearsay issue and the statement must fall into a hearsay exception. The hearsay statement is admissible under past recollection recorded because it carries sufficient circumstantial guarantees of trustworthiness that are derived from the fact that the statement was made at or near the time of the incident. It is important to note that the witness on the stand need not necessarily have been the one who made the writing. As long as the witness adopted the written document it suffices for purposes of FRE 803(5). The test is whether the witness adopted the record, if made at or near the time of the event, and the witness testifies, the record accurately reflects the facts.

When dealing with these issues it always looks better to the jury if your witness can testify from present memory. If the witness cannot remember, first try to refresh their memory. If the witness still cannot remember, then lay the foundation for past recollection recorded. When you refresh memory keep in mind that although the witness may read from the document, the evidence is testimonial – the oral statement of the witness – not documentary. The writing itself should not be admitted into evidence unless offered by the opposing counsel. However, if you have to use past recollection recorded then the document is the evidence, not the testimony of the witness.

FRE 803(6)

The business records exception rests in part on necessity. Modern business depends on recorded data, electronic entries, or written documents. The record is often a composite of information gleaned from many sources, and admitting it obviates the need to take the time for testimony from all who participated in making it, and spares the hours of business and working people who would otherwise spend time in court to give evidence on narrow points. A witness who made the record, who maintains the record, or one who uses the record can authenticate the business record.

The reason counsel want to introduce business records at trial is, most often, to get the jury to believe -- or at least to see -- facts contained within those records. Thus, counsel need to call a witness who can explain how those records are kept to support the inference that the information contained in those records is accurate. The witness does not need to be aware of the specific assertions contained within the records; he simply has to be able to identify the record and the reasons for which it was kept.

It may be that counsel seeks to introduce a record the authenticity of which is *presumed*. The drill here is simpler, and does not require a sponsoring witness.

Once counsel establishes the authenticity of a ***record***, counsel must establish that the contents of the report are admissible as an exception to the hearsay rule. Moreover, counsel will see that there is a good deal of overlap between the foundations for authentication and for the hearsay exception. Indeed, laying the hearsay foundation usually serves to authenticate the record.

This rule excludes secondary evidence of a writing's contents. Where a writing's terms are in issue. In that instance counsel must either produce an original or duplicate or show the excuse for the non-production of the originals and present an admissible type of secondary evidence. While this rule is not applicable simply because a document may be offered into evidence, counsel must consider this rule whenever a document may be used.

Counsel should remember, as part of their case preparation, to think through the items of evidence they intend to introduce, the reason that they intend to introduce such evidence, and possible objections. Obviously, counsel must be able to describe an item of evidence and explain its relevance to the court, yet counsel must always remember that relevance is not the only test for admissibility. Counsel should remember that they can use the absence of information that would normally be present in the business record as proof that the test, event or issue in question did not occur.

In the case of business and government records, the rules of evidence impose several requirements. First, the records must be authenticated: That is, counsel must demonstrate that the records are what counsel says that they are. Second, counsel must remember that the declarations contained within a business record are out-of-court declarations offered to prove the truth of the matter contained in those records, and, thus, hearsay. Consequently, counsel must establish that the records meet an applicable hearsay exception. Finally, if the terms of the record itself are in issue, the Best Evidence ("original document") Rule may apply.

Counsel come across these rules when trying to introduce a commonly used law enforcement document such as a chain-of-custody form typically offered through the police evidence custodian. The chain-of-custody form is the document that goes with an item of evidence through the various stages of the investigation (seizure, testing, etc.). The chain-of-custody helps to show relevance and to show that the item being offered in court is the item that was seized and tested by the government (identifying the item is easy if it is something distinctive, like a gun or a knife; more difficult if the item is more generic, like drugs).

Remember that fungible, otherwise referred to as non-unique evidence, requires a chain of custody. It becomes admissible after a showing of continuous custody that preserves the evidence in an unaltered state. For unique evidence, so long as your witness testifies to the unique characteristic, "I scratched my initials and date on the handle of the knife," you don't need a chain of custody. **Lab tests** are presumed to be trustworthy under the business records exception (FRE 803(6)) because the lab applies independent standards and is not part of a "prosecution team." However, there maybe confrontation issues with the results of the lab test as discussed in the previous chapter concerning hearsay and confrontation.

When dealing with lab reports and fungible evidence the chain of custody must link the fungible evidence to the document. Though lab reports are admissible under FRE 902(4a) they do not have probative value -- they are not authenticated as pertaining to a particular person or item of evidence -- until they are **linked** with the evidence identified on the chain of custody form. Ensure you cross-reference the specimen or evidence number on the chain of custody with the report received from the lab.

Example: Chain-of-custody using a lab report

Have counsel lay a foundation first for the chain-of-custody document. They should authenticate the baggies of heroin and then satisfy the hearsay requirements by asking the witness appropriate questions. After doing this counsel lays a foundation for the lab report through a self-**authenticating** certificate. Counsel should lay a foundation for the lab report as a self-authenticating report. They should then realize they must draft a self-authenticating certificate, attach it to the exhibit, and then offer it with the proper foundation. A sample certificate is also attached.

The facts: The accused, Mr. James, is charged with drug distribution. On July 15th of last year, James sold heroin to an undercover agent, Bond. The state has the drugs, in a baggie marked with Bond's initials. The state wishes to offer the chain-of-custody; the document that tracks the substance from the seizure by undercover agent Bond through the evidence custodian, detective Bean, to the drug lab back to detective Bean. It also has the laboratory report, describing the results of tests done on the heroin.

Q. As the evidence custodian, did you receive the bag of heroin in this case?
A. Yes.

Q. From whom?
A. Agent Bond.

Q. When?
A. On July 15th of last year, the night of the drug bust.

Q. Did you make a record when you received the evidence?
A. Yes.

Q. What did you do with it after you received it?
A. I placed it in the evidence room.

Q. Who has access to that room?
A. I do. It's locked when I'm not there. Everyone has to sign out evidence from me if they want to take it from the evidence room

Q. Did you at some point send the evidence to the Crime Lab?
A. Yes, I did.

Q. How did you send it to the lab?
A. I sent it by registered mail.

Q. Did you make a record when you sent the drugs to the laboratory?
A. Yes.

Q. Did you later receive the evidence back from the lab?
A. Yes.

Q. Did you record that as well?
A. Yes.

Q. Did you record all of this information regarding the movement of the evidence on the same document?
A. Yes.

Q. What is that document?
A. It's a CoC Form 92, an evidence/property document or a chain-of-custody document.

Q. What's the purpose of this form?
A. To track a piece of evidence as it goes from one person or one office to the next.

Q. Is such a form used for every piece of evidence processed by your office?
A. Yes.

Q.   ***I'm handing you Prosecution Exhibit 10 for Identification. What is that?***
A.   *It's CoC Form 92, the chain-of-custody document for the heroin.*

Q.   ***Does your name appear on this document?***
A.   *Yes.*

Q.   ***Where does it appear the first time?***
A.   *The first time it appears is in the right column on the first line, under the "received by" column.*

Q.   ***Is that your name and signature?***
A.   *Yes, it is.*

Q.   ***Did you enter your name and signature when you received the evidence from Agent Bond?***
A.   *Yes, I did.*

Q.   ***Is that the normal procedure -- to make the entry each time the evidence is transferred?***
A.   *Yes, it is.*

Q.   ***What is the entry to the left of yours?***
A.   *It's the name and signature of Agent Bond.*

Q.   ***What do these two entries mean?***
A.   *They mean that Agent Bond handed the suspected heroin to me on the fifteenth of July.*

Q.   ***You mentioned that you later sent the evidence to the laboratory. Is that reflected on the form?***
A.   *Yes, it is.*

Q.   ***Please explain.***
A.   *Notice on the next line I placed the evidence in the evidence room. Then you see the entry with my name showing it was shipped by registered mail with the registered mail number and the notation in the right column "transmitted to crime lab for examination."*

Q.   ***And then you mentioned you later received the evidence again. Is that reflected on this form?***
A.   *Yes.*

Q.   ***Where?***
A.   *If you look on the back of the form, after all of the notations made at the lab, you notice that I received the evidence in registered mail and placed it in the evidence room.*

Q.   ***Again your signature appears next to those entries. Did you make the entries at the time?***
A.   *Yes.*

Q. **When the evidence came back from the lab with the chain-of-custody document, Prosecution Exhibit 10 for Identification, did any other documents come with it?**
A. Yes.

Q. **What other documents?**
A. A laboratory report showing the results of testing performed on the evidence.

Q. **Did that document come with a certification letter?**
A. Yes.

Q. **What letterhead appeared on that certificate?**
A. The letterhead is from the State Criminal Investigation Laboratory.

Q. **Who signed the certificate?**
A. Mr. Ferguson.

Q. **What is his position?**
A. He's the records custodian at the lab.

Q. **Was anything attached to the certificate signed by Mr. Ferguson?**
A. Yes.

Q. **What was attached?**
A. A laboratory report showing the results of testing done on the suspected heroin.

Q. **Do you normally receive such reports in response to a request for testing of evidence?**
A. Yes.

Q. **Was the report you received on this occasion similar in format to other such reports you have received from the laboratory in the past?**
A. Yes.

Q. **Did you personally open the envelope containing the evidence, the chain-of-custody document and the report from the lab?**
A. Yes.

Q. **I'm now handing you Prosecution Exhibit 11 for Identification, a two page document. What is it?**
A. It's the certificate from Mr. Ferguson showing that the laboratory report is attached.

Q. **What does the lab report pertain to?**
A. It pertains to the bag of suspected heroin we sent to the lab.

Q. **How do you know this?**
A. Compare the specimen number noted in the top right hand corner of the chain-of-custody document.

Q. **Prosecution Exhibit 10 for Identification?**
A. Yes. Compare that specimen number on the chain-of-custody document with the specimen number mentioned in the cover letter from the lab and on the lab report that is attached to that letter.

Q. On Prosecution Exhibit 11 for Identification?

A. *Yes. They are the same, meaning it's the same piece of evidence.*

Q. I'm withdrawing Prosecution Exhibits 10 and 11 from the witness Your Honor, the state asks that these two exhibits be admitted into evidence as Prosecution Exhibits 10 and 11.

J. *Defense, any objection?*

DC.*Yes, Your Honor. I object on the ground that there has been insufficient authentication of the lab report. No sponsoring witness from the lab has verified the authenticity of this lab report.*

J. *State?*

C. Your Honor, testimony from a lab expert is unnecessary. The law generally presumes that public officials have properly performed their duties and that their purported signatures and seals are presumed genuine. This lab report is authenticated through the evidence custodian and under FRE 902(4a) by the attesting certificate attached to the document that indicates that the report is a true and accurate copy.

J. *Objection overruled. Prosecution Exhibit 10 for ID is admitted as P.E. 10.*

C. Your Honor, at this point I would like to hand prosecution exhibits 10 and 11 to the jury members and inform them of the results of the test on the heroin.

J. *Go ahead.*

C. Please note that the lab report states that the substance in the evidence pouch numbered 200xx-STA96523 tested by the laboratory was heroin.

HEARSAY EXCEPTIONS – DECLARANT UNAVAILABLE
Rule 804. Exceptions to the Rule Against Hearsay--When the Declarant Is Unavailable as a Witness

> (a) Criteria for Being Unavailable. A declarant is considered to be unavailable as a witness if the declarant:
>
> (1) is exempted from testifying about the subject matter of the declarant's statement because the court rules that a privilege applies;
>
> (2) refuses to testify about the subject matter despite a court order to do so;
>
> (3) testifies to not remembering the subject matter;
>
> (4) cannot be present or testify at the trial or hearing because of death or a then-existing infirmity, physical illness, or mental illness; or
>
> (5) is absent from the trial or hearing and the statement's proponent has not been able, by process or other reasonable means, to procure:

(A) the declarant's attendance, in the case of a hearsay exception under Rule 804(b)(1) or (6); or

(B) the declarant's attendance or testimony, in the case of a hearsay exception under Rule 804(b)(2), (3), or (4).

But this subdivision (a) does not apply if the statement's proponent procured or wrongfully caused the declarant's unavailability as a witness in order to prevent the declarant from attending or testifying.

(b) The Exceptions. The following are not excluded by the rule against hearsay if the declarant is unavailable as a witness:

(1) Former Testimony. Testimony that:

(A) was given as a witness at a trial, hearing, or lawful deposition, whether given during the current proceeding or a different one; and

(B) is now offered against a party who had--or, in a civil case, whose predecessor in interest had--an opportunity and similar motive to develop it by direct, cross-, or redirect examination.

(2) Statement Under the Belief of Imminent Death. In a prosecution for homicide or in a civil case, a statement that the declarant, while believing the declarant's death to be imminent, made about its cause or circumstances.

(3) Statement Against Interest. A statement that:

(A) a reasonable person in the declarant's position would have made only if the person believed it to be true because, when made, it was so contrary to the declarant's proprietary or pecuniary interest or had so great a tendency to invalidate the declarant's claim against someone else or to expose the declarant to civil or criminal liability; and

(B) is supported by corroborating circumstances that clearly indicate its trustworthiness, if it is offered in a criminal case as one that tends to expose the declarant to criminal liability.

(4) Statement of Personal or Family History. A statement about:

(A) the declarant's own birth, adoption, legitimacy, ancestry, marriage, divorce, relationship by blood, adoption, or marriage, or similar facts of personal or family history, even though the declarant had no way of acquiring personal knowledge about that fact; or

(B) another person concerning any of these facts, as well as death, if the declarant was related to the person by blood, adoption, or marriage or was so intimately associated with the person's family that the declarant's information is likely to be accurate.

(5) [Other Exceptions.] [Transferred to Rule 807.]

(6) Statement Offered Against a Party That Wrongfully Caused the Declarant's Unavailability. A statement offered against a party that wrongfully caused--or acquiesced in wrongfully causing--the declarant's unavailability as a witness, and did so intending that result.

The primary rationale for the hearsay rule is that the opponent has not had an opportunity to test the out of court statement by cross-examination. However, when the opponent of the statement had an opportunity and similar motive to develop the testimony by direct, cross, or direct examination in a prior trial or hearing, former testimony is admissible as an exception to hearsay.

The first step is to establish unavailability. Federal rule of Evidence 804(a) defines "unavailability." Under FRE 804, there are two categories of unavailable witnesses: (1) the witness is absent from the trial; or (2) the witness is present but provides no testimony. These two categories are furthered divided into six situations concerning hearings.

- **Situation 1**: The declarant is exempted by ruling of the judge on the ground of privilege from testifying concerning the subject matter of the declarant's statement.

- **Situation 2**: The declarant persists in refusing to testify concerning the subject matter of the declarant's statement despite an order of the military judge to do so.

- **Situation 3**: The declarant testifies to a lack of memory of the subject matter of the declarant's statement.

- **Situation 4**: The declarant is unable to be present to testify at the hearing because of death or then existing physical or mental illness or infirmity.

- **Situation 5**: The declarant is absent from the hearing and the proponent of the statement has been unable to procure the declarant's attendance (or in the case of FRE 804b(2), (3), or (4), the proponent has been unable to procure the declarant's attendance or testimony) by process or other reasonable means.

- **Situation 6**: The declarant is unavailable for reasons of "death, age, sickness, bodily infirmity, imprisonment, non amenability to process, or other reasonable cause, inability or refusal to appear and testify in person at the trial or hearing."

When the witness' absence from trial is caused by the proponent in an attempt to prevent the witness from attending or testifying at the trial, the witness will not be considered unavailable under FRE 804(b)(4)-(6). Once unavailability is established: (1) a witness' testimony from a prior hearing of the same or different proceeding, or in a deposition taken in compliance with law in the course of the same or another proceeding, is admissible into evidence; (2) if the party against whom the testimony is now offered had an opportunity and similar motive to develop the testimony by direct, cross, or redirect examination.

The opponent in the current trial (second hearing) must have had the opportunity to question the witness in the prior hearing (first hearing). How does it work? Consider the following:

At a deposition, a witness testified that he saw the accused when he stole several CDs from the store. The accused and lawyer were present at the deposition and defense lawyer thoroughly cross-examined the witness on his testimony. On the date of the trial the witness was unavailable under FRE 804(a). The prosecution can use the earlier deposition testimony against the accused at trial because the accused had a fair opportunity for confrontation and cross-examination of the witness at the earlier deposition. Under FRE 804(b)(1), the identity of the parties must be the same. The defense lawyer had an opportunity and similar motive to develop witness A's testimony by cross-examination.

The foundation for unavailability is relatively easy to establish. Lawyers should ensure that the declarant in the first three instances, or a third party witness in the last thee situations 4-6 provides the evidence supporting unavailability. This prevents the counsel from assuming the role of a witness in the case. Under FRE 804(a)(4)-(6), the counsel should assign the duty of locating a potentially unavailable witness to another counsel or a legal clerk. They should keep detailed records of the steps taken to produce the witness in order meet the Confrontation Clause requirement that the prosecution make a good faith effort to obtain the witness for trial.

Elements of the foundation for unavailability in FRE 803(4)(a) (1)–(3)

For the first three situations in Rule 804(a), the witnesses are technically unavailable because they provide no testimony but are physically present at the second hearing, just not legally present.

- *Under FRE 804(a)(1), the witness is deemed unavailable because the judge has recognized his or her assertion of a privilege from testifying. In this case, the witness from hearing #1 takes the stand in hearing #2, but the witness properly refuses to testify on the ground of privilege.*

- *Under FRE 804(a)(2), the witness is considered unavailable if he or she persists in refusing to testify despite an order from the court to do so. In this case, the witness does not have a legitimate ground for refusing to answer.*

- *Under FRE 804(a)(3), the witness is unavailable when he or she testifies to a lack of memory of the subject matter of the declarant's statement. The witness is physically present, but is unavailable because he or she has no recall regarding the declarant's statement.*

In all the situations listed above the proponent must ensure that the record reflects the witness' refusal or inability to testify.

FRE 804(a)(4) establishes that a witness is unavailable to be present or to testify because of "death or then existing physical or mental illness or infirmity." The following issues apply when dealing with FRE 804(a)(4):

- *If the witness is dead, the proponent may prove this fact by introducing a properly certified death certificate.*

- *If the witness is ill, under FRE 104(a), the court may permit the proponent to prove the illness by a physician's affidavit, declaration or letter. Otherwise, the proponent may call the physician to prove the witness' illness, after laying the expert opinion testimony foundation.*

FRE 804(a)(5) provides that a declarant is considered unavailable when the witness "is absent from the hearing and the proponent has been unable to procure their attendance … by process or other reasonable means." The trick is in identifying the proper witness and laying the correct foundation. The witness to lay the foundation is either (1) the process server that could not locate the witness despite several attempts to contact said witness at their last known address, or (2) another individual that can testify that the witness lives in another jurisdiction, cannot be compelled to appear at in court, and refuses to appear voluntarily, despite several offers to pay her expenses to return.

FRE 804(a)(6) indicates that a declarant may be unavailable by reason of "death, age, sickness, bodily infirmity, imprisonment, nonamenability to process or other reasonable cause, an inability or refusal to appear and testify in person at the place of the trial or hearing...." In this case, the evidence depends on the specific reason for the unavailability.

When the state is attempting to offer the statement of the witness pursuant to FRE 804(a)(4)-(6), potential confrontation clauses may be implicated. When the declarant does not testify at trial, the proponent must make sure the statements satisfy the accused's Sixth Amendment right to confront witnesses. The Sixth Amendment requires that the state make a good faith effort to produce a witness at trial to satisfy the Confrontation Clause where the use of these exceptions is contemplated. At a minimum the proponent of the evidence may overcome the potential confrontation clause issues by showing that:

- If there is no possibility of procuring a witness, good faith demands nothing further of the prosecution.

- If, however, a remote possibility exists that a witness may be procured, the state must take affirmative measures to produce the declarant.

  - The proponent must argue:

  - The out of court statement is firmly rooted in an 804 exception, or

  - It passes the residual trustworthiness test.

It is not necessary to use live testimony to authenticate the transcript from the first hearing if the record is authenticated under FRE 902. A court reporter can prepare a certificate of authentication for a verbatim transcript of any of the above records prior to trial. The verbatim transcript does not go with the jury to the deliberation room. The proponent could use the testimony of someone who heard firsthand the testimony in the first hearing.

To rely on this evidence for unavailability, the state must show that good faith efforts have been used to produce the declarant. The proponent can show that there was no compulsory process to compel the former witness' attendance at trial. At trial, the judge can take judicial notice of the constitutional and statutory provisions setting out the territorial limits of the court's compulsory process. The proponent must also show that the proponent unsuccessfully attempted to persuade the former witness to voluntarily attend the hearing or that any attempt would probably be futile. Note that FRE 804(a)(5) expressly requires the proponent to attempt to use "other reasonable means."

Example: Foundation for Unavailability in a child abuse prosecution

The facts: The accused is on trial for child abuse. The former witness, Ms. Tanya Chapman, is the accused's girl friend and the mother of the child victim. She testified at a preliminary hearing in the same case. Since testifying at that investigation she has vehemently refused to testify against the accused. She has taken a trip to the Caribbean and is outside the jurisdiction of the court for compulsory process. The prosecution calls the clerk of the prosecution office, Mr. Doug Smith, to establish Ms. Chapman's refusal to voluntarily appear and the state's inability to subpoena her.

Q.   Where does Ms. Chapman live now?

A.   In Houston, Texas.

Q.   How do you know that?

A.   She provided her forwarding address when she left after the preliminary hearing.

Q.   How do you know that she resides at this address?

A.   I contacted her by telephone after the trial date was set and attempted to get her to return.

Q.   How do you know that you spoke with her on the telephone?

A.   She identified herself and I recognized her voice. A few days before the preliminary hearing she came into our office for an appointment with the Victim-Witness Liaison and I directed her to his office.

Q.   Where is Ms. Chapman today?

A.   I can't say for sure but I believe she is in the Caribbean.

Q.   Why isn't Ms. Chapman here today?

A.   She refused to come and we could not subpoena her.

Q.   What attempts did you make to get her to return?

A.   I contacted her on three separate occasions before trial. Each time I told her that the state would pay her expenses if she would return to testify at the trial. Each time she refused the offer to return. She said,

DC: Objection.

At this point, defense may object that the witness' next answer provides hearsay. Counsel should respond that the testimony is not offered to prove the truth of the matter asserted but to show the effect on the state of mind of the witness. The issue is whether the clerk acted reasonably and made good faith efforts to procure the witness' attendance at trial. The objection should be overruled.

Q.   *What did she say?*
A.   *She said she would never testify against the accused again.*

Q.   *Was Ms. Chapman actually issued any tickets to return?*
A.   *Yes, I told her that we would be sending her some tickets. Our office obtained the tickets and tickets were sent. I mailed them to Ms. Chapman, with a letter stating that the state would pay her expenses. She returned the contents of that letter to our office in another envelope.*

Q.   *Thank you. I have no further questions.*

J: *Defense?*

DC: No questions, Your Honor.

C: Your Honor, we request that you find that Ms. Chapman is unavailable for purposes of Rule 804(a). We have made reasonable and diligent attempts to get Ms. Chapman to return. She is simply not available to us as a witness. We have her deposition testimony and if you find her unavailable, we intend to offer that prior testimony under FRE 804(b)(1).

J: *I find that Ms. Chapman is unavailable for trial. Any other attempts would most likely be futile. We cannot subpoena her, therefore, I cannot issue a warrant of attachment and she has verbally expressed her intent not to return verbally and by returning the invitational tickets.*

Now that the prosecution has established unavailability under FRE 804, they want to offer Ms.

Chapman's verbatim preliminary hearing testimony by seeking to introduce a verbatim transcript of her testimony. The prosecution calls the clerk who transcribed the preliminary hearing, Ms. Cheryl Chandler. She prepared the transcript.

Q.   **Ms. Chandler, Where were you on the afternoon of September 7, of last year?**
A.   *I was the court reporter at a hearing in this case.*

Q.   **Who was present at this hearing?**
A.   *The accused, his defense counsel, the prosecutor, and myself.*

Q.   **Is the accused present here today?**
A.   *Yes.*

C: *Let the record reflect that the witness has identified the accused.*

Q.   **What happened at this hearing that you attended on September 7th?**
A.   *The prosecution called witnesses to testify.*

Q.   **What did the state do when they first called the witnesses to the stand?**
A.   *They would swear the witnesses.*

Q.   **Who questioned the witnesses?**
A.   *Both the state and the defense counsel.*

Q.   **What was the counsel's name that cross-examined the witnesses?**
A.   *Mr. Grant, the defense counsel.*

Q.   **Who were the witnesses that day?**
A.   *A doctor, a psychologist, Ms. Chapman, and her daughter.*

Q.   **How long was Ms. Chapman on the stand?**
A.   *About two hours.*

Q.   **Was Ms. Chapman put under oath?**
A.   *Yes.*

Q.   **Did the DC cross-examine her?**
A.   *Yes.*

Q.   **How long did defense counsel cross-examine Ms. Chapman?**
A.   *About seventy minutes.*

Q.   **How much of her testimony did you hear?**
A.   *All of it. I was present during her entire testimony.*

Q. **What happened after you closed the hearing?**
A. *I transcribed the recorded tapes of the hearing.*

C: *(Taking prosecution exhibit #2 for identification and showing it to defense counsel and the judge.)*
Your honor may I approach the witness?

J: *Yes, you may counsel.*

Q. **Ms. Chandler, I am showing you what has been marked as prosecution exhibit number two for identification, do you recognize it?**
A. *Yes, I do. It is a portion of the transcript. It is Mrs. Chapman's testimony from that hearing.*

Q. **How do you recognize it?**
A. *It is exactly the same transcript of her testimony that I transcribed and read.*

Q. **Does the transcript accurately reflect what Ms. Chapman said during her testimony?**
A. *Yes.*

Q. **Is the transcript verbatim?**
A. *Yes.*

Q. **Is the transcript in the same condition as when you received it?**
A. *Yes, it appears exactly as it did when I made it.*

C: *Your honor, I offer prosecution exhibit number two for identification into evidence as prosecution exhibit number two.*

DC: *Your Honor, I object to the introduction of the exhibit on the ground that the exhibit is hearsay.*

J: *Counsel approach the bench.*

C: *Your Honor, I concede that the exhibit is hearsay. However, it falls within the former testimony exception under FRE 804 and is admissible into evidence. It is a copy of the verbatim transcript of Ms. Chapman's preliminary hearing testimony. Ms. Chandler has testified that it is a verbatim copy of the testimony that she heard and later transcribed.*

J: *Where is the foundation for the former testimony exception?*

C: *The transcription is a record of Ms. Chapman's prior testimony. The parties were the same as ones as in this hearing. The accused and counsel were present as shown by the transcription. I've already introduced evidence to show that she is unavailable under FRE 804(a). The transcription shows that Ms. Chapman was sworn before she testified. The seventy-minute cross-examination shows that the defense had an opportunity and motive to cross-examine Ms. Chapman.*

J: *The objection will be overruled, and the exhibit will be received.*

FRE 804(b)(1)

FRE 804(b)(1) creates an exception for prior testimony by someone who is unavailable at trial where two conditions are satisfied. First, the exception only reaches testimony given in a proceeding. Second, the party against whom that testimony is now offered must have had an opportunity and similar motive to "develop" the testimony by examining the witness at the earlier time. In criminal cases, use of the former testimony exception against the accused raises constitutional issues.

Consider the following case that dealt with the application of a hearsay exception where the declarant must be unavailable for admissibility to occur.

AN APPELLATE COURT SPEAKS

296 F.3d 1, United States Court of Appeals, First Circuit
Theodore TRIGONES, Petitioner, Appellant,
v.
Lynn BISSONNETTE, Superintendent, North Central Correctional Institution,
Respondent, Appellee.
No. 00-2504.Heard March 5, 2002.Decided July 10, 2002

Opinion

LYNCH, Circuit Judge.

This is a habeas corpus case involving a state prisoner and raising Confrontation Clause questions. The district court denied habeas relief; we find the question closer, but affirm the denial of relief because the state court decision affirming petitioner's murder conviction cannot be said to be an unreasonable application of clearly established federal law, as determined by the Supreme Court.

I.

On July 1, 1983, a thirteen-year-old babysitter, Erica Forestiere, was stabbed to death between 12:30 a.m. and 2:30 a.m. while her two young charges slept upstairs. In 1984, a state court jury convicted Theodore J. Trigones of the crime, finding him guilty of first degree murder. He was sentenced to life imprisonment without parole.

Trigones's defense at trial was that the father of the children, Leo Trzcinski Jr., intending to kill his estranged wife, had mistakenly killed Forestiere, the babysitter. Trigones testified that, on the night of the murder, he went to the Trzcinski residence, where he encountered Trzcinski sitting near the already dead babysitter.

Later that night, Trigones spoke with his stepfather, Roland Weed. At a pretrial hearing on Trigones's motion to suppress, Weed testified that Trigones, in the early morning hours following the murder, had said "I've done something terrible" or "I did something terrible." At that same hearing, Weed also testified that he understood Trigones to say "I killed someone," and that Trigones said something like "[t]here's a lot of hate in me" and "if it wasn't her it would have been somebody else."

The only purpose of this pretrial hearing was to determine whether Trigones's statements to Weed were voluntary and products of a rational intellect, given Trigones's contemporaneous drug and alcohol ingestion. The trial court found the statements voluntary and admissible.

Trigones was denied the opportunity to confront Weed at trial. An edited version of the transcript of Weed's suppression hearing testimony was read to the jury, over Trigones's objection, when Weed exercised his Fifth Amendment rights by refusing to testify at trial. Trigones sought interlocutory relief on the question of the admissibility of the Weed testimony and lost.

At trial, Trigones testified and pointed the finger at Trzcinski. Trigones also attempted to counter Weed's statement. He testified that what he had said to Weed was not that he, Trigones, had killed someone, but that it was Trzcinski who had killed someone, although, in the conversation with Weed, Trigones did not name Trzcinski as the killer. Trigones testified that he had told Weed that there is a lot of hate in him, meaning Trzcinski, and that, if it wasn't her (the babysitter), he, again meaning Trzcinski, would have killed someone else. Trzcinski also testified and provided a version of the facts which, if credited, exculpated him. The jury had the opportunity to hear from both Trigones and Trzcinski and to evaluate which witness to believe and who was the killer.

Weed's testimony, read into evidence at trial, was an important element of the Commonwealth's case. Trigones's alleged confession, as recounted by Weed, was a significant part of the evidence tending to show that Trigones, rather than Trzcinski, committed the murder. Indeed, as the federal district court that heard this habeas petition noted, "Weed's testimony recounting [Trigones's] alleged confession was likely some of the most damning evidence." _Trigones v. Hall,_ 115 F.Supp.2d 158, 171 (D.Mass.2000). The differences between Trigones's version of his statement to Weed and Weed's version of Trigones's statement make all the difference, according to Trigones, because Trigones's version is an admission only to being an accessory after the fact, whereas Weed's version is an admission that Trigones committed the murder himself.

The jury convicted Trigones, and the Supreme Judicial Court of Massachusetts ("SJC") affirmed the jury's verdict on appeal, _Commonwealth v. Trigones, 397 Mass. 633, 492 N.E.2d 1146 (1986)._ The SJC rejected Trigones's argument that, under the Confrontation Clause, the court should not have admitted Weed's statement. *5 _Id._ at 1150. It concluded that, under _Ohio v. Roberts, 448 U.S. 56, 100 S.Ct. 2531, 65 L.Ed.2d 597 (1980),_ the testimony was admissible because Weed was unavailable2 to testify at trial and his suppression hearing testimony bore adequate indicia of reliability. _Trigones,_ 492 N.E.2d at 1149-50.

In 1991 Trigones filed a new trial motion based on ineffective assistance of counsel. The trial court initially denied the motion without a hearing. A single justice of the SJC then denied Trigones's motion for leave to appeal the denial, but remanded to the trial court for an evidentiary hearing because the justice could not make the requisite ineffective assistance of counsel determination on the record as it existed at the time. The trial court held an evidentiary hearing at which Trigones's trial counsel testified. After this hearing, the trial court again denied the motion and a single justice of the SJC then denied Trigones's motion for leave to appeal. Trigones next filed an unsuccessful action in the SJC for a declaration that it was unconstitutional to deny him the right to appeal from the denial of the new trial motion. _Trigones v. Attorney Gen., 420 Mass. 859, 652 N.E.2d 893 (1995)._

In 1997, some thirteen years after his conviction, Trigones sought federal habeas corpus relief. He argues that the admission into evidence of the transcript of Weed's testimony denied him his rights under the Confrontation Clause of the Sixth Amendment to cross-examine Weed at trial. The district court denied the writ, holding 1) that it was bound by what it considered the SJC's not-clearly-erroneous factual conclusion that Trigones abandoned his bias line of questioning at the suppression hearing and 2) that Trigones had failed to raise before the state courts his argument that his counsel had lacked a similar motive to cross-examine at the suppression hearing. *Trigones,* 115 F.Supp.2d at 172-73.

Although Trigones's argument is far from frivolous, we affirm the district court's denial. In light of the particular circumstances of this case, we cannot say that the SJC's conclusion was unreasonable.

II.

Trigones makes a two-part argument: (1) that admission at trial of the Weed transcript violated his Sixth Amendment right to confront Weed; and (2) that the SJC's decision that there was no Sixth Amendment violation was either "contrary to, or involved an unreasonable application of, clearly established Federal law, as determined by the Supreme Court of the United States." 28 U.S.C. § 2254(d)(1) (2000).

There is no credible argument that this case fits within the "contrary to" framework of analysis. *See Williams v. Taylor,* 529 U.S. 362, 405-06, 120 S.Ct. 1495, 146 L.Ed.2d 389 (2000); *Hurtado v. Tucker,* 245 F.3d 7, 15 (1st Cir.), *cert. denied,* 534 U.S. 925, 122 S.Ct. 282, 151 L.Ed.2d 208 (2001). This is simply because Trigones has not shown that the SJC's decision "arrives at a conclusion opposite to that reached by [the Supreme] Court on a question of law." *Williams,* 529 U.S. at 405, 120 S.Ct. 1495; *see also Bell v. Cone,* 535 U.S. 685, 122 S.Ct. 1843, 1850, 152 L.Ed.2d 914 (2002). Nor has he shown that the SJC "confront[ed] facts that are materially indistinguishable from a relevant Supreme Court precedent and arrive [d] at a[n opposite] result." *Williams,* 529 U.S. at 405, 120 S.Ct. 1495; *see also Bell,* 122 S.Ct. at 1850. Because the SJC adjudicated the constitutional claim on its merits, we apply the deferential, statutory "unreasonable application" test, 28 U.S.C. § 2254(d)(1),4 and do not review the SJC's constitutional conclusion de novo. *Cf. Fortini v. Murphy,* 257 F.3d 39, 47 (1st Cir.2001) (stating that "we can hardly defer to the state court on an issue that the state court did not address"), *cert. denied,* 535 U.S. 1018, 122 S.Ct. 1609, 152 L.Ed.2d 623 (2002). Even an incorrect state court decision is not necessarily an "unreasonable" one for habeas purposes. *Williams,* 529 U.S. at 410, 120 S.Ct. 1495 (stating that "an *unreasonable* application of federal law is different from an *incorrect* application of federal law"); *see also Bell,* 122 S.Ct. at 1850.

The "unreasonable application" issue is measured against the Sixth Amendment's requirements for the admission of prior preliminary judicial hearing testimony of a witness who is unavailable at trial. The Sixth Amendment's Confrontation Clause states that "[i]n all criminal prosecutions, the accused shall enjoy the right ... to be confronted with the witnesses against him." U.S. Const. amend. VI. It applies to the states through the Fourteenth Amendment's Due Process Clause. *Pointer v. Texas,* 380 U.S. 400, 403, 85 S.Ct. 1065, 13 L.Ed.2d 923 (1965).

The Confrontation Clause does not prohibit the admission of all hearsay evidence. *Idaho v. Wright,* 497 U.S. 805, 813-14, 110 S.Ct. 3139, 111 L.Ed.2d 638 (1990); *Mattox v. United States,* 156 U.S. 237, 15 S.Ct. 337, 39 L.Ed. 409 (1895). Although "a literal interpretation of the Confrontation Clause could bar the use of any out-of-court statements when the declarant is unavailable, [the Supreme] Court has rejected that view as 'unintended and too extreme.' " *Bourjaily v. United States,* 483 U.S. 171, 182, 107 S.Ct. 2775, 97 L.Ed.2d 144 (1987) (quoting *Roberts,* 448 U.S. at 63, 100 S.Ct. 2531). "[T]here has traditionally been an exception to the confrontation requirement where a witness is unavailable and has given testimony at previous judicial proceedings against the same defendant which was subject to cross-examination by that defendant." *Barber v. Page,* 390 U.S. 719, 722, 88 S.Ct. 1318, 20 L.Ed.2d 255 (1968). That is because "the right of cross-examination initially afforded provides substantial compliance with the purposes behind the confrontation requirement." *Id.*5

Where hearsay evidence is offered, and that evidence consists of testimony by an unavailable declarant, the Confrontation Clause requires that the proponent (here the Commonwealth) show that the transcribed testimony from the preliminary judicial hearing bears adequate "indicia of reliability," sufficient to offset the lack of cross-examination. *Roberts,* 448 U.S. at 65-66, 100 S.Ct. 2531 (quoting *Dutton v. Evans,* 400 U.S. 74, 89, 91 S.Ct. 210, 27 L.Ed.2d 213 (1970) (plurality)); *see also Wright,* 497 U.S. at 815-25, 110 S.Ct. 3139 (applying the *Roberts* framework); *2 McCormick on Evidence §* *252, at 123-24 (J.W. Strong ed., 5th ed.1999)* (outlining the Confrontation Clause's standard for admission of prior testimony). Adequate indicia are shown if the proffered testimony "falls within a firmly rooted ... exception" to the hearsay prohibition or if the proponent of the evidence makes a showing of "particularized guarantees of trustworthiness." *Roberts,* 448 U.S. at 66, 100 S.Ct. 2531. If the testimony is within a firmly rooted hearsay exception, then it has adequate indicia of reliability, without more. *White v. Illinois,* 502 U.S. 346, 355 n. 8, 112 S.Ct. 736, 116 L.Ed.2d 848 (1992); *Roberts,* 448 U.S. at 66, 100 S.Ct. 2531.

The federal and state hearsay rules, although they do not control the constitutional inquiry, are instructive because they outline the contours of the firmly rooted hearsay exception at issue in this case. We have previously concluded that Fed.R.Evid. 804(b)(1) codifies a firmly rooted exception to the hearsay prohibition, and so evidence admissible under Rule 804(b)(1) is, "by definition, not vulnerable to a challenge based upon the Confrontation Clause." *United States v. McKeeve,* 131 F.3d 1, 9 (1st Cir.1997).

The Federal Rules provide that former testimony is not excluded by the hearsay prohibition if the declarant is unavailable as a witness and "the party against whom the testimony is now offered ... had an opportunity and similar motive to develop the testimony." Fed.R.Evid. 804(b)(1); *see generally 2 McCormick on Evidence, supra, §* *304, at 296-97* (stating that "the issues in the first proceeding, and hence the purpose for which the testimony was offered, must have been such as to produce an adequate motive for testing on cross-examination the credibility of the testimony"). The Massachusetts rule is similar. *See Commonwealth v. Meech,* 380 Mass. 490, 403 N.E.2d 1174, 1177-78 (1980); *Trigones,* 492 N.E.2d at 1149-50; P.J. Liacos et al., *Handbook of Massachusetts Evidence* § 8.7.1, at 489 (7th ed.1999) (stating that "[p]rior testimony ... is admissible if it was given under oath in a proceeding where the issues were substantially the same as in the current proceeding and the party against whom it is offered had an opportunity and a similar motive to cross-examine the witness").

Even if the motives to develop the testimony are dissimilar, that does not end the Confrontation Clause inquiry. Although a showing of sufficiently dissimilar motives removes the testimony from the "firmly rooted ... exception" analysis by placing the testimony outside of Rule 804(b)(1) or any other firmly rooted hearsay exception, the testimony may still be analyzed for "particularized guarantees of trustworthiness" and, if such guarantees are found, admitted into evidence. *Roberts,* 448 U.S. at 66, 100 S.Ct. 2531; *see also Lee v. Illinois,* 476 U.S. 530, 543, 106 S.Ct. 2056, 90 L.Ed.2d 514 (1986) (stating that hearsay evidence that does not fall within a firmly rooted exception may nonetheless be admitted without violating the Confrontation Clause upon a showing that it has particularized guarantees of trustworthiness). If the testimony is not within a firmly rooted exception, then the proponent must show particularized guarantees of trustworthiness rendering the contested hearsay statement at least as reliable as a statement admissible under a firmly rooted exception. *Wright,* 497 U.S. at 821, 110 S.Ct. 3139 (citing *Roberts,* 448 U.S. at 66, 100 S.Ct. 2531).6

The SJC correctly articulated the federal constitutional standards; the only issue, then, on federal habeas review is whether the SJC unreasonably applied those standards.

III.

Trigones, in his habeas appeal, argues that the admission of the Weed transcript violated his Sixth Amendment rights because he was unable to cross-examine Weed on two issues: (1) pro-Commonwealth bias and (2) Weed's ability to recollect accurately the statements Weed recounted. We address bias below, and find that Trigones has failed to exhaust his argument pertaining to Weed's ability to recollect (except to the extent that he is alleging an inaccuracy in Weed's recollection due to bias, as distinguished from inaccuracies resulting from other imperfections in Weed's ability to have perceived and recalled Trigones's statement, such as lack of memory or inability to hear the statements at the time they were allegedly made). The SJC concluded that Trigones's "sole argument" was that "Weed's testimony lacked reliability because he was not fully cross-examined on the possibility that he may have lied in order to protect his wife and himself from prosecution as accessories to the crime." *Trigones,* 492 N.E.2d at 1150. After closely examining Trigones's arguments presented to the SJC, we agree that Trigones did not make his "inability to recollect" argument before the SJC and hence, for reasons of lack of exhaustion, he may not raise it now. *Scarpa v. DuBois,* 38 F.3d 1, 6 (1st Cir.1994).7

Trigones argued before the SJC that the admission of the Weed transcript violated his Sixth Amendment rights because he was unable to cross-examine Weed on the bias issue. He claimed that his suppression motion sought to exclude Weed's testimony-recounting Trigones's statements after the murder-because Weed's testimony also showed that Trigones was intoxicated on drugs and alcohol and could not have made a voluntary statement. Bias, Trigones argued to the SJC, was not an issue at the suppression hearing, but would have been an issue at trial if Weed had testified. The asserted bias was in favor of the Commonwealth, and brought about by the interests of Weed and his wife in avoiding being charged "as accessories after the fact to murder." *Trigones,* 492 N.E.2d at 1148.

The SJC addressed three issues: (1) "the extent of the asserted restriction of cross-examination," (2) the "Sixth Amendment principles governing the admission of Weed's recorded testimony," and (3) "whether ... the constitutional standard was satisfied." *Id.* It concluded there was no constitutional violation, *id.* at 1150, finding that Trigones had an opportunity to cross-examine Weed on bias, although, "[p]erhaps for tactical reasons, defense counsel ... acquiesced in the judge's suggestion of irrelevance and abandoned that line of questioning," *id.* at 1149. The SJC noted that there had been some limited examination on bias at the suppression hearing. *Id.* at 1148-49. As to motive, the SJC concluded that Trigones "should have had the same motive to cross-examine Weed at the pretrial hearing on the relevant issue of bias ... as he would have had if Weed had testified in person at trial." *Id.* at 1150.

These conclusions, if correct (or, for habeas purposes, at least reasonable), were sufficient under clearly established Supreme Court law for the SJC to reject Trigones's Confrontation Clause argument. The SJC, however, proceeded to address whether Weed's testimony should nonetheless be excluded because Trigones did not adequately pursue his opportunity to cross-examine Weed on bias, and concluded that cross-examination on this point would not have made a difference. *Id.* We hold that the SJC's conclusions on opportunity and similar motive were not unreasonable and therefore conclude that Weed's testimony fell within a firmly rooted hearsay exception. Because it would not have been unreasonable for the SJC to stop the analysis there, given that the Supreme Court has not resolved whether an unexercised opportunity is sufficient to satisfy the Confrontation Clause's requirements, *Roberts,* 448 U.S. at 61-62, 70-71, 100 S.Ct. 2531, we conclude without the need to address the SJC's holding that cross-examination on bias at trial would not have made a difference.

A. Opportunity to Cross-Examine Weed on Bias

The question whether Trigones had an opportunity to pursue his bias line of questioning at the suppression hearing is a very close one. Even if, faced with the issue on direct appeal, we would have resolved the issue differently, we cannot say that the SJC's conclusion as to opportunity was unreasonable.

The question whether Trigones's counsel, regardless of his motive, had a sufficient opportunity to cross-examine Weed at the suppression hearing turns on one's interpretation of the following exchange, which occurred at the suppression hearing, between counsel (Mr. Delinsky) and Weed, immediately followed by an exchange between counsel and the trial judge:

Q: Were you told at that time that Mrs. Weed could not be prosecuted ... for helping somebody after a crime was committed because she was a blood relative and a mother? Were you told that by the Police?

A: No, I wasn't.

Q: Were you told that by the District Attorney?

THE COURT: Now wait, Mr. Delinsky, please. Let's assume that all of this happened that you're asking him. What relevance does it have to this hearing?

DELINSKY: I'll go on.

Q: Now,-

THE COURT: No, I mean tell me. What relevance does it have? The only thing that I've got to decide in this is was his statement that of a rational intellect and I'm going to let the jury listen.

DELINSKY: I agree.

THE COURT: And what he told his wife and what his wife did or what he did has got absolutely nothing to do with this hearing. Now when we get in front of the jury as to what caused him to make this statement, that's a different story. I'm not going to stop you there.

DELINSKY: Okay, thank you.

One view of this colloquy, not unreasonable, is that counsel had an opportunity to engage in the bias line of questioning, but chose not to pursue it. When the trial judge first asked counsel "[w]hat relevance does [this line of questioning] have to this hearing?" counsel's only response was "I'll go on," apparently meaning that he would proceed to a different topic. The judge, refusing to permit counsel to abandon his line of questioning so easily, asked counsel a second time, "[w]hat relevance does [this line of questioning] have?" The judge explained his own reason for thinking that the bias-related question was not relevant, stating "[t]he only thing that I've got to decide in this is was his statement that of a rational intellect." At this point, counsel did not rebut the judge's suggestion of lack of relevance, but instead stated "I agree."

As the SJC concluded, _Trigones, 492 N.E.2d at 1149,_ Weed's purported pro-Commonwealth bias was of course relevant at the suppression hearing, even though the suppression hearing was limited to the rational intellect question. Pro-Commonwealth bias would tend to diminish the credibility of any of Weed's statements favoring the

Commonwealth, and to enhance the force of any of Weed's statements favoring Trigones. Upon prompting by the trial judge to describe the relevance of the bias line of questioning to the suppression hearing, counsel could have pointed this out. Instead, counsel acquiesced.

We might have decided the opportunity issue differently were it raised on direct appeal, given that counsel might plausibly be understood to have acquiesced not in the face of an invitation to explain the relevance of his inquiry, but rather in light of the trial judge's final conclusion that the line of questioning was not relevant. This alternative characterization of the colloquy is strengthened by the trial judge's reassuring statement to counsel that "when we get in front of the jury as to what caused him to make this statement, that's a different story. I'm not going to stop you there."

But the SJC's conclusion that defense counsel, perhaps for tactical reasons, acquiesced and abandoned the bias line of questioning despite the trial judge's invitation to explain its relevance is not "unreasonable" as that term has been interpreted under § 2254. Similarly, the conclusion that an opportunity, though hardly used, is sufficient to qualify as an "opportunity" to cross-examine for purposes of the Confrontation Clause is not unreasonable. *See Roberts,* 448 U.S. at 61-62, 70-71, 73 n. 12, 100 S.Ct. 2531; *Siegfriedt v. Fair,* 982 F.2d 14, 19 (1st Cir.1992) (citing *Delaware v. Fensterer,* 474 U.S. 15, 20, 106 S.Ct. 292, 88 L.Ed.2d 15 (1985) (per curiam), and *Roberts,* 448 U.S. at 73 n. 12, 100 S.Ct. 2531); Fed.R.Evid. 804 advisory committee's note (stating "no unfairness is apparent in requiring [a party] to accept his own prior ... decision not to cross-examine").

B. Similarity of Motive to Cross-Examine Weed on Bias

In this case, the similarity of motive question is a complicated one. Our analysis differs substantially from the SJC's, but we again conclude that the SJC's position was not unreasonable.

At first cut, there appears to be a substantial argument that Trigones's motive to cross-examine Weed on bias at the suppression hearing was significantly different from the motive he would have had at trial. Weed's suppression hearing testimony that Trigones was incoherent and irrational tended to favor Trigones, who was then trying to prove that his confession was not the product of a rational intellect and, for that reason, should be suppressed. At the suppression hearing, the truth of Weed's rendition of Trigones's statement was not at issue. The only issue was whether Trigones's alcohol and drug intoxication rendered whatever statements he made involuntary. The limited scope of the suppression hearing is evident from the text of Trigones's original motion to suppress, the trial judge's statements at the suppression hearing, and the trial judge's ruling on the motion to suppress, all of which were limited to the issue of voluntariness.

At trial, in contrast, the truth of Weed's testimony about the content of the inculpatory statements was certainly at issue and, when credited, that testimony hurt Trigones. It formed an important part of the evidence tending to implicate Trigones, rather than Trzcinski, in the murder. At trial, one could argue that Trigones had an incentive to attack Weed's credibility and thereby undermine his harmful testimony, whereas at the suppression hearing Trigones had an incentive to defend Weed's credibility and thereby bolster his helpful testimony. Such differences can make for *12 dissimilar motives. *Cf. United States v. Bartelho,* 129 F.3d 663, 672 (1st Cir.1997) (concluding that similar motive to cross-examine did not exist when, "[a]lthough [the witness's] credibility was generally at issue in each proceeding, ... the more particular points [counsel] sought to make were quite different").

But the SJC's contrary position, that Trigones "should have had the same motive to cross-examine Weed at the pretrial hearing on the relevant issue of bias in favor of the

Commonwealth as he would have had if Weed had testified in person at trial," *Trigones, 492 N.E.2d at 1150,* is not unreasonable. At both the suppression hearing and at trial Trigones had an incentive to paint Weed as biased in favor of the Commonwealth. Such a characterization would tend to diminish the credibility of any of Weed's statements favoring the Commonwealth. It would also tend to enhance the force of any of Weed's statements favoring Trigones because any such statements, made despite pressure to testify unfavorably to Trigones, could be characterized as all the more believable in light of Weed's incentive to testify contrary to Trigones's interests. At the suppression hearing, showing Weed's pro-Commonwealth bias could only have helped Trigones, by showing that Weed was willing to describe Trigones as unable to make rational statements-testimony helping Trigones-despite his incentive to provide testimony favoring the Commonwealth, and perhaps by casting doubt on whether Trigones even made the exact statements that Weed recounted.

For these reasons, it is not unreasonable to conclude that Trigones had a motive at the suppression hearing to cross-examine Weed on the issue of pro-Commonwealth bias similar to the motive he would have had at trial. True, the stakes at trial would have been higher, but the stakes are almost always higher then (or at least different), and it is clear that in many cases the motive at a preliminary hearing is sufficiently similar to the motive at trial to bring the evidence within the Confrontation Clause's requirements, *e.g., Roberts,* 448 U.S. at 72-73, 100 S.Ct. 2531; *California v. Green,* 399 U.S. 149, 165, 90 S.Ct. 1930, 26 L.Ed.2d 489 (1970). *See generally* 5 *Weinstein's Federal Evidence* § 804.04[5] (J.M. McLaughlin ed., 2d ed.2002) (stating that "similar motive does not mean identical motive"). In addition, the stakes were also high at the suppression hearing, where, if Trigones had successfully asserted his involuntariness argument, the inculpatory statements could have been kept out altogether. Trigones could only have been helped by showing Weed's bias against him.

The more simplistic characterization-that Trigones had a motive to paint Weed as truthful at the suppression hearing, but as a liar at trial-is not necessarily the best characterization because it fails adequately to account for the nuances of Trigones's bias argument. Trigones's argument was never that Weed was a liar. Rather, his argument was that the import of Weed's testimony turned on the small details, those small details were matters of recollection, and Weed's recollection could easily have been tilted against him as a result of Weed's desire to please the Commonwealth and thereby avoid prosecution of himself or his wife as an accessory after the fact to murder. Trigones had a motive to cross-examine Weed on this subtle pro-Commonwealth bias at the suppression hearing and would have had a similar motive to cross-examine on this point at trial. It was not unreasonable to conclude that he had a motive to cross-examine on this subject matter at the suppression hearing similar to the motive he would have had at trial.

In light of this conclusion, we hold that the SJC reasonably concluded that Weed's testimony was admissible under the firmly rooted exception to the hearsay rule for prior recorded testimony. This finding alone suffices to reject Trigones's Confrontation Clause challenge and we need not address the SJC's resolution of whether Trigones's pursuit of the bias point would have made a difference.

IV.

The Supreme Court's Confrontation Clause cases have sought to accommodate competing interests. Those interests include both allowing the prosecution to present material, reliable evidence and preserving the accuracy of the judicial process through the defendant's exercise of his rights to confront and cross-examine adverse witnesses. The SJC's conclusion that there was no Confrontation Clause violation is within the range of reasonable judgments which may be reached. The state court decision is not an unreasonable application of clearly established federal law, as determined by the Supreme Court.

We *affirm* the district court order denying the writ of habeas corpus.

FOR DISCUSSION

1. Now that you have read both the Confrontation clause cases and this case are you convinced that the Supreme Court's Confrontation Clause doctrine works?

2. What are the problems with it?

3. How would you fashion a better rule?

CONCLUSION

In the last three chapters we have discussed the fundamental precepts of Hearsay doctrine, to include what is a statement, how the confrontation clause works, and when statements that qualify as hearsay are nonetheless admissible at trial.

Chapter 14: The Federal Rules of Evidence

Article I: General Provisions

Rule 101. Scope; Definitions

(a) Scope. These rules apply to proceedings in United States courts. The specific courts and proceedings to which the rules apply, along with exceptions, are set out in Rule 1101.

(b) Definitions. In these rules:

(1) "civil case" means a civil action or proceeding;

(2) "criminal case" includes a criminal proceeding;

(3) "public office" includes a public agency;

(4) "record" includes a memorandum, report, or data compilation;

(5) a "rule prescribed by the Supreme Court" means a rule adopted by the Supreme Court under statutory authority; and

(6) a reference to any kind of written material or any other medium includes electronically stored information.

Credits (Pub.L. 93-595, § 1, Jan. 2, 1975, 88 Stat. 1929; Mar. 2, 1987, eff. Oct. 1, 1987; Apr. 25, 1988, eff. Nov. 1, 1988; Apr. 22, 1993, eff. Dec. 1, 1993; Apr. 26, 2011, eff. Dec. 1, 2011.)

ADVISORY COMMITTEE NOTES
(Edited for clarity and current applicability)
1972 Proposed Rules

Rule 1101 specifies in detail the courts, proceedings, questions, and stages of proceedings to which the rules apply in whole or in part (now including bankruptcy judges).

2011 Amendments
The language of Rule 101 has been amended, and definitions have been added, as part of the general restyling of the Evidence Rules to make them more easily understood and to make style and terminology consistent throughout the rules. These changes are intended to be stylistic only. There is no intent to change any result in any ruling on evidence admissibility.

The reference to electronically stored information is intended to track the language of Fed. R. Civ. P. 34.

The Style Project
The Evidence Rules are the fourth set of national procedural rules to be restyled. The restyled Rules of Appellate Procedure took effect in 1998. The restyled Rules of Criminal Procedure took effect in 2002. The restyled Rules of Civil Procedure took effect in 2007. The restyled Rules of Evidence apply the same general drafting guidelines and principles used in restyling the Appellate, Criminal, and Civil Rules.

Formatting Changes.
Many of the changes in the restyled Evidence Rules result from using format to achieve clearer presentations. The rules are broken down into constituent parts, using progressively indented

subparagraphs with headings and substituting vertical for horizontal lists. "Hanging indents" are used throughout. These formatting changes make the structure of the rules graphic and make the restyled rules easier to read and understand even when the words are not changed. Rules 103, 404(b), 606(b), and 612 illustrate the benefits of formatting changes.

No Substantive Change.
The Committee made special efforts to reject any purported style improvement that might result in a substantive change in the application of a rule. The Committee considered a change to be "substantive" if any of the following conditions were met:

a. Under the existing practice in any circuit, the change could lead to a different result on a question of admissibility (e.g., a change that requires a court to provide either a less or more stringent standard in evaluating the admissibility of particular evidence);

b. Under the existing practice in any circuit, it could lead to a change in the procedure by which an admissibility decision is made (e.g., a change in the time in which an objection must be made, or a change in whether a court must hold a hearing on an admissibility question);

c. The change would restructure a rule in a way that would alter the approach that courts and litigants have used to think about, and argue about, questions of admissibility (e.g., merging Rules 104(a) and 104(b) into a single subdivision); or

d. It changes a "sacred phrase"--one that has become so familiar in practice that to alter it would be unduly disruptive to practice and expectations. Examples in the Evidence Rules include "unfair prejudice" and "truth of the matter asserted."

Rule 102. Purpose

These rules should be construed so as to administer every proceeding fairly, eliminate unjustifiable expense and delay, and promote the development of evidence law, to the end of ascertaining the truth and securing a just determination.

Credits (Pub.L. 93-595, § 1, Jan. 2, 1975, 88 Stat.1929; Apr. 26, 2011, eff. Dec. 1, 2011.)

ADVISORY COMMITTEE NOTES
(Edited for clarity and current applicability)
1972 Proposed Rules
The purpose clause is modeled on other procedural rules. For similar provisions see Rule 2 of the Federal Rules of Criminal Procedure, Rule 1 of the Federal Rules of Civil Procedure, California Evidence Code § 2, and New Jersey Evidence Rule 5.

2011 Amendments
The language of Rule 102 has been amended as part of the restyling of the Evidence Rules to make them more easily understood and to make style and terminology consistent throughout the rules. These changes are intended to be stylistic only. There is no intent to change any result in any ruling on evidence admissibility.

Rule 103. Rulings on Evidence

(a) Preserving a Claim of Error. A party may claim error in a ruling to admit or exclude evidence only if the error affects a substantial right of the party and:

(1) if the ruling admits evidence, a party, on the record:

(A) timely objects or moves to strike; and

(B) states the specific ground, unless it was apparent from the context; or

(2) if the ruling excludes evidence, a party informs the court of its substance by an offer of proof, unless the substance was apparent from the context.

(b) Not Needing to Renew an Objection or Offer of Proof. Once the court rules definitively on the record--either before or at trial--a party need not renew an objection or offer of proof to preserve a claim of error for appeal.

(c) Court's Statement About the Ruling; Directing an Offer of Proof. The court may make any statement about the character or form of the evidence, the objection made, and the ruling. The court may direct that an offer of proof be made in question-and-answer form.

(d) Preventing the Jury from Hearing Inadmissible Evidence. To the extent practicable, the court must conduct a jury trial so that inadmissible evidence is not suggested to the jury by any means.

(e) Taking Notice of Plain Error. A court may take notice of a plain error affecting a substantial right, even if the claim of error was not properly preserved.

Credits (Pub.L. 93-595, § 1, Jan. 2, 1975, 88 Stat. 1929; Apr. 17, 2000, eff. Dec. 1, 2000; Apr. 26, 2011, eff. Dec. 1, 2011.)

ADVISORY COMMITTEE NOTES
(Edited for clarity and current applicability)
FRE 103(a) establishes that rulings on evidence cannot be assigned as error unless (1) a substantial right is affected, and (2) the nature of the error was called to the attention of the judge, so as to alert him to the proper course of action and enable opposing counsel to take proper corrective measures. The objection and the offer of proof are the techniques for accomplishing these objectives. The status of constitutional error as harmless or not is treated in Chapman v. California, 386 U.S. 18, 87 S.Ct. 824, 17 L.Ed.2d 705 (1967).

The purpose of 103(b) is to reproduce for an appellate court, insofar as possible, a true reflection of what occurred in the trial court. The second sentence is in part derived from the final sentence of Rule 43(c). It is designed to resolve doubts as to what testimony the witness would have in fact given, and, in nonjury cases, to provide the appellate court with material for a possible final disposition of the case in the event of reversal of a ruling which excluded evidence.

FRE 103[c] works on the assumption that a ruling which excludes evidence in a jury case is likely to be a pointless procedure if the excluded evidence nevertheless comes to the attention of the jury. See Bruton v. United States, 389 U.S. 818, 88 S.Ct. 126, There is no requirement that the issue be preserved in the presence of the jury. In fact, the judge can foreclose a particular line of testimony and counsel can protect the record without a series of questions before the jury, designed at best to waste time and at worst "to waft into the jury box" the very matter sought to be excluded.

FRE 103(d) is a plain error rule, restated from Rule 52(b) of the Federal Rules of Criminal Procedure. It is a principle that has been applied in both criminal and civil cases. Generally speaking the plain error rule will be more likely with respect to the admission of evidence than to exclusion, since failure to comply with normal requirements of offers of proof is likely to produce a record which simply does not disclose the error.

The 2000 amendment to this rule made it clear that this rule applies to all rulings on evidence whether they occur at or before trial, including so-called "in limine" rulings. Prior to the 2000 amendment it was not clear whether or not counsel would have to raise an objection again during trial to preserve it on appeal. It is now clear that raises the issue during a motion in limine is sufficient. The amendment provides that a claim of error with respect to a definitive ruling is preserved for review when the party has otherwise satisfied the objection or offer of proof requirements of Rule 103(a). When the ruling is definitive, a renewed objection or offer of proof at the time the evidence is to be offered is more a formalism than a necessity and is therefore not required to preserve the issue. Counsel must make certain that the judge has definitively ruled on the motion, and not merely "reserved ruling" depending upon the testimony of witnesses. If the court has reserved ruling then the objection must be made again to preserve the issue for appeal. Counsel are also responsible for seeking clarification as to whether an in limine or other evidentiary ruling is definitive when there is doubt on that point.

Counsel should note that even where the court's ruling is definitive, nothing in the amendment prohibits the court from revisiting its decision when the evidence is to be offered. If the court changes its initial ruling, or if the opposing party violates the terms of the initial ruling, objection must be made when the evidence is offered to preserve the claim of error for appeal. The error, if any, in such a situation occurs only when the evidence is offered and admitted.

A definitive advance ruling is reviewed in light of the facts and circumstances before the trial court at the time of the ruling. If the relevant facts and circumstances change materially after the advance ruling has been made, those facts and circumstances cannot be relied upon on appeal unless they have been brought to the attention of the trial court by way of a renewed, and timely, objection, offer of proof, or motion to strike.

Rule 104. Preliminary Questions

(a) In General. The court must decide any preliminary question about whether a witness is qualified, a privilege exists, or evidence is admissible. In so deciding, the court is not bound by evidence rules, except those on privilege.

(b) Relevance That Depends on a Fact. When the relevance of evidence depends on whether a fact exists, proof must be introduced sufficient to support a finding that the fact does exist. The court may admit the proposed evidence on the condition that the proof be introduced later.

(c) Conducting a Hearing So That the Jury Cannot Hear It. The court must conduct any hearing on a preliminary question so that the jury cannot hear it if:

(1) the hearing involves the admissibility of a confession;

(2) a defendant in a criminal case is a witness and so requests; or

(3) justice so requires.

(d) Cross-Examining a Defendant in a Criminal Case. By testifying on a preliminary question, a defendant in a criminal case does not become subject to cross-examination on other issues in the case.

(e) Evidence Relevant to Weight and Credibility. This rule does not limit a party's right to introduce before the jury evidence that is relevant to the weight or credibility of other evidence.

Credits (Pub.L. 93-595, § 1, Jan. 2, 1975, 88 Stat.1930; Mar. 2, 1987, eff. Oct. 1, 1987; Apr. 26, 2011, eff. Dec. 1, 2011.)

ADVISORY COMMITTEE NOTES
(Edited for clarity and current applicability)

FRE 104(a) addresses preliminary questions. The applicability of a particular rule of evidence often depends upon the existence of a condition. Is the alleged expert a qualified physician? Is a witness whose former testimony is offered unavailable? Was a stranger present during a conversation between attorney and client? In each instance the admissibility of evidence will turn upon the answer to the question of the existence of the condition. The judge is responsible for making these determinations.

When necessary to determine preliminary questions the judge acts as a trier of fact. Usually rulings on evidence call for an evaluation in terms of a legal standard. For example, when a hearsay statement is offered as a declaration against interest, the court must decide whether the statement possesses the required against-interest characteristics. FRE 104 places that decision in the hands of the judge.

When the question is factual the court will receive evidence on both sides of the issue prior to ruling. When doing so the court is not generally bound by the rules of evidence, given that the jury is not present and therefore the concerns about poisoning the jury's deliberations are not relevant. This view is reinforced by practical necessity in certain situations. An item, offered and objected to, may itself be considered in ruling on admissibility, though not yet admitted in evidence. Thus, the content of an asserted declaration against interest must be considered in ruling whether it is against interest. Finally, when applying FRE 104(a) the court must also consider the specific provisions for conditional relevancy.

FRE 104(b) addresses the concept of conditional relevancy. In some situations, the relevancy of an item of evidence, in the large sense, depends upon the existence of a particular preliminary fact. Thus when a spoken statement is relied upon to prove notice to X, it is without probative value unless X heard it. Or if a letter purporting to be from Y is relied upon to establish an admission by him, it has no probative value unless Y wrote or authorized it. Relevance in this sense has been labelled "conditional relevancy." The judge makes a preliminary determination whether the foundation evidence is sufficient to support a finding of fulfillment of the condition. If so, the item is admitted. If after all the evidence on the issue is in, pro and con, the jury could reasonably conclude that fulfillment of the condition is not established, the issue is for them. If the evidence is not such as to allow a finding, the judge withdraws the matter from their consideration by instructing them to disregard the testimony in question. Counsel should always keep in mind that the judge has the ability to control the order of proof at trial.

FRE 104[c] deals with the problems presented when a criminal defendant wishes to testify during a preliminary hearing on an issue relating to the exclusion of evidence. In that case, the testimony is offered for the limited purpose of of the hearing, and will not necessarily be admissible at trial. The situation is different when dealing with other witnesses.

When the witness at the preliminary hearing is not the defendant, a detailed treatment of when preliminary matters should be heard outside the hearing of the jury is not feasible. The procedure is time consuming. Not infrequently the same evidence which is relevant to the issue of establishment of fulfillment of a condition precedent to admissibility is also relevant to weight or credibility, and time is saved by taking foundation proof in the presence of the jury. Much evidence on preliminary questions, though not relevant to jury issues, may be heard by the jury with no adverse effect. A great deal must be left to the discretion of the judge who will act as the interests of justice require.

The limitation upon cross-examination is designed to encourage participation by the accused in the determination of preliminary matters. He may testify concerning them without exposing himself to cross-examination generally. The provision is necessary because of the breadth of cross-examination under Rule 611(b).

Under rule 104(c) the hearing on a preliminary matter may at times be conducted in front of the jury. Should an accused testify in such a hearing, waiving his privilege against self-incrimination as to the preliminary issue, rule 104(d) provides that he will not generally be subject to cross-examination as to any other issue. This rule is not, however, intended to immunize the accused from cross-examination where, in testifying about a preliminary issue, he injects other issues into the hearing. If he could not be cross-examined about any issues gratuitously raised by him beyond the scope of the preliminary matters, injustice might result. Accordingly, in order to prevent any such unjust result, the committee intends the rule to be construed to provide that the accused may subject himself to cross-examination as to issues raised by his own testimony upon a preliminary matter before a jury.

Rule 105. Limiting Evidence That Is Not Admissible Against Other Parties or for Other Purposes

If the court admits evidence that is admissible against a party or for a purpose-- but not against another party or for another purpose--the court, on timely request, must restrict the evidence to its proper scope and instruct the jury accordingly.

Credits (Pub.L. 93-595, § 1, Jan. 2, 1975, 88 Stat. 1930; Apr. 26, 2011, eff. Dec. 1, 2011.)

ADVISORY COMMITTEE NOTES
(Edited for clarity and current applicability)
A close relationship exists between this rule and Rule 403 which requires exclusion when "probative value is substantially outweighed by the danger of unfair prejudice, confusion of the issues, or misleading the jury." The present rule recognizes the practice of admitting evidence for a limited purpose and instructing the jury accordingly. The availability and effectiveness of this practice must be taken into consideration in reaching a decision whether to exclude for unfair prejudice under Rule 403.

Rule 106. Remainder of or Related Writings or Recorded Statements

If a party introduces all or part of a writing or recorded statement, an adverse party may require the introduction, at that time, of any other part--or any other writing or recorded statement--that in fairness ought to be considered at the same time.

Credits (Pub.L. 93-595, § 1, Jan. 2, 1975, 88 Stat. 1930; Mar. 2, 1987, eff. Oct. 1, 1987; Apr. 26, 2011, eff. Dec. 1, 2011.)

ADVISORY COMMITTEE NOTES
(Edited for clarity and current applicability)
The rule is an expression of the rule of completeness. It is, for the most part, a restatement of Rule 32(a)(4) of the Federal Rules of Civil Procedure. The rule is based on two considerations. The first is the misleading impression created by taking matters out of context. The second is the inadequacy of repair work when delayed to a point later in the trial. The rule does not in any way circumscribe the right of the adversary to develop the matter on cross-examination or as part of his own case. While the rule is limited to writings and recorded statements and does not apply to conversations, the common law has applied the same concepts to conversations

Article II: Judicial Notice

Rule 201. Judicial Notice of Adjudicative Facts

(a) Scope. This rule governs judicial notice of an adjudicative fact only, not a legislative fact.

(b) Kinds of Facts That May Be Judicially Noticed. The court may judicially notice a fact that is not subject to reasonable dispute because it:

(1) is generally known within the trial court's territorial jurisdiction; or

(2) can be accurately and readily determined from sources whose accuracy cannot reasonably be questioned.

(c) Taking Notice. The court:

(1) may take judicial notice on its own; or

(2) must take judicial notice if a party requests it and the court is supplied with the necessary information.

(d) Timing. The court may take judicial notice at any stage of the proceeding.

(e) Opportunity to Be Heard. On timely request, a party is entitled to be heard on the propriety of taking judicial notice and the nature of the fact to be noticed. If the court takes judicial notice before notifying a party, the party, on request, is still entitled to be heard.

(f) Instructing the Jury. In a civil case, the court must instruct the jury to accept the noticed fact as conclusive. In a criminal case, the court must instruct the jury that it may or may not accept the noticed fact as conclusive.

Credits (Pub.L. 93-595, § 1, Jan. 2, 1975, 88 Stat. 1930; Apr. 26, 2011, eff. Dec. 1, 2011.)

ADVISORY COMMITTEE NOTES
(Edited for clarity and current applicability)
Note to Subdivision (a). This is the only evidence rule on the subject of judicial notice. It deals only with judicial notice of "adjudicative" facts. No rule deals with judicial notice of "legislative" facts. Judicial notice of matters of foreign law is treated in Rule 44.1 of the Federal Rules of Civil Procedure and Rule 26.1 of the Federal Rules of Criminal Procedure.

The omission of any treatment of legislative facts results from fundamental differences between adjudicative facts and legislative facts. Adjudicative facts are simply the facts of the particular case. Legislative facts, on the other hand, are those which have relevance to legal reasoning and the lawmaking process, whether in the formulation of a legal principle or ruling by a judge or court or in the enactment of a legislative body. The terminology was coined by Professor Kenneth Davis in his article An Approach to Problems of Evidence in the Administrative Process, 55 Harv.L.Rev. 364, 404-407 (1942). The following discussion draws extensively upon his writings. In addition, see the same author's Judicial Notice, 55 Colum.L.Rev. 945 (1955); Administrative Law Treatise, ch. 15 (1958); A System of Judicial Notice Based on Fairness and Convenience, in Perspectives of Law 69 (1964).

The usual method of establishing adjudicative facts is through the introduction of evidence, ordinarily consisting of the testimony of witnesses. If particular facts are outside the area of reasonable controversy, this process is dispensed with as unnecessary. A high degree of indisputability is the essential prerequisite.

Legislative facts are quite different. As Professor Davis says:

"My opinion is that judge-made law would stop growing if judges, in thinking about questions of law and policy, were forbidden to take into account the facts they believe, as distinguished from facts which are 'clearly * * * within the domain of the indisputable.' Facts most needed in thinking about difficult problems of law and policy have a way of being outside the domain of the clearly indisputable." A System of Judicial Notice Based on Fairness and Convenience, supra, at 82.

An illustration is Hawkins v. United States, 358 U.S. 74, 79 S.Ct. 136, 3 L.Ed.2d 125 (1958), in which the Court refused to discard the common law rule that one spouse could not testify against the other, saying, "Adverse testimony given in criminal proceedings would, we think, be likely to destroy almost any marriage." This conclusion has a large intermixture of fact, but the factual aspect is scarcely "indisputable." See Hutchins and Slesinger, Some Observations on the Law of Evidence--Family Relations, 13 Minn.L.Rev. 675 (1929). If the destructive effect of the giving of adverse testimony by a spouse is not indisputable, should the Court have refrained from considering it in the absence of supporting evidence?

"If the Model Code or the Uniform Rules had been applicable, the Court would have been barred from thinking about the essential factual ingredient of the problems before it, and such a result would be obviously intolerable. What the law needs at its growing points is more, not less, judicial thinking about the factual ingredients of problems of what the law ought to be, and the needed facts are seldom 'clearly' indisputable." Davis, supra, at 83.

Professor Morgan gave the following description of the methodology of determining domestic law:

"In determining the content or applicability of a rule of domestic law, the judge is unrestricted in his investigation and conclusion. He may reject the propositions of either party or of both parties. He may consult the sources of pertinent data to which they refer, or he may refuse to do so. He may make an independent search for persuasive data or rest content with what he has or what the parties present. * * * [T]he parties do no more than to assist; they control no part of the process." Morgan, Judicial Notice, 57 Harv.L.Rev. 269, 270-271 (1944).

This is the view which should govern judicial access to legislative facts. It renders inappropriate any limitation in the form of indisputability, any formal requirements of notice other than those already inherent in affording opportunity to hear and be heard and exchanging briefs, and any requirement of formal findings at any level. It should, however leave open the possibility of introducing evidence through regular channels in appropriate situations. See Borden's Farm Products Co. v. Baldwin, 293 U.S. 194, 55 S.Ct. 187, 79 L.Ed. 281 (1934), where the cause was remanded for the taking of evidence as to the economic conditions and trade practices underlying the New York Milk Control Law.

Similar considerations govern the judicial use of non-adjudicative facts in ways other than formulating laws and rules. Thayer described them as a part of the judicial reasoning process.

"In conducting a process of judicial reasoning, as of other reasoning, not a step can be taken without assuming something which has not been proved; and the capacity to do this with competent judgment and efficiency, is imputed to judges and juries as part of their necessary mental outfit." Thayer, Preliminary Treatise on Evidence 279-280 (1898).

As Professor Davis points out, A System of Judicial Notice Based on Fairness and Convenience, in Perspectives of Law 69, 73 (1964), every case involves the use of hundreds or thousands of non-evidence facts. When a witness in an automobile accident case says "car," everyone, judge and jury included, furnishes, from non-evidence sources within himself, the supplementing information that the "car" is an automobile, not a railroad car, that it is self-propelled, probably by an internal combustion engine, that it may be assumed to have four wheels with pneumatic rubber tires, and so on. The judicial process cannot construct every case from scratch, like Descartes creating a world based on the postulate Cogito, ergo sum. These items could not possibly be introduced into evidence, and no one suggests that they be. Nor are they appropriate subjects for any formalized treatment of judicial notice of facts. See Levin and Levy, Persuading the Jury with Facts Not in Evidence: The Fiction-Science Spectrum, 105 U.Pa.L.Rev. 139 (1956).

Another aspect of what Thayer had in mind is the use of non-evidence facts to appraise or assess the adjudicative facts of the case. Pairs of cases from two jurisdictions illustrate this use and also the difference between non-evidence facts thus used and adjudicative facts. In People v. Strook, 347 Ill. 460, 179 N.E. 821 (1932), venue in Cook County had been held not established by testimony that the crime was committed at 7956 South Chicago Avenue, since judicial notice would not be taken that the address was in Chicago. However, the same court subsequently ruled that venue in Cook County was established by testimony that a crime occurred at 8900 South Anthony Avenue, since notice would be taken of the common practice of omitting the name of the city when speaking of local addresses, and the witness was testifying in Chicago. People v. Pride, 16 Ill.2d 82, 156 N.E. 2d 551 (1951). And in Hughes v. Vestal, 264 N.C. 500, 142 S.E.2d 361 (1965), the Supreme Court of North Carolina disapproved the trial judge's admission in evidence of a state-published table of automobile stopping distances on the basis of judicial notice, though the court itself had referred to the same table in an earlier case in a "rhetorical and illustrative" way in determining that the defendant could not have stopped her car in time to avoid striking a child who suddenly appeared in the highway and that a nonsuit was properly granted. Ennis v. Dupree, 262 N.C. 224, 136 S.E.2d 702 (1964). See also Brown v. Hale, 263 N.C. 176, 139 S.E.2d 210 (1964); Clayton v. Rimmer, 262 N.C. 302, 136 S.E.2d 562 (1964). It is apparent that this use of non-evidence facts in evaluating the adjudicative facts of the case is not an appropriate subject for a formalized judicial notice treatment.

In view of these considerations, the regulation of judicial notice of facts by the present rule extends only to adjudicative facts.

What, then, are "adjudicative" facts? Davis refers to them as those "which relate to the parties," or more fully:

"When a court or an agency finds facts concerning the immediate parties--who did what, where, when, how, and with what motive or intent--the court or agency is performing an adjudicative function, and the facts are conveniently called adjudicative facts. * * *

"Stated in other terms, the adjudicative facts are those to which the law is applied in the process of adjudication. They are the facts that normally go to the jury in a jury case. They relate to the parties, their activities, their properties, their businesses." 2 Administrative Law Treatise 353.

Note to Subdivision (b). With respect to judicial notice of adjudicative facts, the tradition has been one of caution in requiring that the matter be beyond reasonable controversy. This tradition of circumspection appears to be soundly based, and no reason to depart from it is apparent. As Professor Davis says:

"The reason we use trial-type procedure, I think, is that we make the practical judgment, on the basis of experience, that taking evidence, subject to cross-examination and rebuttal, is the best way to resolve controversies involving disputes of adjudicative facts, that is, facts pertaining to the parties. The reason we require a determination on the record is that we think fair procedure in resolving disputes of adjudicative facts calls for giving each party a chance to meet in the appropriate fashion the facts that come to the tribunal's attention, and the appropriate fashion for meeting disputed adjudicative facts includes rebuttal evidence, cross-examination, usually confrontation, and argument (either written or oral or both). The key to a fair trial is opportunity to use the appropriate weapons (rebuttal evidence, cross-examination, and argument) to meet adverse materials that come to the tribunal's attention." A System of Judicial Notice Based on Fairness and Convenience, in Perspectives of Law 69, 93 (1964).

The rule proceeds upon the theory that these considerations call for dispensing with traditional methods of proof only in clear cases. Compare Professor Davis' conclusion that judicial notice should be a matter of convenience, subject to requirements of procedural fairness. Id., 94.

This rule is consistent with Uniform Rule 9(1) and (2) which limit judicial notice of facts to those "so universally known that they cannot reasonably be the subject of dispute," those "so generally known or of such common notoriety within the territorial jurisdiction of the court that they cannot reasonably be the subject of dispute," and those "capable of immediate and accurate determination by resort to easily accessible sources of indisputable accuracy." The traditional textbook treatment has included these general categories (matters of common knowledge, facts capable of verification), McCormick §§ 324, 325, and then has passed on into detailed treatment of such specific topics as facts relating to the personnel and records of the court, Id. § 327, and other governmental facts, Id. § 328. The California draftsmen, with a background of detailed statutory regulation of judicial notice, followed a somewhat similar pattern. California Evidence Code §§ 451, 452. The Uniform Rules, however, were drafted on the theory that these particular matters are included within the general categories and need no specific mention. This approach is followed in the present rule.

The phrase "propositions of generalized knowledge," found in Uniform Rule 9(1) and (2) is not included in the present rule. It was, it is believed, originally included in Model Code Rules 801 and 802 primarily in order to afford some minimum recognition to the right of the judge in his "legislative" capacity (not acting as the trier of fact) to take judicial notice of very limited categories of generalized knowledge. The limitations thus imposed have been discarded herein as undesirable, unworkable, and contrary to existing practice. What is left, then, to be considered, is the status of a "proposition of generalized knowledge" as an "adjudicative" fact to be noticed judicially and communicated by the judge to the jury. Thus viewed, it is considered to be lacking practical significance. While judges use judicial notice of "propositions of generalized knowledge" in a variety of situations: determining the validity and meaning of statutes, formulating common law rules, deciding whether evidence should be admitted, assessing the sufficiency and effect of evidence, all are essentially nonadjudicative in nature. When judicial notice is seen as a significant vehicle for progress in the law, these are the areas involved, particularly in developing fields of scientific knowledge. See McCormick 712. It is not believed that judges now instruct juries as to "propositions of generalized knowledge" derived from encyclopedias or other sources, or that they are likely to do so, or, indeed, that it is desirable that they do so. There is a vast difference between ruling on the basis of judicial notice that radar evidence of speed is admissible and explaining to the jury its principles and degree of accuracy, or between using a table of stopping distances of automobiles at various speeds in a judicial evaluation of testimony and telling the jury its precise application in the case. For cases raising doubt as to the propriety of the use of medical texts by lay triers of fact in passing on disability claims in administrative proceedings, see Sayers v. Gardner, 380 F.2d 940 (6th Cir.1967); Ross v. Gardner, 365 F.2d 554 (6th Cir.1966); Sosna v. Celebrezze, 234 F.Supp. 289 (E.D.Pa.1964); Glendenning v. Ribicoff, 213 F.Supp. 301 (W.D.Mo.1962).

Notes to Subdivisions (c) and (d). Under subdivision (c) the judge has a discretionary authority to take judicial notice, regardless of whether he is so requested by a party. The taking of judicial notice is mandatory, under subdivision (d), only when a party requests it and the necessary information is supplied. This scheme is believed to reflect existing practice. It is simple and workable. It avoids troublesome distinctions in the many situations in which the process of taking judicial notice is not recognized as such.

Compare Uniform Rule 9 making judicial notice of facts universally known mandatory without request, and making judicial notice of facts generally known in the jurisdiction or capable of determination by resort to accurate sources discretionary in the absence of request but mandatory if request is made and the information furnished. But see Uniform Rule 10(3), which directs the judge to decline to take judicial notice if available information fails to convince him that the matter falls clearly within Uniform Rule 9 or is insufficient to enable him to notice it judicially. Substantially the same approach is found in California Evidence Code §§ 451-453 and in New Jersey Evidence Rule 9. In contrast, the present rule treats alike all adjudicative facts which are subject to judicial notice.

Note to Subdivision (e). Basic considerations of procedural fairness demand an opportunity to be heard on the propriety of taking judicial notice and the tenor of the matter noticed. The rule requires the granting of that opportunity upon request. No formal scheme of giving notice is provided. An adversely affected party may learn in advance that judicial notice is in contemplation, either by virtue of being served with a copy of a request by another party under subdivision (d) that judicial notice be taken, or through an advance indication by the judge. Or he may have no advance notice at all. The likelihood of the latter is enhanced by the frequent failure to recognize judicial notice as such. And in the absence of advance notice, a request made after the fact could not in fairness be considered untimely. See the provision for hearing on timely request in the Administrative

Procedure Act, 5 U.S.C. § 556(e). See also Revised Model State Administrative Procedure Act (1961), 9C U.L.A. § 10(4) (Supp.1967).

Note to Subdivision (f). In accord with the usual view, judicial notice may be taken at any stage of the proceedings, whether in the trial court or on appeal. Uniform Rule 12; California Evidence Code § 459; Kansas Rules of Evidence § 60-412; New Jersey Evidence Rule 12; McCormick § 330, p. 712.

Note to Subdivision (g). Much of the controversy about judicial notice has centered upon the question whether evidence should be admitted in disproof of facts of which judicial notice is taken.

The writers have been divided. Favoring admissibility are Thayer, Preliminary Treatise on Evidence 308 (1898); 9 Wigmore § 2567; Davis, A System of Judicial Notice Based on Fairness and Convenience, in Perspectives of Law, 69, 76-77 (1964). Opposing admissibility are Keeffe, Landis and Shaad, Sense and Nonsense about Judicial Notice, 2 Stan.L.Rev. 664, 668 (1950); McNaughton, Judicial Notice--Excerpts Relating to the Morgan-Whitmore Controversy, 14 Vand.L.Rev. 779 (1961); Morgan, Judicial Notice, 57 Harv.L.Rev. 269, 279 (1944); McCormick 710-711. The Model Code and the Uniform Rules are predicated upon indisputability of judicially noticed facts.

The proponents of admitting evidence in disproof have concentrated largely upon legislative facts. Since the present rule deals only with judicial notice of adjudicative facts, arguments directed to legislative facts lose their relevancy.

Within its relatively narrow area of adjudicative facts, the rule contemplates there is to be no evidence before the jury in disproof. The judge instructs the jury to take judicially noticed facts as established. This position is justified by the undesirable effects of the opposite rule in limiting the rebutting party, though not his opponent, to admissible evidence, in defeating the reasons for judicial notice, and in affecting the substantive law to an extent and in ways largely unforeseeable. Ample protection and flexibility are afforded by the broad provision for opportunity to be heard on request, set forth in subdivision (e).

Authority upon the propriety of taking judicial notice against an accused in a criminal case with respect to matters other than venue is relatively meager. Proceeding upon the theory that the right of jury trial does not extend to matters which are beyond reasonable dispute, the rule does not distinguish between criminal and civil cases. People v. Mayes, 113 Cal. 618, 45 P. 860 (1896); Ross v. United States, 374 F.2d 97 (8th Cir.1967). Cf. State v. Main, 94 R.I. 338, 180 A.2d 814 (1962); State v. Lawrence, 120 Utah 323, 234 P.2d 600 (1951).

Note on Judicial Notice of Law. By rules effective July 1, 1966, the method of invoking the law of a foreign country is covered elsewhere. Rule 44.1 of the Federal Rules of Civil Procedure; Rule 26.1 of the Federal Rules of Criminal Procedure. These two new admirably designed rules are founded upon the assumption that the manner in which law is fed into the judicial process is never a proper concern of the rules of evidence but rather of the rules of procedure. The Advisory Committee on Evidence, believing that this assumption is entirely correct, proposes no evidence rule with respect to judicial notice of law, and suggests that those matters of law which, in addition to foreign-country law, have traditionally been treated as requiring pleading and proof and more recently as the subject of judicial notice be left to the Rules of Civil and Criminal Procedure.

1974 Enactment
Rule 201(g) as received from the Supreme Court provided that when judicial notice of a fact is taken, the court shall instruct the jury to accept that fact as established. Being of the view that mandatory instruction to a jury in a criminal case to accept as conclusive any fact judicially noticed is inappropriate because contrary to the spirit of the Sixth Amendment right to a jury trial, the Committee adopted the 1969 Advisory Committee draft of this subsection, allowing a mandatory instruction in civil actions and proceedings and a discretionary instruction in criminal cases. House Report No. 93-650.

2011 Amendments

The language of Rule 201 has been amended as part of the restyling of the Evidence Rules to make them more easily understood and to make style and terminology consistent throughout the rules. These changes are intended to be stylistic only. There is no intent to change any result in any ruling on evidence admissibility.

Article III: Presumptions in Civil Cases

Rule 301. Presumptions in Civil Cases Generally

In a civil case, unless a federal statute or these rules provide otherwise, the party against whom a presumption is directed has the burden of producing evidence to rebut the presumption. But this rule does not shift the burden of persuasion, which remains on the party who had it originally.

Credits

(Pub.L. 93-595, § 1, Jan. 2, 1975, 88 Stat. 1931; Apr. 26, 2011, eff. Dec. 1, 2011.)

Editors' Notes

ADVISORY COMMITTEE NOTES

1972 Proposed Rules

This rule governs presumptions generally. See Rule 302 for presumptions controlled by state law and Rule 303 [deleted] for those against an accused in a criminal case.

Presumptions governed by this rule are given the effect of placing upon the opposing party the burden of establishing the nonexistence of the presumed fact, once the party invoking the presumption establishes the basic facts giving rise to it. The same considerations of fairness, policy, and probability which dictate the allocation of the burden of the various elements of a case as between the prima facie case of a plaintiff and affirmative defenses also underlie the creation of presumptions. These considerations are not satisfied by giving a lesser effect to presumptions. Morgan and Maguire, Looking Backward and Forward at Evidence, 50 Harv.L.Rev. 909, 913 (1937); Morgan, Instructing the Jury upon Presumptions and Burden of Proof, 47 Harv.L.Rev. 59, 82 (1933); Cleary, Presuming and Pleading: An Essay on Juristic Immaturity, 12 Stan.L.Rev. 5 (1959).

The so-called "bursting bubble" theory, under which a presumption vanishes upon the introduction of evidence which would support a finding of the nonexistence of the presumed fact, even though not believed, is rejected as according presumptions too "slight and evanescent" an effect. Morgan and Maguire, supra, at p. 913.

In the opinion of the Advisory Committee, no constitutional infirmity attends this view of presumptions. In Mobile, J. & K. C. R. Co. v. Turnipseed, 219 U.S. 35, 31 S.Ct. 136, 55 L.Ed. 78 (1910), the Court upheld a Mississippi statute which provided that in actions against railroads proof of injury inflicted by the running of trains should be prima facie evidence of negligence by the railroad. The injury in the case had resulted from a derailment. The opinion made the points (1) that the only effect of the statute was to impose on the railroad the duty of producing some evidence to the contrary, (2) that an inference may be supplied by law if there is a rational connection between the fact proved and the fact presumed, as long as the opposite party is not precluded from presenting his evidence to the contrary, and (3) that considerations of public policy arising from the character of the business justified the application in question. Nineteen years later, in Western & Atlantic R. Co. v. Henderson, 279 U.S. 639, 49 S.Ct. 445, 73 L.Ed. 884 (1929), the Court overturned a Georgia statute making railroads liable for damages done by trains, unless the railroad made it appear that reasonable care had been used, the presumption being against the railroad. The declaration alleged the death of plaintiff's husband from a grade crossing collision, due to specified acts of negligence by defendant. The jury were instructed that proof of the injury raised a presumption of negligence; the burden shifted to the railroad to prove ordinary care; and unless it did so, they should find for plaintiff. The instruction was held erroneous in an opinion stating (1) that there was no rational connection between the mere fact of collision and negligence on the part of anyone, and (2) that the statute was different from that in Turnipseed in imposing a burden upon the railroad. The reader is left in a state of some confusion. Is the difference between a derailment and a grade crossing collision of no significance? Would the Turnipseed presumption have been bad if it had imposed a burden of persuasion on defendant, although that would in nowise have impaired its "rational connection"? If Henderson forbids imposing a burden of persuasion on defendants, what happens to affirmative defenses?

Two factors serve to explain Henderson. The first was that it was common ground that negligence was indispensable to liability. Plaintiff thought so, drafted her complaint accordingly, and relied upon the presumption. But how in logic could the same presumption establish her alternative grounds of negligence that the engineer was so blind he could not see decedent's truck and that he failed to stop after he saw it? Second, take away the basic assumption of no liability without fault, as Turnipseed intimated might be done ("considerations of public policy arising out of the character of the business"), and the structure of the decision in Henderson fails. No question of logic would have arisen if the statute had simply said: a prima facie case of liability is made by proof of injury by a train; lack of negligence is an affirmative defense, to be pleaded and proved as other affirmative defenses. The problem would be one of economic due process only. While it seems likely that the Supreme Court of 1929 would have voted that due process was denied, that result today would be unlikely. See, for example, the shift in the direction of absolute liability in the consumer cases. Prosser, The Assault upon the Citadel (Strict Liability to the Consumer), 69 Yale L.J. 1099 (1960).

Any doubt as to the constitutional permissibility of a presumption imposing a burden of persuasion of the nonexistence of the presumed fact in civil cases is laid at rest by Dick v. New York Life Ins. Co., 359 U.S. 437, 79 S.Ct. 921, 3 L.Ed.2d 935 (1959). The Court unhesitatingly applied the North Dakota rule that the presumption against suicide imposed on defendant the burden of proving that the death of insured, under an accidental death clause, was due to suicide.

"Proof of coverage and of death by gunshot wound shifts the burden to the insurer to establish that the death of the insured was due to his suicide." 359 U.S. at 443, 79 S.Ct. at 925.

"In a case like this one, North Dakota presumes that death was accidental and places on the insurer the burden of proving that death resulted from suicide." Id. at 446, 79 S.Ct. at 927.

The rational connection requirement survives in criminal cases, Tot v. United States, 319 U.S. 463, 63 S.Ct. 1241, 87 L.Ed. 1519 (1943), because the Court has been unwilling to extend into that area the greater-includes-the-lesser theory of Ferry v. Ramsey, 277 U.S. 88, 48 S.Ct. 443, 72 L.Ed. 796 (1928). In that case the Court sustained a Kansas statute under which bank directors were personally liable for deposits made with their assent and with knowledge of insolvency, and the fact of insolvency was prima facie evidence of assent and knowledge of insolvency. Mr. Justice Holmes pointed out that the state legislature could have made the directors personally liable to depositors in every case. Since the statute imposed a less stringent liability, "the thing to be considered is the result reached, not the possibly inartificial or clumsy way of reaching it." Id. at 94, 48 S.Ct. at 444. Mr. Justice Sutherland dissented: though the state could have created an absolute liability, it did not purport to do so; a rational connection was necessary, but lacking, between the liability created and the prima facie evidence of it; the result might be different if the basis of the presumption were being open for business.

The Sutherland view has prevailed in criminal cases by virtue of the higher standard of notice there required. The fiction that everyone is presumed to know the law is applied to the substantive law of crimes as an alternative to complete unenforceability. But the need does not extend to criminal evidence and procedure, and the fiction does not encompass them. "Rational connection" is not fictional or artificial, and so it is reasonable to suppose that Gainey should have known that his presence at the site of an illicit still could convict him of being connected with (carrying on) the business, United States v. Gainey, 380 U.S. 63, 85 S.Ct. 754, 13 L.Ed.2d 658 (1965), but not that Romano should have known that his presence at a still could convict him of possessing it, United States v. Romano, 382 U.S. 136, 86 S.Ct. 279, 15 L.Ed.2d 210 (1965).

In his dissent in Gainey, Mr. Justice Black put it more artistically:

"It might be argued, although the Court does not so argue or hold, that Congress if it wished could make presence at a still a crime in itself, and so Congress should be free to create crimes which are called 'possession' and 'carrying on an illegal distillery business' but which are defined in such a way that unexplained presence is sufficient and indisputable evidence in all cases to support conviction for those offenses. See Ferry v. Ramsey, 277 U.S. 88, 48 S.Ct. 443, 72 L.Ed. 796. Assuming for the sake of argument that Congress could make unexplained presence a criminal act, and ignoring also the refusal of this Court in other cases to uphold a statutory presumption on such a theory, see Heiner v. Donnan, 285 U.S. 312, 52 S.Ct. 358, 76 L.Ed. 772, there is no indication here that Congress intended to adopt such a misleading method of draftsmanship, nor in my judgment could the statutory provisions if so construed escape condemnation for vagueness, under the principles applied in Lanzetta v. New Jersey, 306 U.S. 451, 59 S.Ct. 618, 83 L.Ed. 888, and many other cases." 380 U.S. at 84, n. 12, 85 S.Ct. at 766.

And the majority opinion in Romano agreed with him:

"It may be, of course, that Congress has the power to make presence at an illegal still a punishable crime, but we find no clear indication that it intended to so exercise this power. The crime remains possession, not presence, and with all due deference to the judgment of Congress, the former may not constitutionally be inferred from the latter." 382 U.S. at 144, 86 S.Ct. at 284.

The rule does not spell out the procedural aspects of its application. Questions as to when the evidence warrants submission of a presumption and what instructions are proper under varying states of fact are believed to present no particular difficulties.

1974 Enactment
Rule 301 as submitted by the Supreme Court provided that in all cases a presumption imposes on the party against whom it is directed the burden of proving that the nonexistence of the presumed fact is more probable than its existence. The Committee limited the scope of Rule 301 to "civil actions and proceedings" to effectuate its decision not to deal with the question of presumptions in criminal cases. (See note on [proposed] Rule 303 in discussion of Rules deleted). With respect to the weight to be given a presumption in a civil case, the Committee agreed with the judgment implicit in the Court's version that the so-called "bursting bubble" theory of presumptions, whereby a presumption vanishes upon the appearance of any contradicting evidence by the other party, gives to presumptions too slight an effect. On the other hand, the Committee believed that the Rule proposed by the Court, whereby a presumption permanently alters the burden of persuasion, no matter how much contradicting evidence is introduced--a view shared by only a few courts--lends too great a force to presumptions. Accordingly, the Committee amended the Rule to adopt an intermediate position under which a presumption does not vanish upon the introduction of contradicting evidence, and does not change the burden of persuasion; instead it is merely deemed sufficient evidence of the fact presumed, to be considered by the jury or other finder of fact. House Report No. 93-650.

The rule governs presumptions in civil cases generally. Rule 302 provides for presumptions in cases controlled by State law.

As submitted by the Supreme Court, presumptions governed by this rule were given the effect of placing upon the opposing party the burden of establishing the nonexistence of the presumed fact, once the party invoking the presumption established the basic facts giving rise to it.

Instead of imposing a burden of persuasion on the party against whom the presumption is directed, the House adopted a provision which shifted the burden of going forward with the evidence. They further provided that "even though met with contradicting evidence, a presumption is sufficient evidence of the fact presumed, to be considered by the trier of fact." The effect of the amendment is that presumptions are to be treated as evidence.

The committee feels the House amendment is ill-advised. As the joint committees (the Standing Committee on Practice and Procedure of the Judicial Conference and the Advisory Committee on the Rules of Evidence) stated: "Presumptions are not evidence, but ways of dealing with evidence." This treatment requires juries to perform the task of considering "as evidence" facts upon which they have no direct evidence and which may confuse them in performance of their duties. California had a rule much like that contained in the House amendment. It was sharply criticized by Justice Traynor in Speck v. Sarver [20 Cal.2d 585, 128 P.2d 16, 21 (1942)] and was repealed after 93 troublesome years [Cal.Ev.Code 1965 § 600].

Professor McCormick gives a concise and compelling critique of the presumption as evidence rule: "Another solution, formerly more popular than now, is to instruct the jury that the presumption is 'evidence', to be weighed and considered with the testimony in the case. This avoids the danger that the jury may infer that the presumption is conclusive, but it probably means little to the jury, and certainly runs counter to accepted theories of the nature of evidence." [McCormick, Evidence, 669 (1954); Id. 825 (2d ed. 1972)].

For these reasons the committee has deleted that provision of the House-passed rule that treats presumptions as evidence. The effect of the rule as adopted by the committee is to make clear that while evidence of facts giving rise to a presumption shifts the burden of coming forward with evidence to rebut or meet the presumption, it does not shift the burden of persuasion on the existence of the presumed facts. The burden of persuasion remains on the party to whom it is allocated under the rules governing the allocation in the first instance.

The court may instruct the jury that they may infer the existence of the presumed fact from proof of the basic facts giving rise to the presumption. However, it would be inappropriate under this rule to instruct the jury that the inference they are to draw is conclusive. Senate Report 93-1277.

The House bill provides that a presumption in civil actions and proceedings shifts to the party against whom it is directed the burden of going forward with evidence to meet or rebut it. Even though evidence contradicting the presumption is offered, a presumption is considered sufficient evidence of the presumed fact to be considered by the jury. The Senate amendment provides that a presumption shifts to the party against whom it is directed the burden of going forward with evidence to meet or rebut the presumption, but it does not shift to that party the burden of persuasion on the existence of the presumed fact.

Under the Senate amendment, a presumption is sufficient to get a party past an adverse party's motion to dismiss made at the end of his case-in-chief. If the adverse party offers no evidence contradicting the presumed fact, the court will instruct the jury that if it finds the basic facts, it may presume the existence of the presumed fact. If the adverse party does offer evidence contradicting the presumed fact, the court cannot instruct the jury that it may presume the existence of the presumed fact from proof of the basic facts. The court may, however, instruct the jury that it may infer the existence of the presumed fact from proof of the basic facts.

The conference adopts the Senate amendment. House Conference Report No. 93-1597.

2011 Amendments
The language of Rule 301 has been amended as part of the restyling of the Evidence Rules to make them more easily understood and to make style and terminology consistent throughout the rules. These changes are intended to be stylistic only. There is no intent to change any result in any ruling on evidence admissibility.

Rule 302. Applying State Law to Presumptions in Civil Cases

In a civil case, state law governs the effect of a presumption regarding a claim or defense for which state law supplies the rule of decision.

Credits

(Pub.L. 93-595, § 1, Jan. 2, 1975, 88 Stat. 1931; Apr. 26, 2011, eff. Dec. 1, 2011.)

Editors' Notes

ADVISORY COMMITTEE NOTES

1972 Proposed Rules

A series of Supreme Court decisions in diversity cases leaves no doubt of the relevance of Erie Railroad Co. v. Tompkins, 304 U.S. 64, 58 S.Ct. 817, 82 L.Ed. 1188 (1938), to questions of burden of proof. These decisions are Cities Service Oil Co. v. Dunlap, 308 U.S. 208, 60 S.Ct. 201, 84 L.Ed. 196 (1939), Palmer v. Hoffman, 318 U.S. 109, 63 S.Ct. 477, 87 L.Ed. 645 (1943), and Dick v. New York Life Ins. Co., 359 U.S. 437, 79 S.Ct. 921, 3 L.Ed.2d 935 (1959). They involved burden of proof, respectively, as to status as bona fide purchaser, contributory negligence, and nonaccidental death (suicide) of an insured. In each instance the state rule was held to be applicable. It does not follow, however, that all presumptions in diversity cases are governed by state law. In each case cited, the burden of proof question had to do with a substantive element of the claim or defense. Application of the state law is called for only when the presumption operates upon such an element. Accordingly the rule does not apply state law when the presumption operates upon a lesser aspect of the case, i.e. "tactical" presumptions.

The situations in which the state law is applied have been tagged for convenience in the preceding discussion as "diversity cases." The designation is not a completely accurate one since Erie applies to any claim or issue having its source in state law, regardless of the basis of federal jurisdiction, and does not apply to a federal claim or issue, even though jurisdiction is based on diversity. Vestal, Erie R.R. v. Tompkins: A Projection, 48 Iowa L.Rev. 248, 257 (1963); Hart and Wechsler, The Federal Courts and the Federal System, 697 (1953); 1A Moore, Federal Practice ¶ 0.305[3] (2d ed. 1965); Wright, Federal Courts, 217-218 (1963). Hence the rule employs, as appropriately descriptive, the phrase "as to which state law supplies the rule of decision." See A.L.I. Study of the Division of Jurisdiction Between State and Federal Courts, § 2344(c), p. 40, P.F.D. No. 1 (1965).

2011 Amendments

The language of Rule 302 has been amended as part of the restyling of the Evidence Rules to make them more easily understood and to make style and terminology consistent throughout the rules. These changes are intended to be stylistic only. There is no intent to change any result in any ruling on evidence admissibility.

Article IV: Relevancy and Its Limits

Rule 401. Test for Relevant Evidence

Evidence is relevant if:

(a) it has any tendency to make a fact more or less probable than it would be without the evidence; and

(b) the fact is of consequence in determining the action.

Credits
(Pub.L. 93-595, § 1, Jan. 2, 1975, 88 Stat.1931; Apr. 26, 2011, eff. Dec. 1, 2011.)

Editors' Notes
ADVISORY COMMITTEE NOTES
1972 Proposed Rules
Problems of relevancy call for an answer to the question whether an item of evidence, when tested by the processes of legal reasoning, possesses sufficient probative value to justify receiving it in evidence. Thus, assessment of the probative value of evidence that a person purchased a revolver shortly prior to a fatal shooting with which he is charged is a matter of analysis and reasoning.

The variety of relevancy problems is coextensive with the ingenuity of counsel in using circumstantial evidence as a means of proof. An enormous number of cases fall in no set pattern, and this rule is designed as a guide for handling them. On the other hand, some situations recur with sufficient frequency to create patterns susceptible of treatment by specific rules. Rule 404 and those following it are of that variety; they also serve as illustrations of the application of the present rule as limited by the exclusionary principles of Rule 403.

Passing mention should be made of so-called "conditional" relevancy. Morgan, Basic Problems of Evidence 45-46 (1962). In this situation, probative value depends not only upon satisfying the basic requirement of relevancy as described above but also upon the existence of some matter of fact. For example, if evidence of a spoken statement is relied upon to prove notice, probative value is lacking unless the person sought to be charged heard the statement. The problem is one of fact, and the only rules needed are for the purpose of determining the respective functions of judge and jury. See Rules 104(b) and 901. The discussion which follows in the present note is concerned with relevancy generally, not with any particular problem of conditional relevancy.

Relevancy is not an inherent characteristic of any item of evidence but exists only as a relation between an item of evidence and a matter properly provable in the case. Does the item of evidence tend to prove the matter sought to be proved? Whether the relationship exists depends upon principles evolved by experience or science, applied logically to the situation at hand. James, Relevancy, Probability and the Law, 29 Calif.L.Rev. 689, 696, n. 15 (1941), in Selected Writings on Evidence and Trial 610, 615, n. 15 (Fryer ed. 1957). The rule summarizes this relationship as a "tendency to make the existence" of the fact to be proved "more probable or less probable." Compare Uniform Rule 1(2) which states the crux of relevancy as "a tendency in reason," thus perhaps emphasizing unduly the logical process and ignoring the need to draw upon experience or science to validate the general principle upon which relevancy in a particular situation depends.

The standard of probability under the rule is "more * * * probable than it would be without the evidence." Any more stringent requirement is unworkable and unrealistic. As McCormick § 152, p. 317, says, "A brick is not a wall," or, as Falknor, Extrinsic Policies Affecting Admissibility, 10 Rutgers L.Rev. 574, 576 (1956), quotes Professor McBaine, " * * * [I]t is not to be supposed that every witness can make a home run." Dealing with probability in the language of the rule has the added virtue of avoiding confusion between questions of admissibility and questions of the sufficiency of the evidence.

The rule uses the phrase "fact that is of consequence to the determination of the action" to describe the kind of fact to which proof may properly be directed. The language is that of California Evidence Code § 210; it has the advantage of avoiding the loosely used and ambiguous word "material." Tentative Recommendation and a Study Relating to the Uniform Rules of Evidence (Art. I. General Provisions), Cal.Law Revision Comm'n, Rep., Rec. & Studies, 10-11 (1964). The fact to be proved may be ultimate, intermediate, or evidentiary; it matters not, so long as it is of consequence in the determination of the action. Cf. Uniform Rule 1(2) which requires that the evidence relate to a "material" fact.

The fact to which the evidence is directed need not be in dispute. While situations will arise which call for the exclusion of evidence offered to prove a point conceded by the opponent, the ruling should be made on the basis of such considerations as waste of time and undue prejudice (see Rule 403), rather than under any general requirement that evidence is admissible only if directed to matters in dispute. Evidence which is essentially background in nature can scarcely be said to involve disputed matter, yet it is universally offered and admitted as an aid to understanding. Charts, photographs, views of real estate, murder weapons, and many other items of evidence fall in this category. A rule limiting admissibility to evidence directed to a controversial point would invite the exclusion of this helpful evidence, or at least the raising of endless questions over its admission. Cf. California Evidence Code § 210, defining relevant evidence in terms of tendency to prove a disputed fact.

2011 Amendments
The language of Rule 401 has been amended as part of the restyling of the Evidence Rules to make them more easily understood and to make style and terminology consistent throughout the rules. These changes are intended to be stylistic only. There is no intent to change any result in any ruling on evidence admissibility.

Rule 402. General Admissibility of Relevant Evidence

Relevant evidence is admissible unless any of the following provides otherwise:

• the United States Constitution;

• a federal statute;

• these rules; or

• other rules prescribed by the Supreme Court.

Irrelevant evidence is not admissible.

Credits
(Pub.L. 93-595, § 1, Jan. 2, 1975, 88 Stat. 1931; Apr. 26, 2011, eff. Dec. 1, 2011.)

Editors' Notes
ADVISORY COMMITTEE NOTES
1972 Proposed Rules
The provisions that all relevant evidence is admissible, with certain exceptions, and that evidence which is not relevant is not admissible are "a presupposition involved in the very conception of a rational system of evidence." Thayer, Preliminary Treatise on Evidence 264 (1898). They constitute the foundation upon which the structure of admission and exclusion rests. For similar provisions see California Evidence Code §§ 350, 351. Provisions that all relevant evidence is admissible are found in Uniform Rule 7(f); Kansas Code of Civil Procedure § 60-407(f); and New Jersey Evidence Rule 7(f); but the exclusion of evidence which is not relevant is left to implication.

Not all relevant evidence is admissible. The exclusion of relevant evidence occurs in a variety of situations and may be called for by these rules, by the Rules of Civil and Criminal Procedure, by Bankruptcy Rules, by Act of Congress, or by constitutional considerations.

Succeeding rules in the present article, in response to the demands of particular policies, require the exclusion of evidence despite its relevancy. In addition, Article V recognizes a number of privileges; Article VI imposes limitations upon witnesses and the manner of dealing with them; Article VII specifies requirements with respect to opinions and expert testimony; Article VIII excludes hearsay not falling within an exception; Article IX spells out the handling of authentication and identification; and Article X restricts the manner of proving the contents of writings and recordings.

The Rules of Civil and Criminal Procedure in some instances require the exclusion of relevant evidence. For example, Rules 30(b) and 32(a)(3) of the Rules of Civil Procedure, by imposing requirements of notice and unavailability of the deponent, place limits on the use of relevant depositions. Similarly, Rule 15 of the Rules of Criminal Procedure restricts the use of depositions in criminal cases, even though relevant. And the effective enforcement of the command, originally statutory and now found in Rule 5(a) of the Rules of Criminal Procedure, that an arrested person be taken without unnecessary delay before a commissioner or other similar officer is held to require the exclusion of statements elicited during detention in violation thereof. Mallory v. United States, 354 U.S. 449, 77 S.Ct. 1356, 1 L.Ed.2d 1479 (1957); 18 U.S.C. § 3501(c).

While congressional enactments in the field of evidence have generally tended to expand admissibility beyond the scope of the common law rules, in some particular situations they have restricted the admissibility of relevant evidence. Most of this legislation has consisted of the formulation of a privilege or of a prohibition against disclosure. 8 U.S.C. § 1202(f), records of refusal of visas or permits to enter United States confidential, subject to discretion of Secretary of State to make available to court upon certification of need; 10 U.S.C. § 3693, replacement certificate of honorable discharge from Army not admissible in evidence; 10 U.S.C. § 8693, same as to Air Force; 11 U.S.C. § 25(a)(10), testimony given by bankrupt on his examination not admissible in criminal proceedings against him, except that given in hearing upon objection to discharge; 11 U.S.C. § 205(a), railroad reorganization petition, if dismissed, not admissible in evidence; 11 U.S.C. § 403(a), list of creditors filed with municipal composition plan not an admission; 13 U.S.C. § 9(a), census information confidential, retained copies of reports privileged; 47 U.S.C. § 605, interception and divulgence of wire or radio communications prohibited unless authorized by sender. These statutory provisions would remain undisturbed by the rules.

The rule recognizes but makes no attempt to spell out the constitutional considerations which impose basic limitations upon the admissibility of relevant evidence. Examples are evidence obtained by unlawful search and seizure. Weeks v. United States, 232 U.S. 383, 34 S.Ct. 341, 58 L.Ed. 652 (1914); Katz v. United States, 389 U.S. 347, 88 S.Ct. 507, 19 L.Ed.2d 576 (1967); incriminating statement elicited from an accused in violation of right to counsel. Massiah v. United States, 377 U.S. 201, 84 S.Ct. 1199, 12 L.Ed.2d 246 (1964).

1974 Enactment
Rule 402 as submitted to the Congress contained the phrase "or by other rules adopted by the Supreme Court". To accommodate the view that the Congress should not appear to acquiesce in the Court's judgment that it has authority under the existing Rules Enabling Acts to promulgate Rules of Evidence, the Committee amended the above phrase to read "or by other rules prescribed by the Supreme Court pursuant to statutory authority" in this and other Rules where the reference appears. House Report No. 93-650.

2011 Amendments
The language of Rule 402 has been amended as part of the restyling of the Evidence Rules to make them more easily understood and to make style and terminology consistent throughout the rules. These changes are intended to be stylistic only. There is no intent to change any result in any ruling on evidence admissibility.

Rule 403. Excluding Relevant Evidence
for Prejudice, Confusion, Waste of Time, or Other Reasons

The court may exclude relevant evidence if its probative value is substantially outweighed by a danger of one or more of the following: unfair prejudice, confusing the issues, misleading the jury, undue delay, wasting time, or needlessly presenting cumulative evidence.

Credits

(Pub.L. 93-595, § 1, Jan. 2, 1975, 88 Stat. 1932; Apr. 26, 2011, eff. Dec. 1, 2011.)

Editors' Notes
ADVISORY COMMITTEE NOTES
1972 Proposed Rules
The case law recognizes that certain circumstances call for the exclusion of evidence which is of unquestioned relevance. These circumstances entail risks which range all the way from inducing decision on a purely emotional basis, at one extreme, to nothing more harmful than merely wasting time, at the other extreme. Situations in this area call for balancing the probative value of and need for the evidence against the harm likely to result from its admission. Slough, Relevancy Unraveled, 5 Kan.L.Rev. 1, 12-15 (1956); Trautman, Logical or Legal Relevancy--A Conflict in Theory, 5 Van.L.Rev. 385, 392 (1952); McCormick § 152, pp. 319-321. The rules which follow in this Article are concrete applications evolved for particular situations. However, they reflect the policies underlying the present rule, which is designed as a guide for the handling of situations for which no specific rules have been formulated.

Exclusion for risk of unfair prejudice, confusion of issues, misleading the jury, or waste of time, all find ample support in the authorities. "Unfair prejudice" within its context means an undue tendency to suggest decision on an improper basis, commonly, though not necessarily, an emotional one.

The rule does not enumerate surprise as a ground for exclusion, in this respect following Wigmore's view of the common law. 6 Wigmore § 1849. Cf. McCormick § 152, p. 320, n. 29, listing unfair surprise as a ground for exclusion but stating that it is usually "coupled with the danger of prejudice and confusion of issues." While Uniform Rule 45 incorporates surprise as a ground and is followed in Kansas Code of Civil Procedure § 60-445, surprise is not included in California Evidence Code § 352 or New Jersey Rule 4, though both the latter otherwise substantially embody Uniform Rule 45. While it can scarcely be doubted that claims of unfair surprise may still be justified despite procedural requirements of notice and instrumentalities of discovery, the granting of a continuance is a more appropriate remedy than exclusion of the evidence. Tentative Recommendation and a Study Relating to the Uniform Rules of Evidence (Art. VI. Extrinsic Policies Affecting Admissibility), Cal.Law Revision Comm'n, Rep., Rec. & Studies, 612 (1964). Moreover, the impact of a rule excluding evidence on the ground of surprise would be difficult to estimate.

In reaching a decision whether to exclude on grounds of unfair prejudice, consideration should be given to the probable effectiveness or lack of effectiveness of a limiting instruction. See Rule 106 [now 105] and Advisory Committee's Note thereunder. The availability of other means of proof may also be an appropriate factor.

2011 Amendments
The language of Rule 403 has been amended as part of the restyling of the Evidence Rules to make them more easily understood and to make style and terminology consistent throughout the rules. These changes are intended to be stylistic only. There is no intent to change any result in any ruling on evidence admissibility.

Rule 404. Character Evidence; Crimes or Other Acts

(a) Character Evidence.

(1) Prohibited Uses. Evidence of a person's character or character trait is not admissible to prove that on a particular occasion the person acted in accordance with the character or trait.

(2) Exceptions for a Defendant or Victim in a Criminal Case. The following exceptions apply in a criminal case:

(A) a defendant may offer evidence of the defendant's pertinent trait, and if the evidence is admitted, the prosecutor may offer evidence to rebut it;

(B) subject to the limitations in Rule 412, a defendant may offer evidence of an alleged victim's pertinent trait, and if the evidence is admitted, the prosecutor may:

(i) offer evidence to rebut it; and

(ii) offer evidence of the defendant's same trait; and

(C) in a homicide case, the prosecutor may offer evidence of the alleged victim's trait of peacefulness to rebut evidence that the victim was the first aggressor.

(3) Exceptions for a Witness. Evidence of a witness's character may be admitted under Rules 607, 608, and 609.

(b) Crimes, Wrongs, or Other Acts.

(1) Prohibited Uses. Evidence of a crime, wrong, or other act is not admissible to prove a person's character in order to show that on a particular occasion the person acted in accordance with the character.

(2) Permitted Uses; Notice in a Criminal Case. This evidence may be admissible for another purpose, such as proving motive, opportunity, intent, preparation, plan, knowledge, identity, absence of mistake, or lack of accident. On request by a defendant in a criminal case, the prosecutor must:

(A) provide reasonable notice of the general nature of any such evidence that the prosecutor intends to offer at trial; and

(B) do so before trial--or during trial if the court, for good cause, excuses lack of pretrial notice.

Credits

(Pub.L. 93-595, § 1, Jan. 2, 1975, 88 Stat.1932; Mar. 2, 1987, eff. Oct. 1, 1987; Apr. 30, 1991, eff. Dec. 1, 1991; Apr. 17, 2000, eff. Dec. 1, 2000; Apr. 12, 2006, eff. Dec. 1, 2006; Apr. 26, 2011, eff. Dec. 1, 2011.)

Editors' Notes
ADVISORY COMMITTEE NOTES
1972 Proposed Rules

Note to Subdivision (a). This subdivision deals with the basic question whether character evidence should be admitted. Once the admissibility of character evidence in some form is established under this rule, reference must then be made to Rule 405, which follows, in order to determine the appropriate method of proof. If the character is that of a witness, see Rules 608 and 610 for methods of proof.

Character questions arise in two fundamentally different ways. (1) Character may itself be an element of a crime, claim, or defense. A situation of this kind is commonly referred to as "character in issue." Illustrations are: the chastity of the victim under a statute specifying her chastity as an element of the crime of seduction, or the competency of the driver in an action for negligently entrusting a motor vehicle to an incompetent driver. No problem of the general relevancy of character evidence is involved, and the present rule therefore has no provision on the subject. The only question relates to allowable methods of proof, as to which see Rule 405, immediately following. (2) Character evidence is susceptible of being used for the purpose of suggesting an inference that the person acted on the occasion in question consistently with his character. This use of character is often described as "circumstantial." Illustrations are: evidence of a violent disposition to prove that the person was the aggressor in an affray, or evidence of honesty in disproof of a charge of theft. This circumstantial use of character evidence raises questions of relevancy as well as questions of allowable methods of proof.

In most jurisdictions today, the circumstantial use of character is rejected but with important exceptions: (1) an accused may introduce pertinent evidence of good character (often misleadingly described as "putting his character in issue"), in which event the prosecution may rebut with evidence of bad character; (2) an accused may introduce pertinent evidence of the character of the victim, as in support of a claim of self-defense to a charge of homicide or consent in a case of rape, and the prosecution may introduce similar evidence in rebuttal of the character evidence, or, in a homicide case, to rebut a claim that deceased was the first aggressor, however proved; and (3) the character of a witness may be gone into as bearing on his credibility. McCormick §§ 155-161. This pattern is incorporated in the rule. While its basis lies more in history and experience than in logic an underlying justification can fairly be found in terms of the relative presence and absence of prejudice in the various situations. Falknor, Extrinsic Policies Affecting Admissibility, 10 Rutgers L.Rev. 574, 584 (1956); McCormick § 157. In any event, the criminal rule is so deeply imbedded in our jurisprudence as to assume almost constitutional proportions and to override doubts of the basic relevancy of the evidence.

The limitation to pertinent traits of character, rather than character generally, in paragraphs (1) and (2) is in accordance with the prevailing view. McCormick § 158, p. 334. A similar provision in Rule 608, to which reference is made in paragraph (3), limits character evidence respecting witnesses to the trait of truthfulness or untruthfulness.

The argument is made that circumstantial use of character ought to be allowed in civil cases to the same extent as in criminal cases, i.e. evidence of good (nonprejudicial) character would be admissible in the first instance, subject to rebuttal by evidence of bad character. Falknor, Extrinsic Policies Affecting Admissibility, 10 Rutgers L.Rev. 574, 581-583 (1956); Tentative Recommendation and a Study Relating to the Uniform Rules of Evidence (Art. VI. Extrinsic Policies Affecting Admissibility), Cal.Law Revision Comm'n, Rep., Rec. & Studies, 657-658 (1964). Uniform Rule 47 goes farther, in that it assumes that character evidence in general satisfies the conditions of relevancy, except as provided in Uniform Rule 48. The difficulty with expanding the use of character evidence in civil cases is set forth by the California Law Revision Commission in its ultimate rejection of Uniform Rule 47, id., 615:

"Character evidence is of slight probative value and may be very prejudicial. It tends to distract the trier of fact from the main question of what actually happened on the particular occasion. It subtly permits the trier of fact to reward the good man and to punish the bad man because of their respective characters despite what the evidence in the case shows actually happened."

Much of the force of the position of those favoring greater use of character evidence in civil cases is dissipated by their support of Uniform Rule 48 which excludes the evidence in negligence cases, where it could be expected to achieve its maximum usefulness. Moreover, expanding concepts of "character," which seem of necessity to extend into such areas as psychiatric evaluation and psychological testing, coupled with expanded admissibility, would open up such vistas of mental examinations as caused the Court concern in Schlagenhauf v. Holder, 379 U.S. 104, 85 S.Ct. 234, 13 L.Ed.2d 152 (1964). It is believed that those espousing change have not met the burden of persuasion.

Note to Subdivision (b). Subdivision (b) deals with a specialized but important application of the general rule excluding circumstantial use of character evidence. Consistently with that rule, evidence of other crimes, wrongs, or acts is not admissible to prove character as a basis for suggesting the inference that conduct on a particular occasion was in conformity with it. However, the evidence may be offered for another purpose, such as proof of motive, opportunity, and so on, which does not fall within the prohibition. In this situation the rule does not require that the evidence be excluded. No mechanical solution is offered. The determination must be made whether the danger of undue prejudice outweighs the probative value of the evidence in view of the availability of other means of proof and other facts appropriate for making decision of this kind under Rule 403. Slough and Knightly, Other Vices, Other Crimes, 41 Iowa L.Rev. 325 (1956).

1974 Enactment
Note to Subdivision (b). The second sentence of Rule 404(b) as submitted to the Congress began with the words "This subdivision does not exclude the evidence when offered". The Committee amended this language to read "It may, however, be admissible", the words used in the 1971 Advisory Committee draft, on the ground that this formulation properly placed greater emphasis on admissibility than did the final Court version. House Report No. 93-650.

Note to Subdivision (b). This rule provides that evidence of other crimes, wrongs, or acts is not admissible to prove character but may be admissible for other specified purposes such as proof of motive.

Although your committee sees no necessity in amending the rule itself, it anticipates that the use of the discretionary word "may" with respect to the admissibility of evidence of crimes, wrongs, or acts is not intended to confer any arbitrary discretion on the trial judge. Rather, it is anticipated that with respect to permissible uses for such evidence, the trial judge may exclude it only on the basis of those considerations set forth in Rule 403, i.e., prejudice, confusion or waste of time. Senate Report No. 93-1277.

1987 Amendments
The amendments are technical. No substantive change is intended.

1991 Amendments
Rule 404(b) has emerged as one of the most cited Rules in the Rules of Evidence. And in many criminal cases evidence of an accused's extrinsic acts is viewed as an important asset in the prosecution's case against an accused. Although there are a few reported decisions on use of such evidence by the defense, see, e.g., United States v. McClure, 546 F.2d 670 (5th Cir.1990) (acts of informant offered in entrapment defense), the overwhelming number of cases involve introduction of that evidence by the prosecution.

The amendment to Rule 404(b) adds a pretrial notice requirement in criminal cases and is intended to reduce surprise and promote early resolution on the issue of admissibility. The notice requirement thus places Rule 404(b) in the mainstream with notice and disclosure provisions in other rules of evidence. See, e.g., Rule 412 (written motion of intent to offer evidence under rule), Rule 609 (written notice of intent to offer conviction older than 10 years), Rule 803(24) and 804(b)(5) (notice of intent to use residual hearsay exceptions).

The Rule expects that counsel for both the defense and the prosecution will submit the necessary request and information in a reasonable and timely fashion. Other than requiring pretrial notice, no specific time limits are stated in recognition that what constitutes a reasonable request or disclosure will depend largely on the circumstances of each case. Compare Fla.Stat.Ann. § 90.404(2)(b) (notice must be given at least 10 days before trial) with Tex.R.Evid. 404(b) (no time limit).

Likewise, no specific form of notice is required. The Committee considered and rejected a requirement that the notice satisfy the particularity requirements normally required of language used in a charging instrument. Cf. Fla.Stat.Ann. § 90.404(2)(b) (written disclosure must describe uncharged misconduct with particularity required of an indictment or information). Instead, the Committee opted for a generalized notice provision which requires the prosecution to apprise the defense of the general nature of the evidence of extrinsic acts. The Committee does not intend that the amendment will supercede other rules of admissibility or disclosure, such as the Jencks Act, 18 U.S.C. § 3500, et. seq. nor require the prosecution to disclose directly or indirectly the names and addresses of its witnesses, something it is currently not required to do under Federal Rule of Criminal Procedure 16.

The amendment requires the prosecution to provide notice, regardless of how it intends to use the extrinsic act evidence at trial, i.e., during its case-in-chief, for impeachment, or for possible rebuttal. The court in its discretion may, under the facts, decide that the particular request or notice was not reasonable, either because of the lack of timeliness or completeness. Because the notice requirement serves as condition precedent to admissibility of 404(b) evidence, the offered evidence is inadmissible if the court decides that the notice requirement has not been met.

Nothing in the amendment precludes the court from requiring the government to provide it with an opportunity to rule in limine on 404(b) evidence before it is offered or even mentioned during trial. When ruling in limine, the court may require the government to disclose to it the specifics of such evidence which the court must consider in determining admissibility.

The amendment does not extend to evidence of acts which are "intrinsic" to the charged offense, see United States v. Williams, 900 F.2d 823 (5th Cir.1990) (noting distinction between 404(b) evidence and intrinsic offense evidence). Nor is the amendment intended to redefine what evidence would otherwise be admissible under Rule 404(b). Finally, the Committee does not intend through the amendment to affect the role of the court and the jury in considering such evidence. See United States v. Huddleston, 485 U.S. 681, 108 S.Ct. 1496 (1988).

2000 Amendments
Rule 404(a)(1) has been amended to provide that when the accused attacks the character of an alleged victim under subdivision (a)(2) of this Rule, the door is opened to an attack on the same character trait of the accused. Current law does not allow the government to introduce negative character evidence as to the accused unless the accused introduces evidence of good character. See, e.g., United States v. Fountain, 768 F.2d 790 (7th Cir. 1985) (when the accused offers proof of self-defense, this permits proof of the alleged victim's character trait for peacefulness, but it does not permit proof of the accused's character trait for violence).

The amendment makes clear that the accused cannot attack the alleged victim's character and yet remain shielded from the disclosure of equally relevant evidence concerning the same character trait of the accused. For example, in a murder case with a claim of self-defense, the accused, to bolster this defense, might offer evidence of the alleged victim's violent disposition. If the government has evidence that the accused has a violent character, but is not allowed to offer this evidence as part of its rebuttal, the jury has only part of the information it needs for an informed assessment of the probabilities as to who was the initial aggressor. This may be the case even if evidence of the accused's prior violent acts is admitted under Rule 404(b), because such evidence can be admitted only for limited purposes and not to show action in conformity with the accused's character on a specific occasion. Thus, the amendment is designed to permit a more balanced presentation of character evidence when an accused chooses to attack the character of the alleged victim.

The amendment does not affect the admissibility of evidence of specific acts of uncharged misconduct offered for a purpose other than proving character under Rule 404(b). Nor does it affect the standards for proof of character by evidence of other sexual behavior or sexual offenses under

Rules 412-415. By its placement in Rule 404(a)(1), the amendment covers only proof of character by way of reputation or opinion.

The amendment does not permit proof of the accused's character if the accused merely uses character evidence for a purpose other than to prove the alleged victim's propensity to act in a certain way. See United States v. Burks, 470 F.2d 432, 434-5 (D.C.Cir. 1972) (evidence of the alleged victim's violent character, when known by the accused, was admissible "on the issue of whether or not the defendant reasonably feared he was in danger of imminent great bodily harm"). Finally, the amendment does not permit proof of the accused's character when the accused attacks the alleged victim's character as a witness under Rule 608 or 609.

The term "alleged" is inserted before each reference to "victim" in the Rule, in order to provide consistency with Evidence Rule 412.

GAP Report--Proposed Amendment to Rule 404(a)
The Committee made the following changes to the published draft of the proposed amendment to Evidence Rule 404(a):
1. The term "a pertinent trait of character" was changed to "the same trait of character," in order to limit the scope of the government's rebuttal. The Committee Note was revised to accord with this change in the text.

2. The word "alleged" was added before each reference in the Rule to a "victim" in order to provide consistency with Evidence Rule 412. The Committee Note was amended to accord with this change in the text.

3. The Committee Note was amended to clarify that rebuttal is not permitted under this Rule if the accused proffers evidence of the alleged victim's character for a purpose other than to prove the alleged victim's propensity to act in a certain manner.

2006 Amendments
The Rule has been amended to clarify that in a civil case evidence of a person's character is never admissible to prove that the person acted in conformity with the character trait. The amendment resolves the dispute in the case law over whether the exceptions in subdivisions (a)(1) and (2) permit the circumstantial use of character evidence in civil cases. Compare Carson v. Polley, 689 F. 2d 562, 576 (5th Cir. 1982) ("when a central issue in a case is close to one of a criminal nature, the exceptions to the Rule 404(a) ban on character evidence may be invoked"), with SEC v. Towers Financial Corp., 966 F.Supp. 203 (S.D.N.Y. 1997) (relying on the terms "accused" and "prosecution" in Rule 404(a) to conclude that the exceptions in subdivisions (a)(1) and (2) are inapplicable in civil cases). The amendment is consistent with the original intent of the Rule, which was to prohibit the circumstantial use of character evidence in civil cases, even where closely related to criminal charges. See Ginter v. Northwestern Mut. Life Ins. Co., 576 F.Supp. 627, 629-30 (D. Ky.1984) ("It seems beyond peradventure of doubt that the drafters of F.R.Evi. 404(a) explicitly intended that all character evidence, except where 'character is at issue' was to be excluded" in civil cases).

The circumstantial use of character evidence is generally discouraged because it carries serious risks of prejudice, confusion and delay. See Michelson v. United States, 335 U.S. 469, 476 (1948) ("The overriding policy of excluding such evidence, despite its admitted probative value, is the practical experience that its disallowance tends to prevent confusion of issues, unfair surprise and undue prejudice."). In criminal cases, the so-called "mercy rule" permits a criminal defendant to introduce evidence of pertinent character traits of the defendant and the victim. But that is because the accused, whose liberty is at stake, may need "a counterweight against the strong investigative and prosecutorial resources of the government." C. Mueller & L. Kirkpatrick, Evidence: Practice Under the Rules, pp. 264-5 (2d ed. 1999). See also Richard Uviller, Evidence of Character to Prove Conduct: Illusion, Illogic, and Injustice in the Courtroom, 130 U.Pa.L.Rev. 845, 855 (1982) (the rule prohibiting circumstantial use of character evidence "was relaxed to allow the criminal defendant with so much at stake and so little available in the way of conventional proof to have special dispensation to tell the factfinder just what sort of person he really is"). Those concerns do not apply to parties in civil cases.

The amendment also clarifies that evidence otherwise admissible under Rule 404(a)(2) may nonetheless be excluded in a criminal case involving sexual misconduct. In such a case, the admissibility of evidence of the victim's sexual behavior and predisposition is governed by the more stringent provisions of Rule 412.

Nothing in the amendment is intended to affect the scope of Rule 404(b). While Rule 404(b) refers to the "accused," the "prosecution," and a "criminal case," it does so only in the context of a notice requirement. The admissibility standards of Rule 404(b) remain fully applicable to both civil and criminal cases.

2011 Amendments
The language of Rule 404 has been amended as part of the restyling of the Evidence Rules to make them more easily understood and to make style and terminology consistent throughout the rules. These changes are intended to be stylistic only. There is no intent to change any result in any ruling on evidence admissibility.

Rule 405. Methods of Proving Character

(a) By Reputation or Opinion. When evidence of a person's character or character trait is admissible, it may be proved by testimony about the person's reputation or by testimony in the form of an opinion. On cross- examination of the character witness, the court may allow an inquiry into relevant specific instances of the person's conduct.

(b) By Specific Instances of Conduct. When a person's character or character trait is an essential element of a charge, claim, or defense, the character or trait may also be proved by relevant specific instances of the person's conduct.

Credits

(Pub.L. 93-595, § 1, Jan. 2, 1975, 88 Stat. 1932; Mar. 2, 1987, eff. Oct. 1, 1987; Apr. 26, 2011, eff. Dec. 1, 2011.)

Editors' Notes
ADVISORY COMMITTEE NOTES
1972 Proposed Rules
The rule deals only with allowable methods of proving character, not with the admissibility of character evidence, which is covered in Rule 404.

Of the three methods of proving character provided by the rule, evidence of specific instances of conduct is the most convincing. At the same time it possesses the greatest capacity to arouse prejudice, to confuse, to surprise, and to consume time. Consequently the rule confines the use of evidence of this kind to cases in which character is, in the strict sense, in issue and hence deserving of a searching inquiry. When character is used circumstantially and hence occupies a lesser status in the case, proof may be only by reputation and opinion. These latter methods are also available when character is in issue. This treatment is, with respect to specific instances of conduct and reputation, conventional contemporary common law doctrine. McCormick § 153.

In recognizing opinion as a means of proving character, the rule departs from usual contemporary practice in favor of that of an earlier day. See 7 Wigmore § 1986, pointing out that the earlier practice permitted opinion and arguing strongly for evidence based on personal knowledge and belief as contrasted with "the secondhand, irresponsible product of multiplied guesses and gossip which we term 'reputation'." It seems likely that the persistence of reputation evidence is due to its largely being opinion in disguise. Traditionally character has been regarded primarily in moral overtones of good and bad: chaste, peaceable, truthful, honest. Nevertheless, on occasion nonmoral considerations crop up, as in the case of the incompetent driver, and this seems bound to happen increasingly. If character is defined as the kind of person one is, then account must be taken of varying ways of arriving at the estimate. These may range from the opinion of the employer who has found the man honest to the opinion of the psychiatrist based upon examination and testing. No effective dividing line exists between character and mental capacity, and the latter traditionally has been provable by opinion.

According to the great majority of cases, on cross-examination inquiry is allowable as to whether the reputation witness has heard of particular instances of conduct pertinent to the trait in question. Michelson v. United States, 335 U.S. 469, 69 S.Ct. 213, 93 L.Ed. 168 (1948); Annot., 47 A.L.R.2d 1258. The theory is that, since the reputation witness relates what he has heard, the inquiry tends to shed light on the accuracy of his hearing and reporting. Accordingly, the opinion witness would be asked whether he knew, as well as whether he had heard. The fact is, of course, that these distinctions are of slight if any practical significance, and the second sentence of subdivision (a) eliminates them as a factor in formulating questions. This recognition of the propriety of inquiring into specific instances of conduct does not circumscribe inquiry otherwise into the bases of opinion and reputation testimony.

The express allowance of inquiry into specific instances of conduct on cross-examination in subdivision (a) and the express allowance of it as part of a case in chief when character is actually in issue in subdivision (b) contemplate that testimony of specific instances is not generally permissible on the direct examination of an ordinary opinion witness to character. Similarly as to witnesses to the character of witnesses under Rule 608(b). Opinion testimony on direct in these situations ought in general to correspond to reputation testimony as now given, i.e., be confined to the nature and extent of observation and acquaintance upon which the opinion is based. See Rule 701.

1974 Enactment
Note to Subdivision (a). Rule 405(a) as submitted proposed to change existing law by allowing evidence of character in the form of opinion as well as reputation testimony. Fearing, among other reasons, that wholesale allowance of opinion testimony might tend to turn a trial into a swearing contest between conflicting character witnesses, the Committee decided to delete from this Rule, as well as from Rule 608(a) which involves a related problem, reference to opinion testimony. House Report No. 93-650.

The Senate makes two language changes in the nature of conforming amendments. The Conference adopts the Senate amendments. House Report No. 93-1597.

1987 Amendments
The amendment is technical. No substantive change is intended.

2011 Amendments
The language of Rule 405 has been amended as part of the restyling of the Evidence Rules to make them more easily understood and to make style and terminology consistent throughout the rules. These changes are intended to be stylistic only. There is no intent to change any result in any ruling on evidence admissibility.

Rule 406. Habit; Routine Practice

Evidence of a person's habit or an organization's routine practice may be admitted to prove that on a particular occasion the person or organization acted in accordance with the habit or routine practice. The court may admit this evidence regardless of whether it is corroborated or whether there was an eyewitness.

Credits

(Pub.L. 93-595, § 1, Jan. 2, 1975, 88 Stat. 1932; Apr. 26, 2011, eff. Dec. 1, 2011.)

Editors' Notes

ADVISORY COMMITTEE NOTES

1972 Proposed Rules
An oft-quoted paragraph, McCormick, § 162, p. 340, describes habit in terms effectively contrasting it with character:

"Character and habit are close akin. Character is a generalized description of one's disposition, or of one's disposition in respect to a general trait, such as honesty, temperance, or peacefulness. 'Habit,' in modern usage, both lay and psychological, is more specific. It describes one's regular response to a repeated specific situation. If we speak of character for care, we think of the person's tendency to act prudently in all the varying situations of life, in business, family life, in handling automobiles and in walking across the street. A habit, on the other hand, is the person's regular practice of meeting a particular kind of situation with a specific type of conduct, such as the habit of going down a particular stairway two stairs at a time, or of giving the hand-signal for a left turn, or of alighting from railway cars while they are moving. The doing of the habitual acts may become semi-automatic."

Equivalent behavior on the part of a group is designated "routine practice of an organization" in the rule.

Agreement is general that habit evidence is highly persuasive as proof of conduct on a particular occasion. Again quoting McCormick § 162, p. 341:

"Character may be thought of as the sum of one's habits though doubtless it is more than this. But unquestionably the uniformity of one's response to habit is far greater than the consistency with which one's conduct conforms to character or disposition. Even though character comes in only exceptionally as evidence of an act, surely any sensible man in investigating whether X did a particular act would be greatly helped in his inquiry by evidence as to whether he was in the habit of doing it."

When disagreement has appeared, its focus has been upon the question what constitutes habit, and the reason for this is readily apparent. The extent to which instances must be multiplied and consistency of behavior maintained in order to rise to the status of habit inevitably gives rise to differences of opinion. Lewan, Rationale of Habit Evidence, 16 Syracuse L.Rev. 39, 49 (1964). While adequacy of sampling and uniformity of response are key factors, precise standards for measuring their sufficiency for evidence purposes cannot be formulated.

The rule is consistent with prevailing views. Much evidence is excluded simply because of failure to achieve the status of habit. Thus, evidence of intemperate "habits" is generally excluded when offered as proof of drunkenness in accident cases, Annot., 46 A.L.R.2d 103, and evidence of other assaults is inadmissible to prove the instant one in a civil assault action, Annot., 66 A.L.R.2d 806. In Levin v. United States, 119 U.S.App.D.C. 156, 338 F.2d 265 (1964), testimony as to the religious "habits" of the accused, offered as tending to prove that he was at home observing the Sabbath rather than out obtaining money through larceny by trick, was held properly excluded:

"It seems apparent to us that an individual's religious practices would not be the type of activities which would lend themselves to the characterization of 'invariable regularity.' [1 Wigmore 520.] Certainly the very volitional basis of the activity raises serious questions as to its invariable nature, and hence its probative value." Id. at 272.

These rulings are not inconsistent with the trend towards admitting evidence of business transactions between one of the parties and a third person as tending to prove that he made the same bargain or proposal in the litigated situation. Slough, Relevancy Unraveled, 6 Kan.L.Rev. 38-41 (1957). Nor are they inconsistent with such cases as Whittemore v. Lockheed Aircraft Corp., 65 Cal.App.2d 737, 151 P.2d 670 (1944), upholding the admission of evidence that plaintiff's intestate had on four other occasions flown planes from defendant's factory for delivery to his employer airline, offered to prove that he was piloting rather than a guest on a plane which crashed and killed all on board while en route for delivery.

A considerable body of authority has required that evidence of the routine practice of an organization be corroborated as a condition precedent to its admission in evidence. Slough, Relevancy Unraveled, 5 Kan.L.Rev. 404, 449 (1957). This requirement is specifically rejected by the rule on the ground that it relates to the sufficiency of the evidence rather than admissibility. A similar position is taken in New Jersey Rule 49. The rule also rejects the requirement of the absence of eyewitnesses, sometimes encountered with respect to admitting habit evidence to prove freedom from contributory negligence in wrongful death cases. For comment critical of the requirements see Frank, J., in Cereste v. New York, N.H. & H.R. Co., 231 F.2d 50 (2d Cir.1956), cert. denied 351 U.S. 951, 76 S.Ct. 848, 100 L.Ed. 1475, 10 Vand.L.Rev. 447 (1957); McCormick § 162, p. 342. The omission of the requirement from the California Evidence Code is said to have effected its elimination. Comment, Cal.Ev.Code § 1105.

2011 Amendments
The language of Rule 406 has been amended as part of the restyling of the Evidence Rules to make them more easily understood and to make style and terminology consistent throughout the rules. These changes are intended to be stylistic only. There is no intent to change any result in any ruling on evidence admissibility.

Rule 407. Subsequent Remedial Measures

When measures are taken that would have made an earlier injury or harm less likely to occur, evidence of the subsequent measures is not admissible to prove:

• negligence;

• culpable conduct;

• a defect in a product or its design; or

• a need for a warning or instruction.

But the court may admit this evidence for another purpose, such as impeachment or--if disputed--proving ownership, control, or the feasibility of precautionary measures.

Credits

(Pub.L. 93-595, § 1, Jan. 2, 1975, 88 Stat. 1932; Apr. 11, 1997, eff. Dec. 1, 1997; Apr. 26, 2011, eff. Dec. 1, 2011.)

Editors' Notes

ADVISORY COMMITTEE NOTES

1972 Proposed Rules

The rule incorporates conventional doctrine which excludes evidence of subsequent remedial measures as proof of an admission of fault. The rule rests on two grounds. (1) The conduct is not in fact an admission, since the conduct is equally consistent with injury by mere accident or through contributory negligence. Or, as Baron Bramwell put it, the rule rejects the notion that "because the world gets wiser as it gets older, therefore it was foolish before." Hart v. Lancashire & Yorkshire Ry. Co., 21 L.T.R. N.S. 261, 263 (1869). Under a liberal theory of relevancy this ground alone would not support exclusion as the inference is still a possible one. (2) The other, and more impressive, ground for exclusion rests on a social policy of encouraging people to take, or at least not discouraging them from taking, steps in furtherance of added safety. The courts have applied this principle to exclude evidence of subsequent repairs, installation of safety devices, changes in company rules, and discharge of employees, and the language of the present rule is broad enough to encompass all of them. See Falknor, Extrinsic Policies Affecting Admissibility, 10 Rutgers L.Rev. 574, 590 (1956).

The second sentence of the rule directs attention to the limitations of the rule. Exclusion is called for only when the evidence of subsequent remedial measures is offered as proof of negligence or culpable conduct. In effect it rejects the suggested inference that fault is admitted. Other purposes are, however, allowable, including ownership or control, existence of duty, and feasibility of precautionary measures, if controverted, and impeachment. 2 Wigmore § 283; Annot., 64 A.L.R.2d 1296. Two recent federal cases are illustrative. Boeing Airplane Co. v. Brown, 291 F.2d 310 (9th Cir.1961), an action against an airplane manufacturer for using an allegedly defectively designed alternator shaft which caused a plane crash, upheld the admission of evidence of subsequent design modification for the purpose of showing that design changes and safeguards were feasible. And Powers v. J.B. Michael & Co., 329 F.2d 674 (6th Cir.1964), an action against a road contractor for negligent failure to put out warning signs, sustained the admission of evidence that defendant subsequently put out signs to show that the portion of the road in question was under defendant's control. The requirement that the other purpose be controverted calls for automatic exclusion unless a genuine issue be present and allows the opposing party to lay the groundwork for exclusion by making an admission. Otherwise the factors of undue prejudice, confusion of issues, misleading the jury, and waste of time remain for consideration under Rule 403.

For comparable rules, see Uniform Rule 51; California Evidence Code § 1151; Kansas Code of Civil Procedure § 60-451; New Jersey Evidence Rule 51.

1997 Amendments
The amendment to Rule 407 makes two changes in the rule. First, the words "an injury or harm allegedly caused by" were added to clarify that the rule applies only to changes made after the occurrence that produced the damages giving rise to the action. Evidence of measures taken by the defendant prior to the "event" causing "injury or harm" do not fall within the exclusionary scope of Rule 407 even if they occurred after the manufacture or design of the product. See Chase v. General Motors Corp., 856 F.2d 17, 21-22 (4th Cir. 1988).

Second, Rule 407 has been amended to provide that evidence of subsequent remedial measures may not be used to prove "a defect in a product or its design, or that a warning or instruction should have accompanied a product." This amendment adopts the view of a majority of the circuits that have interpreted Rule 407 to apply to products liability actions. See Raymond v. Raymond Corp., 938 F.2d 1518, 1522 (1st Cir. 1991); In re Joint Eastern District and Southern District Asbestos Litigation v. Armstrong World industries, Inc., 995 F.2d 343 (2d Cir. 1993); Cann v. Ford Motor Co., 658 F.2d 54, 60 (2d Cir. 1981), cert. denied, 456 U.S. 960 (1982); Kelly v. Crown Equipment Co., 970 F.2d 1273, 1275 (3d Cir. 1992); Werner v. Upjohn, Inc., 628 F.2d 848 (4th Cir. 1980); cert. denied, 449 U.S. 1080 (1981); Grenada Steel Industries, Inc. v. Alabama Oxygen Co., Inc., 695 F. 2d 883 (5th Cir. 1983); Bauman v. Volkswagenwerk Aktiengesellschaft, 621 F.2d 230, 232 (6th Cir. 1980); Flaminio v. Honda Motor Company, Ltd., 733 F.2d 463, 469 (7th Cir. 1984); Gauthier v. AMF, Inc., 788 F.2d 634, 636-37 (9th Cir. 1986).

Although this amendment adopts a uniform federal rule, it should be noted that evidence of subsequent remedial measures may be admissible pursuant to the second sentence of Rule 407. Evidence of subsequent measures that is not barred by Rule 407 may still be subject to exclusion on Rule 403 grounds when the dangers of prejudice or confusion substantially outweigh the probative value of the evidence.

GAP Report on Rule 407. The words "injury or harm" were substituted for the word "event " in line 3. The stylization changes in the second sentence of the rule were eliminated. The words "causing 'injury or harm' " were added to the Committee Note.

2011 Amendments

The language of Rule 407 has been amended as part of the general restyling of the Evidence Rules to make them more easily understood and to make style and terminology consistent throughout the rules. These changes are intended to be stylistic only. There is no intent to change any result in any ruling on evidence admissibility.

Rule 407 previously provided that evidence was not excluded if offered for a purpose not explicitly prohibited by the Rule. To improve the language of the Rule, it now provides that the court may admit evidence if offered for a permissible purpose. There is no intent to change the process for admitting evidence covered by the Rule. It remains the case that if offered for an impermissible purpose, it must be excluded, and if offered for a purpose not barred by the Rule, its admissibility remains governed by the general principles of Rules 402, 403, 801, etc.

Rule 408. Compromise Offers and Negotiations

(a) Prohibited Uses. Evidence of the following is not admissible--on behalf of any party--either to prove or disprove the validity or amount of a disputed claim or to impeach by a prior inconsistent statement or a contradiction:

(1) furnishing, promising, or offering--or accepting, promising to accept, or offering to accept--a valuable consideration in compromising or attempting to compromise the claim; and

(2) conduct or a statement made during compromise negotiations about the claim--except when offered in a criminal case and when the negotiations related to a claim by a public office in the exercise of its regulatory, investigative, or enforcement authority.

(b) Exceptions. The court may admit this evidence for another purpose, such as proving a witness's bias or prejudice, negating a contention of undue delay, or proving an effort to obstruct a criminal investigation or prosecution.

Credits

(Pub.L. 93-595, § 1, Jan. 2, 1975, 88 Stat. 1933; Apr. 12, 2006, eff. Dec. 1, 2006; Apr. 26, 2011, eff. Dec. 1, 2011.)

Editors' Notes

ADVISORY COMMITTEE NOTES

1972 Proposed Rules

As a matter of general agreement, evidence of an offer to compromise a claim is not receivable in evidence as an admission of, as the case may be, the validity or invalidity of the claim. As with evidence of subsequent remedial measures, dealt with in Rule 407, exclusion may be based on two grounds. (1) The evidence is irrelevant, since the offer may be motivated by a desire for peace rather than from any concession of weakness of position. The validity of this position will vary as the amount of the offer varies in relation to the size of the claim and may also be influenced by other circumstances. (2) A more consistently impressive ground is promotion of the public policy favoring the compromise and settlement of disputes. McCormick §§ 76, 251. While the rule is ordinarily phrased in terms of offers of compromise, it is apparent that a similar attitude must be taken with respect to completed compromises when offered against a party thereto. This latter situation will not, of course, ordinarily occur except when a party to the present litigation has compromised with a third person.

The same policy underlies the provision of Rule 68 of the Federal Rules of Civil Procedure that evidence of an unaccepted offer of judgment is not admissible except in a proceeding to determine costs.

The practical value of the common law rule has been greatly diminished by its inapplicability to admissions of fact, even though made in the course of compromise negotiations, unless hypothetical, stated to be "without prejudice," or so connected with the offer as to be inseparable from it. McCormick § 251, pp. 540-541. An inevitable effect is to inhibit freedom of communication with respect to compromise, even among lawyers. Another effect is the generation of controversy over whether a given statement falls within or without the protected area. These considerations account for the expansion of the rule herewith to include evidence of conduct or statements made in compromise negotiations, as well as the offer or completed compromise itself. For similar provisions see California Evidence Code §§ 1152, 1154.

The policy considerations which underlie the rule do not come into play when the effort is to induce a creditor to settle an admittedly due amount for a lesser sum. McCormick § 251, p. 540. Hence the rule requires that the claim be disputed as to either validity or amount.

The final sentence of the rule serves to point out some limitations upon its applicability. Since the rule excludes only when the purpose is proving the validity or invalidity of the claim or its amount, an offer for another purpose is not within the rule. The illustrative situations mentioned in the rule are supported by the authorities. As to proving bias or prejudice of a witness, see Annot., 161 A.L.R. 395, contra, Fenberg v. Rosenthal, 348 Ill.App. 510, 109 N.E.2d 402 (1952), and negativing a contention of lack of due diligence in presenting a claim, 4 Wigmore § 1061. An effort to "buy off" the prosecution or a prosecuting witness in a criminal case is not within the policy of the rule of exclusion. McCormick § 251, p. 542.

For other rules of similar import, see Uniform Rules 52 and 53; California Evidence Code §§ 1152, 1154; Kansas Code of Civil Procedure §§ 60-452, 60-453; New Jersey Evidence Rules 52 and 53.

1974 Enactment
Under existing federal law evidence of conduct and statements made in compromise negotiations is admissible in subsequent litigation between the parties. The second sentence of Rule 408 as submitted by the Supreme Court proposed to reverse that doctrine in the interest of further promoting non-judicial settlement of disputes. Some agencies of government expressed the view that the Court formulation was likely to impede rather than assist efforts to achieve settlement of disputes. For one thing, it is not always easy to tell when compromise negotiations begin, and informal dealings end. Also, parties dealing with government agencies would be reluctant to furnish factual information at preliminary meetings; they would wait until "compromise negotiations" began and thus hopefully effect an immunity for themselves with respect to the evidence supplied. In light of these considerations, the Committee recast the Rule so that admissions of liability or opinions given during compromise negotiations continue inadmissible, but evidence of unqualified factual assertions is admissible. The latter aspect of the Rule is drafted, however, so as to preserve other possible objections to the introduction of such evidence. The Committee intends no modification of current law whereby a party may protect himself from future use of his statements by couching them in hypothetical conditional form. House Report No. 93-650.

This rule as reported makes evidence of settlement or attempted settlement of a disputed claim inadmissible when offered as an admission of liability or the amount of liability. The purpose of this rule is to encourage settlements which would be discouraged if such evidence were admissible.

Under present law, in most jurisdictions, statements of fact made during settlement negotiations, however, are excepted from this ban and are admissible. The only escape from admissibility of statements of fact made in a settlement negotiation is if the declarant or his representative expressly states that the statement is hypothetical in nature or is made without prejudice. Rule 408 as submitted by the Court reversed the traditional rule. It would have brought statements of fact within the ban and made them, as well as an offer of settlement, inadmissible.

The House amended the rule and would continue to make evidence of facts disclosed during compromise negotiations admissible. It thus reverted to the traditional rule. The House committee report states that the committee intends to preserve current law under which a party may protect himself by couching his statements in hypothetical form [See House Report No. 93-650 above]. The real impact of this amendment, however, is to deprive the rule of much of its salutary effect. The exception for factual admissions was believed by the Advisory Committee to hamper free communication between parties and thus to constitute an unjustifiable restraint upon efforts to negotiate settlements--the encouragement of which is the purpose of the rule. Further, by protecting hypothetically phrased statements, it constituted a preference for the sophisticated, and a trap for the unwary.

Three States which had adopted rules of evidence patterned after the proposed rules prescribed by the Supreme Court opted for versions of rule 408 identical with the Supreme Court draft with respect to the inadmissibility of conduct or statements made in compromise negotiations [Nev.Rev.Stats. § 48.105; N.Mex.Stats.Anno. (1973 Supp.) § 20-4-408; West's Wis.Stats.Anno. (1973 Supp.) § 904.08].

For these reasons, the committee has deleted the House amendment and restored the rule to the version submitted by the Supreme Court with one additional amendment. This amendment adds a sentence to insure that evidence, such as documents, is not rendered inadmissible merely because it is presented in the course of compromise negotiations if the evidence is otherwise discoverable. A party should not be able to immunize from admissibility documents otherwise discoverable merely by offering them in a compromise negotiation. Senate Report No. 93-1277.

The House bill provides that evidence of admissions of liability or opinions given during compromise negotiations is not admissible, but that evidence of facts disclosed during compromise negotiations is not inadmissible by virtue of having been first disclosed in the compromise negotiations. The Senate amendment provides that evidence of conduct or statements made in compromise negotiations is not admissible. The Senate amendment also provides that the rule does not require the exclusion of any evidence otherwise discoverable merely because it is presented in the course of compromise negotiations.

The House bill was drafted to meet the objection of executive agencies that under the rule as proposed by the Supreme Court, a party could present a fact during compromise negotiations and thereby prevent an opposing party from offering evidence of that fact at trial even though such evidence was obtained from independent sources. The Senate amendment expressly precludes this result.

The Conference adopts the Senate amendment. House Report No. 93-1597.

2006 Amendment
Rule 408 has been amended to settle some questions in the courts about the scope of the Rule, and to make it easier to read. First, the amendment provides that Rule 408 does not prohibit the introduction in a criminal case of statements or conduct during compromise negotiations regarding a civil dispute by a government regulatory, investigative, or enforcement agency. See, e.g., United States v. Prewitt, 34 F.3d 436, 439 (7th Cir. 1994) (admissions of fault made in compromise of a civil securities enforcement action were admissible against the accused in a subsequent criminal action for mail fraud). Where an individual makes a statement in the presence of government agents, its subsequent admission in a criminal case should not be unexpected. The individual can seek to protect against subsequent disclosure through negotiation and agreement with the civil regulator or an attorney for the government.

Statements made in compromise negotiations of a claim by a government agency may be excluded in criminal cases where the circumstances so warrant under Rule 403. For example, if an individual was unrepresented at the time the statement was made in a civil enforcement proceeding, its probative value in a subsequent criminal case may be minimal. But there is no absolute exclusion imposed by Rule 408.

In contrast, statements made during compromise negotiations of other disputed claims are not admissible in subsequent criminal litigation, when offered to prove liability for, invalidity of, or amount of those claims. When private parties enter into compromise negotiations they cannot protect against the subsequent use of statements in criminal cases by way of private ordering. The inability to guarantee protection against subsequent use could lead to parties refusing to admit fault, even if by doing so they could favorably settle the private matter. Such a chill on settlement negotiations would be contrary to the policy of Rule 408.

The amendment distinguishes statements and conduct (such as a direct admission of fault) made in compromise negotiations of a civil claim by a government agency from an offer or acceptance of a compromise of such a claim. An offer or acceptance of a compromise of any civil claim is excluded under the Rule if offered against the defendant as an admission of fault. In that case, the predicate for the evidence would be that the defendant, by compromising with the government agency, has admitted the validity and amount of the civil claim, and that this admission has sufficient probative value to be considered as evidence of guilt. But unlike a direct statement of fault, an offer or acceptance of a compromise is not very probative of the defendant's guilt. Moreover, admitting such an offer or acceptance could deter a defendant from settling a civil regulatory action, for fear of evidentiary use in a subsequent criminal action. See, e.g., Fishman, Jones on Evidence, Civil and Criminal, § 22:16 at 199, n.83 (7th ed. 2000) ("A target of a potential criminal investigation may be unwilling to settle civil claims against him if by doing so he increases the risk of prosecution and conviction.").

The amendment retains the language of the original rule that bars compromise evidence only when offered as evidence of the "validity," "invalidity," or "amount" of the disputed claim. The intent is to retain the extensive case law finding Rule 408 inapplicable when compromise evidence is offered for a purpose other than to prove the validity, invalidity, or amount of a disputed claim. See, e.g., Athey v. Farmers Ins. Exchange, 234 F.3d 357 (8th Cir. 2000) (evidence of settlement offer by insurer was properly admitted to prove insurer's bad faith); Coakley & Williams v. Structural Concrete Equip., 973 F.2d 349 (4th Cir. 1992) (evidence of settlement is not precluded by Rule 408 where offered to prove a party's intent with respect to the scope of a release); Cates v. Morgan Portable Bldg. Corp., 708 F.2d 683 (7th Cir. 1985) (Rule 408 does not bar evidence of a settlement when offered to prove a breach of the settlement agreement, as the purpose of the evidence is to prove the fact of settlement as opposed to the validity or amount of the underlying claim); Uforma/ Shelby Bus. Forms, Inc. v. NLRB, 111 F.3d 1284 (6th Cir. 1997) (threats made in settlement negotiations were admissible; Rule 408 is inapplicable when the claim is based upon a wrong that is committed during the course of settlement negotiations). So for example, Rule 408 is inapplicable if offered to show that a party made fraudulent statements in order to settle a litigation.

The amendment does not affect the case law providing that Rule 408 is inapplicable when evidence of the compromise is offered to prove notice. See, e.g., United States v. Austin, 54 F.3d 394 (7th Cir. 1995) (no error to admit evidence of the defendant's settlement with the FTC, because it was offered to prove that the defendant was on notice that subsequent similar conduct was wrongful); Spell v. McDaniel, 824 F.2d 1380 (4th Cir. 1987) (in a civil rights action alleging that an officer used excessive force, a prior settlement by the City of another brutality claim was properly admitted to prove that the City was on notice of aggressive behavior by police officers).

The amendment prohibits the use of statements made in settlement negotiations when offered to impeach by prior inconsistent statement or through contradiction. Such broad impeachment would tend to swallow the exclusionary rule and would impair the public policy of promoting settlements. See McCormick on Evidence at 186 (5th ed. 1999) ("Use of statements made in compromise negotiations to impeach the testimony of a party, which is not specifically treated in Rule 408, is fraught with danger of misuse of the statements to prove liability, threatens frank interchange of information during negotiations, and generally should not be permitted."). See also EEOC v. Gear Petroleum, Inc., 948 F.2d 1542 (10th Cir.1991) (letter sent as part of settlement negotiation cannot be used to impeach defense witnesses by way of contradiction or prior inconsistent statement; such broad impeachment would undermine the policy of encouraging uninhibited settlement negotiations).

The amendment makes clear that Rule 408 excludes compromise evidence even when a party seeks to admit its own settlement offer or statements made in settlement negotiations. If a party were to reveal its own statement or offer, this could itself reveal the fact that the adversary entered into settlement negotiations. The protections of Rule 408 cannot be waived unilaterally because the Rule, by definition, protects both parties from having the fact of negotiation disclosed to the jury. Moreover, proof of statements and offers made in settlement would often have to be made through the testimony of attorneys, leading to the risks and costs of disqualification. See generally Pierce v. F.R. Tripler & Co., 955 F.2d 820, 828 (2d Cir. 1992) (settlement offers are excluded under Rule 408 even if it is the offeror who seeks to admit them; noting that the "widespread admissibility of the substance of settlement offers could bring with it a rash of motions for disqualification of a party's chosen counsel who would likely become a witness at trial").

The sentence of the Rule referring to evidence "otherwise discoverable" has been deleted as superfluous. See, e.g., Advisory Committee Note to Maine Rule of Evidence 408 (refusing to include the sentence in the Maine version of Rule 408 and noting that the sentence "seems to state what the law would be if it were omitted"); Advisory Committee Note to Wyoming Rule of Evidence 408 (refusing to include the sentence in Wyoming Rule 408 on the ground that it was "superfluous"). The intent of the sentence was to prevent a party from trying to immunize admissible information, such as a pre-existing document, through the pretense of disclosing it during compromise negotiations. See Ramada Development Co. v. Rauch, 644 F.2d 1097 (5th Cir. 1981). But even without the sentence, the Rule cannot be read to protect pre-existing information simply because it was presented to the adversary in compromise negotiations.

2011 Amendments
The language of Rule 408 has been amended as part of the general restyling of the Evidence Rules to make them more easily understood and to make style and terminology consistent throughout the rules. These changes are intended to be stylistic only. There is no intent to change any result in any ruling on evidence admissibility.

Rule 408 previously provided that evidence was not excluded if offered for a purpose not explicitly prohibited by the Rule. To improve the language of the Rule, it now provides that the court may admit evidence if offered for a permissible purpose. There is no intent to change the process for admitting evidence covered by the Rule. It remains the case that if offered for an impermissible purpose, it must be excluded, and if offered for a purpose not barred by the Rule, its admissibility remains governed by the general principles of Rules 402, 403, 801, etc.

The Committee deleted the reference to "liability" on the ground that the deletion makes the Rule flow better and easier to read, and because "liability" is covered by the broader term "validity." Courts have not made substantive decisions on the basis of any distinction between validity and liability. No change in current practice or in the coverage of the Rule is intended.

Rule 409. Offers to Pay Medical and Similar Expenses
Evidence of furnishing, promising to pay, or offering to pay medical, hospital, or similar expenses resulting from an injury is not admissible to prove liability for the injury.

Credits

(Pub.L. 93-595, § 1, Jan. 2, 1975, 88 Stat.1933; Apr. 26, 2011, eff. Dec. 1, 2011.)

Editors' Notes

ADVISORY COMMITTEE NOTES

1972 Proposed Rules

The considerations underlying this rule parallel those underlying Rules 407 and 408, which deal respectively with subsequent remedial measures and offers of compromise. As stated in Annot., 20 A.L.R.2d 291, 293:

"[G]enerally, evidence of payment of medical, hospital, or similar expenses of an injured party by the opposing party, is not admissible, the reason often given being that such payment or offer is usually made from humane impulses and not from an admission of liability, and that to hold otherwise would tend to discourage assistance to the injured person."

Contrary to Rule 408, dealing with offers of compromise, the present rule does not extend to conduct or statements not a part of the act of furnishing or offering or promising to pay. This difference in treatment arises from fundamental differences in nature. Communication is essential if compromises are to be effected, and consequently broad protection of statements is needed. This is not so in cases of payments or offers or promises to pay medical expenses, where factual statements may be expected to be incidental in nature.

For rules on the same subject, but phrased in terms of "humanitarian motives," see Uniform Rule 52; California Evidence Code § 1152; Kansas Code of Civil Procedure § 60-452; New Jersey Evidence Rule 52.

2011 Amendments

The language of Rule 409 has been amended as part of the restyling of the Evidence Rules to make them more easily understood and to make style and terminology consistent throughout the rules. These changes are intended to be stylistic only. There is no intent to change any result in any ruling on evidence admissibility.

Rule 410. Pleas, Plea Discussions, and Related Statements

(a) Prohibited Uses. In a civil or criminal case, evidence of the following is not admissible against the defendant who made the plea or participated in the plea discussions:

(1) a guilty plea that was later withdrawn;

(2) a nolo contendere plea;

(3) a statement made during a proceeding on either of those pleas under Federal Rule of Criminal Procedure 11 or a comparable state procedure; or

(4) a statement made during plea discussions with an attorney for the prosecuting authority if the discussions did not result in a guilty plea or they resulted in a later-withdrawn guilty plea.

(b) Exceptions. The court may admit a statement described in Rule 410(a)(3) or (4):

(1) in any proceeding in which another statement made during the same plea or plea discussions has been introduced, if in fairness the statements ought to be considered together; or

(2) in a criminal proceeding for perjury or false statement, if the defendant made the statement under oath, on the record, and with counsel present.

Credits

(Pub.L. 93-595, § 1, Jan. 2, 1975, 88 Stat. 1933; Pub.L. 94-149, § 1(9), Dec. 12, 1975, 89 Stat. 805; Apr. 30, 1979, eff. Dec. 1, 1980; Apr. 26, 2011, eff. Dec. 1, 2011.)

Editors' Notes

ADVISORY COMMITTEE NOTES

1972 Proposed Rules

Withdrawn pleas of guilty were held inadmissible in federal prosecutions in Kercheval v. United States, 274 U.S. 220, 47 S.Ct. 582, 71 L.Ed. 1009 (1927). The Court pointed out that to admit the withdrawn plea would effectively set at naught the allowance of withdrawal and place the accused in a dilemma utterly inconsistent with the decision to award him a trial. The New York Court of Appeals, in People v. Spitaleri, 9 N.Y.2d 168, 212 N.Y.S.2d 53, 173 N.E.2d 35 (1961), reexamined and overturned its earlier decisions which had allowed admission. In addition to the reasons set forth in Kercheval, which was quoted at length, the court pointed out that the effect of admitting the plea was to compel defendant to take the stand by way of explanation and to open the way for the prosecution to call the lawyer who had represented him at the time of entering the plea. State court decisions for and against admissibility are collected in Annot., 86 A.L.R.2d 326.

Pleas of nolo contendere are recognized by Rule 11 of the Rules of Criminal Procedure, although the law of numerous States is to the contrary. The present rule gives effect to the principal traditional characteristic of the nolo plea, i.e. avoiding the admission of guilt which is inherent in pleas of guilty. This position is consistent with the construction of Section 5 of the Clayton Act, 15 U.S.C. § 16(a), recognizing the inconclusive and compromise nature of judgments based on nolo pleas. General Electric Co. v. City of San Antonio, 334 F.2d 480 (5th Cir.1964); Commonwealth Edison Co. v. Allis-Chalmers Mfg. Co., 323 F.2d 412 (7th Cir.1963), cert. denied 376 U.S. 939, 84 S.Ct. 794, 11 L.Ed.2d 659; Armco Steel Corp. v. North Dakota, 376 F.2d 206 (8th Cir.1967); City of Burbank v. General Electric Co., 329 F.2d 825 (9th Cir.1964). See also state court decisions in Annot., 18 A.L.R.2d 1287, 1314.

Exclusion of offers to plead guilty or nolo has as its purpose the promotion of disposition of criminal cases by compromise. As pointed out in McCormick § 251, p. 543.

"Effective criminal law administration in many localities would hardly be possible if a large proportion of the charges were not disposed of by such compromises."

See also People v. Hamilton, 60 Cal.2d 105, 32 Cal.Rptr. 4, 383 P.2d 412 (1963), discussing legislation designed to achieve this result. As with compromise offers generally, Rule 408, free communication is needed, and security against having an offer of compromise or related statement admitted in evidence effectively encourages it.

Limiting the exclusionary rule to use against the accused is consistent with the purpose of the rule, since the possibility of use for or against other persons will not impair the effectiveness of withdrawing pleas or the freedom of discussion which the rule is designed to foster. See A.B.A. Standards Relating to Pleas of Guilty § 2.2 (1968). See also the narrower provisions of New Jersey Evidence Rule 52(2) and the unlimited exclusion provided in California Evidence Code § 1153.

1974 Enactment
The Committee added the phrase "Except as otherwise provided by Act of Congress" to Rule 410 as submitted by the Court in order to preserve particular congressional policy judgments as to the effect of a plea of guilty or of nolo contendere. See 15 U.S.C. 16(a). The Committee intends that its amendment refers to both present statutes and statutes subsequently enacted. House Report No. 93-650.

As adopted by the House, rule 410 would make inadmissible pleas of guilty or nolo contendere subsequently withdrawn as well as offers to make such pleas. Such a rule is clearly justified as a means of encouraging pleading. However, the House rule would then go on to render inadmissible for any purpose statements made in connection with these pleas or offers as well.

The committee finds this aspect of the House rule unjustified. Of course, in certain circumstances such statements should be excluded. If, for example, a plea is vitiated because of coercion, statements made in connection with the plea may also have been coerced and should be inadmissible on that basis. In other cases, however, voluntary statements of an accused made in court on the record, in connection with a plea, and determined by a court to be reliable should be admissible even though the plea is subsequently withdrawn. This is particularly true in those cases where, if the House rule were in effect, a defendant would be able to contradict his previous statements and thereby lie with impunity [See Harris v. New York, 401 U.S. 222 (1971)]. To prevent such an injustice, the rule has been modified to permit the use of such statements for the limited purposes of impeachment and in subsequent perjury or false statement prosecutions. Senate Report No. 93-1277.

The House bill provides that evidence of a guilty or nolo contendere plea, of an offer of either plea, or of statements made in connection with such pleas or offers of such pleas, is inadmissible in any civil or criminal action, case or proceeding against the person making such plea or offer. The Senate amendment makes the rule inapplicable to a voluntary and reliable statement made in court on the record where the statement is offered in a subsequent prosecution of the declarant for perjury or false statement.

The issues raised by Rule 410 are also raised by proposed Rule 11(e)(6) of the Federal Rules of Criminal Procedure presently pending before Congress. This proposed rule, which deals with the admissibility of pleas of guilty or nolo contendere, offers to make such pleas, and statements made in connection with such pleas, was promulgated by the Supreme Court on April 22, 1974, and in the absence of congressional action will become effective on August 1, 1975. The conferees intend to make no change in the presently-existing case law until that date, leaving the courts free to develop rules in this area on a case-by-case basis.

The Conferees further determined that the issues presented by the use of guilty and nolo contendere pleas, offers of such pleas, and statements made in connection with such pleas or offers, can be explored in greater detail during Congressional consideration of Rule 11(e)(6) of the Federal Rules of Criminal Procedure. The Conferees believe, therefore, that it is best to defer its effective date until August 1, 1975. The Conferees intend that Rule 410 would be superseded by any subsequent Federal Rule of Criminal Procedure or act of Congress with which it is inconsistent, if the Federal Rule of Criminal Procedure or Act of Congress takes effect or becomes law after the date of the enactment of the act establishing the rules of evidence.

The conference adopts the Senate amendment with an amendment that expresses the above intentions. House Report No. 93-1597.

1979 Amendments
Present rule 410 conforms to rule 11(e)(6) of the Federal Rules of Criminal Procedure. A proposed amendment to rule 11(e)(6) would clarify the circumstances in which pleas, plea discussions and related statements are inadmissible in evidence: see Advisory Committee Note thereto. The amendment proposed above would make comparable changes in rule 410.

2011 Amendments
The language of Rule 410 has been amended as part of the restyling of the Evidence Rules to make them more easily understood and to make style and terminology consistent throughout the rules. These changes are intended to be stylistic only. There is no intent to change any result in any ruling on evidence admissibility.

Rule 411. Liability Insurance

Evidence that a person was or was not insured against liability is not admissible to prove whether the person acted negligently or otherwise wrongfully. But the court may admit this evidence for another purpose, such as proving a witness's bias or prejudice or proving agency, ownership, or control.

Credits

(Pub.L. 93-595, § 1, Jan. 2, 1975, 88 Stat.1933; Mar. 2, 1987, eff. Oct. 1, 1987; Apr. 26, 2011, eff. Dec. 1, 2011.)

Editors' Notes

ADVISORY COMMITTEE NOTES

1972 Proposed Rules

The courts have with substantial unanimity rejected evidence of liability insurance for the purpose of proving fault, and absence of liability insurance as proof of lack of fault. At best the inference of fault from the fact of insurance coverage is a tenuous one, as is its converse. More important, no doubt, has been the feeling that knowledge of the presence or absence of liability insurance would induce juries to decide cases on improper grounds. McCormick § 168; Annot., 4 A.L.R.2d 761. The rule is drafted in broad terms so as to include contributory negligence or other fault of a plaintiff as well as fault of a defendant.

The second sentence points out the limits of the rule, using well established illustrations. Id.

For similar rules see Uniform Rule 54; California Evidence Code § 1155; Kansas Code of Civil Procedure § 60-454; New Jersey Evidence Rule 54.

1987 Amendments
The amendment is technical. No substantive change is intended.

2011 Amendments
The language of Rule 411 has been amended as part of the general restyling of the Evidence Rules to make them more easily understood and to make style and terminology consistent throughout the rules. These changes are intended to be stylistic only. There is no intent to change any result in any ruling on evidence admissibility.

Rule 411 previously provided that evidence was not excluded if offered for a purpose not explicitly prohibited by the Rule. To improve the language of the Rule, it now provides that the court may admit evidence if offered for a permissible purpose. There is no intent to change the process for admitting evidence covered by the Rule. It remains the case that if offered for an impermissible purpose, it must be excluded, and if offered for a purpose not barred by the Rule, its admissibility remains governed by the general principles of Rules 402, 403, 801, etc.

Rule 412. Sex-Offense Cases:
The Victim's Sexual Behavior or Predisposition

(a) Prohibited Uses. The following evidence is not admissible in a civil or criminal proceeding involving alleged sexual misconduct:

(1) evidence offered to prove that a victim engaged in other sexual behavior; or

(2) evidence offered to prove a victim's sexual predisposition.

(b) Exceptions.

(1) Criminal Cases. The court may admit the following evidence in a criminal case:

(A) evidence of specific instances of a victim's sexual behavior, if offered to prove that someone other than the defendant was the source of semen, injury, or other physical evidence;

(B) evidence of specific instances of a victim's sexual behavior with respect to the person accused of the sexual misconduct, if offered by the defendant to prove consent or if offered by the prosecutor; and

(C) evidence whose exclusion would violate the defendant's constitutional rights.

(2) Civil Cases. In a civil case, the court may admit evidence offered to prove a victim's sexual behavior or sexual predisposition if its probative value substantially outweighs the danger of harm to any victim and of unfair prejudice to any party. The court may admit evidence of a victim's reputation only if the victim has placed it in controversy.

(c) Procedure to Determine Admissibility.

(1) Motion. If a party intends to offer evidence under Rule 412(b), the party must:

(A) file a motion that specifically describes the evidence and states the purpose for which it is to be offered;

(B) do so at least 14 days before trial unless the court, for good cause, sets a different time;

(C) serve the motion on all parties; and

(D) notify the victim or, when appropriate, the victim's guardian or representative.

(2) Hearing. Before admitting evidence under this rule, the court must conduct an in camera hearing and give the victim and parties a right to attend and be heard. Unless the court orders otherwise, the motion, related materials, and the record of the hearing must be and remain sealed.

(d) Definition of "Victim." In this rule, "victim" includes an alleged victim.

Credits

(Added Pub.L. 95-540, § 2(a), Oct. 28, 1978, 92 Stat. 2046; amended Pub.L. 100-690, Title VII, § 7046(a), Nov. 18, 1988, 102 Stat. 4400; Apr. 29, 1994, eff. Dec. 1, 1994; Pub.L. 103-322, Title IV, § 40141(b), Sept. 13, 1994, 108 Stat. 1919; Apr. 26, 2011, eff. Dec. 1, 2011.)

Editors' Notes

ADVISORY COMMITTEE NOTES

1994 Amendments

Rule 412 has been revised to diminish some of the confusion engendered by the original rule and to expand the protection afforded alleged victims of sexual misconduct. Rule 412 applies to both civil and criminal proceedings. The rule aims to safeguard the alleged victim against the invasion of privacy, potential embarrassment and sexual stereotyping that is associated with public disclosure of intimate sexual details and the infusion of sexual innuendo into the factfinding process. By affording victims protection in most instances, the rule also encourages victims of sexual misconduct to institute and to participate in legal proceedings against alleged offenders

Rule 412 seeks to achieve these objectives by barring evidence relating to the alleged victim's sexual behavior or alleged sexual predisposition, whether offered as substantive evidence of for impeachment, except in designated circumstances in which the probative value of the evidence significantly outweighs possible harm to the victim.

The revised rule applies in all cases involving sexual misconduct without regard to whether the alleged victim or person accused is a party to the litigation. Rule 412 extends to "pattern" witnesses in both criminal and civil cases whose testimony about other instances of sexual misconduct by the person accused is otherwise admissible. When the case does not involve alleged sexual misconduct, evidence relating to a third-party witness' alleged sexual activities is not within the ambit of Rule 412. The witness will, however, be protected by other rules such as Rules 404 and 608, as well as Rule 403.

The terminology "alleged victim" is used because there will frequently be a factual dispute as to whether sexual misconduct occurred. It does not connote any requirement that the misconduct be alleged in the pleadings. Rule 412 does not, however, apply unless the person against whom the evidence is offered can reasonably be characterized as a "victim of alleged sexual misconduct." When this is not the case, as for instance in a defamation action involving statements concerning sexual misconduct in which the evidence is offered to show that the alleged defamatory statements were true or did not damage the plaintiff's reputation, neither Rule 404 nor this rule will operate to bar the evidence; Rule 401 and 403 will continue to control. Rule 412 will, however, apply in a Title VII action in which the plaintiff has alleged sexual harassment.

The reference to a person "accused" is also used in a non-technical sense. There is no requirement that there be a criminal charge pending against the person or even that the misconduct would constitute a criminal offense. Evidence offered to prove allegedly false prior claims by the victim is not barred by Rule 412. However, the evidence is subject to the requirements of Rule 404.

Subdivision (a). As amended, Rule 412 bars evidence offered to prove the victim's sexual behavior and alleged sexual predisposition. Evidence, which might otherwise be admissible under Rules 402, 404(b), 405, 607, 608, 609 of some other evidence rule, must be excluded if Rule 412 so requires. The word "other" is used to suggest some flexibility in admitting evidence "intrinsic" to the alleged sexual misconduct. Cf. Committee Note to 1991 amendment to Rule 404(b)

Past sexual behavior connotes all activities that involve actual physical conduct, i.e. sexual intercourse or sexual contact. See, e.g., United States v. Galloway, 937 F.2d 542 (10th Cir. 1991), cert. denied, 113 S.Ct. 418 (1992) (use of contraceptives inadmissible since use implies sexual activity); United States v. One Feather, 702 F.2d 736 (8th Cir. 1983) (birth of an illegitimate child inadmissible); State v. Carmichael, 727 P.2d 918, 925 (Kan. 1986) (evidence of venereal disease inadmissible). In addition, the word "behavior" should be construed to include activities of the mind, such as fantasies of dreams. See 23 C. Wright and K. Graham, Jr., Federal Practice and Procedure, § 5384 at p. 548 (1980) ("While there may be some doubt under statutes that require 'conduct,' it would seem that the language of Rule 412 is broad enough to encompass the behavior of the mind.").

The rule has been amended to also exclude all other evidence relating to an alleged victim of sexual misconduct that is offered to prove a sexual predisposition. This amendment is designed to exclude evidence that does not directly refer to sexual activities or thoughts but that the proponent believes may have a sexual connotation for the factfinder. Admission of such evidence would contravene Rule 412's objectives of shielding the alleged victim from potential embarrassment and safeguarding the victim against stereotypical thinking. Consequently, unless the (b)(2) exception is satisfied, evidence such as that relating to the alleged victim's mode of dress, speech, or life-style will not be admissible.

The introductory phrase in subdivision (a) was deleted because it lacked clarity and contained no explicit reference to the other provisions of the law that were intended to be overridden. The conditional clause, "except as provided in subdivisions (b) and (c)" is intended to make clear that evidence of the types described in subdivision (a) is admissible only under the strictures of those sections.

The reason for extending the rule to all criminal cases is obvious. The strong social policy of protecting a victim's privacy and encouraging victims to come forward to report criminal acts is not confined to cases that involve a charge of sexual assault. The need to protect the victim is equally great when a defendant is charged with kidnapping, and evidence is offered, either to prove motive or as background, that the defendant sexually assaulted the victim.

The reason for extending Rule 412 to civil cases is equally obvious. The need to protect alleged victims against invasions of privacy, potential embarrassment, and unwarranted sexual stereotyping, and the wish to encourage victims to come forward when they have been sexually molested do not disappear because the context has shifted from a criminal prosecution to a claim for damages or injunctive relief. There is a strong social policy in not only punishing those who engage in sexual misconduct, but in also providing relief to the victim. Thus, Rule 412 applies in any civil case in which a person claims to be the victim of sexual misconduct, such as actions for sexual battery or sexual harassment.

Subdivision (b). Subdivision (b) spells out the specific circumstances in which some evidence may be admissible that would otherwise be barred by the general rule expressed in subdivision (a). As amended, Rule 412 will be virtually unchanged in criminal cases, but will provide protection to any person alleged to be a victim of sexual misconduct regardless of the charge actually brought against an accused. A new exception has been added for civil cases.

In a criminal case, evidence may be admitted under subdivision (b)(1) pursuant to three possible exceptions, provided the evidence also satisfies other requirements for admissibility specified in the Federal Rules of Evidence, including Rule 403. Subdivisions (b)(1)(A) and (b)(1)(B) require proof in the form of specific instances of sexual behavior in recognition of the limited probative value and dubious reliability of evidence of reputation or evidence in the form of an opinion.

Under subdivision (b)(1)(A), evidence of specific instances of sexual behavior with persons other than the person whose sexual misconduct is alleged may be admissible if it is offered to prove that another person was the source of semen, injury or other physical evidence. Where the prosecution has directly or indirectly asserted that the physical evidence originated with the accused, the defendant must be afforded an opportunity to prove that another person was responsible. See United States v. Begay, 937 F.2d 515, 523 n. 10 (10th Cir. 1991). Evidence offered for the specific purpose identified in this subdivision may still be excluded if it does not satisfy Rules 401 or 403. See, e.g., United States v. Azure, 845 F.2d 1503, 1505-06 (8th Cir. 1988) (10 year old victim's injuries indicated recent use of force; court excluded evidence of consensual sexual activities with witness who testified at in camera hearing that he had never hurt victim and failed to establish recent activities).

Under the exception in subdivision (b)(1)(B), evidence of specific instances of sexual behavior with respect to the person whose sexual misconduct is alleged is admissible if offered to prove consent, or offered by the prosecution. Admissible pursuant to this exception might be evidence of prior instances of sexual activities between the alleged victim and the accused, as well as statements in which the alleged victim expresses an intent to engage in sexual intercourse with the accused, or voiced sexual fantasies involving that specific accused. In a prosecution for child sexual abuse, for example, evidence of uncharged sexual activity between the accused and the alleged victim offered by the prosecution may be admissible pursuant to Rule 404(b) to show a pattern of behavior. Evidence relating to the victim's alleged sexual predisposition is not admissible pursuant to this exception.

Under subdivision (b)(1)(C), evidence of specific instances of conduct may not be excluded if the result would be to deny a criminal defendant the protections afforded by the Constitution. For example, statements in which the victim has expressed an intent to have sex with the first person encountered on a particular occasion might not be excluded without violating the due process right of a rape defendant seeking to prove consent. Recognition of this basic principle was expressed on subdivision (b)(1) of the original rule. The United States Supreme Court has recognized that in various circumstances a defendant may have a right to introduce evidence otherwise precluded by an evidence rule under the Confrontation Clause. See, e.g., Olden v. Kentucky, 488 U.S. 227 (1988) (defendant in rape cases had right to inquire into alleged victim's cohabitation with another man to show bias).

Subdivision (b)(2) governs the admissibility of otherwise proscribed evidence in civil cases. It employs a balancing test rather than the specific exceptions stated in subdivision (b)(1) in recognition of the difficulty of foreseeing future developments in the law. Greater flexibility is needed to accommodate evolving causes of action such as claims for sexual harassment.

The balancing test requires the proponent of the evidence, whether plaintiff or defendant, to convince the court that the probative value of the proffered evidence "substantially outweighs the danger of harm to any victim and of unfair prejudice of any party." This test for admitting evidence offered to prove sexual behavior or sexual propensity in civil cases differs in three respects from the general rule governing admissibility set forth in Rule 403. First, it Reverses that usual procedure spelled out in Rule 403 by shifting the burden to the proponent to demonstrate admissibility rather than making the opponent justify exclusion of the evidence. Second, the standard expressed in subdivision (b)(2) is more stringent than in the original rule; it raises the threshold for admission by requiring that the probative value of the evidence substantially outweigh the specified dangers. Finally, the Rule 412 test puts "harm to the victim" on the scale in addition to prejudice to the parties.

Evidence of reputation may be received in a civil case only if the alleged victim has put his or her reputation into controversy. The victim may do so without making a specific allegation in a pleading. Cf. Fed.R.Civ.P. 35(a).

Subdivision (c). Amended subdivision (c) is more concise and understandable than the subdivision it replaces. The requirement of a motion before trial is continued in the amended rule, as is the provision that a late motion may be permitted for good cause shown. In deciding whether to permit late filing, the court may take into account the conditions previously included in the rule: namely whether the evidence is newly discovered and could not have been obtained earlier through the existence of due diligence, and whether the issue to which such evidence relates has newly arisen in the case. The rule recognizes that in some instances the circumstances that justify an application to introduce evidence otherwise barred by Rule 412 will not become apparent until trial.

The amended rule provides that before admitting evidence that falls within that prohibition of Rule 412(a), the court must hold a hearing in camera at which the alleged victim and any party must be afforded the right to be present and an opportunity to be heard. All papers connected with the motion must be kept and remain under seal during the course of trial and appellate proceedings unless otherwise ordered. This is to assure that the privacy of the alleged victim is preserved in all cases in which the court rules that proffered evidence is not admissible, and in which the hearing refers to matters that are not received, or are received in another form.

The procedures set forth in subdivision (c) do not apply to discovery of a victim's past sexual conduct or predisposition in civil cases, which will be continued to be governed by Fed. R. Civ. P. 26. In order not to undermine the rationale of Rule 412, however, courts should enter appropriate orders pursuant to Fed. R. Civ. P. 26 (c) to protect the victim against unwarranted inquiries and to ensure confidentiality. Courts should presumptively issue protective orders barring discovery unless the party seeking discovery makes a showing that the evidence sought to be discovered would be relevant under the facts and theories of the particular case, and cannot be obtained except through discovery. In an action for sexual harassment, for instance, while some evidence of the alleged victim's sexual behavior and/or predisposition in the workplace may perhaps be relevant, non-work place conduct will usually be irrelevant. Cf. Burns v. McGregor Electronic Industries, Inc., 989 F. 2d 959, 962-63 (8th Cir. 1993) (posing for a nude magazine outside work hours is irrelevant to issue of unwelcomeness of sexual advances at work). Confidentiality orders should be presumptively granted as well.

One substantive change made in subdivision (c) is the elimination of the following sentence: "Notwithstanding subdivision (b) of Rule 104, if the relevancy of the evidence which the accused seeks to offer in trial depends upon the fulfillment of a condition of fact, the court, at the hearing in chambers or at a subsequent hearing in chambers scheduled for such purpose, shall accept evidence on the issue of whether such condition of fact is fulfilled and shall determine such issue." On its face, this language would appear to authorize a trial judge to exclude evidence of past sexual conduct between alleged victim and an accused or a defendant in a civil case based upon the judge's belief that such past acts did not occur. Such an authorization raises questions of invasion of the right to a jury trial under the Sixth and Seventh Amendments. See 1 S. Saltzburg & M. Martin, Federal Rules of Evidence Manual, 396-97 (5th ed. 1990).

The Advisory Committee concluded that the amended rule provided adequate protection for all persons claiming to be the victims of sexual misconduct, and that it was inadvisable to continue to include a provision in the rule that has been confusing and that raises substantial constitutional issues.

[Advisory Committee Note adopted by Congressional Conference Report accompanying Pub.L. 103-322. See H.R. Conf. Rep. No. 103-711, 103rd Cong., 2nd Sess., 383 (1994).]

Congressional Discussion

The following discussion in the House of Representatives of October 10, 1978, preceded passage of H.R. 4727, which enacted Rule 412. The discussion appears in 124 Cong.Record, at page H. 11944.

Mr. MANN. Mr. Speaker, I yield myself such time as I may consume.

Mr. Speaker, for many years in this country, evidentiary rules have permitted the introduction of evidence about a rape victim's prior sexual conduct. Defense lawyers were permitted great latitude in bringing out intimate details about a rape victim's life. Such evidence quite often serves no real purpose and only results in embarrassment to the rape victim and unwarranted public intrusion into her private life.

The evidentiary rules that permit such inquiry have in recent years come under question; and the States have taken the lead to change and modernize their evidentiary rules about evidence of a rape victim's prior sexual behavior. The bill before us similarly seeks to modernize the Federal Evidentiary rules.

The present Federal Rules of Evidence reflect the traditional approach. If a defendant in a rape case raises the defense of consent, that defendant may then offer evidence about the victim's prior sexual behavior. Such evidence may be in the form of opinion evidence, evidence of reputation, or evidence of specific instances of behavior. Rule 404(a)(2) of the Federal Rules of Evidence permits the introduction of evidence of a "pertinent character trait." The advisory committee note to that rule cites, as an example of what the rule covers, the character of a rape victim when the issue is consent. Rule 405 of the Federal Rules of Evidence permits the use of opinion or reputation evidence or the use of evidence of specific behavior to show a character trait.

Thus, Federal evidentiary rules permit a wide ranging inquiry into the private conduct of a rape victim, even though that conduct may have at best a tenuous connection to the offense for which the defendant is being tried.

H.R. 4727 amends the Federal Rules of Evidence to add a new rule, applicable only in criminal cases, to spell out when, and under what conditions, evidence of a rape victim's prior sexual behavior can be admitted. The new rule provides that reputation or opinion evidence about a rape victim's prior sexual behavior is not admissible. The new rule also provides that a court cannot admit evidence of specific instances of a rape victim's prior sexual conduct except in three circumstances.

The first circumstance is where the Constitution requires that the evidence be admitted. This exception is intended to cover those infrequent instances where, because of an unusual chain of circumstances, the general rule of inadmissibility, if followed, would result in denying the defendant a constitutional right.

The second circumstance in which the defendant can offer evidence of specific instances of a rape victim's prior sexual behavior is where the defendant raises the issue of consent and the evidence is of sexual behavior with the defendant. To admit such evidence, however, the court must find that the evidence is relevant and that its probative value outweighs the danger of unfair prejudice.

The third circumstance in which a court can admit evidence of specific instances of a rape victim's prior sexual behavior is where the evidence is of behavior with someone other than the defendant and is offered by the defendant on the issue of whether or not he was the source of semen or injury. Again, such evidence will be admitted only if the court finds that the evidence is relevant and that its probative value outweighs the danger of unfair prejudice.

The new rule further provides that before evidence is admitted under any of these exceptions, there must be an in camera hearing--that is, a proceeding that takes place in the judge's chambers out of the presence of the jury and the general public. At this hearing, the defendant will present the evidence he intends to offer and be able to argue why it should be admitted. The prosecution, of course, will be able to argue against that evidence being admitted.

The purpose of the in camera hearing is twofold. It gives the defendant an opportunity to demonstrate to the court why certain evidence is admissible and ought to be presented to the jury. At the same time, it protects the privacy of the rape victim in those instances when the court finds that evidence is inadmissible. Of course, if the court finds the evidence to be admissible, the evidence will be presented to the jury in open court.

The effect of this legislation, therefore, is to preclude the routine use of evidence of specific instances of a rape victim's prior sexual behavior. Such evidence will be admitted only in clearly and narrowly defined circumstances and only after an in camera hearing. In determining the admissibility of such evidence, the court will consider all of the facts and circumstances surrounding the evidence, such as the amount of time that lapsed between the alleged prior act and the rape charged in the prosecution. The greater the lapse of time, of course, the less likely it is that such evidence will be admitted.

Mr. Speaker, the principal purpose of this legislation is to protect rape victims from the degrading and embarrassing disclosure of intimate details about their private lives. It does so by narrowly circumscribing when such evidence may be admitted. It does not do so, however, by sacrificing any constitutional right possessed by the defendant. The bill before us fairly balances the interests involved--the rape victim's interest in protecting her private life from unwarranted public exposure; the defendant's interest in being able adequately to present a defense by offering relevant and probative evidence; and society's interest in a fair trial, one where unduly prejudicial evidence is not permitted to becloud the issues before the jury.

I urge support of the bill.

Mr. WIGGINS. Mr. Speaker, I yield myself such time as I may consume.

(Mr. WIGGINS asked and was given permission to revise and extend his remarks.)

Mr. WIGGINS. Mr. Speaker, this legislation addresses itself to a subject that is certainly a proper one for our consideration. Many of us have been troubled for years about the indiscriminate and prejudicial use of testimony with respect to a victim's prior sexual behavior in rape and similar cases. This bill deals with that problem. It is not, in my opinion, Mr. Speaker, a perfect bill in the manner in which it deals with the problem, but my objections are not so fundamental as would lead me to oppose the bill.

I think, Mr. Speaker, that it is unwise to adopt a per se rule absolutely excluding evidence of reputation and opinion with respect to the victim--and this bill does that--but it is difficult for me to foresee the specific case in which such evidence might be admissible. The trouble is this, Mr. Speaker: None of us can foresee perfectly all of the various circumstances under which the propriety of evidence might be before the court. If this bill has a defect, in my view it is because it adopts a per se rule with respect to opinion and reputation evidence.

Alternatively we might have permitted that evidence to be considered in camera as we do other evidence under the bill.

I should note, however, in fairness, having expressed minor reservations, that the bill before the House at this time does improve significantly upon the bill which was presented to our committee.

I will not detail all of those improvements but simply observe that the bill upon which we shall soon vote is a superior product to that which was initially considered by our subcommittee.

Mr. Speaker, I ask my colleagues to vote for this legislation as being, on balance, worthy of their support, and urge its adoption.

I reserve the balance of my time.

Mr. MANN. Mr. Speaker, this legislation has more than 100 cosponsors, but its principal sponsor, as well as its architect is the gentlewoman from New York (Ms. Holtzman). As the drafter of the legislation she will be able to provide additional information about the probable scope and effect of the legislation.

I yield such time as she may consume to the gentlewoman from New York (Ms. Holtzman).

(Ms. HOLTZMAN asked and was given permission to revise and extend her remarks.)

Ms. HOLTZMAN. Mr. Speaker, I would like to begin first by complimenting the distinguished gentleman from South Carolina (Mr. Mann), the chairman of the subcommittee, for his understanding of the need for corrective legislation in this area and for the fairness with which he has conducted the subcommittee hearings. I would like also to compliment the other members of the subcommittee, including the gentleman from California (Mr. Wiggins).

Too often in this country victims of rape are humiliated and harassed when they report and prosecute the rape. Bullied and cross-examined about their prior sexual experiences, many find the trial almost as degrading as the rape itself. Since rape trials become inquisitions into the victim's morality, not trials of the defendant's innocence or guilt, it is not surprising that it is the least reported crime. It is estimated that as few as one in ten rapes is ever reported.

Mr. Speaker, over 30 States have taken some action to limit the vulnerability of rape victims to such humiliating cross-examination of their past sexual experiences and intimate personal histories. In federal courts, however, it is permissible still to subject rape victims to brutal cross-examination about their past sexual histories. H.R. 4727 would rectify this problem in Federal courts and I hope, also serve as a model to suggest to the remaining states that reform of existing rape laws is important to the equity of our criminal justice system.

H.R. 4727 applies only to criminal rape cases in Federal courts. The bill provides that neither the prosecution nor the defense can introduce any reputation or opinion evidence about the victim's past sexual conduct. It does permit, however, the introduction of specific evidence about the victim's past sexual conduct in three very limited circumstances.

First, this evidence can be introduced if it deals with the victim's past sexual relations with the defendant and is relevant to the issue of whether she consented. Second, when the defendant claims he had no relations with the victim, he can use evidence of the victim's past sexual relations with others if the evidence rebuts the victim's claim that the rape caused certain physical consequences, such as semen or injury. Finally, the evidence can be introduced if it is constitutionally required. This last exception, added in subcommittee, will insure that the defendant's constitutional rights are protected.

Before any such evidence can be introduced, however, the court must determine at a hearing in chambers that the evidence falls within one of the exceptions.

Furthermore, unless constitutionally required, the evidence of specific instances of prior sexual conduct cannot be introduced at all it if would be more prejudicial and inflammatory that probative.

Mr. Speaker, I urge adoption of this bill. It will protect women from both injustice and indignity.

Mr. MANN. Mr. Speaker, I have no further requests for time, and I yield back the balance of my time.

Mr. WIGGINS. Mr. Speaker, I have no further requests for time, and yield back the balance of my time.

The SPEAKER pro tempore. The question is on the motion offered by the gentleman from South Carolina (Mr. Mann) that the House suspend the rules and pass the bill H.R. 4727, as amended.

The question was taken; and (two-thirds having voted in favor thereof) the rules were suspended and the bill, as amended, was passed.

A motion to reconsider was laid on the table.

2011 Amendment
The language of Rule 412 has been amended as part of the restyling of the Evidence Rules to make them more easily understood and to make style and terminology consistent throughout the rules. These changes are intended to be stylistic only. There is no intent to change any result in any ruling on evidence admissibility.

Rule 413. Similar Crimes in Sexual-Assault Cases

(a) Permitted Uses. In a criminal case in which a defendant is accused of a sexual assault, the court may admit evidence that the defendant committed any other sexual assault. The evidence may be considered on any matter to which it is relevant.

(b) Disclosure to the Defendant. If the prosecutor intends to offer this evidence, the prosecutor must disclose it to the defendant, including witnesses' statements or a summary of the expected testimony. The prosecutor must do so at least 15 days before trial or at a later time that the court allows for good cause.

(c) Effect on Other Rules. This rule does not limit the admission or consideration of evidence under any other rule.

(d) Definition of "Sexual Assault." In this rule and Rule 415, " sexual assault" means a crime under federal law or under state law (as " state" is defined in 18 U.S.C. § 513) involving:

(1) any conduct prohibited by 18 U.S.C. chapter 109A;

(2) contact, without consent, between any part of the defendant's body--or an object--and another person's genitals or anus;

(3) contact, without consent, between the defendant's genitals or anus and any part of another person's body;

(4) deriving sexual pleasure or gratification from inflicting death, bodily injury, or physical pain on another person; or

(5) an attempt or conspiracy to engage in conduct described in subparagraphs (1)-(4).

Credits

(Added Pub.L. 103-322, Title XXXII, § 320935(a), Sept. 13, 1994, 108 Stat. 2136; amended Apr. 26, 2011, eff. Dec. 1, 2011.)

Editors' Notes

ADVISORY COMMITTEE NOTES

2011 Amendments

The language of Rule 413 has been amended as part of the restyling of the Evidence Rules to make them more easily understood and to make style and terminology consistent throughout the rules. These changes are intended to be stylistic only. There is no intent to change any result in any ruling on evidence admissibility.

Rule 414. Similar Crimes in Child-Molestation Cases

(a) Permitted Uses. In a criminal case in which a defendant is accused of child molestation, the court may admit evidence that the defendant committed any other child molestation. The evidence may be considered on any matter to which it is relevant.

(b) Disclosure to the Defendant. If the prosecutor intends to offer this evidence, the prosecutor must disclose it to the defendant, including witnesses' statements or a summary of the expected testimony. The prosecutor must do so at least 15 days before trial or at a later time that the court allows for good cause.

(c) Effect on Other Rules. This rule does not limit the admission or consideration of evidence under any other rule.

(d) Definition of "Child" and "Child Molestation." In this rule and Rule 415:

(1) "child" means a person below the age of 14; and

(2) "child molestation" means a crime under federal law or under state law (as "state" is defined in 18 U.S.C. § 513) involving:

(A) any conduct prohibited by 18 U.S.C. chapter 109A and committed with a child;

(B) any conduct prohibited by 18 U.S.C. chapter 110;

(C) contact between any part of the defendant's body--or an object--and a child's genitals or anus;

(D) contact between the defendant's genitals or anus and any part of a child's body;

(E) deriving sexual pleasure or gratification from inflicting death, bodily injury, or physical pain on a child; or

(F) an attempt or conspiracy to engage in conduct described in subparagraphs (A)-(E).

Credits

(Added Pub.L. 103-322, Title XXXII, § 320935(a), Sept. 13, 1994, 108 Stat. 2135; amended Apr. 26, 2011, eff. Dec. 1, 2011.)

Editors' Notes

ADVISORY COMMITTEE NOTES

2011 Amendments

The language of Rule 414 has been amended as part of the restyling of the Evidence Rules to make them more easily understood and to make style and terminology consistent throughout the rules. These changes are intended to be stylistic only. There is no intent to change any result in any ruling on evidence admissibility.

Rule 415. Similar Acts in Civil Cases Involving Sexual Assault or Child Molestation

(a) Permitted Uses. In a civil case involving a claim for relief based on a party's alleged sexual assault or child molestation, the court may admit evidence that the party committed any other sexual assault or child molestation. The evidence may be considered as provided in Rules 413 and 414.

(b) Disclosure to the Opponent. If a party intends to offer this evidence, the party must disclose it to the party against whom it will be offered, including witnesses' statements or a summary of the expected testimony. The party must do so at least 15 days before trial or at a later time that the court allows for good cause.

(c) Effect on Other Rules. This rule does not limit the admission or consideration of evidence under any other rule.

Credits

(Added Pub.L. 103-322, Title XXXII, § 320935(a), Sept. 13, 1994, 108 Stat. 2137; amended Apr. 26, 2011, eff. Dec. 1, 2011.)

Editors' Notes

ADVISORY COMMITTEE NOTES

2011 Amendments

The language of Rule 415 has been amended as part of the restyling of the Evidence Rules to make them more easily understood and to make style and terminology consistent throughout the rules. These changes are intended to be stylistic only. There is no intent to change any result in any ruling on evidence admissibility.

Article V: Privileges

Rule 501. Privilege in General

The common law--as interpreted by United States courts in the light of reason and experience--governs a claim of privilege unless any of the following provides otherwise:

• the United States Constitution;

• a federal statute; or

• rules prescribed by the Supreme Court.

But in a civil case, state law governs privilege regarding a claim or defense for which state law supplies the rule of decision.

Credits

(Pub.L. 93-595, § 1, Jan. 2, 1975, 88 Stat. 1933; Apr. 26, 2011, eff. Dec. 1, 2011.)

Editors' Notes

ADVISORY COMMITTEE NOTES

1974 Enactment

Article V as submitted to Congress contained thirteen Rules. Nine of those Rules defined specific non-constitutional privileges which the federal courts must recognize (i.e. required reports, lawyer-client, psychotherapist-patient, husband-wife, communications to clergymen, political vote, trade secrets, secrets of state and other official information, and identity of informer.) Another Rule provided that only those privileges set forth in Article V or in some other Act of Congress could be recognized by the federal courts. The three remaining Rules addressed collateral problems as to waiver of privilege by voluntary disclosure, privileged matter disclosed under compulsion or without opportunity to claim privilege, comment upon or inference from a claim of privilege, and jury instruction with regard thereto.

The Committee amended Article V to eliminate all of the Court's specific Rules on privileges. Instead, the Committee, through a single Rule, 501, left the law of privileges in its present state and further provided that privileges shall continue to be developed by the courts of the United States under a uniform standard applicable both in civil and criminal cases. That standard, derived from Rule 26 of the Federal Rules of Criminal Procedure, mandates the application of the principles of the common law as interpreted by the courts of the United States in the light of reason and experience. The words "person, government, State, or political subdivision thereof" were added by the Committee to the lone term "witnesses" used in Rule 26 to make clear that, as under present law, not only witnesses may have privileges. The Committee also included in its amendment a proviso modeled after Rule 302 and similar to language added by the Committee to Rule 601 relating to the competency of witnesses. The proviso is designed to require the application of State privilege law in civil actions and proceedings governed by Erie R. Co. v. Tompkins, 304 U.S. 64 (1938), a result in accord with current federal court decisions. See Republic Gear Co. v. Borg-Warner Corp., 381 F.2d 551, 555-556 n. 2 (2nd Cir.1967). The Committee deemed the proviso to be necessary in the light of the Advisory Committee's view (see its note to Court [proposed] Rule 501) that this result is not mandated under Erie.

The rationale underlying the proviso is that federal law should not supersede that of the States in substantive areas such as privilege absent a compelling reason. The Committee believes that in civil cases in the federal courts where an element of a claim or defense is not grounded upon a federal question, there is no federal interest strong enough to justify departure from State policy. In addition, the Committee considered that the Court's proposed Article V would have promoted forum shopping in some civil actions, depending upon differences in the privilege law applied as among the State and federal courts. The Committee's proviso, on the other hand, under which the federal courts are bound to apply the State's privilege law in actions founded upon a State-created right or defense, removes the incentive to "shop". House Report No. 93-650.

Article V as submitted to Congress contained 13 rules. Nine of those rules defined specific nonconstitutional privileges which the Federal courts must recognize (i.e., required reports, lawyer-client, psychotherapist-patient, husband-wife, communications to clergymen, political vote, trade secrets, secrets of state and other official information, and identity of informer). Many of these rules contained controversial modifications or restrictions upon common law privileges. As noted supra, the House amended article V to eliminate all of the Court's specific rules on privileges. Through a single rule, 501, the House provided that privileges shall be governed by the principles of the common law as interpreted by the courts of the United States in the light of reason and experience (a standard derived from rule 26 of the Federal Rules of Criminal Procedure) except in the case of an element of a civil claim or defense as to which State law supplies the rule of decision, in which event state privilege law was to govern.

The committee agrees with the main thrust of the House amendment: that a federally developed common law based on modern reason and experience shall apply except where the State nature of the issues renders deference to State privilege law the wiser course, as in the usual diversity case. The committee understands that thrust of the House amendment to require that State privilege law be applied in "diversity" cases (actions on questions of State law between citizens of different States arising under 28 U.S.C. § 1332). The language of the House amendment, however, goes beyond this in some respects, and falls short of it in others: State privilege law applies even in nondiversity, Federal question civil cases, where an issue governed by State substantive law is the object of the evidence (such issues do sometimes arise in such cases); and, in all instances where State privilege law is to be applied, e.g., on proof of a State issue in a diversity case, a close reading reveals that State privilege law is not to be applied unless the matter to be proved is an element of that state claim or defense, as distinguished from a step along the way in the proof of it.

The committee is concerned that the language used in the House amendment could be difficult to apply. It provides that "in civil actions * * * with respect to an element of a claim or defense as to which State law supplies the rule of decision," State law on privilege applies. The question of what is an element of a claim or defense is likely to engender considerable litigation. If the matter in question constitutes an element of a claim, State law supplies the privilege rule; whereas if it is a mere item of proof with respect to a claim, then, even though State law might supply the rule of decision, Federal law on the privilege would apply. Further, disputes will arise as to how the rule should be applied in an antitrust action or in a tax case where the Federal statute is silent as to a particular aspect of the substantive law in question, but Federal cases had incorporated State law by reference to State law. [For a discussion of reference to State substantive law, see note on Federal Incorporation by Reference of State Law, Hart & Wechsler, The Federal Courts and the Federal System, pp. 491-494 (2d ed. 1973).] Is a claim (or defense) based on such a reference a claim or defense as to which federal or State law supplies the rule of decision?

Another problem not entirely avoidable is the complexity or difficulty the rule introduces into the trial of a Federal case containing a combination of Federal and State claims and defenses, e.g. an action involving Federal antitrust and State unfair competition claims. Two different bodies of privilege law would need to be consulted. It may even develop that the same witness-testimony might be relevant on both counts and privileged as to one but not the other. [The problems with the House formulation are discussed in Rothstein, The Proposed Amendments to the Federal Rules of Evidence, 62 Georgetown University Law Journal 125 (1973) at notes 25, 26 and 70-74 and accompanying text.]

The formulation adopted by the House is pregnant with litigious mischief. The committee has, therefore, adopted what we believe will be a clearer and more practical guideline for determining when courts should respect State rules of privilege. Basically, it provides that in criminal and Federal question civil cases, federally evolved rules on privilege should apply since it is Federal policy which is being enforced. [It is also intended that the Federal law of privileges should be applied with respect to pendent State law claims when they arise in a Federal question case.] Conversely, in diversity cases where the litigation in question turns on a substantive question of State law, and is brought in the Federal courts because the parties reside in different States, the committee believes it is clear that State rules of privilege should apply unless the proof is directed at a claim or defense for which Federal law supplies the rule of decision (a situation which would not commonly arise.) [While such a situation might require use of two bodies of privilege law, federal and state, in the same case, nevertheless the occasions on which this would be required are considerably reduced as compared with the House version, and confined to situations where the Federal and State interests are such as to justify application of neither privilege law to the case as a whole. If the rule proposed here results in two conflicting bodies of privilege law applying to the same piece of evidence in the same case, it is contemplated that the rule favoring reception of the evidence should be applied. This policy is based on the present rule 43(a) of the Federal Rules of Civil Procedure which provides: In any case, the statute or rule which favors the reception of the evidence governs and the evidence shall be presented according to the most convenient method prescribed in any of the statutes or rules to which reference is herein made.] It is intended that the State rules of privilege should apply equally in original diversity actions and diversity actions removed under 28 U.S.C. § 1441(b).

Two other comments on the privilege rule should be made. The committee has received a considerable volume of correspondence from psychiatric organizations and psychiatrists concerning the deletion of rule 504 of the rule submitted by the Supreme Court. It should be clearly understood that, in approving this general rule as to privileges, the action of Congress should not be understood as disapproving any recognition of a psychiatrist-patient, or husband-wife, or any other of the enumerated privileges contained in the Supreme Court rules. Rather, our action should be understood as reflecting the view that the recognition of a privilege based on a confidential relationship and other privileges should be determined on a case-by-case basis.

Further, we would understand that the prohibition against spouses testifying against each other is considered a rule of privilege and covered by this rule and not by rule 601 of the competency of witnesses. Senate Report No. 93-1277.

Rule 501 deals with the privilege of a witness not to testify. Both the House and Senate bills provide that federal privilege law applies in criminal cases. In civil actions and proceedings, the House bill provides that state privilege law applies "to an element of a claim or defense as to which State law supplies the rule of decision." The Senate bill provides that "in civil actions and proceedings arising under 28 U.S.C. § 1332 or 28 U.S.C. § 1335, or between citizens of different States and removed under 28 U.S.C. § 1441(b) the privilege of a witness, person, government, State or political subdivision thereof is determined in accordance with State law, unless with respect to the particular claim or defense, Federal law supplies the rule of decision."

The wording of the House and Senate bills differs in the treatment of civil actions and proceedings. The rule in the House bill applies to evidence that relates to "an element of a claim or defense." If an item of proof tends to support or defeat a claim or defense, or an element of a claim or defense, and if state law supplies the rule of decision for that claim or defense, then state privilege law applies to that item of proof.

Under the provision in the House bill, therefore, state privilege law will usually apply in diversity cases. There may be diversity cases, however, where a claim or defense is based upon federal law. In such instances, federal privilege law will apply to evidence relevant to the federal claim or defense. See Sola Electric Co. v. Jefferson Electric Co., 317 U.S. 173 (1942).

In nondiversity jurisdiction civil cases, federal privilege law will generally apply. In those situations where a federal court adopts or incorporates state law to fill interstices or gaps in federal statutory phrases, the court generally will apply federal privilege law. As Justice Jackson has said:
A federal court sitting in a non-diversity case such as this does not sit as a local tribunal. In some cases it may see fit for special reasons to give the law of a particular state highly persuasive or even controlling effect, but in the last analysis its decision turns upon the law of the United States, not that of any state.

D'Oench, Duhme & Co. v. Federal Deposit Insurance Corp., 315 U.S. 447, 471 (1942) (Jackson, J., concurring). When a federal court chooses to absorb state law, it is applying the state law as a matter of federal common law. Thus, state law does not supply the rule of decision (even though the federal court may apply a rule derived from state decisions), and state privilege law would not apply. See C.A. Wright, Federal Courts 251-252 (2d ed. 1970); Holmberg v. Armbrecht, 327 U.S. 392 (1946); DeSylva v. Ballentine, 351 U.S. 570, 581 (1956); 9 Wright & Miller, Federal Rules and Procedure § 2408.

In civil actions and proceedings, where the rule of decision as to a claim or defense or as to an element of a claim or defense is supplied by state law, the House provision requires that state privilege law apply.

The Conference adopts the House provision. House Report No. 93-1597.

2011 Amendments

The language of Rule 501 has been amended as part of the restyling of the Evidence Rules to make them more easily understood and to make style and terminology consistent throughout the rules. These changes are intended to be stylistic only. There is no intent to change any result in any ruling on evidence admissibility.

Rule 502. Attorney-Client Privilege and Work Product; Limitations on Waiver

The following provisions apply, in the circumstances set out, to disclosure of a communication or information covered by the attorney-client privilege or work-product protection.

(a) Disclosure Made in a Federal Proceeding or to a Federal Office or Agency; Scope of a Waiver. When the disclosure is made in a federal proceeding or to a federal office or agency and waives the attorney-client privilege or work-product protection, the waiver extends to an undisclosed communication or information in a federal or state proceeding only if:

(1) the waiver is intentional;

(2) the disclosed and undisclosed communications or information concern the same subject matter; and

(3) they ought in fairness to be considered together.

(b) Inadvertent Disclosure. When made in a federal proceeding or to a federal office or agency, the disclosure does not operate as a waiver in a federal or state proceeding if:

(1) the disclosure is inadvertent;

(2) the holder of the privilege or protection took reasonable steps to prevent disclosure; and

(3) the holder promptly took reasonable steps to rectify the error, including (if applicable) following Federal Rule of Civil Procedure 26(b)(5)(B).

(c) Disclosure Made in a State Proceeding. When the disclosure is made in a state proceeding and is not the subject of a state-court order concerning waiver, the disclosure does not operate as a waiver in a federal proceeding if the disclosure:

(1) would not be a waiver under this rule if it had been made in a federal proceeding; or

(2) is not a waiver under the law of the state where the disclosure occurred.

(d) Controlling Effect of a Court Order. A federal court may order that the privilege or protection is not waived by disclosure connected with the litigation pending before the court--in which event the disclosure is also not a waiver in any other federal or state proceeding.

(e) Controlling Effect of a Party Agreement. An agreement on the effect of disclosure in a federal proceeding is binding only on the parties to the agreement, unless it is incorporated into a court order.

(f) Controlling Effect of This Rule. Notwithstanding Rules 101 and 1101, this rule applies to state proceedings and to federal court-annexed and federal court-mandated arbitration proceedings, in the circumstances set out in the rule. And notwithstanding Rule 501, this rule applies even if state law provides the rule of decision.

(g) Definitions. In this rule:

(1) "attorney-client privilege" means the protection that applicable law provides for confidential attorney-client communications; and

(2) "work-product protection" means the protection that applicable law provides for tangible material (or its intangible equivalent) prepared in anticipation of litigation or for trial.

Credits

(Pub.L. 110-322, § 1(a), Sept. 19, 2008, 122 Stat. 3537; Apr. 26, 2011, eff. Dec. 1, 2011.)

Editors' Notes

ADVISORY COMMITTEE NOTES

2011 Amendments

Rule 502 has been amended by changing the initial letter of a few words from uppercase to lowercase as part of the restyling of the Evidence Rules to make style and terminology consistent throughout the rules. There is no intent to change any result in any ruling on evidence admissibility.

ADVISORY COMMITTEE NOTES
Explanatory Note (Revised 11/28/2007)
This new rule has two major purposes:
1) It resolves some longstanding disputes in the courts about the effect of certain disclosures of communications or information protected by the attorney-client privilege or as work product--specifically those disputes involving inadvertent disclosure and subject matter waiver.

2) It responds to the widespread complaint that litigation costs necessary to protect against waiver of attorney-client privilege or work product have become prohibitive due to the concern that any disclosure (however innocent or minimal) will operate as a subject matter waiver of all protected communications or information. This concern is especially troubling in cases involving electronic discovery. See, e.g., Hopson v. City of Baltimore, 232 F.R.D. 228, 244 (D.Md. 2005) (electronic discovery may encompass "millions of documents" and to insist upon "record-by-record pre-production privilege review, on pain of subject matter waiver, would impose upon parties costs of production that bear no proportionality to what is at stake in the litigation").

The rule seeks to provide a predictable, uniform set of standards under which parties can determine the consequences of a disclosure of a communication or information covered by the attorney-client privilege or work-product protection. Parties to litigation need to know, for example, that if they exchange privileged information pursuant to a confidentiality order, the court's order will be enforceable. Moreover, if a federal court's confidentiality order is not enforceable in a state court then the burdensome costs of privilege review and retention are unlikely to be reduced.

The rule makes no attempt to alter federal or state law on whether a communication or information is protected under the attorney-client privilege or work-product immunity as an initial matter.

Moreover, while establishing some exceptions to waiver, the rule does not purport to supplant applicable waiver doctrine generally.

The rule governs only certain waivers by disclosure. Other common-law waiver doctrines may result in a finding of waiver even where there is no disclosure of privileged information or work product. See, e.g., Nguyen v. Excel Corp., 197 F.3d 200 (5th Cir. 1999) (reliance on an advice of counsel defense waives the privilege with respect to attorney-client communications pertinent to that defense); Ryers v. Burleson, 100 F.R.D. 436 (D.D.C. 1983) (allegation of lawyer malpractice constituted a waiver of confidential communications under the circumstances). The rule is not intended to displace or modify federal common law concerning waiver of privilege or work product where no disclosure has been made.

Subdivision (a). The rule provides that a voluntary disclosure in a federal proceeding or to a federal office or agency, if a waiver, generally results in a waiver only of the communication or information disclosed; a subject matter waiver (of either privilege or work product) is reserved for those unusual situations in which fairness requires a further disclosure of related, protected information, in order to prevent a selective and misleading presentation of evidence to the disadvantage of the adversary. See, e.g., In re United Mine Workers of America Employee Benefit Plans Litig., 159 F.R.D. 307, 312 (D.D.C. 1994) (waiver of work product limited to materials actually disclosed, because the party did not deliberately disclose documents in an attempt to gain a tactical advantage). Thus, subject matter waiver is limited to situations in which a party intentionally puts protected information into the litigation in a selective, misleading and unfair manner. It follows that an inadvertent disclosure of protected information can never result in a subject matter waiver. See Rule 502(b). The rule rejects the result in In re Sealed Case, 877 F.2d 976 (D.C.Cir. 1989), which held that inadvertent disclosure of documents during discovery automatically constituted a subject matter waiver.

The language concerning subject matter waiver--"ought in fairness"--is taken from Rule 106, because the animating principle is the same. Under both Rules, a party that makes a selective, misleading presentation that is unfair to the adversary opens itself to a more complete and accurate presentation.

To assure protection and predictability, the rule provides that if a disclosure is made at the federal level, the federal rule on subject matter waiver governs subsequent state court determinations on the scope of the waiver by that disclosure.

Subdivision (b). Courts are in conflict over whether an inadvertent disclosure of a communication or information protected as privileged or work product constitutes a waiver. A few courts find that a disclosure must be intentional to be a waiver. Most courts find a waiver only if the disclosing party acted carelessly in disclosing the communication or information and failed to request its return in a timely manner. And a few courts hold that any inadvertent disclosure of a communication or information protected under the attorney-client privilege or as work product constitutes a waiver without regard to the protections taken to avoid such a disclosure. See generally Hopson v. City of Baltimore, 232 F.R.D. 228 (D.Md. 2005), for a discussion of this case law.

The rule opts for the middle ground: inadvertent disclosure of protected communications or information in connection with a federal proceeding or to a federal office or agency does not constitute a waiver if the holder took reasonable steps to prevent disclosure and also promptly took reasonable steps to rectify the error. This position is in accord with the majority view on whether inadvertent disclosure is a waiver.

Cases such as Lois Sportswear, U.S.A., Inc. v. Levi Strauss & Co., 104 F.R.D. 103, 105 (S.D.N.Y. 1985) and Hartford Fire Ins. Co. v. Garvey, 109 F.R.D. 323, 332 (N.D.Cal. 1985), set out a multi-factor test for determining whether inadvertent disclosure is a waiver. The stated factors (none of which is dispositive) are the reasonableness of precautions taken, the time taken to rectify the error, the scope of discovery, the extent of disclosure and the overriding issue of fairness. The rule does not explicitly codify that test, because it is really a set of non-determinative guidelines that vary from case to case. The rule is flexible enough to accommodate any of those listed factors. Other considerations bearing on the reasonableness of a producing party's efforts include the number of documents to be reviewed and the time constraints for production. Depending on the circumstances, a party that uses advanced analytical software applications and linguistic tools in screening for privilege and work product may be found to have taken "reasonable steps" to prevent inadvertent disclosure. The implementation of an efficient system of records management before litigation may also be relevant.

The rule does not require the producing party to engage in a post-production review to determine whether any protected communication or information has been produced by mistake. But the rule does require the producing party to follow up on any obvious indications that a protected communication or information has been produced inadvertently.

The rule applies to inadvertent disclosures made to a federal office or agency, including but not limited to an office or agency that is acting in the course of its regulatory, investigative or enforcement authority. The consequences of waiver, and the concomitant costs of pre-production privilege review, can be as great with respect to disclosures to offices and agencies as they are in litigation.

Subdivision (c). Difficult questions can arise when 1) a disclosure of a communication or information protected by the attorney-client privilege or as work product is made in a state proceeding, 2) the communication or information is offered in a subsequent federal proceeding on the ground that the disclosure waived the privilege or protection, and 3) the state and federal laws are in conflict on the question of waiver. The Committee determined that the proper solution for the federal court is to apply the law that is most protective of privilege and work product. If the state law is more protective (such as where the state law is that an inadvertent disclosure can never be a waiver), the holder of the privilege or protection may well have relied on that law when making the disclosure in the state proceeding. Moreover, applying a more restrictive federal law of waiver could impair the state objective of preserving the privilege or work-product protection for disclosures made in state proceedings. On the other hand, if the federal law is more protective, applying the state law of waiver to determine admissibility in federal court is likely to undermine the federal objective of limiting the costs of production.

The rule does not address the enforceability of a state court confidentiality order in a federal proceeding, as that question is covered both by statutory law and principles of federalism and comity. See 28 U.S.C. § 1738 (providing that state judicial proceedings "shall have the same full faith and credit in every court within the United States . . . as they have by law or usage in the courts of such State . . . from which they are taken"). See also Tucker v. Ohtsu Tire & Rubber Co., 191 F.R.D. 495, 499 (D.Md. 2000) (noting that a federal court considering the enforceability of a state confidentiality order is "constrained by principles of comity, courtesy, and . . . federalism"). Thus, a state court order finding no waiver in connection with a disclosure made in a state court proceeding is enforceable under existing law in subsequent federal proceedings.

Subdivision (d). Confidentiality orders are becoming increasingly important in limiting the costs of privilege review and retention, especially in cases involving electronic discovery. But the utility of a confidentiality order in reducing discovery costs is substantially diminished if it provides no protection outside the particular litigation in which the order is entered. Parties are unlikely to be able to reduce the costs of pre-production review for privilege and work product if the consequence of disclosure is that the communications or information could be used by non-parties to the litigation.

There is some dispute on whether a confidentiality order entered in one case is enforceable in other proceedings. See generally Hopson v. City of Baltimore, 232 F.R.D. 228 (D.Md. 2005), for a discussion of this case law. The rule provides that when a confidentiality order governing the consequences of disclosure in that case is entered in a federal proceeding, its terms are enforceable against non-parties in any federal or state proceeding. For example, the court order may provide for return of documents without waiver irrespective of the care taken by the disclosing party; the rule contemplates enforcement of "claw-back" and "quick peek" arrangements as a way to avoid the excessive costs of pre-production review for privilege and work product. See Zubulake v. UBS

Warburg LLC, 216 F.R.D. 280, 290 (S.D.N.Y. 2003) (noting that parties may enter into "so-called 'claw-back' agreements that allow the parties to forego privilege review altogether in favor of an agreement to return inadvertently produced privilege documents"). The rule provides a party with a predictable protection from a court order--predictability that is needed to allow the party to plan in advance to limit the prohibitive costs of privilege and work product review and retention.

Under the rule, a confidentiality order is enforceable whether or not it memorializes an agreement among the parties to the litigation. Party agreement should not be a condition of enforceability of a federal court's order.

Under subdivision (d), a federal court may order that disclosure of privileged or protected information "in connection with" a federal proceeding does not result in waiver. But subdivision (d) does not allow the federal court to enter an order determining the waiver effects of a separate disclosure of the same information in other proceedings, state or federal. If a disclosure has been made in a state proceeding (and is not the subject of a state-court order on waiver), then subdivision (d) is inapplicable. Subdivision (c) would govern the federal court's determination whether the state-court disclosure waived the privilege or protection in the federal proceeding.

Subdivision (e). Subdivision (e) codifies the well-established proposition that parties can enter an agreement to limit the effect of waiver by disclosure between or among them. Of course such an agreement can bind only the parties to the agreement. The rule makes clear that if parties want protection against non-parties from a finding of waiver by disclosure, the agreement must be made part of a court order.

Subdivision (f). The protections against waiver provided by Rule 502 must be applicable when protected communications or information disclosed in federal proceedings are subsequently offered in state proceedings. Otherwise the holders of protected communications and information, and their lawyers, could not rely on the protections provided by the Rule, and the goal of limiting costs in discovery would be substantially undermined. Rule 502(f) is intended to resolve any potential tension between the provisions of Rule 502 that apply to state proceedings and the possible limitations on the applicability of the Federal Rules of Evidence otherwise provided by Rules 101 and 1101.

The rule is intended to apply in all federal court proceedings, including court-annexed and court-ordered arbitrations, without regard to any possible limitations of Rules 101 and 1101. This provision is not intended to raise an inference about the applicability of any other rule of evidence in arbitration proceedings more generally.

The costs of discovery can be equally high for state and federal causes of action, and the rule seeks to limit those costs in all federal proceedings, regardless of whether the claim arises under state or federal law. Accordingly, the rule applies to state law causes of action brought in federal court.

Subdivision (g). The rule's coverage is limited to attorney-client privilege and work product. The operation of waiver by disclosure, as applied to other evidentiary privileges, remains a question of federal common law. Nor does the rule purport to apply to the Fifth Amendment privilege against compelled self-incrimination.

The definition of work product "materials" is intended to include both tangible and intangible information. See In re Cendant Corp. Sec. Litig., 343 F.3d 658, 662 (3d Cir. 2003) ("work product protection extends to both tangible and intangible work product").

Committee Letter

The letter from the Committee on Rules of Practice and Procedure of the Judicial Conference of the United States to the Committee on the Judiciary of the U.S. Senate and House of Representatives, dated September 26, 2007, provided:

On behalf of the Judicial Conference of the United States, I respectfully submit a proposed addition to the Federal Rules of Evidence. The Conference recommends that Congress adopt this proposed rule as Federal Rule of Evidence 502.

The Rule provides for protections against waiver of the attorney-client privilege or work product immunity. The Conference submits this proposal directly to Congress because of the limitations on the rulemaking function of the federal courts in matters dealing with evidentiary privilege. Unlike all other federal rules of procedure prescribed under the Rules Enabling Act, those rules governing evidentiary privilege must by approved by an Act of Congress, 28 U.S.C. § 2074(b).

Description of the Process Leading to the Proposed Rule

The Judicial Conference Rules Committees have long been concerned about the rising costs of litigation, much of which has been caused by the review, required under current law, of every document produced in discovery, in order to determine whether the document contains privileged information. In 2006, the House Judiciary Committee Chair suggested that the Judicial Conference consider proposing a rule dealing with waiver of attorney-client privilege and work product, in order to limit these rising costs. The Judicial Conference was urged to proceed with rulemaking that would:
•protect against the forfeiture of privilege when a disclosure in discovery is the result of an innocent mistake; and

•permit parties, and courts, to protect against the consequences of waiver by permitting disclosures of privileged information between the parties to litigation.

The task of drafting a proposed rule was referred to the Advisory Committee on Evidence Rules (the "Advisory Committee"). The Advisory Committee prepared a draft Rule 502 and invited a select group of judges, lawyers, and academics to testify before the Advisory Committee about the need for the rule, and to suggest any improvements. The Advisory Committee considered all the testimony presented by these experts and redrafted the rule accordingly. At its Spring 2006 meeting, the Advisory Committee approved for release for public comment a proposed Rule 502 that would provide certain exceptions to the federal common law on waiver of privileges and work product. That rule was approved for release for public comment by the Committee on Rules of Practice and Procedure ("the Standing Committee"). The public comment period began in August 2006 and ended February 15, 2007. The Advisory Committee received more that [sic] 70 public comments, and also heard the testimony of more than 20 witnesses at two public hearings. The rule released for public comment was also carefully reviewed by the Standing Committee's Subcommittee on Style. In April 2007, the Advisory Committee issued a revised proposed Rule 502 taking into account the public comment, the views of the Subcommittee on Style, and its own judgment. The revised rule was approved by the Standing Committee and the Judicial Conference. It is enclosed with this letter.

In order to inform Congress of the legal issues involved in this rule, the proposed Rule 502 also includes a proposed Committee Note of the kind that accompanies all rules adopted through the Rules Enabling Act. This Committee Note may be incorporated as all or part of the legislative history of the rule if it is adopted by Congress. See, e.g., House Conference Report 103-711 (stating that the "Conferees intend that the Advisory Committee Note on [Evidence] Rule 412, as transmitted by the Judicial Conference of the United States to the Supreme Court on October 25, 1993, applies to Rule 412 as enacted by this section" of the Violent Crime Control and Law Enforcement Act of 1994).

Problems Addressed by the Proposed Rule

In drafting the proposed Rule, the Advisory Committee concluded that the current law on waiver of privilege and work product is responsible in large part for the rising costs of discovery, especially discovery of electronic information. In complex litigation the lawyers spend significant amounts of time and effort to preserve the privilege and work product. The reason is that if a protected document is produced, there is a risk that a court will find a subject matter waiver that will apply not only to the instant case and document but to other cases and documents as well. Moreover, an enormous amount of expense is put into document production in order to protect against inadvertent disclosure of privileged information, because the producing party risks a ruling that even a mistaken disclosure can result in a subject matter waiver. Advisory Committee members also expressed the view that the fear of waiver leads to extravagant claims of privilege. Members concluded that if there were a way to produce documents in discovery without risking subject matter waiver, the discovery process could be made much less expensive. The Advisory Committee noted that the existing law on the effect of inadvertent disclosures and on the scope of waiver is far from consistent or certain. It also noted that agreements between parties with regard to the effect of disclosure on privilege are common, but are unlikely to decrease the costs of discovery due to the ineffectiveness of such agreements as to persons not party to them.

Proposed Rule 502 does not attempt to deal comprehensively with either attorney-client privilege or work-product protection. It also does not purport to cover all issues concerning waiver or forfeiture of either the attorney-client privilege or work-product protection. Rather, it deals primarily with issues involved in the disclosure of protected information in federal court proceedings or to a federal public office or agency. The rule binds state courts only with regard to disclosures made in federal proceedings. It deals with disclosures made in state proceedings only to the extent that the effect of those disclosures becomes an issue in federal litigation. The Rule covers issues of scope of waiver, inadvertent disclosure, and the controlling effect of court orders and agreements.

Rule 502 provides the following protections against waiver of privilege or work product:

•Limitations on Scope of Waiver. Subdivision (a) provides that if a waiver is found, it applies only to the information disclosed, unless a broader waiver is made necessary by the holder's intentional and misleading use of privileged or protected communications or information.

•Protections Against Inadvertent Disclosure. Subdivision (b) provides that an inadvertent disclosure of privileged or protected communications or information, when made at the federal level, does not operate as a waiver if the holder took reasonable steps to prevent such a disclosure and employed reasonably prompt measures to retrieve the mistakenly disclosed communications or information.

•Effect on State Proceedings and Disclosures Made in State Courts. Subdivision (c) provides that 1) if there is a disclosure of privileged or protected communications or information at the federal level, then state courts must honor Rule 502 in subsequent state proceedings; and 2) if there is a disclosure of privileged or protected communications or information in a state proceeding, then admissibility in a subsequent federal proceeding is determined by the law that is most protective against waiver.

•Orders Protecting Privileged Communications Binding on Non-Parties. Subdivision (d) provides that if a federal court enters an order providing that a disclosure of privileged or protected communications or information does not constitute a waiver, that order is enforceable against all persons and entities in any federal or state proceeding. This provision allows parties in an action in which such an order is entered to limit their costs of pre-production privilege review.

•Agreements Protecting Privileged Communications Binding on Parties. Subdivision (e) provides that parties in a federal proceeding can enter into a confidentiality agreement providing for mutual protection against waiver in that proceeding. While those agreements bind the signatory parties, they are not binding on non-parties unless incorporated into a court order.

Drafting Choices Made by the Advisory Committee

The Advisory Committee made a number of important drafting choices in Rule 502. This section explains those choices.

1) The effect in state proceedings of disclosures initially made in state proceedings. Rule 502 does not apply to a disclosure made in a state proceeding when the disclosed communication or information is subsequently offered in another state proceeding. The first draft of Rule 502 provided for uniform waiver rules in federal and state proceedings, regardless of where the initial disclosure was made. This draft raised the objections of the Conference of State Chief Justices. State judges argued that the Rule as drafted offended principles of federalism and comity, by superseding state law of privilege waiver, even for disclosures that are made initially in state proceedings--and even when the disclosed material is then offered in a state proceeding (the so-called "state-to-state" problem). In response to these objections, the Advisory Committee voted unanimously to scale back the Rule, so that it would not cover the "state-to-state" problem. Under the current proposal state courts are bound by the Federal Rule only when a disclosure is made at the federal level and the disclosed communication or information is later offered in a state proceeding (the so-called "federal-to-state" problem).

During the public comment period on the scaled-back rule, the Advisory Committee received many requests from lawyers and lawyer groups to return to the original draft and provide a uniform rule of privilege waiver that would bind both state and federal courts, for disclosures made in either state or federal proceedings. These comments expressed the concern that if states were not bound by a uniform federal rule on privilege waiver, the protections afforded by Rule 502 would be undermined; parties and their lawyers might not be able to rely on the protections of the Rule, for fear that a state law would find a waiver even though the Federal Rule would not.

The Advisory Committee determined that these comments raised a legitimate concern, but decided not to extend Rule 502 to govern a state court's determination of waiver with respect to disclosures made in state proceedings. The Committee relied on the following considerations:
•Rule 502 is located in the Federal Rules of Evidence, a body of rules determining the admissibility of evidence in federal proceedings. Parties in a state proceeding determining the effect of a disclosure made in that proceeding or in other state courts would be unlikely to look to the Federal Rules of Evidence for the answer.

•In the Advisory Committee's view, Rule 502, as proposed herein, does fulfill its primary goal of reducing the costs of discovery in federal proceedings. Rule 502 by its terms governs state courts with regard to the effect of disclosures initially made in federal proceedings or to federal offices or agencies. Parties and their lawyers in federal proceedings can therefore predict the consequences of disclosure by referring to Rule 502; there is no possibility that a state court could find a waiver when Rule 502 would not, when the disclosure is initially made at the federal level.

The Judicial Conference has no position on the merits of separate legislation to cover the problem of waiver of privilege and work product when the disclosure is made at the state level and the consequence is to be determined in a state court.

2) Other applications of Rule 502 to state court proceedings. Although disclosures made in state court proceedings and later offered in state proceedings would not be covered, Rule 502 would have an effect on state court proceedings where the disclosure is initially made in a federal proceeding or to a federal office or agency. Most importantly, state courts in such circumstances would be bound by federal protection orders. The other protections against waiver in Rule 502-- against mistaken disclosure and subject matter waiver--would also bind state courts as to disclosures initially made at the federal level. The Rule, as submitted, specifically provides that it applies to state proceedings under the circumstances set out in the Rule. This protection is needed, otherwise parties could not rely on Rule 502 even as to federal disclosures, for fear that a state court would find waiver even when a federal court would not.

3) Disclosures made in state proceedings and offered in a subsequent federal proceeding. Earlier drafts of proposed Rule 502 did not determine the question of what rule would apply when a disclosure is made in state court and the waiver determination is to be made in a subsequent federal proceeding. Proposed Rule 502 as submitted herein provides that all of the provisions of Rule 502 apply unless the state law of privilege is more protective (less likely to find waiver) than the federal law. The Advisory Committee determined that this solution best preserved federal interests in

protecting against waiver, and also provided appropriate respect for state attempts to give greater protection to communications and information covered by the attorney-client privilege or work-product doctrine.

4) Selective waiver. At the suggestion of the House Judiciary Committee Chair, the Advisory Committee considered a rule that would allow persons and entities to cooperate with government agencies without waiving all privileges as to other parties in subsequent litigation. Such a rule is known as a "selective waiver" rule, meaning that disclosure of protected communications or information to the government waives the protection only selectively--to the government--and not to any other person or entity.

The selective waiver provision proved to be very controversial. The Advisory Committee determined that it would not propose adoption of a selective waiver provision; but in light of the request from the House Judiciary Committee, the Advisory Committee did prepare language for a selective waiver provision should Congress decide to proceed. The draft language for a selective waiver provision is available on request.

Conclusion
Proposed Rule 502 is respectfully submitted for consideration by Congress as a rule that will effectively limit the skyrocketing costs of discovery. Members of the Standing Committee, the Advisory Committee, as well as their reporters and consultants, are ready to assist Congress in any way it sees fit.

Sincerely,

Lee H. Rosenthal
Chair, Committee on Rules of Practice and Procedure

Addendum to Advisory Committee Notes
STATEMENT OF CONGRESSIONAL INTENT REGARDING RULE 502 OF THE FEDERAL RULES OF EVIDENCE
During consideration of this rule in Congress, a number of questions were raised about the scope and contours of the effect of the proposed rule on current law regarding attorney-client privilege and work-product protection. These questions were ultimately answered satisfactorily, without need to revise the text of the rule as submitted to Congress by the Judicial Conference.

In general, these questions are answered by keeping in mind the limited though important purpose and focus of the rule. The rule addresses only the effect of disclosure, under specified circumstances, of a communication that is otherwise protected by attorney-client privilege, or of information that is protected by work-product protection, on whether the disclosure itself operates as a waiver of the privilege or protection for purposes of admissibility of evidence in a federal or state judicial or administrative proceeding. The rule does not alter the substantive law regarding attorney-client privilege or work-product protection in any other respect, including the burden on the party invoking the privilege (or protection) to prove that the particular information (or communication) qualifies for it. And it is not intended to alter the rules and practices governing use of information outside this evidentiary context.

Some of these questions are addressed more specifically below, in order to help further avoid uncertainty in the interpretation and application of the rule.

Subdivision (a)--Disclosure vs. Use

This subdivision does not alter the substantive law regarding when a party's strategic use in litigation of otherwise privileged information obliges that party to waive the privilege regarding other information concerning the same subject matter, so that the information being used can be fairly considered in context. One situation in which this issue arises, the assertion as a defense in patent-infringement litigation that a party was relying on advice of counsel, is discussed elsewhere in this Note. In this and similar situations, under subdivision (a)(1) the party using an attorney-client communication to its advantage in the litigation has, in so doing, intentionally waived the privilege as to other communications concerning the same subject matter, regardless of the circumstances in which the communication being so used was initially disclosed.

Subdivision (b)--Fairness Considerations

The standard set forth in this subdivision for determining whether a disclosure operates as a waiver of the privilege or protection is, as explained elsewhere in this Note, the majority rule in the federal courts. The majority rule has simply been distilled here into a standard designed to be predictable in its application. This distillation is not intended to foreclose notions of fairness from continuing to inform application of the standard in all aspects as appropriate in particular cases--for example, as to whether steps taken to rectify an erroneous inadvertent disclosure were sufficiently prompt under subdivision (b)(3) where the receiving party has relied on the information disclosed.

Subdivisions (a) and (b)--Disclosures to Federal Office or Agency

This rule, as a Federal Rule of Evidence, applies to admissibility of evidence. While subdivisions (a) and (b) are written broadly to apply as appropriate to disclosures of information to a federal office or agency, they do not apply to uses of information--such as routine use in government publications--that fall outside the evidentiary context. Nor do these subdivisions relieve the party seeking to protect the information as privileged from the burden of proving that the privilege applies in the first place.

Subdivision (d)--Court Orders

This subdivision authorizes a court to enter orders only in the context of litigation pending before the court. And it does not alter the law regarding waiver of privilege resulting from having acquiesced in the use of otherwise privileged information. Therefore, this subdivision does not provide a basis for a court to enable parties to agree to a selective waiver of the privilege, such as to a federal agency conducting an investigation, while preserving the privilege as against other parties seeking the information. This subdivision is designed to enable a court to enter an order, whether on motion of one or more parties or on its own motion, that will allow the parties to conduct and respond to discovery expeditiously, without the need for exhaustive pre-production privilege reviews, while still preserving each party's right to assert the privilege to preclude use in litigation of information disclosed in such discovery. While the benefits of a court order under this subdivision would be equally available in government enforcement actions as in private actions, acquiescence by the disclosing party in use by the federal agency of information disclosed pursuant to such an order would still be treated as under current law for purposes of determining whether the acquiescence in use of the information, as opposed to its mere disclosure, effects a waiver of the privilege. The same applies to acquiescence in use by another private party.

Moreover, whether the order is entered on motion of one or more parties, or on the court's own motion, the court retains its authority to include the conditions it deems appropriate In the circumstances.

Subdivision (e)--Party Agreements

This subdivision simply makes clear that while parties to a case may agree among themselves regarding the effect of disclosures between each other in a federal proceeding, it is not binding on others unless it is incorporated into a court order. This subdivision does not confer any authority on a court to enter any order regarding the effect of disclosures. That authority must be found in subdivision (d), or elsewhere.

Rules 503 to 600. Reserved for future legislation

Article VI: Witnesses

Rule 601. Competency to Testify in General

Every person is competent to be a witness unless these rules provide otherwise. But in a civil case, state law governs the witness's competency regarding a claim or defense for which state law supplies the rule of decision.

Credits

(Pub.L. 93-595, § 1, Jan. 2, 1975, 88 Stat.1934; Apr. 26, 2011, eff. Dec. 1, 2011.)

Editors' Notes

ADVISORY COMMITTEE NOTES

1972 Proposed Rules

This general ground-clearing eliminates all grounds of incompetency not specifically recognized in the succeeding rules of this Article. Included among the grounds thus abolished are religious belief, conviction of crime, and connection with the litigation as a party or interested person or spouse of a party or interested person. With the exception of the so-called Dead Man's Acts, American jurisdictions generally have ceased to recognize these grounds.

The Dead Man's Acts are surviving traces of the common law disqualification of parties and interested persons. They exist in variety too great to convey conviction of their wisdom and effectiveness. These rules contain no provision of this kind. For the reasoning underlying the decision not to give effect to state statutes in diversity cases, see the Advisory Committee's Note to Rule 501.

No mental or moral qualifications for testifying as a witness are specified. Standards of mental capacity have proved elusive in actual application. A leading commentator observes that few witnesses are disqualified on that ground. Weihofen, Testimonial Competence and Credibility, 34 Geo.Wash.L.Rev. 53 (1965). Discretion is regularly exercised in favor of allowing the testimony. A witness wholly without capacity is difficult to imagine. The question is one particularly suited to the jury as one of weight and credibility, subject to judicial authority to review the sufficiency of the evidence. 2 Wigmore §§ 501, 509. Standards of moral qualification in practice consist essentially of evaluating a person's truthfulness in terms of his own answers about it. Their principal utility is in affording an opportunity on voir dire examination to impress upon the witness his moral duty. This result may, however, be accomplished more directly, and without haggling in terms of legal standards, by the manner of administering the oath or affirmation under Rule 603.

Admissibility of religious belief as a ground of impeachment is treated in Rule 610. Conviction of crime as a ground of impeachment is the subject of Rule 609. Marital relationship is the basis for privilege under Rule 505. Interest in the outcome of litigation and mental capacity are, of course, highly relevant to credibility and require no special treatment to render them admissible along with other matters bearing upon the perception, memory, and narration of witnesses.

1974 Enactment

Rule 601 as submitted to the Congress provided that "Every person is competent to be a witness except as otherwise provided in these rules." One effect of the Rule as proposed would have been to abolish age, mental capacity, and other grounds recognized in some State jurisdictions as making a person incompetent as a witness. The greatest controversy centered around the Rule's rendering inapplicable in the federal courts the so-called Dead Man's Statutes which exist in some States. Acknowledging that there is substantial disagreement as to the merit of Dead Man's Statutes, the

Committee nevertheless believed that where such statutes have been enacted they represent State policy which should not be overturned in the absence of a compelling federal interest. The Committee therefore amended the Rule to make competency in civil actions determinable in accordance with State law with respect to elements of claims or defenses as to which State law supplies the rule of decision. Cf. Courtland v. Walston & Co., Inc., 340 F.Supp. 1076, 1087-1092 (S.D.N.Y.1972). House Report No. 93-650.

The amendment to rule 601 parallels the treatment accorded Rule 501 discussed immediately above. Senate Report No. 93-1277.

Rule 601 deals with competency of witnesses. Both the House and Senate bills provide that federal competency law applies in criminal cases. In civil actions and proceedings, the House bill provides that state competency law applies "to an element of a claim or defense as to which State law supplies the rule of decision." The Senate bill provides that "in civil actions and proceedings arising under 28 U.S.C. § 1332 or 28 U.S.C. § 1335, or between citizens of different States and removed under 28 U.S.C. § 1441(b) the competency of a witness, person, government, State or political subdivision thereof is determined in accordance with State law, unless with respect to the particular claim or defense, Federal law supplies the rule of decision."

The wording of the House and Senate bills differs in the treatment of civil actions and proceedings. The rule in the House bill applies to evidence that relates to "an element of a claim or defense." If an item of proof tends to support or defeat a claim or defense, or an element of a claim or defense, and if state law supplies the rule of decision for that claim or defense, then state competency law applies to that item of proof.

For reasons similar to those underlying its action on Rule 501, the Conference adopts the House provision. House Report No. 93-1597.

2011 Amendments
The language of Rule 601 has been amended as part of the restyling of the Evidence Rules to make them more easily understood and to make style and terminology consistent throughout the rules. These changes are intended to be stylistic only. There is no intent to change any result in any ruling on evidence admissibility.

Rule 602. Need for Personal Knowledge

A witness may testify to a matter only if evidence is introduced sufficient to support a finding that the witness has personal knowledge of the matter. Evidence to prove personal knowledge may consist of the witness' s own testimony. This rule does not apply to a witness's expert testimony under Rule 703.

Credits

(Pub.L. 93-595, § 1, Jan. 2, 1975, 88 Stat. 1934; Mar. 2, 1987, eff. Oct. 1, 1987; Apr. 25, 1988, eff. Nov. 1, 1988; Apr. 26, 2011, eff. Dec. 1, 2011.)

Editors' Notes

ADVISORY COMMITTEE NOTES

1972 Proposed Rules

" * * * [T]he rule requiring that a witness who testifies to a fact which can be perceived by the senses must have had an opportunity to observe, and must have actually observed the fact" is a "most pervasive manifestation" of the common law insistence upon "the most reliable sources of information." McCormick § 10, p. 19. These foundation requirements may, of course, be furnished by the testimony of the witness himself; hence personal knowledge is not an absolute but may consist of what the witness thinks he knows from personal perception. 2 Wigmore § 650. It will be observed that the rule is in fact a specialized application of the provisions of Rule 104(b) on conditional relevancy.

This rule does not govern the situation of a witness who testifies to a hearsay statement as such, if he has personal knowledge of the making of the statement. Rules 801 and 805 would be applicable. This rule would, however, prevent him from testifying to the subject matter of the hearsay statement, as he has no personal knowledge of it.

The reference to Rule 703 is designed to avoid any question of conflict between the present rule and the provisions of that rule allowing an expert to express opinions based on facts of which he does not have personal knowledge.

1987 Amendments
The amendments are technical. No substantive change is intended.

1988 Amendments
The amendment is technical. No substantive change is intended.

2011 Amendments
The language of Rule 602 has been amended as part of the restyling of the Evidence Rules to make them more easily understood and to make style and terminology consistent throughout the rules. These changes are intended to be stylistic only. There is no intent to change any result in any ruling on evidence admissibility.

Rule 603. Oath or Affirmation to Testify Truthfully

Before testifying, a witness must give an oath or affirmation to testify truthfully. It must be in a form designed to impress that duty on the witness's conscience.

Credits

(Pub.L. 93-595, § 1, Jan. 2, 1975, 88 Stat. 1934; Mar. 2, 1987, eff. Oct. 1, 1987; Apr. 26, 2011, eff. Dec. 1, 2011.)

Editors' Notes

ADVISORY COMMITTEE NOTES

1972 Proposed Rules

The rule is designed to afford the flexibility required in dealing with religious adults, atheists, conscientious objectors, mental defectives, and children. Affirmation is simply a solemn undertaking to tell the truth; no special verbal formula is required. As is true generally, affirmation is recognized by federal law. "Oath" includes affirmation, 1 U.S.C. § 1; judges and clerks may administer oaths and affirmations, 28 U.S.C. §§ 459, 953; and affirmations are acceptable in lieu of oaths under Rule 43(d) of the Federal Rules of Civil Procedure. Perjury by a witness is a crime, 18 U.S.C. § 1621.

1987 Amendments
The amendments are technical. No substantive change is intended.

2011 Amendments
The language of Rule 603 has been amended as part of the restyling of the Evidence Rules to make them more easily understood and to make style and terminology consistent throughout the rules. These changes are intended to be stylistic only. There is no intent to change any result in any ruling on evidence admissibility.

Rule 604. Interpreter

An interpreter must be qualified and must give an oath or affirmation to make a true translation.

Credits

(Pub.L. 93-595, § 1, Jan. 2, 1975, 88 Stat. 1934; Mar. 2, 1987, eff. Oct. 1, 1987; Apr. 26, 2011, eff. Dec. 1, 2011.)

Editors' Notes

ADVISORY COMMITTEE NOTES

1972 Proposed Rules

The rule implements Rule 43(f) of the Federal Rules of Civil Procedure and Rule 28(b) of the Federal Rules of Criminal Procedure, both of which contain provisions for the appointment and compensation of interpreters.

1987 Amendments
The amendment is technical. No substantive change is intended.

2011 Amendments
The language of Rule 604 has been amended as part of the restyling of the Evidence Rules to make them more easily understood and to make style and terminology consistent throughout the rules. These changes are intended to be stylistic only. There is no intent to change any result in any ruling on evidence admissibility.

Rule 605. Judge's Competency as a Witness

The presiding judge may not testify as a witness at the trial. A party need not object to preserve the issue.

Credits

(Pub.L. 93-595, § 1, Jan. 2, 1975, 88 Stat. 1934; Apr. 26, 2011, eff. Dec. 1, 2011.)

Editors' Notes

ADVISORY COMMITTEE NOTES

1972 Proposed Rules

In view of the mandate of 28 U.S.C. § 455 that a judge disqualify himself in "any case in which he * * * is or has been a material witness," the likelihood that the presiding judge in a federal court might be called to testify in the trial over which he is presiding is slight. Nevertheless the possibility is not totally eliminated.

The solution here presented is a broad rule of incompetency, rather than such alternatives as incompetency only as to material matters, leaving the matter to the discretion of the judge, or recognizing no incompetency. The choice is the result of inability to evolve satisfactory answers to questions which arise when the judge abandons the bench for the witness stand. Who rules on objections? Who compels him to answer? Can he rule impartially on the weight and admissibility of his own testimony? Can he be impeached or cross-examined effectively? Can he, in a jury trial, avoid conferring his seal of approval on one side in the eyes of the jury? Can he, in a bench trial, avoid an involvement destructive of impartiality? The rule of general incompetency has substantial support. See Report of the Special Committee on the Propriety of Judges Appearing as Witnesses, 36 A.B.A.J. 630 (1950); cases collected in Annot. 157 A.L.R. 311; McCormick § 68, p. 147; Uniform Rule 42; California Evidence Code § 703; Kansas Code of Civil Procedure § 60-442; New

Jersey Evidence Rule 42. Cf. 6 Wigmore § 1909, which advocates leaving the matter to the discretion of the judge, and statutes to that effect collected in Annot. 157 A.L.R. 311.

The rule provides an "automatic" objection. To require an actual objection would confront the opponent with a choice between not objecting, with the result of allowing the testimony, and objecting, with the probable result of excluding the testimony but at the price of continuing the trial before a judge likely to feel that his integrity had been attacked by the objector.

2011 Amendments
The language of Rule 605 has been amended as part of the restyling of the Evidence Rules to make them more easily understood and to make style and terminology consistent throughout the rules. These changes are intended to be stylistic only. There is no intent to change any result in any ruling on evidence admissibility.

Rule 606. Juror's Competency as a Witness

(a) At the Trial. A juror may not testify as a witness before the other jurors at the trial. If a juror is called to testify, the court must give a party an opportunity to object outside the jury's presence.

(b) During an Inquiry Into the Validity of a Verdict or Indictment.

(1) Prohibited Testimony or Other Evidence. During an inquiry into the validity of a verdict or indictment, a juror may not testify about any statement made or incident that occurred during the jury's deliberations; the effect of anything on that juror's or another juror's vote; or any juror's mental processes concerning the verdict or indictment. The court may not receive a juror's affidavit or evidence of a juror's statement on these matters.

(2) Exceptions. A juror may testify about whether:

(A) extraneous prejudicial information was improperly brought to the jury's attention;

(B) an outside influence was improperly brought to bear on any juror; or

(C) a mistake was made in entering the verdict on the verdict form.

Credits

(Pub.L. 93-595, § 1, Jan. 2, 1975, 88 Stat. 1934; Pub.L. 94-149, § 1(10), Dec. 12, 1975, 89 Stat. 805; Mar. 2, 1987, eff. Oct. 1, 1987; Apr. 12, 2006, eff. Dec. 1, 2006; Apr. 26, 2011, eff. Dec. 1, 2011.

Editors' Notes

ADVISORY COMMITTEE NOTES

1972 Proposed Rules

Note to Subdivision (a). The considerations which bear upon the permissibility of testimony by a juror in the trial in which he is sitting as juror bear an obvious similarity to those evoked when the judge is called as a witness. See Advisory Committee's Note to Rule 605. The judge is not, however in this instance so involved as to call for departure from usual principles requiring objection to be made; hence the only provision on objection is that opportunity be afforded for its making out of the presence of the jury. Compare Rule 605.

Note to Subdivision (b). Whether testimony, affidavits, or statements of jurors should be received for the purpose of invalidating or supporting a verdict or indictment, and if so, under what circumstances, has given rise to substantial differences of opinion. The familiar rubric that a juror may not impeach his own verdict, dating from Lord Mansfield's time, is a gross oversimplification. The values sought to be promoted by excluding the evidence include freedom of deliberation, stability and finality of verdicts, and protection of jurors against annoyance and embarrassment. McDonald v. Pless, 238 U.S. 264, 35 S.Ct. 783, 59 L.Ed. 1300 (1915). On the other hand, simply putting verdicts beyond effective reach can only promote irregularity and injustice. The rule offers an accommodation between these competing considerations.

The mental operations and emotional reactions of jurors in arriving at a given result would, if allowed as a subject of inquiry, place every verdict at the mercy of jurors and invite tampering and harassment. See Grenz v. Werre, 129 N.W.2d 681 (N.D.1964). The authorities are in virtually complete accord in excluding the evidence. Fryer, Note on Disqualification of Witnesses, Selected Writings on Evidence and Trial 345, 347 (Fryer ed. 1957); Maguire, Weinstein, et al., Cases on Evidence 887 (5th ed. 1965); 8 Wigmore § 2349 (McNaughton Rev.1961). As to matters other than mental operations and emotional reactions of jurors, substantial authority refuses to allow a juror to disclose irregularities which occur in the jury room, but allows his testimony as to irregularities occurring outside and allows outsiders to testify as to occurrences both inside and out. 8 Wigmore § 2354 (McNaughton Rev.1961). However, the door of the jury room is not necessarily a satisfactory dividing point, and the Supreme Court has refused to accept it for every situation. Mattox v. United States, 146 U.S. 140, 13 S.Ct. 50, 36 L.Ed. 917 (1892).

Under the federal decisions the central focus has been upon insulation of the manner in which the jury reached its verdict, and this protection extends to each of the components of deliberation, including arguments, statements, discussions, mental and emotional reactions, votes, and any other feature of the process. Thus testimony or affidavits of jurors have been held incompetent to show a compromise verdict, Hyde v. United States, 225 U.S. 347, 382 (1912); a quotient verdict, McDonald v. Pless, 238 U.S. 264 (1915); speculation as to insurance coverage, Holden v. Porter, 405 F.2d 878 (10th Cir.1969); Farmers Coop. Elev. Ass'n v. Strand, 382 F.2d 224, 230 (8th Cir. 1967), cert. denied 389 U.S. 1014; misinterpretation of instructions, Farmers Coop. Elev. Ass'n v. Strand, supra; mistake in returning verdict, United States v. Chereton, 309 F.2d 197 (6th Cir.1962); interpretation of guilty plea by one defendant as implicating others, United States v. Crosby, 294 F. 2d 928, 949 (2d Cir.1961). The policy does not, however, foreclose testimony by jurors as to prejudicial extraneous information or influences injected into or brought to bear upon the deliberative process. Thus a juror is recognized as competent to testify to statements by the bailiff or the introduction of a prejudicial newspaper account into the jury room, Mattox v. United States, 146 U.S. 140 (1892). See also Parker v. Gladden, 385 U.S. 363 (1966).

This rule does not purport to specify the substantive grounds for setting aside verdicts for irregularity; it deals only with the competency of jurors to testify concerning those grounds. Allowing them to testify as to matters other than their own inner reactions involves no particular hazard to the values sought to be protected. The rule is based upon this conclusion. It makes no attempt to specify the substantive grounds for setting aside verdicts for irregularity.

See also Rule 6(e) of the Federal Rules of Criminal Procedure and 18 U.S.C. § 3500, governing the secrecy of grand jury proceedings. The present rule does not relate to secrecy and disclosure but to the competency of certain witnesses and evidence.

1974 Enactment
Note to Subdivision (b). As proposed by the Court, Rule 606(b) limited testimony by a juror in the course of an inquiry into the validity of a verdict or indictment. He could testify as to the influence of extraneous prejudicial information brought to the jury's attention (e.g. a radio newscast or a newspaper account) or an outside influence which improperly had been brought to bear upon a juror (e.g. a threat to the safety of a member of his family), but he could not testify as to other irregularities which occurred in the jury room. Under this formulation a quotient verdict could not be attacked through the testimony of a juror, nor could a juror testify to the drunken condition of a fellow juror which so disabled him that he could not participate in the jury's deliberations.

The 1969 and 1971 Advisory Committee drafts would have permitted a member of the jury to testify concerning these kinds of irregularities in the jury room. The Advisory Committee note in the 1971 draft stated that " * * * the door of the jury room is not a satisfactory dividing point, and the Supreme Court has refused to accept it." The Advisory Committee further commented that--
The trend has been to draw the dividing line between testimony as to mental processes, on the one hand, and as to the existence of conditions or occurrences of events calculated improperly to influence the verdict on the other hand, without regard to whether the happening is within or without the jury room. * * * The jurors are the persons who know what really happened. Allowing them to testify as to matters other than their own reactions involves no particular hazard to the values sought to be protected. The rule is based upon this conclusion. It makes no attempt to specify the substantive grounds for setting aside verdicts for irregularity.

Objective jury misconduct may be testified to in California, Florida, Iowa, Kansas, Nebraska, New Jersey, North Dakota, Ohio, Oregon, Tennessee, Texas, and Washington.

Persuaded that the better practice is that provided for in the earlier drafts, the Committee amended subdivision (b) to read in the text of those drafts. House Report No. 93-650.

Note to Subdivision (b). As adopted by the House, this rule would permit the impeachment of verdicts by inquiry into, not the mental processes of the jurors, but what happened in terms of conduct in the jury room. This extension of the ability to impeach a verdict is felt to be unwarranted and ill-advised.

The rule passed by the House embodies a suggestion by the Advisory Committee of the Judicial Conference that is considerably broader than the final version adopted by the Supreme Court, which embodied long-accepted Federal law. Although forbidding the impeachment of verdicts by inquiry into the jurors' mental processes, it deletes from the Supreme Court version the proscription against testimony "as to any matter or statement occurring during the course of the jury's deliberations." This deletion would have the effect of opening verdicts up to challenge on the basis of what happened during the jury's internal deliberations, for example, where a juror alleged that the jury refused to follow the trial judge's instructions or that some of the jurors did not take part in deliberations.

Permitting an individual to attack a jury verdict based upon the jury's internal deliberations has long been recognized as unwise by the Supreme Court. In McDonald v. Pless, the Court stated:

* * * *

[L]et it once be established that verdicts solemnly made and publicly returned into court can be attacked and set aside on the testimony of those who took part in their publication and all verdicts could be, and many would be, followed by an inquiry in the hope of discovering something which might invalidate the finding. Jurors would be harassed and beset by the defeated party in an effort to secure from them evidence of facts which might establish misconduct sufficient to set aside a verdict. If evidence thus secured could be thus used, the result would be to make what was intended to be a private deliberation, the constant subject of public investigation--to the destruction of all frankness and freedom of discussion and conference [238 U.S. 264, at 267 (1914)].

* * * *

As it stands then, the rule would permit the harassment of former jurors by losing parties as well as the possible exploitation of disgruntled or otherwise badly-motivated ex-jurors.

Public policy requires a finality to litigation. And common fairness requires that absolute privacy be preserved for jurors to engage in the full and free debate necessary to the attainment of just verdicts. Jurors will not be able to function effectively if their deliberations are to be scrutinized in post-trial litigation. In the interest of protecting the jury system and the citizens who make it work, rule 606 should not permit any inquiry into the internal deliberations of the jurors. Senate Report No. 93-1277.

Note to Subdivision (b). Rule 606(b) deals with juror testimony in an inquiry into the validity of a verdict or indictment. The House bill provides that a juror cannot testify about his mental processes or about the effect of anything upon his or another juror's mind as influencing him to assent to or dissent from a verdict or indictment. Thus, the House bill allows a juror to testify about objective matters occurring during the jury's deliberation, such as the misconduct of another juror or the reaching of a quotient verdict. The Senate bill does not permit juror testimony about any matter or statement occurring during the course of the jury's deliberations. The Senate bill does provide, however, that a juror may testify on the question whether extraneous prejudicial information was improperly brought to the jury's attention and on the question whether any outside influence was improperly brought to bear on any juror.

The Conference adopts the Senate amendment. The Conferees believe that jurors should be encouraged to be conscientious in promptly reporting to the court misconduct that occurs during jury deliberations. House Report No. 93-1597.

1987 Amendments
The amendments are technical. No substantive change is intended.

2006 Amendments
Rule 606(b) has been amended to provide that juror testimony may be used to prove that the verdict reported was the result of a mistake in entering the verdict on the verdict form. The amendment responds to a divergence between the text of the Rule and the case law that has established an exception for proof of clerical errors. See, e.g., Plummer v. Springfield Term. Ry., 5 F.3d 1, 3 (1st Cir. 1993) ("A number of circuits hold, and we agree, that juror testimony regarding an alleged clerical error, such as announcing a verdict different than that agreed upon, does not challenge the validity of the verdict or the deliberation of mental processes, and therefore is not subject to Rule 606(b)."); Teevee Toons, Inc., v. MP3.Com, Inc., 148 F.Supp.2d 276, 278 (S.D.N.Y. 2001) (noting that Rule 606(b) has been silent regarding inquiries designed to confirm the accuracy of a verdict).

In adopting the exception for proof of mistakes in entering the verdict on the verdict form, the amendment specifically rejects the broader exception, adopted by some courts, permitting the use of juror testimony to prove that the jurors were operating under a misunderstanding about the consequences of the result that they agreed upon. See, e.g., Attridge v. Cencorp Div. of Dover Techs. Int'l, Inc., 836 F.2d 113, 116 (2d Cir. 1987); Eastridge Development Co., v. Halpert Associates, Inc., 853 F.2d 772 (10th Cir. 1988). The broader exception is rejected because an inquiry into whether the jury misunderstood or misapplied an instruction goes to the jurors' mental processes underlying the verdict, rather than the verdict's accuracy in capturing what the jurors had agreed upon. See, e.g. , Karl v. Burlington Northern R.R., 880 F.2d 68, 74 (8th Cir. 1989) (error to receive juror testimony on whether verdict was the result of jurors' misunderstanding of instructions: "The jurors did not state that the figure written by the foreman was different from that which they agreed upon, but indicated that the figure the foreman wrote down was intended to be a net figure, not a gross figure. Receiving such statements violates Rule 606(b) because the testimony relates to how the jury interpreted the court's instructions, and concerns the jurors' 'mental processes,' which is forbidden by the rule."); Robles v. Exxon Corp., 862 F.2d 1201, 1208 (5th Cir. 1989) ("the alleged error here goes to the substance of what the jury was asked to decide, necessarily implicating the jury's mental processes insofar as it questions the jury's understanding of the court's instructions and application of those instructions to the facts of the case"). Thus, the exception established by the amendment is limited to cases such as "where the jury foreperson wrote down, in response to an interrogatory, a number different from that agreed upon by the jury, or mistakenly stated that the defendant was 'guilty' when the jury had actually agreed that the defendant was not guilty." Id.

It should be noted that the possibility of errors in the verdict form will be reduced substantially by polling the jury. Rule 606(b) does not, of course, prevent this precaution. See 8 C. Wigmore, Evidence, § 2350 at 691 (McNaughten ed. 1961) (noting that the reasons for the rule barring juror testimony, "namely, the dangers of uncertainty and of tampering with the jurors to procure testimony, disappear in large part if such investigation as may be desired is made by the judge and takes place before the jurors' discharge and separation") (emphasis in original). Errors that come to light after polling the jury "may be corrected on the spot, or the jury may be sent out to continue deliberations, or, if necessary, a new trial may be ordered." C. Mueller & L. Kirkpatrick, Evidence Under the Rules at 671 (2d ed. 1999) (citing Sincox v. United States, 571 F.2d 876, 878-79 (5th Cir. 1978)).

2011 Amendments
The language of Rule 606 has been amended as part of the restyling of the Evidence Rules to make them more easily understood and to make style and terminology consistent throughout the rules. These changes are intended to be stylistic only. There is no intent to change any result in any ruling on evidence admissibility.

Rule 607. Who May Impeach a Witness

Any party, including the party that called the witness, may attack the witness's credibility.

Credits

(Pub.L. 93-595, § 1, Jan. 2, 1975, 88 Stat.1934; Mar. 2, 1987, eff. Oct. 1, 1987; Apr. 26, 2011, eff. Dec. 1, 2011.)

Editors' Notes

ADVISORY COMMITTEE NOTES

1972 Proposed Rules

The traditional rule against impeaching one's own witness is abandoned as based on false premises. A party does not hold out his witnesses as worthy of belief, since he rarely has a free choice in selecting them. Denial of the right leaves the party at the mercy of the witness and the adversary. If the impeachment is by a prior statement, it is free from hearsay dangers and is excluded from the category of hearsay under Rule 801(d)(1). Ladd, Impeachment of One's Own Witness--New Developments, 4 U.Chi.L.Rev. 69 (1936); McCormick § 38; 3 Wigmore §§ 896-918. The substantial inroads into the old rule made over the years by decisions, rules, and statutes are evidence of doubts as to its basic soundness and workability. Cases are collected in 3 Wigmore § 905. Revised Rule 32(a)(1) of the Federal Rules of Civil Procedure allows any party to impeach a witness by means of his deposition, and Rule 43(b) has allowed the calling and impeachment of an adverse party or person identified with him. Illustrative statutes allowing a party to impeach his own witness under varying circumstances are Ill.Rev.Stats.1967, c. 110, § 60; Mass.Laws Annot. 1959, c. 233, § 23; 20 N.M.Stats.Annot. 1953, § 20-2-4; N.Y. CPLR § 4514 (McKinney 1963); 12 Vt.Stats.Annot.1959, §§ 1641a, 1642. Complete judicial rejection of the old rule is found in United States v. Freeman, 302 F.2d 347 (2d Cir.1962). The same result is reached in Uniform Rule 20; California Evidence Code § 785; Kansas Code of Civil Procedure § 60-420. See also New Jersey Evidence Rule 20.

1987 Amendments
The amendment is technical. No substantive change is intended.

2011 Amendments
The language of Rule 607 has been amended as part of the restyling of the Evidence Rules to make them more easily understood and to make style and terminology consistent throughout the rules. These changes are intended to be stylistic only. There is no intent to change any result in any ruling on evidence admissibility.

Rule 608. A Witness's Character for Truthfulness or Untruthfulness

(a) Reputation or Opinion Evidence. A witness's credibility may be attacked or supported by testimony about the witness's reputation for having a character for truthfulness or untruthfulness, or by testimony in the form of an opinion about that character. But evidence of truthful character is admissible only after the witness's character for truthfulness has been attacked.

(b) Specific Instances of Conduct. Except for a criminal conviction under Rule 609, extrinsic evidence is not admissible to prove specific instances of a witness's conduct in order to attack or support the witness's character for truthfulness. But the court may, on cross-examination, allow them to be inquired into if they are probative of the character for truthfulness or untruthfulness of:

(1) the witness; or

(2) another witness whose character the witness being cross-examined has testified about.

By testifying on another matter, a witness does not waive any privilege against self-incrimination for testimony that relates only to the witness's character for truthfulness.

Credits

(Pub.L. 93-595, § 1, Jan. 2, 1975, 88 Stat.1935; Mar. 2, 1987, eff. Oct. 1, 1987; Apr. 25, 1988, eff. Nov. 1, 1988; Mar. 27, 2003, eff. Dec. 1, 2003; Apr. 26, 2011, eff. Dec. 1, 2011.)

Editors' Notes

ADVISORY COMMITTEE NOTES

1972 Proposed Rules

Note to Subdivision (a). In Rule 404(a) the general position is taken that character evidence is not admissible for the purpose of proving that the person acted in conformity therewith, subject, however, to several exceptions, one of which is character evidence of a witness as bearing upon his credibility. The present rule develops that exception.

In accordance with the bulk of judicial authority, the inquiry is strictly limited to character for veracity, rather than allowing evidence as to character generally. The result is to sharpen relevancy, to reduce surprise, waste of time, and confusion, and to make the lot of the witness somewhat less unattractive. McCormick § 44.

The use of opinion and reputation evidence as means of proving the character of witnesses is consistent with Rule 405(a). While the modern practice has purported to exclude opinion, witnesses who testify to reputation seem in fact often to be giving their opinions, disguised somewhat misleadingly as reputation. See McCormick § 44. And even under the modern practice, a common relaxation has allowed inquiry as to whether the witnesses would believe the principal witness under oath. United States v. Walker, 313 F.2d 236 (6th Cir.1963), and cases cited therein; McCormick § 44, pp. 94-95, n. 3.

Character evidence in support of credibility is admissible under the rule only after the witness' character has first been attacked, as has been the case at common law. Maguire, Weinstein, et al., Cases on Evidence 295 (5th ed. 1965); McCormick § 49, p. 105; 4 Wigmore § 1104. The enormous needless consumption of time which a contrary practice would entail justifies the limitation. Opinion or reputation that the witness is untruthful specifically qualifies as an attack under the rule, and evidence of misconduct, including conviction of crime, and of corruption also fall within this category. Evidence of bias or interest does not. McCormick § 49; 4 Wigmore §§ 1106, 1107. Whether evidence in the form of contradiction is an attack upon the character of the witness must depend upon the circumstances. McCormick § 49. Cf. 4 Wigmore §§ 1108, 1109.

As to the use of specific instances on direct by an opinion witness, see the Advisory Committee's Note to Rule 405, supra.

Note to Subdivision (b). In conformity with Rule 405, which forecloses use of evidence of specific incidents as proof in chief of character unless character is an issue in the case, the present rule generally bars evidence of specific instances of conduct of a witness for the purpose of attacking or supporting his credibility. There are, however, two exceptions: (1) specific instances are provable when they have been the subject of criminal conviction, and (2) specific instances may be inquired into on cross-examination of the principal witness or of a witness giving an opinion of his character for truthfulness.

(1) Conviction of crime as a technique of impeachment is treated in detail in Rule 609, and here is merely recognized as an exception to the general rule excluding evidence of specific incidents for impeachment purposes.

(2) Particular instances of conduct, though not the subject of criminal conviction, may be inquired into on cross-examination of the principal witness himself or of a witness who testifies concerning his character for truthfulness. Effective cross-examination demands that some allowance be made for going into matters of this kind, but the possibilities of abuse are substantial. Consequently safeguards are erected in the form of specific requirements that the instances inquired into be probative of truthfulness or its opposite and not remote in time. Also, the overriding protection of Rule 403 requires that probative value not be outweighed by danger of unfair prejudice, confusion of issues, or misleading the jury, and that of Rule 611 bars harassment and undue embarrassment.

The final sentence constitutes a rejection of the doctrine of such cases as People v. Sorge, 301 N.Y. 198, 93 N.E.2d 637 (1950), that any past criminal act relevant to credibility may be inquired into on cross-examination, in apparent disregard of the privilege against self-incrimination. While it is clear that an ordinary witness cannot make a partial disclosure of incriminating matter and then invoke the privilege on cross-examination, no tenable contention can be made that merely by testifying he waives his right to foreclose inquiry on cross-examination into criminal activities for the purpose of attacking his credibility. So to hold would reduce the privilege to a nullity. While it is true that an accused, unlike an ordinary witness, has an option whether to testify, if the option can be exercised only at the price of opening up inquiry as to any and all criminal acts committed during his lifetime, the right to testify could scarcely be said to possess much vitality. In Griffin v. California, 380 U.S. 609, 85 S.Ct. 1229, 14 L.Ed.2d 106 (1965), the Court held that allowing comment on the election of an accused not to testify exacted a constitutionally impermissible price, and so here. While no specific provision in terms confers constitutional status on the right of an accused to take the stand in his own defense, the existence of the right is so completely recognized that a denial of it or substantial infringement upon it would surely be of due process dimensions. See Ferguson v. Georgia, 365 U.S. 570, 81 S.Ct. 756, 5 L.Ed.2d 783 (1961); McCormick § 131; 8 Wigmore § 2276 (McNaughton Rev.1961). In any event, wholly aside from constitutional considerations, the provision represents a sound policy.

1974 Enactment
Note to Subdivision (a). Rule 608(a) as submitted by the Court permitted attack to be made upon the character for truthfulness or untruthfulness of a witness either by reputation or opinion testimony. For the same reason underlying its decision to eliminate the admissibility of opinion testimony in Rule 405(a), the Committee amended Rule 608(a) to delete the reference to opinion testimony.

Note to Subdivision (b). The second sentence of Rule 608(b) as submitted by the Court permitted specific instances of misconduct of a witness to be inquired into on cross-examination for the purpose of attacking his credibility, if probative of truthfulness or untruthfulness, "and not remote in time". Such cross-examination could be of the witness himself or of another witness who testifies as to "his" character for truthfulness or untruthfulness.

The Committee amended the Rule to emphasize the discretionary power of the court in permitting such testimony and deleted the reference to remoteness in time as being unnecessary and confusing (remoteness from time of trial or remoteness from the incident involved?). As recast, the Committee amendment also makes clear the antecedent of "his" in the original Court proposal. House Report No. 93-650.

The Senate amendment adds the words "opinion or" to conform the first sentence of the rule with the remainder of the rule.

The Conference adopts the Senate amendment. House Report No. 93-1597.

1987 Amendments
The amendments are technical. No substantive change is intended.

1988 Amendments
The amendment is technical. No substantive change is intended.

2003 Amendments
The Rule has been amended to clarify that the absolute prohibition on extrinsic evidence applies only when the sole reason for proffering that evidence is to attack or support the witness' character for truthfulness. See United States v. Abel, 469 U.S. 45 (1984); United States v. Fusco, 748 F.2d 996 (5th Cir. 1984) (Rule 608(b) limits the use of evidence "designed to show that the witness has done things, unrelated to the suit being tried, that make him more or less believable per se"); Ohio R.Evid. 608(b). On occasion the Rule's use of the overbroad term "credibility" has been read "to bar extrinsic evidence for bias, competency and contradiction impeachment since they too deal with credibility." American Bar Association Section of Litigation, Emerging Problems Under the Federal Rules of Evidence at 161 (3d ed. 1998). The amendment conforms the language of the Rule to its original intent, which was to impose an absolute bar on extrinsic evidence only if the sole purpose for offering the evidence was to prove the witness' character for veracity. See Advisory Committee Note to Rule 608(b) (stating that the Rule is "[i]n conformity with Rule 405, which forecloses use of evidence of specific incidents as proof in chief of character unless character is in issue in the case ... ").

By limiting the application of the Rule to proof of a witness' character for truthfulness, the amendment leaves the admissibility of extrinsic evidence offered for other grounds of impeachment (such as contradiction, prior inconsistent statement, bias and mental capacity) to Rules 402 and 403. See, e.g., United States v. Winchenbach, 197 F.3d 548 (1st Cir. 1999) (admissibility of a prior inconsistent statement offered for impeachment is governed by Rules 402 and 403, not Rule 608(b)); United States v. Tarantino, 846 F.2d 1384 (D.C. Cir. 1988) (admissibility of extrinsic evidence offered to contradict a witness is governed by Rules 402 and 403); United States v. Lindemann, 85 F.3d 1232 (7th Cir. 1996) (admissibility of extrinsic evidence of bias is governed by Rules 402 and 403).

It should be noted that the extrinsic evidence prohibition of Rule 608(b) bars any reference to the consequences that a witness might have suffered as a result of an alleged bad act. For example, Rule 608(b) prohibits counsel from mentioning that a witness was suspended or disciplined for the conduct that is the subject of impeachment, when that conduct is offered only to prove the character of the witness. See United States v. Davis, 183 F.3d 231, 257 n.12 (3d Cir. 1999) (emphasizing that in attacking the defendant's character for truthfulness "the government cannot make reference to Davis's forty-four day suspension or that Internal Affairs found that he lied about" an incident because "[s]uch evidence would not only be hearsay to the extent it contains assertion of fact, it would be inadmissible extrinsic evidence under Rule 608(b)"). See also Stephen A. Saltzburg,

Impeaching the Witness: Prior Bad Acts and Extrinsic Evidence, 7 Crim. Just. 28, 31 (Winter 1993) ("counsel should not be permitted to circumvent the no-extrinsic-evidence provision by tucking a third person's opinion about prior acts into a question asked of the witness who has denied the act").

For purposes of consistency the term "credibility" has been replaced by the term "character for truthfulness" in the last sentence of subdivision (b). The term "credibility" is also used in subdivision (a). But the Committee found it unnecessary to substitute "character for truthfulness" for "credibility" in Rule 608(a), because subdivision (a)(1) already serves to limit impeachment to proof of such character.

Rules 609(a) and 610 also use the term "credibility" when the intent of those Rules is to regulate impeachment of a witness' character for truthfulness. No inference should be derived from the fact that the Committee proposed an amendment to Rule 608(b) but not to Rules 609 and 610.

2011 Amendments
The language of Rule 608 has been amended as part of the general restyling of the Evidence Rules to make them more easily understood and to make style and terminology consistent throughout the rules. These changes are intended to be stylistic only. There is no intent to change any result in any ruling on evidence admissibility.

The Committee is aware that the Rule's limitation of bad-act impeachment to "cross-examination" is trumped by Rule 607, which allows a party to impeach witnesses on direct examination. Courts have not relied on the term "on cross-examination" to limit impeachment that would otherwise be permissible under Rules 607 and 608. The Committee therefore concluded that no change to the language of the Rule was necessary in the context of a restyling project.

Rule 609. Impeachment by Evidence of a Criminal Conviction

(a) In General. The following rules apply to attacking a witness's character for truthfulness by evidence of a criminal conviction:

(1) for a crime that, in the convicting jurisdiction, was punishable by death or by imprisonment for more than one year, the evidence:

(A) must be admitted, subject to Rule 403, in a civil case or in a criminal case in which the witness is not a defendant; and

(B) must be admitted in a criminal case in which the witness is a defendant, if the probative value of the evidence outweighs its prejudicial effect to that defendant; and

(2) for any crime regardless of the punishment, the evidence must be admitted if the court can readily determine that establishing the elements of the crime required proving--or the witness's admitting--a dishonest act or false statement.

(b) Limit on Using the Evidence After 10 Years. This subdivision (b) applies if more than 10 years have passed since the witness's conviction or release from confinement for it, whichever is later. Evidence of the conviction is admissible only if:

(1) its probative value, supported by specific facts and circumstances, substantially outweighs its prejudicial effect; and

(2) the proponent gives an adverse party reasonable written notice of the intent to use it so that the party has a fair opportunity to contest its use.

(c) Effect of a Pardon, Annulment, or Certificate of Rehabilitation. Evidence of a conviction is not admissible if:

(1) the conviction has been the subject of a pardon, annulment, certificate of rehabilitation, or other equivalent procedure based on a finding that the person has been rehabilitated, and the person has not been convicted of a later crime punishable by death or by imprisonment for more than one year; or

(2) the conviction has been the subject of a pardon, annulment, or other equivalent procedure based on a finding of innocence.

(d) Juvenile Adjudications. Evidence of a juvenile adjudication is admissible under this rule only if:

(1) it is offered in a criminal case;

(2) the adjudication was of a witness other than the defendant;

(3) an adult's conviction for that offense would be admissible to attack the adult's credibility; and

(4) admitting the evidence is necessary to fairly determine guilt or innocence.

(e) Pendency of an Appeal. A conviction that satisfies this rule is admissible even if an appeal is pending. Evidence of the pendency is also admissible.

Credits

(Pub.L. 93-595, § 1, Jan. 2, 1975, 88 Stat.1935; Mar. 2, 1987, eff. Oct. 1, 1987; Jan. 26, 1990, eff. Dec. 1, 1990; Apr. 12, 2006, eff. Dec. 1, 2006; Apr. 26, 2011, eff. Dec. 1, 2011.)

Editors' Notes

ADVISORY COMMITTEE NOTES

1972 Proposed Rules

As a means of impeachment, evidence of conviction of crime is significant only because it stands as proof of the commission of the underlying criminal act. There is little dissent from the general proposition that at least some crimes are relevant to credibility but much disagreement among the cases and commentators about which crimes are usable for this purpose. See McCormick § 43; 2 Wright, Federal Practice and Procedure: Criminal § 416 (1969). The weight of traditional authority has been to allow use of felonies generally, without regard to the nature of the particular offense, and of crimen falsi without regard to the grade of the offense. This is the view accepted by Congress in the 1970 amendment of § 14-305 of the District of Columbia Code, P.L. 91-358, 84 Stat. 473. Uniform Rule 21 and Model Code Rule 106 permit only crimes involving "dishonesty or false statement." Others have thought that the trial judge should have discretion to exclude convictions if the probative value of the evidence of the crime is substantially outweighed by the danger of unfair prejudice. Luck v. United States, 121 U.S.App.D.C. 151, 348 F.2d 763 (1965); McGowan, Impeachment of Criminal Defendants by Prior Convictions, 1970 Law & Soc.Order 1. Whatever may be the merits of those views, this rule is drafted to accord with the Congressional policy manifested in the 1970 legislation.

The proposed rule incorporates certain basic safeguards, in terms applicable to all witnesses but of particular significance to an accused who elects to testify. These protections include the imposition of definite time limitations, giving effect to demonstrated rehabilitation, and generally excluding juvenile adjudications.

Note to Subdivision (a). For purposes of impeachment, crimes are divided into two categories by the rule: (1) those of what is generally regarded as felony grade, without particular regard to the nature of the offense, and (2) those involving dishonesty or false statement, without regard to the grade of the offense. Probable convictions are not limited to violations of federal law. By reason of our constitutional structure, the federal catalog of crimes is far from being a complete one, and resort must be had to the laws of the states for the specification of many crimes. For example, simple theft as compared with theft from interstate commerce. Other instances of borrowing are the Assimilative Crimes Act, making the state law of crimes applicable to the special territorial and maritime jurisdiction of the United States, 18 U.S.C. § 13, and the provision of the Judicial Code disqualifying persons as jurors on the grounds of state as well as federal convictions, 28 U.S.C. § 1865. For evaluation of the crime in terms of seriousness, reference is made to the congressional measurement of felony (subject to imprisonment in excess of one year) rather than adopting state definitions which vary considerably. See 28 U.S.C. § 1865, supra, disqualifying jurors for conviction in state or federal court of crime punishable by imprisonment for more than one year.

Note to Subdivision (b). Few statutes recognize a time limit on impeachment by evidence of conviction. However, practical considerations of fairness and relevancy demand that some boundary be recognized. See Ladd, Credibility Tests--Current Trends, 89 U.Pa.L.Rev. 166, 176-177 (1940). This portion of the rule is derived from the proposal advanced in Recommendation Proposing in Evidence Code, § 788(5), p. 142, Cal.Law Rev.Comm'n (1965), though not adopted. See California Evidence Code § 788.

Note to Subdivision (c). A pardon or its equivalent granted solely for the purpose of restoring civil rights lost by virtue of a conviction has no relevance to an inquiry into character. If, however, the pardon or other proceeding is hinged upon a showing of rehabilitation the situation is otherwise. The result under the rule is to render the conviction inadmissible. The alternative of allowing in evidence both the conviction and the rehabilitation has not been adopted for reasons of policy, economy of time, and difficulties of evaluation.

A similar provision is contained in California Evidence Code § 788. Cf. A.L.I. Model Penal Code, Proposed Official Draft § 306.6(3)(e) (1962), and discussion in A.L.I. Proceedings 310 (1961).

Pardons based on innocence have the effect, of course, of nullifying the conviction ab initio.

Note to Subdivision (d). The prevailing view has been that a juvenile adjudication is not usable for impeachment. Thomas v. United States, 74 App.D.C. 167, 121 F.2d 905 (1941); Cotton v. United States, 355 F.2d 480 (10th Cir.1966). This conclusion was based upon a variety of circumstances. By virtue of its informality, frequently diminished quantum of required proof, and other departures from accepted standards for criminal trials under the theory of parens patriae, the juvenile adjudication was considered to lack the precision and general probative value of the criminal conviction. While In re Gault, 387 U.S. 1, 87 S.Ct. 1428, 18 L.Ed.2d 527 (1967), no doubt eliminates these characteristics insofar as objectionable, other obstacles remain. Practical problems of administration are raised by the common provisions in juvenile legislation that records be kept confidential and that they be destroyed after a short time. While Gault was skeptical as to the realities of confidentiality of juvenile records, it also saw no constitutional obstacles to improvement. 387 U.S. at 25, 87 S.Ct. 1428. See also Note, Rights and Rehabilitation in the Juvenile Courts, 67 Colum.L.Rev. 281, 289 (1967). In addition, policy considerations much akin to those which dictate exclusion of adult convictions after rehabilitation has been established strongly suggest a rule of excluding juvenile adjudications. Admittedly, however, the rehabilitative process may in a given case be a demonstrated failure, or the strategic importance of a given witness may be so great as to require the overriding of general policy in the interests of particular justice. See Giles v. Maryland, 386 U.S. 66, 87 S.Ct. 793, 17 L.Ed.2d 737 (1967). Wigmore was outspoken in his condemnation of the disallowance of juvenile adjudications to impeach, especially when the witness is the complainant in a case of molesting a minor. 1 Wigmore § 196; 3 Id. §§ 924a, 980. The rule recognizes discretion in the judge to effect an accommodation among these various factors by departing from the general principle of exclusion. In deference to the general pattern and policy of juvenile statutes, however, no discretion is accorded when the witness is the accused in a criminal case.

Note to Subdivision (e). The presumption of correctness which ought to attend judicial proceedings supports the position that pendency of an appeal does not preclude use of a conviction for impeachment. United States v. Empire Packing Co., 174 F.2d 16 (7th Cir.1949), cert. denied 337 U.S. 959, 69 S.Ct. 1534, 93 L.Ed. 1758; Bloch v. United States, 226 F.2d 185 (9th Cir.1955), cert. denied 350 U.S. 948, 76 S.Ct. 323, 100 L.Ed. 826 and 353 U.S. 959, 77 S.Ct. 868, 1 L.Ed.2d 910; and see Newman v. United States, 331 F.2d 968 (8th Cir.1964). Contra, Campbell v. United States, 85 U.S.App.D.C. 133, 176 F.2d 45 (1949). The pendency of an appeal is, however, a qualifying circumstance properly considerable.

1974 Enactment
Note to Subdivision (a). Rule 609(a) as submitted by the Court was modeled after Section 133(a) of Public Law 91-358, 14 D.C.Code 305(b)(1), enacted in 1970. The Rule provided that:
For the purpose of attacking the credibility of a witness, evidence that he has been convicted of a crime is admissible but only if the crime (1) was punishable by death or imprisonment in excess of one year under the law under which he was convicted or (2) involved dishonesty or false statement regardless of the punishment.

As reported to the Committee by the Subcommittee, Rule 609(a) was amended to read as follows:
For the purpose of attacking the credibility of a witness, evidence that he has been convicted of a crime is admissible only if the crime (1) was punishable by death or imprisonment in excess of one year, unless the court determines that the danger of unfair prejudice outweighs the probative value of the evidence of the conviction, or (2) involved dishonesty or false statement.

In full committee, the provision was amended to permit attack upon the credibility of a witness by prior conviction only if the prior crime involved dishonesty or false statement. While recognizing that the prevailing doctrine in the federal courts and in most States allows a witness to be impeached by evidence of prior felony convictions without restriction as to type, the Committee was of the view that, because of the danger of unfair prejudice in such practice and the deterrent effect upon an accused who might wish to testify, and even upon a witness who was not the accused, cross-examination by evidence of prior conviction should be limited to those kinds of convictions bearing directly on credibility, i.e., crimes involving dishonesty or false statement.

Note to Subdivision (b). Rule 609(b) as submitted by the Court was modeled after Section 133(a) of Public Law 91-358, 14 D.C.Code 305(b)(2)(B), enacted in 1970. The Rule provided:
Evidence of a conviction under this rule is not admissible if a period of more than ten years has elapsed since the date of the release of the witness from confinement imposed for his most recent conviction, or the expiration of the period of his parole, probation, or sentence granted or imposed with respect to his most recent conviction, whichever is the later date.

Under this formulation, a witness' entire past record of criminal convictions could be used for impeachment (provided the conviction met the standard of subdivision (a)), if the witness had been most recently released from confinement, or the period of his parole or probation had expired, within ten years of the conviction.

The Committee amended the Rule to read in the text of the 1971 Advisory Committee version to provide that upon the expiration of ten years from the date of a conviction of a witness, or of his release from confinement for that offense, that conviction may no longer be used for impeachment. The Committee was of the view that after ten years following a person's release from confinement (or from the date of his conviction) the probative value of the conviction with respect to that person's credibility diminished to a point where it should no longer be admissible.

Note to Subdivision (c). Rule 609(c) as submitted by the Court provided in part that evidence of a witness' prior conviction is not admissible to attack his credibility if the conviction was the subject of a pardon, annulment, or other equivalent procedure, based on a showing of rehabilitation, and the witness has not been convicted of a subsequent crime. The Committee amended the Rule to provide that the "subsequent crime" must have been "punishable by death or imprisonment in excess of one year", on the ground that a subsequent conviction of an offense not a felony is insufficient to rebut the finding that the witness has been rehabilitated. The Committee also intends that the words "based on a finding of the rehabilitation of the person convicted" apply not only to "certificate of rehabilitation, or other equivalent procedure", but also to "pardon" and "annulment.". House Report No. 93-650.

Note to Subdivision (a). As proposed by the Supreme Court, the rule would allow the use of prior convictions to impeach if the crime was a felony or a misdemeanor if the misdemeanor involved dishonesty or false statement. As modified by the House, the rule would admit prior convictions for impeachment purposes only if the offense, whether felony or misdemeanor, involved dishonesty or false statement.

The committee has adopted a modified version of the House-passed rule. In your committee's view, the danger of unfair prejudice is far greater when the accused, as opposed to other witnesses, testifies, because the jury may be prejudiced not merely on the question of credibility but also on the ultimate question of guilt or innocence. Therefore, with respect to defendants, the committee agreed with the House limitation that only offenses involved false statement or dishonesty may be used. By that phrase, the committee means crimes such as perjury or subornation of perjury, false statement, criminal fraud, embezzlement or false pretense, or any other offense, in the nature of crimen falsi the commission of which involves some element of untruthfulness, deceit or falsification bearing on the accused's propensity to testify truthfully.

With respect to other witnesses, in addition to any prior conviction involving false statement or dishonesty, any other felony may be used to impeach if, and only if, the court finds that the probative value of such evidence outweighs its prejudicial effect against the party offering that witness.

Notwithstanding this provision, proof of any prior offense otherwise admissible under Rule 404 could still be offered for the purposes sanctioned by that rule. Furthermore, the committee intends that notwithstanding this rule, a defendant's misrepresentation regarding the existence or nature of prior convictions may be met by rebuttal evidence, including the record of such prior convictions. Similarly, such records may be offered to rebut representations made by the defendant regarding his attitude toward or willingness to commit a general category of offense, although denials or other representations by the defendant regarding the specific conduct which forms the basis of the charge against him shall not make prior convictions admissible to rebut such statement.

In regard to either type of representation, of course, prior convictions may be offered in rebuttal only if the defendant's statement is made in response to defense counsel's questions or is made gratuitously in the course of cross-examination. Prior convictions may not be offered as rebuttal evidence if the prosecution has sought to circumvent the purpose of this rule by asking questions which elicit such representations from the defendant.

One other clarifying amendment has been added to this subsection, that is, to provide that the admissibility of evidence of a prior conviction is permitted only upon cross-examination of a witness. It is not admissible if a person does not testify. It is to be understood, however, that a court record of a prior conviction is admissible to prove that conviction if the witness has forgotten or denies its existence.

Note to Subdivision (b). Although convictions over ten years old generally do not have much probative value, there may be exceptional circumstances under which the conviction substantially bears on the credibility of the witness. Rather than exclude all convictions over 10 years old, the committee adopted an amendment in the form of a final clause to the section granting the court discretion to admit convictions over 10 years old, but only upon a determination by the court that the probative value of the conviction supported by specific facts and circumstances, substantially outweighs its prejudicial effect.

It is intended that convictions over 10 years old will be admitted very rarely and only in exceptional circumstances. The rules provide that the decision be supported by specific facts and circumstances thus requiring the court to make specific findings on the record as to the particular facts and circumstances it has considered in determining that the probative value of the conviction substantially outweighs its prejudicial impact. It is expected that, in fairness, the court will give the party against whom the conviction is introduced a full and adequate opportunity to contest its admission. Senate Report No. 93-1277.

Rule 609 defines when a party may use evidence of a prior conviction in order to impeach a witness. The Senate amendments make changes in two subsections of Rule 609.

Note to Subdivision (a). The House bill provides that the credibility of a witness can be attacked by proof of prior conviction of a crime only if the crime involves dishonesty or false statement. The Senate amendment provides that a witness' credibility may be attacked if the crime (1) was punishable by death or imprisonment in excess of one year under the law under which he was convicted or (2) involves dishonesty or false statement, regardless of the punishment.

The Conference adopts the Senate amendment with an amendment. The Conference amendment provides that the credibility of a witness, whether a defendant or someone else, may be attacked by proof of a prior conviction but only if the crime: (1) was punishable by death or imprisonment in excess of one year under the law under which he was convicted and the court determines that the probative value of the conviction outweighs its prejudicial effect to the defendant; or (2) involved dishonesty or false statement regardless of the punishment.

By the phrase "dishonesty and false statement" the Conference means crimes such as perjury or subornation of perjury, false statement, criminal fraud, embezzlement, or false pretense, or any other offense in the nature of crimen falsi, the commission of which involves some element of deceit, untruthfulness, or falsification bearing on the accused's propensity to testify truthfully.

The admission of prior convictions involving dishonesty and false statement is not within the discretion of the Court. Such convictions are peculiarly probative of credibility and, under this rule, are always to be admitted. Thus, judicial discretion granted with respect to the admissibility of other prior convictions is not applicable to those involving dishonesty or false statement.

With regard to the discretionary standard established by paragraph (1) of Rule 609(a), the Conference determined that the prejudicial effect to be weighed against the probative value of the conviction is specifically the prejudicial effect to the defendant. The danger of prejudice to a witness other than the defendant (such as injury to the witness' reputation in his community) was considered and rejected by the Conference as an element to be weighed in determining admissibility. It was the judgment of the Conference that the danger of prejudice to a nondefendant witness is outweighed by the need for the trier of fact to have as much relevant evidence on the issue of credibility as possible. Such evidence should only be excluded where it presents a danger of improperly influencing the outcome of the trial by persuading the trier of fact to convict the defendant on the basis of his prior criminal record.

Note to Subdivision (b). The House bill provides in subsection (b) that evidence of conviction of a crime may not be used for impeachment purposes under subsection (a) if more than ten years have elapsed since the date of the conviction or the date the witness was released from confinement imposed for the conviction, whichever is later. The Senate amendment permits the use of convictions older than ten years, if the court determines, in the interests of justice, that the probative value of the conviction, supported by specific facts and circumstances, substantially outweighs its prejudicial effect.

The Conference adopts the Senate amendment with an amendment requiring notice by a party that he intends to request that the court allow him to use a conviction older than ten years. The Conferees anticipate that a written notice, in order to give the adversary a fair opportunity to contest the use of the evidence, will ordinarily include such information as the date of the conviction, the jurisdiction, and the offense or statute involved. In order to eliminate the possibility that the flexibility of this provision may impair the ability of a party-opponent to prepare for trial, the Conferees intend that the notice provision operate to avoid surprise. House Report No. 93-1597.

1987 Amendments
The amendments are technical. No substantive change is intended.

1990 Amendments
The amendment to Rule 609(a) makes two changes in the rule. The first change removes from the rule the limitation that the conviction may only be elicited during cross-examination, a limitation that virtually every circuit has found to be inapplicable. It is common for witnesses to reveal on direct examination their convictions to "remove the sting" of the impeachment. See e.g., United States v. Bad Cob, 560 F.2d 877 (8th Cir.1977). The amendment does not contemplate that a court will necessarily permit proof of prior convictions through testimony, which might be time-consuming and more prejudicial than proof through a written record. Rules 403 and 611(a) provide sufficient authority for the court to protect against unfair or disruptive methods of proof.

The second change effected by the amendment resolves an ambiguity as to the relationship of Rules 609 and 403 with respect to impeachment of witnesses other than the criminal defendant. See, Green v. Bock Laundry Machine Co., 109 S.Ct. 1981, 490 U.S. 504 (1989). The amendment does not disturb the special balancing test for the criminal defendant who chooses to testify. Thus, the rule recognizes that, in virtually every case in which prior convictions are used to impeach the testifying defendant, the defendant faces a unique risk of prejudice--i.e., the danger that convictions that would be excluded under Fed.R.Evid. 404 will be misused by a jury as propensity evidence despite their introduction solely for impeachment purposes. Although the rule does not forbid all use of convictions to impeach a defendant, it requires that the government show that the probative value of convictions as impeachment evidence outweighs their prejudicial effect.

Prior to the amendment, the rule appeared to give the defendant the benefit of the special balancing test when defense witnesses other than the defendant were called to testify. In practice, however, the concern about unfairness to the defendant is most acute when the defendant's own convictions are offered as evidence. Almost all of the decided cases concern this type of impeachment, and the amendment does not deprive the defendant of any meaningful protection, since Rule 403 now clearly protects against unfair impeachment of any defense witness other than the defendant. There are cases in which a defendant might be prejudiced when a defense witness is impeached. Such cases may arise, for example, when the witness bears a special relationship to the defendant such that the defendant is likely to suffer some spill-over effect from impeachment of the witness.

The amendment also protects other litigants from unfair impeachment of their witnesses. The danger of prejudice from the use of prior convictions is not confined to criminal defendants. Although the danger that prior convictions will be misused as character evidence is particularly acute when the defendant is impeached, the danger exists in other situations as well. The amendment reflects the view that it is desirable to protect all litigants from the unfair use of prior convictions, and that the ordinary balancing test of Rule 403, which provides that evidence shall not be excluded unless its prejudicial effect substantially outweighs its probative value, is appropriate for assessing the admissibility of prior convictions for impeachment of any witness other than a criminal defendant.

The amendment reflects a judgment that decisions interpreting Rule 609(a) as requiring a trial court to admit convictions in civil cases that have little, if anything, to do with credibility reach undesirable results. See, e.g., Diggs v. Lyons, 741 F.2d 577 (3d Cir.1984), cert. denied, 105 S.Ct. 2157 (1985). The amendment provides the same protection against unfair prejudice arising from prior convictions used for impeachment purposes as the rules provide for other evidence. The amendment finds support in decided cases. See, e.g., Petty v. Ideco, 761 F.2d 1146 (5th Cir.1985); Czaka v. Hickman, 703 F.2d 317 (8th Cir.1983).

Fewer decided cases address the question whether Rule 609(a) provides any protection against unduly prejudicial prior convictions used to impeach government witnesses. Some courts have read Rule 609(a) as giving the government no protection for its witnesses. See, e.g., United States v.

Thorne, 547 F.2d 56 (8th Cir.1976); United States v. Nevitt, 563 F.2d 406 (9th Cir.1977), cert. denied, 444 U.S. 847 (1979). This approach also is rejected by the amendment. There are cases in which impeachment of government witnesses with prior convictions that have little, if anything, to do with credibility may result in unfair prejudice to the government's interest in a fair trial and unnecessary embarrassment to a witness. Fed.R.Evid. 412 already recognizes this and excluded certain evidence of past sexual behavior in the context of prosecutions for sexual assaults.

The amendment applies the general balancing test of Rule 403 to protect all litigants against unfair impeachment of witnesses. The balancing test protects civil litigants, the government in criminal cases, and the defendant in a criminal case who calls other witnesses. The amendment addresses prior convictions offered under Rule 609, not for other purposes, and does not run afoul, therefore, of Davis v. Alaska, 415 U.S. 308 (1974). Davis involved the use of a prior juvenile adjudication not to prove a past law violation, but to prove bias. The defendant in a criminal case has the right to demonstrate the bias of a witness and to be assured a fair trial, but not to unduly prejudice a trier of fact. See generally Rule 412. In any case in which the trial court believes that confrontation rights require admission of impeachment evidence, obviously the Constitution would take precedence over the rule.

The probability that prior convictions of an ordinary government witness will be unduly prejudicial is low in most criminal cases. Since the behavior of the witness is not the issue in dispute in most cases, there is little chance that the trier of fact will misuse the convictions offered as impeachment evidence as propensity evidence. Thus, trial courts will be skeptical when the government objects to impeachment of its witnesses with prior convictions. Only when the government is able to point to a real danger of prejudice that is sufficient to outweigh substantially the probative value of the conviction for impeachment purposes will the conviction be excluded.

The amendment continues to divide subdivision (a) into subsections (1) and (2) thus facilitating retrieval under current computerized research programs which distinguish the two provisions. The Committee recommended no substantive change in subdivision (a)(2), even though some cases raise a concern about the proper interpretation of the words "dishonesty or false statement." These words were used but not explained in the original Advisory Committee Note accompanying Rule 609. Congress extensively debated the rule, and the Report of the House and Senate Conference Committee states that "[b]y the phrase 'dishonesty and false statement,' the Conference means crimes such as perjury, subornation of perjury, false statement, criminal fraud, embezzlement, or false pretense, or any other offense in the nature of crimen falsi, commission of which involves some element of deceit, untruthfulness, or falsification bearing on the accused's propensity to testify truthfully." The Advisory Committee concluded that the Conference Report provides sufficient guidance to trial courts and that no amendment is necessary, notwithstanding some decisions that take an unduly broad view of "dishonesty," admitting convictions such as for bank robbery or bank larceny. Subsection (a)(2) continues to apply to any witness, including a criminal defendant.

Finally, the Committee determined that it was unnecessary to add to the rule language stating that, when a prior conviction is offered under Rule 609, the trial court is to consider the probative value of the prior conviction for impeachment, not for other purposes. The Committee concluded that the title of the rule, its first sentence, and its placement among the impeachment rules clearly establish that evidence offered under Rule 609 is offered only for purposes of impeachment.

2006 Amendments
The amendment provides that Rule 609(a)(2) mandates the admission of evidence of a conviction only when the conviction required the proof of (or in the case of a guilty plea, the admission of) an act of dishonesty or false statement. Evidence of all other convictions is inadmissible under this subsection, irrespective of whether the witness exhibited dishonesty or made a false statement in the process of the commission of the crime of conviction. Thus, evidence that a witness was convicted for a crime of violence, such as murder, is not admissible under Rule 609(a)(2), even if the witness acted deceitfully in the course of committing the crime.

The amendment is meant to give effect to the legislative intent to limit the convictions that are to be automatically admitted under subdivision (a)(2). The Conference Committee provided that by "dishonesty and false statement" it meant "crimes such as perjury, subornation of perjury, false statement, criminal fraud, embezzlement, or false pretense, or any other offense in the nature of crimen falsi, the commission of which involves some element of deceit, untruthfulness, or falsification bearing on the [witness's] propensity to testify truthfully." Historically, offenses classified as crimina falsi have included only those crimes in which the ultimate criminal act was itself an act of deceit. See Green, Deceit and the Classification of Crimes: Federal Rule of Evidence 609(a)(2) and the Origins of Crimen Falsi, 90 J. Crim. L. & Criminology 1087 (2000).

Evidence of crimes in the nature of crimina falsi must be admitted under Rule 609(a)(2), regardless of how such crimes are specifically charged. For example, evidence that a witness was convicted of making a false claim to a federal agent is admissible under this subdivision regardless of whether the crime was charged under a section that expressly references deceit (e.g., 18 U.S.C. § 1001, Material Misrepresentation to the Federal Government) or a section that does not (e.g., 18 U.S.C. § 1503, Obstruction of Justice).

The amendment requires that the proponent have ready proof that the conviction required the factfinder to find, or the defendant to admit, an act of dishonesty or false statement. Ordinarily, the statutory elements of the crime will indicate whether it is one of dishonesty or false statement. Where the deceitful nature of the crime is not apparent from the statute and the face of the judgment -- as, for example, where the conviction simply records a finding of guilt for a statutory offense that does not reference deceit expressly -- a proponent may offer information such as an indictment, a statement of admitted facts, or jury instructions to show that the factfinder had to find, or the defendant had to admit, an act of dishonesty or false statement in order for the witness to have been convicted. Cf. Taylor v. United States, 495 U.S. 575, 602 (1990) (providing that a trial court may look to a charging instrument or jury instructions to ascertain the nature of a prior offense where the statute is insufficiently clear on its face); Shepard v. United States, 125 S.Ct. 1254 (2005) (the inquiry to determine whether a guilty plea to a crime defined by a nongeneric statute necessarily admitted elements of the generic offense was limited to the charging document's terms, the terms of a plea agreement or transcript of colloquy between judge and defendant in which the factual basis for the plea was confirmed by the defendant, or a comparable judicial record). But the amendment does not contemplate a "mini-trial" in which the court plumbs the record of the previous proceeding to determine whether the crime was in the nature of crimen falsi.

The amendment also substitutes the term "character for truthfulness" for the term "credibility" in the first sentence of the Rule. The limitations of Rule 609 are not applicable if a conviction is admitted for a purpose other than to prove the witness's character for untruthfulness. See, e.g., United States v. Lopez, 979 F.2d 1024 (5th Cir. 1992) (Rule 609 was not applicable where the conviction was offered for purposes of contradiction). The use of the term "credibility" in subdivision (d) is retained, however, as that subdivision is intended to govern the use of a juvenile adjudication for any type of impeachment.

2011 Amendments
The language of Rule 609 has been amended as part of the restyling of the Evidence Rules to make them more easily understood and to make style and terminology consistent throughout the rules. These changes are intended to be stylistic only. There is no intent to change any result in any ruling on evidence admissibility.

Rule 610. Religious Beliefs or Opinions
Evidence of a witness's religious beliefs or opinions is not admissible to attack or support the witness's credibility.

Credits

(Pub.L. 93-595, § 1, Jan. 2, 1975, 88 Stat.1936; Mar. 2, 1987, eff. Oct. 1, 1987; Apr. 26, 2011, eff. Dec. 1, 2011.)

Editors' Notes

ADVISORY COMMITTEE NOTES

1972 Proposed Rules

While the rule forecloses inquiry into the religious beliefs or opinions of a witness for the purpose of showing that his character for truthfulness is affected by their nature, an inquiry for the purpose of showing interest or bias because of them is not within the prohibition. Thus disclosure of affiliation with a church which is a party to the litigation would be allowable under the rule. Cf. Tucker v. Reil, 51 Ariz. 357, 77 P.2d 203 (1938). To the same effect, though less specifically worded, is California Evidence Code § 789. See 3 Wigmore § 936.

1987 Amendments
The amendment is technical. No substantive change is intended.

2011 Amendments
The language of Rule 610 has been amended as part of the restyling of the Evidence Rules to make them more easily understood and to make style and terminology consistent throughout the rules. These changes are intended to be stylistic only. There is no intent to change any result in any ruling on evidence admissibility.

Rule 611. Mode and Order of Examining Witnesses and Presenting Evidence

(a) Control by the Court; Purposes. The court should exercise reasonable control over the mode and order of examining witnesses and presenting evidence so as to:

(1) make those procedures effective for determining the truth;

(2) avoid wasting time; and

(3) protect witnesses from harassment or undue embarrassment.

(b) Scope of Cross-Examination. Cross-examination should not go beyond the subject matter of the direct examination and matters affecting the witness's credibility. The court may allow inquiry into additional matters as if on direct examination.

(c) Leading Questions. Leading questions should not be used on direct examination except as necessary to develop the witness's testimony. Ordinarily, the court should allow leading questions:

(1) on cross-examination; and

(2) when a party calls a hostile witness, an adverse party, or a witness identified with an adverse party.

Credits

(Pub.L. 93-595, § 1, Jan. 2, 1975, 88 Stat. 1936; Mar. 2, 1987, eff. Oct. 1, 1987; Apr. 26, 2011, eff. Dec. 1, 2011.)

Editors' Notes

ADVISORY COMMITTEE NOTES

1972 Proposed Rules

Note to Subdivision (a). Spelling out detailed rules to govern the mode and order of interrogating witnesses and presenting evidence is neither desirable nor feasible. The ultimate responsibility for the effective working of the adversary system rests with the judge. The rule sets forth the objectives which he should seek to attain.

Item (1) restates in broad terms the power and obligation of the judge as developed under common law principles. It covers such concerns as whether testimony shall be in the form of a free narrative or responses to specific questions, McCormick § 5, the order of calling witnesses and presenting evidence, 6 Wigmore § 1867, the use of demonstrative evidence, McCormick § 179, and the many other questions arising during the course of a trial which can be solved only by the judge's common sense and fairness in view of the particular circumstances.

Item (2) is addressed to avoidance of needless consumption of time, a matter of daily concern in the disposition of cases. A companion piece is found in the discretion vested in the judge to exclude evidence as a waste of time in Rule 403(b).

Item (3) calls for a judgment under the particular circumstances whether interrogation tactics entail harassment or undue embarrassment. Pertinent circumstances include the importance of the testimony, the nature of the inquiry, its relevance to credibility, waste of time, and confusion. McCormick § 42. In Alford v. United States, 282 U.S. 687, 694, 51 S.Ct. 218, 75 L.Ed. 624 (1931), the Court pointed out that, while the trial judge should protect the witness from questions which "go beyond the bounds of proper cross-examination merely to harass, annoy or humiliate," this protection by no means forecloses efforts to discredit the witness. Reference to the transcript of the prosecutor's cross-examination in Berger v. United States, 295 U.S. 78, 55 S.Ct. 629, 79 L.Ed. 1314 (1935), serves to lay at rest any doubts as to the need for judicial control in this area.

The inquiry into specific instances of conduct of a witness allowed under Rule 608(b) is, of course, subject to this rule.

Note to Subdivision (b). The tradition in the federal courts and in numerous state courts has been to limit the scope of cross-examination to matters testified to on direct, plus matters bearing upon the credibility of the witness. Various reasons have been advanced to justify the rule of limited cross-examination. (1) A party vouches for his own witness but only to the extent of matters elicited on direct. Resurrection Gold Mining Co. v. Fortune Gold Mining Co., 129 F. 668, 675 (8th Cir.1904), quoted in Maguire, Weinstein, et al., Cases on Evidence 277, n. 38 (5th ed. 1965). But the concept of vouching is discredited, and Rule 607 rejects it. (2) A party cannot ask his own witness leading questions. This is a problem properly solved in terms of what is necessary for a proper development of the testimony rather than by a mechanistic formula similar to the vouching concept. See discussion under subdivision (c). (3) A practice of limited cross-examination promotes orderly presentation of the case. Finch v. Weiner, 109 Conn. 616, 145 A. 31 (1929). While this latter reason has merit, the matter is essentially one of the order of presentation and not one in which involvement at the appellate level is likely to prove fruitful. See, for example, Moyer v. Aetna Life Ins. Co., 126 F.2d 141 (3rd Cir.1942); Butler v. New York Central R. Co., 253 F.2d 281 (7th Cir. 1958); United States v. Johnson, 285 F.2d 35 (9th Cir.1960); Union Automobile Indemnity Ass'n v. Capitol Indemnity Ins. Co., 310 F.2d 318 (7th Cir.1962). In evaluating these considerations, McCormick says:

"The foregoing considerations favoring the wide-open or restrictive rules may well be thought to be fairly evenly balanced. There is another factor, however, which seems to swing the balance overwhelmingly in favor of the wide-open rule. This is the consideration of economy of time and energy. Obviously, the wide-open rule presents little or no opportunity for dispute in its application. The restrictive practice in all its forms, on the other hand, is productive in many court rooms, of continual bickering over the choice of the numerous variations of the 'scope of the direct' criterion, and of their application to particular cross-questions. These controversies are often reventilated on appeal, and reversals for error in their determination are frequent. Observance of these vague and ambiguous restrictions is a matter of constant and hampering concern to the cross-examiner. If these efforts, delays and misprisions were the necessary incidents to the guarding of substantive rights or the fundamentals of fair trial, they might be worth the cost. As the price of the choice of an obviously debatable regulation of the order of evidence, the sacrifice seems misguided. The American Bar Association's Committee for the Improvement of the Law of Evidence for the year 1937-38 said this:

'The rule limiting cross-examination to the precise subject of the direct examination is probably the most frequent rule (except the Opinion rule) leading in the trial practice today to refined and technical quibbles which obstruct the progress of the trial, confuse the jury, and give rise to appeal on technical grounds only. Some of the instances in which Supreme Courts have ordered new trials for the mere transgression of this rule about the order of evidence have been astounding.

'We recommend that the rule allowing questions upon any part of the issue known to the witness * * * be adopted. * * * ' " McCormick, § 27, p. 51. See also 5 Moore's Federal Practice ¶ 43.10 (2nd ed. 1964).

The provision of the second sentence, that the judge may in the interests of justice limit inquiry into new matters on cross-examination, is designed for those situations in which the result otherwise would be confusion, complication, or protraction of the case, not as a matter of rule but as demonstrable in the actual development of the particular case.

The rule does not purport to determine the extent to which an accused who elects to testify thereby waives his privilege against self-incrimination. The question is a constitutional one, rather than a mere matter of administering the trial. Under Simmons v. United States, 390 U.S. 377, 88 S.Ct. 967, 19 L.Ed.2d 1247 (1968), no general waiver occurs when the accused testifies on such preliminary matters as the validity of a search and seizure or the admissibility of a confession. Rule 104(d), supra. When he testifies on the merits, however, can he foreclose inquiry into an aspect or element of the crime by avoiding it on direct? The affirmative answer given in Tucker v. United States, 5 F.2d 818 (8th Cir.1925), is inconsistent with the description of the waiver as extending to "all other relevant facts" in Johnson v. United States, 318 U.S. 189, 195, 63 S.Ct. 549, 87 L.Ed. 704 (1943). See also Brown v. United States, 356 U.S. 148, 78 S.Ct. 622, 2 L.Ed.2d 589 (1958). The situation of an accused who desires to testify on some but not all counts of a multiple-count indictment is one to be approached, in the first instance at least, as a problem of severance under Rule 14 of the Federal Rules of Criminal Procedure. Cross v. United States, 118 U.S.App.D.C. 324, 335 F.2d 987 (1964). Cf. United States v. Baker, 262 F.Supp. 657, 686 (D.D.C.1966). In all events, the extent of the waiver of the privilege against self-incrimination ought not to be determined as a by-product of a rule on scope of cross-examination.

Note to Subdivision (c). The rule continues the traditional view that the suggestive powers of the leading question are as a general proposition undesirable. Within this tradition, however, numerous exceptions have achieved recognition: The witness who is hostile, unwilling, or biased; the child witness or the adult with communication problems; the witness whose recollection is exhausted; and undisputed preliminary matters. 3 Wigmore §§ 774-778. An almost total unwillingness to reverse for infractions has been manifested by appellate courts. See cases cited in 3 Wigmore § 770. The matter clearly falls within the area of control by the judge over the mode and order of interrogation and presentation and accordingly is phrased in words of suggestion rather than command.

The rule also conforms to tradition in making the use of leading questions on cross-examination a matter of right. The purpose of the qualification "ordinarily" is to furnish a basis for denying the use of leading questions when the cross-examination is cross-examination in form only and not in fact, as for example the "cross-examination" of a party by his own counsel after being called by the opponent (savoring more of re-direct) or of an insured defendant who proves to be friendly to the plaintiff.

The final sentence deals with categories of witnesses automatically regarded and treated as hostile. Rule 43(b) of the Federal Rules of Civil Procedure has included only "an adverse party or an officer, director, or managing agent of a public or private corporation or of a partnership or association which is an adverse party." This limitation virtually to persons whose statements would stand as admissions is believed to be an unduly narrow concept of those who may safely be regarded as hostile without further demonstration. See, for example, Maryland Casualty Co. v. Kador, 225 F.2d 120 (5th Cir.1955), and Degelos v. Fidelity and Casualty Co., 313 F.2d 809 (5th Cir.1963), holding despite the language of Rule 43(b) that an insured fell within it, though not a party in an action under the Louisiana direct action statute. The phrase of the rule, "witness identified with" an adverse party, is designed to enlarge the category of persons thus callable.

1974 Enactment
Note to Subdivision (b). As submitted by the Court, Rule 611(b) provided:
A witness may be cross-examined on any matter relevant to any issue in the case, including credibility. In the interests of justice, the judge may limit cross-examination with respect to matters not testified to on direct examination.

The Committee amended this provision to return to the rule which prevails in the federal courts and thirty-nine State jurisdictions. As amended, the Rule is in the text of the 1969 Advisory Committee draft. It limits cross-examination to credibility and to matters testified to on direct examination, unless the judge permits more, in which event the cross-examiner must proceed as if on direct examination. This traditional rule facilitates orderly presentation by each party at trial. Further, in light of existing discovery procedures, there appears to be no need to abandon the traditional rule.

Note to Subdivision (c). The third sentence of Rule 611(c) as submitted by the Court provided that:

In civil cases, a party is entitled to call an adverse party or witness identified with him and interrogate by leading questions.

The Committee amended this Rule to permit leading questions to be used with respect to any hostile witness, not only an adverse party or person identified with such adverse party. The Committee also substituted the word "When" for the phrase "In civil cases" to reflect the possibility that in criminal cases a defendant may be entitled to call witnesses identified with the government, in which event the Committee believed the defendant should be permitted to inquire with leading questions. House Report No. 93-650.

Note to Subdivision (b). Rule 611(b) as submitted by the Supreme Court permitted a broad scope of cross-examination: "cross-examination on any matter relevant to any issue in the case" unless the judge, in the interests of justice, limited the scope of cross-examination.

The House narrowed the Rule to the more traditional practice of limiting cross-examination to the subject matter of direct examination (and credibility), but with discretion in the judge to permit inquiry into additional matters in situations where that would aid in the development of the evidence or otherwise facilitate the conduct of the trial.

The committee agrees with the House amendment. Although there are good arguments in support of broad cross-examination from perspectives of developing all relevant evidence, we believe the factors of insuring an orderly and predictable development of the evidence weigh in favor of the narrower rule, especially when discretion is given to the trial judge to permit inquiry into additional matters. The committee expressly approves this discretion and believes it will permit sufficient flexibility allowing a broader scope of cross-examination whenever appropriate.

The House amendment providing broader discretionary cross-examination permitted inquiry into additional matters only as if on direct examination. As a general rule, we concur with this limitation, however, we would understand that this limitation would not preclude the utilization of leading questions if the conditions of subsection (c) of this rule were met, bearing in mind the judge's discretion in any case to limit the scope of cross-examination [see McCormick on Evidence, §§ 24-26 (especially 24) (2d ed. 1972)].

Further, the committee has received correspondence from Federal judges commenting on the applicability of this rule to section 1407 of title 28. It is the committee's judgment that this rule as reported by the House is flexible enough to provide sufficiently broad cross-examination in appropriate situations in multidistrict litigation.

Note to Subdivision (c). As submitted by the Supreme Court, the rule provided: "In civil cases, a party is entitled to call an adverse party or witness identified with him and interrogate by leading questions."

The final sentence of subsection (c) was amended by the House for the purpose of clarifying the fact that a "hostile witness"--that is a witness who is hostile in fact--could be subject to interrogation by leading questions. The rule as submitted by the Supreme Court declared certain witnesses hostile as a matter of law and thus subject to interrogation by leading questions without any showing of hostility in fact. These were adverse parties or witnesses identified with adverse parties. However, the wording of the first sentence of subsection (c) while generally prohibiting the use of leading questions on direct examination, also provides "except as may be necessary to develop his testimony." Further, the first paragraph of the Advisory Committee note explaining the subsection makes clear that they intended that leading questions could be asked of a hostile witness or a witness who was unwilling or biased and even though that witness was not associated with an adverse party. Thus, we question whether the House amendment was necessary.

However, concluding that it was not intended to affect the meaning of the first sentence of the subsection and was intended solely to clarify the fact that leading questions are permissible in the interrogation of a witness, who is hostile in fact, the committee accepts that House amendment.

The final sentence of this subsection was also amended by the House to cover criminal as well as civil cases. The committee accepts this amendment, but notes that it may be difficult in criminal cases to determine when a witness is "identified with an adverse party," and thus the rule should be applied with caution. Senate Report No. 93-1277.

1987 Amendments
The amendment is technical. No substantive change is intended.

2011 Amendments
The language of Rule 611 has been amended as part of the restyling of the Evidence Rules to make them more easily understood and to make style and terminology consistent throughout the rules. These changes are intended to be stylistic only. There is no intent to change any result in any ruling on evidence admissibility.

Rule 612. Writing Used to Refresh a Witness's Memory

(a) Scope. This rule gives an adverse party certain options when a witness uses a writing to refresh memory:

(1) while testifying; or

(2) before testifying, if the court decides that justice requires the party to have those options.

(b) Adverse Party's Options; Deleting Unrelated Matter. Unless 18 U.S.C. § 3500 provides otherwise in a criminal case, an adverse party is entitled to have the writing produced at the hearing, to inspect it, to cross-examine the witness about it, and to introduce in evidence any portion that relates to the witness's testimony. If the producing party claims that the writing includes unrelated matter, the court must examine the writing in camera, delete any unrelated portion, and order that the rest be delivered to the adverse party. Any portion deleted over objection must be preserved for the record.

(c) Failure to Produce or Deliver the Writing. If a writing is not produced or is not delivered as ordered, the court may issue any appropriate order. But if the prosecution does not comply in a criminal case, the court must strike the witness's testimony or--if justice so requires--declare a mistrial.

Credits

(Pub.L. 93-595, § 1, Jan. 2, 1975, 88 Stat. 1936; Mar. 2, 1987, eff. Oct. 1, 1987; Apr. 26, 2011, eff. Dec. 1, 2011.)

Editors' Notes
ADVISORY COMMITTEE NOTES
1972 Proposed Rules
The treatment of writings used to refresh recollection while on the stand is in accord with settled doctrine. McCormick § 9, p. 15. The bulk of the case law has, however, denied the existence of any right to access by the opponent when the writing is used prior to taking the stand, though the judge may have discretion in the matter. Goldman v. United States, 316 U.S. 129, 62 S.Ct. 993, 86 L.Ed. 1322 (1942); Needelman v. United States, 261 F.2d 802 (5th Cir.1958), cert. dismissed 362 U.S. 600, 80 S.Ct. 960, 4 L.Ed.2d 980, rehearing denied 363 U.S. 858, 80 S.Ct. 1606, 4 L.Ed.2d 1739, Annot., 82 A.L.R.2d 473, 562 and 7 A.L.R.3d 181, 247. An increasing group of cases has repudiated the distinction. People v. Scott, 29 Ill.2d 97, 193 N.E.2d 814 (1963); State v. Mucci, 25 N.J. 423, 136 A.2d 761 (1957); State v. Hunt, 25 N.J. 514, 138 A.2d 1 (1958); State v. Deslovers, 40 R.I. 89, 100 A. 64 (1917), and this position is believed to be correct. As Wigmore put it, "the risk of imposition and the need of safeguard is just as great" in both situations. 3 Wigmore § 762, p. 111. To the same effect is McCormick, § 9, p. 17.

The purpose of the phrase "for the purpose of testifying" is to safeguard against using the rule as a pretext for wholesale exploration of an opposing party's files and to insure that access is limited only to those writings which may fairly be said in fact to have an impact upon the testimony of the witness.

The purpose of the rule is the same as that of the Jencks statute, 18 U.S.C. § 3500: to promote the search of credibility and memory. The same sensitivity to disclosure of government files may be involved; hence the rule is expressly made subject to the statute, subdivision (a) of which provides: "In any criminal prosecution brought by the United States, no statement or report in the possession of the United States which was made by a Government witness or prospective Government witness (other than the defendant) shall be the subject of subpena, discovery, or inspection until said witness has testified on direct examination in the trial of the case." Items falling within the purview of the statute are producible only as provided by its terms, Palermo v. United States, 360 U.S. 343, 351 (1959), and disclosure under the rule is limited similarly by the statutory conditions. With this limitation in mind, some differences of application may be noted. The Jencks statute applies only to statements of witnesses; the rule is not so limited. The statute applies only to criminal cases; the rule applies to all cases. The statute applies only to government witnesses; the rule applies to all witnesses. The statute contains no requirement that the statement be consulted for purposes of refreshment before or while testifying; the rule so requires. Since many writings would qualify under either statute or rule, a substantial overlap exists, but the identity of procedures makes this of no importance.

The consequences of nonproduction by the government in a criminal case are those of the Jencks statute, striking the testimony or in exceptional cases a mistrial. 18 U.S.C. § 3500(d). In other cases these alternatives are unduly limited, and such possibilities as contempt, dismissal, finding issues against the offender, and the like are available. See Rule 16(g) of the Federal Rules of Criminal Procedure and Rule 37(b) of the Federal Rules of Civil Procedure for appropriate sanctions.

1974 Enactment

As submitted to Congress, Rule 612 provided that except as set forth in 18 U.S.C. 3500, if a witness uses a writing to refresh his memory for the purpose of testifying, "either before or while testifying," an adverse party is entitled to have the writing produced at the hearing, to inspect it, to cross-examine the witness on it, and to introduce in evidence those portions relating to the witness' testimony. The Committee amended the Rule so as still to require the production of writings used by a witness while testifying, but to render the production of writings used by a witness to refresh his memory before testifying discretionary with the court in the interests of justice, as is the case under existing federal law. See Goldman v. United States, 316 U.S. 129 (1942). The Committee considered that permitting an adverse party to require the production of writings used before testifying could result in fishing expeditions among a multitude of papers which a witness may have used in preparing for trial.

The Committee intends that nothing in the Rule be construed as barring the assertion of a privilege with respect to writings used by a witness to refresh his memory. House Report No. 93-650.

1987 Amendments

The amendment is technical. No substantive change is intended.

2011 Amendments

The language of Rule 612 has been amended as part of the restyling of the Evidence Rules to make them more easily understood and to make style and terminology consistent throughout the rules. These changes are intended to be stylistic only. There is no intent to change any result in any ruling on evidence admissibility.

Rule 613. Witness's Prior Statement

(a) Showing or Disclosing the Statement During Examination. When examining a witness about the witness's prior statement, a party need not show it or disclose its contents to the witness. But the party must, on request, show it or disclose its contents to an adverse party's attorney.

(b) Extrinsic Evidence of a Prior Inconsistent Statement. Extrinsic evidence of a witness's prior inconsistent statement is admissible only if the witness is given an opportunity to explain or deny the statement and an adverse party is given an opportunity to examine the witness about it, or if justice so requires. This subdivision (b) does not apply to an opposing party's statement under Rule 801(d)(2).

Credits

(Pub.L. 93-595, § 1, Jan. 2, 1975, 88 Stat.1936; Mar. 2, 1987, eff. Oct. 1, 1987; Apr. 25, 1988, eff. Nov. 1, 1988; Apr. 26, 2011, eff. Dec. 1, 2011.)

Editors' Notes

ADVISORY COMMITTEE NOTES

1972 Proposed Rules

Note to Subdivision (a). The Queen's Case, 2 Br. & B. 284, 129 Eng.Rep. 976 (1820), laid down the requirement that a cross-examiner, prior to questioning the witness about his own prior statement in writing, must first show it to the witness. Abolished by statute in the country of its origin, the requirement nevertheless gained currency in the United States. The rule abolishes this useless impediment, to cross-examination. Ladd, Some Observations on Credibility: Impeachment of Witnesses, 52 Cornell L.Q. 239, 246-247 (1967); McCormick § 28; 4 Wigmore §§ 1259-1260. Both oral and written statements are included.

The provision for disclosure to counsel is designed to protect against unwarranted insinuations that a statement has been made when the fact is to the contrary.

The rule does not defeat the application of Rule 1002 relating to production of the original when the contents of a writing are sought to be proved. Nor does it defeat the application of Rule 26(b)(3) of the Rules of Civil Procedure, as revised, entitling a person on request to a copy of his own statement, though the operation of the latter may be suspended temporarily.

Note to Subdivision (b). The familiar foundation requirement that an impeaching statement first be shown to the witness before it can be proved by extrinsic evidence is preserved but with some modifications. See Ladd, Some Observations on Credibility: Impeachment of Witnesses, 52 Cornell L.Q. 239, 247 (1967). The traditional insistence that the attendance of the witness be directed to the statement on cross-examination is relaxed in favor of simply providing the witness an opportunity to explain and the opposite party an opportunity to examine on the statement, with no specification of any particular time or sequence. Under this procedure, several collusive witnesses can be examined before disclosure of a joint prior inconsistent statement. See Comment to California Evidence Code § 770. Also, dangers of oversight are reduced. See McCormick § 37, p. 68.

In order to allow for such eventualities as the witness becoming unavailable by the time the statement is discovered, a measure of discretion is conferred upon the judge. Similar provisions are found in California Evidence Code § 770 and New Jersey Evidence Rule 22(b).

Under principles of expression unius the rule does not apply to impeachment by evidence of prior inconsistent conduct. The use of inconsistent statements to impeach a hearsay declaration is treated in Rule 806.

1987 Amendments
The amendments are technical. No substantive change is intended.

1988 Amendments
The amendment is technical. No substantive change is intended.

2011 Amendments
The language of Rule 613 has been amended as part of the restyling of the Evidence Rules to make them more easily understood and to make style and terminology consistent throughout the rules. These changes are intended to be stylistic only. There is no intent to change any result in any ruling on evidence admissibility.

Rule 614. Court's Calling or Examining a Witness

(a) Calling. The court may call a witness on its own or at a party's request. Each party is entitled to cross-examine the witness.

(b) Examining. The court may examine a witness regardless of who calls the witness.

(c) Objections. A party may object to the court's calling or examining a witness either at that time or at the next opportunity when the jury is not present.

Credits

(Pub.L. 93-595, § 1, Jan. 2, 1975, 88 Stat.1937; Apr. 26, 2011, eff. Dec. 1, 2011.)

Editors' Notes
ADVISORY COMMITTEE NOTES
1972 Proposed Rules

Note to Subdivision (a). While exercised more frequently in criminal than in civil cases, the authority of the judge to call witnesses is well established. McCormick § 8, p. 14; Maguire, Weinstein, et al., Cases on Evidence 303-304 (5th ed. 1965); 9 Wigmore § 2484. One reason for the practice, the old rule against impeaching one's own witness, no longer exists by virtue of Rule 607, supra. Other reasons remain, however, to justify the continuation of the practice of calling court's witnesses. The right to cross-examine, with all it implies, is assured. The tendency of juries to associate a witness with the party calling him, regardless of technical aspects of vouching, is avoided. And the judge is not imprisoned within the case as made by the parties.

Note to Subdivision (b). The authority of the judge to question witnesses is also well established. McCormick § 8, pp. 12-13; Maguire, Weinstein, et al., Cases on Evidence 737-739 (5th ed. 1965); 3 Wigmore § 784. The authority is, of course, abused when the judge abandons his proper role and assumes that of advocate, but the manner in which interrogation should be conducted and the proper extent of its exercise are not susceptible of formulation in a rule. The omission in no sense precludes courts of review from continuing to reverse for abuse.

Note to Subdivision (c). The provision relating to objections is designed to relieve counsel of the embarrassment attendant upon objecting to questions by the judge in the presence of the jury, while at the same time assuring that objections are made in apt time to afford the opportunity to take possible corrective measures. Compare the "automatic" objection feature of Rule 605 when the judge is called as a witness.

2011 Amendments

The language of Rule 614 has been amended as part of the restyling of the Evidence Rules to make them more easily understood and to make style and terminology consistent throughout the rules. These changes are intended to be stylistic only. There is no intent to change any result in any ruling on evidence admissibility.

Rule 615. Excluding Witnesses

At a party's request, the court must order witnesses excluded so that they cannot hear other witnesses' testimony. Or the court may do so on its own. But this rule does not authorize excluding:

(a) a party who is a natural person;

(b) an officer or employee of a party that is not a natural person, after being designated as the party's representative by its attorney;

(c) a person whose presence a party shows to be essential to presenting the party's claim or defense; or

(d) a person authorized by statute to be present.

Credits

(Pub.L. 93-595, § 1, Jan. 2, 1975, 88 Stat.1937; Mar. 2, 1987, eff. Oct. 1, 1987; Apr. 25, 1988, eff. Nov. 1, 1988; Pub.L. 100-690, Nov. 18, 1988, Title VII, § 7075(a), 102 Stat. 4405; Apr. 24, 1998, eff. Dec. 1, 1998; Apr. 26, 2011, eff. Dec. 1, 2011.)

Editors' Notes

ADVISORY COMMITTEE NOTES

1972 Proposed Rules

The efficacy of excluding or sequestering witnesses has long been recognized as a means of discouraging and exposing fabrication, inaccuracy, and collusion. 6 Wigmore §§ 1837-1838. The authority of the judge is admitted, the only question being whether the matter is committed to his discretion or one of right. The rule takes the latter position. No time is specified for making the request.

Several categories of persons are excepted. (1) Exclusion of persons who are parties would raise serious problems of confrontation and due process. Under accepted practice they are not subject to exclusion. 6 Wigmore § 1841. (2) As the equivalent of the right of a natural-person party to be present, a party which is not a natural person is entitled to have a representative present. Most of the cases have involved allowing a police officer who has been in charge of an investigation to remain in court despite the fact that he will be a witness. United States v. Infanzon, 235 F.2d 318, (2d Cir.1956); Portomene v. United States, 221 F.2d 582 (5th Cir.1955); Powell v. United States, 208 F.2d 618 (6th Cir.1953); Jones v. United States, 252 F.Supp. 781 (W.D.Okl.1966). Designation of the representative by the attorney rather than by the client may at first glance appear to be an inversion of the attorney-client relationship, but it may be assumed that the attorney will follow the wishes of the client, and the solution is simple and workable. See California Evidence Code § 777. (3) The category contemplates such persons as an agent who handled the transaction being litigated or an expert needed to advise counsel in the management of the litigation. See 6 Wigmore § 1841, n. 4.

1974 Enactment
Many district courts permit government counsel to have an investigative agent at counsel table throughout the trial although the agent is or may be a witness. The practice is permitted as an exception to the rule of exclusion and compares with the situation defense counsel finds himself in--he always has the client with him to consult during the trial. The investigative agent's presence may be extremely important to government counsel, especially when the case is complex or involves some specialized subject matter. The agent, too, having lived with the case for a long time, may be able to assist in meeting trial surprises where the best-prepared counsel would otherwise have difficulty. Yet, it would not seem the Government could often meet the burden under rule 615 of showing that the agent's presence is essential. Furthermore, it could be dangerous to use the agent as a witness as early in the case as possible, so that he might then help counsel as a nonwitness, since the agent's testimony could be needed in rebuttal. Using another, nonwitness agent from the same investigative agency would not generally meet government counsel's needs.

This problem is solved if it is clear that investigative agents are within the group specified under the second exception made in the rule, for "an officer or employee of a party which is not a natural person designated as its representative by its attorney." It is our understanding that this was the intention of the House committee. It is certainly this committee's construction of the rule. Senate Report No. 93-1277.

1987 Amendments
The amendment is technical. No substantive change is intended.

1988 Amendments
The amendment is technical. No substantive change is intended.

1998 Amendments
The amendment is in response to: (1) the Victim's Rights and Restitution Act of 1990, 42 U.S.C. § 10606, which guarantees, within certain limits, the right of a crime victim to attend the trial; and (2) the Victim Rights Clarification Act of 1997 (18 U.S.C. § 3510).

2011 Amendments
The language of Rule 615 has been amended as part of the restyling of the Evidence Rules to make them more easily understood and to make style and terminology consistent throughout the rules. These changes are intended to be stylistic only. There is no intent to change any result in any ruling on evidence admissibility.

Article VII: Opinions and Expert Testimony

Rule 701. Opinion Testimony by Lay Witnesses

If a witness is not testifying as an expert, testimony in the form of an opinion is limited to one that is:

(a) rationally based on the witness's perception;

(b) helpful to clearly understanding the witness's testimony or to determining a fact in issue; and

(c) not based on scientific, technical, or other specialized knowledge within the scope of Rule 702.

Credits

(Pub.L. 93-595, § 1, Jan. 2, 1975, 88 Stat.1937; Mar. 2, 1987, eff. Oct. 1, 1987; Apr. 17, 2000, eff. Dec. 1, 2000; Apr. 26, 2011, eff. Dec. 1, 2011.)

Editors' Notes
ADVISORY COMMITTEE NOTES
1972 Proposed Rules
The rule retains the traditional objective of putting the trier of fact in possession of an accurate reproduction of the event.

Limitation (a) is the familiar requirement of first-hand knowledge or observation.

Limitation (b) is phrased in terms of requiring testimony to be helpful in resolving issues. Witnesses often find difficulty in expressing themselves in language which is not that of an opinion or conclusion. While the courts have made concessions in certain recurring situations, necessity as a standard for permitting opinions and conclusions has proved too elusive and too unadaptable to particular situations for purposes of satisfactory judicial administration. McCormick § 11. Moreover, the practical impossibility of determining by rule what is a "fact," demonstrated by a century of litigation of the question of what is a fact for purposes of pleading under the Field Code, extends into evidence also. 7 Wigmore § 1919. The rule assumes that the natural characteristics of the adversary system will generally lead to an acceptable result, since the detailed account carries more conviction than the broad assertion, and a lawyer can be expected to display his witness to the best advantage. If he fails to do so, cross-examination and argument will point up the weakness. See Ladd, Expert Testimony, 5 Vand.L.Rev. 414, 415-417 (1952). If, despite these considerations, attempts are made to introduce meaningless assertions which amount to little more than choosing up sides, exclusion for lack of helpfulness is called for by the rule.

The language of the rule is substantially that of Uniform Rule 56(1). Similar provisions are California Evidence Code § 800; Kansas Code of Civil Procedure § 60-456(a); New Jersey Evidence Rule 56(1).

1987 Amendments
The amendments are technical. No substantive change is intended.

2000 Amendments
Rule 701 has been amended to eliminate the risk that the reliability requirements set forth in Rule 702 will be evaded through the simple expedient of proffering an expert in lay witness clothing. Under the amendment, a witness' testimony must be scrutinized under the rules regulating expert opinion to the extent that the witness is providing testimony based on scientific, technical, or other specialized knowledge within the scope of Rule 702. See generally Asplundh Mfg. Div. v. Benton Harbor Eng'g, 57 F.3d 1190 (3d Cir. 1995). By channeling testimony that is actually expert testimony to Rule 702, the amendment also ensures that a party will not evade the expert witness

disclosure requirements set forth in Fed.R.Civ.P. 26 and Fed.R.Crim.P. 16 by simply calling an expert witness in the guise of a layperson. See Joseph, Emerging Expert Issues Under the 1993 Disclosure Amendments to the Federal Rules of Civil Procedure, 164 F.R.D. 97, 108 (1996) (noting that "there is no good reason to allow what is essentially surprise expert testimony." and that "the Court should be vigilant to preclude manipulative conduct designed to thwart the expert disclosure and discovery process"). See also United States v. Figueroa-Lopez, 125 F.3d 1241, 1246 (9th Cir. 1997) (law enforcement agents testifying that the defendant's conduct was consistent with that of a drug trafficker could not testify as lay witnesses; to permit such testimony under Rule 701 "subverts the requirements of Federal Rule of Criminal Procedure 16(a)(1)(E)").

The amendment does not distinguish between expert and lay witnesses, but rather between expert and lay testimony. Certainly it is possible for the same witness to provide both lay and expert testimony in a single case. See, e.g, United States v. Figueroa-Lopez, 125 F.3d 1241, 1246 (9th Cir. 1997) (law enforcement agents could testify that the defendant was acting suspiciously, without being qualified as experts; however, the rules on experts were applicable where the agents testified on the basis of extensive experience that the defendant was using code words to refer to drug quantities and prices). The amendment makes clear that any part of a witness' testimony that is based upon scientific, technical, or other specialized knowledge within the scope of Rule 702 is governed by the standards of Rule 702 and the corresponding disclosure requirements of the Civil and Criminal Rules.

The amendment is not intended to affect the "prototypical example[s] of the type of evidence contemplated by the adoption of Rule 701 relat[ing] to the appearance of persons or things, identity, the manner of conduct, competency of a person, degrees of light or darkness, sound, size, weight, distance, and an endless number of items that cannot be described factually in words apart from inferences." Asplundh Mfg. Div. v. Benton Harbor Eng' g, 57 F.3d 1190, 1196 (3d Cir. 1995).

For example, most courts have permitted the owner or officer of a business to testify to the value or projected profits of the business, without the necessity of qualifying the witness as an accountant, appraiser, or similar expert. See, e.g., Lightning Lube, Inc. v. Witco Corp. 4 F.3d 1153 (3d Cir. 1993) (no abuse of discretion in permitting the plaintiff's owner to give lay opinion testimony as to damages, as it was based on his knowledge and participation in the day-to-day affairs of the business). Such opinion testimony is admitted not because of experience, training or specialized knowledge within the realm of an expert, but because of the particularized knowledge that the witness has by virtue of his or her position in the business. The amendment does not purport to change this analysis. Similarly, courts have permitted lay witnesses to testify that a substance appeared to be a narcotic, so long as a foundation of familiarity with the substance is established. See, e.g., United States v. Westbrook, 896 F.2d 330 (8th Cir. 1990) (two lay witnesses who were heavy amphetamine users were properly permitted to testify that a substance was amphetamine; but it was error to permit another witness to make such an identification where she had no experience with amphetamines). Such testimony is not based on specialized knowledge within the scope of Rule 702, but rather is based upon a layperson's personal knowledge. If, however, that witness were to describe how a narcotic was manufactured, or to describe the intricate workings of a narcotic distribution network, then the witness would have to qualify as an expert under Rule 702. United States v . Figueroa-Lopez, supra.

The amendment incorporates the distinctions set forth in State v. Brown, 836 S.W.2d 530, 549 (1992), a case involving former Tennessee Rule of Evidence 701, a rule that precluded lay witness testimony based on "special knowledge." In Brown, the court declared that the distinction between lay and expert witness testimony is that lay testimony "results from a process of reasoning familiar in everyday life," while expert testimony "results from a process of reasoning which can be mastered only by specialists in the field." The court in Brown noted that a lay witness with experience could testify that a substance appeared to be blood, but that a witness would have to qualify as an expert before he could testify that bruising around the eyes is indicative of skull trauma. That is the kind of distinction made by the amendment to this Rule.

GAP Report--Proposed Amendment to Rule 701

The Committee made the following changes to the published draft of the proposed amendment to Evidence Rule 701:

1. The words "within the scope of Rule 702" were added at the end of the proposed amendment, to emphasize that the Rule does not require witnesses to qualify as experts unless their testimony is of the type traditionally considered within the purview of Rule 702. The Committee Note was amended to accord with this textual change.

2. The Committee Note was revised to provide further examples of the kind of testimony that could and could not be proffered under the limitation imposed by the proposed amendment.

2011 Amendments

The language of Rule 701 has been amended as part of the general restyling of the Evidence Rules to make them more easily understood and to make style and terminology consistent throughout the rules. These changes are intended to be stylistic only. There is no intent to change any result in any ruling on evidence admissibility.

The Committee deleted all reference to an "inference" on the grounds that the deletion made the Rule flow better and easier to read, and because any "inference" is covered by the broader term "opinion." Courts have not made substantive decisions on the basis of any distinction between an opinion and an inference. No change in current practice is intended.

Rule 702. Testimony by Expert Witnesses

A witness who is qualified as an expert by knowledge, skill, experience, training, or education may testify in the form of an opinion or otherwise if:

(a) the expert's scientific, technical, or other specialized knowledge will help the trier of fact to understand the evidence or to determine a fact in issue;

(b) the testimony is based on sufficient facts or data;

(c) the testimony is the product of reliable principles and methods; and

(d) the expert has reliably applied the principles and methods to the facts of the case.

Credits

(Pub.L. 93-595, § 1, Jan. 2, 1975, 88 Stat. 1937; Apr. 17, 2000, eff. Dec. 1, 2000; Apr. 26, 2011, eff. Dec. 1, 2011.)

Editors' Notes

ADVISORY COMMITTEE NOTES

1972 Proposed Rules

An intelligent evaluation of facts is often difficult or impossible without the application of some scientific, technical, or other specialized knowledge. The most common source of this knowledge is the expert witness, although there are other techniques for supplying it.

Most of the literature assumes that experts testify only in the form of opinions. The assumption is logically unfounded. The rule accordingly recognizes that an expert on the stand may give a dissertation or exposition of scientific or other principles relevant to the case, leaving the trier of fact to apply them to the facts. Since much of the criticism of expert testimony has centered upon the hypothetical question, it seems wise to recognize that opinions are not indispensable and to encourage the use of expert testimony in non-opinion form when counsel believes the trier can itself draw the requisite inference. The use of opinions is not abolished by the rule, however. It will continue to be permissible for the experts to take the further step of suggesting the inference which should be drawn from applying the specialized knowledge to the facts. See Rules 703 to 705.

Whether the situation is a proper one for the use of expert testimony is to be determined on the basis of assisting the trier. "There is no more certain test for determining when experts may be used than the common sense inquiry whether the untrained layman would be qualified to determine intelligently and to the best possible degree the particular issue without enlightenment from those having a specialized understanding of the subject involved in the dispute." Ladd, Expert Testimony, 5 Vand.L.Rev. 414, 418 (1952). When opinions are excluded, it is because they are unhelpful and therefore superfluous and a waste of time. 7 Wigmore § 1918.

The rule is broadly phrased. The fields of knowledge which may be drawn upon are not limited merely to the "scientific" and "technical" but extend to all "specialized" knowledge. Similarly, the expert is viewed, not in a narrow sense, but as a person qualified by "knowledge, skill, experience, training or education." Thus within the scope of the rule are not only experts in the strictest sense of the word, e.g., physicians, physicists, and architects, but also the large group sometimes called "skilled" witnesses, such as bankers or landowners testifying to land values.
2000 Amendments

Rule 702 has been amended in response to Daubert v. Merrell Dow Pharmaceuticals, Inc., 509 U.S. 579 (1993), and to the many cases applying Daubert, including Kumho Tire Co. v. Carmichael, 119 S.Ct. 1167 (1999). In Daubert the Court charged trial judges with the responsibility of acting as gatekeepers to exclude unreliable expert testimony, and the Court in Kumho clarified that this gatekeeper function applies to all expert testimony, not just testimony based in science. See also Kumho, 119 S.Ct. at 1178 (citing the Committee Note to the proposed amendment to Rule 702, which had been released for public comment before the date of the Kumho decision). The amendment affirms the trial court's role as gatekeeper and provides some general standards that the trial court must use to assess the reliability and helpfulness of proffered expert testimony. Consistently with Kumho, the Rule as amended provides that all types of expert testimony present questions of admissibility for the trial court in deciding whether the evidence is reliable and helpful. Consequently, the admissibility of all expert testimony is governed by the principles of Rule 104(a). Under that Rule, the proponent has the burden of establishing that the pertinent admissibility requirements are met by a preponderance of the evidence. See Bourjaily v. United States, 483 U.S. 171 (1987).

Daubert set forth a non-exclusive checklist for trial courts to use in assessing the reliability of scientific expert testimony. The specific factors explicated by the Daubert Court are (1) whether the expert's technique or theory can be or has been tested---that is, whether the expert's theory can be challenged in some objective sense, or whether it is instead simply a subjective, conclusory approach that cannot reasonably be assessed for reliability; (2) whether the technique or theory has been subject to peer review and publication; (3) the known or potential rate of error of the technique or theory when applied; (4) the existence and maintenance of standards and controls; and (5) whether the technique or theory has been generally accepted in the scientific community. The Court in Kumho held that these factors might also be applicable in assessing the reliability of non-scientific expert testimony, depending upon "the particular circumstances of the particular case at issue." 119 S.Ct. at 1175.

No attempt has been made to "codify" these specific factors. Daubert itself emphasized that the factors were neither exclusive nor dispositive. Other cases have recognized that not all of the specific Daubert factors can apply to every type of expert testimony. In addition to Kumho, 119 S.Ct. at 1175, see Tyus v. Urban Search Management, 102 F.3d 256 (7th Cir. 1996) (noting that the factors mentioned by the Court in Daubert do not neatly apply to expert testimony from a sociologist). See also Kannankeril v. Terminix Int'l, Inc., 128 F.3d 802, 809 (3d Cir. 1997) (holding that lack of peer review or publication was not dispositive where the expert's opinion was supported by "widely accepted scientific knowledge"). The standards set forth in the amendment are broad enough to require consideration of any or all of the specific Daubert factors where appropriate.

Courts both before and after Daubert have found other factors relevant in determining whether expert testimony is sufficiently reliable to be considered by the trier of fact. These factors include:
(1) Whether experts are "proposing to testify about matters growing naturally and directly out of research they have conducted independent of the litigation, or whether they have developed their opinions expressly for purposes of testifying." Daubert v. Merrell Dow Pharmaceuticals, Inc., 43 F. 3d 1311, 1317 (9th Cir. 1995).

(2) Whether the expert has unjustifiably extrapolated from an accepted premise to an unfounded conclusion. See General Elec. Co. v. Joiner, 522 U.S. 136, 146 (1997) (noting that in some cases a trial court "may conclude that there is simply too great an analytical gap between the data and the opinion proffered").

(3) Whether the expert has adequately accounted for obvious alternative explanations. See Claar v. Burlington N.R.R., 29 F.3d 499 (9th Cir. 1994) (testimony excluded where the expert failed to consider other obvious causes for the plaintiff's condition). Compare Ambrosini v. Labarraque, 101 F.3d 129 (D.C. Cir. 1996) (the possibility of some uneliminated causes presents a question of weight, so long as the most obvious causes have been considered and reasonably ruled out by the expert).

(4) Whether the expert "is being as careful as he would be in his regular professional work outside his paid litigation consulting." Sheehan v. Daily Racing Form, Inc., 104 F.3d 940, 942 (7th Cir. 1997). See Kumho Tire Co. v. Carmichael, 119 S.Ct. 1167, 1176 (1999) (Daubert requires the trial court to assure itself that the expert "employs in the courtroom the same level of intellectual rigor that characterizes the practice of an expert in the relevant field").

(5) Whether the field of expertise claimed by the expert is known to reach reliable results for the type of opinion the expert would give. See Kumho Tire Co. v. Carmichael, 119 S.Ct.1167, 1175 (1999) (Daubert's general acceptance factor does not "help show that an expert's testimony is reliable where the discipline itself lacks reliability, as for example, do theories grounded in any so-called generally accepted principles of astrology or necromancy."), Moore v. Ashland Chemical, Inc., 151 F.3d 269 (5th Cir. 1998) (en banc) (clinical doctor was properly precluded from testifying to the toxicological cause of the plaintiff's respiratory problem, where the opinion was not sufficiently grounded in scientific methodology); Sterling v. Velsicol Chem. Corp., 855 F.2d 1188 (6th Cir. 1988) (rejecting testimony based on "clinical ecology" as unfounded and unreliable).

All of these factors remain relevant to the determination of the reliability of expert testimony under the Rule as amended. Other factors may also be relevant. See Kumho, 119 S.Ct. 1167, 1176 ("[W]e conclude that the trial judge must have considerable leeway in deciding in a particular case how to go about determining whether particular expert testimony is reliable."). Yet no single factor is necessarily dispositive of the reliability of a particular expert's testimony. See, e.g., Heller v. Shaw Industries, Inc., 167 F.3d 146, 155 (3d Cir. 1999) ("not only must each stage of the expert's testimony be reliable, but each stage must be evaluated practically and flexibly without bright-line exclusionary (or inclusionary) rules."); Daubert v. Merrell Dow Pharmaceuticals, Inc., 43 F.3d 1311, 1317, n.5 (9th Cir. 1995) (noting that some expert disciplines "have the courtroom as a principal theatre of operations" and as to these disciplines "the fact that the expert has developed an expertise principally for purposes of litigation will obviously not be a substantial consideration.").

A review of the caselaw after Daubert shows that the rejection of expert testimony is the exception rather than the rule. Daubert did not work a "seachange over federal evidence law," and "the trial court's role as gatekeeper is not intended to serve as a replacement for the adversary system." United States v. 14.38 Acres of Land Situated in Leflore County, Mississippi, 80 F.3d 1074, 1078 (5th Cir. 1996). As the Court in Daubert stated: "Vigorous cross-examination, presentation of contrary evidence, and careful instruction on the burden of proof are the traditional and appropriate means of attacking shaky but admissible evidence." 509 U.S. at 595. Likewise, this amendment is not intended to provide an excuse for an automatic challenge to the testimony of every expert. See Kumho Tire Co. v . Carmichael, 119 S.Ct.1167, 1176 (1999) (noting that the trial judge has the discretion "both to avoid unnecessary 'reliability' proceedings in ordinary cases where the reliability of an expert's methods is properly taken for granted, and to require appropriate proceedings in the less usual or more complex cases where cause for questioning the expert's reliability arises.").

When a trial court, applying this amendment, rules that an expert's testimony is reliable, this does not necessarily mean that contradictory expert testimony is unreliable. The amendment is broad enough to permit testimony that is the product of competing principles or methods in the same field of expertise. See, e.g., Heller v. Shaw Industries, Inc., 167 F.3d 146, 160 (3d Cir. 1999) (expert testimony cannot be excluded simply because the expert uses one test rather than another, when both tests are accepted in the field and both reach reliable results). As the court stated in In re Paoli R.R. Yard PCB Litigation, 35 F.3d 717, 744 (3d Cir. 1994), proponents "do not have to demonstrate to the judge by a preponderance of the evidence that the assessments of their experts are correct, they only have to demonstrate by a preponderance of evidence that their opinions are reliable.... The evidentiary requirement of reliability is lower than the merits standard of correctness." See also Daubert v. Merrell Dow Pharmaceuticals, Inc., 43 F.3d 1311, 1318 (9th Cir. 1995) (scientific experts might be permitted to testify if they could show that the methods they used were also employed by "a recognized minority of scientists in their field."); Ruiz-Troche v. Pepsi Cola, 161 F. 3d 77, 85 (1st Cir. 1998) ("Daubert neither requires nor empowers trial courts to determine which of several competing scientific theories has the best provenance.").

The Court in Daubert declared that the "focus, of course, must be solely on principles and methodology, not on the conclusions they generate." 509 U.S. at 595. Yet as the Court later recognized, "conclusions and methodology are not entirely distinct from one another." General Elec. Co. v. Joiner, 522 U.S. 136, 146 (1997). Under the amendment, as under Daubert, when an expert purports to apply principles and methods in accordance with professional standards, and yet reaches a conclusion that other experts in the field would not reach, the trial court may fairly suspect that the principles and methods have not been faithfully applied. See Lust v. Merrell Dow Pharmaceuticals, Inc., 89 F.3d 594, 598 (9th Cir. 1996). The amendment specifically provides that the trial court must scrutinize not only the principles and methods used by the expert, but also whether those principles and methods have been properly applied to the facts of the case. As the court noted in In re Paoli R.R. Yard PCB Litig., 35 F.3d 717, 745 (3d Cir. 1994), "any step that renders the analysis unreliable ... renders the expert's testimony inadmissible. This is true whether the step completely changes a reliable methodology or merely misapplies that methodology."

If the expert purports to apply principles and methods to the facts of the case, it is important that this application be conducted reliably. Yet it might also be important in some cases for an expert to educate the factfinder about general principles, without ever attempting to apply these principles to the specific facts of the case. For example, experts might instruct the factfinder on the principles of thermodynamics, or bloodclotting, or on how financial markets respond to corporate reports, without ever knowing about or trying to tie their testimony into the facts of the case. The amendment does not alter the venerable practice of using expert testimony to educate the factfinder on general principles. For this kind of generalized testimony, Rule 702 simply requires that: (1) the expert be qualified; (2) the testimony address a subject matter on which the factfinder can be assisted by an expert; (3) the testimony be reliable; and (4) the testimony "fit" the facts of the case.

As stated earlier, the amendment does not distinguish between scientific and other forms of expert testimony. The trial court's gatekeeping function applies to testimony by any expert. See Kumho Tire Co. v. Carmichael, 119 S.Ct. 1167, 1171 (1999) ("We conclude that Daubert's general holding--setting forth the trial judge's general 'gatekeeping' obligation--applies not only to testimony based on 'scientific' knowledge, but also to testimony based on 'technical' and 'other specialized' knowledge."). While the relevant factors for determining reliability will vary from expertise to expertise, the amendment rejects the premise that an expert's testimony should be treated more permissively simply because it is outside the realm of science. An opinion from an expert who is not a scientist should receive the same degree of scrutiny for reliability as an opinion from an expert who purports to be a scientist. See Watkins v. Telsmith, Inc., 121 F.3d 984, 991 (5th Cir. 1997) ("[I]t seems exactly backwards that experts who purport to rely on general engineering principles and practical experience might escape screening by the district court simply by stating that their conclusions were not reached by any particular method or technique."). Some types of expert testimony will be more objectively verifiable, and subject to the expectations of falsifiability, peer review, and publication, than others. Some types of expert testimony will not rely on anything like a scientific method, and so will have to be evaluated by reference to other standard principles attendant to the particular area of expertise. The trial judge in all cases of proffered expert testimony must find that it is properly grounded, well-reasoned, and not speculative before it can be admitted. The expert's testimony must be grounded in an accepted body of learning or experience in the expert's field, and the expert must explain how the conclusion is so grounded. See, e.g., American College of Trial Lawyers, Standards and Procedures for Determining the Admissibility of Expert Testimony after Daubert, 157 F.R.D. 571, 579 (1994) ("[W] hether the testimony concerns economic principles, accounting standards, property valuation or other non-scientific subjects, it should be evaluated by reference to the 'knowledge and experience' of that particular field.").

The amendment requires that the testimony must be the product of reliable principles and methods that are reliably applied to the facts of the case. While the terms "principles" and "methods" may convey a certain impression when applied to scientific knowledge, they remain relevant when applied to testimony based on technical or other specialized knowledge. For example, when a law enforcement agent testifies regarding the use of code words in a drug transaction, the principle used by the agent is that participants in such transactions regularly use code words to conceal the nature of their activities. The method used by the agent is the application of extensive experience to analyze the meaning of the conversations. So long as the principles and methods are reliable and applied reliably to the facts of the case, this type of testimony should be admitted.

Nothing in this amendment is intended to suggest that experience alone--or experience in conjunction with other knowledge, skill, training or education--may not provide a sufficient foundation for expert testimony. To the contrary, the text of Rule 702 expressly contemplates that an expert may be qualified on the basis of experience. In certain fields, experience is the predominant, if not sole, basis for a great deal of reliable expert testimony. See, e.g., United States v. Jones, 107 F.3d 1147 (6th Cir. 1997) (no abuse of discretion in admitting the testimony of a handwriting examiner who had years of practical experience and extensive training, and who explained his methodology in detail); Tassin v. Sears Roebuck, 946 F.Supp. 1241, 1248 (M.D.La. 1996) (design engineer's testimony can be admissible when the expert's opinions "are based on facts, a reasonable investigation, and traditional technical/mechanical expertise, and he provides a reasonable link between the information and procedures he uses and the conclusions he reaches"). See also Kumho Tire Co. v. Carmichael, 119 S.Ct. 1167, 1178 (1999) (stating that "no one denies that an expert might draw a conclusion from a set of observations based on extensive and specialized experience.").

If the witness is relying solely or primarily on experience, then the witness must explain how that experience leads to the conclusion reached, why that experience is a sufficient basis for the opinion, and how that experience is reliably applied to the facts. The trial court's gatekeeping function requires more than simply "taking the expert's word for it." See Daubert v. Merrell Dow Pharmaceuticals, Inc., 43 F.3d 1311, 1319 (9th Cir. 1995) ("We've been presented with only the experts' qualifications, their conclusions and their assurances of reliability. Under Daubert, that's not enough."). The more subjective and controversial the expert's inquiry, the more likely the testimony should be excluded as unreliable. See O'Conner v. Commonwealth Edison Co., 13 F.3d 1090 (7th Cir. 1994) (expert testimony based on a completely subjective methodology held properly excluded). See also Kumho Tire Co. v. Carmichael, 119 S.Ct . 1167, 1176 (1999) ("[I]t will at times be useful to ask even of a witness whose expertise is based purely on experience, say, a perfume tester able to distinguish among 140 odors at a sniff, whether his preparation is of a kind that others in the field would recognize as acceptable.").

Subpart (1) of Rule 702 calls for a quantitative rather than qualitative analysis. The amendment requires that expert testimony be based on sufficient underlying "facts or data." The term "data" is intended to encompass the reliable opinions of other experts. See the original Advisory Committee Note to Rule 703. The language "facts or data" is broad enough to allow an expert to rely on hypothetical facts that are supported by the evidence. Id.

When facts are in dispute, experts sometimes reach different conclusions based on competing versions of the facts. The emphasis in the amendment on " sufficient facts or data" is not intended to authorize a trial court to exclude an expert's testimony on the ground that the court believes one version of the facts and not the other.

There has been some confusion over the relationship between Rules 702 and 703. The amendment makes clear that the sufficiency of the basis of an expert' s testimony is to be decided under Rule 702. Rule 702 sets forth the overarching requirement of reliability, and an analysis of the sufficiency of the expert's basis cannot be divorced from the ultimate reliability of the expert's opinion. In contrast, the "reasonable reliance" requirement of Rule 703 is a relatively narrow inquiry. When an expert relies on inadmissible information, Rule 703 requires the trial court to determine whether that information is of a type reasonably relied on by other experts in the field. If so, the expert can rely on the information in reaching an opinion. However, the question whether the expert is relying on a sufficient basis of information--whether admissible information or not--is governed by the requirements of Rule 702.

The amendment makes no attempt to set forth procedural requirements for exercising the trial court's gatekeeping function over expert testimony. See Daniel J. Capra, The Daubert Puzzle, 38 Ga.L.Rev. 699, 766 (1998) ("Trial courts should be allowed substantial discretion in dealing with Daubert questions; any attempt to codify procedures will likely give rise to unnecessary changes in practice and create difficult questions for appellate review."). Courts have shown considerable ingenuity and flexibility in considering challenges to expert testimony under Daubert, and it is contemplated that this will continue under the amended Rule. See, e.g., Cortes-Irizarry v. Corporacion Insular, 111 F.3d 184 (1st Cir. 1997) (discussing the application of Daubert in ruling on a motion for summary judgment); In re Paoli R.R. Yard PCB Litig., 35 F.3d 717, 736, 739 (3d Cir. 1994) (discussing the use of in limine hearings); Claar v. Burlington N.R.R., 29 F.3d 499, 502-05 (9th Cir. 1994) (discussing the trial court's technique of ordering experts to submit serial affidavits explaining the reasoning and methods underlying their conclusions).

The amendment continues the practice of the original Rule in referring to a qualified witness as an "expert." This was done to provide continuity and to minimize change. The use of the term "expert" in the Rule does not, however, mean that a jury should actually be informed that a qualified witness is testifying as an "expert." Indeed, there is much to be said for a practice that prohibits the use of the term "expert" by both the parties and the court at trial. Such a practice "ensures that trial courts do not inadvertently put their stamp of authority" on a witness's opinion, and protects against the jury's being "overwhelmed by the so-called 'experts'." Hon. Charles Richey, Proposals to Eliminate the Prejudicial Effect of the Use of the Word "Expert" Under the Federal Rules of Evidence in Criminal and Civil Jury Trials, 154 F.R.D. 537, 559 (1994) (setting forth limiting instructions and a standing order employed to prohibit the use of the term " expert" injury trials).

GAP Report--Proposed Amendment to Rule 702
The Committee made the following changes to the published draft of the proposed amendment to Evidence Rule 702:
1. The word "reliable" was deleted from Subpart (1) of the proposed amendment, in order to avoid an overlap with Evidence Rule 703, and to clarify that an expert opinion need not be excluded simply because it is based on hypothetical facts. The Committee Note was amended to accord with this textual change.

2. The Committee Note was amended throughout to include pertinent references to the Supreme Court's decision in Kumho Tire Co. v. Carmichael, which was rendered after the proposed amendment was released for public comment. Other citations were updated as well.

3. The Committee Note was revised to emphasize that the amendment is not intended to limit the right to jury trial, nor to permit a challenge to the testimony of every expert, nor to preclude the testimony of experience-based experts, nor to prohibit testimony based on competing methodologies within a field of expertise.

4. Language was added to the Committee Note to clarify that no single factor is necessarily dispositive of the reliability inquiry mandated by Evidence Rule 702.

2011 Amendments

The language of Rule 702 has been amended as part of the restyling of the Evidence Rules to make them more easily understood and to make style and terminology consistent throughout the rules. These changes are intended to be stylistic only. There is no intent to change any result in any ruling on evidence admissibility.

Rule 703. Bases of an Expert's Opinion Testimony

An expert may base an opinion on facts or data in the case that the expert has been made aware of or personally observed. If experts in the particular field would reasonably rely on those kinds of facts or data in forming an opinion on the subject, they need not be admissible for the opinion to be admitted. But if the facts or data would otherwise be inadmissible, the proponent of the opinion may disclose them to the jury only if their probative value in helping the jury evaluate the opinion substantially outweighs their prejudicial effect.

Credits

(Pub.L. 93-595, § 1, Jan. 2, 1975, 88 Stat.1937; Mar. 2, 1987, eff. Oct. 1, 1987; Apr. 17, 2000, eff. Dec. 1, 2000; Apr. 26, 2011, eff. Dec. 1, 2011.)

Editors' Notes
ADVISORY COMMITTEE NOTES
1972 Proposed Rules
Facts or data upon which expert opinions are based may, under the rule, be derived from three possible sources. The first is the firsthand observation of the witness with opinions based thereon traditionally allowed. A treating physician affords an example. Rheingold, The Basis of Medical Testimony, 15 Vand.L.Rev. 473, 489 (1962). Whether he must first relate his observations is treated in Rule 705. The second source, presentation at the trial, also reflects existing practice. The technique may be the familiar hypothetical question or having the expert attend the trial and hear the testimony establishing the facts. Problems of determining what testimony the expert relied upon, when the latter technique is employed and the testimony is in conflict, may be resolved by resort to Rule 705. The third source contemplated by the rule consists of presentation of data to the expert outside of court and other than by his own perception. In this respect the rule is designed to broaden the basis for expert opinions beyond that current in many jurisdictions and to bring the judicial practice into line with the practice of the experts themselves when not in court. Thus a physician in his own practice bases his diagnosis on information from numerous sources and of considerable variety, including statements by patients and relatives, reports and opinions from nurses, technicians and other doctors, hospital records, and X rays. Most of them are admissible in evidence, but only with the expenditure of substantial time in producing and examining various authenticating witnesses. The physician makes life-and-death decisions in reliance upon them. His validation, expertly performed and subject to cross-examination, ought to suffice for judicial purposes. Rheingold, supra, at 531; McCormick § 15. A similar provision is California Evidence Code § 801(b).

The rule also offers a more satisfactory basis for ruling upon the admissibility of public opinion poll evidence. Attention is directed to the validity of the techniques employed rather than to relatively fruitless inquiries whether hearsay is involved. See Judge Feinberg's careful analysis in Zippo Mfg. Co. v. Rogers Imports, Inc., 216 F.Supp. 670 (S.D.N.Y.1963). See also Blum et al., The Art of Opinion Research: A Lawyer's Appraisal of an Emerging Service, 24 U.Chi.L.Rev. 1 (1956); Bonynge Trademark Surveys and Techniques and Their Use in Litigation, 48 A.B.A.J. 329 (1962); Zeisel, The Uniqueness of Survey Evidence, 45 Cornell L.Q. 322 (1960); Annot., 76 A.L.R.2d 919.

If it be feared that enlargement of permissible data may tend to break down the rules of exclusion unduly, notice should be taken that the rule requires that the facts or data "be of a type reasonably relied upon by experts in the particular field." The language would not warrant admitting in evidence the opinion of an "accidentologist" as to the point of impact in an automobile collision based on statements of bystanders since this requirement is not satisfied. See Comment, Cal.Law Rev.Comm'n, Recommendation Proposing an Evidence Code 148-150 (1965).

1987 Amendments
The amendment is technical. No substantive change is intended.

2000 Amendments
Rule 703 has been amended to emphasize that when an expert reasonably relies on inadmissible information to form an opinion or inference, the underlying information is not admissible simply because the opinion or inference is admitted. Courts have reached different results on how to treat inadmissible information when it is reasonably relied upon by an expert in forming an opinion or drawing an inference. Compare United States v. Rollins, 862 F.2d 1282 (7th Cir. 1988) (admitting, as part of the basis of an FBI agent's expert opinion on the meaning of code language, the hearsay statements of an informant), with United States v. 0.59 Acres of Land, 109 F.3d 1493 (9th Cir. 1997) (error to admit hearsay offered as the basis of an expert opinion, without a limiting instruction). Commentators have also taken differing views. See e.g., Ronald Carlson, Policing the Bases of Modern Expert Testimony, 39 Vand.L.Rev. 577 (1986) (advocating limits on the jury's consideration of otherwise inadmissible evidence used as the basis for an expert opinion); Paul Rice, Inadmissible Evidence as a Basis for Expert Testimony: A Response to Professor Carlson, 40 Vand.L.Rev. 583 (1987) (advocating unrestricted use of information reasonably relied upon by an expert).

When information is reasonably relied upon by an expert and yet is admissible only for the purpose of assisting the jury in evaluating an expert's opinion, a trial court applying this Rule must consider the information's probative value in assisting the jury to weigh the expert's opinion on the one hand, and the risk of prejudice resulting from the jury's potential misuse of the information for substantive purposes on the other. The information may be disclosed to the jury, upon objection, only if the trial court finds that the probative value of the information in assisting the jury to evaluate the expert's opinion substantially outweighs its prejudicial effect. If the otherwise inadmissible information is admitted under this balancing test, the trial judge must give a limiting instruction upon request, informing the jury that the underlying information must not be used for substantive purposes. See Rule 105. In determining the appropriate course, the trial court should consider the probable effectiveness or lack of effectiveness of a limiting instruction under the particular circumstances.

The amendment governs only the disclosure to the jury of information that is reasonably relied on by an expert, when that information is not admissible for substantive purposes. It is not intended to affect the admissibility of an expert's testimony. Nor does the amendment prevent an expert from relying on information that is inadmissible for substantive purposes.

Nothing in this Rule restricts the presentation of underlying expert facts or data when offered by an adverse party. See Rule 705. Of course, an adversary's attack on an expert's basis will often open the door to a proponent's rebuttal with information that was reasonably relied upon by the expert, even if that information would not have been discloseable initially under the balancing test provided by this amendment. Moreover, in some circumstances the proponent might wish to disclose information that is relied upon by the expert in order to "remove the sting" from the opponent's anticipated attack, and thereby prevent the jury from drawing an unfair negative inference. The trial court should take this consideration into account in applying the balancing test provided by this amendment.

This amendment covers facts or data that cannot be admitted for any purpose other than to assist the jury to evaluate the expert's opinion. The balancing test provided in this amendment is not applicable to facts or data that are admissible for any other purpose but have not yet been offered for such a purpose at the time the expert testifies.

The amendment provides a presumption against disclosure to the jury of information used as the basis of an expert's opinion and not admissible for any substantive purpose, when that information is offered by the proponent of the expert. In a multi-party case, where one party proffers an expert whose testimony is also beneficial to other parties, each such party should be deemed a "proponent" within the meaning of the amendment.

GAP Report--Proposed Amendment to Rule 703
The Committee made the following changes to the published draft of the proposed amendment to Evidence Rule 703:
1. A minor stylistic change was made in the text, in accordance with the suggestion of the Style Subcommittee of the Standing Committee on Rules of Practice and Procedure.

2. The words "in assisting the jury to evaluate the expert's opinion" were added to the text, to specify the proper purpose for offering the otherwise inadmissible information relied on by an expert. The Committee Note was revised to accord with this change in the text.

3. Stylistic changes were made to the Committee Note.

4. The Committee Note was revised to emphasize that the balancing test set forth in the proposal should be used to determine whether an expert's basis may be disclosed to the jury either (1) in rebuttal or (2) on direct examination to "remove the sting" of an opponent's anticipated attack on an expert's basis.

2011 Amendments
The language of Rule 703 has been amended as part of the general restyling of the Evidence Rules to make them more easily understood and to make style and terminology consistent throughout the rules. These changes are intended to be stylistic only. There is no intent to change any result in any ruling on evidence admissibility.

The Committee deleted all reference to an "inference" on the grounds that the deletion made the Rule flow better and easier to read, and because any "inference" is covered by the broader term "opinion." Courts have not made substantive decisions on the basis of any distinction between an opinion and an inference. No change in current practice is intended.

Rule 704. Opinion on an Ultimate Issue

(a) In General--Not Automatically Objectionable. An opinion is not objectionable just because it embraces an ultimate issue.

(b) Exception. In a criminal case, an expert witness must not state an opinion about whether the defendant did or did not have a mental state or condition that constitutes an element of the crime charged or of a defense. Those matters are for the trier of fact alone.

Credits

(Pub.L. 93-595, § 1, Jan. 2, 1975, 88 Stat. 1937; Pub.L. 98-473, Title IV, § 406, Oct. 12, 1984, 98 Stat. 2067; Apr. 26, 2011, eff. Dec. 1, 2011.)

Editors' Notes
ADVISORY COMMITTEE NOTES
1972 Proposed Rules
The basic approach to opinions, lay and expert, in these rules is to admit them when helpful to the trier of fact. In order to render this approach fully effective and to allay any doubt on the subject, the so-called "ultimate issue" rule is specifically abolished by the instant rule.

The older cases often contained strictures against allowing witnesses to express opinions upon ultimate issues, as a particular aspect of the rule against opinions. The rule was unduly restrictive, difficult of application, and generally served only to deprive the trier of fact of useful information. 7 Wigmore §§ 1920, 1921; McCormick § 12. The basis usually assigned for the rule, to prevent the witness from "usurping the province of the jury," is aptly characterized as "empty rhetoric." 7 Wigmore § 1920, p. 17. Efforts to meet the felt needs of particular situations led to odd verbal circumlocutions which were said not to violate the rule. Thus a witness could express his estimate of the criminal responsibility of an accused in terms of sanity or insanity, but not in terms of ability to tell right from wrong or other more modern standard. And in cases of medical causation, witnesses were sometimes required to couch their opinions in cautious phrases of "might or could," rather than "did," though the result was to deprive many opinions of the positiveness to which they were entitled, accompanied by the hazard of a ruling of insufficiency to support a verdict. In other instances the rule was simply disregarded, and, as concessions to need, opinions were allowed upon such matters as intoxication, speed, handwriting, and value, although more precise coincidence with an ultimate issue would scarcely be possible.

Many modern decisions illustrate the trend to abandon the rule completely. People v. Wilson, 25 Cal.2d 341, 153 P.2d 720 (1944), whether abortion necessary to save life of patient; Clifford-Jacobs Forging Co. v. Industrial Comm., 19 Ill.2d 236, 166 N.E.2d 582 (1960), medical causation; Dowling v. L. H. Shattuck, Inc., 91 N.H. 234, 17 A.2d 529 (1941), proper method of shoring ditch; Schweiger v. Solbeck, 191 Or. 454, 230 P.2d 195 (1951), cause of landslide. In each instance the opinion was allowed.

The abolition of the ultimate issue rule does not lower the bars so as to admit all opinions. Under Rules 701 and 702, opinions must be helpful to the trier of fact, and Rule 403 provides for exclusion of evidence which wastes time. These provisions afford ample assurances against the admission of opinions which would merely tell the jury what result to reach, somewhat in the manner of the oath-helpers of an earlier day. They also stand ready to exclude opinions phrased in terms of inadequately explored legal criteria. Thus the question, "Did T have capacity to make a will?" would be excluded, while the question, "Did T have sufficient mental capacity to know the nature and extent of his property and the natural objects of his bounty and to formulate a rational scheme of distribution?" would be allowed. McCormick § 12.

For similar provisions see Uniform Rule 56(4); California Evidence Code § 805; Kansas Code of Civil Procedure § 60-456(d); New Jersey Evidence Rule 56(3).

2011 Amendments

The language of Rule 704 has been amended as part of the general restyling of the Evidence Rules to make them more easily understood and to make style and terminology consistent throughout the rules. These changes are intended to be stylistic only. There is no intent to change any result in any ruling on evidence admissibility.

The Committee deleted all reference to an "inference" on the grounds that the deletion made the Rule flow better and easier to read, and because any "inference" is covered by the broader term "opinion." Courts have not made substantive decisions on the basis of any distinction between an opinion and an inference. No change in current practice is intended.

Rule 705. Disclosing the Facts or Data Underlying an Expert's Opinion

Unless the court orders otherwise, an expert may state an opinion--and give the reasons for it--without first testifying to the underlying facts or data. But the expert may be required to disclose those facts or data on cross- examination.

Credits

(Pub.L. 93-595, § 1, Jan. 2, 1975, 88 Stat. 1938; Mar. 2, 1987, eff. Oct. 1, 1987; Apr. 22, 1993, eff. Dec. 1, 1993; Apr. 26, 2011, eff. Dec. 1, 2011.)

Editors' Notes
ADVISORY COMMITTEE NOTES
1972 Proposed Rules
The hypothetical question has been the target of a great deal of criticism as encouraging partisan bias, affording an opportunity for summing up in the middle of the case, and as complex and time consuming. Ladd, Expert Testimony, 5 Vand.L.Rev. 414, 426-427 (1952). While the rule allows counsel to make disclosure of the underlying facts or data as a preliminary to the giving of an expert opinion, if he chooses, the instances in which he is required to do so are reduced. This is true whether the expert bases his opinion on data furnished him at secondhand or observed by him at firsthand.

The elimination of the requirement of preliminary disclosure at the trial of underlying facts or data has a long background of support. In 1937 the Commissioners on Uniform State Laws incorporated a provision to this effect in their Model Expert Testimony Act, which furnished the basis for Uniform Rules 57 and 58. Rule 4515, N.Y. CPLR (McKinney 1963), provides:

"Unless the court orders otherwise, questions calling for the opinion of an expert witness need not be hypothetical in form, and the witness may state his opinion and reasons without first specifying the data upon which it is based. Upon cross-examination, he may be required to specify the data * * *."

See also California Evidence Code § 802; Kansas Code of Civil Procedure §§ 60-456, 60-457; New Jersey Evidence Rules 57, 58.

If the objection is made that leaving it to the cross-examiner to bring out the supporting data is essentially unfair, the answer is that he is under no compulsion to bring out any facts or data except those unfavorable to the opinion. The answer assumes that the cross-examiner has the advance knowledge which is essential for effective cross-examination. This advance knowledge has been afforded, though imperfectly, by the traditional foundation requirement. Rule 26(b)(4) of the Rules of Civil Procedure, as revised, provides for substantial discovery in this area, obviating in large measure the obstacles which have been raised in some instances to discovery of findings, underlying data, and even the identity of the experts. Friedenthal Discovery and Use of an Adverse Party's Expert Information, 14 Stan.L.Rev. 455 (1962).

These safeguards are reinforced by the discretionary power of the judge to require preliminary disclosure in any event.

1987 Amendment
The amendment is technical. No substantive change is intended.

1993 Amendment
This rule, which relates to the manner of presenting testimony at trial, is revised to avoid an arguable conflict with revised Rules 26(a)(2)(B) and 26(e)(1) of the Federal Rules of Civil Procedure or with revised Rule 16 of the Federal Rules of Criminal Procedure, which require disclosure in advance of trial of the basis and reasons for an expert's opinions.

If a serious question is raised under Rule 702 or 703 as to the admissibility of expert testimony, disclosure of the underlying facts or data on which opinions are based may, of course, be needed by the court before deciding whether, and to what extent, the person should be allowed to testify. This rule does not preclude such an inquiry.

2011 Amendments
The language of Rule 705 has been amended as part of the general restyling of the Evidence Rules to make them more easily understood and to make style and terminology consistent throughout the

rules. These changes are intended to be stylistic only. There is no intent to change any result in any ruling on evidence admissibility.

The Committee deleted all reference to an "inference" on the grounds that the deletion made the Rule flow better and easier to read, and because any "inference" is covered by the broader term "opinion." Courts have not made substantive decisions on the basis of any distinction between an opinion and an inference. No change in current practice is intended.

Rule 706. Court-Appointed Expert Witnesses

(a) Appointment Process. On a party's motion or on its own, the court may order the parties to show cause why expert witnesses should not be appointed and may ask the parties to submit nominations. The court may appoint any expert that the parties agree on and any of its own choosing. But the court may only appoint someone who consents to act.

(b) Expert's Role. The court must inform the expert of the expert's duties. The court may do so in writing and have a copy filed with the clerk or may do so orally at a conference in which the parties have an opportunity to participate. The expert:

(1) must advise the parties of any findings the expert makes;

(2) may be deposed by any party;

(3) may be called to testify by the court or any party; and

(4) may be cross-examined by any party, including the party that called the expert.

(c) Compensation. The expert is entitled to a reasonable compensation, as set by the court. The compensation is payable as follows:

(1) in a criminal case or in a civil case involving just compensation under the Fifth Amendment, from any funds that are provided by law; and

(2) in any other civil case, by the parties in the proportion and at the time that the court directs--and the compensation is then charged like other costs.

(d) Disclosing the Appointment to the Jury. The court may authorize disclosure to the jury that the court appointed the expert.

(e) Parties' Choice of Their Own Experts. This rule does not limit a party in calling its own experts.

Credits

(Pub.L. 93-595, § 1, Jan. 2, 1975, 88 Stat.1938; Mar. 2, 1987, eff. Oct. 1, 1987; Apr. 26, 2011, eff. Dec. 1, 2011.)

Editors' Notes
ADVISORY COMMITTEE NOTES
1972 Proposed Rules
The practice of shopping for experts, the venality of some experts, and the reluctance of many reputable experts to involve themselves in litigation, have been matters of deep concern. Though the contention is made that court appointed experts acquire an aura of infallibility to which they are not entitled, Levy, Impartial Medical Testimony--Revisited, 34 Temple L.Q. 416 (1961), the trend is

increasingly to provide for their use. While experience indicates that actual appointment is a relatively infrequent occurrence, the assumption may be made that the availability of the procedure in itself decreases the need for resorting to it. The ever-present possibility that the judge may appoint an expert in a given case must inevitably exert a sobering effect on the expert witness of a party and upon the person utilizing his services.

The inherent power of a trial judge to appoint an expert of his own choosing is virtually unquestioned. Scott v. Spanjer Bros., Inc., 298 F.2d 928 (2d Cir.1962); Danville Tobacco Assn. v. Bryant-Buckner Associates, Inc., 333 F.2d 202 (4th Cir.1964); Sink, The Unused Power of a Federal Judge to Call His Own Expert Witnesses, 29 S.Cal.L.Rev. 195 (1956); 2 Wigmore § 563, 9 id. § 2484; Annot., 95 A.L.R.2d 383. Hence the problem becomes largely one of detail.

The New York plan is well known and is described in Report by Special Committee of the Association of the Bar of the City of New York: Impartial Medical Testimony (1956). On recommendation of the Section of Judicial Administration, local adoption of an impartial medical plan was endorsed by the American Bar Association. 82 A.B.A.Rep. 184-185 (1957). Descriptions and analyses of plans in effect in various parts of the country are found in Van Dusen, A United States District Judge's View of the Impartial Medical Expert System, 32 F.R.D. 498 (1963); Wick and Kightlinger, Impartial Medical Testimony Under the Federal Civil Rules: A Tale of Three Doctors, 34 Ins. Counsel J. 115 (1967); and numerous articles collected in Klein, Judicial Administration and the Legal Profession 393 (1963). Statutes and rules include California Evidence Code §§ 730-733; Illinois Supreme Court Rule 215(d), Ill.Rev.Stat.1969, c. 110A, § 215(d); Burns Indiana Stats.1956, § 9-1702; Wisconsin Stats.Annot.1958, § 957.27.

In the federal practice, a comprehensive scheme for court appointed experts was initiated with the adoption of Rule 28 of the Federal Rules of Criminal Procedure in 1946. The Judicial Conference of the United States in 1953 considered court appointed experts in civil cases, but only with respect to whether they should be compensated from public funds, a proposal which was rejected. Report of the Judicial Conference of the United States 23 (1953). The present rule expands the practice to include civil cases.

Note to Subdivision (a). Subdivision (a) is based on Rule 28 of the Federal Rules of Criminal Procedure, with a few changes, mainly in the interest of clarity. Language has been added to provide specifically for the appointment either on motion of a party or on the judge's own motion. A provision subjecting the court appointed expert to deposition procedures has been incorporated. The rule has been revised to make definite the right of any party, including the party calling him, to cross-examine.

Note to Subdivision (b). Subdivision (b) combines the present provision for compensation in criminal cases with what seems to be a fair and feasible handling of civil cases, originally found in the Model Act and carried from there into Uniform Rule 60. See also California Evidence Code §§ 730-731. The special provision for Fifth Amendment compensation cases is designed to guard against reducing constitutionally guaranteed just compensation by requiring the recipient to pay costs. See Rule 71A(l) of the Rules of Civil Procedure.

Note to Subdivision (c). Subdivision (c) seems to be essential if the use of court appointed experts is to be fully effective. Uniform Rule 61 so provides.

Note to Subdivision (d). Subdivision (d) is in essence the last sentence of Rule 28(a) of the Federal Rules of Criminal Procedure.

1987 Amendment
The amendments are technical. No substantive change is intended.

2011 Amendments
The language of Rule 706 has been amended as part of the restyling of the Evidence Rules to make them more easily understood and to make style and terminology consistent throughout the rules.

These changes are intended to be stylistic only. There is no intent to change any result in any ruling on evidence admissibility.

Article VIII: Hearsay

Rule 801. Definitions
That Apply to This Article; Exclusions from Hearsay

(a) Statement. "Statement" means a person's oral assertion, written assertion, or nonverbal conduct, if the person intended it as an assertion.

(b) Declarant. "Declarant" means the person who made the statement.

(c) Hearsay. "Hearsay" means a statement that:

(1) the declarant does not make while testifying at the current trial or hearing; and

(2) a party offers in evidence to prove the truth of the matter asserted in the statement.

(d) Statements That Are Not Hearsay. A statement that meets the following conditions is not hearsay:

(1) A Declarant-Witness's Prior Statement. The declarant testifies and is subject to cross-examination about a prior statement, and the statement:

(A) is inconsistent with the declarant's testimony and was given under penalty of perjury at a trial, hearing, or other proceeding or in a deposition;

(B) is consistent with the declarant's testimony and is offered to rebut an express or implied charge that the declarant recently fabricated it or acted from a recent improper influence or motive in so testifying; or

(C) identifies a person as someone the declarant perceived earlier.

(2) An Opposing Party's Statement. The statement is offered against an opposing party and:

(A) was made by the party in an individual or representative capacity;

(B) is one the party manifested that it adopted or believed to be true;

(C) was made by a person whom the party authorized to make a statement on the subject;

(D) was made by the party's agent or employee on a matter within the scope of that relationship and while it existed; or

(E) was made by the party's coconspirator during and in furtherance of the conspiracy.

The statement must be considered but does not by itself establish the declarant's authority under (C); the existence or scope of the relationship under (D); or the existence of the conspiracy or participation in it under (E).

Credits

(Pub.L. 93-595, § 1, Jan. 2, 1975, 88 Stat.1938; Pub.L. 94-113, § 1, Oct. 16, 1975, 89 Stat. 576; Mar. 2, 1987, eff. Oct. 1, 1987; Apr. 11, 1997, eff. Dec. 1, 1997; Apr. 26, 2011, eff. Dec. 1, 2011.)

Editors' Notes
ADVISORY COMMITTEE NOTES
1972 Proposed Rules
Note to Subdivision (a). The definition of "statement" assumes importance because the term is used in the definition of hearsay in subdivision (c). The effect of the definition of "statement" is to exclude from the operation of the hearsay rule all evidence of conduct, verbal or nonverbal, not intended as an assertion. The key to the definition is that nothing is an assertion unless intended to be one.

It can scarcely be doubted that an assertion made in words is intended by the declarant to be an assertion. Hence verbal assertions readily fall into the category of "statement." Whether nonverbal conduct should be regarded as a statement for purposes of defining hearsay requires further consideration. Some nonverbal conduct, such as the act of pointing to identify a suspect in a lineup, is clearly the equivalent of words, assertive in nature, and to be regarded as a statement. Other nonverbal conduct, however, may be offered as evidence that the person acted as he did because of his belief in the existence of the condition sought to be proved, from which belief the existence of the condition may be inferred. This sequence is, arguably, in effect an assertion of the existence of the condition and hence properly includable within the hearsay concept. See Morgan, Hearsay Dangers and the Application of the Hearsay Concept, 62 Harv.L.Rev. 177, 214, 217 (1948), and the elaboration in Finman, Implied Assertions as Hearsay: Some Criticisms of the Uniform Rules of Evidence, 14 Stan.L.Rev. 682 (1962). Admittedly evidence of this character is untested with respect to the perception, memory, and narration (or their equivalents) of the actor, but the Advisory Committee is of the view that these dangers are minimal in the absence of an intent to assert and do not justify the loss of the evidence on hearsay grounds. No class of evidence is free of the possibility of fabrication, but the likelihood is less with nonverbal than with assertive verbal conduct. The situations giving rise to the nonverbal conduct are such as virtually to eliminate questions of sincerity. Motivation, the nature of the conduct, and the presence or absence of reliance will bear heavily upon the weight to be given the evidence. Falknor, The "Hear-Say" Rule as a "See-Do" Rule: Evidence of Conduct, 33 Rocky Mt.L.Rev. 133 (1961). Similar considerations govern nonassertive verbal conduct and verbal conduct which is assertive but offered as a basis for inferring something other than the matter asserted, also excluded from the definition of hearsay by the language of subdivision (c).

When evidence of conduct is offered on the theory that it is not a statement, and hence not hearsay, a preliminary determination will be required to determine whether an assertion is intended. The rule is so worded as to place the burden upon the party claiming that the intention existed; ambiguous and doubtful cases will be resolved against him and in favor of admissibility. The determination involves no greater difficulty than many other preliminary questions of fact. Maguire, The Hearsay System: Around and Through the Thicket, 14 Vand.L.Rev. 741, 765-767 (1961).

For similar approaches, see Uniform Rule 62(1); California Evidence Code §§ 225, 1200; Kansas Code of Civil Procedure § 60-459(a); New Jersey Evidence Rule 62(1).

Note to Subdivision (c). The definition follows along familiar lines in including only statements offered to prove the truth of the matter asserted. McCormick § 225; 5 Wigmore § 1361, 6 id. § 1766. If the significance of an offered statement lies solely in the fact that it was made, no issue is raised as to the truth of anything asserted, and the statement is not hearsay. Emich Motors Corp. v. General Motors Corp., 181 F.2d 70 (7th Cir.1950), rev'd on other grounds 340 U.S. 558, 71 S.Ct. 408, 95 L.Ed. 534, letters of complaint from customers offered as a reason for cancellation of dealer's franchise, to rebut contention that franchise was revoked for refusal to finance sales through affiliated finance company. The effect is to exclude from hearsay the entire category of "verbal acts" and "verbal parts of an act," in which the statement itself affects the legal rights of the parties or is a circumstance bearing on conduct affecting their rights.

The definition of hearsay must, of course, be read with reference to the definition of statement set forth in subdivision (a).

Testimony given by a witness in the course of court proceedings is excluded since there is compliance with all the ideal conditions for testifying.

Note to Subdivision (d). Several types of statements which would otherwise literally fall within the definition are expressly excluded from it:

(1) Prior statement by witness. Considerable controversy has attended the question whether a prior out-of-court statement by a person now available for cross-examination concerning it, under oath and in the presence of the trier of fact, should be classed as hearsay. If the witness admits on the stand that he made the statement and that it was true, he adopts the statement and there is no hearsay problem. The hearsay problem arises when the witness on the stand denies having made the statement or admits having made it but denies its truth. The argument in favor of treating these latter statements as hearsay is based upon the ground that the conditions of oath, cross-examination, and demeanor observation did not prevail at the time the statement was made and cannot adequately be supplied by the later examination. The logic of the situation is troublesome. So far as concerns the oath, its mere presence has never been regarded as sufficient to remove a statement from the hearsay category, and it receives much less emphasis than cross-examination as a truth-compelling device. While strong expressions are found to the effect that no conviction can be had or important right taken away on the basis of statements not made under fear of prosecution for perjury, Bridges v. Wixon, 326 U.S. 135, 65 S.Ct. 1443, 89 L.Ed. 2103 (1945), the fact is that, of the many common law exceptions to the hearsay rule, only that for reported testimony has required the statement to have been made under oath. Nor is it satisfactorily explained why cross-examination cannot be conducted subsequently with success. The decisions contending most vigorously for its inadequacy in fact demonstrate quite thorough exploration of the weaknesses and doubts attending the earlier statement. State v. Saporen, 205 Minn. 358, 285 N.W. 898 (1939); Ruhala v. Roby, 379 Mich. 102, 150 N.W.2d 146 (1967); People v. Johnson, 68 Cal.2d 646, 68 Cal.Rptr. 599, 441 P.2d 111 (1968). In respect to demeanor, as Judge Learned Hand observed in Di Carlo v. United States, 6 F.2d 364 (2d Cir.1925), when the jury decides that the truth is not what the witness says now, but what he said before, they are still deciding from what they see and hear in court. The bulk of the case law nevertheless has been against allowing prior statements of witnesses to be used generally as substantive evidence. Most of the writers and Uniform Rule 63(1) have taken the opposite position.

The position taken by the Advisory Committee in formulating this part of the rule is funded upon an unwillingness to countenance the general use of prior prepared statements as substantive evidence, but with a recognition that particular circumstances call for a contrary result. The judgment is one more of experience than of logic. The rule requires in each instance, as a general safeguard, that the declarant actually testify as a witness, and it then enumerates three situations in which the statement is excepted from the category of hearsay. Compare Uniform Rule 63(1) which allows any out-of-court statement of a declarant who is present at the trial and available for cross-examination.

(A) Prior inconsistent statements traditionally have been admissible to impeach but not as substantive evidence. Under the rule they are substantive evidence. As has been said by the California Law Revision Commission with respect to a similar provision:

"Section 1235 admits inconsistent statements of witnesses because the dangers against which the hearsay rule is designed to protect are largely nonexistent. The declarant is in court and may be examined and cross-examined in regard to his statements and their subject matter. In many cases, the inconsistent statement is more likely to be true than the testimony of the witness at the trial because it was made nearer in time to the matter to which it relates and is less likely to be influenced by the controversy that gave rise to the litigation. The trier of fact has the declarant before it and can observe his demeanor and the nature of his testimony as he denies or tries to explain away the inconsistency. Hence, it is in as good a position to determine the truth or falsity of the prior statement as it is to determine the truth or falsity of the inconsistent testimony given in court. Moreover, Section 1235 will provide a party with desirable protection against the 'turncoat' witness who changes his story on the stand and deprives the party calling him of evidence essential to his case." Comment, California Evidence Code § 1235. See also McCormick § 39. The Advisory Committee finds these views more convincing than those expressed in People v. Johnson, 68 Cal.2d 646, 68 Cal.Rptr. 599, 441 P.2d 111 (1968). The constitutionality of the Advisory Committee's view was upheld in California v. Green, 399 U.S. 149, 90 S.Ct. 1930, 26 L.Ed.2d 489 (1970). Moreover, the requirement that the statement be inconsistent with the testimony given assures a thorough exploration of both versions while the witness is on the stand and bars any general and indiscriminate use of previously prepared statements.

(B) Prior consistent statements traditionally have been admissible to rebut charges of recent fabrication or improper influence or motive but not as substantive evidence. Under the rule they are substantive evidence. The prior statement is consistent with the testimony given on the stand, and, if the opposite party wishes to open the door for its admission in evidence, no sound reason is apparent why it should not be received generally.

(C) The admission of evidence of identification finds substantial support, although it falls beyond a doubt in the category of prior out-of-court statements. Illustrative are People v. Gould, 54 Cal.2d 621, 7 Cal.Rptr. 273, 354 P.2d 865 (1960); Judy v. State, 218 Md. 168, 146 A.2d 29 (1958); State v. Simmons, 63 Wash.2d 17, 385 P.2d 389 (1963); California Evidence Code § 1238; New Jersey Evidence Rule 63(1)(c); N.Y.Code of Criminal Procedure § 393-b. Further cases are found in 4 Wigmore § 1130. The basis is the generally unsatisfactory and inconclusive nature of courtroom identifications as compared with those made at an earlier time under less suggestive conditions. The Supreme Court considered the admissibility of evidence of prior identification in Gilbert v. California, 388 U.S. 263, 87 S.Ct. 1951, 18 L.Ed.2d 1178 (1967). Exclusion of lineup identification was held to be required because the accused did not then have the assistance of counsel. Significantly, the Court carefully refrained from placing its decision on the ground that testimony as to the making of a prior out-of-court identification ("That's the man") violated either the hearsay rule or the right of confrontation because not made under oath, subject to immediate cross-examination, in the presence of the trier. Instead the Court observed:

"There is a split among the States concerning the admissibility of prior extra-judicial identifications, as independent evidence of identity, both by the witness and third parties present at the prior identification. See 71 ALR2d 449. It has been held that the prior identification is hearsay, and, when admitted through the testimony of the identifier, is merely a prior consistent statement. The recent trend, however, is to admit the prior identification under the exception that admits as substantive evidence a prior communication by a witness who is available for cross-examination at the trial. See 5 ALR2d Later Case Service 1225-1228. * * * " 388 U.S. at 272, n. 3, 87 S.Ct. at 1956.

(2) Admissions. Admissions by a party-opponent are excluded from the category of hearsay on the theory that their admissibility in evidence is the result of the adversary system rather than satisfaction of the conditions of the hearsay rule. Strahorn, A Reconsideration of the Hearsay Rule and Admissions, 85 U.Pa.L.Rev. 484, 564 (1937); Morgan, Basic Problems of Evidence 265 (1962); 4 Wigmore § 1048. No guarantee of trustworthiness is required in the case of an admission. The freedom which admissions have enjoyed from technical demands of searching for an assurance of truthworthiness in some against-interest circumstance, and from the restrictive influences of the opinion rule and the rule requiring firsthand knowledge, when taken with the apparently prevalent satisfaction with the results, calls for generous treatment of this avenue to admissibility.

The rule specifies five categories of statements for which the responsibility of a party is considered sufficient to justify reception in evidence against him:

(A) A party's own statement is the classic example of an admission. If he has a representative capacity and the statement is offered against him in that capacity, no inquiry whether he was acting in the representative capacity in making the statement is required; the statement need only be relevant to represent affairs. To the same effect in California Evidence Code § 1220. Compare Uniform Rule 63(7), requiring a statement to be made in a representative capacity to be admissible against a party in a representative capacity.

(B) Under established principles an admission may be made by adopting or acquiescing in the statement of another. While knowledge of contents would ordinarily be essential, this is not inevitably so: "X is a reliable person and knows what he is talking about." See McCormick § 246, p. 527, n. 15. Adoption or acquiescence may be manifested in any appropriate manner. When silence is relied upon, the theory is that the person would, under the circumstances, protest the statement made in his presence, if untrue. The decision in each case calls for an evaluation in terms of probable human behavior. In civil cases, the results have generally been satisfactory. In criminal cases, however, troublesome questions have been raised by decisions holding that failure to deny is an admission: the inference is a fairly weak one, to begin with; silence may be motivated by advice of counsel or realization that "anything you say may be used against you"; unusual opportunity is afforded to manufacture evidence; and encroachment upon the privilege against self-incrimination seems inescapably to be involved. However, recent decisions of the Supreme Court relating to custodial interrogation and the right to counsel appear to resolve these difficulties. Hence the rule contains no special provisions concerning failure to deny in criminal cases.

(C) No authority is required for the general proposition that a statement authorized by a party to be made should have the status of an admission by the party. However, the question arises whether only statements to third persons should be so regarded, to the exclusion of statements by the agent to the principal. The rule is phrased broadly so as to encompass both. While it may be argued that the agent authorized to make statements to his principal does not speak for him, Morgan, Basic Problems of Evidence 273 (1962), communication to an outsider has not generally been thought to be an essential characteristic of an admission. Thus a party's books or records are usable against him, without regard to any intent to disclose to third persons. 5 Wigmore § 1557. See also McCormick § 78, pp. 159-161. In accord is New Jersey Evidence Rule 63(8)(a). Cf. Uniform Rule 63(8)(a) and California Evidence Code § 1222 which limit status as an admission in this regard to statements authorized by the party to be made "for" him, which is perhaps an ambiguous limitation to statements to third persons. Falknor, Vicarious Admissions and the Uniform Rules, 14 Vand.L.Rev. 855, 860-861 (1961).

(D) The tradition has been to test the admissibility of statements by agents, as admissions, by applying the usual test of agency. Was the admission made by the agent acting in the scope of his employment? Since few principals employ agents for the purpose of making damaging statements, the usual result was exclusion of the statement. Dissatisfaction with this loss of valuable and helpful evidence has been increasing. A substantial trend favors admitting statements related to a matter within the scope of the agency or employment. Grayson v. Williams, 256 F.2d 61 (10th Cir. 1958); Koninklijke Luchtvaart Maatschappij N.V. KLM Royal Dutch Airlines v. Tuller, 110 U.S.App.D.C. 282, 292 F.2d 775, 784 (1961); Martin v. Savage Truck Lines, Inc., 121 F.Supp. 417 (D.D.C.1954), and numerous state court decisions collected in 4 Wigmore, 1964 Supp. pp. 66-73, with comments by the editor that the statements should have been excluded as not within scope of agency. For the traditional view see Northern Oil Co. v. Socony Mobil Oil Co., 347 F.2d 81, 85 (2d Cir.1965) and cases cited therein. Similar provisions are found in Uniform Rule 63(9)(a), Kansas Code of Civil Procedure § 60-460(i)(1), and New Jersey Evidence Rule 63(9)(a).

(E) The limitation upon the admissibility of statements of co-conspirators to those made "during the course and in furtherance of the conspiracy" is in the accepted pattern. While the broadened view of agency taken in item (iv) might suggest wider admissibility of statements of co-conspirators, the agency theory of conspiracy is at best a fiction and ought not to serve as a basis for admissibility beyond that already established. See Levie, Hearsay and Conspiracy, 52 Mich.L.Rev. 1159 (1954); Comment, 25 U.Chi.L.Rev. 530 (1958). The rule is consistent with the position of the Supreme Court in denying admissibility to statements made after the objectives of the conspiracy have either failed or been achieved. Krulewitch v. United States, 336 U.S. 440, 69 S.Ct. 716, 93 L.Ed. 790 (1949); Wong Sun v. United States, 371 U.S. 471, 490, 83 S.Ct. 407, 9 L.Ed.2d 441 (1963). For similarly limited provisions see California Evidence Code § 1223 and New Jersey Rule 63(9)(b). Cf. Uniform Rule 63(9)(b).

1974 Enactment

Note to Subdivision (d)(1). Present federal law, except in the Second Circuit, permits the use of prior inconsistent statements of a witness for impeachment only. Rule 801(d)(1) as proposed by the Court would have permitted all such statements to be admissible as substantive evidence, an approach followed by a small but growing number of State jurisdictions and recently held constitutional in California v. Green, 399 U.S. 149 (1970). Although there was some support expressed for the Court Rule, based largely on the need to counteract the effect of witness intimidation in criminal cases, the Committee decided to adopt a compromise version of the Rule similar to the position of the Second Circuit. The Rule as amended draws a distinction between types of prior inconsistent statements (other than statements of identification of a person made after perceiving him which are currently admissible, see United States v. Anderson, 406 F.2d 719, 720 (4th Cir.), cert. denied, 395 U.S. 967 (1969)) and allows only those made while the declarant was subject to cross-examination at a trial or hearing or in a deposition, to be admissible for their truth. Compare United States v. DeSisto, 329 F.2d 929 (2nd Cir.), cert. denied, 377 U.S. 979 (1964); United States v. Cunningham, 446 F.2d 194 (2nd Cir.1971) (restricting the admissibility of prior inconsistent statements as substantive evidence to those made under oath in a formal proceeding, but not requiring that there have been an opportunity for cross-examination). The rationale for the Committee's decision is that (1) unlike in most other situations involving unsworn or oral statements, there can be no dispute as to whether the prior statement was made; and (2) the context of a formal proceeding, an oath, and the opportunity for cross-examination provide firm additional assurances of the reliability of the prior statement. House Report No. 93-650.

Note to Subdivision (d)(1)(A). Rule 801 defines what is and what is not hearsay for the purpose of admitting a prior statement as substantive evidence. A prior statement of a witness at a trial or hearing which is inconsistent with his testimony is, of course, always admissible for the purpose of impeaching the witness' credibility.

As submitted by the Supreme Court, subdivision (d)(1)(A) made admissible as substantive evidence the prior statement of a witness inconsistent with his present testimony.

The House severely limited the admissibility of prior inconsistent statements by adding a requirement that the prior statement must have been subject to cross-examination, thus precluding even the use of grand jury statements. The requirement that the prior statement must have been subject to cross-examination appears unnecessary since this rule comes into play only when the witness testifies in the present trial. At that time, he is on the stand and can explain an earlier position and be cross-examined as to both.

The requirement that the statement be under oath also appears unnecessary. Notwithstanding the absence of an oath contemporaneous with the statement, the witness, when on the stand, qualifying or denying the prior statement, is under oath. In any event, of all the many recognized exceptions to the hearsay rule, only one (former testimony) requires that the out-of-court statement have been made under oath. With respect to the lack of evidence of the demeanor of the witness at the time of the prior statement, it would be difficult to improve upon Judge Learned Hand's observation that when the jury decides that the truth is not what the witness says now but what he said before, they are still deciding from what they see and hear in court. [Di Carlo v. U.S., 6 F.2d 364 (2d Cir. 1925)].

The rule as submitted by the Court has positive advantages. The prior statement was made nearer in time to the events, when memory was fresher and intervening influences had not been brought into play. A realistic method is provided for dealing with the turncoat witness who changes his story on the stand [see Comment, California Evidence Code § 1235; McCormick, Evidence, § 38 (2nd ed. 1972)].

New Jersey, California, and Utah have adopted a rule similar to this one; and Nevada, New Mexico, and Wisconsin have adopted the identical Federal rule.

For all of these reasons, we think the House amendment should be rejected and the rule as submitted by the Supreme Court reinstated. [It would appear that some of the opposition to this Rule is based on a concern that a person could be convicted solely upon evidence admissible under this Rule. The Rule, however, is not addressed to the question of the sufficiency of evidence to send a case to the jury, but merely as to its admissibility. Factual circumstances could well arise where, if this were the sole evidence, dismissal would be appropriate.]

Note to Subdivision (d)(1)(C). As submitted by the Supreme Court and as passed by the House, subdivision (d)(1)(C) of rule 801 made admissible the prior statement identifying a person made after perceiving him. The committee decided to delete this provision because of the concern that a person could be convicted solely upon evidence admissible under this subdivision.

Note to Subdivision 801(d)(2)(E). The House approved the long-accepted rule that "a statement by a coconspirator of a party during the course and in furtherance of the conspiracy" is not hearsay as it was submitted by the Supreme Court. While the rule refers to a coconspirator, it is this committee's understanding that the rule is meant to carry forward the universally accepted doctrine that a joint venturer is considered as a coconspirator for the purposes of this rule even though no conspiracy has been charged. United States v. Rinaldi, 393 F.2d 97, 99 (2d Cir.), cert. denied 393 U.S. 913 (1968); United States v. Spencer, 415 F.2d 1301, 1304 (7th Cir., 1969). Senate Report No. 93-1277.

Rule 801 supplies some basic definitions for the rules of evidence that deal with hearsay. Rule 801(d)(1) defines certain statements as not hearsay. The Senate amendments make two changes in it.

Note to Subdivision (d)(1)(A). The House bill provides that a statement is not hearsay if the declarant testifies and is subject to cross-examination concerning the statement and if the statement is inconsistent with his testimony and was given under oath subject to cross-examination and subject to the penalty of perjury at a trial or hearing or in a deposition. The Senate amendment drops the requirement that the prior statement be given under oath subject to cross-examination and subject to the penalty of perjury at a trial or hearing or in a deposition.

The Conference adopts the Senate amendment with an amendment, so that the rule now requires that the prior inconsistent statement be given under oath subject to the penalty of perjury at a trial, hearing, or other proceeding, or in a deposition. The rule as adopted covers statements before a grand jury. Prior inconsistent statements may, of course, be used for impeaching the credibility of a witness. When the prior inconsistent statement is one made by a defendant in a criminal case, it is covered by Rule 801(d)(2).

Note to Subdivision (d)(1)(C). The House bill provides that a statement is not hearsay if the declarant testifies and is subject to cross-examination concerning the statement and the statement is one of identification of a person made after perceiving him. The Senate amendment eliminated this provision.

The Conference adopts the Senate amendment. House Report No. 93-1597.

1987 Amendment
The amendments are technical. No substantive change is intended.

1997 Amendment
Rule 801(d)(2) has been amended in order to respond to three issues raised by Bourjaily v. United States, 483 U.S. 171 (1987). First, the amendment codifies the holding in Bourjaily by stating expressly that a court shall consider the contents of a coconspirator's statement in determining "the existence of the conspiracy and the participation therein of the declarant and the party against whom the statement is offered." According to Bourjaily, Rule 104(a) requires these preliminary questions to be established by a preponderance of the evidence.

Second, the amendment resolves an issue on which the Court had reserved decision. It provides that the contents of the declarant's statement do not alone suffice to establish a conspiracy in which the declarant and the defendant participated. The court must consider in addition the circumstances surrounding the statement, such as the identity of the speaker, the context in which the statement was made, or evidence corroborating the contents of the statement in making its determination as to each preliminary question. This amendment is in accordance with existing practice. Every court of appeals that has resolved this issue requires some evidence in addition to the contents of the statement. See, e.g., United States v. Beckham, 968 F.2d 47, 51 (D.C.Cir.1992); United States v. Sepulveda, 15 F.3d 1161, 1181-82 (1st Cir.1993), cert. denied, 114 S.Ct. 2714 (1994); United States v. Daly, 842 F.2d 1380, 1386 (2d Cir.), cert. denied, 488 U.S. 821 (1988); United States v. Clark, 18 F.3d 1337, 1341-42 (6th Cir.), cert. denied, 115 S.Ct. 152 (1994); United States v. Zambrana, 841 F. 2d 1320, 1344-45 (7th Cir.1988); United States v. Silverman, 861 F.2d 571, 577 (9th Cir.1988); United States v. Gordon, 844 F.2d 1397, 1402 (9th Cir.1988); United States v. Hernandez, 829 F.2d 988, 993 (10th Cir.1987), cert. denied, 485 U.S. 1013 (1988); United States v. Byrom, 910 F.2d 725, 736 (11th Cir.1990).

Third, the amendment extends the reasoning of Bourjaily to statements offered under subdivisions (C) and (D) of Rule 801(d)(2). In Bourjaily, the Court rejected treating foundational facts pursuant to the law of agency in favor of an evidentiary approach governed by Rule 104(a). The Advisory Committee believes it appropriate to treat analogously preliminary questions relating to the declarant's authority under subdivision (C), and the agency or employment relationship and scope thereof under subdivision (D).

GAP Report on Rule 801. The word "shall" was substituted for the word "may" in line 19. The second sentence of the committee note was changed accordingly.

2011 Amendments
The language of Rule 801 has been amended as part of the general restyling of the Evidence Rules to make them more easily understood and to make style and terminology consistent throughout the rules. These changes are intended to be stylistic only. There is no intent to change any result in any ruling on evidence admissibility.

Statements falling under the hearsay exclusion provided by Rule 801(d)(2) are no longer referred to as "admissions" in the title to the subdivision. The term "admissions" is confusing because not all statements covered by the exclusion are admissions in the colloquial sense--a statement can be within the exclusion even if it "admitted" nothing and was not against the party's interest when made. The term "admissions" also raises confusion in comparison with the Rule 804(b)(3) exception for declarations against interest. No change in application of the exclusion is intended.

Rule 802. The Rule Against Hearsay
Hearsay is not admissible unless any of the following provides otherwise:

• a federal statute;

• these rules; or

• other rules prescribed by the Supreme Court.

Credits

(Pub.L. 93-595, § 1, Jan. 2, 1975, 88 Stat. 1939; Apr. 26, 2011, eff. Dec. 1, 2011.)

Editors' Notes
ADVISORY COMMITTEE NOTES
1972 Proposed Rules
The provision excepting from the operation of the rule hearsay which is made admissible by other rules adopted by the Supreme Court or by Act of Congress continues the admissibility thereunder

of hearsay which would not qualify under these Evidence Rules. The following examples illustrate the working of the exception:

Federal Rules of Civil Procedure

Rule 4(g): proof of service by affidavit.

Rule 32: admissibility of depositions.

Rule 43(e): affidavits when motion based on facts not appearing of record.

Rule 56: affidavits in summary judgment proceedings.

Rule 65(b): showing by affidavit for temporary restraining order.
Federal Rules of Criminal Procedure

Rule 4(a): affidavits to show grounds for issuing warrants.

Rule 12(b)(4): affidavits to determine issues of fact in connection with motions.
Acts of Congress

10 U.S.C. § 7730: affidavits of unavailable witnesses in actions for damages caused by vessel in naval service, or towage or salvage of same, when taking of testimony or bringing of action delayed or stayed on security grounds.

29 U.S.C. § 161(4): affidavit as proof of service in NLRB proceedings.

38 U.S.C. § 5206: affidavit as proof of posting notice of sale of unclaimed property by Veterans Administration.

2011 Amendments
The language of Rule 802 has been amended as part of the restyling of the Evidence Rules to make them more easily understood and to make style and terminology consistent throughout the rules. These changes are intended to be stylistic only. There is no intent to change any result in any ruling on evidence admissibility.

Rule 803. Exceptions to the Rule Against Hearsay
--Regardless of Whether the Declarant Is Available as a Witness
The following are not excluded by the rule against hearsay, regardless of whether the declarant is available as a witness:

(1) Present Sense Impression. A statement describing or explaining an event or condition, made while or immediately after the declarant perceived it.

(2) Excited Utterance. A statement relating to a startling event or condition, made while the declarant was under the stress of excitement that it caused.

(3) Then-Existing Mental, Emotional, or Physical Condition. A statement of the declarant's then-existing state of mind (such as motive, intent, or plan) or emotional, sensory, or physical condition (such as mental feeling, pain, or bodily health), but not including a statement of memory or belief to prove the fact remembered or believed unless it relates to the validity or terms of the declarant's will.

(4) Statement Made for Medical Diagnosis or Treatment. A statement that:

(A) is made for--and is reasonably pertinent to--medical diagnosis or treatment; and

(B) describes medical history; past or present symptoms or sensations; their inception; or their general cause.

(5) Recorded Recollection. A record that:

(A) is on a matter the witness once knew about but now cannot recall well enough to testify fully and accurately;

(B) was made or adopted by the witness when the matter was fresh in the witness's memory; and

(C) accurately reflects the witness's knowledge.

If admitted, the record may be read into evidence but may be received as an exhibit only if offered by an adverse party.

(6) Records of a Regularly Conducted Activity. A record of an act, event, condition, opinion, or diagnosis if:

(A) the record was made at or near the time by--or from information transmitted by--someone with knowledge;

(B) the record was kept in the course of a regularly conducted activity of a business, organization, occupation, or calling, whether or not for profit;

(C) making the record was a regular practice of that activity;

(D) all these conditions are shown by the testimony of the custodian or another qualified witness, or by a certification that complies with Rule 902(11) or (12) or with a statute permitting certification; and

(E) neither the source of information nor the method or circumstances of preparation indicate a lack of trustworthiness.

(7) Absence of a Record of a Regularly Conducted Activity. Evidence that a matter is not included in a record described in paragraph (6) if:

(A) the evidence is admitted to prove that the matter did not occur or exist;

(B) a record was regularly kept for a matter of that kind; and

(C) neither the possible source of the information nor other circumstances indicate a lack of trustworthiness.

(8) Public Records. A record or statement of a public office if:

(A) it sets out:

(i) the office's activities;

(ii) a matter observed while under a legal duty to report, but not including, in a criminal case, a matter observed by law-enforcement personnel; or

(iii) in a civil case or against the government in a criminal case, factual findings from a legally authorized investigation; and

(B) neither the source of information nor other circumstances indicate a lack of trustworthiness.

(9) Public Records of Vital Statistics. A record of a birth, death, or marriage, if reported to a public office in accordance with a legal duty.

(10) Absence of a Public Record. Testimony--or a certification under Rule 902-- that a diligent search failed to disclose a public record or statement if the testimony or certification is admitted to prove that:

(A) the record or statement does not exist; or

(B) a matter did not occur or exist, if a public office regularly kept a record or statement for a matter of that kind.

(11) Records of Religious Organizations Concerning Personal or Family History. A statement of birth, legitimacy, ancestry, marriage, divorce, death, relationship by blood or marriage, or similar facts of personal or family history, contained in a regularly kept record of a religious organization.

(12) Certificates of Marriage, Baptism, and Similar Ceremonies. A statement of fact contained in a certificate:

(A) made by a person who is authorized by a religious organization or by law to perform the act certified;

(B) attesting that the person performed a marriage or similar ceremony or administered a sacrament; and

(C) purporting to have been issued at the time of the act or within a reasonable time after it.

(13) Family Records. A statement of fact about personal or family history contained in a family record, such as a Bible, genealogy, chart, engraving on a ring, inscription on a portrait, or engraving on an urn or burial marker.

(14) Records of Documents That Affect an Interest in Property. The record of a document that purports to establish or affect an interest in property if:

(A) the record is admitted to prove the content of the original recorded document, along with its signing and its delivery by each person who purports to have signed it;

(B) the record is kept in a public office; and

(C) a statute authorizes recording documents of that kind in that office.

(15) Statements in Documents That Affect an Interest in Property. A statement contained in a document that purports to establish or affect an interest in property if the matter stated was relevant to the document's purpose--unless later dealings with the property are inconsistent with the truth of the statement or the purport of the document.

(16) Statements in Ancient Documents. A statement in a document that is at least 20 years old and whose authenticity is established.

(17) Market Reports and Similar Commercial Publications. Market quotations, lists, directories, or other compilations that are generally relied on by the public or by persons in particular occupations.

(18) Statements in Learned Treatises, Periodicals, or Pamphlets. A statement contained in a treatise, periodical, or pamphlet if:

(A) the statement is called to the attention of an expert witness on cross-examination or relied on by the expert on direct examination; and

(B) the publication is established as a reliable authority by the expert's admission or testimony, by another expert's testimony, or by judicial notice.

If admitted, the statement may be read into evidence but not received as an exhibit.

(19) Reputation Concerning Personal or Family History. A reputation among a person's family by blood, adoption, or marriage--or among a person's associates or in the community--concerning the person's birth, adoption, legitimacy, ancestry, marriage, divorce, death, relationship by blood, adoption, or marriage, or similar facts of personal or family history.

(20) Reputation Concerning Boundaries or General History. A reputation in a community--arising before the controversy--concerning boundaries of land in the community or customs that affect the land, or concerning general historical events important to that community, state, or nation.

(21) Reputation Concerning Character. A reputation among a person's associates or in the community concerning the person's character.

(22) Judgment of a Previous Conviction. Evidence of a final judgment of conviction if:

(A) the judgment was entered after a trial or guilty plea, but not a nolo contendere plea;

(B) the conviction was for a crime punishable by death or by imprisonment for more than a year;

(C) the evidence is admitted to prove any fact essential to the judgment; and

(D) when offered by the prosecutor in a criminal case for a purpose other than impeachment, the judgment was against the defendant.

The pendency of an appeal may be shown but does not affect admissibility.

(23) Judgments Involving Personal, Family, or General History, or a Boundary. A judgment that is admitted to prove a matter of personal, family, or general history, or boundaries, if the matter:

(A) was essential to the judgment; and

(B) could be proved by evidence of reputation.

(24) [Other Exceptions.] [Transferred to Rule 807.]

Credits

(Pub.L. 93-595, § 1, Jan. 2, 1975, 88 Stat. 1939; Pub.L. 94-149, § 1(11), Dec. 12, 1975, 89 Stat. 805; Mar. 2, 1987, eff. Oct. 1, 1987; Apr. 11, 1997, eff. Dec. 1, 1997; Apr. 17, 2000, eff. Dec. 1, 2000; Apr. 26, 2011, eff. Dec. 1, 2011.)

Editors' Notes
ADVISORY COMMITTEE NOTES
1972 Proposed Rules
The exceptions are phrased in terms of nonapplication of the hearsay rule, rather than in positive terms of admissibility, in order to repel any implication that other possible grounds for exclusion are eliminated from consideration.

The present rule proceeds upon the theory that under appropriate circumstances a hearsay statement may possess circumstantial guarantees of trustworthiness sufficient to justify nonproduction of the declarant in person at the trial even though he may be available. The theory finds vast support in the many exceptions to the hearsay rule developed by the common law in which unavailability of the declarant is not a relevant factor. The present rule is a synthesis of them, with revision where modern developments and conditions are believed to make that course appropriate.

In a hearsay situation, the declarant is, of course, a witness, and neither this rule nor Rule 804 dispenses with the requirement of firsthand knowledge. It may appear from his statement or be inferable from circumstances. See Rule 602.

Note to Paragraphs (1) and (2). In considerable measure these two examples overlap, though based on somewhat different theories. The most significant practical difference will lie in the time lapse allowable between event and statement.

The underlying theory of Exception [paragraph] (1) is that substantial contemporaneity of event and statement negate the likelihood of deliberate or conscious misrepresentation. Moreover, if the witness is the declarant, he may be examined on the statement. If the witness is not the declarant, he may be examined as to the circumstances as an aid in evaluating the statement. Morgan, Basic Problems of Evidence 340-341 (1962).

The theory of Exception [paragraph] (2) is simply that circumstances may produce a condition of excitement which temporarily stills the capacity of reflection and produces utterances free of conscious fabrication. 6 Wigmore § 1747, p. 135. Spontaneity is the key factor in each instance, though arrived at by somewhat different routes. Both are needed in order to avoid needless niggling.

While the theory of Exception [paragraph] (2) has been criticized on the ground that excitement impairs accuracy of observation as well as eliminating conscious fabrication, Hutchins and Slesinger, Some Observations on the Law of Evidence: Spontaneous Exclamations, 28 Colum.L.Rev. 432 (1928), it finds support in cases without number. See cases in 6 Wigmore § 1750; Annot. 53 A.L.R.2d 1245 (statements as to cause of or responsibility for motor vehicle accident); Annot., 4 A.L.R.3d 149 (accusatory statements by homicide victims). Since unexciting events are less likely to evoke comment, decisions involving Exception [paragraph] (1) are far less numerous. Illustrative are Tampa Elec. Co. v. Getrost, 151 Fla. 558, 10 So.2d 83 (1942); Houston Oxygen Co. v. Davis, 139 Tex. 1, 161 S.W.2d 474 (1942); and cases cited in McCormick § 273, p. 585, n. 4.

With respect to the time element, Exception [paragraph] (1) recognizes that in many, if not most, instances precise contemporaneity is not possible and hence a slight lapse is allowable. Under Exception [paragraph] (2) the standard of measurement is the duration of the state of excitement. "How long can excitement prevail? Obviously there are no pat answers and the character of the transaction or event will largely determine the significance of the time factor." Slough, Spontaneous Statements and State of Mind, 46 Iowa L.Rev. 224, 243 (1961); McCormick § 272, p. 580.

Participation by the declarant is not required: a non-participant may be moved to describe what he perceives, and one may be startled by an event in which he is not an actor. Slough, supra; McCormick, supra; 6 Wigmore § 1755; Annot. 78 A.L.R.2d 300.

Whether proof of the startling event may be made by the statement itself is largely an academic question, since in most cases there is present at least circumstantial evidence that something of a startling nature must have occurred. For cases in which the evidence consists of the condition of the declarant (injuries, state of shock), see Insurance Co. v. Mosely, 75 U.S. (8 Wall.) 397, 19 L.Ed. 437 (1869); Wheeler v. United States, 93 U.S. App.D.C. 159, 211 F.2d 19 (1953), cert. denied 347 U.S. 1019, 74 S.Ct. 876, 98 L.Ed. 1140; Wetherbee v. Safety Casualty Co., 219 F.2d 274 (5th Cir. 1955); Lampe v. United States, 97 U.S.App.D.C. 160, 229 F.2d 43 (1956). Nevertheless, on occasion the only evidence may be the content of the statement itself, and rulings that it may be sufficient are described as "increasing," Slough, supra at 246, and as the "prevailing practice," McCormick § 272, p. 579. Illustrative are Armour & Co. v. Industrial Commission, 78 Colo. 569, 243 P. 546 (1926); Young v. Stewart, 191 N.C. 297, 131 S.E. 735 (1926). Moreover, under Rule 104(a) the judge is not limited by the hearsay rule in passing upon preliminary questions of fact.

Proof of declarant's perception by his statement presents similar considerations when declarant is identified. People v. Poland, 22 Ill.2d 175, 174 N.E.2d 804 (1961). However, when declarant is an unidentified bystander, the cases indicate hesitancy in upholding the statement alone as sufficient, Garrett v. Howden, 73 N.M. 307, 387 P.2d 874 (1963); Beck v. Dye, 200 Wash. 1, 92 P.2d 1113 (1939), a result which would under appropriate circumstances be consistent with the rule.

Permissible subject matter of the statement is limited under Exception [paragraph] (1) to description or explanation of the event or condition, the assumption being that spontaneity, in the absence of a startling event, may extend no farther. In Exception [paragraph] (2), however, the statement need only "relate" to the startling event or condition, thus affording a broader scope of subject matter coverage. 6 Wigmore §§ 1750, 1754. See Sanitary Grocery Co. v. Snead, 67 App.D.C. 129, 90 F.2d 374 (1937), slip-and-fall case sustaining admissibility of clerk's statement. "That has been on the floor for a couple of hours," and Murphy Auto Parts Co., Inc. v. Ball, 101 U.S.App.D.C. 416, 249 F.2d 508 (1957), upholding admission, on issue of driver's agency, of his statement that he had to call on a customer and was in a hurry to get home. Quick, Hearsay, Excitement, Necessity and the Uniform Rules: A Reappraisal of Rule 63(4), 6 Wayne L.Rev. 204, 206-209 (1960).

Similar provisions are found in Uniform Rule 63(4)(a) and (b); California Evidence Code § 1240 (as to Exception (2) only); Kansas Code of Civil Procedure § 60-460(d)(1) and (2); New Jersey Evidence Rule 63(4).

Note to Paragraph (3). Exception [paragraph] (3) is essentially a specialized application of Exception [paragraph] (1), presented separately to enhance its usefulness and accessibility. See McCormick §§ 265, 268.

The exclusion of "statements of memory or belief to prove the fact remembered or believed" is necessary to avoid the virtual destruction of the hearsay rule which would otherwise result from allowing state of mind, provable by a hearsay statement, to serve as the basis for an inference of the happening of the event which produced the state of mind. Shepard v. United States, 290 U.S. 96, 54 S.Ct. 22, 78 L.Ed. 196 (1933); Maguire, The Hillmon Case--Thirty-three Years After, 38 Harv.L.Rev. 709, 719-731 (1925); Hinton, States of Mind and the Hearsay Rule, 1 U.Chi.L.Rev. 394, 421-423 (1934). The rule of Mutual Life Ins. Co. v. Hillmon, 145 U.S. 285, 12 S.Ct. 909, 36 L.Ed. 706 (1892), allowing evidence of intention as tending to prove the doing of the act intended, is, of course, left undisturbed.

The carving out, from the exclusion mentioned in the preceding paragraph, of declarations relating to the execution, revocation, identification, or terms of declarant's will represents and ad hoc judgment which finds ample reinforcement in the decisions, resting on practical grounds of necessity and expediency rather than logic. McCormick § 271, pp. 577-578; Annot. 34 A.L.R.2d

588, 62 A.L.R.2d 855. A similar recognition of the need for and practical value of this kind of evidence is found in California Evidence Code § 1260.

Note to Paragraph (4). Even those few jurisdictions which have shied away from generally admitting statements of present condition have allowed them if made to a physician for purposes of diagnosis and treatment in view of the patient's strong motivation to be truthful. McCormick § 266, p. 563. The same guarantee of trustworthiness extends to statements of past conditions and medical history, made for purposes of diagnosis or treatment. It also extends to statements as to causation, reasonably pertinent to the same purposes, in accord with the current trend. Shell Oil Co. v. Industrial Commission, 2 Ill.2d 590, 119 N.E.2d 224 (1954); McCormick § 266, p. 564; New Jersey Evidence Rule 63(12)(c). Statements as to fault would not ordinarily qualify under this latter language. Thus a patient's statement that he was struck by an automobile would qualify but not his statement that the car was driven through a red light. Under the exception the statement need not have been made to a physician. Statements to hospital attendants, ambulance drivers, or even members of the family might be included.

Conventional doctrine has excluded from the hearsay exception, as not within its guarantee of truthfulness, statements to a physician consulted only for the purpose of enabling him to testify. While these statements were not admissible as substantive evidence, the expert was allowed to state the basis of his opinion, including statements of this kind. The distinction thus called for was one most unlikely to be made by juries. The rule accordingly rejects the limitation. This position is consistent with the provision of Rule 703 that the facts on which expert testimony is based need not be admissible in evidence if of a kind ordinarily relied upon by experts in the field.

Note to Paragraph (5). A hearsay exception for recorded recollection is generally recognized and has been described as having "long been favored by the federal and practically all the state courts that have had occasion to decide the question." United States v. Kelly, 349 F.2d 720, 770 (2d Cir. 1965), citing numerous cases and sustaining the exception against a claimed denial of the right of confrontation. Many additional cases are cited in Annot., 82 A.L.R.2d 473, 520. The guarantee of trustworthiness is found in the reliability inherent in a record made while events were still fresh in mind and accurately reflecting them. Owens v. State, 67 Md. 307, 316, 10 A. 210, 212 (1887).

The principal controversy attending the exception has centered, not upon the propriety of the exception itself, but upon the question whether a preliminary requirement of impaired memory on the part of the witness should be imposed. The authorities are divided. If regard be had only to the accuracy of the evidence, admittedly impairment of the memory of the witness adds nothing to it and should not be required. McCormick § 277, p. 593; 3 Wigmore § 738, p. 76; Jordan v. People, 151 Colo. 133, 376 P.2d 699 (1962), cert. denied 373 U.S. 944, 83 S.Ct. 1553, 10 L.Ed.2d 699; Hall v. State, 223 Md. 158, 162 A.2d 751 (1960); State v. Bindhammer, 44 N.J. 372, 209 A.2d 124 (1965). Nevertheless, the absence of the requirement, it is believed, would encourage the use of statements carefully prepared for purposes of litigation under the supervision of attorneys, investigators, or claim adjusters. Hence the example includes a requirement that the witness not have "sufficient recollection to enable him to testify fully and accurately." To the same effect are California Evidence Code § 1237 and New Jersey Rule 63(1)(b), and this has been the position of the federal courts. Vicksburg & Meridian R.R. v. O'Brien, 119 U.S. 99, 7 S.Ct. 118, 30 L.Ed. 299 (1886); Ahern v. Webb, 268 F.2d 45 (10th Cir.1959); and see N.L.R.B. v. Hudson Pulp and Paper Corp., 273 F.2d 660, 665 (5th Cir.1960); N.L.R.B. v. Federal Dairy Co., 297 F.2d 487 (1st Cir. 1962). But cf. United States v. Adams, 385 F.2d 548 (2d Cir.1967).

No attempt is made in the exception to spell out the method of establishing the initial knowledge or the contemporaneity and accuracy of the record, leaving them to be dealt with as the circumstances of the particular case might indicate. Multiple person involvement in the process of observing and recording, as in Rathbun v. Brancatella, 93 N.J.L. 222, 107 A. 279 (1919), is entirely consistent with the exception.

Locating the exception at this place in the scheme of the rules is a matter of choice. There were two other possibilities. The first was to regard the statement as one of the group of prior statements of a testifying witness which are excluded entirely from the category of hearsay by Rule 801(d)(1). That category, however, requires that declarant be "subject to cross-examination," as to which the impaired memory aspect of the exception raises doubts. The other possibility was to include the exception among those covered by Rule 804. Since unavailability is required by that rule and lack of memory is listed as a species of unavailability by the definition of the term in Rule 804(a)(3), that treatment at first impression would seem appropriate. The fact is, however, that the unavailability requirement of the exception is of a limited and peculiar nature. Accordingly, the exception is located at this point rather than in the context of a rule where unavailability is conceived of more broadly.

Note to Paragraph (6). Exception [paragraph] (6) represents an area which has received much attention from those seeking to improve the law of evidence. The Commonwealth Fund Act was the result of a study completed in 1927 by a distinguished committee under the chairmanship of Professor Morgan. Morgan et al., The Law of Evidence: Some Proposals for its Reform 63 (1927). With changes too minor to mention, it was adopted by Congress in 1936 as the rule for federal courts. 28 U.S.C. § 1732. A number of states took similar action. The Commissioners on Uniform State Laws in 1936 promulgated the Uniform Business Records as Evidence Act, 9A U.L.A. 506, which has acquired a substantial following in the states. Model Code Rule 514 and Uniform Rule 63(13) also deal with the subject. Difference of varying degrees of importance exist among these various treatments.

These reform efforts were largely within the context of business and commercial records, as the kind usually encountered, and concentrated considerable attention upon relaxing the requirement of producing as witnesses, or accounting for the nonproduction of, all participants in the process of gathering, transmitting, and recording information which the common law had evolved as a burdensome and crippling aspect of using records of this type. In their areas of primary emphasis on witnesses to be called and the general admissibility of ordinary business and commercial records, the Commonwealth Fund Act and the Uniform Act appear to have worked well. The exception seeks to preserve their advantages.

On the subject of what witnesses must be called, the Commonwealth Fund Act eliminated the common law requirement of calling or accounting for all participants by failing to mention it. United States v. Mortimer, 118 F.2d 266 (2d Cir.1941); La Porte v. United States, 300 F.2d 878 (9th Cir.1962); McCormick § 290, p. 608. Model Code Rule 514 and Uniform Rule 63(13) did likewise. The Uniform Act, however, abolished the common law requirement in express terms, providing that the requisite foundation testimony might be furnished by "the custodian or other qualified witness." Uniform Business Records as Evidence Act, § 2; 9A U.L.A. 506. The exception follows the Uniform Act in this respect.

The element of unusual reliability of business records is said variously to be supplied by systematic checking, by regularity and continuity which produce habits of precision, by actual experience of business in relying upon them, or by a duty to make an accurate record as part of a continuing job or occupation. McCormick §§ 281, 286, 287; Laughlin, Business Entries and the Like, 46 Iowa L.Rev. 276 (1961). The model statutes and rules have sought to capture these factors and to extend their impact by employing the phrase "regular course of business," in conjunction with a definition of "business" far broader than its ordinarily accepted meaning. The result is a tendency unduly to emphasize a requirement of routineness and repetitiveness and an insistence that other types of records be squeezed into the fact patterns which give rise to traditional business records. The rule therefore adopts the phrase "the course of a regularly conducted activity" as capturing the essential basis of the hearsay exception as it has evolved and the essential element which can be abstracted from the various specifications of what is a "business."

Amplification of the kinds of activities producing admissible records has given rise to problems which conventional business records by their nature avoid. They are problems of the source of the recorded information, of entries in opinion form, of motivation, and of involvement as participant in the matters recorded.

Sources of information presented no substantial problem with ordinary business records. All participants, including the observer or participant furnishing the information to be recorded, were acting routinely, under a duty of accuracy, with employer reliance on the result, or in short "in the regular course of business." If, however, the supplier of the information does not act in the regular course, an essential link is broken; the assurance of accuracy does not extend to the information itself, and the fact that it may be recorded with scrupulous accuracy is of no avail. An illustration is the police report incorporating information obtained from a bystander: the officer qualifies as acting in the regular course but the informant does not. The leading case, Johnson v. Lutz, 253 N.Y. 124, 170 N.E. 517 (1930), held that a report thus prepared was inadmissible. Most of the authorities have agreed with the decision. Gencarella v. Fyfe, 171 F.2d 419 (1st Cir.1948); Gordon v. Robinson, 210 F.2d 192 (3d Cir.1954); Standard Oil Co. of California v. Moore, 251 F.2d 188, 214 (9th Cir.1957), cert. denied 356 U.S. 975, 78 S.Ct. 1139, 2 L.Ed.2d 1148; Yates v. Bair Transport, Inc., 249 F.Supp. 681 (S.D.N.Y.1965); Annot., 69 A.L.R.2d 1148. Cf. Hawkins v. Gorea Motor Express, Inc., 360 F.2d 933 (2d Cir.1966); Contra, 5 Wigmore § 1530a, n. 1, pp. 391-392. The point is not dealt with specifically in the Commonwealth Fund Act, the Uniform Act, or Uniform Rule 63(13). However, Model Code Rule 514 contains the requirement "that it was the regular course of that business for one with personal knowledge * * * to make such a memorandum or record or to transmit information thereof to be included in such a memorandum or record * * *." The rule follows this lead in requiring an informant with knowledge acting in the course of the regularly conducted activity.

Entries in the form of opinions were not encountered in traditional business records in view of the purely factual nature of the items recorded, but they are now commonly encountered with respect to medical diagnoses, prognoses, and test results, as well as occasionally in other areas. The Commonwealth Fund Act provided only for records of an "act, transaction, occurrence, or event," while the Uniform Act, Model Code Rule 514, and Uniform Rule 63(13) merely added the ambiguous term "condition." The limited phrasing of the Commonwealth Fund Act, 28 U.S.C. § 1732, may account for the reluctance of some federal decisions to admit diagnostic entries. New York Life Ins. Co. v. Taylor, 79 U.S.App.D.C. 66, 147 F.2d 297 (1945); Lyles v. United States, 103 U.S.App.D.C. 22, 254 F.2d 725 (1957), cert. denied 356 U.S. 961, 78 S.Ct. 997, 2 L.Ed.2d 1067; England v. United States, 174 F.2d 466 (5th Cir.1949); Skogen v. Dow Chemical Co., 375 F.2d 692 (8th Cir.1967). Other federal decisions, however, experienced no difficulty in freely admitting diagnostic entries. Reed v. Order of United Commercial Travelers, 123 F.2d 252 (2d Cir.1941); Buckminster's Estate v. Commissioner of Internal Revenue, 147 F.2d 331 (2d Cir.1944); Medina v. Erickson, 226 F.2d 475 (9th Cir.1955); Thomas v. Hogan, 308 F.2d 355 (4th Cir.1962); Glawe v. Rulon, 284 F.2d 495 (8th Cir.1960). In the state courts, the trend favors admissibility. Borucki v. MacKenzie Bros. Co., 125 Conn. 92, 3 A.2d 224 (1938); Allen v. St. Louis Public Service Co., 365 Mo. 677, 285 S.W.2d 663, 55 A.L.R.2d 1022 (1956); People v. Kohlmeyer, 284 N.Y. 366, 31 N.E. 2d 490 (1940); Weis v. Weis, 147 Ohio St. 416, 72 N.E.2d 245 (1947). In order to make clear its adherence to the latter position, the rule specifically includes both diagnoses and opinions, in addition to acts, events, and conditions, as proper subjects of admissible entries.

Problems of the motivation of the informant have been a source of difficulty and disagreement. In Palmer v. Hoffman, 318 U.S. 109, 63 S.Ct. 477, 87 L.Ed. 645 (1943), exclusion of an accident report made by the since deceased engineer, offered by defendant railroad trustees in a grade crossing collision case, was upheld. The report was not "in the regular course of business," not a record of the systematic conduct of the business as a business, said the Court. The report was prepared for use in litigating, not railroading. While the opinion mentions the motivation of the engineer only obliquely, the emphasis on records of routine operations is significant only by virtue of impact on motivation to be accurate. Absence of routineness raises lack of motivation to be accurate. The opinion of the Court of Appeals had gone beyond mere lack of motive to be accurate: the engineer's statement was "dripping with motivations to misrepresent." Hoffman v. Palmer, 129 F.2d 976, 991 (2d Cir.1942). The direct introduction of motivation is a disturbing factor, since absence of motive to misrepresent has not traditionally been a requirement of the rule; that records might be self-serving has not been a ground for exclusion. Laughlin, Business Records and the Like, 46 Iowa L.Rev. 276, 285 (1961). As Judge Clark said in his dissent, "I submit that there is hardly a grocer's account book which could not be excluded on that basis." 129 F.2d at 1002. A physician's evaluation report of a personal injury litigant would appear to be in the routine of his business. If the report is offered by the party at whose instance it was made, however, it has been held inadmissible, Yates v. Bair Transport, Inc., 249 F.Supp. 681 (S.D.N.Y.1965), otherwise if offered by the opposite party, Korte v. New York, N.H. & H.R. Co., 191 F.2d 86 (2d Cir.1951), cert. denied 342 U.S. 868, 72 S.Ct. 108, 96 L.Ed. 652.

The decisions hinge on motivation and which party is entitled to be concerned about it. Professor McCormick believed that the doctor's report or the accident report were sufficiently routine to justify admissibility. McCormick § 287, p. 604. Yet hesitation must be experienced in admitting everything which is observed and recorded in the course of a regularly conducted activity. Efforts to set a limit are illustrated by Hartzog v. United States, 217 F.2d 706 (4th Cir.1954), error to admit worksheets made by since deceased deputy collector in preparation for the instant income tax evasion prosecution, and United States v. Ware, 247 F.2d 698 (7th Cir.1957), error to admit narcotics agents' records of purchases. See also Exception [paragraph] (8), infra, as to the public record aspects of records of this nature. Some decisions have been satisfied as to motivation of an accident report if made pursuant to statutory duty, United States v. New York Foreign Trade Zone Operators, 304 F.2d 792 (2d Cir.1962); Taylor v. Baltimore & O.R. Co., 344 F.2d 281 (2d Cir. 1965), since the report was oriented in a direction other than the litigation which ensued. Cf. Matthews v. United States, 217 F.2d 409 (5th Cir.1954). The formulation of specific terms which would assure satisfactory results in all cases is not possible. Consequently the rule proceeds from the base that records made in the course of a regularly conducted activity will be taken as admissible but subject to authority to exclude if "the sources of information or other circumstances indicate lack of trustworthiness."

Occasional decisions have reached for enhanced accuracy by requiring involvement as a participant in matters reported. Clainos v. United States, 82 U.S.App.D.C. 278, 163 F.2d 593 (1947), error to admit police records of convictions; Standard Oil Co. of California v. Moore, 251 F.2d 188 (9th Cir. 1957), cert. denied 356 U.S. 975, 78 S.Ct. 1139, 2 L.Ed.2d 1148, error to admit employees' records of observed business practices of others. The rule includes no requirement of this nature. Wholly acceptable records may involve matters merely observed, e.g. the weather.

The form which the "record" may assume under the rule is described broadly as a "memorandum, report, record, or data compilation, in any form." The expression "data compilation" is used as broadly descriptive of any means of storing information other than the conventional words and figures in written or documentary form. It includes, but is by no means limited to, electronic computer storage. The term is borrowed from revised Rule 34(a) of the Rules of Civil Procedure.

Note to Paragraph (7). Failure of a record to mention a matter which would ordinarily be mentioned is satisfactory evidence of its nonexistence. Uniform Rule 63(14), Comment. While probably not hearsay as defined in Rule 801, supra, decisions may be found which class the evidence not only as hearsay but also as not within any exception. In order to set the question at rest in favor of admissibility, it is specifically treated here. McCormick § 289, p. 609; Morgan, Basic Problems of Evidence 314 (1962); 5 Wigmore § 1531; Uniform Rule 63(14); California Evidence Code § 1272; Kansas Code of Civil Procedure § 60-460(n); New Jersey Evidence Rule 63(14).

Note to Paragraph (8). Public records are a recognized hearsay exception at common law and have been the subject of statutes without number. McCormick § 291. See, for example, 28 U.S.C. § 1733, the relative narrowness of which is illustrated by its nonapplicability to nonfederal public agencies, thus necessitating resort to the less appropriate business record exception to the hearsay rule. Kay v. United States, 255 F.2d 476 (4th Cir.1958). The rule makes no distinction between federal and nonfederal offices and agencies.

Justification for the exception is the assumption that a public official will perform his duty properly and the unlikelihood that he will remember details independently of the record. Wong Wing Foo v. McGrath, 196 F.2d 120 (9th Cir.1952), and see Chesapeake & Delaware Canal Co. v. United States, 250 U.S. 123, 39 S.Ct. 407, 63 L.Ed. 889 (1919). As to items (a) and (b), further support is found in the reliability factors underlying records of regularly conducted activities generally. See Exception [paragraph] (6), supra.

(a) Cases illustrating the admissibility of records of the office's or agency's own activities are numerous. Chesapeake & Delaware Canal Co. v. United States, 250 U.S. 123, 39 S.Ct. 407, 63

L.Ed. 889 (1919), Treasury records of miscellaneous receipts and disbursements; Howard v. Perrin, 200 U.S. 71, 26 S.Ct. 195, 50 L.Ed. 374 (1906), General Land Office records; Ballew v. United States, 160 U.S. 187, 16 S.Ct. 263, 40 L.Ed. 388 (1895). Pension Office records.

(b) Cases sustaining admissibility of records of matters observed are also numerous. United States v. Van Hook, 284 F.2d 489 (7th Cir.1960), remanded for resentencing 365 U.S. 609, 81 S.Ct. 823, 5 L.Ed.2d 821, letter from induction officer to District Attorney, pursuant to army regulations, stating fact and circumstances of refusal to be inducted; T'Kach v. United States, 242 F.2d 937 (5th Cir. 1957), affidavit of White House personnel officer that search of records showed no employment of accused, charged with fraudulently representing himself as an envoy of the President; Minnehaha County v. Kelley, 150 F.2d 356 (8th Cir.1945); Weather Bureau records of rainfall; United States v. Meyer, 113 F.2d 387 (7th Cir.1940), cert. denied 311 U.S. 706, 61 S.Ct. 174, 85 L.Ed. 459, map prepared by government engineer from information furnished by men working under his supervision.

(c) The more controversial area of public records is that of the so-called "evaluative" report. The disagreement among the decisions has been due in part, no doubt, to the variety of situations encountered, as well as to differences in principle. Sustaining admissibility are such cases as United States v. Dumas, 149 U.S. 278, 13 S.Ct. 872, 37 L.Ed. 734 (1893), statement of account certified by Postmaster General in action against postmaster; McCarty v. United States, 185 F.2d 520 (5th Cir. 1950), reh. denied 187 F.2d 234, Certificate of Settlement of General Accounting Office showing indebtedness and letter from Army official stating Government had performed, in action on contract to purchase and remove waste food from Army camp; Moran v. Pittsburgh-Des Moines Steel Co., 183 F.2d 467 (3d Cir.1950), report of Bureau of Mines as to cause of gas tank explosion; Petition of W___, 164 F.Supp. 659 (E.D.Pa.1958), report by Immigration and Naturalization Service investigator that petitioner was known in community as wife of man to whom she was not married. To the opposite effect and denying admissibility are Franklin v. Skelly Oil Co., 141 F.2d 568 (10th Cir.1944), State Fire Marshal's report of cause of gas explosion; Lomax Transp. Co. v. United States, 183 F.2d 331 (9th Cir.1950), Certificate of Settlement from General Accounting Office in action for naval supplies lost in warehouse fire; Yung Jin Teung v. Dulles, 229 F.2d 244 (2d Cir. 1956), "Status Reports" offered to justify delay in processing passport applications. Police reports have generally been excluded except to the extent to which they incorporate firsthand observations of the officer. Annot., 69 A.L.R.2d 1148. Various kinds of evaluative reports are admissible under federal statutes: 7 U.S.C. § 78, findings of Secretary of Agriculture prima facie evidence of true grade of grain; 7 U.S.C. § 210(f), findings of Secretary of Agriculture prima facie evidence in action for damages against stockyard owner; 7 U.S.C. § 292, order by Secretary of Agriculture prima facie evidence in judicial enforcement proceedings against producers association monopoly; 7 U.S.C. § 1622(h), Department of Agriculture inspection certificates of products shipped in interstate commerce prima facie evidence; 8 U.S.C. § 1440(c), separation of alien from military service on conditions other than honorable provable by certificate from department in proceedings to revoke citizenship; 18 U.S.C. § 4245, certificate of Director of Prisons that convicted person has been examined and found probably incompetent at time of trial prima facie evidence in court hearing on competency; 42 U.S.C. § 269(b), bill of health by appropriate official prima facie evidence of vessel's sanitary history and condition and compliance with regulations; 46 U.S.C. § 679, certificate of consul presumptive evidence of refusal of master to transport destitute seamen to United States. While these statutory exceptions to the hearsay rule are left undisturbed, Rule 802, the willingness of Congress to recognize a substantial measure of admissibility for evaluative reports is a helpful guide.

Factors which may be of assistance in passing upon the admissibility of evaluative reports include: (1) the timeliness of the investigation, McCormick, Can the Courts Make Wider Use of Reports of Official Investigations? 42 Iowa L.Rev. 363 (1957); (2) the special skill or experience of the official, id., (3) whether a hearing was held and the level at which conducted, Franklin v. Skelly Oil Co., 141 F.2d 568 (10th Cir.1944); (4) possible motivation problems suggested by Palmer v. Hoffman, 318 U.S. 109, 63 S.Ct. 477, 87 L.Ed. 645 (1943). Others no doubt could be added.

The formulation of an approach which would give appropriate weight to all possible factors in every situation is an obvious impossibility. Hence the rule, as in Exception [paragraph] (6), assumes admissibility in the first instance but with ample provision for escape if sufficient negative factors are present. In one respect, however, the rule with respect to evaluative reports under item (c) is very specific: they are admissible only in civil cases and against the government in criminal cases in view of the almost certain collision with confrontation rights which would result from their use against the accused in a criminal case.

Note to Paragraph (9). Records of vital statistics are commonly the subject of particular statutes making them admissible in evidence, Uniform Vital Statistics Act, 9C U.L.A. 350 (1957). The rule is in principle narrower than Uniform Rule 63(16) which includes reports required of persons performing functions authorized by statute, yet in practical effect the two are substantially the same. Comment Uniform Rule 63(16). The exception as drafted is in the pattern of California Evidence Code § 1281.

Note to Paragraph (10). The principle of proving nonoccurrence of an event by evidence of the absence of a record which would regularly be made of its occurrence, developed in Exception [paragraph] (7) with respect to regularly conducted activities, is here extended to public records of the kind mentioned in Exceptions [paragraphs] (8) and (9). 5 Wigmore § 1633(6), p. 519. Some harmless duplication no doubt exists with Exception [paragraph] (7). For instances of federal statutes recognizing this method of proof, see 8 U.S.C. § 1284(b), proof of absence of alien crewman's name from outgoing manifest prima facie evidence of failure to detain or deport, and 42 U.S.C. § 405(c)(3), (4)(B), (4)(C), absence of HEW [Department of Health, Education, and Welfare] record prima facie evidence of no wages or self-employment income.

The rule includes situations in which absence of a record may itself be the ultimate focal point of inquiry, e.g. People v. Love, 310 Ill. 558, 142 N.E. 204 (1923), certificate of Secretary of State admitted to show failure to file documents required by Securities Law, as well as cases where the absence of a record is offered as proof of the nonoccurrence of an event ordinarily recorded.

The refusal of the common law to allow proof by certificate of the lack of a record or entry has no apparent justification, 5 Wigmore § 1678(7), p. 752. The rule takes the opposite position, as to Uniform Rule 63(17); California Evidence Code § 1284; Kansas Code of Civil Procedure § 60-460(c); New Jersey Evidence Rule 63(17). Congress has recognized certification as evidence of the lack of a record. 8 U.S.C. § 1360(d), certificate of Attorney General or other designated officer that no record of Immigration and Naturalization Service of specified nature or entry therein is found, admissible in alien cases.

Note to Paragraph (11). Records of activities of religious organizations are currently recognized as admissible at least to the extent of the business records exception to the hearsay rule, 5 Wigmore § 1523, p. 371, and Exception [paragraph] (6) would be applicable. However, both the business record doctrine and Exception [paragraph] (6) require that the person furnishing the information be one in the business or activity. The result is such decisions as Daily v. Grand Lodge, 311 Ill. 184, 142 N.E. 478 (1924), holding a church record admissible to prove fact, date, and place of baptism, but not age of child except that he had at least been born at the time. In view of the unlikelihood that false information would be furnished on occasions of this kind, the rule contains no requirement that the informant be in the course of the activity. See California Evidence Code § 1315 and Comment.

Note to Paragraph (12). The principle of proof by certification is recognized as to public officials in Exceptions [paragraphs] (8) and (10), and with respect to authentication in Rule 902. The present exception is a duplication to the extent that it deals with a certificate by a public official, as in the case of a judge who performs a marriage ceremony. The area covered by the rule is, however, substantially larger and extends the certification procedure to clergymen and the like who perform marriages and other ceremonies or administer sacraments. Thus certificates of such matters as baptism or confirmation, as well as marriage, are included. In principle they are as acceptable evidence as certificates of public officers. See 5 Wigmore § 1645, as to marriage certificates. When the person executing the certificate is not a public official, the self-authenticating character of documents purporting to emanate from public officials, see Rule 902, is lacking and proof is required that the person was authorized and did make the certificate. The time element, however, may safely be taken as supplied by the certificate, once authority and authenticity are established, particularly in view of the presumption that a document was executed on the date it bears.

For similar rules, some limited to certificates of marriage, with variations in foundation requirements, see Uniform Rule 63(18); California Evidence Code § 1316; Kansas Code of Civil Procedure § 60-460(p); New Jersey Evidence Rule 63(18).

Note to Paragraph (13). Records of family history kept in family Bibles have by long tradition been received in evidence. 5 Wigmore §§ 1495, 1496, citing numerous statutes and decisions. See also Regulations, Social Security Administration, 20 C.F.R. § 404.703(c), recognizing family Bible entries as proof of age in the absence of public or church records. Opinions in the area also include inscriptions on tombstones, publicly displayed pedigrees, and engravings on rings. Wigmore, supra. The rule is substantially identical in coverage with California Evidence Code § 1312.

Note to Paragraph (14). The recording of title documents is a purely statutory development. Under any theory of the admissibility of public records, the records would be receivable as evidence of the contents of the recorded document, else the recording process would be reduced to a nullity. When, however, the record is offered for the further purpose of proving execution and delivery, a problem of lack of firsthand knowledge by the recorder, not present as to contents, is presented. This problem is solved, seemingly in all jurisdictions, by qualifying for recording only those documents shown by a specified procedure, either acknowledgement or a form of probate, to have been executed and delivered. 5 Wigmore §§ 1647-1651. Thus what may appear in the rule, at first glance, as endowing the record with an effect independently of local law and inviting difficulties of an Erie nature under Cities Service Oil Co. v. Dunlap, 308 U.S. 208, 60 S.Ct. 201, 84 L.Ed. 196 (1939), is not present, since the local law in fact governs under the example.

Note to Paragraph (15). Dispositive documents often contain recitals of fact. Thus a deed purporting to have been executed by an attorney in fact may recite the existence of the power of attorney, or a deed may recite that the grantors are all the heirs of the last record owner. Under the rule, these recitals are exempted from the hearsay rule. The circumstances under which dispositive documents are executed and the requirement that the recital be germane to the purpose of the document are believed to be adequate guarantees of trustworthiness, particularly in view of the nonapplicability of the rule if dealings with the property have been inconsistent with the document. The age of the document is of no significance, though in practical application the document will most often be an ancient one. See Uniform Rule 63(29), Comment.

Similar provisions are contained in Uniform Rule 63(29); California Evidence Code § 1330; Kansas Code of Civil Procedure § 60-460(aa); New Jersey Evidence Rule 63(29).

Note to Paragraph (16). Authenticating a document as ancient, essentially in the pattern of the common law, as provided in Rule 901(b)(8), leaves open as a separate question the admissibility of assertive statements contained therein as against a hearsay objection. 7 Wigmore § 2145a. Wigmore further states that the ancient document technique of authentication is universally conceded to apply to all sorts of documents, including letters, records, contracts, maps, and certificates, in addition to title documents, citing numerous decisions. Id. § 2145. Since most of these items are significant evidentially only insofar as they are assertive, their admission in evidence must be as a hearsay exception. But see 5 id. § 1573, p. 429, referring to recitals in ancient deeds as a "limited" hearsay exception. The former position is believed to be the correct one in reason and authority. As pointed out in McCormick § 298, danger of mistake is minimized by authentication requirements, and age affords assurance that the writing antedates the present controversy. See Dallas County v. Commercial Union Assurance Co., 286 F.2d 388 (5th Cir.1961), upholding admissibility of 58-year-old newspaper story. Cf. Morgan, Basic Problems of Evidence 364 (1962), but see id. 254.

For a similar provision, but with the added requirement that "the statement has since generally been acted upon as true by persons having an interest in the matter," see California Evidence Code § 1331.

Note to Paragraph (17). Ample authority at common law supported the admission in evidence of items falling in this category. While Wigmore's text is narrowly oriented to lists, etc., prepared for the use of a trade or profession, 6 Wigmore § 1702, authorities are cited which include other kinds of publications, for example, newspaper market reports, telephone directories, and city directories. Id. §§ 1702-1706. The basis of trustworthiness is general reliance by the public or by a particular segment of it, and the motivation of the compiler to foster reliance by being accurate.

For similar provisions, see Uniform Rule 63(30); California Evidence Code § 1340; Kansas Code of Civil Procedure § 60-460(bb); New Jersey Evidence Rule 63(30). Uniform Commercial Code § 2-724 provides for admissibility in evidence of "reports in official publications or trade journals or in newspapers or periodicals of general circulation published as the reports of such [established commodity] market."

Note to Paragraph (18). The writers have generally favored the admissibility of learned treatises, McCormick § 296, p. 621; Morgan, Basic Problems of Evidence 366 (1962); 6 Wigmore § 1692, with the support of occasional decisions and rules, City of Dothan v. Hardy, 237 Ala. 603, 188 So. 264 (1939); Lewandowski v. Preferred Risk Mut. Ins. Co., 33 Wis.2d 69, 146 N.W.2d 505 (1966), 66 Mich.L.Rev. 183 (1967); Uniform Rule 63(31); Kansas Code of Civil Procedure § 60-460(cc), but the great weight of authority has been that learned treatises are not admissible as substantive evidence though usable in the cross-examination of experts. The foundation of the minority view is that the hearsay objection must be regarded as unimpressive when directed against treatises since a high standard of accuracy is engendered by various factors: the treatise is written primarily and impartially for professionals, subject to scrutiny and exposure for inaccuracy, with the reputation of the writer at stake. 6 Wigmore § 1692. Sound as this position may be with respect to trustworthiness, there is, nevertheless, an additional difficulty in the likelihood that the treatise will be misunderstood and misapplied without expert assistance and supervision. This difficulty is recognized in the cases demonstrating unwillingness to sustain findings relative to disability on the basis of judicially noticed medical texts. Ross v. Gardner, 365 F.2d 554 (6th Cir.1966); Sayers v. Gardner, 380 F.2d 940 (6th Cir.1967); Colwell v. Gardner, 386 F.2d 56 (6th Cir.1967); Glendenning v. Ribicoff, 213 F.Supp. 301 (W.D.Mo.1962); Cook v. Celebrezze, 217 F.Supp. 366 (W.D.Mo. 1963); Sosna v. Celebrezze, 234 F.Supp. 289 (E.D.Pa.1964); and see McDaniel v. Celebrezze, 331 F.2d 426 (4th Cir.1964). The rule avoids the danger of misunderstanding and misapplication by limiting the use of treatises as substantive evidence to situations in which an expert is on the stand and available to explain and assist in the application of the treatise if desired. The limitation upon receiving the publication itself physically in evidence, contained in the last sentence, is designed, to further this policy.

The relevance of the use of treatises on cross-examination is evident. This use of treatises has been the subject of varied views. The most restrictive position is that the witness must have stated expressly on direct his reliance upon the treatise. A slightly more liberal approach still insists upon reliance but allows it to be developed on cross-examination. Further relaxation dispenses with reliance but requires recognition as an authority by the witness, developable on cross-examination. The greatest liberality is found in decisions allowing use of the treatise on cross-examination when its status as an authority is established by any means. Annot., 60 A.L.R.2d 77. The exception is hinged upon this last position, which is that of the Supreme Court, Reilly v. Pinkus, 338 U.S. 269, 70 S.Ct. 110, 94 L.Ed. 63 (1949), and of recent well considered state court decisions, City of St. Petersburg v. Ferguson, 193 So.2d 648 (Fla.App.1967), cert. denied Fla., 201 So.2d 556; Darling v. Charleston Memorial Community Hospital, 33 Ill.2d 326, 211 N.E.2d 253 (1965); Dabroe v. Rhodes Co., 64 Wash.2d 431, 392 P.2d 317 (1964).

In Reilly v. Pinkus, supra, the Court pointed out that testing of professional knowledge was incomplete without exploration of the witness' knowledge of and attitude toward established treatises in the field. The process works equally well in reverse and furnishes the basis of the rule.

The rule does not require that the witness rely upon or recognize the treatise as authoritative, thus avoiding the possibility that the expert may at the outset block cross-examination by refusing to concede reliance or authoritativeness. Dabroe v. Rhodes Co., supra. Moreover, the rule avoids the unreality of admitting evidence for the purpose of impeachment only, with an instruction to the jury not to consider it otherwise. The parallel to the treatment of prior inconsistent statements will be apparent. See Rules 613(b) and 801(d)(1).

Note to Paragraphs (19), (20) and (21). Trustworthiness in reputation evidence is found "when the topic is such that the facts are likely to have been inquired about and that persons having personal knowledge have disclosed facts which have thus been discussed in the community; and thus the community's conclusion, if any has been formed, is likely to be a trustworthy one." 5 Wigmore § 1580, p. 444, and see also § 1583. On this common foundation, reputation as to land boundaries, customs, general history, character, and marriage have come to be regarded as admissible. The breadth of the underlying principle suggests the formulation of an equally broad exception, but tradition has in fact been much narrower and more particularized, and this is the pattern of these exceptions in the rule.

Exception [paragraph] (19) is concerned with matters of personal and family history. Marriage is universally conceded to be a proper subject of proof by evidence of reputation in the community. 5 Wigmore § 1602. As to such items as legitimacy, relationship, adoption, birth, and death, the decisions are divided. Id. § 1605. All seem to be susceptible to being the subject of well founded repute. The "world" in which the reputation may exist may be family, associates, or community. This world has proved capable of expanding with changing times from the single uncomplicated neighborhood, in which all activities take place, to the multiple and unrelated worlds of work, religious affiliation, and social activity, in each of which a reputation may be generated. People v. Reeves, 360 Ill. 55, 195 N.E. 443 (1935); State v. Axilrod, 248 Minn. 204, 79 N.W.2d 677 (1956); Mass.Stat.1947, c. 410, M.G.L.A. c. 233 § 21A; 5 Wigmore § 1616. The family has often served as the point of beginning for allowing community reputation. 5 Wigmore § 1488. For comparable provisions see Uniform Rule 63(26), (27)(c); California Evidence Code §§ 1313, 1314; Kansas Code of Civil Procedure § 60-460(x), (y)(3); New Jersey Evidence Rule 63(26), (27)(c).

The first portion of Exception [paragraph] (20) is based upon the general admissibility of evidence of reputation as to land boundaries and land customs, expanded in this country to include private as well as public boundaries. McCormick § 299, p. 625. The reputation is required to antedate the controversy, though not to be ancient. The second portion is likewise supported by authority, id., and is designed to facilitate proof of events when judicial notice is not available. The historical character of the subject matter dispenses with any need that the reputation antedate the controversy with respect to which it is offered. For similar provisions see Uniform Rule 63(27)(a), (b); California Evidence Code §§ 1320-1322; Kansas Code of Civil Procedure § 60-460(y), (1), (2); New Jersey Evidence Rule 63(27)(a), (b).

Exception [paragraph] (21) recognizes the traditional acceptance of reputation evidence as a means of proving human character. McCormick §§ 44, 158. The exception deals only with the hearsay aspect of this kind of evidence. Limitations upon admissibility based on other grounds will be found in Rules 404, relevancy of character evidence generally, and 608, character of witness. The exception is in effect a reiteration, in the context of hearsay, of Rule 405(a). Similar provisions are contained in Uniform Rule 63(28); California Evidence Code § 1324; Kansas Code of Civil Procedure § 60-460(z); New Jersey Evidence Rule 63(28).

Note to Paragraph (22). When the status of a former judgment is under consideration in subsequent litigation, three possibilities must be noted: (1) the former judgment is conclusive under the doctrine of res judicata, either as a bar or a collateral estoppel; or (2) it is admissible in evidence for what it is worth; or (3) it may be of no effect at all. The first situation does not involve any problem of evidence except in the way that principles of substantive law generally bear upon the relevancy and materiality of evidence. The rule does not deal with the substantive effect of the judgment as a bar or collateral estoppel. When, however, the doctrine of res judicata does not apply to make the judgment either a bar or a collateral estoppel, a choice is presented between the second and third alternatives. The rule adopts the second for judgments of criminal conviction of felony grade. This is the direction of the decisions, Annot., 18 A.L.R.2d 1287, 1299, which manifest an increasing reluctance to reject in toto the validity of the law's factfinding processes outside the confines of res judicata and collateral estoppel. While this may leave a jury with the evidence of conviction but without means to evaluate it, as suggested by Judge Hinton, Note 27 Ill.L.Rev. 195 (1932), it seems safe to assume that the jury will give it substantial effect unless defendant offers a satisfactory explanation, a possibility not foreclosed by the provision. But see North River Ins. Co. v. Militello, 104 Colo. 28, 88 P.2d 567 (1939), in which the jury found for plaintiff on a fire policy despite the introduction of his conviction for arson. For supporting federal decisions see Clark, J., in New York & Cuba Mail S.S. Co. v. Continental Cas. Co., 117 F.2d 404, 411 (2d Cir.1941); Connecticut Fire Ins. Co. v. Farrara, 277 F.2d 388 (8th Cir.1960).

Practical considerations require exclusion of convictions of minor offenses, not because the administration of justice in its lower echelons must be inferior, but because motivation to defend at this level is often minimal or nonexistent. Cope v. Goble, 39 Cal.App.2d 448, 103 P.2d 598 (1940); Jones v. Talbot, 87 Idaho 498, 394 P.2d 316 (1964); Warren v. Marsh, 215 Minn. 615, 11 N.W.2d 528 (1943); Annot., 18 A.L.R.2d 1287, 1295-1297; 16 Brooklyn L.Rev. 286 (1950); 50 Colum.L.Rev. 529 (1950); 35 Cornell L.Q. 872 (1950). Hence the rule includes only convictions of felony grade, measured by federal standards.

Judgments of conviction based upon pleas of nolo contendere are not included. This position is consistent with the treatment of nolo pleas in Rule 410 and the authorities cited in the Advisory Committee's Note in support thereof.

While these rules do not in general purport to resolve constitutional issues, they have in general been drafted with a view to avoiding collision with constitutional principles. Consequently the exception does not include evidence of the conviction of a third person, offered against the accused in a criminal prosecution to prove any fact essential to sustain the judgment of conviction. A contrary position would seem clearly to violate the right of confrontation. Kirby v. United States, 174 U.S. 47, 19 S.Ct. 574, 43 L.Ed. 890 (1899), error to convict of possessing stolen postage stamps with the only evidence of theft being the record of conviction of the thieves. The situation is to be distinguished from cases in which conviction of another person is an element of the crime, e.g. 15 U.S.C. § 902(d), interstate shipment of firearms to a known convicted felon, and, as specifically provided, from impeachment.

For comparable provisions see Uniform Rule 63(20); California Evidence Code § 1300; Kansas Code of Civil Procedure § 60-460(r); New Jersey Evidence Rule 63(20).

Note to Paragraph (23). A hearsay exception in this area was originally justified on the ground that verdicts were evidence of reputation. As trial by jury graduated from the category of neighborhood inquests, this theory lost its validity. It was never valid as to chancery decrees. Nevertheless the rule persisted, though the judges and writers shifted ground and began saying that the judgment or decree was as good evidence as reputation. See City of London v. Clerke, Carth. 181, 90 Eng.Rep. 710 (K.B. 1691); Neill v. Duke of Devonshire, 8 App.Cas. 135 (1882). The shift appears to be correct, since the process of inquiry, sifting, and scrutiny which is relied upon to render reputation reliable is present in perhaps greater measure in the process of litigation. While this might suggest a broader area of application, the affinity to reputation is strong, and paragraph [paragraph] (23) goes no further, not even including character.

The leading case in the United States, Patterson v. Gaines, 47 U.S. (6 How.) 550, 599, 12 L.Ed. 553 (1847), follows in the pattern of the English decisions, mentioning as illustrative matters thus provable: manorial rights, public rights of way, immemorial custom, disputed boundary, and pedigree. More recent recognition of the principle is found in Grant Bros. Construction Co. v. United States, 232 U.S. 647, 34 S.Ct. 452, 58 L.Ed. 776 (1914), in action for penalties under Alien Contract Labor Law, decision of board of inquiry of Immigration Service admissible to prove alienage of laborers, as a matter of pedigree; United States v. Mid-Continent Petroleum Corp., 67 F. 2d 37 (10th Cir.1933), records of commission enrolling Indians admissible on pedigree; Jung Yen Loy v. Cahill, 81 F.2d 809 (9th Cir.1936), board decisions as to citizenship of plaintiff's father admissible in proceeding for declaration of citizenship. Contra, In re Estate of Cunha, 49 Haw. 273, 414 P.2d 925 (1966).

1974 Enactment

Note to Paragraph (3). Rule 803(3) was approved in the form submitted by the Court to Congress. However, the Committee intends that the Rule be construed to limit the doctrine of Mutual Life Insurance Co. v. Hillmon, 145 U.S. 285, 295-300 (1892), so as to render statements of intent by a declarant admissible only to prove his future conduct, not the future conduct of another person.

Note to Paragraph (4). After giving particular attention to the question of physical examination made solely to enable a physician to testify, the Committee approved Rule 803(4) as submitted to Congress, with the understanding that it is not intended in any way to adversely affect present privilege rules or those subsequently adopted.

Note to Paragraph (5). Rule 803(5) as submitted by the Court permitted the reading into evidence of a memorandum or record concerning a matter about which a witness once had knowledge but now has insufficient recollection to enable him to testify accurately and fully, "shown to have been made when the matter was fresh in his memory and to reflect that knowledge correctly." The Committee amended this Rule to add the words "or adopted by the witness" after the phrase "shown to have been made", a treatment consistent with the definition of "statement" in the Jencks Act, 18 U.S.C. 3500. Moreover, it is the Committee's understanding that a memorandum or report, although barred under this Rule, would nonetheless be admissible if it came within another hearsay exception. This last stated principle is deemed applicable to all the hearsay rules.

Note to Paragraph (6). Rule 803(6) as submitted by the Court permitted a record made "in the course of a regularly conducted activity" to be admissible in certain circumstances. The Committee believed there were insufficient guarantees of reliability in records made in the course of activities falling outside the scope of "business" activities as that term is broadly defined in 28 U.S.C. 1732. Moreover, the Committee concluded that the additional requirement of Section 1732 that it must have been the regular practice of a business to make the record is a necessary further assurance of its trustworthiness. The Committee accordingly amended the Rule to incorporate these limitations.

Note to Paragraph (7). Rule 803(7) as submitted by the Court concerned the absence of entry in the records of a "regularly conducted activity." The Committee amended this Rule to conform with its action with respect to Rule 803(6).

Note to Paragraph (8). The Committee approved Rule 803(8) without substantive change from the form in which it was submitted by the Court. The Committee intends that the phrase "factual findings" be strictly construed and that evaluations or opinions contained in public reports shall not be admissible under this Rule.

Note to Paragraph (13). The Committee approved this Rule in the form submitted by the Court, intending that the phrase "Statements of fact concerning personal or family history" be read to include the specific types of such statements enumerated in Rule 803(11). House Report No. 93-650.

Note to Paragraph (4). The House approved this rule as it was submitted by the Supreme Court "with the understanding that it is not intended in any way to adversely affect present privilege rules." We also approve this rule, and we would point out with respect to the question of its relation to privileges, it must be read in conjunction with rule 35 of the Federal Rules of Civil Procedure which provides that whenever the physical or mental condition of a party (plaintiff or defendant) is in controversy, the court may require him to submit to an examination by a physician. It is these examinations which will normally be admitted under this exception.

Note to Paragraph (5). Rule 803(5) as submitted by the Court permitted the reading into evidence of a memorandum or record concerning a matter about which a witness once had knowledge but now has insufficient recollection to enable him to testify accurately and fully, "shown to have been made when the matter was fresh in his memory and to reflect that knowledge correctly." The House amended the rule to add the words "or adopted by the witness" after the phrase "shown to have been made," language parallel to the Jencks Act [18 U.S.C. § 3500].

The committee accepts the House amendment with the understanding and belief that it was not intended to narrow the scope of applicability of the rule. In fact, we understand it to clarify the rule's applicability to a memorandum adopted by the witness as well as one made by him. While the rule as submitted by the Court was silent on the question of who made the memorandum, we view the House amendment as a helpful clarification, noting, however, that the Advisory Committee's note to this rule suggests that the important thing is the accuracy of the memorandum rather than who made it.

The committee does not view the House amendment as precluding admissibility in situations in which multiple participants were involved.

When the verifying witness has not prepared the report, but merely examined it and found it accurate, he has adopted the report, and it is therefore admissible. The rule should also be interpreted to cover other situations involving multiple participants, e.g., employer dictating to secretary, secretary making memorandum at direction of employer, or information being passed along a chain of persons, as in Curtis v. Bradley [65 Conn. 99, 31 Atl. 591 (1894); see, also, Rathbun v. Brancatella, 93 N.J.L. 222, 107 Atl. 279 (1919); see, also, McCormick on Evidence, § 303 (2d ed. 1972)].

The committee also accepts the understanding of the House that a memorandum or report, although barred under this rule, would nonetheless be admissible if it came within another hearsay exception. We consider this principle to be applicable to all the hearsay rules.

Note to Paragraph (6). Rule 803(6) as submitted by the Supreme Court permitted a record made in the course of a regularly conducted activity to be admissible in certain circumstances. This rule constituted a broadening of the traditional business records hearsay exception which has been long advocated by scholars and judges active in the law of evidence.

The House felt there were insufficient guarantees of reliability of records not within a broadly defined business records exception. We disagree. Even under the House definition of "business" including profession, occupation, and "calling of every kind," the records of many regularly conducted activities will, or may be, excluded from evidence. Under the principle of ejusdem generis, the intent of "calling of every kind" would seem to be related to work-related endeavors-- e.g., butcher, baker, artist, etc.

Thus, it appears that the records of many institutions or groups might not be admissible under the House amendments. For example, schools, churches, and hospitals will not normally be considered businesses within the definition. Yet, these are groups which keep financial and other records on a regular basis in a manner similar to business enterprises. We believe these records are of equivalent trustworthiness and should be admitted into evidence.

Three states, which have recently codified their evidence rules, have adopted the Supreme Court version of rule 803(6), providing for admission of memoranda of a "regularly conducted activity." None adopted the words "business activity" used in the House amendment. [See Nev.Rev.Stats. § 15.135; N.Mex.Stats. (1973 Supp.) § 20-4-803(6); West's Wis.Stats.Anno. (1973 Supp.) § 908.03(6).]

Therefore, the committee deleted the word "business" as it appears before the word "activity". The last sentence then is unnecessary and was also deleted.

It is the understanding of the committee that the use of the phrase "person with knowledge" is not intended to imply that the party seeking to introduce the memorandum, report, record, or data compilation must be able to produce, or even identify, the specific individual upon whose first-hand knowledge the memorandum, report, record or data compilation was based. A sufficient foundation for the introduction of such evidence will be laid if the party seeking to introduce the evidence is able to show that it was the regular practice of the activity to base such memorandums, reports, records, or data compilations upon a transmission from a person with knowledge, e.g., in the case of the content of a shipment of goods, upon a report from the company's receiving agent or in the case of a computer printout, upon a report from the company's computer programmer or one who has knowledge of the particular record system. In short, the scope of the phrase "person with knowledge" is meant to be coterminous with the custodian of the evidence or other qualified witness. The committee believes this represents the desired rule in light of the complex nature of modern business organizations.

Note to Paragraph (8). The House approved rule 803(8), as submitted by the Supreme Court, with one substantive change. It excluded from the hearsay exception reports containing matters observed by police officers and other law enforcement personnel in criminal cases. Ostensibly, the reason for this exclusion is that observations by police officers at the scene of the crime or the apprehension of the defendant are not as reliable as observations by public officials in other cases because of the adversarial nature of the confrontation between the police and the defendant in criminal cases.

The committee accepts the House's decision to exclude such recorded observations where the police officer is available to testify in court about his observation. However, where he is unavailable as unavailability is defined in rule 804(a)(4) and (a)(5), the report should be admitted as the best available evidence. Accordingly, the committee has amended rule 803(8) to refer to the provision of [proposed] rule 804(b)(5) [deleted], which allows the admission of such reports, records or other statements where the police officer or other law enforcement officer is unavailable because of death, then existing physical or mental illness or infirmity, or not being successfully subject to legal process.

The House Judiciary Committee report contained a statement of intent that "the phrase 'factual findings' in subdivision (c) be strictly construed and that evaluations or opinions contained in public reports shall not be admissible under this rule." The committee takes strong exception to this limiting understanding of the application of the rule. We do not think it reflects an understanding of the intended operation of the rule as explained in the Advisory Committee notes to this subsection. The Advisory Committee notes on subsection (c) of this subdivision point out that various kinds of evaluative reports are now admissible under Federal statutes. 7 U.S.C. § 78, findings of Secretary of Agriculture prima facie evidence of true grade of grain; 42 U.S.C. § 269(b), bill of health by appropriate official prima facie evidence of vessel's sanitary history and condition and compliance with regulations. These statutory exceptions to the hearsay rule are preserved. Rule 802. The willingness of Congress to recognize these and other such evaluative reports provides a helpful guide in determining the kind of reports which are intended to be admissible under this rule. We think the restrictive interpretation of the House overlooks the fact that while the Advisory Committee assumes admissibility in the first instance of evaluative reports, they are not admissible if, as the rule states, "the sources of information or other circumstances indicate lack of trustworthiness."

The Advisory Committee explains the factors to be considered:

* * * *

Factors which may be assistance in passing upon the admissibility of evaluative reports include: (1) the timeliness of the investigation, McCormick, Can the Courts Make Wider Use of Reports of Official Investigations? 42 Iowa L.Rev. 363 (1957); (2) the special skill or experience of the official, id.; (3) whether a hearing was held and the level at which conducted, Franklin v. Skelly Oil Co., 141 F.2d 568 (19th Cir.1944); (4) possible motivation problems suggested by Palmer v. Hoffman, 318 U.S. 109, 63 S.Ct. 477, 87 L.Ed. 645 (1943). Others no doubt could be added.

* * * *

The committee concludes that the language of the rule together with the explanation provided by the Advisory Committee furnish sufficient guidance on the admissibility of evaluative reports.

Note to Paragraph (24). The proposed Rules of Evidence submitted to Congress contained identical provisions in rules 803 and 804 (which set forth the various hearsay exceptions), admitting any hearsay statement not specifically covered by any of the stated exceptions, if the hearsay statement was found to have "comparable circumstantial guarantees of trustworthiness." The House deleted these provisions (proposed rules 803(24) and 804(b)(6)[(5)]) as injecting "too much uncertainty" into the law of evidence and impairing the ability of practitioners to prepare for trial. The House felt that rule 102, which directs the courts to construe the Rules of Evidence so as to promote growth and development, would permit sufficient flexibility to admit hearsay evidence in appropriate cases under various factual situations that might arise.

We disagree with the total rejection of a residual hearsay exception. While we view rule 102 as being intended to provide for a broader construction and interpretation of these rules, we feel that, without a separate residual provision, the specifically enumerated exceptions could become tortured beyond any reasonable circumstances which they were intended to include (even if broadly construed). Moreover, these exceptions, while they reflect the most typical and well recognized exceptions to the hearsay rule, may not encompass every situation in which the reliability and appropriateness of a particular piece of hearsay evidence make clear that it should be heard and considered by the trier of fact.

The committee believes that there are certain exceptional circumstances where evidence which is found by a court to have guarantees of trustworthiness equivalent to or exceeding the guarantees reflected by the presently listed exceptions, and to have a high degree of prolativeness [sic] and necessity could properly be admissible.

The case of Dallas County v. Commercial Union Assoc. Co., Ltd., 286 F.2d 388 (5th Cir.1961) illustrates the point. The issue in that case was whether the tower of the county courthouse collapsed because it was struck by lightning (covered by insurance) or because of structural weakness and deterioration of the structure (not covered). Investigation of the structure revealed the presence of charcoal and charred timbers. In order to show that lightning may not have been the cause of the charring, the insurer offered a copy of a local newspaper published over 50 years earlier containing an unsigned article describing a fire in the courthouse while it was under construction. The court found that the newspaper did not qualify for admission as a business record or an ancient document and did not fit within any other recognized hearsay exception. The court concluded, however, that the article was trustworthy because it was inconceivable that a newspaper reporter in a small town would report a fire in the courthouse if none had occurred. See also United States v. Barbati, 284 F.Supp. 409 (E.D.N.Y.1968).

Because exceptional cases like the Dallas County case may arise in the future, the committee has decided to reinstate a residual exception for rules 803 and 804(b).

The committee, however, also agrees with those supporters of the House version who felt that an overly broad residual hearsay exception could emasculate the hearsay rule and the recognized exceptions or vitiate the rationale behind codification of the rules.

Therefore, the committee has adopted a residual exception for rules 803 and 804(b) of much narrower scope and applicability than the Supreme Court version. In order to qualify for admission, a hearsay statement not falling within one of the recognized exceptions would have to satisfy at least four conditions. First, it must have "equivalent circumstantial guarantees of trustworthiness." Second, it must be offered as evidence of a material fact. Third, the court must determine that the statement "is more probative on the point for which it is offered than any other evidence which the proponent can procure through reasonable efforts." This requirement is intended to insure that only statements which have high probative value and necessity may qualify for admission under the residual exceptions. Fourth, the court must determine that "the general purposes of these rules and the interests of justice will best be served by admission of the statement into evidence."

It is intended that the residual hearsay exceptions will be used very rarely, and only in exceptional circumstances. The committee does not intend to establish a broad license for trial judges to admit hearsay statements that do not fall within one of the other exceptions contained in rules 803 and 804(b). The residual exceptions are not meant to authorize major judicial revisions of the hearsay rule, including its present exceptions. Such major revisions are best accomplished by legislative action. It is intended that in any case in which evidence is sought to be admitted under these subsections, the trial judge will exercise no less care, reflection and caution than the courts did under the common law in establishing the now-recognized exceptions to the hearsay rule.

In order to establish a well-defined jurisprudence, the special facts and circumstances which, in the court's judgment, indicates that the statement has a sufficiently high degree of trustworthiness and necessity to justify its admission should be stated on the record. It is expected that the court will give the opposing party a full and adequate opportunity to contest the admission of any statement sought to be introduced under these subsections. Senate Report No. 93-1277.

Rule 803 defines when hearsay statements are admissible in evidence even though the declarant is available as a witness. The Senate amendments make three changes in this rule.

Note to Paragraph (6). The House bill provides in subsection (6) that records of a regularly conducted "business" activity qualify for admission into evidence as an exception to the hearsay rule. "Business" is defined as including "business, profession, occupation and calling of every kind." The Senate amendment drops the requirement that the records be those of a "business" activity and eliminates the definition of "business." The Senate amendment provides that records are admissible if they are records of a regularly conducted "activity."

The Conference adopts the House provision that the records must be those of a regularly conducted "business" activity. The Conferees changed the definition of "business" contained in the House provision in order to make it clear that the records of institutions and associations like schools, churches and hospitals are admissible under this provision. The records of public schools and hospitals are also covered by Rule 803(8), which deals with public records and reports.

Note to Paragraph (8). The Senate amendment adds language, not contained in the House bill, that refers to another rule that was added by the Senate in another amendment ([proposed] Rule 804(b) (5)--Criminal law enforcement records and reports [deleted]).

In view of its action on [proposed] Rule 804(b)(5) (Criminal law enforcement records and reports) [deleted], the Conference does not adopt the Senate amendment and restores the bill to the House version.

Note to Paragraph (24). The Senate amendment adds a new subsection, (24), which makes admissible a hearsay statement not specifically covered by any of the previous twenty-three subsections, if the statement has equivalent circumstantial guarantees of trustworthiness and if the court determines that (A) the statement is offered as evidence of a material fact; (B) the statement is more probative on the point for which it is offered than any other evidence the proponent can procure through reasonable efforts; and (C) the general purposes of these rules and the interests of justice will best be served by admission of the statement into evidence.

The House bill eliminated a similar, but broader, provision because of the conviction that such a provision injected too much uncertainty into the law of evidence regarding hearsay and impaired the ability of a litigant to prepare adequately for trial.

The Conference adopts the Senate amendment with an amendment that provides that a party intending to request the court to use a statement under this provision must notify any adverse party of this intention as well as of the particulars of the statement, including the name and address of the declarant. This notice must be given sufficiently in advance of the trial or hearing to provide any adverse party with a fair opportunity to prepare to contest the use of the statement. House Report No. 93-1597.

1987 Amendment
The amendments are technical. No substantive change is intended.

1997 Amendment

The contents of Rule 803(24) and Rule 804(b)(5) have been combined and transferred to a new Rule 807. This was done to facilitate additions to Rules 803 and 804. No change in meaning is intended.

GAP Report on Rule 803. The words "Transferred to Rule 807" were substituted for "Abrogated."

2000 Amendment
The amendment provides that the foundation requirements of Rule 803(6) can be satisfied under certain circumstances without the expense and inconvenience of producing time-consuming foundation witnesses. Under current law, courts have generally required foundation witnesses to testify. See, e.g., Tongil Co., Ltd. v. Hyundai Merchant Marine Corp., 968 F.2d 999 (9th Cir. 1992) (reversing a judgment based on business records where a qualified person filed an affidavit but did not testify). Protections are provided by the authentication requirements of Rule 902(11) for domestic records, Rule 902(12) for foreign records in civil cases, and 18 U.S.C. § 3505 for foreign records in criminal cases.

GAP Report--Proposed Amendment to Rule 803(6)

The Committee made no changes to the published draft of the proposed amendment to Evidence Rule 803(6).

2011 Amendments
The language of Rule 803 has been amended as part of the restyling of the Evidence Rules to make them more easily understood and to make style and terminology consistent throughout the rules. These changes are intended to be stylistic only. There is no intent to change any result in any ruling on evidence admissibility.

Rule 804. Exceptions to the Rule Against Hearsay--When the Declarant Is Unavailable as a Witness

(a) Criteria for Being Unavailable. A declarant is considered to be unavailable as a witness if the declarant:

(1) is exempted from testifying about the subject matter of the declarant's statement because the court rules that a privilege applies;

(2) refuses to testify about the subject matter despite a court order to do so;

(3) testifies to not remembering the subject matter;

(4) cannot be present or testify at the trial or hearing because of death or a then-existing infirmity, physical illness, or mental illness; or

(5) is absent from the trial or hearing and the statement's proponent has not been able, by process or other reasonable means, to procure:

(A) the declarant's attendance, in the case of a hearsay exception under Rule 804(b)(1) or (6); or

(B) the declarant's attendance or testimony, in the case of a hearsay exception under Rule 804(b)(2), (3), or (4).

But this subdivision (a) does not apply if the statement's proponent procured or wrongfully caused the declarant's unavailability as a witness in order to prevent the declarant from attending or testifying.

(b) The Exceptions. The following are not excluded by the rule against hearsay if the declarant is unavailable as a witness:

(1) Former Testimony. Testimony that:

(A) was given as a witness at a trial, hearing, or lawful deposition, whether given during the current proceeding or a different one; and

(B) is now offered against a party who had--or, in a civil case, whose predecessor in interest had--an opportunity and similar motive to develop it by direct, cross-, or redirect examination.

(2) Statement Under the Belief of Imminent Death. In a prosecution for homicide or in a civil case, a statement that the declarant, while believing the declarant's death to be imminent, made about its cause or circumstances.

(3) Statement Against Interest. A statement that:

(A) a reasonable person in the declarant's position would have made only if the person believed it to be true because, when made, it was so contrary to the declarant's proprietary or pecuniary interest or had so great a tendency to invalidate the declarant's claim against someone else or to expose the declarant to civil or criminal liability; and

(B) is supported by corroborating circumstances that clearly indicate its trustworthiness, if it is offered in a criminal case as one that tends to expose the declarant to criminal liability.

(4) Statement of Personal or Family History. A statement about:

(A) the declarant's own birth, adoption, legitimacy, ancestry, marriage, divorce, relationship by blood, adoption, or marriage, or similar facts of personal or family history, even though the declarant had no way of acquiring personal knowledge about that fact; or

(B) another person concerning any of these facts, as well as death, if the declarant was related to the person by blood, adoption, or marriage or was so intimately associated with the person's family that the declarant's information is likely to be accurate.

(5) [Other Exceptions.] [Transferred to Rule 807.]

(6) Statement Offered Against a Party That Wrongfully Caused the Declarant's Unavailability. A statement offered against a party that wrongfully caused--or acquiesced in wrongfully causing--the declarant's unavailability as a witness, and did so intending that result.

Credits

(Pub.L. 93-595, § 1, Jan. 2, 1975, 88 Stat. 1942; Pub.L. 94-149, § 1(12), (13), Dec. 12, 1975, 89 Stat. 806; Mar. 2, 1987, eff. Oct. 1, 1987; Pub.L. 100-690, Title VII, § 7075(b), Nov. 18, 1988, 102 Stat. 4405; Apr. 11, 1997, eff. Dec. 1, 1997; Apr. 28, 2010, eff. Dec. 1, 2010; Apr. 26, 2011, eff. Dec. 1, 2011.)

Editors' Notes

ADVISORY COMMITTEE NOTES

1972 Proposed Rules

As to firsthand knowledge on the part of hearsay declarants, see the introductory portion of the Advisory Committee's Note to Rule 803.

Note to Subdivision (a). The definition of unavailability implements the division of hearsay exceptions into two categories by Rules 803 and 804(b).

At common law the unavailability requirement was evolved in connection with particular hearsay exceptions rather than along general lines. For example, see the separate explications of unavailability in relation to former testimony, declarations against interest, and statements of pedigree, separately developed in McCormick §§ 234, 257, and 297. However, no reason is apparent for making distinctions as to what satisfies unavailability for the different exceptions. The treatment in the rule is therefore uniform although differences in the range of process for witnesses between civil and criminal cases will lead to a less exacting requirement under item (5). See Rule 45(e) of the Federal Rules of Civil Procedure and Rule 17(e) of the Federal Rules of Criminal Procedure.

Five instances of unavailability are specified:

(1) Substantial authority supports the position that exercise of a claim of privilege by the declarant satisfies the requirement of unavailability (usually in connection with former testimony). Wyatt v. State, 35 Ala.App. 147, 46 So.2d 837 (1950); State v. Stewart, 85 Kan. 404, 116 P. 489 (1911); Annot., 45 A.L.R.2d 1354; Uniform Rule 62(7)(a); California Evidence Code § 240(a)(1); Kansas Code of Civil Procedure § 60-459(g)(1). A ruling by the judge is required, which clearly implies that an actual claim of privilege must be made.

(2) A witness is rendered unavailable if he simply refuses to testify concerning the subject matter of his statement despite judicial pressures to do so, a position supported by similar considerations of practicality. Johnson v. People, 152 Colo. 586, 384 P.2d 454 (1963); People v. Pickett, 339 Mich. 294, 63 N.W.2d 681, 45 A.L.R.2d 1341 (1954). Contra, Pleau v. State, 255 Wis. 362, 38 N.W.2d 496 (1949).

(3) The position that a claimed lack of memory by the witness of the subject matter of his statement constitutes unavailability likewise finds support in the cases, though not without dissent. McCormick § 234, p. 494. If the claim is successful, the practical effect is to put the testimony beyond reach, as in the other instances. In this instance, however, it will be noted that the lack of memory must be established by the testimony of the witness himself, which clearly contemplates his production and subjection to cross-examination.

(4) Death and infirmity find general recognition as grounds. McCormick §§ 234, 257, 297; Uniform Rule 62(7)(c); California Evidence Code § 240(a)(3); Kansas Code of Civil Procedure § 60-459(g)(3); New Jersey Evidence Rule 62(6)(c). See also the provisions on use of depositions in Rule 32(a)(3) of the Federal Rules of Civil Procedure and Rule 15(e) of the Federal Rules of Criminal Procedure.

(5) Absence from the hearing coupled with inability to compel attendance by process or other reasonable means also satisfies the requirement. McCormick § 234; Uniform Rule 62(7)(d) and (e); California Evidence Code § 240(a)(4) and (5); Kansas Code of Civil Procedure § 60-459(g)(4) and (5); New Jersey Rule 62(6)(b) and (d). See the discussion of procuring attendance of witnesses who are nonresidents or in custody in Barber v. Page, 390 U.S. 719, 88 S.Ct. 1318, 20 L.Ed.2d 255 (1968).

If the conditions otherwise constituting unavailability result from the procurement or wrongdoing of the proponent of the statement, the requirement is not satisfied. The rule contains no requirement that an attempt be made to take the deposition of a declarant.

Note to Subdivision (b). Rule 803, supra, is based upon the assumption that a hearsay statement falling within one of its exceptions possesses qualities which justify the conclusion that whether the declarant is available or unavailable is not a relevant factor in determining admissibility. The instant rule proceeds upon a different theory: hearsay which admittedly is not equal in quality to testimony of the declarant on the stand may nevertheless be admitted if the declarant is unavailable and if his statement meets a specified standard. The rule expresses preferences: testimony given on the stand in person is preferred over hearsay, and hearsay, if of the specified quality, is preferred over complete loss of the evidence of the declarant. The exceptions evolved at common law with respect to declarations of unavailable declarants furnish the basis for the exceptions enumerated in the proposal. The term "unavailable" is defined in subdivision (a).

Exception (1). Former testimony does not rely upon some set of circumstances to substitute for oath and cross-examination, since both oath and opportunity to cross-examine were present in fact. The only missing one of the ideal conditions for the giving of testimony is the presence of trier and opponent ("demeanor evidence"). This is lacking with all hearsay exceptions. Hence it may be argued that former testimony is the strongest hearsay and should be included under Rule 803, supra. However, opportunity to observe demeanor is what in a large measure confers depth and meaning upon oath and cross-examination. Thus in cases under Rule 803 demeanor lacks the significance which it possesses with respect to testimony. In any event, the tradition, founded in experience, uniformly favors production of the witness if he is available. The exception indicates continuation of the policy. This preference for the presence of the witness is apparent also in rules and statutes on the use of depositions, which deal with substantially the same problem.

Under the exception, the testimony may be offered (1) against the party against whom it was previously offered or (2) against the party by whom it was previously offered. In each instance the question resolves itself into whether fairness allows imposing, upon the party against whom now offered, the handling of the witness of the earlier occasion. (1) If the party against whom now offered is the one against whom the testimony was offered previously, no unfairness is apparent in requiring him to accept his own prior conduct of cross-examination or decision not to cross-examine. Only demeanor has been lost, and that is inherent in the situation. (2) If the party against whom now offered is the one by whom the testimony was offered previously, a satisfactory answer becomes somewhat more difficult. One possibility is to proceed somewhat along the line of an adoptive admission, i.e. by offering the testimony proponent in effect adopts it. However, this theory savors of discarded concepts of witnesses' belonging to a party, of litigants' ability to pick and choose witnesses, and of vouching for one's own witnesses. Cf. McCormick § 246, pp. 526-527; 4 Wigmore § 1075. A more direct and acceptable approach is simply to recognize direct and redirect examination of one's own witness as the equivalent of cross-examining an opponent's witness. Falknor, Former Testimony and the Uniform Rules: A Comment, 38 N.Y.U.L.Rev. 651, n. 1 (1963); McCormick § 231, p. 483. See also 5 Wigmore § 1389. Allowable techniques for dealing with hostile, double-crossing, forgetful, and mentally deficient witnesses leave no substance to a claim that one could not adequately develop his own witness at the former hearing. An even less appealing argument is presented when failure to develop fully was the result of a deliberate choice.

The common law did not limit the admissibility of former testimony to that given in an earlier trial of the same case, although it did require identity of issues as a means of insuring that the former handling of the witness was the equivalent of what would now be done if the opportunity were presented. Modern decisions reduce the requirement to "substantial" identity. McCormick § 233. Since identity of issues is significant only in that it bears on motive and interest in developing fully the testimony of the witness, expressing the matter in the latter terms is preferable. Id. Testimony given at a preliminary hearing was held in California v. Green, 399 U.S. 149, 90 S.Ct. 1930, 26 L.Ed.2d 489 (1970), to satisfy confrontation requirements in this respect.

As a further assurance of fairness in thrusting upon a party the prior handling of the witness, the common law also insisted upon identity of parties, deviating only to the extent of allowing substitution of successors in a narrowly construed privity. Mutuality as an aspect of identity is now generally discredited, and the requirement of identity of the offering party disappears except as it might affect motive to develop the testimony. Falknor, supra, at 652; McCormick § 232, pp.

487-488. The question remains whether strict identity, or privity, should continue as a requirement with respect to the party against whom offered. The rule departs to the extent of allowing substitution of one with the right and opportunity to develop the testimony with similar motive and interest. This position is supported by modern decisions. McCormick § 232, pp. 489-490; 5 Wigmore § 1388.

Provisions of the same tenor will be found in Uniform Rule 63(3)(b); California Evidence Code §§ 1290-1292; Kansas Code of Civil Procedure § 60-460(c)(2); New Jersey Evidence Rule 63(3). Unlike the rule, the latter three provide either that former testimony is not admissible if the right of confrontation is denied or that it is not admissible if the accused was not a party to the prior hearing. The genesis of these limitations is a caveat in Uniform Rule 63(3) Comment that use of former testimony against an accused may violate his right of confrontation. Mattox v. United States, 156 U.S. 237, 15 S.Ct. 337, 39 L.Ed. 409 (1895), held that the right was not violated by the Government's use, on a retrial of the same case, of testimony given at the first trial by two witnesses since deceased. The decision leaves open the questions (1) whether direct and redirect are equivalent to cross-examination for purposes of confrontation, (2) whether testimony given in a different proceeding is acceptable, and (3) whether the accused must himself have been a party to the earlier proceeding or whether a similarly situated person will serve the purpose. Professor Falknor concluded that, if a dying declaration untested by cross-examination is constitutionally admissible, former testimony tested by the cross-examination of one similarly situated does not offend against confrontation. Falknor, supra, at 659-660. The constitutional acceptability of dying declarations has often been conceded. Mattox v. United States, 156 U.S. 237, 243, 15 S.Ct. 337, 39 L.Ed. 409 (1895); Kirby v. United States, 174 U.S. 47, 61, 19 S.Ct. 574, 43 L.Ed. 890 (1899); Pointer v. Texas, 380 U.S. 400, 407, 85 S.Ct. 1065, 13 L.Ed.2d 923 (1965).

Exception (2). The exception is the familiar dying declaration of the common law, expanded somewhat beyond its traditionally narrow limits. While the original religious justification for the exception may have lost its conviction for some persons over the years, it can scarcely be doubted that powerful psychological pressures are present. See 5 Wigmore § 1443 and the classic statement of Chief Baron Eyre in Rex v. Woodcock, 1 Leach 500, 502, 168 Eng.Rep. 352, 353 (K.B.1789).

The common law required that the statement be that of the victim, offered in a prosecution for criminal homicide. Thus declarations by victims in prosecutions for other crimes, e.g. a declaration by a rape victim who dies in childbirth, and all declarations in civil cases were outside the scope of the exception. An occasional statute has removed these restrictions, as in Colo.R.S. § 52-1-20, or has expanded the area of offenses to include abortions, 5 Wigmore § 1432, p. 224, n. 4. Kansas by decision extended the exception to civil cases. Thurston v. Fritz, 91 Kan. 468, 138 P. 625 (1914). While the common law exception no doubt originated as a result of the exceptional need for the evidence in homicide cases, the theory of admissibility applies equally in civil cases and in prosecutions for crimes other than homicide. The same considerations suggest abandonment of the limitation to circumstances attending the event in question, yet when the statement deals with matters other than the supposed death, its influence is believed to be sufficiently attenuated to justify the limitation. Unavailability is not limited to death. See subdivision (a) of this rule. Any problem as to declarations phrased in terms of opinion is laid at rest by Rule 701, and continuation of a requirement of firsthand knowledge is assured by Rule 602.

Comparable provisions are found in Uniform Rule 63(5); California Evidence Code § 1242; Kansas Code of Civil Procedure § 60-460(e); New Jersey Evidence Rule 63(5).

Exception (3). The circumstantial guaranty of reliability for declarations against interest is the assumption that persons do not make statements which are damaging to themselves unless satisfied for good reason that they are true. Hileman v. Northwest Engineering Co., 346 F.2d 668 (6th Cir. 1965). If the statement is that of a party, offered by his opponent, it comes in as an admission, Rule 803(d)(2) [sic; probably should be "Rule 801(d)(2)"], and there is no occasion to inquire whether it is against interest, this not being a condition precedent to admissibility of admissions by opponents.

The common law required that the interest declared against be pecuniary or proprietary but within this limitation demonstrated striking ingenuity in discovering an against-interest aspect. Higham v.

Ridgway, 10 East 109, 103 Eng.Rep. 717 (K.B.1808); Reg. v. Overseers of Birmingham, 1 B. & S. 763, 121 Eng.Rep. 897 (Q.B.1861); McCormick, § 256, p. 551, nn. 2 and 3.

The exception discards the common law limitation and expands to the full logical limit. One result is to remove doubt as to the admissibility of declarations tending to establish a tort liability against the declarant or to extinguish one which might be asserted by him, in accordance with the trend of the decisions in this country. McCormick § 254, pp. 548-549. Another is to allow statements tending to expose declarant to hatred, ridicule, or disgrace, the motivation here being considered to be as strong as when financial interests are at stake. McCormick § 255, p. 551. And finally, exposure to criminal liability satisfies the against-interest requirement. The refusal of the common law to concede the adequacy of a penal interest was no doubt indefensible in logic, see the dissent of Mr. Justice Holmes in Donnelly v. United States, 228 U.S. 243, 33 S.Ct. 449, 57 L.Ed. 820 (1913), but one senses in the decisions a distrust of evidence of confessions by third persons offered to exculpate the accused arising from suspicions of fabrication either of the fact of the making of the confession or in its contents, enhanced in either instance by the required unavailability of the declarant. Nevertheless, an increasing amount of decisional law recognizes exposure to punishment for crime as a sufficient stake. People v. Spriggs, 60 Cal.2d 868, 36 Cal.Rptr. 841, 389 P.2d 377 (1964); Sutter v. Easterly, 354 Mo. 282, 189 S.W.2d 284 (1945); Band's Refuse Removal, Inc. v. Fairlawn Borough, 62 N.J.Super. 522, 163 A.2d 465 (1960); Newberry v. Commonwealth, 191 Va. 445, 61 S.E.2d 318 (1950); Annot., 162 A.L.R. 446. The requirement of corroboration is included in the rule in order to effect an accommodation between these competing considerations. When the statement is offered by the accused by way of exculpation, the resulting situation is not adapted to control by rulings as to the weight of the evidence, and hence the provision is cast in terms of a requirement preliminary to admissibility. Cf. Rule 406(a). The requirement of corroboration should be construed in such a manner as to effectuate its purpose of circumventing fabrication.

Ordinarily the third-party confession is thought of in terms of exculpating the accused, but this is by no means always or necessarily the case: it may include statements implicating him, and under the general theory of declarations against interest they would be admissible as related statements. Douglas v. Alabama, 380 U.S. 415, 85 S.Ct. 1074, 13 L.Ed.2d 934 (1965), and Bruton v. United States, 389 U.S. 818, 88 S.Ct. 126, 19 L.Ed.2d 70 (1968), both involved confessions by codefendants which implicated the accused. While the confession was not actually offered in evidence in Douglas, the procedure followed effectively put it before the jury, which the Court ruled to be error. Whether the confession might have been admissible as a declaration against penal interest was not considered or discussed. Bruton assumed the inadmissibility, as against the accused, of the implicating confession of his codefendant, and centered upon the question of the effectiveness of a limiting instruction. These decisions, however, by no means require that all statements implicating another person be excluded from the category of declarations against interest. Whether a statement is in fact against interest must be determined from the circumstances of each case. Thus a statement admitting guilt and implicating another person, made while in custody, may well be motivated by a desire to curry favor with the authorities and hence fail to qualify as against interest. See the dissenting opinion of Mr. Justice White in Bruton. On the other hand, the same words spoken under different circumstances, e.g., to an acquaintance, would have no difficulty in qualifying. The rule does not purport to deal with questions of the right of confrontation.

The balancing of self-serving against dissenting aspects of a declaration is discussed in McCormick § 256.

For comparable provisions, see Uniform Rule 63(10); California Evidence Code § 1230; Kansas Code of Civil Procedure § 60-460(j); New Jersey Evidence Rule 63(10).

Exception (4). The general common law requirement that a declaration in this area must have been made ante litem motam has been dropped, as bearing more appropriately on weight than admissibility. See 5 Wigmore § 1483. Item (i)[(A)] specifically disclaims any need of firsthand knowledge respecting declarant's own personal history. In some instances it is self-evident (marriage) and in others impossible and traditionally not required (date of birth). Item (ii)[(B)] deals with declarations concerning the history of another person. As at common law, declarant is qualified if related by blood or marriage. 5 Wigmore § 1489. In addition, and contrary to the common law, declarant qualifies by virtue of intimate association with the family. Id., § 1487. The requirement sometimes encountered that when the subject of the statement is the relationship between two other persons the declarant must qualify as to both is omitted. Relationship is reciprocal. Id., § 1491.

For comparable provisions, see Uniform Rule 63(23), (24), (25); California Evidence Code §§ 1310, 1311; Kansas Code of Civil Procedure § 60-460(u), (v), (w); New Jersey Evidence Rules 63-23), 63(24), 63(25).

1974 Enactment

Note to Subdivision (a)(3). Rule 804(a)(3) was approved in the form submitted by the Court. However, the Committee intends no change in existing federal law under which the court may choose to disbelieve the declarant's testimony as to his lack of memory. See United States v. Insana, 423 F.2d 1165, 1169-1170 (2nd Cir.), cert. denied, 400 U.S. 841 (1970).

Note to Subdivision (a)(5). Rule 804(a)(5) as submitted to the Congress provided, as one type of situation in which a declarant would be deemed "unavailable", that he be "absent from the hearing and the proponent of his statement has been unable to procure his attendance by process or other reasonable means." The Committee amended the Rule to insert after the word "attendance" the parenthetical expression "(or, in the case of a hearsay exception under subdivision (b)(2), (3), or (4), his attendance or testimony)". The amendment is designed primarily to require that an attempt be made to depose a witness (as well as to seek his attendance) as a precondition to the witness being deemed unavailable. The Committee, however, recognized the propriety of an exception to this additional requirement when it is the declarant's former testimony that is sought to be admitted under subdivision (b)(1).

Note to Subdivision (b)(1). Rule 804(b)(1) as submitted by the Court allowed prior testimony of an unavailable witness to be admissible if the party against whom it is offered or a person "with motive and interest similar" to his had an opportunity to examine the witness. The Committee considered that it is generally unfair to impose upon the party against whom the hearsay evidence is being offered responsibility for the manner in which the witness was previously handled by another party. The sole exception to this, in the Committee's view, is when a party's predecessor in interest in a civil action or proceeding had an opportunity and similar motive to examine the witness. The Committee amended the Rule to reflect these policy determinations.

Note to Subdivision (b)(2). Rule 804(b)(3) as submitted by the Court (now Rule 804(b)(2) in the bill) proposed to expand the traditional scope of the dying declaration exception (i.e. a statement of the victim in a homicide case as to the cause or circumstances of his believed imminent death) to allow such statements in all criminal and civil cases. The Committee did not consider dying declarations as among the most reliable forms of hearsay. Consequently, it amended the provision to limit their admissibility in criminal cases to homicide prosecutions, where exceptional need for the evidence is present. This is existing law. At the same time, the Committee approved the expansion to civil actions and proceedings where the stakes do not involve possible imprisonment, although noting that this could lead to forum shopping in some instances.

Note to Subdivision (b)(3). Rule 804(b)(4) as submitted by the Court (now Rule 804(b)(3) in the bill) provided as follows:

Statement against interest.--A statement which was at the time of its making so far contrary to the declarant's pecuniary or proprietary interest or so far tended to subject him to civil or criminal liability or to render invalid a claim by him against another or to make him an object of hatred, ridicule, or disgrace, that a reasonable man in his position would not have made the statement unless he believed it to be true. A statement tending to exculpate the accused is not admissible unless corroborated.

The Committee determined to retain the traditional hearsay exception for statements against pecuniary or proprietary interest. However, it deemed the Court's additional references to statements tending to subject a declarant to civil liability or to render invalid a claim by him against another to be redundant as included within the scope of the reference to statements against pecuniary or proprietary interest. See Gichner v. Antonio Triano Tile and Marble Co., 410 F.2d 238 (D.C.Cir.1968). Those additional references were accordingly deleted.

The Court's Rule also proposed to expand the hearsay limitation from its present federal limitation to include statements subjecting the declarant to criminal liability and statements tending to make him an object of hatred, ridicule, or disgrace. The Committee eliminated the latter category from the subdivision as lacking sufficient guarantees of reliability. See United States v. Dovico, 380 F.2d 325, 327 nn. 2, 4 (2nd Cir.), cert. denied, 389 U.S. 944 (1967). As for statements against penal interest, the Committee shared the view of the Court that some such statements do possess adequate assurances of reliability and should be admissible. It believed, however, as did the Court, that statements of this type tending to exculpate the accused are more suspect and so should have their admissibility conditioned upon some further provision insuring trustworthiness. The proposal in the Court Rule to add a requirement of simple corroboration was, however, deemed ineffective to accomplish this purpose since the accused's own testimony might suffice while not necessarily increasing the reliability of the hearsay statement. The Committee settled upon the language "unless corroborating circumstances clearly indicate the trustworthiness of the statement" as affording a proper standard and degree of discretion. It was contemplated that the result in such cases as Donnelly v. United States, 228 U.S. 243 (1912), where the circumstances plainly indicated reliability, would be changed. The Committee also added to the Rule the final sentence from the 1971 Advisory Committee draft, designed to codify the doctrine of Bruton v. United States, 391 U.S. 123 (1968). The Committee does not intend to affect the existing exception to the Bruton principle where the codefendant takes the stand and is subject to cross-examination, but believed there was no need to make specific provision for this situation in the Rule, since in that event the declarant would not be "unavailable". House Report No. 93-650.

Note to Subdivision (a)(5). Subdivision (a) of rule 804 as submitted by the Supreme Court defined the conditions under which a witness was considered to be unavailable. It was amended in the House.

The purpose of the amendment, according to the report of the House Committee on the Judiciary, is "primarily to require that an attempt be made to depose a witness (as well as to seek his attendance) as a precondition to the witness being unavailable."

Under the House amendment, before a witness is declared unavailable, a party must try to depose a witness (declarant) with respect to dying declarations, declarations against interest, and declarations of pedigree. None of these situations would seem to warrant this needless, impractical and highly restrictive complication. A good case can be made for eliminating the unavailability requirement entirely for declarations against interest cases. [Uniform rule 63(10); Kan.Stat.Anno. 60-460(j); 2A N.J.Stats.Anno. 84-63(10).]

In dying declaration cases, the declarant will usually, though not necessarily, be deceased at the time of trial. Pedigree statements which are admittedly and necessarily based largely on word of mouth are not greatly fortified by a deposition requirement.

Depositions are expensive and time-consuming. In any event, deposition procedures are available to those who wish to resort to them. Moreover, the deposition procedures of the Civil Rules and Criminal Rules are only imperfectly adapted to implementing the amendment. No purpose is served unless the deposition, if taken, may be used in evidence. Under Civil Rule (a)(3) the Criminal Rule 15(e), a deposition, though taken, may not be admissible, and under Criminal Rule 15(a) substantial obstacles exist in the way of even taking a deposition.

For these reasons, the committee deleted the House amendment.

The committee understands that the rule as to unavailability, as explained by the Advisory Committee "contains no requirement that an attempt be made to take the deposition of a declarant." In reflecting the committee's judgment, the statement is accurate insofar as it goes. Where, however, the proponent of the statement, with knowledge of the existence of the statement, fails to confront the declarant with the statement at the taking of the deposition, then the proponent should not, in fairness, be permitted to treat the declarant as "unavailable" simply because the declarant was not amenable to process compelling his attendance at trial. The committee does not consider it necessary to amend the rule to this effect because such a situation abuses, not conforms to, the rule. Fairness would preclude a person from introducing a hearsay statement on a particular issue if the person taking the deposition was aware of the issue at the time of the deposition but failed to depose the unavailable witness on that issue.

Note to Subdivision (b)(1). Former testimony.--Rule 804(b)(1) as submitted by the Court allowed prior testimony of an unavailable witness to be admissible if the party against whom it is offered or a person "with motive and interest similar" to his had an opportunity to examine the witness.

The House amended the rule to apply only to a party's predecessor in interest. Although the committee recognizes considerable merit to the rule submitted by the Supreme Court, a position which has been advocated by many scholars and judges, we have concluded that the difference between the two versions is not great and we accept the House amendment.

Note to Subdivision (b)(3). The rule defines those statements which are considered to be against interest and thus of sufficient trustworthiness to be admissible even though hearsay. With regard to the type of interest declared against, the version submitted by the Supreme Court included inter alia, statements tending to subject a declarant to civil liability or to invalidate a claim by him against another. The House struck these provisions as redundant. In view of the conflicting case law construing pecuniary or proprietary interests narrowly so as to exclude, e.g., tort cases, this deletion could be misconstrued.

Three States which have recently codified their rules of evidence have followed the Supreme Court's version of this rule, i.e., that a statement is against interest if it tends to subject a declarant to civil liability. [Nev.Rev.Stats. § 51.345; N.Mex.Stats. (1973 Supp.) § 20-4-804(4); West's Wis.Stats.Anno. (1973 Supp.) § 908.045(4).]

The committee believes that the reference to statements tending to subject a person to civil liability constitutes a desirable clarification of the scope of the rule. Therefore, we have reinstated the Supreme Court language on this matter.

The Court rule also proposed to expand the hearsay limitation from its present federal limitation to include statements subjecting the declarant to statements tending to make him an object of hatred, ridicule, or disgrace. The House eliminated the latter category from the subdivision as lacking sufficient guarantees of reliability. Although there is considerable support for the admissibility of such statements (all three of the State rules referred to supra, would admit such statements), we accept the deletion by the House.

The House amended this exception to add a sentence making inadmissible a statement or confession offered against the accused in a criminal case, made by a codefendant or other person implicating both himself and the accused. The sentence was added to codify the constitutional principle announced in Bruton v. United States, 391 U.S. 123 (1968). Bruton held that the admission of the extrajudicial hearsay statement of one codefendant inculpating a second codefendant violated the confrontation clause of the sixth amendment.

The committee decided to delete this provision because the basic approach of the rules is to avoid codifying, or attempting to codify, constitutional evidentiary principles, such as the fifth amendment's right against self-incrimination and, here, the sixth amendment's right of confrontation. Codification of a constitutional principle is unnecessary and, where the principle is under development, often unwise. Furthermore, the House provision does not appear to recognize the exceptions to the Bruton rule, e.g. where the codefendant takes the stand and is subject to cross examination; where the accused confessed, see United States v. Mancusi, 404 F.2d 296 (2d Cir. 1968), cert. denied 397 U.S. 942 (1907); where the accused was placed at the scene of the crime, see United States v. Zelker, 452 F.2d 1009 (2d Cir.1971). For these reasons, the committee decided to delete this provision.

Note to Subdivision (b)(5). See Note to Paragraph (24), Notes of Committee on the Judiciary, Senate Report No. 93-1277, set out as a note under rule 803 of these rules. Senate Report No. 93-1277.

Rule 804 defines what hearsay statements are admissible in evidence if the declarant is unavailable as a witness. The Senate amendments make four changes in the rule.

Note to Subdivision (a)(5). Subsection (a) defines the term "unavailability as a witness". The House bill provides in subsection (a)(5) that the party who desires to use the statement must be unable to procure the declarant's attendance by process or other reasonable means. In the case of dying declarations, statements against interest and statements of personal or family history, the House bill requires that the proponent must also be unable to procure the declarant's testimony (such as by deposition or interrogatories) by process or other reasonable means. The Senate amendment eliminates this latter provision.

The Conference adopts the provision contained in the House bill.

Note to Subdivision (b)(3). The Senate amendment to subsection (b)(3) provides that a statement is against interest and not excluded by the hearsay rule when the declarant is unavailable as a witness, if the statement tends to subject a person to civil or criminal liability or renders invalid a claim by him against another. The House bill did not refer specifically to civil liability and to rendering invalid a claim against another. The Senate amendment also deletes from the House bill the provision that subsection (b)(3) does not apply to a statement or confession, made by a codefendant or another, which implicates the accused and the person who made the statement, when that statement or confession is offered against the accused in a criminal case.

The Conference adopts the Senate amendment. The Conferees intend to include within the purview of this rule, statements subjecting a person to civil liability and statements rendering claims invalid. The Conferees agree to delete the provision regarding statements by a codefendant, thereby reflecting the general approach in the Rules of Evidence to avoid attempting to codify constitutional evidentiary principles.

Note to Subdivision (b)(5). The Senate amendment adds a new subsection, (b)(6) [now (b)(5)], which makes admissible a hearsay statement not specifically covered by any of the five previous subsections, if the statement has equivalent circumstantial guarantees of trustworthiness and if the court determines that (A) the statement is offered as evidence of a material fact; (B) the statement is more probative on the point for which it is offered than any other evidence the proponent can procure through reasonable efforts; and (C) the general purposes of these rules and the interests of justice will best be served by admission of the statement into evidence.

The House bill eliminated a similar, but broader, provision because of the conviction that such a provision injected too much uncertainty into the law of evidence regarding hearsay and impaired the ability of a litigant to prepare adequately for trial.

The Conference adopts the Senate amendment with an amendment that renumbers this subsection and provides that a party intending to request the court to use a statement under this provision must notify any adverse party of this intention as well as of the particulars of the statement, including the name and address of the declarant. This notice must be given sufficiently in advance of the trial or hearing to provide any adverse party with a fair opportunity to prepare to contest the use of the statement. House Report No. 93-1597.

1987 Amendments
The amendments are technical. No substantive change is intended.

1997 Amendments

Subdivision (b)(5). The contents of Rule 803(24) and Rule 804(b)(5) have been combined and transferred to a new Rule 807. This was done to facilitate additions to Rules 803 and 804. No change in meaning is intended.

Subdivision (b)(6). Rule 804(b)(6) has been added to provide that a party forfeits the right to object on hearsay grounds to the admission of a declarant's prior statement when the party's deliberate wrongdoing or acquiescence therein procured the unavailability of the declarant as a witness. This recognizes the need for a prophylactic rule to deal with abhorrent behavior "which strikes at the heart of the system of justice itself." United States v. Mastrangelo, 693 F.2d 269, 273 (2d Cir.1982), cert. denied, 467 U.S. 1204 (1984). The wrongdoing need not consist of a criminal act. The rule applies to all parties, including the government.

Every circuit that has resolved the question has recognized the principle of forfeiture by misconduct, although the tests for determining whether there is a forfeiture have varied. See, e.g., United States v. Aguiar, 975 F.2d 45, 47 (2d Cir.1992); United States v. Potamitis, 739 F.2d 784, 789 (2d Cir.), cert. denied, 469 U.S. 918 (1984); Steele v. Taylor, 684 F.2d 1193, 1199 (6th Cir. 1982), cert. denied, 460 U.S. 1053 (1983); United States v. Balano, 618 F.2d 624, 629 (10th Cir. 1979), cert. denied, 449 U.S. 840 (1980); United States v. Carlson, 547 F.2d 1346, 1358-59 (8th Cir.), cert. denied, 431 U.S. 914 (1977). The foregoing cases apply a preponderance of the evidence standard. Contra United States v. Thevis, 665 F.2d 616, 631 (5th Cir.) (clear and convincing standard), cert. denied, 459 U.S. 825 (1982). The usual Rule 104(a) preponderance of the evidence standard has been adopted in light of the behavior the new Rule 804(b)(6) seeks to discourage.

GAP Report on Rule 804(b)(5). The words "Transferred to Rule 807" were substituted for "Abrogated".

GAP Report on Rule 804(b)(6). The title of the rule was changed to "Forfeiture by wrongdoing." The word "who" in line 24 was changed to "that" to indicate that the rule is potentially applicable against the government. Two sentences were added to the first paragraph of the committee note to clarify that the wrongdoing need not be criminal in nature, and to indicate the rule's potential applicability to the government. The word "forfeiture" was substituted for "waiver" in the note.

2010 Amendments

Subdivision (b)(3). Rule 804(b)(3) has been amended to provide that the corroborating circumstances requirement applies to all declarations against penal interest offered in criminal cases. A number of courts have applied the corroborating circumstances requirement to declarations against penal interest offered by the prosecution, even though the text of the Rule did not so provide. See, e.g., United States v. Alvarez, 584 F.2d 694, 701 (5th Cir. 1978) ("by transplanting the language governing exculpatory statements onto the analysis for admitting inculpatory hearsay, a unitary standard is derived which offers the most workable basis for applying Rule 804(b)(3)"); United States v. Shukri, 207 F.3d 412 (7th Cir. 2000) (requiring corroborating circumstances for against-penal-interest statements offered by the government). A unitary approach to declarations against penal interest assures both the prosecution and the accused that the Rule will not be abused and that only reliable hearsay statements will be admitted under the exception.

All other changes to the structure and wording of the Rule are intended to be stylistic only. There is no intent to change any other result in any ruling on evidence admissibility.

The amendment does not address the use of the corroborating circumstances for declarations against penal interest offered in civil cases.

In assessing whether corroborating circumstances exist, some courts have focused on the credibility of the witness who relates the hearsay statement in court. But the credibility of the witness who relates the statement is not a proper factor for the court to consider in assessing corroborating circumstances. To base admission or exclusion of a hearsay statement on the witness's credibility would usurp the jury's role of determining the credibility of testifying witnesses.

2011 Amendments

The language of Rule 804 has been amended as part of the general restyling of the Evidence Rules to make them more easily understood and to make style and terminology consistent throughout the rules. These changes are intended to be stylistic only. There is no intent to change any result in any ruling on evidence admissibility.

No style changes were made to Rule 804(b)(3), because it was already restyled in conjunction with a substantive amendment, effective December 1, 2010.

Rule 805. Hearsay Within Hearsay

Hearsay within hearsay is not excluded by the rule against hearsay if each part of the combined statements conforms with an exception to the rule.

Credits

(Pub.L. 93-595, § 1, Jan. 2, 1975, 88 Stat. 1943; Apr. 26, 2011, eff. Dec. 1, 2011.)

Editors' Notes
ADVISORY COMMITTEE NOTES
1972 Proposed Rules
On principle it scarcely seems open to doubt that the hearsay rule should not call for exclusion of a hearsay statement which includes a further hearsay statement when both conform to the requirements of a hearsay exception. Thus a hospital record might contain an entry of the patient's age based on information furnished by his wife. The hospital record would qualify as a regular entry except that the person who furnished the information was not acting in the routine of the business. However, her statement independently qualifies as a statement of pedigree (if she is unavailable) or as a statement made for purposes of diagnosis or treatment, and hence each link in the chain falls under sufficient assurances. Or, further to illustrate, a dying declaration may incorporate a declaration against interest by another declarant. See McCormick § 290, p. 611.

2011 Amendments
The language of Rule 805 has been amended as part of the restyling of the Evidence Rules to make them more easily understood and to make style and terminology consistent throughout the rules. These changes are intended to be stylistic only. There is no intent to change any result in any ruling on evidence admissibility.

Rule 806. Attacking and Supporting the Declarant's Credibility

When a hearsay statement--or a statement described in Rule 801(d)(2)(C), (D), or (E)--has been admitted in evidence, the declarant's credibility may be attacked, and then supported, by any evidence that would be admissible for those purposes if the declarant had testified as a witness. The court may admit evidence of the declarant's inconsistent statement or conduct, regardless of when it occurred or whether the declarant had an opportunity to explain or deny it. If the party against whom the statement was admitted calls the declarant as a witness, the party may examine the declarant on the statement as if on cross-examination.

Credits

(Pub.L. 93-595, § 1, Jan. 2, 1975, 88 Stat. 1943; Mar. 2, 1987, eff. Oct. 1, 1987; Apr. 11, 1997, eff. Dec. 1, 1997; Apr. 26, 2011, eff. Dec. 1, 2011.)

Editors' Notes

ADVISORY COMMITTEE NOTES
1972 Proposed Rules

The declarant of a hearsay statement which is admitted in evidence is in effect a witness. His credibility should in fairness be subject to impeachment and support as though he had in fact testified. See Rules 608 and 609. There are however, some special aspects of the impeaching of a hearsay declarant which require consideration. These special aspects center upon impeachment by inconsistent statement, arise from factual differences which exist between the use of hearsay and an actual witness and also between various kinds of hearsay, and involve the question of applying to declarants the general rule disallowing evidence of an inconsistent statement to impeach a witness unless he is afforded an opportunity to deny or explain. See Rule 613(b).

The principal difference between using hearsay and an actual witness is that the inconsistent statement will in the case of the witness almost inevitably of necessity in the nature of things be a prior statement, which it is entirely possible and feasible to call to his attention, while in the case of hearsay the inconsistent statement may well be a subsequent one, which practically precludes calling it to the attention of the declarant. The result of insisting upon observation of this impossible requirement in the hearsay situation is to deny the opponent, already barred from cross-examination, any benefit of this important technique of impeachment. The writers favor allowing the subsequent statement. McCormick § 37, p. 69; 3 Wigmore § 1033. The cases, however, are divided. Cases allowing the impeachment include People v. Collup, 27 Cal.2d 829, 167 P.2d 714 (1946); People v. Rosoto, 58 Cal.2d 304, 23 Cal.Rptr. 779, 373 P.2d 867 (1962); Carver v. United States, 164 U.S. 694, 17 S.Ct. 228, 41 L.Ed. 602 (1897). Contra, Mattox v. United States, 156 U.S. 237, 15 S.Ct. 337, 39 L.Ed. 409 (1895); People v. Hines, 284 N.Y. 93, 29 N.E.2d 483 (1940). The force of Mattox, where the hearsay was the former testimony of a deceased witness and the denial of use of a subsequent inconsistent statement was upheld, is much diminished by Carver, where the hearsay was a dying declaration and denial of use of a subsequent inconsistent statement resulted in reversal. The difference in the particular brand of hearsay seems unimportant when the inconsistent statement is a subsequent one. True, the opponent is not totally deprived of cross-examination when the hearsay is former testimony or a deposition but he is deprived of cross-examining on the statement or along lines suggested by it. Mr. Justice Shiras, with two justices joining him, dissented vigorously in Mattox.

When the impeaching statement was made prior to the hearsay statement, differences in the kinds of hearsay appear which arguably may justify differences in treatment. If the hearsay consisted of a simple statement by the witness, e.g. a dying declaration or a declaration against interest, the feasibility of affording him an opportunity to deny or explain encounters the same practical impossibility as where the statement is a subsequent one, just discussed, although here the impossibility arises from the total absence of anything resembling a hearing at which the matter could be put to him. The courts by a large majority have ruled in favor of allowing the statement to be used under these circumstances. McCormick § 37, p. 69; 3 Wigmore § 1033. If, however, the hearsay consists of former testimony or a deposition, the possibility of calling the prior statement to the attention of the witness or deponent is not ruled out, since the opportunity to cross-examine was available. It might thus be concluded that with former testimony or depositions the conventional foundation should be insisted upon. Most of the cases involve depositions, and Wigmore describes them as divided. 3 Wigmore § 1031. Deposition procedures at best are cumbersome and expensive, and to require the laying of the foundation may impose an undue burden. Under the federal practice, there is no way of knowing with certainty at the time of taking a deposition whether it is merely for discovery or will ultimately end up in evidence. With respect to both former testimony and depositions the possibility exists that knowledge of the statement might not be acquired until after the time of the cross-examination. Moreover, the expanded admissibility of former testimony and depositions under Rule 804(b)(1) calls for a correspondingly expanded approach to impeachment. The rule dispenses with the requirement in all hearsay situations, which is readily administered and best calculated to lead to fair results.

Notice should be taken that Rule 26(f) of the Federal Rules of Civil Procedure, as originally submitted by the Advisory Committee, ended with the following:

" * * * and, without having first called them to the deponent's attention, may show statements contradictory thereto made at any time by the deponent."

This language did not appear in the rule as promulgated in December, 1937. See 4 Moore's Federal Practice ¶¶ 26.01[9], 26.35 (2d ed.1967). In 1951, Nebraska adopted a provision strongly resembling the one stricken from the federal rule:

"Any party may impeach any adverse deponent by self-contradiction without having laid foundation for such impeachment at the time such deposition was taken." R.S.Neb. § 25-1267.07.

For similar provisions, see Uniform Rule 65; California Evidence Code § 1202; Kansas Code of Civil Procedure § 60-462; New Jersey Evidence Rule 65.

The provision for cross-examination of a declarant upon his hearsay statement is a corollary of general principles of cross-examination. A similar provision is found in California Evidence Code § 1203.

1974 Enactment
Rule 906, as passed by the House and as proposed by the Supreme Court provides that whenever a hearsay statement is admitted, the credibility of the declarant of the statement may be attacked, and if attacked may be supported, by any evidence which would be admissible for those purposes if the declarant had testified as a witness. Rule 801 defines what is a hearsay statement. While statements by a person authorized by a party-opponent to make a statement concerning the subject, by the party-opponent's agent or by a coconspirator of a party--see rule 801(d)(2)(c), (d) and (e)--are traditionally defined as exceptions to the hearsay rule, rule 801 defines such admission by a party-opponent as statements which are not hearsay. Consequently, rule 806 by referring exclusively to the admission of hearsay statements, does not appear to allow the credibility of the declarant to be attacked when the declarant is a coconspirator, agent or authorized spokesman. The committee is of the view that such statements should open the declarant to attacks on his credibility. Indeed, the reason such statements are excluded from the operation of rule 806 is likely attributable to the drafting technique used to codify the hearsay rule, viz. some statements, instead of being referred to as exceptions to the hearsay rule, are defined as statements which are not hearsay. The phrase "or a statement defined in rule 801(d)(2)(c), (d) and (e)" is added to the rule in order to subject the declarant of such statements, like the declarant of hearsay statements, to attacks on his credibility. [The committee considered it unnecessary to include statements contained in rule 801(d)(2)(A) and (B)--the statement by the party-opponent himself or the statement of which he has manifested his adoption--because the credibility of the party-opponent is always subject to an attack on his credibility]. Senate Report No. 93-1277.

The Senate amendment permits an attack upon the credibility of the declarant of a statement if the statement is one by a person authorized by a party-opponent to make a statement concerning the subject, one by an agent of a party-opponent, or one by a coconspirator of the party-opponent, as these statements are defined in Rules 801(d)(2)(C), (D) and (E). The House bill has no such provision.

The Conference adopts the Senate amendment. The Senate amendment conforms the rule to present practice. House Report No. 93-1597.

1987 Amendments
The amendments are technical. No substantive change is intended.

1997 Amendments
The amendment is technical. No substantive change is intended.

GAP Report. Restylization changes in the rule were eliminated.

2011 Amendments

The language of Rule 806 has been amended as part of the restyling of the Evidence Rules to make them more easily understood and to make style and terminology consistent throughout the rules. These changes are intended to be stylistic only. There is no intent to change any result in any ruling on evidence admissibility.

Rule 807. Residual Exception

(a) In General. Under the following circumstances, a hearsay statement is not excluded by the rule against hearsay even if the statement is not specifically covered by a hearsay exception in Rule 803 or 804:

(1) the statement has equivalent circumstantial guarantees of trustworthiness;

(2) it is offered as evidence of a material fact;

(3) it is more probative on the point for which it is offered than any other evidence that the proponent can obtain through reasonable efforts; and

(4) admitting it will best serve the purposes of these rules and the interests of justice.

(b) Notice. The statement is admissible only if, before the trial or hearing, the proponent gives an adverse party reasonable notice of the intent to offer the statement and its particulars, including the declarant's name and address, so that the party has a fair opportunity to meet it.

Credits
(Added Apr. 11, 1997, eff. Dec. 1, 1997; Apr. 26, 2011, eff. Dec. 1, 2011.)

Editors' Notes
ADVISORY COMMITTEE NOTES
1997 Amendments
The contents of Rule 803(24) and Rule 804(b)(5) have been combined and transferred to a new Rule 807. This was done to facilitate additions to Rules 803 and 804. No change in meaning is intended.

GAP Report on Rule 807. Restylization changes in the rule were eliminated.

2011 Amendments
The language of Rule 807 has been amended as part of the restyling of the Evidence Rules to make them more easily understood and to make style and terminology consistent throughout the rules. These changes are intended to be stylistic only. There is no intent to change any result in any ruling on evidence admissibility.

Article IX: Authentication and Identification

Rule 901. Authenticating or Identifying Evidence

(a) In General. To satisfy the requirement of authenticating or identifying an item of evidence, the proponent must produce evidence sufficient to support a finding that the item is what the proponent claims it is.

(b) Examples. The following are examples only--not a complete list--of evidence that satisfies the requirement:

(1) Testimony of a Witness with Knowledge. Testimony that an item is what it is claimed to be.

(2) Nonexpert Opinion About Handwriting. A nonexpert's opinion that handwriting is genuine, based on a familiarity with it that was not acquired for the current litigation.

(3) Comparison by an Expert Witness or the Trier of Fact. A comparison with an authenticated specimen by an expert witness or the trier of fact.

(4) Distinctive Characteristics and the Like. The appearance, contents, substance, internal patterns, or other distinctive characteristics of the item, taken together with all the circumstances.

(5) Opinion About a Voice. An opinion identifying a person's voice--whether heard firsthand or through mechanical or electronic transmission or recording--based on hearing the voice at any time under circumstances that connect it with the alleged speaker.

(6) Evidence About a Telephone Conversation. For a telephone conversation, evidence that a call was made to the number assigned at the time to:

(A) a particular person, if circumstances, including self- identification, show that the person answering was the one called; or

(B) a particular business, if the call was made to a business and the call related to business reasonably transacted over the telephone.

(7) Evidence About Public Records. Evidence that:

(A) a document was recorded or filed in a public office as authorized by law; or

(B) a purported public record or statement is from the office where items of this kind are kept.

(8) Evidence About Ancient Documents or Data Compilations. For a document or data compilation, evidence that it:

(A) is in a condition that creates no suspicion about its authenticity;

(B) was in a place where, if authentic, it would likely be; and

(C) is at least 20 years old when offered.

(9) Evidence About a Process or System. Evidence describing a process or system and showing that it produces an accurate result.

(10) Methods Provided by a Statute or Rule. Any method of authentication or identification allowed by a federal statute or a rule prescribed by the Supreme Court.

Credits

(Pub.L. 93-595, § 1, Jan. 2, 1975, 88 Stat.1943; Apr. 26, 2011, eff. Dec. 1, 2011.)

Editors' Notes
ADVISORY COMMITTEE NOTES

1972 Proposed Rules
Note to Subdivision (a). Authentication and identification represent a special aspect of relevancy. Michael and Adler, Real Proof, 5 Vand.L.Rev. 344, 362 (1952); McCormick §§ 179, 185; Morgan, Basic Problems of Evidence 378 (1962). Thus a telephone conversation may be irrelevant because on an unrelated topic or because the speaker is not identified. The latter aspect is the one here involved. Wigmore describes the need for authentication as "an inherent logical necessity." 7 Wigmore § 2129, p. 564.

This requirement of showing authenticity or identity falls in the category of relevancy dependent upon fulfillment of a condition of fact and is governed by the procedure set forth in Rule 104(b).

The common law approach to authentication of documents has been criticized as an "attitude of agnosticism," McCormick, Cases on Evidence 388, n. 4 (3rd ed. 1956), as one which "departs sharply from men's customs in ordinary affairs," and as presenting only a slight obstacle to the introduction of forgeries in comparison to the time and expense devoted to proving genuine writings which correctly show their origin on their face, McCormick § 185, pp. 395, 396. Today, such available procedures as requests to admit and pretrial conference afford the means of eliminating much of the need for authentication or identification. Also, significant inroads upon the traditional insistence on authentication and identification have been made by accepting as at least prima facie genuine items of the kind treated in Rule 902, infra. However, the need for suitable methods of proof still remains, since criminal cases pose their own obstacles to the use of preliminary procedures, unforeseen contingencies may arise, and cases of genuine controversy will still occur.

Note to Subdivision (b). The treatment of authentication and identification draws largely upon the experience embodied in the common law and in statutes to furnish illustrative applications of the general principle set forth in subdivision (a). The examples are not intended as an exclusive enumeration of allowable methods but are meant to guide and suggest, leaving room for growth and development in this area of the law.

The examples relate for the most part to documents, with some attention given to voice communications and computer printouts. As Wigmore noted, no special rules have been developed for authenticating chattels. Wigmore, Code of Evidence § 2086 (3rd ed. 1942).

It should be observed that compliance with requirements of authentication or identification by no means assures admission of an item into evidence, as other bars, hearsay for example, may remain.

Example (1). Example (1) contemplates a broad spectrum ranging from testimony of a witness who was present at the signing of a document to testimony establishing narcotics as taken from an accused and accounting for custody through the period until trial, including laboratory analysis. See California Evidence Code § 1413, eyewitness to signing.

Example (2). Example (2) states conventional doctrine as to lay identification of handwriting, which recognizes that a sufficient familiarity with the handwriting of another person may be acquired by seeing him write, by exchanging correspondence, or by other means, to afford a basis for identifying it on subsequent occasions. McCormick § 189. See also California Evidence Code § 1416. Testimony based upon familiarity acquired for purposes of the litigation is reserved to the expert under the example which follows.

Example (3). The history of common law restrictions upon the technique of proving or disproving the genuineness of a disputed specimen of handwriting through comparison with a genuine specimen, by either the testimony of expert witnesses or direct viewing by the triers themselves, is detailed in 7 Wigmore §§ 1991-1994. In breaking away, the English Common Law Procedure Act of 1854, 17 and 18 Vict., c. 125, § 27, cautiously allowed expert or trier to use exemplars "proved to the satisfaction of the judge to be genuine" for purposes of comparison. The language found its way into numerous statutes in this country, e.g., California Evidence Code §§ 1417, 1418. While explainable as a measure of prudence in the process of breaking with precedent in the handwriting situation, the reservation to the judge of the question of the genuineness of exemplars and the imposition of an unusually high standard of persuasion are at variance with the general treatment of relevancy which depends upon fulfillment of a condition of fact. Rule 104(b). No similar attitude is found in other comparison situations, e.g., ballistics comparison by jury, as in Evans v. Commonwealth, 230 Ky. 411, 19 S.W.2d 1091 (1929), or by experts, Annot., 26 A.L.R.2d 892, and no reason appears for its continued existence in handwriting cases. Consequently Example (3) sets no higher standard for handwriting specimens and treats all comparison situations alike, to be governed by Rule 104(b). This approach is consistent with 28 U.S.C. § 1731: "The admitted or proved handwriting of any person shall be admissible, for purposes of comparison, to determine genuineness of other handwriting attributed to such person."

Precedent supports the acceptance of visual comparison as sufficiently satisfying preliminary authentication requirements for admission in evidence. Brandon v. Collins, 267 F.2d 731 (2d Cir. 1959); Wausau Sulphate Fibre Co. v. Commissioner of Internal Revenue, 61 F.2d 879 (7th Cir. 1932); Desimone v. United States, 227 F.2d 864 (9th Cir.1955).

Example (4). The characteristics of the offered item itself, considered in the light of circumstances, afford authentication techniques in great variety. Thus a document or telephone conversation may be shown to have emanated from a particular person by virtue of its disclosing knowledge of facts known peculiarly to him; Globe Automatic Sprinkler Co. v. Braniff, 89 Okl. 105, 214 P. 127 (1923); California Evidence Code § 1421; similarly, a letter may be authenticated by content and circumstances indicating it was in reply to a duly authenticated one. McCormick § 192; California Evidence Code § 1420. Language patterns may indicate authenticity or its opposite. Magnuson v. State, 187 Wis. 122, 203 N.W. 749 (1925); Arens and Meadow, Psycholinguistics and the Confession Dilemma, 56 Colum.L.Rev. 19 (1956).

Example (5). Since aural voice identification is not a subject of expert testimony, the requisite familiarity may be acquired either before or after the particular speaking which is the subject of the identification, in this respect resembling visual identification of a person rather than identification of handwriting. Cf. Example (2), supra, People v. Nichols, 378 Ill. 487, 38 N.E.2d 766 (1942); McGuire v. State, 200 Md. 601, 92 A.2d 582 (1952); State v. McGee, 336 Mo. 1082, 83 S.W.2d 98 (1935).

Example (6). The cases are in agreement that a mere assertion of his identity by a person talking on the telephone is not sufficient evidence of the authenticity of the conversation and that additional evidence of his identity is required. The additional evidence need not fall in any set pattern. Thus the content of his statements or the reply technique, under Example (4), supra, or voice identification under Example (5), may furnish the necessary foundation. Outgoing calls made by the witness involve additional factors bearing upon authenticity. The calling of a number assigned by the telephone company reasonably supports the assumption that the listing is correct and that the number is the one reached. If the number is that of a place of business, the mass of authority allows an ensuing conversation if it relates to business reasonably transacted over the telephone, on the theory that the maintenance of the telephone connection is an invitation to do business without further identification. Matton v. Hoover Co., 350 Mo. 506, 166 S.W.2d 557 (1942); City of Pawhuska v. Crutchfield, 147 Okl. 4, 293 P. 1095 (1930); Zurich General Acc. & Liability Ins. Co. v. Baum, 159 Va. 404, 165 S.E. 518 (1932). Otherwise, some additional circumstance of identification of the speaker is required. The authorities divide on the question whether the self-identifying statement of the person answering suffices. Example (6) answers in the affirmative on the assumption that usual conduct respecting telephone calls furnish adequate assurances of regularity, bearing in mind that the entire matter is open to exploration before the trier of fact. In general, see McCormick § 193; 7 Wigmore § 2155; Annot., 71 A.L.R. 5, 105 id. 326.

Example (7). Public records are regularly authenticated by proof of custody, without more. McCormick § 191; 7 Wigmore §§ 2158, 2159. The example extends the principle to include data stored in computers and similar methods, of which increasing use in the public records area may be expected. See California Evidence Code §§ 1532, 1600.

Example (8). The familiar ancient document rule of the common law is extended to include data stored electronically or by other similar means. Since the importance of appearance diminishes in this situation, the importance of custody or place where found increases correspondingly. This expansion is necessary in view of the widespread use of methods of storing data in forms other than conventional written records.

Any time period selected is bound to be arbitrary. The common law period of 30 years is here reduced to 20 years, with some shift of emphasis from the probable unavailability of witnesses to the unlikeliness of a still viable fraud after the lapse of time. The shorter period is specified in the English Evidence Act of 1938, 1 & 2 Geo. 6, c. 28, and in Oregon R.S.1963, § 41.360(34). See also the numerous statutes prescribing periods of less than 30 years in the case of recorded documents. 7 Wigmore § 2143.

The application of Example (8) is not subject to any limitation to title documents or to any requirement that possession, in the case of a title document, has been consistent with the document. See McCormick § 190.

Example (9). Example (9) is designed for situations in which the accuracy of a result is dependent upon a process or system which produces it. X rays afford a familiar instance. Among more recent developments is the computer, as to which see Transport Indemnity Co. v. Seib, 178 Neb. 253, 132 N.W.2d 871 (1965); State v. Veres, 7 Ariz.App. 117, 436 P.2d 629 (1968); Merrick v. United States Rubber Co., 7 Ariz.App. 433, 440 P.2d 314 (1968); Freed, Computer Print-Outs as Evidence, 16 Am.Jur.Proof of Facts 273; Symposium, Law and Computers in the Mid-Sixties, ALI-ABA (1966); 37 Albany L.Rev. 61 (1967). Example (9) does not, of course, foreclose taking judicial notice of the accuracy of the process or system.

Example (10). The example makes clear that methods of authentication provided by Act of Congress and by the Rules of Civil and Criminal Procedure or by Bankruptcy Rules are not intended to be superseded. Illustrative are the provisions for authentication of official records in Civil Procedure Rule 44 and Criminal Procedure Rule 27, for authentication of records of proceedings by court reporters in 28 U.S.C. § 753(b) and Civil Procedure Rule 80(c), and for authentication of depositions in Civil Procedure Rule 30(f).

2011 Amendments

The language of Rule 901 has been amended as part of the restyling of the Evidence Rules to make them more easily understood and to make style and terminology consistent throughout the rules. These changes are intended to be stylistic only. There is no intent to change any result in any ruling on evidence admissibility.

Rule 902. Evidence That Is Self-Authenticating

The following items of evidence are self-authenticating; they require no extrinsic evidence of authenticity in order to be admitted:

(1) Domestic Public Documents That Are Sealed and Signed. A document that bears:

(A) a seal purporting to be that of the United States; any state, district, commonwealth, territory, or insular possession of the United States; the former Panama Canal Zone; the Trust Territory of the Pacific Islands; a political subdivision of any of these entities; or a department, agency, or officer of any entity named above; and

(B) a signature purporting to be an execution or attestation.

(2) Domestic Public Documents That Are Not Sealed but Are Signed and Certified. A document that bears no seal if:

(A) it bears the signature of an officer or employee of an entity named in Rule 902(1)(A); and

(B) another public officer who has a seal and official duties within that same entity certifies under seal--or its equivalent--that the signer has the official capacity and that the signature is genuine.

(3) Foreign Public Documents. A document that purports to be signed or attested by a person who is authorized by a foreign country's law to do so. The document must be accompanied by a final certification that certifies the genuineness of the signature and official position of the signer or attester--or of any foreign official whose certificate of genuineness relates to the signature or attestation or is in a chain of certificates of genuineness relating to the signature or attestation. The certification may be made by a secretary of a United States embassy or legation; by a consul general, vice consul, or consular agent of the United States; or by a diplomatic or consular official of the foreign country assigned or accredited to the United States. If all parties have been given a reasonable opportunity to investigate the document's authenticity and accuracy, the court may, for good cause, either:

(A) order that it be treated as presumptively authentic without final certification; or

(B) allow it to be evidenced by an attested summary with or without final certification.

(4) Certified Copies of Public Records. A copy of an official record--or a copy of a document that was recorded or filed in a public office as authorized by law--if the copy is certified as correct by:

(A) the custodian or another person authorized to make the certification; or

(B) a certificate that complies with Rule 902(1), (2), or (3), a federal statute, or a rule prescribed by the Supreme Court.

(5) Official Publications. A book, pamphlet, or other publication purporting to be issued by a public authority.

(6) Newspapers and Periodicals. Printed material purporting to be a newspaper or periodical.

(7) Trade Inscriptions and the Like. An inscription, sign, tag, or label purporting to have been affixed in the course of business and indicating origin, ownership, or control.

(8) Acknowledged Documents. A document accompanied by a certificate of acknowledgment that is lawfully executed by a notary public or another officer who is authorized to take acknowledgments.

(9) Commercial Paper and Related Documents. Commercial paper, a signature on it, and related documents, to the extent allowed by general commercial law.

(10) Presumptions Under a Federal Statute. A signature, document, or anything else that a federal statute declares to be presumptively or prima facie genuine or authentic.

(11) Certified Domestic Records of a Regularly Conducted Activity. The original or a copy of a domestic record that meets the requirements of Rule 803(6)(A)-(C), as shown by a certification of the custodian or another qualified person that complies with a federal statute or a rule prescribed by the Supreme Court. Before the trial or hearing, the proponent must give an adverse party reasonable written notice of the intent to offer the record--and must make the record and certification available for inspection--so that the party has a fair opportunity to challenge them.

(12) Certified Foreign Records of a Regularly Conducted Activity. In a civil case, the original or a copy of a foreign record that meets the requirements of Rule 902(11), modified as follows: the certification, rather than complying with a federal statute or Supreme Court rule, must be signed in a manner that, if falsely made, would subject the maker to a criminal penalty in the country where the certification is signed. The proponent must also meet the notice requirements of Rule 902(11).

Credits

(Pub.L. 93-595, § 1, Jan. 2, 1975, 88 Stat. 1944; Mar. 2, 1987, eff. Oct. 1, 1987; Apr. 25, 1988, eff. Nov. 1, 1988; Apr. 17, 2000, eff. Dec. 1, 2000; Apr. 26, 2011, eff. Dec. 1, 2011.)

Editors' Notes
ADVISORY COMMITTEE NOTES
1972 Proposed Rules
Case law and statutes have, over the years, developed a substantial body of instances in which authenticity is taken as sufficiently established for purposes of admissibility without extrinsic evidence to that effect, sometimes for reasons of policy but perhaps more often because practical considerations reduce the possibility of unauthenticity to a very small dimension. The present rule collects and incorporates these situations, in some instances expanding them to occupy a larger area which their underlying considerations justify. In no instance is the opposite party foreclosed from disputing authenticity.

Note to Paragraph (1). The acceptance of documents bearing a public seal and signature, most often encountered in practice in the form of acknowledgments or certificates authenticating copies of public records, is actually of broad application. Whether theoretically based in whole or in part upon judicial notice, the practical underlying considerations are that forgery is a crime and detection is fairly easy and certain. 7 Wigmore § 2161, p. 638; California Evidence Code § 1452. More than 50 provisions for judicial notice of official seals are contained in the United States Code.

Note to Paragraph (2). While statutes are found which raise a presumption of genuineness of purported official signatures in the absence of an official seal, 7 Wigmore § 2167; California Evidence Code § 1453, the greater ease of effecting a forgery under these circumstances is apparent. Hence this paragraph of the rule calls for authentication by an officer who has a seal. Notarial acts by members of the armed forces and other special situations are covered in paragraph (10).

Note to Paragraph (3). Paragraph (3) provides a method for extending the presumption of authenticity to foreign official documents by a procedure of certification. It is derived from Rule 44(a)(2) of the Rules of Civil Procedure but is broader in applying to public documents rather than being limited to public records.

Note to Paragraph (4). The common law and innumerable statutes have recognized the procedure of authenticating copies of public records by certificate. The certificate qualifies as a public document, receivable as authentic when in conformity with paragraph (1), (2), or (3). Rule 44(a) of the Rules of Civil Procedure and Rule 27 of the Rules of Criminal Procedure have provided authentication procedures of this nature for both domestic and foreign public records. It will be observed that the certification procedure here provided extends only to public records, reports, and recorded documents, all including data compilations, and does not apply to public documents generally. Hence documents provable when presented in original form under paragraphs (1), (2), or (3) may not be provable by certified copy under paragraph (4).

Note to Paragraph (5). Dispensing with preliminary proof of the genuineness of purportedly official publications, most commonly encountered in connection with statutes, court reports, rules, and regulations, has been greatly enlarged by statutes and decisions. 5 Wigmore § 1684. Paragraph (5), it will be noted, does not confer admissibility upon all official publications; it merely provides a means whereby their authenticity may be taken as established for purposes of admissibility. Rule 44(a) of the Rules of Civil Procedure has been to the same effect.

Note to Paragraph (6). The likelihood of forgery of newspapers or periodicals is slight indeed. Hence no danger is apparent in receiving them. Establishing the authenticity of the publication may, of course, leave still open questions of authority and responsibility for items therein contained. See 7 Wigmore § 2150. Cf. 39 U.S.C. § 4005(b), public advertisement prima facie evidence of agency of person named, in postal fraud order proceeding; Canadian Uniform Evidence Act, Draft of 1936, printed copy of newspaper prima facie evidence that notices or advertisements were authorized.

Note to Paragraph (7). Several factors justify dispensing with preliminary proof of genuineness of commercial and mercantile labels and the like. The risk of forgery is minimal. Trademark infringement involves serious penalties. Great efforts are devoted to inducing the public to buy in reliance on brand names, and substantial protection is given them. Hence the fairness of this treatment finds recognition in the cases. Curtiss Candy Co. v. Johnson, 163 Miss. 426, 141 So. 762 (1932), Baby Ruth candy bar; Doyle v. Continental Baking Co., 262 Mass. 516, 160 N.E. 325 (1928), loaf of bread; Weiner v. Mager & Throne, Inc., 167 Misc. 338, 3 N.Y.S.2d 918 (1938), same. And see W.Va.Code 1966, § 47-3-5, trademark on bottle prima facie evidence of ownership. Contra, Keegan v. Green Giant Co., 150 Me. 283, 110 A.2d 599 (1954); Murphy v. Campbell Soup Co., 62 F.2d 564 (1st Cir.1933). Cattle brands have received similar acceptance in the western states. Rev.Code Mont.1947, § 46-606, State v. Wolfley, 75 Kan. 406, 89 P. 1046 (1907); Annot., 11 L.R.A.(N.S.) 87. Inscriptions on trains and vehicles are held to be prima facie evidence of ownership or control. Pittsburgh, Ft. W. & C. Ry. v. Callaghan, 157 Ill. 406, 41 N.E. 909 (1895); 9 Wigmore § 2510a. See also the provision of 19 U.S.C. § 1615(2) that marks, labels, brands, or stamps indicating foreign origin are prima facie evidence of foreign origin of merchandise.

Note to Paragraph (8). In virtually every state, acknowledged title documents are receivable in evidence without further proof. Statutes are collected in 5 Wigmore § 1676. If this authentication suffices for documents of the importance of those affecting titles, logic scarcely permits denying this method when other kinds of documents are involved. Instances of broadly inclusive statutes are California Evidence Code § 1451 and N.Y.CPLR 4538, McKinney's Consol.Laws 1963.

Note to Paragraph (9). Issues of the authenticity of commercial paper in federal courts will usually arise in diversity cases, will involve an element of a cause of action or defense, and with respect to presumptions and burden of proof will be controlled by Erie Railroad Co. v. Tompkins, 304 U.S. 64, 58 S.Ct. 817, 82 L.Ed. 1188 (1938). Rule 302, supra. There may, however, be questions of authenticity involving lesser segments of a case or the case may be one governed by federal common law. Clearfield Trust Co. v. United States, 318 U.S. 363, 63 S.Ct. 573, 87 L.Ed. 838 (1943). Cf. United States v. Yazell, 382 U.S. 341, 86 S.Ct. 500, 15 L.Ed.2d 404 (1966). In these situations, resort to the useful authentication provisions of the Uniform Commercial Code is provided for. While the phrasing is in terms of "general commercial law," in order to avoid the potential complications inherent in borrowing local statutes, today one would have difficulty in determining the general commercial law without referring to the Code. See Williams v. Walker-Thomas Furniture Co., 121 U.S.App.D.C. 315, 350 F.2d 445 (1965). Pertinent Code provisions are sections 1-202, 3-307, and 3-510, dealing with third-party documents, signatures on negotiable instruments, protests, and statements of dishonor.

Note to Paragraph (10). The paragraph continues in effect dispensations with preliminary proof of genuineness provided in various Acts of Congress. See, for example, 10 U.S.C. § 936, signature, without seal, together with title, prima facie evidence of authenticity of acts of certain military personnel who are given notarial powers; 15 U.S.C. § 77f(a), signature on SEC registration presumed genuine; 26 U.S.C. § 6064, signature to tax return prima facie genuine.

1974 Enactment
Note to Paragraph (8). Rule 902(8) as submitted by the Court referred to certificates of acknowledgment "under the hand and seal of" a notary public or other officer authorized by law to take acknowledgments. The Committee amended the Rule to eliminate the requirement, believed to be inconsistent with the law in some States, that a notary public must affix a seal to a document acknowledged before him. As amended the Rule merely requires that the document be executed in the manner prescribed by State law.

Note to Paragraph (9). The Committee approved Rule 902(9) as submitted by the Court. With respect to the meaning of the phrase "general commercial law", the Committee intends that the Uniform Commercial Code, which has been adopted in virtually every State, will be followed generally, but that federal commercial law will apply where federal commercial paper is involved. See Clearfield Trust Co. v. United States, 318 U.S. 363 (1943). Further, in those instances in which the issues are governed by Erie R. Co. v. Tompkins, 304 U.S. 64 (1938), State law will apply irrespective of whether it is the Uniform Commercial Code. House Report No. 93-650.

1987 Amendments
The amendments are technical. No substantive change is intended.

1988 Amendments
These two sentences were inadvertently eliminated from the 1987 amendments. The amendment is technical. No substantive change is intended.

2000 Amendments
The amendment adds two new paragraphs to the rule on self-authentication. It sets forth a procedure by which parties can authenticate certain records of regularly conducted activity, other than through the testimony of a foundation witness. See the amendment to Rule 803(6). 18 U.S.C. § 3505 currently provides a means for certifying foreign records of regularly conducted activity in criminal cases, and this amendment is intended to establish a similar procedure for domestic records, and for foreign records offered in civil cases.

A declaration that satisfies 28 U.S.C. § 1746 would satisfy the declaration requirement of Rule 902(11), as would any comparable certification under oath.

The notice requirement in Rules 902(11) and (12) is intended to give the opponent of the evidence a full opportunity to test the adequacy of the foundation set forth in the declaration.

GAP Report--Proposed Amendment to Rule 902
The Committee made the following changes to the published draft of the proposed amendment to Evidence Rule 902:
1. Minor stylistic changes were made in the text, in accordance with suggestions of the Style Subcommittee of the Standing Committee on Rules of Practice and Procedure.

2. The phrase "in a manner complying with any Act of Congress or rule prescribed by the Supreme Court pursuant to statutory authority" was added to proposed Rule 902(11), to provide consistency with Evidence Rule 902(4). The Committee Note was amended to accord with this textual change.

3. Minor stylistic changes were made in the text to provide a uniform construction of the terms "declaration" and "certifying."

4. The notice provisions in the text were revised to clarify that the proponent must make both the declaration and the underlying record available for inspection.

2011 Amendments
The language of Rule 902 has been amended as part of the restyling of the Evidence Rules to make them more easily understood and to make style and terminology consistent throughout the rules. These changes are intended to be stylistic only. There is no intent to change any result in any ruling on evidence admissibility.

Rule 903. Subscribing Witness's Testimony

A subscribing witness's testimony is necessary to authenticate a writing only if required by the law of the jurisdiction that governs its validity.
Credits

(Pub.L. 93-595, § 1, Jan. 2, 1975, 88 Stat.1945; Apr. 26, 2011, eff. Dec. 1, 2011.)

Editors' Notes
ADVISORY COMMITTEE NOTES
1972 Proposed Rules
The common law required that attesting witnesses be produced or accounted for. Today the requirement has generally been abolished except with respect to documents which must be attested to be valid, e.g. wills in some states. McCormick § 188. Uniform Rule 71; California Evidence Code § 1411; Kansas Code of Civil Procedure § 60-468; New Jersey Evidence Rule 71; New York CPLR Rule 4537.

2011 Amendments
The language of Rule 903 has been amended as part of the restyling of the Evidence Rules to make them more easily understood and to make style and terminology consistent throughout the rules. These changes are intended to be stylistic only. There is no intent to change any result in any ruling on evidence admissibility.

Article X: Contents of Writings, Recordings, and Photographs

Rule 1001. Definitions That Apply to This Article

In this article:

(a) A "writing" consists of letters, words, numbers, or their equivalent set down in any form.

(b) A "recording" consists of letters, words, numbers, or their equivalent recorded in any manner.

(c) A "photograph" means a photographic image or its equivalent stored in any form.

(d) An "original" of a writing or recording means the writing or recording itself or any counterpart intended to have the same effect by the person who executed or issued it. For electronically stored information, "original" means any printout-- or other output readable by sight--if it accurately reflects the information. An "original" of a photograph includes the negative or a print from it.

(e) A "duplicate" means a counterpart produced by a mechanical, photographic, chemical, electronic, or other equivalent process or technique that accurately reproduces the original.

Credits

(Pub.L. 93-595, § 1, Jan. 2, 1975, 88 Stat. 1945; Apr. 26, 2011, eff. Dec. 1, 2011.)

Editors' Notes
ADVISORY COMMITTEE NOTES
1972 Proposed Rules
In an earlier day, when discovery and other related procedures were strictly limited, the misleading named "best evidence rule" afforded substantial guarantees against inaccuracies and fraud by its insistence upon production or original documents. The great enlargement of the scope of discovery and related procedures in recent times has measurably reduced the need for the rule. Nevertheless important areas of usefulness persist: discovery of documents outside the jurisdiction may require substantial outlay of time and money; the unanticipated document may not practically be discoverable; criminal cases have built-in limitations on discovery. Cleary and Strong, The Best Evidence Rule: An Evaluation in Context, 51 Iowa L.Rev. 825 (1966).

Note to Paragraph (1). Traditionally the rule requiring the original centered upon accumulations of data and expressions affecting legal relations set forth in words and figures. this meant that the rule was one essentially related to writings. Present day techniques have expanded methods of storing data, yet the essential form which the information ultimately assumes for usable purposes is words and figures. Hence the considerations underlying the rule dictate its expansion to include computers, photographic systems, and other modern developments.

Note to Paragraph (3). In most instances, what is an original will be self-evident and further refinement will be unnecessary. However, in some instances particularized definition is required. A carbon copy of a contract executed in duplicate becomes an original, as does a sales ticket carbon copy given to a customer. While strictly speaking the original of a photograph might be thought to be only the negative, practicality and common usage require that any print from the negative be regarded as an original. Similarly, practicality and usage confer the status of original upon any computer printout. Transport Indemnity Co. v. Seib, 178 Neb. 253, 132 N.W.2d 871 (1965).

Note to Paragraph (4). The definition describes "copies" produced by methods possessing an accuracy which virtually eliminates the possibility of error. Copies thus produced are given the status of originals in large measure by Rule 1003, infra. Copies subsequently produced manually, whether handwritten or typed, are not within the definition. It should be noted that what is an original for some purposes may be a duplicate for others. Thus a bank's microfilm record of checks cleared is the original as a record. However, a print offered as a copy of a check whose contents are in controversy is a duplicate. This result is substantially consistent with 28 U.S.C. § 1732(b). Compare 26 U.S.C. § 7513(c), giving full status as originals to photographic reproductions of tax returns and other documents, made by authority of the Secretary of the Treasury, and 44 U.S.C. § 399(a), giving original status to photographic copies in the National Archives.

1974 Enactment
Note to Paragraph (2). The Committee amended this Rule expressly to include "video tapes" in the definition of "photographs." House Report No. 93-650.

2011 Amendments
The language of Rule 1001 has been amended as part of the restyling of the Evidence Rules to make them more easily understood and to make style and terminology consistent throughout the rules. These changes are intended to be stylistic only. There is no intent to change any result in any ruling on evidence admissibility.

Rule 1002. Requirement of the Original

An original writing, recording, or photograph is required in order to prove its content unless these rules or a federal statute provides otherwise.

CREDIT(S)
(Pub.L. 93-595, § 1, Jan. 2, 1975, 88 Stat. 1946; Apr. 26, 2011, eff. Dec. 1, 2011.)

ADVISORY COMMITTEE NOTES
1972 Proposed Rules
The rule is the familiar one requiring production of the original of a document to prove its contents, expanded to include writings, recordings, and photographs, as defined in Rule 1001(1) and (2), *supra*.

Application of the rule requires a resolution of the question whether contents are sought to be proved. Thus an event may be proved by nondocumentary evidence, even though a written record of it was made. If, however, the event is sought to be proved by the written record, the rule applies. For example, payment may be proved without producing the written receipt which was given. Earnings may be proved without producing books of account in which they are entered. McCormick § 198; 4 Wigmore § 1245. Nor does the rule apply to testimony that books or records have been examined and found not to contain any reference to a designated matter.

The assumption should not be made that the rule will come into operation on every occasion when use is made of a photograph in evidence. On the contrary, the rule will seldom apply to ordinary photographs. In most instances a party *wishes* to introduce the item and the question raised is the propriety of receiving it in evidence. Cases in which an offer is made of the testimony of a witness as to what he saw in a photograph or motion picture, without producing the same, are most unusual. The usual course is for a witness on the stand to identify the photograph or motion picture as a correct representation of events which he saw or of a scene with which he is familiar. In fact he adopts the picture as his testimony, or, in common parlance, uses the picture to illustrate his testimony. Under these circumstances, no effort is made to prove the contents of the picture, and the rule is inapplicable. Paradis, The Celluloid Witness, 37 U.Colo.L.Rev. 235, 249-251 (1965).

On occasion, however, situations arise in which contents are sought to be proved. Copyright, defamation, and invasion of privacy by photograph or motion picture falls in this category. Similarly as to situations in which the picture is offered as having independent probative value, e.g. automatic photograph of bank robber. See *People v. Doggett,* 83 Cal.App.2d 405, 188 P.2d 792 (1948), photograph of defendants engaged in indecent act; Mouser and Philbin, Photographic Evidence--Is There a Recognized Basis for Admissibility? 8 Hastings L.J. 310 (1957). the most commonly encountered of this latter group is of course, the X ray, with substantial authority calling for production of the original. *Daniels v. Iowa City,* 191 Iowa 811, 183 N.W. 415 (1921); *Cellamare v. Third Acc. Transit Corp.,* 273 App.Div. 260, 77 N.Y.S.2d 91 (1948); *Patrick & Tilman v. Matkin,* 154 Okl. 232, 7 P.2d 414 (1932); *Mendoza v. Rivera,* 78 P.R.R. 569 (1955).

It should be noted, however, that Rule 703, *supra*, allows an expert to give an opinion based on matters not in evidence, and the present rule must be read as being limited accordingly in its application. Hospital records which may be admitted as business records under Rule 803(6) commonly contain reports interpreting X-rays by the staff radiologist, who qualifies as an expert, and these reports need not be excluded from the records by the instant rule.

The reference to Acts of Congress is made in view of such statutory provisions as 26 U.S.C. § 7513, photographic reproductions of tax returns and documents, made by authority of the Secretary of the Treasury, treated as originals, and 44 U.S.C. § 399(a), photographic copies in National Archives treated as originals.

2011 Amendments
The language of Rule 1002 has been amended as part of the restyling of the Evidence Rules to make them more easily understood and to make style and terminology consistent throughout the rules. These changes are intended to be stylistic only. There is no intent to change any result in any ruling on evidence admissibility.

Rule 1003. Admissibility of Duplicates

A duplicate is admissible to the same extent as the original unless a genuine question is raised about the original's authenticity or the circumstances make it unfair to admit the duplicate.

CREDIT(S)
(Pub.L. 93-595, § 1, Jan. 2, 1975, 88 Stat. 1946; Apr. 26, 2011, eff. Dec. 1, 2011.)

ADVISORY COMMITTEE NOTES
1972 Proposed Rules
When the only concern is with getting the words or other contents before the court with accuracy and precision, then a counterpart serves equally as well as the original, if the counterpart is the product of a method which insures accuracy and genuineness. By definition in Rule 1001(4), *supra,* a "duplicate" possesses this character.

Therefore, if no genuine issue exists as to authenticity and no other reason exists for requiring the original, a duplicate is admissible under the rule. This position finds support in the decisions, *Myrick v. United States,* 332 F.2d 279 (5th Cir.1964), no error in admitting photostatic copies of checks instead of original microfilm in absence of suggestion to trial judge that photostats were incorrect; *Johns v. United States,* 323 F.2d 421 (5th Cir.1963), not error to admit concededly accurate tape recording made from original wire recording; *Sauget v. Johnston,* 315 F.2d 816 (9th Cir.1963), not error to admit copy of agreement when opponent had original and did not on appeal claim any discrepancy. Other reasons for acquiring the original may be present when only a part of the original is reproduced and the remainder is needed for cross-examination or may disclose matters qualifying the part offered or otherwise useful to the opposing party. *United States v. Alexander,* 326 F.2d 736 (4th Cir.1964). And see *Toho Bussan Kaisha, Ltd. v. American President Lines, Ltd.,* 265 F.2d 418, 76 A.L.R.2d 1344 (2d Cir.1959).

1974 Enactment
The Committee approved this Rule in the form submitted by the Court, with the expectation that the courts would be liberal in deciding that a "genuine question is raised as to the authenticity of the original." House Report No. 93-650.

2011 Amendments
The language of Rule 1003 has been amended as part of the restyling of the Evidence Rules to make them more easily understood and to make style and terminology consistent throughout the rules. These changes are intended to be stylistic only. There is no intent to change any result in any ruling on evidence admissibility.

Rule 1004. Admissibility of Other Evidence of Content

An original is not required and other evidence of the content of a writing, recording, or photograph is admissible if:

(a) all the originals are lost or destroyed, and not by the proponent acting in bad faith;

(b) an original cannot be obtained by any available judicial process;

(c) the party against whom the original would be offered had control of the original; was at that time put on notice, by pleadings or otherwise, that the original would be a subject of proof at the trial or hearing; and fails to produce it at the trial or hearing; or

(d) the writing, recording, or photograph is not closely related to a controlling issue.

CREDIT(S)
(Pub.L. 93-595, § 1, Jan. 2, 1975, 88 Stat. 1946; Mar. 2, 1987, eff. Oct. 1, 1987; Apr. 26, 2011, eff. Dec. 1, 2011.)

ADVISORY COMMITTEE NOTES
1972 Proposed Rules
Basically the rule requiring the production of the original as proof of contents has developed as a rule of preference: if failure to produce the original is satisfactorily explained, secondary evidence is admissible. The instant rule specifies the circumstances under which production of the original is excused.

The rule recognizes no "degrees" of secondary evidence. While strict logic might call for extending the principle of preference beyond simply preferring the original, the formulation of a hierarchy of preferences and a procedure for making it effective is believed to involve unwarranted complexities. Most, if not all, that would be accomplished by an extended scheme of preferences will, in any event, be achieved through the normal motivation of a party to present the most convincing evidence possible and the arguments and procedures available to his opponent if he does not. Compare McCormick § 207.

Note to Paragraph (1). Loss or destruction of the original, unless due to bad faith of the proponent, is a satisfactory explanation of nonproduction. McCormick § 201.

Note to Paragraph (2). When the original is in the possession of a third person, inability to procure it from him by resort to process or other judicial procedure is a sufficient explanation of nonproduction. Judicial procedure includes subpoena duces tecum as an incident to the taking of a deposition in another jurisdiction. No further showing is required. See McCormick § 202.

Note to Paragraph (3). A party who has an original in his control has no need for the protection of the rule if put on notice that proof of contents will be made. He can ward off secondary evidence by offering the original. The notice procedure here provided is not to be confused with orders to produce or other discovery procedures, as the purpose of the procedure under this rule is to afford the opposite party an opportunity to produce the original, not to compel him to do so. McCormick § 203.

Note to Paragraph (4). While difficult to define with precision, situations arise in which no good purpose is served by production of the original. Examples are the newspaper in an action for the price of publishing defendant's advertisement, *Foster-Holcomb Investment Co. v. Little Rock Publishing Co.,* 151 Ark. 449, 236 S.W. 597 (1922), and the streetcar transfer of plaintiff claiming status as a passenger, *Chicago City Ry. Co. v. Carroll,* 206 Ill. 318, 68 N.E. 1087 (1903). Numerous cases are collected in McCormick § 200, p. 412, n. 1.

1974 Enactment
Note to Paragraph (1). The Committee approved Rule 1004(1) in the form submitted to Congress. However, the Committee intends that loss or destruction of an original by another person at the

instigation of the proponent should be considered as tantamount to loss or destruction in bad faith by the proponent himself. House Report No. 93-650.

1987 Amendments
The amendments are technical. No substantive change is intended.

2011 Amendments

The language of Rule 1004 has been amended as part of the restyling of the Evidence Rules to make them more easily understood and to make style and terminology consistent throughout the rules. These changes are intended to be stylistic only. There is no intent to change any result in any ruling on evidence admissibility.

Rule 1005. Copies of Public Records to Prove Content

The proponent may use a copy to prove the content of an official record--or of a document that was recorded or filed in a public office as authorized by law--if these conditions are met: the record or document is otherwise admissible; and the copy is certified as correct in accordance with Rule 902(4) or is testified to be correct by a witness who has compared it with the original. If no such copy can be obtained by reasonable diligence, then the proponent may use other evidence to prove the content.

CREDIT(S)
(Pub.L. 93-595, § 1, Jan. 2, 1975, 88 Stat. 1946; Apr. 26, 2011, eff. Dec. 1, 2011.)

ADVISORY COMMITTEE NOTES
1972 Proposed Rules
Public records call for somewhat different treatment. Removing them from their usual place of keeping would be attended by serious inconvenience to the public and to the custodian. As a consequence judicial decisions and statutes commonly hold that no explanation need be given for failure to produce the original of a public record. McCormick § 204; 4 Wigmore §§ 1215-1228. This blanket dispensation from producing or accounting for the original would open the door to the introduction of every kind of secondary evidence of contents of public records were it not for the preference given certified or compared copies. Recognition of degrees of secondary evidence in this situation is an appropriate *quid pro quo* for not applying the requirement of producing the original.

The provisions of 28 U.S.C. § 1733(b) apply only to departments or agencies of the United States. The rule, however, applies to public records generally and is comparable in scope in this respect to Rule 44(a) of the Rules of Civil Procedure.

2011 Amendments
The language of Rule 1005 has been amended as part of the restyling of the Evidence Rules to make them more easily understood and to make style and terminology consistent throughout the rules. These changes are intended to be stylistic only. There is no intent to change any result in any ruling on evidence admissibility.

Rule 1006. Summaries to Prove Content

The proponent may use a summary, chart, or calculation to prove the content of voluminous writings, recordings, or photographs that cannot be conveniently examined in court. The proponent must make the originals or duplicates available for examination or copying, or both, by other parties at a reasonable time and place. And the court may order the proponent to produce them in court.

CREDIT(S)

(Pub.L. 93-595, § 1, Jan. 2, 1975, 88 Stat. 1946; Apr. 26, 2011, eff. Dec. 1, 2011.)

ADVISORY COMMITTEE NOTES
1972 Proposed Rules
The admission of summaries of voluminous books, records, or documents offers the only practicable means of making their contents available to judge and jury. The rule recognizes this practice, with appropriate safeguards. 4 Wigmore § 1230.

2011 Amendments
The language of Rule 1006 has been amended as part of the restyling of the Evidence Rules to make them more easily understood and to make style and terminology consistent throughout the rules. These changes are intended to be stylistic only. There is no intent to change any result in any ruling on evidence admissibility.

Rule 1007. Testimony or Statement of a Party to Prove Content

The proponent may prove the content of a writing, recording, or photograph by the testimony, deposition, or written statement of the party against whom the evidence is offered. The proponent need not account for the original.

Credits

(Pub.L. 93-595, § 1, Jan. 2, 1975, 88 Stat. 1947; Mar. 2, 1987, eff. Oct. 1, 1987; Apr. 26, 2011, eff. Dec. 1, 2011.)

Editors' Notes
ADVISORY COMMITTEE NOTES
1972 Proposed Rules
While the parent case, Slatterie v. Pooley, 6 M. & W. 664, 151 Eng.Rep. 579 (Exch.1840), allows proof of contents by evidence of an oral admission by the party against whom offered, without accounting for nonproduction of the original, the risk of inaccuracy is substantial and the decision is at odds with the purpose of the rule giving preference to the original. See 4 Wigmore § 1255. The instant rule follows Professor McCormick's suggestion of limiting this use of admissions to those made in the course of giving testimony or in writing. McCormick § 208, p. 424. The limitation, of course, does not call for excluding evidence of an oral admission when nonproduction of the original has been accounted for and secondary evidence generally has become admissible. Rule 1004, supra.
A similar provision is contained in New Jersey Evidence Rule 70(1)(h)

1987 Amendments

The amendment is technical. No substantive change is intended.

2011 Amendments

The language of Rule 1007 has been amended as part of the restyling of the Evidence Rules to make them more easily understood and to make style and terminology consistent throughout the rules. These changes are intended to be stylistic only. There is no intent to change any result in any ruling on evidence admissibility.

Rule 1008. Functions of the Court and Jury

Ordinarily, the court determines whether the proponent has fulfilled the factual conditions for admitting other evidence of the content of a writing, recording, or photograph under Rule 1004 or 1005. But in a jury trial, the jury determines--in accordance with Rule 104(b)--any issue about whether:

(a) an asserted writing, recording, or photograph ever existed;

(b) another one produced at the trial or hearing is the original; or

(c) other evidence of content accurately reflects the content.

Credits

(Pub.L. 93-595, § 1, Jan. 2, 1975, 88 Stat. 1947; Apr. 26, 2011, eff. Dec. 1, 2011.)

Editors' Notes

ADVISORY COMMITTEE NOTES

1972 Proposed Rules

Most preliminary questions of fact in connection with applying the rule preferring the original as evidence of contents are for the judge, under the general principles announced in Rule 104, supra. Thus, the question whether the loss of the originals has been established, or of the fulfillment of other conditions specified in Rule 1004, supra, is for the judge. However, questions may arise which go beyond the mere administration of the rule preferring the original and into the merits of the controversy. For example, plaintiff offers secondary evidence of the contents of an alleged contract, after first introducing evidence of loss of the original, and defendant counters with evidence that no such contract was ever executed. If the judge decides that the contract was never executed and excludes the secondary evidence, the case is at an end without ever going to the jury on a central issue. Levin, Authentication and Content of Writings, 10 Rutgers L.Rev. 632, 644 (1956). The latter portion of the instant rule is designed to insure treatment of these situations as raising jury questions. The decision is not one for uncontrolled discretion of the jury but is subject to the control exercised generally by the judge over jury determinations. See Rule 104(b), supra.

For similar provisions, see Uniform Rule 70(2); Kansas Code of Civil Procedure § 60-467(b); New Jersey Evidence Rule 70(2), (3).

2011 Amendments

The language of Rule 1008 has been amended as part of the restyling of the Evidence Rules to make them more easily understood and to make style and terminology consistent throughout the rules. These changes are intended to be stylistic only. There is no intent to change any result in any ruling on evidence admissibility.

Article XI: Miscellaneous Rules

Rule 1101. Applicability of the Rules

(a) To Courts and Judges. These rules apply to proceedings before:

• United States district courts;

• United States bankruptcy and magistrate judges;

• United States courts of appeals;

• the United States Court of Federal Claims; and

• the district courts of Guam, the Virgin Islands, and the Northern Mariana Islands.

(b) To Cases and Proceedings. These rules apply in:

• civil cases and proceedings, including bankruptcy, admiralty, and maritime cases;

• criminal cases and proceedings; and

• contempt proceedings, except those in which the court may act summarily.

(c) Rules on Privilege. The rules on privilege apply to all stages of a case or proceeding.

(d) Exceptions. These rules--except for those on privilege--do not apply to the following:

(1) the court's determination, under Rule 104(a), on a preliminary question of fact governing admissibility;

(2) grand-jury proceedings; and

(3) miscellaneous proceedings such as:

• extradition or rendition;

• issuing an arrest warrant, criminal summons, or search warrant;

• a preliminary examination in a criminal case;

• sentencing;

• granting or revoking probation or supervised release; and

• considering whether to release on bail or otherwise.

(e) Other Statutes and Rules. A federal statute or a rule prescribed by the Supreme Court may provide for admitting or excluding evidence independently from these rules.

Credits

(Pub.L. 93-595, § 1, Jan. 2, 1975, 88 Stat. 1947; Pub.L. 94-149, § 1(14), Dec. 12, 1975, 89 Stat. 806; Pub.L. 95-598, Title II, § 251, Nov. 6, 1978, 92 Stat. 2673; Pub.L. 97-164, Title I, § 142, Apr. 2, 1982, 96 Stat. 45; Mar. 2, 1987, eff. Oct. 1, 1987; Apr. 25, 1988, eff. Nov. 1, 1988; Pub.L. 100-690, Title VII, § 7075(c), Nov. 18, 1988, 102 Stat. 4405; Apr. 22, 1993, eff. Dec. 1, 1993; Apr. 26, 2011, eff. Dec. 1, 2011.)

Editors' Notes
ADVISORY COMMITTEE NOTES
1972 Proposed Rules
Note to Subdivision (a). The various enabling acts contain differences in phraseology in their descriptions of the courts over which the Supreme Court's power to make rules of practice and procedure extends. The act concerning civil actions, as amended in 1966, refers to "the district courts * * * of the United States in civil actions, including admiralty and maritime cases. * * *" 28 U.S.C. § 2072, Pub.L. 89-773, § 1, 80 Stat. 1323. The bankruptcy authorization is for rules of practice and procedure "under the Bankruptcy Act." 28 U.S.C. § 2075, Pub.L. 88-623, § 1, 78 Stat. 1001. The Bankruptcy Act in turn creates bankruptcy courts of "the United States district courts and the district courts of the Territories and possessions to which this title is or may hereafter be applicable." 11 U.S.C. §§ 1(10), 11(a). The provision as to criminal rules up to and including verdicts applies to "criminal cases and proceedings to punish for criminal contempt of court in the United States district courts, in the district courts for the districts of the Canal Zone and Virgin Islands, in the Supreme Court of Puerto Rico, and in proceedings before United States magistrates." 18 U.S.C. § 3771.

These various provisions do not in terms describe the same courts. In congressional usage the phrase "district courts of the United States," without further qualification, traditionally has included the district courts established by Congress in the states under Article III of the Constitution, which are "constitutional" courts, and has not included the territorial courts created under Article IV, Section 3, clause 2, which are "legislative" courts. Hornbuckle v. Toombs, 85 U.S. 648, 21 L.Ed. 966 (1873). However, any doubt as to the inclusion of the District Court for the District of Columbia in the phrase is laid at rest by the provisions of the Judicial Code constituting the judicial districts, 28 U.S.C. § 81 et seq., creating district courts therein, id. § 132, and specifically providing that the term "district court of the United States" means the court so constituted. Id. § 451. The District of Columbia is included. Id. § 88. Moreover, when these provisions were enacted, reference to the District of Columbia was deleted from the original civil rules enabling act. 28 U.S.C. § 2072. Likewise Puerto Rico is made a district, with a district court, and included in the term. Id. § 119. The question is simply one of the extent of the authority conferred by Congress. With respect to civil rules it seems clearly to include the district courts in the states, the District Court for the District of Columbia, and the District Court for the District of Puerto Rico.

The bankruptcy coverage is broader. The bankruptcy courts include "the United States district courts," which includes those enumerated above. Bankruptcy courts also include "the district courts of the Territories and possessions to which this title is or may hereafter be applicable." 11 U.S.C. §§ 1(10), 11(a). These courts include the district courts of Guam and the Virgin Islands. 48 U.S.C. §§ 1424(b), 1615. Professor Moore points out that whether the District Court for the District of the Canal Zone is a court of bankruptcy "is not free from doubt in view of the fact that no other statute expressly or inferentially provides for the applicability of the Bankruptcy Act in the Zone." He further observes that while there seems to be little doubt that the Zone is a territory or possession within the meaning of the Bankruptcy Act, 11 U.S.C. § 1(10), it must be noted that the appendix to the Canal Zone Code of 1934 did not list the Act among the laws of the United States applicable to the Zone. 1 Moore's Collier on Bankruptcy ¶ 1.10, pp. 67, 72, n. 25 (14th ed. 1967). The Code of 1962 confers on the district court jurisdiction of:

"(4) actions and proceedings involving laws of the United States applicable to the Canal Zone; and

"(5) other matters and proceedings wherein jurisdiction is conferred by this Code or any other law." Canal Zone Code, 1962, Title 3, § 141.

Admiralty jurisdiction is expressly conferred. Id. § 142. General powers are conferred on the district court, "if the course of proceeding is not specifically prescribed by this Code, by the statute, or by applicable rule of the Supreme Court of the United States * * *" Id. § 279. Neither these provisions nor § 1(10) of the Bankruptcy Act ("district courts of the Territories and possessions to which this title is or may hereafter be applicable") furnishes a satisfactory answer as to the status of the District Court for the District of the Canal Zone as a court of bankruptcy. However, the fact is that this court exercises no bankruptcy jurisdiction in practice.

The criminal rules enabling act specified United States district courts, district courts for the districts of the Canal Zone and the Virgin Islands, the Supreme Court of the Commonwealth of Puerto Rico, and proceedings before United States commissioners. Aside from the addition of commissioners, now magistrates, this scheme differs from the bankruptcy pattern in that it makes no mention of the District Court of Guam but by specific mention removes the Canal Zone from the doubtful list.

The further difference in including the Supreme Court of the Commonwealth of Puerto Rico seems not to be significant for present purposes, since the Supreme Court of the Commonwealth of Puerto Rico is an appellate court. The Rules of Criminal Procedure have not been made applicable to it, as being unneeded and inappropriate, Rule 54(a) of the Federal Rules of Criminal Procedure, and the same approach is indicated with respect to rules of evidence.

If one were to stop at this point and frame a rule governing the applicability of the proposed rules of evidence in terms of the authority conferred by the three enabling acts, an irregular pattern would emerge as follows:

Civil actions, including admiralty and maritime cases--district courts in the states, District of Columbia, and Puerto Rico.

Bankruptcy--same as civil actions, plus Guam and Virgin Islands.

Criminal cases--same as civil actions, plus Canal Zone and Virgin Islands (but not Guam).

This irregular pattern need not, however, be accepted. Originally the Advisory Committee on the Rules of Civil Procedure took the position that, although the phrase "district courts of the United States" did not include territorial courts, provisions in the organic laws of Puerto Rico and Hawaii would make the rules applicable to the district courts thereof, though this would not be so as to Alaska, the Virgin Islands, or the Canal Zone, whose organic acts contained no corresponding provisions. At the suggestion of the Court, however, the Advisory Committee struck from its notes a statement to the above effect. 2 Moore's Federal Practice ¶ 1.07 (2nd ed. 1967); 1 Barron and Holtzoff, Federal Practice and Procedure § 121 (Wright ed. 1960). Congress thereafter by various enactments provided that the rules and future amendments thereto should apply to the district courts of Hawaii, 53 Stat. 841 (1939), Puerto Rico, 54 Stat. 22 (1940), Alaska, 63 Stat. 445 (1949), Guam, 64 Stat. 384-390 (1950), and the Virgin Islands, 68 Stat. 497, 507 (1954). The original enabling act for rules of criminal procedure specifically mentioned the district courts of the Canal Zone and the Virgin Islands. The Commonwealth of Puerto Rico was blanketed in by creating its court a "district court of the United States" as previously described. Although Guam is not mentioned in either the enabling act or in the expanded definition of "district court of the United States," the Supreme Court in 1956 amended Rule 54(a) to state that the Rules of Criminal Procedure are applicable in Guam. The Court took this step following the enactment of legislation by Congress in 1950 that rules theretofore or thereafter promulgated by the Court in civil cases, admiralty, criminal cases and bankruptcy should apply to the District Court of Guam, 48 U.S.C. § 1424(b), and two Ninth Circuit decisions upholding the applicability of the Rules of Criminal Procedure to Guam. Pugh v. United States, 212 F.2d 761 (9th Cir.1954); Hatchett v. Guam, 212 F.2d 767 (9th Cir.1954); Orfield, The Scope of the Federal Rules of Criminal Procedure, 38 U. of Det.L.J. 173, 187 (1960).

From this history, the reasonable conclusion is that Congressional enactment of a provision that rules and future amendments shall apply in the courts of a territory or possession is the equivalent of mention in an enabling act and that a rule on scope and applicability may properly be drafted accordingly. Therefore the pattern set by Rule 54 of the Federal Rules of Criminal Procedure is here followed.

The substitution of magistrates in lieu of commissioners is made in pursuance of the Federal Magistrates Act, P.L. 90-578, approved October 17, 1968, 82 Stat. 1107.

Note to Subdivision (b). Subdivision (b) is a combination of the language of the enabling acts, supra, with respect to the kinds of proceedings in which the making of rules is authorized. It is subject to the qualifications expressed in the subdivisions which follow.

Note to Subdivision (c). Subdivision (c) singling out the rules of privilege for special treatment, is made necessary by the limited applicability of the remaining rules.

Note to Subdivision (d). The rule is not intended as an expression as to when due process or other constitutional provisions may require an evidentiary hearing. Paragraph (1) restates, for convenience, the provisions of the second sentence of Rule 104(a), supra. See Advisory Committee's Note to that rule.

(2) While some states have statutory requirements that indictments be based on "legal evidence," and there is some case law to the effect that the rules of evidence apply to grand jury proceedings, 1 Wigmore § 4(5), the Supreme Court has not accepted this view. In Costello v. United States, 350 U.S. 359, 76 S.Ct. 406, 100 L.Ed. 397 (1965), the Court refused to allow an indictment to be attacked, for either constitutional or policy reasons, on the ground that only hearsay evidence was presented.

"It would run counter to the whole history of the grand jury institution, in which laymen conduct their inquiries unfettered by technical rules. Neither justice nor the concept of a fair trial requires such a change." Id. at 364. The rule as drafted does not deal with the evidence required to support an indictment.

(3) The rule exempts preliminary examinations in criminal cases. Authority as to the applicability of the rules of evidence to preliminary examinations has been meagre and conflicting. Goldstein, The State and the Accused: Balance of Advantage in Criminal Procedure, 69 Yale L.J. 1149, 1168, n. 53 (1960); Comment, Preliminary Hearings on Indictable Offenses in Philadelphia, 106 U. of Pa.L.Rev. 589, 592-593 (1958). Hearsay testimony is, however, customarily received in such examinations. Thus in a Dyer Act case, for example, an affidavit may properly be used in a preliminary examination to prove ownership of the stolen vehicle, thus saving the victim of the crime the hardship of having to travel twice to a distant district for the sole purpose of testifying as to ownership. It is believed that the extent of the applicability of the Rules of Evidence to preliminary examinations should be appropriately dealt with by the Federal Rules of Criminal Procedure which regulate those proceedings.

Extradition and rendition proceedings are governed in detail by statute. 18 U.S.C. §§ 3181-3195. They are essentially administrative in character. Traditionally the rules of evidence have not applied. 1 Wigmore § 4(6). Extradition proceedings are accepted from the operation of the Rules of Criminal Procedure. Rule 54(b)(5) of Federal Rules of Criminal Procedure.

The rules of evidence have not been regarded as applicable to sentencing or probation proceedings, where great reliance is placed upon the presentence investigation and report. Rule 32(c) of the Federal Rules of Criminal Procedure requires a presentence investigation and report in every case unless the court otherwise directs. In Williams v. New York, 337 U.S. 241, 69 S.Ct. 1079, 93 L.Ed. 1337 (1949), in which the judge overruled a jury recommendation of life imprisonment and imposed a death sentence, the Court said that due process does not require confrontation or cross-examination in sentencing or passing on probation, and that the judge has broad discretion as to the sources and types of information relied upon. Compare the recommendation that the substance of all derogatory information be disclosed to the defendant, in A.B.A. Project on Minimum Standards for Criminal Justice, Sentencing Alternatives and Procedures § 4.4, Tentative Draft (1967, Sobeloff, Chm.). Williams was adhered to in Specht v. Patterson, 386 U.S. 605, 87 S.Ct. 1209, 18 L.Ed.2d 326 (1967), but not extended to a proceeding under the Colorado Sex Offenders Act, which was said to be a new charge leading in effect to punishment, more like the recidivist statutes where opportunity must be given to be heard on the habitual criminal issue.

Warrants for arrest, criminal summonses, and search warrants are issued upon complaint or affidavit showing probable cause. Rules 4(a) and 41(c) of the Federal Rules of Criminal Procedure. The nature of the proceedings makes application of the formal rules of evidence inappropriate and impracticable.

Criminal contempts are punishable summarily if the judge certifies that he saw or heard the contempt and that it was committed in the presence of the court. Rule 42(a) of the Federal Rules of Criminal Procedure. The circumstances which preclude application of the rules of evidence in this situation are not present, however, in other cases of criminal contempt.

Proceedings with respect to release on bail or otherwise do not call for application of the rules of evidence. The governing statute specifically provides:

"Information stated in, or offered in connection with, any order entered pursuant to this section need not conform to the rules pertaining to the admissibility of evidence in a court of law." 18 U.S.C.A. § 3146(f). This provision is consistent with the type of inquiry contemplated in A.B.A. Project on Minimum Standards for Criminal Justice, Standards Relating to Pretrial Release, § 4.5(b), (c), p. 16 (1968). The references to the weight of the evidence against the accused, in Rule 46(a)(1), (c) of the Federal Rules of Criminal Procedure and in 18 U.S.C.A. § 3146(b), as a factor to be considered, clearly do not have in view evidence introduced at a hearing under the rules of evidence.

The rule does not exempt habeas corpus proceedings. The Supreme Court held in Walker v. Johnston, 312 U.S. 275, 61 S.Ct. 574, 85 L.Ed. 830 (1941), that the practice of disposing of matters of fact on affidavit, which prevailed in some circuits, did not "satisfy the command of the statute that the judge shall proceed 'to determine the facts of the case, by hearing the testimony and arguments.' " This view accords with the emphasis in Townsend v. Sain, 372 U.S. 293, 83 S.Ct. 745, 9 L.Ed.2d 770 (1963), upon trial-type proceedings, id. 311, 83 S.Ct. 745, with demeanor evidence as a significant factor, id. 322, 83 S.Ct. 745, in applications by state prisoners aggrieved by unconstitutional detentions. Hence subdivision (3) applies the rules to habeas corpus proceedings to the extent not inconsistent with the statute.

Note to Subdivision (e). In a substantial number of special proceedings, ad hoc evaluation has resulted in the promulgation of particularized evidentiary provisions, by Act of Congress or by rule adopted by the Supreme Court. Well adapted to the particular proceedings, though not apt candidates for inclusion in a set of general rules, they are left undisturbed. Otherwise, however, the rules of evidence are applicable to the proceedings enumerated in the subdivision.

1974 Enactment
Note to Subdivision (a). Subdivision (a) as submitted to the Congress, in stating the courts and judges to which the Rules of Evidence apply, omitted the Court of Claims and commissioners of that Court. At the request of the Court of Claims, the Committee amended the Rule to include the Court and its commissioners within the purview of the Rules.

Note to Subdivision (b). Subdivision (b) was amended merely to substitute positive law citations for those which were not. House Report No. 93-650.

1987 Amendments
Subdivision (a) is amended to delete the reference to the District Court for the District of the Canal Zone, which no longer exists, and to add the District Court for the Northern Mariana Islands. The United States bankruptcy judges are added to conform the subdivision with Rule 1101(b) and Bankruptcy Rule 9017.

1988 Amendments
The amendments are technical. No substantive change is intended.

1993 Amendments
This revision is made to conform the rule to changes in terminology made by Rule 58 of the Federal Rules of Criminal Procedure and to the changes in the title of United States magistrates made by the Judicial Improvements Act of 1990.

2011 Amendments
The language of Rule 1101 has been amended as part of the restyling of the Evidence Rules to make them more easily understood and to make style and terminology consistent throughout the rules. These changes are intended to be stylistic only. There is no intent to change any result in any ruling on evidence admissibility.

Rule 1102. Amendments

These rules may be amended as provided in 28 U.S.C. § 2072.

Credits

(Pub.L. 93-595, § 1, Jan. 2, 1975, 88 Stat.1948; Apr. 30, 1991, eff. Dec. 1, 1991; Apr. 26, 2011, eff. Dec. 1, 2011.)

Editors' Notes
ADVISORY COMMITTEE NOTES

1991 Amendments
The amendment is technical. No substantive change is intended.

2011 Amendments
The language of Rule 1102 has been amended as part of the restyling of the Evidence Rules to make them more easily understood and to make style and terminology consistent throughout the rules. These changes are intended to be stylistic only. There is no intent to change any result in any ruling on evidence admissibility.

Rule 1103. Title

These rules may be cited as the Federal Rules of Evidence.

Credits

(Pub.L. 93-595, § 1, Jan. 2, 1975, 88 Stat.1948; Apr. 26, 2011, eff. Dec. 1, 2011.)

Editors' Notes

ADVISORY COMMITTEE NOTES

2011 Amendments

The language of Rule 1103 has been amended as part of the restyling of the Evidence Rules to make them more easily understood and to make style and terminology consistent throughout the rules. These changes are intended to be stylistic only. There is no intent to change any result in any ruling on evidence admissibility.

FRE Legislative History

House Report (Judiciary Committee) No. 93-650, Nov. 15, 1973 [To accompany H.R. 5463]
Senate Report (Judiciary Committee) No. 93-1277, Oct. 11, 1974 [To accompany H.R. 5463]

House Conference Report No. 93-1597, Dec. 14, 1974 [To accompany H.R. 5463]
Cong. Record Vol. 120 (1974)

DATES OF CONSIDERATION AND PASSAGE
House February 6, December 18, 1974
Senate November 22, December 16, 1974
The Senate Report, the House Report, and the House Conference Report are set out.
SENATE REPORT NO. 93-1277
The Committee on the Judiciary, to which was referred the bill (H.R. 5463) to establish rules of evidence for certain courts and proceedings, having considered the same, reports favorably thereon with amendments and recommends that the bill as amended do pass.

BACKGROUND

H.R. 5463 is the culmination of 13 years of study by distinguished judges, Members of Congress, lawyers, and others interested in and affected by the administration of justice in the Federal courts.

In 1961, the Judicial Conference of the United States authorized the Honorable Earl Warren, then Chief Justice of the United States, to appoint an advisory committee to study the advisability and feasibility of uniform rules of evidence for use in the Federal courts. The Conference expressed the view that if uniform rules were found to be advisable and feasible, they should be promulgated.

The Chief Justice decided to move first toward a determination of whether uniform rules were advisable and feasible. He appointed a Special Committee on Evidence to make this initial exploration.

Because of the importance of the project and the fact that matters of evidence and proof cross the jurisdictional and interest lines of all of the Judicial Conference Advisory Committees, Chief Justice Warren designated the chairmen of the Civil, Criminal, Bankruptcy, Admiralty and Appellate Advisory Committees to serve on the Special Committee on Evidence.

By December 11, 1961, the Special Committee on Evidence submitted its preliminary report to the Judicial Conference Standing Committee on Rules of Practice and Procedure. In that report the Special Committee on Evidence concluded that uniform rules of evidence were advisable and feasible, and recommended that such rules should be promulgated promptly.

This preliminary report of the Special Committee was circulated for approximately one year with an invitation to the "bench and bar for consideration and suggestions." Thereafter, at its March, 1963, meeting, the Judicial Conference approved the final report of the Special Committee and recommended the appointment of an Advisory Committee on Rules of Evidence to prepare uniform rules of evidence for adoption and promulgation by the Supreme Court of the United States.

A distinguished Advisory Committee composed of judges, lawyers and teachers was appointed on March 8, 1965, and assigned the monumental task of developing a uniform code of evidence for use in the Federal courts.

Approximately 4 years later, in March, 1969, the Judicial Conference Standing Committee on Rules of Practice and Procedure printed and circulated widely for comment a preliminary draft of proposed rules of evidence which had been developed by the Advisory Committee. The draft was accompanied by detailed Advisory Committee notes.

After reviewing the numerous comments, suggestions and proposals received on the preliminary draft, the Advisory Committee and, in turn, the Judicial Conference, approved a revised draft which it submitted to the Supreme Court for promulgation in October, 1970.

The Court, however, returned the draft to the Judicial Conference for further public circulation and opportunity to comment, and in March, 1971, that draft was printed and widely circulated. The final work product of the Advisory Committee of the Judicial Conference and the Standing Committee on Rules of Practice and Procedure, was forwarded to the Supreme Court in October, 1971.

On November 20, 1972, the Supreme Court promulgated the Federal Rules of Evidence pursuant to the various enabling acts in the United States Code (18 U.S.C. 3402, 3771, 3772; 28 U.S.C. 2072, 2075) to take effect on July 1, 1973.

On February 5, 1973, Chief Justice Warren Burger, acting pursuant to the Supreme Court order of November 20, 1972, transmitted the proposed rules to the Congress.

Because of the general importance of these Rules as well as serious questions which were raised with respect to certain Rules of Privilege in particular, the Congress enacted Public Law 93-12 to insure that Congress had a full opportunity to review them. This law deferred the effectiveness of the Rules until expressly approved by Congress.

The Subcommittee on Criminal Justice of the House Judiciary Committee held 6 days of hearings on the proposed rules and after extensive consideration in executive session published a committee print of H.R. 5463, the legislative embodiment of the proposed rules, in June of 1973. The subcommittee exerted extensive efforts to circulate widely its subcommittee print to the bench and bar for consideration and suggestions. After receiving further comments which were carefully evaluated by the subcommittee, H.R. 5463 was approved by the full committee and subsequently passed by the House on February 6, 1974.

NOTE ON PRIVILEGE

Clearly, the most far-reaching House change in the rules as promulgated, was the elimination of the Court's proposed rules on privilege contained in article V. Article V purported to define the privileges to be recognized in the Federal courts in all actions, cases, and proceedings; any alleged privilege not enumerated in article V (e.g., that of a news reporter) was deemed not to exist and could not be given effect unless of constitutional dimension. The privileges recognized included trade secret, lawyer-client, husband-wife, doctor-patient (but applicable only to psychotherapists), identity of informer, secrets of state, and official information.

From the outset, it was clear that the content of the proposed privilege provisions was extremely controversial. Critics attacked, and proponents defended, the secrets of state and official information privileges, with the nub of the disagreement being whether the rule defining them was merely codifying existing law. In addition, the husband-wife privilege drew fire as a result of the conscious decision of the Court to narrow its scope from that recognized under present Federal decisions. The partial doctor-patient privilege seemed to satisfy no one, either doctors or patients; and even the attorney-client privilege as drafted came in for its share of criticism because of its failure to define representative of the client, a critical issue for corporations and organizations. Much controversy also attended the failure to include a newsman's privilege. Further, there was dissatisfaction with the policy of the Court's rule not to require application of State privilege in civil actions where the underlying issues were governed by substantive State law, a result which many legal scholars deemed mandated by Erie R. Co. v. Tompkins.1 Finally, some commentators questioned the wisdom of promulgating rules of privilege under the rules Enabling Act, on the ground that in their view, the codification of the law of privilege should be left to the regular legislative process.

Since it was clear that no agreement was likely to be possible as to the content of specific privilege rules, and since the inability to agree threatened to forestall or prevent passage of an entire rules package, the determination was made that the specific privilege rules proposed by the Court should be eliminated and a single rule (rule 501) substituted, leaving the law in its current condition to be developed by the courts of the United States utilizing the principles of the common law. In addition, a proviso was approved requiring Federal courts to recognize and apply state privilege law in civil cases governed by Erie R. Co. v. Tompkins, supra, as under present Federal case law.2

The rationale underlying the proviso as passed by the House is that Federal law should not supersede that of the States in substantive areas such as privilege absent a compelling reason. This reflects the view that in civil cases in the Federal courts, where a claim or defense asserted is not grounded upon a Federal question, there is no Federal interest in the application, or in its resolution, of a uniform law of Federal privilege strong enough to justify departure from State policy.3 Another rationale for the proviso is that the Court's proposal would have prompted forum shopping in some civil actions, depending upon differences in the privilege law applied as among the State and Federal courts. The House provision, on the other hand, under which the Federal court is bound to apply the State's privilege law in actions founded on a State-created right, might limit the incentive to shop.

Your committee is in accord with the approach of the House with respect to article V. Therefore, save for a technical amendment which is discussed infra., rule 501, as passed by the House, was left undisturbed.

OVERVIEW

On February 7, H.R. 5463 was referred to the Committee on the Judiciary. In order to allow several interested subcommittees to participate in the processing of the Rules, an agreement was reached to retain the bill in full committee. Additionally, it was thought that this approach would likely serve to expedite the measure.

Hearings on the subject bill were held by your committee on June 4 and 5, during which testimony and statements were presented by a score of interested organizations and individuals.4

At the outset, it was evident that the members of the committee viewed with general favor efforts of the House with respect to the subject bill. In this regard, Senator Ervin, at the opening of the hearings, noted:

While I have not as yet studied H.R. 5463 sufficiently to have reached a final conclusion as to the wisdom of each particular rule, I am familiar enough with the bill to suggest that the House Judiciary Committee has drafted a set of rules, which, in my judgment, is greatly improved over what was originally promulgated by the Supreme Court.5

This view was echoed by Senator Hruska who observed:

This Senator is hopeful that this Committee will act promptly on ... [H.R. 5463] ... to ensure the emergence of a public law codifying Federal rules of evidence prior to the close of the 93d Congress. Towards this end, I would hope that our hearings ... will logically build upon the substantial efforts of the House ...6

Therefore, rather than returning to the Rules as promulgated as a work basis for Senate action, your committee focused upon the subject bill as passed by the House.

Although arguments to the contrary have been heard,7 the committee is of the view that there is a real need for a comprehensive code of evidence intended to govern the admissibility of proof in all trials before the Federal courts because of the lack of uniformity and clarity in the present law of evidence on the Federal level.

In criminal cases and civil cases based on Federal question jurisdiction, the Federal courts now apply Federal statutes, rulings on evidence previously decided in suits in equity or general common law as interpreted by the Federal courts.

In civil cases based on diversity of citizenship, the courts apply State rules of evidence contained in State statutes, and sometimes State decisional law, unless there is an overriding Federal policy to the contrary.

Consequently, the law of evidence varies from case to case, court to court, and circuit to circuit.

Rules would provide uniformity, accessibility, intelligibility and a basis for reform and growth. Therefore, arguments against codification were by and large inapposite to the review by your committee.

Perhaps the most fundamental question considered by the committee relevant to the subject bill revolved around the appropriate congressional role in the rulemaking process (Sec. 2).

The general principle that day-to-day judicial procedure and practice is best regulated by the courts, subject only to general oversight by legislative bodies, is a principle which is firmly rooted in Federal statutory law and dates back to the Judiciary Act of 1789. That act gave the Federal courts power to make necessary rules for the orderly conduct of business.

For the purpose of rulemaking, this existing relationship between Congress and the Federal courts is not unlike the relationship between principal and agent. As Leland L. Tollman, one of the principal architects of the Rules of Civil Procedure, succinctly put it in testimony before the House in 1938:

Court rule gets its vitality from Congress, and what Congress may do, it may undo. (House Hearing on Civil Rules, 75th Cong., 1st Sess. 67 (1938).)

As discussed infra, the Congress must ensure that the rule-making process is not delegated to the unbridled discretion of the courts--not because of any distrust of the courts but because of the dictates of sound government.

Other amendments adopted by the committee involve the appropriate scope of judicial discretion, the furtherance of compromise by litigants, the necessity of growth in the law and notions of fundamental fairness within our criminal process. Hopefully, this attempt by the committee to balance competing interests in the context of the subject bill will meet with the general approval of members of the bench and bar and litigants within the Federal system.

COMMITTEE AMENDMENTS

The committee has amended the subject bill in the following respects:

Rule 301. Presumptions in General Civil Actions and Proceedings

This rule governs presumptions in civil cases generally. Rule 302 provides for presumptions in cases controlled by State law.

As submitted by the Supreme Court, presumptions governed by this rule were given the effect of placing upon the opposing party the burden of establishing the nonexistence of the presumed fact, once the party invoking the presumption established the basic facts giving rise to it.

Instead of imposing a burden of persuasion on the party against whom the presumption is directed, the House adopted a provision which shifted the burden of going forward with the evidence. They further provided that "even though met with contradicting evidence, a presumption is sufficient evidence of the fact presumed, to be considered by the trier of fact." The effect of the amendment is that presumptions are to be treated as evidence.

The committee feels the House amendment is ill-advised. As the joint committees (the Standing Committee on Practice and Procedure of the Judicial Conference and the Advisory Committee on the Rules of Evidence) stated: "Presumptions are not evidence, but ways of dealing with evidence."8 This treatment requires juries to perform the task of considering "as evidence" facts upon which they have no direct evidence and which may confuse them in performance of their duties. California had a rule much like that contained in the House amendment. It was sharply criticized by Justice Traynor in Speck v. Sarver9 and was repealed after 93 troublesome years.10

Professor McCormick gives a concise and compelling critique of the presumption as evidence rule:

Another solution, formerly more popular than now, is to instruct the jury that the presumption is 'evidence', to be weighed and considered with the testimony in the case. This avoids the danger that the jury may infer that the presumption is conclusive, but it probably means little to the jury, and certainly runs counter to accepted theories of the nature of evidence.11

For these reasons the committee has deleted that provision of the House-passed rule that treats presumptions as evidence. The effect of the rule as adopted by the committee is to make clear that while evidence of facts giving rise to a presumption shifts the burden of coming forward with evidence to rebut or meet the presumption, it does not shift the burden of persuasion on the existence of the presumed facts. The burden of persuasion remains on the party to whom it is allocated under the rules governing the allocation in the first instance.

The court may instruct the jury that they may infer the existence of the presumed fact from proof of the basic facts giving rise to the presumption. However, it would be inappropriate under this rule to instruct the jury that the inference they are to draw is conclusive.

Rule 408. Compromise and offers to compromise

This rule as reported makes evidence of settlement or attempted settlement of a disputed claim inadmissible when offered as an admission of liability or the amount of liability. The purpose of this rule is to encourage settlements which would be discouraged if such evidence were admissible.

Under present law, in most jurisdictions, statements of fact made during settlement negotiations, however, are excepted from this ban and are admissible. The only escape from admissibility of statements of fact made in a settlement negotiation is if the declarant or his representative expressly states that the statement is hypothetical in nature or it made without prejudice. Rule 408 as submitted by the Court reversed the traditional rule. It would have brought statements of fact within the ban and made them, as well as an offer of settlement, inadmissible.

The House amended the rule and would continue to make evidence of facts disclosed during compromise negotiations admissible. It thus reverted to the traditional rule. The House committee report states that the committee intends to preserve current law under which a party may protect himself by couching his statements in hypothetical form.12 The real impact of this amendment, however, is to deprive the rule of much of its salutary effect. The exception for factual admissions was believed by the Advisory Committee to hamper free communication between parties and thus to constitute an unjustifiable restraint upon efforts to negotiate settlements--the encouragement of which is the purpose of the rule. Further, by protecting hypothetically phrased statements, it constituted a preference for the sophisticated, and a trap for the unwary.

Three States which had adopted rules of evidence patterned after the proposed rules prescribed by the Supreme Court opted for versions of rule 408 identical with the Supreme Court draft with respect to the inadmissibility of conduct or statements made in compromise negotiations.13

For these reasons, the committee has deleted the House amendment and restored the rule to the version submitted by the Supreme Court with one additional amendment. This amendment adds a sentence to insure that evidence, such as documents, is not rendered inadmissible merely because it is presented in the course of compromise negotiations if the evidence is otherwise discoverable. A party should not be able to immunize from admissibility documents otherwise discoverable merely by offering them in a compromise negotiation.

Rule 410. Offer to plead guilty; nolo contendere; withdrawn plea of guilty

As adopted by the House, rule 410 would make inadmissible pleas of guilty or nolo contendere subsequently withdrawn as well as offers to make such pleas. Such a rule is clearly justified as a means of encouraging pleading. However, the House rule would then go on to render inadmissible for any purpose statements made in connection with these pleas or offers as well.

The committee finds this aspect of the House rule unjustified. Of course, in certain circumstances such statements should be excluded. If, for example, a plea is vitiated because of coercion, statements made in connection with the plea may also have been coerced and should be inadmissible on that basis. In other cases, however, voluntary statements of an accused made in court on the record, in connection with a plea, and determined by a court to be reliable should be admissible even though the plea is subsequently withdrawn. This is particularly true in those cases where, if the House rule were in effect, a defendant would be able to contradict his previous statements and thereby lie with impunity.14 To prevent such an injustice, the rule has been modified to permit the use of such statements for the limited purposes of impeachment and in subsequent perjury or false statement prosecutions.

Rule 501. Privileges--General rule

Article V as submitted to Congress contained 13 rules. Nine of those rules defined specific nonconstitutional privileges which the Federal courts must recognize (i.e., required reports, lawyer-client, psychotherapist-patient, husband-wife, communications to clergymen, political vote, trade secrets, secrets of state and other official information, and identity of informer). Many of these rules contained controversial modifications or restrictions upon common law privileges. As noted supra, the House amended article V to eliminate all of the Court's specific rules on privileges. Through a single rule, 501, the House provided that privileges shall be governed by the principles of the common law as interpreted by the courts of the United States in the light of reason and experience (a standard derived from rule 26 of the Federal Rules of Criminal Procedure) except in the case of an element of a civil claim or defense as to which State law supplies the rule of decision, in which event state privilege law was to govern.

The committee agrees with the main thrust of the House amendment: that a federally developed common law based on modern reason and experience shall apply except where the State nature of the issues renders deference to State privilege law the wiser course, as in the usual diversity case. The committee understands that thrust of the House amendment to require that State privilege law be applied in "diversity" cases (actions on questions of State law between citizens of different States arising under 28 U.S.C. § 1332). The language of the House amendment, however, goes beyond this in some respects, and falls short of it in others: State privilege law applies even in nondiversity, Federal question civil cases, where an issue governed by State substantive law is the object of the evidence (such issues do sometimes arise in such cases); and, in all instances where State privilege law is to be applied, e.g., on proof of a State issue in a diversity case, a close reading reveals that State privilege law is not to be applied unless the matter to be proved is an element of that state claim or defense, as distinguished from a step along the way in the proof of it.

The committee is concerned that the language used in the House amendment could be difficult to apply. It provides that "in civil actions ... with respect to an element of a claim or defense as to which State law supplies the rule of decision," State law on privilege applies. The question of what is an element of a claim or defense is likely to engender considerable litigation. If the matter in question constitutes an element of a claim, State law supplies the privilege rule; whereas if it is a mere item of proof with respect to a claim, then, even though State law might supply the rule of decision, Federal law on the privilege would apply. Further, disputes will arise as to how the rule should be applied in an antitrust action or in a tax case where the Federal statute is silent as to a particular aspect of the substantive law in question, but Federal cases had incorporated State law by reference to State law.15 Is a claim (or defense) based on such a reference a claim or defense as to which federal or State law supplies the rule of decision?

Another problem not entirely avoidable is the complexity or difficulty the rule introduces into the trial of a Federal case containing a combination of Federal and State claims and defenses, e.g. an action involving Federal antitrust and State unfair competition claims. Two different bodies of privilege law would need to be consulted. It may even develop that the same witness-testimony might be relevant on both counts and privileged as to one but not the other.15a

The formulation adopted by the House is pregnant with litigious mischief. The committee has, therefore, adopted what we believe will be a clearer and more practical guideline for determining when courts should respect State rules of privilege. Basically, it provides that in criminal and Federal question civil cases, federally evolved rules on privilege should apply since it is Federal policy which is being enforced.16 Conversely, in diversity cases where the litigation in question turns on a substantive question of State law, and is brought in the Federal courts because the parties reside in different States, the committee believes it is clear that State rules of privilege should apply unless the proof is directed at a claim or defense for which Federal law supplies the rule of decision (a situation which would not commonly arise.)17 It is intended that the State rules of privilege should apply equally in original diversity actions and diversity actions removed under 28 U.S.C. § 1441(b).

Two other comments on the privilege rule should be made. The committee has received a considerable volume of correspondence from psychiatric organizations and psychiatrists concerning the deletion of rule 504 of the rule submitted by the Supreme Court. It should be clearly understood that, in approving this general rule as to privileges, the action of Congress should not be understood as disapproving any recognition of a psychiatrist-patient, or husband-wife, or any other of the enumerated privileges contained in the Supreme Court rules. Rather, our action should be understood as reflecting the view that the recognition of a privilege based on a confidential relationship and other privileges should be determined on a case-by-case basis.

Further, we would understand that the prohibition against spouses testifying against each other is considered a rule of privilege and covered by this rule and not by rule 601 of the competency of witnesses.

Rule 601. General Rule of Competency

The amendment to rule 601 parallels the treatment accorded rule 501 discussed immediately above.

Rule 606(b). Competency of Juror as a Witness: Inquiry into Validity of Verdict or Indictment

As adopted by the House, this rule would permit the impeachment of verdicts by inquiry into, not the mental processes of the jurors, but what happened in terms of conduct in the jury room. This extension of the ability to impeach a verdict is felt to be unwarranted and ill-advised.

The rule passed by the House embodies a suggestion by the Advisory Committee of the Judicial Conference that is considerably broader than the final version adopted by the Supreme Court, which embodied long-accepted Federal law. Although forbidding the impeachment of verdicts by inquiry into the jurors' mental processes, it deletes from the Supreme Court version the proscription against testimony "as to any matter or statement occurring during the course of the jury's deliberations." This deletion would have the effect of opening verdicts up to challenge on the basis of what happened during the jury's internal deliberations, for example, where a juror alleged that the jury refused to follow the trial judge's instructions or that some of the jurors did not take part in deliberations.

Permitting an individual to attack a jury verdict based upon the jury's internal deliberations has long been recognized as unwise by the Supreme Court. In McDonald v. Pless, the Court stated:

[L]et it once be established that verdicts solemnly made and publicly returned into court can be attacked and set aside on the testimony of those who took part in their publication and all verdicts could be, and many would be, followed by an inquiry in the hope of discovering something which might invalidate the finding. Jurors would be harassed and beset by the defeated party in an effort to secure from them evidence of facts which might establish misconduct sufficient to set aside a verdict. If evidence thus secured could be thus used, the result would be to make what was intended to be a private deliberation, the constant subject of public investigation--to the destruction of all frankness and freedom of discussion and conference.18

As it stands then, the rule would permit the harassment of former jurors by losing parties as well as the possible exploitation of disgruntled or otherwise badly-motivated ex-jurors.

Public policy requires a finality to litigation. And common fairness requires that absolute privacy be preserved for jurors to engage in the full and free debate necessary to the attainment of just verdicts. Jurors will not be able to function effectively if their deliberations are to be scrutinized in post-trial litigation. In the interest of protecting the jury system and the citizens who make it work, rule 606 should not permit any inquiry into the internal deliberations of the jurors.

Rule 609(a). Impeachment by Evidence of Conviction

As proposed by the Supreme Court, the rule would allow the use of prior convictions to impeach if the crime was a felony or a misdemeanor if the misdemeanor involved dishonesty or false statement. As modified by the House, the rule would admit prior convictions for impeachment purposes only if the offense, whether felony or misdemeanor, involved dishonesty or false statement.

The committee has adopted a modified version of the House-passed rule. In your committee's view, the danger of unfair prejudice is far greater when the accused, as opposed to other witnesses, testifies, because the jury may be prejudiced not merely on the question of credibility but also on the ultimate question of guilt or innocence. Therefore, with respect to defendants, the committee agreed with the House limitation that only offenses involving false statement or dishonesty may be used. By that phrase, the committee means crimes such as perjury or subornation of perjury, false statement, criminal fraud, embezzlement or false pretense, or any other offense, in the nature of crimen falsi the commission of which involves some element of untruthfulness, deceit or falsification bearing on the accused's propensity to testify truthfully.

With respect to other witnesses, in addition to any prior conviction involving false statement or dishonesty, any other felony may be used to impeach if, and only if, the court finds that the probative value of such evidence outweighs its prejudicial effect against the party offering that witness.

Notwithstanding this provision, proof of any prior offense otherwise admissible under rule 404 could still be offered for the purposes sanctioned by that rule. Furthermore, the committee intends that notwithstanding this rule, a defendant's misrepresentation regarding the existence or nature of prior convictions may be met by rebuttal evidence, including the record of such prior convictions. Similarly, such records may be offered to rebut representations made by the defendant regarding his attitude toward or willingness to commit a general category of offense, although denials or other representations by the defendant regarding the specific conduct which forms the basis of the charge against him shall not make prior convictions admissible to rebut such statement.

In regard to either type of representation, of course, prior convictions may be offered in rebuttal only if the defendant's statement is made in response to defense counsel's questions or is made gratuitously in the course of cross-examination. Prior convictions may not be offered as rebuttal evidence if the prosecution has sought to circumvent the purpose of this rule by asking questions which elicit such representations from the defendant.

One other clarifying amendment has been added to this subsection, that is, to provide that the admissibility of evidence of a prior conviction is permitted only upon cross-examination of a witness. It is not admissible if a person does not testify. It is to be understood, however, that a court record of a prior conviction is admissible to prove that conviction if the witness has forgotten or denies its existence.

Rule 609(b). Impeachment by Evidence of Conviction of Crime; Time Limit

Although convictions over ten years old generally do not have much probative value, there may be exceptional circumstances under which the conviction substantially bears on the credibility of the witness. Rather than exclude all convictions over 10 years old, the committee adopted an amendment in the form of a final clause to the section granting the court discretion to admit convictions over 10 years old, but only upon a determination by the court that the probative value of the conviction supported by specific facts and circumstances, substantially outweighs its prejudicial effect.

It is intended that convictions over 10 years old will be admitted very rarely and only in exceptional circumstances. The rules provide that the decision be supported by specific facts and circumstances thus requiring the court to make specific findings on the record as to the particular facts and circumstances it has considered in determining that the probative value of the conviction substantially outweighs its prejudicial impact. It is expected that, in fairness, the court will give the party against whom the conviction is introduced a full and adequate opportunity to contest its admission.

Rule 801(d)(1)(A). Hearsay definitions; Prior Statement by Witness

Rule 801 defines what is and what is not hearsay for the purpose of admitting a prior statement as substantive evidence. A prior statement of a witness at a trial or hearing which is inconsistent with his testimony is, of course, always admissible for the purpose of impeaching the witness' credibility.

As submitted by the Supreme Court, subdivision (d)(1)(A) made admissible as substantive evidence the prior statement of a witness inconsistent with his present testimony.

The House severely limited the admissibility of prior inconsistent statements by adding a requirement that the prior statement must have been subject to cross-examination, thus precluding even the use of grand jury statements. The requirement that the prior statement must have been subject to cross-examination appears unnecessary since this rule comes into play only when the witness testifies in the present trial. At that time, he is on the stand and can explain an earlier position and be cross-examined as to both.

The requirement that the statement be under oath also appears unnecessary. Notwithstanding the absence of an oath contemporaneous with the statement, the witness, when on the stand, qualifying or denying the prior statement, is under oath. In any event, of all the many recognized exceptions to the hearsay rule, only one (former testimony) requires that the out-of-court statement have been made under oath. With respect to the lack of evidence of the demeanor of the witness at the time of the prior statement, it would be difficult to improve upon Judge Learned Hand's observation that when the jury decides that the truth is not what the witness says now but what he said before, they are still deciding from what they see and hear in court.19

The rule as submitted by the Court has positive advantages. The prior statement was made nearer in time to the events, when memory was fresher and intervening influences had not been brought into play. A realistic method is provided for dealing with the turncoat witness who changes his story on the stand.20

New Jersey, California, and Utah have adopted a rule similar to this one; and Nevada, New Mexico, and Wisconsin have adopted the identical Federal rule.

For all of these reasons, we think the House amendment should be rejected and the rule as submitted by the Supreme Court reinstated.21

As submitted by the Supreme Court and as passed by the House, subdivision (d)(1)(c) of rule 801 made admissible the prior statement identifying a person made after perceiving him. The committee decided to delete this provision because of the concern that a person could be convicted solely upon evidence admissible under this subdivision.

Rule 803(6). Hearsay Exceptions; Records of Regularly Conducted Activity

Rule 803(6) as submitted by the Supreme Court permitted a record made in the course of a regularly conducted activity to be admissible in certain circumstances. This rule constituted a broadening of the traditional business records hearsay exception which has been long advocated by scholars and judges active in the law of evidence.

The House felt there were insufficient guarantees of reliability of records not within a broadly defined business records exception. We disagree. Even under the House definition of "business" including profession, occupation, and "calling of every kind," the records of many regularly conducted activities will, or may be, excluded from evidence. Under the principle of ejusdem generis, the intent of "calling of every kind" would seem to be related to work-related endeavors-- e.g., butcher, baker, artist, etc.

Thus, it appears that the records of many institutions or groups might not be admissible under the House amendments. For example, schools, churches, and hospitals will not normally be considered businesses within the definition. Yet, these are groups which keep financial and other records on a regular basis in a manner similar to business enterprises. We believe these records are of equivalent trustworthiness and should be admitted into evidence.

Three states, which have recently codified their evidence rules, have adopted the Supreme Court version of rule 803(6), providing for admission of memoranda of a "regularly conducted activity." None adopted the words "business activity" used in the House amendment.22

Therefore, the committee deleted the word "business" as it appears before the word "activity". The last sentence then is unnecessary and was also deleted.

It is the understanding of the committee that the use of the phrase "person with knowledge" is not intended to imply that the party seeking to introduce the memorandum, report, record, or data compilation must be able to produce, or even identify, the specific individual upon whose first-hand knowledge the memorandum, report, record or data compilation was based. A sufficient foundation for the introduction of such evidence will be laid if the party seeking to introduce the evidence is able to show that it was the regular practice of the activity to base such memorandums, reports, records, or data compilations upon a transmission from a person with knowledge, e.g., in the case of the content of a shipment of goods, upon a report from the company's receiving agent or in the case of a computer printout, upon a report from the company's computer programmer or one who has knowledge of the particular record system. In short, the scope of the phrase "person with knowledge" is meant to be coterminous with the custodian of the evidence or other qualified witness. The committee believes this represents the desired rule in light of the complex nature of modern business organizations.

Rules 803(8) and 804(b)(5). Hearsay Exceptions; Public Records and reports

The House approved rule 803(8), as submitted by the Supreme Court, with one substantive change. It excluded from the hearsay exception reports containing matters observed by police officers and other law enforcement personnel in criminal cases. Ostensibly, the reason for this exclusion is that observations by police officers at the scene of the crime or the apprehension of the defendant are not as reliable as observations by public officials in other cases because of the adversarial nature of the confrontation between the police and the defendant in criminal cases.

The committee accepts the House's decision to exclude such recorded observations where the police officer is available to testify in court about his observation. However, where he is unavailable as unavailability is defined in rule 804(a)(4) and (a)(5), the report should be admitted as the best available evidence. Accordingly, the committee has amended rule 803(8) to refer to the provision of rule 804(b)(5), which allows the admission of such reports, records or other statements where the police officer or other law enforcement officer is unavailable because of death, then existing physical or mental illness or infirmity, or not being successfully subject to legal process.

The House Judiciary Committee report contained a statement of intent that "the phrase 'factual findings' in subdivision (c) be strictly construed and that evaluations or opinions contained in public reports shall not be admissible under this rule." The committee takes strong exception to this limiting understanding of the application of the rule. We do not think it reflects an understanding of the intended operation of the rule as explained in the Advisory Committee notes to this subsection. The Advisory Committee notes on subsection (c) of this subdivision point out that various kinds of evaluative reports are now admissible under Federal statutes. 7 U.S.C. § 78, findings of Secretary of Agriculture prima facie evidence of true grade of grain; 42 U.S.C. § 269(b), bill of health by appropriate official prima facie evidence of vessel's sanitary history and condition and compliance with regulations. These statutory exceptions to the hearsay rule are preserved. Rule 802. The willingness of Congress to recognize these and other such evaluative reports provides a helpful guide in determining the kind of reports which are intended to be admissible under this rule. We think the restrictive interpretation of the House overlooks the fact that while the Advisory Committee assumes admissibility in the first instance of evaluative reports, they are not admissible if, as the rule states, "the sources of information or other circumstances indicate lack of trustworthiness."

The Advisory Committee explains the factors to be considered:

Factors which may be assistance in passing upon the admissibility of evaluative reports include: (1) the timeliness of the investigation, McCormick, Can the Courts Make Wider Use of Reports of Official Investigations? 42 Iowa L.Rev. 363 (1957); (2) the special skill or experience of the official, id.; (3) whether a hearing was held and the level at which conducted, Franklin v. Skelly Oil Co., 141 F.2d 568 (19th Cir.1944); (4) possible motivation problems suggested by Palmer v. Hoffman, 318 U.S. 109, 63 S.Ct. 477, 87 L.Ed. 645 (1943). Others no doubt could be added.23

The committee concludes that the language of the rule together with the explanation provided by the Advisory Committee furnish sufficient guidance on the admissibility of evaluative reports.

Rules 803(24) and 804(b)(6). Hearsay Exceptions; Other Exceptions

The proposed Rules of Evidence submitted to Congress contained identical provisions in rules 803 and 804 (which set forth the various hearsay exceptions), admitting any hearsay statement not specifically covered by any of the stated exceptions, if the hearsay statement was found to have "comparable circumstantial guarantees of trustworthiness." The House deleted these provisions (proposed rules 803(24) and 804(b)(6)) as injecting "too much uncertainty" into the law of evidence and impairing the ability of practitioners to prepare for trial. The House felt that rule 102, which directs the courts to construe the Rules of Evidence so as to promote growth and development, would permit sufficient flexibility to admit hearsay evidence in appropriate cases under various factual situations that might arise.

We disagree with the total rejection of a residual hearsay exception. While we view rule 102 as being intended to provide for a broader construction and interpretation of these rules, we feel that, without a separate residual provision, the specifically enumerated exceptions could become tortured beyond any reasonable circumstances which they were intended to include (even if broadly construed). Moreover, these exceptions, while they reflect the most typical and well recognized exceptions to the hearsay rule, may not encompass every situation in which the reliability and appropriateness of a particular piece of hearsay evidence make clear that it should be heard and considered by the trier of fact.

The committee believes that there are certain exceptional circumstances where evidence which is found by a court to have guarantees of trustworthiness equivalent to or exceeding the guarantees reflected by the presently listed exceptions, and to have a high degree of prolativeness and necessity could properly be admissible.

The case of Dallas County v. Commercial Union Assoc. Co., Ltd., 286 F.2d 388 (5th Cir.1961) illustrates the point. The issue in that case was whether the tower of the county courthouse collapsed because it was struck by lightning (covered by insurance) or because of structural weakness and deterioration of the structure (not covered). Investigation of the structure revealed the presence of charcoal and charred timbers. In order to show that lightning may not have been the cause of the charring, the insurer offered a copy of a local newspaper published over 50 years earlier containing an unsigned article describing a fire in the courthouse while it was under construction. The Court found that the newspaper did not qualify for admission as a business record or an ancient document and did not fit within any other recognized hearsay exception. The court concluded, however, that the article was trustworthy because it was inconceivable that a newspaper reporter in a small town would report a fire in the courthouse if none had occurred. See also United States v. Barbati, 284 F.Supp. 409 (E.D.N.Y.1968).

Because exceptional cases like the Dallas County case may arise in the future, the committee has decided to reinstate a residual exception for rules 803 and 804(b).

The committee, however, also agrees with those supporters of the House version who felt that an overly broad residual hearsay exception could emasculate the hearsay rule and the recognized exceptions or vitiate the rationale behind codification of the rules.

Therefore, the committee has adopted a residual exception for rules 803 and 804(b) of much narrower scope and applicability than the Supreme Court version. In order to qualify for admission, a hearsay statement not falling within one of the recognized exceptions would have to satisfy at least four conditions. First, it must have "equivalent circumstantial guarantees of trustworthiness." Second, it must be offered as evidence of a material fact. Third, the court must determine that the statement "is more probative on the point for which it is offered than any other evidence which the proponent can procure through reasonable efforts." This requirement is intended to insure that only statements which have high probative value and necessity may qualify for admission under the residual exceptions. Fourth, the court must determine that "the general purposes of these rules and the interests of justice will best be served by admission of the statement into evidence."

It is intended that the residual hearsay exceptions will be used very rarely, and only in exceptional circumstances. The committee does not intend to establish a broad license for trial judges to admit hearsay statements that do not fall within one of the other exceptions contained in rules 803 and 804(b). The residual exceptions are not meant to authorize major judicial revisions of the hearsay rule, including its present exceptions. Such major revisions are best accomplished by legislative action. It is intended that in any case in which evidence is sought to be admitted under these subsections, the trial judge will exercise no less care, reflection and caution than the courts did under the common law in establishing the now-recognized exceptions to the hearsay rule.

In order to establish a well-defined jurisprudence, the special facts and circumstances which, in the court's judgment, indicates that the statement has a sufficiently high degree of trustworthiness and necessity to justify its admission should be stated on the record. It is expected that the court will give the opposing party a full and adequate opportunity to contest the admission of any statement sought to be introduced under these subsections.

Rule 804(a)(5). Hearsay Exceptions; Declarant Unavailable; Definition of Unavailability

Subdivision (a) of rule 804 as submitted by the Supreme Court defined the conditions under which a witness was considered to be unavailable. It was amended in the House.

The purpose of the amendment, according to the report of the House Committee on the Judiciary, is "primarily to require that an attempt be made to depose a witness (as well as to seek his attendance) as a precondition to the witness being unavailable."25

Under the House amendment, before a witness is declared unavailable, a party must try to depose a witness (declarant) with respect to dying declarations, declarations against interest, and declarations of pedigree. None of these situations would seem to warrant this needless, impractical and highly restrictive complication. A good case can be made for eliminating the unavailability requirement entirely for declarations against interest cases.26

In dying declaration cases, the declarant will usually, though not necessarily, be deceased at the time of trial. Pedigree statements which are admittedly and necessarily based largely on word of mouth are not greatly fortified by a deposition requirement.

Depositions are expensive and time-consuming. In any event, deposition procedures are available to those who wish to resort to them. Moreover, the deposition procedures of the Civil Rules and Criminal Rules are only imperfectly adapted to implementing the amendment. No purpose is served unless the deposition, if taken, may be used in evidence. Under Civil Rule (a)(3) and Criminal Rule 15(e), a deposition, though taken, may not be admissible, and under Criminal Rule 15(a) substantial obstacles exist in the way of even taking a deposition.

For these reasons, the committee deleted the House amendment.

The committee understand that the rule as to unavailability, as explained by the Advisory Committee "contains no requirement that an attempt be made to take the deposition of a declarant." In reflecting the committee's judgment, the statement is accurate insofar as it goes. Where, however, the proponent of the statement, with knowledge of the existence of the statement, fails to confront the declarant with the statement at the taking of the deposition, then the proponent should not, in fairness, be permitted to treat the declarant as "unavailable" simply because the declarant was not amenable to process compelling his attendance at trial. The committee does not consider it necessary to amend the rule to this effect because such a situation abuses, not conforms to, the rule. Fairness would preclude a person from introducing a hearsay statement on a particular issue if the person taking the deposition was aware of the issue at the time of the deposition but failed to depose the unavailable witness on that issue.

Rule 804(b)(3). Hearsay Exceptions; Declarant Unavailable; Statement Against Interest

The rule defines those statements which are considered to be against interest and thus of sufficient trustworthiness to be admissible even though hearsay. With regard to the type of interest declared against, the version submitted by the Supreme Court included inter alia, statements tending to subject a declarant to civil liability or to invalidate a claim by him against another. The House struck these provisions as redundant. In view of the conflicting case law construing pecuniary or proprietary interests narrowly so as to exclude, e.g., tort cases, this deletion could be misconstrued.

Three States which have recently codified their rules of evidence have followed the Supreme Court's version of this rule, i.e., that a statement is against interest if it tends to subject a declarant to civil liability.27

The committee believes that the reference to statements tending to subject a person to civil liability constitutes a desirable clarification of the scope of the rule. Therefore, we have reinstated the Supreme Court language on this matter.

The Court rule also proposed to expand the hearsay limitation from its present federal limitation to include statements subjecting the declarant to statements tending to make him an object of hatred, ridicule, or disgrace. The House eliminated the latter category from the subdivision as lacking sufficient guarantees of reliability. Although there is considerable support for the admissibility of such statements (all three of the State rules referred to supra, would admit such statements), we accept the deletion by the House.

Rule 804(b)(3). Hearsay Exceptions; statement against interest

The House amended this exception to add a sentence making inadmissible a statement or confession offered against the accused in a criminal case, made by a codefendant or other person implicating both himself and the accused. The sentence was added to codify the constitutional principle announced in Bruton v. United States, 391 U.S. 123 (1968). Bruton held that the admission of the extrajudicial hearsay statement of one codefendant inculpating a second codefendant violated the confrontation clause of the sixth amendment.

The committee decided to delete this provision because the basic approach of the rules is to avoid codifying, or attempting to codify, constitutional evidentiary principles, such as the fifth amendment's right against self-incrimination and, here, the sixth amendment's right of confrontation. Codification of a constitutional principle is unnecessary and, where the principle is under development, often unwise. Furthermore, the House provision does not appear to recognize the exceptions to the Bruton rule, e.g. where the codefendant takes the stand and is subject to cross examination; where the accused confessed, see United States v. Mancusi, 404 F.2d 296 (2d Cir. 1968), cert. denied 397 U.S. 942 (1907); where the accused was placed at the scene of the crime, see United States v. Zelker, 452 F.2d 1009 (2d Cir.1971). For these reasons, the committee decided to delete this provision.

Rule 806. Attacking and Supporting Credibility of Declarant

Rule 906, as passed by the House and as proposed by the Supreme Court provides that whenever a hearsay statement is admitted, the credibility of the declarant of the statement may be attacked, and if attacked may be supported, by any evidence which would be admissible for those purposes if the declarant had testified as a witness. Rule 801 defines what is a hearsay statement. While statements by a person authorized by a party-opponent to make a statement concerning the subject, by the party-opponent's agent or by a coconspirator of a party--see rule 801(d)(2)(c), (d) and (e)--are traditionally defined as exceptions to the hearsay rule, rule 801 defines such admission by a party-opponent as statements which are not hearsay. Consequently, rule 806 by referring exclusively to the admission of hearsay statements, does not appear to allow the credibility of the declarant to be attacked when the declarant is a coconspirator, agent or authorized spokesman. The committee is of the view that such statements should open the declarant to attacks on his credibility. Indeed, the reason such statements are excluded from the operation of rule 806 is likely attributable to the drafting technique used to codify the hearsay rule, viz some statements, instead of being referred to as exceptions to the hearsay rule, are defined as statements which are not hearsay. The phrase "or a statement defined in rule 801(d)(2)(c), (d) and (e)" is added to the rule in order to subject the declarant of such statements, like the declarant of hearsay statements, to attacks on his credibility. 28

SECTION 2. ENABLING ACT

The House, in order to clarify the power of the Supreme Court to issue Rules of Evidence or amendments to them, added a new section 2076 to title 28, United States Code, specifying the Supreme Court's 3402; 28 U.S.C. 2072, 2075), which the Supreme Court invoked as the authority pursuant to which it promulgated the Rules of Evidence, provide that the Court may prescribe rules of "practice and procedure" and submit them to Congress. The rules then take effect automatically either at such time as the Court directs, or after 90 days following their submission. An act of Congress is necessary to prevent any rule so submitted from taking effect.

The House believed that the Rules of Evidence involve policy judgments as to which it is appropriate for the Congress to play a greater role than that provided in the present Enabling Acts. Accordingly, the bill provides for a new statutory procedure by which amendments to the Rules of Evidence may be made, designed to insure adequate congressional participation in the evidence rulemaking process. Section 2(a) adds a new section, 2076, to title 28, United States Code, permitting the Court to prescribe amendments to the Rules of Evidence, which amendments must be reported to the Congress. However, three changes were made with respect to the role of Congress. First, any rule, rather than the entire package of rules may be disapproved. Second, either House of Congress, rather than the both Houses acting together, can prevent a rule from becoming operative. Third, rather than the 90-day period allowed in the existing Rules Enabling Acts, a 180-day period is prescribed for congressional action.

In order to augment the power of Congress to review rules of evidence, the committee made two additional amendments. It decided to extend the review period to 365 days--1 full year--and adopted a provision under which either House of Congress can defer the effective date of a rule to permit further study, either until a later date or until approved by Act of Congress. Thus, either House of Congress can disapprove or defer consideration of any proposed rule or combination of rules. The committee also added one clarifying amendment which provides that either a proposed rule or a rule already in effect may be amended by act of Congress. While this has been generally understood, the committee feels it should be made clear.

The committee considered the possibility of requiring congressional approval of any rule of evidence submitted to it by the Court. We determined, however, that while requiring affirmative congressional action was appropriate to this first effort at codifying the Rules of Evidence, it was not needed with respect to subsequent amendments which would likely be of more modest dimension. Indeed, the committee believed that to require affirmative congressional action with respect to amendments might well result in some worthwhile amendments not being approved because of other pressing demands on the Congress. The committee thus concluded that the system of allowing Court-proposed amendments to the Rules of Evidence to take effect automatically unless disapproved by either House strikes a sound balance between the proper role of Congress in the amendatory process and the dictates of convenience and legislative priorities.

For the same reasons, the committee has deleted an amendment made no [on] the floor of the House providing that no amendment creating, abolishing or modifying a privilege could take effect until approved by act of Congress. The basis for the House action was the belief that rules of privilege constitute matters of substance that require affirmative congressional approval. While matters of privilege are, in a sense, substantive, and also involve particularly sensitive issues, the committee does not believe that privileges necessarily require different treatment from other rules, provided there are adequate safeguards so that the Congress retains sufficient review power to review effectively proposed changes in this area, as well as in others. By extending the period of review from 90 to 365 days and by providing that any proposed rule may be disapproved or its effective date deferred by either House of Congress, the committee believes that the Congress does, in fact retain sufficient review power to reflect its views on such matters.

Subsection (b) strikes out section 1732(a) of title 28, United States Code, since its subject matter is covered in rule 803(b) relating to records of a regularly conducted activity.

Subsection (c) amends section 1733 of title 28, United States Code, since that section is largely, if not entirely, encompassed by rule 803(8) relating to public records and reports. Because of the possibility that section 1733 may reach some matters not touched by rule 803(9), subsection (c) does not repeal section 1733 but merely provides that the section does not apply to actions, cases, and proceedings to which the Rules of Evidence are applicable.

ADDITIONAL COMMENTARIES

Additional commentary was deemed appropriate by the committee with respect to certain rules left undisturbed in the subject bill.

Rule 104(d). Preliminary Questions: Testimony by accused

Under rule 104(c) the hearing on a preliminary matter may at times be conducted in front of the jury. Should an accused testify in such a hearing, waiving his privilege against self-incrimination as to the preliminary issue, rule 104(d) provides that he will not generally be subject to cross-examination as to any other issue. This rule is not, however, intended to immunize the accused from cross-examination where, in testifying about a preliminary issue, he injects other issues into the hearing. If he could not be cross-examined about any issues gratuitously raised by him beyond the scope of the preliminary matters, injustice might result. Accordingly, in order to prevent any such unjust result, the committee intends the rule to be construed to provide that the accused may subject himself to cross-examination as to issues raised by his own testimony upon a preliminary matter before a jury.

Rule 105. Summing Up and Comment by Judge

This rule as submitted by the Supreme Court permitted the judge to sum up and comment on the evidence. The House struck the rule.

The committee accepts the House action with the understanding that the present Federal practice, taken from the common law, of the trial judge's discretionary authority to comment on and summarize the evidence is left undisturbed.

Rule 404(b). Character Evidence Not Admissible To Prove Conduct; Other crimes, wrongs, or acts

This rule provides that evidence of other crimes, wrongs, or acts is not admissible to prove character but may be admissible for other specified purposes such as proof of motive.

Although your committee sees no necessity in amending the rule itself, it anticipates that the use of the discretionary word "may" with respect to the admissibility of evidence of crimes, wrongs, or acts is not intended to confer any arbitrary discretion on the trial judge. Rather, it is anticipated that with respect to permissible uses for such evidence, the trial judge may exclude it only on the basis of those considerations set forth in Rule 403, i.e. prejudice, confusion or waste of time.

Rule 611(b). Mode and Order of Interrogation and Presentation; Scope of Cross-examination

Rule 611(b) as submitted by the Supreme Court permitted a broad scope of cross-examination: "cross-examination on any matter relevant to any issue in the case" unless the judge, in the interests of justice, limited the scope of cross-examination.

The House narrowed the Rule to the more traditional practice of limiting cross-examination to the subject matter of direct examination (and credibility), but with discretion in the judge to permit inquiry into additional matters in situations where that would aid in the development of the evidence or otherwise facilitate the conduct of the trial.

The committee agrees with the House amendment. Although there are good arguments in support of broad cross-examination from prospectives of developing all relevant evidence, we believe the factors of insuring an orderly and predictable development of the evidence weigh in favor of the narrower rule, especially when discreation is given to the trial judge to permit inquiry into additional matters. The committee expressly approves this discretion and believes it will permit sufficient flexibility allowing a broader scope of cross-examination whenever appropriate.

The House amendment providing broader discretionary cross-examination permitted inquiry into additional matters only as if on direct examination. As a general rule, we concur with this limitation, however, we would understand that this limitation would not preclude the utilization of leading questions if the conditions of subsection (c) of this rule were met, bearing in mind the judge's discretion in any case to limit the scope of cross-examination.29

Further, the committee has received correspondence from Federal judges commenting on the applicability of this rule to section 1407 of title 28. It is the committee's judgment that this rule as reported by the House is flexible enough to provide sufficiently broad cross-examination in appropriate situations in multidistrict litigation.

Rule 611(c). Mode and Order of Interrogation and Presentation; Leading Questions

As submitted by the Supreme Court, the rule provided: "In civil cases, a party is entitled to call an adverse party or witness identified with him and interrogate by leading questions."

The final sentence of subsection (c) was amended by the House for the purpose of clarifying the fact that a "hostile witness"--that is a witness who is hostile in fact--could be subject to interrogation by leading questions. The rule as submitted by the Supreme Court declared certain witnesses hostile as a matter of law and thus subject to interrogation by leading questions without any showing of hostility in fact. These were adverse parties or witnesses identified with adverse parties. However, the wording of the first sentence of subsection (c) while generally prohibiting the use of leading questions on direct examination, also provides "except as may be necessary to develop his testimony." Further, the first paragraph of the Advisory Committee note explaining the subsection makes clear that they intended that leading questions could be asked of a hostile witness or a witness who was unwilling or biased and even though that witness was not associated with an adverse party. Thus, we question whether the House amendment was necessary.

However, concluding that it was not intended to affect the meaning of the first sentence of the subsection and was intended solely to clarify the fact that leading questions are permissible in the interrogation of a witness, who is hostile in fact, the committee accepts that House amendment.

The final sentence of this subsection was also amended by the House to cover criminal as well as civil cases. The committee accepts this amendment, but notes that it may be difficult in criminal cases to determine when a witness is "identified with an adverse party," and thus the rule should be applied with caution.

Rule 615. Exclusion of Witnesses

Many district courts permit government counsel to have an investigative agent at counsel table throughout the trial although the agent is or may be a witness. The practice is permitted as an exception to the rule of exclusion and compares with the situation defense counsel finds himself in--he always has the client with him to consult during the trial. The investigative agent's presence may be extremely important to government counsel, especially when the case is complex or involves some specialized subject matter. The agent, too, having lived with the case for a long time, may be able to assist in meeting trial surprises where the best-prepared counsel would otherwise have difficulty. Yet, it would not seem the Government could often meet the burden under rule 615 of showing that the agent's presence is essential. Furthermore, it could be dangerous to use the agent as a witness as early in the case as possible, so that he might then help counsel as a nonwitness, since the agent's testimony could be needed in rebuttal. Using another, nonwitness agent from the same investigative agency would not generally meet government counsel's needs.

This problem is solved if it is clear that investigative agents are within the group specified under the second exception made in the rule, for "an officer or employee of a party which is not a natural person designated as its representative by its attorney." It is our understanding that this was the intention of the House committee. It is certainly this committee's construction of the rule.

Rule 801(d)(2)(E). Hearsay Definitions: Statements Which Are Not Hearsay

The House approved the long-accepted rule that "a statement by a coconspirator of a party during the course and in furtherance of the conspiracy" is not hearsay as it was submitted by the Supreme Court. While the rule refers to a coconspirator, it is this committee's understanding that the rule is meant to carry forward the universally accepted doctrine that a joint venturer is considered as a coconspirator for the purposes of this rule even though no conspiracy has been charged. United States v. Rinaldi, 393 F.2d 97, 99 (2d Cir.), cert. denied 393 U.S. 913 (1968); United States v. Spencer, 415 F.2d 1301, 1304 (7th Cir., 1969).

Rule 803(4). Hearsay Exceptions; Statements for the Purposes of Medical Diagnosis or Treatment

The House approved this rule as it was submitted by the Supreme Court "with the understanding that it is not intended in any way to adversely affect present privilege rules." We also approve this rule, and we would point out with respect to the question of its relation to privileges, it must be read in conjunction with rule 35 of the Federal Rules of Civil Procedure which provides that whenever the physical or mental condition of a party (plaintiff or defendant) is in controversy, the court may require him to submit to an examination by a physician. It is these examinations which will normally be admitted under this exception.

Rule 803(5). Hearsay Exceptions; Recorded recollection

Rule 803(5) as submitted by the Court permitted the reading into evidence of a memorandum or record concerning a matter about which a witness once had knowledge but now has insufficient recollection to enable him to testify accurately and fully, "shown to have been made when the matter was fresh in his memory and to reflect that knowledge correctly." The House amended the rule to add the words "or adopted by the witness" after the phrase "shown to have been made," language parallel to the Jencks Act.30

The committee accepts the House amendment with the understanding and belief that it was not intended to narrow the scope of applicability of the rule. In fact, we understand it to clarify the rule's applicability to a memorandum adopted by the witness as well as one made by him. While the rule as submitted by the Court was silent on the question of who made the memorandum, we view the House amendment as a helpful clarification, noting, however, that the Advisory Committee's note to this rule suggests that the important thing is the accuracy of the memorandum rather than who made it.

The committee does not view the House amendment as precluding admissibility in situations in which multiple participants were involved.

When the verifying witness has not prepared the report, but merely examined it and found it accurate, he has adopted the report, and it is therefore admissible. The rule should also be interpreted to cover other situations involving multiple participants, e.g., employer dictating to secretary, secretary making memorandum at direction of employer, or information being passed along a chain of persons, as in Curtis v. Bradley.31

The committee also accepts the understanding of the House that a memorandum or report, although barred under this rule, would nonetheless be admissible if it came within another hearsay exception. We consider this principle to be applicable to all the hearsay rules.

Rule 804(b)(1). Hearsay Exceptions; Declarant unavailable; Former testimony

Former testimony.--Rule 804(b)(1) as submitted by the Court allowed prior testimony of an unavailable witness to be admissible if the party against whom it is offered or a person "with motive and interest similar" to his had an opportunity to examine the witness.

The House amended the rule to apply only to a party's predecessor in interest. Although the committee recognizes considerable merit to the rule submitted by the Supreme Court, a position which has been advocated by many scholars and judges, we have concluded that the difference between the two versions is not great and we accept the House amendment.

Section 3

Section 3 affirmatively approves conforming amendments, proposed by the Court to the Federal Rules of Civil Procedure and the Federal Rules of Criminal Procedure, which will be necessitated by the enactment into law of the Federal Rules of Evidence. These amendments were submitted by the Court to Congress along with the proposed Rules of Evidence. Affirmative congressional approval of them in order to render them effective is required by the terms of Public Law 93-12.

COST

Enactment of H.R. 5463 will entail no cost to the Government of the United States.

COMMUNICATION FROM THE CHIEF JUSTICE OF THE UNITED STATES

Supreme Court of the United States,
Washington D.C., February 5, 1973.
To the Senate and House of Representatives of the United States of America in Congress Assembled:

By direction of the Supreme Court, I have the honor to submit to the Congress the Rules of Evidence of the United States Courts and Magistrates, amendments and further amendments to the Federal Rules of Civil Procedures and amendments to the Federal Rules of Criminal Procedures which have been adopted by the Supreme Court, pursuant to Title 28, United States Code, Sections 2072 and 2075 and Title 18, United States Code, Sections 3402, 3771 and 3772. Mr. Justice Douglas dissents from the adoption of these rules and amendments.

Accompanying these amendments is the report of the Judicial Conference of the United States submitted to the Court for its consideration, pursuant to Title 28, United States Code, Section 331.

Respectfully.

"WARREN E. BURGER
"
"Chief Justice of the United States.
"

HOUSE REPORT NO. 93-650
The Committee on Judiciary, to whom was referred the bill (H.R. 5463) to establish rules of evidence for certain courts and proceedings, having considered the same, report favorably thereon with an amendment, and recommend that the bill as amended do pass.

The amendment strikes out all after the enacting clause and inserts in lieu thereof a substitute text which appears in italic type in the reported bill.

PURPOSE
The purpose of this legislation is to provide a uniform code of evidence for use in the Federal courts, and to make conforming amendments to the Federal Rules of Civil Procedure and the Federal Rules of Criminal Procedure.

STATEMENT
Judge Albert B. Maris, then Chairman of the Standing Committee on Rules of Practice and Procedure of the Judicial Conference of the United States, testified on February 7, 1973. He said: "[T]he adoption of the Federal Rules of Evidence represents, and in the future will be regarded as, a significant milestone on the road to the better administration of justice in the Federal courts, by providing clear, precise, and readily available rules for trial judges and trial lawyers to follow, which will be uniformly applicable throughout the Federal judicial system."

This view was echoed by Mr. Albert E. Jenner, Jr., Chairman of the Advisory Committee on Rules of Evidence, Judicial Conference of the United States. In his words: "I point to my own experience as a trial lawyer throughout the Nation in the trial of cases, that really this is what brought about the demand of the American Bar Association, its Special Committee on Rules of Evidence that we must have, in order to administer justice in the Federal Courts, uniform rules of evidence that are applicable to all district courts." Mr. Jenner also suggested that the uniform rules would be of particular assistance to judges who are assigned to districts or circuits other than their own to assist with congested calendars, and to the younger members of the bar. As he said, we will for the first time in the history of the nation have a pamphlet of rules in the "hands of the gladiators trying the case in the courtroom" and on the judge's bench.

The case against an evidence code was ably stated by a number of witnesses, including former Supreme Court Justice Arthur J. Goldberg and Chief Judge Henry J. Friendly of the United States Court of Appeals for the Second Circuit. Judge Friendly voiced three major objections--there is no need for the proposed rules, evidence is a subject which does not lend itself to codification but is peculiarly apt for case-by-case development, and uniform rules in the Federal courts which may overturn State social policies with respect to inter-personal relationships may well render equal protection of the law impossible.

After six days of hearings, the Subcommittee on Criminal Justice concluded that, on balance, there should be an evidence code.

However, recognizing that rules of evidence are in large measure substantive in their nature or impact, the Subcommittee and the Full Committee concluded they were not within the scope of the enabling acts which authorize the Supreme Court to promulgate rules of "practice and procedure" (18 USC 3771, 3772, 3402; 28 USC 2072, 2075).

H.R. 5463 constitutes the Committee's demonstration of these two conclusions, as well as its view as to what should be the content and scope of a uniform code of evidence.

Within the Subcommittee and the Full Committee there was no dispute with respect to many of the Rules. As a matter of fact, 27 of the Rules were not amended at all. Non-substantive changes were made to another 14. Thus, more than 50% of the Rules are substantively unchanged from those submitted by the Supreme Court.

HISTORICAL BACKGROUND
H.R. 5463 is the culmination of almost thirteen years of study by distinguished judges, Members of Congress, lawyers and others interested in and affected by the administration of justice in the Federal courts.

In 1961, the Judicial Conference of the United States authorized Earl Warren, then Chief Justice of the United States, to appoint an advisory committee to study the advisability and feasibility of uniform rules of evidence for use in the Federal courts. The Conference expressed the view that if uniform rules were found to be advisable and feasible, they should be promulgated.

The Chief Justice decided to move first toward a determination of whether uniform rules were advisable and feasible. He appointed a Special Committee on Evidence to make this initial exploration.

Because of the importance of the project and the fact that matters of evidence and proof cross the jurisdictional and interest lines of all of the Judicial Conference Advisory Committee, Chief Justice Warren designated the chairmen of the Civil, Criminal, Bankruptcy, Admiralty and Appellate Advisory Committees to serve on the Special Committee on Evidence.

By December 11, 1961, the Special Committee on Evidence submitted its preliminary report to the Judicial Conference Standing Committee on Rules of Practice and Procedure. In that report the Special Committee on Evidence concluded that uniform rules of evidence were advisable and feasible, and recommended that such rules should be promulgated promptly.

This preliminary report of the Special Committee was circulated for approximately one year with an invitation to the "bench and bar for consideration and suggestions." Thereafter, at its March, 1963 meeting, the Judicial Conference approved the final report of the Special Committee and recommended the appointment of an Advisory Committee on Rules of Evidence to prepare uniform rules of evidence for adoption and promulgation by the Supreme Court of the United States.

A distinguished Advisory Committee composed of judges, lawyers and teachers was appointed on March 8, 1965, and assigned the monumental task of developing a uniform code of evidence for use in the Federal courts.

Approximately four years later, in March, 1969, the Judicial Conference Standing Committee on Rules of Practice and Procedure printed and circulated widely for comment a preliminary draft of proposed rules of evidence which had been developed by the Advisory Committee. The draft was accompanied by detailed Advisory Committee notes.

After reviewing the numerous comments, suggests, and proposals received on the preliminary draft, the Advisory Committee and, in turn, the Judicial Conference, approved a revised draft which it submitted to the Supreme Court for promulgation in October, 1970.

The Court, however, returned the draft to the Judicial Conference for further public circulation and opportunity to comment, and in March, 1971, that draft was printed and widely circulated. The final work product of the Advisory Committee of the Judicial Conference and the Standing Committee on Rules of Practice and Procedure, was forwarded to the Supreme Court in October, 1971.

On November 20, 1972, the Supreme Court promulgated the Federal Rules of Evidence pursuant to the various enabling acts in title 18 and 28 of the United States Code, to take effect on July 1, 1973.

On February 5, 1973, Chief Justice Warren Burger, acting pursuant to the Supreme Court order of November 20, 1972, transmitted the proposed rules to the Congress. As transmitted, the proposed rules and accompanying Advisory Committee notes occupied 168 closely printed pages.

CONGRESSIONAL CONSIDERATION
Recognizing the importance and the enormity of the task before it, and in light of the serious question raised by Mr. Justice Douglas, in dissenting to the Supreme Court Order, as to the authority of the Supreme Court to promulgate rules of evidence, the Congress promptly enacted Public Law 93-12. This Public Law (which passed the House 399 to 1) deferred the effectiveness of the rules until expressly approved by the Congress.

Two days after receipt of the proposed rules, on February 7, 1973, the Subcommittee on Criminal Justice opened hearings and began to take testimony on the desirability of a uniform code of evidence and the merits of each individual rule. H.R. 5463 was introduced by the Chairman of the Subcommittee, Congressman William L. Hungate, and other Members, so that the proposed rules would be before the Committee in legislative form.

The Subcommittee held six days of hearings, heard twenty-eight witnesses, received numerous written communications, and developed a hearing record of approximately 600 pages. By March 21, the Subcommittee was ready to begin its markup sessions with a view to developing a Subcommittee draft. Between March 21 and June 22, the Subcommittee held 17 markup sessions which culminated in a Committee Print of H.R. 5463 dated June 28, 1973. The Committee Print was circulated nationwide for comment and printed in the Congressional Record to assure the widest distribution. Over the course of the next six weeks, approximately 90 comments were received by the Subcommittee. By and large, the Committee Print was well received, even by those individuals and organizations objecting to the Subcommittee treatment of specific rules and those who objected to having uniform rules of any kind. The American Bar Association House of Delegates, for example, endorsed most of the provisions generally and "concurs in the Hungate Subcommittee's Report ... insofar as it omits Rules 803(24), 804(b)(6); all of the rules pertaining to privilege ...; and the rule on summing up and comment by judges (105)". The American College of Trial Lawyers "approves thoroughly". From the Association of the Bar of the City of New York, "The Committee is to be commended for a most thorough, scholarly revision of the Federal Rules of Evidence". Chief Judge Friendly wrote "... if there are to be Federal rules of evidence, I do not see how there could be much better ones than your Subcommittee has proposed". Assistant Attorney General Robert Repasky of Wisconsin advised that "the balance the Committee has arrived at is a most reasonable balance between the rather clear interest of the individual States and the interest of the Federal courts in having some formalized Rules of Evidence to guide their decisions." Similar comments were received from numerous other individuals and organizations in the legal field. Laudatory comments were also received from non-legal groups, for example, the communications media, the American Hospital Association, the National Association of Social Workers, Inc., and others.

All comments were thoroughly considered and the Subcommittee developed a revised Committee Print in the course of five additional markup sessions. This Print, dated October 10, 1973, was approved by the Subcommittee and reported to the full Judiciary Committee for its consideration.

On October 16 and 18 and on November 6, 1973, the full Committee thoroughly debated H.R. 5463, amended it in several respects, and ordered it favorably reported.

COMMITTEE AMENDMENTS
In some instances, the Committee has deleted entire rules or parts of rules proposed by the Supreme Court; in other instances, rules have been retained but significantly amended. The following explanatory information reflects the Committee views in taking each individual action.

PROPOSED RULES DELETED BY COMMITTEE
Proposed Rule 105

Rule 105 as submitted by the Supreme Court concerned the issue of summing up and comment by the judge. It provided that after the close of the evidence and the arguments of counsel, the presiding judge could fairly and impartially sum up the evidence and comment to the jury upon its weight and the credibility of the witnesses, if he also instructed the jury that it was not bound thereby and must make its own determination of those matters. The Committee recognized that the Rule as submitted is consistent with long standing and current federal practice. However, the aspect of the Rule dealing with the authority of a judge to comment on the weight of the evidence and the credibility of witnesses--an authority not granted to judges in most State courts--was highly controversial. After much debate the Committee determined to delete the entire Rule, intending that its action be understood as reflecting no conclusion as to the merits of the proposed Rule and that the subject should be left for separate consideration at another time.

Proposed Rule 303

Rule 303, as submitted by the Supreme Court was directed to the issues of when, in criminal cases, a court may submit a presumption to a jury and the type of instruction it should give. The Committee deleted this Rule since the subject of presumptions in criminal cases is addressed in detail in bills now pending before the Committee to revise the federal criminal code. The Committee determined to consider this question in the course of its study of these proposals.

Proposed Rule 406(b)

Rule 406 as submitted to Congress contained a subdivision (b) providing that the method of proof of habit or routine practice could be "in the form of an opinion or by specific instances of conduct sufficient in number to warrant a finding that the habit existed or that the practice was routine." The Committee deleted this subdivision believing that the method of proof of habit and routine practice should be left to the courts to deal with on a case-by-case basis. At the same time, the Committee does not intend that its action be construed as sanctioning a general authorization of opinion evidence in this area.

Proposed Rules 803(24) and 804(b)(6)

The proposed Rules of Evidence submitted to Congress contained identical provisions in Rules 803 and 804 (which set forth the various hearsay exceptions), to the effect that the federal courts could admit any hearsay statement not specifically covered by any of the stated exceptions, if the hearsay statement was found to have "comparable circumstantial guarantees of trustworthiness."

The Committee deleted these provisions (proposed Rules 803(24) and 804(b)(6)) as injecting too much uncertainty into the law of evidence and impairing the ability of practitioners to prepare for trial. It was noted that Rule 102 directs the courts to construe the Rules of Evidence so as to promote "growth and development." The Committee believed that if additional hearsay exceptions are to be created, they should be by amendments to the Rules, not on a case-by-case basis.

Proposed Rule 804(b)(2)

Rule 804(b)(2), a hearsay exception submitted by the Court, titled "Statement of recent perception", read as follows:

A statement, not in response to the instigation of a person engaged in investigating, litigating, or settling a claim, which narrates, describes, or explains an event or condition recently perceived by the declarant, made in good faith, not in contemplation of pending or anticipated litigation in which he was interested, and while his recollection was clear.

The Committee eliminated this Rule as creating a new and unwarranted hearsay exception of great potential breadth. The Committee did not believe that statements of the type referred to bore sufficient guarantees of trustworthiness to justify admissibility.

RULES SIGNIFICANTLY AMENDED
Rule 104(c)

Rule 104(c) as submitted to the Congress provided that hearings on the admissibility of confessions shall be conducted outside the presence of the jury and hearings on all other preliminary matters should be so conducted when the interests of justice require. The Committee amended the Rule to provide that where an accused is a witness as to a preliminary matter, he has the right, upon his request, to be heard outside the jury's presence. Although recognizing that in some cases duplication of evidence would occur and that the procedure could be subject to abuse, the Committee believed that a proper regard for the right of an accused not to testify generally in the case dictates that he be given an option to testify out of the presence of the jury on preliminary matters.

The Committee construes the second sentence of subdivision (c) as applying to civil actions and proceedings as well as to criminal cases, and on this assumption has left the sentence unamended.

Rule 106

Rule 106 as submitted by the Supreme Court (now Rule 105 in the bill) dealt with the subject of evidence which is admissible as to one party or for one purpose but is not admissible against another party or for another purpose. The Committee adopted this Rule without change on the understanding that it does not affect the authority of a court to order a severance in a multi-defendant case.

Rule 201(g)

Rule 201(g) as received from the Supreme Court provided that when judicial notice of a fact is taken, the court shall instruct the jury to accept that fact as established. Being of the view that mandatory instruction to a jury in a criminal case to accept as conclusive any fact judicially noticed is inappropriate because contrary to the spirit of the Sixth Amendment right to a jury trial, the Committee adopted the 1969 Advisory Committee draft of this subsection, allowing a mandatory instruction in civil actions and proceedings and a discretionary instruction in criminal cases.

Rule 301

Rule 301 as submitted by the Supreme Court provided that in all cases a presumption imposes on the party against whom it is directed the burden of proving that the nonexistence of the presumed fact is more probable than its existence. The Committee limited the scope of Rule 301 to "civil actions and proceedings" to effectuate its decision not to deal with the question of presumptions in criminal cases. (See note on Rule 303 in discussion of Rules deleted). With respect to the weight to be given a presumption in a civil case, the Committee agreed with the judgment implicit in the Court's version that the so-called "bursting bubble" theory of presumptions, whereby a presumption vanishes upon the appearance of any contradicting evidence by the other party, gives to presumptions too slight an effect. On the other hand, the Committee believed that the Rule proposed by the Court, whereby a presumption permanently alters the burden of persuasion, no matter how much contradicting evidence is introduced--a view shared by only a few courts--lends too great a force to presumptions. Accordingly, the Committee amended the Rule to adopt an intermediate position under which a presumption does not vanish upon the introduction of contradicting evidence, and does not change the burden of persuasion; Instead it is merely deemed sufficient evidence of the fact presumed, to be considered by the jury or other finder of fact.

Rule 402

Rule 402 as submitted to the Congress contained the phrase "or by other rules adopted by the Supreme Court". To accommodate the view that the Congress should not appear to acquiesce in the Court's judgment that it has authority under the existing Rules Enabling Acts to promulgate Rules of Evidence, the Committee amended the above phrase to read "or by other rules prescribed by the Supreme Court pursuant to statutory authority" in this and other Rules where the reference appears.

Rule 404(b)

The second sentence of Rule 404(b) as submitted to the Congress began with the words "This subdivision does not exclude the evidence when offered". The Committee amended this language to read "It may, however, be admissible", the words used in the 1971 Advisory Committee draft, on the ground that this formulation properly placed greater emphasis on admissibility than did the final Court version.

Rule 405(a)

Rule 405(a) as submitted proposed to change existing law by allowing evidence of character in the form of opinion as well as reputation testimony. Fearing, among other reasons, that wholesale allowance of opinion testimony might tend to turn a trial into a swearing contest between conflicting character witnesses, the Committee decided to delete from this Rule, as well as from Rule 608(a) which involves a related problem, reference to opinion testimony.

Rule 408

Under existing federal law evidence of conduct and statements made in compromise negotiations is admissible in subsequent litigation between the parties. The second sentence of Rule 408 as submitted by the Supreme Court proposed to reverse that doctrine in the interest of further promoting non-judicial settlement of disputes. Some agencies of government expressed the view that the Court formulation was likely to impede rather than assist efforts to achieve settlement of disputes. For one thing, it is not always easy to tell when compromise negotiations begin, and informal dealings end. Also, parties dealing with government agencies would be reluctant to furnish factual information at preliminary meetings; they would wait until "compromise negotiations" began and thus hopefully effect an immunity for themselves with respect to the evidence supplied. In light of these considerations, the Committee recast the Rule so that admissions of liability or opinions given during compromise negotiations continue inadmissible, but evidence of unqualified factual assertions is admissible. The latter aspect of the Rule is drafted, however, so as to preserve other possible objections to the introduction of such evidence. The Committee intends no modification of current law whereby a party may protect himself from future use of his statements by couching them in hypothetical conditional form.

Rule 410

The Committee added the phrase "Except as otherwise provided by Act of Congress" to Rule 410 as submitted by the Court in order to preserve particular congressional policy judgments as to the effect of a plea of guilty or of nolo contendere. See 15 U.S.C. 16(a). The Committee intends that its amendment refers to both present statutes and statutes subsequently enacted.

Article V

Article V as submitted to Congress contained thirteen Rules. Nine of those Rules defined specific non-constitutional privileges which the federal courts must recognize (i.e. required reports, lawyer-client, psychotherapist-patient, husband-wife, communications to clergymen, political vote, trade secrets, secrets of state and other official information, and identity of informer). Another Rule provided that only those privileges set forth in Article V or in some other Act of Congress could be recognized by the federal courts. The three remaining Rules addressed collateral problems as to waiver of privilege by voluntary disclosure, privileged matter disclosed under compulsion or without opportunity to claim privilege, comment upon or inference from a claim of privilege, and jury instruction with regard thereto.

The Committee amended Article V to eliminate all of the Court's specific Rules on privileges. Instead, the Committee, through a single Rule, 501, left the law of privileges in its present state and further provided that privileges shall continue to be developed by the courts of the United States under a uniform standard applicable both in civil and criminal cases. That standard, derived from Rule 26 of the Federal Rules of Criminal Procedure, mandates the application of the principles of the common law as interpreted by the courts of the United States in the light of reason and experience. The words "person, government, State, or political subdivision thereof" were added by the Committee to the lone term "witnesses" used in Rule 26 to make clear that, as under present law, not only witnesses may have privileges. The Committee also included in its amendment a proviso modeled after Rule 302 and similar to language added by the Committee to Rule 601 relating to the competency of witnesses. The proviso is designed to require the application of State privilege law in civil actions and proceedings governed by Erie R. Co. v. Tompkins, 304 U.S. 64 (1938), a result in accord with current federal court decisions. See Republic Gear Co. v. Borg-Warner Corp., 381 F2d 551, 555-556 n. 2 (2nd Cir.1967). The Committee deemed the proviso to be necessary in the light of the Advisory Committee's view (see its note to Court Rule 501) that this result is not mandated under Erie.

The rationale underlying the proviso is that federal law should not supersede that of the States in substantive areas such as privilege absent a compelling reason. The Committee believes that in civil cases in the federal courts where an element of a claim or defense is not grounded upon a federal question, there is no federal interest strong enough to justify departure from State policy. In addition, the Committee considered that the Court's proposed Article V would have promoted forum shopping in some civil actions, depending upon differences in the privilege law applied as among the State and federal courts. The Committee's proviso, on the other hand, under which the federal courts are bound to apply the State's privilege law in actions founded upon a State-created right or defense, removes the incentive to "shop".

Rule 601

Rule 601 as submitted to the Congress provided that "Every person is competent to be a witness except as otherwise provided in these rules." One effect of the Rule as proposed would have been to abolish age, mental capacity, and other grounds recognized in some State jurisdictions as making a person incompetent as a witness. The greatest controversy centered around the Rule's rendering inapplicable in the federal courts the so-called Dead Man's Statutes which exist in some States. Acknowledging that there is substantial disagreement as to the merit of Dead Man's Statutes, the Committee nevertheless believed that where such statutes have been enacted they represent State policy which should not be overturned in the absence of a compelling federal interest. The Committee therefore amended the Rule to make competency in civil actions determinable in accordance with State law with respect to elements of claims or defenses as to which State law supplies the rule of decision. Cf. Courtland v. Walston & Co., Inc., 340 F.Supp. 1076, 1087-1092 (S.D.N.Y.1972).

Rule 606(b)

As proposed by he [the] Court, Rule 606(b) limited testimony by a juror in the course of an inquiry into the validity of a verdict or indictment. He could testify as to the influence of extraneous prejudicial information brought to the jury's attention (e.g. a radio newscast or a newspaper account) or an outside influence which improperly had been brought to bear upon a juror (e.g. a threat to the safety of a member of his family), but he could not testify as to other irregularities which occurred in the jury room. Under this formulation a quotient verdict could not be attacked through the testimony of a juror, nor could a juror testify to the drunken condition of a fellow juror which so disabled him that he could not participate in the jury's deliberations.

The 1969 and 1971 Advisory Committee drafts would have permitted a member of the jury to testify concerning these kinds of irregularities in the jury room. The Advisory Committee note in the 1971 draft stated that " * * * the door of the jury room is not a satisfactory dividing point, and the Supreme Court has refused to accept it." The Advisory Committee further commented that--

The trend has been to draw the dividing line between testimony as to mental processes, on the one hand, and as to the existence of conditions or occurrences of events calculated improperly to influence the verdict, on the other hand, without regard to whether the happening is within or without the jury room. * * * The jurors are the persons who know what really happened. Allowing them to testify as to matters other than their own reactions involves no particular hazard to the values sought to be protected. The rule is based upon this conclusion. It makes no attempt to specify the substantive grounds for setting aside verdicts for irregularity.

Objective jury misconduct may be testified to in California, Florida, Iowa, Kansas, Nebraska, New Jersey, North Dakota, Ohio, Oregon, Tennessee, Texas, and Washington.

Persuaded that the better practice is that provided for in the earlier drafts, the Committee amended subdivision (b) to read in the text of those drafts.

Rule 608(a)

Rule 608(a) as submitted by the Court permitted attack to be made upon the character for truthfulness or untruthfulness of a witness either by reputation or opinion testimony. For the same reasons underlying its decision to eliminate the admissibility of opinion testimony in Rule 405(a), the Commttee [committee] amended Rule 608(a) to delete the reference to opinion testimony.

Rule 608(b)

The second sentence of Rule 608(b) as submitted by the Court permitted specific instances of misconduct of a witness to be inquired into on cross-examination for the purpose of attacking his credibility, if probative of truthfulness or untruthfulness, "and not remote in time". Such cross-examination could be of the witness himself or of another witness who testifies as to "his" character for truthfulness or untruthfulness.

The Committee amended the Rule to emphasize the discretionary power of the court in permitting such testimony and deleted the reference to remoteness in time as being unnecessary and confusing (remoteness from time of trial or remoteness from the incident involved?). As recast, the Committee amendment also makes clear the antecedent of "his" in the original Court proposal.

Rule 609(a)

Rule 609(a) as submitted by the Court was modeled after Section 133(a) of Public Law 91-358. 14 D.C.Code 305(b)(1), enacted in 1970. The Rule provided that:

For the purpose of attacking the credibility of a witness, evidence that he has been convicted of a crime is admissible but only if the crime (1) was punishable by death or imprisonment in excess of one year under the law under which he was convicted or (2) involved dishonesty or false statement regardless of the punishment.

As reported to the Committee by the Subcommittee, Rule 609(a) was amended to read as follows:

For the purpose of attacking the credibility of a witness, evidence that he has been convicted of a crime is admissible only if the crime (1) was punishable by death or imprisonment in excess of one year, unless the court determines that the danger of unfair prejudice outweighs the probative value of the evidence of the conviction, or (2) involved dishonesty or false statement.

In full committee, the provision was amended to permit attack upon the credibility of a witness by prior conviction only if the prior crime involved dishonesty or false statement. While recognizing that the prevailing doctrine in the federal courts and in most States allows a witness to be impeached by evidence of prior felony convictions without restriction as to type, the Committee was of the view that, because of the danger of unfair prejudice in such practice and the deterrent effect upon an accused who might wish to testify, and even upon a witness who was not the accused, cross-examination by evidence of prior conviction should be limited to those kinds of convictions bearing directly on credibility, i.e., crimes involving dishonesty or false statement.

Rule 609(b)

Rule 609(b) as submitted by the Court was modeled after Section 133(a) of Public Law 91-358, 14 D.C.Code 305(b)(2)(B), enacted in 1970. The Rule provided:

Evidence of a conviction under this rule is not admissible if a period of more than ten years has elapsed since the date of the release of the witness from confinement imposed for his most recent conviction, or the expiration of the period of his parole, probation, or sentence granted or imposed with respect to his most recent conviction, whichever is the later date.

Under this formulation, a witness' entire past record of criminal convictions could be used for impeachment (provided the conviction met the standard of subdivision (a), if the witness had been most recently released from confinement, or the period of his parole or probation had expired, within ten years of the conviction.

The Committee amended the Rule to read in the text of the 1971 Advisory Committee version to provide that upon the expiration of ten years from the date of a conviction of a witness, or of his release from confinement for that offense, that conviction may no longer be used for impeachment. The Committee was of the view that after ten years following a person's release from confinement (or from the date of his conviction) the probative value of the conviction with respect to that person's credibility diminished to a point where it should no longer be admissible.

Rule 609(c)

Rule 609(c) as submitted by the Court provided in part that evidence of a witness' prior conviction is not admissible to attack his credibility if the conviction was the subject of a pardon, annulment, or other equivalent procedure, based on a showing of rehabilitation, and the witness has not been convicted of a subsequent crime. The Committee amended the Rule to provide that the "subsequent crime" must have been "punishable by death or imprisonment in excess of one year", on the ground that a subsequent conviction of an offense not a felony is insufficient to rebut the finding that the witness has been rehabilitated. The Committee also intends that the words "based on a finding of the rehabilitation of the person convicted" apply not only to "certificate of rehabilitation, or other equivalent procedure", but also to "pardon" and "annulment."

Rule 611(b)

As submitted by the Court, Rule 611(b) provided:

A witness may be cross-examined on any matter relevant to any issue in the case, including credibility. In the interests of justice, the judge may limit cross-examination with respect to matters not testified to on direct examination.

The Committee amended this provision to return to the rule which prevails in the federal courts and thirty-nine State jurisdictions. As amended, the Rule is in the text of the 1969 Advisory Committee draft. It limits cross-examination to credibility and to matters testified to on direct examination, unless the judge permits more, in which event the cross-examiner must proceed as if on direct examination. This traditional rule facilitates orderly presentation by each party at trial. Further, in light of existing discovery procedures, there appears to be no need to abandon the traditional rule.

Rule 611(c)

The third sentence of Rule 611(c) as submitted by the Court provided that:

In civil cases, a party is entitled to call an adverse party or witness identified with him and interrogate by leading questions.

The Committee amended this Rule to permit leading questions to be used with respect to any hostile witness, not only an adverse party or person identified with such adverse party. The Committee also substituted the word "When" for the phrase "In civil cases" to reflect the possibility that in criminal cases a defendant may be entitled to call witnesses identified with the government, in which event the Committee believed the defendant should be permitted to inquire with leading questions.

Rule 612

As submitted to Congress, Rule 612 provided that except as set forth in 18 U.S.C. 3500, if a witness uses a writing to refresh his memory for the purpose of testifying, "either before or while testifying," an adverse party is entitled to have the writing produced at the hearing, to inspect it, to cross-examine the witness on it, and to introduce in evidence those portions relating to the witness' testimony. The Committee amended the Rule so as still to require the production of writings used by a witness while testifying, but to render the production of writings used by a witness to refresh his memory before testifying discretionary with the court in the interests of justice, as is the case under existing federal law. See Goldman v. United States, 316 U.S. 129 (1942). The Committee considered that permitting an adverse party to require the production of writings used before testifying could result in fishing expeditions among a multitude of papers which a witness may have used in preparing for trial.

The Committee intends that nothing in the Rule be construed as barring the assertion of a privilege with respect to writings used by a witness to refresh his memory.

Rule 801(d)(1)

Present federal law, except in the Second Circuit, permits the use of prior inconsistent statements of a witness for impeachment only. Rule 801(d)(1) as proposed by the Court would have permitted all such statements to be admissible as substantive evidence, an approach followed by a small but growing number of State jurisdictions and recently held constitutional in California v. Green, 399 U.S. 149 (1970). Although there was some support expressed for the Court Rule, based largely on the need to counteract the effect of witness intimidation in criminal cases, the Committee decided to adopt a compromise version of the Rule similar to the position of the Second Circuit. The Rule as amended draws a distinction between types of prior inconsistent statements (other than statements of identification of a person made after perceiving him which are currently admissible, see United States v. Anderson, 406 F.2d 719, 720 (4th Cir.), cert. denied, 395 U.S. 967 (1969)) and allows only those made while the declarant was subject to cross-examination at a trail or hearing or in a deposition, to be admissible for their truth. Compare United States v. DeSisto, 329 F.2d 929 (2nd Cir.), cert. denied, 377 U.S. 979 (1964); United States v. Cunningham, 446 F.2d 194 (2nd Cir. 1971) (restricting the admissibility of prior inconsistent statements as substantive evidence to those made under oath in a formal proceeding, but not requiring that there have been an opportunity for cross-examination). The rationale for the Committee's decision is that (1) unlike in most other situations involving unsworn or oral statements, there can be no dispute as to whether the prior statement was made; and (2) the context of a formal proceeding, an oath, and the opportunity for cross-examination provide firm additional assurances of the reliability of the prior statement.

Rule 803(3)

Rule 803(3) was approved in the form submitted by the Court to Congress. However, the Committee intends that the Rule be construed to limit the doctrine of Mutual Life Insurance Co. v. Hillmon, 145 U.S. 285, 295-300 (1892), so as to render statements of intent by a declarant admissible only to prove his future conduct, not the future conduct of another person.

Rule 803(4)

After giving particular attention to the question of physical examination made solely to enable a physician to testify, the Committee approved Rule 803(4) as submitted to Congress, with the understanding that it is not intended in any way to adversely affect present privilege rules or those subsequently adopted.

Rule 803(5)

Rule 803(5) as submitted by the Court permitted the reading into evidence of a memorandum or record concerning a matter about which a witness once had knowledge but now has insufficient recollection to enable him to testify accurately and fully, "shown to have been made when the matter was fresh in his memory and to reflect that knowledge correctly." The Committee amended this Rule to add the words "or adopted by the witness" after the phrase "shown to have been made", a treatment consistent with the definition of "statement" in the Jencks Act, 18 U.S.C. 3500. Moreover, it is the Committee's understanding that a memorandum or report, although barred under this Rule, would nonetheless be admissible if it came within another hearsay exception. This last stated principle is deemed applicable to all the hearsay rules.

Rule 803(6)

Rule 803(6) as submitted by the Court permitted a record made "in the course of a regularly conducted activity" to be admissible in certain circumstances. The Committee believed there were insufficient guarantees of reliability in records made in the course of activities falling outside the scope of "business" activities as that term is broadly defined in 28 U.S.C. 1732. Moreover, the Committee concluded that the additional requirement of Section 1732 that it must have been the regular practice of a business to make the record is a necessary further assurance of its trustworthiness. The Committee accordingly amended the Rule to incorporate these limitations.

Rule 803(7)

Rule 803(7) as submitted by the Court concerned the absence of entry in the records of a "regularly conducted activity." The Committee amended this Rule to conform with its action with respect to Rule 803(6).

Rule 803(8)

The Committee approved Rule 803(8) without substantive change from the form in which it was submitted by the Court. The Committee intends that the phrase "factual findings" be strictly construed and that evaluations or opinions contained in public reports shall not be admissible under this Rule.

Rule 803(13)

The Committee approved this Rule in the form submitted by the Court, intending that the phrase "Statements of fact concerning personal or family history" be read to include the specific types of such statements enumerated in Rule 803(11).

Rule 804(a)(3)

Rule 804(a)(3) was approved in the form submitted by the Court. However, the Committee intends no change in existing federal law under which the court may choose to disbelieve the declarant's testimony as to his lack of memory. See United States v. Insana, 423 F.2d 1165, 1169-1170 (2nd Cir.), cert. denied, 400 U.S. 841 (1970).

Rule 804(a)(5)

Rule 804(a)(5) as submitted to the Congress provided, as one type of situation in which a declarant would be deemed "unavailable", that he be "absent from the hearing and the proponent of his statement has been unable to procure his attendance by process or other reasonable means." The Committee amended the Rule to insert after the word "attendance" the parenthetical expression" (or, in the case of a hearsay exception under subdivision (b)(2), (3), or (4), his attendance or testimony)". The amendment is designed primarily to require that an attempt be made to depose a witness (as well as to seek his attendance) as a precondition to the witness being deemed unavailable. The Committee, however, recognized the propriety of an exception to this additional requirement when it is the declarant's former testimony that is sought to be admitted under subdivision (b)(1).

Rule 804(b)(1)

Rule 804(b)(1) as submitted by the Court allowed prior testimony of an unavailable witness to be admissible if the party against whom it is offered or a person "with motive and interest similar" to his had an opportunity to examine the witness. The Committee considered that it is generally unfair to impose upon the party against whom the hearsay evidence is being offered responsibility for the manner in which the witness was previously handled by another party. The sole exception to this, in the Committee's view, is when a party's predecessor in interest in a civil action or proceeding had an opportunity and similar motive to examine the witness. The Committee amended the Rule to reflect these policy determinations.

Rule 804(b)(2)

Rule 804(b)(3) as submitted by the Court (now Rule 804(b)(2) in the bill) proposed to expand the traditional scope of the dying declaration exception (i.e. a statement of the victim in a homicide case as to the cause or circumstances of his believed imminent death) to allow such statements in all criminal and civil cases. The Committee did not consider dying declarations as among the most reliable forms of hearsay. Consequently, it amended the provision to limit their admissibility in criminal cases to homicide prosecutions, where exceptional need for the evidence is present. This is existing law. At the same time, the Committee approved the expansion to civil actions and proceedings where the stakes do not involve possible imprisonment, although noting that this could lead to forum shopping in some instances.

Rule 804(b)(3)

Rule 804(b)(4) as submitted by the Court (now Rule 804(b)(3) in the bill) provided as follows:

Statement against interest.--A statement which was at the time of its making so far contrary to the declarant's pecuniary or proprietary interest or so far tended to subject him to civil or criminal liability or to render invalid a claim by him against another or to make him an object of hatred, ridicule, or disgrace, that a reasonable man in his position would not have made the statement unless he believed it to be true. A statement tending to exculpate the accused is not admissible unless corroborated.

The Committee determined to retain the traditional hearsay exception for statements against pecuniary or proprietary interest. However, it deemed the Court's additional references to statements tending to subject a declarant to civil liability or to render invalid a claim by him against another to be redundant as included within the scope of the reference to statements against pecuniary or proprietary interest. See Gichner v. Antonio Triano Tile and Marble Co., 410 F.2d 238 (D.C.Cir.1968). Those additional references were accordingly deleted.

The Court's Rule also proposed to expand the hearsay limitation from its present federal limitation to include statements subjecting the declarant to criminal liability and statements tending to make him an object of hatred, ridicule, or disgrace. The Committee eliminated the latter category from the subdivision as lacking sufficient guarantees of reliability. See United States v. Dovico, 380 F.2d 325, 327 nn. 2, 4 (2nd Cir.), cert. denied, 389 U.S. 944 (1967). As for statements against penal interest, the Committee shared the view of the Court that some such statements do possess adequate assurances of reliability and should be admissible. It believed, however, as did the Court, that statements of this type tending to exculpate the accused are more suspect and so should have their admissibility conditioned upon some further provision insuring trustworthiness. The proposal in the Court Rule to add a requirement of simple corroboration was, however, deemed ineffective to accomplish this purpose since the accused's own testimony might suffice while not necessarily increasing the reliability of the hearsay statement. The Committee settled upon the language "unless corroborating circumstances clearly indicate the trustworthiness of the statement" as affording a proper standard and degree of discretion. It was contemplated that the result in such cases as Donnelly v. United States, 228 U.S. 243 (1912), where the circumstances plainly indicated reliability, would be changed. The Committee also added to the Rule the final sentence from the 1971 Advisory Committee draft, designed to codify the doctrine of Bruton v. United States, 391 U.S. 123 (1968). The Committee does not intend to affect the existing exception to the Bruton principle where the codefendant takes the stand and is subject to cross-examination, but believed there was no need to make specific provision for this situation in the Rule, since in that even the declarant would not be "unavailable".

Rule 902(8)

Rule 902(8) as submitted by the Court referred to certificates of acknowledgment "under the hand and seal of" a notary public or other officer authorized by law to take acknowledgments. The Committee amended the Rule to eliminate the requirement, believed to be inconsistent with the law in some States, that a notary public must affix a seal to a document acknowledged before him. As amended the Rule merely requires that the document be executed in the manner prescribed by State law.

Rule 902(9)

The Committee approved Rule 902(9) as submitted by the Court. With respect to the meaning of the phrase "general commercial law", the Committee intends that the Uniform Commercial Code, which has been adopted in virtually every State, will be followed generally, but that federal commercial law will apply where federal commercial paper is involved. See Clearfield Trust Co. v. United States, 318 U.S. 363 (1943). Further, in those instances in which the issues are governed by Erie R. Co. v. Tompkins, 304 U.S. 64 (1938), State law will apply irrespective of whether it is the Uniform Commercial Code.

Rule 1001(2)

The Committee amended this Rule expressly to include "video tapes" in the definition of "photographs."

Rule 1003

The Committee approved this Rule in the form submitted by the Court, with the expectation that the courts would be liberal in deciding that a "genuine question is raised as to the authenticity of the original."

Rule 1004(1)

The Committee approved Rule 1004(1) in the form submitted to Congress. However, the Committee intends that loss or destruction of an original by another person at the instigation of the proponent should be considered as tantamount to loss or destruction in bad faith by the proponent himself.

Rule 1101

Subdivision (a) as submitted to the Congress, in stating the courts and judges to which the Rules of Evidence apply, omitted the Court of Claims and commissioners of that Court. At the request of the Court of Claims, the Committee amended the Rule to include the Court and its commissioners within the purview of the Rules.

Subdivision (b) was amended merely to substitute positive law citations for those which were not.

ANALYSIS OF SECTIONS 2 AND 3 OF THE BILL
Section 2

Subsection (a) sets forth the method by which future amendments may be made to the Rules of Evidence. The present Rules Enabling Acts (18 U.S.C. 3771, 3772, 3402; 28 U.S.C. 2072, 2075), which the Supreme Court invoked as the authority pursuant to which it promulgated the Rules of Evidence, provide that the Court may prescribe rules of "practice and procedure" and submit them to Congress. The rules then take effect automatically either at such time as the Court directs, or after ninety days following their submission. An Act of Congress is necessary to prevent any rule so submitted from taking effect.

The Committee believed that many of the Rules of Evidence, particularly in the privilege and hearsay fields, involve substantive policy judgments as to which it is appropriate that the Congress play a greater role than that provided for in the present Enabling Acts. Accordingly, the Committee concluded that it should provide for a new statutory procedure by which amendments to the Rules of Evidence may be made, designed to insure adequate congressional participation in the evidence rule-making process. Section 2(a) as adopted by the Committee adds a new section, 2076, to title 28, United States Code, permitting the Court to prescribe amendments to the Rules of Evidence, which amendments must be reported to the Congress. However, unlike the situation under the present Rules Enabling Acts, either House of Congress may, by resolution, prevent a rule from becoming operative. Moreover, rather than the ninety-day period allowed in the existing Rules Enabling Acts, a one hundred and eighty day period is prescribed for Congressional action.

The committee considered the possibility of requiring congressional approval of any rule of evidence submitted to it by the Court, and recognized that a similar judgment inhered in Public Law 93-12, pursuant to which the Court's proposed Rules of Evidence were barred from taking effect until approved by Congress. However, the Committee determined that requiring affirmative congressional action was appropriate to this first effort at codifying the Rules of Evidence, but was not needed with respect to subsequent amendments which would likely be of more modest dimension. Indeed, it believed that to require affirmative congressional action with respect to amendments might well result in some worthwhile amendments not being approved because of other pressing demands on the Congress. The Committee thus concluded that the system of allowing Court-proposed amendments to the Rules of Evidence to take effect automatically unless disapproved by either House strikes a sound balance between the proper role of Congress in the amendatory process and the dictates of convenience and legislative priorities.

Subsection (b) strikes out Section 1732(a) of title 28, United States Code, since its subject matter is covered in Rule 803(6) relating to records of a regularly conducted business activity.

Subsection (c) amends Section 1733 of title 28, United States Code, since that section is largely, if not entirely, encompassed by Rule 803(8) relating to public records and reports. Because of the possibility that Section 1733 may reach some matters not touched by Rule 803(8), subsection (c) does not repeal Section 1733 but merely provides that the Section does not apply to actions, cases, and proceedings to which the Rules of Evidence are applicable.

Section 3

Section 3 affirmatively approves conforming amendments, proposed by the Court to the Federal Rules of Civil Procedure and the Federal Rules of Criminal Procedure, which will be necessitated by the enactment into law of the Federal Rules of Evidence. These amendments were submitted by the Court to Congress along with the proposed Rules of Evidence. Affirmative congressional approval of them in order to render them effective is required by the terms of Public Law 93-12.

COST
Enactment of H.R. 5463 will entail no cost to the Government of the United States.

COMMUNICATION FROM THE CHIEF JUSTICE OF THE UNITED STATES
SUPREME COURT OF THE UNITED STATES,
Washington, D.C., February 5, 1973.
To the Senate and House of Representatives of the United States of America in Congress assembled:

By direction of the Supreme Court, I have the honor to submit to the Congress the Rules of Evidence1 of the United States Courts and Magistrates, amendments and further amendments to the Federal Rules of Civil Procedure and amendments to the Federal Rules of Criminal Procedure which have been adopted by the Supreme Court, pursuant to Title 28, United States Code, Sections 2072 and 2075 and Title 18, United States Code, Sections 3402, 3771 and 3772. Mr. Justice Douglas dissents from the adoption of these rules and amendments.

Accompanying these amendments is the report of the Judicial Conference of the United States submitted to the Court for its consideration, pursuant to Title 28, United States Code, Section 331.

Respectfully.

"WARREN E. BURGER,
"
"Chief Justice of the United States.
"

ADDITIONAL VIEWS OF HON. LAWRENCE J. HOGAN

While I consider codification of the Proposed Federal Rules of Evidence of highest importance, I nonetheless feel compelled to set forth in these dissenting views my strenuous objection to the majority of the Judiciary Committee's reformulation of Rule 609.

There are, of course, some other proposed rules which, in my opinion, might have been improved upon but I want to focus in these dissenting views on my objection to Rule 609--Impeachment by Evidence of Conviction of Crime. My objection extends not only to the fact that the rule as drafted by the Judiciary Committee not only rejects the version of the Rule recommended by the Advisory Committee on Rules of Evidence of the Judicial Conference of the United States, but also abrogates the prevailing view in the Federal and State courts, but I object even more to the Judiciary Committee's clear disavowal of the Congressional mandate expressed as recently as 1970 on the principle underlying this rule.

I offered an amendment before the Subcommittee and full Committee to restore the version of the rule recommended by the Advisory Committee on the Rules of Evidence of the Judicial Conference of the United States. I believe it important to look at the policy behind the formulations and reformulations which this impeachment rule has undergone throughout the course of consideration of these Proposed Federal Rules. There is set forth below the precise language of each of these formulations:

March 1969 Draft: Rule 609(a) General Rule. For the purpose of attacking the credibility of a witness, evidence that he has been convicted of a crime is admissible but only if the crime, (1) was punishable by death or imprisonment in excess of one year under the law under which he was convicted, or (2) involved dishonesty or false statement regardless of the punishment.

March 1971 Draft: Rule 609(a) General Rule. For the purpose of attacking the credibility of a witness, evidence that he has been convicted of a crime, except on a plea of nolo contendere, is admissible but only if the crime (1) was punishable by death or imprisonment in excess of one year under the law under which he was convicted or (2) involved dishonesty or false statement regardless of the punishment, unless (3), in either case, the judge determines that the probative value of the evidence of the crime is substantially outweighed by the danger of unfair prejudice.

December 1972 Draft: Identical with March 1969 Draft.

Subcommittee Draft: Rule 609(a) General Rule. For the purpose of attacking the credibility of a witness, evidence that he has been convicted of a crime is admissible only if the crime (1) was punishable by death or imprisonment in excess of one year, unless the court determines that the danger of unfair prejudice outweighs the probative value of the evidence of the conviction, or (2) involved dishonesty or false statement.

Judiciary Committee Draft: Rule 609(a) General Rule. For the purpose of attacking the credibility of a witness, evidence that he has been convicted of a crime is admissible only if the crime involved dishonesty or false statement.

The conventional and majority judicial view of the impeachment rule has been that an accused who elects to take the stand is subject to impeachment as any other witnesses, including impeachment by proof of conviction. The raging debate over impeachment of the accused's credibility by conviction of crime exemplifies the continual attempt by all involved with the judicial system to balance the scales of justice between the rights of the individual and the rights of society.

It is for this very reason that the draftsmen of the March 1969 draft of the Proposed Rules specifically undertook to study and evaluate every formulation of the impeachment rule brought to their attention. Reduced to their essentials, these included the following six alternatives:

(1) Allow no impeachment by conviction when the witness is the accused.

(2) Allow only crimen falsi.

(3) Exclude if the crime is similar.

(4) Allow conviction evidence only if the accused first introduces evidence of character for truthfulness.

(5) Leave the matter to the discretion of the trial judge.

(6) Allow impeachment by conviction when the witness is the accused--the traditional and majority rule among the State and Federal Courts.

After giving consideration to each of these six proposals, and concluding that each was only a partial solution or, at the least, no clear improvement, the Advisory Committee chose to promulgate the sixth possibility, thereby retaining the rule of the overwhelming majority of Federal and State courts as well as the views unhesitatingly exposed [espoused] by Dean Wigmore, renowned expert on evidence (See 3 Wigmore, §§ 889-891). This formulation adopts the prevailing prosecutorial view that it would be misleading to permit the accused to appear as a witness of blameless life on those occasions when the accused chooses to take the stand.

The first alternative above, that of excluding all convictions of the accused for impeachment purposes, has been given short shrift because there is little dissent from the proposition that at least some crimes are relevant to credibility. (See McCormick § 43 (2nd ed. (1972); 2 Wright, Federal Practice and Procedure: Criminal § 416 (1969).

In the second draft disseminated in March 1971, the Advisory Committee on the Rules of Evidence, totally without explanation, reversed its earlier position adopting the majority rule of Courts throughout the country and instead adopted the fifth alternative above. In effect, this was a particularized application of the Luck rule, expounded by the United States Court of Appeals for the District of Columbia in Luck v. U.S., (121 U.S.App.D.C. 151, 348 F.2d 763) in 1965. The most significant feature of the rule is the requirement that the evidence of conviction be excluded if the judge determines that its probative value is outweighed by the danger of unfair prejudice. In July, 1969, the Congress specifically repudiated the Luck rule when it enacted the traditional rule as the impeachment rule to be followed in all criminal trials in the District of Columbia. The D.C. Court Reorganization and Criminal Procedure Act of 1970, incorporating the traditional impeachment rule, was approved by the House by a vote of 294-47.

The Advisory Committee took note of the 1969 Congressional pronouncement on the impeachment question and returned to its original position in endorsing the traditional rule in the third and final version which was submitted to this Congress for our consideration and enactment in December 1972.

In spite of the fact that the eminent members of the Bench and Bar who made up the Advisory Committee on the Rules of Evidence made their position clear, the majority of the House Committee on the Judiciary rejected the majority rule in the State and Federal courts and have changed the rule once again. But with this change the dimensions of the rule are totally immeasurable either from a prosecutorial or from a defense viewpoint. The Judiciary Committee has seen fit not only to renounce the traditional rule which is that under which their fellow members of the Bar labor in the majority of their Federal courts and in 90% of their State courts but the majority of the full Judiciary Committee has also defeated the compromise effected by the Subcommittee on Criminal Justice after many hours of arguing the merits and demerits of the various alternative formulations.

The rule which the majority has now settled upon is, of all the alternatives set out above, the most unsettling. Allowing only evidence of the crimen falsi to impeach the credibility of the accused adopts only the worst feature of the Luck rule, i.e., unpredictability, without bestowing upon the Bench and Bar any useful new tool for coping with the evidentiary problem which is at the heart of this debate.

When the draftsmen of the Advisory Committee on the Rules of Evidence originally rejected the crimen falsi alternative for Rule 609, they did so because most of the crimes regarded as having a substantial impeaching effect would be excluded, resulting in virtually the same effect as if the alternative allowing no prior convictions for impeachment purposes were adopted.

In the commentaries to the first draft, the Advisory Committee on the Rules of Evidence noted:

"While it may be argued that considerations of relevancy should limit provable convictions to those of crimes of untruthfulness, acts are constituted major crimes because they entail substantial injury to and disregard of the rights of other persons or the public. A demonstrated instance of willingness to engage in conduct in disregard of accepted patterns is translatable into willingness to give false testimony.

A further argument against adoption of the crimen falsi alternative, as noted above, is that of its unpredictability and its uneven application to criminal defendants across the board. One of the major objections to the Luck rule in the District of Columbia, and one of the major reasons that it has failed to be adopted in most of the other Federal circuit courts, is that the discretionary authority which Luck vests in the trial judge imposes another discriminatory element into an already overly-criticized criminal justice system in this country.

Even more so is this true of the crimen falsi alternative. What, really, is dishonesty or false statement in judicial or legal terms? Unless one practices in a jurisdiction which has statutorily defined crimen falsi, the common law definition of "any crime which may injuriously affect the administration of justice, by the introduction of falsehood and fraud" is applicable. This definition has been held to include forgery, perjury, subornation of perjury, suppression of testimony by bribery, conspiracy to procure the absence of a witness or to accuse of crime, obtaining money under false pretenses, stealing, moral turpitude, shoplifting, intoxication, petit larceny, jury tampering, embezzlement and filing a false estate tax return. In other jurisdictions, some of these same offenses have been found not to fit the crimen falsi definition.

From the foregoing analyses undertaken by the eminent professors, jurists and lawyers of the Advisory Committee, as well as by my colleagues on the Committee on the Judiciary, I am convinced that the only viable alternative is that which has stood the test of time. If for no other reason than that the other considered alternatives are no improvement over the shortcomings of the traditional, I shall offer an amendment on the floor to reinstate the traditional, majority rule as promulgated by the Advisory Committee on the Rules of Evidence of the Judicial Conferences of the United States, and as it is known in the majority of our American courts. I am hopeful that this amendment will receive the support of the House as it did in 1970 when the crimen falsi alternative was specifically voted down in the D.C. Court Reorganization and Criminal Procedure Act of 1970.

Lawrence J. Hogan.
SEPARATE VIEWS OF HON. ELIZABETH HOLTZMAN
The code of evidence proposed by the Judiciary Committee marks a substantial improvement over the rules initially promulgated by the Supreme Court--a fact attributable to the excellent and conscientious work done by the Subcommittee on Criminal Justice chaired by Congressman Hungate.

Although the Subcommittee did an extremely commendable job, I still have substantial reservations about the final product.

1. IS THERE A NEED TO CODIFY RULES OF EVIDENCE?
At the present time, the rules of evidence in the federal courts are not codified. Evidentiary matters are governed essentially by the common law, with a few exceptions, and rules have been developed on a case-by-case basis.

Eminent jurists and lawyers have objected to any codification of rules of evidence--or freezing them into black letter law. Judge Friendly, former Chief Judge of the Court of Appeals for the Second Circuit stated:

"Evidence to me seems just not the kind of subject that lends itself very well to codification."

His position was supported by the Chairman of the Association of Trial Lawyers of America and representatives of the American College of Trial Lawyers.

I think it is fair to say that the testimony as a whole before the subcommittee showed no overwhelming need to codify the rules. Instead, the dangers of codification became apparent.

Black letter rules will make evidentiary points high profile. Presently, evidentiary rulings are generally not considered critical at a trial. Once we adopt a "black letter" code, lawyers will have a field day determining how many evidentiary angels can dance on the top of a pin. A number of witnesses testified that the rules will generate appeals and increase reversals on evidentiary rulings. (This is especially true with the highly confused legislative history of these rules: three advisory committee drafts, two subcommittee drafts, comments on subcommittee drafts, etc.).

Another thorny problem this codification will produce is forum shopping. Because this code substantially liberalizes the hearsay rules, federal courts may become a more attractive forum for litigation. This is not, however, a time to increase the work load of the already congested federal courts. Nor is there any substantial justification on a hearsay issue for a different outcome in a federal court when state law is involved.

In short, many have argued that adoption of a rigid black letter evidentiary code might constitute a step backwards. Problems might include prolongation of trials, an increase in appellate reversals, the denial to trial judges of flexibility, the difficulty of dealing with evidentiary issues by black letter law and the disadvantage of cutting off the development of the law in many areas where such development on a case basis was presently desirable.

2. OBJECTIONS TO PARTICULAR RULES

The Committee's action on most of the controversial rules--privileges, impeachment by prior convictions, use of opinion evidence and the like--was in my opinion eminently correct. Part of the reason for this was the fact that most of the comments we received were directed to these rules.

Unfortunately, however, many of the other "minor" rules did not receive very much attention from commentators or witnesses and Committee action on these was, in my opinion, much less persuasive.

I will cite a few examples.

Rule 803(8)(b) permits an exception to the hearsay rule for records of public officers or agencies "setting forth matters observed pursuant to duty imposed by law." It would allow reports by police officers, social workers, building inspectors and the like--instead of direct testimony--as substantive evidence in criminal or civil trials. Thus, a social worker's report of a random observation of a marital relationship could be introduced in a criminal case against one of the spouses. Similarly, a policeman's report containing an observation of an alleged criminal offense could be used in the criminal trial instead of having the police officer himself testify. This represents an extraordinary departure from existing law. It gives more credibility to the observations of government employees than are given to observations of private citizens.

There are also problems with rules concerning the admission of unfairly prejudicial evidence (Rule 403), best evidence rule (Article 10), use of accused is testimony on preliminary matters (Rule 104(d)), statements in documents affecting an interest in property (Rule 803(15)), authenticity of commercial paper (Rule 902(9)), authenticity of handwriting (Rule 901), hearsay use of telephone directories and similar publications (Rule 803(17)), and use of court appointed expert witnesses (Rule 706).

3. THE PROCEDURE FOR AMENDING THESE RULES IS UNWISE

Under the committee bill, the Supreme Court may propose an amendment which becomes law unless the House or Senate vetoes that amendment.

The dangers in this procedure are particularly apparent with respect to evidentiary privileges: husband-wife, lawyer-client, doctor-patient privilege. Decisions regarding privileges necessarily entail policy considerations because, unlike most evidentiary rules, privileges protect interpersonal relationships outside of the courtroom. Clearly, by creating a newspaperman's privilege or defining the limits of confidential communications, we are expressing a desire to promote a social objective: e.g., promoting a free press, encouraging clients to be candid with their lawyers, etc.

Rules creating, abolishing or limiting privileges are legislative. Nonetheless, under the committee bill we would be allowing the Supreme Court to legislate in the area of privilege subject only to a congressional veto. This procedure is unwise since rules concerning privilege, if enacted, should be done through an affirmative vote by Congress.

The process is, I submit, unconstitutional as well. The Supreme Court is not given the power under Article III of the Constitution to legislate rules on substantive matters. It can pass such judgments only in the context of a particular case or controversy. Yet, H.R. 5453 allows the Court to promulgate a rule in a substantive policy area without the benefit of an adversary proceeding. We cannot (and should not) delegate such rule-making power to the Supreme Court.

CONCLUSION

Unquestionably if we enact these rules of evidence we will be enacting a code substantially better than the one confronting Congress earlier this year. Yet, we must balance the fine work done by the subcommittee and the proported benefits of a uniform federal code of evidence against the dangers of codification and the problems outlined above.

In making our decision we should bear in mind the testimony of Judge Friendly:

"(T)here is no need for [the proposed Rules]. Someone once said that, in legal matters, when it is not necessary to do anything, it is necessary to do nothing. I find that a profoundly wise remark. We know we are now having almost no serious problems with respect to evidence; we cannot tell how many the Proposed Rules will bring."

ELIZABETH HOLTZMAN.
CONFERENCE REPORT NO. 93-1597
JOINT EXPLANATORY STATEMENT OF THE COMMITTEE OF CONFERENCE
The managers on the part of the House and the Senate at the conference on the disagreeing votes of the two houses on the amendments of the Senate to the bill (H.R. 5463) to establish rules of evidence1 for certain courts and proceedings, submit the following joint statement to the House and the Senate in explanation of the effect of the action agreed upon by the managers and recommended in the accompanying conference report:

The House and Senate conferees met twice to discuss the differences in the Senate and House versions of H.R. 5463. The first meeting took place in the afternoon of Wednesday, December 11, 1974, and the second took place in the afternoon of Thursday, December 12, 1974.

The Senate made 44 amendments to the House bill, seven of which are of a technical or conforming nature. Of these seven, the Conference adopts 5, the Senate recedes from 1, and the Conference adopts one of the technical amendments with an amendment.

The more significant differences in the House and Senate versions of the bill were resolved as follows:

RULE 103. RULINGS ON EVIDENCE
The House bill contains the word "judge". The Senate amendment substitutes the word "court" in order to conform with usage elsewhere in the House bill.

The Conference adopts the Senate amendment.

RULE 301. PRESUMPTIONS IN GENERAL IN CIVIL ACTIONS AND PROCEEDINGS
The House bill provides that a presumption in civil actions and proceedings shifts to the party against whom it is directed the burden of going forward with evidence to meet or rebut it. Even though evidence contradicting the presumption is offered, a presumption is considered sufficient evidence of the presumed fact to be considered by the jury. The Senate amendment provides that a presumption shifts to the party against whom it is directed the burden of going forward with evidence to meet or rebut the presumption, but it does not shift to that party the burden of persuasion on the existence of the presumed fact.

Under the Senate amendment, a presumption is sufficient to get a party past an adverse party's motion to dismiss made at the end of his case-in-chief. If the adverse party offers no evidence contradicting the presumed fact, the court will instruct the jury that if it finds the basic facts, it may presume the existence of the presumed fact. If the adverse party does offer evidence contradicting the presumed fact, the court cannot instruct the jury that it may presume the existence of the presumed fact from proof of the basic facts. The court may, however, instruct the jury that it may infer the existence of the presumed fact from proof of the basic facts.

The Conference adopts the Senate amendment.

RULE 405. METHODS OF PROVING CHARACTER
The Senate makes two language changes in the nature of conforming amendments. The Conference adopts the Senate amendments.

RULE 408. COMPROMISE AND OFFERS TO COMPROMISE
The House bill provides that evidence of admissions of liability or opinions given during compromise negotiations is not admissible, but that evidence of facts disclosed during compromise negotiations is not inadmissible by virtue of having been first disclosed in the compromise negotiations. The Senate amendment provides that evidence of conduct or statements made in compromise negotiations is not admissible. The Senate amendment also provides that the rule does not require the exclusion of any evidence otherwise discoverable merely because it is presented in the course of compromise negotiations.

The House bill was drafted to meet the objection of executive agencies that under the rule as proposed by the Supreme Court, a party could present a fact during compromise negotiations and thereby prevent an opposing party from offering evidence of that fact at trial even though such evidence was obtained from independent sources. The Senate amendment expressly precludes this result.

The Conference adopts the Senate amendment.

RULE 410. OFFER TO PLEAD GUILTY; NOLO CONTENDERE; WITHDRAWN PLEA OF GUILTY
The House bill provides that evidence of a guilty or nolo contendere plea, of an offer of either plea, or of statements made in connection with such pleas or offers of such pleas, is inadmissible in any civil or criminal action, case or proceeding against the person making such plea or offer. The Senate amendment makes the rule inapplicable to a voluntary and reliable statement made in court on the record where the statement is offered in a subsequent prosecution of the declarant for perjury or false statement.

The issues raised by Rule 410 are also raised by proposed Rule 11(e)(6) of the Federal Rules of Criminal Procedure presently pending before Congress. This proposed rule, which deals with the admissibility of pleas of guilty or nolo contendere, offers to make such pleas, and statements made in connection with such pleas, was promulgated by the Supreme Court on April 22, 1974, and in the absence of congressional action will become effective on August 1, 1975. The conferees intend to make no change in the presently-existing case law until that date, leaving the courts free to develop rules in this area on a case-by-case basis.

The Conferees further determined that the issues presented by the use of guilty and nolo contendere pleas, offers of such pleas, and statements made in connection with such pleas or offers, can be explored in greater detail during Congressional consideration of Rule 11(e)(6) of the Federal Rules of Criminal Procedure. The Conferees believe, therefore, that it is best to defer its effective date until August 1, 1975. The Conferees intend that Rule 410 would be superseded by any subsequent Federal Rule of Criminal Procedure or Act of Congress with which it is inconsistent, if the Federal Rule of Criminal Procedure or Act of Congress takes effect or becomes law after the date of the enactment of the act establishing the rules of evidence.

The conference adopts the Senate amendment with an amendment that expresses the above intentions.

RULE 501. GENERAL RULE (OF PRIVILEGE)
Rule 501 deals with the privilege of a witness not to testify. Both the House and Senate bills provide that federal privilege law applies in criminal cases. In civil actions and proceedings, the

House bill provides that state privilege law applies "to an element of a claim or defense as to which State law supplies the rule of decision." The Senate bill provides that "in civil actions and proceedings arising under 28 U.S.C. § 1332 or 28 U.S.C. § 1335, or between citizens of different States and removed under 28 U.S.C. § 1441(b) the privilege of a witness, person, government, State or political subdivision thereof is determined in accordance with State law, unless with respect to the particular claim or defense, Federal law supplies the rule of decision."

The wording of the House and Senate bills differs in the treatment of civil actions and proceedings. The rule in the House bill applies to evidence that relates to "an element of a claim or defense." If an item of proof tends to support or defeat a claim or defense, or an element of a claim or defense, and if state law supplies the rule of decision for that claim or defense, then state privilege law applies to that item of proof.

Under the provision in the House bill, therefore, state privilege law will usually apply in diversity cases. There may be diversity cases, however, where a claim or defense is based upon federal law. In such instances, federal privilege law will apply to evidence relevant to the federal claim or defense. See Sola Electric Co. v. Jefferson Electric Co., 317 U.S. 173 (1942).

In nondiversity jurisdiction civil cases, federal privilege law will generally apply. In those situations where a federal court adopts or incorporates state law to fill interstices or gaps in federal statutory phrases, the court generally will apply federal privilege law. As Justice Jackson has said:

A federal court sitting in a non-diversity case such as this does not sit as a local tribunal. In some cases it may see fit for special reasons to give the law of a particular state highly persuasive or even controlling effect, but in the last analysis its decision turns upon the law of the United States, not that of any state.

D'Oench, Duhme & Co. v. Federal Deposit Insurance Corp., 315 U.S. 447, 471 (1942) (Jackson, J., concurring). When a federal court chooses to absorb state law, it is applying the state law as a matter of federal common law. Thus, state law does not supply the rule of decision (even though the federal court may apply a rule derived from state decisions), and state privilege law would not apply. See C.A. Wright, Federal Courts 251-252 (2d ed. 1970); Holmberg v. Armbrecht, 327 U.S. 392 (1946); DeSylva v. Ballentine, 351 U.S. 570, 581 (1956); 9 Wright & Miller, Federal Rules and Procedure § 2408.

In civil actions and proceedings, where the rule of decision as to a claim or defense or as to an element of a claim or defense is supplied by state law, the House provision requires that state privilege law apply.

The Conference adopts the House provision.

RULE 601. GENERAL RULE OF COMPETENCY

Rule 601 deals with competency of witnesses. Both the House and Senate bills provide that federal competency law applies in criminal cases. In civil actions and proceedings, the House bill provides that state competency law applies "to an element of a claim or defense as to which State law supplies the rule of decision." The Senate bill provides that "in civil actions and proceedings arising under 28 U.S.C. § 1332 or 28 U.S.C. § 1335, or between citizens of different States and removed under 28 U.S.C. § 1441(b) the competency of a witness, person, government, State or political subdivision thereof is determined in accordance with State law, unless with respect to the particular claim or defense, Federal law supplies the rule of decision."

The wording of the House and Senate bills differs in the treatment of civil actions and proceedings. The rule in the House bill applies to evidence that relates to "an element of a claim or defense." If an item of proof tends to support or defeat a claim or defense, or an element of a claim or defense, and if state law supplies the rule of decision for that claim or defense, then state competency law applies to that item of proof.

For reasons similar to those underlying its action on Rule 501, the Conference adopts the House provision.

RULE 606. COMPETENCY OF JUROR AS WITNESS

Rule 606(b) deals with juror testimony in an inquiry into the validity of a verdict or indictment. The House bill provides that a juror cannot testify about his mental processes or about the effect of anything upon his or another juror's mind as influencing him to assent to or dissent from a verdict or indictment. Thus, the House bill allows a juror to testify about objective matters occurring during the jury's deliberation, such as the misconduct of another juror or the reaching of a quotient verdict. The Senate bill does not permit juror testimony about any matter or statement occurring during the course of the jury's deliberations. The Senate bill does provide, however, that a juror may testify on the question whether extraneous prejudicial information was improperly brought to the jury's attention and on the question whether any outside influence was improperly brought to bear on any juror.

The Conference adopts the Senate amendment. The Conferees believe that jurors should be encouraged to be conscientious in promptly reporting to the court misconduct that occurs during jury deliberations.

RULE 608. EVIDENCE OF CHARACTER AND CONDUCT OF WITNESS

The Senate amendment adds the words "opinion or" to conform the first sentence of the rule with the remainder of the rule.

The Conference adopts the Senate amendment.

RULE 609. IMPEACHMENT BY EVIDENCE OF CONVICTION OF CRIME

Rule 609 defines when a party may use evidence of a prior conviction in order to impeach a witness. The Senate amendments make changes in two subsections of Rule 609.

A. Rule 609(a)--General Rule

The House bill provides that the credibility of a witness can be attacked by proof of prior conviction of a crime only if the crime involves dishonesty or false statement. The Senate amendment provides that a witness' credibility may be attacked if the crime (1) was punishable by death or imprisonment in excess of one year under the law under which he was convicted or (2) involves dishonesty or false statement, regardless of the punishment.

The Conference adopts the Senate amendment with an amendment. The Conference amendment provides that the credibility of a witness, whether a defendant or someone else, may be attacked by proof of a prior conviction but only if the crime: (1) was punishable by death or imprisonment in excess of one year under the law under which he was convicted and the court determines that the probative value of the conviction outweighs its prejudicial effect to the defendant; or (2) involved dishonesty or false statement regardless of the punishment.

By the phrase "dishonesty and false statement" the Conference means crimes such as perjury or subornation of perjury, false statement, criminal fraud, embezzlement, or false pretense, or any other offense in the nature of crimen falsi, the commission of which involves some element of deceit, untruthfulness, or falsification bearing on the accused's propensity to testify truthfully.

The admission of prior convictions involving dishonesty and false statement is not within the discretion of the Court. Such convictions are peculiarly probative of credibility and, under this rule, are always to be admitted. Thus, judicial discretion granted with respect to the admissibility of other prior convictions is not applicable to those involving dishonesty or false statement.

With regard to the discretionary standard established by paragraph (1) of rule 609(a), the Conference determined that the prejudicial effect to be weighed against the probative value of the conviction is specifically the prejudicial effect to the defendant. The danger of prejudice to a witness other than the defendant (such as injury to the witness' reputation in his community) was considered and rejected by the Conference as an element to be weighed in determining admissibility. It was the judgment of the Conference that the danger of prejudice to a nondefendant witness is outweighed by the need for the trier of fact to have as much relevant evidence on the issue of credibility as possible. Such evidence should only be excluded where it presents a danger of improperly influencing the outcome of the trial by persuading the trier of fact to convict the defendant on the basis of his prior criminal record.

B. Rule 609(b)--Time Limit

The House bill provides in subsection (b) that evidence of conviction of a crime may not be used for impeachment purposes under subsection (a) if more than ten years have elapsed since the date of the conviction or the date the witness was released from confinement imposed for the conviction, whichever is later. The Senate amendment permits the use of convictions older than ten years, if the court determines, in the interests of justice, that the probative value of the conviction, supported by specific facts and circumstances, substantially outweighs its prejudicial effect.

The Conference adopts the Senate amendment with an amendment requiring notice by a party that he intends to request that the court allow him to use a conviction older than ten years. The Conferees anticipate that a written notice, in order to give the adversary a fair opportunity to contest the use of the evidence, will ordinarily include such information as the date of the conviction, the jurisdiction, and the offense or statute involved. In order to eliminate the possibility that the flexibility of this provision may impair the ability of a party-opponent to prepare for trial, the Conferees intend that the notice provision operate to avoid surprise.

RULE 801. DEFINITIONS

Rule 801 supplies some basic definitions for the rules of evidence that deal with hearsay. Rule 801(d)(1) defines certain statements as not hearsay. The Senate amendments make two changes in it.

A. Rule 801(d)(1)(A)

The House bill provides that a statement is not hearsay if the declarant testifies and is subject to cross-examination concerning the statement and if the statement is inconsistent with his testimony and was given under oath subject to cross-examination and subject to the penalty of perjury at a trial or hearing or in a deposition. The Senate amendment drops the requirement that the prior statement be given under oath subject to cross-examination and subject to the penalty of perjury at a trial or hearing or in a deposition.

The Conference adopts the Senate amendment with an amendment, so that the rule now requires that the prior inconsistent statement be given under oath subject to the penalty of perjury at a trial, hearing, or other proceeding, or in a deposition. The rule as adopted covers statements before a grand jury. Prior inconsistent statements may, of course, be used for impeaching the credibility of a witness. When the prior inconsistent statement is one made by a defendant in a criminal case, it is covered by Rule 801(d)(2).

B. Rule 801(d)(1)(C)

The House bill provides that a statement is not hearsay if the declarant testifies and is subject to cross-examination concerning the statement and the statement is one of identification of a person made after perceiving him. The Senate amendment eliminated this provision.

The Conference adopts the Senate amendment.

RULE 803. HEARSAY EXCEPTIONS; AVAILABILITY OF DECLARANT IMMATERIAL

Rule 803 defines when hearsay statements are admissible in evidence even though the declarant is available as a witness. The Senate amendments make three changes in this rule.

A. Rule 803(6)--Records of Regularly Conducted Activity

The House bill provides in subsection (6) that records of a regularly conducted "business" activity qualify for admission into evidence as an exception to the hearsay rule. "Business" is defined as including "business, profession, occupation and calling of every kind." The Senate amendment drops the requirement that the records be those of a "business" activity and eliminates the definition of "business." The Senate amendment provides that records are admissible if they are records of a regularly conducted "activity."

The Conference adopts the House provision that the records must be those of a regularly conducted "business" activity. The Conferees changed the definition of "business" contained in the House provision in order to make it clear that the records of institutions and associations like schools, churches and hospitals are admissible under this provision. The records of public schools and hospitals are also covered by Rule 803(8), which deals with public records and reports.

B. Rule 803(8)--Public Records and Reports

The Senate amendment adds language, not contained in the House bill, that refers to another rule that was added by the Senate in another amendment (Rule 804(b)(5)--Criminal law enforcement records and reports).

In view of its action on Rule 804(b)(5) (Criminal law enforcement records and reports), the Conference does not adopt the Senate amendment and restores the bill to the House version.

C. Rule 803(24)--Other exceptions

The Senate amendment adds a new subsection, (24), which makes admissible a hearsay statement not specifically covered by any of the previous twenty-three subsections, if the statement has equivalent circumstantial guarantees of trustworthiness and if the court determines that (A) the statement is offered as evidence of a material fact; (B) the statement is more probative on the point for which it is offered than any other evidence the proponent can procure through reasonable efforts; and (C) the general purposes of these rules and the interests of justice will best be served by admission of the statement into evidence.

The House bill eliminated a similar, but broader, provision because of the conviction that such a provision injected too much uncertainty into the law of evidence regarding hearsay and impaired the ability of a litigant to prepare adequately for trial.

The Conference adopts the Senate amendment with an amendment that provides that a party intending to request the court to use a statement under this provision must notify any adverse party of this intention as well as of the particulars of the statement, including the name and address of the declarant. This notice must be given sufficiently in advance of the trial or hearing to provide any adverse party with a fair opportunity to prepare to contest the use of the statement.

RULE 804. HEARSAY EXCEPTIONS: DECLARANT UNAVAILABLE

Rule 804 defines what hearsay statements are admissible in evidence if the declarant is unavailable as a witness. The Senate amendments make four changes in the rule.

A. Rule 804(a)(5)--Definition of Unavailability

Subsection (a) defines the term "unavailability as a witness". The House bill provides in subsection (a)(5) that the party who desires to use the statement must be unable to procure the declarant's attendance by process or other reasonable means. In the case of dying declarations, statements against interest and statements of personal or family history, the House bill requires that the proponent must also be unable to procure the declarant's testimony (such as by deposition or interrogatories) by process or other reasonable means. The Senate amendment eliminates this latter provision.

The Conference adopts the provision contained in the House bill.

B. Rule 804(b)(3)--Statement against Interest

The Senate amendment to subsection (b)(3) provides that a statement is against interest and not excluded by the hearsay rule when the declarant is unavailable as a witness, if the statement tends to subject a person to civil or criminal liability or renders invalid a claim by him against another. The House bill did not refer specifically to civil liability and to rendering invalid a claim against another. The Senate amendment also deletes from the House bill the provision that subsection (b) (3) does not apply to a statement or confession, made by a codefendant or another, which implicates the accused and the person who made the statement, when that statement or confession is offered against the accused in a criminal case.

The Conference adopts the Senate amendment. The Conferees intend to include within the purview of this rule, statements subjecting a person to civil liability and statements rendering claims invalid. The Conferees agree to delete the provision regarding statements by a codefendant, thereby reflecting the general approach in the Rules of Evidence to avoid attempting to codify constitutional evidentiary principles.

C. Rule 804(b)(5)--Criminal Law Enforcement Records and Reports

The Senate amendment adds a new hearsay exception, not contained in the House bill, which provides that certain law enforcement records are admissible if the officer-declarant is unavailable to testify or be present because of (1) death or physical or mental illness or infirmity or (2) absence from the proceeding and the proponent of the statement has been unable to procure his attendance by process or other reasonable means.

The Conference does not adopt the Senate amendment, preferring instead to leave the bill in the House version, which contained no such provision.

D. Rule 804(b)(6)--Other Exceptions

The Senate amendment adds a new subsection, (b)(6), which makes admissible a hearsay statement not specifically covered by any of the five previous subsections, if the statement has equivalent circumstantial guarantees of trustworthiness and if the court determines that (A) the statement is offered as evidence of a material fact; (B) the statement is more probative on the point for which it is offered than any other evidence the proponent can procure through reasonable efforts; and (C) the general purposes of these rules and the interests of justice will best be served by admission of the statement into evidence.

The House bill eliminated a similar, but broader, provision because of the conviction that such a provision injected too much uncertainty into the law of evidence regarding hearsay and impaired the ability of a litigant to prepare adequately for trial.

The Conference adopts the Senate amendment with an amendment that renumbers this subsection and provides that a party intending to request the court to use a statement under this provision must notify any adverse party of this intention as well as of the particulars of the statement, including the name and address of the declarant. This notice must be given sufficiently in advance of the trial or hearing to provide any adverse party with a fair opportunity to prepare to contest the use of the statement.

RULE 806. ATTACKING AND SUPPORTING CREDIBILITY OF DECLARANT
The Senate amendment permits an attack upon the credibility of the declarant of a statement if the statement is one by a person authorized by a party-opponent to make a statement concerning the subject, one by an agent of a party-opponent, or one by a coconspirator of the party-opponent, as these statements are defined in Rules 801(d)(2)(C), (D) and (E). The House bill has no such provision.

The Conference adopts the Senate amendment. The Senate amendment conforms the rule to present practice.

SECTION 2. ENABLING ACT

Section 2 of the bill adds a new section to title 28 of the United States Code that establishes a procedure for amending the rules of evidence in the future. The House bill provides that the Supreme Court may promulgate amendments, and these amendments become effective 180 days after being reported to Congress, However, any amendment that creates, abolishes or modifies a rule of privilege does not become effective until approved by Act of Congress. The Senate amendments changed the length of time that must elapse before an amendment becomes effective to 365 days. The Senate amendments also added language, not contained in the House provision, that (1) either House can defer the effective date of a proposed amendment to a later date or until approved by Act of Congress and (2) an Act of Congress can amend any rule of evidence, whether proposed or in effect. Finally, the Senate amendments struck the provision requiring that amendments creating, abolishing or modifying a privilege be approved by Act of Congress.

The Conference adopts the House provision on the time period (180 days) and the House provision requiring that an amendment creating, abolishing or modifying a rule of privilege cannot become effective until approved by Act of Congress. The Conference adopts the Senate amendment providing that either House can defer the effective date of an amendment to the rules of evidence and that any rule, either proposed or in effect, can be amended by Act of Congress. In making these changes in the enabling Act, Conference recognizes the continuing role of the Supreme Court in promulgating rules of evidence.

"WILLIAM L. HUNGATE,"
"BOB KASTENMEIER,"
"DON EDWARDS,"
"HENRY P. SMITH III,"
"DAVID W. DENNIS,"
"Managers on the part of the House."

"JAMES O. EASTLAND,"
"JOHN L. MCCLELLAN,"
"P.A. HART,"
"SAM J. ERVIN, JR.,"
"QUENTIN N. BURDICK,"
"ROMAN L. HRUSKA,"
"STROM THURMOND,"
"HUGH SCOTT,"
"Managers on the part of the Senate."

STATEMENT BY HOUSE SUBCOMMITTEE CHAIRMAN
STATEMENT BY THE HON. WILLIAM L. HUNGATE, CHAIRMAN OF THE HOUSE JUDICIARY SUBCOMMITTEE ON CRIMINAL JUSTICE, UPON PRESENTING THE CONFERENCE REPORT ON H.R. 5463 TO THE HOUSE FOR FINAL CONSIDERATION.
December 18, 1974, 120 Congressional Record H 12253
Mr. HUNGATE. Mr. Speaker, I yield 30 minutes to the gentleman from New York, pending which I yield myself such time as I may consume.

Mr. Speaker, the bill now before the body, H.R. 5463, is the culmination of 13 years of work, which began in March 1961 when then Chief Justice Earl Warren appointed a committee to study the feasibility of developing uniform rules of evidence. The special committee reported favorably, and Chief Justice Earl Warren then appointed an Advisory Committee on Rules of Evidence to go about drafting rules of evidence. This committee completed its work and in February 1973 the Supreme Court promulgated a code of evidence that was to become effective on July 1, 1973, unless disapproved by Congress before that date.

It soon became apparent that the issues raised by the evidence code were of such magnitude that Congress could not properly dispose of the matter before the July 1, 1973 deadline. Consequently, legislation was enacted to delay the effective date of the rules of evidence until they were "expressly approved by Act of Congress"--Public Law 93-12. The bill now before the House, H.R. 5463, constitutes the congressional approval required by Public Law 93-12.

The Subcommittee on Criminal Justice gave extensive consideration to the rules of evidence. We held 6 days of hearings and compiled a hearing record of about 600 pages. Based on this, this subcommittee then discussed each and every one of the rules promulgated by the Supreme Court. This took 22 markup sessions. The full committee then held 3 markup sessions to consider the bill. On November 15, 1973, the bill was reported favorably to the House.

This body took up the bill on February 6 and passed it by a vote of 377 to 13.

The Supreme Court promulgated 77 proposed rules of evidence. Of these 77, the House bill made no changes in 27 and only minor, nonsubstantive changes in 14. Thus, over half of the rules were not substantively changed. Many of the substantive amendments were relatively noncontroversial and easily agreed upon. A few, of course, generated a great deal of controversy.

The Senate received the House bill, and in June of this year the Senate Judiciary Committee held two hearings on the House bill. In October 1974, the Senate Judiciary Committee reported the bill favorably with amendments. The Senate passed the bill on November 22 by a vote of 69 to 0.

The House and Senate appointed conferees to resolve the differences in the two bills. House conferees were Representatives Kastenmeier, Edwards of California, Smith of New York, Dennis, and myself. Senate conferees were Senators Eastland, McClellan, Ervin, Hart, Burdick, Hruska, Thurmond, and Scott of Pennsylvania. The conferees met twice--on the afternoon of Wednesday, December 11, and on the afternoon of Thursday, December 12. The conferees were able to reach to resolve all the differences unanimously.

The Senate made 44 numbered amendments to the House bill. Seven of these were of a technical or conforming nature and were easily disposed of. Of the remainder, only a few amendments raised difficult problems. The Senate receded from 14 of its amendments, and the House receded from its disagreement with 21 of the Senate amendments. The House and Senate agreed to modify the language of 9 Senate amendments. These 9 amendments, as amended, were then adopted by the conference.

I must say that, in all fairness, neither the House nor the Senate "won" at the conference. The real winner is the Federal judicial system. A spirit of compromise and accommodation ran throughout the conference sessions and enabled us to do our work quickly, yet thoroughly and fairly.

Let me now discuss a few of the more important matters and how the conference handled them.

RULE 410--OFFER TO PLEAD GUILTY; NOLO CONTENDERE; WITHDRAWN PLEA OF GUILTY
This rule deals with the admissibility of pleas of guilty or nolo contendere, offers of such pleas, and statements made in connection with such pleas or offers of such pleas. The Senate had proposed to make such evidence admissible for purposes of impeachment and for perjury or false statement prosecutions.

This same subject is covered by proposed rule 11(e)(6) of the Federal Rules of Criminal Procedure. Pursuant to Public Law 93-361, proposed rule 11(e)(6) will become effective on August 1, 1975. Proposed rule 11(e)(6) will be the subject of congressional scrutiny. In fact, the Subcommittee on Criminal Justice has already had one day of hearings on this and other proposed changes in the Federal Rules of Criminal Procedure.

The conference decided that the issues raised by rule 410 could better be considered in connection with proposed rule 11(e)(6) of the Federal Rules of Criminal Procedure. Therefore, the conference added language to the bill that, in effect, strikes rule 410 from the rules of evidence. Specifically, the new language provides that rule 410 will become effective on August 1, 1975. The language further provides that rule 410 will be superseded by any amendment to the Federal Rules of Criminal Procedure with which it, rule 410, is inconsistent, if that amendment takes effect after enactment of this legislation establishing the rules of evidence. Thus, if the presently proposed rule 11(e)(6) becomes effective on August 1, 1975, then this rule, rule 410, does not go into effect. In fact, any amendment to the Federal Rules of Criminal Procedure that is inconsistent with rule 410 and that becomes effective after this legislation is enacted, renders rule 410 ineffective and inoperable.

RULE 501--GENERAL RULE OF PRIVILEGE

This rule deals with when a witness is privileged not to testify--that is, when a witness may decline to give evidence that is otherwise relevant, material and probative. The Senate receded from its amendments to this rule. Under the House rule, which was adopted by the conference, the Federal law of privilege will apply in Federal criminal cases. The Federal law of privilege will apply to civil actions and proceedings, unless State law supplies the rule of decision for a claim or defense, or for an element of a claim or defense. When State law does supply the rule of decision, then State privilege law applies.

The rule uses the term "element of a claim or defense." This term means that the evidence in question must tend to support or defeat a claim or defense. If the evidence does tend to support or defeat a claim or defense, then the evidence is an "element of a claim or defense."

The rules promulgated by the Supreme Court contained 11 specific rules of privilege. Without doubt, the privilege section of the rules of evidence generated more comment or controversy than any other section. I would say that 50 percent of the complaints received by the Criminal Justice Subcommittee related to the privilege section. The House rule on privilege is intended to leave the Federal law of privilege where we found it. The Federal courts are to develop the law of privilege on a case-by-case basis.

Rule 501 is not intended to freeze the law of privilege as it now exists. The phrase "governed by the principles of the common law as they may be interpreted by the courts of the United States in the light of reason and experience," is intended to provide the courts with the flexibility to develop rules of privilege on a case-by-case basis. For example, the Supreme Court's rules of evidence contained no rule of privilege for a newspaperperson. The language of rule 501 permits the courts to develop a privilege for newspaperpeople on a case-by-case basis. The language cannot be interpreted as a congressional expression in favor of having no such privilege, nor can the conference action be interpreted as denying to newspeople any protection they may have from State newsperson's privilege laws.

RULE 609(a)--IMPEACHMENT BY EVIDENCE OF PRIOR CONVICTION

This rule provides when evidence of a prior conviction may be used to impeach the credibility of a witness. The House version of the rule permitted the use of convictions for crimes of dishonesty or false statement. The Senate version permitted the use of convictions for any felony or for any crime of dishonesty or false statement. Thus, the Senate version permitted greater latitude in the use of prior convictions than did the House version.

The conference rule strikes a middle ground between the two versions, but a ground as close or closer to the House version than to the Senate's. The conference rule provides that evidence of a conviction of a crime involving dishonesty or false statement may always be used to impeach-- subject, of course, to the time limitation of subsection (b). This constitutes no change from either the House or Senate version. The conference rule further provides that evidence of a prior felony conviction may be used for impeachment but only if the court determines that the probative value of the conviction outweighs its prejudicial effect to the defendant. Thus, the rule puts the burden on the proponent of such evidence to show that it should be used--to show that the probative value of the evidence outweighs its prejudicial effect to the defendant. The rule, in practical effect, means that in a criminal case the prior felony conviction of a prosecution witness may always be used. There can be no prejudicial effect to the defendant if he, the defendant, impeaches the credibility of a prosecution witness. The prior conviction of a defense witness, on the other hand, may have a prejudicial effect to the defendant.

RULE 804(b)(5)--CRIMINAL LAW ENFORCEMENT REPORTS AND RECORDS
This was added by the Senate to establish a new hearsay exception for police reports. It made police reports admissible when the officer-declarant was unavailable as a witness. The conference deleted this provision. As the rules of evidence now stand, police and law enforcement reports are not admissible against defendants in criminal cases. This is made quite clear by the provisions of rule 803(8)(B) and (C). Police reports, especially in criminal cases, tend to be one-sided and self-serving. They are frequently prepared for the use of prosecutors, who use such reports in deciding whether to prosecute. The danger of unfair prejudice inherent in such reports is heightened where-- as proposed in the Senate's rule 804(b)(5)--the officer who prepared the report is not available to take the stand and be cross-examined about it. There was some thought that the Senate's rule would raise a constitutional question of the right of confrontation.

Section 2 of the bill establishes a procedure by which the rules of evidence can be amended. The Senate made three changes in the House bill. The House bill provided that the Supreme Court could promulgate amendments to the rules of evidence and that such amendments would become effective 180 days after being reported to the Congress. The Senate increased the time period to 365 days. The conferees adopted the House provision.

The Senate added new language that permits either House of Congress to defer any proposed amendment. The deferral can be indefinite or to a date certain. The Senate language also provided that an act of Congress could amend any rule of evidence, proposed or in effect. The House conferees agreed to accept this language.

The House version required that any amendment to the rules of evidence that creates, abolishes, or modifies a rule of privilege must be approved by act of Congress. The Senate deleted this provision. The Senate receded from this amendment.

Rules of privilege keep out of litigation relevant and material information. They do so because of a substantive policy judgment that certain values--such as preserving confidential relationships-- outweigh the detrimental effect that excluding the information has on the judicial truthfinding process. In short, rules of privilege reflect a substantive policy choice between competing values, and his policy choice is legislative in nature. The legislative character of the policy choice is particularly clear with governmental privileges. Because of the legislative character of rules of privilege, there is a need for affirmative congressional action in formulating them.

As I said earlier, this bill is the culmination of over 13 years of work by people in all three branches of Government. The bill is a wholly nonpartisan effort to develop the best possible set of evidence rules to use nationwide in Federal courts. I urge the House to pass this legislation.

Footnotes
1   "304 U.S. 64 (1938)."
2   "See Republic Gear Co. v. Borg-Warner Corp., 381 F.2d 551, 555-556 n. 2 (2d Cir.1967)."
3   "Just the reverse is, of course, true in Federal criminal cases, all of which are of necessity grounded upon Federal statutes."
4   ""Rules of Evidence." Hearings Before the Committee on the Judiciary, U.S. Senate, 93d Cong., 2d Sess. (1974) (Hereinafter cited as Hearings.)."
5   "See Opening Statement of Senator Sam J. Ervin, Hearings at p. 2."
6   "See Opening Statement of Senator Roman L. Hruska, Hearings at p. 3."
7   "See Testimony of George A. Spiegelberg, Hearings at p. 96."
8   "Ibid."
9   "20 Cal.2d 585, 594, 128 P.2d 16, 21 (1942)."
10   "Cal.Ev.Code 1965 § 600."

11   "McCormick, Evidence, 669 (1954); id. 825 (2d ed. 1972)."

12   "See Report No. 93-650, dated November 15, 1973."

13   "Nev.Rev.Stats. § 48.105; N.Mex.Stats.Anno. (1973 Supp.) § 20-4-408; West's Wis.Stats.Anno. (1973 Supp.) § 904.08."

14   "See Harris v. New York, 401 U.S. 222 (1971)."

15   "For a discussion of reference to State substantive law, see note on Federal Incorporation by Reference of State Law, Hart & Wechsler, The Federal Courts and the Federal System, pp. 491-94 (2d ed. 1973)."

15a   "The problems with the House formulation are discussed in Rothstein. The Proposed Amendments to the Federal Rules of Evidence, 62 Georgetown University Law Journal 125 (1973) at notes 25, 26 and 70-74 and accompanying text."

16   "It is also intended that the Federal law of privileges should be applied with respect to pendant State law claims when they arise in a Federal question case."

17   "While such a situation might require use of two bodies of privilege law, federal and state, in the same case, nevertheless the occasions on which this would be required are considerably reduced as compared with the House version, and confined to situations where the Federal and State interests are such as to justify application of neither privilege law to the case as a whole. If the rule proposed here results in two conflicting bodies of privilege law applying to the same piece of evidence in the same case, it is contemplated that the rule favoring reception of the evidence should be applied. This policy is based on the present rule 43(a) of the Federal Rules of Civil Procedure which provides: In any case, the statute or rule which favors the reception of the evidence governs and the evidence shall be presented according to the most convenient method prescribed in any of the statutes or rules to which reference is herein made."

18   "238 U.S. 264, at 267 (1914)."

19   "Di Carlo v. United States, 6 F.2d 364 (2d Cir.1925)."

20   "See Comment, California Evidence Code § 1235; McCormick, Evidence, § 38 (2nd ed. 1972)."

21   "It would appear that some of the opposition to this Rule is based on a concern that a person could be convicted solely upon evidence admissible under this Rule. The Rule, however, is not addressed to the question of the sufficiency of evidence to send a case to the jury, but merely as to its admissibility. Factual circumstances could well arise where, if this were the sole evidence, dismissal would be appropriate."

22   "See Nev.Rev.Stats. § 15.135; N.Mex.Stats. (1973 Supp.) § 20-4-803(6); West's Wis.Stats.Anno. (1973 Supp.) § 908.03(6)."

23   "Advisory Committee's notes, to rule 803(8)(c)."

25   "H.Rept. 93-650, at p. 15. [So in original. No footnote 24 appears.]"

26   "Uniform rule 63(10); Kan.Stat.Anno. 60-460(j); 2A N.J.Stats.Anno. 84-63(10)."

27   "Nev.Rev.Stats. § 51.345; N.Mex.Stats. (1973 supp.) § 20-4-804(4); West's Wis.Stats.Anno. (1973 supp.) § 908.045(4)."

28   "The committee considered it unnecessary to include statements contained in rule 801(d)(2) (A) and (B)--the statement by the party-opponent himself or the statement of which he has manifested his adoption--because the credibility of the party-opponent is always subject to an attack on his credibility."

29   "See McCormick on Evidence, §§ 24-26 (especially 24) (2d ed. 1972)."

30   "18 U.S.C. § 3500."

31   "65 Conn. 99, 31 Atl. 591 (1894). See also, Rathbun v. Brancatella, 93 N.J.L. 222, 107 Atl. 279 (1919); see also McCormick on Evidence, § 303 (2d ed. 1972)."

1   ". The Rules of Evidence to which the Chief Justice refers have been printed as H. Doc. 93-46."

Copyright

EVERYDAY EVIDENCE: A PRACTICAL APPROACH, 2nd Edition

2nd Editions
Print Edition (c) December 2016
ISBN-10:
ISBN-13:

Publisher

Practice Ready Press
United States
6261 14th Avenue South
Suite 201
Gulfport, Florida 33707
www.practice-ready-press.com
Phone: 813-924-4717

Copyright

This book is a work of non-fiction. The teaching scenarios used to demonstrate the relevant advocacy skills are based upon archetypal situations familiar to all attorneys that practice in this area. They are not intended to represent actual clients and are based upon fictional scenarios. Any resemblance to actual events or persons, living or dead, is entirely coincidental.

ISBN-13: 978-0-9896667-6-3

Publisher

Practice Ready Press
United States
6261 14th Avenue South
Suite 201
Gulfport, Florida 33707
www.practice-ready-press.com
Phone: 813-924-4717

By the Author

Books with Practice Ready Press

Everyday Evidence: A Practical Approach (enhanced ebook)
Persuasive Openings: Storytelling in the Courtroom (enhanced ebook)
Everyday Evidence: A Practical Approach 1st Edition
Everyday Evidence: A Practical Approach 2nd Edition
Federal Criminal Procedure: Cases that Matter, 1st Edition
Federal Criminal Procedure: Cases that Matter, 2nd Edition
Federal Criminal Procedure: Cases that Matter, 3rd Edition

Books with WEST Publishing

Fundamental Trial Advocacy, 3rd Edition
Fundamental Trial Advocacy, 2nd Edition
Fundamental Trial Advocacy, 1st Edition
Fundamental Pretrial Advocacy, 2nd Edition
Fundamental Pretrial Advocacy, 1st Edition
Advocacy Case Files, 1st Edition
Evidence in Context: Evidentiary Problems & Exercises, 1st Edition
Jury Selection: The Law, Art and Science of Jury Selection, 3rd Edition (co-author)

Books with Matthew Bender

Military Crimes & Defenses, 2nd Edition (co-author)
Military Crimes & Defenses, 1st Edition (co-author)

Books with ASPEN Publishing

Evidence Practice Under the Rules, 4th Edition (co-author)
Evidence Practice Under the Rules, 3rd Edition (co-author

Made in the USA
Charleston, SC
03 January 2017